Using

Word and Excel® in Office 97

Special Edition

Using

QUE®

Special Edition

Using

Using Word and Excel® in Office 97

que®

Ron Person, Rob Tidrow,
Rick Winter, et al.

Contents at a Glance

Table of Contents

III Mail Merging with Word

IV Using Tables, Outlines, Lists, and Field Codes

Credits

PUBLISHER
John Pierce

EXECUTIVE EDITOR
Jim Minatel

DIRECTOR OF EDITORIAL SERVICES
Carla Hall

MANAGING EDITOR
Thomas F. Hayes

ACQUISITIONS EDITOR
Jill Byus

DEVELOPMENT EDITOR
Rick Kughen

PRODUCTION EDITOR
Heather E. Butler

EDITORS
Kate O. Givens
Katie Purdum
Colleen Williams

PRODUCTION TEAM SUPERVISOR
Andrew Stone

PRODUCTION TEAM
Cyndi Davis-Hubler
Chris Livengood

INDEXERS
Chris Barrick
Nadia Ibrahim

Composed in *Century Old Style* and *ITC Franklin Gothic* by Que Corporation.

About the Authors

Ron Person has written more than 18 books for Que Corporation, including *Special Edition Using Excel for Windows 95*, *Web Publishing with Word for Windows*, and *Special Edition Using Windows 3.11*. He is the lead author of *Special Edition Using Windows 95*. He has an M.S. in physics from The Ohio State University and an MBA from Hardin-Simmons University. Ron was one of Microsoft's original 12 Consulting Partners and is a Microsoft Solutions Partner.

Rob Tidrow is an author, Web site designer, trainer, and president of Tidrow Communications, Inc., a firm specializing in content creation and delivery. Rob has authored or co-authored more than 25 books on a wide variety of computer topics, including eight books on Windows 95. He authored *Windows 95 Installation and Configuration Handbook, First Edition*, *MCSE Training Guide Windows 95*, *Windows 95 Registry Troubleshooting*, *Windows NT Registry Troubleshooting*, and *Microsoft Outlook 97 Essentials*, all published by Macmillan Computer Publishing. He also is a contributing author to several books, including New Riders's *Official World Wide Web Yellow Pages*, *Special Edition Using Microsoft Office 97*, *Inside Windows 95, Deluxe Edition*, *Platinum Edition Using Windows 95*, *Inside the World Wide Web*, and *Windows 95 for Network Administrators*, all published by Macmillan Computer Publishing. He lives in Indianapolis, Indiana, with his wife, Tammy, and their two sons, Adam and Wesley.

Rick Winter welcomes any comments or suggestions you have on this book. His email address is **prwtrain@compuserve.com**.

Rick is a senior partner at PRW Computer Training and Services. Rick is a Microsoft Certified Trainer and Certified Professional for Access and has trained thousands of adults on personal computers. He is lead author of *Microsoft Access 97 Quick Reference*; lead author of *Special Edition Using Microsoft Office 97* and *Special Editon Using Microsoft Office Professional for Windows 95*; co-author of Que's *Excel for Windows SureSteps*, *Look Your Best with Excel*, and *Q&A QueCards*. He has also contributed to more than 20 books for Que. Rick is past president and currently involved with Information Systems Trainers, a professional training organization based in Denver, Colorado (**http://www.istrn.org**). Rick has a B.A. from Colorado College and an M.A. from the University of Colorado at Denver.

PRW Computer Training and Services, based in Idaho Springs, Colorado, is a recognized leader in training, consulting, and developing training materials. PRW won the prestigious Rocky Mountain Chapter Society for Technical Communication's Distinguished Award for its work on Que's *Excel for Windows SureSteps* in 1994. If your company needs training or programming on any of the Microsoft Office applications, you can contact PRW.

For information on course content, on-site corporate classes, or consulting, contact PRW at the following address:

PRW Computer Training and Services, 491 Highway 103, Idaho Springs, CO 80452; (303) 567-4943 (8-5 MST)

Patty Winter is a senior partner at PRW Computer and Training Services. She has worked with computers since 1982, training adults, testing programs, developing course material, and creating solutions for user productivity. She has trained thousands of adults. Her emphasis has been on peopleware. She is lead author of *Special Edition Using Microsoft Office 97* and *Special Edition Using Microsoft Office Professional for Windows 95*; author of *Excel 5 for Windows Essentials*; contributing author of *Special Edition Using Microsoft Office*; and co-author of *Excel for Windows SureSteps*, *Look Your Best with Excel*, and *Q&A QueCards*.

Joseph Lowery has been writing about computers and new technology since 1981. He is the co-author of *HTML 3.2 Manual of Style* by Ziff-Davis Press and a contributor to *Microsoft Office 97 Small Business Edition 6-in-1* by Que Publishing. Joseph is currently developing the Web site for the MCP Office 97 Resource Center as well as other sites for a variety of clients, including a managed health care organization, a stock market research firm, and a bar. Joseph and his wife, the dancer/choreographer Debra Wanner, have a daughter, Margot, who hogs the computer.

We'd Like to Hear from You!

Que Corporation has a long-standing reputation for high-quality books and products. To ensure your continued satisfaction, we also understand the importance of customer service and support.

Tech Support

If you need assistance with the information in this book or with a CD/disk accompanying the book, please access Macmillan Computer Publishing's online Knowledge Base at

http://www.superlibrary.com/general/support

You may contact Macmillan Technical Support by phone at **317-581-3833** or via email at **support@mcp.com**.

Also be sure to visit Que's Web resource center for all the latest information, enhancements, errata, downloads, and more. It's located at

http://www.mcp.com/

Orders, Catalogs, and Customer Service

To order other Que or Macmillan Computer Publishing books, catalogs, or products, please contact our Customer Service Department:

Phone: 800/428-5331
Fax: 800/882-8583
International Fax: 317/228-4400

or visit our online bookstore at

http://www.mcp.com/

Comments and Suggestions

We want you to let us know what you like or dislike most about this book or other Que products. Your comments will help us to continue publishing the best books available on computer topics in today's market.

Rick Kughen
Que Corporation
201 West 103rd Street, 4B
Indianapolis, Indiana 46290 USA
Fax: 317/581-4663

Please be sure to include the book's title and author as well as your name and phone or fax number. We will carefully review your comments and share them with the author. Please note that due to the high volume of mail we receive, we may not be able to reply to every message.

Thank you for choosing Que!

Introduction

Each new version of the applications in the Microsoft Office Suite introduces a wealth of new features designed to make the software easier to use and more powerful. Word 97 and Excel 97 are no exceptions to this. These are easily the most powerful versions ever of these products. They incorporate Internet publishing functions, data sharing features, and advanced document tools that hadn't even been conceived of in prior versions.

But with that new functionality comes a price. If you use Word and Excel in your job or at home, it's unlikely that you can be a master of all the features in the program. Even if you have used previous versions of the programs and are skilled with them, there's a good chance that you won't know all the things you can do with these new versions. And you certainly don't have the time to experiment with the programs in hope that you will find the answer to the problem you need to solve.

So, if you want to be productive with Office, you really need a good reference book. This book takes the approach that Word and Excel are the workhorse applications of the Office Suite. These are the programs that most people using Office use the most and depend on most in their jobs. If you find that you spend most of your Office time using these two applications, then this book is probably the right book for you.

Furthermore, we recognize that if you are looking at this book, there's a good chance you've already used Word or Excel. So by limiting the coverage to Word and Excel, we can give you more in-depth coverage of the intermediate and advanced features and capabilities of Word and Excel than you will find in other Office books without coverage of some of the most basic features that you already know. This book should be especially useful for you if you have some experience with either Word or Excel and need a reference that covers both of these programs in depth.

But, this book is not for all Office users. If you have never used Word or Excel before, this may not be the best book for you. This book does not cover some of the most introductory elements of typing and editing in Word or data entry in Excel so it is not ideal for someone learning the basics of these programs for the first time. Likewise, if you don't think you will ever need coverage of the intermediate and advanced features of Word and Excel and would prefer to get some coverage of PowerPoint, Outlook, and Access, you may want to choose one of Que's other Office books. These include the following:

- *Special Edition Using Microsoft Office 97 Bestseller Edition*: This book covers Word, Excel, PowerPoint, Access, and Outlook. It is suitable for you if you use either the "Standard" or "Professional" version of Office 97.

- *Special Edition Using Microsoft Office Small Business Edition*: This book covers the new Office Small Business version that includes Word, Excel, Publisher, and Outlook.

- If you are looking for a book about one of the individual Office applications to complement this book, you should consider:

  - *Special Edition Using Microsoft Word 97 Bestseller Edition*
  - *Special Edition Using Microsoft Excel 97 Bestseller Edition*

- *Special Edition Using Microsoft PowerPoint 97*
- *Special Edition Using Microsoft Access 97*
- *Special Edition Using Microsoft Outlook 97*

Any of these books can be purchased or ordered through your local bookstore, computer retailer, or the Macmillan Computer Publishing Web site.

We hope that by offering you this new book choice with a new combination of coverage that you can find a book that best fits the way you use Office. But regardless of which Office or Office application book you choose, we hope that you find the *Special Edition Using* books about Office to be the most comprehensive and useful reference books available for these important programs.

Conventions Used in This Book

This book uses various stylistic and typographic conventions to make it easier to use.

Shortcut key combinations are joined by + (plus) signs; for example, Ctrl+X means to hold down the Ctrl key, press the X key, and then release both simultaneously.

Menu items and dialog box selections often have a mnemonic key associated with them. This key is indicated by an underline on the item onscreen. To use these mnemonic keys, you press the Alt key and then the shortcut key. In this book, mnemonic keys are underlined like this: File.

This book uses the following typeface conventions:

Typeface	Meaning
Italic	Italics indicate new terms. They also indicate variables in commands and addresses.
Bold	Bold indicates text you type. It also indicates Internet addresses.
Computer type	Commands.

N O T E Notes provide additional information related to the topic at hand.

 T I P Tips provide quick and helpful information to assist you along the way.

CAUTION
Cautions alert you to potential pitfalls or dangers in the operations discussed.

TROUBLESHOOTING

What are Troubleshooting notes?   Troubleshooting notes answer questions that might arise while following the procedures in this book.

Special Edition Using Word and Excel in Office 97 uses references to point you to other places in the book with additional information relevant to the topic.

▶ **See** "Section Title," **p. xxx**

Using Word's Editing and Printing Tools

CHAPTER 1

Using Templates and Wizards for Frequently Created Documents

In this chapter

Working with Templates

A *template* is a file that contains the parts of a document and features used for a specific type of document. Word templates can contain text, pictures, graphs, formatting, styles, macros, AutoText, buttons on the toolbar, field codes, custom menu commands, and shortcut keys. You can put text, formatting, and settings you use repeatedly for a specific task into a template.

When you open a new document, all the contents and features of the template are transferred to the new untitled document. The original template remains unaltered on disk.

Add-ins are supplemental programs that extend the functionality of Word 97. You can purchase add-ins from software vendors. Once installed, an add-in acts as if it is a part of Word and may add a new menu command or toolbar, for example. At the end of this chapter, you learn more about add-in programs, where you can find them, and what they can do for you.

Figures 1.1, 1.2, and 1.3 show some examples of templates in use.

FIG. 1.1

Everyday blank documents are based on the Normal template, which includes font selections and other formatting settings, but no text.

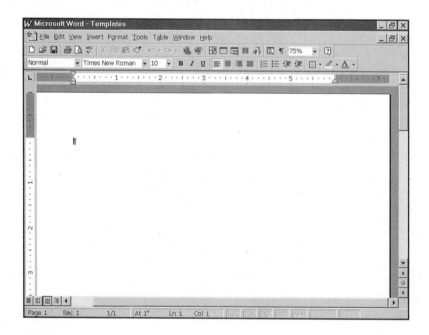

FIG. 1.2
You can base frequently used documents, such as forms, memos, and invoices, on a custom template.

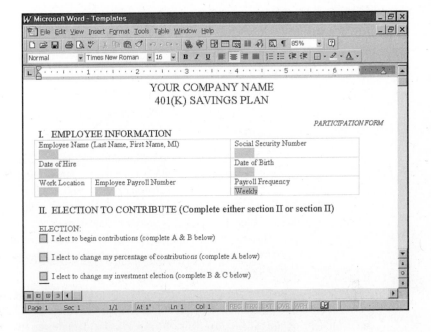

FIG. 1.3
Template wizards guide you through document creation for documents such as résumés, legal pleadings, and newsletters.

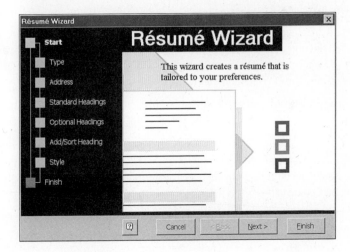

You can use templates to simplify the creation of any frequently used document. You may find templates useful for these types of documents:

- Invoices, employee records, or any standardized form
- Web pages
- Proposals and reports
- Newsletters
- Memos and fax sheets

Using templates to create Web pages and preprinted forms can significantly reduce your company's costs. Attaching templates to reports ensures that all reports have the same format and layout. You can build into the template special commands or macros needed to produce a report, such as integrating Excel charts, so that they are readily available. When certain phrases and names are stored in AutoText, you can more easily keep the spelling and formatting the same across documents. All table and figure formatting, tables of contents, and indexes look the same from report to report because they are created and formatted with macros and styles attached to the template.

From the Help menu in Word, you can access the World Wide Web. And, you can use Word to create Web pages. Word comes with a template to help you create a blank Web page that you can then fill in, or you can use Word's Web Page Wizard to guide you through the process of creating a Web page.

Many companies use templates to prepare interoffice memos and fax cover letters. The headings and document formatting are predefined and, therefore, are standardized. ASK or FILLIN fields prompt the operator for entries. The DATE and AUTHOR fields can be used to enter automatically the current date and name of the operator.

Word comes with several predesigned templates that you can use as a basis for your own business documents. You can modify the Word templates to meet your needs, or you can create your own templates from scratch.

In addition, Word provides *wizards* to automate customizing your documents. The wizard you select, such as Letter or Fax, displays a series of dialog boxes in which you make selections. Word uses your responses to design your document.

Templates remove some of the tedium that comes with typing the same text repeatedly. Rather than retyping a memo heading, for example, you can create or modify a template to include the repeated text. Many of the templates are automated and require only that you point, click, and type to fill out a form. Figure 1.4 shows an example of an easy-to-use memo template.

What You Need to Know About Templates

Word normally saves templates as files with the DOT file extension in the Templates subfolder under the folder that contains Word. DOT files in this subfolder appear as choices in each category of the New dialog box. This accessibility makes templates readily available regardless of which folder you are working in.

FIG. 1.4
This memo template provides on-screen instructions and requires only that you point, click, and type.

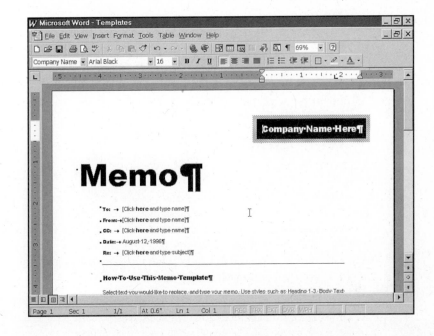

N O T E If you're using Word as part of Microsoft Office, you'll find the Templates folder located under the folder in which you installed Office. In Office 97, all of Office is installed in the Program Files folder. ■

Word normally looks to the Templates folder when it searches for the templates used in the New dialog box. The tabs that appear in the New dialog box are determined by the structure of the folder that contains the template files. Each tab corresponds to the name of a subfolder in the Templates folder. To change the folder Word uses for templates, choose Tools, Options, and select the File Locations tab. Double-click User Templates and select a new template folder.

All documents in Word are based on a template. Even the default new document is based on a template, NORMAL.DOT. The NORMAL.DOT file contains the formatting and default settings for the new document you open when you choose File, New.

Styles, macros, AutoText, and other items stored in the NORMAL.DOT template are available to all documents at all times. Because the information stored in NORMAL.DOT is available to all documents all the time, they are said to be available *globally*.

Templates can contain the following:

■ Body text, headers, footers, footnotes, and graphics with formatting

■ Page and paper layouts

■ Styles

■ AutoText entries

■ Bookmarks

■ Custom menus and commands

■ Tools

■ Shortcut keys

Word uses a different format for its files than previous versions of Word. You can open and use templates you created in prior versions, but remember that menu commands may have moved or changed. Word may display a warning to let you know that some elements contained in those templates, such as macros, may not work properly.

When you create a document based on a template, the document opens to show the body text, graphics, and formatting contained in the template. All the styles, macros, tools, and so on that are in the template are available for use with the document.

After you create a document, you can attach the document to a different template so that you can use the features (but not the text or page formatting) found in that template. Later sections of this chapter show you how you can transfer features between templates so that a style or macro you create in one template can be copied into another.

Using Templates as a Pattern for Documents

Most people use only a few templates. The templates they use may include the NORMAL.DOT template for everyday work or one of a few custom templates for use in memos or reports. Many people use the NORMAL.DOT template to create the blank document with which they normally work. Examine the predefined templates that come with Word, because you may find one appropriate to your particular task.

Using Word's Predefined Templates

Word for Windows comes with predefined templates you can use to create many typical business documents. Many of the templates contain special tools, formatting styles, custom menus, macros, and AutoText for frequently used procedures. The template layouts fall into three categories: *contemporary, elegant,* and *professional,* and use similar design principles within each group. You can select a style that suits your needs. Using the templates from that group, be assured that all your documents will have a harmonious, professional appearance. Many of the templates include on-screen instructions that guide you step-by-step in creating some very sophisticated effects.

The predefined templates are organized on different tabs in the New dialog box and are described in Table 1.1.

Table 1.1 Predefined Word Templates

Category	Template
General	Normal (default document)
Other Documents	Contemporary Resumé Elegant Resumé Professional Resumé

Category	Template
Letters & Faxes	Contemporary Letter
	Elegant Letter
	Professional Letter
	Contemporary Fax
	Elegant Fax
	Professional Fax
Memos	Contemporary Memo
	Elegant Memo
	Professional Memo
Reports	Contemporary Report
	Elegant Report
	Professional Report
Publications	Newsletter
Web Pages	Blank Web Page
Office 95 Templates	Templates you created or modified in Office 95

Opening a New Document Based on a Template

Opening a new document is easy. To do so, follow these steps:

1. Choose File, New. The New dialog box opens to the General tab with the NORMAL.DOT template selected (see Figure 1.5).

FIG. 1.5
Most documents
are based on the
NORMAL.DOT template.

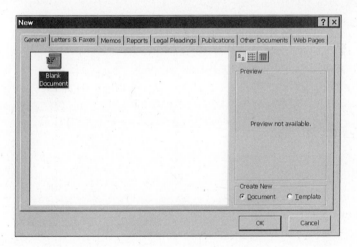

2. Select a tab, then click the name or icon of the template you want to use. The Preview box shows a sample document for which the template is designed.

3. Choose OK.

N O T E   If you select the Blank Document icon in the New dialog box, you are actually selecting the Normal template. In this case, because the document is blank, Word doesn't offer a preview, as you can see in Figure 1.5. ▪

T I P   To open a new document based on NORMAL.DOT using a tool, click the New button in the Standard toolbar or press Ctrl+N.

Opening a Template on Startup   You can make Word open a specific template when it starts by following these steps:

1. Open the NORMAL.DOT template.

2. With the NORMAL.DOT template active, record a macro and assign it the name **AutoExec**.

3. While the macro recorder is on, create a new document based on the template you want Word to open automatically. Then, turn off the macro recorder.

4. You can close the new document you started to create without saving it, but save the Normal template and exit from Word.

From this point on, when you start Word, it automatically opens a new document based on the template you specified. Remember, if that template contained text, you'll see that text in Document 1 *every time you start Word.*

N O T E   If you make a mistake and want Word to open the Normal template at startup, reopen the Normal template. Then, open the Macro dialog box and delete the AutoExec macro. Don't forget to save the Normal template. ▪

T I P   If Word doesn't find a Normal template, it automatically creates a new one, with the same settings Word had when you first installed it. Use this information to re-create a Normal template if yours becomes corrupted.

N O T E   If you frequently use the same templates, you can save yourself time by creating a tool or menu command that opens a new document from each of these templates. Use the macro recorder to record a macro when you open a template. Assign this macro to a button on a toolbar or to a menu command. ▪

Opening Word 7 Templates   Templates created for Word 7 can be opened and used in Word. When you close a document based on the old template, Word automatically saves the document in Word format. If you edit and save the old template, it is saved in the Word format. The file is no longer compatible with Word 7, however. In addition, some of your macros may not convert or function properly because menu commands have changed.

Using Information from Another Template

If you are working on a document and decide you want to have access to all the features in another template, you can attach that template to the document. Attaching a new template does not change the existing document text, but it does change specified settings, such as macros, AutoText, menu commands, margins, shortcut key assignments, and buttons.

To attach another template to a document, follow these steps:

1. Open the document to which you want to attach a template.

2. Choose Tools, Templates and Add-Ins. The Templates and Add-ins dialog box appears. Notice that the Document Template edit box displays the name of the template currently attached to the document (see Figure 1.6).

FIG. 1.6

Use features from other templates by attaching a different template containing those features to a document.

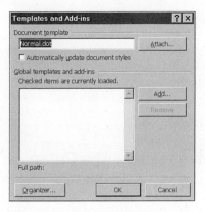

3. Choose the Attach button to display the Attach Template dialog box (see Figure 1.7).

FIG. 1.7

From the Attach Template dialog box, choose the template to which you want to attach the document.

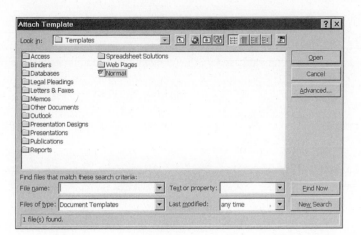

4. Double-click the folder that contains the template you want. Select the template or type the template name in the File Name box.

5. Choose Open. The Attach Template dialog box closes, and the template name you selected replaces the selection in the Document Template edit box of the Templates and Add-ins dialog box.

6. Choose OK.

For a single Word session, you can load several templates simultaneously and make the features of those templates available globally, similar to the way features in the Normal template are available globally. In the Templates and Add-ins dialog box, choose the Add button to display the Add Template dialog box. Navigate to the folder containing the template whose features you want available. When you choose Open, Word redisplays the Templates and Add-ins dialog box. The template you selected appears in the Global Templates and Add-ins list box—preceded by a check to indicate its features are available. The features of all selected templates that appear in this list box are available to you for the rest of the Word session. When you start your next session, the templates still appear in the list box, but they aren't selected. You can select them to make the settings available to you.

 T I P If you want the features of a particular template or several templates available *every time* you start Word, copy the template to your \WinWord\Startup folder. The Startup folder is the default folder used for startup files. If you do not have a Startup folder, choose Tools, Options and select the File Locations tab. Select the Startup folder in the File Types list, and then choose Modify to set a new folder as the startup folder.

Transferring Template Contents Using the Organizer

As you work, you may find that you need a style, macro, toolbar, or AutoText entry that is stored in another template. Or you may develop a style, macro, toolbar, or AutoText entry in one document and want to use it with other documents. After you learn how to use the Organizer, you'll be able to transfer features between templates so that they are available wherever you need them.

To copy a style, macro, toolbar, or AutoText entry from one template to another, follow these steps:

1. Open a document based on the template that contains the feature you want to copy.

2. Choose Tools, Templates and Add-Ins, then choose the Organizer button. The Organizer, shown in Figure 1.8, appears. The left side of the dialog box shows the template of the current document, and the right side of the dialog box shows the Normal template.

FIG. 1.8

Use the Organizer to transfer styles, macros, AutoText, or toolbars between templates and documents.

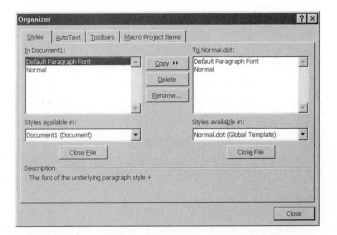

3. If you want to transfer an entry to some other template, choose the Close File button. Word then replaces Close File with an Open File button. Choose the Open File button to display the Open dialog box. Navigate to the folder containing the template you want to receive the feature. Choose Open to display the contents of that template in the right side of the Organizer dialog box.

4. Select the tab for the type of feature you want to transfer.

5. From the lists on the left, select the feature you want to copy.

6. Choose the Copy button.

7. Repeat steps 4–6 to transfer additional features, or choose Close at the bottom of the dialog box to close the Organizer.

Transferring styles, macros, AutoText, or toolbars is described in more detail in the specific chapters that discuss those features.

▶ **See** "Creating an AutoText Entry," **p. 51**

Storing Summary Information About a Document

Each Word document can have summary and other information attached. This information can remind you about the source or contents of a document, when the document was created, how much time you've spent creating it, and more. You can also search for keywords, which can be very helpful if you forget a file's name or need a list of all files that have similar keywords in the summary.

If you want to attach summary information to a document, choose File, Properties, and complete the Properties dialog box. When you save the document you have opened, the property information is saved with the file. You can edit the property information for the active document by choosing File, Properties.

The Properties dialog box includes the following tabs:

Tab	Description
General	Provides information about the file's location, size, and save dates.
Summary	Provides space for you to note important information about the document itself, such as who wrote it, keywords (for document searches), and comments.
Statistics	Includes information such as the number of pages, lines, words, and so forth.
Contents	Provides space for you to describe the document's contents.
Custom	Provides space for you to customize the information you save with the document.

TROUBLESHOOTING

The template on which my document was originally based is no longer available. What happened?
It may have been erased, renamed, or moved to a different folder. You cannot use the macros, AutoText, or toolbars that were assigned to that template. You do, however, still have the styles that were in that template.

You can attach another template to the document to gain the use of the other template's features by opening the document and choosing File, Templates. Follow the description in the section "Using Information from Another Template" earlier in this chapter.

I don't see Word's predefined templates in the New dialog box. If Word's predefined templates do not appear in the New dialog box, the templates may not have been installed when you installed Word for Windows. You can rerun the installation procedure and choose to install only the templates.

I created a custom template, but it doesn't appear in the New dialog box. Templates use a DOT extension and are stored in the template folder. The folder to which Word normally looks for template files is C:\WinWord\Templates or C:\Office95\Templates. Choose Tools, Options, and select the File Locations tab. Confirm that User Templates shows the correct folder. If it does not, choose Modify and correct the folder name. Click Close.

Modifying Templates

The templates that come with Word for Windows are designed to handle many daily business transactions; however, you may need to modify the template to fit your business formats more closely or to add AutoText and styles specific to your needs. For example, you may want to use the Contemporary Fax template as your standard cover sheet, but the original form of the template doesn't contain your company's address and phone information, nor does it contain your name as the sender. You don't want to type this information each time you need to send a fax. You can edit the Contemporary Fax template to include your standardized information, change the format to fit your needs, and even include your own AutoText entries.

You can modify templates to incorporate the specific text, graphics, styles, formatting, macros, and AutoText you need for your documents. In other words, you can modify templates to fit your needs, even if the template came with Word or was given to you by another Word user.

What You Need to Know About Changing a Template

After you make changes to a template, all new documents using that template include the modifications or edits you've made to the template. Documents created from the template before it was modified, however, have access to only some of the changes to the template. For example, styles, text, graphics, page formatting, or print formatting added to the template do not transfer to existing documents. The following template changes *do* transfer to documents that were created from an earlier template:

- AutoText entries
- Shortcut keys
- Macros
- Toolbar buttons
- Menus

CAUTION

If you change a template and preserve the original name, the original template is replaced. To ensure that you will always have the original template available, consider using a new name for the modified template or giving the original template a new name.

Changing a Template

When you need to make just a few modifications to a template, you can easily modify the template with the method described in this section. However, if you have many changes to make to a template, it might be easier to use one of the methods described later in this chapter to create a new template from scratch or to use an existing document as the basis for the new template.

To change an existing template, follow these steps:

1. Choose File, Open; click the Open button; or press Ctrl+O. The Open dialog box appears (see Figure 1.9).
2. By using the Look In box, navigate to the Templates folder or the folder containing your template.

FIG. 1.9

Use the Open dialog
box to select the
template file you want
to modify.

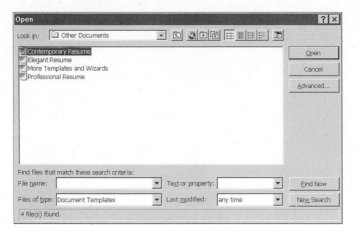

3. Select Document Templates (*.DOT) from the Files of Type box.

4. Select the template you want to modify and choose Open.

5. Change the template by adding or modifying text or graphics; changing formats; redefining styles or AutoText entries; or adding or changing macros, shortcut keys, or buttons.

6. Choose File, Save to save the template back to the same folder with the same name.

Setting Default Formats in the Normal Template

Word for Windows bases its default settings for a new document on a template stored in the file NORMAL.DOT. All documents you create by choosing File, New and pressing Enter are based on the Normal template. Settings, such as the style, font type and size, margins, and other formats, are stored in this file.

You can change default settings for new documents in two ways. In the more powerful method, you can set new defaults for styles, AutoText, page formatting, and so on by changing the setting in the NORMAL.DOT template. If you need to change only the default for a font, style, or page layout, you can change them while editing a document using the method described later in the section "Changing Template Features from Within a Document."

If you want to change any of the default formatting or features controlled by a template, open the NORMAL.DOT template and change the appropriate format or settings. Save the NORMAL.DOT template back to the same folder with the same name.

Making Template Features Available to All Documents

If you have macros, AutoText, buttons, or styles that you want to be available to all documents, put them in the NORMAL.DOT template. However, be aware that a conflict might occur if the active document is based on a template that has styles, macros, or AutoText with the same names as those in the NORMAL.DOT template.

Whenever a conflict occurs between styles, macros, or AutoText with the same name, the template that created the document takes priority over the NORMAL.DOT template. For example, if your report is based on the ELEGANT REPORT.DOT template that contains a style named List Bullet, and the NORMAL.DOT template also contains a style named List Bullet, your document uses the List Bullet style found in ELEGANT REPORT.DOT.

Changing Template Features from Within a Document

Default settings are format settings specified when a document opens—settings such as which font and font size are used when you first begin to type. You can change default settings in two ways: You can open and modify the template that creates a type of document, or you can change some formats within a document and transfer the changes back to the template so that the changes become new defaults.

The types of changes you can transfer from a document back to its template are found in these menu choices: Format, Font; Format, Style; and File, Page Setup.

To transfer a format change from the document back to the template, follow these steps:

1. Open a new or existing document based on the template you want to change.
2. Choose Format, Font or Format, Style or File, Page Setup, depending on the type of default change you want to make.
3. Select the style or tab, if any, for the type of formatting you want to change, then select the formatting options you want to define as default settings on the template.
4. If you change the font or page setup, choose the Default button. A dialog box appears asking you to confirm the update to the template.

   Or, if you change or add a style, choose the Modify button and select the Add to Template check box in the Modify Style dialog box.
5. Choose Yes or press Enter to update the document's template file with the selected default settings.

You may be able to save yourself some work when modifying a template by copying existing styles, macros, AutoText, or buttons from another template. Use the Organizer to copy template items. The Organizer is described in each chapter that deals with a feature you can transfer. The feature is covered lightly in the section "Using Information from Another Template" earlier in this chapter.

N O T E The changes you make to default fonts, styles, or page setup affect only the current document and all new documents you subsequently create based on the current template. Old default formats remain in any existing documents. ■

 T I P If you open a document you created before changing defaults, Word may update the document for you automatically, or you can update the document quickly by choosing Tools, Templates and Add-Ins, and placing a check in the Automatically Update Document Styles check box.

Creating a New Template

Although Word comes with many predesigned templates, you probably have many documents or forms that do not fit any of the templates. You can create a completely new template based on an existing template or document.

Creating a New Template Based on an Existing Template

You can create a template in much the same way you create any document. If you have a template that already has most of the features you want, you can save time by creating the new template based on the existing one.

To create a new template based on an existing template, follow these steps:

1. Choose File, New.
2. Choose the Template button.
3. Choose the tab that contains the template on which you want to base the new template.
4. Select the template you want. Select the Normal template if you want to start with a blank template and the default settings.
5. Choose OK. Note that the title bar now displays Template rather than Document (see Figure 1.10).

FIG. 1.10

The title bar indicates that you are creating a template. This one is based on the NORMAL.DOT template.

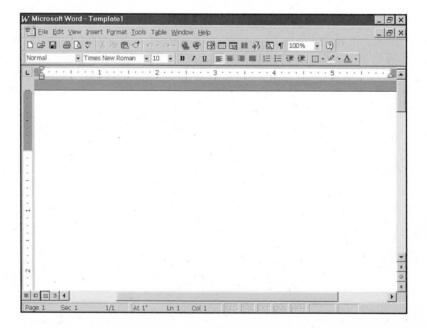

6. Lay out and format the template as you would a document. Include text that will not change between documents. The template can contain text and graphics you want to appear on all documents, formatting and styles, macros, bookmarks, AutoText entries, new commands, shortcut keys, and new toolbar buttons.

To save a template, follow these steps:

1. Choose File, Save As.
2. Select the folder in which you want to save the template. The folder you select determines the tab on which the template appears when you choose File, New.
3. Enter a name for the template in the File Name box. The extension DOT is assigned to templates.
4. Choose OK.

Creating a Template Based on an Existing Document

You already may have a document that contains most of the text, formatting, and settings you want to use in a template. Rather than re-create the document on a template, Word for Windows enables you to create a template based on the existing document.

To create a template based on an existing document, follow these steps:

1. Choose File, Open and open the document you want to use as the basis for a template.
2. Modify this document by editing text and adding graphics, styles, macros, AutoText, or buttons that you want to include in the template.
3. Choose File, Save As.
4. Select Document Template from the Save as Type pull-down list.
5. Select the folder in which you want to save the template. The folder you select determines the tab on which the template appears when you choose File, New.
6. Type the template's file name in the File Name box (see Figure 1.11). You do not have to type the DOT extension. The template file automatically is saved to the folder that contains templates.

FIG. 1.11

If you create a particular document frequently, you should save it as a template.

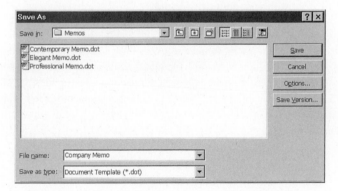

7. Choose OK.

N O T E Templates are a key to creating forms that you use repeatedly. Word has the capability to create forms that include edit fields, drop-down lists, and check boxes. To use Word's Form Fill-in feature, you need to save forms as templates. Users can create forms easily by opening a new document based on the form template. You don't have to worry about the form being accidentally changed, because the original template stays on disk and the user works with a copy of the form. ■

Adding Power and Features with Add-Ins

Add-ins are a way of extending the capabilities of Word. An add-in program is not part of Word but behaves as if it is a part of Word. An add-in program may add new menu choices to Word or add new toolbars to Word. Like a template, the add-in program remains available until you exit Word. Add-in programs for various tasks are available from a variety of third-party vendors. For specific information about using a particular add-in, consult the documentation provided with the add-in program.

Loading Add-Ins

Add-in programs end with the file extension WLL. Follow the installation instructions provided with the add-in program for help in installing an add-in. To load an add-in program, follow these steps:

1. Choose Tools, Templates and Add-Ins. The Templates and Add-ins dialog box appears.
2. Choose the Add button in the Global Templates and Add-ins section. The Add Template dialog box appears.
3. Choose Word Add-ins in the Files of Type list box.
4. Select the add-in you want. If the add-in you want is not listed, change the folder or drive in the Look In box. (If you don't know the name of the add-in, consult the documentation provided with your add-in program.)
5. Choose OK. Word loads the add-in program.

You also can load add-ins automatically, every time Word starts. To load an add-in program on startup, simply copy the add-in WLL file into the Startup subfolder located in the WinWord folder. The Startup folder is the default folder used for startup files. If you do not have a Startup folder, choose Tools, Options and select the File Locations tab (see Figure 1.12). Select the Startup folder in the File Types list and then choose the Modify button to set a new folder as the Startup folder.

FIG. 1.12
Modify the location of
the Startup folder in the
Options dialog box.

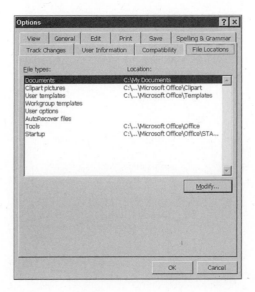

Removing Add-Ins

After an add-in is loaded, it remains available until you quit Word or explicitly remove the add-in. You may want to remove an add-in to make more system memory available.

To remove an add-in, follow these steps:

1. Choose Tools, Templates and Add-Ins. The Templates and Add-ins dialog box appears.
2. Select the add-in you want to remove in the Global Templates and Add-ins list.
3. Click the Remove button. The add-in is unloaded.
4. Choose OK.

Using Editing and Proofing Tools

Word's Editing Tools

With Word 97, you can use the Find and Replace feature to change text, formatting, special characters, and styles.

Before you print your document, you should check its spelling. Your eyes are trained to correct obvious spelling errors when you read them. However, you can still overlook a mistake when you proof a document. Use the spelling checker to catch mistakes that you missed and to correct spelling when you make an error. Use the Word 97 grammar checker to correct faulty sentence construction and style. You can use the thesaurus to find just the right word or to define a term you're unsure about.

If you need to know how many words your document contains, use the Word Count feature. This feature enables you to gather information about the number of words, lines, paragraphs, and more. For example, term papers and magazine articles typically require accurate word counts.

The following two figures show a document before (see Figure 2.1) and after (see Figure 2.2) Word checked its spelling and grammar. The user also used the thesaurus to improve some of the language.

FIG. 2.1
This rough draft of a document has not been revised using Word's editing and proofing tools.

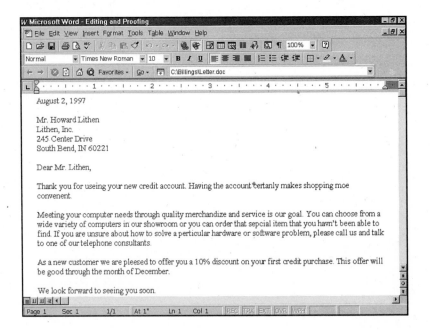

FIG. 2.2
You can polish your writing with the editing and proofing tools.

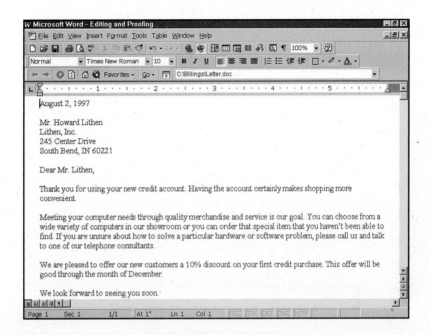

All the editing and proofing tools combine to help you hone the language of your documents. Use the tools to do the following:

- Catch typos and spelling errors.
- Make sure that your grammatical usage fits the type of document you're working on.
- Use the thesaurus to find the right replacement word. Then, choose Edit, Replace to exchange the new word for the original word.

Using Find and Replace

Being able to find and replace text, formatting, styles, and special characters is an important time-saver. (This feature helps ensure that you catch every occurrence of whatever you need to find or replace.) The Edit, Find command finds and selects the text, formatting, style, or special character that you specify, enabling you to locate a certain phrase or a particular type of formatting easily. The Edit, Replace command enables you to find and replace the item in question. You can replace items selectively or globally (changing all occurrences at the same time).

Finding Text

With the Word Find feature, you can quickly locate a specific word or phrase or a special formatting character in a document that is many pages long. The text can be as brief as a single letter or as long as a sentence containing up to 255 characters. You can also search for special characters, such as tabs, page breaks, extra spaces, line numbers, footnotes, or revision marks within your document. Alternatively, you might want to search for a particular format or style.

To find text (containing as many as 255 characters) or special characters, follow these steps:

1. Choose Edit, Find, or press Ctrl+F. The Find and Replace dialog box appears with the Find tab selected (see Figure 2.3).

FIG. 2.3

Use the Find and Replace dialog box to search through your document quickly.

2. In the Find What text box, type the text or special characters you want to search for. (For a list of special characters, see Table 2.2 in the section "Finding and Replacing Special Characters.")

The text scrolls to the right if you enter more text than will fit in the box. You can enter as many as 255 characters.

3. Choose the More button to display selectable search options (see Figure 2.4).

FIG. 2.4

Use the search options to find a specific word, phrase, formatting, style, or special character.

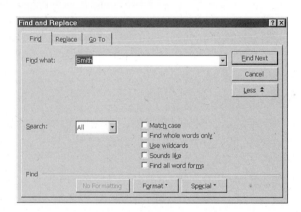

4. Select one or more of the following options in the Find and Replace dialog box:

Option	Effect
Search	Determines the direction of the search. *Down* searches from the insertion point to the end of the document or selection. *Up* searches from the insertion point to the beginning of the document or selection. *All* searches the entire document or selection.

Option	Effect
Match Case	Matches the text exactly as you have typed it including capital letters. Word doesn't consider the use of small caps or all uppercase letters, but it examines the case of the letters just as you originally typed them. Do not select this option if you want to find all occurrences of the text regardless of case.
Find Whole Words Only	Finds whole words only, not parts of words. Select this option if you want to find all occurrences of the text.
Use Wildcards	Uses special search operators and expressions with which to search. See the section "Finding and Replacing Special Characters" later in this chapter.
Sounds Like	Matches words that sound alike but are spelled differently, such as *seize* and *sees*.
Find All Word Forms	Finds all forms of a word, such as *entry* and *entries*.
Format	Displays the Format options, including Font, Paragraph, Language, and Style. Depending on your selection, the dialog box displays the tab that contains the various types of formatting for each formatting option. (For more information on these options, refer to the section "Finding and Replacing Formats" later in this chapter.)
Special	Enables you to search for special codes in the text, such as paragraph marks and tab characters (see Figure 2.5). You can also type these codes. (See "Finding and Replacing Special Characters" later in this chapter.)
No Formatting	Removes any formatting codes displayed beneath the text box from a previous Find operation.

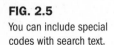

FIG. 2.5

You can include special codes with search text.

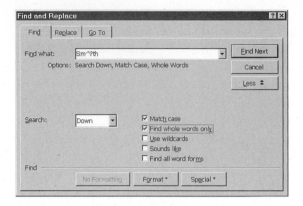

5. Choose the Find Next button to begin the search, or choose the Replace tab to display the Replace With text box.

Word finds the first occurrence of the text or special character and then moves to and selects that occurrence. The dialog box remains open so you can immediately continue to search for other occurrences of the text or special character by choosing Find Next.

When you're finished with your search, close the Find and Replace dialog box by choosing Cancel or pressing Esc. For example, close the dialog box if you want to edit the found text.

 You can leave the dialog box open while editing the found text by clicking in the document window or pressing Ctrl+Tab.

After closing the Find and Replace dialog box, you can repeat the search by pressing Shift+F4. Alternatively, you can choose Edit, Find again and then choose Find Next.

If Word cannot find the text, the program displays a dialog box that indicates Word has finished searching the document. Choose OK and try again.

 You can display the Find and Replace dialog box by pressing Ctrl+F.

If you're unsure of how to spell the word you want to find, try using *special characters* in place of letters that you're not sure about. If you want to find *Smith*, for example, but aren't sure whether to spell it with an *i* or a *y*, search for **Sm^?th** (refer to Figure 2.5). You can insert the question mark by typing **^?** (the caret character followed by the question mark) or by choosing Any Letter from the Special pop-up menu. Alternatively, you can search for part of a word, such as *Smi*.

TIP If you are searching for part of a word such as Smi, make sure that the Find Whole Words Only check box in the Find and Replace dialog box is not selected.

If you want to search for or replace text in only a portion of your document, select that portion. Then follow the general instructions for finding or replacing.

Replacing Text

Besides searching for text, formatting, or special characters, you also can replace them automatically. If you finish your document and realize that *Smythe* really should have been *Smith*, you can use a simple menu command to search for every occurrence of the incorrect spelling and replace it with the correct version. Or if your typist underlined every title in a long list of books and you decide that you want to italicize book titles, you can search for every occurrence of underlining and replace it with italic.

Replacing text works much the same way as finding text. The only major difference is that, in addition to the Find What text box in the Find and Replace dialog box, the Replace tab includes a Replace With text box. In this box, you enter the text to replace the text that you find. The Find and Replace dialog box enables you to confirm each replacement. Alternatively, you can replace all occurrences of the text with a single command.

To replace text, follow these steps:

1. Choose Edit, Replace or press Ctrl+H. The Find and Replace dialog box appears (see Figure 2.6).

FIG. 2.6

Use the Find and Replace dialog box to change one word or phrase to another throughout your document.

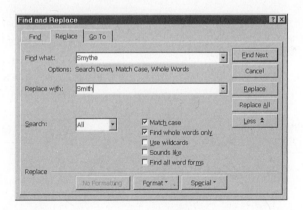

2. In the Find What text box, type the text that you want to replace.

3. In the Replace With text box, type the new text.

4. Select one or more options in the Find and Replace dialog box:

Option	Effect
Search	Determines the direction of the search. *Down* searches from the insertion point to the end of the document or selection. *Up* searches from the insertion point to the beginning of the document or selection. *All* searches the entire document or selection.
Match Case	Matches the text exactly as you have typed it—including capital letters. Word doesn't consider the use of small caps or all uppercase letters, but it examines the case of the letters just as you originally typed them. Do not select this option if you want to find all occurrences of the text regardless of case.
Find Whole Words Only	Finds whole words only, not parts of words. Do not select this option if you want to find all occurrences of the text.
Use Wildcards	Uses special search operators and expressions with which to search. See the section "Finding and Replacing Special Characters" later in this chapter.
Sounds Like	Matches words that sound alike but are spelled differently, such as *seize* and *sees*.
Find All Word Forms	Finds all forms of a word, such as *entry* and *entries*.
Format	Displays Format options, including Font, Paragraph, Language, and Style. Depending on your selection, the dialog box displays the tab that contains the various types of formatting for each formatting option. (For more information on these options, see the section "Finding and Replacing Formats" later in this chapter.)
Special	Enables you to search for special codes in the text, such as paragraph

Option	Effect
	marks and tab characters (refer to Figure 2.5). You also can type these codes. See "Finding and Replacing Special Characters" later in this chapter.
No Formatting	Removes any formatting codes displayed beneath the text box from a previous Find operation (unless you want these codes to affect the current search).

5. Choose the Find Next or Replace All button.

If you want to confirm each change, choose Find Next. When Word finds an occurrence of the text, choose the Replace button to change the text. Or choose the Find Next button again to continue the search without altering the selected occurrence.

If you want to change all occurrences of the specified text without confirmation, choose the Replace All button.

6. Choose Cancel to return to the document.

If Word cannot find the text, you see a dialog box that indicates that Word has finished searching the document without finding the search item.

If you want to search for or replace text in only a portion of your document, select that portion. Then follow the general instructions for finding and replacing.

To cancel a Replace operation, press Esc or click the Cancel button.

CAUTION

Choosing the Replace All button saves time but can be risky. You need to be absolutely certain that you want to replace *every* occurrence of a word before you use this feature. You might want to start by confirming the first few replacements. When you are sure that you want to change all remaining occurrences of the text, choose Replace All. If you choose Replace All and then realize that you made a mistake, immediately choose Edit, Undo Replace.

Unless you specify otherwise, Word applies the original formatting to the new replacement text. If you replace the boldface word *Roger* with the name *Mr. Smith* that is not bold, for example, the replacement is a boldface *Mr. Smith*. To override this feature, specify formatting as part of your replacement (see this chapter's section "Finding and Replacing Formatting and Styles").

You can undo a replacement by choosing Edit, Undo Replace. If you have confirmed each replacement, Edit, Undo Replace undoes only the last replacement (however, you can choose Edit, Undo Replace repeatedly to undo replacements sequentially, starting with the last replacement). If you choose the Replace All button and make all the replacements at once, Edit, Undo Replace undoes all the replacements.

You can use the Undo button on the Standard toolbar to undo all the replacements.

To undo all replacements using the Undo button, follow these steps:

1. Click the down arrow of the Undo button on the Standard toolbar. The box containing all the actions appears.
2. Drag to select all the Replace items listed on the Undo button's pull-down menu.
3. Release the mouse button. All the replacements revert to the original text.

If you are searching for or replacing long phrases, you can easily copy and paste the text into the Find and Replace dialog box. Highlight the text and choose Edit, Copy or press Ctrl+C to copy the text to the Clipboard. Position the insertion point in the Find What or Replace With text box. Paste the text by choosing Edit, Paste or pressing Ctrl+V.

Finding and Replacing Formatting and Styles

Finding and replacing formatting is similar to finding and replacing text. Suppose that you have a document in which you have underlined many titles, and you decide to italicize them instead. Or suppose that you have sprinkled an article with boldface phrases and decide to remove the boldface formatting. You can change the text, the formatting, or both text and formatting.

You can also find and replace paragraph formats, languages, and styles. For example, if your document has centered paragraphs, you can replace the centered formatting with right-aligned formatting. If you want to check the spelling in a French paragraph, you can assign a French language dictionary rather than an English (U.S.) language dictionary. Or you can replace a style such as Heading 1 with another style, such as Heading 2.

Finding and Replacing Formats   You can find and replace text (or special characters), formatting, or both. For example, you can find text and replace it with different text, as described in the preceding section, or you can find formatting and replace it with different formatting. Or you can find formatted text and replace it with different text and different formatting.

To find or replace formatting, follow these steps:

1. Choose Edit, Find or Edit, Replace. The Find and Replace dialog box appears.
2. In the Find What box, type the text that you want to locate, or leave the box empty to find only formatting.
3. Select the font, character, paragraph, language, or style formatting that you want to find or replace, as described in the following list:

   - To find a font or character formatting, choose the Format button and select Font from the menu that appears. The Find Font dialog box appears (see Figure 2.7). This dialog box looks the same as the Font dialog box that you use to format characters. Select the font or other options that you want to find. Then choose OK or press Enter.

FIG. 2.7
You can include character formatting as a Find What option or Replace With option in the Find Font dialog box.

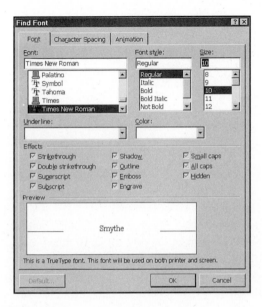

- To find paragraph formatting, choose the Format button and select Paragraph from the menu that appears. The Find Paragraph dialog box appears. This dialog box resembles the Paragraph dialog box that you use to format paragraphs. Select the paragraph formatting options that you want to find. Then choose OK or press Enter.

- To find language formatting (areas of the document to which you assign a dictionary for another language), choose the Format button and select Language from the menu that appears. The Find Language dialog box displays (see Figure 2.8). Select the language assignment that you want to use in your Find and Replace operations.

FIG. 2.8
Use the Find Language dialog box to search for or replace an area of text that has a foreign language dictionary assigned to it.

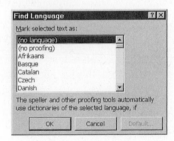

- To find style formatting, choose the Format button and select Style from the menu that appears. The Find Style dialog box appears (see Figure 2.9). Select the style that you want to find or replace. Choose OK or press Enter.

FIG. 2.9

In the Find Style dialog box, choose the styles that you want to find or replace.

The font, paragraph, language, or style options that you select are listed beneath the Find What or Replace With text boxes.

4. To replace formatting, select the Replace With text box. Then type the replacement text or leave the box empty to replace the contents of the Find What text box with formatting only.

5. To add formatting to the replacement text, choose the Format button. Then choose Font, Paragraph, Language, or Style. The Replace Font, Replace Paragraph, Replace Language, or Replace Style dialog box appears. Select the options you want. Choose OK or press Enter.

The formatting options that you select are listed under the Replace With text box.

6. Choose Find Next to find the next occurrence of the specified text, formatting, or both.

If you're replacing formatting, choose Find Next to find the next occurrence. Then choose Replace, or choose Replace All to find and replace all occurrences.

7. When the Find or Replace operation is complete, click Cancel (or press Esc) to close the Find and Replace dialog box.

Initially, check boxes are gray and text boxes are blank on the format dialog boxes. This indicates that these fields are not involved in the Find or Replace operation. Clicking a check box option one time selects it; a check appears in the box. Clicking a second time clears the option. In this case, the option is still involved in the Find or Replace operation. However, you have specifically cleared that option, removing the format. Clicking a third time grays the option again so that it is no longer involved in the Find or Replace operation.

If you want to remove small caps from all occurrences of a certain word, for example, follow these steps:

1. Choose Edit, Replace and then type the word into the Find What text box.

2. Choose the Format button. Then choose Font.

3. Choose the Small Caps option to select it. Choose OK to return to the Find and Replace dialog box. Then type the same word into the Replace With box.

4. Choose the Format button then choose Font. Select the Small Caps check box twice to clear this option. If you leave this box grayed, the operation does not remove the formatting.

5. Choose OK, then choose the Find Next button.

The formatting selections that you make for the Find What and the Replace With text boxes remain in effect until you change them. In other words, the selections are in effect the next time you open the Find and Replace dialog box. To remove all formatting options, select Find What or Replace With, and then choose the No Formatting button until you end the editing session. (Each time you start Word 97, the dialog box appears with no formatting.)

You can use the shortcut keys for formatting characters and paragraphs in the Find and Replace dialog box. To specify bold formatting, for example, press Ctrl+B. To specify a font, press Ctrl+Shift+F repeatedly until the font you want is selected. See the reference card for a list of the shortcut keys.

Part

I

Ch

2

The Find and Replace feature in Word is flexible, enabling you to replace text regardless of formatting, to replace just formatting, or to replace both text and formatting. You also can replace text with nothing (that is, delete specified text) or remove formatting. Table 2.1 outlines replacement options available when you use the Find and Replace commands.

Table 2.1   Find and Replace Options

If You Replace	With	You Get
Text	Format	Old text and format, plus new format
Format or text and format	Format	Old text, new format
Text	Text and format	New text, old format, plus new format
Text	Nothing	Deleted text
Format or text and format	Nothing	Deleted text and formatting

Finding and Replacing Styles   A *style* is a combination of several formatting commands. You can have a style called Title, for example, that includes the formatting commands for Times New Roman font, 24-point size, centered, underlined, and bold. A style enables you to apply all these formats with a single command. You can use the Word Replace command to replace a format with a style or to replace one style with another. When you replace formatting or a style with a style, all paragraphs formatted by the replacement style take on its formatting.

▶ **See** "Creating Styles," **p. 147**

The procedure to replace a format with a style, or one style with another, is identical to the procedure you use for finding and replacing formats. When you choose the Format button and select Style in the Find and Replace dialog box, the Find Style or Replace Style dialog box displays all the defined styles (refer to Figure 2.9). When you select the style in the Find What Style or Replace With Style list, the formatting commands that compose the selected style appear below the list.

Finding and Replacing Special Characters

Finding and replacing text in your document is handy and easy. Sometimes, however, you want to search for and replace other items. You can find and replace many special characters, including a wildcard character (?), a tab mark, a paragraph mark, section marks, a blank space, and many more. If you open a text (or ASCII) file with carriage returns at the end of every line, for example, you can replace each of those paragraph marks with a space. Alternatively, if you have a list that contains spaces rather than tabs, you can replace those spaces with tabs. Always be careful to confirm your changes at least once so that you don't inadvertently make an incorrect replacement.

You can find or replace special characters by using the Special button in the Find and Replace dialog box or by using the keyboard. Table 2.2 lists the codes that you can type from the keyboard.

Table 2.2 Codes for Special Characters

Code	Special Character
^p	Paragraph mark (¶)
^t	Tab character (®)
^a	Comment mark (Find only)
^?	Any character (Find only)
^#	Any digit (Find only)
^$	Any letter (Find only)
^^	Caret character (^)
^n	Column break
^+	Em dash (—)
^=	En dash (–)
^e	Endnote mark (Find only)
^d	Field (Find only)
^f	Footnote mark (Find only)
^g	Graphic (Find only)
^l	Manual line break
^m	Manual page break
^~	Nonbreaking hyphen
^s	Nonbreaking space
^-	Optional hyphen

Code	Special Character
^b	Section break (Find only)
^w	Whitespace (any space—one space, multiple spaces, tab spaces—bordered by characters) (Find only)
^c	Clipboard contents (Replace only)
^&	Find What text (Replace only)
^0nnn	ANSI or ASCII characters (n is the character number) (Replace only)

To insert special codes by choosing the Special button, follow these steps:

1. Choose Edit, Find or Edit, Replace.
2. Select the Find What or Replace With text box.
3. Choose the Special button.
4. Select the command that you want to find or replace.

To insert special codes from the keyboard, follow these steps:

1. Choose Edit, Find or Edit, Replace.
2. Type the appropriate code in the Find What or the Replace With text box. Enter the caret character (^) by pressing Shift+6.
3. Choose the No Formatting button if you do not want the formats to affect the action of the Find or Replace command.

If you want to find or replace special characters, you should display nonprinting characters, such as paragraph marks and tab marks. To display nonprinting characters from the toolbar, click the Show/Hide ¶ button on the Standard toolbar.

To display nonprinting characters from the menu, follow these steps:

1. Choose Tools, Options.
2. Select the View tab.
3. Select the All check box in the Nonprinting Characters group.
4. Choose OK.

Checking Your Spelling

After you enter your text and you're fairly sure that the words are correct, check your document's spelling.

The Word spelling checker quickly pinpoints words in your document that don't match those in its or the user's dictionary, or in your own custom dictionary. When you aren't sure about a word, you can ask Word to suggest alternative spellings. The program searches its dictionary for a match and offers you a list of other spellings. It can even suggest a spelling as the most likely choice.

When automatic spell checking is turned on, Word uses a red wavy line to underline words it thinks are misspelled, which makes them easy to spot when you proofread your document. An icon of an open book with a red <u>X</u> also appears at the bottom-right portion of the screen indicating spelling errors in your document.

> **N O T E** The Word spelling checker also searches for several other problems: double words (*the the*), oddly capitalized words (*mY*), words that should be capitalized (*california*), and words that should be all capitals (*dos*). You also can set additional options in the Spelling dialog box. ▪

Spell checking begins at the beginning of your document and works through your document, checking its entire contents. You can check spelling in a smaller section of text by first selecting that area (it can be as little as a single word). Then you can check the spelling as usual.

A good spelling checker gives you the confidence of knowing that your work is accurate. However, be careful: No spelling checker can tell you when you have misused words, perhaps typing *for* when you mean *four*, or *thought* when the word should be *though*. A spelling checker is an important tool but cannot replace thorough proofreading.

Checking Your Document's Spelling Automatically

Word 97 automatically underlines misspelled words with a wavy red line. Spell checking and underlining occur as you type. Automatic spell checking works only when the feature is enabled. To turn on automatic spell checking, choose <u>T</u>ools, <u>O</u>ptions, select the Spelling tab, and then select the <u>A</u>utomatic Spell Checking check box. If you find that your system becomes unacceptably slow when using automatic spell checking, disable this option and use the command method of spell checking that is described in the next section.

To check spelling of words with a wavy underline, follow these steps:

1. Double-click the open book icon in the status bar at the bottom of the screen to find the next underlined word in the document. Or, right-click an underlined word.

    A pop-up menu appears showing a list of suggested words and additional options.

2. You have four choices for correcting the misspelled word:

    - Correct the word if it is misspelled.
    - Select a word from the list shown in the pop-up menu.
    - Select Ignore All to ignore all occurrences of the word in your document.
    - Select Add to add the word to the selected dictionary displayed in the Custom Dictionary in the Spelling dialog box.

3. Repeat this procedure for each word you want to check.

Using the Spelling Command to Check Spelling

To check spelling in your document using commands, follow these steps:

1. Select the word or section of your document that you want to check for spelling. If you select nothing, Word checks the entire document.

2. Choose Tools, Spelling and Grammar, or click the Spelling button on the Standard toolbar. Alternatively, press F7.

   Word scrolls through your document, matching each word against the main dictionary. The program selects words that it does not recognize, and the Spelling and Grammar dialog box appears. The unrecognized word is highlighted in the text and displayed in the Not In Dictionary box (see Figure 2.10). You can move the Spelling and Grammar dialog box if it is hiding the selected word.

FIG. 2.10

You can choose Spelling to find misspellings and typos throughout your document.

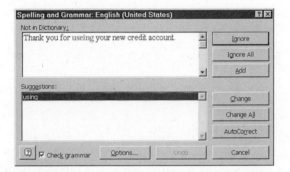

3. Select the correct word from the Suggestions list.

   If the Always Suggest Corrections option is turned on in the Spelling Options, and Word can suggest an alternative spelling, that suggestion appears in the Suggestions list. Other possible words appear in the Suggestions list. (For more information on using Always Suggest Corrections, see the section "Setting Spelling Options" later in this chapter.)

   If the Always Suggest Corrections option is turned off, the Suggestions list is empty. Press Alt+E to display a list of possible words, and then select the correct word from the list.

4. If the correct spelling appears in the Suggestions list, select the correct word from the Suggestions list, then choose the Change button. The selected word changes to the spelling displayed in the Suggestions list. Choose Change All to change all occurrences of the misspelled word in your document.

   Alternatively, choose Ignore to leave the word as is. Choose Ignore All to ignore all future occurrences of the word in your document.

   If Word finds a word that it thinks is misspelled and you want to add that word to the dictionary, choose the Add button. The program then adds the word to the selected dictionary displayed in the Custom Dictionary box.

5. Word continues searching. Choose Cancel to discontinue the spell checking. You also can undo as many as five previous corrections by choosing the Undo command.

6. A dialog box appears when the spell checker reaches the end of the document or the selection. If you are checking a word or a selected section, a dialog box asks whether you want to check the remainder of the document. Choose Yes or No.

If you start spell checking in the middle of the document, the spell checker completes checking of the document, then returns to the beginning and continues checking to the point at which you began.

You can halt the spelling check to edit your document without closing the Spelling and Grammar dialog box. Drag the Spelling and Grammar dialog box away from the area that you want to edit. Then click in the document or press Ctrl+Tab to activate the document window. After editing your document, choose the Resume button in the Spelling and Grammar dialog box to resume spell checking where you stopped. (If you're using a keyboard rather than a mouse, press Ctrl+Tab to reactivate the Spelling and Grammar dialog box.)

If no words in the Suggestions list are correct, you can edit the word from within the Not in Dictionary box. After you've edited the word, choose the Change button to update the document window, or choose the Undo Edit button to undo the spelling change.

You also can undo all spelling changes made during a spell check in two other ways. To undo all spelling changes from a menu command, choose Edit, Undo Spelling Change immediately after you complete the spell checking. To undo all spelling changes with the Undo button, follow these steps:

1. Click the Undo button on the Standard toolbar.
2. Drag down through all the Spelling edits.
3. Release the mouse button.

Correcting Double Words   When the Word spelling checker finds double words, the Not In Dictionary box changes to the Repeated Word box, and the repeated word is highlighted in red (see Figure 2.11).

To delete the repeated word, choose the Delete button. Be sure to delete unwanted spaces.

Adding Words to a Dictionary   The spell-checking process enables you to add words to a custom dictionary. When Word selects an unrecognized word that you use often, choose the dictionary to which you want to add it. Thereafter, the spell checker will bypass the word.

To add words to a custom dictionary, select a dictionary by choosing the Options button in the Spelling and Grammar dialog box. Select a dictionary from the Custom Dictionary list in the Spelling & Grammar tab of the Options dialog box, then click the OK button. Then choose the Add button in the Options dialog box.

> **CAUTION**
>
> Be careful not to accidentally add misspelled words to the dictionary. If you want to delete a misspelled word from a dictionary, use Windows WordPad to open the dictionary and delete the word. Dictionaries are located in the Proof folder, found in the C:\Program Files\Common Files\Microsoft Shared folder.

FIG. 2.11
Word indicates double occurrences during a spelling check.

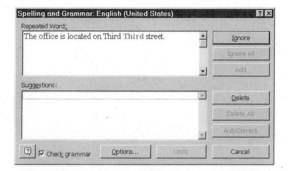

Setting Spelling Options

The Spelling and Grammar dialog box includes the <u>O</u>ptions button. Choosing this button enables you to use a non-English dictionary or to check spelling against a custom dictionary that you create. (See the next section for information on creating a custom dictionary.) The button also enables you to select automatic spell checking.

You can set options at any time by following these steps:

1. To set options before you check spelling, choose <u>T</u>ools, <u>O</u>ptions. Then select the Spelling & Grammar tab.

   To set options while checking spelling, choose the <u>O</u>ptions button in the Spelling and Grammar dialog box to open the Options dialog box. The Spelling & Grammar tab for adjusting spelling options appears (see Figure 2.12).

FIG. 2.12
In the Spelling & Grammar tab of the Options dialog box, you can customize a spelling check.

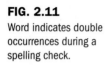

2. Under Spelling, select among the following options:

Option	Function
Check Spelling as You Type	Automatically identifies words not found in the dictionary by placing a red wavy line under each.
Hide Spelling Errors in This Document	Hides red wavy lines from beneath words not found in the dictionary.
Always Suggest Corrections	Word will always suggest corrections. Clear this option if you don't always want suggestions (and if you want the spelling checker to work faster).
Suggest from Main Dictionary Only	Suggestions will come from the Main dictionary only, not from any open custom dictionaries.
Ignore Words in UPPERCASE	Ignores words in all uppercase letters.
Ignore Words with Numbers	Ignores words that include numbers.
Ignore Internet and File Addresses	Ignores Internet and file addresses.

3. Choose the Dictionaries button to open the Custom Dictionaries dialog box (see Figure 2.13). As many as ten custom dictionaries can be open during a spelling check. You may have many custom dictionaries available. However, Word checks spelling against only custom dictionaries that are open.

FIG. 2.13

You can select a custom dictionary in the Custom Dictionaries dialog box.

4. Choose OK.

Creating a Custom Dictionary

Each time you run the spelling checker, it compares the words in your document with those in the dictionary. The Word 97 standard dictionary contains thousands of commonly used words. However, this dictionary may not include certain words that you frequently use—for example, terms specific to your profession, your company's name, or the names of products that your firm sells. You can create custom dictionaries and specify that Word 97 consult them each time you check spelling. To learn how to open these dictionaries so that Word uses them when you check spelling, see the preceding section, "Setting Spelling Options." To learn how to add words to your custom dictionary, refer to the earlier section, "Adding Words to a Dictionary."

To create a new custom dictionary, follow these steps:

1. Choose Tools, Options. Then select the Spelling & Grammar tab.
2. Choose the Dictionaries button.
3. Choose the New button in the Custom Dictionaries dialog box. A dialog box prompts you for the name of the dictionary file.
4. In the File Name box, type a name for the new dictionary ending with the extension **DIC**. Your dictionary is stored in the C:\Program Files\Common Files\Microsoft Shared\Proof folder. You can select another folder in which Word is to store the dictionary.
5. Choose Save.
6. To close the Custom Dictionaries dialog box, choose OK.
7. To close the Options dialog box, choose OK in the Spelling & Grammar tab.

You can edit or remove a word from a custom dictionary by selecting the dictionary in the Custom Dictionaries list in the Custom Dictionaries dialog box and then choosing the Edit button. Choose OK to close the Custom Dictionaries dialog box. Then choose OK to close the Options dialog box. The file lists all dictionary entries alphabetically. Delete the words that you no longer want or edit words that need changes. Then save the file in Text Only format (don't change the file's name or location).

The following table describes the options in the Custom Dictionaries group:

Option	Function
Edit	Makes changes to the custom dictionary that you select. You must confirm that you want to open the dictionary as a Word document. Word warns you that it will stop automatic spell checking when you edit a dictionary. You must select the Check Spelling as You Type check box to enable automatic spell checking. This check box is accessed by choosing Tools, Options, then selecting the Spelling & Grammar tab.
Add	Adds a custom dictionary from another directory or disk.

Option	Function
<u>R</u>emove	Removes a dictionary from the Custom <u>D</u>ictionaries list. You must select the dictionary before you can remove it.
Language	Adds language formatting to a custom dictionary. Word will use that custom dictionary only when checking the spelling of text formatted in that language. (See "Proofing in Other Languages" later in this chapter.) If you select (none), Word uses the dictionary to check spelling of text formatted in any language.

TROUBLESHOOTING

I tried to run the Spelling option, and a dialog box appeared indicating that Word 97 cannot locate that feature from the <u>T</u>ools menu. Many Word 97 features, such as the spelling checker, are optional during the Word 97 installation process. If a feature or command that you want to use is not installed, you can click Add/Remove Office Programs on the Office Shortcut bar menu, and then select the options you want. For example, select Proofing Tools if you want to install the spelling checker. You will need your installation CD-ROM or disks. To complete the installation process, follow the instructions that appear. If you do not use the full Office suite, follow your original installation procedure and select the Add/Remove button when the Setup dialog box appears. You will be given the opportunity to select features that are not installed.

Checking Your Grammar

While writing a document, you may be uncertain whether your sentence structure is grammatically correct. You might use the phrase *between you and I*, for example, when the grammatically correct version is *between you and me*. Use the Word grammar checker to spot grammatical errors and receive suggestions on how to correct them. The Spelling and Grammar dialog box provides several choices for making changes (see Figure 2.14).

FIG. 2.14
Use the grammar checker to flag possible errors in spelling and grammar.

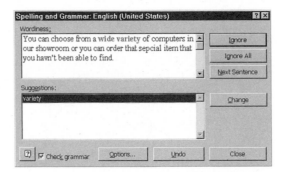

If you do not select any text before using the grammar checker, Word checks the entire document, beginning at the insertion point. If you select text, Word checks only the selection. A selection must contain at least one sentence.

By default, Word checks spelling and grammar. If you want to check only grammar, turn off the Check Grammar with Spelling option in the Spelling & Grammar tab of the Options dialog box. (To learn how to do this, see the upcoming section, "Selecting Grammar Rules.")

To check a document's grammar, follow these steps:

1. Choose Tools, Spelling and Grammar.

   The Spelling and Grammar dialog box appears when Word finds a sentence with a possible grammatical error or questionable style (refer to Figure 2.14). The grammatically questionable construction appears highlighted in the upper text box.

   If Word can offer any suggestions for replacement text, it lists them in the Suggestions text box. (If the Change button is grayed, the Grammar checker cannot suggest a change.) An explanation of the error or questionable style appears just above the upper text box. For a more detailed explanation, click the question mark located in the lower left corner of the Spelling and Grammar dialog box.

2. Correct the sentence by selecting a suggestion in the Suggestions box and then choosing the Change button.

   or

   Correct the sentence by editing it in the upper text box, then choosing the Change button.

   The grammar check resumes at the insertion point.

You also can choose from these Spelling and Grammar dialog box options:

Option	Function
Ignore	Ignores the questioned word or phrase.
Ignore All	Skips other similar occurrences that break the same grammar or style rule.
Undo Edit	Undoes all edits made in the upper text box.
Next Sentence	Leaves the sentence unchanged and moves to the next sentence.
Question Mark button	Provides more information about the error. A window appears describing the relevant grammar or style rule. After you read the information, click the window's X button to clear the window and return to the Spelling and Grammar dialog box.
Options	Selects different rules of grammar and style. The Spelling & Grammar Options tab that appears enables you to select an option button for the rule group that you want to observe for the remainder of the check. (See "Selecting Grammar Rules" later in this chapter.)

Part

I

Ch

2

After reaching the end of the document, the grammar checker continues checking from the beginning. When Word finishes checking the entire document, you see a message indicating that the grammar check is completed. Choose OK to return to your document.

If you select the Show Readability Statistics option in the Options dialog box, a dialog box displays the information about the document. (The section "Testing the Readability of a Document," later in this chapter, covers readability.) Choose OK to return to your document.

Selecting Grammar Rules

You can choose the rules of style and grammar that Word uses during grammar checks. Depending on your audience, your style, and the material, you may want to follow some rules and disregard others. Choose Tools, Options and select the Spelling & Grammar tab. You can then choose among five predefined rule groups: Casual, Standard, Formal, Technical, or Custom. Table 2.3 describes these rule groups. You also can create as many as three custom rule groups or customize the predefined rule groups by selecting or clearing grammar and style options.

Table 2.3 Grammar Checker's Rule Groups

Rule Group	Rules Applied
Casual	Only those rules appropriate for informal written communication (the fewest number of rules)
Standard	Only those rules appropriate for written business communication
Formal (all rules)	All grammar and style rules except gender-specific words
Technical	Only those rules appropriate for technical communication
Custom	Rules that you apply

To customize a rule group, follow these steps:

1. Choose Tools, Options and select the Spelling & Grammar tab. If you have already started grammar checking, choose the Options button in the Spelling and Grammar dialog box. The Spelling & Grammar tab of the Options dialog box appears (see Figure 2.15).
2. Select from the Writing Style list the rule group that you want to change.
3. Choose the Settings button. The Grammar Settings dialog box appears (see Figure 2.16).
4. If you base a custom rule group on an existing rule group, select the existing rule group from the Writing Style list.
5. Choose the Settings button and then select the check boxes for the rules that you want Word 97 to observe. Clear the check boxes for rules that you want Word to ignore.
6. Choose OK to return to the Options dialog box.
7. Choose OK to return to the document or grammar checking.

FIG. 2.15
Use the Spelling & Grammar tab in the Options dialog box to choose the grammatical rules and styles that you want to apply to your documents.

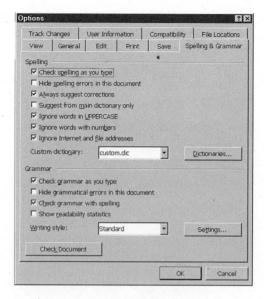

FIG. 2.16
You can customize the grammatical rules that Word 97 uses to check your document.

Testing the Readability of a Document

Readability statistics measure how easy your writing is to read. Writing that is easier to read communicates more clearly. *The Wall Street Journal*, for example, is written at the eighth-grade level. Hemingway wrote at the sixth-grade level. Writing need not be boring to be readable. To make his writing interesting, Hemingway used intriguing subject matter, active writing, colorful descriptions, and variable sentence lengths.

If you choose to display readability statistics, they appear at the end of grammar checking.

To display readability statistics after you use the Spelling and Grammar command, follow these steps:

1. Choose Tools, Options.
2. Select the Spelling & Grammar tab.
3. Select the Show Readability Statistics check box.
4. Choose OK.

The Word 97 readability statistics are based on the Flesch-Kincaid index. This index assigns a reading-ease score and grade level based on the average number of words per sentence and syllables per 100 words.

Using the Thesaurus

When you're not sure of a word's meaning, when you think you're using a certain term too often, or when you can't come up with the right word, take advantage of the Word 97 thesaurus. It defines selected words and offers alternative terms (synonyms). For example, Word 97 synonyms for the word *information* include *intelligence, data,* and *facts.*

The thesaurus looks up one word at a time. You can specify the word by selecting it. Otherwise, the thesaurus looks up the word that the insertion point indicates. If the insertion point is within a word, the thesaurus looks up that word. If the insertion point is outside a word, the thesaurus looks up the word preceding the insertion point.

To display a list of synonyms and definitions for a word in your document, follow these steps:

1. Select the word for which you want to locate a synonym.
2. Choose Tools, Language, Thesaurus, or press Shift+F7. The Thesaurus dialog box appears (see Figure 2.17).

FIG. 2.17

In the Thesaurus dialog box, you can find a list of meanings for almost any word you select.

The Looked Up text box displays the selected word. The Replace with Synonym text box displays the first synonym, followed by a list of other synonyms. The word's definition appears in the Meanings box.

3. You have several options:

Action	Result
Choose a synonym in the Replace with Synonym list.	The word moves into the Replace with Synonym box.
Select a different meaning from the Meanings list.	A new list of synonyms appears in the Replace With Synonym list. You can select a word from this list.
Select related words or antonyms in the Meanings list.	The Replace With Synonym list displays related words or antonyms.
Select the word from the Meanings or Replace with Synonym list, or type a word and choose Look Up.	Meanings of the new words appear.
Select the word from the Meanings or Replace with Synonym list, or type a word and choose Look Up.	Meanings of those new words appear.
Choose Previous.	The word that the thesaurus previously looked up appears.

4. Choose the Replace button to replace the selected word in the document with the word in the Replace with Synonym, Replace with Antonym, or Replace with Related Word box, or click the Cancel button.

Proofing in Other Languages

If you're reading the English language edition of this book, most of your typing is probably in this language. However, your document may contain some text in Spanish, French, or another language. You can select that text, assign to it a language other than English, and all the Word 97 proofing tools—the spell checker, hyphenation, thesaurus, and grammar checker—will use the other language dictionary that you specify to proof that text.

Before the Language command is available, you must purchase and install the appropriate language-proofing tools for the language you want to use. If you want to check the spelling of French text, for example, you must install a French dictionary. Contact Microsoft Corporation or other vendors for information on the many language-proofing tools available.

To proof text in another language, follow these steps:

1. Select the text written in another language.
2. Choose Tools, Language, Set Language to display the Language dialog box.

3. Select the language from the Mark Selected Text As list. To change the language for all the text that you proof, choose the Default button.

You can choose (no proofing) from the list if you want the proofing tools to skip the selected text. This feature is useful for technical material that contains terms not listed in any of the standard spelling dictionaries.

4. Choose OK.

Counting Words

The Tools, Word Count command counts the number of pages, words, characters, paragraphs, and lines in a document (see Figure 2.18). You can choose to include footnotes and endnotes in the count.

FIG. 2.18
The Word Count dialog box provides statistics about a document.

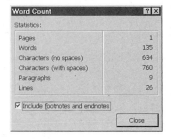

To use the word count feature for the document on-screen, follow these steps:

1. Choose Tools, Word Count. The Word Count dialog box appears. Word performs the count and displays the results.

2. Choose Include Footnotes and Endnotes if you want to include these items in the count. Word redoes the count and the new results appear.

3. Choose the Close button.

Inserting Frequently Used Material

The Word AutoText feature is like word-processing shorthand. It saves you time by storing selected text and graphics (and their formatting) that are used repeatedly. If you have a long company name that you frequently must type in documents, for example, you can abbreviate it as AutoText and insert it with only a few keystrokes. AutoText also ensures that repetitive material is typed correctly and consistently. If you create templates for standardized documents, you should consider including AutoText entries in the templates for frequently used words, phrases, formats, or pictures. (A *template* provides a guide or pattern for creating specific types of documents.)

▶ **See** "Using Templates and Wizards for Frequently Created Documents," **p. 3**

AutoText is not limited to text. It can contain pictures and graphics of digitized signatures, graphic letterheads, logos, or symbols. If you frequently use a table with special formatting, you can make it an AutoText entry.

Word 97 contains more than 40 predefined AutoText entries used frequently by most users. These entries include, among other things, letter closings (such as Sincerely or Best regards) and Mailing Instructions (such as Confidential and Via Airmail). To see the predefined entries, choose Insert, AutoText and scroll through the various menus for the predefined entries. Under certain conditions, the predefined entries may not be visible on the AutoText menu; "Inserting AutoText" later in this chapter discusses these conditions in detail and provides instructions for viewing all AutoText entries.

In the previous version of Word, AutoText was located on the Edit menu. AutoText can be found on the Insert menu in Word 97 and can also be accessed in the AutoCorrect dialog box (Tools, AutoCorrect).

Another new feature in Word 97 is the AutoText toolbar, which provides quick access to AutoText entries for mouse users.

Creating an AutoText Entry

You can use the AutoText command to store text or graphics as AutoText entries by choosing Insert, AutoText.

To create an AutoText entry, follow these steps:

1. Select the text, graphic, table, or combination of items that you want to add as an AutoText entry.

2. Choose Insert, AutoText, and then select New from the AutoText menu, or press Alt+F3. The Create AutoText dialog box appears (see Figure 2.19).

   Word suggests a name for your entry based on the selected text.

FIG. 2.19
Use the Create AutoText dialog box to create an AutoText entry.

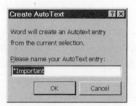

3. You can change the suggested name by deleting it and typing in a logical name for this entry.

   An AutoText entry name can contain spaces and special characters such as * or %. Try to keep AutoText entry names short to minimize the number of keystrokes needed to insert them.

If you type a name that is already in use for another entry, Word will warn you before you proceed.

4. Choose OK.

AutoText entries can be stored with the document template or with NORMAL.DOT (to make them accessible in all documents). Using the above method does not give you control over where your AutoText entry is stored (it is stored in the template that was last accessed by Word; that might be the document template *or* NORMAL.DOT).

To change the default storage location, follow these steps:

1. Choose Insert, AutoText, and then select AutoText from the AutoText menu. The AutoCorrect dialog box appears with the AutoText tab selected. A suggested name appears in the Enter AutoText Entries Here text box (see Figure 2.20).

2. Select the template you want in the Look In list box (select Normal or All Active Templates to store future entries in NORMAL.DOT), and then choose OK.

   The selected template will only remain as the default until another template is selected when inserting or creating an AutoText entry.

Storing an entry in NORMAL.DOT enables you to access the entry from any document. Storing an entry in a document template other than NORMAL.DOT will enable you to access the entry *only* when working in a document based on that template.

▶ **See** "Working with Templates," **p. 4**

To control the storage location when creating an AutoText entry, follow these steps:

1. Select the text, graphic, table, or combination of items that you want to add as an AutoText entry.

2. Choose Insert, AutoText, and then select AutoText from the AutoText menu. The AutoCorrect dialog box appears with the AutoText tab selected. A suggested name appears in the Enter AutoText Entries Here text box.

3. Type a name for your entry into the Enter AutoText Entries Here text box.

4. Select the template in which you want to store this entry in the Look In list box. Choose All Active Templates or NORMAL.DOT to make this entry available in all documents. Selecting a template other than NORMAL.DOT will make this entry *only* available in documents based on that template.

▶ **See** "Opening a New Document Based on a Template," **p. 9**

5. Choose Add. The entry is stored to the selected template. The AutoText entry is added and the AutoCorrect dialog box closes.

Depending on how the Word's Save options have been customized, you may or may not be prompted to save NORMAL.DOT after an AutoText entry has been added; Word may save it automatically. If you store an AutoText entry to a template other than NORMAL.DOT, Word will prompt you to save the template when you next save or close the document; at that time, you can choose to save the newly created entries or discard them.

FIG. 2.20
The AutoText tab of the AutoCorrect dialog box enables you to control where AutoText entries are stored.

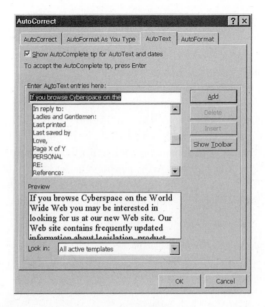

Part

I

Ch

2

Inserting AutoText

Once you've created an AutoText entry, it's easy to use it in your document.

To insert an AutoText entry into your text, follow these steps:

1. Position the insertion point where you want the AutoText entry to appear.
2. Type the abbreviation you gave the AutoText entry.
3. Press F3 (the Insert AutoText key).

When you press F3, Word replaces the AutoText abbreviation with the AutoText. (The AutoText abbreviation you type in your document must be at the beginning of a line or preceded by a space. Otherwise, the AutoText abbreviation will not be replaced with the AutoText.)

If you cannot remember the AutoText abbreviation, or if you want to insert one of the predefined AutoText entries, you can access a list of entries in the Insert menu.

To insert an AutoText entry from the Insert menu, follow these steps:

1. Position the insertion point where you want the AutoText entry to appear.
2. Choose Insert, AutoText. The AutoText menu appears.

▶ **See** "Opening a New Document Based on a Template," **p. 9**
▶ **See** "Applying Paragraph Styles," **p. 144**

Entries listed will depend on the currently selected style or template. For example, assume you are working in a letter. If the insertion point is positioned in a paragraph that is formatted with the Body Text style, you will see different options on this menu than you will see if the insertion point is in a paragraph that is formatted with the Normal style.

The selected option in the Look In list box on the AutoText tab of the AutoCorrect dialog box will also control what is displayed on the AutoText menu. For example, if you are working in a letter and All Active Templates has been selected in the Look In list box, and if you have positioned the insertion point within the salutation of the letter (so Salutation is the active style), various salutations will be displayed. However, if the letter template is the selected template in the Look In list box, different options will appear on the AutoText menu. You can change the selection in the Look In list box by choosing Insert, AutoText. Choose AutoText to display the AutoCorrect dialog box with the AutoText tab selected. Select the option you want in the Look In list box, and then choose OK.

N O T E   To list *all* AutoText entries on the AutoText menu, hold down Shift while pressing Alt+A to access AutoText or while clicking AutoText on the insert menu. ▪

3. Select the AutoText entry from the AutoText menu. The entry is inserted.

Understanding the AutoText Toolbar

You can use the AutoText toolbar to quickly create and insert AutoText entries.

To display the AutoText toolbar on-screen, choose View, Toolbars, and choose AutoText from the Toolbars menu. Figure 2.21 shows the AutoText toolbar displayed on the screen.

You can also display the toolbar by choosing Show Toolbar from the AutoText tab in the AutoCorrect dialog box.

To create an AutoText entry using the AutoText toolbar, select the text for your entry and click New on the AutoText toolbar. Enter the name for your entry and choose OK.

 T I P   You can press Alt+N to access the New option on the AutoText toolbar.

To insert an entry using the AutoText toolbar, click "All Entries." In Figure 2.21, the AutoText toolbar menu reads All Entries. However, the wording of this menu may vary depending on the selected style or template. To see all AutoText entries, hold down Shift and then click the toolbar menu. Click the AutoText you want inserted.

You can display the AutoText tab of the AutoCorrect dialog box by clicking the AutoText icon on the AutoText toolbar.

FIG. 2.21
The AutoText toolbar provides quick access to AutoText entries.

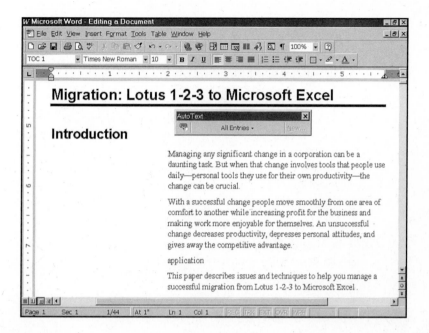

Deleting AutoText

You may want to delete an AutoText entry if you no longer use it.

To delete an AutoText entry, follow these steps:

1. Choose Insert, AutoText and choose AutoText from the AutoText menu, or click the AutoText icon on the AutoText toolbar.

2. Type the name of the AutoText entry you want to delete in the Enter AutoText Entries Here text box, or select the name from the list.

3. Choose the Delete button.

You may or may not be prompted to save NORMAL.DOT after an AutoText entry has been deleted; if you have set up Word to automatically save NORMAL.DOT, you will not be prompted. If you delete an AutoText entry from a template other than NORMAL.DOT, Word will prompt you to save the template when you next save or close the document; at that time, you can choose to either save the changes you made or discard them.

Using AutoComplete

A new feature in Word 97 is the AutoComplete tip. If you select this option, Word will suggest a complete word or phrase when you type the first three or more letters of a common item, such as a date (day of the week or month) or an AutoText entry.

To turn on and use AutoComplete, follow these steps:

1. Choose Insert, AutoText and choose AutoText from the AutoText menu, or click the AutoText icon on the AutoText toolbar. The AutoCorrect dialog box appears with the AutoText tab selected.

2. Select Show AutoComplete Tip for AutoText and Dates.

3. Type a date or the beginning of an AutoText entry name into your document. A tip will appear as soon as Word recognizes the text as a date or AutoText entry.

   When you type the name of an AutoText entry that is three characters or longer, the tip will display the first several words of the entry; press Enter to insert the suggested entry. Tips are not displayed for entry names of fewer than three characters.

4. Press Enter (or F3) to accept the suggested text or continue typing to ignore it.

Printing AutoText Entries

If you do not use certain AutoText entries regularly, you may soon forget what the abbreviation in the AutoText list does. To see a more complete view of each AutoText entry, including its format, print a list of AutoText entries.

To print a list of AutoText entries, follow these steps:

1. Open a document based on the template containing the AutoText entries.

2. Choose File, Print, and select AutoText Entries from the Print What drop-down list box.

3. Choose OK.

▶ **See** "Using Templates as a Pattern for Documents," **p. 8**

Correcting Spelling Errors as You Type

Almost every typist makes at least one or two typing mistakes frequently. The Word AutoCorrect feature recognizes common typing mistakes and automatically substitutes the correct spelling for you. You also can use AutoCorrect to automatically type long words from an abbreviation. You could use AutoCorrect to automatically type the phrase **not applicable**, for example, every time you type the abbreviation **na**.

The AutoCorrect feature can also correct accidental usage of the Caps Lock key, automatically capitalize the first word of every sentence, and automatically capitalize the names of days of the week.

N O T E As you type, you may see words with a wavy red underline. These words do not appear in Word's spelling dictionary. You can right-click them to display a list of suggested corrections. ■

Creating AutoCorrect Entries

You can create AutoCorrect entries in two ways:

- You can manually add entries using menu commands.
- You can add an AutoCorrect entry while you perform a spelling check.

Adding AutoCorrect Entries with Menu Commands   To add an AutoCorrect entry using the menu commands, follow these steps:

1. Choose Tools, AutoCorrect. Word displays the AutoCorrect dialog box with the AutoCorrect tab selected.

   Select the AutoCorrect tab if it is not selected.

2. In the Replace text box, type the misspelling or abbreviation that you want to have corrected automatically.

3. In the With text box, type the correct spelling of the word or phrase (see Figure 2.22).

TIP Select long phrases in the document before accessing the AutoCorrect dialog box to have Word automatically insert the selected text into the With text box.

FIG. 2.22

Use the AutoCorrect dialog box to create new AutoCorrect entries and to set the AutoCorrect options.

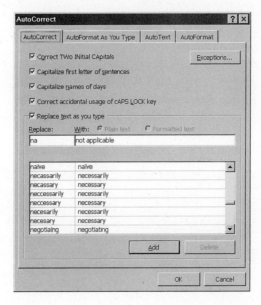

4. Choose Add to add the new entry to the list of AutoCorrect entries.

   If an AutoCorrect entry of the same name as that in the Replace text box already exists, the Add button will read Replace. Word will prompt you for confirmation before replacing the selection. Choose Yes to replace the existing entry, or No to cancel the action; you can then type a different AutoCorrect entry name in the Replace text box.

5. Choose OK.

Part

I

Ch

2

To have AutoCorrect automatically replace the misspelling or abbreviation with the correct spelling or complete phrase, make sure to select the Replace Text as You Type option.

You cannot use the Enter key within the AutoCorrect dialog box (pressing Enter activates the OK button). If your phrase contains a paragraph return, you must select the text prior to selecting the AutoCorrect dialog box. Word will insert the phrase and the return(s) into the With text box.

AutoCorrect entries are limited to 255 characters. If you need a longer phrase, you can use AutoText along with the AutoComplete feature to create an effective shortcut (see "Using AutoComplete" in the previous section).

Adding AutoCorrect Entries During a Spelling Check   You also can add AutoCorrect entries as you perform spelling checks on your document. To add an AutoCorrect entry during a spelling check, follow these steps:

1. Choose Tools, Spelling and Grammar, to start the spelling check if you have not already done so.

2. Choose the AutoCorrect button to add the misspelled word in the Not in Dictionary: text box and the selected spelling in the Suggestions list box to the list of AutoCorrect entries.

    You can only add entries from the Suggestions list box to AutoCorrect. If you type in a correction, it cannot be added.

    If an AutoCorrect entry of the same name as that in the Suggestions list box already exists, Word will prompt you and ask if you want to redefine the entry. Choose Yes to replace the existing entry, or No to correct the spelling in the document, but not to create an AutoCorrect entry.

3. Continue the spelling check.

Using AutoCorrect

The AutoCorrect feature works automatically as you type, without any special actions on your part. AutoCorrect offers several options that you can change to suit your working style and preferences.

To change the AutoCorrect options, follow these steps:

1. Choose Tools, AutoCorrect. The AutoCorrect dialog box appears (refer to Figure 2.22).

2. Choose any combination of the available options. Each option is described in the following table:

Option	Result	Example
Correct TWo INitial CApitals	Changes the second of two capital letters at the beginning of a word to lowercase	"THe" becomes "The"
Capitalize First Letter of Sentences	Changes the first letter of a word beginning a sentence to uppercase	"now is the time..." becomes "Now is the time..."
Capitalize Names of Days	Capitalizes the first letter of names of days of the week	"monday" becomes "Monday"
Correct Accidental Usage of cAPS LOCK key	Corrects the case of text accidentally typed while the Caps Lock key is on (automatically turns off the Caps Lock key after the first correction)	"wORD FOR wINDOWS" becomes "Word for Windows"
Replace Text as You Type	Replaces misspelled words with correct spellings, based on the list of entries maintained by AutoCorrect	"teh" becomes "the"

Word performs the corrections listed in the Result column when the spacebar is pressed after a word is completed.

Creating AutoCorrect Exceptions

Sometimes you will have words that should not be capitalized, even if they appear at the beginning of a sentence. For example, you will often have abbreviations that end in periods that you do not want capitalized. You may also have exceptions for "Correct TWo INitial Capitals," such as trademarked names that may use nonstandard capitalization. To accommodate these, you can set up exceptions in the AutoCorrect Exceptions dialog box.

To set up exceptions, follow these steps:

1. Choose Tools, AutoCorrect. The AutoCorrect dialog box appears (refer to Figure 2.22).
2. Choose Exceptions. The AutoCorrect Exceptions dialog box appears (see Figure 2.23).

FIG. 2.23

Use the AutoCorrect Exceptions dialog box to keep Word from correcting certain abbreviations and spellings.

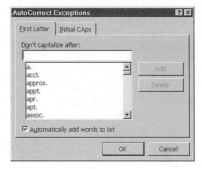

3. To prevent Word from capitalizing a first letter, select the First Letter tab.

4. Type the exception into the Don't Capitalize After text box and choose Add.

   If you want to set up an exception for initial caps, select the INitial CAps tab. Type the exception into the Don't Correct text box and choose Add.

5. Select Automatically Add Words To list if you would like Word to automatically add words to the exceptions list.

   Words are added to the exception list if you use Backspace to erase the word immediately after a correction is made by AutoCorrect, and then you retype the original word into the document.

   If you use Edit, Undo (or press Ctrl+Z), Word will restore the original word, but will *not* add it to the exceptions list.

6. When you are finished adding exceptions, choose OK.

Deleting an AutoCorrect Entry or Exception

Occasionally, you may want to remove an AutoCorrect entry because you no longer use an abbreviation or because the AutoCorrect entry conflicts with a legitimately spelled word (it doesn't always make sense to have AutoCorrect replace misspellings such as *tow* for *two*, because *tow* is actually a correctly spelled word). Likewise, you may find that you want to remove an exception from the Exceptions list.

To delete an AutoCorrect entry, follow these steps:

1. Choose Tools, AutoCorrect to display the AutoCorrect dialog box.

2. Select the entry you want to delete in the list at the bottom of the dialog box.

3. Choose the Delete button.

4. Choose OK.

When you choose Delete, Word leaves the deleted entry in the Replace and With text boxes. If you decide you would rather not delete this entry, simply choose Add to once again add this item to the list.

To delete an AutoCorrect exception, follow these steps:

1. Choose Tools, AutoCorrect to display the AutoCorrect dialog box.
2. Choose Exceptions to display the AutoCorrect Exceptions dialog box.
3. Select either the First Letter or INitial CAps tab.
4. Select the entry you want to delete in the list at the bottom of the dialog box.
5. Choose the Delete button.
6. Choose OK.

Part

I

Ch

2

Previewing and Printing a Document

Previewing Pages Before Printing

Word offers you two alternatives for viewing your document before you print. These alternatives are the Page Layout and Print Preview views.

In Page Layout view, you can select text or graphics and enclose the selected item in a frame, and then drag the text or graphics to new locations. You can also drag page breaks to new locations.

The primary advantage of using the Print Preview view is the Preview screen's toolbar, which contains convenient buttons for zooming and displaying multiple pages.

Using Page Layout View

Different document views in Word show different perspectives on your margins. In Normal view, you don't see the margins, but you see the space between them where your text appears. In Page Layout view, you see the page as it will print, margins and all. Select this view if you want to see headers, footers, page numbers, footnotes, and anything else that appears within the margins.

At the left of the horizontal scroll bar are three buttons offering different views of documents. (If your horizontal scroll bar is not displayed, choose Tools, Options, select the View tab, and in the Window group, select Horizontal Scroll Bar.) The Standard toolbar includes a button that displays the Print Preview view. Table 3.1 summarizes the effects of the document view icons.

Table 3.1   Effects of Document View Icons

Button	Name	Effect
	Normal	Displays a document in Normal view.
	Online Layout	Displays a document in Online Layout view.
	Page Layout	Displays a document in Page Layout view.
	Outline	Displays a document in Outline view.
	Print Preview	Displays a document in Print Preview view.

To view the document in Page Layout view, follow these steps:

1. Open the document you want to preview.
2. Choose View, Page Layout (if you haven't already selected the command). Alternatively, click the Page Layout button in the horizontal scroll bar.
3. If you want, adjust the magnification by choosing View, Zoom.

To return to Normal view, choose View, Normal or click the Normal button at the left of the horizontal scroll bar.

Using Print Preview

The other method of seeing how your document will print is to use the Print Preview view.

To see the entire document in print preview, you first must open the document you want to preview. Then choose File, Print Preview or click the Print Preview button on the Standard toolbar. You then see a screen like the one shown in Figure 3.1.

FIG. 3.1
Display a screen representation of your printed document by using the Preview screen.

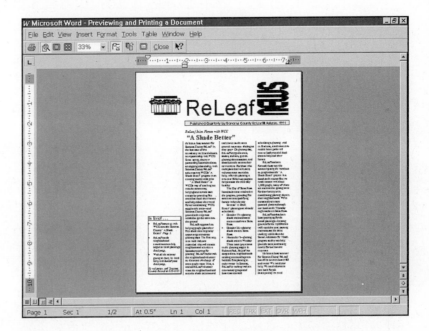

Part

I

Ch

3

Across the top of the Preview screen is a toolbar with buttons that make it easier to work with your document in Print Preview. You can use the buttons on the toolbar to perform the actions listed in Table 3.2.

Table 3.2 Preview Screen Buttons

Button	Name	Effect
🖨	Print	Prints the document using the printing options set in the Print dialog box.
🔍	Magnifier	Toggles the mouse pointer between a magnifying glass (for examining the document) and the normal mouse pointer (for editing the document).

continues

Table 3.2 Continued

Button	Name	Effect
	One Page	Displays document in single-page view.
	Multiple Pages	Displays document in multiple-page view.
41% ▾	Zoom Control	Displays a list box of zoom magnification percentages and options.
	View Ruler	Toggles the ruler display on and off.
	Shrink to Fit	When the last page of the document contains very little text, it tries to "shrink" the document to fit on one less page.
	Toggle Full Screen	Toggles between full-screen display (which View removes everything but the document and the toolbar) and normal display.
Close	Close Preview	Returns to your document.
▶?	Context-Sensitive Help	Provides context-sensitive help.

In Print Preview, you also have access to the normal, page layout, and outline icons at the extreme left of the horizontal scroll bar (if the bar is displayed). Clicking any of these buttons closes the preview screen and displays the document in the view mode you selected.

You can move around in the document in the Preview screen by using your keyboard's Page Up and Page Down keys and the scroll bars. When the rulers are displayed, you adjust margins in the same manner as in Page Layout view. You can also edit the document.

To edit a document in Print Preview, follow these steps:

1. Click the Magnifier button on the Standard toolbar. The mouse pointer changes to a magnifying lens.
2. Click the part of the document you want to edit. Word displays the document at 100 percent magnification.
3. Click the Magnifier button again to restore the normal Word mouse pointer.
4. Edit the document, revising text and repositioning margins on the page.

After you make your changes, you can reduce the document to the previous magnification by clicking the Magnifier button again and then clicking the document with the magnifying glass icon.

Printing from Print Preview　You can print all or part of your document from the Print Preview screen. To do so, you can use the Standard toolbar's Print button or the Print dialog box.

To print using the Standard toolbar, click the Print button to print the document using the current print settings. (The Print dialog box does not appear when you click this toolbar button.)

To print using the Print dialog box, follow these steps:

1. Choose File, Print.
2. Make the appropriate printing selections in the Print dialog box.
3. Choose OK.

Viewing One or Two Pages　You can view as many as 18 pages at once in 640×480 resolution— although you might not find it practical to display more than six or eight at the same time.

To view multiple pages, follow these steps:

1. Click the Standard toolbar's Multiple Pages button.
2. Move the mouse pointer over the upper-left portion of the grid that appears below the Multiple Pages button.
3. Drag the mouse pointer down and to the right until the highlighted portion of the grid reflects the number of pages you want to display. If you continue dragging, the grid expands to display additional pages to a maximum of three rows and six columns in 640×480 resolution.
4. Release the mouse button. The Preview screen now displays the arrangement of pages that the grid represented when you released the button.

To change back to single-page view again, click the Standard toolbar's One Page button.

Canceling or Closing the Print Preview Screen　To return to your editable document, click Close Preview from the Standard toolbar.

Printing the Current Document

The simplest way to print is to open a document and choose File, Print. By default, Word prints one copy of all pages of the currently open document on the currently selected printer without printing hidden text.

To print one copy of a document, follow these steps:

1. Open the document you want to print.
2. Choose File, Print or press Ctrl+Shift+F12. The Print dialog box appears.
3. Choose OK. The Print dialog box closes, and a printer icon in the status bar displays the process of the print job.

Part

I

Ch

3

To cancel printing while the Print icon is displayed, follow these steps:

1. Press Esc.

2. When the Windows 97 printer icon appears in the taskbar, you can double-click it to open the Printers folder.

3. Select the document you want to cancel printing, and then choose Document, Cancel Printing. If the Printer icon is no longer displayed in the Windows taskbar, Word may have already sent the print job to the printer.

You can bypass the Print dialog box and print your document quickly by clicking the Print button on the Standard toolbar. Word prints your document using settings previously selected in the Print dialog box.

Printing the Current Web Page

As you view or create World Wide Web pages in Word, you may want to print them. Use the same process you would use to print a Word document. While the HTML page (Web page) is active, choose File, Print Preview to see a preview like that shown in Figure 3.2. For more information on using Word to create web pages, see Chapter 51, "Creating Word Documents for the Web."

FIG. 3.2

See a preview of how the Web page will print using Word's File, Print Preview command.

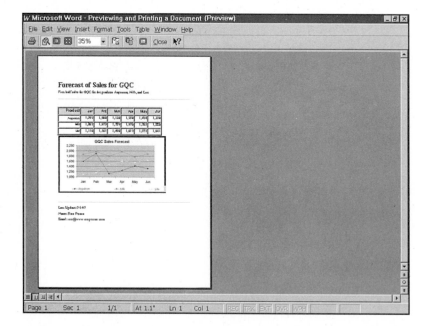

Print your Web pages as you would a normal Word document by pressing the File, Print command or the Print button on the Standard toolbar. You will find that many Web pages appear better on-screen than they do printed. If you need a higher-quality print, see if the Web page can be downloaded as a Word DOC file or an Adobe Acrobat PDF file.

Printing Multiple Copies

With Word's Print dialog box, you can print more than one copy of your document. In fact, you can print 32,767 copies of your document (but you may want to plan a trip to Hawaii while all those copies print). By default, Word collates the copies—a handy feature for long documents.

To print multiple copies of your document, follow these steps:

1. Open the document you want to print.

2. Choose File, Print, or press Ctrl+Shift+F12. The Print dialog box appears (see Figure 3.3).

FIG. 3.3

You can print multiple copies of your document by changing the number in the Number of Copies box of the Print dialog box.

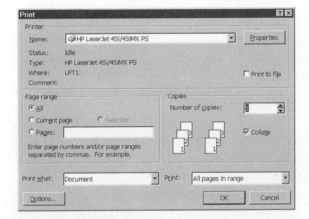

Part

I

Ch

3

3. Select the Number of Copies box in the Print dialog box and enter the number of copies you want to print. (Alternatively, use the increment/decrement arrows to increase or decrease the specified number of copies.)

4. Choose OK.

If print time is important, you can deselect the Collate option in the bottom-right corner of the dialog box. This step enables Word to run multiple documents through the printer faster. You pay for choosing this option later, however, when you have to collate all the copies by hand.

Printing Part of a Document

Word provides two ways to print part of a document. You can select the portion of your document you want to print and then choose File, Print. You can also print by indicating specific page numbers in various ways. Also, you can print on both sides of the paper even if you don't have a duplex printer. Printing a selected area is useful when you want to print a section of a larger document but don't know on which page or pages the section is located.

To print a selected area of text, follow these steps:

1. Select the text to print.

2. Choose File, Print, or press Ctrl+Shift+F12.

3. Choose the <u>S</u>election option in the Page Range area of the dialog box.

4. Choose OK.

If you know exactly which pages you want to print, you can print a range of pages. Suppose you make changes to the first three pages of a long document. In that case, you might want to print from pages 1–3.

To print a specific range of pages, follow these steps:

1. Choose <u>F</u>ile, <u>P</u>rint or press Ctrl+Shift+F12.

2. In the Pages box of the Page Range area, enter the range of pages you want to print. (For instance, to print pages 1 through 3, enter **1–3**.)

3. Choose OK.

In the Pages box, you can specify multiple page ranges (such as **1–7,8–13,14–20**) or multiple discontinuous pages (**1,2,8,13**). You can combine ranges with individual page numbers, as shown in Figure 3.4.

FIG. 3.4

Enter groups of page ranges and selected pages in the Pages box of the Print dialog box.

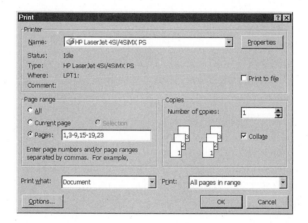

You can also print pages in a certain section. To print the second section in your document, type **s2** in the Pages box. If you want to print from page 7 in the second section to page 10 in the third section, type **p7s2–p10s3** in the Pages box.

In a long document, it's sometimes helpful to simply print the page on which you're working. To do so, follow these steps:

1. Position the insertion point on the page you want to print.

2. Choose <u>F</u>ile, <u>P</u>rint, or press Ctrl+Shift+F12.

3. Choose Curr<u>e</u>nt Page.

4. Choose OK.

If you want to print on both sides of the paper and don't have a duplex printer, you should print the odd-numbered pages in one print run and the even-numbered pages in another. To print only the odd- or even-numbered pages, follow these steps:

1. Choose File, Print or press Ctrl+Shift+F12.

2. In the Print box, select the Odd Pages or Even Pages option.

3. Choose OK.

Printing Different Types of Document Information

Word documents contain associated information such as document properties, field codes, and data for forms. You can print this information with the document or separately. The first method that this section presents describes how to print the ancillary hidden information with the document. The second method describes how to print the hidden information separately.

Word enables you to include the following hidden attributes as part of your printed document:

- Document properties
- Hidden text
- Field codes
- Drawing objects
- Comments

To print hidden information with your document, follow these steps:

1. Choose Tools, Options, then select the Print tab if it is not already displayed (see Figure 3.5).

FIG. 3.5
Choose Tools, Options and display the Print tab to specify a variety of printing options, including printing "nondisplaying" information when you print the document.

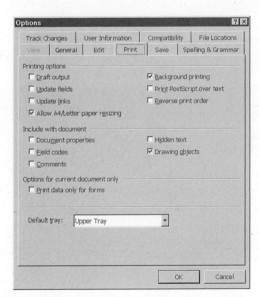

Part
I

Ch
3

2. In the Include with Document Print options, select the options you want to print (see Table 3.3). If you choose Comments, for example, Word prints a list of the comments associated with your document. (You can use this option to display a list of the comments that a reviewer has made to your document.)

3. Choose OK.

Table 3.3   Include Associated Document Information with Document

Option	Effect
Document properties	Prints a summary of information about the document—including author, subject, print date, and number of pages, words, and characters—on separate pages at the end of the document.
Field Codes	Prints field codes rather than their results.
Comments	Prints at the end of the document a list of comments that reviewers have attached to your document, with page number headings indicating where each comment occurs.
Hidden Text	Prints any hidden text, such as table of contents entries, where text appears in document.
Drawing Objects	Prints drawing objects you created in Word.

Alternatively, you can print hidden information separately from the document itself, although you can select only one of the following items at a time:

- Document properties
- AutoText entries
- Comments
- Key assignments
- Styles

To print only a document's hidden information without printing the document, follow these steps:

1. Choose File, Print.

2. Select Print What to open the drop-down list.

3. Select one of the options from the list.

4. Choose OK.

Controlling Printing Options

Word offers you many printing options. You can print the pages in reverse order or save time by printing a draft copy (on some printers). You can print text that usually is hidden, separately or as part of your document. You can update fields as you print, or you can print on paper from a specified bin if your printer has more than one paper source.

To set printing options, follow these steps:

1. Choose Tools, Options, and select the Print tab.
2. Select the desired options.
3. Choose OK.

The following sections describe the available printing options.

Printing a Draft

Sometimes you need a quick, plain printed copy of your document. Perhaps someone else must edit the copy, or you want to take the copy home from work to review. For a quick, unadorned print, choose a draft copy. A *draft* prints quickly without formatting. Word underlines enhanced characters instead of boldfacing or italicizing them, and prints graphics as empty boxes. (The exact result of a draft print depends on your printer. For example, a Hewlett-Packard LaserJet prints formatted text but no graphics in Draft mode, but a PostScript printer does not support Draft mode.)

If you select draft printing as your default, all printing is in Draft mode until you deselect that option. Alternatively, on some printers, you can print in Draft mode only once without changing the default (this option is not available for laser printers).

To select draft as your default print-quality mode, follow these steps:

1. Choose Tools, Options. Select the Print tab.
2. In the Print tab of the Options dialog box, select the Draft Output check box.
3. Choose OK.

To print a draft copy of a document one time using a dot-matrix printer, follow these steps:

1. Choose File, Print.
2. In the Print dialog box, choose Options. The Options dialog box appears with the Print tab opened.
3. In the Printing Options area, select Draft Output.
4. Choose OK.
5. In the Print dialog box, choose OK.

Part
I

Ch
3

Printing Pages in Reverse Order

Some printers have a collator that produces printed pages stacked in the correct order. Other printers stack pages with the last page on top. If your printer stacks with the last page on top, you might want to select the Reverse Print Order option to stack your pages in the correct order.

To print in reverse order, select the Reverse Print Order check box in the Print tab of the Options dialog box; then choose OK.

Updating Fields

Word files can include field codes that instruct Word to insert special information into the document. A date field, for example, inserts the current date when Word prints the document. But some fields cannot be updated during the printing process. To update those fields when you print, you must choose a special option. In most cases, you want this option turned on.

To update fields when you print, select the Update Fields check box in the Print tab of the Options dialog box. Choose OK.

▶ **See** "Viewing Fields," **p. 348**

Updating Links

The Update Links option updates any linked information in the document before printing. To update links before you print, select the Update Links check box in the Print tab of the Options dialog box. Then choose OK.

Background Printing

The Background Printing option enables you to continue working in Word while you print a document. To print in the background while performing other operations in Word, select the Background Printing check box in the Print tab of the Options dialog box. Then choose OK.

Printing Form Input Data Only

If you have entered data into fields on a form, printing only the input data might make it easier to compare the data in Word to the source document. To print the input data only, select the Print Data Only for Forms check box in the Print tab of the Options dialog box. Then choose OK.

Selecting the Paper Source

If you want to always print from a particular bin on your printer, you can change the default paper source. To do so, follow these steps:

1. Choose Tools, Options.
2. In the Print tab of the Options dialog box, choose Default Tray to open the drop-down list (see Figure 3.6).
3. Select the paper source by selecting the option you want from the Default Tray list box.

FIG. 3.6

You can change the paper source with the Default Tray option in the Print tab.

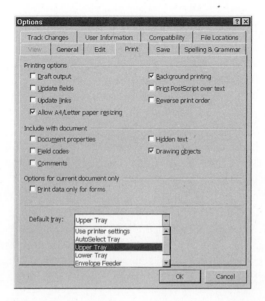

You also can set the paper source for your document by choosing File, Page Setup; selecting the Paper Source tab; and selecting the First Page and Other Pages options.

In most single-bin laser printers, you can slide your letterhead into the manual tray as far as the letterhead goes and leave your bond paper in the paper bin. After you choose OK from the Print dialog box, the printer first pulls in the letterhead and then pulls in the bond for following sheets. As a result, on printers such as the HP LaserJet Series II, III, or IV, you do not need to go through a series of steps. Just print.

Printing Multiple Unopened Documents

Occasionally, you might want to print an unopened document or several documents simultaneously. File, Print in the Windows Explorer enables you to open and print several documents at once.

To print one (or more) unopened documents, follow these steps:

1. Right-click the Start menu, and choose Explore to open the Explorer. If you prefer to use My Computer, open a window into My Computer.

2. Select the files you want to print. Click the first file; then hold down the Shift key, and click the last file to select contiguous files. Or, click the first file, then Ctrl+click other files to select non-contiguous files.

3. Move the pointer over a selected file and right-click to display the Send To shortcut menu.

4. Select the printer or fax where you want to send the files.

Part

I

Ch

3

Printing to a File

Someday you might need to print a Word document from a printer that doesn't have Word installed. You have two options. You can take a copy of the Word Viewer, a free subset of Word that displays and prints DOC files, or you can print the document to a printer file and take this printer file with you. The printer file you create must be made for the printer you will actually print on.

 TIP Before you create a Word document that will be sent to a typesetter, check with the typesetter to learn the fonts that are compatible with their typesetting equipment. Some typesetters can suggest alternative fonts that can be substituted in the original Word document.

One use for printing to a file is when you need a Word document typeset. To create a print file for typesetting, set up Word for a PostScript printer, usually a Linotronic printer, to a file. You can then take the resulting encapsulated PostScript (EPS) file to a printer (or service bureau) to be printed on a Linotronic typesetting machine for high-quality documents. Try a test file with the printer before you get down to a deadline. In some cases, alternative settings or the original DOC file may be needed.

Another use for printing to a file is to create a file you can print on a computer that has no copy of Word. If you create the file for that model of printer, you can open an MS-DOS window and use the DOS COPY command to copy the Word file to the LPT1 printer port. The file prints even though Word is not running.

To print the resulting printer file to a printer without using Word, open a DOS window by clicking Start, Programs, MS-DOS Prompt. In the DOS window use the CD, Change Directory, command to change to the folder (directory) where you saved the printer file created by Word. If your printer is connected to the LPT1 port, you will enter a command such as

```
COPY LETTER.PRN LTP1:
```

CAUTION

When you create a print file, Word must be set up for the specific printer that will be used to print the file. The print file contains the same codes and printer commands that would have been sent to the printer. The print file cannot be edited in Word.

To print to a file, ensure that Word is set up for the printer to be used to print the file, then follow these steps:

1. Choose File, Print.
2. Select the Print to File option, and then choose OK.

   The Print to File dialog box appears.
3. Change to the folder where you want to save the printer file. In the File Name box, type the name of the file to contain the document. Then choose OK.

When you want to resume printing to your printer, deselect the Print to File option in the Print dialog box.

N O T E You can create a text file easily in Word. Just choose File, Save As; then select the Save as Type pull-down list and select one of the text file format files that Word creates. In most cases, you should choose the Text Only (*.TXT) format. ▨

Styling Your Word Documents

Formatting Lines and Paragraphs

Understanding Paragraph Formats

In Word, a paragraph is a formatting unit. Just as you format individual characters with character formatting options, such as bold and italic, you can format paragraphs with paragraph, tab, and border formatting options, such as the following:

- *Alignment.* Line up the text of a paragraph to the left, center, right, or both margins.
- *Indents.* Indent the left edge, right edge, or first line of a paragraph.
- *Tabs.* Create columns of text that line up perfectly and can be adjusted easily.
- *Spacing.* Add spaces between lines and paragraphs.
- *Lines, borders, and shading.* Add graphic interest to paragraphs with lines next to paragraphs, borders surrounding paragraphs, and shading to fill borders.

New paragraphs formed when you press Enter carry over the formatting from the previous paragraph. After you format a paragraph, you can continue that format into subsequent paragraphs simply by pressing Enter (see Figures 4.1 and 4.2).

FIG. 4.1

The formatting is specified in the first paragraph of this document.

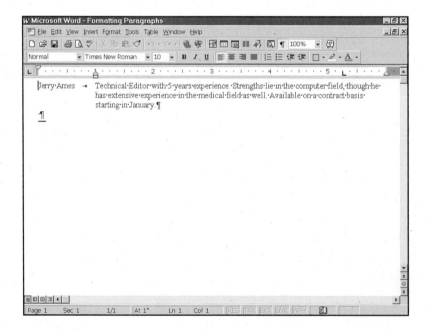

Paragraph formatting affects the entire paragraph and is stored in the paragraph mark that ends each paragraph. If you delete the paragraph mark between paragraphs, the text preceding the mark becomes part of the following paragraph. What was the second paragraph takes on the formatting of the first paragraph, as shown in Figures 4.3 and 4.4.

FIG. 4.2
When you press Enter, the paragraph formatting is carried forward to the new paragraph. Paragraph formatting is stored in the paragraph marks, shown in this figure.

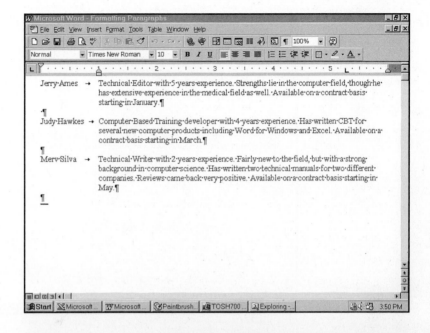

FIG. 4.3
Display paragraph marks to avoid accidentally including them with selected text.

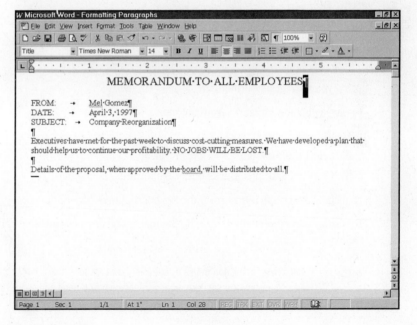

Part

II

Ch

4

FIG. 4.4

Delete the paragraph mark between paragraphs and the following paragraph takes on the format and style of the first.

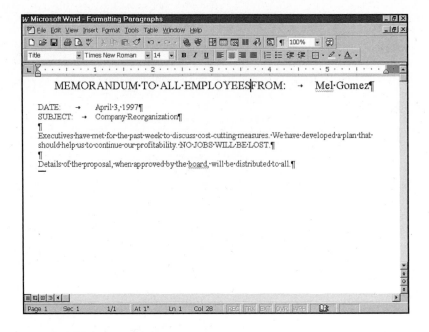

Displaying Paragraph Marks

When paragraph marks are hidden, you don't see them at the end of a paragraph. You can display paragraph marks, however (refer to Figure 4.4). If you expect to do much text editing, you should display paragraph marks to avoid accidentally deleting one of them and thereby losing your paragraph formatting.

To display paragraph marks from the menu, follow these steps:

1. Choose Tools, Options.
2. Select the View tab.
3. Choose Paragraph Marks under Nonprinting characters.

To display paragraph marks from the keyboard, press Ctrl+Shift+8.

To display paragraph marks from the Standard toolbar, click the Show/Hide ¶ button on the Standard toolbar.

N O T E　If you turn on paragraph marks by choosing Tools, Options, then selecting the Paragraph Marks check box, you can turn on and off the display of tabs and spaces only by clicking the Show/Hide ¶ button. Paragraph marks remain on.

Using Paragraph Formatting Techniques

Every new document you create based on the default Normal template is controlled by the Normal style. The Normal style formats paragraphs as left-aligned and single-spaced, with left-aligned tab stops every half-inch. If you usually choose different paragraph formatting selections, change the Normal style to reflect your preferences.

▶ **See** "Applying Paragraph Styles," **p. 144**

You can format a paragraph at two times—before you begin typing and after you finish typing. To format after typing, you must select the paragraph or paragraphs you want to format. If you are formatting only one paragraph instead of selecting the entire paragraph, you can position the insertion point anywhere inside the paragraph before making your formatting selections. Paragraph formatting commands apply to the entire paragraph.

Word offers several alternative techniques for formatting paragraphs:

- Choose Format, Paragraph to select many formatting options at once and to get the widest possible range of paragraph formatting options.
- Select the Formatting toolbar to access paragraph formatting commands individually.
- Use the ruler to set tabs and indents quickly.

With keyboard shortcuts, you can format as you type. Figures 4.5 and 4.6 show examples of selecting and formatting text from the Formatting toolbar.

FIG. 4.5

Select the paragraphs you want to format.

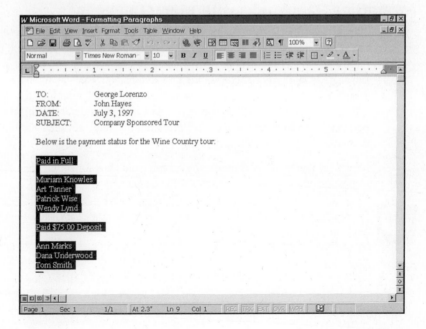

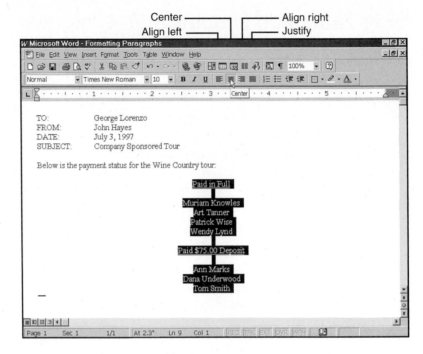

FIG. 4.6
Click the button for the
formatting you want. The
Center button is
selected in this
example, and the
selected text is
centered.

Formatting Paragraphs with Menu Commands

The Paragraph dialog box offers the greatest number of options for formatting paragraphs and shows a sample of how the formatting you choose affects your paragraph in the Preview box (see Figure 4.7). You can choose the Indents and Spacing tab to change indentation, spacing, and alignment, or you can choose the Line and Page Breaks tab to change pagination and suppress line numbers and hyphenation. Because the Paragraph dialog box provides quick access to the Tabs dialog box, you also can do quite a bit of formatting at once by choosing Format, Paragraph. See Chapter 7, "Formatting the Page Layout, Alignment, and Numbering," for more details on pagination.

Specific instructions on using the Paragraph dialog box for setting indentation, spacing, and pagination options appear throughout this chapter.

 You also can access the Paragraph dialog box by clicking the right mouse button and choosing Paragraph from the shortcut menu.

FIG. 4.7

Use the Paragraph dialog box to change the formatting of the selected text or the paragraph that contains the insertion point.

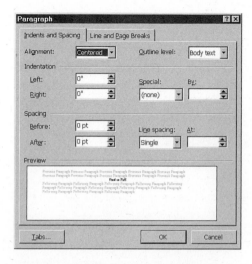

Formatting Paragraphs with Shortcut Keys

You can choose from several shortcut keys for quick formatting changes, which you can make directly from the keyboard. To use a shortcut key for formatting, first select the paragraph or paragraphs you want to change or place the insertion point in the paragraph you want to change, then choose one of the following commands:

To Do This	Press
Left-align text	Ctrl+L
Center text	Ctrl+E
Right-align text	Ctrl+R
Justify text	Ctrl+J
Indent from left margin	Ctrl+M
Create a hanging indent out one tab stop	Ctrl+T
Reduce a hanging indent by one tab stop	Ctrl+Shift+T
Single-space text	Ctrl+1
Change to 1.5 line spacing	Ctrl+5
Double-space text	Ctrl+2
Add 12 points of space before a paragraph	Ctrl+0 (zero)
Remove space before a paragraph	Ctrl+Shift+0 (zero)

To Do This	Press
Remove paragraph formatting that isn't part of the paragraph's assigned style	Ctrl+Q
Restore default formatting (from the Normal style)	Ctrl+Shift+N

Formatting Paragraphs with the Formatting Toolbar

The Word Formatting toolbar, shown in Figure 4.8, provides a quick way to choose certain paragraph formatting options using the mouse. Default paragraph formatting buttons on the Formatting toolbar include buttons for creating numbered lists and bulleted lists, indenting and unindenting, and controlling a paragraph's alignment. You also can access a special toolbar for creating lines and borders in your document.

FIG. 4.8
You can change the format of selected paragraphs from the Formatting toolbar.

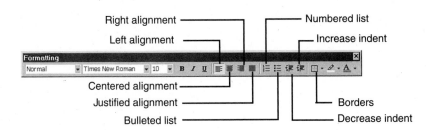

Right alignment — Numbered list
Left alignment — Increase indent
Centered alignment
Justified alignment — Borders
Bulleted list — Decrease indent

TIP Displaying toolbars is optional but useful if you do a lot of formatting. If you want more typing space on-screen, however, remove the toolbar by placing the mouse pointer between buttons or list boxes, clicking the right mouse button, then clicking the name of the toolbar in the drop-down list.

To use the Formatting toolbar for alignment, follow these steps:

1. Select the paragraph or paragraphs you want to align, or place the insertion point in the paragraph you want to align.

2. Choose the appropriate alignment button: Left, Center, Right, or Justify (both margins aligned).

Formatting Paragraphs with the Ruler

The *ruler*, shown in Figure 4.9, is useful for quickly setting paragraph indentations and tabs with a click of the mouse. By default, tabs are left aligned; if you want a different tab style, you must select that style and then position the tab on the ruler.

FIG. 4.9

The ruler provides quick access to some formatting options.

First-line Indent marker

Left Indent marker

Tab Alignment button

Right Indent marker

Displaying the ruler, like the toolbar, is also optional. To display or remove the ruler, choose View, Ruler. The Ruler command has a check mark to its left when displayed. Choose the command again to remove the ruler.

TIP Displaying the ruler can speed up formatting if you have a mouse; however, removing the ruler gives you more room on-screen.

The sections "Setting Tabs" and "Setting Indents," later in this chapter, discuss using ruler options.

Duplicating Formats

The easiest way to duplicate paragraph formatting is to carry the formatting forward as you type. As you arrive at the end of the current paragraph and press Enter, the current paragraph ends and a new one begins—using the same formatting as the preceding paragraph. If, however, you use the mouse or arrow keys to move out of the current paragraph, you move into a different paragraph, which may have different formatting.

Another way to duplicate formatting is to choose Edit, Repeat, or press F4. Remember that the Repeat command duplicates only your most recent action. The command works best when you format with the Paragraph, Tabs, or Borders dialog boxes, making multiple formatting choices at once.

To duplicate paragraph formatting using a mouse, follow these steps:

1. Select the text containing the formatting you want to duplicate.
2. Click the Format Painter button in the Standard toolbar. The pointer changes to a combination insertion point and paintbrush.
3. Drag across the text you want formatted.

When you release the mouse button, the text over which you dragged changes to the copied format.

To duplicate paragraph formatting from the keyboard, follow these steps:

1. Select the paragraph whose format you want to copy.
2. Press Ctrl+Shift+C.
3. Select the paragraph(s) whose format you want to change.
4. Press Ctrl+Shift+V.

Part
II

Ch
4

Probably the most powerful way to duplicate paragraph formatting is to use styles. A *style* is a set of formatting commands that you can apply all at once and can change globally later. Styles are easy to use and create—especially when you use the "styles by example" technique. Styles are explained in detail in Chapter 5, "Using Styles for Repetitive Formats."

If you deleted a paragraph mark and you need to reapply the previous formatting, reformat it or copy a paragraph mark from a paragraph that has the formatting you want to apply, and paste it at the end of the problem paragraph.

 To avoid deleting a paragraph mark inadvertently, turn on paragraph marks by clicking the paragraph mark button at the right end of the Standard toolbar. Or turn on paragraph marks by choosing Tools, Options and selecting the Paragraph Marks option in the View tab.

TROUBLESHOOTING

I set up formatting in a paragraph and then moved to the next paragraph, but the formatting didn't carry over.   You must press the Enter key at the end of the paragraph whose formatting you want to carry over to a new paragraph. If there is already a paragraph mark following the formatted paragraph and you use the mouse or arrow keys to move into this paragraph, the new paragraph will not necessarily have the same formatting as the previous paragraph.

Aligning Paragraphs

Paragraph alignment refers to how the left and right edges of a paragraph line up (see Figure 4.10). Left-aligned paragraphs line up on the left edge but are ragged on the right (the Word default). Left-aligned text is commonly used in informal letters or in the body text in a book, such as this book. Right-aligned paragraphs line up on the right edge but are ragged on the left. Right-aligned text can be used in headers and footers in a document—for example, page numbering—or when you are creating a list and want the items in the right column to line up along the right margin. Centered paragraphs are ragged on both edges and centered between the margins. Centered paragraphs are most often used for headings. Justified paragraphs are aligned on both edges and are often used in formal business letters and in text that appears in columns, as in a newsletter.

Paragraphs are aligned to the margins if no indentations are set for them. If paragraphs are indented, they align to the indentation.

You can set paragraph alignment while you're typing or editing your document. If you set alignment as you type, the alignment carries forward when you press Enter (as do all paragraph formatting selections). If you set alignment later, your setting applies only to the selected paragraph or paragraphs.

FIG. 4.10

You can choose from four styles of alignment: left, centered, right, and justified.

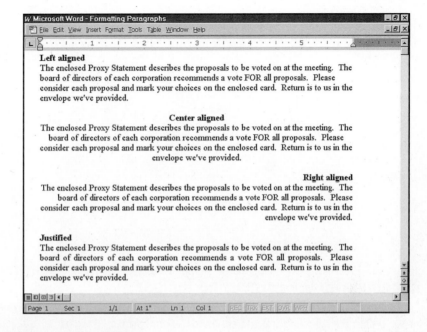

Aligning with Menu Commands

You can choose Format, Paragraph to set alignment with a mouse or your keyboard.

 T I P   To justify the last line of a paragraph, end the line with a soft return (Shift+Enter) rather than Enter.

To set alignment using the menu command, follow these steps:

1. Select the paragraph or paragraphs to align, or position the insertion point where you want the new alignment to begin.

2. Choose Format, Paragraph. The Paragraph dialog box appears.

3. Select the Alignment option from the Indents and Spacing tab.

4. Select Left, Centered, Right, or Justified from the Alignment pull-down list, as shown in Figure 4.11.

5. Click OK.

N O T E   You can choose formatting commands from the shortcut menu. Select the text you want to format, click the right mouse button, and choose Paragraph. The Paragraph dialog box appears.

FIG. 4.11

You can choose paragraph alignment from the Alignment list box in the Paragraph dialog box.

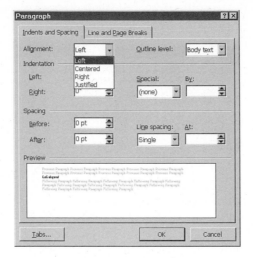

Aligning with the Formatting Toolbar

If you have a mouse, a quicker way to set alignment is to display the Formatting toolbar and click the appropriate alignment button. If the Formatting toolbar isn't displayed, choose View, Toolbars, and specify the toolbar(s) you want to display.

To align paragraphs with the Formatting toolbar, follow these steps:

1. Select the paragraph or paragraphs to align, or position the insertion point where you want the new alignment to begin.

2. Click the Align Left, Center, Align Right, or Justify Alignment button.

Aligning with Keyboard Shortcuts

One of the quickest ways to align selected paragraphs is to use keyboard shortcuts. With this technique, you also can save screen space by not displaying the Formatting toolbar.

To align paragraphs using keyboard shortcuts, follow these steps:

1. Select the paragraph or paragraphs to align, or position the insertion point where you want the new alignment to begin.

2. Press the appropriate Ctrl+key combination:

Paragraph Alignment	Shortcut
Left	Ctrl+L
Centered	Ctrl+E
Right	Ctrl+R
Justified	Ctrl+J

TROUBLESHOOTING

When I insert a page break immediately after a justified paragraph, Word justifies the words in the last line of the paragraph, resulting in very wide spacing between the words. This problem occurs because the insertion point is located at the end of the justified paragraph when you insert the page break. Be sure to press Enter at the end of the paragraph before you insert the page break.

Setting Tabs

Working with tabs is a two-part process. First, you must set the tab stops, or you must plan to use the Word default left-aligned tab stops at every 0.5". Setting the tab stops includes selecting the type of tab—left, centered, right, decimal, or bar—and specifying where the tab stops must appear. The second step in using tabs is to press the Tab key as you type your document to move the insertion point forward to the next tab stop. You also have three leader style options including dotted, dashed, or solid.

A wonderful advantage to working with tabs is that after the tabs are in your document, you can move or change the tab stops, and the selected text moves or realigns with the stops.

You can set tabs in one of two ways. You can use the Tabs dialog box, which gives you precise control over where each tab is to appear and enables you to customize tabs by adding tab leaders. Alternatively, you can use the ruler to select a tab style and then to set the tab's position using the mouse.

When you work with a table or list made up of tabs, displaying the tab characters in your document is helpful. The tab characters appear as right-pointing arrows.

To display the tab characters from the Standard toolbar, click the Show/Hide ¶ button at the right end of the Standard toolbar. To display the tab characters using menu commands, follow these steps:

1. Choose Tools, Options.
2. Select the View tab.
3. Select the Tab Characters option from the Nonprinting characters group.

You must understand that, like all paragraph formatting options, tabs belong to paragraphs. If you set tab stops as you type text and then press Enter, the tab settings are carried forward to the next paragraph. If you add tabs later, however, they apply only to the paragraph or paragraphs selected when you set the tab stops.

Figure 4.12 shows how each of the different tab styles affects the text to which they're applied; Figure 4.13 shows the three different tab leader styles.

FIG. 4.12

You can select from five tab styles: left, centered, right, decimal, or bar. This example includes bar tabs set between and around the other tab styles.

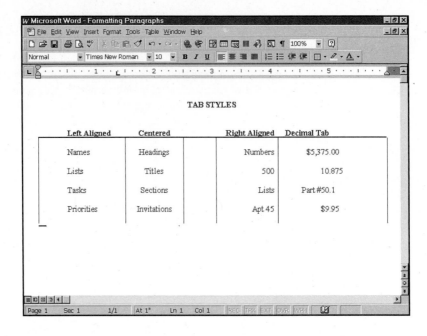

Although tabs are useful for lists, menus, tables of contents, and anything requiring tab leaders, a table sometimes works better for lists. A table contains *cells* formed by rows and columns, and it is the best choice when you have many columns or when the text in each cell varies in length.

▶ **See** "Creating Tables," **p. 275**

▶ **See** "Formatting a Table," **p. 301**

Using the Tabs Dialog Box

Using the Tabs dialog box to set tabs has several advantages. You can set each tab's position precisely by typing in decimal numbers, and you can add dotted, dashed, or underlined tab leaders. (A *tab leader* "leads" up to tabbed text on the left side; see Figure 4.13.) With a mouse or a keyboard, you can quickly clear existing tabs and change the default tab settings for the rest of your document. You can even reformat existing tabs.

To set tabs using the menu command, follow these steps:

1. Select the paragraph or paragraphs for which you want to set tabs, or position the insertion point where you want the tab settings to begin.

2. Choose F̲ormat, T̲abs. The Tabs dialog box appears, as shown in Figure 4.14.

3. Using decimal numbers, type the position of the tab stop you want to set in the T̲ab Stop Position box.

FIG. 4.13
Use any of the three leader styles to "lead" the eye to tabbed text.

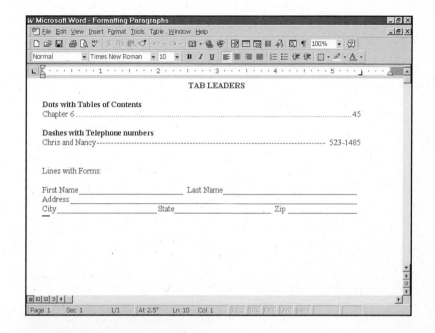

FIG. 4.14
You can set tabs at precise locations and include leaders from the Tabs dialog box.

4. From the Alignment group, select the tab style you want: Left, Center, Right, Decimal, or Bar.

5. In the Leader group, select the tab leader style you want (if any): 1 for no leader, 2 for a dotted leader, 3 for a dashed leader, or 4 for an underlined leader.

6. Click the Set button to set the tab stop.

7. Repeat steps 3 through 6 to set additional tab stops.

8. Click OK.

The Tab Stop Position list box displays your tab stops after you set them. You can reformat existing tab stops by following the same general procedure for setting tabs.

To reformat existing tab stops, follow these steps:

1. Select the tab to reformat in the Tab Stop Position list box.
2. Select the new formatting options for the selected tab stop in the Alignment and Leader groups.
3. Click Set.

You can access the Tabs dialog box through the Paragraph dialog box. Choose Format, Paragraph or click the right mouse button and choose Paragraph in the shortcut menu; then click the Tabs button. Alternatively, you can double-click any tab set on the ruler to display the Tabs dialog box.

Clearing Tabs

After you set tabs, you can *clear* (remove) them individually or as a group. The following technique works whether you set the tabs through the Tabs dialog box or use the ruler.

To clear tab stops with the menu command, follow these steps:

1. Select the paragraph or paragraphs from which you want to clear tabs, or position the insertion point where you want to begin working with the new tab settings.
2. Choose Format, Tabs.
3. Click the Clear All button to clear all the tabs.

    You can also select the tab from the Tab Stop Position list box and click the Clear button to clear one tab. Repeat this process to clear additional tab stops.
4. Click OK.

As you clear tab stops with the Clear button in step 3, the tab stops are listed in the Tab Stops to Be Cleared area at the bottom of the Tabs dialog box.

Using the Ruler to Set Tabs

If you have a mouse, you can use the ruler to set, move, and remove left, center, right, or decimal tabs quickly. (Bar tabs are not available from the ruler.) This task involves two steps— selecting the tab style by clicking the Tab Alignment button on the ruler, and then setting the tabs where you want them on the ruler.

The ruler displays Word's default tab stops (set every 0.5", unless you change the interval) as tiny vertical lines along the bottom of the ruler. When you set your own tab stops, all default tab stops to the left are removed from the ruler (see Figure 4.15). To display the ruler, choose View, Ruler.

To set tabs using the ruler, follow these steps:

FIG. 4.15

This ruler shows the symbols for the various kinds of tabs.

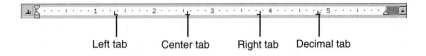

Left tab   Center tab   Right tab   Decimal tab

1. Select the paragraph or paragraphs for which you want to set tabs, or position the insertion point where you want the new tab settings to begin.

2. Click the Tab Alignment button at the far left of the ruler until the symbol for the tab style you want to use is selected—Left, Centered, Right, or Decimal. (Refer to Figure 4.12 to see how each Tab Alignment style looks on-screen.)

3. Position the pointer just below the tick mark on the ruler where you want the tab stop to appear. Click the left mouse button to place the tab stop on the ruler.

Repeat steps 2 and 3 to add various kinds of tab stops to the ruler, or just step 3 to add more tab stops of the same style.

The tab stop appears as a marker in the same style as the tab style you selected from the ruler. If you don't get the tab marker in just the right place on the ruler, position the mouse pointer on the marker, hold down the left mouse button to select the marker, and drag the tab marker to the correct position.

To use the ruler to change a tab stop's alignment or to add a leader, double-click the tab stop to display the Tabs dialog box. Select the tab stop you want to change in the Tab Stop Position list box, make whatever changes you want, and click OK.

To use the mouse to quickly remove a tab from the ruler, follow these steps:

1. Drag the tab off the ruler onto the document.

2. Release the mouse button.

Resetting the Default Tab Stops

If you do not set custom tabs, Word has preset tabs every 0.5". When you set a custom tab, all preset tabs to the left of the custom tab are cleared. You can use the Tabs dialog box to change the default tab stop interval if you routinely use the preset tabs and do not like the default tab setting. Any custom tab stops you may have set for existing paragraphs are not affected.

To change the default tab stops, follow these steps:

1. Choose Format, Tabs.

2. In the Default Tab Stops text box, type in a new default tab interval or click the up or down arrow to change the number in the box.

3. Click OK.

Part
II

Ch
4

Setting Default Tabs

Default tabs are set every 0.5". If you find that you are changing them frequently, you can change the default tab settings in NORMAL.DOT, the template on which most documents are based. You first need to retrieve NORMAL.DOT, then change the tabs, and finally save the template.

▶ **See** "Setting Default Formats in the Normal Template," **p. 16**

To retrieve NORMAL.DOT, follow these steps:

1. Choose File, Open.
2. Open the OFFICE folder.
3. Open the TEMPLATE folder.
4. Click the down arrow of Files of Type and choose Document Templates (*.dot).
5. Choose NORMAL.
6. Click Open.

If you have never made any changes to the default settings in NORMAL.DOT, NORMAL.DOT will not appear in the TEMPLATE folder. If this is the case, you can create NORMAL.DOT, which can then be modified as described. To create NORMAL.DOT, open a new document, choose Format, Font, and then click the Default button. When asked if you want to change the default font, choose Yes. Because you didn't actually select a new font, you haven't really changed the default font. The idea is to trick Word into thinking you made a change in the default settings, so it will create a NORMAL.DOT file. Choose File, Save All. Click Cancel when the Save As dialog box appears, because you don't need to save the blank document. Word then automatically saves NORMAL.DOT, and NORMAL.DOT appears in the TEMPLATE folder, as described earlier.

To change the default tabs, follow these steps:

1. Choose Format, Tabs.
2. Change the setting in the Default Tab Stops text box to the interval you prefer.
3. Click OK.

To save and exit NORMAL.DOT, follow these steps:

1. Choose File, Close. You are asked whether you want to save the changes.
2. Click Yes to save the changes you have made.

The next time you create a document using NORMAL.DOT, the default tab settings will match the changes you've made to the template.

TROUBLESHOOTING

When I tried to adjust the column in a table created with tabs by dragging the tab stop on the ruler, only one row in the table changed.   Tab settings are a paragraph characteristic and are stored in the paragraph mark at the end of a paragraph. To adjust the columns in a table, you must select all of the rows (paragraphs) in the table and then drag the tab stops on the ruler.

When I select the rows in a table created with tabs, some of the tab stops are grayed on the ruler. When you select a group of paragraphs that don't all have exactly the same tab settings, the tab stops that are not common to all of the paragraphs will appear in gray. You can drag a tab stop to a new setting, and it will then be applied to all of the paragraphs in the selection. This is a good way to synchronize the tab stops in a group of paragraphs if you accidentally change a tab setting in just one of the paragraphs.

Setting Indents

A document's margins are determined by selections made in the File Page Setup dialog box. Margins apply to the entire document or to sections within the document. But individual paragraphs or groups of paragraphs can be indented from those margins and therefore appear to have their own margin settings.

Although only two side margins (left and right) are available, you can indent a paragraph in many ways, as shown in Figure 4.16. You can indent from the left, right, or both margins. You can indent just the first line of a paragraph, a technique that often substitutes for pressing Tab at the beginning of each new paragraph. You can create a *hanging indent*, which "hangs" the first line of a paragraph to the left of the rest of the paragraph; hanging indents often are used for bulleted or numbered lists. You also can create *nested indents*—indentations within indentations.

Part

II

Ch

4

FIG. 4.16
You can use various levels of indenting to achieve various effects.

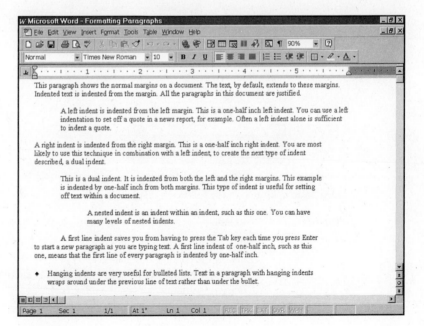

Several techniques exist for creating indents. You can use the Paragraph dialog box and enter the amount of indent for the selected paragraph or paragraphs. You can use the ruler, dragging indent icons left and right. You can use a button on the toolbar to indent or un-indent paragraphs quickly or to create lists with a hanging indent. You also can use keyboard shortcuts.

Whichever technique you use, indenting is stored in the paragraph mark and is carried forward when you press Enter at the end of a paragraph. Alternatively, you can return to a paragraph later and format the text with an indent.

N O T E   Numbered and bulleted lists are a special type of indented list. ■

▶ **See** "Creating Bulleted Lists," **p. 313**

▶ **See** "Creating Numbered Lists," **p. 320**

Using the Paragraph Command to Set Indents

You can use the Paragraph dialog box to precisely set any type of indent. The Indentation list in the Paragraph dialog box lists three options: Left, Right, and Special, as shown in Figure 4.17.

FIG. 4.17
Use the Indents and Spacing tab to change paragraph indentation.

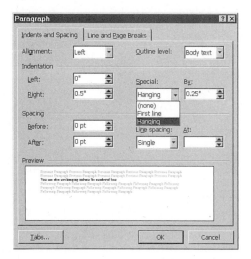

The indentation options give the following results:

Option	Result
Left	Indents selected paragraph or paragraphs from the left margin. If the number is positive, the paragraph is indented inside the left margin; if the number is negative, the paragraph is indented outside the left margin (sometimes termed *outdenting*).

Option	Result
Right	Indents selected paragraph or paragraphs from the right margin. If the number is positive, the paragraph is indented inside the right margin; if the number is negative, the paragraph is indented outside the right margin.
Special	Indents the first line or lines of selected paragraph or paragraphs from left indent (or margin, if no indent is made). Click the down arrow to select either First Line or Hanging. First Line indents inside the left indent. Hanging Indent indents outside the left indent. The default indent is 0.5". Change the indent by typing a new number or by using the up or down arrow to change the number.

To set indentations using the Paragraph dialog box, follow these steps:

1. Select the paragraph or paragraphs to indent, or position the insertion point where you want the new indentation to begin.
2. Choose Format, Paragraph. The Paragraph dialog box opens.
3. Select the Indents and Spacing tab.
4. Type or select a value in the Left or Right Indentation text box. You also can select First Line or Hanging from the Special list box and type or select a value in the By text box. Or, you can preview the effects of the choices you make in the Preview box.
5. Click OK.

You can create indents in measurements other than decimal inches. To create a 6-point indent, for example, type **6 pt** in either indentation box. (An inch consists of 72 points.) To create an indent of 2 centimeters, type **2 cm**; to create an indent of 1 pica, type **1 pi** (six picas per inch; 12 points per pica).

Creating a Hanging Indent

A hanging indent is used for items such as bulleted and numbered lists, glossary items, and bibliographic entries (see Figure 4.18).

To create a hanging indent, follow these steps:

1. Choose Format, Paragraph.
2. Select the Special box by clicking its down arrow.
3. Choose Hanging.
4. Type the amount you want the first line of the paragraph to extend to the left of the rest of the paragraph.
5. Click OK.

Part

II

Ch

4

FIG. 4.18

Hanging indents can be used for creating bulleted and numbered lists and bibliographic entries.

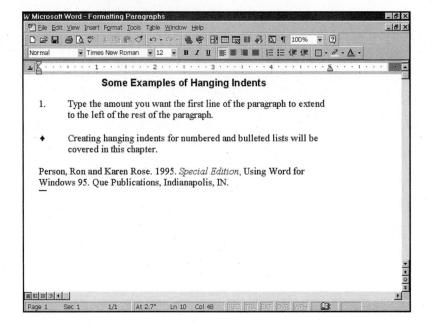

To use a hanging indent, type a number or bullet at the left margin, press Tab to advance to the left indent, and then begin typing the text of the paragraph. When text reaches the end of the line, the paragraph wraps around to the left indent, not the left margin. This technique is useful for numbered and bulleted lists. (You can create hanging indents for numbered and bulleted lists automatically with the toolbar or the Bullets and Numbering dialog box.) See Chapter 12, "Creating Bulleted or Numbered Lists," for further information.

N O T E Symbol fonts such as Symbol and Zapf Dingbats are full of interesting characters you can use as bullets in a list. ▪

Using the Ruler or Formatting Toolbar to Set Indents

With the ruler, you easily can create indents of any kind. With the Formatting toolbar, you can indent a selected paragraph to the next available tab stop.

The ruler contains triangular markers, called *indent markers*, at the left and right margins. You can drag them left and right on the ruler to set indents. The top triangle at the left margin represents the first-line indent. The bottom triangle represents the left indent. Both the top and bottom triangles move independently. You use the square below the bottom triangle to move both the first-line and left paragraph indents at once. The triangle at the right margin represents the paragraph's right indent. Figure 4.19 shows the indent markers on the ruler.

First-line Indent marker

Left Indent marker

Right Indent marker

First-line and Left Indent marker

FIG. 4.19

Use the indent markers to set left and right indentations.

Left and right indents are measured from the left and right margins, respectively. First-line indents are measured relative to the left indent. In Figures 4.20, 4.21, and 4.22, you can see that the position of the indent markers reflects the indentation settings for the selected paragraph.

FIG. 4.20

The first-line, left, and right indent markers are set even with the left and right margins.

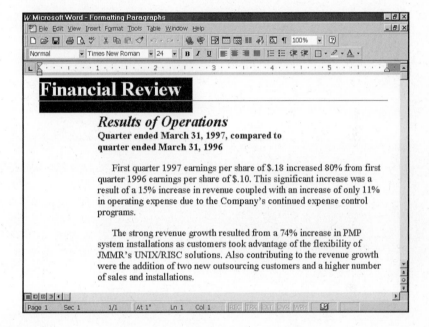

To set indentations with the ruler, first display the ruler by choosing <u>V</u>iew, <u>R</u>uler, and then follow these steps:

1. Select the paragraph or paragraphs to indent, or position the insertion point where you want the new indentation to begin.

2. To set a left indent, drag the square below the left indent marker to the ruler position where you want the indentation. (Notice that the top triangle moves also.)

    To set a right indent, drag the right indent marker to the position where you want the indentation.

    To set a first-line indent, drag the first-line indent marker to the position where you want the first-line indentation.

    To set a hanging indent with the first line at the left margin, drag the left indent marker to a new position on the ruler.

Part

II

Ch

4

FIG. 4.21

The first-line and left indent markers are set at 1.0", and the right indent marker has been moved to 6".

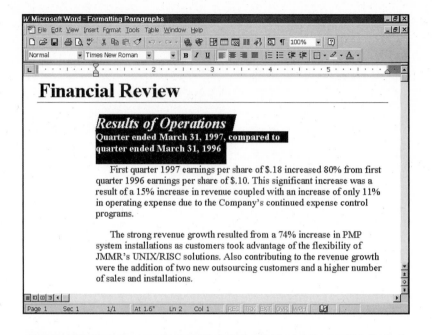

FIG. 4.22

The first-line indent marker is set to .25" from the left indent marker to create a first-line indentation.

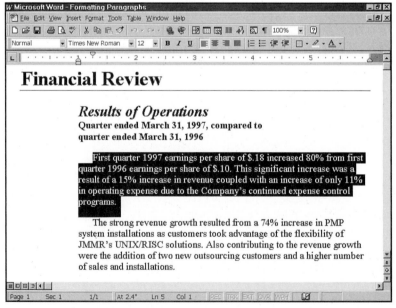

N O T E While in Normal view, when you drag the left or first-line indent to the left of the left margin, the ruler automatically scrolls to the left. If you want to scroll on the ruler into the left margin without moving the indent markers, however, hold down the Shift key while you click the left scroll arrow in the horizontal scroll bar.

The Formatting toolbar includes two buttons for indenting a selected paragraph to the next tab stop: the Increase Indent and Decrease Indent buttons. Increase Indent is used to indent to the next tab stop. Decrease Indent is used to decrease the indent to the previous tab stop. You use these buttons to create left indents only—not first-line or hanging indents—and to indent to tab stops already set in the current paragraph(s). To use this technique, be sure the Formatting toolbar is displayed by choosing View, Toolbars.

To indent or un-indent paragraphs using the Formatting toolbar, follow these steps:

1. Select the paragraph or paragraphs to indent, or position the insertion point where you want the new indentation to begin.

2. To indent the paragraph, click the Increase Indent button.

   To un-indent the paragraph, click the Decrease Indent button.

You can click the Increase Indent button as many times as you want to continue moving the left indentation to the right. The Increase Indent button, therefore, is an easy way to create nested paragraphs, which are like indents within indents (refer to Figure 4.16).

Using Keyboard Shortcuts to Set Indents

If you're a touch typist, you might appreciate being able to create indents by using keyboard shortcuts. Just as when you use the Formatting toolbar to create indents, keyboard shortcuts rely on existing tab settings to determine the position of indents. If you haven't changed Word default tab stops, for example—and therefore they still are set every 0.5"—using the shortcut keys to create a hanging indent leaves the first line of the paragraph at the margin but moves the left edge for the remaining lines of the paragraph to one-half inch.

To set indents by using keyboard shortcuts, follow these steps:

1. Select the paragraph or paragraphs to indent, or position the insertion point where you want the new indentation to begin.

2. Use one of the following keyboard shortcuts to indent your text:

Shortcut	Indentation Type
Ctrl+M	Moves the left indent to the next tab stop
Ctrl+Shift+M	Moves the left indent to the preceding tab stop (but not beyond the left margin)
Ctrl+T	Creates a hanging indent
Ctrl+Shift+T	Removes an existing hanging indent

N O T E Just as you use shortcuts to format a paragraph, you can use a shortcut to remove formatting. Select a paragraph and press Ctrl+Spacebar to remove all character formatting and return a paragraph to only the formatting specified by the paragraph's style. ■

Part

II

Ch

4

Setting Default Indents

One of the most commonly used letter-writing styles is modified-block style, with indented paragraphs. If you find that you are frequently changing indentations to indent paragraphs, for example, you can change the default indentation settings in NORMAL.DOT, the template on which most documents are based. You first need to retrieve NORMAL.DOT, then change the indentation, and finally save the template.

Refer to "Setting Default Tabs" earlier in this chapter for information about changing default indentation settings in NORMAL.DOT.

Numbering Lines

Line numbers are useful in preparing manuscripts or legal documents, for reference, or if you simply need to know how many lines of text are on a page, in a poem, or in a document. You can choose the starting number for line numbering, the distance between numbers and text, the interval at which line numbers appear, and whether line numbering restarts with every new page or section or continues throughout your section. You can suppress line numbering for a specific paragraph or paragraphs.

Adding Line Numbers

You can add line numbers to sections of a document or to the entire document if it isn't formatted into sections. For information about formatting a document in sections, see Chapter 7, "Formatting the Page Layout, Alignment, and Numbering."

To number lines, follow these steps:

1. Position the insertion point inside the section in which you want line numbers, or anywhere in the document to number a document that hasn't been split into sections. To number an entire document that has been divided into sections, select the entire document.
2. Choose File, Page Setup. The Page Setup dialog box appears.
3. Select the Layout tab.
4. Click Line Numbers.
5. Select the Add Line Numbering option (see Figure 4.23). Change the following default line numbering settings if you want:

Option	Description	Then Type
Start At	Starting line number	A new starting number in the box, or click the up or down arrow to increase or decrease the starting number. (By default, line numbering begins with 1.)

Option	Description	Then Type
From Text	Distance between line numbers and text	A distance in the box or click the up or down arrow to increase or decrease the distance by tenths of an inch. (The Auto option places line numbers .25" to the left of single-column text or .13" to the left of newspaper-style columns.) If the margin or the space between columns is too small, line numbers do not print.
Count By	Interval between printed line numbers (all lines are numbered but only those numbers specified here print)	An interval in the box, or click the up or down arrow to increase or decrease the interval.

FIG. 4.23
Choose line numbering options from the Line Numbers dialog box.

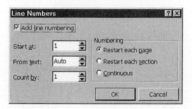

6. Select an option from the Numbering group to establish when line numbers restart at the first number (but only those numbers specified here print):

Option	Restart Point
Restart Each Page	Beginning of each new page
Restart Each Section	Beginning of each new section
Continuous	None; number lines continuously through document

7. Click OK twice.

You cannot see line numbering in Normal view. To see line numbers, choose View, Page Layout, or File, Print Preview. You also can print your document.

N O T E You can change the formatting of line numbers by redefining the Line Number style. Refer to Chapter 5 for information about redefining styles. ▪

Removing or Suppressing Line Numbers

You can remove line numbers entirely. Also, you have the chance to suppress line numbers by selecting the Suppress Line Numbers option in the Paragraph dialog box. This option clears line numbering from selected paragraphs or the paragraph containing the insertion point. (This option doesn't suppress line numbers applied in creating a numbered list, described in Chapter 12.)

To remove line numbers, follow these steps:

1. Position the insertion point in the section from which you want to remove line numbers, or select the entire document if it's formatted into more than one section.
2. Choose File, Page Setup.
3. Select the Layout tab.
4. Click the Line Numbers button.
5. Choose Add Line Numbering to remove the check mark.
6. Click OK or press Enter twice to return to the document.

To suppress line numbers, follow these steps:

1. Select the paragraphs for which you want to suppress line numbering.
2. Choose Format, Paragraph.
3. Select the Line and Page Breaks tab.
4. Click the Suppress Line Numbers option.
5. Click OK.

▶ **See** "Creating Numbered Lists" **p. 320**

Adjusting Line and Paragraph Spacing

Like all word processing and typesetting programs, Word spaces lines of text far enough apart so that lines don't crash into each other. If something large is on the line, such as a graphic or an oversized character or word, Word leaves extra space.

You're not limited to using Word automatic spacing, however. You can add extra space between lines and paragraphs.

N O T E Using styles is an excellent way to ensure that adjustments made to line and paragraph spacing are consistent throughout your document. If your document's format includes subheadings preceded by extra space, for example, create a style for your subheadings that includes the extra space, and apply the style to each subheading. For details about using styles, see Chapter 5. ■

Adjusting Paragraph Spacing

You can adjust paragraph spacing by adding extra lines before or after the selected paragraphs. After you press Enter, Word skips the specified amount of space before starting the next paragraph. This technique is useful when your document's format requires extra spacing between paragraphs, before new sections, or around graphics. Adding extra spacing before or after paragraphs is like pressing Enter a second time each time you finish typing a paragraph (see Figure 4.24).

FIG. 4.24
Use paragraph spacing to add extra spacing around headings and paragraphs.

10 points of space before; 14 points of space after

0 points of space before; 0 points of space after

0 points of space before; 12 points of space after

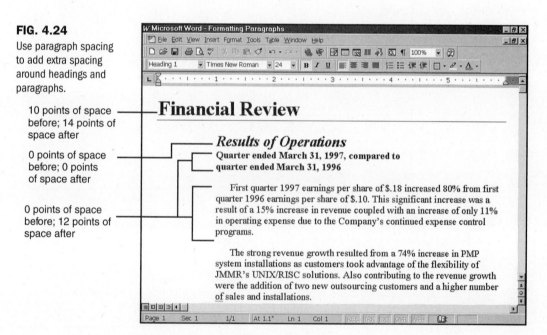

Part
II

Ch
4

The Preview section of the Paragraph dialog box shows the effect of your selected spacing.

N O T E When you're printing, if you format a paragraph to include extra space before and the paragraph appears at the top of a new page, Word ignores the extra space so that the top margins of your document always remain even. ■

To adjust paragraph spacing, follow these steps:

1. Select the paragraph or paragraphs to add spacing before or after, or position the insertion point where you want the new spacing to begin.

2. Choose Format, Paragraph.

3. Select the Indents and Spacing tab.

4. To add line spacing before the selected paragraph or paragraphs, type a number in the Spacing Before text box or click the up or down arrow to increase or decrease the spacing amount in increments of half a line (see Figure 4.25).

FIG. 4.25

Use the Paragraph Indents and Spacing tab to set paragraph spacing options.

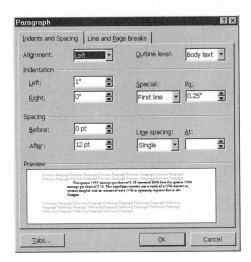

5. To add line spacing after the selected paragraph or paragraphs, type a number in the Spacing After text box or click the up or down arrow to increase or decrease the spacing amount in increments of half a line.

You can use measurements other than decimal inches to specify spacing. To add six-point spacing, for example, type **6 pt** in the Before or After box. To add spacing of two centimeters, type **2 cm**, and to add spacing of one pica, type **1 pi**.

6. Click OK.

Adjusting Line Spacing

Typesetters and desktop publishers call the spacing between lines in a document *leading* (pronounced "ledding"). Typesetters have great control over precisely how much space appears between lines. They know that long lines need more spacing so that the eye doesn't lose its place in moving from the right margin back to the left. They know that font styles with small letters require less spacing between lines than fonts with big letters.

Word gives you a typesetter's control over spacing between lines in your document. The feature begins with automatic spacing and enables you to increase spacing, reduce spacing, or permit extra spacing for a large character or superscript on the line.

Spacing is measured by lines. Normal text has single spacing of one line, but if you request spacing of .5, you get half-line spacing. Lines formatted this way are *condensed*. If you request spacing of 1.5, the paragraph has an extra half line of space between lines of text (see Figure 4.26).

FIG. 4.26

The line spacing is set at 1.5 to put more space between the lines of the selected text.

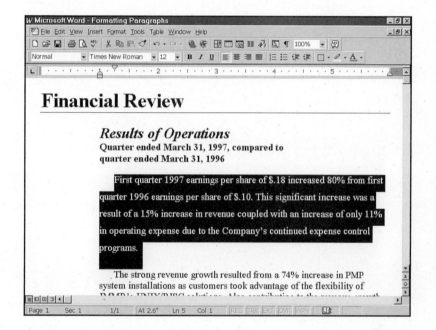

You can be very specific about line spacing. If your page design requires 10-point type with 12 points of leading, for example, type **12 pt** in the At box on the Indents and Spacing tab in the Paragraph dialog box. Word automatically changes the Line Spacing setting to Multiple and inserts a comparable number in inches.

N O T E You can include line spacing with styles so that when you press Enter to end a paragraph, the exact spacing is inserted automatically for each style of text you type, whether it's a heading that requires 14 points of space before the next line of text or body text that requires only 12 points of space between lines. ■

▶ **See** "Applying, Copying, and Removing Styles," **p. 144**

Part

II

Ch

4

To adjust spacing between lines using the menu commands, follow these steps:

1. Select the paragraph(s) to space, or position the insertion point where you want the new spacing to begin.

2. Choose Format, Paragraph to open the Paragraph dialog box.

3. Select the Indents and Spacing tab.

4. Choose one of the following options in the Line Spacing box:

Option	Description
Single	Single-line spacing. Line height automatically adjusts to accommodate the size of the font and any graphics or formulas that have been inserted into a line.
1.5 Lines	Line-and-a-half spacing. Puts an extra half line between lines.
Double	Double-spacing. Puts an extra full line between lines.
At Least	At least the amount of spacing you specify in the At text box. Word adds extra spacing, if necessary, for tall characters, big graphics, or super/subscript.
Exactly	The exact amount of spacing you specify in the At text box. All lines are exactly the same height, regardless of the size of the characters in the line. Word doesn't add extra spacing for anything. Some text may be cut off if enough space isn't available. Increase the amount of spacing if characters are cut off.
Multiple	Multiples of single-line spacing, such as triple (3) or quadruple (4).

5. If you want to specify your own line spacing, type the spacing amount in the At text box (with decimal numbers, such as **1.25** for an extra quarter-line of space between lines) or click the up or down arrow to increase or decrease the amount.

   You can choose a spacing amount in the At text box without first choosing from the Line Spacing list box. Word assumes that you want at least this spacing and provides extra spacing if needed for large characters, superscript, and so on.

6. Click OK.

If you want to return to single-line spacing, select the paragraph or paragraphs, choose Format, Paragraph, and then choose Single Line Spacing.

You can change line spacing to single, 1.5, or double from the keyboard. You can also add or remove 12 points of space before a paragraph.

To adjust spacing between lines from the keyboard, follow these steps:

1. Select the paragraph or paragraphs, or place the insertion point in the paragraph in which you want to change the spacing.

2. Press one of the following key combinations:

Press	To Do This
Ctrl+1	Single-space text
Ctrl+5	1.5 line space text
Ctrl+2	Double-space text
Ctrl+0 (zero)	Add 12 points of space before a paragraph
Ctrl+Shift+0 (zero)	Remove any space before a paragraph

Inserting a Line Break

▶ **See** "Changing Styles," **p. 156**

When you type a paragraph formatted by a style that is automatically followed by a different style and then press Enter, the next paragraph is formatted with the next style. Sometimes, however, you may not be ready to change to the next style. If you have a two-line subheading, for example, you may want to press Enter after the first line and still be in the subheading style, rather than switch to the next style. In this case, you want to insert a line break, or *soft return*, rather than a new paragraph. To end a line without inserting a paragraph mark, press Shift+Enter.

Pressing Shift+Enter breaks a line without breaking the paragraph. After you finish typing your two-line subheading, press Enter in the usual way to end the paragraph and begin the following paragraph with the next style.

If you click the Show/Hide ¶ button to display paragraph marks, you see that the line end marks at the ends of lines where you pressed Shift+Enter look like left-facing arrows rather than paragraph marks (see Figure 4.27).

Part

II

Ch

4

FIG. 4.27
Press Shift+Enter to create a new line without creating a new paragraph. Line end marks display as left-facing arrows rather than paragraph marks.

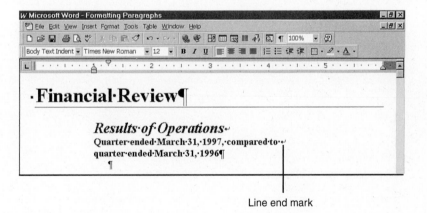

Line end mark

Shading and Bordering Paragraphs

For a finishing touch, you can add paragraph borders and shading to your document. A *border* may be a box surrounding a paragraph (or paragraphs) on all sides or a line that sets a paragraph off on one or more sides. A border can include *shading*, which fills a paragraph with a pattern. Boxes and lines can be solid black and shading can be gray, or, if you have a color monitor, they can be more colorful than a rainbow.

Borders are particularly useful in setting special paragraphs apart from the rest of your text for emphasis (see Figure 4.28) or for wonderful graphic effects. If you use Word for desktop publishing, you may find boxes, lines, and shading to be helpful.

FIG. 4.28

Borders, lines, and shading can set paragraphs apart.

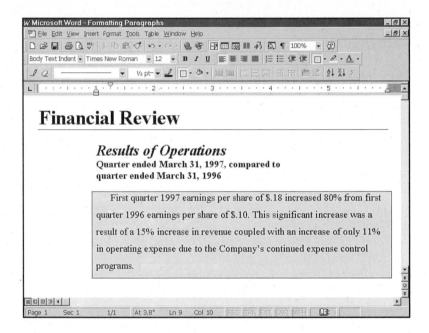

N O T E Creating colored lines, boxes, and shading is easy if you have a color monitor. If you have a color printer, you also can print colored lines, boxes, and shading. Service bureaus in many cities offer color printing for a per-page fee. If you want to print your document with colored lines, boxes, and shading, use your own printer to proof the pages and then take a floppy disk containing your file to the service bureau to have the final pages printed in color. Before you go to the service bureau, check to see if they have Word. You may need to reformat your document slightly for their printer. ▪

Borders, like all forms of paragraph formatting, belong to the paragraphs to which they are applied. They are carried forward when you press Enter at the end of a paragraph. Thus, if a group of paragraphs is formatted with a box around them and you press Enter at the end of the last paragraph, your new paragraph falls within the box. To create a new paragraph outside the border, move the insertion point outside the border before you press Enter. If you're at the end of the document and have nowhere to go outside of the border, create a new paragraph and remove the border.

TROUBLESHOOTING

The text changes its formatting when you press the Delete or Backspace key. Word stores paragraph formatting in the paragraph mark at the end of each paragraph. If you delete the paragraph mark of a particular paragraph, it takes on the format of the following paragraph. Choose Edit, Undo immediately to reverse the deletion and restore the paragraph formatting.

N O T E Sometimes the screen display inaccurately shows text extending beyond borders or shading. This situation results from screen fonts and screen resolutions that differ from the printer's fonts and resolution. Your printed text formats within the border or shading. ▪

Enclosing Paragraphs in Boxes and Lines

A box fully surrounds a paragraph or selected group of paragraphs. Two types of preset boxes are available: box and shadow. A line appears on one or more sides of a paragraph or selected paragraphs, or may appear between selected paragraphs. You have 11 line styles to choose from and can use any line style to create a line, a box, or a shadowed box.

You use the Borders and Shading dialog box to create boxes, lines, and shadows. Choose Format, Borders and Shading to access the dialog box. In the dialog box, you can choose either the Borders tab, Page Border tab, or Shading tab. The Borders tab shown in Figure 4.29 offers the following choices:

FIG. 4.29

The Borders tab in the Borders and Shading dialog box offers options for adding lines to any and all sides of a paragraph.

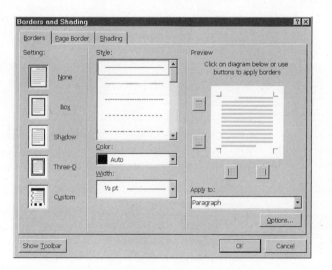

Part
II

Ch
4

Borders Option	Effect
None	No box. Use this option to remove an existing box. (This option is used often with the Shading options to create a shaded box with no border.)
Box	A box with identical lines on all four sides.
Shadow	A box with a drop shadow on the bottom right corner.
3-D	A "picture frame" box. You must select an asymmetric line style such as thin-thick, thick-thin, embossed, or engraved lines for this function to work.
Custom	Custom design borders on one or more sides of the selected paragraph(s) using Preview buttons.
Preview	A line on one or more sides of the selected paragraph(s). Dotted lines at the corners and sides of the sample indicate where the lines appear; when they are selected, arrows point to these dotted lines. The sample displays each border as added (see Figure 4.30).

FIG. 4.30

The Preview box in the Borders tab shows you which line is currently selected and gives you a preview of the lines you have inserted.

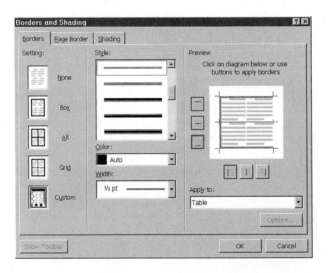

From Text	(Select the Options button.) The distance between the line or box and the text, measured in points. Because 72 points make up an inch, select 9 points for a .125" distance or 18 points for a .25" distance.
Style	A line or box in the selected line style. Options listed show exact point size and a sample display.
Color	A line or box in the selected color. Sixteen colors and gray shades are available. If you select the Auto option, the default color for text is used. This is usually black, but can be changed in the Windows Control Panel.

Width	A line or box in the selected width. Sixteen colors and gray shades are available. Options listed show exact point size and a sample display.
Apply to	Apply border and shade formatting to selected paragraphs or to selected text.

You also can use the Tables and Borders toolbar to add borders and shading to selected paragraphs (see Figures 4.31 and 4.32). Display the Tables and Borders toolbar by choosing View, Toolbars, or by clicking the Borders button on the Formatting toolbar.

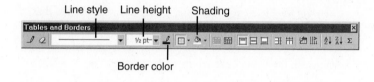

FIG. 4.31
You can add borders and shading from the Tables and Borders toolbar.

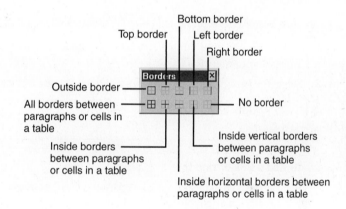

FIG. 4.32
The Tables and Borders toolbar can be torn off and placed with the other displayed toolbars, or it can be left to float in the document window.

Part
II

Ch
4

To create a box or line from the menu command, follow these steps:

1. Select the paragraph or paragraphs for which you want to create a box or line.

   If you create a box for more than one paragraph, the box encloses the paragraphs as a group, with no borders between them.

To Add a Box or Line to	Select
A paragraph, including paragraphs inside a table cell or frame	The paragraph
A table cell	The entire cell, including the end-of-cell marker
A frame	The frame

2. Choose Format, Borders and Shading. The Borders and Shading dialog box appears.

3. Select the Borders tab.

4. To create a box, choose Box, Shadow, or 3-D from the Setting group.

   To create a line using the mouse, do the following:

   Click the side of the paragraph where you want the line in the Preview group or click the preview button corresponding to the line you want. The preview buttons appear depressed when a line is selected. If a style has already been selected from the Style group, a line with that style will be inserted. You can continue inserting using this approach. If multiple paragraphs are selected, you can create a line between them by clicking the horizontal line between paragraphs in the Preview box.

   Choosing the line style before you create borders ensures that borders take on the appearance of the selected line style.

5. To set the spacing between a box and the text, select the Options button and specify a distance in the From Text group, and then click OK.

6. To apply color to all your boxes and lines, choose a color from the Color list.

7. Click OK.

To create a box or line from the Tables and Borders toolbar, follow these steps:

1. Display the Tables and Borders toolbar by choosing View, Toolbars and specifying the Tables and Borders toolbar.

2. Select the paragraph or paragraphs for which you want to create a box or line.

TIP If you create a box for more than one paragraph, the box encloses the paragraphs as a group with no borders between them.

To Add a Box or Line to	Select
A paragraph, including paragraphs inside a table	The paragraph cell or frame
A table cell	The entire cell, including the end-of-cell marker
A frame	The frame

3. Select the Line Style list box by clicking the down arrow, and choose a line style.

4. Select the Line Weight list box by clicking the down arrow, and choose a line weight.

5. Select the Border list box by clicking the down arrow, and choose the border you want to add by clicking one of the following buttons:

Choose This Button	To Do This
	Add a box border
	Add a border along the top
	Add a border along the bottom

Add a border along the left edge

Add a border along the right edge

Add all borders

Add inside borders

Add inside horizontal border

Add inside vertical border

Remove all borders

6. Choose shading or a pattern from the Shading list box, if you want shading or a pattern added.

The width of a paragraph border (box or line) is determined by the paragraph indent. (If no indent exists, width is determined by the page margins.) If you want a paragraph's border (or line) to be narrower than the margins, indent the paragraph (see Figures 4.33 and 4.34).

Part

II

Ch

4

FIG. 4.33
With indents set to the left and right margins, borders extend the full width of the page.

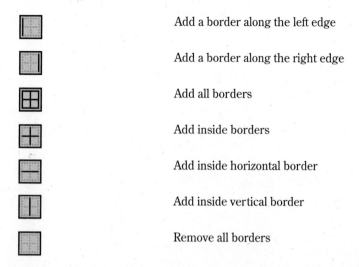

Left indent marker

Right indent marker

FIG. 4.34
To create a shorter border, move in the left and right indent markers.

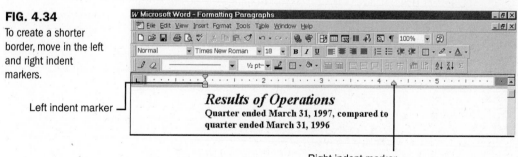

Left indent marker

Right indent marker

If you select and box several paragraphs that have different indents, each paragraph appears in its own separate box (instead of all appearing together in one box). To make paragraphs with different indents appear within a single box, you must create a table and put each paragraph in a row by itself and then select the table and format the outside border of the table (see Chapter 10, "Creating and Editing Tables").

When paragraphs extend exactly to the margins of your page (as they always do if you don't indent the paragraphs), borders extend slightly outside the margins. If you want borders to fall within or exactly on the margins, you must indent the paragraph. To make borders fall on the margins, indent the paragraph by the width of the border.

For example, if the border is the double 1.5-point line, the line width totals 4.5 points including the space between the double lines, indent the paragraph by 4.5 points. Type **4.5 pt** in the L̲eft and R̲ight indentation boxes in the Paragraph dialog box.

N O T E If you format groups of paragraphs to have lines between them, those lines apply to blank spaces between paragraphs if you create those blank spaces by pressing Enter an extra time. To avoid extra lines between paragraphs, use the Spacing Aft̲er option in the Paragraph dialog box to add blank space between paragraphs. (See "Adjusting Line and Paragraph Spacing" earlier in this chapter.)

You can remove borders all at once or line-by-line. Changing the line style of existing borders is essentially the same process.

To remove or change a box or line from the menu command, follow these steps:

1. Select the paragraph or paragraphs for which you want to remove or change boxes or lines.
2. Choose Fo̲rmat, B̲orders and Shading.
3. Select the B̲orders tab.
4. Select the N̲one option in the Setting group to remove all borders.
5. Select the line you want to change and choose a different option from the Style box. You also can select a different line color from the C̲olor list box.
6. Select Bo̲x, Sha̲dow, 3-D̲, or Cu̲stom to change the Setting border style.
7. Click OK.

To remove or change a line or box from the Tables and Borders toolbar, follow these steps:

1. Select the paragraph or paragraphs for which you want to remove or change boxes or lines.
2. Click the Borders button on the Formatting toolbar to display the Tables and Borders toolbar.
3. Click the No Border button to remove all borders.
4. Choose a new line style.
5. Click the button(s) for the box(es) or border(s) you want to add.

TIP Before you concoct patterns that you hope to use behind text, be sure to test whether the text is readable with that pattern behind it.

Shading Paragraphs

Paragraphs can be shaded, as well as bordered. Shading comes in various percentages of black or the selected color, and in patterns (see Figure 4.35). Percentages of black appear as grays of various intensities. For each shade or pattern, you can select a foreground or background color. *Shades* create a blended effect: A foreground of yellow and a background of blue creates the effect of green.

FIG. 4.35

The Shading tab from the Borders and Shading dialog box offers options for adding varying degrees of shading and/or color to a paragraph.

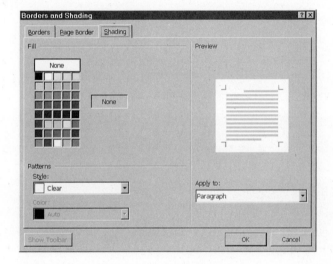

Part

II

Ch

4

But in *patterns*, the effect is more dramatic: In a Lt Grid pattern, for example, the yellow foreground forms a light grid pattern over a blue background. With some experimentation, you can create eye-catching results that can add visual impact to documents used for presentations or overhead transparencies. Colors are converted to shades of gray or patterns on a black-and-white printer.

You can use shading with borders so that a paragraph is surrounded by a line and filled with shading, or you can use shading alone so that no border goes around the shaded paragraph. Watch the Preview box on the Shading tab to see the effect of the patterns and colors you select. To add shading, choose the Shading tab in the Borders and Shading dialog box. You have the following options:

Shading Option	Effect
Fill	A background color for the selected shading pattern. Auto selects the best color, usually white. Select from 16 colors, including black and white.

None	No shading in selected paragraph(s).
Style	Shading in the selected custom darkness or pattern. Options include increasing degrees of shading and various patterns. Clear applies the selected background color; Solid applies the selected foreground color.
Color	A foreground color for the selected shading pattern. Auto selects the best color, usually black. You can select from 16 colors, including black and white.

To shade paragraphs with the menu command, follow these steps:

1. Select the paragraph or paragraphs you want to shade:

    | **To Shade** | **Select** |
    | A paragraph | The paragraph, including paragraphs inside a table cell or frame |
    | A table cell | The entire cell, including the end-of-cell marker |
    | A frame | The frame |

2. Choose Format, Borders and Shading.

 TIP If you want borders around your selected paragraph, select the Borders tab and choose border options.

3. Select the Shading tab.

4. Select the Style pattern you want. Options include Clear (uses the background color), Solid (uses the foreground color), percentages, and striped and checkered patterns such as Dk Horizontal (for dark horizontal stripes) and Lt Grid (for a grid made of light cross-hatching).

 TIP Percentage patterns consist of foreground and background colors. The result appears in the Preview box. For best results in creating colors, however, look first for the color you want in the Color list.

5. Select a color from the Color list to color a percentage pattern or a pattern foreground.

6. Select a color from the Fill list to color a percentage pattern or a pattern background.

7. Click OK.

To shade paragraphs using the Tables and Borders toolbar, follow these steps:

1. Select the paragraph or paragraphs you want to shade:

To Shade	Select
A paragraph	The paragraph, including paragraphs inside a table cell or frame
A table cell	The entire cell, including the end-of-cell marker
A frame	The frame

2. Click the Borders button on the Formatting toolbar to display the Tables and Borders toolbar.

3. Choose the shading or pattern you want from the Shading Color box.

To remove shading using the menu command, follow these steps:

1. Select the paragraph or paragraphs from which you want to remove shading.

2. Choose Format, Borders and Shading.

3. Click the Shading button.

4. Choose None from the Fill group.

5. Click OK.

To remove shading with the Tables and Borders toolbar, follow these steps:

1. Select the paragraph or paragraphs from which you want to remove shading.

2. Click the Borders button on the Formatting toolbar to display the Tables and Borders toolbar.

3. Choose the Clear setting from the Shading box.

Part

II

Ch

4

Using Styles for Repetitive Formats

Using Styles Versus Direct Formatting

What gives your document style? For the most part, style is the appearance of your document: the arrangement of text on pages, the shape of the paragraphs, the characteristics of the letters, and the use of lines and borders to give your document emphasis. All these elements of style are formatting choices you make while working with Word.

Style involves more than just appearance, however. Style is also readability and consistency. When your document's style is appropriate to its content and is consistent from one section to the next, the reader's job of gleaning information from your text becomes much easier.

Word offers you tools designed to make the task of developing and maintaining your document's style much easier. Appropriately, these tools are called *styles*. In Word 97, a style is a set of formatting instructions you save with a name in order to use them again and again. All text formatted with the same style has exactly the same formatting. If you make a formatting change to a style, all the text formatted with that style will reformat to match the new formatting.

You can create and apply two types of styles: character styles and paragraph styles. *Character styles* include any of the options available from the Font dialog box, such as bold, italic, and small caps. Character styles store only character formatting, and apply to selected text or to the word containing the insertion point. *Paragraph styles* include character and paragraph formatting, tab settings, paragraph positioning, borders and shading, and language used for spell checking. Paragraph styles can store both character and paragraph formatting, and apply to selected paragraphs or the paragraph containing the insertion point.

You can type a plain business letter and then apply a set of styles automatically with the AutoFormat command on the Format menu to give it a professional appearance. Word applies styles to common text elements, such as bulleted and numbered lists and headings. In addition, Word makes small improvements, such as changing straight quotation marks (") to curved typesetting quotation marks, often called "smart quotes" (" "). You can review and undo the changes Word has made and make further changes of your own.

You can also choose from among many available style groups to change the document format automatically to the style you want. The Style Gallery command displays your document in other styles and lets you select from among them the one you most like.

See Figures 5.1 and 5.2 for an example of how automatic formatting can quickly change your document's appearance with styles.

Instead of directly formatting each word, phrase, paragraph, or page individually, using styles offers several benefits:

■ *Saves time.* You can format one word or paragraph the way you like it and copy that formatting to other words or paragraphs. The AutoFormat command applies styles automatically, quickly formatting a simple document into a professional-appearing document.

FIG. 5.1

You can choose between different families of styles. This letter uses the Contemporary Letter template.

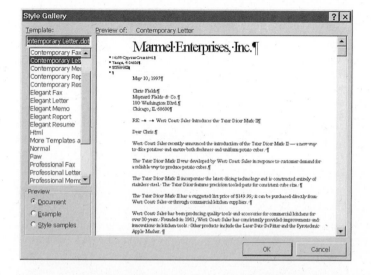

FIG. 5.2

This is the same letter, previewed with the Professional Letter template.

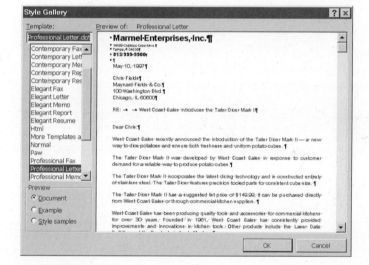

Part
II

Ch
5

- *Preserves consistency.* By using styles to format your document, you can be sure that each selected item or paragraph looks the same as others of its type.

- *Reduces the effort required to change your document's appearance.* By changing a style, you also change all the selected text or paragraphs associated with that style. For example, you can easily change styles used in a proposal or marketing letter to see which gives the appearance you want. Literature produced by a committee can be changed as quickly as the committee changes members.

Choosing a Formatting Method

You're always using at least one style when you work with Word. The *Normal style*, built into Word, gives your document its default formatting choices. If you have the Formatting toolbar displayed when you start a new document, you can see the Normal style in the Style Preview box, already selected (see Figure 5.3). The Normal style's formatting selections are basic: they include a font and font size (12-point MS Serif, 10-point Times New Roman, or a different font, depending on your printer), left alignment, and single-line spacing. Word also makes other styles available for items like page numbers, headers, and footers. You learn how to change the Normal style in the section "Redefining Standard Styles" later in this chapter.

FIG. 5.3

The Normal style is displayed in the Formatting toolbar when you start a new document.

N O T E Style information for a paragraph, such as alignment, is stored in the paragraph mark at the end of each paragraph. If you delete a paragraph mark, that paragraph assumes the style of the next paragraph. If the next paragraph has a different style, you will see a formatting change.

Be aware when deleting paragraph marks. Because of the danger in losing a paragraph's formatting, some Word users prefer to work with paragraph marks showing. You can display paragraph marks in your document by clicking the Show/Hide Paragraph button in the Standard toolbar. When displayed, paragraph marks appear like a reversed bold P (¶), at the end of each paragraph.

The list of styles from which you can select depends on the *template* you select when you create a document. The default template is Normal. In addition to the Normal style, a template may contain styles for indents, tables of contents, titles, headings, lists, envelopes, and many more. You can use the styles built into a template as they come, you can modify them, or you can create your own styles.

▶ **See** "Using Templates as a Pattern for Documents," **p. 8**

Except for the Normal template, which is designed for general use, each template's styles have been designed to suit one particular application, such as a memo, a fax cover sheet, or a résumé. The Normal style in one template may be 10-point Times New Roman, while in another template it may be 12-point Century Schoolbook. Changing the template may change the formatting of the style. Word provides a Style Gallery in which you can preview the effects of changing a template and its resultant changes to the styles you use. The Style Gallery is covered later in this chapter, in the section "Using the Style Gallery."

You can apply and change styles in three ways. Each method has advantages and disadvantages, as described in the following paragraphs.

■ *Method 1.* The fastest formatting method is formatting automatically with Format, AutoFormat.

Advantage: The formatting is done automatically without having to select styles.

Disadvantage: You have less control over the selection of styles, although you can manually override any style selections.

■ *Method 2.* The method that allows you the greatest control over the format of the text is manually formatting by creating, selecting, and/or modifying those styles available in the template on which your document is based.

Advantage: You can make your document appear any way you choose by creating and selecting suitable styles.

Styles you create can be based on existing styles and/or followed by other styles. For example, you can follow a heading style with a body text style, automatically incorporating consistent spacing and other formatting.

Disadvantage: You have to create and/or select a style for each element of your document.

■ *Method 3.* The third formatting method is selecting a new template with Format, Style Gallery.

Advantage: You can preview your document as it will appear based on each of many other templates, and then select and apply that template. For example, you can choose from three different letter styles.

Disadvantage: You have less control over the selection of styles, although you can manually override any style selections.

The following sections describe in detail each method of formatting.

Formatting a Document Automatically

Imagine that you quickly dash off an important business letter, paying no special attention to the letter's formatting. Then with a click of the mouse, the letter suddenly takes the shape of the formal business letter you had in mind. The Format, AutoFormat command gives you that power.

When you choose Format, AutoFormat, Word goes through your document paragraph by paragraph, applying appropriate styles. If you've included a list of items, each preceded with an asterisk, for example, Word reformats the list, replacing asterisks with bullets and adding the bulleted list style. If you've only formatted some of the text, AutoFormat completes the job. AutoFormat ensures that the formatting is consistent throughout the document and also improves the appearance. The styles Word applies come from the template that is currently attached to the document. See Figures 5.4 and 5.5 for an example of a document that has been formatted with AutoFormat.

Part
II

Ch
5

FIG. 5.4

You can type letters, documents, and memos without worrying about formatting.

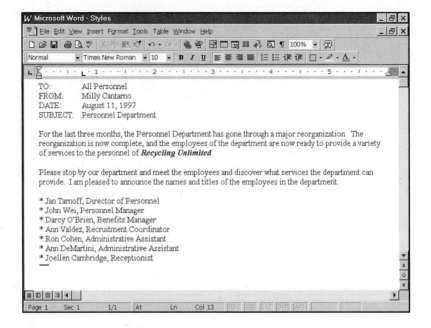

FIG. 5.5

The AutoFormat command uses its rules to apply formats, such as bullets, to your documents.

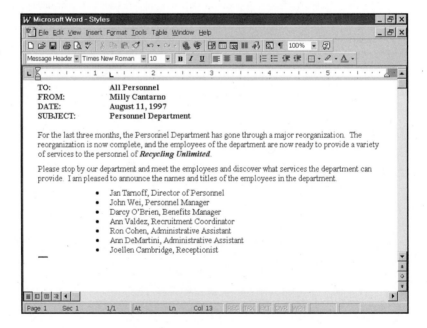

After the text has been formatted with AutoFormat, you can polish the document's appearance by manually applying styles or formatting to any elements of the document. You can also choose a new template from the Style Gallery to change the overall design of the document. Each of these topics is covered later in this chapter, in the sections "Using the Style Gallery" and "Applying, Copying, and Removing Styles."

TROUBLESHOOTING

As I type, Word automatically inserts bullets, changes my tabbed lists to tables, indents lines, or starts automatically numbering lists. It's driving me crazy. How do I turn it off? Word is attempting to help you by automatically formatting as you type. But you're right, it can be very annoying when you don't want its help. There are two ways to handle this feature. If you want automatic formatting most of the time, but just not for this one instance, then backspace over the automatic formatting and retype it as you want it. Word will "learn" that you want it that way and leave it. If you want to turn portions of AutoFormatting off, choose Format, AutoFormat. When the AutoFormat dialog box displays, click Options. Select the AutoFormat as You Type tab from the AutoCorrect dialog box. Clear options for AutoFormatting that you do not want.

Applying Styles with AutoFormat

AutoFormat analyzes the document in the active window and applies a style to each paragraph that is currently formatted with either the Normal or Body Text style. The styles AutoFormat applies are designed to format common writing elements such as quotations, bulleted lists, headings, and more. AutoFormat applies styles and makes corrections as described in the following list:

- Uses its formatting rules to find and format such items as headings, body text, lists, superscript and subscript, addresses, and letter closings.
- Removes extra paragraph marks.
- Replaces straight quotation marks (") and apostrophes (') with typesetting quotation marks (" ") and apostrophes (' ').
- Replaces "(c)," "(R)," and "(TM)" with copyright ©, registered trademark ®, and trademark ™ symbols.
- Replaces asterisks, hyphens, or other characters used to list items with a bullet character (■).
- Replaces horizontal spaces inserted with the Tab key or the space bar with indents.

To format text automatically with the menu command, follow these steps:

1. Select the text you want to format. If you want to format the entire document, position the insertion point anywhere in the document.

2. Choose Format, AutoFormat. The AutoFormat dialog box appears (see Figure 5.6).

Part
II

Ch
5

FIG. 5.6

You can automatically format a document by choosing Format, AutoFormat.

You can determine which changes AutoFormat makes by clicking the Options button in the AutoFormat dialog box or by changing the settings in the AutoFormat tab of the Options dialog box. See the section "Setting AutoFormat Options," later in this chapter, for more information.

3. Select AutoFormat Now to format the document and not review formatting changes.

or

Select AutoFormat and Review Each Change to accept or reject formatting after this procedure is complete.

To improve AutoFormat's accuracy when selecting formats, open the list box and choose the type of document you are formatting: General document, Letter, or Email.

4. Choose OK to begin formatting. Word reviews the text and selects styles from the current template.

5. When AutoFormat is finished, the document will have the new format. If you selected the AutoFormat and Review option then another dialog box appears, and you have four choices (see Figure 5.7):

FIG. 5.7

When AutoFormat is complete, you can choose to accept or reject all changes, to review the changes, or to change templates in the Style Gallery.

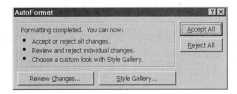

- Choose Accept All to accept all the changes.

- Choose Reject All to reject all the changes.

- Choose Review Changes to examine changes one by one, accepting or rejecting individual changes. See "Reviewing Format Changes" in this section for more information.

- Choose Style Gallery to apply styles from another template. See "Using the Style Gallery" later in this chapter for more information.

If you don't like the result of the AutoFormatting, you can undo the formatting changes you've made.

To undo all changes after accepting them, click the down-arrow button next to the Undo button on the Standard toolbar and undo AutoFormat Begin.

> **CAUTION**
>
> You may have noticed, in the AutoFormat dialog box, the AutoFormat Now option. If you choose this option, Word doesn't prompt you to review the changes it makes—you simply see them on-screen. If you don't like what you see, click the Undo button.

 TIP You can automatically format tables with AutoFormat on the Table menu.

▶ **See** "Formatting a Table with Table AutoFormat," **p. 301**

Reviewing Format Changes

After a document has been automatically formatted, you may want to review the changes and possibly make some alterations. You can choose the Review Changes button in the AutoFormat dialog box to review the changes one by one (refer to Figure 5.7). As you review each change, you can accept or reject it. You can also scroll through the document and select specific changes for review.

Word indicates changes to text and formatting with temporary revision marks and color. With paragraph marks displayed, Word highlights the extra paragraph marks it deleted and also those to which a style was applied.

To display paragraph marks, click the Show/Hide ¶ button on the Standard toolbar.

You can also review the document with the revision marks hidden. To hide revision marks, choose the Hide Marks button in the Review AutoFormat Changes dialog box.

Table 5.1 describes Word's revision marks.

Part

II

Ch

5

Table 5.1 AutoFormat Revision Marks

Visual Change	Meaning
Blue paragraph mark (¶)	Applied a style to that paragraph
Red paragraph mark (¶)	Deleted that paragraph mark
Strikethrough character (–)	Deleted text or spaces (indicated in red)
Underline (_)	Added the underlined characters (indicated in blue)
Vertical bar in the left margin	Changed the text or formatting in that line of text

To review changes made by AutoFormat, follow these steps:

1. After Word completes the AutoFormat, choose the Review Changes button. The Review AutoFormat Changes dialog box appears (see Figure 5.8).

FIG. 5.8

Use options in the Review AutoFormat Changes dialog box to reject or accept the changes made by AutoFormat.

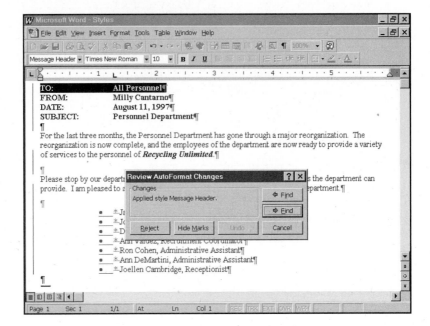

2. Choose from among the following options to target the change(s) you want to review:

   To see text under the dialog box, drag the box by its title bar to a new location.

   To see the entire document, use the vertical scroll bar in the document window to scroll through the document.

   To see changes one by one, use the Find buttons in the Review AutoFormat Changes dialog box.

   To see the effect of another style, select the text and then select another style from the Style Preview box on the Formatting toolbar.

3. Choose from among the following options to alter the selected change:

   To undo the displayed change, choose Reject.

   To undo the last rejected change, choose Undo.

   To view the document with all remaining changes and revision marks turned off, choose Hide Marks.

4. Click the Cancel button to accept all remaining changes. Any text for which you rejected returns to its original appearance, but Word applies all remaining changes. The AutoFormat dialog box is displayed again.

5. Choose <u>A</u>ccept All to accept all changes.

   Or, you can choose <u>R</u>eject All to reject all changes.

   You can even choose <u>S</u>tyle Gallery to select a different AutoFormat style.

 T I P   AutoFormat can format a document with styles you've designed if you redefine the built-in styles. See "Getting the Most from AutoFormat" and "Creating Styles" later in this chapter.

Setting AutoFormat Options

You can change the rules that Word follows each time it performs an AutoFormat. You can choose whether to apply styles to headings and lists, for example.

To change the AutoFormat formatting rules, follow these steps:

1. Choose F<u>o</u>rmat, <u>A</u>utoFormat and select the <u>O</u>ptions button to display the AutoCorrect dialog box. Then, choose the Auto Format tab (see Figure 5.9).

FIG. 5.9

Specify the settings you want to control the changes Word makes during an AutoFormat.

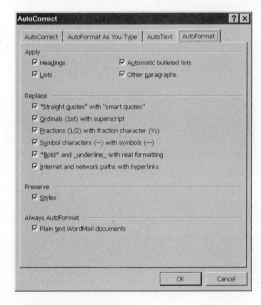

2. Select from the Apply group the document parts to which you want Word to apply styles (selected options are marked with a ✓).

3. Select from the Replace group the characters or symbols you want Word to replace (selected options are marked with a ✓).

4. Click OK.

The options for AutoFormat As You Type now appear on their own tab in the AutoCorrect dialog box. Choose F<u>o</u>rmat, <u>A</u>utoFormat, and then select AutoFormat As You Type.

T I P To speed up the formatting process, have Word automatically format as you type. Set the options for this type of automatic formatting on the AutoFormat As You Type tab in the AutoCorrect dialog box. This tab contains three sections: Apply As You Type, Replace As You Type, and Automatically As You Type.

Getting the Most from AutoFormat

Any formatting you have applied using commands on the Format menu helps Word determine which styles to apply during AutoFormat. For example, styles previously applied can be preserved or changed, depending on the settings you establish on the AutoFormat tab (see the preceding section). In addition, the following tips will help you maximize the results you get from the AutoFormat command.

- *Use a larger font for level 1 headings than you use for subordinate level headings.* Higher heading style levels are applied to larger point sizes.
- *Clear all the check boxes on the AutoFormat tab, choose OK, and then do an AutoFormat.* Extra hard returns will be removed from files, such as those you've converted from another file format.
- *Type (c), (R), or (TM).* Word converts this text to the appropriate ©, ®, or ™ symbol.
- *Redefine built-in styles.* Word assigns styles, such as heading styles, formatted as you want them.

▶ **See** "Checking Your Grammar," **p. 44**

Using the Style Gallery

Each document you create is based on a template. When you create a new document, the styles that are part of the template you select are copied into that document. Each template contains a set of standard styles, most of which are available with all Word's templates. Styles in one template may differ from those in another. For example, Heading 1 in the Normal template uses Arial 14-point, whereas in the Professional Fax template, Heading 1 is Arial MT Black 11-point. You can use Format, Style Gallery to preview and then change the appearance of a document by switching the style definitions to those of another template.

You can choose from any of the document templates that appear in the New dialog box when you start a new document. You'll find templates in the following categories—fax cover sheet, legal pleading, letter, memo, report, resume, newsletter, and Web page—and, of course, any existing templates from Word 7. Many of Word's templates fit into one of three families:

- Contemporary
- Professional
- Elegant

▶ **See** "Using Word's Predefined Templates," **p. 8**

Starting in Word 7, you'll find a template name preceded by its family name; for example, the fax template in the Contemporary style family is named CONTEMPORARY FAX.DOT. In Word 6, each template name was followed by a number to indicate the family into which it fit, but the long file names feature of Windows 95 lets Microsoft eliminate the use of this coding system.

To preview and change styles in the Style Gallery, follow these steps:

1. Display in the active window the document whose styles you want to change.

2. Choose F̲ormat, Style G̲allery. The Style Gallery dialog box appears (see Figure 5.10).

FIG. 5.10

Use the Style Gallery to preview your document with styles from other templates.

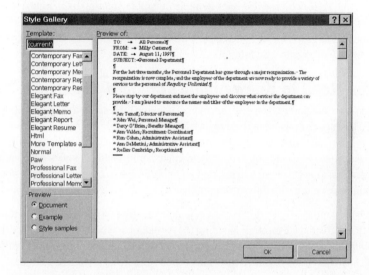

3. Select one of the following in the Preview group:

  Select D̲ocument to see the active document formatted with the styles from the template you select.

  Select E̲xample to see sample text formatted with the styles from the template you select.

  Select S̲tyle Samples to see a list of styles available in the selected template including text samples of each style.

4. Select the T̲emplate you want to preview. Continue to preview other templates by selecting them.

5. Choose OK to accept the selected template. Word copies the styles from the template you selected to the active document.

  Or, choose Cancel to return to your document with its original template intact.

When you change the styles in the Style Gallery, you are copying the style formatting from the new template into the active document. You aren't replacing the template; you're replacing the style definitions in the current document only. For example, the original Body Text style of

Part
II

Ch
5

Times New Roman 10-point may be replaced by Times New Roman 12-point. In addition, any styles that exist in the new template and not in the one attached to the document are added to the document. Any styles that are unique to the document aren't affected by the change.

▶ **See** "Modifying Templates," **p. 14**

Using Word Standard Styles

Word includes a great number of *standard*, or *built-in styles*. You already are familiar with the Normal style, which Word uses to apply default formatting to all new documents based on the default Normal template. Other standard styles include those that provide formatting for outline headings, headers, footers, page numbers, line numbers, index entries, table of contents entries, comments, and footnotes.

What You Need to Know About Standard Styles

In a new document, you see the styles Heading 1, Heading 2, Heading 3, Normal, and Default Paragraph Font listed in the Formatting toolbar's Style Preview box. Word applies these styles automatically when you use the AutoFormat feature, and you can apply these styles to selected paragraphs yourself. You are likely to apply some standard styles automatically by creating headers, footers, index entries, and so on. After you use these styles in your document, their names appear in the Formatting toolbar's Style Preview box.

Many standard styles do more than just format text. When you use the automatic heading styles (Heading 1 through Heading 9), for example, you later can collect these headings into a table of contents. Or, if you insert table of contents entries (formatted with the styles TOC 1 through TOC 9), you later can collect these entries as a table of contents. Similarly, if you insert index or footnote entries into your document, Word collects them where you have specified they are to appear in your document.

▶ **See** "Formatting an Index," **p. 476**

▶ **See** "Creating a Table of Contents Using Any Style," **p. 487**

▶ **See** "Formatting Cross-References," **p. 525**

▶ **See** "Formatting Captions," **p. 532**

To apply standard styles from the menu command, follow these steps:

1. Position the insertion point where you want the new style to begin or select the text or paragraph(s) you want formatted in the new style. (To format a single paragraph, you can position the insertion point anywhere in the paragraph.)

2. Choose Format, Style. The Style dialog box opens (see Figure 5.11).

3. Choose All Styles in the List drop-down list. All styles are displayed in the Styles list.

4. Select a style from the Styles list and choose the Apply button.

FIG. 5.11

Select any of the standard styles from the Style dialog box.

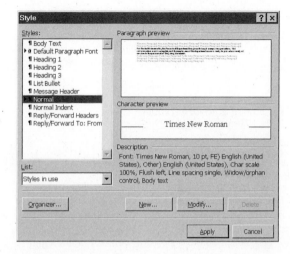

To apply standard styles from the Formatting toolbar, follow these steps:

1. Position the insertion point where you want the new style to begin or select the text or paragraph(s) you want formatted in the new style. (To format a single paragraph, you can position the insertion point anywhere in the paragraph.)

2. Click the down arrow next to the Style Preview box in the Formatting toolbar. Each style in the list appears formatted using the attributes it will apply to your document (see Figure 5.12).

FIG. 5.12

When you display styles from the Formatting Toolbar, you'll see them using the formatting they will apply to your document.

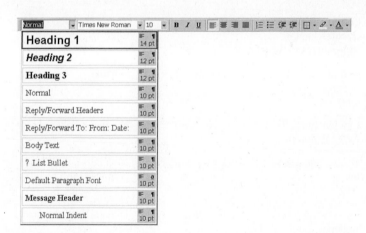

Styles appear in the Style Preview box using the formatting they will apply to your document. The gray box at the right edge of the line shows you the font size of the style. You can tell the style's alignment by the four horizontal lines that appear in the same gray box. And, the symbol in the gray box (either a or ¶) identifies the type of style—character or paragraph.

3. Click the style you want to apply.

N O T E The Style Preview box in the Formatting toolbar shows the style at the position of the insertion point or of the selected text. If the text selection includes text formatted with more than one style, the Style Preview box is blank. ■

Table 5.2 describes some of the Word standard styles.

Table 5.2 Word Standard Styles

Standard Style or Style Family	Style Type	Default Formatting	How Applied
Normal (used by default to format all new text)	Paragraph	10- or 12-point serif font (varies with printer), left-aligned, single line spacing, widow/orphan control	Applied to all text in automatically document that is based on the Normal template
Normal Indent (indents paragraphs)	Paragraph	Normal + 1/2-inch left indent	Manually
Heading 1 through Heading 9 (formats outline headings)	Paragraph	Formatting ranges from large and bold (Heading 1) to small and italic	Outline view
Comment Reference (creates hidden comment references)	Character	Normal + 8 point Font	Insert, Comment
Comment Text (formats comment text)	Paragraph	Normal	Typing annotation text in the comment pane
Caption (formats figure captions)	Paragraph	Normal + bold	Insert, Caption
Footer (formats footers)	Paragraph	Normal + 3-inch centered tab, 6-inch right tab	View, Header and Footer
Footnote Reference (formats footnote references)	Character	Default Paragraph Font	Insert, Footnote
Endnote Reference (formats endnote references)	Character	Default Paragraph Font	Insert, Endnote

Standard Style or Style Family	Style Type	Default Formatting	How Applied
Footnote text (formats footnote text)	Paragraph	Normal	Typing footnote text
Endnote text (formats endnote text)	Paragraph	Normal	Typing endnote text
Header (formats headers)	Paragraph	Normal + 3-inch centered tab, 6-inch right tab	View, Header and Footer command
Index 1 through Index 9 (formats index entries)	Paragraph	Varies with selection of index formats	Insert, Index and Tables, Index tab
Index Heading (formats optional heading separators in index)	Paragraph	Varies with selection of index formats	Insert, Index and Tables, Index tab
Line Number (formats line numbers)	Character	Normal	File, Page Setup Layout tab, Line Numbers
Page Number	Character	Normal	Insert, Page Numbers
TOC 1 through TOC 9 (formats table of contents entries)	Paragraph	Varies with selection of Table of Contents formats	Insert, Index and Tables, Table of Contents tab

Notice that the formatting for many standard styles is based on the Normal style. In other words, many styles include all the formatting contained in the Normal style plus additional formatting choices. The header and footer styles, for example, are Normal style plus tab settings.

N O T E If you change the Normal style, any other style based on the Normal style also changes. If you change the Normal style to double spacing, for example, headers, footers, index entries, and all other styles based on Normal also will include double spacing. If the other style includes its own definition for line spacing, then that definition takes precedence over the Normal line spacing. ■

T I P You can redefine a standard style except the Default Paragraph Font, but you cannot delete a standard style.

Part
II

Ch
5

Redefining Standard Styles

Standard styles come with predefined formatting, but you can easily redefine them. Suppose that you want to use the standard heading styles (Heading 1 through Heading 9) to format your document because you can use the Outline view to apply these styles and because you want to collect the headings later as a table of contents. Unfortunately, you don't like the default formatting choices Word has made for the heading styles. Redefine the styles, using either the styles-by-example techniques, or by using Format, Style; both methods are described later in this chapter.

Displaying Styles with the Style Area

If you're working with styles extensively, you can display the style area on your screen to list each paragraph's style name in the left margin (see Figure 5.13).

FIG. 5.13

Use the Style Area to display the names of the styles currently in use.

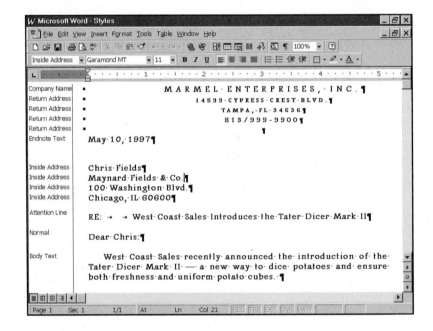

Using the style area, you can see at a glance which style is applied to each paragraph. With your mouse, you also can use the style area to quickly access the Style dialog box.

To apply and redefine styles quickly, double-click the style name in the style area to display the Style dialog box. From there, you can apply, create, or redefine a style.

The width of the style area varies. When you first display the style area, you set its width. After it's displayed, however, you can change its width by using a mouse to drag the line separating the style area from the text to the left or right. You can close the style area entirely by dragging the arrow all the way to the left edge of the screen, or by resetting the style area width to zero.

To display or remove the style area, follow these steps:

1. Choose Tools, Options.
2. Select the View tab. The View dialog box lists all the view settings you can modify.
3. Type the style area width you want in decimal inches in the Style Area Width box.

   Or, click the up or down arrows at the right end of the Style Area Width spin box to increase or decrease the style area width by tenths of an inch.

   Or, type **0** (zero) to remove the style area from the screen.
4. Choose OK.

 By single-clicking the style name in the style area, you quickly can select an entire paragraph.

Overriding Styles with Manual Formatting

Although you can do most of your formatting with styles, at times you will need to override the formatting in a style you have already applied. You may want to do something simple, like making one word in a paragraph bold, or maybe something more substantial, like italicizing a whole paragraph. You can modify the formatting in a paragraph without changing the style.

Be aware, however, of the effect your formatting will have on the paragraph if you later reapply the style. Reapplying the style may cancel some of the manual formatting changes you have made. Manual formatting works with styles as follows:

- If the reapplied style contains formatting choices in the same category as those you have applied manually, the style's choices override the manual formatting. If you have manually applied double line spacing, but the style specifies single line spacing, for example, then the double line spacing is canceled when you apply the style.
- If the reapplied style contains formatting choices unrelated to the formatting you have applied manually, the style won't affect manual formatting. If you add a border to a paragraph and then reapply a style that doesn't specify borders, for example, the border will remain.
- Some character formatting choices toggle on and off—you select bold to turn it on and select it again to turn it off. If you apply a style containing bold to a paragraph with one or two words that are bold, for example, then all of the paragraph will be bold except the one or two words that you manually formatted as bold (the style toggles them off). On the other hand, if you make a whole paragraph bold, then reapply a style that contains bold, Word leaves the paragraph bold rather than toggling off the bold.
- If you want to remove all manually applied character formatting from a word formatted with a style, move the insertion point into the word that was manually formatted, then press Ctrl+Spacebar.
- If you want to remove all manually applied paragraph formatting from a paragraph formatted with a style, place the insertion point anywhere in that paragraph and press Ctrl+Q.

Part

II

Ch

5

Applying, Copying, and Removing Styles

The power of styles becomes apparent when you use them to apply consistent formatting to paragraph after paragraph in your document. You can apply styles to text as you type or to selected text by choosing a style from a menu command, from the Formatting toolbar, or with a keyboard shortcut. You will mostly use the Formatting toolbar.

By default, the Formatting toolbar appears when you start Word. If you don't see it, you can display the Formatting toolbar by following these steps:

1. Choose View, Toolbars.
2. Select Formatting from the Toolbars list. A checkmark appears in the box to indicate that it is selected.

Resolving Conflicts Between Paragraph and Character Style

When you first begin to work with styles, you may not realize that there are two types of styles—paragraph and character. It is important to understand how these two styles interact. Because characters are within paragraphs, applying a paragraph style to a paragraph can change the appearance of the characters with a character style.

N O T E Remember that paragraph styles can include both paragraph-level formatting commands and character-level formatting. Character styles include only character-level formatting commands. Any paragraph style you apply to text formats the entire paragraph (or the group of selected paragraphs). If a paragraph style includes character formatting, it too is applied to the entire paragraph. If you apply a character style, such as bold, to text in a paragraph, and then apply a paragraph style that includes bold, the text you boldfaced with the character style appears normal, rather than bold, because the paragraph style toggles off bold.

Applying Paragraph Styles

To apply a paragraph style to a single paragraph, the insertion point must first be positioned anywhere in that paragraph. You can apply a paragraph style to a group of paragraphs by first selecting those paragraphs, or at least part of each paragraph (see Figure 5.14).

Applying Character Styles

To apply a character style, you must first select the text to which you want to apply the character style. The formatting of the new style will be added to those formats already in effect on the selected text. For example, a character style that adds bold and italic doesn't change the font or point size or other formatting applied by the paragraph style in use.

To apply a style from the menu, follow these steps:

1. Position the insertion point inside the paragraph, or select text in the paragraph(s) you want to format with a style.

FIG. 5.14

All of these paragraphs will change with a new style selection because at least part of each paragraph has been selected.

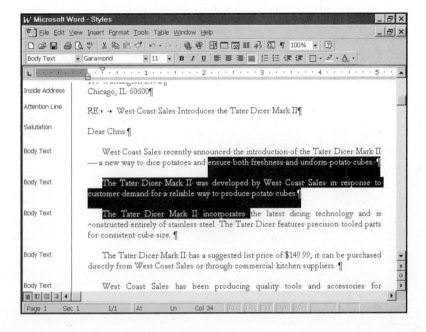

2. Choose Format, Style. The Style dialog box appears.

3. Click the down arrow to the right of the List box and select one of the following options:

   Select the Styles in Use option to list standard styles and those you've created or modified for the current document.

   Select the All Styles option to list all styles available in the document.

   Select the User-Defined Styles option to list non-standard styles that you have created for the document.

4. Select the style you want from the Styles list box. Paragraph styles are preceded by the ¶ symbol; character styles are preceded by the a symbol. The Paragraph Preview and Character Preview boxes provide a sample of how the style appears.

5. Choose Apply.

To apply a style from the Formatting toolbar, follow these steps:

1. Position the insertion point inside the paragraph, or select text in the paragraph(s) you want to format with a style.

   In Word 97, you can distinguish a character style from a paragraph style by the symbol that appears in the same box where you see the style's point size.

2. Click the down arrow at the right side of the Style Preview box in the Formatting toolbar to display a list of available styles. In the box at the right that identifies the font size for the style, you'll see the ¶ symbol for paragraph styles and the a symbol for character styles (see Figure 5.15).

Part
II
Ch
5

FIG. 5.15

You can distinguish paragraph styles from character styles by looking for the symbols in the box that displays the style's font size.

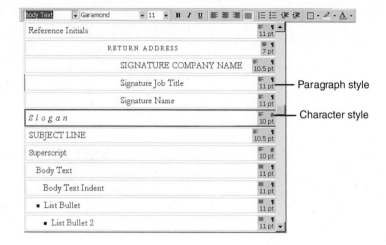

3. Select the style you want to apply to the paragraph(s) or selected text (scroll the list if necessary).

TIP The styles listed in the Style Preview box are only a partial list of what's available. To see the entire list, hold down the Shift key while you click the down arrow next to the Style Preview box.

To apply a style from the keyboard, follow these steps:

1. Position the insertion point inside the paragraph, or select text in the paragraph(s) you want to format with a style.

2. Press any of the following key combinations:

Press This	To Apply This Style
Ctrl+Alt+1	Heading 1
Ctrl+Alt+2	Heading 2
Ctrl+Alt+3	Heading 3
Ctrl+Shift+L	List Bullet (bulleted list style)
Ctrl+Shift+N	Normal
Ctrl+Shift+S	Activates the Style Preview box on the Formatting toolbar; choose the style you want from the list

When you press Ctrl+Shift+S, Word selects the currently displayed style in the Style Preview box in the Formatting toolbar. To select another, either type a different name in the Style Preview box, or use the arrow keys to highlight another style and then press Enter. If you type the name of a style that doesn't exist, you will create a style based on the example of the selected paragraph or paragraphs, rather than applying a style.

You can assign shortcut keys to other styles, as well. See "Creating Style Shortcut Keys" later in this chapter.

Copying Styles

You can apply the same style several times consecutively. Apply the style the first time, then select the additional text you want to format with that style, and press F4 or Ctrl+Y. Continue the procedure to apply the style in other locations. This method works for both paragraph styles and character styles.

You also can use the Format Painter button on the Standard toolbar to copy character styles to paragraphs or selected text, one or several times.

To copy character styles with the Format Painter button, follow these steps:

1. Select the text or paragraph mark (¶) that has the formatting you want to copy.
2. Click the Format Painter button on the Standard toolbar.
3. Select the text you want to format with the character style. The new character style is applied to the selected text.

To copy character styles multiple times with the Format Painter button, repeat the steps above but double-click in step 2. To turn off the copy process, click the Format Painter button again.

 TIP If there are a lot of instances where you want to replace one style with another, then use Word's Edit, Replace command to replace all or selectively replace one style with another.

▶ **See** " Finding and Replacing Formatting and Styles," **p. 32**

Removing Character Styles

You can remove a character style and reapply the default character formatting, which will match the character formats defined for the selected paragraph style.

To remove a character style, place the insertion point in the word or select the text formatted with the character style you want to remove, and press Ctrl+Spacebar.

Creating Styles

The process of using styles of your own involves two steps. First, you create the style, specifying formatting choices like paragraph indentations, line spacing, font, and font size. Then you apply that style—along with all your formatting choices—to other characters or paragraphs in your document.

You can create paragraph styles in two ways: by example (using the Formatting toolbar or a keyboard shortcut) or by menu command. Creating a style by example is a good method for a beginner to use; because creating a style by example is so easy, many advanced users also prefer this technique. Alternatively, using a menu command gives you more options, including creating character styles, and isn't difficult when you understand the concept of styles. (See "Creating Styles with a Menu Command" later in this chapter.)

Part
II
Ch
5

N O T E Styles are saved with the document or template in which you create them. You can share styles with other documents, however. (See the section "Copying Styles Between Documents" later in this chapter.)

Naming the New Style

A new style name must be unique. If you try to create a new style with an existing name, you apply the existing style to your paragraph instead of creating a new style. If that happens, choose Edit, Undo and try again. Be aware that Word includes quite a few built-in styles (like Normal and Heading 1 through Heading 9); don't create new styles using the names of these built-in styles. For a list of built-in styles, refer to the section "Using Word Standard Styles" earlier in this chapter.

As you're naming your style, remember these rules:

- A style name can contain as many as 253 characters. Try, however, to use simple, memorable style names.
- The name can contain spaces, commas, and aliases. An *alias* is an optional, shorter name (see "Giving a Style a New Name or Alias" later in this chapter).
- Style names are case-sensitive—you can use uppercase and lowercase letters.
- Illegal characters include backslash (\), braces ({ or }), and semicolon (;).

Choose a style name that makes sense to you so that you will remember it later and use it consistently in other documents. If you frequently use small caps in your documents, for example, create a style called Small Caps and use it to quickly format text.

Creating a Style by Example

To create a style by example, you format a paragraph the way you want it, and then create a style based on the formatting contained in that paragraph. If your sample paragraph contains left and right indents and a border, those formatting choices will also be part of your style. As you format your first paragraph (the one you will use as an example to create a style), remember that although paragraph styles are paragraph-level formatting commands, they also can contain character formatting. The character-level formatting is defined by the font, size, and other character formats of the first character of the selected text.

To create a style by example, follow these steps:

1. Choose View, Toolbars and select the Formatting toolbar (if it isn't already displayed).
2. Format your sample paragraph.

   You can include character or paragraph formatting, borders and shading, frames and positioning, tabs, and a language for spell checking.
3. With the insertion point still in your sample paragraph, select the entire name of the existing style in the Formatting toolbar's Style Preview box, or press Ctrl+Shift+S to select the name of the style in the Style Preview box (see Figure 5.16).

FIG. 5.16

Select the current style name in the Formatting toolbar's Style Preview box.

4. Type the name of the style you want to create (see Figure 5.17).

FIG. 5.17

Type the new style name to create a style by example.

5. Press Enter to create the style.

After you create your style, look in the Formatting toolbar's Style Preview box. You see your new style name displayed, indicating that its formatting choices control the appearance of your sample paragraph.

You also can use a menu command to create a style by example. You might do this, for example, if you want to use a formatted paragraph as the basis for a style, but you also want to add additional formatting choices to the style.

To create a style by example using the menu command, follow these steps:

1. Format the paragraph you want to use as an example for your style, and leave the insertion point inside the paragraph.
2. Choose Format, Style and choose the New button. (See "Creating a Style with a Menu Command" for details on using this dialog box.)
3. In the Name box, type the name of your new style.
4. Choose Format and make additional formatting choices, if necessary.
5. Choose OK to return to the Style dialog box.
6. Choose Close.

Creating a Style with a Menu Command

If you want to create styles before you use them, rather than creating them by example, use Format, Style. Using this command, you name a style, define its formatting characteristics, and select options such as whether to base the style on another style, whether to follow it with another style, and whether to add the style to the current template. You can also import and export styles to and from other documents and templates. Also, using this method, you can create both types of styles: paragraph and character.

When you create a style by using the menu command, you have the option to apply the style to the currently selected paragraph or simply to add it to the list of styles you created for your document (or for your template).

All new styles you create are based on the style of the currently selected paragraph in your document. In the next section, you learn how you can base your new style on any other style.

 T I P If you plan to use your styles over and over in the same type of document, as in a monthly newsletter, create them in a new template.

▶ **See** "Creating a New Template," **p. 18**

 T I P If you want to print a list of a document's styles (along with a description of each style), choose File, Print, select Styles in the Print What box, and then choose OK.

To create a style from the menu command, follow these steps:

1. Choose Format, Style. The Style dialog box appears.

   Notice that the preview boxes display both the paragraph and character formatting of the currently selected paragraph. The Description box indicates the precise characteristics of the formatting.

2. Click the New button. The New Style dialog box appears (see Figure 5.18).

FIG. 5.18

You can create styles in the New Style dialog box.

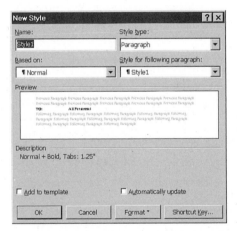

3. In the Name box, type the name of your new style. Use a unique, brief, and easy-to-recall name. Refer to "Naming the New Style," earlier in this chapter, for style naming rules.

4. In the Style Type box, select Character to create a character style, or Paragraph to create a paragraph style.

5. Click the Format button to display the list of format options and select the one you want (if you want to include bold formatting as part of your style, for example, select Font to display the Font dialog box, then select the Bold option from the Font Style group):

Select This	To Select These Formatting Options
Font	Font, style (bold, italic, underline), size, color, super/subscript, and character spacing
Paragraph	Paragraph alignment, spacing, indentation, and line spacing (not available for character styles)
Tabs	Tab stop position, alignment, and leaders, or clear tabs (not available for character styles)
Border	Border location, style, color, and paragraph shading (not available for character styles)
Language	The language that the spell checker, thesaurus, and grammar checker should use for the current paragraph
Frame	Text wrapping, frame size or position, or remove frame (not available for character styles)
Numbering	Bulleted and Numbered paragraphs in various styles (not available for character styles)

Repeat this step to include as much formatting as you want.

6. Choose OK.

   To create additional styles, you can repeat steps 2 through 5 before closing the dialog box.

7. To apply your new style to the currently selected paragraph, choose Apply.

   Or, to exit the Style dialog box without applying the style to any paragraph, choose Close.

> **CAUTION**
>
> When you type the name of your new style in step 2, be sure that it is a unique name. If you type the name of an existing style and then make formatting choices, you will redefine the existing style. Any text formatted with the existing style then takes on this redefined formatting.

Part
II

Ch
5

As part of the process of creating a style, you can assign shortcut keys to make the style easy to apply. See the later section "Creating Style Shortcut Keys."

Creating a Style Based on an Existing Style

You may need a group of styles that are similar to each other but have slight variations. For example, you may need a Table Body style for the contents of a table, and you also may need a Table Heading style and a Table Last Row style. Using the following technique, you can create a "family" of styles based on one foundation style.

To base one style on another style, follow these steps:

1. Choose Format, Style.

2. Choose New.

3. Choose <u>N</u>ame and type the name of your new style.

4. Specify the name of the style on which you want to base your style in the <u>B</u>ased On box. To display a list of styles, click the down arrow to the right of the <u>B</u>ased On box.

   When you select a style name, you see the name of the style plus any formatting attributes from the selected paragraph in the Description box. Your new style automatically is based on that existing style, unless you specify a different style.

5. Choose any of the F<u>o</u>rmat button options to add formatting options to your style.

6. Choose OK to return to the Style dialog box.

7. Choose Close.

   Or, choose <u>A</u>pply if you want to apply your new style to the currently selected paragraph.

▶ **See** "Creating a New Template," **p. 18**

Creating Style Shortcut Keys

A fast way to apply a style is with a shortcut key, which you can assign as part of the process of creating or redefining a style. The shortcut keys usually include pressing the Alt key plus a letter that you designate. You could assign the shortcut Alt+S, for example, to a style called Sub. You can use other key combinations if you want, but they may conflict with shortcut keys preassigned to Word built-in functions. (Word uses Ctrl+Shift+S, for example, to enable you to create or apply a style quickly, so you wouldn't want to assign Ctrl+Shift+S to your style Sub.)

To create shortcut keys for styles, follow these steps:

1. Choose F<u>o</u>rmat, <u>S</u>tyle.

2. From the <u>S</u>tyles list, highlight the style for which you want to create shortcut keys.

3. Click the <u>M</u>odify button.

4. Click the Shortcut <u>K</u>ey button. The Customize Keyboard dialog box opens (see Figure 5.19).

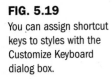

FIG. 5.19

You can assign shortcut keys to styles with the Customize Keyboard dialog box.

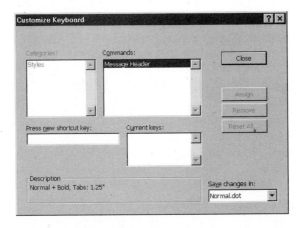

5. Select the Press New Shortcut Key text box, and press the shortcut key combination you want to use. You can use the letters A through Z, the numbers 0 through 9, Insert, and Delete, combined with Ctrl, Alt, and Shift.

If the shortcut key combination you selected is already in use, Word displays the message Currently Assigned To and the command or function to which the shortcut key is assigned. If the shortcut key isn't assigned, the Currently Assigned To message line displays [unassigned].

TIP To try another combination, press the Backspace key to delete the combination you initially selected.

6. Click the Assign button.
7. Click the Close button to return to the Modify Style dialog box.
8. Choose OK to return to the Style dialog box.
9. Choose Close.

To remove a shortcut key, follow these steps:

1. Choose Format, Style.
2. From the Styles list, highlight the style for which you want to remove the shortcut key.
3. Click the Modify button.
4. Click the Shortcut Key button.
5. Select the shortcut key you want to remove in the Current Keys box.
6. Click the Remove button.
7. Click Close to return to the Modify Style dialog box.
8. Choose OK to return to the Style dialog box.
9. Choose Close.

To apply a style with a shortcut key you have assigned, follow these steps:

1. Select the paragraph (or paragraphs) to which you want to apply the style.
2. Press the key combination you assigned to the style. (If your shortcut is Alt+C, for example, hold down Alt while you press C.)

Following One Style with the Next Style

One of the most useful style options is the ability to follow one style with another. Suppose that you're editing a complex document with many subheadings, all formatted with styles. You want the text following each subheading to be formatted with the Normal style. You would save considerable time and effort if you didn't have to manually apply the Normal style to the paragraph following each subheading. Setting one style to follow another saves you that time and effort. If you tell Word that the Normal style should follow the subheading style, then, when you finish typing a subheading and press Enter, Word automatically applies the Normal style to the next paragraph.

Part
II

Ch
5

By default, Word follows each style with that same style so that when you press Enter, the style carries forward. In many cases, that's what you want. When you finish typing a paragraph formatted with the Normal style, typically you want the next paragraph also to be formatted with the Normal style.

To follow one style with another style, follow these steps:

1. Choose Format, Style.

2. Click the New button to create a new style. The New Style dialog box appears.

   Or, highlight an existing style from the list and click Modify. The Modify Style dialog box appears.

3. Select from the Style for Following Paragraph list box the style that you want to follow the current style. To display a list of styles, click the down arrow to the right of the Style for Following Paragraph box.

   If you select no style, your style will be followed by itself.

4. Choose OK to return to the Style dialog box.

5. Choose Close.

Copying Styles Between Documents

Every document you create includes styles—even if it's only the Normal style and Word's other standard styles. Each document's group of styles is provided by its template—either the Normal template, one of the other templates provided with Word, or a custom template you create.

In its simplest sense, using a template is the basic way you can share styles among documents. You create a template that contains certain styles you need, and then base your documents on that template. You may, for example, have a template called Letters that contains styles for formatting letters to be printed on your company's letterhead. If you regularly produce several different types of documents, you may create a template for each of them.

▶ **See** "Creating a New Template," **p. 18**

At some point, however, you may want to use the styles from one document or template in a different document or template. You can do that by copying styles from one document or template to another. For example, you might create a template that includes styles for a sales letter that you frequently write. You notice a coworker's letter that includes a nice style. Using the following technique, you can copy the style you want from your coworker's template to your sales letter template.

You can copy styles to or from any document or template. If you copy an identically named style, it replaces the one in the document or template you're copying to (you will be asked to confirm the replacement); new styles are added to the document or template to which you're copying.

To copy styles from a document or template, follow these steps:

1. Choose Format, Style.

2. Click the Organizer button. The Organizer dialog box appears.

   The In box on the left displays a list of the styles in the currently open document or template. The To box on the right displays a list of the styles of the NORMAL.DOT template.

3. Select Close File (below the appropriate list) to close the current document style list or the Normal template style list. When you close either the current document or the Normal template, the Close File button changes to an Open File button and you can open a different document or template.

4. Select Open File (below the appropriate list) to open a different document or template to copy its styles. The Open dialog box appears; select the document you want to use. If you want to select a template, open the Files of Type in the Open dialog box to choose Document Templates (*.dot). If necessary, change folders or drives. When you find the document or template you want to open, choose the Open button to return to the Organizer dialog box.

5. Select the styles you want to copy from the In or To lists. The Copy button arrows change direction to indicate the direction the styles will be copied.

   You can select a contiguous group of styles by clicking the first one you want to copy, then holding down Shift while you click the last one you want to copy. To select noncontiguous styles, hold down Ctrl while you click each one.

6. Choose Copy.

7. Choose Close.

Another way to merge a *single* style into a document is to copy into your document a paragraph formatted with a different style from another document. Be careful, though. Copying styles into your document this way doesn't override existing styles, as does copying styles through the Organizer dialog box. If you copy a paragraph formatted with a style called First Item, for example, and your existing document also contains a style called First Item, the new paragraph will take on the formatting of the existing First Item style.

 TIP You can avoid copying the style along with the paragraph into the new document by not including the paragraph mark with the text you're copying.

Other commands for inserting text into a document, such as AutoText, Paste, and Paste Special, also can bring in new styles. You can copy in as many as 50 paragraphs that contain unique style names—if you copy in more than 50, Word merges in the document's entire style sheet.

Part

II

Ch

5

Changing Styles

You can change any style, including standard styles. This capability makes it easy to adapt to the changing tasks you have to do. For example, suppose you defined a style for closing signatures and your company develops a new format. You don't need to define a new style; you can simply redefine the style you previously created. All you need to do is continue working like you did before; the new style definition takes care of the changes.

There are many ways to change a style. To name just a few, you can redefine the style to incorporate new or different characteristics, or you can delete or rename the style. To make assigning styles easier, provide an alias for a style. The following sections discuss these and other techniques for changing styles.

> **CAUTION**
>
> Make sure you save the template containing the styles you have modified. If you do not save the template, your changes will not be available next time you use the template.

Deleting a Style

At some point, you may decide you no longer need a style. You can delete it, and all text associated with the deleted style will revert to the Normal style. The list of styles will become shorter, making it easier to look through the Styles list. You cannot delete built-in styles.

To delete a style, follow these steps:

1. Choose Format, Style.
2. Select the style you want to delete from the Styles list.

    If you have selected a paragraph containing the style you want to delete, the style already will be selected in the Styles list box.

3. Click the Delete button. You see a message asking whether you want to delete the style.
4. Choose Yes.

You also can delete several styles at once. Choose the Organizer button in the Style dialog box. Select the styles you want to delete and click the Delete button.

 TIP   You can select a group of contiguous files by clicking the first one, and then holding down Shift while you click the last one. To select noncontiguous files, hold down Ctrl while you click each one.

N O T E   You can choose Edit, Replace to delete text that has been formatted with a particular style. In the Find box, click the More button. Then, click the Format button and choose Style. Word displays the Find Style dialog box. Choose the name of the style whose text you want to delete from the Find What Style list and choose OK to return to the Find and Replace dialog box. Leave the

Replace With box empty. Click the Find Next button. If the text you find is text you want to delete, click the Replace button. If you don't want to delete the text, proceed through the document with the Find Next button to the next item. Choose Close when you are finished deleting text. ▪

Giving a Style a New Name or Alias

You can rename a style, which doesn't affect the associated text, but changes the style name throughout your document. You can choose to rename a style for two purposes: to give it a new name or to add an optional name, or alias. An *alias* is a shorter name or abbreviation that you can type quickly in the Style Preview box in the Formatting toolbar. For example, if you're using the Heading 1 style frequently, and applying it from the keyboard, you can give the style an alias of h1. Then to apply the Heading 1 style you press Ctrl+Shift+S, type **h1** (rather than the full name), and press Enter.

Standard styles cannot be renamed, but you can add an alias to them. Also, you cannot use a standard style name as an alias for another style.

To rename a style or add an alias, follow these steps:

1. Choose Format, Style.
2. In the Styles list, highlight the style you want to change.
3. Click the Modify button. The Modify Style dialog box appears.
4. Type the new name in the Name text box. To include an alias, type a comma after the new name and then type the alias.

   Or, to add an alias, type a comma after the current style name, and then type the alias.
5. Choose OK to return to the Style dialog box.
6. Choose Close.

Redefining a Style

When you *redefine* a style, all the text formatted with that style updates to reflect the changes you have made. Suppose that you finish a 35-page report with many subheadings formatted with a style called Subhead which includes 18-point, bold, Helvetica, centered text. Now your company's publications committee decides subheadings should be smaller and underlined. Just redefine the style Subhead to reflect the new formatting, and all the subheadings in your text will change.

It is as easy to modify a style by example as it is to create a style by example.

To redefine a style by example, follow these steps:

1. Choose View, Toolbars and select the Formatting toolbar if it isn't currently displayed.
2. Reformat the paragraph you will use as a sample for the redefined style.
3. Select the paragraph (or some portion of the paragraph).

4. In the Formatting toolbar, select the current style name, or just position the insertion point to its right.

Or, press Ctrl+Shift+S and select or type the name of the style you want to redefine.

5. Press Enter. The Modify Style dialog box appears (see Figure 5.20). You have the following options:

Choose Update the Style to Reflect Recent Changes? to change the formatting of the current style to match the formatting of the selected text.

Choose Reapply the Formatting of the Style to the Selection? To reapply the formatting of the style to the selected text.

If you want Word to change style definitions to match current selections *without displaying this dialog box*, place a check in the Automatically Update The Style From Now On check box. If you decide later that you don't want automatic updating, open the Style dialog box, click Modify, and then clear the Automatically Update check box.

FIG. 5.20

The Modify Style dialog box appears when you redefine a style by example.

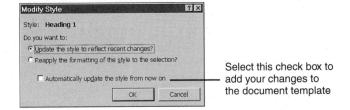

Select this check box to add your changes to the document template

6. Choose OK or press Enter to redefine the style.

The Format, Style command gives you the greatest flexibility for changing a style. You can make a change and add that change to the template on which you based the document. That way, each time you use the template in the future, the particular style will reflect the change.

To redefine a style using the menu command, follow these steps:

1. Choose Format, Style.

2. From the Styles list, select the style you want to redefine. If the style isn't included in the list, select a different option from the List drop-down list.

3. Click the Modify button. The Modify Style dialog box appears (see Figure 5.21).

4. Click the Format button and select any formatting options you want to add to your style. Remove any other options as needed.

5. Select the Add to Template check box to make the change in the document's template, as well as in the document.

6. Select the Automatically Update check box if you want Word to automatically redefine this style in the future based on any manual formatting you apply to any paragraph formatted with this style.

FIG. 5.21

You can change a style's formatting in the Modify Style dialog box.

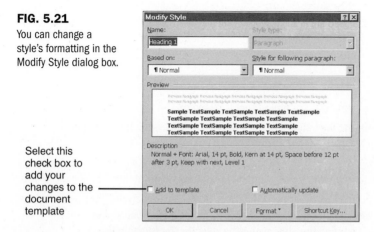

Select this check box to add your changes to the document template

7. Choose OK to return to the Style dialog box.

   Repeat steps 2 through 6 if you want to redefine additional styles.

8. Choose Close.

Changing the Normal Style

Each time you begin a new document based on the Normal template, Word uses the Normal style to determine the font, font size, line spacing, and other formats. If you find that you are always changing the font, the point size, or some other aspect of the Normal style, you can change its default format settings.

Changing the formats defined for the Normal style in your document affects only the current document. Modify the style and update the template to apply the change to future documents. Existing documents are not changed unless you specifically have Word update their styles. See "Updating Styles" later in this chapter.

Remember that any change you make to the Normal style will be reflected in all styles that are based on that style, which includes most styles.

To change the default settings for the Normal style with the menu command, follow these steps:

1. Choose File, New and double-click the Blank Document template.

   The Style Preview box on the Formatting toolbar should show Normal. In a new document based on the Normal template, the first paragraph will automatically use the Normal style.

2. Choose Format, Style and choose Modify. The Normal style should be selected in the Name box. If it isn't, type **Normal**.

3. Make the changes you want to the style, using the Format options.

Part
II

Ch
5

4. When you return to the Modify Style dialog box, select the Add to Template check box.

5. Choose OK to return to the Style dialog box.

6. Choose Close.

To change the default settings for the Normal style by example, follow these steps:

1. Choose File, Open and select a document that is based on the Normal template.

2. Select text or position the insertion point in a paragraph that is formatted with the Normal style.

3. Select commands on the Format menu, from the Formatting toolbar, or with shortcut keys to make formatting changes you want applied to most documents. For example, you might want to indent the first line of each paragraph by .5".

4. Click the Style Preview box in the Formatting toolbar and press Enter. Word asks whether you want to redefine the style using the selection as an example.

5. Choose OK.

6. Choose Format, Style. The Style dialog box opens with the Normal style selected in the Styles list. Select Normal if it isn't selected.

7. Click Modify, select the Add to Template check box, and choose OK.

8. Choose Close.

 Choose Format, Font to make changes to the default font of the Normal style. In the Font dialog box, make the changes you want and then click the Default button. Word displays a dialog box indicating that the changes you made will affect all new documents based on the Normal template. Choose Yes.

Updating Styles

If you create a group of documents, each based on the same template, you'll want to make sure that any change to a style is reflected in each of the documents. For example, if you're writing a book with each chapter in a separate file, you want any changes to headers, footers, and headings to be copied to each of the document files. Another example is familiar to anyone working in a large corporation where styles are set and then reset by a committee. At the beginning of a project, the committee might decide on a template containing styles for formatting each document. Because all documents are based on the same template, they contain identical formatting, which preserves consistency. Later, the committee issues major design changes. Those design changes must now be incorporated throughout all the other documents that were based on the original templates. To insure that a document updates to match changes in the template, use the Automatically Update Document Styles command.

 If you want to copy just a few styles from one template to another, see the previous section titled "Copying Styles Between Documents."

When you select the Automatically Update Document Styles command, Word copies the attached template's styles to the document each time you open it. The Update feature follows these rules:

- A style in the template that has the same name as a style in the document overrides the document style. The formatting from the template's style replaces the formatting from the document's style.
- Styles not found in the document are copied from the template to the document.
- Styles found in the document, but not in the template, are left unchanged.

Make sure that you use identically named styles in each of the documents. Otherwise, Word will not properly update the styles.

To update a document's styles each time you open it, follow these steps:

1. Place the insertion point anywhere in the file whose styles you want to update automatically.

N O T E Prior to Word 97, this command was the Templates command and appeared on the File menu. ■

2. Choose Tools, Templates and Add-Ins. The Templates and Add-ins dialog box appears (see Figure 5.22). The template attached to the current document is named in the Document Template box.

FIG. 5.22
Select Automatically Update Document Styles, and each time you open the document its styles will be updated from the attached template.

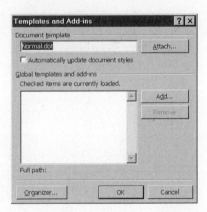

Part
II

Ch
5

3. Select the Automatically Update Document Styles check box.
4. Choose OK.

Changing the Base of a Style

Unless you specify otherwise, a new style is based on the style of the currently selected paragraph. Often, that's the Normal style. You have the option, however, to base any style on any other style. When you do, any changes you make to the base style carry through to all styles based on that style. If you change Normal, those changes are reflected in any style based on the Normal style.

This often can be to your advantage. Suppose that you work in a legal office and you regularly type certain court documents that must always be double-spaced, in a certain font and size, and have specific margins. To help automate this task, you can create a template with the correct margins, and then modify the template's Normal style to include the correct font and size and double-spacing. You then can create additional styles based on that redefined Normal style, and they too will use the specified font and size and be double-spaced.

Keep in mind that Word's standard styles are based on the Normal style, and if you alter the Normal style, your alterations will apply to all the standard styles as well.

If you don't want to alter your Normal style, you can create a base style in your document and use it as the basis for additional styles. By changing that base style, you can make extensive changes throughout a document.

To base one style on another style, follow these steps:

1. Choose Format, Style.

2. From the Styles list, select a style whose base style you want to change.

3. Click the Modify button. The Modify Style dialog box appears.

4. Specify the name of the style on which you want to base your style in the Based On box. To display a list of styles, click the down arrow to the right of the Based On box.

   If you want the selected style to remain unaffected by changes to any other style, select (no style) from the top of the list in the Based On box.

   When you select a style name, you see the name of the style plus any formatting attributes from the selected style in the Description box. Your new style automatically is based on that existing style, unless you specify a different style.

5. Select any of the Format button options to add additional formatting options to your style.

6. Choose OK to return to the Style dialog box.

7. Choose Close.

   Or, choose Apply if you want to apply your new style to the currently selected paragraph.

TROUBLESHOOTING

I attached the wrong template to my document and updated the styles. Now, all the styles in my document look wrong. What can I do?   If you have not made changes to the document, a safe approach is to close the document without saving it, then reopen and attach the correct template. If you don't want to close the document without saving, then repeat the process using the correct template or the original template. Attach either the original template or the correct template to your document and again update styles. The styles in your document should return to their original appearance or to the appearance of the styles in the correct template.

Checking Formats

Formatting can be applied from a style or manually from the Format menu commands. You can quickly determine how formatting was applied to any text with the Help button on the Standard toolbar.

To determine how formatting was added, follow these steps:

1. Press Shift+F1 or open the Help menu and choose What's This?. The pointer changes to an arrow with a question mark attached.

2. Click the text you want to check. A formatting box appears, showing paragraph and font formatting (see Figure 5.23). You can continue to click other locations to see the formatting of other text.

3. Press Esc to turn off the Help feature.

FIG. 5.23
Use the What's This? Help feature to quickly check the formatting of any text.

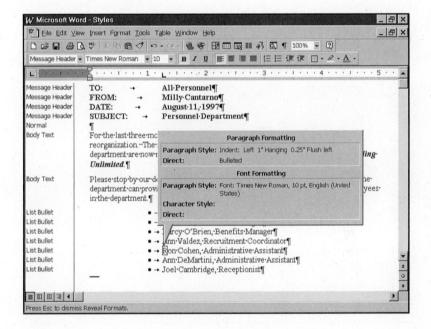

Part

II

Ch

5

Working with Columns

Creating a Newsletter the Easy Way

In Word 97, you can create two types of columns—the *snaking columns* of text you see in newspapers, magazines, and newsletters, and the *parallel columns* of text and numbers you see in lists and tables. Tables (which consist of columns and rows of text, numbers, or dates) work well for parallel columns or for data that you want to keep aligned. This chapter discusses snaking columns (sometimes called *newspaper columns*) in which the text wraps continuously from the bottom of one column to the top of the next column. To learn more about parallel columns, refer to Chapter 10, "Creating and Editing Tables."

If you've been using Word 6 or 7, you know about wizards. If you read Chapter 1, "Using Templates and Wizards for Frequently Created Documents," you know about wizards. In Word 7, Microsoft introduced the Newsletter Wizard, which makes creating a truly professional-looking newsletter a breeze (see Figure 6.1).

FIG. 6.1.

Use the Newsletter Wizard to easily create a newsletter designed to your specifications.

Published Quarterly by Sonoma County ReLeaf § Autumn, 1997

ReLeaf Joins Forces with WCG

"A Shade Better"

It's been a busy summer for Sonoma County ReLeaf. In the last issue of this newsletter, we hinted about a new partnership with WCG. Since spring, that new partnership has evolved into an ongoing relationship, with Sonoma County ReLeaf administering WCG's "A Shade Better" program in an exciting county-wide pilot.

"A Shade Better" is WCG's way of reaching out into the community, helping homeowners save energy by providing free trees that shade their homes and help reduce their need for air conditioning. WCG supplies the trees—and Sonoma County ReLeaf provides the expertise needed to get the trees into the ground.

ReLeaf's approach to helping people plant their free shade trees begins by organizing community planting days. The first step is to work with one individual who will contact neighbors and schedule a Saturday morning for planting. ReLeaf works with the neighborhood volunteer to determine which type of trees people want. Next, a trained ReLeaf volunteer

visits the neighborhood and sites the shade trees around each home so the trees provide maximum shading as they grow. On planting day, ReLeaf brings the trees, stakes, and ties, gives a planting demonstration, and distributes the trees to their new owners. For those who can't plant their own trees, volunteers are trained to help. After the planting, a two-year follow-up program helps ensure the trees stay healthy.

The City of Santa Rosa has also become involved in the program, providing free street trees to qualifying homes within the city.

Several "A Shade Better" plantings are already scheduled:

October 19—planting shade trees and street trees in northwest Santa Rosa.

October 26—planting shade trees in Santa Rosa.

November 9—planting shade trees in Windsor.

Three more projects are in the planning stages. In Rohnert Park, ReLeaf has targeted two neighborhoods needing trees and hopes to hold the first planting in early winter. In Sonoma,

ReLeaf is working with ten community groups and businesses toward scheduling a planting. And in Petaluma, residents in two mobile home parks will receive badly-needed shade trees to help cool their homes.

ReLeaf has been furiously busy over the summer getting the word out to people about the "A Shade Better" project. In a booth at the county fair, we made contact with about 1,000 people, many of whom are interested in getting trees for their homes, or in coordinating planting days in their neighborhoods. We've contacted even more potential planters through our booth at the Thursday night market in Santa Rosa.

ReLeaf has also been busy gearing up for the actual plantings—locating growers for the 15,000 trees we'll need this year; training interns to site the trees; working with kids in the Social Advocates for Youth program so they can help plant the trees; and raising money for our non-tree expenses.

It's been a busy summer for Sonoma County ReLeaf, but it'll be an even busier fall

In Brief . . .

ReLeaf teams up with WCG to make Sonoma County "A Shade Better." *Page 1.*

ReLeaf needs neighborhood coordinators to help organize local plantings. *Back page.*

With all the activity going on now, we need help with lots of jobs. *Back page.*

To volunteer, call Sonoma County ReLeaf at 323-4321

To select the Newsletter Wizard, follow these steps:

1. Choose File, New. You'll see the General tab of the New dialog box.

2. Click the Publications tab. Word displays the available templates and wizards that relate to producing publications (see Figure 6.2).

FIG. 6.2.

In the New dialog box, you see templates and wizards available for several different categories of documents.

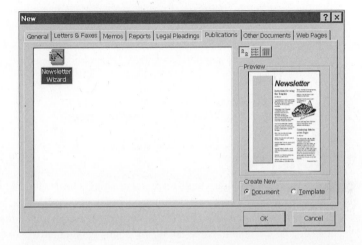

3. Click the Newsletter Wizard, and choose OK. Word displays the Newsletter Wizard (see Figure 6.3). Click Next to move to the Style & Color step in the Newsletter Wizard.

FIG. 6.3.

In the second dialog box of the Newsletter Wizard, choose the style of newsletter you want to create.

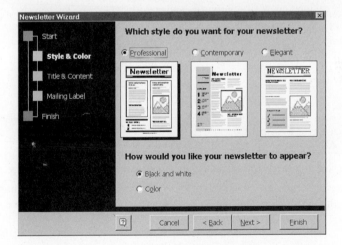

Part

II

Ch

6

To design your newsletter with the Newsletter Wizard, follow these steps:

1. Choose the style of newsletter you want to create—Classic or Modern. As you click each of the option buttons, the Preview box changes to show you examples.

2. Click the <u>N</u>ext button. In the second Newsletter Wizard dialog box, choose the number of columns you want for your newsletter—<u>O</u>ne, <u>T</u>wo, Th<u>r</u>ee, or Fo<u>ur</u>. If you click each option button, you'll see the changes in the layout.

3. Click the <u>N</u>ext button. In the third Newsletter Wizard dialog box, type the name of your newsletter. You can edit the name later.

4. Click the <u>N</u>ext button. In the fourth Newsletter Wizard dialog box, type the number of pages you want for your newsletter. Again, you can change this later.

5. Click the <u>N</u>ext button. In the fifth Newsletter Wizard dialog box, select the options you want to include in your newsletter—<u>T</u>able of Contents, Fancy First <u>L</u>etters, <u>D</u>ate, <u>V</u>olume, and Issue.

6. Click the <u>N</u>ext button.

7. Click the Finish button. Word displays a skeleton newsletter.

Creating Columns

If you need to work with columns and you're *not* creating a newsletter, Word's column features help you in your task. You can create columns of equal or unequal width. You also can include a vertical line between columns. You can include different numbers or styles of columns in different sections of your document. Newsletters, for example, often have two or more sections. The first section contains a large one-column banner, and the remaining text is divided into multiple columns.

On a page with left and right margins of one inch each, you can include up to 13 columns in portrait orientation or 18 columns in landscape orientation. You can also include different numbers or styles of columns in different parts of your document, as long as you divide your document into sections. You learn more about sections later in this chapter.

> **CAUTION**
>
> From a readability standpoint, including too many columns on the page can make your document difficult to read. As a rule of thumb, try to include no more than three columns on a portrait-oriented sheet of paper, or five columns on a landscape-oriented sheet of paper.

Word gives you two methods of creating columns: choosing F<u>o</u>rmat, <u>C</u>olumns and clicking the Columns button on the Standard toolbar. In Normal view, you see columns in their correct width, but not side by side; only in Page Layout or Print Preview views do you see columns side by side.

Calculating the Number and Length of Columns

Word determines how many columns you can have on a page based on three factors: page width, margin widths, and size and spacing of your columns. On a wide landscape-oriented page, for example, you have more room for columns than on a narrower portrait-oriented page.

Similarly, if your margins are narrow, there's more room for text on the page, and thus you can have more columns. If columns are narrow, you can fit more of them on a page than if they are wide. But remember, more isn't necessarily better; too many columns on a page can make reading difficult.

In Word, columns must be at least half an inch (.5″) wide. If you try to fit too many on a page, Word displays a message reading Column widths cannot be less than 0.5". You might see this message if you change your margins, for example, making them wider so that there is less room on the page for columns. If you see the message, change either your page layout or the number, width, or spacing of your columns.

Columns are the length of the current section or of the current page if there are no sections.

Understanding Sections

A new document based on the default Normal template is a single section with a one-column format. *Sections* are divisions within a document that can be formatted independently. If you want different numbers or styles of columns in different parts of your document, you must divide it into sections.

▶ **See** "Working with Sections in Your Document," **p. 196**

With columns, there are three ways you can insert section breaks:

- Choose Format, Columns to create columns and specify that columns apply not to the whole document, but to "this point forward" in your document; Word adds a section break before the insertion point.
- Select the text that you want to appear in different columns before you create or change the columns; a section break is added before and after the selected text (or just after the selected text if it falls at the beginning of a document).
- Choose Insert, Break to display the Break dialog box (see Figure 6.4).

Using the Break dialog box, you can specify that sections run continuously so that you can have a different number of columns on the same page, or you can specify that each section start on a new page or on the next even-numbered or odd-numbered page.

In Normal view, section breaks appear in your document as a double-dotted line containing the words Section Break.

TIP All column formatting is stored in the section break mark at the end of a section. If you delete this mark, that section takes on the column formatting and section formatting of the section after it.

FIG. 6.4
You can insert section
breaks using the Insert,
Break command.

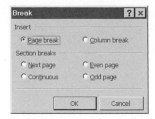

Formatting Columns

When formatting your document into columns, remember the following tips:

- If you want to format the entire document into columns, and your document has only one section, position the insertion point anywhere in your document.

- If you want to format only one section into columns and you've already divided your document into sections, position the insertion point inside the section you want formatted into columns. (Columns apply to multiple sections if multiple sections are selected.)

- If you want columns to start at a certain point in your document and you haven't divided your document into sections, position the insertion point where you want columns to start. You can apply columns from that point forward. Word inserts a section break at the insertion point.

- If you want to format selected text into columns and you haven't divided your document into sections, select the text that you want in columns. Word inserts a section break before and after the selected text.

 TIP If you don't like the number of columns you've created or don't like their widths, choose Edit, Undo Columns to return to your original number of columns.

Creating Columns of Equal Width

The width of the columns in your document depends on the number of columns you choose, your margins, and the amount of space you set between columns. For example, if you have one-inch left and right margins on a standard 8 1/2-inch paper width, and you divide your text into three columns with one-quarter inch between them, you get three two-inch-wide columns.

Remember that only in Page Layout view (or Print Preview) will you see your columns side by side.

To create equal-width columns with the menu or with the Columns button, follow these steps:

1. Specify which part of your document you want divided into columns (see "Formatting Columns" earlier in this chapter).

2. On the Standard toolbar, click the Columns button to display the column drop-down box. Drag right to select the number of columns you want (up to six). Figure 6.5 shows the Columns button drop-down box with three columns selected.

FIG. 6.5

The quickest way to format your document with columns is to use the Columns button on the Standard toolbar.

You also can choose F<u>o</u>rmat, <u>C</u>olumns. The Columns dialog box appears (see Figure 6.6).

FIG. 6.6

Use presets to quickly format your text into columns, or select the number of columns you want.

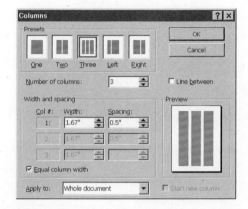

3. In the Presets group, select <u>O</u>ne, T<u>w</u>o, or <u>T</u>hree columns. You also can select <u>N</u>umber of Columns, and type or select the number of columns you want. If you want columns to start at the insertion point, click the <u>A</u>pply To drop-down list arrow and select This Point Forward from the list. Choose OK.

Creating Columns of Unequal Width

Although you can easily format your document with columns by clicking the Columns button, you can use more options when you use the Columns dialog box. You can define your own columns, or you can choose preset columns. *Preset columns* include a wide and a narrow column (the wide column is twice as wide as the narrow column). Preset columns make a good starting point for defining your own columns. Using them ensures that your columns are a consistent width.

When you create columns by choosing F<u>o</u>rmat, <u>C</u>olumns, you can specify whether columns apply to the whole document, the current section(s), the insertion point forward, or the selected text (if text is selected) (see "Formatting Columns," earlier in this chapter). By choosing F<u>o</u>rmat, <u>C</u>olumn, you also can specify how wide you want your columns and how much space you want between them.

Part

II

Ch

6

To create columns of unequal width, follow these steps:

1. Select the text you want to format into multiple columns, or position the insertion point inside the section you want to format or at the point where you want a new number of columns to begin.

2. Choose Format, Columns. The Columns dialog box appears (see Figure 6.7).

FIG. 6.7
To create columns of unequal width, use presets or define your own columns.

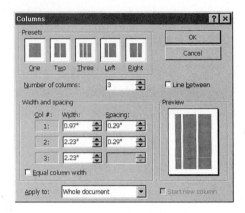

3. Optionally, from the Presets group, select Left if you want a narrow column on the left, or Right if you want a narrow column on the right.

4. Select Number of Columns, and type or select the number of columns you want. Look at the Preview box to see how your columns will appear.

5. Clear the Equal Column Width check box if it is selected.

6. If you want to define the width or spacing for individual columns, place the insertion point in the Width or Spacing box for the column you want to change. The dialog box has space for only three column numbers; click or press the down arrow to display additional column numbers.

7. Type or select the width you want for the selected column.

   You can also type or select the spacing you want to the right of the selected column (there is no space to the right of the rightmost column).

8. From the Apply To drop-down list, select the amount of text you want to format. The options shown in the Apply To list change depending on whether text is selected or whether your document contains multiple sections. Usually Word correctly guesses where you want to apply your columns, based on the location of the insertion point.

   • The Selected Sections option appears only when multiple sections are selected. It formats the sections you selected with columns.

   • The Selected Text option appears only when text is selected. This option formats the text you selected with columns. It also puts a section break before and after the selection.

- The This Point Forward option appears only when no text is selected. This option formats with columns from the insertion point forward. It puts a section break at the location of the insertion point.
- The This Section option appears only when the insertion point is inside one of multiple sections. This option formats with columns the section containing the insertion point.
- The Whole Document option formats the entire document with columns.

9. Choose OK.

Typing and Editing Text in Columns

Typing, editing, and formatting text in columns follows all the same rules and takes advantage of the same shortcuts for typing, selecting, and editing any other text. The following two tips will help you as you move around in and select columnar text:

- To move from one column to the top of the next column on the current page using the keyboard, press Alt+down-arrow key. To move to the top of the previous column, press Alt+up-arrow key.
- In a single-column document, the selection bar, an invisible column you use to select text, is normally positioned at the left margin of a page. When you move the mouse pointer into this area, the mouse pointer turns into an arrow you can use to select lines and paragraphs. In a multi-column document, you'll find a selection bar at the left margin of each column in Page Layout view.

TROUBLESHOOTING

My text seems narrower than the columns.   This condition may appear if the text is indented. Use the ruler or choose Format, Paragraph to eliminate or change the indentation settings for selected text. Also check the margin settings within each column.

Adding a Line Between Columns

Adding a vertical line between columns can add interest to your page. Lines are the length of the longest column in the section. You can see lines in the Page Layout view or in Print Preview.

To add lines between columns, follow these steps:

1. Click in the section containing columns where you want vertical lines.
2. Choose Format, Columns.
3. In the Columns dialog box, check the Line Between check box.
4. Choose OK.

To remove lines between columns, remove the check from the Line Between check box in the Columns dialog box. You can also add vertical lines on your page by choosing Format, Borders and Shading. If you do, and you also add lines between columns, you may see two lines between columns. For columns, the Line Between option is a better choice than Format, Borders and Shading because it creates lines of uniform length in the section, even if one column of text is shorter than the others.

Viewing Columns

Word enables you to view a document in several ways. Views include Normal, Outline, Page Layout, Master Document, and Print Preview. Depending on which view you use, columns appear differently on-screen.

Normal view is faster for text entry but does not display columns side by side as they will appear when printed. The text appears in the same width as the column, but in one continuous column. In Online Layout, Outline, and Master Document views, columns also appear in one continuous column. Page Layout view displays columns side by side, with vertical lines between columns if you've selected that option. Section and column breaks appear only when you've displayed paragraph marks. Print Preview gives an overview of the page as it will appear when printed. In Normal, Page Layout, and Print Preview views, you can change column width using the ruler, and in all views, you can display the Column dialog box to edit columns.

 T I P   You can switch between Normal, Online Layout, Page Layout, and Outline views using the four icons that appear at the left edge of the horizontal scroll bar.

When you are editing a document, you may need to view a particular section up close. At other times, you may need an overview of the entire page. When you work in Page Layout view, the Zoom Control box on the Standard toolbar includes three choices that enable you to magnify or reduce the size of the display:

- *Whole Page*. Shows you a miniature view of the whole page. The view you see is very similar to Print Preview.
- *Page Width*. Shows you the full width of the page.
- *Two Pages*. Lays out your document so that you can see a miniature view of two pages simultaneously.

The Zoom Control box also has, on its drop-down list, several percentages at which you can view your page. You can also select magnification by choosing View, Zoom.

Changing Columns

Once you format your document with columns, you can change the columns in many ways:

- You can change the number of columns, or switch between equal- and unequal-width columns.
- You can change the width of columns or the spacing between them.

■ You can force text to move to the top of the next column, and you can force a column to start on a new page.

■ You can balance columns on a page so that they are as close to the same length as possible.

You can make some changes to columns using the ruler; for example, you can change their width or the spacing between them. Other changes are made using the Columns dialog box.

TIP You can quickly display the Columns dialog box by double-clicking the gray area between columns on the horizontal ruler.

Before you change columns, make sure you select the text you want to change, and be sure, in the Columns dialog box, to apply the changes where you want them (use the Apply To list). Follow these rules for selecting text and applying the changes:

■ If you want to change columns for the entire document and your document has only one section, position the insertion point anywhere in your document. In the Apply To list of the Columns dialog box, choose Whole Document.

■ If you want to change columns in only one section and you've already divided your document into sections, position the insertion point inside the section you want to change. In the Apply To list of the Columns dialog box, choose This Section.

■ If you want columns to start at a certain point in your document and you haven't divided your document into sections, position the insertion point where you want columns to start. In the Apply To list of the Columns dialog box, choose This Point Forward.

■ If you want to change columns in only part of your document and you haven't divided your document into sections, select the text that you want in columns. In the Apply To list of the Columns dialog box, choose Selected Text.

■ If you want to change columns in multiple existing sections, select the sections. In the Apply To list of the Columns dialog box, choose Selected Sections.

Most of the time, Word understands where you want to apply changes by where you've positioned the insertion point, and you don't need to make a selection in the Apply To list.

Because you can format text in columns in the same way you can format text that is not in columns, you may create some unexpected results. If your column is too narrow, for example, you may find yourself with a vertical strip of text that isn't very readable. Try widening the column, lessening the space between the columns, reducing the number of columns, or reducing the size of the text.

Changing the Number of Columns

You can change the number of columns using either the ruler or the Columns dialog box. You can also change between equal- and unequal-width columns. If you want to change from equal-width to unequal-width columns, you must use the Columns dialog box, but you can change from unequal-width to equal-width columns using the ruler.

To change the number of equal-width columns, or to change from unequal-width to equal-width columns, follow these steps:

1. Position the insertion point or select the text where you want changes to apply.

2. On the Standard toolbar, click the Columns button and select the number of columns you want from the drop-down box (drag right in the box to display up to seven columns).

   You also can choose Format, Columns to display the Columns dialog box. From the Presets group, select One, Two, or Three. Or select Number of Columns, and type or select the number of columns you want. If you are changing from unequal-width to equal-width columns, select the Equal Column Width check box. Choose OK.

To change the number of unequal-width columns, or to change from equal-width to unequal-width columns, follow these steps:

1. Position the insertion point or select the text where you want changes to apply.

2. Choose Format, Columns to display the Columns dialog box. If you want two preset columns of unequal width, select Left or Right from the Presets group. Or, select Number of Columns, and type or select the number of columns you want.

3. If you're changing from equal-width to unequal-width columns, clear the check from the Equal Column Width check box.

4. Choose OK.

Changing the Width of Columns and the Spacing Between Columns

When you first create columns, Word determines their width based on your margins and the number of columns you want. You can change the width of all or some columns.

You can also change the spacing between columns. By default, columns have a half inch (.5") of spacing between them, but you may want to decrease or increase this distance. You may want to decrease the distance if you have many columns, because the greater number of columns you have, the narrower they are, and the less space you need between them. You may want to increase the distance with fewer columns, as you might in a three-column brochure printed sideways on the page, for example.

You can change the width of columns or the space between columns in two ways: using the ruler or using the Columns dialog box. Using the ruler, you drag column margin markers to change the width and spacing at the same time.

If your columns are currently equal-width and you want to change them to unequal-width, you must use the Columns dialog box.

To change the width of columns or the space between columns using the ruler, follow these steps:

1. Make sure the ruler is displayed; if it is not, choose View, Ruler.

2. Position the insertion point inside the section containing the columns you want to change.

3. The gray areas in the horizontal ruler indicate the spaces between columns. Move the mouse pointer into one of these gray areas. Choose any gray area if your columns are all the same width; choose the gray area above the space you want to change if your columns are different widths. After you slide the mouse pointer into a gray area, the pointer will turn into a two-headed arrow, and you'll see a text tip on-screen. What you see in the text tip depends on whether your columns are all the same width or whether they are different widths:

- If your columns are all the same width, you won't see any text tip when you slide the mouse pointer into the middle of the gray area, but the text tip will display either Right Margin or Left Margin as you slide the mouse pointer over the left or right edge of the gray area (see Figure 6.8).

FIG. 6.8

Using the ruler, you can change the width of columns and the spacing between them. If your columns are all the same width, changing one changes them all identically.

- When your columns are different widths, the middle of the gray area contains a grid-like icon. You'll see the same text tip (Right Margin or Left Margin) if you move the mouse pointer over the right or left edge of the gray area; in the center of the gray area, however, you'll see Move Column in the text tip (see Figure 6.9).

4. Hold down the mouse button and drag the edge of the gray area away from the center to widen the space between columns, or drag it toward the center to lessen the space between columns. If columns are different widths, you can drag either side of the gray area to change the spacing in either direction.

Part

II

Ch

6

FIG. 6.9

When columns are of unequal widths, or if they were created using the Columns button, the gray area of the ruler contains a grid-like icon.

Grid-like icon

N O T E When dragging the unequal columns marker, remember that it functions two ways, depending upon how you drag it:

Dragging the edge of the marker changes the widths of unequal columns.

Dragging the grid-like icon to move the column changes the space between unequal columns. ▪

 T I P If columns are all the same width, changing the spacing for one changes the spacing for them all. If columns are different widths, changing the spacing for one affects only that column.

To change the width of columns or the space between columns using the Columns dialog box, or to change columns of equal width into columns of unequal width, follow these steps:

1. Position the insertion point inside the section containing the columns you want to change.

2. Choose Format, Columns.

3. If you are changing equal-width columns to unequal-width columns, remove the checkmark from the Equal Column Width check box.

 T I P If your columns are all the same width, change the width of column 1 only; all the rest use the same measurements.

4. In the Width and Spacing group, place the insertion point in the Width box of the column you want to change and type or select the width you want for your column or columns. Word then automatically recalculates the dimensions of the remaining columns to fit within the margins of the page.

5. In the Width and Spacing group, place the insertion point in the Spacing box of the column you want to change and type or select the spacing you want between your columns.

6. Choose OK.

Removing Columns

If your document is formatted into columns, you can remove them easily using either the Columns button or the Columns dialog box.

To remove columns, follow these steps:

1. Position the insertion point or select text where you want to remove columns.

2. Use the Columns button to select one column.

   You also can choose Format, Columns. From the Presets group, select One. Choose OK.

Starting a New Column

When Word creates columns, it automatically breaks the columns to fit on the page. Sometimes, the column may break inappropriately. On a three-column page, for example, column 2 may end with a heading that should be at the top of column 3. By inserting a column break directly before the heading, you shift the heading to the top of the next column, keeping the heading and its following text together.

If you want a column to start on a new page, you can insert a page break.

To insert a column break, press Ctrl+Shift+Enter or follow these steps:

1. Position the insertion point at the beginning of the line where you want the new column to start.

2. Choose Insert, Break. The Break dialog box appears (see Figure 6.10).

FIG. 6.10

Inserting a column break causes text to move to the top of the next column.

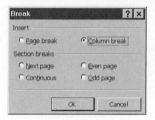

3. Select the Column Break option.

4. Choose OK.

To insert a page break, press Ctrl+Enter or repeat the steps above, choosing Page Break in step 3.

Balancing Column Lengths

On pages where the text in columns continues to the next page, Word automatically balances (lines up) the last line of text at the bottom of each column. But when columnar text runs out on a page, you may be left with two full-length columns and a third column that's only partially filled. You can balance column lengths so that the bottoms of all the columns are within one line of each other. Figures 6.11 and 6.12 show unbalanced and balanced columns.

Part

II

Ch

6

FIG. 6.11
These columns have not been balanced.

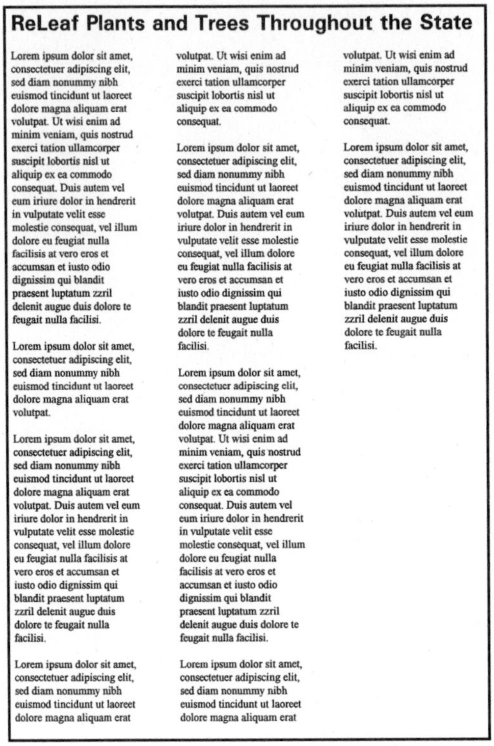

ReLeaf Plants and Trees Throughout the State

Lorem ipsum dolor sit amet, consectetuer adipiscing elit, sed diam nonummy nibh euismod tincidunt ut laoreet dolore magna aliquam erat volutpat. Ut wisi enim ad minim veniam, quis nostrud exerci tation ullamcorper suscipit lobortis nisl ut aliquip ex ea commodo consequat. Duis autem vel eum iriure dolor in hendrerit in vulputate velit esse molestie consequat, vel illum dolore eu feugiat nulla facilisis at vero eros et accumsan et iusto odio dignissim qui blandit praesent luptatum zzril delenit augue duis dolore te feugait nulla facilisi.

Lorem ipsum dolor sit amet, consectetuer adipiscing elit, sed diam nonummy nibh euismod tincidunt ut laoreet dolore magna aliquam erat volutpat.

Lorem ipsum dolor sit amet, consectetuer adipiscing elit, sed diam nonummy nibh euismod tincidunt ut laoreet dolore magna aliquam erat volutpat. Duis autem vel eum iriure dolor in hendrerit in vulputate velit esse molestie consequat, vel illum dolore eu feugiat nulla facilisis at vero eros et accumsan et iusto odio dignissim qui blandit praesent luptatum zzril delenit augue duis dolore te feugait nulla facilisi.

Lorem ipsum dolor sit amet, consectetuer adipiscing elit, sed diam nonummy nibh euismod tincidunt ut laoreet dolore magna aliquam erat volutpat. Ut wisi enim ad minim veniam, quis nostrud exerci tation ullamcorper suscipit lobortis nisl ut aliquip ex ea commodo consequat.

Lorem ipsum dolor sit amet, consectetuer adipiscing elit, sed diam nonummy nibh euismod tincidunt ut laoreet dolore magna aliquam erat volutpat. Duis autem vel eum iriure dolor in hendrerit in vulputate velit esse molestie consequat, vel illum dolore eu feugiat nulla facilisis at vero eros et accumsan et iusto odio dignissim qui blandit praesent luptatum zzril delenit augue duis dolore te feugait nulla facilisi.

Lorem ipsum dolor sit amet, consectetuer adipiscing elit, sed diam nonummy nibh euismod tincidunt ut laoreet dolore magna aliquam erat volutpat. Ut wisi enim ad minim veniam, quis nostrud exerci tation ullamcorper suscipit lobortis nisl ut aliquip ex ea commodo consequat. Duis autem vel eum iriure dolor in hendrerit in vulputate velit esse molestie consequat, vel illum dolore eu feugiat nulla facilisis at vero eros et accumsan et iusto odio dignissim qui blandit praesent luptatum zzril delenit augue duis dolore te feugait nulla facilisi.

Lorem ipsum dolor sit amet, consectetuer adipiscing elit, sed diam nonummy nibh euismod tincidunt ut laoreet dolore magna aliquam erat volutpat. Ut wisi enim ad minim veniam, quis nostrud exerci tation ullamcorper suscipit lobortis nisl ut aliquip ex ea commodo consequat.

Lorem ipsum dolor sit amet, consectetuer adipiscing elit, sed diam nonummy nibh euismod tincidunt ut laoreet dolore magna aliquam erat volutpat. Duis autem vel eum iriure dolor in hendrerit in vulputate velit esse molestie consequat, vel illum dolore eu feugiat nulla facilisis at vero eros et accumsan et iusto odio dignissim qui blandit praesent luptatum zzril delenit augue duis dolore te feugait nulla facilisi.

FIG. 6.12
You can balance columns by adding a section break at the end of your document.

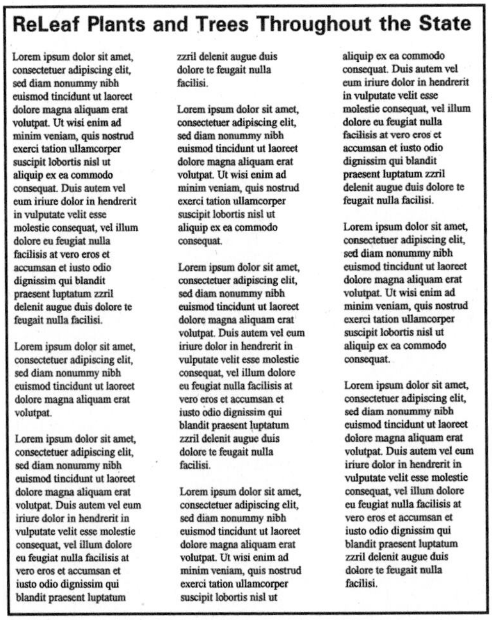

ReLeaf Plants and Trees Throughout the State

Lorem ipsum dolor sit amet, consectetuer adipiscing elit, sed diam nonummy nibh euismod tincidunt ut laoreet dolore magna aliquam erat volutpat. Ut wisi enim ad minim veniam, quis nostrud exerci tation ullamcorper suscipit lobortis nisl ut aliquip ex ea commodo consequat. Duis autem vel eum iriure dolor in hendrerit in vulputate velit esse molestie consequat, vel illum dolore eu feugiat nulla facilisis at vero eros et accumsan et iusto odio dignissim qui blandit praesent luptatum zzril delenit augue duis dolore te feugait nulla facilisi.

Lorem ipsum dolor sit amet, consectetuer adipiscing elit, sed diam nonummy nibh euismod tincidunt ut laoreet dolore magna aliquam erat volutpat.

Lorem ipsum dolor sit amet, consectetuer adipiscing elit, sed diam nonummy nibh euismod tincidunt ut laoreet dolore magna aliquam erat volutpat. Duis autem vel eum iriure dolor in hendrerit in vulputate velit esse molestie consequat, vel illum dolore eu feugiat nulla facilisis at vero eros et accumsan et iusto odio dignissim qui blandit praesent luptatum zzril delenit augue duis dolore te feugait nulla facilisi.

Lorem ipsum dolor sit amet, consectetuer adipiscing elit, sed diam nonummy nibh euismod tincidunt ut laoreet dolore magna aliquam erat volutpat. Ut wisi enim ad minim veniam, quis nostrud exerci tation ullamcorper suscipit lobortis nisl ut aliquip ex ea commodo consequat.

Lorem ipsum dolor sit amet, consectetuer adipiscing elit, sed diam nonummy nibh euismod tincidunt ut laoreet dolore magna aliquam erat volutpat. Duis autem vel eum iriure dolor in hendrerit in vulputate velit esse molestie consequat, vel illum dolore eu feugiat nulla facilisis at vero eros et accumsan et iusto odio dignissim qui blandit praesent luptatum zzril delenit augue duis dolore te feugait nulla facilisi.

Lorem ipsum dolor sit amet, consectetuer adipiscing elit, sed diam nonummy nibh euismod tincidunt ut laoreet dolore magna aliquam erat volutpat. Ut wisi enim ad minim veniam, quis nostrud exerci tation ullamcorper suscipit lobortis nisl ut aliquip ex ea commodo consequat. Duis autem vel eum iriure dolor in hendrerit in vulputate velit esse molestie consequat, vel illum dolore eu feugiat nulla facilisis at vero eros et accumsan et iusto odio dignissim qui blandit praesent luptatum zzril delenit augue duis dolore te feugait nulla facilisi.

Lorem ipsum dolor sit amet, consectetuer adipiscing elit, sed diam nonummy nibh euismod tincidunt ut laoreet dolore magna aliquam erat volutpat. Ut wisi enim ad minim veniam, quis nostrud exerci tation ullamcorper suscipit lobortis nisl ut aliquip ex ea commodo consequat.

Lorem ipsum dolor sit amet, consectetuer adipiscing elit, sed diam nonummy nibh euismod tincidunt ut laoreet dolore magna aliquam erat volutpat. Duis autem vel eum iriure dolor in hendrerit in vulputate velit esse molestie consequat, vel illum dolore eu feugiat nulla facilisis at vero eros et accumsan et iusto odio dignissim qui blandit praesent luptatum zzril delenit augue duis dolore te feugait nulla facilisi.

To balance the length of multiple columns, follow these steps:

1. Position the insertion point at the end of the text in the last column of the section you want to balance.
2. Choose Insert, Break.
3. Select the Continuous option in the Section Breaks group.
4. Choose OK.

TROUBLESHOOTING

I have several columns and I want to change their width and spacing, but in the Columns dialog box I can select only column 1. Your columns are currently of equal width. Clear the Equal Column Width check box if you want to make them different widths.

Product lists, date schedules, and the dialogue for plays all appear to use columns, but it's impossible to keep related items lined up across the columns. Adding or editing in one column changes the position of items in following columns. Use Word's table feature to create scripts for plays, procedural steps, duty rosters, product catalogs, and so on. Tables are grids of rows and columns. Information within a cell in a table will stay adjacent or parallel to other information in the same row, even when you add lines in the cell. Cells can contain entire paragraphs, math calculations, field codes, and even pictures. Tables are described in detail in Chapter 10, "Creating and Editing Tables."

Formatting the Page Layout, Alignment, and Numbering

In this chapter

Understanding Page Formats

Of the four levels of formatting—page, section, paragraph, and character—page layout is the broadest. Page layout often encompasses formatting choices that affect the entire document— for most documents, page layout choices such as margins and page size do apply to the whole document. In a change from tradition, however, Word 97 also enables you to apply page-level formatting to portions of the document known as sections.

Page layout options include margins, vertical alignment on the page, page and paragraph breaks, section breaks, page numbers, headers and footers, paper size and orientation, and the paper source. By default, many page setup options, such as margins, headers and footers, and page numbers, apply to the entire document. Alternatively, you can apply these options to a designated section of text or from the position of the insertion point forward in your document.

You can include an envelope and a letter in a single document, for example, by specifying different margins, paper size, paper orientation, and paper source for the first page of the document—the envelope—than you specify for the remaining pages—the letter. Or you can create different headers and footers for different parts of a long document. Being able to divide your document into sections and specify where page layout options apply gives you great flexibility in designing your document.

Setting Margins

Margins are the borders on all four sides of a page, within which the text of your document is confined. Margins aren't necessarily blank, however; they may contain headers, footers, page numbers, footnotes, or even text and graphics.

Word default margins are 1 inch at the top and bottom and 1.25 inches on the left and right. You can change the margins for the entire document or for parts of the document (if you divide the document into sections). See Figure 7.1. If you use different margin settings regularly, you can modify the Normal template so that they become the new defaults.

▶ **See** "Setting Default Formats in the Normal Template," **p. 16**

Different views in Word show different perspectives on your margins. In Normal and Online Layout view, you don't see the margins, but you see the space between them, where your text appears. In Page Layout view, you see the page as it will print, margins and all. Select that view if you want to see headers, footers, page numbers, footnotes, and anything else that appears within the margins.

To select a view, choose View, Normal; View, Online Layout; or View, Page Layout; you can also click the appropriate icon at the left edge of the horizontal scroll bar.

You can change the margins in your document in two ways. First, you can make selections from the Page Setup dialog box. When you set margins this way, you control margin settings precisely. A second technique for setting margins is to use the ruler. Using this technique, you can see how margin settings affect the appearance of your page.

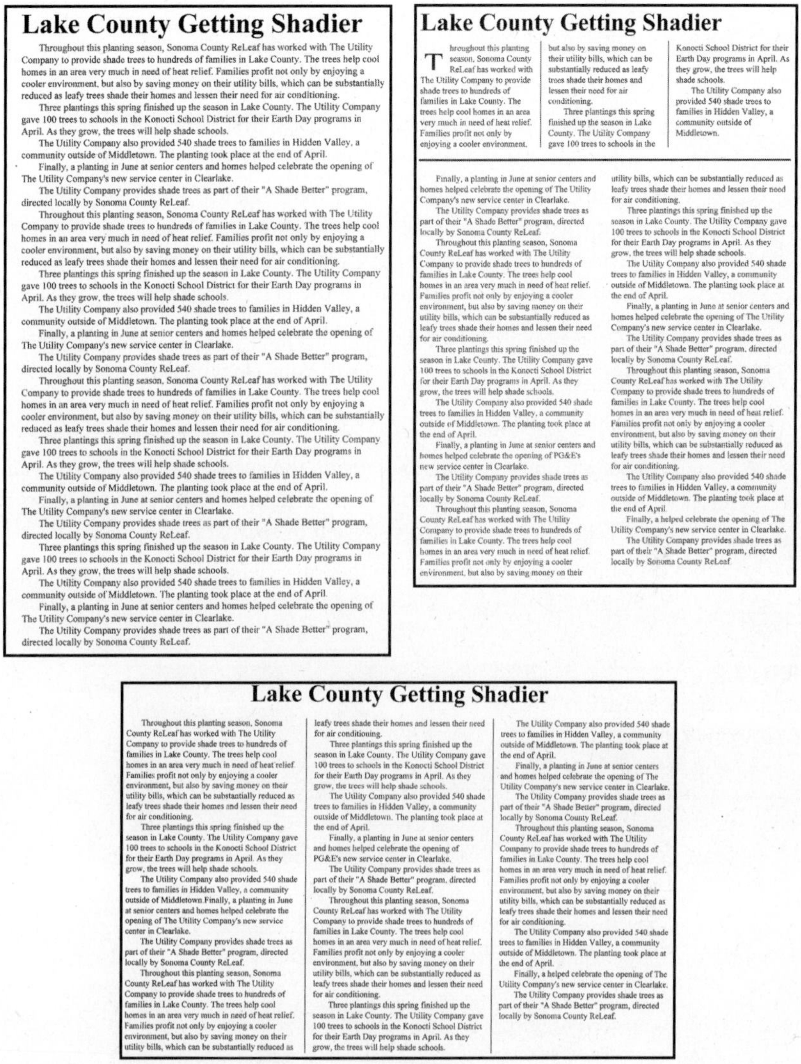

FIG. 7.1

You can set margins however you want.

Setting Margins with a Precise Measurement

Using the Page Setup command to set margins gives you the greatest number of options. You can set the margins to precise measurements, establish facing pages and gutters for binding (discussed later in this chapter), set varying margins for different sections of your document, and apply your margin settings to the Normal template so that they become the new default settings.

To apply margin settings to your entire document, you can locate the insertion point anywhere in the document when you set your margins. If you want to apply margins to only one part of your document, however, you must do one of three things:

■ To apply margins to a selected portion of your text, select that text before you set the margins. If you apply margins to selected text, Word automatically inserts section breaks before and after the selected text.

■ To apply margins to existing sections, first place the insertion point in the section, or select those sections whose margins you want to change.

■ To apply margins from a specific point forward in your document, position the insertion point where you want the new margins to start and then specify that the margins apply to the text from This Point Forward. If you apply margins from the insertion point forward, Word inserts a section break at the insertion point.

Setting different margins for different parts of your document is covered in a later section in this chapter, "Working with Sections in Your Document."

To set measured margins, follow these steps:

1. Position the insertion point inside the section for which you want to set margins. (The margins apply to the entire document unless the document has multiple sections.) Or select the text for which you want to set margins.

2. Choose File, Page Setup. In the Page Setup dialog box, select the Margins tab (see Figure 7.2).

FIG. 7.2

Set precisely measured margins using the Page Setup dialog box.

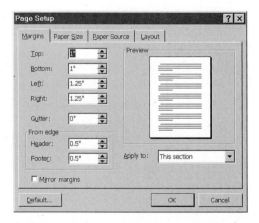

3. Choose your margin settings. Your options include Top, Bottom, Left, Right, and Gutter. Gutter controls extra spacing on pages for binding (see the section "Creating Facing Pages and Gutters"). For each setting, type the amount of the margin or use the spinner (or press the up- or down-arrow key) to increase or decrease the margin setting by tenths of an inch.

4. Choose OK.

N O T E As you select your margin settings, notice that the Preview box in the Page Setup dialog box shows you how a typical page will look. ■

Margins usually are measured in decimal inches, unless you change your default measurement system by using Tools, Options (General tab). You can create margins in a different measurement system by typing in amounts such as **36 pt** for 36 points (72 points equal one inch), **3 cm** for 3 centimeters, or **9 pi** for 9 picas (6 picas equal an inch). If you use the inch measurement system, the next time you open the Page Layout dialog box you see that your measurements have been converted back to the equivalent in inches.

Setting Different Margins for Different Parts of Your Document   To vary the margin settings in different parts of your document, you must divide the document into sections. You can create sections with unique margins in several ways. You can insert section breaks manually and then format the text between the breaks, or before or after a break, with different margin settings. Alternatively, you can select text and choose File, Page Setup to apply margins to only the selected text or from the insertion point forward in your document. When necessary, Word inserts section breaks.

The Apply To list in the Page Setup dialog box, which determines where margins are applied, changes depending on two factors:

- Whether your document is divided into sections
- Whether you've selected text before choosing File, Page Setup

Word tries to apply your margin settings logically; for example, if your document is divided into sections, and the insertion point is inside one of those sections when you set margins, then, in the Apply To list, Word proposes applying those margin settings to This Section. You can select a different option in the list, however.

You learn more about creating sections later in this chapter in the section "Working with Sections in Your Document."

To set different margins for specific parts of your document, follow these steps:

1. Position the insertion point inside the section or sections for which you want to set margins.

   You can also select the text for which you want to set margins.

   Or, you can position the insertion point where you want new margins to begin in your document.

2. Choose File, Page Setup, and in the Page Setup dialog box, select the Margins tab.

3. Type or select Top, Bottom, Left, and Right margin amounts.

4. From the Apply To list, select the section to which you want to apply margins (choices on the list vary depending on the amount of text currently selected):

Option	Applies Margins To	When
This Section	Current section (No section break is inserted)	Insertion point is located within a section
Selected Sections	Multiple sections (No section breaks are inserted)	At least part of more than one section is selected

continues

continued

Option	Applies Margins To	When
This Point Forward	Insertion point (Inserts new-page section break at insertion point)	Insertion point is where you want new margin to start
Selected Text	Selected text (Inserts new page section breaks at beginning and end of text)	Text is selected
Whole Document	Entire document (No section breaks inserted)	Insertion point is anywhere

5. Choose OK.

 TIP If you include sections with different margins in your document, remember that you delete the section (and thus lose its margins) if you delete the section break. If you accidentally delete a section break, choose Edit, Undo.

Creating Facing Pages and Gutters   *Facing pages* in a document are the left and right pages of a double-sided document, as in a book or magazine. You can set up your document for facing pages by selecting the Mirror Margins check box in the Page Setup dialog box (see Figure 7.3). When you do, you no longer have left and right margins; instead, you have inside and outside margins. Facing pages are ideal when you plan to print your document on both sides of the paper and want wider margins on the inside than on the outside edges.

FIG. 7.3

When you select Mirror Margins, you create facing pages with inside and outside margins, rather than left and right margins.

Check this box to format margins for facing pages

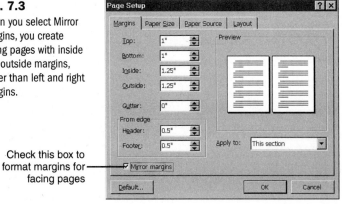

With facing pages, you can have different headers and footers on each page and can position page numbers on opposite sides of the facing pages. In a newsletter footer, for example, you may want to position page numbers below the outside margins and the date below the inside margins.

Like margins, facing pages apply to sections. You can insert section breaks before you select facing pages, or you can create sections as part of the process. (For details, see "Setting Different Margins for Different Parts of Your Document" earlier in this chapter.)

To create facing pages, follow these steps:

1. Position the insertion point or select the text where you want facing pages.
2. Choose File, Page Setup and select the Margins tab.
3. Select the Mirror Margins check box.
4. Choose OK.

Adding Extra Margin Space in Gutters   Whether you're working with normal pages that have left and right margins or facing pages that have inside and outside (mirror) margins, you can add a *gutter* to leave extra space for binding. A gutter on normal pages adds space at the left edge of the page; a gutter on facing pages adds space at the inside edges of each page. To leave an extra half-inch for binding, for example, include a gutter of 0.5". A gutter doesn't change your document's margins, but it does reduce the printing area.

Like margins, gutters apply to sections. You can insert section breaks before you select gutters, or you can create sections as part of the process. (For details, see "Setting Different Margins for Different Parts of Your Document" earlier in this chapter.)

To set a gutter, follow these steps:

1. Position the insertion point or select the text where you want a gutter.
2. Choose File, Page Setup and select the Margins tab.
3. Select Gutter and type or select the amount by which you want to increase the left margin (if you have left and right margins) or the inside margin (if you select mirror margins so that you have inside and outside margins). The Preview box shows a shaded area where the gutter appears (see Figure 7.4).
4. Choose OK.

FIG. 7.4

Gutters appear as a shaded area in the Preview box.

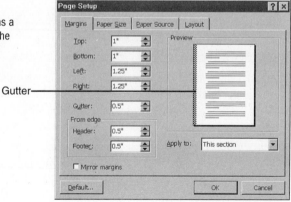

Part

II

Ch

7

Setting Margins Visually

A quick way to set margins for your document or for a section in your document is to click the ruler.

You must display a ruler to set margins with a mouse. In Page Layout or Print Preview view, Word has two rulers:

- A horizontal ruler, which appears at the top of your document and can be used to set left and right (or inside and outside) margins

- A vertical ruler, which appears at the left side of your document and can be used to set top and bottom margins (see Figure 7.5)

FIG. 7.5
You can set left and right (or inside and outside) margins with the horizontal ruler, and you can set top and bottom margins with the vertical ruler.

Margin boundaries
Horizontal ruler
Vertical ruler

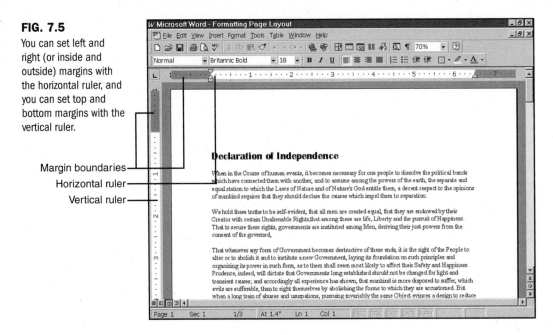

> **TIP** Only the horizontal ruler is available in Normal view.

On each ruler is a gray area and a white area. The gray area indicates the margins; the white area indicates the space between the margins. The line where the gray and the white areas connect is the *margin boundary*. You can drag the margin boundaries on either ruler to change the margins for the currently selected section or sections. To make the left margin smaller, for example, you can drag the left margin boundary toward the left edge of the page.

The ruler doesn't insert any section breaks into your document; it sets the margins for the entire document or for the section containing the insertion point. If you want to use the ruler to create margins for multiple sections in your document, insert section breaks before you begin. Then you can select the sections and use the ruler to change their margins.

T I P Choose File, Page Setup if you want to change margins in the Outline, Online Layout, or Master Document view.

If you want to change the margins for just one or a few paragraphs, use indents instead of the ruler. Use the ruler to change margins only when you want to change margins for the entire document or for a large section.

▶ **See** "Setting Indents," **p. 99**

To change margins with a ruler, follow these steps:

1. If the ruler is not displayed, choose View, Ruler.

2. Switch to Page Layout view by clicking the appropriate icon at the left edge of the horizontal scroll bar or by choosing View, Page Layout.

N O T E If you don't see the vertical ruler in Page Layout view, choose Tools, Options, then select the View tab, and in the Window group select the Vertical Ruler option. In Print Preview view, click the Ruler button to display rulers. ▪

3. Position the mouse pointer between the indent markers of the margin boundary that you want to change. When the arrow turns into a two-headed arrow and the text tip (telling which margin you're changing) appears, you can drag the boundary (see Figure 7.6).

FIG. 7.6
When you see a two-headed arrow and a text tip, you are ready to drag the margin boundary.

Two-headed arrow

CAUTION

Be sure you're pointing at the margin boundaries on the ruler. If you see the one-headed mouse arrow instead of the two-headed arrow, you're pointing to something other than the margin boundary—probably an indent marker. At the left margin boundary, for example, if you haven't set indents for your document, it's easy to point at the indent markers because they are right on top of the margin boundary. Watch the text tip to be sure you're pointing at the margin boundary.

4. Drag the margin boundary toward the edge of the page to make the margin smaller or toward the center of the page to make the margin wider. A dotted line on your document shows you where the new margin will appear (see Figure 7.7).

 T I P You can hold down the Alt key as you drag a margin boundary to see margin measurements in the ruler.

Part
II

Ch
7

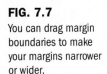

FIG. 7.7
You can drag margin boundaries to make your margins narrower or wider.

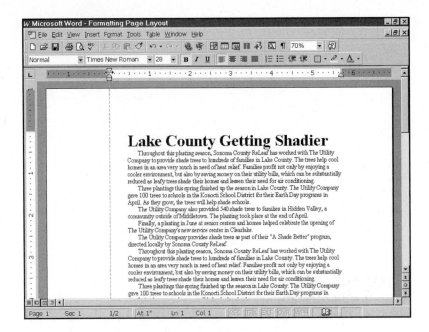

If you change your mind about dragging a margin, you can cancel your change by pressing Esc before you release the mouse button, by choosing <u>E</u>dit, <u>U</u>ndo Formatting, or by clicking the Undo button after you release the mouse button.

N O T E   If your document has facing pages (mirror margins), display multiple pages in Print Preview view so that you can see the effect of any change you make to the inside margins. If you change the inside margin on one page, all pages in the section reflect that change. ▪

Aligning Text Vertically

Text is normally aligned to the top margin in your document. But you may want to align it differently—in the center of the page or justified on the page (see Figure 7.8). When you justify text, the paragraphs (not the lines within paragraphs) on the page are spread evenly between the top and bottom margins.

Text alignment applies to sections (you learn more about sections in "Working with Sections in Your Document," later in this chapter). If you haven't divided your document into sections, it applies to the entire document. If text fills each page, changing its vertical alignment does not make much difference; reserve this technique for pages that are not full or for sections that are less than a page in length.

FIG. 7.8
You can align text in the center of the page or justify it.

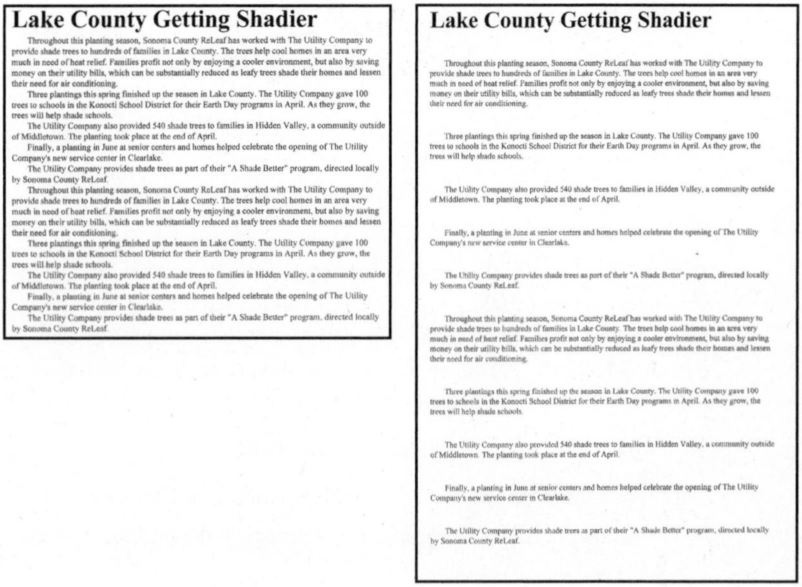

Lake County Getting Shadier

Throughout this planting season, Sonoma County ReLeaf has worked with The Utility Company to provide shade trees to hundreds of families in Lake County. The trees help cool homes in an area very much in need of heat relief. Families profit not only by enjoying a cooler environment, but also by saving money on their utility bills, which can be substantially reduced as leafy trees shade their homes and lessen their need for air conditioning.

Three plantings this spring finished up the season in Lake County. The Utility Company gave 100 trees to schools in the Konocti School District for their Earth Day programs in April. As they grow, the trees will help shade schools.

The Utility Company also provided 540 shade trees to families in Hidden Valley, a community outside of Middletown. The planting took place at the end of April.

Finally, a planting in June at senior centers and homes helped celebrate the opening of The Utility Company's new service center in Clearlake.

The Utility Company provides shade trees as part of their "A Shade Better" program, directed locally by Sonoma County ReLeaf.

Throughout this planting season, Sonoma County ReLeaf has worked with The Utility Company to provide shade trees to hundreds of families in Lake County. The trees help cool homes in an area very much in need of heat relief. Families profit not only by enjoying a cooler environment, but also by saving money on their utility bills, which can be substantially reduced as leafy trees shade their homes and lessen their need for air conditioning.

Three plantings this spring finished up the season in Lake County. The Utility Company gave 100 trees to schools in the Konocti School District for their Earth Day programs in April. As they grow, the trees will help shade schools.

The Utility Company also provided 540 shade trees to families in Hidden Valley, a community outside of Middletown. The planting took place at the end of April.

Finally, a planting in June at senior centers and homes helped celebrate the opening of The Utility Company's new service center in Clearlake.

The Utility Company provides shade trees as part of their "A Shade Better" program, directed locally by Sonoma County ReLeaf.

Lake County Getting Shadier

Throughout this planting season, Sonoma County ReLeaf has worked with The Utility Company to provide shade trees to hundreds of families in Lake County. The trees help cool homes in an area very much in need of heat relief. Families profit not only by enjoying a cooler environment, but also by saving money on their utility bills, which can be substantially reduced as leafy trees shade their homes and lessen their need for air conditioning.

Three plantings this spring finished up the season in Lake County. The Utility Company gave 100 trees to schools in the Konocti School District for their Earth Day programs in April. As they grow, the trees will help shade schools.

The Utility Company also provided 540 shade trees to families in Hidden Valley, a community outside of Middletown. The planting took place at the end of April.

Finally, a planting in June at senior centers and homes helped celebrate the opening of The Utility Company's new service center in Clearlake.

The Utility Company provides shade trees as part of their "A Shade Better" program, directed locally by Sonoma County ReLeaf.

Throughout this planting season, Sonoma County ReLeaf has worked with The Utility Company to provide shade trees to hundreds of families in Lake County. The trees help cool homes in an area very much in need of heat relief. Families profit not only by enjoying a cooler environment, but also by saving money on their utility bills, which can be substantially reduced as leafy trees shade their homes and lessen their need for air conditioning.

Three plantings this spring finished up the season in Lake County. The Utility Company gave 100 trees to schools in the Konocti School District for their Earth Day programs in April. As they grow, the trees will help shade schools.

The Utility Company also provided 540 shade trees to families in Hidden Valley, a community outside of Middletown. The planting took place at the end of April.

Finally, a planting in June at senior centers and homes helped celebrate the opening of The Utility Company's new service center in Clearlake.

The Utility Company provides shade trees as part of their "A Shade Better" program, directed locally by Sonoma County ReLeaf.

To vertically align text on the page, follow these steps:

1. Position the insertion point inside the section where you want to align text.
2. Choose File, Page Setup. The Page Setup dialog box appears.
3. Select the Layout tab.
4. In the Vertical Alignment list, select Center to center text on the page.

   You can also select Justify to spread paragraphs between the top and bottom margins on the page.

   Or, you can select Top to align text to the top margin.
5. Choose OK.

Controlling Where Paragraphs and Pages Break

As you type your document, Word automatically breaks text at the bottom margin of each page. Text continues on the next page, unless you specify otherwise. Word determines how much text appears on a page based on many factors, including margins, type size, paragraph specifications, and the size of footnotes. Displaying hidden text and field codes also can affect page breaks—hide them to see accurately how your pages will break.

You have many ways to control how text breaks on a page. You can specify that paragraphs stay together, for example, or with other paragraphs. You can also specify at which line a page will break.

Controlling Paragraph Breaks

By default, paragraphs break at the bottom margin of a page and continue at the top margin of the next page. Many times you might want to prevent paragraphs from breaking arbitrarily at the bottom of the page. You may want to keep a heading paragraph together with the paragraph that follows it, for example. Or you may want certain paragraphs not to break at all. You may want to avoid widows and orphans, single lines of text that appear at the top or bottom of the page.

Regardless of how you format paragraphs to control paragraph breaks, hard page breaks that you insert manually take precedence. If you format a paragraph to stay together on a page but insert a hard page break inside the paragraph, for example, the paragraph always breaks at the line containing the hard page break. You must remove the hard page break if you want the paragraph to stay together (see the next section).

To control paragraph breaks, follow these steps:

1. Position the insertion point inside the paragraph you want to affect.

2. Choose F<u>o</u>rmat, <u>P</u>aragraph. The Paragraph dialog box appears. Select the Line and <u>P</u>age Breaks tab (see Figure 7.9).

FIG. 7.9
In the Paragraph dialog box, you can control how paragraphs break—or don't break—at the bottom of a page.

3. Select the following options you want from the Pagination group:

Select this option	To get this result
<u>W</u>idow/Orphan Control	Prevents single lines in selected paragraphs from appearing alone at the top or bottom of a page.
<u>K</u>eep Lines Together	Prevents a page break inside a selected paragraph. Moves the paragraph to the next page if there's not room on the current page for all of it.

Select this option	To get this result
Keep with Next	Ensures that the selected paragraph always appears on the same page as the next paragraph. Moves the paragraph to the next page if there's not room on the current page for it and the next paragraph.
Page Break Before	Starts the selected paragraph at the top of the next page. Inserts a page break before selected paragraph.

4. Choose OK.

A nonprinting square selection handle appears in the left margin next to any paragraph for which you've selected a pagination option. If text breaks on the page in a way you don't like, look for these squares to see whether the page break is caused by a pagination option. If it is, you can remove it by following the preceding steps and clearing the offending pagination option.

Inserting Page Breaks

Word inserts soft page breaks at the end of every page and adjusts them as necessary when you edit, add, or remove text. If you want to force a page to break at a particular place in your document, you can insert a hard page break. Word always starts text following a hard page break at the top of the next page.

In Normal view, a soft page break appears as a dotted line; in Page Layout or Print Preview view, you see the page as it will print. In Outline and Online Layout views, you don't see soft page breaks. Hard page breaks appear in the Normal and Outline views as a dotted line containing the words Page Break; they appear this way in the Page Layout and Master Document views when you display nonprinting characters. In Online Layout view, hard page breaks appear as excessive space between paragraphs.

N O T E   Hard page breaks take priority over paragraph pagination options.

After you insert a hard page break, you can delete it, move it, copy it, or paste it.

You can insert a hard page break by using a command or a keyboard shortcut. You also can insert a page break by inserting a section break that begins on the next page, or on the next odd- or even-numbered page; see "Working with Sections in Your Document" later in this chapter. To insert a hard page break, follow these steps:

1. Position the insertion point at the beginning of the text that you want to start on a new page.
2. Choose Insert, Break. The Break dialog box appears (see Figure 7.10).
3. Select Page Break.
4. Choose OK.

Part

II

Ch

7

FIG. 7.10
In the Break dialog box, you can insert a hard page break by selecting the Page Break option.

 To insert a hard page break using a keyboard shortcut, press Ctrl+Enter.

Working with Sections in Your Document

Initially, in word processing programs, many formatting choices—margins, columns, headers and footers, line numbers, page numbers, and footnotes—applied to the entire document. Later, users' needs grew to require different settings for different parts of the document; Word uses *sections* as its way to divide your document into parts that you can format differently. Each section is like a document within a document.

Sections are especially important in creating two types of documents—those with chapters and those that fall into the desktop publishing category. Sections are useful for chapters because you can force a section to start on a right-facing page (as most chapters do) and can change headers, footers, page numbers, line numbering, and so on for each chapter. Sections also are indispensable for desktop publishing, where you often need to vary the number of columns on a single page.

▶ **See** "Creating Columns," **p. 168**
▶ **See** "Changing Columns," **p. 174**

Dividing a Document into Sections

By default, a document contains only a single section. Section breaks divide your document into sections. The breaks appear as double-dotted lines containing the words `Section Break` in Normal view (the type of section break will appear in parentheses). You'll see section breaks in Page Layout view if all nonprinting characters are displayed (see Figure 7.11). (You can display nonprinting characters by choosing Tools, Options, selecting the View tab, and then selecting All.) The dotted lines do not print.

A *section break* marks the point in your document where new formatting begins. In a newsletter, for example, a section break often follows the title, so that a multiple-column format can begin. The text following the section break, along with its new formatting, can begin in your document immediately, on the next page, or on the next even-numbered or odd-numbered page. You determine where the new section formatting begins when you insert the section break.

FIG. 7.11
Section breaks appear as a double-dotted line in Normal view and in Page Layout view when all nonprinting characters are displayed.

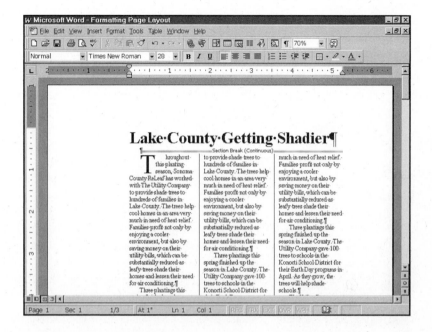

To insert a section break, follow these steps:

1. Position the insertion point where you want the section break.

2. Choose <u>I</u>nsert, <u>B</u>reak. The Break dialog box appears (refer to Figure 7.10).

3. Select from the following Section Breaks options:

Option	Section starts
<u>N</u>ext Page	Top of the next page in document
Con<u>t</u>inuous	Insertion point (causing no apparent break in the document)
<u>E</u>ven Page	Next even-numbered page in the document (generally a left-facing page)
<u>O</u>dd Page	Next odd-numbered page in the document (generally a right-facing page)

4. Choose OK.

Use the <u>N</u>ext Page section break when you want the new section to begin on the next page. Use the Con<u>t</u>inuous section break when you want the new section to begin at the insertion point; for example, when you create a newsletter that has different-width columns on the same page (such as a full-width title followed by a three-column story). Another use for the Continuous section break is to balance columns on a page: Insert a Con<u>t</u>inuous section break at the end of a document that is divided into columns but that doesn't fill the last column of the last page.

Use the <u>O</u>dd Page section break for chapters when you want them to start always on a right-facing page (assuming page numbering in your document starts with page 1 on a right-facing

Part

II

Ch

7

page). Use the Even Page section break to start a section on the next even-numbered page; on facing page layouts with mirror margins, even-numbered pages usually are on the left side of the layout.

Word inserts section breaks for you on some occasions. When you format a document for columns and specify that the columns take effect from This Point Forward, Word inserts a continuous section break at the insertion point. When you select text and format it for columns, Word inserts continuous section breaks both before and after the selected text. The same rule holds true when you make many page setup selections.

▶ **See** "Creating Columns," **p. 168**

Removing Section Breaks

In the same way that paragraph marks store paragraph formatting, section break marks store section formatting. Although you can remove a section break easily, remember that when you do, you also remove all section formatting for the section that precedes the deleted break. The preceding section merges with the following section and takes on its formatting characteristics. If you accidentally delete a section break marker, immediately choose Edit, Undo to retrieve the marker.

To remove a section break, position the insertion point on the section break and press the Delete key. As alternatives, you can position the insertion point just after the section break marker and press Backspace; you can select the section break and click the Cut button or choose Edit, Cut.

To remove all the section breaks in your document, follow these steps:

1. Choose Edit, Replace and choose More.
2. With the insertion point in the Find What box, open the Special list and choose Section Break.
3. Make sure that the Replace With box contains no text, and choose Replace All.

Copying Section Formatting

The section break stores section formatting. You can duplicate (or apply) section formatting quickly by selecting, copying, and then pasting the section break elsewhere. After you paste the section break, the preceding text takes on the formatting of the copied section break.

Another way to duplicate section formatting is to copy and store a section break as AutoText. That way, the break becomes available in all new documents and can be applied quickly and easily.

A final way to duplicate section formatting is to include the formatting in a template—even the Normal template. Remember that by default, a new document includes only one section. That section carries certain default formatting characteristics: one column, a half-inch space between columns (if columns are selected), and no line numbers. If you always format sections differently, modify the Normal template or create a new template that includes your own custom section formatting selections.

▶ **See** "Creating a New Template," **p. 18**

▶ **See** "Changing a Template," **p. 15**

Changing the Section Break Type

If you insert a continuous section break and want to change it to a new page section break, you must delete the existing section break and insert a new one. If you want to make this change without removing the previous section's formatting, insert the new section break so that it appears after the old one and then delete the old page break. The section will then take on the formatting contained in the next section break, which is the new break you added.

Finding Section Breaks

If you want to find section breaks, choose Edit, Find. Next, choose More, select Special, and then select Section Break. Choose Find Next to find the next section break. You can find section breaks this way even if they are not displayed.

You can choose Edit, Replace to find a section break and replace it with something else, but you cannot replace something with a section break. Use this technique if you want to remove all the section breaks in your document: simply replace section breaks with nothing.

▶ **See** "Using Find and Replace," **p. 25**

Creating Headers and Footers

Headers and footers contain information repeated at the top or bottom of the pages of a document. The simplest header or footer may contain only a chapter title and page number. More elaborate headers or footers may contain a company logo (or other graphic), the author's name, the time and date the file was saved or printed, and any other information that may be needed.

You can format headers and footers like any other part of the document, but you usually position them within a page's top and bottom margins, although Word enables you to position them anywhere on the page.

Word also gives you the option of having a different header or footer on the first page of a document or section. You also can have different headers and footers on even and odd pages. This feature is useful for chapter headers in books and manuscripts. Each section of a document—a chapter, for example—can have its own headers and footers.

When you create and edit headers and footers, Word switches you to Page Layout view and displays headers and footers at the top or bottom of the page, just as they appear when you print your document.

Adding Headers and Footers

When you add headers and footers, Word switches you to Page Layout view, activates a pane where you can create your header, displays a special Header and Footer toolbar, and dims the text of your document so that you can't edit it (see Figure 7.12).

Part

II

Ch

7

FIG. 7.12

You create headers and footers in a special pane.

Insert Number of Pages

Show/hide document text

Switch between header and footer

Show previous section's header/footer

Show next section's header/footer

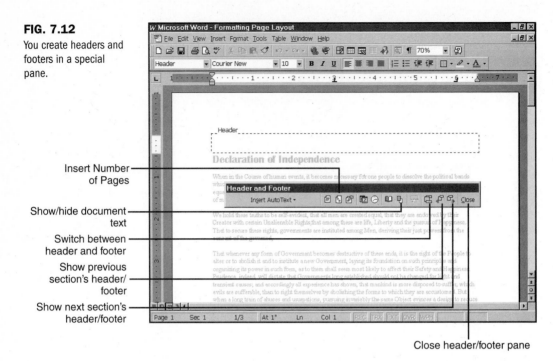

Close header/footer pane

You create your header or footer inside the pane, and you can edit and format it the same way you do any text. After you finish creating the header or footer, close the Header and Footer toolbar. You can move the Header and Footer toolbar by dragging it to a different position on the page.

You can include text or graphics, or both, in a header or footer. If you want, you can insert autotext entries, page numbers, date and time, fields, symbols, cross-references, files, frames, pictures, objects, or a database. Or you can draw a picture using buttons on the Drawing toolbar.

Buttons on the toolbar aid you in creating your header or footer (see Figure 7.13). If the status bar is visible at the bottom of your screen, you can display a message explaining each button by pausing the mouse pointer over the button.

Page number

Format page number

Time

Show/hide document text

Switch between header and footer

Show next section's header/footer

FIG. 7.13

Create a header or footer using the buttons in the Header and Footer toolbar.

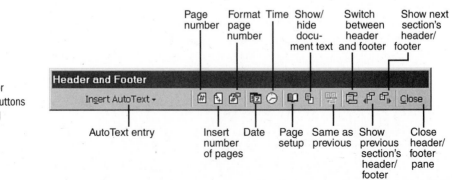

AutoText entry

Insert number of pages

Date

Page setup

Same as previous

Show previous section's header/footer

Close header/footer pane

In Page Layout view, your document appears grayed when you're creating or editing headers or footers; headers and footers appear grayed when you're working on your document. To see both your document and its headers and footers, choose File, Print Preview.

To add a header or footer to your document, follow these steps:

1. Choose View, Header and Footer.
2. Type and format the text of your header. Click the Page Number, Number of Pages, Date, and/or Time buttons to quickly add those elements to your header.
3. Click the Switch Between button to display the footer, and type and format just as you did the header (see step 2). Alternatively, use the scroll bars or press Page Up or Page Down to scroll to the footer.
4. Choose Close or double-click your document to close the header or footer pane and return to your document.

Another way to include an automatic date or time in a header or footer is to insert a date or time field by choosing Insert, Field. Using this command, you can select among different formatting options for your date or time.

If your header or footer is larger than your margin, Word adjusts the margins of your document to make room. If you don't want Word to adjust your margins, make your header or footer smaller or move it closer to the edge of the page (see "Positioning Headers and Footers," later in this chapter). If you want text to overlap a header or footer (as you might if the header or footer is a graphic that is to appear behind text), type a minus sign (–) in front of your margin measurement. If your header is four inches high, for example, and you want a top margin of one inch, and you want the text to overlap the header, type –1" as your top margin. You can use this technique to create a "watermark" that appears behind the text on every page of your document.

Varying Headers and Footers Within a Single Document

Each section in a document can have unique headers and footers. This setup is helpful if you format each chapter in a book as a separate section. Or you can create different headers and footers on odd and even pages. You also can have a different header or footer on the first page of a document. If your document has facing pages and mirror margins, for example, you might want a right-aligned header on odd-numbered pages (which appear on the right side of a facing-page layout) and a left-aligned header on even-numbered pages (which appear on the left). In a newsletter, you might want no header on the first page.

Changing Headers and Footers for Specific Sections   When you first create headers and footers, Word applies them to all the sections in your document. That way, all the headers and footers in your document are the same. Similarly, if you divide into sections a document with existing headers or footers, the headers and footers are the same in all sections.

If you want a different header or footer in a section, you must go to that section and unlink the existing header or footer; then you must create the new header or footer. The new header or footer applies to the current section and to all following sections. Later, if you decide you want your new header or footer to be the same as the previous header or footer, you can relink it.

If you want different headers and footers in different sections of your document, you first must divide your document into sections. To learn how, see "Working with Sections in your Document" earlier in this chapter. To change the header or footer in one section of your document, follow these steps:

1. Position the insertion point inside the section where you want to change the header or footer.

 T I P As a shortcut, activate a header or footer by double-clicking it in Page Layout view.

2. Choose View, Header and Footer. Word selects the header for the section in which you're located. If you want to change the footer for that section, click the Switch Between button instead.

3. To unlink the header or footer, click the Same as Previous button. The Same as Previous line disappears from the top right of the header or footer editing pane.

4. Create the new header or footer.

5. Choose the Close button or double-click your document to close the Header and Footer toolbar.

   You also can click the Show Next button to change the header or footer in the following section.

The new header or footer applies to the current section and to all following sections.

As an alternative to steps 1 and 2, you can choose View, Header and Footer from within any section to activate headers and footers. Then click the Switch Between button to jump between headers and footers, or click the Show Next or Show Previous buttons to activate headers or footers in a different section.

 T I P You can make headers and footers different in all sections of your document. After step 4, click the Show Next button and repeat steps 3 and 4 until you've created all your headers or footers. Then, close the Header and Footer toolbar.

To relink a different header or footer to the previous header or footer, follow these steps:

1. Position the insertion point inside the section containing the header or footer you want to relink.

2. Choose View, Header and Footer. Word selects the header for the section in which you're located. If you want to change the footer for that section, click the Switch Between button.

3. To relink the header or footer, click the Same as Previous button. Word displays a message box asking whether you want to delete the header/footer and connect to the header/footer in the previous section.

4. Choose Yes.

5. Choose Close, or double-click your document to close the Header and Footer toolbar.

By relinking the header or footer to the previous header or footer, you change not only the current header or footer, but also those in all the following sections.

CAUTION

If you change one header or footer without unlinking it, all the headers and footers in all the sections change.

Creating Special First-Page and Odd/Even Page Headers and Footers   Many documents have a different header or footer on the first page—or have no header or footer on the first page. In Word, first-page headers and footers apply to sections, not to the whole document. That way, you can have a different header or footer at the beginning of each section in a document that is divided into sections.

Sometimes you want different headers and footers for the odd- and even-numbered pages in your document. In a document with facing pages (mirror margins), odd-numbered pages appear on the right side and even-numbered pages appear on the left side. You might want left-aligned headers on even-numbered pages and right-aligned headers on odd-numbered pages so that headers always appear on the outside edges of your document.

To specify special headers and footers for first pages or odd and even pages in your document, follow these steps:

1. Choose View, Header and Footer.

2. Click the Show Previous or Show Next button to locate the section in which you want a different first-page header or footer.

3. Click the Page Setup button (or choose File, Page Setup) to display the Page Setup dialog box.

4. Select the Layout tab.

5. In the Headers and Footers group, select Different First Page to create specific first page headers or footers, and then choose OK. The header or footer editing pane for the section you're in is titled First Page Header or First Page Footer.

   Or, in the Headers and Footers group, select Different Odd and Even and choose OK. Word re-titles the header or footer editing box for the section you're in to Even Page Header, Even Page Footer, Odd Page Header, or Odd Page Footer.

6. If you want no header or footer, leave the header or footer editing area blank. If you want a different header or footer on the first page or odd/even pages of the section, create it now.

7. Choose Close or double-click your document.

To remove first-page headers and footers from a section or document, follow these steps:

1. Position the insertion point anywhere inside a document containing only one section.

   You can also position the insertion point inside the section for which you want to remove first-page headers and footers.

2. Choose File, Page Setup.

3. Select the Layout tab.

4. Clear the Different First Page check box in the Headers and Footers group.

5. Choose OK.

Positioning Headers and Footers

By default, headers and footers appear one-half inch from the top or bottom edge of the document page. You can change that distance in the Header and Footer view.

To specify a header's or footer's distance from the edge of the paper, follow these steps:

1. Choose View, Header and Footer.

2. Click the Show Previous or Show Next button to locate the section containing the header or footer you want to affect.

3. Click the Page Setup button (or choose File, Page Setup) to display the Page Setup dialog box.

4. Select the Margins tab.

5. In the From Edge group, select Header and type or select the distance that you want your header from the top edge of the page.

   Or, select Footer and type or select the distance that you want your footer from the bottom edge of the page.

6. Choose OK to close the Page Setup dialog box.

7. Choose Close or double-click your document to return to it.

 Remember that most printers have a quarter-inch nonprinting edge on all sides.

Formatting Headers and Footers

Anything you can do to or in regular text, you can do to a header or footer. You can change the font, reduce or enlarge the size of the text, insert graphics, draw pictures, include a table, add a line or box, or add shading. You also can add tabs, change the alignment or indents, or change line or paragraph spacing. Use any of Word's formatting techniques to make headers and footers look distinct from the text in your document.

▶ **See** "Shading and Bordering Paragraphs," **p. 114**

You can use most of the commands in the Insert, Format, Tools, and Table menus to format headers and footers. You can use the ruler to set tabs and indents.

Editing Headers and Footers

In Normal view, you can't see headers or footers. In Page Layout view, you can see headers and footers, but they appear dimmed. In any view, you must activate a header or footer to edit it. You can activate a header or footer using the same command you used to create it, or in Page Layout view, you can double-click a header or footer to activate it. After it is activated, you edit the header or footer using the same commands you used to create it.

If your document contains only one section, then the headers and footers are the same throughout your document, and you can edit headers and footers with the insertion point anywhere within the document. If your document contains multiple sections with different headers and footers, you must locate the header or footer you want to edit. You can do that two ways:

■ Activate headers and footers and then use the Show Previous and Show Next buttons on the Header and Footer toolbar to move between sections.

■ First locate the header or footer you want to edit and then activate it.

To edit headers and footers, follow these steps:

1. Choose View, Header and Footer. Word activates the header for the section containing the insertion point. Or, in Page Layout view, double-click the header or footer you want to edit.

2. To edit a footer rather than a header, click the Switch Between button or press Page Down to scroll to the bottom of the page.

3. To locate a header or footer in a different section of your document, click the Show Previous or the Show Next button.

4. After you locate the header or footer you want to edit, make the changes you want.

5. Choose Close or double-click the document.

You can delete a header or footer by activating it, selecting all the text or objects contained in the header or footer, pressing Delete, and then choosing Close.

Hiding the Text Layer

Normally, the text layer appears dimmed while you're working on headers and footers. If you want to hide it altogether, you can click a special button on the Header and Footer toolbar. Text is only hidden while you're working on the header or footer.

To hide or display the text layer, follow these steps:

1. Activate headers and footers by choosing View, Header and Footer or by double-clicking an existing header or footer in Page Layout view.

2. Click the Hide/Show Document Text button. The text (grayed already), disappears from your screen. Click the button a second time to display the text.

3. Choose Close or double-click your document to return to it.

Part
II

Ch
7

Working with Page Numbers

Long documents are easier to read and reference when the pages are numbered. In Word, you can insert a page number quickly, and Word formats it as a header or footer for you. That way, you can use all the techniques for working with headers and footers to work with page numbers. See "Creating Headers and Footers" earlier in this chapter.

Inserting Page Numbers

Page numbers can appear at the top or bottom of the page and can be aligned to the center or either side of the page. When you insert a page number, Word includes a PAGE field and frames the page number. Because of the field, Word can update the page number even if you move the page to another portion of the document. Because of the frame, you can move the page number anywhere within the header or footer.

Another way to include page numbers is to insert them as part of creating a header or footer, by clicking the Page Numbers button on the Header and Footer toolbar. This technique is the best if you want to include text with your page number.

To insert page numbers, follow these steps:

1. Choose Insert, Page Numbers. The Page Numbers dialog box appears (see Figure 7.14).

FIG. 7.14

Using the Page Numbers dialog box, you can include page numbers at the top or bottom of the page, in any alignment. You can choose whether to show them on the first page of your document.

2. In the Position list, select Bottom of Page (Footer) to position your page number at the bottom of the page in a footer or choose Top of Page (Header) to position your page number at the top of the page in a header.

3. In the Alignment list, select Left, Center, Right, Inside, or Outside to line up your page number to the center or one side of the page.

4. Select Show Number on First Page if you want a page number to appear on the first page of your document. Clear this check box to prevent the page number from appearing on the first page.

5. Choose OK.

To reposition page numbers, choose Insert, Page Numbers and choose a different option from the Alignment list. Alternatively, in Page Layout view, double-click the page number to activate the Header or Footer editing pane. Select the page number and drag it to a new position (or select the frame and reposition it by choosing F**o**rmat, Fra**m**e and making selections from the Frame dialog box). Then choose **C**lose.

Removing Page Numbers

Because page numbers appear within headers or footers, to remove them you must activate the header or footer, select the page number, and delete it.

To remove page numbers, follow these steps:

1. In Page Layout view, double-click the page number.

   You can also choose **V**iew, **H**eader and Footer and click the Switch Between, Show Next, or Show Previous button to locate the page number.

2. Select the page number.

3. Press Delete.

4. Choose **C**lose or double-click your document.

Formatting Page Numbers

You can format your page numbers in a variety of ways. They can appear as numbers, upper-case or lowercase letters, or uppercase or lowercase Roman numerals.

You can include chapter numbers if your document's chapter numbers are formatted with Word default heading styles (Heading 1 through Heading 9) and if you've formatted the headings by choosing F**o**rmat, Bullets and **N**umbering and making a selection from the O**u**tline Numbered tab. If you include chapter numbers, you can separate them from the page numbers with a hyphen, a period, a colon, or a — (a wide hyphen).

▶ **See** "Creating Numbered Headings," **p. 329**

You can format page numbers at the same time that you insert them, or you can format them later. To format page numbers, follow these steps:

1. If you're creating new page numbers, choose **I**nsert, Page N**u**mbers. Make selections from the **P**osition and **A**lignment lists.

   If you want to format existing page numbers for a single section, you can also position the insertion point inside that section and choose **I**nsert, Page N**u**mbers.

2. Click the **F**ormat button. The Page Number Format dialog box displays (see Figure 7.15).

3. In the Number **F**ormat list, select the style you want your numbers to be.

4. Select Include Chapter **N**umber if you want to include a chapter number before your page number. In the Chapter Starts with Style drop-down list, choose the style (Heading 1 through Heading 9) that you use for chapter numbers in your document.

5. If you want a separator between the chapter number and page number, make a selection from the Use S**e**parator list.

6. Choose OK.

Part

II

Ch

7

FIG. 7.15

You can format your page numbers as you create them or after you've already created them.

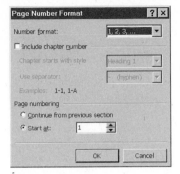

Numbering Different Sections in a Document

Even if your document contains more than a single section, page numbering applies by default to your entire document, and numbers are continuous throughout the document. You can start page numbering at the number you specify in any section, however. You may want page numbering to restart at "1" for each section, for example.

To create page numbering by section, follow these steps:

1. If necessary, divide your document into sections by inserting section breaks.
2. Position the insertion point inside the section for which you want unique page numbering.
3. Unlink the header or footer from previous headers or footers (see the section "Varying Headers and Footers within a Single Document," earlier in this chapter).
4. Choose Insert, Page Numbers, and then choose Format.
5. In the Page Numbering group, select Start At and type or select the starting page number for the current section.
6. Choose OK to return to the Page Numbers dialog box; choose OK again to return to your document.

If headers and footers containing page numbers are unlinked from previous sections but you want page numbering to be continuous from section to section, repeat the steps above, choosing Continue from the Previous Section in the Page Numbering Group. Finally, choose OK.

▶ **See** "Creating Numbered Headings," **p. 329**

Repaginating in the Background

By default, Word automatically calculates page breaks as you work on your document. In the Normal, Outline, Or Master Document view, you can turn off background pagination, but in Online Layout, Page Layout or Print Preview views, you cannot. You may see a slight performance improvement if you turn off background repagination.

TIP   Word always repaginates when you print your document, switch to Online Layout, Page Layout or Print Preview view, or compile an index or table of contents.

To turn off background repagination, follow these steps:

1. Choose <u>V</u>iew, and then choose either <u>N</u>ormal, <u>O</u>utline, or <u>M</u>aster Document.

 TIP Click the appropriate button on the horizontal scroll bar to switch to Normal or Outline view.

2. Choose <u>T</u>ools, <u>O</u>ptions, and select the General Tab.
3. Clear the <u>B</u>ackground Repagination check box.
4. Choose OK.

Inserting a Date and Time

In Word, there are several ways to insert the date and time automatically. You can use a command to insert the current date and time as frozen—that is, the date and time do not change—or you can insert them as a field that you can update to reflect the current date and time. You can choose among many different date and time formats. Or you can include a date and time field in a header or footer. These fields also update to reflect the current date or time.

 TIP To update a date or time field, select the field and press the F9 key. Date and time fields automatically update whenever you open or print a document if you set your options accordingly.

To insert a date or time, follow these steps:

1. Position the insertion point where you want the date or time to appear. You can insert the date or time in your document or in a header or footer.
2. Choose <u>I</u>nsert, Date and <u>T</u>ime. The Date and Time dialog box appears (see Figure 7.16).

FIG. 7.16
Choose <u>I</u>nsert, Date and <u>T</u>ime to insert a date or time.

3. Choose the date and time format you want from the <u>A</u>vailable Formats list.
4. If you want the date and time to update to reflect the current date and time, select <u>U</u>pdate Automatically (Insert as Field).
5. Choose OK.

Part
II

Ch
7

Inserting Line Numbers

If a document is used for reference, it is helpful to readers if the lines are numbered. You can number lines in text that a class shares or in legal briefs, for example.

You can number some or all of the lines in a document. If your document contains no section breaks, line numbers apply to the entire document. If your document contains sections, line numbers apply to the currently selected section. If you select text before you assign line numbers, Word places page section breaks before and after the selected text, isolating it on a page (or pages) by itself. If you want to apply line numbers to an entire document that contains multiple sections, select the entire document before you apply the line numbers.

Word offers many options for controlling how line numbers appear. Numbers can start at 1 or some other number, and they can appear on each line or on only some lines. They can be continuous, or they can restart at each section or page. You can control the distance between text and the line numbers. You also can suppress line numbers for selected paragraphs.

Line numbers appear in the left margin of your page or to the left of text in columns.

To add and format line numbers, follow these steps:

1. Position the insertion point inside the section containing lines you want to number. (Position the insertion point anywhere inside a document that is not divided into sections.)

   You can also select the text whose lines you want to number.

   Or, you can select the entire document if it is divided into sections and you want line numbering for all the sections.

2. Choose File, Page Setup. The Page Setup dialog box appears.

3. Select the Layout tab.

4. Choose Line Numbers. The Line Numbers dialog box appears (see Figure 7.17).

FIG. 7.17

Using the Line Numbers dialog box, you can number the lines of your text for easy reference.

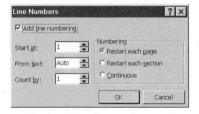

5. Select Add Line Numbering.

6. Make changes to any of the following:

   - Select Start At and type or select the starting line number.
   - Select From Text and type the distance between the line numbers and text. (Be sure your margins are wide enough to accommodate this distance.)

- Select Count <u>B</u>y and type or select the increment by which you want lines to be numbered. Select 3, for example, if you want every third line numbered.

7. In the Numbering group, select any of the following:

- Select Restart Each <u>P</u>age for numbering to start over on each page.
- Select Restart Each <u>S</u>ection to start over in each section.
- Select <u>C</u>ontinuous if you want line numbers continuous throughout the document.

8. Choose OK.

   Choose OK again to close the Page Setup dialog box and return to your document, where you can see the line numbers (see Figure 7.18).

FIG. 7.18

This document is divided into two sections, so that the title line isn't numbered.

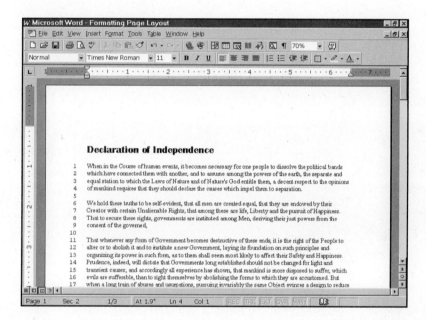

To remove line numbers, follow these steps:

1. Follow steps 1–4 above.
2. Clear the check from the Add <u>L</u>ine Numbering check box.
3. Choose OK. Choose OK again to close the Page Setup dialog box.

To suppress line numbers, follow these steps:

1. Select the paragraphs where you don't want line numbers to appear.
2. Choose F<u>o</u>rmat, <u>P</u>aragraph. The Paragraph dialog box appears.
3. Select the Lines and <u>P</u>age Breaks tab.
4. Select <u>S</u>uppress Line Numbers.
5. Choose OK.

Part

II

Ch

7

Changing Page Setup Defaults

All new documents are based on a template, and unless you choose a different template, Word bases new documents on the Normal template, which contains default page setup choices. Because these default choices may not be exactly what you want, Word gives you the chance to change them by applying your own page setup options to the Normal template and, thus, use your own page setup choices as defaults. You can change the default margins, for example, if you always print on paper that requires different margin settings than those supplied by the Normal template. You can change the paper size if you normally use paper different from standard letter size.

▶ **See** "Setting Default Formats in the Normal Template," **p. 16**

You can change defaults for any option in the Page Setup dialog box. Then each new document you create based on the Normal template has your new defaults. (Your current document—or the text or section you've selected—also uses your new settings.)

To change the default page setup settings, follow these steps:

1. Choose File, Page Setup.
2. On each tab in the Page Setup dialog box, make the page setup selections you want.
3. Click the Default button on any of the tabs. A dialog box asks you to confirm that all new documents based on the Normal template are affected by the change.
4. Choose OK.

Mail Merging with Word

CHAPTER 8

Creating and Managing Data for Mail Merge

In this chapter

Using Word for Data Storage

Word 97 does more than just publish text. Think of it as a report writer or publisher of database information as well. Word has the ability to retrieve, store, and manipulate rows of information such as names and addresses, billing information, invoice data, product catalog information, and so on. Some of the tasks that are commonly relegated to database report applications can be accomplished with Word, and Word can give you a more free-form, publishing-oriented result. For example, you can use data stored or linked into Word to create:

- *Form letters* using name and address information. Other information can be merged into the form letters such as amounts owed, product information, or notes.
- *Envelopes* to go with the form letters. Envelopes can be printed in sorted ZIP code order and include POSTNET and FIM bar codes to save you money.
- *Mailing labels* that even include logos, graphics and bar codes.
- *Product catalogs* that include graphics and a more professionally published appearance than what is normally produced from a database report.
- *Sales report data* in a more free-form layout. Word can publish data using features such as newspaper columns and integrated graphics that are not available in worksheets such as Excel or from database report writers.

Methods of Storing Data

There are three sources of data Word can use for a mail merge—a Word document, an external file, and shared office data.

A Word document can consist of a table containing rows and columns of information, as shown in Figure 8.1. You can also use a tab- or comma-delimited Word document as your data source. Tables are much easier to read and edit than tab- or comma-delimited documents, so you may want to convert a tab- or comma-delimited document into a table. To do this, choose Table, Convert Text to Table. Select how the text is separated, for example by Tabs or Commas. Word will estimate how many columns to use, but you can change this in the Number of Columns box. Choose OK.

An external file can be a file imported from another application, or a database file that was created using Microsoft Access, Microsoft Excel, dBASE, Paradox, and so on. You can also use data from popular database applications if you have installed the appropriate ODBC driver. For more information about database files, see the section, "Inserting a Database from a File."

Shared office data refers to address books created in the Personal Address Book that is part of Word or in the address books available in other Microsoft applications such as Outlook, Schedule+, the Postoffice Address List, and lists for Microsoft Network.

FIG. 8.1

A data source can be as simple as a table in Word containing rows and columns of information.

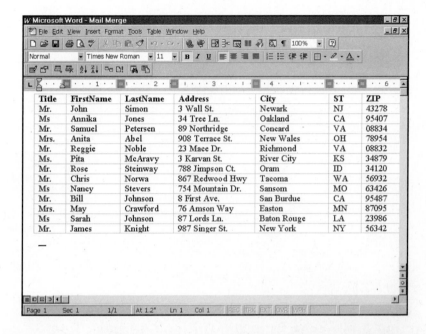

Managing Names and Addresses with Address Books

Managing a list of names and addresses is a simple task if you use an address book application such as the one in Outlook or Schedule+ Personal Address Book. After you have entered names and addresses, you can perform a number of tasks on the information. For example, you can edit, insert, delete, search, and sort the information.

Word 97 enables you to specify the address book in Outlook or Schedule+ as the data source for a mail merge. Because many companies and individuals use Outlook or Schedule+ to manage personal schedules, meeting rooms, and resources, it makes sense to use Outlook or Schedule+ as your address book for names and contacts used by everyone in your workgroup. Names and contact information for your personal use can be stored in the Personal Address Book.

Don't think that you have to enter a zillion names, addresses, and phone numbers manually, especially if you are targeting a set of people or businesses you can define by geographic region, demographic profile, or business profile. There are many sources for computer lists. Table 8.1 lists some of the more popular World Wide Web locations for name and address information.

Table 8.1   Name and Address Resources on the Web

Web Site Name	URL	Description
BigBook	**http://www.bigbook.com**	Searchable business phone directories
BigYellow	**http://s10.bigyellow.com**	Searchable business phone directories along with addresses and ZIP codes
Internet 800	**http://inter800.com**	Search businesses for 800 Directory numbers
Switchboard	**http://www.switchboard.com**	Search for businesses or people
United States Postal Service	**http://www.usps.gov**	Searchable index for ZIP+4 and lots of postal information.

Using Addresses from the Outlook Address Book

Microsoft Outlook is a personal information manager that manages e-mail, appointments, contacts, tasks, documents, and files on your hard disk. Outlook combines e-mail, phone support, group scheduling, public folders, forms, and the Internet capability to increase productivity.

If you did a Typical install of Microsoft Office 97 Suite, then you have Outlook installed. Outlook is easier to use and more robust than Schedule+. Outlook and Schedule+ are not compatible on the same network.

To use data from the Microsoft Outlook Address Book, follow these steps:

1. Choose Tools, Mail Merge. The Mail Merge Helper dialog box appears.
2. Choose Create and then select Form Letters.
3. Click the New Main Document button. This opens a blank document and returns you to the Mail Merge Helper. The Get Data button is now available.
4. Click the Get Data button. Click the Use Address Book item. The Use Address Book dialog box appears, as shown in Figure 8.2.

FIG. 8.2

Select data for use in a mail merge from the Outlook Address Book, Personal Address Book, or from Schedule+ Contacts.

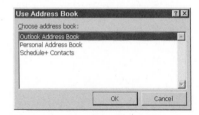

5. Select Outlook Address Book from the list, then click OK.

   You may be prompted to select the user profile you want to use from the Choose Profile dialog box, then click OK.

   If you do not have merge fields in your main document, Word displays a message requesting you to choose the Edit Main Document button and insert merge fields into your document.

To add new data to the existing data, perform these steps:

1. Choose Tools, Mail Merge. The Mail Merge Helper dialog box appears.

2. Click the Edit button next to the Get Data button. Then select the data to edit. The Data Form dialog box appears, as shown in Figure 8.3.

FIG. 8.3

Add new data or edit existing data in the Data Form dialog box.

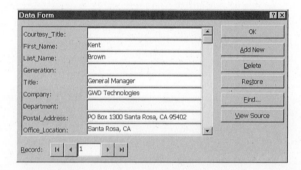

3. Click the Add New button, fill in the text boxes as appropriate, then click OK.

To edit existing data, perform these steps:

1. Choose Tools, Mail Merge. The Mail Merge Helper dialog box appears.

2. Click the Edit button next to the Get Data button. Then select the data to edit. The Data Form dialog box appears, as shown in Figure 8.3.

3. Click the Record arrow buttons to display the first, previous, next, or last record until you find the record you want to edit.

   You also can click the Find button to search for the record you want to edit. Figure 8.4 is an example of the Find in Field dialog box that appears after clicking the Find button.

4. Type the appropriate information in the Find What text box. For example, if you have a last name data field in your data records, find the record to edit by typing the last name.

FIG. 8.4

Use the Find in Field dialog box to find a record.

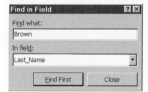

5. Select the appropriate merge field name from the In Field list. Make sure that the field name you select corresponds to the information you typed in the Find What text box.

6. Click the Find First button. The data record appears in the Data Form dialog box.

7. Click the Close button in the Find in Field dialog box.

8. Click the Restore button to revert to the original information.

Entering Addresses in Microsoft Schedule+

Microsoft Schedule+ is a useful scheduling program that you can use for your personal schedules and contact management, or that you can share in your workgroup. It even includes tips and a wizard on how to be more productive. If you work in a corporate network that uses Schedule+, you may be using Schedule+ to maintain your e-mail, calendar, and address books. Although Outlook comes with Microsoft Office 97 Suite, it does not work in a mixed environment with Schedule+.

To enter information into the Schedule+ address book, follow these steps:

1. Click the Start button in the taskbar, then click Programs, Microsoft Schedule+.

TIP   If the taskbar is currently hidden, move the pointer to the bottom of the screen and the taskbar will appear, or press Ctrl+Esc.

2. If you are prompted, type your User Name and logon password in the Schedule+ Logon dialog box, and then choose OK. Schedule+ will display.

3. Click the Contacts tab to view the list of contacts to make changes or add new contacts. Figure 8.5 shows an example of a new Schedule+ Address Book.

FIG. 8.5

Use the Microsoft Schedule+ Address Book to maintain a list of your contacts.

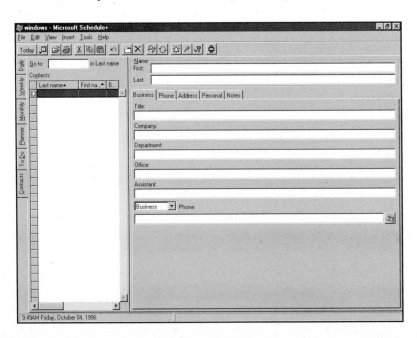

4. In the edit boxes on the right side, type information you want stored in the Schedule+ Address Book.

The contact information you enter in the Schedule+ Address Book will be accessible in Word.

Creating Your Own Data Sources

The Mail Merge Helper allows you the flexibility to create your own data sources from a wide range of applications. You can create a data source from a Word document, spreadsheet application, database file, or some other external application. The obvious benefit to you is that you can create your data source in a familiar application and then use the data to create multiple documents in Word.

Managing Data

Word dialog boxes and the Mail Merge Helper refer to the object containing data as the *data source*. The data source can be in a wide variety of common PC formats, such as Word documents, Excel worksheets, or dBASE-compatible database files. The data source can be on your PC or reside on another computer to which Word is linked via a network. You can also use data from a large database application, such as Oracle or SQL Server. Word can retrieve just the part of the database it needs from these larger databases.

Information stored in the data source is normally laid out in a table format of rows and columns. Each row of information is known as a *record*. If the data source contains the names and addresses of clients, a record contains an individual's name, address, and specific client information. In this case, one record of information is like a card in a card file. Each row in a data source ends with a paragraph mark.

Information is arranged within records by column. These columns are known as *fields*. Each field, or column, contains one specific type of information. For example, the name and address data source might need one field for state and another for ZIP code. A *delimiter* separates each field of data. Delimiters that Word understands are commas, tabs, or separate cells in a table. If a record contains more than 31 fields, then Word cannot use a table; it uses tabs or commas instead.

Data sources need a row of titles at the top that are known as *field names*. The field names should describe the contents of that field in the data source. You refer to these field names when you are searching for or limiting the data used from the data source. Field names are also used to indicate where information goes when it is taken from the data source and placed into the merge document such as a form letter or label.

Field names have specific requirements. They must be no longer than 40 characters, start with a letter, and cannot contain a space. Instead of using a space in a field name, you may want to use an underscore character.

TIP Without spaces between words, a multiple word field name can be difficult to read. To solve this, just capitalize the first letter of each word (for example, **FieldName**).

Word includes a toolbar specifically designed to help you manage tables, databases, and data sources. The Database toolbar displays by selecting Yiew, Toolbars, and selecting Database from the list.

▶ **See** "Selecting a Data Source," **p. 245**

The different buttons in the Database toolbar are as follows:

Icon	Name	Description
	Data Form	Displays the Data Form, which makes adding, editing, and finding information easier in the database.
	Manage Fields	Makes it easy to add, remove, or rename fields (columns) in a database.
	Add New Record	Adds a new record at the current insertion point in a table or database.
	Delete Record	Removes a record at the current insertion point in a table or database.
	Sort Ascending	Sorts the table or database in ascending order on the current field.
	Sort Descending	Sorts the table or database in descending order on the current field.
	Insert Database	Displays the Database dialog box so that you can insert a file containing a database.
	Update Fields	Updates fields and links in the document. Updates databases linked to files.
	Find Record	Displays the Find in Field dialog box to help you search a database.
	Mail Merge	Opens the Main Document Main Document attached to the current data source.

Inserting a Database from a File

Small lists can be managed in a word processor; however, if you have lists or databases larger than a few hundred records, you will want to use a database application such as Microsoft Access in which to store, edit, and retrieve your data. Word makes it easy to store data in many different types of databases and then bring that data into a Word document so that it can be used as a data source for mail merge.

For Word to import or access a database file, it must have the appropriate file converters or Open Database Connectivity (ODBC) drivers installed. Installing converters and drivers can be done after Word has been initially installed. To install converters and drivers, rerun the Office or Word Setup program.

Database files that Word can convert and insert include the following:

Microsoft Word	Microsoft FoxPro
Microsoft Access	Word for Mac 3.x, 4.x, and 5.x
Microsoft Excel	Word for MS-DOS 3.0–6.0
dBASE	WordPerfect 5.x for MS-DOS or Windows
Paradox	Lotus 1-2-3 2.x and 3.x

When you insert a database, you can choose to insert the data or insert a field code, which creates a link to the database file. Inserted data acts just as though it was typed in the document. Inserting a field code enables you to quickly update the database, because it has a link to the file on disk. If the data in the file changes, you can easily update the list.

To insert a database that is in a file on disk, follow these steps:

1. Position the insertion point in the document where you want the database.
2. If the Database toolbar is not displayed, choose View, Toolbars, and click Database.
3. Click the Insert Database icon in the Database toolbar. The Database dialog box is displayed in Figure 8.6.

FIG. 8.6
Use the Database dialog box to insert all or part of a database that is in a file from Word or another application.

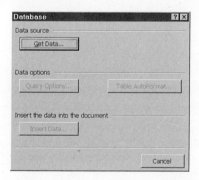

4. Click the Get Data button to display the Open Data Source dialog box, shown in Figure 8.7.

FIG. 8.7
From the Open Data Source dialog box, you can open the file containing your merge data.

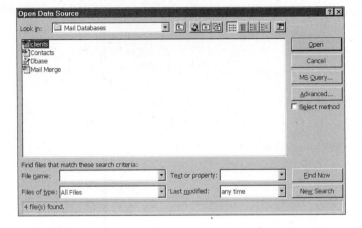

5. Select or type the name of the file in the File Name drop-down list. Choose OK.

    If it is possible to select part of the data source, such as a range on a spreadsheet, a dialog box like the one in Figure 8.8 appears. In this example, the Excel spreadsheet named CONTACTS contains a named range, TopTen. Select the range or query that defines the data you want, then choose OK to return to the Database dialog box.

FIG. 8.8
You can insert a portion of some database files.

6. Click the Query Options button from the Database dialog box if you want the data you insert to meet certain criteria.

7. Select Table AutoFormat if you want to be guided through custom formatting of the table.

8. Click the Insert Data button to display the Insert Data dialog box, shown in Figure 8.9.

FIG. 8.9
From the Insert Data dialog box, you can select the amount of data you want and whether the database should be linked to the file on disk.

9. If you want to limit the number of records inserted, select From and To and enter the starting and ending record numbers.

10. If you want to create a link from your database to the database file on disk, select the Insert Data as Field check box.

11. Choose OK.

If you did not select the Insert Data as Field check box, the data is inserted as if it were typed. If the check box was selected, a link is created between the document and the database file. This link is created with a field code. You can update this field code by highlighting it and pressing F9. You can unlink the field code so that the database becomes fixed text by selecting the table and pressing Shift+Ctrl+F9.

Creating Your Mail Merge Data

The data source you use in Word can come from an existing Word document, be created in Word, or be linked into Word from another application.

If the amount of data you need to store is not extensive and you do not need to share the information with other users, the easiest way for you to store and manage your data is in a Word document. You can create a data source in a Word document either manually or with the guidance of the Mail Merge Helper.

Creating a Data Source Manually   You can manually create a data source document by typing data into a document. The fields of data must be separated into the cells of a table, or separated by tabs or commas. The field names in the first row of the data source document must fit the rules for field names:

- Names must start with a letter.
- Names must not contain a space. Use an underscore if you need to separate words.
- Names must not be longer than 40 characters.
- Names must be unique. You cannot have two field names spelled the same.

You must save the document containing your data source to disk before you can use it. Try to save the document with a file name that will not change frequently. If the file name of the data source changes, you must reconnect the mail merge document to use the data source.

Figure 8.1 illustrated an example of a table that is used as a data source for a mail merge document. Each field (column) in the table contained a type of information and each record (row) contained a group of information about a client. The information in this document could also have been separated by commas or by tabs.

Figure 8.10 shows the same information, written as a data source with the data separated by tabs. If you decide to use commas or tabs to separate data, use one or the other throughout the data source—do not mix them in the same document. End each record (row) with a paragraph mark if it is a comma or tab-delimited record. See the upcoming section "Managing Information in the Data Source."

FIG. 8.10

You can manually create data source documents by typing data into tables or by typing each record in a row and separating the fields with commas or tabs.

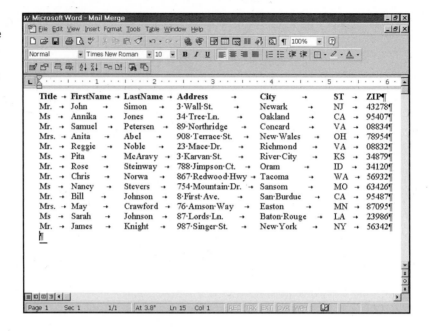

After you have created your data source document, save it and remember its name and folder. When you run a mail merge, the Mail Merge Helper asks you to select the file name of the data source.

▶ **See** "Merging Mailing Lists and Documents," **p. 242**

If you create a comma-delimited data source and some of your data contains commas, Word may be confused as to the fields in which data belongs. To solve this problem, enclose any data that contains commas within quotation marks (" ") when you use commas to separate fields of data. The quotation marks around a piece of data tell Word that any comma within the quotation marks is part of the data. Because of the problems that can occur with comma-delimited data, you may find it easier to work with tables. However, if your data files contain hundreds or thousands of lines, tables may not be practical.

Using the Mail Merge Helper to Create a New Data Source   If you want to be guided through the process of creating a data source document, use the Mail Merge Helper. The Mail Merge Helper is a series of dialog boxes that present options for creating some of the most commonly used field names. After you have created the field names, the Mail Merge Helper gives you a chance to enter data into the new data source. A later section of this chapter, "Finding or Editing Records with the Data Form," describes a convenient way to add more records or find and edit existing records.

The following process helps you create a data source document with the Mail Merge Helper. The Mail Merge Helper assumes you are creating a form letter and the source document at the same time. Because most people create one or the other and then return later to merge the two, the following steps show you how to create only the source document.

To create a new data source with the Mail Merge Helper, follow these steps:

1. Choose Tools, Mail Merge. The Mail Merge Helper dialog box appears.

2. Choose Create and then select Form Letters.

3. Click the New Main Document button. This opens a blank document and returns you to the Mail Merge Helper. The Get Data button is now available.

 TIP The blank document that opened would normally be used to create a new form letter, but you need it open only to appease the Mail Merge Helper while you create a new data source.

4. Click the Get Data button, then select Create Data Source from the list (see Figure 8.11). The Create Data Source dialog box appears, as shown in Figure 8.12.

FIG. 8.11
Choosing Tools, Mail Merge displays the Mail Merge Helper. The Mail Merge Helper guides you through the process of creating data sources, creating main documents, and merging the data and document.

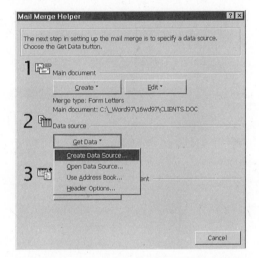

FIG. 8.12
The Create Data Source dialog box gives you the opportunity to accept, add, or remove field names that are used to name each column in the data source.

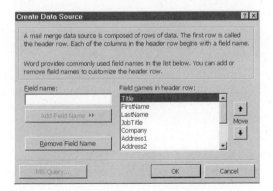

5. In the Create Data Source dialog box, add or remove field names for the columns in your data source. When the Create Data Source dialog box first appears, it shows in the Field Names in Header Row list the most frequently used field names for mail merge. Field names appear left to right across the first row of the data source in the order they are listed in the Field Names in Header Row list. Edit the field names in the list using the following steps:

   ▪ Add a new field name to the list by typing the name in the Field Name edit box and clicking Add Field Name. The name is added to the end of the list.

 TIP   Field names must be 40 characters or less and start with a letter. Spaces are not allowed.

   ▪ Delete a field name from the list by selecting the name in the Field Names in Header Row list, and then click Remove Field Name.

   ▪ Move a field name up or down in the list by selecting the name and then clicking the up or down arrows.

6. Choose OK. The Save As dialog box appears.

7. Type a filename in the File Name edit box. Change to the folder in which you expect to keep the data source.

8. Choose OK to close the Save As dialog box. A dialog box appears warning you that the data source you created contains no data.

9. Click Edit Data Source to display the Data Form dialog box where you can add records to your new data source (see Figure 8.13).

FIG. 8.13
Use the Data Form to add new data to your new data source. You can bring up the Data Form at any time to find or edit data in a data source.

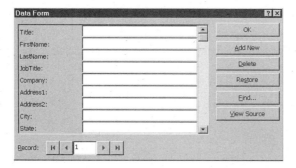

10. Enter data in the Data Form. Press Tab or Enter to move to the next field of data. Click Add New to add another record. The Data Form is described in detail later in this chapter in "Finding or Editing Records in the Data Form."

11. When you are finished entering data and want to save the data source, click the View Source button. When the data source document appears, choose File, Save.

If you do not save the data source document, you will be given a chance to save it when you attempt to close the blank document you opened in step 3.

T I P View more of a wide data source by choosing View, Zoom to fit more fields on the screen.

▶ **See** "Creating Tables," **p. 275**

You can see the paragraph mark that ends a row of comma-delimited data if you click the Show/Hide ¶ button on the Standard toolbar.

Your data source document looks like a table if it has 31 or fewer field names. If it has more than 31 field names, data is separated by commas, and records end with a paragraph mark. The field names will be in the first row and data in the following rows.

Working with an Existing Data Source   You can work with data sources that already exist, even if they aren't Word documents. The data may have come from a worksheet, database, or corporate mainframe.

You may want to work with an existing data source to edit its contents or to build a new main document that contains merge fields. For example, if you want to create a new form letter using a data source you already have, follow this procedure:

1. Choose Tools, Mail Merge.
2. Click the Main Document Create button, then select the type of main document you want to create: Form Letters, Mailing Labels, Envelopes, or Catalog. From the dialog box that appears, choose either Active Window or New Main Document to attach the data source to the existing active document or to open a new document.
3. Click Get Data, and then choose Open Data Source from the pull-down list. The Open Data Source dialog box appears.
4. Change to the folder containing the data source, and then select or type the filename of the data source in the File Name box. Choose OK.
5. Click the Set Up Main Document or Edit Main Document button.

The data source is open but does not appear in a window. If you want to edit the data in the data source, refer to the section, "Finding or Editing Records with the Data Form."

You can use the data source documents you used in previous versions of Word with the Mail Merge Helper in Word 97. Make sure that Word has the converters installed to convert the old document into Word format. After you have resaved the document, you can treat it the same as any data source.

Using Data from Another Application   Word can use the data from other applications as a data source. Your main documents in Word can link to data in other applications such as Access or Excel. The document can read directly from databases such as Access, Paradox, FoxPro, or dBASE through the use of Open Database Connectivity (ODBC) drivers. You also can import and convert data from any files for which you have a converter.

Using the Mail Merge Helper with a Non-Word Data Source   To work with a non-Word data source, follow these steps:

1. Open a main document.

2. Choose Tools, Mail Merge.

3. Choose Main Document Create, and then select the type of main document you want to create: Form Letters, Mailing Labels, Envelopes, or Catalog. From the Help dialog box that appears, choose either Active Window or New Main Document to attach the data source to the existing active document or to open a new document.

4. Choose Get Data, and then select Open Data Source from the drop-down list.

5. Change to the folder containing the data source, and then select or type the filename of the data source in the File Name box. Choose OK.

   Or, if you open an Excel worksheet, you are given an opportunity to specify a range name within the worksheet that describes the data you want to bring in. If you open an Access file, you can open an Access query file and only the data that satisfies that query will be loaded.

   You can also choose MS Query to open Microsoft Query so you can connect to and query an external data source. Microsoft Query is a separate Microsoft application that comes with Excel or Office. When you are finished in Microsoft Query, choose File, Return Data to Microsoft Word.

6. If the active document is not a main document that contains merge fields, Word displays a Mail Merge Helper dialog box. Click the Edit Main Document button.

Managing Information in the Data Source

You can manage the data in your data source just as though you had a small database program built into Word. You can find or edit records using the Data Form. You can also reorganize the columns in a data source or merge together two data source files.

 TIP   When you don't know which field (column) contains the data you need to find, select the entire database and search with Edit, Find.

Finding or Editing Records with the Data Form   The information in your data source is of little value unless it is accurate. Word includes features to help you keep your data source up-to-date.

To quickly find data when the data source is in the active document, follow these steps:

1. Click within a data source.

2. Click the Find Record button on the Database toolbar to display the Find in Field dialog box shown in Figure 8.14.

FIG. 8.14

You can find records that contain information in the field name you select.

3. Select from the In Field list the field name of the column you want to search.

4. Type in the Find What box what you are searching for under the field name.

5. Click Find First.

6. Examine the record found or click the Find Next button to continue.

To find and edit information when a data source is in the active document, follow these steps:

1. Click within a data source.

   The database may have fields in table columns, tab-separated or comma-separated. A main document does not have to be opened or attached. It must have valid data source field names.

2. Click the Data Form button on the Database toolbar.

3. Begin at step 3 in the next procedure to find or edit data using the Data Form.

To find data within the data source when the main document is active, follow these steps:

1. Open a main document that uses your data source.

2. Click the Data Form button in the Database toolbar or choose Tools, Mail Merge, and then click the Edit button and select the data source. The Data Form dialog box appears.

3. Move to the first record in the data source if you want to begin the search from the first data record.

4. Click Find.

5. Select from the In Field list the field name of the column you want to search.

6. Type in the Find What box what you are searching for under the field name.

7. Choose Find First.

When the first record satisfying your request is found, the Find First button changes to a Find Next button. Select this button to find any further occurrences of what you are searching for. A message notifies you when you have reached the last record in the database.

When you find a record you want to edit, choose Close in the Find in Field dialog box and edit the record in the Data Form.

TIP You can delete a record by displaying it in the Data Form and then clicking Delete.

If you delete or edit a record incorrectly, immediately choose Restore to return the record to its original condition. After you move to a new record when editing, you cannot restore previous edits. If the data form is too restrictive (for example, fields contain data that is too long), you can edit the contents of the table directly, as if it was any other Word table.

Sorting a Data Source   Sorting a data source can be useful for a couple of reasons. If you are printing a large volume of mail merge envelopes or labels, you can get a discount on postage if ZIP codes are in sorted order. Another reason for sorting is to create printed lists that will be searched manually.

To quickly sort a data source, follow these steps:

1. Click in the data source in the field (column) that you want to sort.
2. Click the Ascending Sort or Descending Sort button on the Database toolbar.

If you have more complex sorts and your data is in a table, or can be converted to a table, choose Table, Sort.

Renaming, Inserting, or Removing Fields from a Data Source   When you need to change your information, you will probably have to add or remove fields (columns) from your data source. For example, you might want to add a field that includes a customer's automatic reorder date, or you might want to delete an old, unnecessary field such as a Client Priority number.

To add or remove a field in a data source, follow these steps:

1. Save your current data source under a new name. Save this file as a backup in case you make mistakes and need to return to an original copy.
2. Open the data source document and display it in the active window.
3. Click the Manage Fields button in the Database toolbar to display the Manage Fields dialog box, shown in Figure 8.15.

FIG. 8.15.

Use the Manage Fields dialog box to add or remove new fields (columns) in the Data Source as your information needs change.

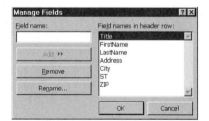

4. If you want to add, remove, or rename a field, follow these steps:

> To add a field, type the new name in the Field Name edit box, then choose the Add button.

To remove a field name and its corresponding data, select the name from the Field Names in Header Row list, then click the Remove button. Choose Yes to confirm that you want to remove the field and data.

To rename a field name, click the Rename button, then type your name in the New Field Name edit box that appears. Choose OK.

5. When you have finished making changes to your data source, choose OK.

Inserting or Removing Records from a Data Source   It seems that the amount of information demanded only seems to grow; however, sometimes you might need to delete a record from your data source. With Word, you can easily insert or delete records.

 TIP If records to be deleted have common data, sort the field containing that data so that you can delete multiple records at one time.

To insert a new blank record at the bottom of the data source, you can use the Data Form as described earlier in this chapter. Alternatively, you can follow these steps:

1. Open and activate the data source document.
2. Click the Add New Record button on the Database toolbar.

To delete a record from the data source, follow these steps:

1. Open and activate the data source document.
2. Click in the record (row) that you want to delete. Select down through many records if you want to delete multiple records.
3. Click the Delete Record button on the Database toolbar. You are not asked to confirm that you want to delete.

If you realize you have accidentally deleted the wrong record, immediately choose Edit, Undo.

Scrolling Through the Data Form   You can browse through records in the data source using the buttons at the bottom of the Data Form. Clicking the left or right button moves the records one at a time. Clicking the left-end or right-end button (VCR end controls, |< and >|) moves to the beginning or end of the data record.

If you do not have a mouse, you can move to a specific record by pressing Alt+R and typing the numeric position of the record you want to see. When you press Enter, the insertion point moves out of the Record Number box and into the first field. ●

CHAPTER 9

Mastering Envelopes, Mail Merge, and Form Letters

Understanding Form Letters

Successful businesses know that staying in touch with their clients and customers is crucial to the success of the business. Staying in touch with many people can be difficult, however, unless you learn how to create personalized form letters and envelopes with Word 97.

To make single letters easier to produce, Word has automated the process of printing an envelope. The envelope printing feature uses the address from a document to print an envelope with or without a return address. The envelope can be printed separately or attached to the document with which it is associated. This feature is covered in the first section of this chapter.

Form letters broadcast information, yet add a personal touch to your work. Even if you generate only a few form letters each day, this feature allows you to automate repetitive parts of your business and gives you time to improve the creative end of your work. You can also generate invoices, appointment reminders, and so on. Learning how to create form letters is challenging, but working through the process will pay great dividends.

You can create two types of form letters with Word: those that are filled in manually and those that are filled in from computer-generated lists. In this chapter, you learn to create an automated form letter that prompts you for information the document needs for creating an invoice. You learn also how to fill in the blanks in a form letter by merging a mailing list with the main document. Finally, you learn advanced Word techniques for document automation, including a form letter that combines manual fill-in with merging of information.

Inserting a Name and an Address from the Address Book

You can use Address Books and lists of contacts to manage the names and addresses of people you write to frequently. After you enter the names, addresses, and email information about people, you can retrieve the information by clicking the Insert Address button in the Standard toolbar, then selecting to use names and addresses from an address book or a contact list. You also can paste a person's address into your document by clicking his or her name.

If the Insert Address button (it looks like an opened address book) is not displayed in the Standard toolbar, choose View, Toolbars, Customize, select Insert from the Categories list, select Address Book from the Commands list, and drag the Address Book icon onto the Standard toolbar.

▶ **See** "Managing Names and Addresses with Address Books," **p. 217**

Before you can use the Address Book on a network or with the Address Book in Outlook or Schedule+, you must gain access to the network and Outlook or Schedule+. If your computer is on a network and you use Outlook or Schedule+, you need to follow these steps:

1. Position the insertion point in the document where you want to paste a person's address.

2. Click the Insert Address button in the Standard toolbar. If you are prompted, select an Exchange profile. The Select Name dialog box appears as shown in Figure 9.1.

FIG. 9.1

The Select Name dialog box gives you access to the address books or contact lists available in Windows.

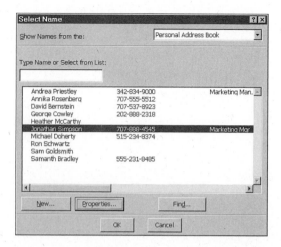

3. Select the Show Names From The list and select the address book or contact list containing the address you want to insert into your document.

   If you have installed Windows 95 and Office 97, the following address books are available:

Address Book	Description
Outlook Address Book	A name, address, and information list stored in Outlook and shared with others on your network
Outlook Contact List	A name, address, and information list stored in Outlook and shared with others on your network
Schedule+ Contact List	A name, address, and information list stored in Schedule+ and shared with others on your network
Personal Address Book	A name, address, and information list used for sending email and faxes from Word through Microsoft Exchange
Postoffice Address List	A name, address, and email address list used for sending email messages from Word through your local network
The Microsoft Network	A name, address, and email address list used for sending email messages from Word over the Microsoft Network

4. Type the name you want into the Type Name or Select From List edit box, or click the name in the list.

5. Choose OK to insert that person's name and address into your Word document.

If you have used the address book before, a shortcut list will be available. Using this shortcut list is a very quick and convenient way to insert names and addresses. To quickly insert a name and address you have used before, follow these steps:

1. Click the drop-down arrow to the right of the Insert Address button to display the list shown in Figure 9.2.

FIG. 9.2

Use the drop-down list to the right of the Insert Address button to insert names and addresses quickly.

2. Click the name and address you want to insert.

Printing an Envelope

Word offers an easy and quick solution to a common word-processing problem: printing envelopes. Word can print envelopes by themselves, attached to a document, or as part of a mass mailing.

To test the envelope feature, create a short letter like the one shown in Figure 9.3.

FIG. 9.3

This figure shows a sample business letter.

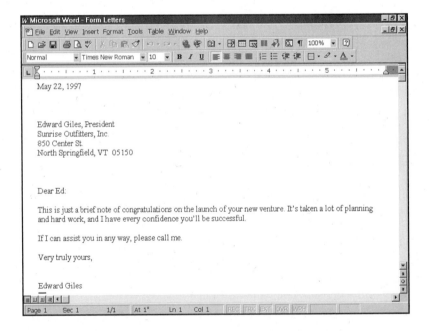

To create an envelope, follow these steps:

1. Select the address in the letter.

   If the address is a contiguous block of three to five short lines near the beginning of the letter, you do not have to select it. Word automatically finds the address.

2. Choose Tools, Envelopes and Labels. Word displays the Envelopes and Labels dialog box (see Figure 9.4).

FIG. 9.4
Word will find the
address in most letters
and display it automati-
cally in the Envelopes
and Labels dialog box.

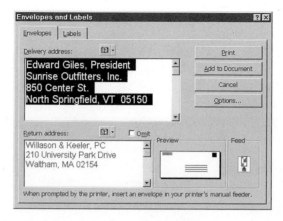

3. Select the Envelopes tab if it is not already active.

4. Edit the Delivery Address information if necessary. To insert line feeds (line breaks without a carriage return), press Shift+Enter.

5. Edit the Return Address information if necessary. If you do not want to print the return address (you may be working with preprinted envelopes, for example), select the Omit check box.

6. Click the Options button to display the Envelopes Options dialog box if you need to select an envelope size (see Figure 9.5); then make your selection from the Envelope Size drop-down list.

FIG. 9.5
Click the Options button
in the Envelopes and
Labels dialog box to
display the Envelope
Options dialog box.

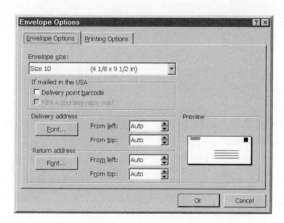

N O T E The Delivery Address and Return Address options enable you to customize the fonts and positions of the addresses. You can read about the postal mailing areas later in this section. ▪

7. Choose OK when you're finished with your selections.

8. Load envelope(s) into your printer's feeder as indicated in the Feed area in the Envelopes and Labels dialog box.

9. Click the Print button to print an envelope immediately.

   You can also click the Add to Document button to add the envelope as a landscape-oriented section before the first page of your document (see Figure 9.6).

FIG. 9.6
The Add to Document button inserts a landscape envelope before the first page of your document.

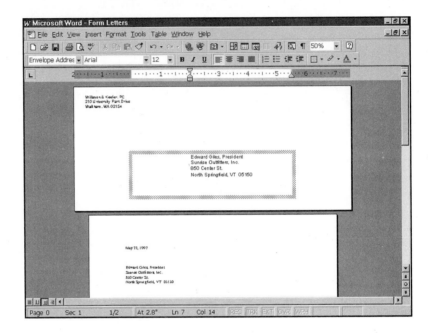

You can change the default Return Address information. Choose Tools, Options, then select User Information tab. In the Mailing Address text box, add or edit the return address. This address becomes the default return address until you change it.

When you click the Print button, many laser printers can immediately print the envelope from the envelope bin. If you do not have an envelope feeder or envelope bin, insert the envelope—narrow side in—in the form-feed guides on top of the primary paper tray. The envelope prints first, followed by the document.

To reposition the Delivery Address area, change to Page Layout view and move the mouse pointer to the striped border until a four-headed arrow appears. Then drag the entire box containing the Delivery Address to a new position (see Figure 9.7).

TROUBLESHOOTING

My address isn't printing properly on the envelopes. If you have trouble printing an envelope with the envelope layout or with envelope and paper feeding, examine the printer driver. Choose File, Print, and look in the Name text box of the Print dialog box to see which printer driver is selected. Make sure you have the correct driver. Check with your printer manufacturer or Microsoft for a more current version of the Windows printer driver program if you continue to have problems. Install a new printer driver by clicking Start, Settings, Printers, then double-clicking the Add Printer icon. Follow the Add Printer Wizard to install a printer driver.

FIG. 9.7
You can drag the address area to a new position in the envelope section.

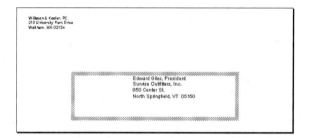

Printing an Envelope with Bar Codes or FIM Codes

Word provides a way to print machine-readable codes on envelopes so that the U.S. Postal Service can process the envelopes by machine. These codes can be used as long as they are sent to addresses within the U.S., thus saving time and money.

You can print *POSTNET* codes (bar code equivalents of U.S. zip codes) and *facing identification marks*, or *FIMs* (vertical lines that indicate the address side of the envelope).

To print POSTNET bar codes and FIMs on envelope(s) attached to the current document, follow these steps:

1. Choose Tools, Envelopes and Labels.

2. Click the Options button in the Envelopes tab of the Envelopes and Labels dialog box. Word displays the Envelope Options dialog box (see Figure 9.8).

FIG. 9.8
Set envelope printing options in the Envelope Options dialog box.

Checking these options adds bar codes and FIMs to your envelopes.

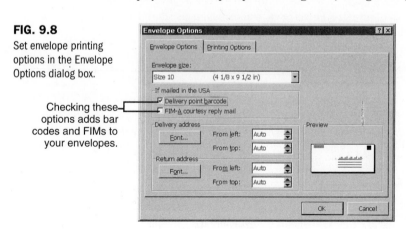

3. Select the Delivery Point <u>B</u>ar Code check box to print POSTNET bar codes.

4. Select the FIM-<u>A</u> Courtesy Reply Mail check box to print FIMs.

5. Choose OK.

Customizing Envelopes with Text and Graphics

You can easily add a graphic—such as a company logo—to your envelopes, whether the graphic consists of formatted text or actual graphics.

To set up envelopes to print your logo, follow these steps:

1. Enter your logo text and graphics in a document.

2. Put the logo in a frame.

3. Choose <u>I</u>nsert, <u>A</u>utoText, <u>N</u>ew.

4. Type the name **EnvelopeExtra** in the Please Name Your AutoText Entry text box.

5. Click OK.

Merging Mailing Lists and Documents

One of the most powerful and time-saving features available in any word processor is mail merge. *Mail merge* enables you to create multiple letters or envelopes by merging a list of names and addresses with letters, envelopes, or address labels. Mail merge can also be used for such tasks as filling in administrative forms and creating invoices from accounting files. Whenever you keep a list or get a list from other programs and you need to put information into a Word document, you should consider using mail merge.

The time you save by using mail merge can be tremendous. Instead of typing or modifying tens or hundreds of documents, Word can make all the documents for you. All you need to do is keep your list (names, addresses, and so on) up-to-date and create a form letter in which to insert the data. In fact, you can even make each document pause during mail merge so that you can enter personalized information.

Understanding the Mail Merge Components Data Sources and Main Documents

You need two documents to create form letters or mailing labels. One document, called the *data source*, contains a precisely laid-out set of data, such as names and addresses. The other document, the *main document*, acts as a form that receives the data. Most forms that receive data are form letters or multicolumn tables for mailing labels.

Although most people would use the term *form letter* to describe a Word main document, a main document can take the form of a mailing list, catalog, mailing labels, or letters.

The main document is like a normal document except that it contains MERGEFIELD field codes that specify the placement of merged data. In a typical form letter, for example, the main document is a form letter in which the names and addresses are inserted, and the data source is the list of those names and addresses.

The data source document must be organized in a very specific way, or the merge process will generate errors. The first row of the data source must be one row of field names. Below the row of names are rows of data. Each row of data is a *record*, and each piece of data in the row, such as a last name, is a *field*. The row of names in the first row of the documents is the *header record*. Each name in the first row is a *field name*. Each field can be referenced by the name for that field in the heading.

▶ **See** "Managing Data," **p. 221**

Part

III

Ch

9

When you merge the documents, Word replaces the merge fields with the appropriate text from the data source. At merge time, you can choose to display the result as a new document on-screen or to print it directly to the current printer.

Understanding Word's Mail Merge Helper

Word's Mail Merge Helper guides you through the three stages of creating a form letter, catalog, or other merged document:

- Creating or identifying the main document
- Creating or identifying the data source
- Merging the data source and main document

To start the Mail Merge Helper, follow these steps:

1. Open the document you want to use as the main document. (If the main document doesn't exist, create a new document.)
2. Choose Tools, Mail Merge.

The Mail Merge Helper dialog box guides you through the three stages of creating a merged document (see Figure 9.9). Notice that the dialog box contains a lot of empty space; this space will fill up with useful information about the merge documents as you proceed.

The Mail Merge Helper is designed to be flexible; you can start setting up the merge at virtually any stage in the document-creation process. At appropriate points, Word requires you to make decisions or reminds you to go back and complete some necessary steps.

You'll see many dialog boxes resembling the one in Figure 9.10. Although this dialog box does not have a name, you might think of it as the "decision" dialog box.

Sometimes the decision box offers a choice between creating a new document or changing the type of the active document. Consider carefully before changing the document type; generally, you'll want to preserve the existing document in its current form.

If you fail to complete a required portion of one of the three stages in the merge process, you see a dialog box like the one shown in Figure 9.11. This type of dialog box essentially forces you to add detail to incomplete documents before going through with the merge. You see this dialog box only if the Mail Merge Helper detects that you have missed a step or incorrectly entered a response.

FIG. 9.9

The Mail Merge Helper dialog box is the central dialog box from which you complete the three stages of form-letter production.

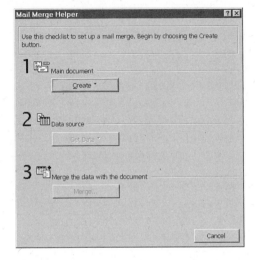

FIG. 9.10

At different points in the merge process, Word asks whether you want to create a new, blank document or use an existing one.

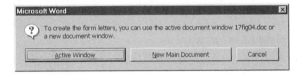

FIG. 9.11

Word's Mail Merge Helper forces you to create complete documents before it will let you begin merging.

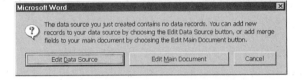

The following sections describe how to proceed through the three stages of creating mail-merge documents. The Mail Merge Helper coordinates the mail-merge documents and the merging process. When you click a button in the Mail Merge Helper, Word displays a series of windows that help you complete the part of the merge process that corresponds to the button.

Selecting the Main Document

You can use any existing document as a main document. Simply open that document before starting the Mail Merge Helper. If you need to create the main document, however, you have the following options:

1. Start Word and make sure you're in a new document.
2. Choose File, New.
3. Make sure that the Document button is selected.
4. Select the tab that contains the template you want to use.
5. Select the template you want to use.
6. Choose OK.

Part
III

Ch
9

It's not necessary to enter any text in the document right now; you can come back to that later.

To create a main document for a form letter, follow these steps:

1. Choose Tools, Mail Merge.
2. Click the Create button under the Main document heading of the Mail Merge Helper dialog box.
3. Choose Form Letters. Word displays a decision dialog box asking what you want to use to create the form letter.
4. Click the Active Window button to use the active document as the main document. Or, click the New Main Document button to open a new document that uses the Normal document template.

Word returns you to the Mail Merge Helper dialog box, which now displays the type of merge and the name and path of the main document under the Main Document heading.

This process illustrates the Mail Merge Helper's flexibility; if you realize by step 4 that you don't want to use the active document, you don't have to start over again.

Selecting a Data Source

Attaching the data source to the main document does three things:

- Shows Word the filename and path where the data will be located
- Attaches a Mail Merge toolbar with merge tools to the top of the main document
- Enables Word to read the field names used in the data source so you can include those field names in your main document

▶ **See** "Managing Data," **p. 221**

If you do not yet have a source for the data that will be merged, read Chapter 8 and create a data source before proceeding. An overview of creating a new data source is presented in the section "Creating a New Data Source" later in this chapter.

Specifying an Address Book as the Data Source   If you have created a list of contacts in a Personal Address Book, Outlook Address Book, or in the Schedule+ Address Book, you already have a data source that you can use for a mail merge by following these steps:

1. Click the Get Data button under the Data Source heading.
2. Choose Use Address Book. Word displays the Use Address Book dialog box, shown in Figure 9.12.

FIG. 9.12
You can select one of the address books available to Word for use in mail merge.

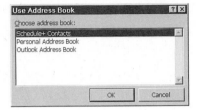

3. Select an address book from the Choose Address Book list, and then choose OK.

The next step depends on whether your main document was complete when you started the merge process. If you have not yet inserted any merge fields in your main document, Word displays the dialog box shown in Figure 9.13.

FIG. 9.13
After attaching the data source, the Mail Merge Helper detects that your main document does not have any merge fields.

To go directly to the main document to add the merge fields, choose Edit Main Document. For instructions on inserting the merge fields in your main document, refer to the section "Editing the Main Document" later in this chapter.

Specifying an Existing File as the Data Source   You can use a data source that you have already created for the mail merge. In the Mail Merge Helper dialog box, you can click the Get Data button to give you access to different sources of data. If you want to use data that is in a file or document, choose the Open Data Source item from the list.

To specify an existing file as a data source, follow these steps:

1. Click the Get Data button under the Data Source heading.

2. Choose Open Data Source. Word displays the Open Data Source dialog box, shown in Figure 9.14.

3. Select the data source from the File Name list. Word can read many different data source formats. Choose from the Files of Type list to see other formats. Choose OK after selecting the file.

   You can also choose the MS_Query button if Microsoft Query is available on your computer. Use Microsoft Query to access specific data in a non-Word database.

N O T E   Use Microsoft Query to retrieve data meeting-specific criteria. The data may be on your computer, network, SQL server, or many types of mainframe databases. Microsoft Query is available as a separate application and comes with Microsoft Excel. ▪

FIG. 9.14
Use the Open Data Source dialog box to access a data source in Word or many other formats.

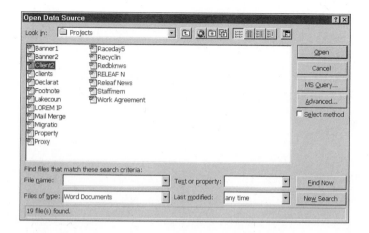

Word automatically converts non-Word files for which it has converters.

Creating a New Data Source

If you did not have a data source that contained your lists of names or database of information to be merged, you need to create one. You also can create a data source in a Word document while you are in the Mail Merge Helper.

▶ **See** "Managing Mail Merge Data," **p. 221**

▶ **See** "Creating Your Own Data Sources," **p. 221**

The Mail Merge Helper guides you through the process of creating a data source in a Word document. It follows a set of rules that you can learn if you want to create a data source document manually. The data source is a grid of rows and columns. The first row in the data source must contain the field names. These names label each column's contents. Only one row of field names can be at the top of the data source. Field names cannot contain blanks and cannot start with a number (although you can include a number in the field name). If you need to use a two-part field name, use an underscore rather than a space. You may want to put words together and capitalize a word's leading letter, such as **RegionManager**. Each field name must be unique.

You can create a new data source within a Word document by using the Create Data Source command. Follow these steps:

1. Click the Get Data button under the Data Source heading in the Mail Merge Helper.

N O T E This button is available only if you attached a main document by clicking the Create button from the Main Document stage. If you want to create a data source and wait to create a main document, just attach a blank document as the main document. ■

2. Choose Create Data Source. Word displays the Create Data Source dialog box (see Figure 9.15).

FIG. 9.15

The Create Data Source dialog box guides you through creating a data source. It even presents the most commonly used headings for mail-merge data sources.

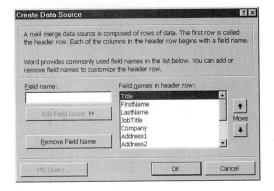

The Field Names in Header Row list box contains names traditionally used for fields in mailing lists. The names in the list box comprise a default list of field names.

3. Edit the list of names in the Field Names in Header Row list box, as described here:

   - If you see any field names you won't use in your main document, select the name from the Field Names in Header Row box, and then choose the Remove Field Name button. Word removes the name from the list.

   - To add a field name, type it in the Field Name box and then choose Add Field Name.

   - When you are satisfied with your list, choose OK.

   - To change the sequence of names (reposition them), select a field name, and then click the up-or down-arrow labeled Move. The top-to-bottom sequence you see in this list box determines the right-to-left sequence of the fields in the data source.

4. Word displays the Save As dialog box. In the File Name text box, enter a name for the data source document and choose Save.

5. Word displays a decision dialog box asking what you want to do next. To enter data in the data source, click the Edit Data Source button. To edit the Main document so that you can insert the merge fields to create a main document, click the Edit Main Document button.

If you click Edit Main Document, Word displays the main document as a normal Word document with one exception: The Mail Merge toolbar is now displayed below the toolbar(s) and above the ruler (see Figure 9.16). With the main document on-screen, you can create a main document in which the data will be inserted.

Merging Data into the Main Document

When you are satisfied with your main document, you can merge it with the data by choosing one of three merge buttons in the Mail Merge toolbar. Table 9.1 shows how these buttons work.

FIG. 9.16
Use the Mail Merge toolbar to insert merge fields as you create the main document.

Mail Merge toolbar——

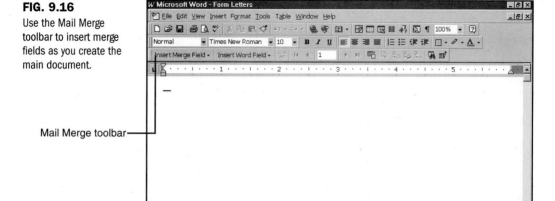

Table 9.1 Merge Buttons in the Mail Merge Toolbar

Button	Name	Description
	Merge to New Document	Creates the merged document and places it in a new Word document
	Merge to Printer	Creates the merged document and prints it on the currently selected printer
	Mail Merge	Displays the Merge dialog box, which provides a wide range of options for record selection and other operations (see the next section for details)

Figure 9.17 shows the merged document. The Form Letters1 document contains the full text of the merged document, with each of the individually addressed letters contained in a section. This document contains no field codes; you can treat it as you would any typed document. Each section break (represented by a double dashed line) starts a new page, so printing the document produces individual letters. Naturally, if you want to make changes to individual letters, you can edit them in the usual manner.

If you merge a large number of records, merge to the printer so that you do not exceed memory limits. You may want to merge a few records to a new document before printing. This enables you to see whether the merge is working correctly.

FIG. 9.17
Merging a form letter to a document can create a long document containing all the individual letters.

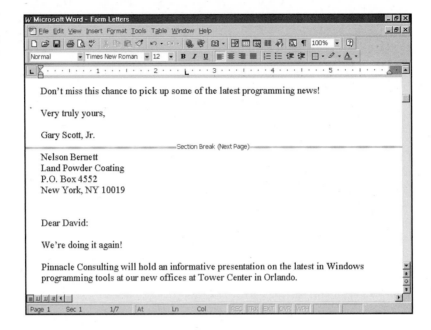

Merging Selected Records Often, you will not want to merge an entire data source into a letter. You may want to merge 20 letters at a time, or limit the merged data to specific zip codes or job titles. Or, you may want to merge one or two letters as a text before running a large merge job.

To control the data that's merged into your main document, follow these steps:

1. Prepare your data source and save it.

2. Open your main document. When it opens, the Mail Merge toolbar also appears.

   If Word cannot find the data source for the main document, it displays a dialog box that you can use to open the correct data source.

3. Choose Tools, Mail Merge to display the Mail Merge Helper, as shown in Figure 9.18.

   In Figure 9.18, you can see that a properly completed Mail Merge Helper displays the type and location of the main document, as well as the data source for that main document and where the data source is located.

4. Click the Merge button to begin the merge process. The Merge dialog box shown in Figure 9.19 appears.

5. Select the Merge To list and select one of the following types of merges:

Merge To:	Effect
Printer	Produces a printed result
New Document	Produces a new document containing all resulting merged documents
Electronic mail	Produces merged documents for electronic mailing

FIG. 9.18
A Mail Merge Helper that is ready to merge data shows both main document and data source types and locations.

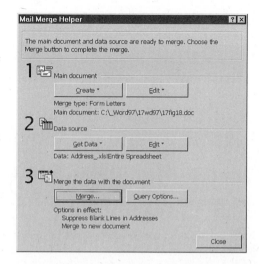

FIG. 9.19
Select how you want Word to perform the merge from the Merge dialog box.

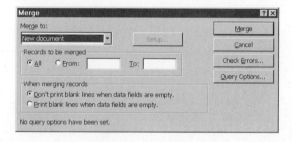

6. Select the number of records to be merged from the Records to be merged group:

Merged Records	Effect
All	Merges all records
From/To	Limits the range of data according to the record (row) numbers in the data source

7. Select from the When merging records group how blank lines will be handled: Don't print blank lines when data fields are empty, or Print blank lines when data fields are empty.

8. Choose Merge.

Creating Mailing Labels

If you are sending many documents, mailing labels can save you lots of time. With Word, you can easily update your mailing lists and print labels on demand.

You can design a form that prints multiple labels on a page in much the same way you create a form letter. If you've designed main documents for mailing labels in a previous version of Word, you can continue to use those documents to print mailing labels. But if you need to create a new label form, Word makes the task quite easy.

Creating a Mailing Label Main Document   The Labels tab of the Envelopes and Labels dialog box automates the process of creating mailing labels. The following example assumes that you have already created a form-letter main document.

To create mailing labels for an existing form letter, follow these steps:

1. Choose Tools, Mail Merge. (You do not need to activate the main document for the form letter.)
2. Click the Create button under the Main Document heading of the Mail Merge Helper dialog box.
3. Select Mailing Labels.
4. Click Active Window if it appears in the Decision dialog box. Otherwise, click New Main Document.
5. Click the Get Data button under the Data Source heading.
6. Select Open Data Source or Use Address Book.
7. Select the appropriate data source.
8. Click Set Up Main Document if Word displays a dialog box.
9. Select a label format from the Label Options dialog box. Label formats are explained in the following section.

Specifying Label Size and Type   The Label Options dialog box (see Figure 9.20) contains specifications for dozens of commercial preprinted label products. You'll probably be able to select the label format you want from this dialog box by following these steps:

1. Select the appropriate label group from the Label Products drop-down list:

Label Products	Comments
Avery standard	Avery U.S. products
Avery A4 and A5 sizes	Avery A4 and A5 size products
MACO standard	MACO standard products
Other	Products from other manufacturers

2. Select your type of label from the Product Number drop-down list. If you are not using labels from any of the commercial products available in this dialog box, use the product number for the same size label. If none of the label formats produces the result you want, you will have to edit the label specifications, as explained in "Creating Custom Mailing Labels" later in this section.
3. If you're not sure which label type is correct, use the arrow keys to browse through the list so that you can view in the Label Information area the label and page dimensions for each type.

FIG. 9.20

Select a label format from the Label Options dialog box.

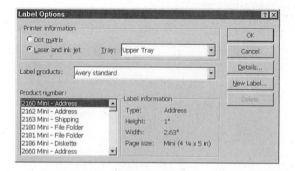

4. If you want to view more details about the selected label type, click the Details button. Word displays a dialog box similar to the one in Figure 9.21. Choose OK to return to the Label Options dialog box. To learn how to create a custom mailing label size, see "Creating Custom Mailing Labels" later in this section.

FIG. 9.21

In this dialog box, you can preview any available label type and set custom sizes.

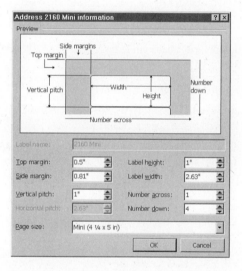

5. Choose OK when you are satisfied with all your selections. Word displays the Create Labels dialog box (see Figure 9.22).

6. Insert the appropriate merge fields in the Sample label box and choose OK. Word then displays the Mail Merge Helper.

7. Click the Merge button to display the Merge dialog box.

8. Select the options you want and then proceed with error checking, query definition, and merging. When you are finished, click the Merge button.

Word creates a new document containing a table formatted for the type of labels you selected. You can merge the labels to a new document or print them in the usual manner.

FIG. 9.22

Use the Create Labels dialog box to build a label by inserting merge field codes.

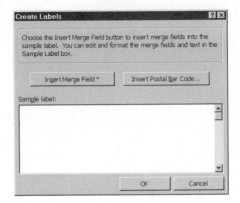

Printing Labels for a Single Address

Naturally, not all your letters will be form letters. In the Labels tab of the Envelopes and Labels dialog box, you can print a single mailing label or several labels containing the same address.

To print one or more mailing labels for a single document, follow these steps:

1. Activate the main document for the form letter.

2. Choose Tools, Envelopes and Labels.

3. Select the Labels tab in the Envelopes and Labels dialog box.

4. Examine the fields displayed in the Address box for accuracy. Or, if you want to print return address labels, select Use Return Address.

5. Print a single address label by selecting Single Label and specifying the location of the label where you want to print. For single-wide, continuous-feed labels for dot-matrix printers, use the defaults (Row 1, Column 1). For labels on cut sheets for laser printers, you will usually have to specify the location of the next available blank label on the page, as shown in Figure 9.23.

FIG. 9.23

In the Print area of the Envelopes and Labels dialog box, you can choose to print a single label. In this example, the address prints on the label in the first column of the first row of the label sheet.

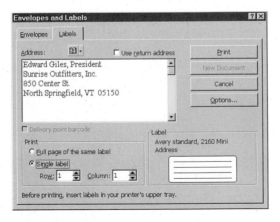

6. Click the <u>O</u>ptions button and make any necessary changes in the Label Options dialog box. Then choose OK.

7. Make sure the label paper is loaded in the printer; then click <u>P</u>rint to print the labels.

Creating Custom Mailing Labels You can design your own labels if you can't find the right size in the Label Options dialog box.

To change the label format to a nonstandard size when creating a mailing label document, follow these steps:

Part

III

Ch

9

1. Select a label format similar to the format you want from the Label Options dialog box.

2. Click the <u>D</u>etails button. Word displays the Label Preview dialog box.

   The Preview window contains a representation of the current label format. In the bottom portion of the dialog box, enter your custom label specifications. (The annotations in the Preview window illustrate the effects of the specifications.) Enter a new value for any of the measurements (or change the amount by clicking the attached arrow buttons) and watch the Preview window reflect the change.

   If you change the specifications in a way that makes it impossible to fit the specified number of labels on a page, Word displays a message.

3. Choose OK when you are satisfied with all your selections.

4. Click OK in the dialog box that appears to confirm that you want to override the existing custom label specifications. In the Label Options dialog box, Word updates the information in the Label Information box.

5. Choose OK to accept the changes.

Word displays the Create Labels dialog box, where you can proceed with label creation, merging, and printing.

CAUTION

Do not use labels with adhesive backing in laser printers. Laser printers operate at high temperatures, which can melt and separate labels, creating a mess in your printer. Suppliers such as Avery manufacture a complete line of labels of different sizes and shapes made especially for laser printers.

Suppressing Blank Lines in Addresses Most business mailings include fields for information such as title, suite number, mail station, and so on. If some information is missing, however, blank lines can show up in your addresses or labels, producing an unfinished, unprofessional appearance. You can make sure that blank lines are skipped by selecting the <u>D</u>on't Print Blank Lines When Data Fields Are Empty option in the Merge dialog box that appears after you choose the <u>M</u>erge button from the Mail Merge Helper. Blank lines involving a MERGEFIELD are skipped if they end with a paragraph mark (¶). Lines ending with a linefeed (Shift+Enter) are not skipped.

Modifying Your Mail Merge

Get in the habit of testing small mail-merge runs before printing a large mail merge involving tens or hundreds of documents. In most cases, you will want to modify your main document, merge fields, or other information. This section contains tips on how to modify mail-merge documents.

Checking for Errors   Browsing through the merged document is a good way to spot problems with the merge, but when the data source contains many records, you might want a higher level of assurance. You can check the entire data source for errors by clicking an error-checking button in the Mail Merge toolbar.

When you click the Check for Errors button, Word reads your data source and checks for errors such as field names that do not meet the rules for bookmarks. Word checks also to ensure that the number of field names and the number of fields in each record (or row) are the same. Word warns you if it cannot find the data source or if the source contains blank records.

To check the main document and data source for errors, follow these steps:

1. Click the Check for Errors button in the Mail Merge toolbar. The Checking and Reporting Errors dialog box appears (see Figure 9.24).

FIG. 9.24

Select the appropriate error-reporting option in the Checking and Reporting Errors dialog box.

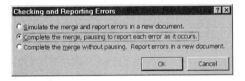

2. Select the error-reporting option you want. The first option simulates the merge, and the second and third complete it. The second option displays messages as errors occur, and the third option puts them in a new document. If you expect some errors, consider simulating the merge first.

3. If you choose to report errors as they occur, the first dialog box displayed might contain an error message, like the one in Figure 9.25. Choose OK to clear the dialog box (or boxes) and proceed accordingly.

FIG. 9.25

This error message appears when Word cannot find a field name in the data source that corresponds to a merge field in the main document.

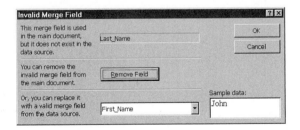

The Invalid Merge Field dialog box assists you in correcting the problem in the merge document. Click the Remove Field button to remove the offending field from the main document. If the field mismatch is the result of a typographical error in the main document, you can correct the error by selecting the valid field name from the list box at the bottom of the dialog box. When you select a field name from this list, the corresponding value from the data source is displayed in the Sample Data box.

The following guidelines can prevent errors that commonly cause problems:

Part
III

Ch
9

- Field names must not have spaces. Use an underscore rather than a space.
- Field names must not start with a number but can have a number in them.
- Field names must be in one row at the top of the data source.
- Field names must be unique (no duplicates).
- Each field (column) of data must have a field name.
- The number of fields in each record must match the number of field names.

N O T E If the records in the data source are not in a table and if commas, tabs, or cells are missing, the number of fields in a record may not match the number of fields in the heading.

Merging to Letterhead   The first page of a form letter is usually on letterhead paper and needs a top margin different from that of the following pages. To compensate for the difference in top margins in your normal documents and form letters, use a different header for the first page.

To create a first-page-only header on the active document, follow these steps:

1. Choose View, Header and Footer.
2. Click the Page Setup button in the Header and Footer toolbar to display the Page Setup dialog box.
3. Select the Layout tab if it is not already selected.
4. Select the Different First Page check box.
5. Choose OK.

In the header-editing box that appears at the top of the document, enter the letterhead text. This header is for the first page; the following pages begin body copy underneath the top margin set by the document format.

If your printer has double paper bins, you can pull letterhead paper from the letterhead bin. If your printer has only one bin, you can stack alternating letterhead and bond in the tray or feed letterhead into the manual feed tray. If you push the letterhead far enough into the manual feed at the appropriate time, the printer often will pull paper from the manual feed before pulling it from the bin.

Merging Envelopes   With the Mail Merge Helper, you can create mail-merge envelopes or a document that merges mail-merge envelopes and documents at the same time.

To create mail-merge envelopes, create a data source and main document, as described in the section "Creating a Form Letter" earlier in this chapter. Attach the data source to the main document. Be sure that the top of the main document contains a three-to-five-line address composed of MERGEFIELD codes. If you are not mailing a main document, create a blank letter with the MERGEFIELD codes in an address block. The automatic envelope maker uses this document as a basis for its MERGEFIELD address information.

To set up a program for creating a mass-mailing envelope based on your main document, follow these steps:

1. Activate the main document.
2. Choose Tools, Mail Merge.

 TIP   If the Mail Merge toolbar is displayed, you can click the Mail Merge Helper dialog box button.

3. Click the Create button under the Main Document heading of the Mail Merge Helper dialog box.
4. Select Envelopes.

   Word displays a decision dialog box. The options offered depend on the condition of the active document when you began the procedure.

5. Click Active Window if it appears in the dialog box. Otherwise, click New Main Document.

   Word displays the Mail Merge Helper dialog box (see Figure 9.26). The information under Main Document reflects the merge type (Envelopes) and new document name.

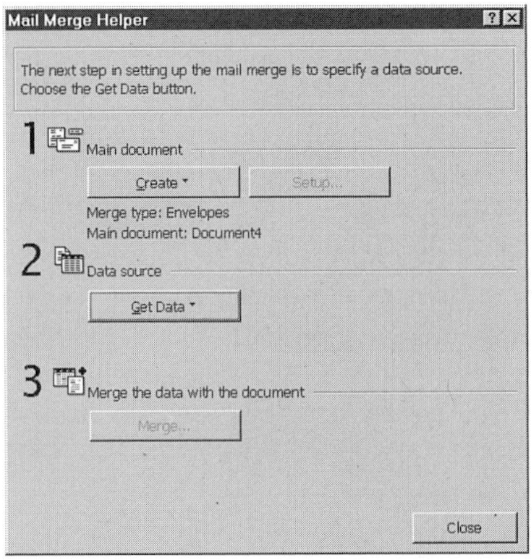

FIG. 9.26

The Mail Merge Helper dialog box changes to reflect the fact that you're creating a new main document.

To finish creating the mass-mailing envelope, follow these steps:

1. Under Data Source, click the Get Data button.

2. Click Open Data Source.

3. Select the data source from the File Name list, and then choose Open. If necessary, browse through the folders in the usual manner. Word then displays the dialog box shown in Figure 9.27.

FIG. 9.27

Word displays this dialog when it needs to set up your main document.

You can also click Use Address Book. Select Schedule+ Contacts, Personal Address Book, or Outlook Address Book, and then choose OK.

4. Click Set Up Main Document.

5. Change any settings in the Envelope Options and Printing Options tabs in the Envelope Options dialog box and then choose OK. Word displays the Envelope Address dialog box (see Figure 9.28).

FIG. 9.28

Use the Envelope Address dialog box to insert the field codes that will insert data into the address area of an envelope.

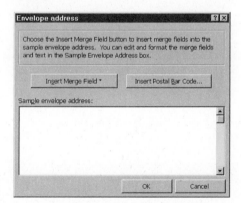

6. Insert the merge fields for names and addresses, adding any necessary spaces and punctuation. You select these fields in the same way as when you created the form letter earlier in this chapter—by clicking the Insert Merge Field button and selecting the field names from the drop-down list.

You can click the Insert Postal Bar Code button to print POSTNET codes on the envelopes. The Insert Postal Bar Code dialog box prompts you for the name of the field containing the postal code.

Choose OK when you finish entering fields. Word returns you to the Mail Merge Helper dialog box.

Part

III

Ch

9

7. In the Mail Merge Helper, click <u>M</u>erge. Your document should look something like that shown in Figure 9.29.

FIG. 9.29

You can create envelopes for mass mailings that use the merge fields you created for the related form-letter document. The envelopes can also include graphics and logos.

Willazon & Keeler, PC
210 University Park Drive
Waltham, MA 02154

John Westgate
Rathbum Import Export
904 Blue Pkwy

8. Select the <u>M</u>erge To list and select one of the following types of merges:

   Select the number of records to be merged from the Records to Be Merged group.

   Select from the When Merging Records group how blank lines will be handled:

   - <u>D</u>on't Print Blank Lines When Data Fields are Empty.
   - <u>P</u>rint Blank Lines When Data Fields Are Empty.

9. Choose <u>M</u>erge.

The envelope is now a new document—separate and distinct from the main document. You should save the envelope main document for later use.

You might ask why steps 5–7 were necessary; that is, why doesn't Word assume that you want to attach the envelope main document to the same data source that's attached to the form letter? Actually, the reason is that your envelope main document rarely changes—unless you change envelope sizes. By contrast, you are likely to generate a variety of form letters, which are saved under different document names. By forcing you to create a "stand alone" envelope, Word relieves you from having to go through the many steps just described for each envelope you create.

Editing the Main Document   After the data source is attached to the main document, you can edit the document by using normal typing and formatting features. Whether you start with an existing document containing body copy or a new blank document, you must enter MERGEFIELD codes to tell Word where to insert specific data from the data source. Once the data source is attached, you can use the Insert Merge Field button in the Mail Merge toolbar to insert these codes.

To insert merge fields in the main document, follow these steps:

1. Place the insertion point where you want the first merged data to appear.
2. Click the Insert Merge Field button from the Mail Merge toolbar that appears under the Formatting toolbar. This displays a list of the fields in your data source.

3. Select the field name from the Print Merge Fields list.

4. Choose OK or press Enter.

5. Move the insertion point to the next location where you want to insert data.

 TIP Make sure to leave a space before or after the merge field just as you would leave a space before or after a word you type.

6. Continue inserting all the merge fields necessary for the form letter. Don't forget, however, to insert needed space—for example, spaces between merge fields for city, state, and zip code.

To add ordinary word fields, such as Date, to main documents, you can choose Insert, Field. You can insert certain Word fields that are directly related to the mail merge—such as Ask, Fill-In, and Next Record—by clicking the Insert Word Field button and selecting the field from the drop-down list. You learn how to do this later in the chapter.

You can delete unwanted fields from main documents in the same way you delete text in any other Word document.

You can get a sneak preview of the merged document by clicking the View Merged Data button in the Mail Merge toolbar. With View Merged Data off, your completed main document resembles the document at the top in Figure 9.30. After you click the View Merged Data button, the document appears as shown at the bottom of that figure.

By default, the main document displays the data from the first record in the data source. You can use the VCR-type control icons in the Mail Merge toolbar to browse through the entire merged document. The controls move backward and forward through records in the data source in the same way VCR controls move through a videotape.

The top screen in Figure 9.30 shows documents with the Field Codes option cleared (found in the View tab of the Options dialog box). When field codes are displayed, the document looks like that shown in Figure 9.31.

Selecting Specific Records to Merge   Word enables you to select the records you want to merge. You can build *rules* that limit which data is merged. The rules form English statements specifying the data you want to merge. You can use this feature if you are doing a targeted mailing to a particular area (selected by zip code). For example, the statement ZIP code is equal to 49217 results in Word merging only those records with that zip code.

To select specific records for merging, follow these steps:

1. Activate the main document.

2. Click the Merge dialog box button from the Mail Merge toolbar or choose Tools, Mail Merge. Click the Merge button to display the Merge dialog box (refer to Figure 9.19).

3. Click the _Query Options button in the Merge dialog box to display the Query Options list, shown in Figure 9.32.

FIG. 9.30

When the document displays the field names (top), click the View Merged Data button to display the data merged from the data source (bottom).

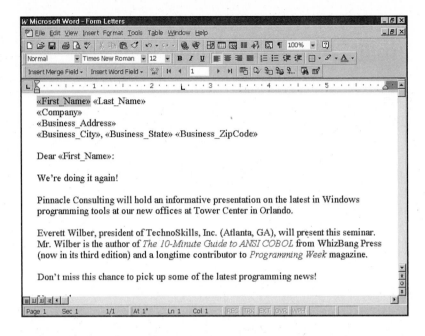

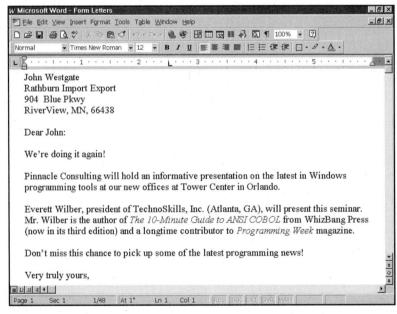

FIG. 9.31
When the Field Codes option is turned on, the document shows the MERGEFIELD field codes.

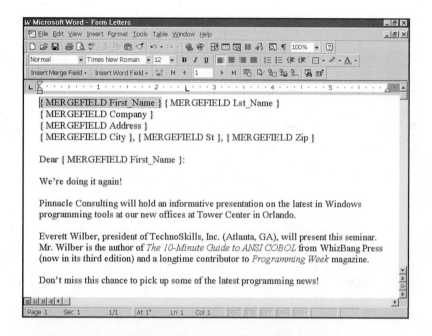

FIG. 9.32
You can use the Query Options dialog box to control the selection of records.

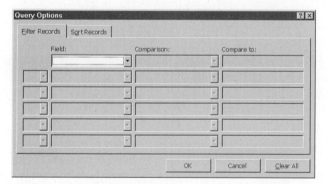

4. Select the first field you want to limit in the Field drop-down list.

5. The phrase Equal to appears in the Comparison list. If you want something other than an exact match, select the type of comparison (such as Less than or Greater than) you want to make.

6. Type the numeric value or text you want compared to the field in the Compare To text box. Figure 9.33 shows an example that merges only those records in which the last name begins with a *P* or a letter following *P*.

FIG. 9.33

To select an alphabetic or numeric range of records, enter the field name, comparison phrase, and comparison value. This rule merges records with last names beginning with P through Z.

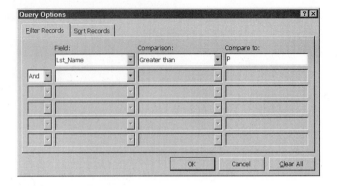

7. After you make an entry in the Compare To box, the word And appears in the leftmost drop-down list in the next row. Select the And or Or option in this box to add another selection rule. If you want to merge only those records that meet both conditions, select And. To merge all records that meet either condition, select Or.

8. To add another rule, repeat steps 4–7.

9. To sort the resulting merged records on any of the selected fields, select the Sort Records tab (see Figure 9.34). You can sort by up to three key fields. Select (or enter) the name of the primary sort field in the Sort By drop-down list box. Enter secondary or tertiary keys, if used, in the Then By and Then By boxes, respectively. You can select the sort order with the option buttons to the right of the list boxes.

FIG. 9.34

Select the Sort Records tab to sort records in a merged document.

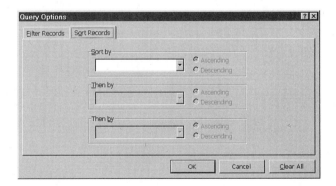

10. Complete the merge by choosing OK. When the merge is complete, click Cancel from the Mail Merge Helper.

If you make a mistake, you can revise any entry or selection at any time. To start over again, click the Clear All button in the Filter Records tab of the Query Options dialog box.

When you build rules, a complete English statement is built that specifies how data from the data source is selected for merging. Figure 9.35, for example, illustrates a rule that would be useful for mailing to a list of contributors. If the data source contains fields for amount pledged

(Pledged) and amount contributed (Paid), this rule selects everyone who pledged $200 or more and paid less than $50.

FIG. 9.35

A completed dialog box selects donors who have yet to fulfill their pledges.

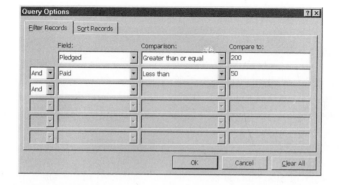

Here are some tips for building rules:

- Text is compared in the same way as numbers. For example, B is less than C.
- Select ranges using And. A numeric range, for example, may be ZIP is Greater than 95400 and ZIP is Less than 95600.
- A text range may be as follows: State is Greater than or Equal to CA and State is Less than or Equal to NY.
- Select individual names or numbers with Or. A numeric selection, for example, may be as follows: ZIP is Equal to 95409 or ZIP is Equal to 95412.
- A text selection may be as follows: Title is Equal to President or Title is Equal to Manager.

 TIP To personally select which records merge, create an extra field (column) with a field name such as **Selection** in your data document. In that column, enter **1** in the row of each record you want to merge. Use the Record Selection dialog box to specify that you want only records with 1 in the Selection field to merge.

Changing the Data Source   Your Main Document Is Attached to You may have one form letter that you use with different mailing lists. In that case, you will want to attach your main document to other data sources. You can use the same procedure that you do for attaching the original data source.

To attach a main document to a different data source, follow these steps:

1. Choose Tools, Mail Merge.
2. Click the Get Data button.
3. Click Open Data Source or Use Address Book if the data source is to be an existing file. Choose Create Data Source or Use Address Book to create a new data source.
4. Select or create the data source file, as appropriate.

CAUTION

Quite often, field headers in the new data source do not match the field codes in the main document. You should always check for errors immediately after you attach a main document to a new data source.

Using One Main Document with Different Data Sources and Field Names   If you use a database program to maintain your mailing lists, you will appreciate this section. Your database program may generate data sources that do not have a *header record*, the top row that contains field names. Instead of opening what may be a huge data source and adding a top row of field names, you can attach a header file. This technique also enables you to use many data sources without having to change the MERGEFIELD in a main document. A *header file* contains a top row of field names, which are used with the data source. The header file can contain a single row of names or be an existing data source with the correct field names. The header file must have the same number of field names as there are fields in the data source.

To create a separate header file, follow these steps:

1. Be sure that the main document is the active document.

2. Choose Tools, Mail Merge.

3. Click the Get Data button.

4. Select Header Options. Word displays the Header Options dialog box.

5. Click Create. Word displays the Create Header Source dialog box (see Figure 9.36).

FIG. 9.36

The Create Header Source dialog box works much like the Create Data Source dialog box.

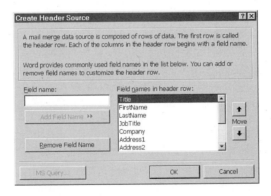

6. Edit the list of field names as you did earlier in the chapter when you created a data source. To remove the selected field name, click Remove Field Name. To add a field name, enter it in the Field Name box and click Add Field Name. When you are satisfied with your list, choose OK. The Save Data Source dialog box appears.

7. Enter a file name for the header source in the File Name box in the Save Data Source dialog box; then choose OK.

Word displays the Mail Merge Helper dialog box, updated for the new header source. The header source you created is attached immediately to the active main document. You still must attach a data source to the main document. The data source itself should not contain a header record because Word will merge the row of names as it would a data record.

> **N O T E**   To print with separate header and data sources, be sure that you attach the header and data sources in the Mail Merge Helper dialog box before you choose the Merge button. ▪

Putting Custom Entries in Mail Merge Documents

Having worked through all the basics of merging documents, you are now ready for a few of the most powerful features of Word. One of these features eliminates blank lines in mail-merge addresses and labels—a feature that gives your labels a more professional appearance. You also learn how to use a main document with different data sources without having to re-create field names. The secret is to use a header file that shows the field names. Another important power feature is making merge documents pause and ask for a customized entry.

Inserting Word Fields in a Main Document   You can insert certain Word fields from the Mail Merge toolbar. Suppose that you want Word to insert one of two different personalized messages in your form letter, depending on whether a condition was satisfied.

To insert an IF field in a main document, follow these steps:

1. Click the Insert Word Field button to display a subset of Word fields.

2. Select If...Then...Else. Word displays the dialog box shown in Figure 9.37. Enter your comparison criteria and the two conditional texts you want in the letter; then choose OK.

FIG. 9.37

Using the Insert Word Field button to insert an IF field displays a helpful dialog box.

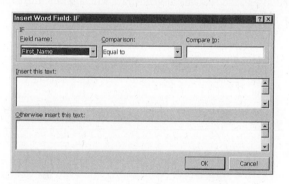

If you then display field codes in the document (by choosing Tools, Options and clicking Field Codes), the IF field will look something like the one in Figure 9.38.

Requesting User Input   During a Mail Merge, Word can automate and personalize your written communication at the same time, but for truly personal form letters, you can put FILLIN fields in form letters so that you can type custom phrases into each mail-merge letter.

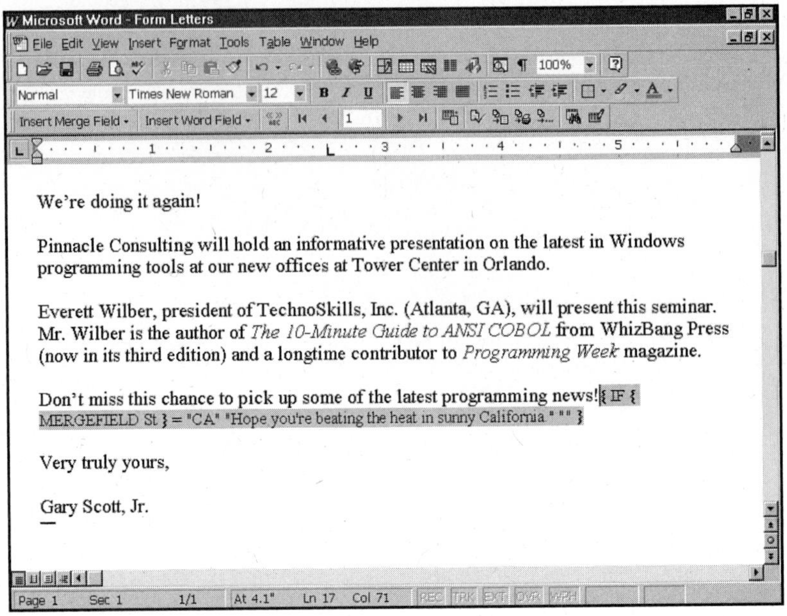
Microsoft Word - Form Letters
File Edit View Insert Format Tools Table Window Help
Normal
Times New Roman
12
Insert Merge Field
Insert Word Field
We're doing it again!
Pinnacle Consulting will hold an informative presentation on the latest in Windows programming tools at our new offices at Tower Center in Orlando.
Everett Wilber, president of TechnoSkills, Inc. (Atlanta, GA), will present this seminar. Mr. Wilber is the author of The 10-Minute Guide to ANSI COBOL from WhizBang Press (now in its third edition) and a longtime contributor to Programming Week magazine.
Don't miss this chance to pick up some of the latest programming news!{ IF { MERGEFIELD St } = "CA" "Hope you're beating the heat in sunny California." "" }
Very truly yours,
Gary Scott, Jr.
Page 1 Sec 1 1/1 At 4.1" Ln 17 Col 71 REC TRK EXT OVR WPH

FIG. 9.38
The IF field shown in this letter will add a personal touch to recipients with a California address.

FILLIN is a Word field (as opposed to a merge field) that can automate document creation. You learn about fields in depth in Chapter 14, "Automating with Field Codes." The following example illustrates how Word fields can be useful in form letters.

Figure 9.39 shows a main document with a FILLIN field in the second paragraph of the body text. During the merge operation, this field displays a dialog box that prompts the user to enter a personalized message to the recipient. The \d switch and the text that follows tell Word to display `Go Blue against the Wildcats in the Silicon Bowl!` as a default response.

To enter the FILLIN field in your document, insert or type the following field code where you want the results to appear:

```
{fillin \d "Go Blue against the Wildcats in the Silicon Bowl!" }
```

Naturally, you can type the FILLIN field code in the document (remember to press Ctrl+F9 to create the field characters {}), or you can insert it by choosing Insert, Field.

To personalize the letter, you need to know to whom you are sending it. To display in the fill-in dialog box the name of the person being addressed, type a prompt in quotes; then in the quotes, use the Insert Merge Field button to insert a MERGEFIELD of the person's name. The field should look like the following:

```
{fillin  "Type a personal message to
➥{mergefield Firstname}   {mergefield Lastname}"
➥\d  "Go Blue against the Wildcats in the Silicon Bowl!" }
```

Notice that the MERGEFIELD code is inside the quotes that enclose the prompt.

FIG. 9.39
Use the FILLIN field when you want to prompt the user to type information in merged letters.

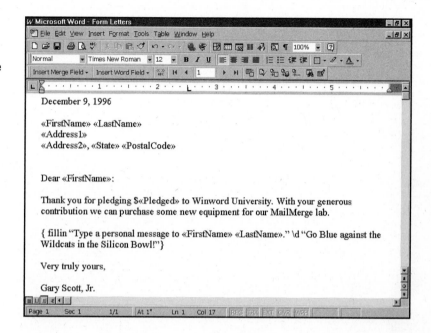

Using Tables, Outlines, Lists, and Field Codes

Creating and Editing Tables

Understanding Tables

If you have worked with a spreadsheet application such as Microsoft Excel or Lotus 1-2-3, you may find working with tables similar to working with a spreadsheet. A *table* is simply a grid of columns and rows. The intersection of a column and a row is a rectangular or square box called a *cell*. Each cell is independent and can be sized or formatted. Figure 10.1 shows an example of a table of data that was created and formatted by using the table feature.

FIG. 10.1

Producing tables with a professional look is simple in Word.

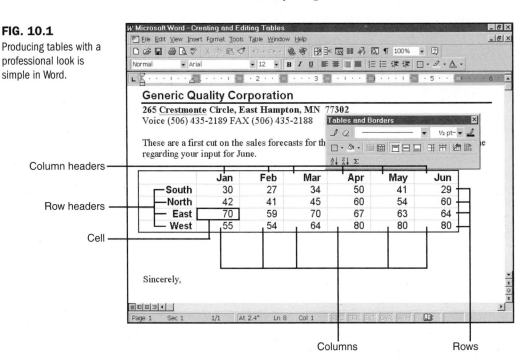

You can insert text, numbers, pictures, or formulas into a cell. If you enter text in a cell, the text wraps to the next line according to the width of the cell. If you adjust the width of the cell or column, the text adjusts to the new width. You can enter or edit text in any cell of the table. A table enables you to present text in columns and align paragraphs or graphics. Figure 10.2 shows text in a table.

FIG. 10.2
You can use tables to create headings to the left of the body text in your documents.

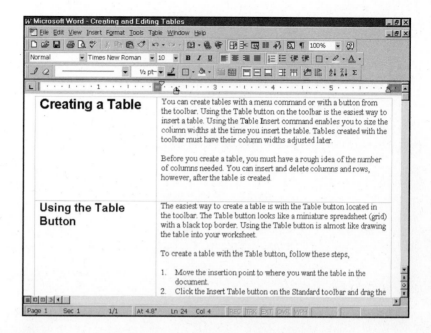

Creating Tables

You can insert a table anywhere in a document. A table can span more than one page, and you can frame a table, resize it, and position it on the page. You can attach a caption to a table and designate headings for the table so that if the table splits between pages, Word automatically repeats the headings at the top of the table.

You can create tables by choosing Table, Insert Table or Draw Table from the pull-down menus, or you can click the Insert Table button on the Standard toolbar. Often, the Insert Table button is the easiest way to create a table because it takes fewer keystrokes. When you click the Insert Table button, Word sets the width of the columns automatically, so you might have to adjust the widths later. When you use the menu command, you can determine the width of the columns when you insert the table.

If the information that you want to include in a table already appears in your document as text, you can convert the text to a table.

▶ **See** "Converting Text to a Table," **p. 308**

 T I P   Before you create a table, it's helpful to have a general idea of the number of columns that you need. You can insert and delete columns and rows, however, after you create the table.

Drawing a Table

The Table, Draw Table command is used to draw a table anywhere within a document. Draw the outer border of the table first. Then draw lines for the cells and columns wherever you want them to be. This makes creating complex tables into a simple task.

To draw a table, follow these steps:

1. Position the cursor on the line in your document where you want to insert the table.
2. Choose Table, Draw Table. The Tables and Borders dialog box appears, as shown in Figure 10.3.

FIG. 10.3

Drawing complex tables is a simple task using the Table, Draw Table command.

Notice that the pointer changes to a pencil.

3. Drag the outline of the table until it is the size you want it to be. You can either drag the pointer downward to the left or right, or upward to the left or right.
4. Position the pointer within the table where you want to draw your first row or column line.
5. Drag the dotted line until it stretches where you want it to go. If the line does not stretch far enough, it will not be drawn.

    For a description on how to use the functions shown in the Table and Borders dialog box, see "Using the Table Toolbar," later in this chapter.

6. When you have finished creating your table, close the Tables and Borders dialog box.

Creating a Table with the Table Wizard

The Table Wizard easily formats tables of any size. The Table Wizard guides you through the table-creation process by displaying a series of boxes that graphically present the most common choices made for preformatted tables. The Table Wizard also makes it easy to handle special situations, such as repeating column headings at the top of pages when a table is longer than a single page. The Table Wizard also formats the headings and table content, and finishes by going directly into AutoFormat, which guides you through the table-formatting process.

Inserting a Table with a Command

Choose Table, Insert Table if you want to specify the width of the columns in the table at the same time you insert the table.

To insert a table in a document, follow these steps:

1. Position the insertion point where you want the top-left corner of the table.
2. Choose Table, Insert Table. The Insert Table dialog box appears, as shown in Figure 10.4.

FIG. 10.4
You can insert a table by using the Insert Table dialog box.

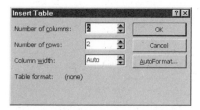

3. Select or type the number of columns that you want in the Number of Columns text box.

4. If you know how many rows you need, select or type the number of rows in the Number of Rows text box.

 T I P If you are unsure how many columns or rows you need, don't worry. You easily can add rows and columns to the end of a table or in the middle of the table.

5. If you know how wide you want all columns, adjust the Column Width box.

You easily can change column widths if you are unsure of the column width or if you later want to adjust the table.

6. Click the Wizard button to be guided through the creation of a table.

7. Click the AutoFormat button to apply predefined formats to the table when Word creates it.

8. Click OK.

Word inserts the table in your document. The table may be visible or invisible depending on whether you have turned on table gridlines (see "Displaying or Hiding Gridlines and End Marks," later in this chapter). The insertion point appears in the first cell.

Using the Insert Table Button

The easiest way to create a table is by using the Insert Table button on the Standard toolbar. Using the Insert Table button is almost like drawing the table into your document.

To create a table using the Insert Table button, follow these steps:

1. Move the insertion point to where you want to insert the table in the document.

2. Click the Insert Table button on the Standard toolbar and drag the mouse pointer within the grid down and to the right.

When you click the button, a grid of rows and columns that looks like a miniature table appears. As long as you continue to hold down the mouse button, you can move the pointer within the grid to select the size of the table that you want to insert. If you move the pointer beyond the right or lower borders, the grid expands. Figure 10.5 shows the Insert Table button expanded and a table size selected.

3. Release the mouse button when the selected grid is the size you want your table to be.

If you have already begun the selection process with the Insert Table button and then decide that you do not want to insert a table, continue to hold down the mouse button and drag the pointer until it is outside the grid and to the left; then release the button. You also can drag up until the pointer is over the button and then release the button.

N O T E   You can store a table, like text, as an AutoText entry. If you use the same type of table repeatedly, you can save considerable time by storing the table as an AutoText entry, then typing the AutoText name in the document where you want it inserted.

To store a table as an AutoText entry, select the entire table and choose Insert, AutoText. Type a name for the entry in the Please Name Your AutoText Entry box, and click OK. To later insert the AutoText entry, type the AutoText Entry name and press F3. ■

FIG. 10.5.
The Insert Table button enables you to draw your table the size that you want.

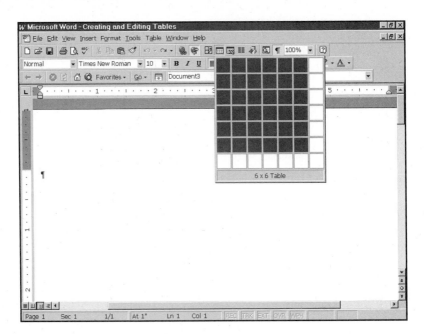

Using the Tables and Borders Toolbar

The Tables and Borders toolbar provides a fast way to create a new table or edit an existing one. Select from a variety of line styles, line weights, border colors, and shading. You also can merge and split cells, align text within a cell or cells, distribute rows and columns evenly, change text rotation within a cell or cells, sort in ascending or descending order, and calculate and display the sum of the values in table cells above or to the left of the cell containing the insertion point.

Choose the Tables and Borders button. The Tables and Borders toolbar appears (see Figure 10.6).

FIG. 10.6
Use the Tables and Borders toolbar to create and edit tables.

Table 10.1 shows the Tables and Borders toolbar functions.

Table 10.1 Tables and Borders Toolbar Functions

Icon	Function
	Selects the Draw Table function for freehand table creation.
	Selects an eraser used to erase borders. Simply drag the eraser over the line you want to erase.
	Selects the line style of border.
	Selects the border color from a color palette.
	Selects the shading from a palette.
	Merges two or more cells.
	Splits a cell.
	Aligns text along the top of the selected cell or cells.
	Aligns text in the center of the selected cell or cells.
	Aligns text along the bottom of the selected cell or cells.
	Distributes selected rows evenly (makes them the same height).
	Distributes selected columns evenly (makes them the same width).
	Selects a predefined table format.
	Changes the text direction.
	Sorts in ascending order.

continues

Table 10.1 Continued

Icon	Function
$\begin{array}{c}\text{Z}\downarrow\\\text{A}\end{array}$	Sorts in descending order.
Σ	Calculates and displays the sum of the values in table cells above or to the left of the cell containing the insertion point.

Displaying or Hiding Gridlines and End Marks

Table gridlines can show you the outline of your cells and table. Such outlines can make working in tables easier. The end-of-cell mark indicates where the contents of a cell end, and the end-of-row mark indicates the end of the row. Figure 10.7 shows a table in which the gridlines and end marks are turned off. Figure 10.8 shows the same table with the gridlines and end marks turned on. As you can see, these lines and marks make it easier to read a table. The gridlines do not print.

If you want gridlines on or off, choose Table, Show Gridlines. This command toggles gridlines on or off. The icon to the left of the menu command is selected if gridlines are turned on and the command changes to Hide Gridlines. To turn end marks on or off quickly, press Shift+Ctrl+8, or click the Show/Hide ¶ button in the Standard toolbar.

FIG. 10.7

In this table, gridlines and end marks are turned off.

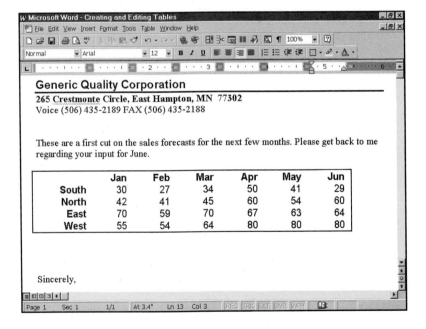

FIG. 10.8

This table is easier to read and edit because gridlines are turned on.

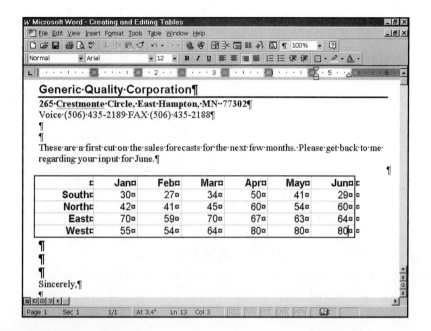

Generic·Quality·Corporation¶

265·Crestmonte·Circle,·East·Hampton,·MN··77302¶
Voice·(506)·435-2189·FAX·(506)·435-2188¶
¶
¶
These·are·a·first·cut·on·the·sales·forecasts·for·the·next·few·months.·Please·get·back·to·me·
regarding·your·input·for·June.¶

¤	Jan¤	Feb¤	Mar¤	Apr¤	May¤	Jun¤	¤
South¤	30¤	27¤	34¤	50¤	41¤	29¤	¤
North¤	42¤	41¤	45¤	60¤	54¤	60¤	¤
East¤	70¤	59¤	70¤	67¤	63¤	64¤	¤
West¤	55¤	54¤	64¤	80¤	80¤	80¤	¤

¶
¶
¶
Sincerely,¶
¶

Typing and Moving in a Table

When you create a new table, the insertion point flashes in the first cell—the cell at the upper-left corner of the table. To insert text or numbers in the cell, just start typing.

As you enter text into a cell, characters will automatically wrap to the next line in the cell as needed. In a Word table, the entire row of cells expands downward to accommodate the text. The same thing happens if you press Enter in a cell. The insertion point moves to the next line down, and the row becomes taller. Each cell acts like a miniature word processing page.

To move forward through the cells in the table, press Tab. Press Shift+Tab to move backward through the cells. When you press Tab to move to a cell, you select any text in the cell. To move with the mouse, click the cell at the point where you want the insertion point to appear.

If you reach the table's last (lower-right) cell and press Tab, you create a new row of cells at the end of the table and move the insertion point into the first cell of that row. To leave the table, you must press an arrow key or use the mouse to move the insertion point outside the table.

Arrow keys also help you move around in a table. Table 18.2 summarizes these keyboard movements and includes several other handy shortcuts to help you move around in a table.

Table 10.2   Shortcut Keys Used to Move in a Table

Key(s)	Function
Tab	Moves the insertion point right one cell; inserts a new row when pressed in the bottom-right cell.

continues

Table 10.2   Continued

Key(s)	Function
Shift+Tab	Moves the insertion point left one cell.
Arrow key	Moves the insertion point character by character through a cell and into the next cell when the insertion point reaches the end of the current cell.
Alt+Home	Moves the insertion point to the first cell in the row.
Alt+End	Moves the insertion point to the last cell in the row.
Alt+Page Up	Moves the insertion point to the top cell in the column.
Alt+Page Down	Moves the insertion point to the bottom cell in the column.

Using Indents and Tabs in a Cell

Just like regular text paragraphs, cells can contain indents. You can format these indents using the same techniques that you use to format a paragraph. Use the ruler or choose Format, Paragraph.

To change the indent or first-line indent within a cell using Format, Paragraph, follow these steps:

1. Select the cell.
2. Choose Format, Paragraph.
3. Set indents in the Paragraph dialog box's Indentation group. Then choose OK.

To change the indent or first-line indent within a cell using the ruler, follow these steps:

1. Select the cell.
2. Click the right mouse button in the selected cell and select Paragraph.
3. Drag the indent and first-line indent markers to the desired position of the new indentation.

▶ **See** "Setting Indents," **p. 99**

Pressing Tab moves you from one cell to the next in a table. Pressing Shift+Tab moves you to the previous cell. You also can set tabs within a cell. Select the cells in which you want tabs, and set the tab stops in the usual way—using the ruler or choosing Format, Tabs. To move the insertion point to the tab stop within the cell, however, press Ctrl+Tab rather than just Tab.

▶ **See** "Setting Tabs," **p. 93**

Attaching Captions to Tables

You can add a caption to a table to identify it, to enable you to cross-reference the table, or to create a list of tables in your document. When you insert a caption, Word uses the SEQ field code to number the table. If you insert a new table before or after an existing table, Word automatically updates the numbering for all the tables.

▶ **See** "Automating with Field Codes," **p. 347**

To attach a caption to a table, follow these steps:

1. Select the entire table by moving the insertion point anywhere in the table and choosing Table, Select Table.
2. Display the Caption dialog box by choosing Insert, Caption (see Figure 10.9).
3. Select Table in the Label list if it isn't already selected.
4. Type text after the caption label in the Caption text box, if you want.
5. Select the position for the label in the Position list.
6. Choose OK.

A caption for the table then appears at the position that you specified (see Figure 10.10). If Word displays the SEQ field code rather than the table number, choose Tools, Options, select the View tab, and clear the Field Codes option. Then choose OK.

▶ **See** "Adding Cross-References and Captions," **p. 519**

FIG. 10.9
You can attach a caption to a table in the Caption dialog box.

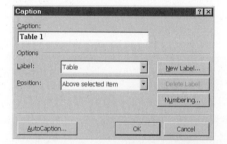

FIG. 10.10
A caption is shown above the table.

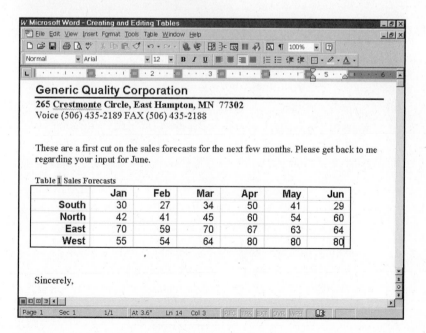

Editing Tables

After you create and fill your table, you probably will have to make changes to the table. You might need to move or copy cells, or insert new cells, rows, or columns to make room for additional text or graphics. Often you must adjust row heights and column widths. In the following sections, you learn how to perform all these tasks.

You can edit the contents within a cell using the same techniques that you use to edit text or graphics in a document. You can delete characters using the Backspace and Delete keys, and move around in the text using the mouse or the arrow keys. To edit the cells, rows, and columns in a table, you use different techniques, which the following sections describe.

By using the shortcut menus, you can quickly access many of the commands that you learn about in the following sections. To use the shortcut menus, point to a cell or selection that you have made in a table, and click the right mouse button. A list of commands that you can use to edit or format the selection appears. Use the mouse to select the appropriate command.

Selecting and Editing Cells

Before you use the table editing commands, you must select the correct cells, rows, or columns for whatever changes you are making to the table. You have two ways to select the contents of a table:

- By character, for which you use Word's usual character-selection techniques
- By cell, for which Word offers special techniques

When you select the entire cell (or cells), the entire cell appears darkened (see Figure 10.11). Word enables you to select an entire row, an entire column, or the entire table easily.

FIG. 10.11

A cell appears darkened when you select it.

	Jan	Feb	Mar	Apr	May	Jun
South	30	27	34	50	41	29
North	42	41	45	60	54	60
East	70	59	70	67	63	64
West	55	54	64	80	80	80

Selecting by Menu   You can select rows, columns, or the entire table by using commands from the menu.

To select cells, rows, or columns, follow these steps:

1. Move the insertion point into the cell that contains the row or column you want to select. To select a table, you can select any cell in that table.

2. Choose Table. Then choose Select Row, Select Column, or Select Table.

Selecting Cells with the Mouse   You also can use a mouse to select a cell's contents. Just drag across characters or double-click words in the usual way.

As you can do with the keyboard, you can use the mouse to extend the selection beyond the cell: As soon as the selection reaches the border of a cell, you begin selecting entire cells rather than characters. In addition, you can use special selection bars with the mouse. When you move the I-beam into a selection bar, the pointer changes to an arrow. You can use the mouse to select a cell, row, or column, depending on where you click the mouse pointer.

Table 10.3 summarizes the mouse selection techniques.

Table 10.3   Using the Mouse to Select Items in a Table

Item to Select	Mouse Action
Characters	Drag across characters.
Cell	Click the cell selection area in the left inside edge of the cell.
Group of cells	Select the first cell or characters; then drag to the last cell or Shift+click the last cell.
Horizontal row	Click the selection area to the left of the table; drag down for multiple rows.
Vertical column	Click the top line of the column; drag to either side for multiple columns. (When positioned correctly, the pointer appears as a solid black down arrow.)
Table	Click the selection area to the left of the top row and drag down to select all rows or Shift+click to the left of the last row.

TROUBLESHOOTING

When I try to drag and drop cells I have selected, it doesn't work. The mouse pointer doesn't change to an arrow when I point to the selected cells. When the drag-and-drop feature is turned off, the mouse pointer does not change to an arrow when you point to a selection, and you cannot drag the selection to a new location. To turn on drag and drop, choose Tools, Options; select the Edit tab; select the Drag-and-Drop text editing option, and then click OK.

Selecting Cells with the Keyboard   Word provides several other keyboard techniques for selecting cells and groups of cells. Table 10.4 lists these methods.

Table 10.4   Using Shortcut Keys to Select Cells

Key(s)	Selects
Tab	The next cell
Shift+Tab	The previous cell
Shift+arrow key	Character by character in the current cell and then the entire adjacent cell

continues

Table 10.4	Continued
Key(s)	**Selects**
F8+up or down arrow	The current cell and the cell above or below (press Esc to end the selection)
F8+left or right arrow	Text in the current cell (character by character) and then all adjacent cells (press Esc to end the selection)
Alt+5 (on the numeric keypad)	An entire table

When you select with an arrow key, you first select each character in the cell. As soon as you go beyond the border of the cell, however, you begin selecting entire cells. If you change arrow directions, you select groups of adjacent cells. If you press Shift+right arrow or F8+right arrow to select three adjacent cells in a row and then press the down-arrow key once, for example, you extend the selection to include the entire contents of the three cells below the original three.

Moving and Copying Cells

Unless you do everything perfectly the first time, you might have to reorganize data in your tables. Word gives you all the flexibility of moving and copying in a table that you have with text.

Using the Mouse to Drag and Drop Cells, Rows, and Columns   The mouse shortcuts that work with text in body copy also work on cell contents, cells, or an entire table.

To move or copy the characters in a cell or one or more cells and their cellular structure, follow these steps:

1. Select the characters, cells, rows, or columns you want to move or copy.

2. Move the mouse pointer over the selected characters until it changes from an I-beam to an arrow pointed upward and to the left. See Figure 10.12. (The pointer might remain an arrow if you don't move it from the selected area.)

FIG. 10.12.

Use the pointer to drag cells, rows, or columns.

	Jan	Feb	Mar	Apr	May	Jun
South	30	27	34	50	41	29
North	42	41	45	60	54	60
East	70	59	70	67	63	64
West	55	54	64	80	80	80

3. To move, hold down the left mouse button. To copy, hold down Ctrl and then the left mouse button. Notice the message in the status bar: Move to where? or Copy to where?

4. Position the grayed insertion point at the location where you want the moved or copied characters or cells to appear. Position the pointer over the top-left cell at the place where

you want a range of cells to appear. The insertion point appears gray and displays a gray box at its bottom end.

5. Release the mouse button.

If you include the end-of-cell mark in your selection, the formatting for your selected cell or cells is moved or copied to the destination, along with the cell contents.

Using Cut, Copy, and Paste   Choosing Edit and then Cut, Copy, or Paste works much the same way in a table as with text outside a table. These commands enable you to move or copy cells within a table or copy a table to another location. You can cut and copy a single cell, multiple cells, or an entire table.

If you select only the text, number, or picture within a cell, you copy or cut only what you have selected, just as you do in a document's body copy. But if you select the entire cell or multiple cells, you copy the cell boundaries as well.

If you select an entire cell, the Copy command copies the entire cell to the Clipboard. The Cut command moves the entire contents of the cell to the Clipboard. The cell's boundaries remain in the table. When you paste cells from the Clipboard, the cell containing the insertion point receives the first cell on the Clipboard. The contents of the cells on the Clipboard replace the table's original cells, as shown in Figures 10.13 and 10.14.

Part

IV

Ch

10

FIG. 10.13

You can copy selected cells.

	Jan	Feb	Mar	Apr	
South	30	27	34	50	
North	42	41	45	60	
East	70	59	70	67	
West	55	54	64	80	

FIG. 10.14

The same cells are pasted into a blank area.

	Jan	Feb	Mar	Apr	Apr	
South	30	27	34	50	50	
North	42	41	45	60	60	
East	70	59	70	67	67	
West	55	54	64	80	80	

When you copy cells, the Paste command becomes Paste Cells, and the command pastes the cells as cells in a table. If you copy an entire row or column, the command becomes Paste Rows or Paste Columns, respectively. When you paste cells into an area not formatted as a table, they arrive as a table. When you paste a group of cells into an existing table, the table expands, if necessary, to accommodate the new cells.

You also can paste text from outside a table into a single cell in a table. Just copy or cut the text, move the insertion point inside a cell, and choose Edit, Paste.

To move or copy cells, follow these steps:

1. Select the cells, rows, or columns that you want to move or copy.

2. To move the cells, choose Edit, Cut, press Ctrl+X, or click the Cut button on the Standard toolbar.

To copy the cells, choose Edit, Copy, press Ctrl+C, or click the Standard toolbar's Copy button.

3. Select an area in the table to which you're moving the cells that match the shape and size of the area that you selected in step 1.

TIP Word warns you if the shape and size of the copied cells do not match the shape and size of the cells into which you're pasting.

4. Choose Edit, Paste Cells, press Ctrl+V, or click the Paste button on the Standard toolbar.

Using the Outliner The Word Outline view provides another option for reorganizing rows, columns, and cells. Switching to Outline view enables you to move an entire row of selected cells by dragging the selection to the location where you want the data to appear.

To move a row of cells using Outline view, follow these steps:

1. Choose View, Outline. A small box, called a *body text symbol*, appears to the left of each row (see Figure 10.15).

FIG. 10.15

To move a row, drag its body text symbol up or down.

This is the body text symbol

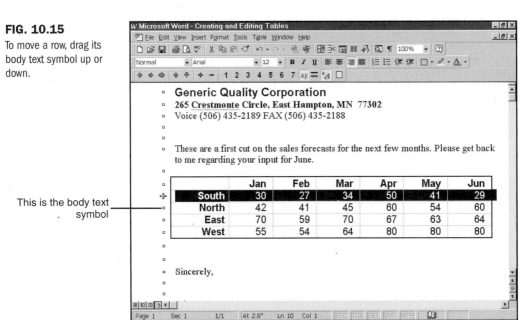

2. Select the row by clicking the body text symbol.

3. Select the up or down arrows in the Outline bar or drag the body text symbol up or down to move the selected row to the desired location.

N O T E A shortcut for moving table rows up or down is to select the entire row and then press Shift+Alt+up or down arrow. You do not have to be in Outline view for this shortcut to work, nor does the document need an outline.

Changing the Column Width

When Word first creates a table, the columns are sized equally to fill the area between the right and left margins. You can change column or cell widths in three ways:

- Drag the right cell border of the column in the table.
- Drag the column marker on the ruler.
- Choose Table, Cell Height and Width.

Dragging Cell Borders or Using the Ruler To change the width of a column with the mouse, position the pointer on the column's right border. The pointer changes to a vertical double bar when you position it properly. (The pointer changes even if the gridlines are turned off.) Figure 10.16 shows the shape of the pointer when it is positioned correctly to drag a cell border.

Part
IV

Ch
10

FIG. 10.16

Drag the border of a cell or selected column to change its width.

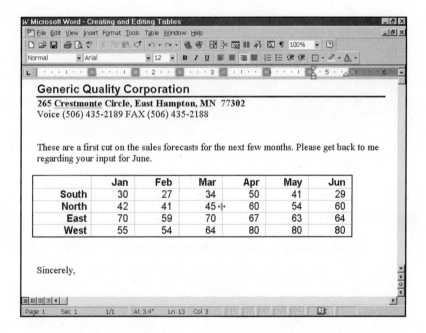

Drag this column marker to the desired column width and release the mouse button. If you have selected either the entire column or nothing in the column, the entire column adjusts to the new width. If you select cells within the column, only the selected cells adjust to the new width.

You can affect the other columns and the overall table width differently by pressing different keys as you drag the border. To see the width measurements of the columns displayed on the ruler, hold down the Alt key as you drag the border. Table 10.5 indicates the different ways that you can adjust the columns.

Table 10.5 Changing Column Widths with the Mouse

Action	Result
Drag the border without holding down any keys	Resizes all columns to the right in proportion to their original width.
Drag the border while holding down Shift	Changes only the width of the column to the left; does not change the table width.
Drag the border while holding down Ctrl	Adjusts all columns to the right equally; does not change the table width.
Drag the border Ctrl+Shift	Leaves columns to the right down unchanged; adjusts the table proportionally.
Double-click the border	Adjusts the column width to fit the widest content.

You can also use the table markers on the ruler to change column widths. Dragging the table markers has the same result as dragging the column borders, as discussed in the preceding paragraphs. If the ruler is not turned on, choose View, Ruler.

Using the Column Width Command   Choosing Table, Cell Height and Width is useful when you want to change the width of multiple columns with a single command or if you want to define the width of columns by specific amounts. The command also enables you to change the distance between columns.

TIP To change the width of an entire column rather than just a cell in a column, be sure to select the entire column first.

To change the column width by choosing Table, Cell Height and Width, follow these steps:

1. Select the columns or cells whose width you want to change.
2. Choose Table, Cell Height and Width, and select the Column tab in the Cell Height and Width dialog box. The Column tab is displayed (see Figure 10.17).
3. Select or type a number in the Width of Column *X* text box, where *X* is the column number.
4. If you want to adjust other columns, click the Previous Column or Next Column buttons to keep the dialog box open, and move to the next column. The Width of Column label changes to tell you which row you are formatting.
5. Choose OK.

FIG. 10.17
You can set the width of any number of columns at one time in the Cell Height and Width dialog box.

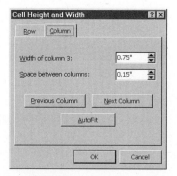

Using the AutoFit Command   You can have Word automatically adjust the width of a column in a table to accommodate the width of the column's longest line of text. One advantage to using AutoFit to adjust the columns in a table is that you ensure the columns are as wide as (but no wider than) they have to be to accommodate the table's data. This feature helps you optimize the use of space on a page.

To AutoFit the column width, follow these steps:

1. Select the columns that you want to AutoFit.

   If you do not select the entire column, only the selected cells are AutoFit.

2. Choose Table, Cell Height and Width, and select the Column tab in the Cell Height and Width dialog box.

3. Click the AutoFit button.

Word then automatically adjusts the column, closes the dialog box, and returns you to the document.

Changing Column Spacing

The Cell Height and Width dialog box also enables you to control the amount of space between columns. When you first create a table, the columns that you choose for the table are the same size and span the distance between page margins. Included in the column width is a default column-spacing setting of 0.15".

To change the spacing between columns, follow these steps:

1. Select the columns you want to adjust. Select a row if you want to adjust all columns in the table.

2. Choose Table, Cell Height and Width and select the Column tab.

3. Select or type a number in the Space Between Columns text box.

   The space that you set in this box is divided by the left and right margins within the cell—just as if the cell were a small page and you were entering the combined value for the left and right margins.

4. Click OK.

Part
IV

Ch
10

The column spacing affects the cell's usable column width. If a column width is 2 inches and the column spacing is set to 0.50 inch, for example, the column width available for text and graphics is 1.5 inches.

Changing Row Height and Position

When you first create a table, each row has the same height. However, the text and amount of paragraph spacing that you add changes the row's height. The Cell Height and Width dialog box enables you to specify how far Word indents a row from the left margin, the row's height, and the row's alignment between margins. You also use the vertical ruler to change the row's height.

Changing Row Height   You can change the height of the rows in a table by using either the Cell Height and Width dialog box or the vertical ruler. If you want to change several rows at the same time to the same height, using the menu command is easier.

To set row height using the Cell Height and Width dialog box, follow these steps:

1. Select the rows whose height you want to adjust.

2. Choose Table, Cell Height and Width, and select the Row tab in the Cell Height and Width dialog box (see Figure 10.18).

FIG. 10.18

You can control the height and indentation of rows in a table.

3. Select the Height of Row option. The following are the available options:

Option	Result
Auto	Automatically adjusts row height to the size of the text or graphic.
At least	Sets the minimum row height. Automatically adjusts the row if text or graphics exceed this minimum.
Exactly	Sets a fixed row height. When printed or displayed on-screen, cuts off text or graphics that exceed the fixed height.

4. If you choose At Least or Exactly in step 3, type or select the row height in points in the At box.

You can also specify the height in lines (**li**) or inches (") by including the abbreviation after the numeric value in the A̲t box.

5. Clear the Allow Row to B̲reak Across Pages option to keep the selected row from splitting at a page break.

   When this option is selected, if the text or graphic in a cell in the row cannot fit on the current page, Word splits the row and continues it on the next page.

6. Click the P̲revious Row or N̲ext Row button if you want to format other rows. The He̲ight of Row label changes to tell you which row you are formatting.

7. Click OK.

To set row height with the vertical ruler, follow these steps:

1. If you are not in Page Layout view, choose V̲iew, P̲age Layout.

   Every row in a table has a corresponding horizontal marker in the vertical ruler (see Figure 10.19). You can adjust the height of a row by dragging its marker.

FIG. 10.19
You can use the vertical ruler on the left to set row heights.

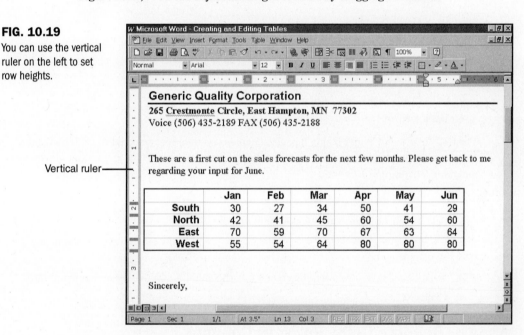

2. Drag the marker to set the height of the row that you want to change.

   If you drag the marker without pressing any keys, you set the row height to at least whatever the new measurement is. The row height automatically adjusts if the text or graphics exceed this minimum setting. If you hold down Ctrl as you drag the marker, you set the row height to exactly the new measurement. When displayed on-screen or printed, text or graphics that exceed the fixed height are cut off.

Changing Row Spacing   A little extra spacing between rows can make your table easier to read. You can adjust the amount of space between rows by choosing Format, Paragraph.

To add space between rows, follow these steps:

1. Select the rows to which you want to add spacing.
2. Choose Format, Paragraph, and select the Indents and Spacing tab in the Paragraph dialog box.
3. Type or select a spacing in the Spacing Before or the Spacing After boxes. You can use lines (**li**) or point (**pt**) measurements by typing the number and space and then the abbreviation.
4. Click OK.

Aligning and Indenting Rows   With Word, you can control a table's position by changing the alignment of rows. You also can indent selected rows to align with other text in your document. Row alignment and indentation does not affect the alignment of text within the cells.

To align rows between page margins, follow these steps:

1. Select the rows that you want to align.
2. Choose Table, Cell Height and Width, and select the Row tab in the Cell Height and Width dialog box (see Figure 10.20).
3. Select Left, Center, or Right alignment.
4. Click OK.

The Cell Height and Width dialog box also enables you to indent selected rows. When you indent a row, the entire row shifts right by the amount that you specify, just as though you were indenting a paragraph.

To indent a row, follow these steps:

1. Select the row or rows that you want to indent.
2. Choose Table, Cell Height and Width, and select the Row tab in the Cell Height and Width dialog box.
3. Type or select in the Indent From Left box the amount of indentation that you want.
4. Click OK.

Adding or Deleting Cells, Rows, or Columns

Word enables you to change a table's structure by adding and deleting cells, rows, and columns. You can add or delete one or many cells, rows, or columns by using a single command. The Table menu changes its Insert and Delete commands depending on what you have selected.

If a cell is selected, the Table menu displays the Insert Cells and Delete Cells commands. If a column is selected, the Table menu displays the Insert Columns and Delete Columns commands. If a row is selected, the menu displays Insert Rows and Delete Rows.

Adding or Deleting Cells   You can add or delete individual cells if you don't want to add or delete entire rows or columns. Word shifts the other cells in the table to accommodate the added or deleted cells.

To add cells to or delete cells from an existing table, follow these steps:

1. Select the cells that you want to delete or position the cursor where you want to add cells.

2. Choose Table, Insert Cells, or Table, Delete Cells. The Insert Cells or Delete Cells dialog box appears, depending on which command you chose (see Figures 10.20 and 10.21).

FIG. 10.20

The Insert Cells dialog box appears if you are inserting cells.

FIG. 10.21

The Delete Cells dialog box appears if you are deleting cells.

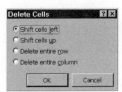

3. Choose the appropriate option button that corresponds to shifting the existing cells to the position that you want. You also have the option of inserting or deleting an entire column or row.

   Choosing Insert Cells inserts blank cells at the location of the selected cells and shifts the selected cells either down or right.

   Choosing Delete Cells deletes the selected cells and shifts adjacent cells either up or left to fill the vacancy.

4. Choose OK.

If you want to delete cell contents without deleting the actual cell, select the cell contents that you want to delete and press Delete or Backspace.

Adding or Deleting Rows and Columns   You can insert and delete columns and rows from a table using the same commands that you use to insert or delete cells. You can add columns and rows to the end of the table or insert them within the table.

To insert a new row at the end of the table, move the insertion point to the last position in the last cell and press Tab.

Part

IV

Ch

10

To insert or delete rows in the middle of an existing table, follow these steps:

1. Select the row or rows where you want to insert or delete.

   When you insert a row, Word shifts the selected row down and inserts a blank row (see Figure 10.22). When you delete a row, Word deletes the selected row and shifts up lower rows.

FIG. 10.22

An inserted row shifts the selected row down.

	Jan	Feb	Mar	Apr	May	Jun
South	30	27	34	50	41	29
North	42	41	45	60	54	60
East	70	59	70	67	63	64
West	55	54	64	80	80	80

2. Choose Table, Insert Rows, or Table, Delete Rows.

   If you are inserting a row or rows, you can click the Insert Table button on the Standard toolbar instead of choosing Table, Insert Rows.

N O T E Word inserts the number of rows you have selected. For example, if you have selected six rows and choose Table, Insert Rows, Word inserts six rows. ■

To insert or delete one or more columns within a table, follow these steps:

1. Select one or more columns where you want to insert or delete columns.

   If you are inserting a column or columns, you can click the Insert Table button on the Standard toolbar instead of choosing Table, Insert Columns.

2. Choose Table and then Insert Columns or Delete Columns.

   When you insert columns, the selected columns shift right to make room for the inserted blank columns. When you're deleting, Word removes the selected columns and shifts columns leftward to fill the gap.

If you insert a column, the table looks like the one shown in Figure 10.23. If you delete a column, the table looks like the one shown in Figure 10.24.

FIG. 10.23

Inserting a column shifts existing columns to the right.

	Jan	Feb	Mar	Apr		May	Jun
South	30	27	34	50		41	29
North	42	41	45	60		54	60
East	70	59	70	67		63	64
West	55	54	64	80		80	80

FIG. 10.24

Deleting a column shifts existing columns to the left to fill the gap.

	Jan	Feb	Mar	Apr	Jun
South	30	27	34	50	29
North	42	41	45	60	60
East	70	59	70	67	64
West	55	54	64	80	80

Inserting a column as the last column requires a different procedure. To insert a column to the right of a table, follow these steps:

1. Position the insertion point at the end of a table row outside the table, which places it in front of an end-of-row mark.

   If gridlines and end marks are not displayed on-screen, see the section "Displaying or Hiding Gridlines and End Marks" earlier in this chapter.

2. Choose T<u>a</u>ble, Select <u>C</u>olumn.

3. Choose T<u>a</u>ble, <u>I</u>nsert Columns, or click the Insert Table button on the Standard toolbar.

To insert additional columns to the right of the table, choose <u>E</u>dit, <u>R</u>epeat, or press F4.

N O T E If you want to insert multiple columns quickly at the right edge of the table, select from the existing table as many columns as you want to insert. (Dragging across with the right mouse button is a quick way to select these columns.) Choose <u>E</u>dit, <u>C</u>opy. Move the insertion point to the end of the first row of the table, and choose <u>E</u>dit, <u>P</u>aste. To clear them, reselect these new columns and press Delete. ■

Part
IV

Ch
10

TROUBLESHOOTING

When I try to insert rows or columns in a table, the <u>I</u>nsert <u>R</u>ows and <u>I</u>nsert <u>C</u>olumns commands do not appear in the T<u>a</u>ble menu. If the T<u>a</u>ble menu doesn't display the <u>I</u>nsert or <u>D</u>elete commands for rows or columns, you have selected only cells. You must select the rows or columns with which you want to work so that Word knows which <u>I</u>nsert or <u>D</u>elete command to add to the menu.

CHAPTER 11

Modifying Tables

In this chapter

Merging and Splitting Cells and Creating Table Headings

Sometimes, you want text or a figure to span the width of multiple cells. A *heading* is an example of text that you might want to stretch across several columns. Word enables you to merge multiple cells in a row into a single cell. Merging cells converts their contents to paragraphs within a single cell.

Merging Cells

You can only merge cells horizontally. Selecting cells in more than one row results in the selected cells in each row being merged horizontally.

To merge multiple cells in a row into a single cell, follow these steps:

1. Select the cells that you want to merge (see Figure 11.1).

FIG. 11.1

Select the cells that you want to merge in the table.

		Sales Forecast					
	Jan	Feb	Mar	Apr	May	Jun
South	30	27	34	50	41	29
North	42	41	45	60	54	60
East	70	59	70	67	63	64
West	55	54	64	80	80	80

2. Choose Table, Merge Cells.

The selected cells condense into a single cell (see Figure 11.2). You might have to reformat the contents so that the cell aligns correctly.

FIG. 11.2

Merge cells to put text such as titles into a single, wider cell.

	Sales Forecast					
	Jan	Feb	Mar	Apr	May	Jun
South	30	27	34	50	41	29
North	42	41	45	60	54	60
East	70	59	70	67	63	64
West	55	54	64	80	80	80

Creating Table Headings

To create table headings, follow these steps:

1. Select the first row and any following rows that you want to use as table headings.

2. Choose Table, Headings.

This command designates the selected rows of a table to be a table heading. However, the selected rows must include the first row of the table in order to be designated as a table heading. Table headings are repeated on subsequent pages if the table spans more than one page.

Splitting Cells

After you have merged cells, you can return them to their original condition. The text in the merged cells is divided among the split cells by paragraph marks. The first paragraph is placed in the first cell, the second paragraph in the second cell, and so on.

To split merged cells, follow these steps:

1. Select a cell that was previously merged.
2. Choose Table, Split Cells.

Text that consists of a single paragraph is inserted into a single cell. If the text consists of multiple paragraphs, each paragraph is inserted into its own cell.

Formatting a Table

You can format the text and cells in a table to produce attractive and professional-looking tables. You can format text and paragraphs just as you do in the body text of your document. To make a table more attractive and more readable, you can add borders and shading around the entire table or to selected cells. You also can draw gridlines within the table. To enhance the appearance or make important data stand out, you can use colored borders or shaded or colored backgrounds. In addition, 40 different shades and patterns are available for black-and-white laser printers—an important feature when you want your document to make a good impression.

You can format the contents in the table's cells by using the same procedures that you use to format regular text. To change the font, font size, and font style, choose Format, Font. To adjust the spacing and indentation of cell contents, choose Format, Paragraph. Remember that you can use the shortcut menus to access these formatting commands. Click the right button after you select the cells, columns, or rows that you want to format, and then choose from the shortcut menu the formatting command that you want to use.

▶ **See** "Using Paragraph Formatting Techniques," **p. 85**

To add borders, shading, and color to a table, choose Format, Borders and Shading. You also can add the Tables and Borders toolbar to the screen to access the border and shading options with a mouse click.

▶ **See** "Shading and Bordering Paragraphs," **p. 114**

 TIP To add the Tables and Borders toolbar to your screen, click an existing toolbar with the right mouse button, and choose Tables and Borders from the menu. Repeat these steps to remove the toolbar.

Formatting a Table with Table AutoFormat

Formatting a table to achieve a professional appearance could take you longer than creating and filling the table—unless you use Table AutoFormat. This feature automatically applies predesigned collections of formatting to the table that you select. The formatting includes

Part

IV

Ch

11

borders, shading, fonts, colors, and AutoFit column widths. If you are familiar with Excel's time-saving AutoFormat command, you already know about this feature's usefulness.

To format a table using Table AutoFormat, follow these steps:

1. Move the insertion point inside the table.
2. Choose Table, Table AutoFormat to display the Table AutoFormat dialog box shown in Figure 11.3.

FIG. 11.3

Apply collections of predefined formats by using the Table AutoFormat dialog box.

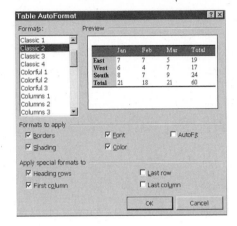

3. Select from the Formats list a predefined format. The Preview box displays an example of the format that you select.
4. If you do not want to lose existing formats in the table, clear the appropriate check box in the Formats to Apply group: Borders, Shading, Font, Color, and AutoFit. The Preview box changes as you select or clear formats.
5. If you want to apply only selected portions of the AutoFormat to your table, select from the Apply Special Formats To check boxes to group the parts of the table that you want to format: Heading Rows, First Column, Last Row, and Last Column.
6. Choose OK.

Selecting Border Formats

With Word, adding borders to a table is easy. You can add borders to individual cells, rows, and columns, or to the entire table. Figure 11.4 shows a table formatted with multiple border styles.

FIG. 11.4

You can format a table with multiple border styles.

	Jan	Feb	Mar	Apr	Jun	May
South	30	27	34	50	29	41
North	42	41	45	60	60	54
East	70	59	70	67	64	63
West	55	54	64	80	80	80

To add borders to all or selected parts of your table, follow these steps:

1. Select the entire table or the cells that you want to shade or border.

2. Choose Format, Borders and Shading, and select the Borders tab in the Borders and Shading dialog box. The Borders tab appears (see Figure 11.5).

FIG. 11.5
Add borders to your table by using the Borders and Shading dialog box.

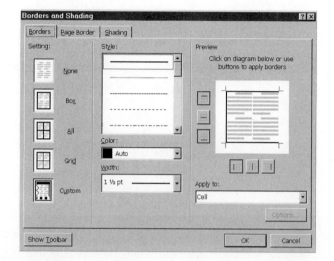

3. Select the line type from the Style box.

4. Select a line color from the Color list.

5. Select the line weight from the Width list.

6. Select one of the border patterns in the Setting group: None, Box, All, or Grid.

7. Choose OK.

If you want to specify custom combinations of border types, weights, and colors, you can select which lines are affected by the Style and Color selections that you make in the Border group.

To specify custom combinations, follow these steps:

1. Select the line type and weight from the Style and Width options as described in the preceding steps.

2. Select the line color from the Color list.

3. Select from the Preview group the line or edge that you want to change. Figure 11.6 shows the border buttons in the Preview group that select the lines to change according to the formatting selections.

   Using the mouse, click the line type shown in the Style box. Click the buttons in the Preview group that correspond to the lines that you want to change.

Part
IV

Ch
11

FIG. 11.6

You can select any combination of individual edges or the interior gridlines to be formatted with borders.

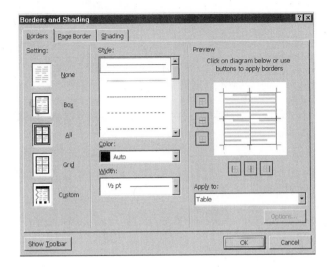

Using the keyboard, press Alt+N to move the focus to the Setting group. Press the up- or down-arrow keys to cycle through combinations of selected lines. Stop on the combination that you want. Press Alt+Y to change the line Style, Alt+C to change the line Color, and Alt+W to change the line Width options until you get the right combination.

4. Watch the sample in the Preview group to see the result of your choices. If you do not like the sample's appearance, choose None from the Presets group and return to step 1.

5. Choose OK.

N O T E The preceding steps show you how to add borders to an entire table or individual cells in a table. You also can add borders to the paragraphs in a cell. Click the Show/Hide button on the Standard toolbar to display paragraph marks, select the paragraph mark for the paragraph to which you want to add borders, and choose Format, Borders, and Shading. You might have to insert a paragraph mark after the text by pressing Enter. ▪

Selecting Shading and Colors

You can enhance a table or selected cells with *shading*. Shading draws attention to a particular section of a table. You also can use it to create reserved areas on office forms.

The selections that you make in the Borders and Shading dialog box can affect the currently selected paragraph, cell or cells, or the entire table.

To add shading to a table, follow these steps:

1. Choose Format, Borders and Shading, and select the Shading tab in the Borders and Shading dialog box. The Shading page appears (see Figure 11.7).

FIG. 11.7

You can add shading and color to a table by using the Shading options.

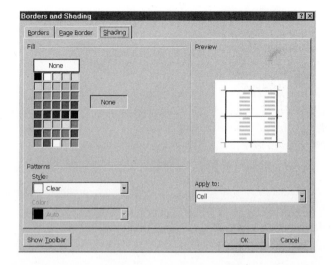

2. In the Fill group, select None to remove shading, or select a shade from the palette.

3. If you choose a shade, select the pattern or percentage of shading from the Style list. Many shades are available.

4. Select a color from the Color list. Select Auto or Black if you are printing to a black-and-white printer.

5. Check the Preview box to see the pattern that you have created. If you like the pattern that you see, choose OK; otherwise, return to step 2 and make other selections.

N O T E When you apply shading, Word shades the background of selected cells. You can control the type of shading by setting the shading percentage. If you want lighter shading, choose a lower shading percentage. A higher percentage applies darker shading. ■

In the Borders and Shading dialog box, experiment with the options by clicking the Shading tab to find the shading pattern that looks best.

Your printer's resolution controls shading patterns. The higher the resolution—measured in *dots per inch* (dpi)—the finer the shading. The resolution at which your printer prints graphics and shading is an option within the Properties dialog box. To access this dialog box, choose File, Print, click the Properties button, and then select the Graphics tab. For more information about this dialog box, access Online help by clicking ?, then clicking the area of interest.

Numbering Rows and Columns

To add numbers to the cells and rows in a table, you can click the Numbering button on the Formatting toolbar or choose Format, Bullets and Numbering. You can add numbers to just the first column in the table, or you can add numbers across rows or down columns in as many cells in the table as you want.

TIP If you frequently use the same collection of formats on a table, learn about styles in Chapter 5, "Using Styles for Repetitive Formats."

Adding Numbers with the Numbering Button

The quickest way to add numbering to a table is to use the Numbering button on the Formatting toolbar. When you use this method, however, you are limited to the numbering style currently selected in the Bullets and Numbering dialog box.

To add numbers to a table using the Numbering button, follow these steps:

1. Select the cells, rows, or columns that you want to number. In most cases, you want a number in the first cell of each row, so select the first column.

2. Click the Numbering button on the Formatting toolbar.

3. Choose OK.

Adding Numbering with the Menu

You can choose Format, Bullets and Numbering to add numbers to a table. When you use this method, you can select from a variety of numbering styles in the Bullets and Numbering dialog box.

To add numbers using the menu, follow these steps:

1. Select the cells, rows, or columns that you want to number.

2. Choose Format, Bullets and Numbering, and select the Numbered tab in the Bullets and Numbering dialog box. The Numbered page appears (see Figure 11.8).

FIG. 11.8

You can select from several numbering styles in the Numbered page of the Bullets and Numbering dialog box.

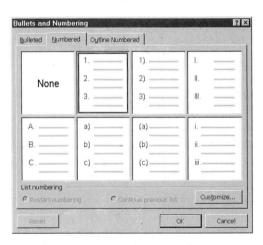

3. Select one of the numbering styles.

4. To modify the predefined style, click the Customize button, and make selections in the Customize Numbered List dialog box to change the format of the numbering.

5. Choose OK.

▶ **See** "Using Bulleted and Numbered Lists," **p. 312**

Splitting a Table

Occasionally, you might want to insert a paragraph or heading between rows in a table. If you start a table at the top of a document and later decide that you need to insert some text before the table, you can do it easily.

To insert text above the table or between rows, follow these steps:

1. Position the insertion point in the row below where you want to insert the text. If you want to enter text above the table, position the insertion point in the first row of the table.

2. Choose Table, Split Table, or press Ctrl+Shift+Enter. A paragraph mark formatted with the Normal style is inserted above the row.

Sorting Tables

Tables often are created to arrange data in columns and rows. You can sort a table that is a database of names and addresses first by the last name, for example, and then within that sort, by the first name. You can sort text, numbers, and dates in either ascending or descending order.

To sort a table, follow these steps:

1. Select the entire table to include all the rows in the sort or select only the rows that you want to sort.

2. Choose Table, Sort. The Sort dialog box appears (see Figure 11.9).

FIG. 11.9
You can sort a table by up to three columns using the Sort dialog box.

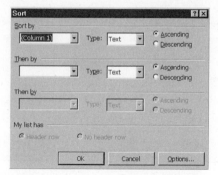

3. Select the first column that you want to sort by in the Sort By list.

4. Select either Text, Number, or Date from the Type list.

5. Select either the Ascending or Descending option.

6. Repeat steps 3 through 5 if you want to sort by additional columns in your table. Make your selections from the Then By lists.

7. If your table has headings that you don't want to include in the search, select the Header Row option in the My List Has group.

8. To make the sort case-sensitive, click the Options button, select the Case Sensitive option, and choose OK.

9. Choose OK.

 TIP Edit, Undo Sort reverses the Sort command if you use it immediately after you sort. You might want to save your document before sorting so that you can return to it if it is sorted incorrectly.

Converting a Table to Text

You can convert a table's cell contents to text separated by commas, tabs, or another single character, or you can convert each cell's contents into one or more paragraphs.

To convert a table to text, follow these steps:

1. Select the rows of the table that you want to convert to text, or select the entire table.

2. Choose Table, Convert Table to Text. The Convert Table to Text dialog box appears.

3. Select a Separate Text With option from the dialog box. You can separate each cell's contents by Paragraph Marks, Tabs, Commas, or Other (Other can be any single character).

4. Choose OK.

Converting Text to a Table

When you copy data from another application or convert a word processing file that does not have tables, your data might be in tabbed columns. To make the data easier to work with, convert the data to Word tables.

To convert text to a table, follow these steps:

1. Select the lines of text or paragraphs that you want to convert to a table.

2. Choose Table, Convert Text to Table. The Convert Text to Table dialog box appears (see Figure 11.10). You also can click the Insert Table button on the Standard toolbar.

   Based on the selected text, Word proposes the number of columns and rows, the width of the columns, and the separator character to use to delineate columns from the text. You can change these settings to suit your own needs.

FIG. 11.10

Use the Convert Text to Table dialog box to separate text at the character that you specify.

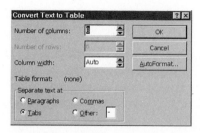

3. Type or select the number of columns in the Number of Columns box to specify a different number of columns.

4. Type or select the number of rows in the Number of Rows box to specify a different number of rows.

5. Type or select an exact column width in the Column Width box if you don't want to use the automatic settings.

6. Select a different separator character if the default character is incorrect.

   Choose one of the following options from the dialog box's Separate Text At group:

Option	Result
Paragraphs	Each paragraph is placed in its own cell.
Tabs	A tab character separates information in a cell. Word converts each paragraph and each line ending in a hard line break (created by pressing Shift+Enter) into a row. The number of columns is determined by the greatest number of tab characters in the paragraphs or lines.
Commas	A comma separates information in a cell. Word for Windows converts each paragraph and each line ending in a hard line break into a row. The number of columns is determined by the greatest number of commas in the paragraphs or lines.
Other	Some other character separates information in a cell. Word converts each paragraph and each line ending in a hard line break into a row. The number of columns is determined by the greatest number of the specified characters in the paragraphs or lines.

7. Choose OK.

CHAPTER 12

Creating Bulleted or Numbered Lists

In this chapter

Using Bulleted and Numbered Lists

A bulleted or numbered list is a special type of list formatted with a *hanging indent*. (A hanging indent occurs when a paragraph's first line goes all the way to the left margin, but all other lines in the paragraph are indented. Chapter 4, "Formatting Lines and Paragraphs," describes hanging indents and other paragraph formatting.) Bulleted lists have a bullet at the left margin; numbered lists have a number and are numbered sequentially. Many writers use bulleted lists to distinguish a series of important items or points from the rest of the text in a document, such as a summary of product features in a sales letter or a list of conclusions reached in a research project. Writers often use numbered lists for step-by-step instructions (as in this book), outlines, or other types of lists in which the specific order of the information is important.

Word 97 provides flexible, easy-to-use methods for creating bulleted or numbered lists with a variety of standardized numbering or bullet formats. You can vary the size of the hanging indent or the space between the numbers or bullets and the following text. You can also create your own custom numbering formats for numbered lists, or you can select characters from any of your installed fonts to use as a bullet in a bulleted list. Word even provides an easy way to remove bullets or numbering (see Figure 12.1).

FIG. 12.1

This figure shows an example of the types of bulleted and numbered lists that you can create.

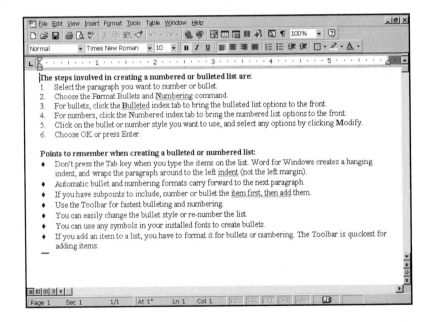

You can type the text for the bulleted or numbered list and then apply the list formatting to the text; alternatively, you can place the insertion point in a blank line, apply the bulleted or numbered list format to that line, and then type the list. Either way, after you select a bulleted or numbered list format, Word sets a 1/4-inch hanging indent and adds the bullets or numbers in front of each paragraph in the selected text, or adds them to each new paragraph that you type.

Like paragraph margin and indent formatting, the bulleted or numbered list format carries forward from paragraph to paragraph. Each time you press Enter to begin a new paragraph, Word adds to the list a new bulleted or numbered paragraph. You can add another bulleted or numbered item anywhere in a list by placing the insertion point where you want to add the new item and then pressing Enter to begin a new paragraph. Word automatically adds a bullet or number sequentially to the beginning of the new paragraph and formats the paragraph with a hanging indent to match the other paragraphs in the bulleted or numbered list. You can also use the AutoFormat feature described in Chapter 5, "Using Styles for Repetitive Formats," to create numbered or bulleted lists automatically.

Creating Bulleted Lists

Word offers seven standard bullet shapes: round, diamond (solid or four small diamonds forming a larger diamond), box (solid or hollow), arrow, and check. If you want to use a heart, pointing hand, or some other symbol as your bullet, Word enables you to select the character for the bullet from any of your installed fonts.

You can create a bulleted list in two ways: with menu commands or with a toolbar shortcut. As usual, you have many more options when you use menu commands.

Creating Bulleted Lists with Menu Commands

To create a bulleted list with menu commands, follow these steps:

1. Type the list at the left margin (without pressing Tab to indent the text) and then select it, or place the insertion point on a blank line.

2. Choose Format, Bullets and Numbering. The Bullets and Numbering dialog box appears (see Figure 12.2).

3. Click the Bulleted tab to display the bulleted list options, if they are not already displayed.

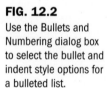

Part
IV

Ch
12

FIG. 12.2
Use the Bullets and Numbering dialog box to select the bullet and indent style options for a bulleted list.

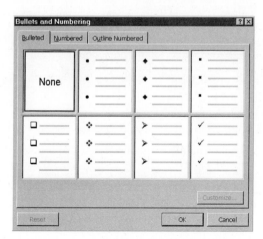

4. Select the bulleted list format that you want from the predefined choices by clicking it with the mouse or using the arrow keys.

   Later in this chapter, the section "Customizing Bulleted Lists" describes how to use the Customize button to customize a bulleted list's formatting.

5. Click OK. Word formats the current line or selected text as a bulleted list.

If you have not yet typed the bulleted list, type it now. Each time you begin a new paragraph, Word formats the paragraph as part of the bulleted list. To end the bulleted list, see "Ending the Bulleted List" later in this chapter.

N O T E You can open the Bullets and Numbering dialog box by placing the pointer over the selected text and then clicking the right mouse button. A context-sensitive menu appears to the right of the insertion point. Choose Bullets and Numbering to display the Bullets and Numbering dialog box.

If you want to replace an existing bulleted list with new bullets or change any of the bulleted list's other formatting properties, select the list, and then follow the instructions in the section "Customizing Bulleted Lists" later in this chapter. If you want to replace bullets with numbers, see the section "Creating Numbered Lists" later in this chapter for instructions on creating a numbered list. Word does not ask you to confirm that you want to replace bullets with numbers. If you inadvertently change a bulleted list to a numbered list, use the Edit, Undo Number Default command.

To add bulleted items anywhere in a bulleted list, position the insertion point where you want to add the new bulleted item, and press Enter to add a new paragraph to the list. Word automatically formats the new paragraph as part of the bulleted list.

Creating Bulleted Lists with the Toolbar

With the Formatting toolbar, you can easily set up a bulleted list by clicking the Bullets button (near the right side of the Formatting toolbar). When you create a bulleted list with the Bullets button, Word uses the bulleted list formatting options selected most recently in the Bullets and Numbering dialog box.

To create a bulleted list with the toolbar, follow these steps:

1. Choose View, Toolbars and select Formatting, if the Formatting toolbar is not already displayed.

2. Type the list at the left margin and select it, or place the text insertion point in a blank line.

3. Choose the Bullets button on the Formatting toolbar. Word formats the current line or selected text as a bulleted list.

If you have not yet typed the bulleted list, type it now. Word formats each new paragraph as part of the bulleted list. The next section explains how to end the bulleted list.

By default, Word uses a small, round bullet and a 1/4-inch hanging indent to format lists that you create with the Formatting toolbar's Bullets button. If you recently selected different options in the Bullets and Numbering dialog box, however, Word uses those selections instead.

Ending the Bulleted List

If you apply bulleted list formatting to a blank line and then type the list, Word continues formatting each new paragraph you type as part of the bulleted list, until you end the bulleted list.

To end a bulleted list, follow these steps:

1. Press Enter to add a bulleted, blank line to the end of the bulleted list.
2. Move the pointer over the blank line and click the right mouse button. Word moves the insertion point to that line and displays a context-sensitive menu to the right of the insertion point.
3. Choose Bullets and Numbering. The Bullets and Numbering dialog box appears.
4. Double-click the None selection to end the bulleted list. Word removes the bullet and hanging indent from the blank line, ending the bulleted list.

Adding Subordinate Paragraphs to a Bulleted List

Sometimes you cannot adequately or gracefully discuss the topic of a bulleted list item within a single paragraph. Usually, if you require more than one paragraph to describe a single topic in a bulleted list, you want only the first paragraph for that topic to have a bullet. The remaining subordinate paragraphs for that topic do not need bullets, although they must have the same hanging indent as the list's bulleted paragraphs.

Whether you are changing an existing bulleted paragraph to a subordinate paragraph or typing the bulleted list as you go along, you can change a bulleted paragraph into a subordinate paragraph by using either a context-sensitive shortcut menu or the Formatting toolbar.

Adding a Subordinate Paragraph with the Menu To change a bulleted list item to a subordinate paragraph, follow these steps:

1. Select the bulleted list items from which you want to remove the bullets.
2. Move the pointer over the selected text, and click the right mouse button. Word moves the insertion point to that line and displays a context-sensitive menu to the right of the insertion point.
3. Choose Bullets and Numbering. The Bullets and Numbering dialog box appears.
4. Double-click the None selection. Word removes the bullet from the selected paragraphs.
5. Choose the Increase Indent button from the Formatting toolbar.

If you added a subordinate paragraph at the end of a bulleted list and you want to add another bulleted list item after the subordinate paragraph, choose the Bullets button from the Formatting toolbar to resume the bulleted list format.

Adding a Subordinate Paragraph with the Toolbar   To use the Formatting toolbar to change a bulleted list item to a subordinate paragraph in the list, follow these steps:

1. Select the bulleted list items from which you want to remove the bullets.

2. Choose the Bullets button from the Formatting toolbar. Word removes the bullet from the selected paragraphs.

3. Choose the Increase Indent button from the Formatting toolbar.

Use the Bullets button to resume formatting the bulleted list on the next line.

Customizing Bulleted Lists

To customize an existing bulleted list or to make your own specifications for the formatting of a new bulleted list, choose the Customize button from the Bullets and Numbering dialog box. Customize enables you to choose a character from any of your installed fonts to use as a bullet, to specify the bullet's point size and color, and to choose from a list of special effects. You can also specify the size of the hanging indent, and how much space appears between the bullet character and the text in the bulleted item.

The only way to customize a bulleted list format is to use menu commands; no toolbar shortcut exists. If your custom bulleted list format is the most recently applied format, however, the Bullets button on the Formatting toolbar applies your custom format.

To create a custom bulleted list format, follow these steps:

1. Select the bulleted list that you want to customize.

2. Choose Format, Bullets and Numbering. The Bullets and Numbering dialog box appears.

3. Choose the Bulleted tab to display the bulleted list options, if that tab is not already up front.

4. Choose the Customize button. The Customize Bulleted List dialog box appears (see Figure 12.3).

5. In the Bullet Character group, select the character that you want to use as a bullet by clicking it or by using the arrow keys.

   The section "Selecting Custom Bullet Character Effects" describes how to use the Font button to select custom bullet character effects.

   The section "Selecting a Custom Bullet Character" describes how to use the Bullet button to select a custom bullet character.

6. Choose any of the following options:

Option	Function
Bullet Position	Choose the bullet's alignment within the space used for the indent. Word offers you the choice of left-aligned, right-aligned, centered, or justified.
Text Position	Type or select a number to set the distance in the bulleted paragraph between the bullet and the text.

FIG. 12.3

The Customize Bulleted List dialog box enables you to select custom bullet characters, colors, and point sizes for the bullet, and to choose the bullet character's alignment with the text.

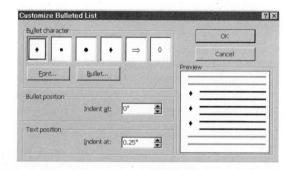

7. Click OK. The Customize Bulleted List dialog box closes, and you are returned immediately to the document.

> **CAUTION**
>
> If you customize or reformat an existing bulleted list that contains subordinate (unbulleted) paragraphs, Word adds bullets to the subordinate paragraphs.

Selecting Custom Bullet Character Effects   Word enables you to customize a selected bullet character by adding a special effect, changing character spacing, or by animating the bullet character.

To select custom font effects, follow these steps:

1. Choose the Font button in the Customize Bulleted List dialog box. Word displays the Font dialog box (see Figure 12.4).

FIG. 12.4

The Font dialog box enables you to choose a different font and add special effects.

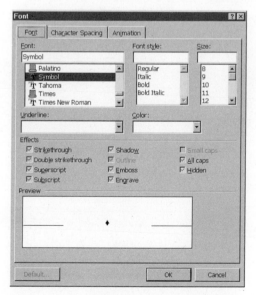

2. Choose any of the following options:

Option	Function
Font	Choose the bullet's font from any of your installed fonts.
Font Style	Choose from Regular, Italic, Bold, or Bold Italic font styles. Notice that the items listed in the Font style list may vary depending on the styles available for the particular font.
Size	Choose the font size.
Underline	Underline the bullet character. Choose from Single, Words only, Double, Dotted, Thick, Dash, Dot Dash, Dot Dot Dash, or Wave.
Color	Choose the bullet's color. Select Auto to have Word for Windows automatically select the color.
Effects	Enhance the bullet by choosing a special effect. Choose from Strikethrough, Double Strikethrough, Superscript, Subscript, Shadow, Outline, Emboss, Engrave, All Caps, or Hidden.

3. Click OK. Word closes the Font dialog box and displays your bullet character in the Bullet character and Preview group of the Customize Bulleted List dialog box.

To select custom character spacing, follow these steps:

1. Choose the Character Spacing tab in the Font dialog box (see Figure 12.5).

FIG. 12.5

The Character Spacing tab enables you to change the bullet's scale, spacing, position, and kerning.

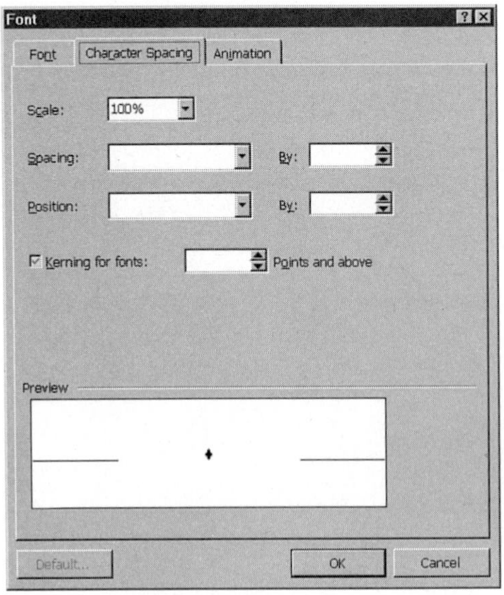

2. Choose any of the following options:

Option	Function
Scale	Stretches or compresses text horizontally by the percentage you choose.
Spacing	Choose Normal, Expanded, or Condensed spacing between characters and specify the amount.
Position	Raises or lowers the bullet character by the amount you specify.
Kerning for Fonts	Adjusts kerning automatically for the font size specified and larger.

3. Click OK. Word closes the Font dialog box and displays your bullet character in the Bullet character and Preview group of the Customize Bulleted List dialog box.

To select animation, follow these steps:

1. Choose the Animation tab in the Font dialog box (see Figure 12.6).

FIG. 12.6

The Animation tab enables you to add predefined animated text effects.

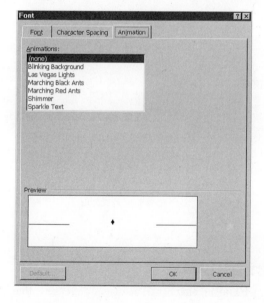

2. Choose an animated text effect from the Animations list box. Choose from Blinking Background, Las Vegas Lights, Marching Black Ants, Marching Red Ants, Shimmer, or Sparkle Text.

3. Click OK. Word closes the Font dialog box and displays your bullet character in the Bullet character and Preview group of the Customize Bulleted List dialog box.

Animated text effects are useful for on-line documentation.

Selecting a Custom Bullet Character Word enables you to select any character from any of your installed fonts to use as the bullet character in a bulleted list.

To select a custom bullet character, follow these steps:

1. Choose the Bullet button in the Customize Bulleted List dialog box. Word displays the Symbol dialog box (see Figure 12.7).

FIG. 12.7

The Symbol dialog box enables you to choose a bullet character from any installed font.

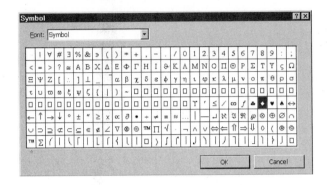

2. Select from the Font list box the font that the Symbol dialog box displays. Select the bullet character that you want from the Symbol dialog box by clicking the character or by using the arrow keys.

3. Select from the Subset list box the character subset you want to jump to in the symbol grid. The subset list is unavailable if the currently selected font does not contain subcategories.

4. Click OK. Word closes the Symbol dialog box and displays your selected bullet character in the Bullet character and Preview group of the Customize Bulleted List dialog box.

 A modified bullet character is not applied to any new lists you create.

Creating Numbered Lists

Numbered lists are much like bulleted lists. The main difference is that a numbered list is numbered sequentially instead of bulleted. If you add a paragraph in the middle of a numbered list or rearrange the order of paragraphs in a numbered list, Word automatically renumbers all the paragraphs in the list so that they retain their sequential numbering.

▶ **See** "Formatting a Document Automatically," **p. 129**

Word offers six standard numbering formats and enables you to customize them. Word also offers a special type of numbered list, called an *outline numbered list*. In an outline numbered list, you can number each successive indentation level in the list. Later in this chapter, the section "Creating Outline Lists" describes outline numbered lists.

You can create a numbered list in two ways: with menu commands or with a toolbar shortcut. As usual, the menu commands offer you many more options.

Creating Numbered Lists with Menu Commands

To create a numbered list with menu commands, follow these steps:

1. Type your list and then select it (don't use the Tab key to indent the items on your list). Or, place the text insertion point on a blank line.

2. Choose Format, Bullets and Numbering. The Bullets and Numbering dialog box appears (refer to Figure 12.2).

3. Choose the Numbered tab to display the numbered list options if they are not already displayed (see Figure 12.8).

FIG. 12.8

Use the Bullets and Numbering dialog box to select the numbered list format.

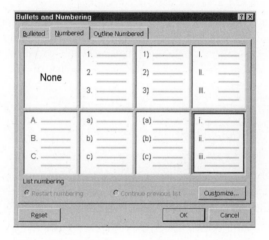

4. Select from the predefined choices the numbering style that you want. Your choices include Arabic numbers, Roman numerals, and letters with either periods or parentheses to separate the numbers from the list text.

    The section "Customizing Numbered Lists" describes how to use the Customize button to customize a numbered list.

5. Click OK. Word formats the selected text or line as a numbered list.

If you have not yet typed the numbered list, type it now. Each time that you begin a new paragraph, Word formats the paragraph as part of the numbered list. The section "Ending the Numbered List," later in this chapter, describes how to end the numbered list.

TIP You can open the Bullets and Numbering dialog box by placing the pointer over the selected text and clicking the right mouse button. A context-sensitive menu appears to the right of the insertion point; choose Bullets and Numbering to display the Bullets and Numbering dialog box.

Part

IV

Ch

12

If you want to replace an existing numbered list with new numbers or change any of the other formatting properties of the numbered list, select the list and then follow the instructions in the section "Customizing Numbered Lists," later in this chapter. If you want to replace numbers with bullets, select the list and see the previous section "Creating Bulleted Lists" for instructions on creating a bulleted list. Word does not ask you to confirm whether you want to replace numbers with bullets. If you inadvertently convert a numbered list to a bulleted list, choose Edit, Undo Bullet Default immediately after the conversion.

To add numbered items anywhere in a numbered list, position the insertion point where you want to add the numbered item, and simply press Enter to add a new paragraph to the list. Word automatically formats the new paragraph as part of the numbered list and renumbers the list's paragraphs so that all the numbers remain sequential.

Creating Numbered Lists with the Toolbar

A quicker way to number a list is to use the Numbering button on the Formatting toolbar. The Numbering button appears near the right side of the Formatting toolbar. When you create a numbered list with the Numbering button, Word uses the numbered list formatting options selected most recently in the Bullets and Numbering dialog box. You can change the numbered list formatting options by choosing Format, Bullets and Numbering.

To create a numbered list with the toolbar, follow these steps:

1. Choose View, Toolbars, and select Formatting. Word displays the Formatting toolbar, if it is not already displayed.

2. At the left margin, type the list and then select it, or place the text insertion point on a blank line.

3. Click the Numbering button on the Formatting toolbar. Word formats the current line or selected text as a numbered list.

If you have not yet typed the numbered list, type it now. Word formats each new paragraph as part of the numbered list. The next section, "Ending the Numbered List," explains how to end the numbered list.

By default, Word uses Arabic numbers and a 1/4-inch hanging indent to format lists with the Formatting toolbar's Numbering button. If you recently selected different options in the Bullets and Numbering dialog box, however, Word uses those selections instead.

Ending the Numbered List

As with bulleted lists, if you apply numbered list formatting to a blank line and then type the list, Word continues formatting each new paragraph that you type as part of the numbered list, until you end the numbered list.

To end a numbered list, follow these steps:

1. Press Enter to add a numbered, blank line to the end of the numbered list.

2. Move the pointer over the blank line, and click the right mouse button. Word moves the insertion point to that line and displays a context-sensitive menu to the right of the insertion point.

3. Choose Bullets and <u>N</u>umbering. The Bullets and Numbering dialog box appears.

4. Double-click the None selection to end the numbered list. Word removes the number and hanging indent from the blank line, ending the numbered list.

Adding Subordinate Paragraphs to a Numbered List

As with bulleted lists, sometimes the topic of a numbered list item requires more than one paragraph. And, as with bulleted lists, you probably want to number only the first of several paragraphs for the same numbered list item.

You can change a numbered paragraph into a subordinate paragraph by using either a context-sensitive shortcut menu or the Formatting toolbar.

Adding a Subordinate Paragraph with the Menu   To use the shortcut menu to change a numbered list item to a subordinate paragraph, follow these steps:

1. Select the numbered list items from which you want to remove the numbers.

2. Move the pointer over the selected text, and click the right mouse button. Word moves the insertion point to that line and displays a context-sensitive menu to the right of the insertion point.

3. Choose Bullets and <u>N</u>umbering. The Bullets and Numbering dialog box appears.

4. Double-click the None selection. Word removes the number from the selected paragraphs.

5. Choose the Increase Indent button from the Formatting toolbar.

If you add a subordinate paragraph at the end of a numbered list and then want to add another numbered list item after the subordinate paragraph, choose the Numbering button from the Formatting toolbar to resume the numbered list format.

Adding a Subordinate Paragraph with the Toolbar   To use the toolbar to change a numbered list item to a subordinate paragraph in the list, follow these steps:

1. Select the numbered list items from which you want to remove the numbers.

2. Choose the Numbering button from the Formatting toolbar. Word removes the number from the selected paragraphs.

3. Choose the Increase Indent button from the Formatting toolbar.

Customizing Numbered Lists

To customize an existing numbered list or to make your own specifications for the number format, choose the Customize button from the Bullets and Numbering dialog box. Customize enables you to specify the text that comes before and after the number, to specify the numbering style, and to choose the font for the numbers. In addition, you can specify the size of the

Part

IV

Ch

12

hanging indent, how much space appears between the bullet character and the text in the bulleted item, and whether the number is right-, left-, or center-aligned within the indent space.

The only way to customize a numbered list format is with the menu commands; no toolbar shortcut exists for altering the format of a numbered list. If your custom numbered-list format is the most recently specified format, however, the Formatting toolbar's Numbering button applies your custom format.

To create a custom numbered-list format, follow these steps:

1. Select the numbered list whose format you want to customize.

2. Choose Format, Bullets and Numbering. The Bullets and Numbering dialog box appears (refer to Figure 12.2).

3. Click the Numbered tab to display the numbered list options, if they are not already displayed.

4. Choose the Customize button. The Customize Numbered List dialog box appears (see Figure 12.9).

FIG. 12.9

Use the Customize Numbered List dialog box to select the format of the number, starting number of the list, the number style, and the number's alignment.

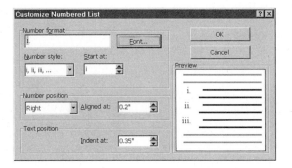

5. Choose any combination of the following numbered list options:

Option	Function
Number Format	Select the Font button to choose from fonts installed on your computer, font attributes, point size, spacing, and add special formatting effects. You can also type text in the edit box to further customize the appearance of the numbering.
Number Style	Select the numbering style that you want. Available choices include Arabic numerals, upper- and lowercase Roman numerals, upper- and lowercase alphabet letters, and word series (1st, One, and First). You can also choose no numbers at all.
Start At	Type the starting number for your list. (If you're creating a series of lists, the starting number can be a number other than 1.)
Number Position	Select the alignment of the number within the space used for the indent. Word offers you the choice of left-aligned, right-aligned, or centered.

Option	Function
Aligned At	Type a number to set the size of the hanging indent.
Text Position	Type a number to set the amount of space between the number and the text in the numbered paragraph.

6. Click OK in the Customize Numbered List dialog box.

> **CAUTION**
>
> If you customize or reformat an existing numbered list that contains subordinate (unnumbered) paragraphs, Word adds numbers to the subordinate paragraphs.

Creating Outline Lists

Outline lists are similar to numbered and bulleted lists, but number or bullet each paragraph in the list according to its indentation level. In outline lists, you can mix numbered and bulleted paragraphs based on indentation level.

▶ **See** "Formatting a Document Automatically," **p. 129**

You can create outline lists with as many as nine levels. You might use an outline list format if you want your list to have numbered items that contain indented, bulleted subparagraphs. Many types of technical or legal documents require that you sequentially number each paragraph and indentation level. You can also use outline lists to create outlines of various types.

Don't confuse outline lists, however, with the outline view and outlining features described in Chapter 13, "Organizing Content with an Outline," or with the heading numbering discussed later in this chapter. In the outline view and heading numbering, only paragraphs that have one of the nine heading styles are numbered. In an outline list, only paragraphs that have a body text style (such as Normal) can be part of the list.

You can create an outline list only by using the menu commands; no toolbar shortcut exists. Although you can customize the numbering formats for the various indentation levels of an outline list, you cannot use more than one outline list format in the same document.

To create an outline list, follow these steps:

1. Type and select your list. Use paragraph indenting to indent text by choosing Format, Paragraph; don't use the Tab key. Alternatively, place the text insertion point on a blank line.

2. Choose Format, Bullets and Numbering. The Bullets and Numbering dialog box appears.

3. Click the Outline Numbered tab to display the multilevel list options, if the options are not already displayed (see Figure 12.10).

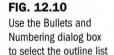

FIG. 12.10

Use the Bullets and Numbering dialog box to select the outline list format that you want.

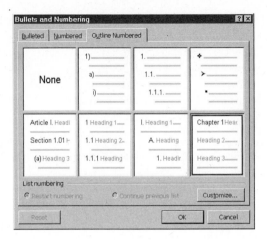

4. Select from the predefined choices the outline numbering style that you want. Your choices include combinations of numbered and lettered paragraphs, and technical and legal numbering styles.

   The section "Customizing Outline Lists," describes how to use the Customize button to customize an outline numbered list.

5. Click OK. Word formats the selected text or line as an outline list.

If you have not yet typed the outline list, type it now. Each time that you begin a new paragraph, Word formats the paragraph as part of the outline list and applies the appropriate numbering for that level of indentation. Use the Formatting toolbar's Increase Indent and Decrease Indent buttons (or the shortcuts Shift+Alt+right arrow and Shift+Alt+left arrow) to set the indentation level of each paragraph in the list. Word automatically adjusts the numbering to accommodate the paragraph's new level of indentation.

Ending an outline list is the same as ending a regular numbered list. For more detailed information, follow the instructions given in the previous section, "Ending a Numbered List." You can also add unnumbered subordinate paragraphs to an outline list the same way that you would for a numbered list.

Making Changes to an Outline List

If you want to replace an existing outline list with new numbers or change any of the other formatting properties of the outline list, select the list and follow the instructions in the next section, "Customizing Outline Lists." If you want to replace an outline list with a numbered or bulleted list, select the list and see the previous sections "Creating a Bulleted List" or "Creating a Numbered List" for instructions on creating a bulleted or numbered list. Word does not ask you to confirm whether you want to replace an outline list with a bulleted or numbered list format. If you inadvertently convert an outline list, choose Edit, Undo immediately after the conversion.

To add a new item to the outline list at any indentation level, position the insertion point where you want to add the item, and press Enter to add a new paragraph to the list. Choose Format, Paragraph to indent the paragraph to the desired level. Word automatically formats the new paragraph as part of the outline list and renumbers the paragraphs in the list so that all the numbers remain sequential.

Customizing Outline Lists

Customizing an outline list format is similar to customizing a numbered or bulleted list. To customize an outline list format, you can only use the menu commands.

To create a custom outline list format, follow these steps:

1. Select the outline list for which you want to customize the format.

2. Choose Format, Bullets and Numbering. The Bullets and Numbering dialog box appears (refer to Figure 12.8).

3. Click the Outline Numbered tab to display the outline list options, if they are not already displayed.

4. Choose the Customize button. The Customize Outline Numbered List dialog box appears (see Figure 12.11).

FIG. 12.11

Use the Customize Outline Numbered List dialog box to customize the numbering or bullet styles, alignment, and indentation levels of an outline list.

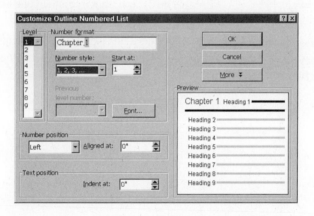

Part
IV

Ch
12

5. Choose the More button to display more options (see Figure 12.12).

6. Use the Level list box to select the indentation level for which you want to adjust the formatting. You must customize each indentation level separately.

7. For each indentation level that you customize, set the following options in any combination:

Option	Function
Number Format	Select the Font button to choose any special font or font attributes (such as bold, italic, and underline), set the point size, spacing, or add special effects and animation for the numbers or bullets used at this indentation level.

continues

continued

Option	Function
Number Style	Select the numbering or bullet style that you want. Available choices include a combination of the numbering choices available for numbered lists and the bullet choices available for bulleted lists, or no number or bullet at all.
Start At	Type the starting number for paragraphs at the selected level of indentation.
Number Position	Select the alignment of the number or bullet within the space used for the indent. Word offers you the choice of left-aligned, right-aligned, or centered.
Aligned At	Type a number to set the size of the hanging indent.
Text Position	Type a number to set the amount of space between the number or bullet and the text in the numbered paragraph.
Link Level To Style	Link the currently selected level to a specific style.
Follow Number With	Select a Tab character or Space to follow each number or bullet at this indentation level.
ListNum Field List Name	Use this field if you want more than one number on a single line.
Legal Style Numbering	Select this check box to use legal style numbering.
Restart Numbering After Higher	Select this check box to restart number-List Leveling when this list level follows a higher list level.

8. Click OK in the Customize Outline Numbered List dialog box.

FIG. 12.12

The dialog box expands to show more options if you click More in step 5.

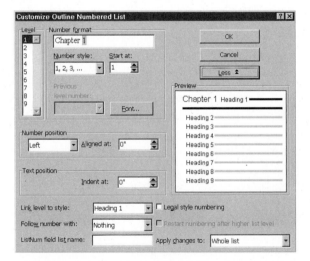

Splitting a Numbered or Bulleted List

You might occasionally want to divide a long numbered or bulleted list into two or more smaller lists. To split a list, follow these steps:

1. Place the insertion point at the place where you want to divide the list.
2. Press Enter to insert a blank line.
3. Remove the bullet or numbering from the blank line by placing the insertion point on the blank line, choosing Format, Bullets and Numbering.
4. Place the insertion point on the bulleted or numbered item following the blank line, and then select the Restart numbering option.

   If you want to rejoin the lists, choose Format, Bullets and Numbering, then select the Continue previous list option.

If you split a numbered or outline list, Word renumbers the list so that both lists start with the starting number (specified in the Customize Numbered List dialog box) and are numbered sequentially.

Removing Bullets or Numbering

You can remove bullets or numbering from a list by using either a menu command or the Formatting toolbar's Numbering and Bullets buttons.

To remove bulleted, numbered, or outline list formatting by using a menu command, follow these steps:

1. Select the list from which you want to remove bullets or numbering.
2. Choose Format, Bullets and Numbering.
3. Double-click the None selection.

To remove list formatting by using the toolbar, do one of the following:

- To remove list formatting from a bulleted list, select the list and click the Bullets button on the Formatting toolbar.
- To remove list formatting from a numbered or outline list, select the list, and click the Numbering button on the Formatting toolbar.

Part IV Ch 12

Creating Numbered Headings

When you number headings, Word looks for different heading styles to determine how to number each heading paragraph. Paragraphs formatted with the heading 1 style, for example, are numbered with the first outline level (I., II., III.); paragraphs with the heading 2 style are numbered with the second level (A., B., C.), and so on. Word provides seven predefined outline numbering formats for these different levels and enables you to establish your own custom numbering formats.

▶ **See** "Numbering an Outline," **p. 344**

Only paragraphs with heading styles are numbered. You can apply heading styles by promoting or demoting the paragraphs in the outline view or by applying the appropriate heading styles. When you delete or rearrange numbered headings, Word automatically renumbers them. You can have only one heading numbering format in your document, although you can set the heading numbering so that numbering starts over at the beginning of each new document section. You can also choose to have headings appear with bullets rather than numbers.

To number headings, follow these steps:

1. Choose Format, Bullets and Numbering. The Bullets and Numbering dialog box appears (see Figure 12.13).

FIG. 12.13
Use the Bullets and Numbering dialog box to choose the numbering or bulleting style for headings.

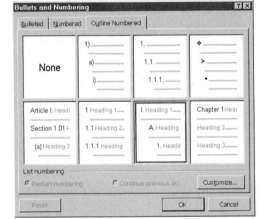

2. Select the Outline Numbered tab.
3. Select from the predefined choices the heading numbering style that you want.

    The next section, "Customizing Numbered Headings," describes how to use the Customize button to customize heading numbering.

4. Click OK.

Word applies your selected numbering format to all paragraphs in your document with a heading style.

Customizing Numbered Headings

To specify your own heading number format, use the Customize option from the Bullets and Numbering dialog box.

The only way to customize heading numbering is with the menu commands; no toolbar shortcut exists.

To create a custom heading number format, follow these steps:

1. Choose F<u>o</u>rmat, Bullets and <u>N</u>umbering. The Bullets and Numbering dialog box appears (refer to Figure 12.13).

2. Choose the O<u>u</u>tline Numbered tab.

3. Select a numbering style.

4. Choose the Cus<u>t</u>omize button, then choose the <u>M</u>ore button. The Customize Outline Numbered List dialog box appears (see Figure 12.14).

FIG. 12.14

By selecting options in the Customize Outline Numbered List dialog box, you can vary the appearance of your heading number formats.

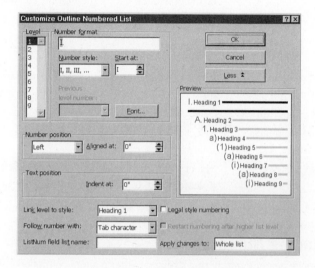

5. In the Le<u>v</u>el list box, select the heading level for which you want to adjust the formatting. You must customize each heading level separately.

6. Choose or set any of the following options, in any combination:

Option	Function
Number F<u>o</u>rmat	Select the <u>F</u>ont button to choose any special font or font attributes (such as bold, italic, and underline); set the point size, spacing, or add special effects and animation for the numbers or bullets used at this indentation level.
<u>N</u>umber Style	Select the numbering or bullet style that you want. Available options include a combination of the numbering choices available for numbered lists and the bullet choices available for bulleted lists, or no number or bullet at all.
<u>S</u>tart At	Type the starting number for paragraphs at the selected level of indentation.

continues

continued

Option	Function
Number Position	Select the alignment of the number or bullet within the space used for the indent. Word offers you the choice of left-aligned, right-aligned, or centered.
Aligned At	Type a number to set the size of the hanging indent.
Text Position	Type a number to set the amount of space between the number or bullet and the text in the numbered paragraph.
Link Level To Style	Link the currently selected level to a specific style.
Follow Number With	Select a Tab character or Space to follow each number or bullet at this indentation level.
ListNum Field List Name	Use this field if you want more than one number on a single line.
Legal Style Numbering	Select this check box to use legal style numbering.
Restart Numbering After Higher List Level	Select this check box to restart numbering when this list level follows a higher list level.
Apply Changes To	Select whether to apply changes to the Whole list, from This point forward, to Selected text, or to the Current Paragraph.

7. Click OK to close the Customize Outline Numbered List dialog box.

Removing Heading Numbers

You can remove heading numbering by using either a menu command or the Formatting toolbar's Numbering and Bullets buttons.

To remove heading numbers by using a menu command, follow these steps:

1. Select the heading from which you want to remove numbering.

2. Choose Format, Bullets and Numbering.

3. Double-click the None selection.

To remove heading numbers by using the toolbar, select the heading and click the Numbering button on the Formatting toolbar.

Organizing Content with an Outline

Using Outlines

In Word 97, an *outline* is a special view of your document that consists of formatted headings and body text. Nine possible outline heading levels are available. Each heading level can have one level of body text. Assigning each heading level a different formatting style enables you and the reader to discern your document's organization quickly.

Having an outline for your document is useful in many ways. For example, an outline can help you organize your thoughts as you compose a new document. At a glance, you can quickly see an overview of your document that shows only the headings. Later, an outline can help you reorganize and edit your document. By "collapsing" parts of your document so that only the headings show, you can easily move an entire section—heading, subheadings, and any associated body text. But Word for Windows has some other not-so-obvious uses for outlines: You can easily number the parts of a document, change heading-level formatting (each heading level has its own specific style), and use headings to generate tables of contents and other lists.

This chapter helps you maintain your documents and manage changes made within a workgroup.

Viewing an Outline

To view an outline, choose View, Outline, or click the Outline View button at the left of the horizontal scroll bar. Figure 13.1 shows the first page of a document in the normal editing view, and Figure 13.2 shows the same document in Outline view with headings displayed. Figure 13.3 shows the document in an expanded outline view, with text and subheadings displayed.

FIG. 13.1
A document in normal view that does not show outline headings.

Outline view

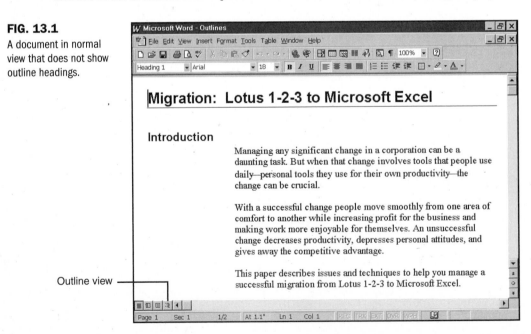

FIG. 13.2
The Outline view shows an overview of contents (headings only).

Outline toolbar—

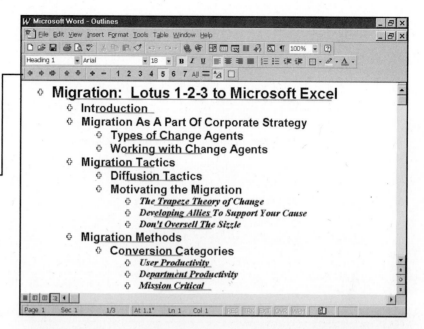

FIG. 13.3
The Outline view showing detailed contents by expanding the outline.

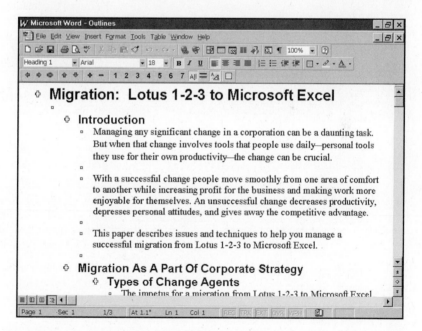

As you can see, Outline view looks different from the normal editing view in several ways. First, the *Outline toolbar* replaces the ruler. Second, Word indents the formatted headings and body text paragraphs to different levels. Third, a + or – icon appears to the left of each heading and paragraph. A plus sign (+) means that subordinate headings (those at a level lower than the heading being examined) or paragraphs of body text are associated with the heading. A minus sign (–) indicates that no headings or paragraphs are beneath the heading.

When you are in Outline view, you have the option of either viewing headings at different levels or viewing the entire document, including all body text. By viewing only the headings of a large document, you can see an overview of your document. You can also see where you have missed or misplaced topics. See the section "Collapsing and Expanding an Outline," later in this chapter, to learn how to change the view of an outline.

The Outline toolbar includes buttons you can use to assign heading levels to text, promote or demote headings, and hide or display headings. Table 13.1 summarizes the functions of the Outline toolbar's buttons.

Table 13.1 The Functions of the Outline Toolbar's Buttons

Icon	Button	Function
	Promote	Promotes the heading by one level, and promotes body text to the heading level of the preceding heading.
	Demote	Demotes the heading by one level, and demotes body text to the heading level below the preceding heading.
	Demote to Body Text	Demotes the heading to body text.
	Move Up	Moves the selected paragraphs before the first visible paragraph that precedes selected paragraphs.
	Move Down	Moves the selected paragraphs after the first visible paragraph that follows selected paragraphs.
	Expand	Expands the first heading level below the currently selected heading; repeated clicks expand through additional heading levels until the body expands.
	Collapse	Collapses body text into headings and then collapses lowest heading levels into higher heading levels.

Icon	Button	Function
1 ↓	Show Heading 1 ↓ Show Heading 7	Displays all headings and text through the lowest level number that you click.
All	Show All Headings	Displays all text if some is collapsed, and displays only headings if all text is already expanded.
=	Show First Line Only	Toggles between displaying all the body text or only the first line of each paragraph.
ᴬA̲	Show Formatting	Toggles between displaying the outline with or without full character formatting.
▢	Master Document View	Changes to Master Document view or back to simple Outline view. If Master Document view is selected, the Master Document toolbar appears.

The next sections teach you how to use these buttons to create and reorganize your outline.

Creating an Outline

Creating an outline does two things: It organizes your work by heading, subheading, and body text, and applies formatting to each heading level. Styles define the formatting applied to each heading level. The style Heading 1 formats the first level of heading, Heading 2 formats the second level, and so on, through Heading 7. The Normal style formats body text. Word has predefined the Heading and Normal styles; however, you can redefine any of those styles by choosing Format, Style.

Word provides two ways to create an outline. The first method is to select the Outline view and then use the Outline toolbar's buttons to assign heading levels to your text (while creating or after creating the document). This chapter describes this method. The second method is to work in Normal view (or Draft or Page Layout view) of your document and assign appropriate styles, such as Heading 1 or Heading 2, to the headings in the document. To learn how to apply styles to text, see Chapter 5, "Using Styles for Repetitive Formats."

Part
IV

Ch

13

To create an outline in a new or existing document, follow these steps:

1. Choose View, Outline.

2. Type a heading or select the text that you want to convert to a heading. Select the heading by moving the insertion point anywhere within the heading's text, or by clicking to the left of the heading (but not clicking the + or – icon).

   If you're creating an outline from scratch (in a new file), Word applies the level 1 heading (Heading 1) as you begin typing.

3. Assign the appropriate heading level by clicking one of the following icons on the Outline toolbar, by clicking the Outline toolbar's arrow buttons with the mouse, or by pressing one of the following shortcut keys:

Icon	Mouse Action	Shortcut Key	Result
⬅	Click the left-arrow button	Press Alt+Shift+ left arrow	Promotes the heading one level
➡	Click the right-arrow button	Press Alt+Shift+ right arrow	Demotes the heading one level
⇥	Click the double-arrow button		Demotes the heading to body text
⬆ ⬇	Click the up- or down-arrow	Press Alt+Shift+ up- or down-arrow	Moves line up or down

4. Press Enter to end the heading (or body text) and start a new heading (or paragraph) at the same level.

N O T E As you work in your document in Normal or Page Layout view, you might reach text that should be a heading in the outline. You can stay in Normal or Page Layout view and create this heading. One way is to format the paragraph with a heading style. Another method is to move the insertion point into the text you want to make into a heading and press Alt+Shift+←. The paragraph containing the insertion point is formatted to the same heading level as the preceding outline heading in the document. Press Alt+Shift+← or Alt+Shift+→ to adjust the heading to the level that you want. ◼

Formatting Your Outline

When you create an outline, you apply styles to the headings in your document. The styles determine your document's formatting. Unless you redefine Heading 1 for your document, for example, the style applies the Arial font in 14-point size, boldface, with extra space before and after the heading.

If you want to format your document's headings differently than the predefined heading styles, you must redefine the heading styles. If you want to format your outline's Level 1 headings differently, for example, you must redefine the Heading 1 style.

▶ **See** "Redefining Standard Styles," **p. 142**

Promoting and Demoting Headings

When you *promote* a heading, you raise its level in the outline. You can promote a Heading 3 to a Heading 2, for example, to make the indent smaller. *Demoting* does just the opposite. When you promote and demote headings, Word for Windows assigns the appropriate heading style for that level.

Using the Mouse to Promote or Demote Headings

You can use the mouse to promote or demote headings in two ways. One method uses the buttons in the Outline toolbar. By using this technique, you promote or demote only the selected heading. In the other method, you drag the heading's + or – icon left or right until the heading is at the level you want; with this technique, you promote or demote the heading and all subordinate text.

If you want to use the mouse to promote or demote only the selected headings or text, follow these steps:

1. Choose View, Outline (if you haven't already).
2. Select the paragraphs to promote or demote.
3. To promote the heading, click the Promote button (the left-arrow button) on the Outline toolbar.

   To demote the heading, click the Demote button (the right-arrow button) on the Outline toolbar.

   To convert the heading to body text, click the Demote to Body Text button (a double-arrow button) on the Outline toolbar.

Word for Windows treats headings independently, and thus does not promote or demote associated subheadings along with the headings. Body text, however, always remains associated with its heading. The preceding mouse method is useful for changing only the selected heading level while leaving subordinate text or levels alone.

To promote or demote a heading and have all subordinate headings and text change at once, follow these steps:

1. Choose View, Outline.
2. Move the mouse pointer over the + or – icon that appears to the left of the heading that you want to promote or demote (the pointer becomes a four-headed arrow). Click and hold down the mouse button.

Part

IV

Ch

13

3. Drag the icon to the left to promote the heading and its subordinate subheadings and body text, or drag the icon to the right to demote them. (Drag to the right edge of the outline to demote a heading to body text.)

As you drag a heading to a new level, the mouse pointer becomes a two-headed arrow, and a gray vertical line appears as you drag across each of the heading levels. When you have aligned the gray vertical line with the new heading level that you want—that is, you have aligned the line with other headings at the level that you want—release the mouse button.

Using Keyboard Shortcuts to Promote or Demote Headings

You can also use keyboard shortcuts to promote and demote individual headings (and body text). You need not be in Outline view to use this method; any view works.

To use shortcut keys to promote or demote a heading or portion of body text, follow these steps:

1. Select the headings or body text to promote or demote.

2. To promote one level, press Alt+Shift+←.

   To demote one level, press Alt+Shift+→.

This method affects only the selected headings and text; Word for Windows does not promote or demote associated subheadings along with the selected headings.

Whichever method you use, when you return to the normal editing view and display the ruler, you see that Word has applied the appropriate heading styles to your outline headings. (You can return to normal editing view by choosing View, Normal; View, Page Layout; or click the Normal View or Page Layout View icons on the horizontal scroll bar.)

Collapsing and Expanding an Outline

A *collapsed* outline shows the headings down to only a specific level. When you *expand* an outline to a specific level, you see all headings down to that level, as well as body text. You can collapse an outline all the way down so that only Level 1 headings show, or you can expand the outline all the way so that all headings and body text show. You also can expand the outline to show all headings and only the first line of each paragraph of body text.

Collapsing and expanding your outline can help you write and edit. By collapsing your outline, you can see an overview of your entire document and can move around quickly in the outline. To move to a particular section, just collapse to the level of the heading to which you want to move, select the heading, and then expand the outline. You can also use shortcuts to move entire headings and all their subordinate headings and text to new locations in the outline.

To collapse or expand the entire outline, use the numeric buttons on the Outline toolbar. Click the lowest level that you want to display in your outline. If you want to show levels 1, 2, and 3, but no lower levels, for example, click the Show Heading 3 button.

To display all levels, including body text, click the Outline toolbar's All button. To display all heading levels but no body text, first click the All button to display all levels and body text (if not already displayed), and click All again to collapse the body text, leaving only the headings for all levels displayed. Clicking one of the Show Heading number buttons on the Outline toolbar collapses or expands your entire outline uniformly. Figure 13.4 shows the outline presented in Figure 13.2 with only two levels of headings displayed.

FIG. 13.4
Collapsing an outline to display only the higher levels of headings.

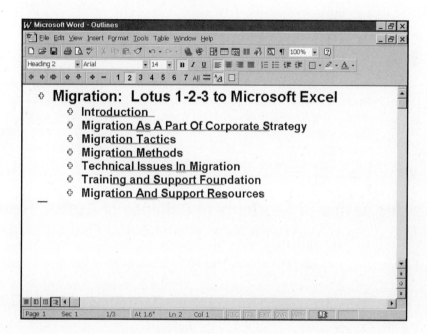

Using the Mouse to Collapse or Expand Headings

You can use the mouse and the Expand (+) and Collapse (–) buttons on the Outline toolbar, as well as the + and – icons in the outline, to collapse or expand headings selectively.

Here are the methods that you can use:

- Collapse headings and body text into the selected heading by clicking the Collapse (–) button on the Outline toolbar.

- Expand contents of selected headings by clicking the Expand (+) button on the Outline toolbar.

- Expand or contract a heading's contents by double-clicking the + icon to the left of the heading in Outline view.

Using the IntelliPoint Mouse to Collapse or Expand Headings

Microsoft's IntelliPoint mouse uses the wheel button located between the left and right mouse buttons to collapse or expand outline headings. This makes it very easy to roll your finger over the wheel and "dial" the level of detail you want to see in an outline.

Part

IV

Ch

13

To collapse or expand an outline with the IntelliPoint mouse, follow these steps:

1. Switch into Outline view by choosing View, Outline.
2. Click the heading level you want to collapse or expand.
3. Hold down the Shift key as you roll the mouse wheel forward to expand the heading's contents and backward to collapse the heading's content.
4. Release the wheel.

TROUBLESHOOTING

When I click the mouse wheel, something unexpected happens—such as Help or the Explorer displays. The mouse wheel can be customized to produce different results. When it has been customized, its normal behavior for outlines is unavailable. To set the mouse wheel back to its default behavior, click Start, Settings, Control Panel. When the Control Panel window appears, double-click the mouse application to display the Mouse Properties dialog box. Select the Mouse tab. Select Default from the Button Assignment list, then choose OK.

Using Keyboard Shortcuts to Collapse or Expand Headings

If you don't have a mouse or if you work faster using the keyboard, you can collapse and expand your outline by using shortcut keys. Table 13.2 lists the shortcut keys available. Before using a shortcut key, you must select the heading or text that you want to collapse or expand.

Table 13.2   Using Shortcut Keys to Collapse and Expand Headings

Shortcut Key	Description
Alt+Shift+ - (hyphen)	Collapses all body text below the heading. Pressing again collapses the heading's lowest level, and repeated presses collapse additional levels.
Alt+Shift++ (+ sign)	Expands the selected heading's next lower level. Repeated presses expand additional levels and, after expanding all headings, the body text.

Fitting More of the Outline into the Window

One of the great benefits of using an outline view of your document is that you get an overview of your document's organization. As you work with an outline to organize a document, you might want to view more of the outline than usually fits into the display window. To enable you to do so, Word for Windows provides two methods that you can use separately or in combination.

If you expand all or some headings to display subordinate body text, you might find that parts of the outline are pushed out of the display window. To view more of the outline, you can display the first line of each body text paragraph only, instead of the entire paragraph. You can also display the outline view without the full character formatting for each heading style. Because the character formatting for many of the heading styles usually uses boldface text and fairly large point sizes, each heading takes up a lot of room on the screen. If you omit the character formatting, the headings take less space.

Displaying an outline without character formatting affects the display in Outline view only; it does not make any permanent changes in the heading styles or their formatting. Figure 13.5 shows the same outline as in Figure 13.2, but without the full character formatting. Notice that you can now see much more of the outline.

FIG. 13.5

By displaying the outline without character formatting in the headings, you can fit more of the outline in the window.

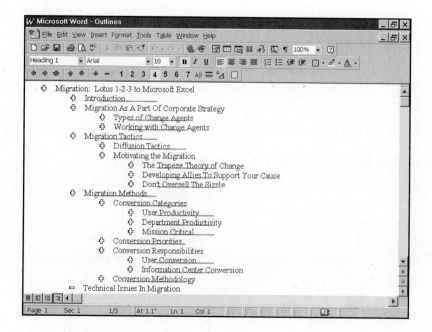

You can use the mouse and the Outline toolbar to fit more of the outline into the display window. Use either of the following methods:

- To show only the first line of expanded body text paragraphs, click the Show First Line Only button on the Outline toolbar. If the body text paragraphs are already showing only the first line, clicking this button causes Word for Windows to display the entire paragraph.

- To display the headings without full character formatting, click the Show Formatting button on the Outline toolbar. If the headings are already shown without character formatting, clicking this button causes Word to redisplay the formatting.

If you prefer to use the keyboard, you can fit more of the outline into the display window by using shortcut keys. Table 13.3 lists the shortcut keys available.

Part
IV

Ch
13

Table 13.3 Using Shortcut Keys to See More of the Outline

Shortcut Key	Description
/ (the slash key on numeric keypad)	Shows or hides character formatting for headings.
Alt+Shift+L	Shows only first line of each paragraph of expanded body text. Pressing this key combination a second time displays all text.

Reorganizing an Outline

By using Word's selection techniques, you can select outline headings in any of the normal ways. Outline view, however, offers a shortcut for selecting that can be a real time-saver. When you select an outline heading by clicking its icon in Outline view, you select the heading and its subordinate headings and body text.

Even if you don't use an outline to organize your thoughts before you begin writing, you can use an outline later to reorganize your document quickly. After you click a heading's + or – icon, you can move all the subordinate headings and text as a unit. (If you select only the words in an expanded heading, you move only the heading.)

N O T E   If you select the paragraph mark for a heading, Word automatically selects the entire heading. If you are editing the text in a heading and inadvertently select the paragraph mark, you could accidentally delete a heading and everything underneath it. If you are paying attention, you'll notice that the entire heading is highlighted if you select the paragraph mark. If this is not what you intended, start your selection again before editing. ▪

You can move selected headings (along with associated subheadings and body text) by using the mouse or the keyboard. To move a selected heading upward (toward the first page) or downward (toward the last page), use any of these methods:

- Press Alt+Shift+up or down arrow.
- Drag the heading's icon up or down.
- Click the Move Up or Move Down button on the Outline toolbar.

By selecting multiple headings and paragraphs, you can move them as a unit. Hold down Shift as you click adjacent headings and paragraphs to select them together.

Numbering an Outline

If you need numbered outlines for legal documents, bids, or proposals, you can have Word add the numbers for you.

To number your outline (from any view), choose Format, Bullets and Numbering. You can then select the type of numbering method. Figure 13.6 shows some of the numbering options available. Figure 13.7 shows an outline that uses the legal numbering style.

FIG. 13.6
Using the Bullets and Numbering option to renumber outlines.

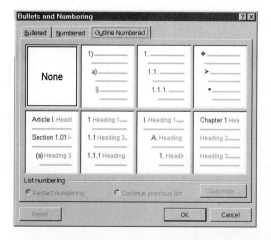

FIG. 13.7
Automatic numbering makes legal and proposal documents easy to construct.

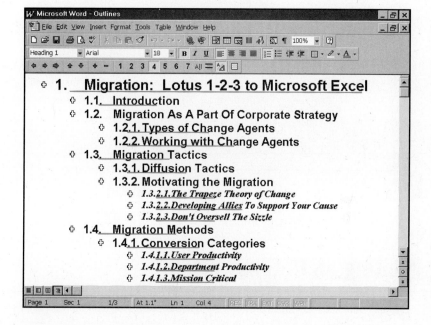

▶ **See** "Creating Numbered Lists," **p. 320**

To apply heading numbering quickly, click with the right mouse button on any heading and select Bullets and Numbering from the shortcut menu that appears.

Using Custom Styles to Create an Outline

If you formatted a document with custom styles and want to convert the document to an outline, you can replace the custom styles with outline styles.

Suppose, for example, that you formatted your document with custom heading styles called title, heading, and subheading. Choose Edit, Replace. With the insertion point in Find What text box, choose More, Format, select Style, select the style title, and then choose OK. Then, in the Replace With text box, choose Format, select Style, select style Heading 1, and then choose OK. (Type no text in either text box.) In the Find and Replace dialog box, choose Replace All to replace all title styles with Heading 1 styles. Do the same for all other headings and subheadings in your document. Then you can view your document as an outline.

Globally Replacing Outline Headings

In your document, you might want to promote or demote heading levels globally. For example, you might want to change all Level 3 headings to Level 4 headings. To do so, replace Heading 3 styles with Heading 4 styles (see the general instructions in the previous section, "Using Custom Styles to Create an Outline").

Removing Text from Within an Outline

You can remove all text from within an outline if the text is formatted with a style. You might want to remove all the text from an outline, for example, so that you can save just the headers. To remove the text instead of replacing the style (or styles) that formats the text with another style, replace the style with nothing. To remove text in an outline formatted with Word's default styles, for example, replace the style Normal with nothing. You might want to save the document first, because you can't undo this procedure. For details, see the general instructions in the previous section "Using Custom Styles to Create an Outline."

 TIP If you want to copy just your outline without any associated text into another document, create a table of contents, as described earlier in this chapter. Select the table of contents, press Ctrl+Shift+F9 to convert it to text, and then copy and paste it into the other document.

Printing an Outline

You can print your document as displayed in Outline view. To print the outline, choose View, Outline, display the levels of headings and body text that you want to print, and then choose File, Print or press Ctrl+P. ●

Automating with Field Codes

What Fields Can Do for You and Your Organization

Here's the technical definition of a field: A *field* is a placeholder for data that Word automatically inserts in your document. Here's the real-world definition: A field is a time-saver. Word 97 automates your document production by placing existing information—whether input by yourself, someone else, or calculated by Word—into designated fields.

You could do everything required of you without ever touching a field, but who has that much time? Sure, you could update the page numbers by hand or retype the document author's name on every page, but there is no reason for you to do so—it's why fields were designed. The time invested in mastering even a few fields and their options is minuscule compared to the amount of time you save with each new document.

Fields are frequently the short answer to the often asked question, "How do I (fill-in-the-blank) in Word 97?" It's not that you have to memorize every field and all of their options. The best course is to familiarize yourself with the possibilities fields offer. Then, when you ask yourself the "How do I" question, you can respond, "Fields, of course." In fact, you'll see in the next section that you're probably already using fields and don't even know it.

Fields You May Already Be Using

One of the most common word processing functions is automatic page numbering. When you choose Insert, Page Number, just what does Word insert? You guessed it, a field. The same is true when you want to indicate the total number of pages in a document as well, such as "Page 1 of 23"—this format uses two fields, one for the current page number and one for the total number of pages.

Another common field used is the date field. When writing repetitive letters or time-stamping documents, it's amazing how much time you can save by letting Word put in the current date and time. Of course, it's essential that your computer be set for the right date and time. Luckily, most of today's computer systems have a built-in clock battery to keep the date current—and even correct for daylight savings time.

Perhaps the single largest application of field codes is the Mail Merge tool. Every merge field that you insert is a specialized field code, as are all of the word fields such as Next Record. Although you could insert all the field codes necessary to create a mail merge main document by hand, it's far simpler to choose Tools, Mail Merge, and use the Mail Merge toolbar.

Viewing Fields

What does a field code look like? Try this: Open a document that uses Automatic Page Numbering. Make sure you're in Page Layout view to see the headers and footers and press Alt+F9. Suddenly your innocuous "Page 3 of 17" is revealed to be something moderately incomprehensible like {PAGE *MERGEFORMAT} of {NUMPAGES *MERGEFORMAT}. Press Alt+F9 again to return to Normal view.

If you want to work with the field codes visible all the time, you can set your options to do so. Choose Tools, Options, and click the View tab of the Option dialog box. Check the Field Codes check box in the Show section. If you pressed Alt+F9 already and are currently showing the field codes in your document, you'll find the Field Codes box already checked.

When you insert a field code, the default is for it to be shaded a medium gray when selected. You can change this by first choosing Tools, Options, and then selecting the View tab. Click the arrow next to the Field Shading drop-down list box to see the other options, as shown in Figure 14.1. You can choose Never to eliminate field code shading entirely—which would mean that you could never distinguish your field codes from the rest of your document. You can choose Always to force the field code to continually show up on-screen (although it never prints).

FIG. 14.1

You set your field codes options in the View tab of the Options dialog box.

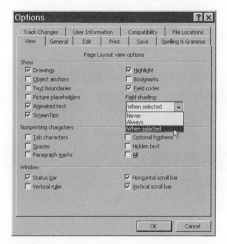

Inserting a Field

There are numerous specialized ways to insert a field—Insert Date, Insert Page Number, and the Mail Merge tools among them—but there's one place where you can find all the field codes and their options. By choosing Insert, Field to open the Field dialog box, you can see the field codes listed by category or alphabetically. The Field dialog box also provides prompts for each field code and its associated options.

Follow these steps to insert a field code into your document:

1. Choose Insert, Field. The Field dialog box opens as shown in Figure 14.2.
2. To choose a field code from an alphabetical list, select All in the Categories column.

Part

IV

Ch

14

FIG. 14.2
Choose from over 75 field codes through the Field dialog box.

3. To choose a field code from a specific kind, select one of the nine named options in the Categories column.

4. Select a field code from the Field Names list in the right column. The field code template is displayed next to Field Codes with available options and switches.

5. Enter any needed text in the Field Code text box.

6. To add any switches, click the Options button.

7. Click OK when you're finished.

Elements of a Field

After you have inserted any field, press Alt+F9 to see its inner workings. All field codes have three basic parts: the delimiters, the field name, and the instructions.

The delimiters are what allow Word to recognize the field code as a field code and they look like curly braces {}. However, the delimiters only look like curly braces—you can't type them in from the keyboard, add the field code information, and expect them to work. To insert a field code by hand, press Ctrl+F9. This places a pair of curly brace field code delimiters in a shaded area, ready for you to put in the other elements.

The second part of a field code is the field code name. Although it is not case sensitive, if you misspell the name (you can put in "AutoNum", "AUTONUM", or "autonum", for example), the field won't work correctly. In fact, it won't work at all.

The instructions are the specifics for each field code. There are four different types of instructions:

■ *Bookmarks* give a field code a reference point in your document. For example, using {INCLUDETEXT *"Filename"* Bookmark} lets you include a bookmarked portion of text from another file.

■ *Expressions* are the mathematical and relational connection to field codes. For example, using {=SubTotal+ShipCost} gives you the total of bookmarked subtotal and shipping cost figures. In this example, the equal sign is actually the field code name.

- *Text* enables you to specify prompts or information to be placed in the document, verbatim. For example, using {FILLIN "Please enter your mother's maiden name."} displays the quoted text as a prompt in a dialog box.

- *Switches* are the options for a field code. For example, using {PAGE * ROMAN} sets the page numbering command to use uppercase Roman numerals (I, II, III, and so on) instead of the default Arabic numerals (1, 2, 3, and so on).

Of the four instructions, switches are by far the most complex. They are covered more extensively in the next section.

 It's a good habit to always put any needed text following the field code word in quotes. Single words and numbers can be entered without quotation marks, but if you put quotes around everything, you won't have to think about it.

Field Switches

Switches are optional instructions that let you customize a field code. Switches begin with a backslash, the (\\) character, followed by a character or letter. What switches do depends entirely on the field code. A field code can have any number of switches or none at all. You can see which switches are available for each field code by selecting the field code and clicking the Option button in the Field dialog box. This opens the Field Option dialog box as shown in Figure 14.3. If the Option button does not become active that means that there are no switches for the selected field code.

FIG. 14.3

Use the Option button in the Field Options dialog box to implement various field code switches.

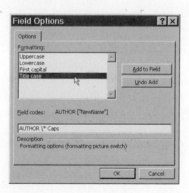

If you make a mistake when choosing your switches, Word lets you know after you confirm your options by closing the Form dialog box. Instead of inserting your field code, Word puts an error code in its place. For example, if you click two different date formats, you'll see `Error! Too many picture switches defined`. Click the Undo button to remove the error code (or highlight and delete it) and insert your field code again.

N O T E The field code options use the term picture when referring to any formatting option. You'll see the references to both Date-Time Picture Switches and Numeric Picture Switches. ▪

Field Characters

Because switches use quotation marks and the backslash character for special functions, you have to take extra steps if you want to use either quotes or a backslash in your field code. The key is to use the backslash character as the escape character to indicate a special circumstance. Here's how it works:

- To include quotation marks as part of a field code, place a backslash character before each quote mark. For example, if you want to prompt your users with a FILLIN field code to put their entries in a particular format, your entry in the Field Code text box would read as follows:

  ```
  FILLIN "Please enter the expiration date in the \"MM-DD\" format."
  ```

- To use the backslash character as part of a field code, place an additional backslash in front of the character. For example to include text with a specific file name, you must use the backslash character to create the path name, like this:

  ```
  INCLUDETEXT "c:\\my documents\\business\\boilerplate1.doc"
  ```

Types of Fields

Field codes are organized according to their function. When you open the Field dialog box by choosing Insert, Field, you'll find nine different groupings in the Categories column. As previously noted, click any of the categories to bring up the corresponding entries in the Field Names column.

Date and Time Fields

As you would expect, the Date and Time fields let you insert the current date and time into your document. What you might not know, however, is that these fields can also tell you when a document was created, saved, printed—even the total amount of time spent editing it. These field codes are often used in headers and footers to differentiate different draft documents. Table 14.1 describes the field codes found under the Date and Time category.

Table 14.1 Date and Time Field Codes

Field Name	Format	Description
CreateDate	CreateDate [\@" Date-Time Picture"]	Inserts the date and time a document was created.
Date	Date [\@"Date-Time Picture"] [Switches]	Inserts the current date.
EditTime	EditTime	Inserts the total editing time in minutes.

Field Name	Format	Description
PrintDate	PrintDate [\@" Date-Time Picture"]	Inserts the date and time the document was last printed.
SaveDate	SaveDate [\@" Date-Time Picture"]	Inserts the date and time the document was last saved.
Time	Time [\@"Date-Time Picture"] [Switches]	Inserts the current time.

Document Automation Fields

The Document Automation fields bring a whole new level of embedded interactivity to your documents. A couple of the field codes (Compare and If) are used to facilitate programming-like branching within the document. Two others (GoToButton and MacroButton) enable you to place command-type buttons in your document. Another (DocVariable) provides a valuable link to VBA programming. Table 14.2 describes the Document Automation fields.

Table 14.2   Document Automation Fields

Field Name	Format	Description
Compare	Compare Expression1 Operator Expression2	Compares the two values using the specified operator and returns 1 if True and 0 if False.
DocVariable	DocVariable "Name"	Inserts the value of the document variable named.
GoToButton	GoToButton Destination DisplayText	Jumps to a new location in the document.
If	If Expression1 Operator Expression2 TrueText FalseText	Compares two values and inserts the appropriate text.
MacroButton	MacroButton MacroName DisplayText	Runs the named macro.
Print	Print "PrintCommands"	Sends printer-control code characters to the selected printer.

Part

IV

Ch

14

In order to see the result from many of the field codes, including those in the Document Automation category, the document must be locked. You do this by either selecting Tools, Protect Document, and choosing the Forms option or by clicking the Protect Form button on the Forms toolbar.

> **CAUTION**
>
> The Print field code works well with a PostScript printer, or a Hewlett-Packard LaserJet Series II or Series III printer, but it may not work properly with another type of laser printer. The Print field code works with a dot-matrix printer only if the printer supports the PassThrough command.

Document Information Fields

Word keeps track of a lot of information about each document. Some of the information requires your input through the Summary tab of the Properties dialog box, such as the Author's name. Other information, such as a document's word count, is calculated by Word and continually updated. All of it can be brought into play through the Document Information field codes.

The Document Information field codes are generally used to make obvious some facet of the document. Quite often a company requires that each document display its path and filename or other such information for easy retrieval. Information that gives a correct updated view of the current document, such as the word count, is also extremely useful. Table 14.3 describes the Document Information field codes.

Table 14.3   Document Information Fields

Field Name	Format	Description
Author	Author ["NewName"]	Inserts Author's name from the Properties dialog box, unless a new name is given.
Comments	Comments ["NewComments"]	Inserts the Comments from the Properties dialog box, unless new comments are given.
DocProperty	DocProperty "Name"	Inserts the value of the property chosen through the Options button.
FileName	FileName [Switches]	Inserts the name and/or path of the file.
FileSize	FileSize [Switches]	Inserts the file size of the current document.
Info	Info [InfoType] [Switches]	Inserts the value of the InfoType as chosen through the Options button.

Field Name	Format	Description
Keywords	Keywords "NewKeywords"	Inserts the keywords from the Properties dialog box, unless new keywords are given.
LastSavedBy	LastSavedBy	Inserts the name of the last person who saved the current document.
NumChars	NumChars	Inserts the total number of characters in the document.
NumPages	NumPages	Inserts the total number of pages in the document.
NumWords	NumWords	Inserts the total number of words in the document.
Subject	Subject "NewSubject"	Inserts the subject from the Properties dialog box, unless a new subject is given.
Template	Template [Switches]	Inserts the name and path of the template, if any, attached to the document.
Title	Title "NewTitle"	Inserts the title from the Properties dialog box, unless a new title is given.

CAUTION

There's a problem with the NumPages field code in Word 97. It doesn't automatically update when you open a previously saved file that includes the field code. If you use a "Page X of X" type footer, you'll get field results like "Page 3 of 1." To work around this problem, switch document views or print the document and the field code will update properly.

Equations and Formulas Fields

If you've ever used a table to calculate a column of numbers, you've used one of the Equations and Formula field codes. When you choose Table, Formula, Word inserts an = (Formula) field code, often in the form "=SUM(ABOVE)". In addition, you can also use an Equations and Formula field code to insert a specialized math element like a fraction or a radical, or completely control the placement of some text.

Use the Equations and Formula field code when you're doing just a little math. If you're doing extensive calculations, you're probably better off building your table in Excel and importing or linking it. Likewise, for complex formula representation, use the Equation Editor.

Part
IV

Ch
14

For straightforward table formulas or simple mathematical equation, however, these math specific fields codes are very quick and useful. Table 14.4 describes the Equations and Formula fields.

Table 14.4 Equation and Formula Fields

Field Name	Format	Description
= (Formula)	= Formula [Bookmark] [*Numeric-Picture]	Calculates a number using a mathematical expression.
Advance	Advance [Switches]	Offsets following text right, left, up, or down, or to a specific horizontal or vertical position.
Eq (Equation)	Eq Instructions	Inserts a mathematical expression.
Symbol	Symbol CharNum [Switches]	Inserts the character specified by the ANSI character number.

CAUTION

There's a bug in the = (Formula) field code that won't let you calculate numbers in more than 85 rows using the ABOVE or BELOW keywords. If, for example, your formula "=SUM(ABOVE)" or "=COUNT(BELOW)" refers to more than 85 numbers, the result will be incorrect. As a workaround, specify the cell range, like this "=SUM(A1:A87)".

Index and Tables Fields

By far the easiest way to create an index, table of contents, or table of authorities is through the Insert, Index and Tables menu option. What you may not realize is that when Word inserts an index or table of contents, it is actually inserting a field code. To verify this, press Alt+F9 while looking at a generated table of contents. All of your text disappears to be replaced by something like {TOC \O "1-4"}, which is field code lingo for a table of contents created by looking at the outline styles and showing levels 1 through 4.

If you do a lot of work with indices, table of contents, or table of authorities, it's a good idea to familiarize yourself with their respective field codes. You can quickly change the field code without having to open the Index and Tables dialog box, make your modification, and then re-insert the table of contents. If, for instance, you wanted to show only the first three levels in the previous example, all you have to do is press Alt+F9, change "1-4" to "1-3", and press F9. You'll get a dialog box asking if you want to update just the pages or the entire table. Choose Entire Table and click OK. The table regenerates.

Table 14.5 lists Index and Tables fields available to Word 97 users.

Table 14.5	Index and Tables Fields	
Field Name	**Format**	**Description**
Index	Index [Switches]	Generates and inserts an index.
RD	RD "FileName"	Includes a file while creating an Index, TOC, or TOA.
TA	TA [Switches]	Marks a table of authorities entry.
TC	TC "Text" [Switches]	Marks a table of contents entry.
TOA	TOA [Switches]	Generates and inserts a table of authorities.
TOC	TOC [Switches]	Generates and inserts a table of contents.
XE	XE "Text" [Switches]	Marks an index entry.

 TIP The TA, TC, and XE field codes are all formatted as hidden text. In order to reveal them, click the Show/Hide ¶ button.

Links and Reference Fields

When your document begins to connect with other documents or use internal cross references, the Links and Reference fields come into play. These fields let you include text, pictures, or links—both from within the document and without—with an added level of flexibility. The AutoText field, for example, lets you insert an AutoText entry as a field rather than as retyped text. This means that if you edit your original AutoText entry and then update the document, all your AutoText fields will reflect the changes.

One of the most used of the Links and Reference fields is the Ref field. The Ref field is used to insert any text marked by a bookmark. For most bookmarks, you can use the abbreviated version of the command and just put the bookmark name in the field delimiters, like this: {Bookmark1}. However, for any bookmark with the same name as a Word field, you must use the Ref keyword. If, for example, your bookmark name were "Author," you would have to use {Ref "Author"} to insert your text; otherwise, Word inserts the text associated with the document property Author. Table 14.6 describes all the Links and Reference fields.

Part
IV

Ch
14

Table 14.6   Links and Reference Fields

Field Name	Format	Description
AutoText	AutoText AutoTextEntry	Inserts a predefined AutoText entry.
AutoTextList	AutoTextList "Literal Text"	Displays a list of AutoText entries for insertion.
Hyperlink	Hyperlink "Filename" [Switches]	Jumps to the specified file or place in document.
IncludePicture	IncludePicture "Filename" [Switches]	Inserts the named image.
IncludeText	IncludeText [Bookmark] "Filename"[Switches]	Inserts the named document or the bookmarked contents.
Link	Link ClassName "FileName" [PlaceReference] [Switches]	Sets up a link with content from another application.
NoteRef	NoteRef Bookmark [Switches]	Inserts the number of a bookmarked footnote or endnote.
PageRef	PageRef Bookmark [Switches]	Inserts the page number of a bookmark.
Quote	Quote "Literal Text"	Inserts the indicated text into the document.
Ref	[Ref] Bookmark [Switches]	Inserts the contents of the named bookmark.
StyleRef	StyleRef StyleIdentifier [Switches]	Inserts text formatted with the specified style.

Two Links and Reference fields, new to Word 97, bring a World Wide Web-like interface to your documents. The AutoTextList field embeds an inline option list that enables the user to choose which AutoText entry to insert. As shown in Figure 14.4, the user right-clicks the field and a list of pertinent AutoText entries appears. The second new field is the Hyperlink field and is what Word 97 puts in your document when you choose Insert, Hyperlink. Hyperlinks let you jump to different places in a document, different documents, or even different Web sites.

Mail Merge Fields

As with the Index and Tables field codes, the best way to use most of the Mail Merge field codes is through the tool designed for their use—the Mail Merge Helper. However, you may encounter situations where you need to tweak the codes inserted by Word to get the results you need. If you press Alt+F9 while looking at your main mail merge document, you'll see a host of field codes, all of which are categorized as Mail Merge field codes.

The Fill-In field can be used outside of a mail merge to automate your documents. This is true of another field, the Ask field. The Ask field puts up a dialog box requesting input like Fill-In, but instead of inserting it, the Ask field code assigns the answer to a bookmark. The bookmark can then be referenced, compared, and otherwise treated like a variable in programming. Another Mail Merge field code, Set, lets you assign bookmarks directly. A description of all the Mail Merge fields can be found in Table 14.7.

FIG. 14.4
The AutoTextList field lets your users choose from a defined list of options.

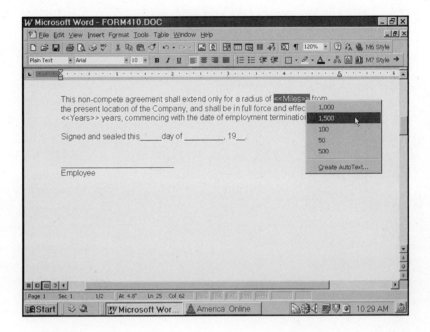

Table 14.7   Mail Merge Fields

Field Name	Format	Description
Ask	Ask Bookmark "Prompt" [Switches]	Displays a dialog box that prompts for text to be assigned to a bookmark.
Compare	Compare Expression1 Operator Expression2	Compares the two values using the specified operator and returns 1 if True and 0 if False.
Database	Database [Switches]	Inserts a Word table containing the result of a database query.
Fill-in	Fillin ["Prompt"] [Switches]	Displays a dialog box that prompts for text to be inserted into the document.

Part

IV

Ch

14

continues

Table 14.7 Continued

Field Name	Format	Description
If	If Expression1 Operator Expression2 TrueText FalseText	Compares two values and inserts the appropriate text.
MergeField	MergeField FieldName	Merges data from the data source into the main document.
MergeRec	MergeRec	Inserts the number of the current data record.
MergeSec	MergeSec	Inserts the number of successfully merged records.
Next	Next	Forces the next data record to be merged in the same document as the previous record.
NextIf	NextIf Expression1 Operator Expression2	Compares two values and merges the next data record in the same document if True.
Set	Set Bookmark "Text"	Assigns named text to a book mark.
SkipIf	SkipIf Expression1 Operator Expression2	Compares two values and skips the next data record if True.

Numbering Fields

One of the most effective time-saving tools in Word 97's repertoire is automatic numbering. Whether you're working from an detailed outline, a legal document, or just an ordinary numbered list, being able to make your additions, deletions, and edits without having to renumber everything is almost worth the price of the program. The Numbering fields embrace and extend the capabilities found under the Numbering button on the Formatting toolbar. Table 14.8 describes the Numbering fields.

Table 14.8 Numbering Fields

Field Name	Format	Description
AutoNum	AutoNum	Automatically numbers paragraphs sequentially.
AutoNumLgl	AutoNumLgl	Automatically numbers paragraphs in legal outline format.

Field Name	Format	Description
AutoNumOut	AutoNumOut	Automatically numbers paragraphs in standard outline format.
Barcode	Barcode \u "LiteralText" or Bookmark \b [Switches]	Inserts a bar code readable by the post office.
ListNum	ListNum ["Name"] [Switches]	Inserts the next number of a named item.
Page	Page [* Format Switch]	Inserts the current page number.
RevNum	RevNum	Inserts the number of document revisions, which is equal to the number of times a document has been saved.
Section	Section	Inserts the current section number.
SectionPages	SectionPages	Inserts the number of pages in the current section.
Seq (Sequence)	Seq Identifier [Bookmark] [Switches]	Inserts the next sequential number for the named item.

New to Word 97's numbering features is the ListNum field. This field combines the functionality of the AutoNum, AutoNumLgl, AutoNumOut, and the Seq fields while adding a few new wrinkles of its own. ListNum enables you to create many different lists and keep track of the numbering for each of them, separately. For example, the same document could have separate lists of figures, illustrations, tables, and graphs.

Moreover, ListNum doesn't just number paragraphs; it lets you put numbers anywhere in a paragraph, like the Seq field. However, unlike the Seq field, ListNum lets you specify the level in the list. ListNum combines the sophisticated level-handling of an outline numbering system with flexible placement control. This is a boon to lawyers and any other business creating contracts where numbering references are essential.

User Information Fields

The User Information fields let you access the name, address, and initials of the currently registered Word 97 user. You can access this data by choosing Tools, Options and clicking the User Information tab as shown in Figure 14.5. Use these fields when you want to easily put your name on a Prepared by: line. Using these fields in templates is a good way to personalize the work of an entire office with just one file. The User Information fields are described in Table 14.9.

Part
IV

Ch
14

FIG. 14.5

The User Information fields pull data from the User Information tab of the Options dialog box.

Table 14.9   User Information Fields

Field Name	Format	Description
UserAddress	UserAddress "NewAddress"	Inserts the user address.
UserInitials	UserInitials "NewInitials"	Inserts the user initials.
UserName	UserName "NewName"	Inserts the user name.

You can override the User Information settings by putting new text following the field code. For example, {UserName "Sherman Hornsworth"} inserts the new name in place of the one currently in the User Information settings.

Updating Fields

Word 97's field capabilities are terrific; you can cross-reference, number, calculate editing time, and so much more. However, if you edit your document, only some changes are incorporated automatically. With few exceptions, fields have to be updated manually.

It's very simple to update a field. Select the field and press F9. To update all the fields in a document, choose Edit, Select All, and then press F9. If you've used the Link field code to update information linked to another Word document, press Ctrl+Shift+F7.

> **CAUTION**
>
> Keep in mind that if you update all the fields in an entire document, you're updating any indexes, tables of contents, tables of authorities, and so on that might be in the document. Unfortunately, if you've tweaked the formatting of any of these items, the formatting is lost during the update. As you'll see in the next section, you can lock a field so that it doesn't update.

There's a way to make sure that you have the most current information anytime you plan to print your document. Choose Tools, Options, and click the Print tab. In the Print Options tab, enable the Update Fields check box. This automatically updates all the fields in the document. While you're in the Print Options tab, if you have any outside files associated with the current document, you might also want to enable the Update Links check box.

Locking, Unlocking, and Unlinking Fields

There are times when you want to lock specific fields and leave others open. Word provides a facility for you to do just that. When you lock a field, you prevent any changes to the field results, not to the field. You can still delete or reformat the field, and even cut it and paste it somewhere else. A locked field is only prevented from being updated by Word.

You lock a field by selecting it and pressing Ctrl+F11. Of course, you can unlock a field to allow updates by pressing Ctrl+Shift+F11 again. Similarly, you can also unlink a field from its original source. Press Ctrl+Shift+F9 to unlink a selected field. However, after a field is unlinked, the current field result becomes regular text. Later, if you want to update the information, you must insert the field again and reestablish the link.

There's a special switch for locking field results. Adding "\!" to a field code prevents it from being updated (unless the field is moved). This Lock Result switch also prohibits any field from being included in the result of a Bookmark, IncludeText, or Ref field. The Lock Result switch is often used when you want to be assured that your referenced or included text is identical to your original text and no codes, such as a date code, have been inadvertently updated.

Fields Shortcut Menu

There are numerous keyboard shortcuts devoted exclusively to fields. One group of shortcuts make it easier to insert commonly used fields, without having to go through the Insert menu; these shortcuts are listed in Table 14.10.

Part

IV

Ch

14

Table 14.10 Keyboard Shortcuts for Commonly Used Fields

Field to Insert	Keyboard Shortcut
Date field	Alt+Shift+D
ListNum Field	Alt+Ctrl+L
Page field	Alt+Shift+P
Time field	Alt+Shift+T
Empty field	Ctrl+F9

Another group of keyboard shortcuts apply to fields in general. Table 14.11 consolidates much of the information about field keyboard shortcuts found throughout this chapter.

Table 14.11 Keyboard Shortcuts for Fields in General

Action	Keyboard Shortcut
Update linked information in another Word document	Ctrl+Shift+F7
Update selected fields	F9
Unlink a field	Ctrl+Shift+F9
Switch between a field code and its result	Shift+F9
Switch between all field codes and their results	Alt+F9
Go to the next field	F11
Go to the previous field	Shift+F11
Lock a field	Ctrl+F11
Unlock a field	Ctrl+Shift+F11

Moving Among Fields

You may have noted in the previous listing of keyboard shortcuts that Word has a facility for moving from one field to the next. Pressing F11 moves you to the next field, and pressing Shift+F11 takes you to the previous one. Word can move from field to field whether or not the field codes are revealed.

You can also locate specific fields using either the Find or the Go To command. To search for a field using the Find command, you first must reveal the codes by pressing Alt+F9. Then choose

Edit, Find, and type ^19 in the Find What text box followed by the field code name—^19 is the special symbol for the opening field brace.

If you don't remember the exact spelling of the field code, it's easy to use the Go To command instead. Follow these steps:

1. Choose Edit, Go To.

2. From the Go to What list, choose Field, as shown in Figure 14.6.

FIG. 14.6.
You can "Go To" any field code in your document.

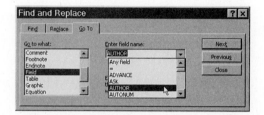

3. Click the arrow next to the Enter Field Name text box and select a field from the drop-down list.

4. Click either the Next or Previous button to find your field in a specific direction.

Note that, unlike with the Find command, you don't have to reveal the field codes when you use the Go To method to locate a specific field.

Formatting Field Results

When it comes to formatting field results, you can affect both style and substance. You can format a field's style just as you would any character—changing its font and its font size, making it bold or italic, and even changing the spacing. Simply highlight the field and make your formatting changes, either through the Formatting toolbar or through the Format menu.

Word also offers another type of formatting through three different general switches. Depending on the type of field code, you can specify:

- The case of text (upper, lower, caps, and so on)
- The style of a number (Arabic, Roman numeral, hexadecimal, and so on)
- The representation of a number (used to specify leading zeros, decimals, and so on)
- The representation of a date or time (used to specify leading zeros, separators, and so on)

Format Switches

Both the text case and number style types of formatting use the Format switch (*) followed by a keyword. Table 14.12 describes all the options.

Part
IV

Ch
14

Table 14.12   Format Switches

Instruction	Description
* caps	Converts the first character of each word to uppercase.
* firstcap	Converts the first character of the first word to uppercase.
* lower	Converts all characters to lowercase.
* upper	Converts all characters to uppercase.
* alphabetic	Converts a number result to lowercase alphabetic characters.
* ALPHABETIC	Converts a number result to uppercase alphabetic characters.
* arabic	Converts a number result to Arabic cardinal form.
* cardtext	Converts a number result to its cardinal text (for example, written word) form.
* dollartext	Converts a number result to cardinal text; inserts "and" at the decimal place and the first two decimals as Arabic numerators over 100 (for example, "Fifteen and $^{23}/_{100}$").
* hex	Converts a number result to hexadecimal numbers.
* ordinal	Converts a number result to Arabic ordinal form (for example, 30th).
* ordtext	Converts a number result to ordinal text form (for example, Seventh).
* roman	Converts a number result to lowercase Roman numerals.
* ROMAN	Converts a number result to uppercase Roman numerals.

Numeric Picture Switches

The Numeric and Date-Time switches are referred to as picture switches because you define a representation for the field result. If you've ever chosen a number format in Excel, you're familiar with picture switches. To represent a number with a dollar sign, a comma for a thousands separator, and two decimals in it, a sample field code looks like this: {=SUM(ABOVE) \# "$#,##0.00"}. Notice that a picture switch starts with a \# character combination.

TIP   It's not necessary to surround a numeric picture switch with quotation marks unless the switch contains spaces.

Certain field codes, such as Seq, make the most common numeric picture switches available through the Options button. However, you can always create your own by using the Numeric Picture switches listed in Table 14.13.

Table 14.13 Numeric Picture Switches

Instruction	Description
0 (zero)	Required digit placeholder. If a digit is not in the result, a zero is displayed.
# (number sign)	Optional digit placeholder. Displays a digit only if the result requires it.
x (truncate)	Truncating digit placeholder. Drops any digit to the left of the placeholder and rounds up when placed to the right of the decimal point.
decimal point	Indicates decimal point placement. The decimal point must match the decimal character in system setting.
thousands separator	Enables thousands separator. Character used must match the thousands separator in system setting.
– (minus sign)	Inserts a minus sign if result is negative, or a space if result is positive or zero.
+ (plus sign)	Inserts a plus sign if the result is positive, a minus sign if it is negative, or a space if it is zero.
postive; negative	Denotes specific number formats for positive and negative numbers, separated by a semicolon.
positive; negative; zero	Denotes specific number formats for positive, negative, and zero results.
'text' (literal text)	Inserts verbatim text in the result. The text must be enclosed with single quotation marks.
'sequence'	Includes the current number in a sequence (previously defined by Seq). The sequence label must be enclosed in accent grave marks.
character	Inserts any character in the result, including percent signs, ampersands, and spaces.

Date-Time Picture Switches

The Date-Time picture switches work much like the Numeric picture switches: You combine certain instructions to get the date and time format you want. Indicate a Date-Time picture switch with a \@ before your format representation. For example, assuming you're in the last month of the year, the field code {Date \@ "MMMM 'yy"} returns December '97. Table 14.14 describes the Date-Time picture switches.

Table 14.14 Date-Time Picture Switches

Instruction	Description
M	Displays the month number without a leading zero.
MM	Displays the month number with a leading zero.
MMM	Displays the month as a three-letter abbreviation.
MMMM	Displays the full name of the month.
d	Displays the day number without a leading zero for single-digit days.
dd	Displays the day number with a leading zero for single-digit days.
ddd	Displays the day as a three-letter abbreviation.
dddd	Displays the full name of the day.
yy	Displays the year as two digits with a leading zero for years 01 through 09.
yyyy	Displays the year as four digits.
h or H	Displays the hour without a leading zero for single-digit hours.
hh or HH	Displays the hour with a leading zero for single-digit hours.
m	Displays the minutes without a leading zero for single-digit minutes.
mm	Displays the minutes with a leading zero for single-digit minutes.
AM/PM	Displays AM or PM in uppercase.
am/pm	Displays am or pm in lowercase.
A/P	Displays abbreviated AM or PM in uppercase (for example, 8 A and 10 P).
a/p	Displays abbreviated AM or PM in lowercase (for example, 8 a and 10 p).
'text' (literal text)	Inserts verbatim text in the result. The text must be enclosed with single quotation marks.
'sequence'	Includes the current number in a sequence (previously defined by Seq). The sequence label must be enclosed in accent grave marks.
character	Inserts any character in the result, including colons, hyphens, and spaces.

 TIP Unlike most of the switches, a couple of the Date-Time picture switches are case sensitive. You have to use an uppercase M to designate months and a lowercase m to indicate minutes. Similarly, when you are dealing with hours, an uppercase H signals a 24-hour clock while a lowercase h means a 12-hour clock.

TROUBLESHOOTING

What kind of trouble can fields lead to? With all the switches possible, both general formatting types and field-specific ones, the everyday typo is a leading source of field-related headaches. Use the Option button whenever possible to have Word insert the proper command. If you are inputting some text with spaces, don't forget to enclose all the text with quotation marks.

My fields won't update. What do I do? As with forms, the mistakes most likely to occur with fields have to do with locking and unlocking. Keep in mind that locking a field only prohibits the result from being updated; it doesn't stop the field from being deleted or typed over. If you press Ctrl+Shift+F11 to unlock a field and it still doesn't update, press Alt+F9 to reveal the field code. You might find a Lock Result switch, \!, in the field; delete it and press F9 to update the field.

I am having trouble viewing my codes. The Word 97 document is composed of layers. There is the normal, the inline text layer, and the drawing layer that many objects, including graphs, equations and charts, use. If you are having trouble viewing your codes, it could be because they are embedded in such an object, which is floating over the text.

To view the field codes in an object, follow these steps:

1. Right-click the object.
2. From the Quick menu, click Format Object.
3. From the Format Object dialog box, click the Position tab.
4. Click the Float Over Text check box to clear it.
5. Click OK.

This makes your floating object an inline object and the fields should display properly.

When I try to number paragraphs in a table cell, I keep getting the number repeated. What's going on? Word exhibits some unexpected behavior when combining tables and the AutoNum field. If you attempt to automatically number several paragraphs within a table cell using AutoNum, Word inserts the same number for each line. The new field code, ListNum, doesn't have the same problem. However, you must remember to indicate a list name for the numbering to work properly, like this, {ListNum "Lots"}.

Building Forms and Fill-In Dialog Boxes

How You Can Use Word's Forms Feature

Interactivity has been a buzzword for so long you may have lost sight of the most basic interactive tool—the form. Word 97 lets you create the following kinds of forms:

- A protected electronic form where the user's answers are limited to specific areas and types of responses.
- A printed form that is intended to be completed with a pen.
- An online form where you can guide the user through a series of questions.

In addition to obvious applications like questionnaires and surveys, forms can also be used in more traditional word processing functions like automated document production. Lawyers use forms to fill out contracts, while realtors use them to complete loan applications. Virtually any document that uses largely repetitive text and distinguishes itself from other documents like it by specific, detailed information can be generated by a form. You even have the options to save or print only the data from a form, which enables you to put the information into a database or fill out preprinted forms.

 TIP The term online refers to all types of electronic forms: those that are used to automate documents as well as those created for use on the Internet.

When it comes to the World Wide Web, forms are definitely cutting-edge. Word 97 lets you gather a full range of feedback from your Web page visitors. You have the option of using traditional input forms like a text area, check box, or option button, or some of the more sophisticated ActiveX controls. After the form has been filled out, it is submitted—generally meaning that the form results are sent to the designated recipient for collection or further processing.

Creating the Skeleton of a Form

No matter what the end-result is for your form—hard-copy, computer file, or Web page—you first have to create the shell in which to place your form elements. You use all the regular text and drawing tools you normally would in making a document, but certain areas are reserved for your *form fields*. A form field is a placeholder, usually indicated by a shaded area, where a particular type of data is input.

Because they are meant to be completed by a number of different people over a period of time, forms generally start as templates. You can also decide to save a regular document as a template.

To create a new, blank template, follow these steps:

1. Choose File, New to open the New dialog box.
2. From the General tab, select the Blank Document file.
3. In the Create New section, click the Template option button.
4. Click OK.

If you were creating a Web page with a form, you could use the same procedure as previously outlined, but instead of the General tab, choose the Web Pages tab, and Blank Web Page instead of Blank Document.

 TIP It's a good idea to lock your form prior to saving. To do this, choose Tools, Protect Document, and then click the Forms option button from the Protect dialog box. This topic is covered in more detail in the section titled "Protecting Your Form from Unauthorized Change."

After you've built the skeleton for your form, make sure you save it as a template. By default, Word saves all templates in the Templates folder; saving your file here will make it appear in the General tab of the New dialog box. You can also save it in any of the Templates subfolders, such as Letters & Faxes, Memos, Publications, and so on, that correspond to the other tabs of the New dialog box. All templates are assigned a .dot file name extension instead of the regular .doc file extension.

When it comes time to edit your form, you must open the template itself, not a document created from the template. To make sure that you're opening a template, you can change the Files of Type to Document Templates in the Open dialog box. If you've protected your document, you'll need to choose Tools, Unprotect Document before proceeding.

Working with the Forms Toolbar

Word 97 has grouped the essential commands for creating and editing a form together in the appropriately named Forms toolbar. Enable this toolbar as you would any other: choose View, Toolbars, and then choose Forms from the submenu. Like any other toolbar that initially "floats" on the screen, you can dock the Forms toolbar by dragging it to any screen edge. As you can see from Figure 15.1, there are nine buttons available:

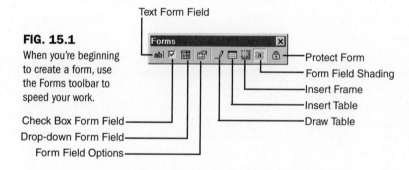

FIG. 15.1
When you're beginning to create a form, use the Forms toolbar to speed your work.

- *Text Form Field* is used for general text entry.
- *Check Box Form Field* enables the user to select one or more options from a series of possibilities.
- *Drop-Down Form Field* lets the user choose one option from several listed possibilities.
- *Form Field Options* is used to specify the conditions for any form field.

- *Draw Table* enables the form designer to drag out a table.

- *Insert Table* puts a table in the form with a set number of columns and rows.

- *Insert Frame* includes a free-floating box in the form for precise placement.

- *Form Field Shading* makes form fields visible in a medium gray.

- *Protect Form* locks the document from any change except entering information into form fields.

Adding Text Form Fields

When it comes to basic forms, by far the most common type of entry is plain text. There are very few forms out there that do not, at a minimum, gather your name and address—and most require everything from your e-mail address to your hat size. Text form fields are the work-horses of forms.

To insert a text form field, first open the Forms toolbar. Make sure your insertion point is where you want the form field to appear and then click the Text Form Field button on the Forms toolbar. By default, you'll see a medium gray rectangle approximately ½-inch wide by one line high. This doesn't indicate how much text you can add; text form fields are initially open ended, meaning that you can insert any number of characters in them.

 If you find the gray shading obtrusive, you can turn it off by clicking the Form Field Shading button on the Forms toolbar. The shading disappears but your fields are still in place. However, unless you're using an alternative way to mark your fields (such as with an underline), it's a good idea to leave the shading enabled.

To remove a text form field from your document, first select it. The field turns a darker shade of gray than normal. Now, press Delete. If your document is protected, you can't delete the form field even though you can access it; you must first choose Tools, Unprotect Document or click the Protect Form button on the Forms toolbar.

Formatting Your Text Form Field You can format your text form field just as you would any other text character—make it bold, italic, or underline, change the font name or size, and so on. The field itself retains the same gray shading. Most formatting, especially anything font-related, isn't evident until some text is placed in the field.

 Adding some additional formatting to your text form fields is a good way to make the form more readable. Use bold rather than italic or a font change to make your text entries stand out.

As with any other editing, you have to add your formatting when the form is in its unprotected state. When the form is locked, you'll find that the entire Formatting toolbar is inactive.

Setting the Text Form Field Options Word 97 gives you a fair amount of flexibility over your text form field. You can set the type of text, determine how many characters can be input, make the field a particular case or format, and even set a default response. All of these characteristics and more are accessed through the Form Field Options button on the Forms toolbar.

As you can see from Figure 15.2, there are four major areas available to alter the appearance of the text form field:

FIG. 15.2

The Text Form Field Options dialog box lets you control a user's input.

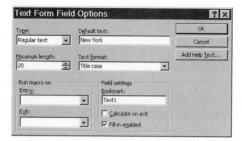

- *Type*. Choose between the following options:

  Regular text—used to allow entry of any key. (Default)

  Number—restricts entry to numeric keys only. If non-numeric keys are used, the field is evaluated to zero when input is confirmed.

  Date—restricts entry to a valid date or time. An error message alerting the user to this restriction appears if an incorrect entry is made.

  Current Date—automatically inserts the current date when the document is opened.

  Current Time—automatically inserts the current time when the document is opened or printed.

  Calculation—sets the field to be equal to equation in the Default Text box.

- *Default text*. This displays the entered text, if any, initially in the text form field. The user can replace the default text with his or her own. This field is not available if either the Current Date or Current Time options are chosen. When Calculation is selected to be the field type, this box is titled "Expression" and starts with an equal sign.

- *Maximum Length*. This sets the number of characters that can be input into the text box. The default is Unlimited. Each click of the spinner arrows increases the character count by one.

- *Format Type*. This determines the formatting applied to the text form field. The options available depend on the Type chosen. If General Text is selected, you can choose between different cases; if Number or Calculation is chosen, the formats are restricted to standard, currency, and other accounting specific number formats; if any of the date or time options are selected, the options are limited to those formats.

CAUTION

When you're creating or editing your form, get in the habit of protecting your document before you test your changes. Otherwise, selecting the form field and then entering some text will potentially erase the field. To quickly lock and unlock your form, use the Protect Form button on the Forms toolbar.

The more advanced features of the Text Form Field Options dialog box such as running macros and adding help text are covered for all the form field elements later in this chapter.

Adding Check Box Form Fields

Check boxes are a very clear and handy method of indicating a selection of one or more options that are not mutually exclusive. Instead of having to type a phrase like "Yes, I agree" or "No thanks, I'm not interested," check boxes let your user to quickly indicate preferences or—by omission—rejections among a series of elements. Check boxes are generally used when it doesn't matter how many of the items in a group your user can select. For example, a check box is the method of choice when you see the phrase "Check all that apply" as in a survey or questionnaire.

To insert a check box, simply click the Check Box Form Field button on the Forms toolbar. By default, a square shaded box the same font size as the current line appears. To see the check box in action, first protect the form. If the check box is the only or first form element on the page, it is highlighted with a slightly thicker border. You check the box by either clicking it once with the mouse or pressing either the Spacebar or the X key; checking the box again by any of the previous methods removes the cross in the box.

Specific options for the check box are limited. To see them, select your check box and then click the Form Field Options button on the Forms toolbar. In the dialog box, you can choose between having the size determined by its surrounding font (the default Auto option) or you can set it by clicking Exactly and setting the size using either the spinner buttons or by typing in a new point size. You can also determine whether the initial condition of the check box is Not Checked or Checked. by choosing the appropriate option button in the Default Value section.

Adding Drop-Down Form Fields

You see examples of drop-down form fields all the time; they're functionally identical to the menus across the top of Word and most other computer programs in use today. Drop-down form fields are used when you want to present your user with a variety of specific options from which only one selection can be made. You might use a drop-down form field in a human resources document where you're asking your applicants to choose between three different dental plans.

This form field is inserted in your document just like the others. Place your insertion point where you want the field to appear. Click the Drop-Down Form Field button from the Forms toolbar. To specify the items in your list, follow these steps:

1. Select the drop-down form field in your document with which you want to work.
2. Click the Form Field Options button on the Forms toolbar.
3. In the Drop-Down Form Options dialog box shown in Figure 15.3, type the first item in your list in the Drop-Down Item box (you may enter a maximum of 50 characters).
4. Click Add or press Enter.

FIG. 15.3
Use the drop-down form field when you want the user to choose from a list of mutually exclusive items.

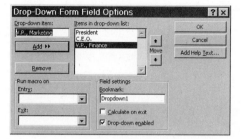

Part
IV
Ch
15

5. Continue steps 3 and 4 until all items are entered.

6. To remove an item from the list, select it, and click the Remove button.

7. To edit an item in the list, select it, and click the Remove button. Make any necessary changes in the Item box and then click Add.

8. To move any item in the list, select the item, and click the up or down arrows to adjust its position.

9. Click OK when you are finished.

10. Click the Protect Form button to see your drop-down form field in action.

Advanced Form Field Features

Word 97 has enabled all the form fields with several enhanced features that can make your forms easier to use and help automate your work. One of these features lets you embed several degrees of guidance for each of your form fields. These can range from a simple message in the status bar like "Enter Your Social Security Number" to a more complex Help message that appears when the user presses the F1 key. Another feature enables you to run specific macros upon entering or exiting the form field, which is a great help when you are completing a document based on user responses! The final feature allows your fields to be calculated after the user has entered the information, which is much nicer than having to remember to press the F9 Update fields key all the time.

Adding Help to Your Forms

One of the most time-consuming tasks faced by any office is training. Whenever you introduce a new procedure that's intended to save time, you run the risk of spending even more time training people how to use it. That's why it's recommended that you always make some form of online help available when you are creating a new form to fill out.

Word 97 makes two levels of help available for every form field: Status Bar and Help Key. When enabled, the Status Bar help displays a line of context-sensitive guidance whenever a form field is entered. The Status Bar help can show up to 83 characters. The Help Key feature kicks in when the user presses the F1 key while on a specific form field. You can be much more explicit with the Help Key; you can enter up to 255 characters to be displayed.

Follow these steps to add help to your form fields:

1. Double-click the desired form field.

2. In the Form Field Options dialog box, click the Add Help Text button
    The Form Field Help Text dialog box opens as shown in Figure 15.4.

FIG. 15.4

Use the form field Help Key option to provide additional details for each field.

3. To have context-sensitive help appear in the status bar, click the Status Bar tab.

4. To use an existing phrase, click the AutoText Entry option button and select the entry from the drop-down list.

5. To create a phrase to be used, click the Type Your Own option button and type into the large text area.

6. To have context-sensitive help appear when the F1 key is pressed, click the Help Key (F1) tab and follow steps 4 and 5.

7. Click OK when you are finished.

8. Lock the form using the Protect Form button on the Forms toolbar.

The Help features can be used in conjunction with each other. For example, you might construct a travel reimbursement form. One form field's status bar might say "Enter total airline ticket cost—Press F1 for necessary departmental approvals"; in the same form field's Help Key section you could list the allowable travel expenses per department.

Calculating Form Input

If you've ever worked with a spreadsheet program like Excel and then had to do calculations in a Word table, you've probably wished that Word had an automatic function that would recalculate the formulas every time a value was changed. Well, sometimes wishes do come true. Normally, if you change any numbers in a Word table, you have to highlight the cell with the formula in it and press F9 to update the fields. With the New Calculate On Exit feature for form fields, you can easily set your Word table so that it automatically recalculates a formula anytime one of the values involved is changed.

The following is a step-by-step example of how you might use this feature:

1. Place text form fields where you want to enter your numbers by clicking the Text Form Field button on the Forms toolbar. Make sure you insert a form field for the total.

2. In all but the final form field (where the total is to appear) first change the Type from General Text to Number in the Text Form Field Options dialog box. Next, check the Calculate on Exit check box. If you like, you can also change the Number Format. Note the name of each form field in the Bookmark text box. (You can also change this to something other than Text1.)

3. In the text form field that is to display the total, first change the Type to Calculation. Next, put your formula in the Expression text box. You refer to the other form field through their Bookmark name. A typical formula that adds the three form fields above it would read "=SUM(TEXT1,TEXT2,TEXT3)". Do not select the Calculate on Exit option for this final form field box.

CAUTION

The Calculate on Exit feature has no effect on a form field whose type is set to Calculation. This means that you can't use one field as a subtotal and then add another number to it to get a total. Microsoft has confirmed this to be a problem in Word 97 that they are researching.

4. After you've closed the text form field dialog boxes, lock the form by clicking the Protect Form button on the Forms toolbar.

Now any time you enter a number into your form fields the formula recalculates.

Creating Printed Forms

Turning your computer-based form into a printed form takes a little bit of work. One of the major problems comes from the Text Form field. Although it enables your user to enter an unlimited number of characters, on-screen—and in print—the Text Form field is barely large enough for a two character state abbreviation. The Drop-Down Form field is another area that suffers in the translation from screen to hard copy.

Designing a printed form depends more on Word's drawing tools than on its form tools. A printed form must be laid out explicitly; the lines for an address block must be long enough and far enough apart to make it possible for the information to be properly entered. Any options normally put in a drop-down list must be stated one-by-one. The check box, which looks okay on the screen, might be too small on the printed form to be noticed.

Here are a number of pointers aimed at making your printed form design work faster and more smoothly:

- If you're designing a form that is intended to be filled out by a typewriter, make the font size 12 or 10 points. The type elements for most typewriters are usually one of these two sizes and it makes aligning the responses much easier.

- Avoid the underscore character when creating multiple long lines. It is much more pleasing to the eye if the line lengths match and much harder to do with the underscore character. Use tabs with the underline attribute instead of the underscore character.

- The Drawing toolbar enables you to create a variety of shapes perfect for forms—straight lines, arrows, boxes, circles, and numerous AutoShapes. Moreover they can all be independently positioned and aligned.

- A table is an easy way to create a series of evenly spaced lines. You can turn off all but the bottom border and set the table height to be exactly a certain point size. The Forms toolbar has both Insert Table and Draw Table buttons.

- If you need to position a element of the form precisely, use a frame. Click the Insert Frame button on the Forms toolbar and drag out the size frame you want. You can specify the size and position by choosing Format, Frame.

- Create a quick list of check box items by choosing Format, Bullets and Numbering and selecting the Open check box bullet. You can select any other symbol as a check box by clicking the Customize button on the Bullets and Numbering dialog box and then selecting the Bullet button. Click the Font button to change the bullet's size. Turn off your check list by clicking the Bullet button on the Formatting toolbar.

Protecting Your Form from Unauthorized Change

By now you're familiar with locking the document through the Protect Form button on the Forms toolbar. It is necessary to protect the form in order to activate many of the form functions such as check boxes and drop-down lists. In some situations, this level of protection is sufficient; however, there are circumstances where access to the form needs to be more rigorously controlled.

A more elaborate method of document protection is available by choosing Tools, Protect Document. From the Protect Document dialog box that opens, (see Figure 15.5) you can protect specifically for forms (or comments or tracked changes) and add a password. After the password is enabled, the document can't be unlocked without it.

FIG. 15.5

The Protect Document dialog box enables you to password-protect specific sections of your document.

Moreover, you can lock specific sections of a document and leave others unlocked. This technique works well when you want to use form fields in part of your document, but leave the remainder open for editing. You separate your document into sections by choosing Insert, Break and selecting Continuous Section Break. To protect a specific section, first choose Tools, Protect Document. Then, after you've clicked Forms in the Protect Document dialog box, click the Sections button. (If the Sections button is not available, either Forms is not selected or you don't have any continuous section breaks in the document). The Sections dialog box lists all available sections by number (Section 1, Section 2, and so on) with a check box next to the name. Check off all the sections to be protected. Click OK when you're done and OK again to close the Protect Document dialog box.

> **CAUTION**
>
> If you enter text in a form field when the form is protected, and then unprotect it and reprotect it, Word clears all form fields and the text is lost. You can preserve text in a field by selecting the field and pressing Ctrl+F11. This locks the selected Text Form field. This works only with Text Form fields.

Saving Your Form

It's essential to remember that forms are best based on templates. While you can make a form from a regular document, you would have to re-create the form each time you used it. If you want your users to be able to access the form by choosing File, New and opening the Template dialog box, you must save the form in the designated Template folder or one of its subfolders.

By default, document templates are stored in the Templates folder of the Microsoft Office (or Microsoft Word) folder. You can verify—and change—that by choosing Tools, Options and clicking the File Locations tab. You'll find the location listed next to the User Templates file type. To change the default template location, select User Templates and click the Modify button. Choose a new directory from the Modify Location dialog box and click OK. If you're on a network, you might also have the Workgroup Templates location set; only your network administrator can change this location.

Where do you save completed forms that are based on the template? Anywhere you like. These are considered to be normal Word documents and can be filed in any manner you see fit.

Saving Only the Data in a Form

One of the key reasons for using a form is to collect data. Data is best accessed through a database where it can be sorted, filtered, and output in various forms. Word 97 gives you an easy method to extract the information from a filled-out form without having to re-enter it into a database; you can save only the data in a form.

To save just the data from a form, follow these steps:

1. After your form has been filled out, click the Save button on the Standard toolbar.
2. Click the Options button on the Save As dialog box.
3. Check the Save Data Only for Forms check box and click OK.
4. Change the file type to Text Only.
5. Choose a file name and folder location for your file. Click OK.

 If you want to save all your forms as data-only, you can choose Tools, Options, click the Save tab and then enable the Save Data Only for Forms check box.

When Word saves just the form data, it uses comma-delimited fields. You might be familiar with the concept of a comma-delimited field if you've worked with mail merges. The information from each field is placed in quotes and separated by commas. For example, one data file might look like this: "John", "Johnson", "123 Somter Street", "Avery", "SC", "29678".

This file format is used for both Text Form fields and Drop-Down Form fields. Information returned from a Check Box Form field is handled slightly differently. A checked box shows up as a 1 while an unchecked box is a 0. Neither is in quotes.

 You can also print just the data from the form; use this feature when you want your data to appear on preprinted forms. To set this up, choose Tools, Options and on the Print tab, check the box next to Print Data Only For Forms. The data prints in the same location on the page as it does on-screen.

After you have saved your forms as data, the information can be imported into an existing database in a program like Microsoft Access. Almost any database program can read comma-delimited fields saved in a text file. If you speak VBA (Visual Basic for Applications) you could write a macro to append the information in each form into one master file to make importing even easier. ●

Inserting Graphics and Special Effects

Inserting Pictures

Inserting Pictures in Word Documents

With Word 97, you can illustrate your ideas by using pictures that come from sources outside Word, such as drawing programs, scanners, and clip art collections. If a picture is worth a thousand words, think how much typing you can save! Even if your picture is worth somewhat less than a thousand words, illustrating your document with graphics can make your pages more appealing—which means that readers pay more attention to your words.

Word can use pictures from many sources. Some may come from an external drawing or painting program, which you can use to create illustrations ranging from the simple to the sophisticated. Some—including photographs—come from scanners that digitize artwork for use in a computer. Some pictures come from clip art packages that provide ready-to-use artwork. Office 97 itself includes many clip art images that you can use in Word.

These pictures come from a source outside of Word. In addition, you can use these pictures in many programs besides Word, which is the feature that distinguishes them from the graphic objects you create using Word's built-in drawing tools: WordArt, AutoShapes, Chart, and the Drawing toolbar. You also can use one of these built-in graphic programs to create a graphic that exists only as a part of your Word document.

Programs you use to create pictures often are more powerful than the simple built-in programs that come with Word. Word gives you the flexibility to include a range of graphics and pictures in your documents—from simple drawings that you create yourself without leaving Word to sophisticated pictures that you can make with a powerful standalone program.

Getting Ready to Insert Pictures

Word is compatible with many of the most frequently used graphics programs and scanner formats. For some formats, you don't need a special import filter. For others you do need a filter, and you must install a filter when you set up Word or Office or rerun the Word or Office Setup program to install them later. From the Options list, select Converters and Filters.

To import pictures into a document, Word uses special *import filters*. One filter is required for each type of file you want to import. If you selected the Complete Setup option when you installed Word, all the graphics import filters were put into your system. If you selected a Custom installation, you might not have installed all the filters. To see which filters are installed (and consequently which types of graphics you are able to import), read the contents of the Files of Type list in the Insert Picture dialog box. This dialog box appears when you choose Insert, Picture, From File.

You can import pictures created with any of the following programs or in any of the formats listed:

Program Format	File Extension
Formats that don't require filters	
Windows Metafile	WMF
Enhanced Windows Metafile	EMF
JPEG Filter	JPG
Portable Network Graphics	PNG
Windows Bitmap	BMP
Formats that do require filters	
PC Paintbrush	PCX
Tagged Image Format	TIF
Encapsulated PostScript	EPS
Computer Graphics Metafile	CGM
WordPerfect Graphics	WPG
Micrografx Designer	DRW
Micrografx Draw	DRW
Targa	TGA
AutoCAD Format 2-D	DXF
CorelDRAW!	CDR
Macintosh PICT	PCT
GIF	GIF
Kodak PhotoCD	PCD

Your favorite graphic program might not be listed. However, many programs easily export graphics (or even part of a graphic) from the native format to a commonly used format. If your program isn't on the preceding list, see whether it can save graphics in one of the formats in the list, so that you can use them in Word.

Inserting and Copying Your Own Pictures into Your Document

You can insert a picture into the text of your document, a text box, or a table. Inserting a picture directly into your text is the simplest way to illustrate your document. You can work with inserted pictures in many ways; for example, you can group them together, wrap text around them, or layer them above or below text and other graphics.

Other techniques, however, sometimes offer advantages. Inserting a picture in one cell of a table enables you to position the picture adjacent to text in the next cell. Inserting a picture in a text box enables you to group the picture with text inside a common border.

Note that if you insert a picture while you're in Normal viewing mode, Word switches you to the Page Layout view. You can't see pictures in your document in Normal view.

You can use one of three methods to insert a picture in your document:

- You can insert pictures by choosing Insert, Picture, From File or by clicking the Insert Picture button on the Picture toolbar. This command asks you to locate the file and then inserts the picture from disk. If you use this method, you don't even need to own the program used to create the picture.

- You can open the program used to create the picture and copy the picture into the Windows Clipboard. Then you can paste the picture into your Word document.

- You can insert picture objects by using Insert, Object to open a graphics program from within Word. You can use this command to insert a picture that you can edit later using the program that created it.

TIP You can automatically include a numbered caption with each picture you insert by choosing Insert, Caption, AutoCaption. For more about captions, see Chapter 22, "Adding Cross-References and Captions."

Use the Insert Picture dialog box when you want to insert pictures that you won't want to edit later.

To quickly insert a picture, position the insertion point where you want it and double-click the picture's file name in the Insert Picture dialog box.

Inserting Pictures into a Document

Although you can insert a picture in your document without ever opening the program used to create the picture, you must first locate the picture file.

Word offers many tools for helping you find a file. You can find files that match a certain name, file type, or property, or files that were modified recently.

You can insert a picture with or without a link to the program used to create the picture. By linking to the graphics program, you might be able to reduce the size of your document (see the upcoming section, "Minimizing File Size through Linking").

To insert a picture, follow these steps:

1. Position the insertion point where you want to insert the picture.

2. Choose Insert, Picture, From File, or click the Insert Picture button on the Picture toolbar.

    The Insert Picture dialog box appears (see Figure 16.1).

FIG. 16.1.
Use the Insert Picture dialog box to locate a picture you want to insert. The preview box shows the selected picture.

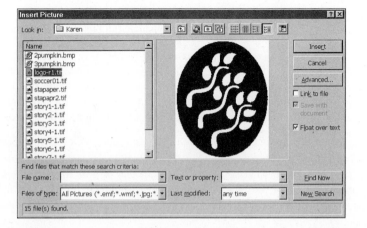

3. Locate your picture file. Use the Look In list to find the folder in which the file is stored and, if necessary, use the matching criteria at the bottom of the dialog box to search for your file.

4. Select the picture file you want to insert from the Name list. Click the Preview button if you want to see a miniature version of your picture.

5. Choose Insert.

When you insert a picture in your Word document, it falls into place at the location of the insertion point and is anchored to its paragraph. The picture stays with that paragraph as you edit surrounding text. You can move the picture by dragging it with the mouse; for details, see the later section, "Working with Pictures."

If you want to embed your picture in the text (so that it is included in the text like a character), rather than allow it to be free floating, clear the Float Over Text option in the Insert Picture dialog box. An embedded picture moves with surrounding text and can even accept paragraph formatting (such as alignment, which you could use to center the picture on the page).

Performing Advanced Picture File Searches   If you're having a hard time locating the picture you want to insert, Word can help you find it. In the Insert Picture dialog box (refer to Figure 16.1), choose Advanced to display the Advanced Find dialog box. Select from the many options to find files matching naming criteria, properties such as the application name or the picture's author, or location.

N O T E   If you cannot insert a picture because it's in a format Word doesn't recognize, try opening the picture in Windows Paint or some other graphics program. Then save the picture in a format Word does recognize, such as BMP. ■

▶ **See** "Formatting Lines and Paragraphs," **p. 81**

Minimizing File Size Through Linking   When you insert a picture in your document, Word usually includes all the information in the picture file, as well as a representation of the picture.

Each time you open your document, you see the picture. However, this method can make your Word file quite large: The file size is increased by the file size of the picture (which can be very large).

Another way to insert a picture is to link the picture to its picture file, but not store a copy of the picture in your Word file. Each time you open your document, Word refers to the original file to draw a representation of the picture. This method has the advantage of minimizing your file size, because Word does not store a copy of the picture in your document.

Minimizing file size in this way is helpful if your graphics files are very large or if you're using the same graphic file repeatedly in different documents (like a logo in your stationery). However, if the file is not available, Word cannot display or print the picture—when you open the Word file, a message box warns you that Word cannot open the picture file. Use this method for minimizing file size only when you are sure Word will be able to locate the picture file.

To minimize file size through linking, follow these steps:

1. Position the insertion point where you want the picture to appear. Then choose Insert, Picture, From File and select the picture you want to insert.

2. In the Insert Picture dialog box, select the Link to File option (at the far right of the dialog box, under the Advanced command button). Then clear the Save with Document option.

3. Choose Insert.

If you move the original picture file, you must update the link by selecting the picture and choosing Edit, Links, Change Source. (You also can use this command to save the picture in the document.)

If you give someone a Word file containing a picture that is linked to the file, be sure to give them a copy of the picture file as well. Have them choose Edit, Links, Change Source to identify the picture file's location on their hard disk.

Another way to minimize file size is to save picture files in a format that creates smaller files, when that is an option. PCX, BMP, and WMF files are usually smaller than EPS or TIF files, for example. You can also minimize document file size by using black-and-white pictures, rather than color, especially if you'll print in black and white anyway.

Copying Pictures into Your Document

Sometimes the easiest way to get a picture you created with a graphics program into Word is to use the Clipboard to copy the picture. You can even link the picture to the original file when you paste it into Word; in this way, you can update the picture if you later make changes to the original.

To copy a picture into your document, follow these steps:

1. Start your graphics or charting program. Then open the file containing the picture you want to copy into your Word document.

2. Select the picture or chart.

3. Choose <u>E</u>dit, <u>C</u>opy.

4. Switch to your Word document.

5. Position the insertion point where you want to insert the picture.

6. Choose <u>E</u>dit, <u>P</u>aste.

   Or, choose <u>E</u>dit, Paste <u>S</u>pecial to link the picture to the original file. Select Paste <u>L</u>ink from the Paste Special dialog box. In the <u>A</u>s list, select the format for your picture (formats vary depending on what type of picture you copied). Select the <u>D</u>isplay as Icon option if you want to display an icon, rather than the picture, in your text. (You can double-click the icon to display and edit the picture.)

7. Click OK.

T I P Images and pictures you see on Web pages can be copied to a file or to the Windows Clipboard. Right-click an image, then choose <u>C</u>opy to copy to the Clipboard or <u>S</u>ave Picture As to display a Save As dialog box. Choose P<u>r</u>operties to see the size and type of file. Insert files and paste Clipboard copies into your documents. Not all images are free for the taking. Do not violate trademark, copyright, and registration laws.

When you paste in a picture with a link, you get some choices. If you paste the picture as an *object*, you can edit it later. If you paste the picture as a *picture*, it might take up less space. To get an idea of the best way to paste in your picture, read the Result box at the bottom of the Paste Special dialog box as you select each of the different formats in the <u>A</u>s list.

Inserting Picture Objects in Your Document

A *picture object* is a picture in your Word document that you can edit. You edit the picture by double-clicking it to display the program used to create the picture, if the program is available. All the data that creates a picture object is contained within the Word document—it is not linked to a file outside the document.

▶ **See** "Inserting Text with Special Effects," **p. 443**

You can insert many types of picture objects in your document. If Adobe Illustrator or another OLE-based graphics program is installed on your computer, you can insert an Illustrator object. If Microsoft Excel is installed, you can embed an Excel chart as an object. You can insert an equation, graph, picture, or WordArt image as an object, and you can insert a Microsoft Word Picture object.

You can insert new or existing picture objects. If you insert new picture objects, Word displays the graphics program you've chosen, and you must draw the picture. For example, if you choose to insert a new Illustrator picture object, Word starts Illustrator and presents you with a blank drawing screen. You draw the picture, and then you choose a command to return to your Word document with the picture.

If you insert existing picture objects, the existing picture appears in your document. Whether you insert new or existing picture objects, you always can double-click one of these objects to display the program used to create the picture. Then you can edit the picture. Alternatively, you can use a command to edit the picture.

To insert a new picture object, follow these steps:

1. Position the insertion point where you want to insert the picture object.
2. Choose Insert, Object. The Object dialog box appears (see Figure 16.2).

FIG. 16.2
When you insert a new picture object, Word displays the program you use to create it.

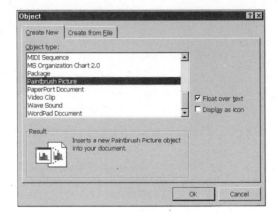

3. Select the Create New tab.
4. Select the type of picture object you want to insert from the Object Type list. For example, to insert a Microsoft Word picture, select Microsoft Word Picture from the list.

   Select the Display as Icon check box if you want to display an icon rather than the picture. Icons can be used if a picture will take too much room in a document. The icon displays on-screen or when printed. You can double-click the icon to see its contents.
5. Choose OK. A rectangular selection appears in your document, and tools from the program you'll use to create the object appear at the edges of the screen.

   For example, if you chose Paintbrush Picture, the screen shown in Figure 16.3 appears. Notice the Drawing tools at the left edge of the screen and the color palette at the bottom.
6. Create the picture.
7. Return to your Word document by clicking your Word document page, outside the object work area.

To insert an existing picture object, follow these steps:

1. Position the insertion point where you want to insert the picture object.
2. Choose Insert, Object. The Object dialog box appears (see Figure 16.4).
3. Select the Create from File tab.
4. Type the path and file name of the picture you want to insert in the File Name box. Locate the file, if necessary, by selecting Browse.

FIG. 16.3
You can insert or draw a picture using Microsoft Paint.

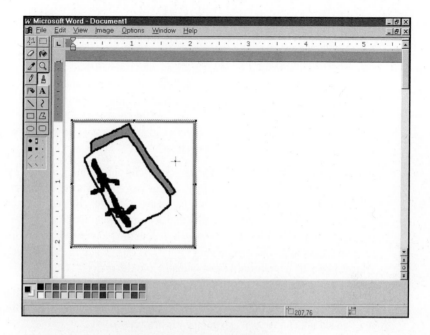

FIG. 16.4
You can insert an existing picture object and edit it later.

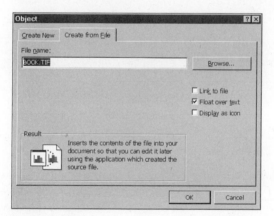

5. Select Link to File if you want the picture in your Word document to update when you change the original picture.

6. Select Display as Icon if you want to display an icon rather than the picture.

7. Click OK.

Read the message in the Result box at the bottom of the Object dialog box to see the results that the currently selected options have produced in your document.

TIP Choose Insert, Object when you want to insert pictures that you can edit later.

Inserting Clip Art in Your Document

Clip art is one of the most economical tools you can use to illustrate a document professionally, and with Word, using clip art is easy. Microsoft Office includes a good collection of more than 1,000 clip art images on disk, and if you're on the Internet, you can download even more. In addition, Word includes a clip art gallery that organizes your clip art into categories and shows you a miniature picture of each piece so you can choose it visually, rather than guessing what a picture looks like by its file name. Word's clip art gallery works equally well with Microsoft clip art and with non-Microsoft clip art packages.

Microsoft Clip Gallery not only manages your clip art, letting you organize, preview, and insert clip art pictures but also is the tool you use in Word to organize and insert sound clips and video clips. The gallery automatically accesses Microsoft clip art that is stored on your Office CD when the CD is in its drive. Other clip art must be added to the gallery—even if the clip art is already on your hard disk—if you want to use the gallery to preview and insert it. If you want to have access to the clip art on your Office CD even when the CD is not in its drive, you must copy the clip art to your hard drive and add it to the gallery.

Many World Wide Web sites contain free graphics, images, and photographs. Stock image companies display on the Web catalogs of the images and photographs they have for sale. To see two sites that have clip art, point your browser to

Web Site	URL	Description
Microsoft's Gallery	http://www.microsoft.com/gallery	Gallery of free images, photos, and multimedia for use in Word and Web pages.
Publisher's Depot	http://www.publishersdepot.com	Desktop publishing software distributor that sells digitized photos, illustrations, and images.

Inserting Clip Art Pictures

Microsoft Clip Gallery is not like a folder that stores files; rather, it is like a pointer that tells Word where to find your clip art files. It organizes your clip art into categories to help you manage them and displays a miniature picture of each clip art image that you can view to select the best picture for your document. If you attempt to insert clip art but find none in the gallery, go to the next section, "Adding Clip Art to the Gallery," to learn how to add your clip art to the gallery.

The gallery dialog box includes two tabs that show different types of clip art. One tab, Clip Art, shows object-based images, some of which you can ungroup and modify using color tools on the Drawing toolbar; the other tab, Pictures, shows bitmap images, some of which you can modify using image, contrast, and brightness tools on the Picture toolbar.

Also included in the Clip Gallery dialog box are two tabs, Sounds and Videos, that display audio and video clips you can include in your documents.

To insert a clip art picture into your document, follow these steps:

1. Position the insertion point where you want the clip art.

2. Choose Insert, Picture, Clip Art to display the Microsoft Clip Gallery 3.0 dialog box, shown in Figure 16.5.

FIG. 16.5
The Microsoft Clip Gallery organizes, previews, and inserts clip art.

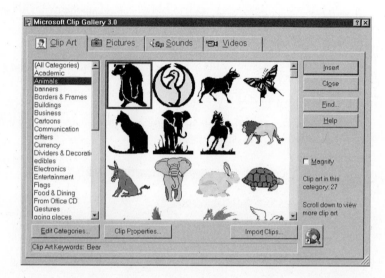

3. Select the Clip Art or the Pictures tab to locate the clip art you want to insert.

4. Scroll through the Categories list and select the category that contains the clip art you want to insert.

5. Click the clip art image you want to insert. If necessary, scroll the viewing screen to see all the art included in the category you selected.

   If you're having trouble locating the image you want, choose Find. In the Find Clip dialog box, type a description of what you're looking for in the Keywords list or type a partial file name in the File Name containing list or select a file type in the Clip Type list. Then choose Find Now. The gallery finds images that match your criteria and displays them in a category called Results of Last Find.

   Choose Magnify if you want to see a magnified view of the selected image, along with its file name.

6. Choose Insert.

Alternatively, you can insert an image by double-clicking it in the gallery.

Creating and Changing Clip Art Categories

The clip art that comes free with Microsoft Office is organized by category for you. Other clip art is not. You can easily create categories or modify existing categories. You should try to create categories, if you need them, before adding new clip art to the gallery, especially when you're adding a whole new package of clip art to the gallery.

To create or change a clip art gallery category, follow these steps:

1. Choose Insert, Picture, Clip Art to display the Microsoft Clip Gallery dialog box.
2. Choose the tab where you want to add a clip art category: Clip Art or Pictures.
3. Choose Edit Categories to display the Edit Category List dialog box, shown in Figure 16.6. Then do one of the following:

   Select New Category to add a category. Then type the new category name and choose OK.

   Select the category you want to delete and choose Delete Category.

   Select the category you want to rename, choose Rename Category, type the new category name, and choose OK.

FIG. 16.6
You can easily add or edit a clip art category.

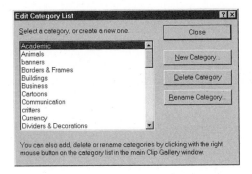

4. Choose Close. Choose Close again if you want to close the gallery.

Adding Clip Art to the Gallery

Although Microsoft Clip Gallery automatically recognizes Microsoft Office clip art, you must add other clip art to the gallery in order for the gallery to recognize it. Clip art might include packages of clip art that you purchase, or it might be art you've drawn yourself using graphics software. Keep in mind that the gallery must always be able to find the clip art files if it is to display them; see the upcoming section, "Relocating Clip Art Files," to learn what to do if you've moved a file.

To add clip art to the gallery, follow these steps:

1. Choose Insert, Picture, Clip Art to open the Microsoft Clip Gallery dialog box.
2. Choose Import Clips to display the Add Clip Art to the Clip Gallery dialog box, shown in Figure 16.7.

FIG. 16.7

Select the clip art files you want to add to the gallery.

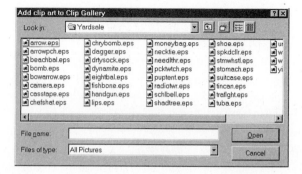

FIG. 16.8

Enter keywords and select categories for the clip art you add to the gallery. You can later search for clip art using keywords.

3. Locate and select the clip art you want to add to the gallery. You can add one at a time or many at once.

4. Choose Open to display the Clip Properties dialog box, shown in Figure 16.8. Notice the preview of the image at the top of the dialog box.

5. Type any keywords you want associated with this clip art in the Keywords box. (You can search for clip art using these keywords.)

6. Select the categories in the Categories list where you want your clip art. Clear categories where you don't want it. (Clip art can go into as many categories as you want.) If you don't have a category for your clip art, choose New Category, type the new category name, and choose OK.

If you're adding many clip art files to the gallery at once and they're all going into the same category or categories, choose Add All Clips to the Selected Categories.

If you're adding many clips at once but they're going to different categories, then don't choose Add All Clips to the Selected Categories; you see in the next step how you can choose categories for each file individually.

7. Choose OK. If you selected multiple clip art files to add all at once but didn't select the Add All Clips to the Selected Categories option, then the Clip Properties dialog box reappears for each clip and gives you the option to change categories, or even to choose Skip This Clip to bypass this particular clip.

Changing Keywords and Categories

Categories help you organize clip art and are especially helpful if you have a lot of clip art. Keywords help you find clip art by using a descriptive word. If you want to change the category a piece of clip art is in, or add or change its keywords, you change its properties. (You can't change properties for the Microsoft Office clip art.)

To change a clip's keywords or category, follow these steps:

1. Select the clip art from the Microsoft Clip Gallery whose keywords or category you want to change.

2. Choose Clip Properties to display the Clip Properties dialog box (refer to Figure 16.8).

3. Type in the Keywords box any new keywords by which you'd like to be able to search for this piece of clip art, or edit existing words. You can separate the words any way you want or even not separate them.

4. Select from the Categories list the category or categories where you want to store this clip art or clear any categories where you don't want to store it.

5. Click OK.

Downloading Clip Art from the Internet

If you have access to the Internet, you can add to your clip art collection by downloading images from Microsoft. The Clip Gallery includes a tool to help you acquire the files and add them to the Clip Gallery. (You must have an Internet connection and browser.)

To download clip art files from the Internet, follow these steps:

1. Choose Insert, Picture, Clip Art to display the Microsoft Clip Gallery.

2. Click the Connect to Web for Additional Clips button, which looks like a globe, at the bottom right of the dialog box. Then choose OK to continue.

3. Choose Accept when the Microsoft Clip Gallery Live screen, shown in Figure 16.9, appears.

4. Click the button that describes the type of clips you want to download: clip art, pictures, sound, or video. Click the leftmost button to download clip art.

5. Define your search criteria by doing one of two things:

   Click Browse and select a clip art category or,

   Click Search and enter keywords.

FIG. 16.9
The Microsoft Clip Gallery Live is a source on the Internet for clip art, pictures, video clips, and sound clips.

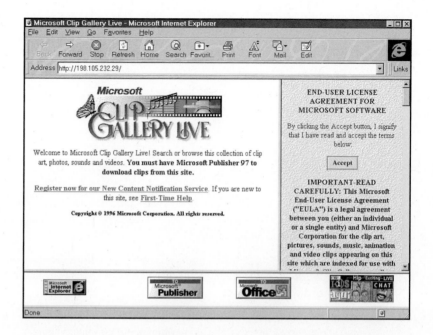

6. Click Go to perform the search. The Gallery returns the results of the search on the left side of the screen, as shown in Figure 16.10.

FIG. 16.10
The Gallery displays images that match your search criteria; you can download them to your Word gallery.

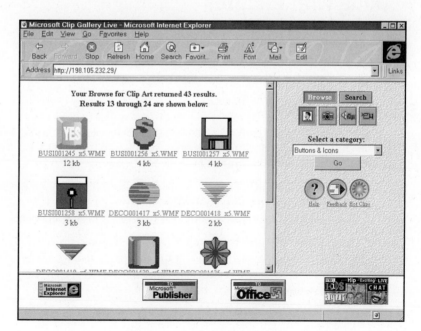

7. Scroll through the images displayed on the screen to decide which image(s) to download. To download an image, click the file name under the preview picture. Your browser returns two options for downloading the image.

8. Choose Open it to install the image in the Microsoft Clip Gallery.

   Or, choose Save It to Disk to copy the file onto your disk. Enter a name and path for the file.

9. Exit your browser.

Relocating Clip Art Files

If you move a clip art file or remove the disk from where Microsoft Clip Gallery expects to find it, then the Gallery cannot find the file and you cannot use the Gallery to insert the clip art into your document. If you try to insert a moved clip art file, you'll get a message saying, Word can't find the file. Choose OK to go on.

The Cannot Insert Picture box recommends that you remove the clip from the Gallery. Choose Remove Preview to remove a single clip art preview or choose Update All to remove all previews whose files have moved.

If you move a clip art file, but still want to use it in the Gallery, first remove it from the Gallery to omit incorrect references to its old location and then import it again.

Working with Pictures

After you insert a picture in your document, you can manipulate it in many ways. You can select and move it, and you can group it with other pictures, with text, or with other objects. You can ungroup pictures that are composed of a group of objects—including some clip art. You can layer pictures in front of or behind text, pictures, and other objects.

Selecting Pictures

Before you change a picture, you must select it. When a picture is selected, it has square selection handles on all four corners and sides—eight in all. You must select a picture before you revise it in any way or before you move, group, or layer it.

To select a picture, simply click it. If you're working with layers, you can use a special tool on the Drawing toolbar to select pictures that are layered behind text or another object; see the later section, "Layering Pictures with Text and Other Objects," for details.

Clicking an inserted picture selects it. Double-clicking a picture often has a very different effect. If it's a picture object, double-clicking will bring up the program used to create the picture; if it's clip art, double-clicking will display the Microsoft Clip Gallery dialog box, which you can use to replace the picture.

▶ **See** "Aligning Paragraphs," **p. 90**

Moving, Positioning, or Copying a Picture

Inserted pictures move easily and freely in a Word document. By simply dragging a picture with a mouse, you can move it anywhere.

To move a picture, follow these steps:

1. Position the insertion point over the picture so that it turns into a pointer arrow over a four-headed arrow.

2. Drag the picture where you want it (see Figure 16.11).

FIG. 16.11

You can drag a picture to move it.

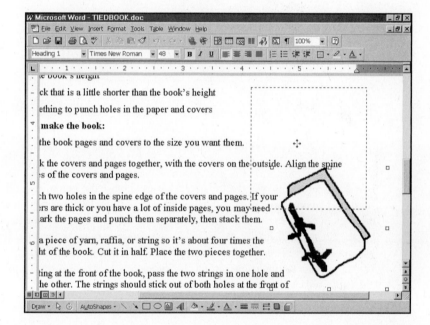

You can also use a command to position a picture in a precise location on the page. The position is horizontally and vertically relative to some edge on your page. Objects are always positioned relative to the left margin, the left edge of a column, the top of the page, or the beginning of a paragraph.

To position a picture precisely, follow these steps:

1. Click the picture to select it.

2. Choose Format, Object or Format, Picture to display the Format dialog box.

3. Select the Position tab, shown in Figure 16.12.

4. Select Horizontal and enter a distance; then select From and select Margin, Page, or Column. The picture will be positioned that distance from the left margin, page edge, or column edge.

FIG. 16.12
You can choose Format, Object, Position or Format, Picture, Position to position a picture precisely.

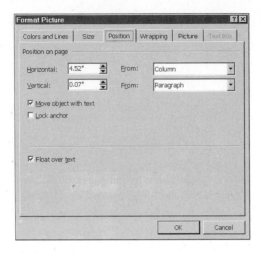

5. Select Vertical and enter a distance; then select From and select Margin, Page, or Paragraph. The picture will be positioned that distance from the top margin, the top of the page, or the beginning of the paragraph.

6. Click OK.

Usually pictures float over the top of text (or can be layered below it; see the upcoming section, "Layering Pictures with Text and Other Objects"). When pictures float in this way, you can move them freely on the page. But there may be times when you want an inserted picture to behave like a text character. Inserted this way, you can move the picture like a text character; you can select it like a text character; you can apply paragraph formatting like a text character. You might want a nonfloating picture, for example, to serve as a small icon that moves with the characters adjacent to it.

To position a picture so that it behaves like text (to anchor it), follow these steps:

1. Select the picture by clicking it.

2. Choose Format, Object, Position or Format, Picture, Position.

3. Clear the Float Over Text option.

4. Click OK.

 If you can't move or position a picture, the picture may have been inserted with the Float Over Text option cleared. To float the picture so you can move or position it in your document, choose Format, Object, Position or Format, Picture, Position and then select the Float Over Text option.

By default, a picture moves along with the text where you inserted it because it is anchored to that text. For example, if you insert it in the third paragraph on a page and then add text above the third paragraph, the picture moves forward along with the paragraph. If you don't want the picture to move with the text, you can override that default.

If you move an anchored picture to another page, the anchor moves with it. You can prevent the picture from moving to another page by locking its anchor.

To change a picture's anchors, follow these steps:

1. Select the picture and choose Format, Object, Position or Format, Picture, Position.

2. Select Move Object with Text to anchor a picture to the paragraph where you insert it; clear this option if you don't want it to move as you edit text.

   Or, select Lock Anchor if you want to keep a picture on the page where it's currently positioned; clear this option to allow the picture to move to another page.

3. Click OK.

You can use a command to move or copy a picture. And here's a trick for copying a picture (or any other object) using the mouse—hold down the Ctrl key on your keyboard while you drag the object with the mouse.

To move or copy a picture using a command, follow these steps:

1. Select the picture.

2. Choose Edit, Cut (Ctrl+X or Shift+Delete) to move a picture, or Edit, Copy (Ctrl+C or Ctrl+Insert) to copy it.

3. Move the insertion point to the place where you want to move the picture. Then choose Edit, Paste (Ctrl+V or Shift+Insert).

Grouping and Ungrouping Pictures

Grouping pictures allows you to move them as a unit and to apply formatting to all the pictures in a group simultaneously. You can group pictures with other pictures or with other objects. For example, you can group a picture with its caption to keep the picture and its caption together.

When you apply formatting to objects in a group, the formatting applies to each individual object. For example, a line border applied to a group appears around the edges of each of the objects in the group, not around the group as a whole. If you want a border or other formatting to apply to the group as a whole, try inserting the objects together in a text or picture box.

To group pictures, follow these steps:

1. Select each of the pictures you want to include in the group by holding the Shift key while you click on each picture. Each picture should show selection handles.

2. Click one of the selected objects with the right mouse button to display the shortcut menu, shown in Figure 16.13.

3. Choose Grouping, Group. Once grouped, the pictures share a single set of selection handles.

Ungrouping a group releases the individual components. Often you can ungroup inserted clip art; if so, you may be able to use individual components in the clip art or modify individual parts of it.

FIG. 16.13

When you group pictures (or other objects), they function as a single unit.

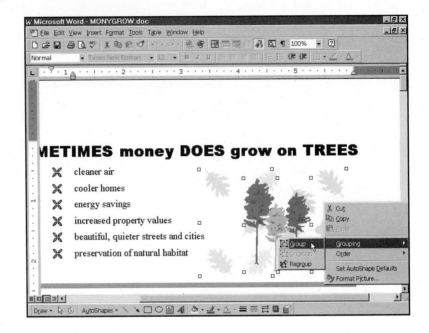

To ungroup pictures or other objects, follow these steps:

1. Click the group with the right mouse button to display the shortcut menu.

2. Choose Grouping, Ungroup.

To regroup a previously grouped collection of objects, you need to select only one of the objects and choose Grouping, Regroup. The objects are regrouped, but not moved—they are grouped in the position they are in when you choose the Regroup command, not in the position they were in the first time you grouped them.

Layering Pictures with Text and Other Objects

Pictures and other Word objects usually are placed in a layer that floats over the top of text. (If you want a picture to be embedded in the text, rather than floating over it, see the earlier section, "Moving, Positioning, or Copying a Picture.") You can layer pictures so that they appear behind text or behind other pictures and objects. You can move a selected object one layer behind or in front of another object, or all the way behind or to the front of several other objects. The Drawing toolbar has a tool to help you select an object that's layered behind text.

Note that you can't layer a picture behind text if you've selected a text wrapping option for the picture. If you can't layer your picture, select the picture and make sure no wrapping is selected. For more information, see the section, "Wrapping Text Around a Picture."

To layer a picture behind or in front of text or another object, follow these steps:

1. Click the picture with the right mouse button to display the shortcut menu.

2. Choose Order and then choose one of the following commands:

Select This Option	To Have This Effect
Bring to Front	Bring to the front of a stack of pictures or objects.
Send to Back	Send to the back of a stack of pictures or objects.
Bring Forward	Bring forward by a single picture or object.
Send Backward	Send backward by a single picture or object.
Bring in Front of Text	Brings a picture in front of text.
Send Behind Text	Sends a picture box behind text.

Be sure to use the Bring in Front of Text and Send Behind Text commands when you want to layer an object with text.

To select a picture that's layered behind text, do the following:

1. Display the Drawing toolbar.
2. Choose the Select Objects tool.
3. Position the Select Objects pointer over the picture and click to select it.
4. Click the Select Objects tool to deselect it when you're finished.

Displaying and Hiding Pictures

Pictures use a lot of your computer's memory (and disk space). Thus they can slow you down when you're working, especially if your document contains several pictures. Hiding pictures is a good way to save time when you don't need to see them. You might display the pictures only while you're inserting and formatting them. Then you can hide them while you work on the text in your document.

To hide pictures, follow these steps:

1. Choose Tools, Options and select the View tab.
2. Clear the Drawings option in the Show group.
3. Click OK.

To display hidden pictures, follow these steps:

1. Choose Tools, Options and select the View tab.
2. Select Drawings in the Show group.
3. Click OK.

Formatting Pictures

Word gives you many ways to format pictures. You can size and crop them; add a border around them; add a fill color to some pictures; place a shadow behind them; or you can wrap text around pictures. Three important tools help you perform all these formatting feats: the Picture toolbar (shown in Figure 16.14), the Format command, and the Drawing toolbar.

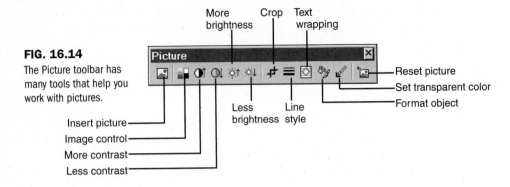

FIG. 16.14

The Picture toolbar has many tools that help you work with pictures.

In the upcoming section, "Modifying Pictures," you learn how to modify the appearance of pictures in other ways, such as by altering a picture's brightness.

You may have to experiment with your picture to find out the ways in which you can change it. Pictures come in one of two formats: bitmap and object. A bitmap picture is like a painting; it is a single layer of varying colors and shapes. An object-oriented picture, on the other hand, is made up of objects that can be moved, layered, grouped, reshaped, and colored. You can change bitmap pictures by altering their brightness and contrast, but you can't change their fill color. You can change the fill color of an object, but you can't alter its brightness or contrast. You can add borders to any picture, size it, crop it, or wrap text around it.

 TIP A quick way to display the Format dialog box is by clicking a picture (or its border, if it's framed) with the right mouse button to display the shortcut menu and then selecting the Format Object or Format Picture command.

Resizing and Cropping Pictures

After you insert a picture in your document, you can scale the picture to a smaller or larger size. You also can size it to the exact dimensions you want, or crop away parts of the picture you don't want to use. Resizing is useful when you need a picture to be a certain size in your document. Cropping helps when you want to zoom in on the most important part of the picture.

You can change the dimensions of a picture in three ways:

- Scale the picture larger or smaller by a percentage (proportionally or nonproportionally)
- Size the picture to an exact width and height
- Crop away part of the picture

You can make any of these changes with the mouse or keyboard commands.

Resizing and Cropping with the Mouse   Using the mouse to scale, size, or crop a picture is a visual process: It enables you to see how your changes look while you're making them. If you use the mouse to change a picture and you later want to see what its dimensions are, select the picture. Then choose Format, Object, Size or Format, Picture, Size. The entries in the Size and Scale groups tell you the picture's current dimensions.

To change a picture, you select it and drag the selection handles that appear on the sides and corners of the picture. After you select the picture and move the mouse pointer over the selection handles, the pointer changes shape: It turns into a two-headed arrow if you're resizing the picture (left side of Figure 16.15) or a cropping tool if you're cropping the picture (right side of Figure 16.15).

FIG. 16.15

You can resize the picture by dragging its handles (left); crop the picture by selecting the Crop tool from the Picture toolbar and then dragging a handle (right).

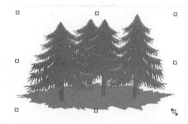 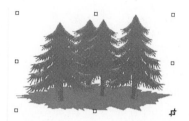

Each of the eight selection handles surrounding a selected picture has a specific purpose. The corner handles enable you to scale or crop from two sides. When you use a corner handle to resize a picture, the picture remains proportional. The side handles enable scaling and cropping from just one side. When you use a side handle to resize, the picture's proportions change. Whenever you drag a handle, the opposite handle stays anchored to its current position.

When you resize a picture by dragging a handle toward the center of the picture, you make the picture smaller. When you crop a picture by dragging toward the center, you cut away part of the picture. When you drag the handle away to resize a picture, you make the picture larger. If you're cropping, you add a blank border after you pass the picture's original edges. Figure 16.16 shows an original picture (on the left) that has been sized smaller (top right example) and cropped (bottom right example).

As you drag the handles to resize or crop the picture, you see a dotted-line box that represents the picture's new size and shape. When you release the mouse button, the picture snaps to fit inside the box.

To resize a picture with the mouse, follow these steps:

1. Select the picture.
2. Move the mouse pointer over a selection handle until it turns into a two-headed arrow.
3. Drag a corner handle to scale the picture proportionally or drag a side handle to scale a picture nonproportionally, distorting it.
4. Release the mouse button when the picture is the size you want.

To crop a picture, follow these steps:

1. Select the picture.
2. Select the Crop tool on the Picture toolbar.

3. Drag any selection handle.

4. Release the mouse button when the picture is cropped the way you want it.

FIG. 16.16

The original picture (left) becomes smaller or larger when you resize it (top right). Some of it is cut away when you crop it (bottom right).

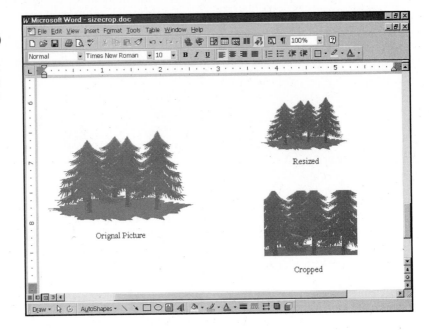

Resizing and Cropping with the Format Dialog Box You can use the Format dialog box to scale, size, or crop a picture. The Format dialog box includes boxes in which you can adjust measurements. Each box has up and down arrows to its right. Click the up arrow to increase the measurement; click the down arrow to decrease it.

Note that the command to format some pictures is Format, Object, while for others it is Format, Picture. The resulting dialog box uses the same name.

 If you want to use a different measurement system in the Format dialog box—for example, points instead of inches—choose Tools, Options, General, and select the system you want in the Measurement Units list.

To size or scale a picture with the Format dialog box, follow these steps:

1. Select the picture.

2. Choose Format, Object, Size or Format, Picture, Size; or click with the right mouse button on the picture and select Format Object or Format Picture, Size.

   The Format dialog box appears (see Figure 16.17).

FIG. 16.17
You can crop, scale, and size a picture to specific dimensions in the Format dialog box.

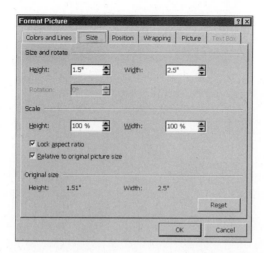

3. If you want to make your picture an exact size, use the Size and Rotate group (even though you can't rotate a picture). Enter the dimensions for your picture in the H̲eight and Wi̲dth boxes.

If you want your picture to be exactly 3 inches high, for example, type **3** in the H̲eight box; if you want the picture to be 2 inches wide, type **2** in the Wi̲dth box.

4. If you want to scale your picture by a percentage, use the Scale group. In the H̲eight or W̲idth box (or both), enter the percentage by which you want to scale the picture.

If you want to scale the picture to half its original height, for example, type **50** (for 50 percent) in the H̲eight box. To double its height, type **200** (for 200 percent) in the H̲eight box.

If you want to scale proportionally (so that the height and widths change to the same percent), select the Lock A̲spect Ratio option. Then you need enter only one value for either height or width to scale the picture.

If you want to scale the picture from its original size, rather than from whatever size you've already scaled it to, select the R̲elative to Original Picture Size option.

5. Click OK.

To crop a picture, follow these steps:

1. Select the picture.

2. Choose F̲ormat, O̲bject, Picture or F̲ormat, Pi̲cture, Picture; or click with the right mouse button on the picture and select Format, O̲bject or Format, Pi̲cture, Picture. The Picture tab in the Format dialog box is shown in Figure 16.18.

3. Enter cropping amounts in the Crop From group, using the L̲eft, R̲ight, T̲op, and B̲ottom list boxes.

To crop 1/2 inch off the bottom of the picture, for example, type **.5** in the B̲ottom box. To crop 1/4 inch off the right side, type **.25** in the R̲ight box.

You can crop by a negative number; in this way, the picture box grows to be larger than the picture.

4. Click OK.

FIG. 16.18

You can use the Format Picture dialog box to crop a picture precisely.

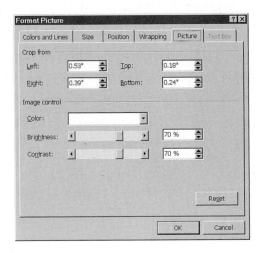

Resetting the Picture to its Original Dimensions   You easily can reset your picture to its original dimensions (even if you changed it with the mouse rather than the Format dialog box). Follow these steps:

1. Select the picture.

2. Choose Format, Object or Format, Picture. Select the Size tab to reset the picture's size; select the Picture tab to undo cropping.

3. Choose the Reset button.

Alternatively, you can reset a picture by selecting it and clicking the Reset Picture button on the Picture toolbar.

Adding Lines, Fills, and Color

Unless a border is part of your original composition, pictures arrive in your document with no lines around their edges. You easily can add a line border around a picture, in any of many line styles and colors. (Whenever you choose a line for a picture, it borders the picture on all four sides.) For some pictures, you can add fill color. Some clip art, for example, can be ungrouped into individual components, and you can change the fill in each piece.

One tool to help you border and color a picture is the Colors and Lines tab in the Format dialog box. Another tool is the Drawing toolbar, which contains tools for quickly changing fill and line color, and style, and for adding a shadow or 3-D effect. You can access the Format dialog box by command, by using the Format button on the Picture toolbar, or by clicking with the right mouse button on the picture and choosing Format Object or Format Picture in the shortcut menu. Display the Drawing toolbar by choosing View, Toolbars, Drawing.

Keep in mind that if you can't change the fill of a picture that looks like an object (for which you should be able to change the fill), you may need to first ungroup the picture and then alter the fill for each individual component. You may need to use this method with clip art included on the Microsoft Office CD.

To add and change colors, borders, shadows, and 3-D settings using the Drawing toolbar, follow these steps:

1. Select the picture. Ungroup it if necessary and select the individual component you want to change.

2. Select one of the following options:

Select This Button		And Do This	For This Result
	Fill Color	Select the fill color you want from the palette or select More Fill colors for more color options, or select Fill Effects to fill a shape with a gradient, texture, pattern, or picture.	Add a fill color or fill effect to an object type picture.
	Line Color	Select the line color you want from the palette or select More Line colors for more color options or select Pattern Fill to fill a line with a pattern.	Add a colored border around the edge of a picture.
	Line Style	Select the line width you want.	Change the width of the line around the border of a picture. (Or change the drawing lines of an ungrouped object.)
	Dash Style	Select the dashed line style you want.	Add a dashed line around a picture. (Or change the drawing lines of an ungrouped object.)
	Shadow	Select the shadow style you want from the palette or select Shadow Settings to display the Shadow Settings toolbar to modify the shadow.	Add a shadowed border to a picture.
	3-D	Select the 3-D style you want from the palette or select 3-D Settings to display the 3-D Settings toolbar to modify the third dimension.	Add a 3-D effect to a picture. (3-D effects are only available for object-oriented pictures, not bitmaps.)

To add and change colors and lines using a command, follow these steps:

1. Select the picture.

2. Choose F_ormat, _Object or F_ormat P_icture; click the Format button on the Picture toolbar; or click with the right mouse button on the object and choose Format _Object or Format P_icture from the shortcut menu.

3. Choose the Colors and Lines tab, shown in Figure 16.19.

FIG. 16.19
You can use the Format dialog box to choose colors and lines.

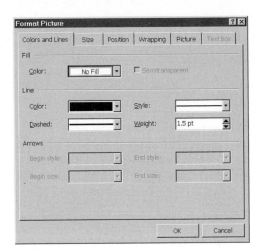

4. In the Fill group, choose _Color and select a fill color. Select _More Colors to choose from a wider range of colors or choose F_ill Effects to select a gradient, texture, pattern, or picture fill.

   Select Semi-T_ransparent to lighten the shade of the color you've chosen.

5. In the Line group, choose C_olor and select a color or select _More Colors to choose from a wider selection of colors or select P_atterned Lines to choose a line pattern.

6. Select a dash style from the _Dashed list if you want a dashed line.

7. Choose _Style and select a line width or style. Line width, called *weight*, is measured in points. A *point* is about 1/72 of an inch; a .25 point line is very thin, like a hairline; while a 4 point line is fairly heavy. (This option is not available for ungrouped objects.)

8. Choose _Weight and enter the line weight, measured in points, to change the width of a line.

9. Click OK.

Removing Lines, Fills, and Color

If you want to remove a line, fill, or color, select the picture and follow the same steps as for adding lines, fills, and colors. To remove a fill, select No Fill; to remove a line, select No Line; to remove a shadow, select No Shadow; to remove a 3-D effect, select No 3-D.

Coloring Bitmap Pictures

You can use a tool on the Picture toolbar to make pictures transparent. This option offers some interesting possibilities for bitmap images, for which you can't alter the fill color: You can layer a transparent bitmap picture over a block of color to change the picture, or some part of it, to the color of the block.

To color a bitmap picture, follow these steps:

1. Select the bitmap picture.
2. Choose the Set Transparent Color button on the Picture toolbar.
3. Click the portion of the picture that you want to make transparent with the Transparent Color pointer.
4. Choose the Rectangle tool on the Drawing toolbar, and use it to draw a rectangle over the picture.
5. Choose a fill color for the rectangle.
6. Layer the colored rectangle behind your picture. The transparent part of the picture changes to the color of the rectangle.

You can change the part of the picture that you want transparent by selecting the Transparent Color button and clicking a different part of your picture.

It might be helpful to group the color rectangle and your transparent picture if you want to move or size them as a unit.

Wrapping Text Around a Picture

Being able to wrap text around pictures opens up a world of design possibilities. You can place a picture anywhere in your document—even in a margin—and wrap text around it in many different ways. You can specify how far from the text the picture will be. And pictures have an extra wrapping option not shared by other objects: the capability to edit the wrap points, available through the Picture toolbar. Consequently, you can shape the text in any way you want around the picture.

To wrap text around a picture using a command (or to remove text wrapping), follow these steps:

1. Select the picture.
2. Choose Format, Object or Format, Picture or click the Format button on the Picture toolbar, or click with the right mouse button on the object and choose Format Object or Format Picture from the shortcut menu.
3. Choose the Wrapping tab, shown in Figure 16.20.
4. In the Wrapping Style group, select the style of text wrap you want. Look at the icons to see the effect of each option. The Square option wraps text around all four sides of a picture in a square shape; the Tight option wraps the text so that it conforms to the shape of the picture.

   Select None to remove text wrapping.

FIG. 16.20
You can use the Format Picture dialog box to wrap text around a picture.

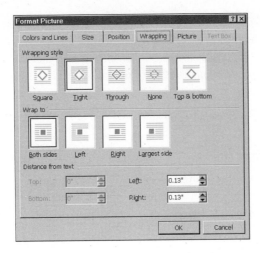

5. In the Wrap To group, select an option for wrapping to both sides or to one side. Look at the icons to see the effect of each option.

6. In the Distance From Text group, select each of the sides listed and enter how far you want the text from that side. Notice that if you choose a <u>T</u>ight wrapping style, the Top and Bottom options are unavailable.

7. Click OK. Figure 16.21 shows text wrapped.

FIG. 16.21
You can create interesting design effects by wrapping text around a picture.

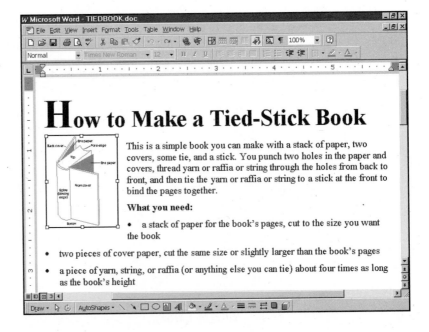

> **TIP** You can choose a text-wrapping style quickly and close the Format dialog box by double-clicking the wrapping style you want.

To select or remove text wrapping using the Picture toolbar, follow these steps:

1. Select the picture.

2. Choose the Text Wrapping button on the Picture toolbar. A list of wrapping styles appears.

3. Choose the wrapping style you want. Choose No Wrapping to remove text wrapping.

Being able to edit wrapping points allows you to shape the text wrap exactly as you want it. *Tight Wrapping* style uses the same number of wrapping points as any other type of wrap: eight. But when you edit the wrapping points, you get any number of wrapping points (depending on the complexity of your picture) that you can drag anywhere.

To edit the wrapping points, follow these steps:

1. Select the picture.

2. Choose the Text Wrapping button on the Picture toolbar.

3. Choose Edit Wrap Points. The picture is surrounded by an irregular wrap shape containing any number of wrap points.

4. Drag any of the wrap points to move the point and thus alter the shape of the text wrap. A special pointer that looks like a small four-sided star lets you know you're in position to drag a wrap point.

5. Click and drag anywhere on the dashed wrapping border when you see the wrap cross hair (a cross hair with a small square at the center) to add wrap points.

6. Click anywhere in the document to deselect the picture and hide the wrap points.

The next time you select the picture, you'll see the usual eight selection handles, though the edited wrapping points are still in place and visible if you choose the Edit Wrap Points command again.

Modifying Pictures

Some of the pictures you include in a Word document are like photographs—they may be scanned photographs or bitmap pictures created with a range of colors and shades. You can modify these pictures in many ways using tools on the Picture toolbar. You can use the Image Control button to change the image type, or you can increase or decrease the contrast and brightness in the picture.

To change the image type, follow these steps:

1. Select the picture.

2. Choose the Image Control button on the Picture toolbar. Select one of these options:

- Automatic is the picture's native type. A color photograph appears in color, for example.
- Grayscale converts a picture to a continuous-tone image made of different shades of gray. It is like a black-and-white photograph rendered as a "halftone" in preparation for offset printing. This option is good for printing color pictures on a black-ink printer.
- Black & White converts a color or grayscale picture to black and white, like a line drawing.
- Watermark changes the picture to a light gray image which you can layer behind text.

To change the contrast or brightness in a picture, follow these steps:

1. Select the picture.
2. Click on one of the following buttons on the Picture toolbar. You can click repeatedly to increase the effect; watch your picture to see how it changes.

   The More Contrast button heightens the differences between the dark and light areas of a picture, moving it closer to black and white. Increasing the contrast usually makes a picture look more dramatic.

   The Less Contrast button reduces the differences between the dark and light areas, making the picture grayer and more monochromatic. Reducing the contrast makes a picture softer.

   The More Brightness button adds light to all areas of the picture, making it brighter.

   The Less Brightness button removes light from all areas of the picture, making it darker.

Another way you can alter a picture's color, brightness, and contrast is through the Format dialog box. Using the command has the same effect as using the tools on the Picture toolbar.

To adjust color, brightness, and contrast with a command, follow these steps:

1. Select the picture.
2. Choose Format, Object, Picture or Format, Picture, Picture (see Figure 16.22).
3. In the Image control group, do the following:

Select this	And do this	To get this result
Color	Select Automatic, Gray scale, Black & White, or Watermark.	Change the picture type.
Brightness	Move the slider left to make the picture darker or right to make it brighter. Or select a percent: a lower number is darker; a higher number is brighter.	Darken or brighten the picture.

Select this	And do this	To get this result
Contrast	Move the slider left for less contrast or right for more contrast. Or select a percent: a lower number has less contrast; a higher number has more contrast.	Adjust the picture's contrast. Less contrast is a grayer picture; greater contrast is more black and white.

You can click the Reset button to reset the picture to its original appearance.

FIG. 16.22
You can use the Format dialog box to adjust color, brightness, and contrast.

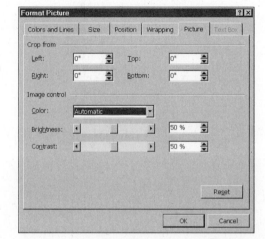

Inserting Text Boxes

In this chapter

Planning Your Document

If you're working with a one-page document, such as an announcement or mailer, consider quickly sketching out your preliminary layout, especially if you're using any kind of graphic such as logos, clip art, or photographs. Getting your ideas on paper, even roughly, can give you a better idea of what size your images should be, how large you can make your headings, and how much room you'll have for your basic text.

When you are putting together a larger publication, such as a newsletter or quarterly report, it's best to gather all your materials before you begin designing the document. One of the biggest problems you'll have as a layout artist is getting the text to fit within a specific number of pages. Whether you have too much text or too little, it is much easier to make it fit when you have all the pieces. If you must lay out a document without all the elements in hand, use rectangles and text boxes of the approximate sizes as placeholders. This gives you a truer picture of how your text is fitting.

 If you want to see how text will flow around a picture or an AutoShape, but don't have the text yet, you can use Word's built-in random text generator. Place your insertion point where you want the text to start, type **=Rand()** and press Enter. Word inserts three paragraphs of repeating phrases.

One final word about planning your document: moderation. When you're choosing fonts, font sizes, and styles for your publication, select the smallest number of options that can do the job. Two fonts and three different font sizes are adequate for a great number of publications. An advertisement or other document with too many changes in fonts and/or font sizes is difficult to read and detracts from your message. Just because you can change fonts every letter doesn't mean you have to.

Quick and Easy Newsletters with the Newsletter Wizard

Word includes a handy template for creating newsletters. The Newsletter Wizard includes most of the standard newsletter features: columns, graphics, wrapping text, headlines, and repeating elements such as headers and footers. In addition to providing a tool that can make your document shine even if you have no layout talent, the Newsletter Wizard also offers a nice tutorial on useful techniques.

To create a publication using the Newsletter Wizard, follow these steps:

1. Choose File, New.
2. From the New dialog box, click the Publications tab.
3. Double-click the Newsletter Wizard icon. In the Create New section, make sure that Document rather than Template is selected.

   You can customize several parts of your newsletter. Click the Next button to begin.

4. On the screen that appears, first select any of the available newsletter styles. Then, select whether your publication is to be in color or black and white. Click Next.

5. On the screen that appears, you can type in a title for your newsletter as well as a date, volume, and issue number. Click the Next button when you are through.

6. On the screen that appears, select whether your newsletter should leave room for a mailing label or not. Click Next to proceed.

7. As with all wizards, you can click the back arrow keys to change your choices. Click Finish when you are ready for Word 97 to create your newsletter.

TIP The Newsletter Wizard automatically creates five pages instead of the four you would expect for an average newsletter. Use the extra page as a work area to temporarily store articles or pictures. Delete the page when you are finished.

A Wizard-created newsletter is shown in Figure 17.1. Each of the different elements, such as main headlines, subheads, body text, and bylines, are set in a particular style, so it's easy to quickly modify the overall look of the newsletter. See Chapter 5, "Using Styles for Repetitive Formats," for more on styles.

Part
V

Ch
17

FIG. 17.1
The Newsletter Wizard can easily create a publication with a professional appearance.

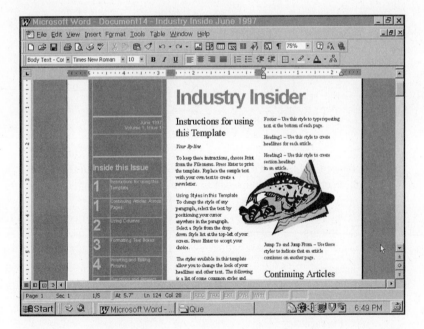

To customize the newsletter, replace the placeholder text with your own. Here's one method you can use if you already have your articles created:

1. After you've built your newsletter with the Newsletter Wizard, open the document with your replacement text.

2. Highlight and copy the text for your first article.

3. Choose <u>W</u>indow, and then your Wizard-created letter document to switch to it.

4. Highlight the placeholder text for the first article. Click the Paste button on the toolbar.

5. Repeat the process to replace additional articles and text.

Figure 17.2 shows how our case study newsletter looks after the placeholder text has been replaced by my newsletter text. The next step is to change the pictures so that they're meaningful to you and your audience.

FIG. 17.2

A wizard-created newsletter with text replaced.

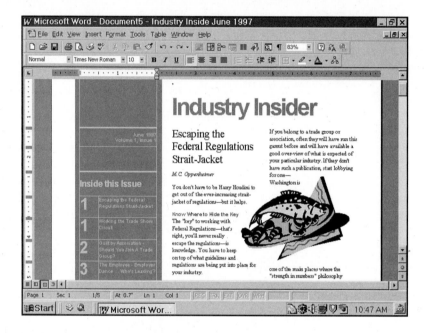

To replace a graphic, it's best to insert your image first and then delete the placeholder image. You can choose from pictures in the Clip Art Gallery, scanned-in photographs you might have, or other original artwork saved on disk. In the next chapter "Inserting Text with Special Effects," you'll learn how to resize and crop pictures to better fit your publication. Figure 17.3 shows the first page of our newsletter, now with an image more suitable to the story.

CAUTION

Don't make the mistake of selecting all the text in your newsletter with the <u>E</u>dit, Select A<u>l</u>l command. Unless every text element is in its own text box, you'll erase your entire template. If this should happen accidentally, click the Undo button from the toolbar.

FIG. 17.3
Completed wizard-
created newsletter with
new graphics and text.

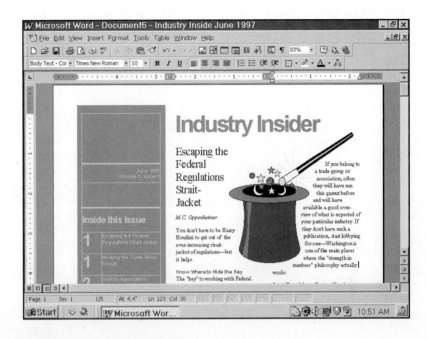

Setting Up Multiple Columns

You may not realize it, but you're already using columns. Regular text layout, as in a letter or report, is in one column. Word 97 has the capacity to produce multiple columns. Multiple columns are used to break up large blocks of text and make them more readable. Although multiple columns are not suitable for most correspondence, they are perfect for newsletters and brochures. You can even use multiple columns within certain reports to offset a particular section of your document. Columns can affect the entire document, one section of a document, or just selected text.

Word uses what are referred to as *newspaper columns*. Text in newspaper columns flows from the bottom of one column to the top of the next. If Columns are turned on for more than one page, text from the bottom of the last column on a page continues at the top of the first column of the next page. For an extra bit of layout definition, Word can automatically draw a vertical line between each column.

There are two main column controls. The first is the Column button on the Standard toolbar. When you click the Column button, a drop-down box offers you an initial choice of one to four columns; you can click and drag to the right to get up to six columns. The Column button quickly produces columns of equal width in the full document, one section (if you are using section breaks), or the selected text. Use this control when you don't need any of the special features of columns such as unequal size or lines drawn between columns.

T I P You must be in Page Layout view to see side-by-side columns. You can get there by choosing View, Page Layout.

Follow these steps to quickly see how columns work:

1. Select a paragraph or more of text.
2. Click the Column button on the Standard toolbar.
3. Choose two or more columns.
4. Release the mouse button.

 T I P The Column button is great for making quick headings that span your columns. Select the text that you want to spread across your columns and click the Column button. Choose 1 Column and you'll get a result like that shown in Figure 17.4.

FIG. 17.4

You can make any text span your columns by using the Column button.

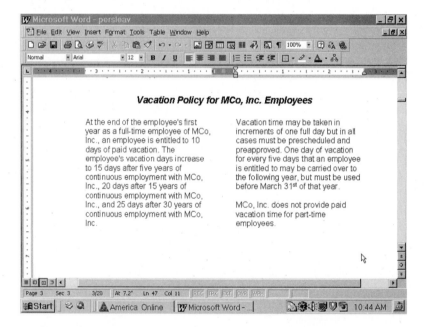

The second way to access column controls, through the Format menu, is covered in the next section.

Using the Format Columns Dialog Box to Control Formatting

To gain complete control over your columns, you have to choose Format, Columns to open the Columns dialog box as shown in Figure 17.5. With this dialog box you can add as many columns as you have room for, customize the size of the columns and the spacing between them, and add vertical lines between columns.

FIG. 17.5
The Columns dialog box gives you total column control.

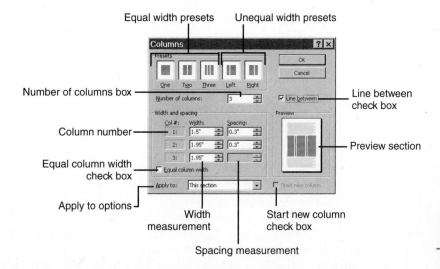

Equal width presets   Unequal width presets

Number of columns box

Column number

Equal column width check box

Apply to options

Width measurement

Spacing measurement

Line between check box

Preview section

Start new column check box

In the Presets section of the Columns dialog box, you can choose between one, two, or three equally divided columns or columns with two different unequal widths. The width of your columns depends on your left and right margins; the wider the margins, the narrower the columns will be. If you choose one of the unequal width presets, Left or Right, the "named" column is set to a little less than one-half the width of the other column. For example, on a page with one-inch left and right margins, selecting the Left preset makes the left column 1.83" and the right column 4.17" with a .5" space in-between; selecting the Right preset switches the widths of the columns.

Columns of unequal width—your first column being narrower than your others, for example—are used to add more visual variety to a large format publication, such as a newsletter. There are no hard-and-fast rules for sizing your columns other than to be sure that your text can still be read. If a large number of the lines in your column end in hyphenated or broken words, your column is too narrow.

To manually create columns of unequal width, follow these steps:

1. Select the document, section, or text that you want to convert to columns.
2. Choose Format, Columns.
3. To create two or three columns, click the corresponding Preset buttons.
4. To create more than three columns, type a value in the Number of Columns text box or use the incrementer arrows.
5. In the Width and Spacing section, remove the check in the Equal Column Width box by clicking the box. The Width text boxes for columns other than Column 1 become active.

6. Type a new value in a Width text box for a particular column or use its incrementer arrows.

   If you use the incrementer arrows, you can see how the other columns shrink or grow according to your choices. The Preview section gives you a general idea of how your columns will appear.

7. Click OK when you have completed your selection.

The gutter between your columns is controlled by the Spacing measurement. Generally, it's a good idea to keep your spacing between .25 and .5 inches. You can use a larger measurement if you decide to use the Line Between option to place vertical line separating each column. Turn on the Line Between by clicking in the check box next to the option.

The Apply To section of the Columns dialog box controls which portions of your document are converted to columns. If you haven't selected any text prior to opening the Columns dialog box, your choices are between Whole Document and This Point Forward. (If you've inserted a continuous section break, you have This Section instead of Whole Document.) This Point Forward creates the columns from the insertion point to the end of the document. When This Point Forward is selected, the Start New Column box becomes active. When checked, Start New Column has the same effect as inserting a column break.

Changing Column Widths with the Ruler

To make quick adjustments when you want to eyeball the changes, you can click and drag new column widths. You can also click and drag the left or right margins for each column, thus affecting the gutter between the columns.

When you want to adjust your column margins by hand, follow these steps:

1. If your Ruler is not visible, select View, Ruler.

2. To change the width of a column and keep the spacing between columns constant, click the center Column Marker (see Figure 17.6) and drag the mouse to a new location when you see a vertical dashed line. Release the mouse button.

3. To adjust the spacing between columns, click either the left or right Column Marker (or the left or right column margin, if your insertion point is in that column) and drag it to a new location when you see the vertical dashed line. Release the mouse button when you are finished.

4. Repeat step 2 and/or step 3 for every column adjustment.

 TIP After you've moved your columns to a new place, use the Undo/Redo buttons to toggle between two different widths for your columns. It's a quick way to compare two choices.

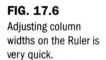

FIG. 17.6
Adjusting column widths on the Ruler is very quick.

Center column marker

Column marker

Left column margin

Right column margin

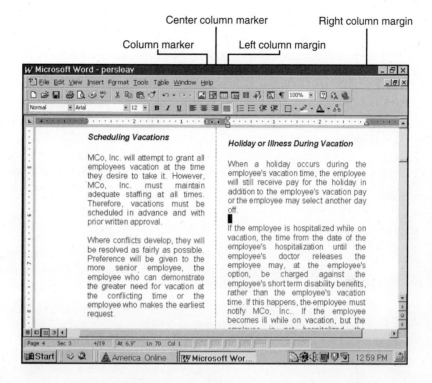

Part
V

Ch
17

Starting a New Column with Column Break

Normally, the text in your columns flows down to the bottom of a page and then continues at the top of the next column. However, there are times when you want to start a new column at a particular place in your text, at a specific paragraph or with a new heading, for example. A column breaks works just like a page break—in fact, you've probably seen the command if you've ever inserted a page break because it's in the same dialog box.

To start a new column with a column break, follow these steps:

1. Place your insertion point in front of the text where you want to start the next column.

2. Select Insert, Break.

3. In the Break dialog box (see Figure 17.7), click the Column Break option in the Insert section.

FIG. 17.7
Column breaks help you control the flow of text.

4. Click OK to close the Break dialog box.

 If you're having trouble seeing where to insert column breaks, you can see—and edit—the whole page at the same time by clicking the arrow next to the Zoom control and selecting Whole Page.

You remove column breaks just as you would a page break. The easiest way to see the break is to switch to Normal view by choosing View, Normal. Then select the Column Break line. Press Delete to remove it.

 If you don't want to switch to Normal view to delete the column break, place your insertion point in front of the line that starts the new column. Press Backspace to remove the column break.

Evening Your Columns

Sometimes you want to balance your columns so that the text is spread evenly over all of your columns. This choice can be made for aesthetic ("It just looks better") or practical ("I couldn't follow the article") reasons. Word has an easy way for you to even out your columns no matter where they end.

Follow these steps to balance text flowing into multiple columns:

1. Create your columns, if you have not already done so.
2. If necessary, switch to Page Layout view by choosing View, Page Layout.
3. At the end of the text that you want to balance, click to place the insertion point.
4. Choose Insert, Break.
5. From the Break dialog box, select a Continuous Section Break.
6. Click OK to close the dialog box.

Figure 17.8 shows a before-and-after view of text that has been balanced using the Continuous Section Break.

CAUTION

Depending on how your document is formatted, you may find that you need to separate the text that follows your balanced columns. One technique for doing this is to select the first blank line after your balanced columns, in the first column, and then click the Column button on the toolbar. Select 1 Column. This makes the blank line span all the other columns and forces a separation.

FIG. 17.8
The text on the right was balanced with a Continuous Section Break.

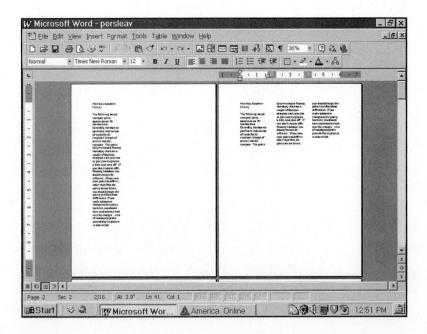

Using Drop Caps

Word can easily create large initial capitals, more commonly known as *drop caps*, that give your documents a distinct, magazine-style appearance. Drop caps work extremely well in newsletters, particularly those formatted with columns.

Drop caps are so named because usually it is the first letter or word of a paragraph, formatted in all capitals, and "dropped" into the paragraph so that the first two or three lines are pushed to one side. Figure 17.9 shows an example of a drop cap as well as the Drop Cap dialog box.

Follow these steps to add a drop cap to any paragraph:

1. Highlight the letter(s) or word(s) you want to convert to a drop cap.

2. Choose Format, Drop Cap.

3. From the Drop Cap dialog box, first select the position you want your drop cap to appear in. Click either Dropped or In Margin.

4. Next, you can select a different font for the drop cap by clicking the arrow next to the Font text box.

5. To change the size of the drop cap, type a new value in the Lines To Drop text box or use the incrementer arrows.

6. To alter the amount of space between the drop cap and the surrounding text, type a new value in the Distance from text box or use the incrementer arrows.

7. Click OK to see the result.

FIG. 17.9

A drop cap adds visual spice to a page.

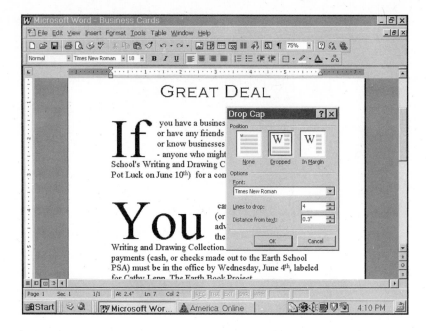

Word makes your drop cap by putting your selected text into a special frame. To alter your options and get a different look, click the frame with the drop cap and select that F<u>o</u>rmat, <u>D</u>rop Cap again. To remove a drop cap, click the frame, select F<u>o</u>rmat, <u>D</u>rop Cap, and choose <u>N</u>one.

 A classic designer's trick is to pick a font for the drop cap that is from a different typeface than the one used for the body of the paragraph. For example, if your paragraph is in a sans-serif font such as Times New Roman, use a serif font such as Arial for your drop cap.

Working with Special Characters and Symbols

If you do any sort of international work, you need to be able to include foreign language characters in your documents. Word can handle a wide range of international characters, as well as special characters, such as the copyright © and trademark ™ symbols.

The primary tool for accessing the special characters is the Symbol dialog box. In addition to selecting symbols and other characters one at a time, the Symbol dialog box also lets you set up a variety of shortcuts for often used characters.

The basic steps for inserting a special character or symbol are as follows:

1. Place your insertion point where you want the special character to appear.

2. Choose Insert, <u>S</u>ymbol.

3. From the Symbol dialog box, as shown in Figure 17.10, click a character box to see the symbol more clearly.

FIG. 17.10
Special characters
magnify when selected.

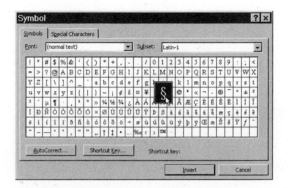

4. To select a character or special symbol from a different font, click the arrow next to the Font text box and choose a font from the drop-down list.

5. Press the Insert button to put the character in your text.

6. Press the Close button to clear the dialog box from the screen.

 TIP If you need to add a series of special characters (for example, when you're typing a foreign language address or phrase), you can keep the Symbol dialog box open. Simply click in your main document to continue typing until you need your next special character.

You can automatically produce certain symbols such as a copyright © or trademark ™ symbol with Microsoft's new AutoCorrect feature.

 TIP To stop AutoCorrect from converting what you type into a symbol on a case-by-case basis, press Backspace after the symbol appears.

Using Text Boxes

The text box is a completely free-floating object, independent of your regular document. The position and size of text boxes is completely user definable, so you decide where to put the text box and how big it should be. You don't have to worry about precisely placing your text box the first time—you can always adjust the size and position later. Text boxes are used to display quotes pulled from an article or any other specially positioned text.

Follow these steps to insert a text box into your document:

1. In your document, go to where you want to place your text box.

2. Choose Insert, Text Box. Your pointer becomes a small crosshair.

3. Click where you want the upper-left corner of your text box to appear and drag out a rectangle.

4. Release the mouse button when your text box is the right size and shape.

When the text box appears, it will look like the one in Figure 17.11. When selected, the text box has a special diagonal line border with eight sizing handles around it. Inside, a new insertion point blinks. The text box also has its own ruler settings, which enable you to set tabs independently from the rest of the document. You can deselect the text box by clicking anywhere outside of it.

FIG. 17.11

The special diagonal line border easily identifies a text box.

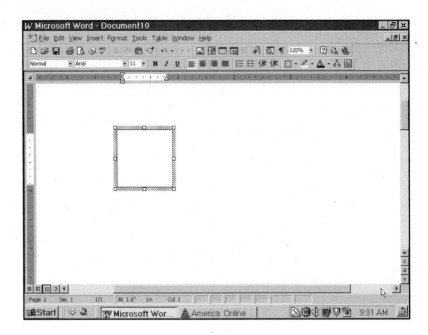

 You can use the default size if you have no idea how large you want your text box to be initially. Choose Insert, Text Box; when you see the pointer become a small crosshair, click once. The default text box appears.

Text boxes can be a little tricky to get rid of. The key is, after you've selected it, click the border of the text box again. The border changes from a diagonal to a dot pattern. Press Delete.

Normally, when you type any new text into your document, its position is dependent upon the margins, and the amount of text and paragraph marks that go before it. Text boxes permit you to place text anywhere on the page, regardless of what else might be there. In Word 97, the capabilities of text boxes have been significantly improved. Some of the new features of text boxes are included in the following list:

- Linking from one text box to another to permit text to flow through the document.

- Creating a watermark image that is visible beneath the regular text.

- Enhanced formatting properties, including control over 3-D effects, shadows, border styles and colors, fills, and backgrounds.

- More text-wrapping options.
- Text boxes can be rotated and flipped.
- The orientation of the text can be adjusted to achieve various effects.
- Text boxes can be layered, aligned, and grouped with each other or with other drawing objects.

N O T E In Word 97, text boxes are used in many of the ways that frames were used in previous versions of Word. However, you still need to use a frame instead of a text box if you need to position text or graphics that include any of the following: a note reference mark, a comment mark, or certain fields, including AUTONUM, AUTONUMLGL, AUTONUMOUT—used for numbering lists and paragraphs in legal documents and outlines—TC (Table of Contents Entry), TOC (Table of Contents), RD (Referenced Document), XE (Index Entry), TA (Table of Authorities Entry), and TOA (Table of Authority) fields. You can convert a text box to a frame by selecting your text box, choosing Format, Text Box from the menu, and clicking the Text Box tab. Click the Convert to Frame button. ■

Formatting a Text Box

Chances are you'll need to format your text box to get exactly the look you want. The default text box has a thin (.75 point) black line surrounding a white-filled interior and the wrapping is set so that text flows across the top and bottom of the box.

The Format Text Box dialog box (see Figure 17.12) has five different main sections: Colors and Lines, Size, Position, Wrapping, and Text Box. The Picture tab is active only when you are inserting a picture.

FIG. 17.12

The Format Text Box dialog box gives you a lot of options.

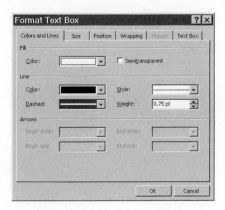

There are two ways to open the Format Text Box dialog box:

- Select your text box. From the menu, choose Format, Text Box.
- Select your text box. Right-click the border of the text box to open the Quick Menu. Choose Format, Text Box.

Working with Text Box Colors and Borders

Until recently, there wasn't much point to using color in your documents. You could change the shading of a table's header row to make it stand out a bit more, but everything was in gray because that's all office printers could handle. That's all changed with the advent of low-cost color inkjet printers, not to mention Word's Web-publishing capabilities. Now, you can (almost) justify using the hot-pink background with a half-inch thick deep-purple border for your semi-annual sales report. Word text boxes give you full color control in addition to the gray shading that the boss still wants.

As mentioned previously, you can independently control the border color and the *fill* or background color of your text boxes. A fill is a solid color; Word can also use color blends called gradients (covered later in this chapter). If you choose the No Fill option, your text box is transparent—a technique used to lay text over a picture. Similarly, you can choose the No Line option to turn off your text box's border entirely. To alter your text box's fill or border color, follow these steps:

1. Select your text box.

2. Choose Format, Text Box.

3. From the Format Text Box dialog box, click the Colors and Lines tab, if necessary.

4. To select a new background color, in the Fill section, click the arrow next to the Color drop-down list box.

5. Choose a new color from the standard color options. To see additional choices, click the More Colors button.

6. To select a new border color, in the Line section, click the arrow next to the Color drop-down list box.

7. Click any of the 40 available colors or click the More Colors button for additional selections.

8. Click OK when you've made your choices.

TIP Clicking the Semitransparent check box in the Fill section gives you a lighter shade of your chosen color that allows anything behind it (text or graphic) to show through. Lighter tones work better than the darker colors.

When you click the More Colors button for either Line or Fill color, you get a dialog box with two tabs: Standard and Custom. Standard shows the normal SVGA 256-color palette arranged in a color hexagon (see Figure 17.13). Standard also features a 16-step grayscale blend of black and white. The Custom tab lets you pick from any of the additional colors available if your Color Palette is set to 16-bit color or higher. In the Custom tab, you can also specify a color by its Red-Green-Blue values or its Hue-Saturation-Luminance numbers.

In addition to changing the color and pattern of a border, you can also control the line's appearance, style, and weight. This is how you make a dashed line to indicate a cutout coupon or a caption box for a legal pleading. All the controls are found in the Format Text Box dialog box.

FIG. 17.13
Additional color options are found under the More Colors button.

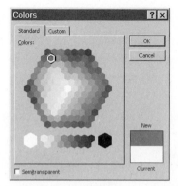

 Word offers 36 different patterns for text box borders. From the Format Text Box dialog box, in the Line section, click the arrow next to the Color drop-down list box. Choose Patterned Lines to select a pattern other than solid. You can also change the Foreground and Background color of the pattern.

Follow these steps to alter the look of a text box border:

1. Select your text box.
2. Choose Format, Text Box.
3. From the Format Text Box dialog box, click the Colors and Lines tab, if necessary.
4. In the Line section, click the arrows next to these options:
   - *Dashed.* Offers eight different appearances ranging from a solid line (the default) to dash-and-dot combinations.
   - *Style.* Gives you nine preset single-line widths (3/4 point is the default) and four multiple-line options.
   - *Weight.* Enables you to type in a new value, in points, or use the incrementer arrows to change the thickness of the line. The default is .75 points.
5. Click OK after you've made your selections.

Selecting a Fill Effect

Solid fills are just the bare bones of what is possible with text boxes backgrounds. Word fill effects include the following:

- *Gradients* are blends between user-selectable or preset colors in a variety of set patterns.
- *Textures* are multicolor designs based on images, such as marble, wood, or denim.
- *Patterns* are repeating designs created from two user-selectable colors.
- *Pictures* allow a text box to have an image as a background.

Follow these steps to select a fill effect:

1. Choose F_ormat, Text B_ox to open the Format Text Box dialog box.
2. In the Fill section of the Colors and Lines tab, click the arrow next to the Color drop-down list box.
3. Select Fill Effects.
4. Click OK on the Fill Effect dialog box after you have made your selections.

Using Word's Built-In Gradients

If you really need to emphasize some text, Word has a collection of very snazzy text box back-grounds, known as gradients. A gradient is a blend that uses two shades of one color, two different colors, or a range of preset colors. You can pick one single color or two colors to use in a gradient; Microsoft includes 24 different preset gradients to choose from in Word.

Gradients are terrific for certificates, special awards, or "plaques" such as the one in Figure 17.14. Some of the preset gradients can even be used thematically, such as Early Sunset, or Rainbow, when coupled with the appropriate text.

FIG. 17.14

Gradients allow subtle blending of two or more colors.

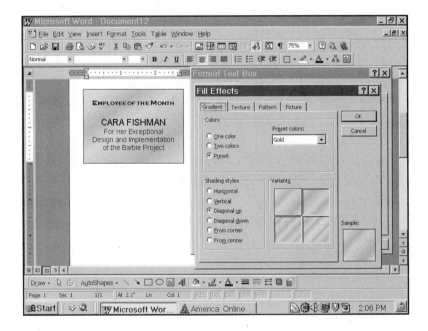

To access the gradient controls, follow the steps for Fill Effects and then click the Gradient tab. When you first bring up the Gradient dialog box, no specific color is selected and the examples shown in the preview section are rendered in grayscale. Click one of the following options to enable additional choices:

- *One Color.* Opens up a selector for choosing the color to blend from dark to light shades. A slider enables you to vary how dark or how light the shades will be.

- *Two Color.* Gives you Color 1 and Color 2 selectors for designing a custom blend. Click the respective arrow to open the Color dialog box.

- *Preset.* Displays the option list for the professionally designed multicolor gradients. Click the arrow to see the drop-down list.

Controlling Shading Styles

The gradient color choices covered in the previous section are used in combination with the shading styles found on the bottom portion of the Gradient tab.

There are six different shading styles that can be selected. All styles have four different options to choose from except for the last one, From Center, which only has two. The six shading styles are Horizontal, Vertical, Diagonal Up, Diagonal Down, From Corner, and From Center.

> **CAUTION**
>
> If you use one of the Gradient Presets and you don't have a color printer—or if the document is going to be photocopied—be sure you can still read the text. Some of the brighter color combinations don't have enough contrast to make text readable when reduced to grayscale.

Adding Textures

Textures are another alternative to filling your text boxes with solid colors or gradients. *Textures* are small pictures that are tiled or repeated as much as necessary to fill out a given text box. A texture can be as subtle as parchment or as broad as a fish fossil—complete with fish! You can even use your own images as a texture.

What distinguishes textures from the other fill effects is that textures can be made from any graphic file, including photographs that have been digitized for use on your computer. A photographic background can give a text box a very realistic look. The various marble and wood textures work well in year-end reports and corporate newsletters.

To include a Texture fill in a text box, follow these steps:

1. Select your text box and open the Fill Effects dialog box by choosing Format, Text Box and clicking the arrow next to the Color drop-down list box in the Fill section of the Colors and Lines tab; then clicking Fill Effects.

2. Click the Texture tab.

3. From the Texture tab (see Figure 17.15), click one of the 32 samples in the scrolling list.

4. If you want to use a file of your own as a texture, click the Other Texture button and open the appropriate file.

5. Click OK on the Fill Effects dialog box when you have finished making your selection.

Part
V

Ch
17

FIG. 17.15
Some of the 32 preset textures available.

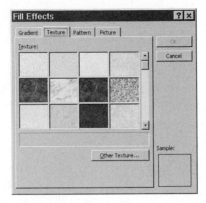

CAUTION

If you use your own file as a texture, you may find unwanted whitespace or lines separating every small image and ruining the overall effect. You probably need to crop your image in a graphics program such as Microsoft Image Composer or Adobe Photoshop to remove any borders.

Adding Patterns

Patterns are two-color repeating designs. Word uses the same 36 patterns for filling a text box as it uses for making a patterned line. The process is identical to choosing a 2-color gradient. Click the Pattern tab of the Fill Effects dialog box. Click one of the available patterns. If you want something other than the black-and-white defaults, you can choose different foreground and background colors. Click OK when you've made your choices.

A word of warning about using a Pattern Fill Effect: Unless you're using very large fonts, you'll probably find that the background fill overwhelms the text rendering it unreadable. The other thing to look out for is the high-contrast default colors. You might like the results more if you choose two colors closer in tone.

Adding a Picture as a Fill Effect

The final Fill Effect option is Picture. Like the Texture effect, this puts any graphic, including photographs, into the background of a text box. There are, however, two differences between Texture and Picture. First, the Picture effect does not tile to fill out the size of the text box as the Texture effect does. Second, the Picture effect stretches the image to fit the text box. After it is filled with a Picture, resizing the text box also resizes the graphic.

One powerful use for the Picture effect is in the development of catalogs. Not only will a smaller text box produce a thumbnail of a larger image, but because it is a text box, important information such as a stock control code or price could easily be overlaid. Figure 17.16 shows a typical use of a Picture Fill Effect.

FIG. 17.16
A Picture Fill Effect provides an effective background for text.

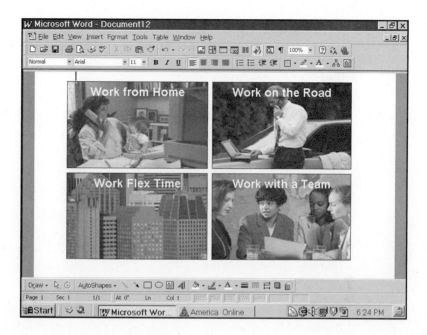

Follow these steps to add a Picture as a Fill Effect:

1. Select your text box and open the Fill Effect dialog box by choosing Format, Text Box and clicking the arrow next to the Color drop-down list box in the Fill section of the Colors and Lines tab and then clicking Fill Effects.

2. Click the Picture tab.

3. Click the Select Picture button.

4. From the Open Picture dialog box, select the picture you want to use as a text box background.

5. The Picture area shows the original file. The Sample area shows the file, stretched to fit a square text box. Note that this does not mean this is how the picture will look in your text box, if your text box is the same aspect ratio as the picture.

6. Click OK to close the Fill Effects dialog box.

Precisely Controlling Text Box Size and Position

How many times have you looked at a document produced in-house and thought, "Something was off, but I can't figure out what it is?" Even a relatively untrained eye notices tiny discrepancies when objects on a page are not perfectly aligned or when one box is slightly larger than another. When precise measurements are essential, Word can size and place objects to within 1/100 of an inch.

Word has added some new facilities to align objects with each other and relative to the page, but you can still use the numeric positioning capabilities when dealing with text boxes on different pages. Repeating elements in exactly the same position, page after page—especially in something like a newsletter or business report—greatly enhances the professional appearance of your documents. This applies to the size of text boxes as well.

To use numeric measurements for text box position and size, follow these steps:

1. Select your text box.

2. Choose Format, Text Box.

3. To alter the size or shape of the Text Box, click the Size tab in the Format Text Box dialog box. You have the following options:

   - In the Size section, type new percentages in the Height and Weight boxes or use the incrementer arrows.

   - In the Scale section, type new percentages in the Height and Weight boxes or use the incrementer arrows.

   - Select the Lock Aspect Ratio to maintain height and width relative to each other.

4. To alter the placement of the text box, click the Position tab in the Format Text Box dialog box.

5. Select the anchor from where the text box is positioned by clicking the arrow next to the From box for both the Horizontal and Vertical directions and selecting one of the options.

6. In the Horizontal and Vertical, type new values or use the incrementer arrows to alter the position of the text box.

7. If you want to make sure that the text box stays with the paragraph it is anchored to, select the Move Object with Text check box.

8. If you want to make sure that the text box stays on the same page as the paragraph it is anchored to, select the Lock Anchor check box.

9. Click OK in the Format Text Box dialog box when you have completed your choices.

 T I P The Format Text Box is also great for checking the exact size and position measurements when you want to duplicate them for another text box, in the same document or another.

Wrapping Text Around a Text Box

I'm sure you've seen magazine articles where a quote from the article is put in a box, in larger type, and the rest of the article flows around the box. If you've ever wondered how they did that, this section is for you. Those effects are known as pull quotes (because they are pulled from the article) and Word handles them with its text box wrapping features.

You get to the Wrapping options by selecting your text box and choosing Format, Text Box. Then click the Wrapping tab. You make your choices from this dialog box as shown in Figure 17.17. Take the three sections one step at a time: first, select the Wrapping Style; then select what you want to Wrap To (from the available choices) and finally change the Distance from text.

FIG. 17.17
Wrapping text around a text box is often used in newsletters and special reports.

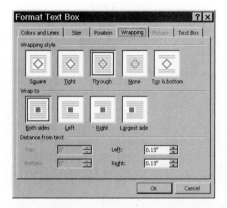

The Tight and Through options work only with pictures or AutoShapes. To enable the Wrap To options, you must have selected either the Square, Tight, or Through wrapping style.

Setting Internal Text Box Margins

Just as you can set the distance between your text box and the text that flows around it, you can also set the distance between the border of your text box and the text inside. The default is to have a .1-inch left and right margin and a .05-inch top and bottom margin. This works well in most circumstances, but there are times where you need to take control of the margins. You could, for instance, need just a little more space on the bottom to make the last line fit correctly. Or, if you use a very heavy border, such as 8 point or higher, you might want to emphasize your text with a little extra whitespace around it.

To alter the internal margins of a text box, follow these steps:

1. Select your text box.
2. Choose Format, Text Box.
3. Click the Text Box tab.
4. In the Internal Margin section, type in new values for the Left, Right, Top, or Bottom margin, or use their respective incrementer arrows.
5. Click OK.

CHAPTER 18

Inserting Text with Special Effects

In this chapter

What You Need to Know About WordArt

You see examples of words used as graphics every day: Pull quotes in magazines lighten a page of text and attract attention to important points; logos turn words into symbols that you recognize without even reading; decorated words embellish the mastheads in newsletters; and special text effects add interest to advertisements.

With WordArt, you can turn ordinary words into graphics. You can pour text into a shape, flip or stretch letters, condense or expand letter spacing, rotate or angle words, or add shading, colors, borders, or shadows to text. By combining your text with WordArt effects and other graphic tools, you can create hundreds of interesting designs.

You can use WordArt with a mouse or your keyboard. Either way, you can create great graphics.

Figure 18.1 shows some examples of finished WordArt objects.

FIG. 18.1
WordArt can create many different graphic effects.

WordArt used to be an OLE-based, add-in program. With Word 97, WordArt has become more closely integrated into the Office package as part of the drawing tools. You can add and edit WordArt objects easily with the new WordArt toolbar. WordArt offers many new styles and formatting options for your text.

Creating a WordArt Object

The process of creating WordArt for your document has changed with Word 97. In the past, you were required to insert a WordArt object and work with it separately. Follow these steps to create a WordArt object:

1. Select the WordArt button from the Drawing or WordArt toolbar or choose Insert, Picture, WordArt. The WordArt Gallery opens.

2. Select a WordArt style (see Figure 18.2) and select OK.

FIG. 18.2
The WordArt Gallery allows you to select from some template styles for your WordArt object.

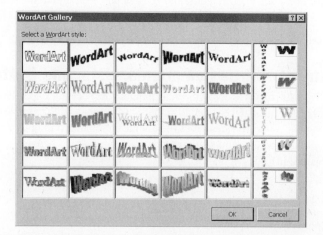

3. Enter your text, make any font or attribute setting changes for the WordArt object, and select OK (see Figure 18.3).

FIG. 18.3
The Edit WordArt Text dialog box is where you enter the text that you want to enhance.

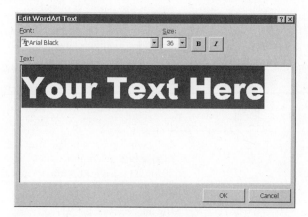

At this point, the WordArt object is placed in your document at the position of your insertion point. You can then treat it like any other drawing object or picture. It behaves the same as other drawing objects. You insert it at the insertion point, and the object moves with the text that surrounds it. You can use many of the drawing format choices to modify the original design. There is also the special WordArt toolbar with some additional formatting features.

▶ **See** "Inserting Pictures into a Document," **p. 388**

Because WordArt graphics are based on text, you also have access to most text formatting tools, such as fonts. Windows comes with some fonts, such as Arial and Times New Roman. Your printer may contain other fonts, and you can purchase additional fonts to install on your computer. Any font installed on your computer is available for use in WordArt.

WordArt will not recognize PostScript fonts.

Understanding WordArt's Commands, Lists, and Buttons

Once the WordArt object is created, you can modify its special effects. WordArt's special effects are available through commands in the Word menus and through lists and buttons on the WordArt toolbar. Table 18.1 describes the unique commands and buttons contained in WordArt. WordArt's commands and buttons are described in detail later in this chapter, in the "Adding Special Effects" section.

Table 18.1   WordArt Commands and Buttons

Menu Command	List or Button	Description
Insert, Picture,	◢	Opens the WordArt Gallery to WordArt, and WordArt begins the process of inserting a WordArt object.
	Edit Text...	Opens the Edit WordArt Text dialog box to edit the text for the WordArt object.
	▤	Opens the WordArt Gallery for an existing WordArt object for modifications.
Format, WordArt	✍	Opens the Format WordArt dialog box to set up the WordArt options.
	Abc	Opens a palette to select the WordArt shape.
	↺	Activates the Free Rotate function. It changes the mouse pointer into the rotate pointer and changes the sizing handles for the object into the rotate handles.
	Aa	Stretches the lowercase letter's height to match that of the uppercase letter's.
	Ab bↄ	Toggles the text between a horizontal and vertical arrangement.

Menu Command	List or Button	Description
	≣	Opens the WordArt alignment menu.
	AV	Opens the WordArt Character spacing menu.

Adding Special Effects

When you add a special effect to a WordArt image, the image changes immediately, and you instantly see the result of each effect you choose. You can experiment with different effects and get quick feedback about how they look. If you decide you do not like an effect, you can use Undo or select another special effect.

You can add many different types of special effects to create a WordArt image. You can combine the effects to develop a look of your own. All the effects apply to the text rather than to the border or background of the text. Figure 18.4 shows just a few of the special effects you can achieve with WordArt.

FIG. 18.4
You can create many special effects with WordArt.

What You Need to Know About WordArt Effects

The effects you apply in WordArt apply to all the text in the dialog box. You cannot apply an effect to just a few of the letters in the dialog box.

TIP If you need to differentiate formatting for a text phrase, you can use more than one WordArt object and place them next to one another.

Choosing some of the commands or buttons displays a dialog box from which you make selections. To remove the effect, choose the same command or button and select a different option. The WordArt toolbar has most of the functions needed to customize the look of your WordArt object.

Editing the Text

The second button on the WordArt toolbar is the Edit Text button. You can change the text of the object at any time without disturbing your formatting. To change the text, select the WordArt object and select the Edit Text button from the toolbar. The Edit WordArt Text dialog box opens (refer to Figure 18.3). You can change the font, size, and font style as well as change the text.

The restrictions of the WordArt object are that it cannot exceed the size of a page, and it starts as a 2-inch wide rectangle, but can resize to hold your text. You can add any text and punctuation. It can also accept a carriage return to break it into multiple lines. In fact, several of the styles expect carriage returns, such as the Button (Pour) shape of the "Shapes and Patterns" example in Figure 28.4.

Selecting a WordArt Style from the Gallery

With WordArt in Office 97, the first step is to select a style from the WordArt Gallery. There are some built-in formats for your WordArt objects. This is always the starting point. You may not find the one that is exactly right for your situation, but try to select the one that will require the least amount of modifications.

Keep in mind that if you select something in the Gallery, you do not have to make modifications to it if it turns out the results were not even close to your expectations. Select the WordArt Gallery button from the WordArt toolbar and select another style.

Once you have an acceptable style from the Gallery, you can start to customize it. You can change the text, its options, its shape, rotation, letter contrast, and arrangement, as well as alignment and character spacing.

Formatting the WordArt Object

The Format WordArt button on the toolbar opens the Format WordArt dialog box, which is identical to the Format AutoShape dialog box except that only some of the options are available. You have access to the Colors and Lines, Size, Position, and Wrapping tabs.

The Colors and Lines tab allows you to modify the fill color of the letters of the WordArt object. You can select a color from the drop-down list; your choices are identical to the Fill Color palette for all other objects. You can fill with a color on the palette or select More Colors to create one of your own. You could also select F̲ill Effects to add a gradient, texture, pattern, or picture fill. You can also change the color, style, and weight of the letter borders.

The Size tab allows you to change the height, width, and rotation of the object. You can also control its scale and aspect ratio to determine its proportion. The Position tab controls the placement of the WordArt object in relation to the document, and the Wrapping tab controls how normal text will wrap around the WordArt object.

Shaping the Text

By applying one special WordArt effect—pouring your text into a shape—you can create an interesting sign or logo. WordArt's toolbar includes a Shapes list that displays a grid of different shapes (see Figure 18.5). When you select one of these shapes, the text in the Enter Your Text Here dialog box "pours" into that shape.

FIG. 18.5
By selecting one of these shapes, you can create an interesting sign or logo.

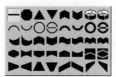

Some shapes produce different results, depending on the number of lines of text you are shaping. The circle shape, for example, turns a single line of text into a circle, but turns multiple lines of text into concentric circles. The button shape turns three lines into a button, but turns a single line into an arch. Experiment to get the result you want.

Adding Additional Text Formatting

The remaining five buttons on the WordArt toolbar adjust the letter height and direction of the text as well as change alignment and spacing. They give you some alternatives to regular text formatting.

The first button is the Free Rotate button. This duplicates the Free Rotate button on the Drawing toolbar. This allows you to use one of the rotation handles and change the direction of the object.

The second button allows you to adjust the character height of the WordArt object. Most fonts' lowercase letters are approximately 50 percent of the height of the uppercase letters. You may want to try to change the effect by using the WordArt Same Letter Heights. Regardless of whether text is upper-or lowercase, each letter will be the same height (see Figure 18.6). If you decide you do not like the effect, you can change it. To remove the effect, select the WordArt Same Letter Height button again.

The third button is the WordArt Vertical Text button. This button takes text and arranges it vertically (see Figure 18.7). If this effect doesn't appeal to you, it can also be removed by selecting the button again.

Part

V

Ch

18

FIG. 18.6
WordArt Same Letter
Height can be used to
modify the top border of
the shape.

FIG. 18.7
The WordArt Vertical Text
button will take the text
and arrange it vertically.

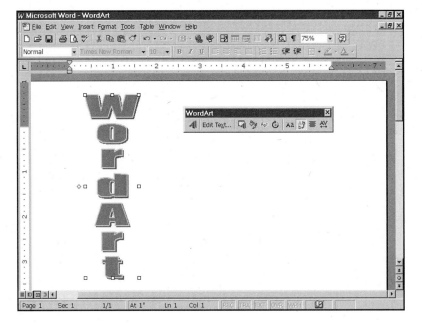

The next button is the WordArt Alignment button. It controls the alignment of the text inside the object. You can align the text using Left Align, Center, Right Align, Word Justify, Letter Justify, and Stretch Justify. Each style in the Gallery has a default alignment.

The last button is WordArt Character Spacing. It controls the amount of white space between the letters. This functions like the Format Paragraph function for regular text. When you select it, a menu pops up that allow you to determine how close together the letters will be.

Using the Draw Toolbar

When the WordArt object is created, it can be treated like any other drawing object. You can take advantage of the functions available on the Drawing toolbar. For example, you can flip, rotate, copy, paste, nudge, and order WordArt with the Draw button on the Drawing toolbar. ●

Part

V

Ch

18

Word's Advanced Editing and Notation Features

Inserting Footnotes and Endnotes

What You Need to Know about Inserting Footnotes and Endnotes

Inserting, editing, and formatting footnotes and endnotes is easy in Word. Basically, a footnote consists of two parts: a footnote reference in the text (usually a superscripted number after the text) and the footnote at the bottom of the page, isolated from the body text by a separator line. An endnote is similar, except that the entry for an endnote appears at the end of the section or document, set apart from the text by a separator.

The process of creating footnotes and endnotes involves two basic steps:

1. Insert the note reference to mark the location in the document where a footnote or endnote is referred to. The note reference is usually a number.

2. After Word inserts the note reference, type the note entry (customizing the separator if you prefer). The note entry is the text information that appears in the footnote or endnote.

Several options are available for specifying where footnotes and endnotes appear, the type of separator line that is used, and the style of numbering used for the reference numbers. Figure 19.1 shows examples of footnotes being placed in a document.

FIG. 19.1

You can add footnotes to a document to provide additional information or to indicate references.

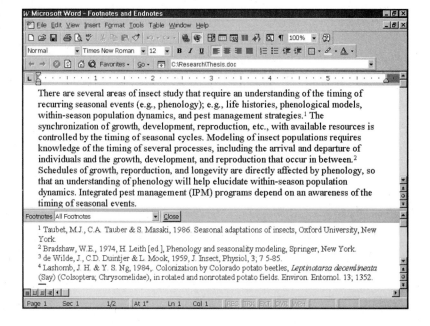

Inserting Footnotes and Endnotes

When you insert a footnote or endnote, Word inserts a reference mark in the text at the current insertion point. The reference mark is usually a sequential number that identifies the note you are adding. You are then given the opportunity to type the text to which the reference mark refers.

If you are in Normal view, a pane opens at the bottom of the window. In that pane, you can type either a footnote or an endnote, depending on the type of note you selected. If you are in Page Layout view, Word moves the insertion point to the bottom of the page for footnotes, or to the end of the document for endnotes. Entering footnotes and endnotes becomes as visual and as easy as if you were manually writing in a notebook. But Word automatically adjusts the page lengths, because footnotes fill up the page. Endnotes at the end of the document are continually pushed to the last page as your document gets longer.

N O T E Footnotes usually make a document more difficult to read because they clutter the bottom of each page. However, many academic institutions require footnotes in their papers. Endnotes are more frequently used in scholarly publications because they do not interfere with reading, but they do make the research accessible for those who need more information. ■

To create a footnote or endnote, follow these steps:

1. Position the insertion point after the text where you want to insert a reference mark.

   Word inserts the reference mark at the insertion point, unless you have selected text, in which case it positions the mark after the selection.

2. Choose Insert, Footnote. The Footnote and Endnote dialog box appears (see Figure 19.2).

FIG. 19.2

In the Footnote and Endnote dialog box, you choose the type of note and how it should be numbered.

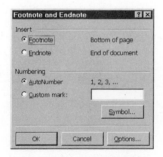

3. Select either the Footnote or the Endnote option.

4. Accept the default AutoNumber to have Word number your footnotes. For custom reference marks, see "Changing the Appearance of Reference Marks" later in this chapter.

5. Choose OK. Word displays the note pane (Normal view) or the bottom margin (Page Layout view) so that you can type your footnote.

6. Type the text of your footnote or endnote.

   If you're in the Normal view of your document, you type in a special note pane, which appears when you choose OK in step 5. At this point, the screen is divided into two parts: the text of your document on top showing the note reference and the note pane below showing the note entry (see Figure 19.3).

FIG. 19.3

The note pane is at the bottom of the screen when you work in Normal view.

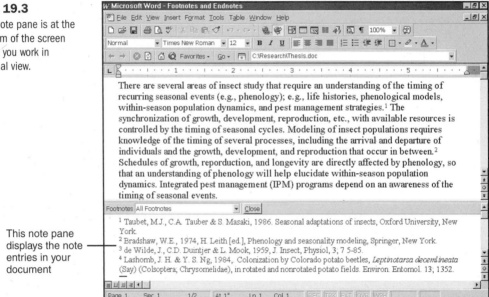

This note pane displays the note entries in your document

If you're in the Page Layout view of your document, you don't see the note pane. Instead, you type the note directly on the page (see Figure 19.4). If you are entering a footnote, you type at the bottom of the page. If you are entering an endnote, you type at the end of the document.

7. If you are in Normal view, leave the note pane visible and press F6 or click the document to move back to the document window. You can also click the document to move the insertion point, or close the note pane by choosing the Close button or View, Footnotes (which is turned on when you insert a footnote).

   Or, if you are in Page Layout view, you can use Shift+F5 (the Go Back key) to return to where you inserted the reference. You can use the mouse to click on any location in the document.

FIG. 19.4

You type footnotes directly on the bottom of the page when you are in the Page Layout view.

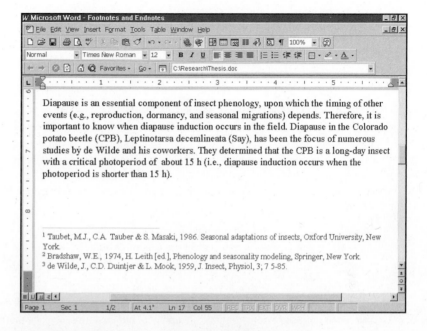

Inserting Multiple References to a Single Note

You can insert multiple references to the same footnote or endnote. For example, you can refer to the same footnote text several times in a document without having to repeat the footnote text.

To insert an additional reference to a note that has already been inserted in your document, follow these steps:

1. Position the insertion point where you want to insert the reference mark, and choose Insert, Cross-Reference.

2. Select either Footnote or Endnote from the Reference Type list box; then select either Footnote Number or Endnote Number from the Insert Reference To list box.

3. Select the footnote or endnote you want to refer to in the For Which Footnote or For Which Endnote list box.

4. Clear the Insert as Hyperlink check box.

5. Choose the Insert button and then click Close.

6. Select the reference mark you just inserted and choose either Footnote Reference or Endnote Reference from the Style drop-down list on the Formatting toolbar to apply the correct formatting to the reference mark.

Part
VI

Ch
19

N O T E   You can insert a cross-reference to another note within the text for a note, using the
procedure just described. ▪

▶ **See** "Adding Cross-References and Captions," **p. 519**

Changing the Appearance of Reference Marks

In the preceding procedure, it is assumed that footnotes and endnotes use the default numbering scheme. You set default numbering by selecting the AutoNumber option when creating a
footnote or endnote. Footnotes are automatically numbered using Arabic numerals (1, 2, 3, and
so on), and endnotes are numbered using Roman numerals (i, ii, iii, and so on). With this option selected, footnotes are renumbered when additional footnotes are added, deleted, moved,
or copied.

You can create footnotes or endnotes with a custom reference mark. To use a custom reference
mark when you create the note, select the Custom Mark option from the Footnote and Endnote
dialog box.

In the Custom Mark text box, you can type up to 10 characters, such as asterisks or daggers; or
you can choose the Symbol button and select a symbol from the Symbol dialog box. Custom
reference marks are not automatically updated, but custom reference marks don't interfere
with any automatically numbered footnote references already in your document.

To change an existing reference mark, follow these steps:

1. Select the mark.
2. Choose Insert, Footnote.
3. Type a new mark in the Custom Mark text box.
4. Choose OK. Word displays the footnote pane (in Normal view, choose Close to close it)
    or the bottom margin (in Page Layout view, press Shift+F5 to return to your document).

Editing and Viewing Footnotes and Endnotes

Research papers, theses, and technical documents are rarely completed in a single pass. They
usually require multiple rewrites and, after review, additional footnotes or endnotes. To make
changes, you need to know how to view and edit existing footnotes and endnotes.

Viewing Footnotes and Endnotes

If you choose to leave the note pane open, it will scroll along with the document to display the
notes that correspond to the note references displayed in the text.

Word offers some handy shortcuts for viewing existing notes. If you have a mouse and are in
Page Layout view, you can open the note pane by double-clicking any note reference in your

document, and you can close the pane and move back to the note reference by double-clicking the reference mark for any note entry in the note pane. You can also open the note pane by holding down the Shift key while you drag the split bar down. (The *split bar* is the narrow gray button above the up arrow in the right scroll bar.) Close the pane by dragging the split bar back up or by double-clicking the split bar.

Once you have opened the note pane, you can switch between viewing footnotes and endnotes by selecting either All Endnotes or All Footnotes from the drop-down list at the top of the pane.

You also can choose <u>V</u>iew, <u>F</u>ootnotes to view footnotes and endnotes. When you are in Normal view, choosing this command will open the note pane. When you are in Page Layout view, a dialog box appears if your document has both footnotes and endnotes, giving you a choice to view either the footnote or endnote area.

Formatting and Editing Footnotes and Endnotes

Footnote and endnote text can be formatted and edited just like any other text. You can use the ruler, toolbars, and menu commands for formatting notes. The default point size is 10 points for the note text and 8 points for the reference mark.

 TIP | Use shortcut menus displayed by clicking the right mouse button to quickly format in the note pane.

▶ **See** "Formatting a Document Automatically," **p. 129**

To change the formatting of all your footnotes by redefining the Footnote and Endnote Reference and Footnote and Endnote Text styles, follow these steps:

1. Choose F<u>o</u>rmat, <u>S</u>tyle, and select the style you want to change from the <u>S</u>tyles list.
2. Choose <u>M</u>odify, and then choose the appropriate command from the F<u>o</u>rmat submenu.
3. Make the desired formatting changes in the dialog box that is displayed and choose OK. Repeat these steps for any other formatting changes you want to make.
4. Choose OK, and then choose Apply.

▶ **See** "Using Word Standard Styles," **p. 138**

Finding Footnotes

If you are in Page Layout view, you can double-click the number to the left of a footnote or endnote reference to return to where you inserted the reference. You can return to the note associated with a reference by double-clicking the reference mark. This method enables you to quickly move back and forth between the document and the note while in Page Layout view. You can edit notes in Page Layout view just like any other text; simply scroll to the note and make the desired changes.

To locate notes, follow these steps:

1. Choose Edit, Go To, or press F5 to display the Find and Replace dialog box.
2. Select either Footnote or Endnote in the Go to What list box, and then enter the number of the note you want to find in the Enter Footnote Number text box.
3. Choose the Next button.

To find the next or previous note, leave the text box blank and click either Next or Previous. Choose Close to close the Go To dialog box.

▶ **See** "Using Find and Replace," **p. 25**

You can also choose Edit, Find to locate notes. Choose Edit, Find, position the insertion point in the Find What text box, select More, and click Special. Select either Endnote Mark or Footnote Mark from the list and click Find Next repeatedly until you find the note you are looking for. Choose Cancel to close the Find and Replace dialog box.

Deleting, Copying, and Moving a Footnote or Endnote

To delete, copy, or move a footnote or endnote, work with the reference mark—not the actual note text. If you delete, copy, or move the actual note text, the reference mark is left in place where it was originally inserted. When you delete, copy, or move a reference mark, Word automatically renumbers all numbered notes.

To delete a footnote or endnote, you must select the reference mark for the footnote and press Delete or Backspace. Deleting the note's text leaves the reference mark in the text.

If you want to remove all the footnotes or endnotes in a document, choose Edit, Replace, More, and click Special. Select Endnote Mark or Footnote Mark from the list, clear any contents in the Replace With text box, and choose Replace All. Choose Close to close the Find and Replace dialog box.

> **CAUTION**
>
> Be careful when deleting text that contains footnotes or endnotes. If you select and delete text that contains a footnote marker, you also delete the footnote or endnote.

To copy or move a note by choosing either Edit, Copy or Edit, Cut, follow these steps:

1. Select the reference mark for the note you want to move.
2. If you want to copy the note, choose Edit, Copy. You can also click the Copy button in the Standard toolbar.

   If you want to move the note, choose Edit, Cut. You can also click the Cut button in the Standard toolbar.

3. Position the insertion point at the new position where you want the note reference.

4. Choose <u>E</u>dit, <u>P</u>aste. You can also click the Paste button in the Standard toolbar.

To copy or move a note with the mouse, follow these steps:

1. Select the reference mark for the note you want to move.

2. To move the note, drag the selected note reference to the new location and release the mouse button.

   To copy the note reference, hold down the Ctrl key and drag and drop the note reference to the location you want to copy it to.

Converting Footnotes and Endnotes

So you've worked and slaved to get an article written for the *Arabian Rain Forest Review*, and it's finally complete. After waiting for three weeks, you get a letter stating that if you resubmit the article by tomorrow, it will be published. But you used footnotes, and they want you to redo your article with endnotes. Because you typed it with Word, you don't have a problem; you can convert existing footnotes to endnotes, or endnotes to footnotes. You can convert all the notes in a document or individual notes.

To convert all notes, follow these steps:

1. Choose <u>I</u>nsert, Foot<u>n</u>ote.

2. Click the <u>O</u>ptions button to display the Note Options dialog box; then click the Conver<u>t</u> button.

3. Select one of the options in the Convert Notes dialog box (see Figure 19.5).

FIG. 19.5

Use the Convert Notes dialog box to convert footnotes to endnotes or endnotes to footnotes.

4. Choose OK to close the Convert Notes dialog box, choose OK to close the Note Options dialog box, and then click the Close button to close the Footnote and Endnote dialog box.

To convert individual notes, follow these steps:

1. Choose <u>V</u>iew, <u>N</u>ormal if you are not already in Normal view.

2. Choose <u>V</u>iew, <u>F</u>ootnotes.

3. Select All Footnotes or All Endnotes in the view drop-down list at the top of the note pane.

4. Select the note you want to convert in the note pane.

5. Click the right mouse button to display the shortcut menu.

6. Choose either Convert to Footnote or Convert to Endnote.

Customizing Note Settings

You can override the default note settings to suit your particular needs in several ways. You can customize the separator—the line that separates notes from the document text and from each other if they continue across more than one page. You also can add a continuation notice specifying that a note continues on the next page.

By default, footnotes appear on the bottom of the page on which their reference marks appear. If you want, you can specify that footnotes are printed directly beneath the document text if the text on a page does not extend to the bottom. Endnotes normally appear at the end of the document. You can specify that they instead appear at the end of each section in a document.

Finally, you can change the numbering scheme for notes. You can change the starting number for notes, or choose to have note numbering restart on each page or at the beginning of each section, rather than having the notes numbered sequentially from the beginning of the document. You can also change the number format used for footnotes and endnotes.

N O T E Word's footnote style is not necessarily the acceptable style for academic institutions. Many universities use Turabian (the author of a manual) as a standard for theses and dissertations. Turabian indents the first line of footnotes and double-spaces between footnotes, for example. You may need to edit the footnote reference and text styles. ▪

Customizing Note Separators

Footnotes and endnotes are separated from the text in a document by a *separator*. When a footnote continues from one page to the next, Word inserts a *continuation separator* line between the document text and the continued footnote.

To customize separators, follow these steps:

1. Choose View, Normal if you are not already in Normal view.

2. Choose View, Footnotes.

3. Select either All Footnotes or All Endnotes from the view drop-down list at the top of the pane.

4. To edit the separator line, select Footnote Separator or Endnote Separator from the view drop-down list.

   The default is a two-inch line. You can keep the line, delete it, or add characters before or after the line. You can change the characters that are used as the separator or use graphics characters if you want.

5. To edit the continuation separator line, select Footnote Continuation Separator or Endnote Continuation Separator from the view list.

The Continuation Separator is the separator between the document text and the remainder of a note that continues across more than one page. Word proposes a margin-to-margin line. You can edit this line the same way as the separator line.

6. Choose the Close button or press Alt+Shift+C to close the note pane.

To reset the default settings for the note separators, follow steps 1 through 5 in the preceding procedure, choose the Reset button and choose Close.

A *continuation notice* is text that explains that footnotes or endnotes continue on the next page. You can add a continuation notice in the note pane.

To add a continuation notice, follow these steps:

1. Choose View, Normal if you are not already in Normal view.
2. Choose View, Footnotes.
3. Select either All Footnotes or All Endnotes from the view drop-down list at the top of the pane.
4. Select either Footnote Continuation Notice or Endnote Continuation Notice from the view drop-down list.
5. Type the text you want to use for the continuation notice.
6. Choose the Close button or press Alt+Shift+C to close the note pane.

To view the text, switch to page layout view. You can only edit the continuation text in the note pane. To reset the default settings for the continuation notice, follow steps 1 through 4 in the preceding procedure, choose the Reset button, and then choose Close.

Placing Footnotes

You can specify where the footnotes or endnotes you create are to appear in your document. Traditionally, footnotes appear at the bottom of the page. Word places them at the bottom margin, below the footnote separator. You can change the placement so that footnotes appear immediately below the text in a document.

Endnotes normally appear at the end of a document. You can choose to have endnotes appear at the end of each section in a document, provided that the document is divided into sections.

To change the position of footnotes, follow these steps:

1. Choose Insert, Footnote.
2. Choose the Options button. The Note Options dialog box appears (see Figure 19.6).

FIG. 19.6

Select the position of notes in the Note Options dialog box.

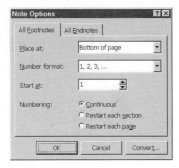

3. Select either the All Footnotes or All Endnotes tab.

4. Select one of the following options from the Place At drop-down list:

Option	Function
Bottom of Page	Places footnotes at the bottom margin of the page on which the footnote references appear (the default setting).
Beneath Text	Prints footnotes after the last line of text. This style is handy when the text is much shorter than a page.
End of Section	Prints the endnotes at the end of the section.
End of Document	Prints endnotes at the end of the document.

5. Choose OK and then choose the Close button.

Figure 19.4, shown earlier in this chapter, shows a document with the footnotes placed at the bottom of the page, just below the document text. Figure 19.7 shows the same document with the endnotes collected at the end of the document.

If you specify endnotes to appear at the end of each section, you can choose to print the endnotes at the end of the current section, or you can save them for a later section. Place the insertion point in the section in which you want to suppress the endnotes. Choose File, Page Setup, and select the Layout tab. Select Suppress Endnotes to save endnotes for the next section, or clear Suppress Endnotes to include the endnotes with the current section.

▶ **See** "Working with Sections in Your Document," **p. 196**

Customizing Numbering

You can change how you number your footnotes. To customize the numbering of footnotes, follow these steps:

1. Choose Insert, Footnote.

2. Choose the Options button. The Note Options dialog box appears.

3. Select either the All Footnotes or All Endnotes tab.

FIG. 19.7

A document in Page Layout view shows endnotes collected at the end of the document.

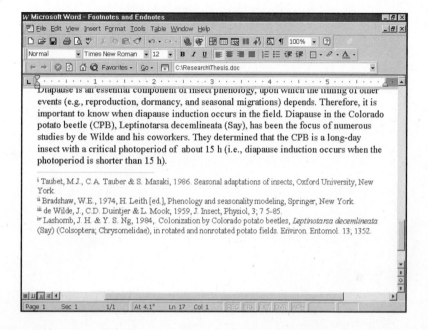

4. To change the starting number, type a new number in the Start At text box, or scroll the spin box arrows to select a new number.

5. Select one of the following Numbering options:

Option	Result
Continuous	Numbering is continuous from beginning to end of document.
Restart Each Section	Numbering is restarted in each section of the document.
Restart Each Page	Numbering is restarted on each page of the document (available only for footnotes).

6. Choose OK and then choose OK in the Footnote and Endnote dialog box.

Part
VI

Ch
19

Creating Indexes and Tables of Contents

Creating Indexes

An index, such as the one found at the end of this book, lists topics covered in a book or document and provides the page numbers where you can find the topics. Without an index, your readers will have difficulty locating information in a long document or in one that is filled with references.

In Word, creating an index involves two steps:

- You must identify each entry you want indexed.
- You must collect these entries into an index.

Word has the capability to create simple indexes, such as the following:

```
Printing, 5, 12, 25
Publishing, 37, 54, 68
```

Word also can create indexes that use subentries so that specific topics are easier to locate:

```
Printing
        Envelopes, 37, 39
        Merge, 43-45
```

If you need more in-depth or complex indexing, Word is capable of creating indexes that include different characters such as separators, unique formatting, and multiple levels of subentries:

```
Printing
        Envelopes: 37, 39-42
        Mail Merge
                Data document: 54-62
                Main document: 50-55, 67, 72
        Summary info, See Properties
```

Creating Index Entries

Identifying an entry, such as a word, to be included in your index can be as simple as selecting the word and choosing a command. As an alternative, you can position the insertion point where you want the entry referenced, choose a command, and type the word to index. This second method gives you the flexibility to decide how the topic will appear in the index.

N O T E   When creating index entries, you should select the entire word or phrase to be indexed. Remember that you can select entire words by double-clicking the word or by moving to the beginning of the word and pressing Shift+Ctrl+right arrow.

To create an index entry in your document, follow these steps:

1. Select the word or words to index, or position the insertion point where you want the entry.
2. Choose Insert, Index and Tables. Word displays the Index and Tables dialog box.

3. Select the Index tab to display the indexing options, if they are not already displayed (see Figure 20.1).

FIG. 20.1

Use the Index and Tables dialog box to create index entries and compile indexes.

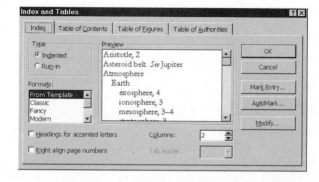

4. Choose the Mark Entry button. Word displays the Mark Index Entry dialog box.

The Mark Index Entry dialog box includes the selected word or words (see Figure 20.2). If no word or words are selected, type the index entry.

FIG. 20.2

Create an index entry in the Mark Index Entry dialog box.

N O T E If the selected text contains a colon (:), Word prefaces the colon with a backslash (\ ). If you type text that contains a colon, you must preface the colon with a backslash yourself. As you learn in "Creating Multiple-Level Index Entries," later in this chapter, the colon has a special meaning in an index entry. The backslash character tells Word to ignore the colon's special meaning and instead to include the colon in the index entry text. ▪

5. In the Main Entry text box, make no change if the index entry looks the way you want it; or type and edit the index entry as you want it to appear in the index.

6. Select among the index entry options:

Select Cross-reference to create a cross-reference index entry. Cross-reference index entries are described later in the section "Creating Cross-Reference Index Entries."

Select Current Page to have the index entry refer only to the current page.

Part
VI

Ch
20

Select Page Range, and type or select the name of a bookmark from the drop-down list if you want the index entry to refer to the range of pages spanned by the bookmark.

7. Select among the Page Number Format options:

Select Bold to print the index page numbers for this entry in boldface text.

Select Italic to print the index page numbers for this entry in italic text.

8. Choose Mark to mark only this entry for inclusion in the index.

Or, choose Mark All to have Word search the entire document and mark all index entries that match the text in the Main Entry text box for inclusion in the index. Mark All is only available if you have preselected text in the document and if you have chosen the Current Page option.

The Mark Index Entry dialog box remains open after you mark the index entry, whether you choose Mark or Mark All. To create additional index entries, scroll your document and select additional text, or move the insertion point to where you want the next index entry and type the entry directly into the Main Entry text box, repeating steps 5 through 8.

N O T E If the Mark Index Entry dialog box is covering your text, you can move the box by dragging the dialog box title bar. ▨

9. Choose Close to close the Mark Index Entry dialog box.

Repeat these steps for every index entry in your document.

N O T E To add character formatting to the index entry—formatting that will be evident in the compiled index—you select text in the Main Entry or Subentry text boxes, and use the character formatting shortcut keys. If you want the main index entry to be in bold, for example, select all the text in the Main Entry text box and press Ctrl+B to apply bold character formatting. When the index is compiled, this entry appears in bold. ▨

Including a Range of Pages

As you create an index, you probably will want to reference a range of pages for an index entry, as in the following example:

```
Desktop Publishing, 51-75
```

To do this, you must first select the range of pages and assign a bookmark to the selection. Then, when you insert the index entry, you select the bookmark name from the Bookmark list box (part of the Page Range option) to indicate the range of pages for the entry.

You need to use a range name to mark the span of pages (rather than an actual number of pages), because editing, insertions, and deletions may move the topic so that it spans different pages than those whose numbers are typed. When using a bookmark, Word calculates the new location of the bookmark so that the index will be up-to-date.

To reference a range of pages, first create the bookmark by following these steps:

1. Select the pages you want to reference in the index entry.
2. Choose Insert, Bookmark (or press Shift+Ctrl+F5).
3. Type a name of up to 40 characters in the Bookmark Name text box.
4. Choose Add.

Now create the index entry, and use the bookmark to describe the page range involved in the reference by following these steps:

1. Position the insertion point where you want to insert the index entry, or select the text you want to index.
2. Choose Insert, Index and Tables.
3. Select the Index tab to display the Index options, if necessary.
4. Choose the Mark Entry button.
5. In the Main Entry text box, make no change if the index entry looks the way you want, or type an index entry.
6. Select Page Range, and type the bookmark name in the Bookmark text box or select it from the drop-down list.
7. Select other options as necessary.
8. Choose Mark to create the index entry (Mark All is not available when working with page ranges because you only need to mark one of the entries within the specified page range). The Mark Index Entry dialog box remains open.
9. Choose Close to close the Mark Index Entry dialog box.

NOTE You can also select text and set bookmarks after you open the Mark Index Entry dialog box. Open the Mark Index Entry dialog box, and then use the usual procedure to set a bookmark; the Mark Index Entry dialog box stays open.

Customizing Index Entries

When you select the Mark Entry option of the Index and Tables dialog box, enter index text, and choose Mark or Mark All, you actually are entering a hidden field code that looks like {XE} into the document at a point directly after the insertion point or the selected text. These field codes are a powerful feature that can help you automate Word and customize the results of some commands, such as Insert, Index and Tables.

To see the hidden text of the field codes inserted by the Mark Entry option, choose Tools, Options, and then select the View tab. Select Hidden Text from the Nonprinting Characters group, and choose OK. The hidden text in the index field is now displayed at all times. Clear this check box when you want to hide the {XE} field text.

TIP You can also display hidden text in {XE} fields by clicking the Show/Hide ¶ button on the Standard toolbar or by pressing Shift+Ctrl+*.

Some examples of field codes for index entries are as follows:

Field Code	Result in Index
{XE "Printing"}	Printing, 56
{XE "Printing" \r "PagesEnv"}	Printing, 72–80
{XE "Printing" \b \i}	Printing, *56*

You can modify and edit these codes to give them more capabilities or formatting than is built into the Mark Index Entry dialog box. The "Formatting an Index" section, later in this chapter, covers formatting in detail.

N O T E Index entries appear in the compiled index capitalized exactly as they are in the {XE} fields. If your document contains index entries for the words *computer* and *Computer*, Word creates a separate entry in the finished index for each word. If you want only one entry for both words, you must edit the text in the {XE} field to have the same capitalization.

Assembling a Simple Index

After you create an entry for each index entry or subentry you want collected into an index, you can compile the index. Follow these steps to create your index:

1. Position the insertion point in your document where you would like the index to appear.

    If you are creating an index for a master document, choose View, Master Document to switch to Master Document view, and make sure that the insertion point is not in a subdocument.

2. Turn off the display of hidden text and field codes so that the document will be repaginated properly as the index is created.

N O T E If you turn off all nonprinting characters, but hidden text is still displayed, then you also must turn off the Hidden Text option in the Options dialog box. Choose Tools, Options and select the View tab. Clear the Hidden Text check box and choose OK.

3. Choose Insert, Index and Tables.

4. Select the Index tab to display the index options, if they are not already displayed (see Figure 20.3).

5. Choose from two types of indexes: indented or run-in. Select Indented to indent subentries under major entries in the index, as in the following example:

```
Printing
        Envelopes, 56
```

Select Run-in to include subentries on the same line as their major entries, with words wrapping to the next line if necessary, as in the following example:

```
Printing: Envelopes, 56
```

FIG. 20.3

You can compile an index with the Index and Tables dialog box.

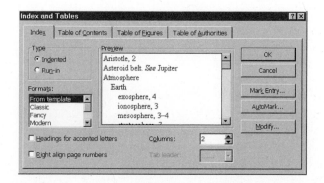

6. Select among seven formats for the index in the Formats list box; a sample of the format you select is shown in the Preview box.

   If you select From Template, the Modify button is enabled. Choose Modify to adjust the style of the text used in the index. Word displays a standard Style dialog box, except that style editing is limited to the Index styles 1 through 9.

▶ **See** "Changing Styles," **p. 156**

7. Select Headings For Accented Letters if you would like words beginning with accented letters to be sorted under a separate heading (for example, words beginning with À would sort under a different heading than words beginning with A).

8. Set the number of columns you want for the index in the Columns spin box.

9. Select Right Align Page Numbers to have page numbers appear right aligned.

   If Right Align Page Numbers is selected, the Tab Leader list box is enabled.

10. Select a leader style (none, dots, dashes, or a solid line) in the Tab Leader list box, if applicable.

11. Choose OK. Word repaginates the document and compiles the index. Figure 20.4 shows a sample index.

When you use choose Insert, Index and Tables to compile an index, you are actually inserting a hidden field code, {INDEX}. Chapter 14, "Automating with Field Codes," describes field codes in detail. The following example shows the field code for the index shown in Figure 20.4:

```
{INDEX \h "A" \c "2" }
```

To view the index field code, place the insertion point in the index and press Shift+F9. Press Shift+F9 while the insertion point is in the field to again view the index text.

FIG. 20.4

This figure shows a sample index.

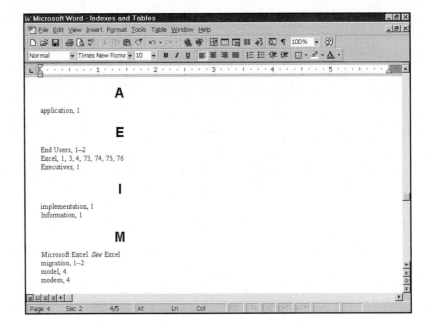

 T I P You can right-click the index with the mouse and choose Toggle Field Codes from the shortcut menu to display the index field code. To display the index text, right-click the index field code and again choose Toggle Field Codes.

The index will not have index headings that separate the index entries (such as separating the A's from the B's) if you choose From Template in the Formats list. Formats list is located on the Index tab in the Index and Tables dialog box. If you want to include a heading in an index with a custom style, you must manually add the \h switch to the {INDEX} field code. In the preceding index field code example, the "A" after the \h indicates that the index heading should contain the letter of the alphabet for the index entries below that heading. To edit the index field code, place the insertion point in the index and press Shift+F9 to display the field code, then edit the text in the field code as you would any other text. To display the index with the new heading, follow the instructions for updating indexes, later in this chapter.

Formatting an Index

You can change the appearance of an index by formatting the index and the individual index entries.

Formatting an Index Using Styles   The easiest and fastest way to change the character and paragraph formatting of an index is to use styles. Word supplies automatic styles for index entries: Index Heading, Index 1, and so on, through Index 9. *Index Heading* is the style Word uses to format the letters at the beginning of each section of an index. In Figure 20.4, the Index

Heading style has been changed to Arial font and a larger point size. To redefine a style, choose Format, Style.

▶ **See** "Redefining a Style," **p. 157**

CAUTION

If you make changes to an index style, you will lose those changes each time you replace the index. This is because Word resets the index styles each time an index is replaced. You can avoid this by using the Update Field command (rather than the Index and Tables dialog box) to update an index when you have made changes to your document. To do this, place the insertion point anywhere in the index and press the F9 (Update Field) key or right-click the index with the mouse and choose Update Field from the shortcut menu.

N O T E You can access several formatting options for indexes by using switches in the {INDEX} field. For example, you can use the \h switch to specify which characters are used to separate index headings. Or with the \e switch, you can change the characters used to separate the index text from the page numbers (the default is a comma followed by a space). To add these switches, place the insertion point within the index, and press Shift+F9 to display the {INDEX} field (or choose Tools, Options; select the View tab, and select the Field Codes check box). Next, type the desired switches. ■

Formatting an Index Directly You can also format your index directly, using the Format menu commands, Formatting toolbar, and the ruler. If you update your index, however, you will lose all direct formatting changes. For this reason, you should redefine the styles for your index to make formatting changes.

Formatting Index Entries You can also apply character formatting to individual index entries by directly formatting the text in the {XE} index entry field. Any character formatting you apply to text in the index entry field is applied to that index entry as Word compiles the index. The character formatting in the index entry field is applied in addition to any formatting dictated by the index style. Character formatting applied directly to text in the {XE} field remains unchanged when you update or replace the index.

You can apply character formatting to individual index entries in two ways:

■ You can format the text in the Mark Index Entry dialog box as you create the index entry.

■ You can edit the index entry field itself.

To format the text as you create the index entry, select text in either the Main Entry or Subentry text boxes, and use the character formatting shortcut keys. To make an entry appear in italics, for example, select the text in the Main Entry text box, and then press Ctrl+I.

To edit the {XE} index field itself, click the Show/Hide ¶ button on the Standard toolbar so that hidden text and nonprinting characters, such as tabs and paragraph marks, are displayed, or choose Tools, Options, and then select Hidden Text on the View tab to display hidden text.

Select all or part of the text in the {XE} field, and use the Formatting toolbar or Format, Font to apply character formatting as you would with any other text.

N O T E   If you choose Insert, Page Numbers to have Word display chapter numbers with page numbers (for example, 4–27), the chapter numbers are also shown with the page numbers in your index.

Updating or Replacing an Index

If you later add index entries to your document and want to update your index, move the insertion point within the {INDEX} field code (or the text that results from the code), and then press F9 (the Update Field command). Word updates the index, adding any new index entries and updating the page numbers for all index entries. Any formatting changes that you made to the index by redefining index styles or formatting individual index entries is kept; any formatting that you performed directly on the index text is lost.

Occasionally, you may want to completely replace an index, especially if you have made extensive changes in a document, or if you want to completely change the appearance of the index. To replace an index, place the insertion point within the {INDEX} field code (or the text that results from the code), and then choose Insert, Index and Tables as you would for compiling a new index. After you choose OK to begin compiling the index, Word asks if you want to replace the existing index. If you choose OK, Word compiles a new index, replacing the existing index. If you choose Cancel, Word still compiles a new index, but adds another {INDEX} field to the document.

> **CAUTION**
>
> If you choose Insert, Index and Tables to replace an index or to compile more than one index, Word resets all the index styles (Index Heading and Index 1 through 9) to have the characteristics of the index format you choose in the Index and Tables dialog box. If you want to keep any changes you have made to the index styles, press the F9 (Update Field) key to update an index instead of replacing it.

Deleting an Index

To delete an index, select the index and press Delete. You can select the entire index quickly by clicking the mouse button in the left margin over the section break at either end of the index. To quickly select and delete an entire index using the keyboard, place the insertion point on either section break, press F8, press the down-arrow key once to select the index, and press Delete.

Another alternative is to choose Tools, Options, and then select Field Codes on the View tab to display field codes (or right-click with the mouse to toggle the field code), select the {INDEX} code, and press Delete.

Locking an Index or Fixing an Index as Text

An index is actually created with a hidden field code, {INDEX}. As long as the field code is there, you can quickly update the index by selecting the code and pressing F9.

There may be times when you will want to lock an index so other users cannot modify it. This is especially helpful when you have applied formatting directly to the index text and do not want it accidentally updated by another user. You can do this by locking the index field code. To do this, place the insertion point anywhere within the index or the index field code and press Ctrl+F11. This will prevent the field from being updated; however, the index can still be replaced via the Index and Tables dialog box. To unlock the index field code so updating can occur, place the insertion point anywhere within the index or the index field code and press Shift+Ctrl+F11.

CAUTION

Word gives no indication that a field has been locked except to sound an audible beep when a user attempts to update a locked field. If users are unfamiliar with this feature, they may fail to realize the index has not been updated or they may delete and reinsert the index out of frustration when Word refuses to update it.

In some cases, you may want to change the field code to its text result so that the index cannot be changed or updated. You may want to fix the field code so that you can reformat the index without losing formatting if someone selects the document and presses F9 to update other fields, or so that you can save the document to another word processing format while preserving the index.

To fix the index field code so that it changes to text, place the insertion point anywhere within the index or the index field code. Then press Shift+Ctrl+F9, the Unlink Field command.

N O T E You cannot change an unlinked field back into a field code; however, you can choose Edit, Undo to undo the Unlink Field command. If you want to reinsert an index field code, but can no longer undo the change, you must delete the text and reinsert the index via the Index and Tables dialog box. ▪

Creating Multiple-Level Index Entries

If you have ever looked up a topic in an index and found the topic listed with a dozen or so page numbers, you know the value of a multiple-level index. When you expect to have several occurrences of a topic, you can help your reader by using categories and subcategories to divide the topic into more specific references. In Word, these entries are called *multiple-level index entries*, and they're easy to create.

The following is an example of the difference between a regular and a multiple-level index:

Index Type	Result
Regular	Computers, 1, 6, 17, 25, 33–37, 54
Multiple-level	Computers
	hard disk drives, 6
	modems, 17
	processor types, 33–37, 54
	software, 1, 25

To create a multiple-level index entry, follow these steps:

1. Position the insertion point where you want the index entry, or select the text you want indexed.

2. Choose Insert, Index and Tables.

3. Select the Index tab to display the index options, if necessary (refer to Figure 20.3).

4. Choose Mark Entry. Word displays the Mark Index Entry dialog box (refer to Figure 20.2).

5. In the Main Entry text box, type the name of the main category, or edit the selected text until the main category item appears how you want it.

6. Type the name of the subcategory in the Subentry text box.

   If you want to create sub-subentries, separate each subentry level in the Subentry text box with a colon (:). (See the example immediately following these steps.)

7. Select other options as needed, and choose Mark.

   The Mark Index Entry dialog box remains open so that you can scroll through your document and create additional index entries. Repeat steps 5 through 7 for each index entry with a subentry.

8. Choose Close when you are finished creating index entries.

Follow this procedure for each index entry and subentry. To create the following multiple-level index entry, for example, you would type **Computers** in the Main Entry text box, and **Hard disk drives** in the Subentry text box (refer to step 6):

```
Computers
      Hard disk drives, 54, 65
```

You also can create sub-subentries, as in the following example:

```
Computers
      Hard disk drives
            Maintenance, 54
            Performance, 65
      Processors, 102
```

All the preceding sub-subentries were made with **Computers** in the Main Entry text box and the following text in the Subentry text box:

```
Hard disk drives:Maintenance
Hard disk drives:Performance
Processors
```

Notice how each subentry level is separated from the previous level by a colon (:). You can have up to six levels of subentries. The index entry fields for these entries would look like this:

```
{XE "Computers:Hard disk drives:Maintenance" }
{XE "Computers:Hard disk drives:Performance" }
{XE "Computers:Processors" }
```

> **CAUTION**
>
> Word will allow you to add more than six levels of subentries when marking an index entry. However, only the first six entries will be used when the index is compiled.

Marking Index Entries for Symbols

Sometimes you may want to index symbols or other special characters.

To create an index entry for a symbol, follow these steps:

1. Select the symbol in your document that you want to index.

2. Choose Insert, Index and Tables. Select the Index tab, if necessary, and then choose Mark Entry. The Mark Index Entry dialog box appears with the selected symbol in the Main Entry text box.

3. Press the right-arrow key or use the mouse to position the insertion point immediately following the symbol in the Main Entry text box.

4. Type a semicolon followed by the number sign (;#) to the right of the symbol.

   Symbols are automatically placed at the beginning of the index. If you choose an index format that includes index headings, the symbols will appear beneath the # heading at the top of the index. You may want to delete the # heading in the final index or replace it with a more meaningful heading such as *Symbols* or *Special Characters*.

N O T E To create index entries for symbols that have been inserted using Insert, Symbol (for example, the ☻ symbol), create the index entry with any symbol or character typed in from the keyboard, then view the {XE} field code and replace the unwanted symbol with the desired symbol from the Symbol dialog box. ▪

5. Choose Mark or Mark All. Continue to mark entries as necessary.

6. When you are finished, choose Close to close the Index and Tables dialog box.

Creating Cross-Reference Index Entries

You can choose Insert, Index and Tables to create cross-reference indexes. A *cross-reference* index gives the reader information such as the following:

```
Modem, see Computers.
```

To create a cross-reference index entry, follow these steps:

1. Select the word or words to index, or position the insertion point where you want the entry placed in your document.

2. Choose Insert, Index and Tables. Word displays the Index and Tables dialog box.

3. Select the Index tab to display the indexing options, if necessary.

4. Choose the Mark Entry button. Word displays the Mark Index Entry dialog box.

   The Mark Index Entry dialog box includes the selected word or words (refer to Figure 20.2). If no word or words are selected, type the index entry in the Main Entry text box.

5. Make no change if the index entry and subentry look the way you want; or type and edit the index entry and subentry as you want them to appear in the index.

6. Select Cross-reference, and type the cross-reference topic after the "See" in the Cross-reference text box. If you want the cross-reference to appear in a different format, press the formatting key command before typing in the cross-reference. For example, if you would like the entire cross-reference italicized, press Ctrl+I to turn on italics and then type the cross-reference.

7. Select among the other options as needed; choose Mark to mark this word in the document. The Mark All button will be disabled because you can only use this feature when page numbers are to be inserted along with an entry; there is no reason to mark all entries when cross-referencing to another entry in the index.

   The Mark Index Entry dialog box remains open so that you can scroll through your document and create additional index entries. Repeat steps 5 through 7 for each index entry.

8. Choose Close when you are finished creating index entries.

Repeat these steps for each index entry. As with all other index entries, Word inserts an {XE} field code each time you mark an index entry. If you view the cross-reference index field, you will notice that it includes a special switch—\t—to create the cross-reference entry. The text preceding the \t switch is the index entry, and the text that follows the \t switch is the cross-reference text. The following line shows a cross-reference index field:

```
{XE "Graphics" \t "See Desktop Publishing" }
```

The preceding index entry field produces the following entry in the compiled index:

```
Graphics. See Desktop Publishing
```

Automatically Creating Index Entries

If you have a large number of index entries to create or you want to standardize the capitalization of your index entries, you can have Word create index entries for you. To automatically create index entries, you must first create a concordance file containing the words or phrases you want to index and their corresponding entries and subentries. After you create the concordance file, you can select the AutoMark option in the Index and Tables dialog box to automatically mark the index entries. You can add index entries to your document automatically or manually, in any combination.

Creating a Concordance File   The *concordance file* is a Word document containing a single, two-column table, and no text outside the table. The first column of the table contains the words and phrases you want to index, and the second column of the table contains the entry and subentry that should appear in the index for the indexed word or phrase.

▶ **See** "Creating Tables," **p. 275**

▶ **See** "Adding or Deleting Cells, Rows, or Columns," **p. 294**

To create a concordance file, follow these steps:

1. Choose File, New, or click the New button to create a new document file.

2. Choose Table, Insert Table, and then choose OK. Word inserts a two-column table into the document. You can also click the Insert Table button to create a two-column table.

3. In the first column of the table, type the word or words you want to index.

4. In the second column of the table, type the text you want to appear in the index for each entry.

   To create an index subentry, separate each subentry level with a colon, as described earlier in this chapter for multi-level indexes. You cannot use a concordance file to create cross-reference index entries.

5. Perform steps 3 and 4 for each word or phrase you want to index, adding additional rows to the table, as necessary (see Figure 20.5). See Chapter 10, "Creating and Editing Tables," for more information about tables.

   If a word needs to be indexed under more than one heading, you must create an entry in the concordance file for each heading.

   The concordance file is case sensitive. You must include both uppercase and lowercase entries if you want them to be included in the index.

   You may find it helpful to sort your table in the order of the words being indexed so you can easily determine if a word has already been added to the concordance file.

▶ **See** "Sorting Tables," **p. 307**

6. Save and close the concordance file.

Creating Index Entries from a Concordance File   To create index entries from the concordance file, follow these steps:

1. Turn off the display of hidden text, if necessary. Click the Show/Hide ¶ button on the Standard toolbar, or choose Tools, Options, select the View tab, and then clear Hidden Text.

2. Choose Insert, Index and Tables.

3. Select the Index tab to display the index options, if necessary.

4. Choose the AutoMark button. Word displays the Open Index AutoMark File dialog box, which operates like the standard Open dialog box.

5. Select the appropriate drive or folder, and then select the concordance file you want to use.

If the concordance file you want is not listed, use the Files of Type list box to change the files displayed in the file list, or try another drive or folder.

6. Choose Open.

Word searches through your document and inserts an index entry at every location where a word or phrase matches a word or phrase in the first column of the table in the concordance file.

FIG. 20.5

You can use a concordance file to automatically insert index entries.

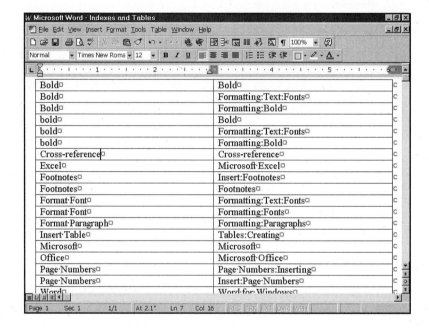

After inserting the index entries, create the index as described in "Assembling a Simple Index" earlier in this chapter. If you later make changes in the concordance file, choose Insert, Index and Tables, AutoMark again. Word adds any new index entries to reflect additions in the concordance file.

CAUTION

Word will not update existing index entries when you choose AutoMark. For example, if you specify "Formatting:Bold" in your concordance file for every occurrence of the word "Bold" and later change this entry in the concordance file to read "Formatting:Bold Text," Word will insert a new index entry reading {XE "Formatting:Bold Text"} for each occurrence of the word "Bold" within your document. However, it will not remove nor change the existing {XE "Formatting:Bold"} entries. Use Edit, Replace to locate and remove unwanted field codes.

Creating Tables of Contents

A table lists selected items included in your document, along with their page numbers. Building a table of contents at the beginning of a document is probably the most common use of this feature. You also can create tables of figures, photos, tables, or other items. Figure 20.6 shows one of the types of tables of contents you can create.

FIG. 20.6
Word can create tables of contents in many formats and for different items.

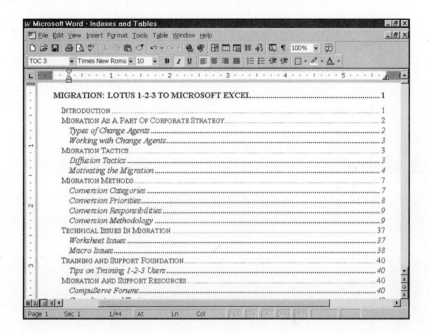

You have two ways to create a table of contents: by using heading styles, or by using special table-of-contents entry fields. The easiest way to create a table of contents is to collect heading styles.

▶ **See** "Applying Paragraph Styles," **p. 144**

Creating a Table of Contents Using Outline Headings

If you know you want a table of contents, you may want to format your document headings by using the built-in heading styles, Heading 1, Heading 2, and so on. When you compile a table of contents, Word recognizes these heading styles and uses the text with those styles to create the table of contents. Word provides nine heading levels, Heading 1 through Heading 9. You choose which heading levels to use when you create a table of contents.

The heading styles used to create tables of contents or lists are the same heading styles used automatically when you create an outline. If you prefer to work with Word's Outliner, you may want to outline your document before or as you write, and then use the outline headings to create your table of contents. Chapter 13, "Organizing Content with an Outline," describes how to create and use outlines.

Part
VI
Ch
20

Before you can create a table of contents, you must apply heading styles to each heading you want to include in the table of contents. (To create tables of figures or other tables, see "Creating Special-Purpose Tables," later in this chapter.) To apply heading styles, move the insertion point into the text and then use one of the following methods, which are listed in order of complexity, beginning with the easiest:

- Select the desired heading style from the style list box on the Formatting toolbar.
- Press Alt+Shift+left arrow or Alt+Shift+right arrow to change a paragraph into a heading style and move it to a higher or lower style.
- Choose Format, Style, select the desired heading style from the Styles list box, and choose Apply.

You can apply heading styles as you type the headings, using either the mouse or keyboard methods.

 TIP You can use keyboard shortcuts to quickly apply Heading 1 through Heading 3 styles. To do this, press Ctrl+Alt+1 to apply Heading 1, Ctrl+Alt+2 to apply Heading 2, and Ctrl+Alt+3 to apply Heading 3.

To create a table of contents from headings formatted with heading styles, follow these steps:

1. Position the insertion point where you want the table of contents to appear in your document.

   If you are creating a table of contents for a master document, choose View, Master Document to switch to Master Document view, and make sure that the insertion point is not in a subdocument.

2. Turn off the display of hidden text and field codes so the document will be repaginated properly as the table of contents is created (see "Assembling a Simple Index," earlier in this chapter, for instructions on how to turn off the display of hidden text and field codes).

3. Choose Insert, Index and Tables.

4. Select the Table of Contents tab to display the table of contents options, if necessary (see Figure 20.7).

FIG. 20.7
Create a table of contents with the Index and Tables dialog box.

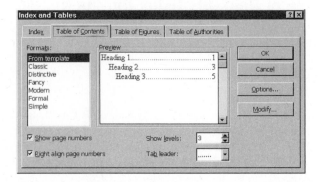

5. Select among seven Forma_t_s for the table of contents; a sample of the format you select is shown in the Pre_v_iew box.

   If you select From Template, the _M_odify button is enabled. Choose _M_odify to adjust the style of the text used in the table of contents. Word displays the standard Style dialog box, except style editing is limited to TOC styles 1 through 9. The TOC styles are used for each of the heading styles; TOC1 for Heading 1, and so on.

▶ **See** "Changing Styles," **p. 156**

6. Select _S_how Page Numbers to turn the display of page numbers on or off.

7. In the Show _L_evels spin box, set the number of heading levels you want to show in the table of contents.

8. Use the _R_ight Align Page Numbers check box to turn the right alignment of page numbers on or off.

   If _R_ight Align Page Numbers is selected, the Ta_b_ Leader list box is enabled.

9. Select the leader style (none, dots, dashes, or a solid line) in the Ta_b_ Leader list box, if applicable.

10. Choose OK. Word repaginates the document and compiles the table of contents.

Figure 20.6, shown earlier, shows a table of contents built from heading styles.

When you choose _I_nsert, In_d_ex and Tables to create a table of contents, you are inserting a hidden field code, {TOC}. Field codes are described in detail in Chapter 14, "Automating with Field Codes." The following example shows the field code for the table of contents shown in Figure 20.6. To view the table of contents field code, place the insertion point in the table of contents and press Shift+F9. Press Shift+F9 while the insertion point is in the field code to view again the table of contents text.

`{TOC \0 "1-9" }`

T I P You can use the mouse to toggle between the table of contents and the {TOC} field. Right-click the table of contents or the field code and choose _T_oggle Field Codes from the shortcut menu.

In the table of contents field, the \0 switch tells Word to create the table of contents from outline headings; the numbers enclosed in quotation marks after the switch indicate the range of heading levels to include in the table of contents.

N O T E Create a table of contents early in your work and use it to navigate through your document. If you put the table of contents at the end of the document, you can press Ctrl+End to go to the end of the document, check the table of contents to identify the page number you want, and then choose _E_dit, _G_o To (or press F5) to quickly go to that page. ■

Creating a Table of Contents Using Any Style

You may want to create a table of contents or some other table for a document that does not contain heading styles, or you may want to include references to items that have a style other than one of the heading styles. You can create a table of contents based on any styles used in the document.

▶ **See** "Creating Styles," **p. 147**

To create a table of contents that includes entries based on styles in addition to (or instead of) the built-in heading styles, follow these steps:

1. Turn off the display of hidden text and field codes so that the document will be repaginated properly as the table of contents is created.

2. Position the insertion point where you want the table of contents to appear in your document.

   If you are creating a table of contents for a master document, choose View, Master Document to switch to Master Document view, and make sure that the insertion point is not in a subdocument.

3. Choose Insert, Index and Tables.

4. Select the Table of Contents tab to display the table of contents options, if necessary (refer to Figure 20.7).

5. Choose Options. The Table of Contents Options dialog box appears (see Figure 20.8).

FIG. 20.8

The Table of Contents Options dialog box enables you to choose which items will be included in a table of contents.

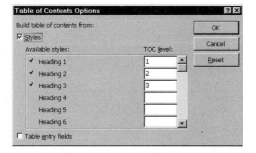

6. To create a table of contents that contains *only* entries compiled from certain styles, select the Styles check box and clear the check box for Table Entry Fields.

   Or, to create a table of contents that contains entries compiled from heading or other styles *as well as* from table entry fields, select Styles and Table Entry Fields.

7. For every style in the Available Styles list that you want included in the table of contents, type the table of contents level for that style in the corresponding TOC Level text box. You can use levels 1 through 9.

   If you don't want a style included in the table of contents, make sure the TOC Level text box for that style is empty.

8. Choose OK to accept the options you set, or choose Cancel to exit the dialog box without saving your changes.

If you have saved changes that you later want to reset, you can choose Reset to return all TOC levels back to their original settings. Reset will also clear the Table Entry Fields check box.

Word closes the Table of Contents Options dialog box when you choose OK or Cancel.

9. Set additional options in the Index and Tables dialog box, as desired.

10. Choose OK to compile the table of contents. Word closes the Index and Tables dialog box and creates the table of contents.

N O T E Word will display Error! No table of contents entries found. if none of the selected styles from the Table of Contents Options dialog box are found in the document. ■

Creating a Table of Contents Using Any Text

You may want to include references to items that don't have heading or other styles. In those cases, you can insert a table of contents entry field {TC}, along with a descriptive entry, at the beginning of each appropriate section in your document (or in the location to be referenced in the table of contents). Word then can collect these fields and descriptions into the table of contents.

A *field* is a hidden code enclosed in special characters that look like braces ({}). Fields are used to automate features of Word. Field codes were used earlier in this chapter for indexes. For more information on fields, see Chapter 14.

Marking Table of Contents Entries   To insert table of contents entry fields into your document, follow these steps:

1. Position the insertion point where you want the table of contents entry.

2. Choose Insert, Field.

3. Select Index and Tables in the Categories list box.

4. Select TC in the Field Names list.

5. Position the insertion point in the Field Codes text box, leaving one space after the TC entry.

6. Type an opening quotation mark ("), type the text of the table of contents entry, and type a closing quotation mark (").

   To create the first entry in the table of contents shown in Figure 20.6, for example, type the following in the Field Codes text box (the \l switch is explained in step 7):

   TC "MIGRATION: LOTUS 1-2-3 TO MICROSOFT EXCEL" \l 1

N O T E You can save time and keystrokes, and avoid typos, by copying the text in your document that will appear in the table of contents entry field (select the text and press Ctrl+C to copy). Then position the insertion point in the Field Codes text box of the Field dialog box and press Ctrl+V to paste the copied text into the text box. ■

Part
VI

Ch
20

7. Type a space, a backslash, and the letter **l** (as shown in the entry line).

8. Type a space and then type the number for the level at which you want this entry to appear in the finished table of contents. You can specify a level of 1 through 9.

9. Choose Options to add additional switches to the TC entry; otherwise, skip to step 11.

10. Select the desired switch in the Switches list box, choose Add to Field to add the switch to the TC field, and then type any additional text needed for the switch in the Field Codes text box.

    Choose Undo Add to remove a switch added with the Add to Field button or select the switch in the Field Codes text box and press the Delete key.

11. Choose OK to close the Field Options dialog box.

12. Choose OK to insert the table of contents entry field and close the Field dialog box.

Repeat these steps for each table of contents entry you want. The field codes you insert will not be visible in your document unless you have turned on the Hidden Text option on the View tab of Tools, Options. You can also click the Show/Hide ¶ button or press Shift+Ctrl+* to toggle on and off the display of hidden text.

N O T E   You can bypass the Insert Field command by using the Insert Field key combination, Ctrl+F9. Position the insertion point where you want the table of contents entry field, press Ctrl+F9 (a pair of field characters will appear), and type

TC "text" switches

where *text* is the text you want to appear in the table of contents and *switches* is the \l switch and level number, followed by any of the optional field code switches you want to use.

You can also copy an existing {TC} field, and then paste it into your document, changing the "text" portion of the field to the appropriate text, see "Editing Table of Contents Entries" in the following section.

If you have several {TC} fields to insert, you might consider creating an AutoText entry.

Editing Table of Contents Entries   You can edit a table of contents entry as you would any other text in your document. Any character formatting that you apply to the text in the table of contents entry will also appear in the finished table of contents. To display the table of contents entry text, use the Show/Hide ¶ button on the Standard toolbar to display the hidden text, or choose Tools, Options, View to turn on the display of Hidden Text.

Creating a Table of Contents Using Table of Contents Entry Fields   To collect {TC} field codes into a table of contents, follow these steps:

1. Turn off the display of hidden text and field codes so that the document will be repaginated properly as the table of contents is created.

2. Position the insertion point where you want the table of contents to appear in your document.

3. Choose Insert, Index and Tables.

4. Select the Table of Contents tab to display the table of contents options, if they are not already displayed (refer to Figure 20.7).

5. Choose Options. The Table of Contents Options dialog box appears (refer to Figure 20.8).

6. To create a table of contents that contains *only* entries compiled from table of contents entry fields, clear the Styles check box and select the check box for Table Entry Fields.

   Or, to create a table of contents that contains entries compiled from heading or other styles *as well as* from table entry fields, select both the Styles and Table Entry Fields check boxes.

 TIP Creating a table of contents based on styles is described earlier in this chapter.

7. Choose OK to accept the options you set. Word closes the Table of Contents Options dialog box.

8. Set additional options in the Index and Tables dialog box, as desired.

9. Choose OK to compile the table of contents. Word closes the Index and Tables dialog box and creates the table of contents.

Creating Special-Purpose Tables

With Word, you can create not only tables of contents, but also tables of figures, photos, charts, equations, tables, or any other items. These tables usually appear in a document after the table of contents.

You can create tables of figures or other special-purpose tables in two ways:

- By compiling the special-purpose tables based on text style
- By manually inserting the table entries into the document

Using Styles to Create Special-Purpose Tables

The easiest way to assemble tables of figures or other special-purpose tables is to use the Figure Caption, Equation, and other styles built into Word. If you choose Insert, Caption to create all your figure captions, for example, you can easily build a table of figures.

▶ **See** "Creating Captions," **p. 525**

To create a table of figures, equations, or tables based on one of Word's caption styles, follow these steps:

1. Position the insertion point where you want the table of figures to appear in your document.

   If you are creating a table of figures for a master document, choose View, Master Document to switch to Master Document view, and make sure that the insertion point is not in a subdocument.

2. Turn off the display of hidden text and field codes so that the document will be repaginated properly as the table of figures is created.

3. Choose Insert, Index and Tables.

4. Select the Table of Figures tab to display the table of figures options, if necessary (see Figure 20.9).

5. Select the appropriate caption in the Caption Label list.

FIG. 20.9

Create a table of figures with the Index and Tables dialog box.

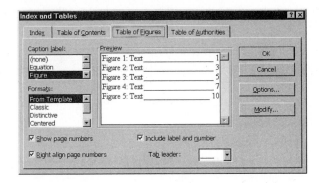

6. Select one of six Formats for the table; a sample of the format you select is shown in the Preview box.

   If you select From Template, the Modify button is enabled. Choose Modify to adjust the style of the text used in the table of figures. A standard Style dialog box appears.

   Choose Cancel or Close when you have finished in the Style dialog box.

   ▶ **See** "Changing Styles," **p. 156**

7. Select Show Page Numbers to turn the display of page numbers on or off.

8. Use the Right Align Page Numbers check box to turn the right alignment of page numbers on or off.

   If Right Align Page Numbers is selected, the Tab Leader list box is enabled.

9. Select a leader style (none, dots, dashes, or a solid line) in the Tab Leader list box, if applicable.

10. Choose Options if you want to change the style on which the table of figures is based (otherwise, skip to step 12). The Table of Figures Options dialog box appears (see Figure 20.10).

FIG. 20.10.

The Table of Figures Options dialog box enables you to choose how the table of figures is constructed.

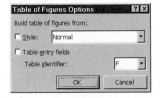

11. To create a table of figures that contains *only* entries compiled from a selected style, select the Style check box, and then select the style in the list box. Also, clear the Table Entry Fields check box if it is selected.

Or, to create a table of figures that contains entries compiled from the selected style *as well as* from table entry fields, select both Styles and Table Entry Fields. Next, select the text style in the Style list box, and select the table identifier in the Table Identifier list box.

Creating a table of figures based on table entries and table identifiers is described in the next section of this chapter.

12. Choose OK. Word repaginates the document and compiles the table of figures.

When you choose Insert, Index and Tables to create a table of figures, you are actually inserting the same {TOC} hidden field code used to create a table of contents. A table of figures is really just a special variety of table of contents. The following is an example of the field code for a table of figures:

```
{TOC \c "Figure" }
```

In this example, the \c switch tells Word to create the table by using the text in paragraphs marked with {SEQ} fields, the text enclosed in quotation marks after the switch indicates which items to group together in the same table. {SEQ} fields are the hidden codes inserted by choosing Insert, Caption. If you choose Insert, Caption to insert a figure caption, for example, the following code is inserted into the document:

```
{SEQ Figure \* ARABIC }
```

▶ **See** "Creating Captions," **p. 525**

Using Any Text to Create Special-Purpose Tables

Another way to collect special tables is to use field codes instead of (or in addition to) styles. These field codes do the following three things:

- They mark the spot in the text you want to reference by page number.
- They include the text you want to appear in the table.
- They include an identifier that defines into which table they should be accumulated.

You can type these field codes directly into a document or choose Insert, Field to insert them. The field codes you insert look similar to the following:

```
{TC "Automated publishing" \f p}
```

In the previous command, TC is the field code, "Automated publishing" is the text that appears in the table, and the \f switch indicates that the table will be built from fields. The p is an identifier that associates this entry with other entries marked with the same identifier. This entry will be accumulated in a table with other field codes that have the p identifier.

The letters you use are up to you. The code for tables, for example, could be simply t. Following are some examples of how you might group items in different tables:

Item	Field Code Identifier
Charts	c
Figures	f
Lists	l
Pictures	p
Tables	t

To insert field codes that mark what will be included in tables, follow these steps:

1. Position the insertion point on the page you want referenced in the table.
2. Choose Insert, Field.
3. Select Index and Tables in the Categories list box.
4. Select TC in the Field Names list box.
5. Position the insertion point in the Field Codes text box, leaving one space after the TC entry.
6. Type an opening quotation mark ("), type the text of the table entry, and type a closing quotation mark (").
7. Press the space bar once, and type \f, (the f indicates that the table is being built from fields).
8. Press the space bar to insert a space, and then type a single-character list identifier, such as **g**, for graphs. Use the same single-letter character for all items to be accumulated in the same table.
9. Choose Options to add additional switches to the TC entry. Choose OK to close the Field Options dialog box.
10. Choose OK to insert the table entry and close the Field dialog box.

Repeat these steps for each entry you want. The field codes you insert do not appear in your document unless you turn on the Hidden Text option on the View tab after choosing Tools, Options. Your TC field code should look similar to the following:

```
{TC "Graph Showing Learning Retention" \f g}
```

Another, and often quicker, way to enter the field code is to position the insertion point in the document, press Ctrl+F9 to insert the field code braces, {}, and then type the code and text inside the braces.

To create a table that accumulates all the items belonging to a single identifier, such as f for figures or g for graphs, follow these steps:

1. Turn off the display of hidden text and field codes so that the document repaginates using only the text that will print.

2. Position the insertion point where you want the table to appear.

3. Choose Insert, Index and Tables.

4. Select the Table of Figures tab to display the table of figures options, if the options are not already displayed (refer to Figure 20.9).

5. Choose Options. Word displays the Table of Figures Options dialog box (refer to Figure 20.10).

6. To create a table that contains *only* entries compiled from table entry fields, select the Table Entry Fields check box and clear the Style check box.

   Or, to create a table that contains entries compiled from a selected style *as well as* from table entry fields, select both the Style and Table Entry Fields check boxes.

   (Creating tables based on styles is described earlier in this chapter.)

7. Select the table identifier in the Table Identifier list box, (for example, g for graphs).

   You must also select a style from the Style list box if you selected the Style check box.

8. Choose OK to accept the options you set. Word closes the Table of Figures Options dialog box.

9. Set additional options in the Index and Tables dialog box, as desired.

10. Choose OK to compile the table. Word closes the Index and Tables dialog box and creates the table.

If you display the resulting field code, it should appear similar to the following:

```
{TOC \f G \c}
```

The preceding {TOC} field produces a table from any TC fields that contain the G identifier. By using different list identifiers, you can include multiple tables for different entries in a document (for example, charts, graphs, lists, and so on).

Creating a Table of Authorities

If you work with legal documents, you are familiar with tables of authorities. A *table of authorities* lists where citations occur in a legal brief; the citations can be references to cases, statutes, treatises, constitutional provisions, and so on.

To create a table of authorities, you first create the citation entries in your document, and then compile the table of authorities.

Creating Citation Entries

To create citation entries in your document, follow these steps:

1. Select the citation text, or position the insertion point where you want the entry.

2. Choose Insert, Index and Tables. The Index and Tables dialog box appears.

3. Select the Table of Authorities tab to display the table of authorities options, if necessary (see Figure 20.11).

FIG. 20.11

Create a table of authorities using the Index and Tables dialog box.

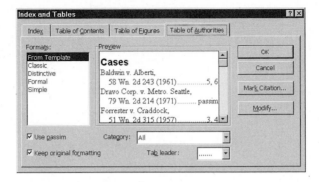

4. Choose Mark Citation. Word displays the Mark Citation dialog box.

   The Mark Citation dialog box includes the selected citation in both the Selected Text box and the Short Citation text box (see Figure 20.12). If no citation is selected, type the citation entry.

FIG. 20.12.

Create a citation entry in the Mark Citation dialog box.

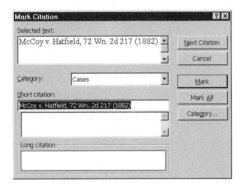

5. In the Selected Text box, edit the text so that the long form of the citation entry looks the way you want it to appear in the table of authorities.

   You can use any of the character formatting shortcut keys (such as Ctrl+B) to apply formatting to the text in the Selected Text box, and press Enter to add line breaks to the text.

6. Select the citation category in the Category list box (see "Customizing Citation Categories," later in this chapter, for information about creating your categories).

7. Edit the text in the Short Citation text box so that it matches the short citation form you use in your document. Because Word searches for and marks short citations in your document by matching the text in the Short Citation text box, be sure that capitalization, punctuation, and abbreviations are the same.

8. Choose Mark to mark only this entry for inclusion in the table of authorities.

You can also choose Mark All to have Word mark the current citation and then search the entire document and mark all long and short citations that match your entries in the Mark Citation dialog box.

N O T E If you mark only one citation now and want to mark additional citations later (after they have been added), you can select the original long citation, press Alt+Shift+I to display the Mark Citation dialog box, and then choose Mark All.

The Mark Citation dialog box remains open after marking the citation, whether you choose Mark or Mark All.

9. To create additional citation entries, scroll your document and select additional text, repeating steps 5 through 8.

   You can also choose Next Citation to have Word search your document for common abbreviations used in legal citations ("in re," "v.," "Ibid., or "Sess."), and then repeat steps 5 through 8.

10. Choose Close to close the Mark Citation dialog box.

Repeat these steps for every citation entry in your document.

Editing and Deleting Citation Entries

After you create a citation entry, you cannot edit it by choosing Insert, Index and Tables. Instead, you must edit the text in the hidden field code that is inserted in the document directly after the selected text whenever you create a citation entry in the Mark Citation dialog box.

To see the hidden text of the field codes inserted by the Mark Citation option, choose Tools, Options, and then select the View tab. Select Hidden Text from the Nonprinting Characters group, and choose OK. The hidden text in the index field is now displayed at all times. Clear this check box when you want to hide the {TA} field codes.

TIP You can also display hidden text in {TA} fields by clicking the Show/Hide ¶ button on the Standard toolbar, or by pressing Shift+Ctrl+*.

Edit and format the hidden text in the citation entry field the same way you would any other text in your document.

To delete a citation entry, simply delete the hidden code from the document. Use Edit, Replace to delete multiple entries quickly.

Assembling a Table of Authorities

After you create an entry for each citation you want collected into the table of authorities, you can compile the table. Follow these steps to create your table of authorities:

Part

VI

Ch

20

1. Position the insertion point where you want the table.

   If you are creating a table of authorities for a master document, choose View, Master Document to switch to Master Document view, and make sure that the insertion point is not in a subdocument.

2. Turn off the display of hidden text and field codes so that the document will be repaginated properly as the table of authorities is created.

3. Choose Insert, Index and Tables.

4. Select the Table of Authorities tab to display the table of authorities options, if necessary.

5. Select among five Formats for the table of authorities; a sample of the format you select is shown in the Preview box.

   If you select From Template, the Modify button is enabled. Choose Modify to adjust the style of the text used in the table of authorities. Word displays a standard Style dialog box. (Refer to Chapter 11, "Modifying Tables," for more information about editing styles.)

   Choose Close to close the Style dialog box and return to the Index and Tables dialog box.

6. Select the Use Passim check box to substitute the term *passim* whenever a citation has five or more different page numbers.

7. Select the Keep Original Formatting check box to retain the character formatting of long citations in the table of authorities.

8. Select the tab leader style (none, dots, dashes, or a solid line) you want to use for the page numbers in the Tab Leader drop-down list box.

9. In the Category list box, select the category for this table of authorities. The All selection includes all the other categories in a single table.

10. Choose OK. Word repaginates the document and compiles the table of authorities.

When you choose Insert, Index and Tables to compile a table of authorities, you are inserting the {TOA} hidden field code. To view the {TOA} field code, place the insertion point in the table of authorities and press Shift+F9. The following is an example of a typical field code for a table of authorities.

```
{TOA \h \c "1" \p}
```

Customizing Citation Categories

You can change Word's predefined citation categories, or add your own categories.

To customize the citation categories, follow these steps:

1. Choose Insert, Index and Tables. The Index and Tables dialog box appears.

2. Select the Table of Authorities tab to display the table of authorities options, if necessary.

3. Choose Mark Citation. The Mark Citation dialog box appears.

4. Choose Category. The Edit Category dialog box appears (see Figure 20.13).

FIG. 20.13.
Create customized
citation categories in
the Edit Category
dialog box.

5. In the Category list box, select the category you want to change.

    Word permits up to 16 categories, and only predefines the first seven. The remaining categories in the Category list box are simply numbered 8 through 16.

6. Type the new category name in the Replace With text box.

7. Choose Replace to change the category name.

8. Repeat steps 5 through 7 for each category you want to customize.

9. Choose OK to close the Edit Category dialog box.

Updating, Replacing, or Deleting Tables of Contents and Other Document Tables

You can easily update, replace, or delete any table of contents, table of figures, table of authorities, or other tables you create by choosing Insert, Index and Tables.

Updating Document Tables

As you add text to or delete it from a document, you also add or delete various table entries. If you add new headings to a document, additional figures, or other items, you will need to update the various tables in your document.

To update any table of contents or other table, follow these steps:

1. Place the insertion point in the table or table field code.

2. Turn off the display of hidden text, so that the document will paginate correctly as the table is updated.

T I P Mouse users can right-click the table and choose Update Field from the shortcut menu.

3. Press F9, the Update Field key. Word displays a dialog box similar to the one shown in Figure 20.14 (the exact title of the dialog box depends on the type of table you are updating).

N O T E If you are updating a table of authorities, Word will automatically update the entire table and will *not* display the Update Table dialog box as shown in Figure 20.14. ■

Part
VI

Ch
20

FIG. 20.14
Word asks you how
extensive the table
update should be.

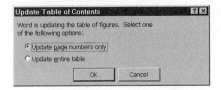

4. Select Update <u>P</u>age Numbers Only if you have only added text to or deleted it from the document, without adding or deleting table entries.

   Select Update <u>E</u>ntire Table if you have added or deleted table entries in the document.

5. Choose OK.

If you choose to update the entire table, any formatting you applied to the table by editing the styles used by the table will remain unchanged. If you formatted the table directly, then updating page numbers leaves that formatting in place, but updating the entire table causes the formatting to be replaced by the style formatting.

Tables that have been unlinked so that their text is fixed cannot be updated; instead, you must reinsert the table if you want an updated version.

Replacing Document Tables

Occasionally, you may want to completely replace a table of contents or other table, especially if you have made extensive changes in a document, or if you want to completely change the appearance of the table. To replace a table of contents or other table, place the insertion point in the table or table field code and then choose <u>I</u>nsert, In<u>d</u>ex and Tables as you would for compiling a new table of contents, table of figures, or table of authorities. After you choose OK to begin assembling the table, Word asks if you want to replace the existing table. Choose <u>Y</u>es to replace the selected table; Word compiles a new table, replacing the selected one. Choose Cancel if you do not want to replace the selected table.

Inserting Additional Document Tables

There may be times when you will want to insert a second table of the same type into your document. For example, you may want to have a different table of contents for different sections of your document (see "Limiting Tables of Contents and Other Tables," later in this chapter). If you want to add an additional table to your document, then position your cursor *outside* of the existing table and choose <u>I</u>nsert, In<u>d</u>ex and Tables. Follow the instructions provided earlier in this chapter to insert the desired type of table. Choose OK and Word asks if you want to replace the selected (existing) table. If you choose <u>N</u>o, then Word compiles a new table using an additional table field ({TOC} or {TOA}. If you do want to replace the existing table, choose <u>Y</u>es when you are prompted.

Deleting Document Tables

To delete any table of contents, table of figures, or table of authorities, just select the table and press Delete, or choose <u>T</u>ools, <u>O</u>ptions to turn on the view of field codes, and then delete the table field.

Limiting Tables of Contents and Other Tables

If you need to create a table of contents or other table for part of a document, you need to modify the field codes with switches. To modify the field codes, choose Tools, Options, select the View tab, and then select Field Codes so that you can see the {TOC} or {TOA} field codes. Type the switches inside the field code braces, as shown in the following table. After modifying the field code, you must update the entire table as described in the preceding section of this chapter.

Switch	Argument	Use
\b	*bookmarkname*	{TOC \o \b NewIdeas} The table of contents that is built is only for the area named NewIdeas.
\o	"1-4"	{TOC \o "1-4"} The table of contents is built from a limited selection of heading styles, Heading 1 through Heading 4.

Formatting Tables of Contents and Other Tables

If you format a table of contents, table of figures, or other table by using the format commands or the Formatting toolbar and ruler, that formatting will be lost if you update the entire table (updating page numbers only does not affect formatting). You can use two methods to format tables of contents, tables of figures, or other tables so that formatting is not lost when tables are updated.

- Apply formatting to the table by editing the styles used by the table.
- Use switches that are inserted in the TOC or TOA field to add or preserve formatting.

The following two sections explain these methods in detail.

Formatting with Styles

Each level in a table of contents has a specific style—TOC1, TOC2, and so on. By redefining these styles, you can change the format of the table of contents, and that new format will still be used when you update the table of contents. For a table of figures or authorities, you change the formatting of the Table of Figures and Table of Authorities styles.

▶ **See** "Redefining a Style," **p. 157**

CAUTION

If you make changes to a table style, you will lose those changes if you choose one of the predefined formats (any format except From Template) from the Formats list box when you insert the table. This is because Word resets the table styles each time a table is replaced. You can avoid this by using the Update Field command (rather than the Index and Tables dialog box) to update a table when you have made changes to your document. To do this, place the insertion point anywhere in the table and press the F9 (Update Field) key or right-click the table with the mouse and choose Update Field from the shortcut menu.

Part
VI

Ch
20

This method of changing styles is useful if you want to format one level of the table of contents differently from other levels. For example, you might want the first level of the table, TOC1, to be in bold 12-point Times Roman without tab leaders (dots or dashes before the page number), and all other levels to use the Normal font with tab leaders.

Word's original TOC (Table of Contents) styles are based on the Normal style, with added indents, so that your table of contents will resemble the rest of your document. To redefine the TOC, Table of Figures, or Table of Authorities styles, choose Format Style, and use the Styles list to select the style you want to redefine (such as TOC1 for the first level of table of contents entries). Next, choose Modify to open the Modify Style dialog box, which gives you options for redefining styles.

Choose Format and select the font, border, and other formatting options for the style you want to change. After making the formatting changes to the style, choose OK; Word applies the changes in style to all text in your document that uses that style. When the original Style dialog box reappears, continue to redefine styles or choose Close.

Formatting with Field Code Switches

The second method of formatting a table of contents or figures so that formatting is preserved when you update the table employs switches you include with the TOC field code. You can use many switches to format the entire table of contents or figures.

To make changes, first display the field code by choosing Tools, Options, selecting the View tab, and then selecting the Field Codes check box. Add your switch(es) inside the field code braces to tell Word how you want the table formatted after it updates. For example, if the TOC field code appears as

```
{TOC \f G \* charformat}
```

the entire table of graphs uses the formatting applied to the first letter of TOC. In this case, the bold and italic on the letter T apply to the entire table. The * charformat switch applies the formatting of the first character in the field code to the entire result.

Some useful switches are listed in the following table:

Switch	Argument	Use
*	charformat	{TOC \o * charformat} Applies the formatting of the first character in the field code to the entire field result. For example, changes the fonts of the entire table of contents.
*	upper	{TOC \f t * upper} Changes all characters in the table of contents to uppercase.
*	lower	{TOC \f g * lower} Changes all characters in the table of contents to lowercase.
*	firstcap	{TOC \o * firstcap} Changes all characters to a title-case format; words such as "and" or "of" are placed in lowercase while other words are initial-capped.

After making changes in the TOC field, you must select the field and press F9 (Update Field) to see the results of the changes. ●

Tracking Revisions and Versions

Using the Track Changes Feature

Revising a document is often a job shared by several people. For example, several coworkers might work together to produce an annual report, or more than one editor might review a book. If a revised document has no marks, it can be hard to find everything that was changed or who did the changes. Revision marks show where the document has been changed and by whom, allowing the originator to accept or reject any of the changes.

Adding revision marks is simple. Before someone makes revisions, turn on the Track Changes feature. Revisions to the document are then marked automatically as the reviewer makes changes (see Figure 21.1).

FIG. 21.1
With Track Changes turned on, you can see exactly what additions and deletions a reviewer has made. The TRK indicator in the status bar tells you that revision marking is on.

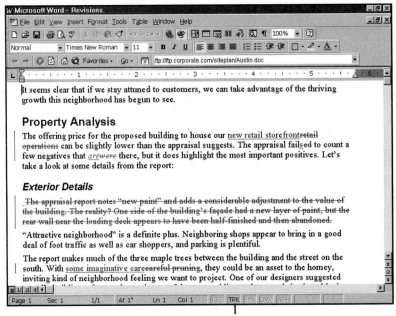

TRK indicator

When you view revision marks, you get a general idea of how much is changed in your document, as well as the details of specific words and letters that were edited. You can also hide revision marks to see exactly what the document would look like if you accepted the changes.

Tracking Changes

When Track Changes is turned on, vertical revision bars appear in the margin next to any lines where text has been inserted or deleted. Revision marks indicate the actual text that has changed—inserted text is underlined, and deleted text has strikethrough formatting. The section "Customizing Revision Marks" later in this chapter tells how you can change these marks.

Before you turn on Track Changes, you should save a copy of the original document. This can help later if incorrect revisions are accepted and you need an original for comparison.

To mark revisions in the active document using menu commands, follow these steps:

1. Choose Tools, Track Changes, Highlight Changes. The Highlight Changes dialog box appears (see Figure 21.2). You turn on the Track Changes feature in the Highlight Changes dialog box.

FIG. 21.2

Mark revisions for working on paper or on screen.

TIP Double-clicking the TRK indicator in the status bar, as shown in Figure 21.1, is a shortcut to display the Highlight Changes dialog box.

---

2. Select the Track Changes While Editing check box.
3. If you do not want to be distracted by revision marks while editing a document, clear the Highlight Changes On Screen check box.
4. Choose OK.

To turn off revision marking, double-click TRK in the status bar, or choose Tools, Track Changes, Highlight Changes, and clear the Track Changes While Editing check box.

To mark revisions in the active document using the Reviewing toolbar, follow these steps:

1. Choose View, Toolbars, then select Reviewing to display the Reviewing toolbar.
2. Click the Track Changes icon. Simply click the Track Changes icon again to turn off revision marking.

The toolbar approach is much faster—you can turn Track Changes on and off with one click.

While Track Changes feature is turned on, any text inserted in the document or deleted from it is marked. If you move a selection of text, two sets of marks appear: The text you moved appears as deleted (strikethrough) text in its original location and as inserted text in its new location. If you delete text marked as inserted, the text simply disappears. Only original text appears in strikethrough format when you delete it.

NOTE You can turn on revision marking for all documents at once, if they are based on the NORMAL.DOT template. Open the NORMAL.DOT template, choose Tools, Track Changes, Highlight Changes, select the Track Changes While Editing check box, and save the template. You can also clear the Highlight Changes On Screen and Highlight Changes in Printed Document check boxes to hide revision marks until you actually review the revisions. ▪

Part

VI

Ch

21

Showing Changes

When a document comes back from your reviewers or you return to a document after editing it yourself, you can look over the changes. If revision marks are not visible in the document, choose Tools, Track Changes, Highlight Changes and select the Highlight Changes On Screen check box.

The document now appears with revision bars in the margin, marking where text has been inserted or deleted. If multiple reviewers made revisions, each reviewer's changes appear in a different color. If you want to continue tracking changes but without seeing revision marks, choose Tools, Track Changes, Highlight Changes, and clear the Highlight Changes On Screen check box.

By default, Word prints documents with revision marks showing. To print a document without revision marks, choose Tools, Track Changes, Highlight Changes, and clear Highlight Changes in Printed Document.

NOTE If you customize your user information, you can keep track of your own editing sessions separately. For each session you want to distinguish, choose Tools, Options, select the User Information tab, and change the Name text box. For example, start with First Draft, then use Style Review for another editing session, and then use Final Draft. Each set of revisions appears in its own color, and the Accept or Reject Changes dialog box shows those names. Also, each time you move your mouse pointer over revised text, Word displays who revised it and when. Be sure to restore your original name later, because other Word features use this information.

Accepting or Rejecting All Changes

Word makes using or discarding changes easy. To incorporate all the changes marked in the document, choose Tools, Track Changes, Accept or Reject Changes, and Accept All. When prompted to accept the revisions, answer Yes and choose Close. All the deleted text disappears, the inserted text is incorporated into the document, and revision bars are removed. Rejecting all changes means restoring your document to its contents before it was reviewed. To reject all revisions, choose Tools, Track Changes, Accept or Reject Changes, and Reject All. When prompted to reject all revisions, answer Yes and choose Close. Inserted text disappears, deleted text is restored, and revision bars are removed.

You can undo these commands. As a safety measure, save your file with a new name before you accept or reject all revisions. You then have a copy of original and revised drafts for later reference or comparison. Remember that any *formatting* changes made by reviewers remain, whether you accept or reject revisions.

Accepting or Rejecting Individual Changes

You'll probably want to use some but not all of the changes made to your document. You can look through the document, jumping directly from change to change, and choose whether to accept or reject each change.

To accept or reject individual changes using menu commands, follow these steps:

1. Choose Tools, Track Changes, Accept or Reject Changes. The Accept or Reject Changes dialog box appears (see Figure 21.3).

FIG. 21.3

The Accept or Reject Changes dialog box helps you move through your document to examine the revisions.

In the Accept or Reject Changes dialog box, you can review all revision marks and see which reviewer made a revision and when.

2. Click one of the Find buttons to find either the next or the previous change in the document and to show which reviewer made the change and when.

3. Select the Changes with Highlighting check box to view original text and highlighted changes.

4. Select the Changes Without Highlighting check box to view only the changes without highlighting.

5. Select the Original check box to view the original text without changes.

6. Click the Accept button to keep the change, or the Reject button to discard it.

7. If you change your mind, click the Undo Last button to restore the most recent revision that you accepted or rejected.

8. Click one of the Find buttons to locate the next revision.

While the Accept or Reject Changes dialog box is on-screen, you can click anywhere in the document to edit the text, or you can select another change to display information about it.

To accept or reject individual changes using the Reviewing toolbar, follow these steps:

1. Choose View, Toolbars, then select Reviewing to display the Reviewing toolbar.

2. Click the Accept Change icon to accept the change.

3. Click the Reject Change icon to reject the change.

4. Click the Next Change icon to find the next change.

5. Click the Previous Change icon to find the previous change.

Customizing Revision Marks

Usually, revision bars in the margins appear black, the revision mark for inserted text is an underline, deleted text has a line through it, and changes made by up to eight reviewers are marked in different colors that Word assigns automatically. (If you have more than eight reviewers, Word reuses the earlier colors.) You can customize each of these marks to your liking. For example, you can mark deleted text as a subdued color, such as light gray, and inserted text as green.

Part

VI

Ch

21

To customize revision marks, follow these steps:

1. Choose Tools, Options, and select the Track Changes tab. You can also choose Tools, Track Changes, Highlight Changes, and then click the Options button to display the tab shown in Figure 21.4.

FIG. 21.4

As you customize revision marks in the Track Changes tab of the Options dialog box, you can preview the appearance of changed text in a document.

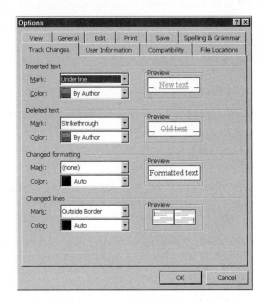

2. Select styles from the Mark list boxes under Inserted Text, Deleted Text, Changed Formatting, and Changed Lines.

3. If you do not need color to distinguish reviewers, select a color from the Color list boxes under Inserted Text and Deleted Text.

4. Choose OK.

If you select By Author under Color in the Inserted Text and Deleted Text sections, each reviewer's changes appear in a different color for up to eight reviewers. The Changed Lines options specify the appearance of the revision bars in the margins of your document. The Changed Formatting options specify the appearance of the revised text.

Protecting Documents for Changes

Protecting a document for changes ensures that changes are being tracked. If a reviewer turns off the Track Changes feature in your document, you could have a good deal of extra work finding where revisions are and who made them. For increased security, you can add a password so that only you can unprotect the document.

When a document is protected for changes, Word tracks all changes and does not allow revision marks to be removed by accepting or rejecting them. Reviewers can add comments as well as revise the document directly. For more information, see the section "Using Comments" later in this chapter.

To protect a document for revisions, follow these steps:

1. Choose Tools, Protect Document. The Protect Document dialog box appears (see Figure 21.5).

FIG. 21.5

Use the Protect Document dialog box to ensure that your document is not changed without your knowledge.

2. Select the Tracked Changes option.

3. If you want to keep other users from unprotecting the document, type a password in the Password text box.

4. Choose OK. If you entered a password, Word prompts you to reenter the password for confirmation.

5. Re-enter the password and choose OK.

> **CAUTION**
>
> It's easy to forget passwords. If you don't remember the password you use, you will have access to the file, but will not have the ability to accept or reject revisions. You might want to jot down the name of the document and the password you assign to it for future reference.

To unprotect a document, choose Tools, Unprotect Document. While the document is protected for changes, any changes made to the document will be tracked until it is unprotected, and you cannot choose to accept or reject any revisions. If you defined a password, you must enter it before the document can be unprotected. If you are using the routing feature of Word, you can protect the document when you add a routing slip.

Merging Changes and Comments

Several different reviewers may have worked on separate copies of a document instead of routing the same copy. If so, filtering through all the revision marks and comments in multiple files can be tedious. To make the work easier, you can combine all the changes into the original document and see them together. To do so, you need the original document and any revised documents from it.

To merge revisions and annotations, follow these steps:

1. Open one of the revised documents.

2. Choose Tools, Merge Documents. The Select File to Merge Into Current Document dialog box appears.

3. Select the original unrevised document and click Open.

4. Repeat these steps for each revised version of the document that you want to merge into the original.

Word merges the revision marks and comments into the original document, where you can see and evaluate them in one place.

TROUBLESHOOTING

I don't have any revision marks in my document. You can see revision marks only if revision marking was turned on while the document was being edited. Choose Tools, Track Changes, Accept or Reject Changes, and then click the Find button. If no revision marks are found, you can add them by comparing your document with the original version of the file. See the section "Comparing Documents" later in this chapter.

I see a revision bar in the margin but no revision marks. There may be revision marks inside hidden text, field codes, or comments. To see these, choose Tools, Options, select the View tab, and then select the Field Codes and Hidden Text check boxes.

I need to see the reviewer name and time information in the Accept or Reject Changes dialog box. Information about each change appears only after you find the change. Choose one of the Find buttons to search for changes.

I can't turn off the option for tracking changes. If the document is protected for revisions, the Track Changes While Editing check box is grayed. To turn off this option, choose Tools, Unprotect Document, asking the document's author for the password if necessary.

Opening, Saving, and Deleting Versions

The File, Versions feature allows a single writer or group of writers to save multiple versions of the same document. By adding detailed comments about each version, you keep a historical record of changes made to a document.

Multiple versions are saved under a single file name. When you open a file having multiple versions, the latest version is opened first. Once opened, you then can open a previous version by clicking the Open button in the Versions dialog box, delete a version, create a new version, or read comments associated with a version.

To open a version of a document, follow these steps:

1. Choose File, Versions. The Versions dialog box appears as shown in Figure 21.6.

2. Highlight the version to open by using the mouse or arrow keys, then click the Open button.

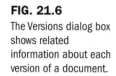

FIG. 21.6

The Versions dialog box shows related information about each version of a document.

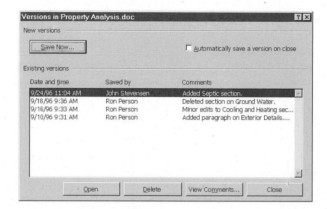

To save a new version or delete an existing version of a document, follow these steps:

1. Choose File, Versions. The Versions dialog box appears as shown in Figure 21.6.

2. If you want to save a version, click the Save Now button, then add related comments in the Save Version dialog box. Then click OK.

3. If you want to delete a version, highlight the version to delete using the mouse or arrow keys, then click the Delete button.

   Click the View Comments button to display the comments related to the highlighted version.

You can save a new version each time you close the document by selecting the Automatically Save A Version On Close check box in the Versions dialog box. In this way, you can avoid overwriting changes that others have made by keeping each user's edits in separate versions.

If you open a version of a document and then save it, the version is saved under a new file name. The new file name includes the version date to aid in tracking versions. You then can open a version directly instead of through the Versions dialog box. Saving a version in this manner removes from the new file the capability to see other versions.

Comparing Documents

You can pinpoint revisions by comparing the current document to an earlier version. When you compare two documents, Word applies revision marks to your current document wherever it differs from the earlier version. The two documents you're comparing must have different names or locations on the disk.

To compare two versions of a document, follow these steps:

1. Open the document where you want the revision marks added.

2. Choose Tools, Track Changes, Compare Documents. The Select File to Compare With Current Document dialog box appears.

3. Select a file to which you want to compare the current file.

4. Click <u>O</u>pen. Word will flag all differences between the two documents, but display them using the formatting settings you've established in the Track Changes tab.

You can select or reject any of the changes by using the following options in the Accept or Reject Changes dialog box:

Choose This	To Do This
<u>A</u>ccept or Reject Changes	Display each revision mark so that you can accept, reject, or ignore it. The Accept or Reject Changes dialog box provides these options.
<u>A</u>ccept All	Leave the selection unchanged and remove the revision marks.
Reject All	Reverse all changes and remove revision marks.

Using Comments

The Track Changes feature is useful for tracking editing changes in a document, whereas Comments are best for attaching comments to a document. Because Comments are linked to specific parts of a document, they are just like notes scribbled in the white space—except that Comments are more convenient.

You may have had the experience of printing a final copy of a document and then noticing a note to yourself that you forgot to delete. The Comment feature takes care of that problem by keeping comments separate from the rest of your text; they aren't printed unless you specifically decide to print them. Comments are the ideal place to store questions and notes to yourself or to an author whose work you're reviewing.

Inserting Comments

When you insert a comment, Word marks the location in the document and opens the Comments pane. Here you can type your comments and even format them.

To insert a comment using menu commands, follow these steps:

1. Select the word or passage you want to comment on, or position the insertion point in the text.

2. Choose <u>I</u>nsert, Co<u>mm</u>ent, or press Alt+Ctrl+M to insert a comment mark and open the Comments pane (see Figure 21.7).

3. Type your comment in the Comments pane. You can use font and paragraph formatting just as you normally would.

FIG. 21.7

The Comments pane shows the reviewer's initials and the text of the annotation. In the main document, the comment is highlighted in yellow.

Insert Sound Object button

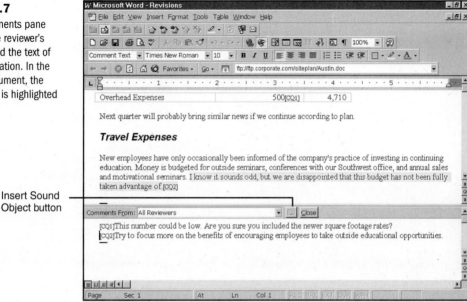

To insert a comment using the Reviewing toolbar, follow these steps:

1. Choose View, Toolbars, then select Reviewing to display the Reviewing toolbar.

2. Click the Insert Comment icon.

3. Type your comment in the Comments pane. You can use font and paragraph formatting just as you normally would.

The comment mark contains the reviewer's initials and a number—for example, [CQ1]. Comments are numbered in sequence. In the Comments pane, a corresponding mark precedes the comment text.

To close the Comments pane, click the Close button or double-click any comment mark in the pane.

Adding Audible Comments

The Insert Sound Object feature enables you to add sound annotations, if your computer has a sound card and microphone installed. You can record an annotation, or use a prerecorded sound file, and insert it in the appropriate location in your document.

To insert a sound annotation, follow these steps:

1. Select the word or passage to which you want to add sound, or position the insertion point at the end of the text.

2. Choose Insert, Comment, or press Alt+Ctrl+M to insert a comment mark and open the Comments pane.

3. If you want to include text with the voice comment, type your comment in the Comments pane. You can use font and paragraph formatting just as you normally would.

4. Position the insertion point at the end of the comment text, then click the Tape icon in the Comments pane. The Sound Object dialog box appears. It uses VCR-like controls.

5. Click the Record button, the red circle, and speak your message into the computer's microphone.

6. Click the Stop button (next to the record function) when you complete your comment.

7. Click File, Exit and Return to Document.

A speaker icon appears in the Comments pane. Double-clicking the Speaker icon will play the voice comment you recorded. To edit the sound object, right-click it, then choose Wave Sound Object, Edit. To delete it, click it once, and then press Delete.

To close the Comments pane, click the Close button or double-click any comment mark in the pane.

N O T E Sound files can get very large. To create them, you must have a sound card and micro-phone. The person reviewing your file must have a PC with a sound card and speakers if they want to play back the recording. ▪

Finding and Viewing Comments

There are several ways to display comment marks in a document. When the Comments pane is open, comment marks always appear. Because comment marks are formatted as hidden text, they appear also when hidden text is showing (when you choose Tools, Options, View and select Hidden Text from the Nonprinting characters group). Finally, you can show comment marks by clicking the Show/Hide ¶ button on the Standard toolbar.

To find a specific comment mark using menu commands, follow these steps:

1. Choose View, Comments. The Comments pane appears.

2. Choose Edit, Go To to display the Find and Replace dialog box. In the Go To tab, you can go to a particular reviewer's next comment or type the number of a comment (see Figure 21.8).

FIG. 21.8

The Go To tab includes a Comment option which lets you go directly to the comment you choose.

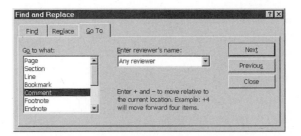

3. Select Comment from the Go To What list box.

4. If you want to find a specific reviewer's comments, type or select the person's name in the Enter Reviewer's Name box.

5. If you want to find a specific comment, type a number in the Enter Reviewer's Name text box. For example, type **3** for the third comment or **+2** for the second comment after the current selection.

6. Click the Next or Previous button. The Next button changes to Go To if you type a number rather than select a reviewer's name.

To find a specific comment mark using the Reviewing toolbar, follow these steps:

1. Choose View, Toolbars, then select Reviewing to display the Reviewing toolbar.

2. Click the Next Comment icon to find the next comment.

3. Click the Previous Comment icon to find the previous comment.

N O T E If you don't need to specify the reviewer, you can find comments quickly by choosing Edit, Find and then selecting Comment Mark from the Special pull-down list. The Comments pane appears automatically when a comment is found. (This pane does not appear when you choose Go To.) ■

When you select a comment in the Comments pane, Word highlights the corresponding document text. This is why it's most useful to select the text in question when you insert comments, rather than simply positioning the cursor in a specific location. You can adjust the size of the Comments pane by dragging the split box—the short, gray button between the vertical scroll bars of the document and Comments panes.

Including or Deleting Comments

A comment often consists of comments or questions about the selected text. If the comment contains suggested text, however, you can easily move the text into your document. Simply select the text in the Comments pane and drag it into your document. Similarly, you can copy the text by holding down the Ctrl key while dragging. (If you cannot drag the text, choose Tools, Options, select the Edit tab, and then choose the Drag-and-Drop text editing check box.)

Comments also can be deleted using the Delete Comment icon in the Reviewing toolbar.

N O T E You can easily remove all comments at once. Choose Edit, Replace, choose Comment Mark in the Special pull-down list, or type **^a** in the Find What text box, leave the Replace With text box empty, and click the Replace All button. ■

If several reviewers added comments to separate copies of an original document, you can merge all the comments into the original document for convenient evaluation. To merge comments, see the section "Merging Changes and Comments" earlier in this chapter.

Protecting Documents for Comments Only

At times, you might want reviewers to comment on your document but not to change it directly. You can allow comments (but no revisions) by protecting your document for comments.

To protect a document for comments, follow these steps:

1. Choose Tools, Protect Document, and select the Comments option.
2. If you want to keep others from unprotecting the document, type a password in the Password text box.
3. Click OK. If you entered a password, Word prompts you to reenter the password for confirmation.
4. Reenter the password and click OK.

No changes except comments can be made to the document until it is unprotected, and menu commands that could make changes are unavailable. When anyone tries to edit the document, a beep warns the user that the document is protected. A message appears in the status bar saying, `This command is not available because the document is locked for edit.`

To unprotect a document, click Tools, Unprotect Document. If you defined a password, you must enter it and click OK before the document can be unprotected.

Printing Comments

To get a printed copy of a commented document, you can either print just the comments or print them at the end of the document.

To print comments only, follow these steps:

1. Choose File, Print.
2. Select Comments from the Print What drop-down list box.
3. Click OK.

Word prints the contents of the Comments pane, adding the page number where each comment mark occurs in the document.

To print a document with comments, follow these steps:

1. Click the Options button in the Print dialog box.
2. Select the Comments check box, which automatically selects the Hidden Text check box, and choose OK.
3. Select Document from the Print What list box.
4. Click OK.

Because comment marks in a document are formatted as hidden text, all hidden text is printed. The comments are printed at the end of the document, along with the page number of the accompanying comment mark.

TROUBLESHOOTING

When I try to delete a comment, the comment mark doesn't go away. To delete a comment, select the comment mark in the document text and press Backspace or Delete. You must select a comment mark first, before pressing Backspace or Delete, because it is a special nontext character.

I don't remember deleting a comment, but now it's gone. Why? If you delete the text surrounding a comment mark in the middle of a document, the mark is deleted, even if the mark is not visible.

How do I change the initials in a comment mark? The initials are taken from the User Information tab of the Options dialog box. If you change your initials there, future comments will contain the new initials.

Adding Cross-References and Captions

Understanding Cross-References and Captions

Cross-references and *captions* simplify your job when you create a document, and they also make your reader's job easier. Cross-references give readers quick access to related information in other parts of your document; captions provide consistent and accurate labeling for the illustrations and tables that augment text.

Figures 22.1 and 22.2 show examples of a cross-reference and a caption.

FIG. 22.1
Both the section title and the page number are cross-references. If either changes, the text on this page reflects that change.

Cross-reference

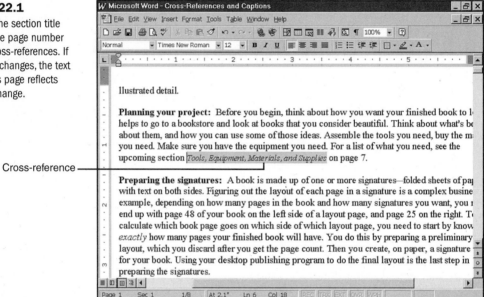

Because cross-references and captions are fields, Word can update them automatically whenever you print the document. (*Fields* are hidden text that perform special functions, such as linking parts of a document together.) Alternatively, you can update fields yourself by selecting them and pressing F9. If you have included page numbers in cross-references throughout your document, for example, and you subsequently add text (so that page numbers change), the cross-references update to show the new page numbers. Or if you include automatically numbered captions for figures and then add more figures, Word renumbers existing figures.

CAUTION

Word 97 does not automatically update fields in your document when you print unless you choose Tools, Options, select the Print tab, and select the Update Fields option.

In a cross-reference, the entire text (except any text you type yourself) is a field result. In a caption, however, only the chapter and caption number are fields. For example, in a caption reading *Figure 1*, the word *Figure* is not a field result, but the number *1* is.

FIG. 22.2
Word numbers captions automatically.

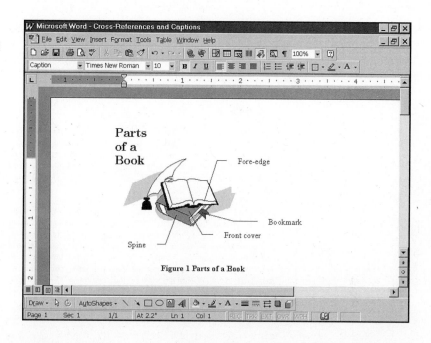

As a rule, you see the results of fields in your document; they look like text (see Figure 22.3). If you choose Tools, Options, however, and on the View tab, select Field Codes in the Show group, you see a code inside braces—the field code—instead of text (see Figure 22.4). Clear this option to see the result of your field, rather than the code.

FIG. 22.3
The cross-reference field code results in text that can be formatted or edited.

Field result

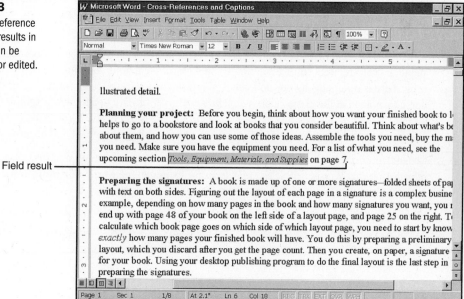

FIG. 22.4
You can choose Tools, Options, the View tab, and the Field Codes option to display field codes.

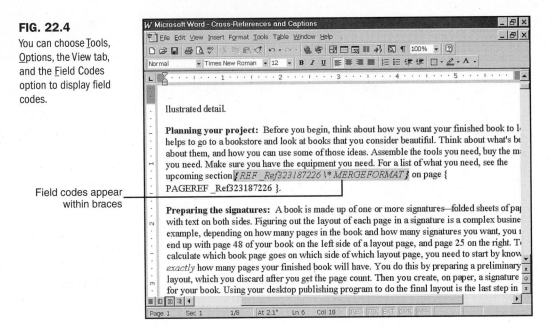

Field codes appear within braces

Creating Cross-References

A cross-reference refers the reader to information in another part of your document (or another document that is part of the same master document). You have the option of including a wide variety of information in your cross-references, depending on the contents of the text or other material you are cross-referencing. If the content or location of the information changes, Word automatically updates the cross-reference to reflect those changes.

Your cross-reference can display several types of information, including headings formatted with Word's built-in heading styles (Heading 1 through Heading 9), page numbers that correspond to cross-referenced text, footnotes and endnotes, captions, and bookmarks. When you apply a cross-reference in your document, Word finds the referenced information and inserts that information at the cross-reference. If you cross-reference a heading, for example, Word inserts the text of that heading at the location of the cross-reference. If you cross-reference text elsewhere in the document, Word displays the page number where that text occurs.

Cross-references generally contain two types of text: text that you type, and the cross-reference information that Word inserts. You may type, for example, the words **For more information see page** and then insert a cross-reference to a page number.

You can include multiple references within a single cross-reference in your document. For example, you may want your cross-reference to read: "For more information see X on page Y," with Word filling in both a heading title and a page number.

Adding Text and Hyperlink Cross-References

Because cross-references contain two kinds of text—the text you type and the cross-reference itself—creating a cross-reference is a two-part process. You type the introductory text and then insert the cross-reference. In many cases, you insert two cross-references—one for a title and one for a page number. Word leaves the Cross-Reference dialog box open so that you can insert as many cross-references as you need. When you use the Cross-Reference dialog box, you make three choices for each cross-reference you insert. This process involves narrowing down your options. First, you select the general category of your cross-reference; for example, you might select Heading if your cross-reference is based on one of Word's built-in heading styles (Heading 1 through Heading 9). You next select what characteristic of that heading you want to reference: the heading text, the page number where that heading appears, or the heading number (if you have included heading numbering). Finally, you select the specific heading you want to reference—the Cross-Reference For Which Heading box lists all the headings. Each reference type (Heading, Bookmark, Footnote, and so on) has specific options.

Two more cross-reference options, Hyperlink and Above/Below, extend the functionality of cross-references. If you select the Insert as Hyperlink option in the Cross-Reference dialog box, you can click the reference to jump to the cross-referenced item. For example, if you create a hyperlinked table of contents, you can jump from any contents heading to that topic in the body of the document. When you position the insertion point over the hyperlinked text, a tip box displays the name of the document you've referenced.

The Above/Below option is available when you reference numbered items. When you select Include Above/Below in the Cross-Reference dialog box, Word automatically inserts the word "above" or "below" in the cross-reference, depending on the position of the cross-referenced item. For example, if you are referring to a figure that is located after the cross-reference, the cross-reference reads, "Figure 1 below."

▶ **See** "Inserting Hyperlinks to Web or Local Files," **p. 1152**

CAUTION

Before you can insert a cross-reference, you must mark the item you want to reference. You can use a heading style, bookmark, footnote, endnote, or caption to mark a location. If you have not marked locations in one of these ways, the lists in the Cross-Reference dialog box will not display items for you to cross-reference.

To add a cross-reference, follow these steps:

1. Type the introductory text preceding the cross-reference. For example, type **"See the following page."** Leave the insertion point where you want the cross-reference to appear.

2. Choose Insert, Cross-Reference. The Cross-Reference dialog box appears (see Figure 22.5).

FIG. 22.5

The Cross-Reference dialog box stays open while you complete your cross-reference.

3. In the Reference Type list, select the type of item you want to reference.

   For example, select Heading if you want to cross-reference to a title or subtitle formatted with a heading style.

4. In the Insert Reference To list, select the information about the item that you want to reference.

   The list varies, according to which reference type you have selected. For example, if you had selected Heading as the Reference type, you could reference the heading's text title, the page number of the heading, or the heading number.

   If you are working in a document that contains numbered paragraphs (as in a legal document), you can select Numbered Item as the Reference Type. Your choices in the Insert Reference To List include Paragraph Number, Paragraph Number (No Context), and Paragraph Number (Full Context). Select *Paragraph Number* to include a relative reference, where shared numbering is not repeated in the reference. For example, a reference to 1.(a)(ii) from 1.(a)(i) refers to (ii) since they both share 1(a). Select *Paragraph Number (No Context)* to include only the last level of numbering in a series, such as a reference to 1.(a)(i) appears as (i), regardless of whether numbering is shared. Select *Paragraph Number (Full Context)* to include the full reference number, regardless of whether any numbering is shared. A reference to 1.(a)(ii) appears anywhere in the document as 1.(a)(ii).

5. In the For Which Numbered Item list box, select the specific item you want to reference.

   Word lists all the items of the selected type that it finds in your document. If you had selected Heading as the Reference type, you would see a list of all headings in the document.

6. Select Insert As Hyperlink to add an on-screen hyperlink from the reference to the cross-referenced item in the document. If the item you are cross-referencing is located in another document, both documents must be part of the same master document.

7. Select Include Above/Below when you are referencing a numbered item if you want Word to add the words "above" or "below" to references.

8. Click Insert to insert the cross-reference.

Part
VI

Ch
22

9. If you want to add additional text in your document before closing the Cross-Reference dialog box, click in your document and type the text. Then you can repeat steps 3 through 6 to insert an additional cross-reference. Choose Close when you are finished. (Close appears after you insert a cross-reference.)

Cross-Referencing Another Document

To include a cross-reference to another document, both documents must be part of a master document. *Master documents* are used to create a large document from many smaller subdocuments. To insert a cross-reference, choose View, Master Document, and in Master Document view, insert cross-references in the usual way. When you are in Master Document view, the Cross-Reference dialog box lists all the headings, bookmarks, and so on, that are contained in the documents linked to this master document.

Updating Cross-References

You can update cross-references and captions by selecting them and pressing the F9 key. To update all the cross-references in your document, select the entire document and press F9. Cross-references update automatically when you print your document.

 T I P   You can include a cross-reference in a header or footer. You may want to include a cross-reference, for example, which displays the title of a chapter inside a header.

▶ **See** "Creating Numbered Headings," **p. 329**

Formatting Cross-References

In your document, a cross-reference looks like text (even though it is a field result), and you can edit it like text. When the insertion point is inside a cross-reference field, the entire cross-reference is highlighted. The field is selected, but the text is not. Within the highlighted field, however, you can select text and edit it using any of Word's usual editing techniques. When you cross-reference a heading, for example, you may want it to appear in italic. After you insert the cross-reference, select the text in the usual way and apply italic using a command or short-cut. For more information about selecting fields, see the section "Editing and Deleting Cross-References and Captions," later in this chapter.

Creating Captions

Captions help readers reference the illustrations you include in your document. In Word, a caption includes a label, a number, and (optionally) a chapter number. A caption may read, for example, `Figure 7` or `Table II-ii`. You can type additional text after the label and number.

When you create a caption, you can select from a list of preexisting labels such as `Figure` or `Table`, or you can create your own labels. You can select from a list of predefined numbering styles, such as `1 2 3`, `A B C`, or `I II III`. You can place a caption above or below your illustration.

You can include captions in your document in one of two ways. You can instruct Word to include a caption each time you insert a particular type of object; for example, you may want a caption for each picture you insert. Or you can select an object and create a caption for it manually.

Captions update automatically when you insert additional captions in your document. The first caption you insert, for example, may read `Figure 1` and the second `Figure 2`. If you insert a new caption between Figure 1 and Figure 2, the new caption is numbered `Figure 2` and the previous Figure 2 becomes `Figure 3`.

Word formats captions with the Caption style. The style that follows Caption is Normal; therefore, when you press Enter after inserting a caption, Word automatically sets the next paragraph's style to Normal. You can change the formatting of the Caption style by using Format, Style, or by defining a new Caption style by example. For details, see Chapter 5, "Using Styles for Repetitive Formats."

Captions work well with cross-references. You can create a cross-reference to any type of caption. If the caption number or label changes, you can update the cross-reference to reflect that change. (For information about updating, see the earlier section, "Creating Cross-References.")

Inserting Captions Manually

You can insert captions manually for figures, tables, objects, and even text. Use this technique when the illustrations are already inserted in your document, or when you include various types of illustrations (pictures and tables, for example), and you want them to have a consistent labeling and numbering scheme.

A caption always includes a label and number, but you also can add text to further explain your illustrations. For example, you may want a caption to read `Table 1 Summary of Annual Sales`. For each type of label you include, Word creates a separate numbering sequence. If you already have inserted Figure 1 and Figure 2, for example, and then insert a caption with the label `Table`, the caption reads `Table 1` rather than `Table 3`.

To insert a caption manually, follow these steps:

1. Select the object for which you want a caption.
2. Choose Insert, Caption.

    The Caption dialog box appears (see Figure 22.6).
3. With the insertion point after the proposed label and number in the Caption text box, type any additional text you want in your caption.
4. You can select a different label from the Label list box. Word numbers each type of label separately.
5. You can select a different location for your caption—above or below the selected item—from the Position list box. Figure 22.7 shows a caption placed below an illustration.
6. Choose OK.

FIG. 22.6
Captions include labels
and numbers, and you
can add additional text
as well. In this example,
Figure is the label
and 1 is the number.

FIG. 22.7
Word inserts the
caption above or below
the selected item.

When you return to your document after inserting a caption, the insertion point flashes at the end of the caption. The caption is formatted with the Caption style. Press Enter to start a new paragraph formatted with the Normal style.

N O T E Because captions are formatted with a style, be sure to put them on a line by themselves; otherwise the entire paragraph where you insert the caption is formatted with Caption style. ▪

Figure captions, unlike the other caption types, are placed in a text box beneath the figure (the Caption style is applied, however). You can manipulate them as you would any other text box. You can, for example, drag the caption to the right of the figure.

Inserting Captions Automatically

If you plan to insert many illustrations of a certain type in your document, you can specify that Word include a caption for each one. If you intend to illustrate your document with many pictures, for example, you can have Word include a caption for each picture. You determine what label Word uses in the captions.

You can include automatic captions for as many different types of document elements, such as pictures or tables, as you want. Either the captions can share a label (and thus share a numbering scheme), or captions for each type of object can have a unique label and a separate sequence of numbers. If you want to add explanatory text after an automatic caption, position the insertion point at the end of the caption and type the text.

Activate automatic captions before you begin inserting your illustrations. If you insert automatic captions after you have inserted some of your illustrations, select the existing illustrations and add their captions manually (see the earlier section, "Inserting Captions Manually," for information on this procedure). If the manually and automatically inserted captions use the same label, Word updates the caption numbers to keep them sequential.

To include automatic captions, follow these steps:

1. Choose Insert, Caption.

2. Click the AutoCaption button.

   The AutoCaption dialog box appears (see Figure 22.8).

FIG. 22.8
You can use automatic captions for many types of document elements.

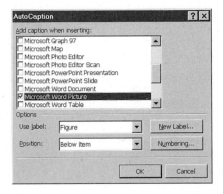

3. In the Add caption when inserting list, select the type of document element for which you want Word to add automatic captions. Select several types of elements if you want them all to have the same label and numbering scheme.

4. Select Options for the type of object you selected. From Use Label, select the type of label for the object; from Position, select Above Item or Below Item.

   To create a unique label, choose New Label (for details, see the next section, "Creating New Caption Labels"). To change the numbering style or include chapter numbers, choose Numbering (see the "Changing Caption Numbering" later in this section).

5. Repeat steps 3 and 4 to add automatic captions for additional types of document elements. By first selecting the element (step 3) and then selecting options (step 4), you can create a separate label and numbering scheme for each type of element for which you insert automatic captions.

6. Choose OK.

Creating New Caption Labels

You can create a new caption label at any of three times when working in your document: when you insert the caption manually, when you insert automatic captions, or after you have inserted your captions.

When you create a new label, Word adds it to the list of existing labels; the new label is available the next time you create a caption.

N O T E   You can't drag across an existing label in the Caption box to select it; to change a label, you must choose Insert, Caption, and then select a caption from the Label list or create a new one by choosing New Label. ■

To create a new label for a manual caption, follow these steps:

1. Select the object for which you want a caption and choose Insert, Caption.

2. Choose New Label. The New Label dialog box opens (see Figure 22.9).

FIG. 22.9
Create your own label by typing it in the Label box.

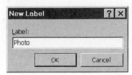

3. In the Label text box, type the text of the label you want. Choose OK to close the New Label dialog box.

4. Choose OK to close the Caption dialog box.

Your new label appears in the Caption list box of the Caption dialog box, as shown in Figure 22.10.

FIG. 22.10
Your new label appears in the Caption box.

To create new labels for automatic captions, follow these steps:

1. Choose Insert, Caption.
2. Click AutoCaption to display the AutoCaption dialog box (refer to Figure 22.8).
3. From the Add Caption When Inserting list box, select the object type for which you want automatic captions.
4. Click New Label.
5. In the Label box, type the text of the label. Choose OK to exit the New Label dialog box.
6. Choose OK.

Changing Caption Labels

You can change the labels for captions you already have inserted in your document. When you change the label for an existing caption, all captions with that label-type change. If you change Figure to Table, for example, all the captions labeled as Figure change to Table.

To change labels for existing captions, follow these steps:

1. Select a caption with the label type you want to change. If you want to change all captions with the label Figure to the label Table, for example, select one *Figure* caption.
2. Choose Insert, Caption.
3. Select a different label from the Label list, or choose New Label and create a new label.
4. Choose OK.

Deleting a Caption Label

When you create new caption labels, they are added to the list of existing labels. You can delete these new labels from the list, but you can't delete Word's built-in labels (such as Figure and Table). To delete the label, choose Insert, Caption, select the label from the Label list, click Delete Label, and then choose Close.

If you delete the label from an existing caption, the caption number remains, and the numbering scheme for that label type is unchanged. To learn about editing captions, see the section "Editing and Deleting Cross-References and Captions" later in this chapter.

Changing Caption Numbering

You can change the caption numbering style for manual or automatic captions when you insert the captions. Alternatively, you can change the numbering style for existing captions in your document. When you change the caption numbering style, the change affects all captions with the same label type as the caption you changed.

To change caption numbering when you insert captions, follow these steps:

1. For manual captions, select the object for which you want to insert a caption and choose Insert, Caption. In the Caption dialog box, click Numbering.

For automatic captions, choose Insert, Caption. In the Caption dialog box, click AutoCaption. Select the type of object for which you want automatic captions, then choose Numbering.

The Caption Numbering dialog box appears (see Figure 22.11).

FIG. 22.11
You can change the format of the caption number, and you can include chapter numbers in your captions.

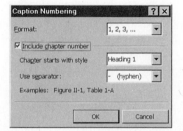

2. To change the style of the numbers, select an option from the Format drop-down list. For example, select 1, 2, 3; or a, b, c; or A, B, C; or i, ii, iii; or I, II, III.

3. Choose OK to return to the previous dialog box.

4. Choose OK to return to your document.

To change caption numbering style for existing captions, follow these steps:

1. Select a caption of the label-type whose numbering style you want to change. For example, if you want to change all the "Figure 1-*x*" captions to "Figure A-*z*" captions, select a single "Figure 1" caption.

2. Choose Insert, Caption.

3. In the Caption dialog box, click Numbering.

4. Select a different numbering style from the Format list.

5. Choose OK to return to the Caption dialog box.

6. Choose Close to return to your document.

All captions using the same label-type reflect your new numbering style.

 You also can change numbering by selecting a captioned object, rather than a caption. If you use this technique, close the Caption dialog box by choosing Close in step 4 rather than OK. If you choose OK, you add an extra caption.

Including Chapter Numbers in a Caption

In a caption, you can include the current chapter number, if you format your chapters with one of Word's built-in heading styles (Heading 1 through Heading 9), and if you have selected a heading numbering style. A caption with a chapter number may read, for example, Figure 1A or Table II:ii.

This technique works well with a document containing several chapters. In a document containing only one chapter, all the chapter numbers would obviously be the same.

To include chapter numbers in your captions, follow these steps:

1. Format all chapter titles and subheadings with built-in heading styles: Heading 1 through Heading 9. Be sure to format the title of each chapter as Heading 1.

2. Choose Format, Bullets and Numbering, and click the Outline Numbered tab. Select a heading numbering style or choose Customize to create your own. (Refer to Chapter 7, "Formatting the Page Layout, Alignment, and Numbering," for more information on numbering.) Choose OK.

3. For manual captions, select the object for which you want to insert a caption and choose Insert, Caption. In the Caption dialog box, choose Numbering.

   For automatic captions, choose Insert, Caption. In the Caption dialog box, choose AutoCaption. Select the type of object for which you want automatic captions, then choose Numbering.

4. In the Caption Numbering dialog box, select the Include Chapter Number option.

5. In the Chapter Starts with Style list box, select the lowest level of heading you want to include in your caption number. If you want only the chapter number, for example, select Heading 1 to get a caption such as Figure 1-3. If you want to include the chapter and first subheading number, however, select Heading 2 for a caption such as Figure 1.2-3.

6. In the Use Separator list, select the punctuation you want to separate the chapter number and the caption number. Options include a hyphen, a period, a colon, an em dash (a wide hyphen), and an en dash (a medium-wide hyphen).

7. Choose OK to return to the previous dialog box.

8. Choose OK to return to your document.

Formatting Captions

The Caption format style is the Normal style, with the addition of bold and a line space before and after the paragraph. You can reformat all your captions automatically by making changes to the Caption style. Alternatively, you can select the caption and apply manual formatting. Because most captions are a single line (and therefore, a single paragraph), you can apply paragraph formatting commands such as indentations and alignment, as well as text formatting commands such as italic or another font.

Editing Captions

You can edit captions in several ways. You can change their labels or numbering styles, as described in the previous sections, "Changing Caption Labels" and "Changing Caption Numbering." You can format captions, as described in the previous section, "Formatting Captions." You can update captions, as described in the upcoming section, "Updating Captions."

You also can edit caption text. Editing a caption's text does not affect other captions of the same type. You can add text to the end of a caption called `Figure 1`, for example, and no other `Figure` captions are affected. You also can edit the field portion of a caption; that edit also does not affect other captions of the same type. To learn how to edit the field, see the section "Editing and Deleting Cross-References and Captions" later in this chapter.

Updating Captions

When you insert new captions using a label you previously have used in your document, Word includes the correct sequential caption number. Word renumbers existing captions when you insert a new caption between existing captions.

When you delete or move something a caption references, however, you must update it by selecting it and pressing F9. To update all the captions in your document at once, select the entire document and press F9.

Framing a Caption with Its Document Element

When you move an element for which you have inserted a caption, the caption does not move with the object. If you want the element and caption to move together, select them and add a text box to contain them as a single object. When an element and caption are both placed in a text box, you can use the mouse to drag them anywhere in your document.

To place a document element and its caption in a text box, follow these steps:

1. Select the element and its caption.
2. Choose Insert, Text Box, or click the Text Box button on the Drawing toolbar.

Alternatively, you can place the element in a text box and *then* insert its caption—the caption is included automatically inside the frame. See Chapter 17, "Inserting Text Boxes," for details on inserting, editing, and moving text boxes.

Editing and Deleting Cross-References and Captions

Cross-references and captions are fields; by default, you see in your document the result of the fields. You may see, for example, a cross-reference such as `Editing Cross- References` or a caption such as `Figure 3`. If you display fields, however, rather than field results, you see field codes, such as `{REF _Ref270669594\* MERGEFORMAT }` or `{ SEQ Figure \* ARABIC }`. Word uses fields so that it can update cross-references and captions if the information changes.

You can edit either the field result or the field code. Editing the field result is the same as editing text; however, the next time the field code is updated, the editing will be lost unless you unlock the results as described in Chapter 14, "Automating with Field Codes." You also can edit the field code when it is displayed. You may want to edit the field code as a quick way of changing a reference or as a means of inserting a special formatting. Chapter 14 describes in detail editing field codes and adding formatting switches. Many cross-references and captions also include normal text preceding or following the field. Edit this text using Word's usual text-editing techniques.

The key to editing a cross-reference or caption is in selecting and displaying the field code that creates the cross-reference or caption. To make selecting a field code easier, you can set viewing options to shade data from field codes.

To shade any data from field codes, follow these steps:

1. Choose Tools, Options and select the View tab.

2. Select one of the following items from the Field Shading drop-down list:

Select this	To get this action
Never	Field codes and results are never shaded.
Always	Field codes and results are always shaded.
When Selected	Field codes and results are shaded only when they are selected or the insertion point is in the field code.

3. Choose OK.

You can switch the entire document between field codes and results by pressing Alt+F9.

To edit or format a field result, move the insertion point within the field result. If the Field Shading option is on, the field results turn light gray (see Figure 22.12). Select the text you want to edit or format. Figure 22.13 shows selected text within a field result.

FIG. 22.12

A field result appears with light shading when the insertion point is inside and Field Shading is turned on.

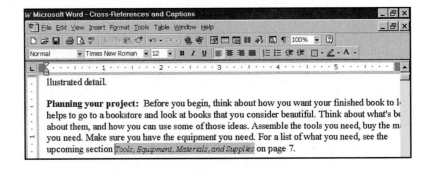

FIG. 22.13

This field result shows darker selected text that can be edited or formatted.

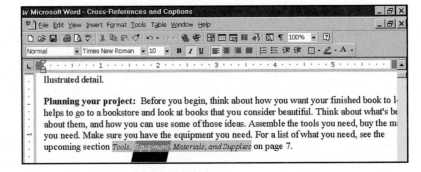

To delete a field code and its result, select across one field code marker or across the entire field result. The entire field result will turn darker (see Figure 22.14). Press the Delete key. It is easier to select and delete field codes if you display the field codes rather than field results.

FIG. 22.14

Selecting the entire field result displays the result with dark shading. The field code can be deleted at this point.

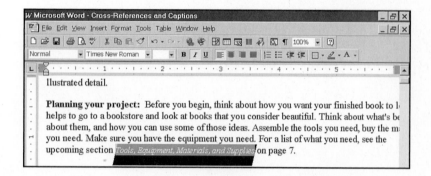

 T I P

To quickly select the next field following the insertion point, press F11. To select the field prior to the insertion point, press Shift+F11.

To update the field, select it and press F9. To update a field, you either can highlight it by positioning the insertion point inside it, or you can select it by dragging across it. ●

Working with Excel Spreadsheets

Formatting Worksheets

Formatting with AutoFormats

Excel's AutoFormat feature lets you create great-looking documents with the click of a few buttons. Even if you are a first-time Excel user, you can create beautifully formatted reports, tables, and lists without resorting to complex formatting operations. If you are an advanced Excel user, you also will appreciate the amount of time you can save by using AutoFormat. Figures 23.1, 23.2, and 23.3 show a few of the 16 formats available through the use of a single Format, AutoFormat command.

Formatting a Table Automatically

With AutoFormat, you can apply preset formats to the labels, backgrounds, lines, totals, and numbers in Excel tables. These formats are designed for tables of information in which labels run down the left column and across the top rows. SUM() functions or totals are expected in the bottom row or right column. These preset formats include formatting for numbers, borders, font, pattern, alignment, column width, and row height. You have the option of selecting which of these formatting elements is used when you format with the Format, AutoFormat command.

FIG. 23.1

The simple AutoFormat gives this table a clean, professional look.

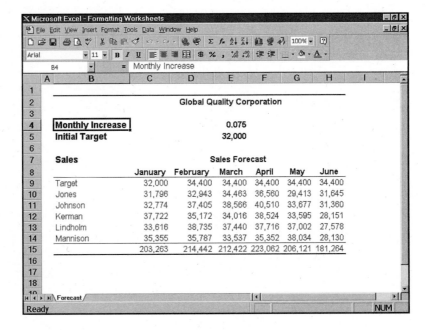

FIG. 23.2
This Classic AutoFormat adds visual impact to a table.

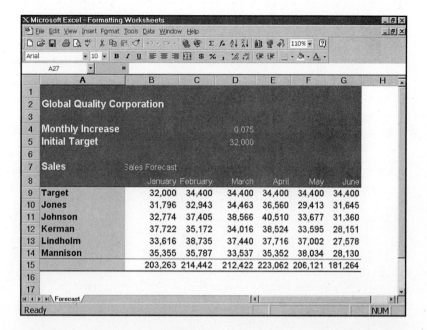

FIG. 23.3
Add another dimension to your tables with one of the 3-D AutoFormats.

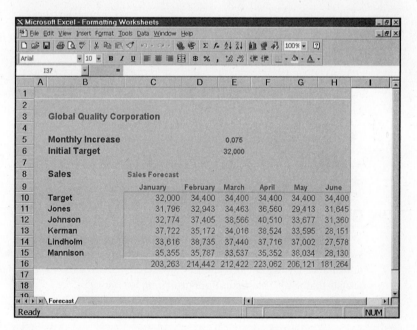

To apply an AutoFormat to a table, follow these steps:

1. Select the range containing the table. If the table is a block of contiguous cells surrounded by clear rows and columns, select a single cell within the table.

2. Choose Format, AutoFormat. The AutoFormat dialog box appears, as shown in Figure 23.4.

FIG. 23.4

You can select and preview from among 16 formats in the AutoFormat dialog box.

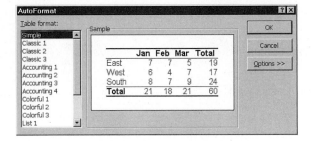

3. Select the format you want from the Table Format list.

4. Review the Sample box to see whether this table format is the one you want. If not, return to step 3 and select a different table format.

5. Choose OK.

If the format does not appear as you expected, immediately choose Edit, Undo AutoFormat to restore the table to its previous format.

After you format a table with AutoFormat, the formatting in the cells is the same as if you had applied normal formatting. Use the techniques described throughout this chapter to change cell formatting to enhance or remove the formatting applied by AutoFormat.

If you decide you want to remove the formatting you applied to a table using the AutoFormat command, select the table and choose Format, AutoFormat. Select None from the Table Format list and choose OK. This procedure also removes any formatting you applied manually to the table.

Using Only Part of an AutoFormat

You don't need to accept the AutoFormat formats exactly as they are. You can decide which types of formatting in the AutoFormat are applied to your table. This capability can be useful, for example, if you have formatted with different colors or have applied custom numeric or date formats that you do not want AutoFormatting to change.

To accept or reject different parts of AutoFormatting, follow these steps:

1. Select the range or a cell within a table.

2. Choose Format, AutoFormat.

3. Select a format from the Table Format list.

4. Choose the Options button. The dialog box expands to include a Formats to Apply group of options as shown in Figure 23.5.

FIG. 23.5
Choose the Options button when you need to apply only parts of an AutoFormat.

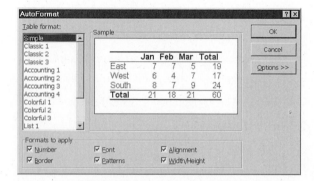

5. Clear formats in the Formats to Apply group that you do not want applied.

6. Review your changes in the Sample box.

7. Choose OK.

N O T E Changes in a format made using the Formats to Apply options do not carry over to the next time you use AutoFormat. Make the changes every time to modify the AutoFormat default settings. ■

Tips About AutoFormatting

If the AutoFormats do not produce the result you need, try creating styles to format your tables or rows or columns within a table. Styles are collections of formats that you assign to a name. You can apply all the formats at one time by selecting the style's name from a list. You might need a combination of styles—one for the table body, one for cells in the total at the bottom of a table, and another for totals at the right edge of a table.

If you need to manually apply a format to a table before you apply the AutoFormat, you can select the entire table with a single keystroke. Select a cell within the table, and then press Shift+Crtl+*. This is the same as choosing the Edit, Go To command, choosing the Special button, and selecting the Current Region option. For this technique to work, the table must be surrounded by a *moat* of blank cells on all sides.

Aligning and Rotating Text and Numbers

In an unformatted cell, text aligns against the left edge of the column, and numbers align against the right edge. To enhance your worksheet, you can align values or formula results so that they are on the left, right, or centered in a cell. You also can align a title across a selection of cells, which enables you to easily center a heading over a table or report. You can fill cells with a character that you specify, such as a dash or an equal sign, to create lines across your worksheet. You can rotate text within a cell. Excel also wraps words within a cell so that you can put a readable paragraph within one cell, or shrinks text to fit within a cell.

Aligning Cell Entries

To align cell contents using the Formatting toolbar, follow these steps:

1. Select the cell or range containing the contents you want to align.
2. Click the Left, Center, or Right Align button in the toolbar.

To align cell contents using the Format menu, follow these steps:

1. Select the cell or range you want to format.
2. Choose Format, Cells.
3. Select the Alignment tab (see Figure 23.6).

FIG. 23.6

Align or rotate text using options in the Alignment tab.

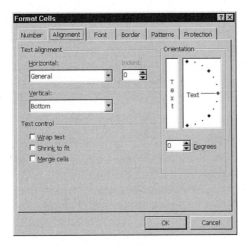

4. Select one of the following alignment options in the Horizontal drop-down list:
   - Select Left (Indent) to align cell contents at the left edge.
   - Select Center to center the cell contents within the cell. Characters may extend outside the cell.
   - Select Right to align cell contents at the right edge.
   - Select Fill to repeat the text to fill the cell.
   - Select Justify to wrap the cell contents into multiple lines within the cell and align cell contents to both edges.
   - Select Center Across Selection to align cell contents in the center of a selected group of cells (see the following section for details).

5. Select one of the following alignment options in the Vertical drop-down list:

- Select Top to align the entry with the top of the cell.
- Select Center to center the entry between the top and bottom edges of the cell.
- Select Bottom to align the entry with the bottom of the cell.
- Select Justify to align cell contents to both edges.

6. Choose OK.

To indent text in a cell, choose the Left (Indent) option in the Horizontal group in step 4 and enter a value in the Indent box. Or you can select the cell whose contents you want to indent and click the Increase Indent button on the Formatting toolbar. Each click will increase the indent by one character. To decrease the indent, click the Decrease Indent button.

Centering Text Across Cells

One problem you may face when building worksheets and databases in other software applications is not being able to center titles across multiple cells. With Excel 97, you can center titles easily using two different methods. The Center Across Selection option in the Alignment tab of the Format Cells dialog box centers the title within a range of selected cells. Alternatively, you can merge a range of selected cells and center a title within the merged cell, using the Merge Cells and Center Alignment options in the Alignment dialog box. The Merge and Center button in the Formatting toolbar accomplishes these two steps with a single mouse click. Note that with the second method, you actually merge multiple cells into one cell and text within that cell can be aligned in any way you want. When you merge selected cells, the original cells become one cell and you can no longer work in the individual cells. The advantage to using the Merge Cells option is that you can align the contents in the merged cell any way you want. Also, editing a title that is centered using the Center Across Selection option can be confusing to a new user because the cell containing the title text is not obvious.

Figure 23.7, for example, shows the new title Sales Forecast entered in cell B8. After centering across the selected cells, the title appears as shown in Figure 23.8.

To center a title using the Merge and Center button from the Formatting toolbar, follow these steps:

1. Type and format the title in the left cell of the range in which you want the title centered.
2. Select the range.
3. Click the Merge and Center button.

The Merge and Center button accomplishes two tasks at once. First, it merges the selected cells, and then it centers the text in the left-most cell within the merged cell.

Part
VII

Ch
23

FIG. 23.7
Select the title and the cells in which you want the title centered.

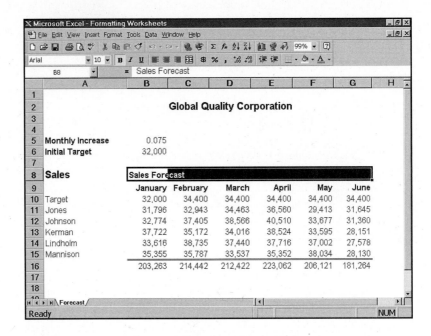

FIG. 23.8
Click the Merge and Center button found on the Formatting toolbar.

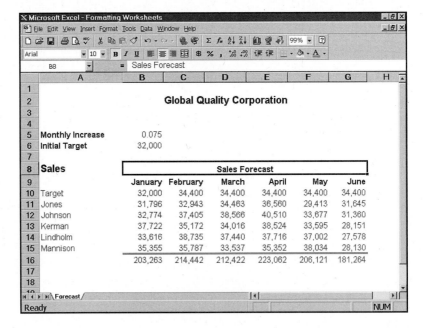

To center a title across multiple cells using the Center Across Selection option, follow these steps:

1. Type and format the title in the left cell of the range in which you want the title centered.
2. Select the cells across which you want the text centered.

3. Choose Format, Cells and select the Alignment tab.

4. Select the Center Across Selection option in the Horizontal drop-down list.

5. Choose OK. The text centers between the cell where the text is entered and the final cell you selected.

Wrapping Text to Fit in a Cell

If you have made a lengthy text entry in a cell, you can have Excel wrap the text so that it forms a paragraph that fits in a cell. The cell's height increases to contain multiple lines. Figure 23.9 illustrates how the Wrap Text option works. Notice that the text in cell B4 extends outside the cell. The text in cell B7, however, where the Wrap Text option has been selected, wraps within the cell to form a single paragraph.

 TIP If you change the width of the column containing the wrapped text, you may want to re-adjust the row height. To re-adjust row height, move the pointer into the header numbers at the windows left edge and double-click the line under the row number.

FIG. 23.9
Wrap long strings of text so that it appears as a paragraph within a single cell.

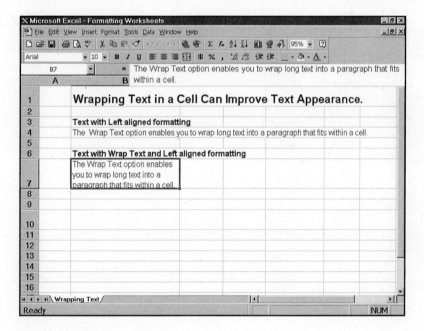

To wrap text within cells, follow these steps:

1. Select the cell or range containing the text you want to wrap.

2. Choose Format, Cells.

3. Select the Alignment tab.

4. Select the Wrap Text check box.

5. Choose OK.

If you change the length of the text in the cell formatted as wrapped text, the row height for the row containing that cell automatically adjusts to accommodate the next text length.

 TIP Another method for wrapping text in a cell is to enter a line break as you type in the text. To enter a line break within text in a cell, begin typing in the formula bar. When you need to break a line, hold down the Alt key as you press Enter. The Wrap Text option is automatically applied to the cell. You can then adjust the column width and row height to wrap the text to your liking.

Shrinking Text to Fit in a Cell

Another way to fit text within a cell is to shrink the size of the text. You can tell Excel to do this automatically, using the Shrink to Fit alignment option. Excel automatically shrinks the size of the text so that it fits within the cell. Figure 23.10 shows how the text size is adjusted in cells formatted with the Shrink to Fit option.

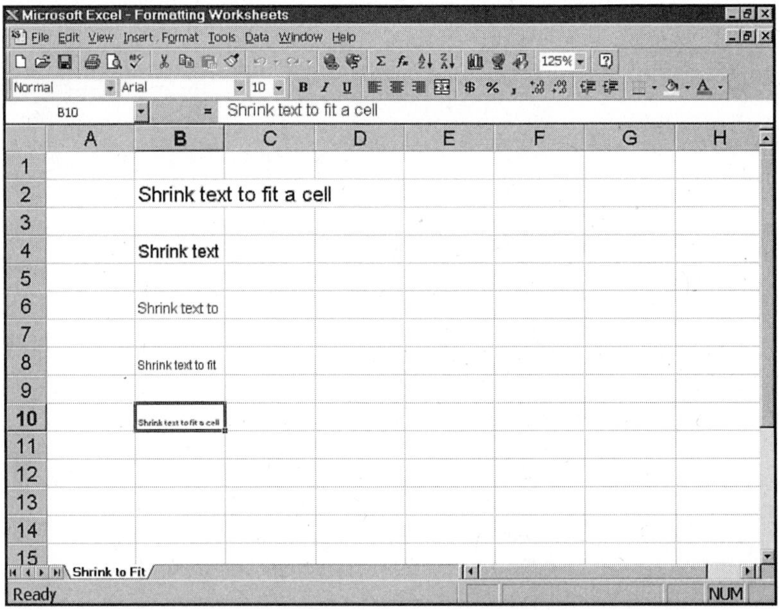

FIG. 23.10

When you apply the Shrink to Fit option to a cell, the text in the cell is reduced in size so that it fits within the cell.

To shrink text to fit within a cell, follow these steps:

1. Select the cell or range containing the text you want to shrink to fit.

2. Choose Format, Cells.

3. Select the Alignment tab.

4. Select the Shrink to Fit check box.

5. Choose OK.

If you add more text to the cell, Excel automatically shrinks the text more so that the text fits in the cell. If you delete some of the text, Excel increases the size of the text. If the text will fit in the cell with the current font size, Excel neither increases nor decreases the size of the text.

Merging Cells

A new option in the Alignment tab of the Format Cells dialog box enables you to select a range of cells and merge them into one cell. One use for merging cells is for creating forms in Excel, as shown in Figure 23.11.

FIG. 23.11

Use the Merge Cells option to create forms in an Excel worksheet.

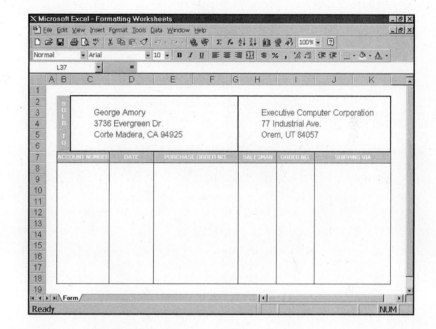

To merge cells, follow these steps:

1. Select the range of cells you want to merge.
2. Choose Format, Cells.
3. Select the Alignment tab.
4. Select the Merge Cells check box.
5. Choose OK.

The selected cells are merged into one cell. The reference for the cell is the reference for the upper-left cell of the original selection. You can enter text into the merged cell and format and align the text as you would in any cell, allowing you to create effects as shown in Figure 23.11.

T I P You can add Merge Cells and Unmerge Cells buttons to the Formatting toolbar. These buttons are found in the Format category in the Commands tab of the Customize dialog box.

Rotating Numbers and Text

When you need vertical titles for reports or to label the sides of drawings or embedded charts, use Excel's Format, Cells command with the Alignment tab to rotate the text or numbers. You can use rotated text effectively beside tables or embedded charts.

The default text orientation is horizontal, reading left to right. You can align text so that the letters are stacked, reading top to bottom, or rotated anywhere from 90 degrees counter-clockwise, reading top to bottom or 90 degrees clockwise, reading top to bottom.

To rotate text or numbers, follow these steps:

1. Select the cells containing the title or label to be rotated.

   Until you are familiar with this feature, you may want to rotate one cell at a time so that you can see what happens step-by-step.

2. Choose Format, Cells.

3. Select the Alignment tab (see Figure 23.12).

FIG. 23.12

Rotate text using the Orientation options in the Alignment tab.

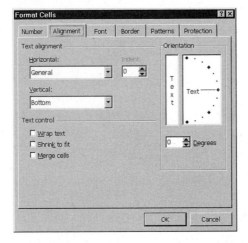

4. Drag the pointer in the Orientation box up or down to change the orientation of the text.

   or

   Specify a value in the Degrees box between 90 and –90 degrees.

   To quickly select a stacked orientation, reading top to bottom, click the box next to the Orientation gauge.

   If you are using the keyboard, press Alt+D, and then use the arrow keys to change the orientation.

5. Choose OK.

Applying Multiple Formats at One Time

Styles are a powerful formatting feature in Excel that can save you time and help you apply a group of formats consistently. By giving a set of combined formats a style name, you can apply that combination to one or more cells by choosing the style name rather than all the individual formats. If you later change the definition of formats associated with that style, all cells having that style immediately change to the new definition. A style name is defined for all sheets in a workbook.

Styles are helpful because they eliminate the need to choose multiple commands for repetitive formats, and they reduce the need to reformat worksheets. If you work in a company in which a standard appearance for proposals and presentations is important, styles can ensure that everyone uses consistent formatting. The company can create preferred styles for titles, headings, bodies of financial reports, and totals. Everyone then can use these styles to reduce the workload and produce a consistent corporate image.

A style can contain all the formatting you use for numbers, font, alignment, borders, patterns, and cell protection. You can even specify not to include a format type in a specific style. A style, for example, can specify a numeric format and font but leave the existing color unchanged.

Part VII Ch 23

Using a Style to Apply a Collection of Formats

You can use styles in different sheets in a workbook. All sheets in a workbook have the same style names available. The default Excel worksheet comes with a few predefined styles: Comma, Comma (0), Currency, Currency (0), Normal, and Percent. Normal is the default style for the entire worksheet. Redefining the formats associated with the Normal style changes the format used throughout a worksheet in those cells not affected by special formatting.

To apply a style, follow these steps:

1. Select the cell(s) to which you want the style applied.
2. Choose Format, Style to display the Style dialog box.
3. Select the Style Name drop-down list box, and then select the style name from the list. Alternatively, you can type the name in the box. When you select or type the name, the Style Includes box shows the formats that are contained in that style.
4. If you want to use some of a styles formatting but exclude some of the formats in a style, deselect the check box of the formats you do not want applied. The check boxes you can deselect are Number, Font, Alignment, Border, Patterns, and Protection.
5. Choose OK.

Whether a style's formats overwrite existing formats in a cell depends on whether check boxes in the Style Includes group were selected to override conflicting styles. For example, in step 4, if you cleared the Patterns check box in the Style Includes group, you can use the style on any cell without changing the existing pattern in the cell.

TIP If you have customized your toolbar to include a Style list, you can see quickly which style was applied to a selected cell by looking at the style listed in the toolbars Style box.

If you use styles often, you should consider customizing your Formatting toolbar so that it includes a Style list. You can use this list to apply styles and to see quickly which styles have been applied. To apply a style using the Style list on the toolbar, follow these steps:

1. Select the cell or range you want to format.
2. Select the Style list in the toolbar by clicking the down arrow.
3. Click the name of the style that defines the formats you want to apply.

Creating Styles

You can create styles in three different ways. You can create them by using the existing format in a cell as an example; you can create them by choosing formats from dialog boxes; or you can merge styles that exist in another workbook.

Creating a Style by Example   If a cell on the sheet already has the formats you want associated with a style, you can use the formats in that cell to define a new style. You can use this method of style by example to create styles with either the toolbar and mouse or with the Format, Style command. If you have multiple cells selected, the style includes only formatting attributes that are common to all the cells.

 TIP It's usually easier to create a style by example than to define it by menu choices. You also see results on the sheet before you create the style.

To use menu commands to create a style by example, follow these steps:

1. Select a cell containing the formats you want to include in a style.
2. Choose Format, Style. The Style dialog box appears (see Figure 23.13).

FIG. 23.13

Type a new style name into the Style Name text box to create a style by example.

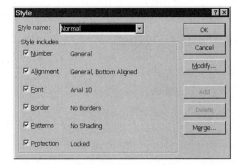

3. Select the Style Name text box and type a new name.
4. Choose OK.

Notice that you can read a description of what the current cell's formatting contains, and what the new style will contain, in the Style Includes box.

Creating a Style by Defining It   If you do not have a mouse or if an example of your style does not exist in the workbook, you can define a style by selecting formats just as you select formats from the Format commands.

To define a style by using the Format, Style command, follow these steps:

1. Choose Format, Style.

2. Select the Style Name list box and type a new name.

> **CAUTION**
>
> Excel does not warn you if you are about to change an existing style. To make sure that you are not using an existing name, click the down arrow and scroll through the list.

3. Choose the Modify button to display the Format Cells dialog box (see Figure 23.14).

FIG. 23.14

Use the tabs in the Format Cells dialog box to define a new style.

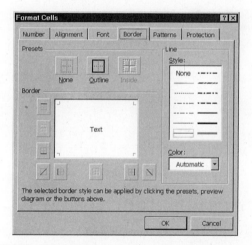

4. Select the formats you want to associate with this style by selecting the appropriate tabs and options from the Format Cells dialog box. Choose OK.

5. If you do not want the style to include a type of formatting, such as patterns, deselect the appropriate check box in the Style Includes box. (The style you are defining changes only the formats that have check boxes selected in the Style Includes box.)

6. If you want to keep this style and define additional styles, choose the Add button. If you want to keep this style and apply it to the selected cells, choose OK. If you want to keep this style but not apply it to the selected cells, choose Add and then Close.

Clearing a format check box in the Style Includes group affects the formats a style changes when applied to a cell. If a check box is deselected when the style is defined, when you apply the style to a cell already containing formats, the cell keeps its original formatting for those deselected formats.

Merging Styles   You may have worksheets or macro sheets that contain styles you want to use on other worksheets and macro sheets. You can copy these styles between workbooks through a process called *merging*. You must take into consideration, however, the fact that *all* styles from the source workbook are merged into the target sheet; they replace styles in the target sheet having the same name.

TIP   When merging styles from another workbook, the source workbook must be open.

To copy styles from a source workbook to a target workbook, follow these steps:

1. Open both workbooks and activate the workbook that will receive the styles.

2. Choose Format, Style.

3. Choose the Merge button. The Merge Styles dialog box is displayed (see Figure 23.15).

FIG. 23.15

Use the Merge Styles dialog box to merge styles from another workbook.

4. Select from the Merge Styles From list the source workbook that contains the styles you want to copy.

5. Choose OK. You may see an alert box as shown in Figure 23.16.

FIG. 23.16

You are warned that styles being copied into a workbook could replace styles with the same names.

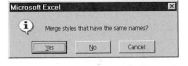

You see the alert box only if the source and target workbooks have styles with the same names and the styles with the same names have different definitions.

6. If the source workbook contains styles with the same names as styles in the target workbook, select one of the following alternatives from the alert box:

Select Yes if you want the source styles to replace styles with the same name in the target workbook.

Select No if you want to merge all styles except those with the same name.

Select Cancel if you don't want to merge styles after all.

Excel returns you to the Style dialog box.

7. Choose the Cancel button in the Style dialog box to close the dialog box without applying a style to the current selection.

Redefining Styles

In addition to saving time used in applying multiple formats, styles also save you time when you need to reformat a document. If your document uses styles, you need only to redefine the style. All cells in the workbook using that style immediately reformat to match the style's new definition.

> **CAUTION**
>
> Be careful when you redefine a style. Redefining the appearance of a style on one sheet redefines the appearance of cells using that same style on other sheets in the same workbook.

If you decide that you need a format different from the one used in an existing style, you have two choices: Create a new style for use with new formatting, or redefine an existing style. The advantage to redefining an existing style is that all cells currently assigned to that style update to use the new formats in the redefined style. This feature makes reformatting all the headings, titles, dates, or totals in a document an easy task. If you redefine the formats associated with a style named Headings, for example, all cells that use the Headings style take on the new format definition.

To redefine a style, follow these steps:

1. Choose Format, Style.
2. Select the style you want to redefine in the Style Name list.
3. Choose the Modify button to display the Format Cells dialog box.

> **CAUTION**
>
> Excel does not warn you if you are about to modify an existing style. Make sure you select the correct style before you choose the Modify button.

4. Select the tab for the type of formatting you want to redefine.
5. Change the options you have selected in the tab to match the changes you want in the style.
6. Choose OK to return to the Style dialog box.
7. Choose OK to redefine the style and apply it to the current cell. Choose Add to redefine the style and keep the dialog box open for more definitions. Choose Close to close the dialog box without applying the style to the selected cell.

Redefining the Default (Normal) Style

The default (standard) format is stored in Excel's Normal style format. If you type in an unformatted cell, Excel uses the Normal style. If you redefine the Normal style, all the cells that you did not format with a style change to match the new Normal definition. If you delete formats from a cell, the cell is reset to the Normal style. Normal style is used also for the column and row headings, fonts, and as the default font for print headers and footers.

To redefine the Normal style and thus the formatting used as the standard when you insert new sheets in the workbook, use one of the previously described methods to redefine the Normal style.

Deleting Styles

If you no longer use a style, delete it to avoid clutter, prevent incorrect use, and to make other styles easier to find.

To delete a style, follow these steps:

1. Choose Format, Style.
2. From the Style Name list, select the style you want to delete. You cannot delete Excel's predefined styles.
3. Choose Delete.
4. If you want the cell to return to Normal style, choose OK or Close. If you want to apply a new style, select the style and choose OK.

Tips About Styles

A style is used by all sheets in a workbook—if you redefine a style in one sheet, you change the definition of that style in other sheets of the same workbook. In some cases, you may have multiple sheets in a workbook that need similar style names, but you don't want the potential problems that can arise if a style in one sheet is redefined. To prevent confusion, assign your style names a prefix that identifies the sheet on which they are to be used. For example, you may have a budget workbook containing sheets from Divisons A, B, and C. This same workbook contains two different final reports. Because subtotals may be formatted in each of these types of sheets, you may want to assign style names of DivSubTotal, YTDSubTotal, and EOMSubTotal.

If most of the sheets in a workbook need Normal style defined one way, but a few sheets need Normal defined a different way, don't despair. You can't have a different Normal style on the few sheets that are different, but you can apply one style to the entire worksheet before you start work. To apply a style to an entire worksheet, click the rectangle that is to the left of the column headings and above the row headings. If you are using the keyboard, press Shift+Ctrl+Spacebar. Now apply a style to the entire worksheet. This has nearly the same effect as redefining Normal for that specific sheet. Be aware that if you clear the formatting from a range, the style for that range returns to the Normal style used in the workbook.

Also note that you can start up Excel with a worksheet customized to your liking preloaded. Simply set the styles on a worksheet the way you want them, and then save the worksheet as a *template* with the filename SHEET1.XLT in the \EXCEL\XLSTART folder. Whenever you launch Excel, the SHEET1.XLT template loads automatically; you can then save the worksheet under a different name when ready. (Any worksheet or template located in the XLSTART folder automatically loads when you launch Excel.)

Part
VII

Ch
23

Protecting Sheets, Workbooks, and Shared Workbooks

If you develop Excel worksheets for use by inexperienced operators, or if you create worksheets for sale, or if you work in the mistake-filled hours after midnight, you will find this section helpful. With Excel, you can protect cells, graphical objects, sheets, windows, and entire workbooks. If you need to protect confidential or proprietary information, you also can hide formulas so that they do not appear in the formula bar. And you can use a password to prevent unauthorized people from changing the protection status or the display of hidden information.

The procedure for protecting a worksheet and its contents involves two commands. The first command formats the cells or objects that you want unprotected. The second command turns on protection for a sheet or the entire workbook.

When you create a shared workbook, you allow other users on your network to work on the workbook, viewing and editing the workbook at the same time. You can merge the changes made by different users and keep a history of changes made. You can apply protection to a shared workbook to prevent other users from removing the workbook from shared use and from turning off the tracking of revisions.

Unprotecting and Hiding Formulas

Cell protection is a valuable feature that prevents someone from accidentally entering data on top of a formula and prevents unauthorized users from changing your formulas. You also can specify whether a cell's contents are visible in the formula bar. Even when the cell contents are hidden from the formula bar, the cell's value or formula results still appear in the worksheet. The default format for all cells is protected and visible. Using the following steps, you can format specific cells that you want users to enter data in or where you want cell contents hidden from the formula bar. Protection and hiding do not take effect until you choose Tools, Protection.

To unprotect a cell so that it can be changed, or to hide a cell's contents from the formula bar, follow these steps:

1. Select the cell or range that you want to unprotect or whose contents you want to hide from the formula bar.
2. Choose Format, Cells.
3. Select the Protection tab of the Format Cells dialog box (see Figure 23.17).

FIG. 23.17

First format cells as unlocked or hidden, and then turn on protection for the entire sheet or workbook.

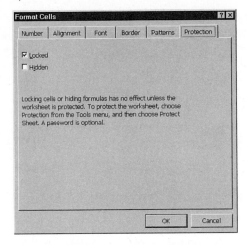

4. Clear the Locked check box to mark the cell or range as one that can be changed, or select the Hidden check box to mark the cell or range as one whose contents do not show in the formula bar.

5. Choose OK.

You can continue to change all cells on the worksheet and see any cell contents until you turn on protection for the worksheet.

Turning On Protection

To turn on protection for a sheet or workbook, follow these steps:

1. Choose Tools, Protection.

2. Choose either Protect Sheet, Protect Workbook or Protect and Share Workbook.

3. If you choose to protect the active sheet, select what you want to protect: Contents, Objects, or Scenarios, or if you choose to protect the workbook, select what you want to protect: Structure or Windows.

   or

   If you choose to protect for sharing, selecting the Sharing with Track Changes protects the sharing and revision history for a shared workbook so that other users can't turn off the change history.

4. If you prefer, enter a password in the Password text box. You can include numbers, spaces, and uppercase and lowercase characters.

5. Choose OK.

Protected windows, contents, and objects cannot be moved, sized, or formatted. Protect objects that you want to lock into place on a worksheet, and protect windows that are prepositioned for use by novice users. Protecting contents prevents the user from changing a cell unless you formatted it as unlocked. Protecting scenarios keeps users from changing the sets of data in scenarios. Protecting a workbook's structure prevents sheets from being inserted, deleted, or moved.

You can turn on protection without using a password. If you do enter a password, you are asked to retype it just to ensure that you typed it correctly the first time. Remember both the spelling and the case you use; the password is case-sensitive.

To unprotect your sheet or workbook, choose Tools, Protection, and then Unprotect Sheet or Unprotect Workbook. If you entered a password, you are asked to type it. Re-enter it exactly the same as the original, including spelling and capitalization.

Part
VII

Ch
23

After you protect the worksheet, look through some of the menus. Notice that most of the commands are grayed and unusable. The only commands available on a protected sheet or workbook are those commands that affect items that are not protected.

If a workbook is already shared, you can protect the workbook for sharing and for the tracking of changes, but you cannot apply a password to this protection. To set a password when you protect for sharing, you must first remove the workbook from sharing.

Tips About Protecting Sheets and Workbooks

You can make data entry forms that are easier to use if you turn off gridlines and unlock cells in which you want users to type data. Before entering data, protect the contents for the sheet. Pressing the Tab or Shift+Tab key moves the active cell only between unlocked cells.

Don't forget your password. If you do, you cannot get back in and make changes. Here are a few helpful hints for choosing passwords:

- Remember the characters that you capitalize in a password. Excel passwords differentiate between uppercase and lowercase letters.
- Avoid using passwords that are easy to figure out, such as the following commonly used choices: your mother's maiden name, your spouse's maiden or middle name, names of your children, your birth date, or your employee number.
- Don't stick your password to the computer with a piece of tape. (Some people do.)
- Use symbols or uncommon capitalization that you will not forget.
- Have a senior officer in the company keep a confidential list of passwords to ensure that a password is accessible if the original guardian is not.
- Change passwords whenever you doubt security.

Checking Spelling

Excel has a built-in spelling checker that gives you confidence that your spelling matches the accuracy of your numbers. With Excel's dictionary, you can check one word, the entire worksheet, or even a chart. When you check the entire worksheet, Excel checks all words on the sheet, including text in charts, text boxes, buttons, headers, footers, and cell comments.

The spelling checker works by comparing the words in your worksheet against the words in the Windows dictionary. Microsoft Office applications all use the same spelling checker and dictionaries. You also can check against a custom dictionary that contains abbreviations or words specific to your clients or industry.

Excel also automatically recognizes common misspellings and makes the corrections as you enter the misspelled word. For example, if you type "teh" instead of "the," Excel will make the correction. This feature is called AutoCorrect. By default, Excel recognizes certain misspellings, plus you can teach Excel the misspellings you often make.

Using the Standard Dictionary

When Excel checks the spelling on a worksheet, it checks more than just cell contents; it checks embedded charts, text boxes, and buttons.

To spell check a document, perform the following steps:

1. Select a single cell if you want to spell check the entire contents of a document. Select a range, embedded chart, or object to limit the check to the selected item. Select a single word or phrase in the formula bar to check individual words.

 TIP To spell check all sheets in the workbook, select them first by right-clicking the sheet tab and then choosing the Select All Sheets command. After all the sheets are selected, start the spell check.

2. Choose the Tools, Spelling command or click the Spelling button on the Standard toolbar.

   If a word cannot be found in the standard or custom dictionary, the Spelling dialog box, shown in Figure 23.18, appears. The word appears at the top-left corner after Not in Dictionary. Depending on the setting of the Always Suggest check box, the suggested alternative spelling may show in the Suggestions list.

FIG. 23.18
When Excel finds a spelling error, you can choose to Ignore, replace with the correct spelling in the Suggestions list, or Add the word to the dictionary.

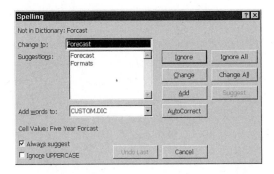

If no misspelled words are found, the Spelling dialog box never appears. A dialog box appears and tells you that the word in the formula bar or the document has no misspelled words.

3. Accept or edit the word in the Change To text box; and then choose the Change button. Choose the Change All button to change this word throughout the document.

Alternatively, select one of the words from the Suggestions list, and then choose the Change button. Choose the Change All button to change this word throughout the document.

You can also choose one of these alternatives:

- *Ignore*. Ignore this word and continue.
- *Ignore All*. Ignore this word throughout the document.
- *Add*. Add this word to the current custom dictionary.
- *Suggest*. Suggest some alternatives from the dictionary.
- *AutoCorrect*. Add this misspelling and the correction to the list of AutoCorrect entries. When you make this same mistake again, Excel automatically replaces the misspelling with the correct spelling.
- *Cancel*. Stop the spelling check.

If Excel did not spell check the contents above the starting point, you are asked whether you want to continue the check from the top of the sheet.

4. If prompted, choose Yes to continue from the top of the document. You can choose Cancel at any time to stop spell checking.

5. When an alert box tells you that the entire worksheet has been checked, choose OK to complete the spelling check.

T I P It's easy to make a mistake when checking words in a spell check. Perhaps you made a change too hastily or weren't paying attention. If you do make a mistake, you can undo the last change made by choosing the Undo Last button in the Spelling dialog box.

If you prefer to see possible correct words in the Suggestion list, select the Always Suggest check box. Spell checking may take longer when you request suggestions. If you want to skip over words that are in uppercase, such as part numbers, account codes, and IDs, select the Ignore UPPERCASE check box.

N O T E To use Excel's built-in spelling checker, you must have installed the spell checking utility. If you did not install spelling checking during initial installation, you can repeat the installation and select to install only spelling checking. ■

Creating Custom Dictionaries

You may need a custom dictionary with your worksheets so that you are not frequently prompted to verify the spelling of client names, abbreviations, product codes, industry terms, and so on. When Excel checks spelling, it looks first at the standard dictionary. If Excel doesn't find the word there, it checks the custom dictionary. You can have multiple custom dictionaries; however, only one can be selected for each spelling check.

TIP Custom dictionary files are stored in a spelling directory specified in the REGISTRY file. The default location for this directory is \Program Files\Common Files\Microsoft Shared\Proof.

Unless you specify otherwise, words you add go into the dictionary named CUSTOM.DIC. This name appears in the Add Words To drop-down list in the Spelling dialog box. You can build your own custom dictionaries and select them from the list. You can have as many custom dictionaries as you like, but only one can operate at a time with the standard dictionary.

To create a new custom dictionary, perform the following steps:

1. Choose Tools, Spelling.
2. Type the dictionary name in the Add Words To text box.
3. Choose Add to add the current word to the dictionary.

At any time when the Spelling dialog box is open, you can change to a different custom dictionary by selecting the dictionary from the Add Words To list.

To add words to your custom dictionary, start the spelling check. When you want to add a word to a custom dictionary, select the dictionary from the Add Words To list and choose the Add button.

Adding Comments

You can attach comments to cells in a worksheet or database. Instead of notes, Excel 97 uses range comments. These comments appear in pop-up text boxes when you move the pointer over the cell containing the comment. You attach comments to cells for two reasons: to preserve your sanity and to preserve your business.

Include in comments any information that helps the next person using the worksheet. That next person might be you in two months, after you have forgotten how and why the worksheet operates.

You can put many things in a comment. In cell A1, you can put the following:

- The author's name
- The auditor's name
- The date the worksheet was last audited

In data-entry cells, you can put the following:

- The worksheet's assumptions
- Any data-entry limits
- The historical significance of a value (such as the high sale of the year)

In formula cells, you can put the following:

- The origin or verification of a formula
- Any analytical comments about a result

Creating Comments

To create a text comment, perform the following steps:

1. Select the cell you want to contain the comment.
2. Choose Insert, Comment or press Shift+F2. You see a pop-up text box with your name.
3. Type the text for the comment within the comment box.

   If you need to move to a new line, press Enter.
4. Click in the worksheet area.

When you click back in the worksheet, the comment box is hidden, but a small red indicator appears at the top-right corner of a cell to show that the cell contains a comment.

 TIP To turn on or off the indicator, choose Tools, Options and select the View tab. Select None to turn off the indicators, Comment Indicator Only to show just the indicator, or Comments & Indicator to show both the indicator and the comment.

Displaying, Finding, and Printing Comments

If either of the Comment Indicator options is selected, a red indicator appears in the top-right corners of cells containing comments. To display the comment behind a cell, move the pointer over the cell. The comment pops up. You can also select the cell and press Shift+F2. Select all the cells that contain comments by choosing the Edit, Go To command and choosing the Special button. Then select the Comments option. Move between the cells containing comments with Tab or Shift+Tab.

Use the Edit, Find command to search quickly through cells and find a comment that contains a pertinent word. Select the Look in Comments option in the Find dialog box.

You can print the comments in a worksheet by choosing the File, Page Setup command. Select the Sheet tab and then the Comments option. Choose whether you want to print the comments at the end of the sheet or as displayed on the sheet. Choose OK and then print the worksheet.

Editing a Text Comment

To edit a comment, select the cell and choose the Insert, Edit Comment command. Edit the comment as you normally edit text in Excel. If you type more text than will fit within the text box, you must resize it. To do so, drag any of the selection handles.

To delete a comment, choose the Insert, Edit Comment command. Then click the text box border to select it. Press the Delete key.

 You can also add or edit a text comment using the New Comment button on the Auditing toolbar.

Working with Formulas

Understanding Formulas

Formulas are the core of an Excel worksheet. Formulas do the work that once required a calculator. Without formulas, there would be no point to using an electronic worksheet such as Excel.

You can use formulas to do simple calculations involving addition, subtraction, multiplication, and division, as well as to carry out very complex financial, statistical, or scientific calculations. You also can use formulas to make comparisons and to manipulate text. When you need to carry out any calculation whose result you want to appear in a worksheet, use a formula.

After you enter a formula in a cell in a worksheet, the results of the formula usually appear on the worksheet. To view the formula that produces the results, select the cell, and the formula appears in the formula bar. To view the formulas in-cell, double-click the cell or select the cell and press F2. Figure 24.1 shows the results of a formula in B8, and the formula that produced the result is in the formula bar.

FIG. 24.1

The formula bar displays the formula in the active cell.

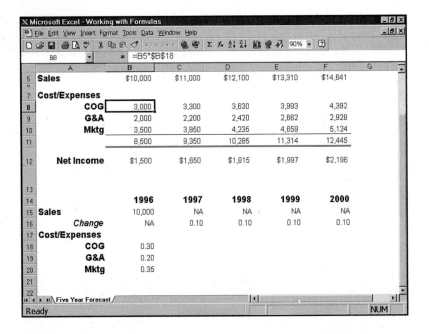

Formulas in Excel always begin with an equal sign (=) and can include numeric and text values (constants), arithmetic operators, comparison operators, text operators, functions, parentheses, cell references, and names. By combining these components, you can calculate the result you want by using the information in the worksheet. A formula's components are discussed in detail in the following section.

N O T E If you are used to working in Lotus 1-2-3, you will probably be in the habit of starting your formulas with a plus sign (+). Excel treats entries starting with a plus sign (+) as a formula and automatically inserts an equal sign (=) at the beginning of the formula. ■

You can display the formulas on a worksheet, instead of the results of the formulas, by choosing Tools, Options, selecting the View tab, selecting the Formulas option, and choosing OK. The shortcut key for toggling between viewing formulas and viewing the results of formulas is Ctrl+` (grave accent). Grave accent is the key co-located with the ~ (tilde) key on most keyboards. When you display formulas, Excel automatically doubles the width of all columns. The column widths will return to their original settings when you return to displaying the formula results. Although you won't usually want to view the formulas in worksheets, it is helpful to do this when debugging a worksheet. Figure 24.2 shows the same worksheet as shown in Figure 24.1, but with the formulas displayed.

FIG. 24.2

You can display formulas in the worksheet by pressing Ctrl+`.

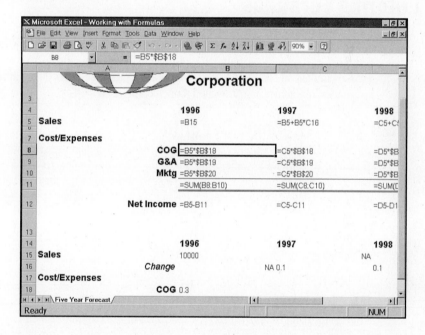

Formulas automatically recalculate and produce current results after you update data used by the formulas. Formulas refer to the contents of a cell by the cell's reference, such as B12. In formulas, you can use math operators such as + or - and also built-in formulas, called *functions*, like SUM() or PMT() (payment).

A simple formula may appear in the *formula bar* under the menu as the following:

=B12*D15

This formula multiplies the contents of cell B12 by the contents of cell D15.

N O T E   Make sure you remember to start the formula with an equal sign (=). If you forget the equal sign, Excel does not interpret the entry as a formula. If you enter B12*D15 (no equal sign), then B12*D15 is actually entered into the cell as text. To get the result of multiplying the contents of cells B12 and D15, you must enter =B12*D15. ■

N O T E   A new feature in Excel 97 helps you avoid making the mistake of forgetting the equal sign. Click the Edit Formula button, which is located at the left end of the formula bar. The formula bar opens and an equal sign is inserted so you can immediately start entering the formula. If in-cell editing is enabled, an equal sign also appears in the active cell, where you can start entering the formula. ■

Entering Formulas

When you enter a formula in Excel, you can work either in the formula bar or in-cell. You begin a formula with an equal sign (=) and then construct the formula piece-by-piece, using values, operators, cell references, functions, and names to calculate the desired result. This section explains in detail the steps involved in entering a formula into a cell, including how to use cell references, operators, functions, and names in formulas.

Working in the Formula Bar or In-Cell

You can enter formulas either in the formula bar or in-cell, in the same way that you enter text or values. You enter a formula using the formula bar by simply typing it in and pressing Enter. You can also enter a formula directly in the cell and bypass the formula bar. The benefit of using in-cell entry is that you don't have to look to the top of the screen—the location of the formula bar—when you are entering the formula.

You enter formulas directly in the cell by simply double-clicking the cell, or by selecting the cell and pressing F2.

To enter a formula in the formula bar, follow these steps:

1. Select the cell to contain the formula.
2. Type an equal sign (=) or click the Edit Formula button.

   If you click the Edit Formula button, Excel automatically inserts an equal sign and displays the results of the formula as you enter it (see Figure 24.3).
3. Type a value, cell reference, function, or name.
4. If the formula is complete, press Enter or click the Enter box (a check mark) in the formula bar. If the formula is incomplete, go to step 5.

   If you clicked the Edit Formula button to open the formula bar, you can also click the OK button in the Formula result bar.

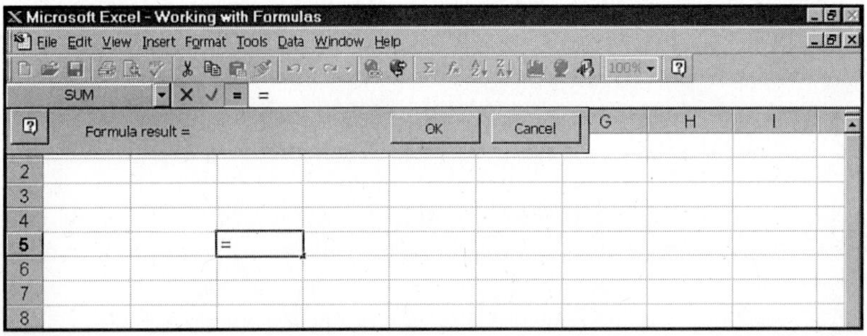

FIG. 24.3

Clicking the Edit Formula button opens the formula bar and enters an equal sign so you can start entering a formula. The results of the formula are displayed as you enter it.

5. Type an operator. There are many types of operators. The most common operators are math symbols, such as + and -.

6. Return to step 3.

To enter a formula in-cell, follow these steps:

1. Double-click the cell in which you want to enter the formula and type an equal sign (=). To use the keyboard, select the cell and press F2.

   or

   Click the Edit Formula button. The cell is opened for editing and an equal sign (=) is inserted.

2. Type a value, cell reference, function, or name.

3. If the formula is complete, press Enter. If the formula is incomplete, go to step 4.

4. Type an operator. There are many types of operators. The most common are math symbols, such as + and -.

5. Return to step 2.

Always separate terms in a formula with operators or parentheses.

Before you enter a formula, you can clear the formula by clicking the Cancel box (an X to the left of the formula bar), or by pressing Esc. Remember that a formula isn't actually put in the cell until you enter it into the cell.

Entering Cell References

Cell references are used in a formula to refer to the contents of a cell or a group of cells. Cell references allow you to use values from different parts of a worksheet and execute a desired calculation. You can use any cell or group of cells in a formula, and any cell or group of cells can be used in as many formulas as you want.

A cell is always referred to by the row and column heading. For example, the cell at the intersection of column A and row 1 has the cell reference of A1. The reference of the active cell is displayed in the name box at the left end of the formula bar.

Part
VII

Ch
24

N O T E You can refer to cells in the same worksheet, in other worksheets in the same workbook, or to cells in other workbooks. You also can enter 3-D references that refer to cells that span a series of worksheets. In this section you learn how to enter and work with all the types of cell references. ▨

Entering Cell References by Pointing   The least error-prone method of entering cell references in a formula is by pointing to the cell you want to include in a formula. Although you can type an entire formula, you often can make a typing error or misread the row or column headings and end up with D52 in a formula when it should be E53. When you point to a cell to include in a formula, you actually move the pointer to the cell you want in the formula. It is obvious when you select the correct cells.

To enter a cell reference into a formula by pointing, follow these steps:

1. Select the cell for the formula.

2. Type an equal sign (=) or click the Edit Formula button.

3. Point to the cell you want in the formula and click, or press the movement keys to move the dashed marquee to the cell you want in the formula.

   The address of the cell you point to appears at the cursor location in the formula bar.

   You also can enter ranges into formulas by pointing. Rather than clicking a cell, point to a corner cell of the range and drag across the range to the opposite corner. To use the keyboard, move to a corner of the range and hold down the Shift key as you move to the opposite corner.

4. Enter an operator, such as the + symbol.

5. Point to the next cell.

6. Repeat the steps from step 4 to continue the formula, or enter the formula by clicking the Enter box or pressing Enter.

Entering Cell References in Existing Formulas   Using the same techniques you used to create formulas, you can edit formulas to change or add new cell references. You can enter new cell references by typing them, pointing to and clicking them or moving to them with the movement keys.

 T I P   You do not need to type the last parenthesis if you are creating a formula composed of a function that encloses all other terms.

To insert a new cell reference or range into an existing formula, follow these steps:

1. Position the insertion point in the formula bar where you want the new cell reference or range.

   You also can double-click the cell that contains the formula you want to edit (or select the cell and press F2) and position the insertion point where you want the new cell reference or range.

When you select a cell containing a formula and open the formula bar (or a cell for in-cell editing), cell references are color-coded. Each cell reference is a different color and the corresponding cell or range on the worksheet is outlined in the same color, as shown in Figure 24.4. This makes it easier to identify the cell references in your formula and to edit them if necessary.

FIG. 24.4

When you edit an existing formula, cell references and their corresponding cells on the worksheet are color-coded to help you identify cell references.

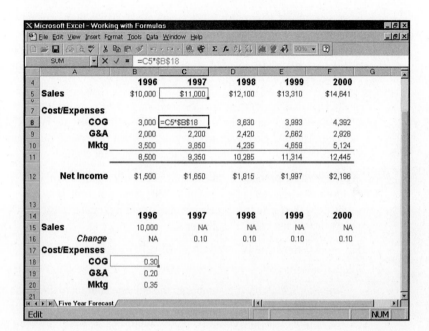

Part
VII

Ch
24

2. Select a cell reference or range you want to replace completely. (Drag across it with the pointer or use Shift+arrow keys.)

3. Type or click the new cell reference. If the new reference is a range, click one corner and drag to the opposite corner. From the keyboard, type the new cell reference or press the movement keys to move to the cell you want as the new reference. To include a range in the formula, press F2 to change to Enter mode, use the movement keys to move to one corner of the range, hold down Shift, and move to the opposite corner of the range. Press F2 again to return to Edit mode.

   Watch the formula bar or in-cell contents as you perform step 3. The new cell reference replaces the old.

4. Add cell references, or choose OK. Press Esc to back out of the changes.

N O T E If you are adding cell references to a formula by pointing to them, you can go to the distant location by pressing the F5 key. Once there, you can select that cell or another one close to it. If the cell or range you want to add is in the Go To dialog box that appears after pressing F5, choose the name from the list box and choose OK. The name appears in the formula, and a marquee appears around the named cells. ■

Using Cell References in Formulas   You can refer to a cell's location in Excel with a relative reference or an absolute reference. Be careful to use the correct type of cell reference in each formula you create. If you understand the difference between the two types of cell references used in Excel, you can avoid creating formulas that change incorrectly when copied to new locations.

You use relative and absolute references in your daily life. Suppose that you are in your office, and you want someone to take a letter to the mailbox. Using a relative reference, you tell the person: "Go out the front door; turn left and go two blocks; turn right and go one block." These directions are relative to your office location at the time you give the instructions. If you move to a different location, these directions no longer work.

To make sure that the letter gets to the mailbox no matter where you are when you give the directions, you must say something like this: "Take this letter to the mailbox at 2700 Mendocino Avenue." No matter where you are when you speak, the mailbox is at one absolute location: 2700 Mendocino Avenue. The address does not change.

Using Relative References   Unless you specify otherwise, Excel uses relative referencing for cell addresses when you enter a formula. This means that cell references in a formula change after you copy the formula to a new location or after you fill a range with a formula. You usually want formulas to use relative cell references.

In Figure 24.5, the formula in cell C5 is =B5+B5*C16. All these references are relative. The formula, translated into English, would read as follows:

> "In cell C5, multiply the number in the cell one column to the left in same row (cell B5 in this example) and the number in the cell 11 rows down in same column (cell C16). Add the number contained in the cell one column to the left in the same row (cell B5)."

When you copy either formula across row 5, the formulas adjust their cell references to their new positions. The copied formulas are as follows:

Cell Containing Formula	A1 Format
D5 or R5C4	=C5+C5*D16
E5 or R5C5	=D5+D5*E16
F5 or R5C6	=E5+E5*F16

Notice how the formula changed to give the cell references the same relative position from the cell that contains the formula.

Usually, you want cell references to change when copied. Occasionally, however, these changes can cause problems. What happens if the worksheet lacks a row of values all the way across row 16? What if row 16 had a single value that each copied formula had to use? What if the worksheet had only a single change number in row 20, used for each year's revenue increase? Each copied formula in these cases would be wrong. If you copy a formula and you want to make sure that some terms in the formula don't adjust to the new locations, you designate those terms as absolute references.

FIG. 24.5

The relative reference formula in C5 is shown in the formula bar.

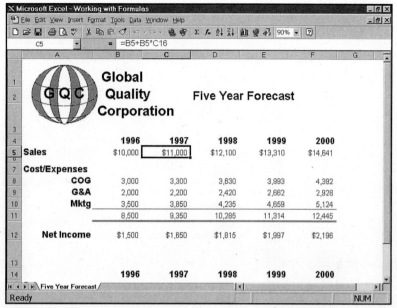

N O T E Users of Multiplan will be accustomed to using the R1C1 style for referencing cells. The R1C1 style indicates a cell by its row number, R1, and its column number, C1. You can also designate a range in R1C1 style. You can view cell references in this style by choosing Tools, Options, selecting the General tab and checking the R1C1 Reference Style box. ■

Using Absolute References   To keep cell references from changing when you copy a formula to new locations, use absolute references. Indicate absolute references by putting a dollar sign ($) in front of the column letter or row number that you want to freeze. Put the dollar sign ($) in front of both the column letter and row number if you want neither to change.

In Figure 24.6, the COG factor is referred to by using an absolute reference address of $B$18. The dollar sign in front of each part of the address, B and 18, prevents the cell reference from changing during a copy.

The formula in B8, for example, was copied into cells C8, D8, E8, and F8. Cell B8's formula is =B5*$B$18. When copied, only the first term changes in each new cell that the formula is copied into. The second term remains absolutely the same. This type of reference was necessary because there was a value in B18, but no corresponding values in C18, D18, E18, and F18. Had the formula used B18 instead of $B$18, all the copied formulas would have referenced the blank cells C18, D18, E18, and F18.

You can enter an absolute reference the following two ways:

■ As you enter the formula, type the dollar sign in front of the row or column that you want to remain the same.

FIG. 24.6

Absolute reference formulas use a $ to freeze a row or column reference.

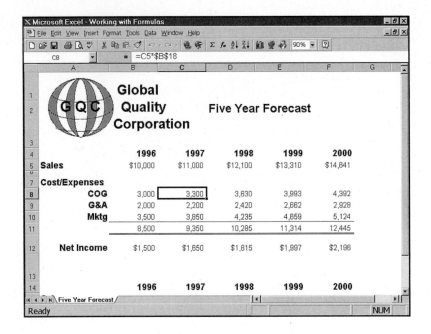

- Move the flashing insertion point in the formula bar so that it is inside the cell reference, and press F4, the absolute reference key. (If the formula was entered already, select its cell and press F2 to edit.) Each time you press F4, the type of reference changes. The first time you press F4, both the column and row reference become absolute. Press F4 again to make only the row reference absolute. Press F4 a third time to make just the column reference absolute.

To enter an absolute reference by using the F4 key, perform the following steps:

1. Type an equal sign (=) and the cell reference you want to be absolute.

2. Press F4, the absolute reference key, until the correct combination of dollar signs appears.

3. Type the next operator and continue to enter the formula.

You can use the F4 key when editing an existing formula.

Using Mixed References   On some occasions, you want only the row to stay fixed or only the column to stay fixed when copied. In these cases, use a mixed reference, one that contains both absolute and relative references. For example, the reference $B5 prevents the column from changing, but the row changes relative to a new copied location; the dollar sign keeps the column from changing. In B$5, just the opposite occurs. The column adjusts to a new location but the row always stays fixed at 5; the dollar sign keeps the row from changing.

You can create mixed references the same way you can create absolute references. Type the dollar signs or specific row and column numbers without brackets or press F4. Each press of F4 cycles the cell reference to a new combination.

Each time you press F4, Excel cycles through all combinations of relative and absolute references. Press F4 four times, for example, and you cycle from B22 through $B$22, B$22, $B22, and B22.

Editing Absolute and Relative References   To change an absolute or relative cell reference that is already entered in a formula, follow these steps:

1. Select the formula (either in the formula bar or in-cell).

2. Move the insertion point so it is within or next to the formula you want to change.

3. Press F4 to cycle through combinations of absolute and relative cell references.

4. When the formula is displayed correctly, press Enter.

Figure 24.7 shows a formula bar with the insertion point in a cell reference before F4 was pressed. Figure 24.8 shows the effect of pressing F4 one time.

FIG. 24.7

Move the insertion point next to the cell reference that you want to change.

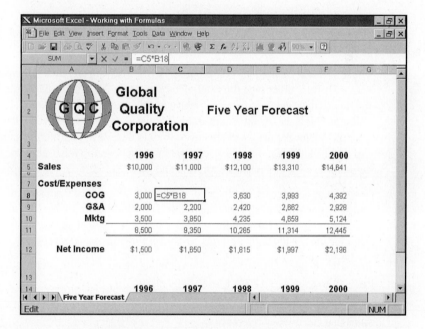

Referring to Other Sheets in a Workbook   You can refer to other sheets in a workbook by including a sheet reference as well as a cell reference in a formula. For example, to refer to cell A1 on Sheet6, you would enter **Sheet6!A1** in the formula. Notice the exclamation mark that separates the sheet reference from the cell reference. If you have named the sheet, simply use the sheet name and then the cell reference. If the sheet name includes spaces, you must surround the sheet reference with single quotation marks.

You also can use the mouse to enter a reference to a cell or range on another worksheet in a workbook. To do this, start entering the formula in the cell where you want the result to appear and then click the tab for the worksheet with the cell or range you want to refer to. Next, select the cell or range that you want to refer to. The complete reference, including the sheet reference, appears in the formula bar. If the sheet name includes spaces, Excel surrounds the sheet reference with single quotation marks. Finish the formula and press Enter.

N O T E   You also can make *external references* to cells in other workbooks. See Chapter 40, "Linking, Embedding, and Consolidating Worksheets," for more information on using external references to link workbooks.

Entering 3-D References   You can use 3-D references to refer to a cell range that includes two or more sheets in a workbook. A 3-D reference consists of a sheet range specifying the beginning and ending sheets, and a cell range specifying the cells being referred to. The following is an example of a 3-D reference:

=SUM(Sheet1:Sheet6!$E$1:$E$6)

This reference sums up the values in the range of cells $E$1:$E$6 in each of the sheets from Sheet1 to Sheet6, and adds the sums together resulting in a grand total.

Using the same techniques you use for entering regular references, you can enter 3-D references. You can either type the references directly in the formula bar (or in-cell), or you can use the mouse to select the worksheet tabs and cell ranges for the reference. To use the mouse to enter the reference, begin entering the formula in the cell where you want the result to appear, click the tab for the first worksheet you want to include in the reference, hold down the Shift key and click the last worksheet you want to include in the reference, and then select the cells you want to refer to. Finish the formula and press Enter.

You can use a 3-D reference to pull together the information from several worksheets into a consolidation worksheet. For example, you may have a worksheet that records sales for each of several regional offices. If these worksheets are arranged identically, you can consolidate the sales for the regional offices into a summary worksheet using 3-D references.

You also can use 3-D references when defining names. See the later section "Naming Cells for Better Worksheets" to learn how to name cells.

Several functions built in to Excel can use 3-D references. The following list shows the functions that can use 3-D references:

AVERAGE	STDEV
COUNT	STDEVP
COUNTA	SUM
MAX	VAR
MIN	VARP
PRODUCT	

Using Operators in Formulas

Operators tell formulas what operations to perform. Excel uses four types of operators:

Operators	Signs
Arithmetic	+, - *, /, %, ^
Text	&
Comparative	=, <, <=, >, >=, <>
Reference	colon (:), comma (,), space ( )

Table 24.1 illustrates how you can use each of the arithmetic operators in formulas.

Table 24.1 Arithmetic Operators

Operator	Formula	Result	Type of Operation
+	=5+2	7	Addition
-	=5-2	3	Subtraction
-	-5	-5	Negation (negative of the number)
*	=5*2	10	Multiplication
/	=5/2	2.5	Division
%	5%	.05	Percentage
^	=5^2	25	Exponentiation (to the power of)

Excel can work with more than just arithmetic formulas. Excel also can manipulate text, perform comparisons, and relate different ranges and cells on the worksheet. The ampersand (&) operator, for example, joins text within quotation marks or text contained in referenced cells. Joining text is known as *concatenation*. Table 24.2 illustrates how you can use text operators.

Table 24.2 Text Operators

Operator	Formula	Result	Type of Operation
&	="Ms. Gibbs" results	Ms. Gibbs	Text is joined
&	=A12&" "&B36	Ms. Gibbs	Text is joined when A12 contains Ms. and B36 contains Gibbs

To compare results, you can create formulas using comparative operators. These operators return a TRUE or FALSE result, depending on how the formula evaluates the condition. Table 24.3 lists the comparative operators.

Table 24.3   Comparative Operators

Operator	Type
=	Equal to
<	Less than
<=	Less than or equal to
>	Greater than
>=	Greater than or equal to
<>	Not equal to

The following are examples of comparative operators in formulas:

Formula	Result
=A12<15	TRUE if the content of A12 is less than 15; FALSE if the content of A12 is 15 or more.
=B36>=15	TRUE if the content of B36 is 15 or more; FALSE if the content of B36 is less than 15.

Another type of operator is the reference operator (see Table 24.4). Reference operators make no changes to constants or cell contents. Instead, they control how a formula groups cells and ranges of cells when the formula calculates. Reference operators enable you to combine absolute and relative references and named ranges. Reference operators are valuable for joining cells (union) or referring to a common area shared between different ranges (intersect).

N O T E   Use the range operator (:) to reduce your work in formulas. If you want a formula to refer to all cells in column B, type B:B. Similarly, the range that includes all cells in rows 5 through 12 is entered as 5:12. ▨

Table 24.4   Reference Operators

Operator	Example	Type	Result
:	SUM(A12:A24)	Range	Evaluates as a single reference the cells in the rectangular area between the two corners.
,	SUM(A12:A24,B36)	Union	Evaluates two references as a single reference.
space	SUM(A12:A24 A16:B20)	Intersect	Evaluates the cells common to both references (if no cells are common to both, then #NULL results).

Operator	Example	Type	Result
space	=Yr92 Sales	Intersect	Cell contents at the intersect of the column named Yr92 and the row named Sales.

N O T E Excel uses a colon (B12:C36) to designate a range like 1-2-3 uses two periods (B12..C36). You can use a comma to select multiple ranges (B12:C36,F14:H26) for many functions. ▪

Excel follows a consistent set of rules when applying operators in a formula. Working from the first calculation to the last, Excel evaluates operators in the order shown in Table 24.5.

Table 24.5 The Order in Which Excel Evaluates Operators

Operator	Definition
:	Range
space	Intersect
,	Union
-	Negation
%	Percentage
^	Exponentiation
* and /	Multiplication and division
+ and -	Addition and subtraction
&	Text joining
=, <, and <=	Comparisons
>, >=, and < >	

You can change the order in which calculations are performed by enclosing in parentheses the terms you want Excel to calculate first. Notice, for instance, the difference between these results:

Formula	Result
=6+21/3	13
=(6+21)/3	9

Pasting Names and Functions into Formulas

You can use English names in formulas to reference cells or ranges. You also can reduce the formula size to operate faster and with less chance of typographical error by using the built-in formulas, called functions, that are part of Excel. Names and functions can be pasted into formulas. Excel enables you to choose the name or function from a list to paste into a formula. This process is easier and more accurate than typing. Naming cells, ranges, formulas, and values is described later in this chapter. For a discussion of functions, see Chapter 25, "Using Functions."

To paste a name into an existing formula, follow these steps:

1. Move the insertion point in the formula bar (or in-cell) to where you want to paste the name.

2. Activate the worksheet or workbook that holds the named reference to paste.

3. Choose Insert, Name, Paste to display the Paste Name dialog box (see Figure 24.9).

   If you have not named any cells, ranges, formulas, or values, the Paste command in the Name submenu is grayed.

4. Select the name you want to paste.

5. Choose OK, then complete the formula with additional terms, if necessary, and press Enter.

To paste a function into a formula, follow these steps:

1. Move the insertion point in the formula bar (or in-cell) to where you want the function.

2. Choose Insert, Function or click the Paste Function button to open the Paste Function dialog box.

   or

   Click the down arrow to the right of the Functions box at the left end of the formula bar to display a list of the most recently used functions (see Figure 24.8).

3. Select a function from the Paste Function dialog box or Most Recently Used Function list.

   If the function you want to insert does not appear in the Most Recently Used Function list, you can select More Functions to open the Paste Function dialog box.

4. Enter the arguments for the function in the Formula Palette that appears.

5. Choose OK.

Entering Text, Dates, and Times in Formulas

Enter text, dates, and times in formulas by including the data in quotation marks. For example:

="The Total Budget is" & TOTAL_BUDGET

displays The Total Budget is $1,200,000 if the number $1,200,000 is in the cell named TOTAL_BUDGET.

FIG. 24.8
Each press of the F4 key changes the mix of absolute and relative cell references.

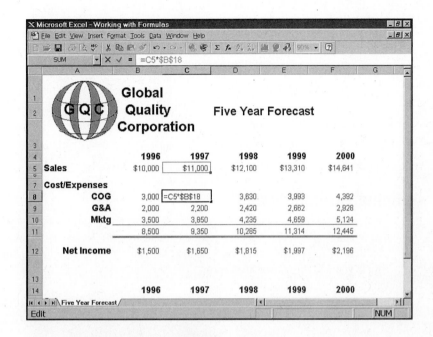

FIG. 24.9
Select a named cell or range to paste into a formula in the Paste Name dialog box.

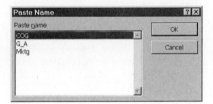

If you want to perform date math on explicit dates, which are dates that are not in cells, use a formula such as

="5/14/98"-"5/14/96"

or

="14 May, 98"-"14 May, 96"

These formulas produce the number of days between the two dates.

When you need numeric or date results from a formula or reference to appear as text, use the TEXT( ) function with a predefined or custom format. For example, use ="Today is" & TEXT(A13,"mmm dd, yy") to produce a text date from the contents of cell A13.

 T I P You can select from most list boxes and choose OK simultaneously by double-clicking a selection in the list.

Changing Formulas to Values

In some situations, you may want to freeze a formula's results so the formula changes to a value. To freeze a formula into its resulting values, follow these steps:

1. Select the cell of an existing formula and press F2 (the Edit key), or click the formula bar, or double-click the cell if you are using in-cell editing.

2. Press F9.

   The formula in the formula bar is replaced by its calculated value.

3. Choose OK or press Enter.

Defining Formula Errors

When Excel cannot evaluate a formula or function, the program displays an error value in the offending cell. Error values begin with a pound sign (#). Excel has seven kinds of error values with self-explanatory names (see Table 24.6). You can choose Tools, Auditing, Trace Error to help you find the source of an error.

Table 24.6. Excel Error Values

Value	Meaning/Solution
#DIV/0!	The formula or macro is attempting to divide by zero.
	Check to see whether cell references are blanks or zeros. You may have accidentally deleted an area of the worksheet needed by this formula. An incorrectly written formula may be attempting to divide by zero.
#N/A	The formula refers to a cell that has a #N/A entry.
	Check to see whether you can type #N/A in mandatory data-entry cells. Then, if data isn't entered to replace the #N/A, formulas that depend on this cell display #N/A. This error value warns that not all the data was entered.
	An array argument is the wrong size, and #N/A is returned in some cells.
	HLOOKUP( ), VLOOKUP( ), LOOKUP( ), MATCH( ), or other functions have incorrect arguments. Often, these functions return an error value when they cannot find a match.
	You omitted an argument from a function. If Excel cannot evaluate the arguments that you entered, some functions return #N/A.
#NAME?	Excel doesn't recognize a name.
	Check by using the Insert, Name, Define command to see if the name exists. Create a name, if necessary.
	Verify the spelling of the name. Make sure that no spaces exist.

Value	Meaning/Solution
	Verify that functions are spelled correctly. Use no spaces between the function name and the opening parenthesis. Novice users frequently type a space between the last character in the function name and the first parenthesis.
	Check whether you used text in a formula without enclosing the text in quotation marks. Excel considers the text as a name rather than as text.
	Check whether you forgot to replace one of the Paste Arguments prompts pasted into a function.
	Check whether you mistyped an address or range, making this information appear to Excel as a name, such as the cell ABB5 (two Bs) or the range B12C45 (a missing :).
	Check whether you referred to an incorrect or nonexistent name in a linked worksheet.
#NULL!	The formula specifies two areas that don't intersect.
	Check to see whether the cell or range reference is entered incorrectly.
#NUM!	The formula has a problem with a number.
	Check to see whether the numeric argument is out of the acceptable range of inputs, or whether the function can find an answer given the arguments you entered.
#REF!	The cell reference is incorrect.
	Check to see whether you deleted cells, rows, or columns referenced by formulas. Other causes may include indexes that exceed a range used in a function or offsets that reach outside worksheet boundaries.
	See whether external worksheet references are still valid. Use the Edit, Links command to open source worksheets. If you need to change a link to a worksheet with a different name or directory, use the Edit, Links command and choose the Change Source button.
	See whether a macro returned a #REF! value from an unopened or incorrect function macro.
	See whether a Dynamic Data Exchange (DDE) topic is incorrectly entered or is unavailable.
#VALUE!	The value is not the type expected by the argument or the result from an intersect operation when the ranges being evaluated do not intersect.

Part
VII

Ch
24

Searching individual formulas for errors or related formulas takes too long. You want to quickly select cells that contain errors, feed into the formula in the active cell, or depend on the result of the active cell.

Another technique is to use the Edit, Go To, Special feature. The Edit, Go To, Special command is a powerful ally in auditing and troubleshooting a worksheet. From the Go To Special dialog box (see Figure 24.10), you can select specific parts of a worksheet of cell contents.

FIG. 24.10

The Edit, Go To, Special command is a valuable ally in troubleshooting worksheets.

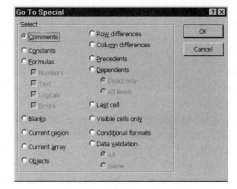

Table 24.7 describes the Edit, Go To, Special options you can use when auditing a worksheet. Finding errors, such as #REF! or #N/A, in a worksheet or in a range is easy. Select the Formulas option and deselect all check boxes except the Errors option.

Table 24.7 Go To Special Options Used in Auditing

Option	Action
Constants	Specifies that constants of the type you identify are selected. Available types are numbers, text, logicals, and errors.
Formulas	Specifies that formulas with results of the type you identify are selected.
Numbers	Selects constants or formulas that result in numbers.
Text	Selects constants or formulas that result in text.
Logicals	Selects constants or formulas that result in logicals (true/false).
Errors	Selects cells with error values.
Precedents	Selects cells that support the active cell.
Dependents	Selects cells that depend on the active cell.
Row Differences	Selects cells in the same row that have a different reference pattern.
Column Differences	Selects cells in the same column that have a different reference pattern.

When debugging a worksheet, find the cells that feed information in the active cell and the cells that depend on the results in the active cell. To see which cells feed into the active cell, select the Precedents option; select the Dependents option to see cells that depend upon the active cell. The Direct Only option selects cells that immediately feed or depend on the active cell. The All Levels option selects cells that feed into or depend on the active cell at all levels. The Direct Only option is like selecting only your parents or your children. The All Levels option is like selecting the entire family tree, backward or forward.

Typing a number over a formula is a common error in worksheets. To see cells that contain formulas and cells that contain values, select the range you want to troubleshoot and select the Constants or Formulas options from the Go To Special dialog box. Usually, you leave all the related check boxes selected. You may be surprised to find a constant value in the middle of what you believed were formulas!

Press Tab or Shift+Tab to move the active cell between the selected cells, while keeping all other cells selected. Read each cell's contents in the formula bar until you find the cell that contains an error.

Locating Formula Errors

In a long formula that contains many parts, you may discover that one of the smaller terms in the formula is incorrect. In this case, it may be difficult to find the part of the formula that produces these incorrect results.

To see how a term or function within a formula evaluates, complete the following steps:

1. Select the cell that produces the incorrect result or an error value.

2. In the formula bar, select the smallest portion of the formula that may cause this problem. The term you select must be a complete function or portion of a formula that is calculated by itself. Figure 24.11 shows a portion of an IF( ) function selected. Notice that the complete AND( ) function, including both parentheses and all arguments, is selected.

3. To calculate the portion you selected, press the F9 key. Figure 24.12 shows how the selected portion in the formula changes to the related calculated result, FALSE. If the selected portion results in a number, text, error, or array, you see these values.

4. Select and calculate other parts of the formula until you find the portion causing the error.

5. To return the formula to the original form, press Esc or click the Cancel box in the formula bar. If you press Enter, the result of the formula replaces the formula.

6. Correct the portion of the formula that returned the incorrect answer.

FIG. 24.11

Select the portion of the formula that you want to check.

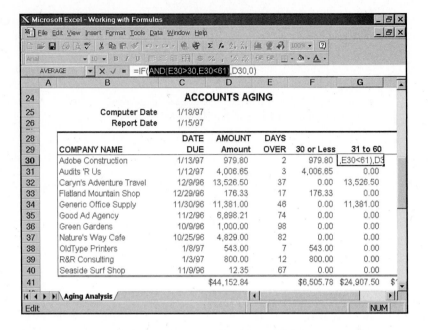

FIG. 24.12

Only the selected portion is calculated.

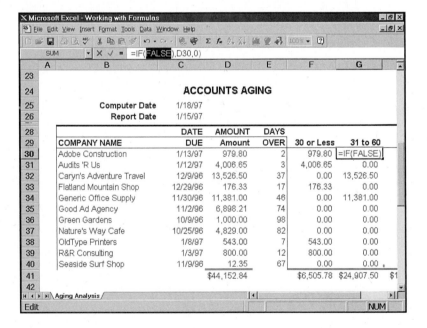

The preceding method of calculating part of a formula displays the contents of arrays. If, in the formula bar, you select a function that returns an array of values and press F9, you see the values within the array, as in the following example:

{2,3,"four";5,6,"seven"}

Commas separate array values into columns. Semicolons separate rows.

You can also check for missing parentheses. Excel highlights matching pairs of parentheses as you move the insertion point across one parenthesis of a pair. To see these highlighted, move the insertion point to the formula bar, and then press the right- or left-arrow keys to move the insertion point across a parenthesis. Watch for an opposing parenthesis to highlight. If the highlighted parenthesis doesn't enclose the correct term in the formula, you have found the terms that require another parenthesis.

▶ **See** "Entering Worksheet Functions," **p. 612**

▶ **See** "Displaying Formulas," **p. 802**

Part

VII

Ch

24

TROUBLESHOOTING

After pressing Enter to enter a formula, Excel beeps and displays an alert box warning that an error exists in the formula. Press the F1 key to display a Help window that lists the most common errors that occur in formulas. If you cannot find the error in the formula, convert the formula to text by deleting the equal sign (=) at the front of the formula and pressing Enter. You can return later and work on it. To turn the text back into a formula, just reenter the equal sign at the front of the formula and press Enter.

Everything within a function appears correct, but Excel doesn't accept the entry. A frequent mistake when typing functions is to miss or delete a comma between arguments. You can reduce the chance of these errors by entering functions using the Paste Function command or the Functions box that appears at the left end of the formula bar when you are entering or editing a formula. Choose Insert, Function (or click the Paste Function button on the toolbar), or click the down arrow next to the Functions box at the left end of the formula bar. Follow the prompts to fill in the arguments for the function.

When auditing a worksheet, you want to see more than one formula or determine the range names that a cell is part of. You can switch the worksheet to display formulas by choosing Tools, Options, selecting the View tab, and selecting the Formulas option. The shortcut key is Ctrl+` (grave accent). Open a second window to the worksheet with the Window, New Window command; then format one worksheet to show results and the other to show formulas. Or, better yet, print the worksheet with formulas displayed and use this printout to audit the worksheet.

If you selected exactly the same cells used by a range name, the name appears in the reference area to the left of the formula bar.

continues

continued

Large Excel worksheets are difficult to understand without a map that shows areas and regions. Use Excel's View, Zoom command to shrink the worksheet so that you can see more. This shows the actual worksheet results. You also can create a map showing text, values, and formulas.

The Circular (Circ) indicator appears at the bottom of the worksheet. Although no data has changed, with every recalculation of the worksheet, some of the results grow larger or grow smaller. The worksheet has a circular error—a formula that refers to another cell that contains a formula that refers to the first. This error may happen through a chain involving many cells. The formula feeds on itself with progressing recalculations. Therefore, like a snake devouring its tail, each recalculation reduces the results, or the results can grow larger, depending on how the formula is built. To find all the cells involved in a circular error, use Excel's auditing tools.

Calculating with Arrays

Arrays are rectangular ranges of formulas or values that Excel treats as a single group. Some array formulas or functions return an array of results that appear in many cells. Other formulas or functions affect an entire array of cells, yet return the result in a single cell.

Arrays are a powerful method of performing a large amount of calculation in a small space. When used to replace repetitive formulas, arrays also can save memory. Some Excel functions, such as the trend analysis functions discussed in Chapter 36, "Manipulating and Analyzing Data," require some knowledge of arrays.

Entering Array Formulas

Rather than entering or copying a repetitive formula in each cell of a range, you can save memory by entering an array formula. Excel stores an array of formulas in memory as a single formula even if the array affects many cells. Some Excel functions also must be entered as arrays that span a range of cells because the function produces multiple results and each result appears only in one cell.

Figure 24.13 shows a worksheet for cost estimating with Price in column D and Quantity in column E. Using standard formulas, you find the result of the products in column D times column E by entering a formula, such as =D5*E5 in F5, and copy it down column F. This method requires a formula for each cell that produced a result.

Instead, you can enter a single array formula in cell F5 that fills the range from F5 through F10 and uses only the memory and storage required for a single formula. Notice that the entire range F5:F10 reflects a different kind of formula shown in the formula bar. This array formula appears enclosed in curly braces ({ }).

To enter a single array formula, follow these steps:

1. Select the range to contain the array formula, which is F5:F10 in this example (see Figure 24.14).

2. Enter the formula that uses ranges by typing the formula or pointing with the mouse. The formula in cell F5 is =D5:D10*E5:E10.

3. To enter the formula or function as an array, press Shift+Ctrl+Enter.

FIG. 24.13

Entering a repetitive formula as an array formula.

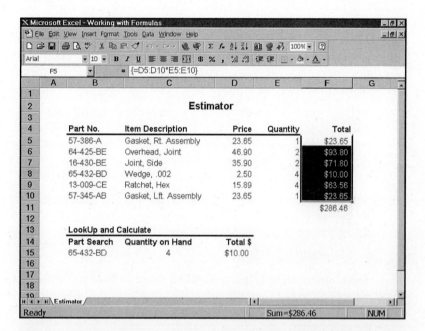

FIG. 24.14

Select the range and then enter the array formula with Shift+Ctrl+Enter.

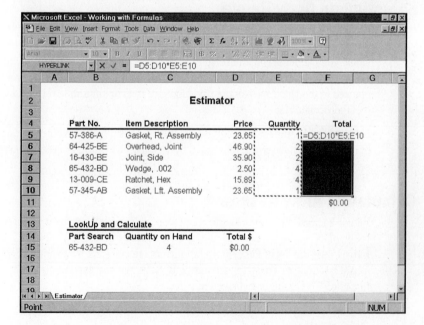

Rather than multiplying two cells, the formula shown in the formula bar of Figure 24.14 multiplies the two arrays D5:D10 and E5:E10 by taking each corresponding element from the two arrays and multiplying them in pairs, for example, D5*E5, then D6*E6, and so on. The corresponding result is placed in each cell of the range F5:F10 that was selected before entry.

Notice that the formula in Figure 24.14 is enclosed in braces ({ }). Each cell in the array range F5:F10 contains the same formula in braces. The braces signify that the formula is an array formula and that the array range must be treated as a single entity. You cannot insert cells or rows within the array range, delete part of the range, or edit a single cell within the range. To change an array, you must select and change the entire array.

You can enter functions that operate on corresponding values in ranges with array math. Array functions use an array of values as input and produce an array of results as output. Enter array functions the same way you enter an array formula. Select a range of the correct size to hold the results of the array function and enter the array formula or function specifying the ranges on which the formula or function works. Then press Shift+Ctrl+Enter.

Suppose that you want only the total in cell F11 of Figure 6.14 and do not need the total price for each part. You can calculate the sum of the products in a single cell with an array formula. To see this result, type the following formula in cell F11:

=SUM(D5:D10*E5:E10)

Enter the formula by pressing Shift+Ctrl+Enter so that Excel treats the formula as an array formula. Excel calculates the sum of the array product. The SUM( ) formula appears in the formula bar, enclosed in braces.

Selecting an Array Range

Usually, the range you select in which to enter an array formula or function should be the same size and shape as the arrays used for input. If the array range you select for the result is too small, you cannot see all the results. If the array range is too large, the unnecessary cells appear with the #N/A message. If an array of a single cell, a single row, or a single column is entered in too large a selection, this element, row, or column is repeated to expand the array to the appropriate size.

In Figure 24.15, the array range for each column is 6-by-1 (six rows by one column). The result of multiplying these two arrays is a 6-by-1 array. Therefore, the range from F5 through F10 is selected.

Calculating Array Results

Figure 24.15 shows how a single array formula can perform the work of multiple formulas in a range of extensive database analysis. The formulas in cells C15 and D15 match the entry in cell B15 against the list of Part No. In the formula in cell C15, for example, when the part number in cell B15 matches a part in the range B5:B10, the corresponding value from E5:E10 is added to a total. The result is displayed in cell C15.

FIG. 24.15
Array formulas can do extensive lookups and calculations in a single cell.

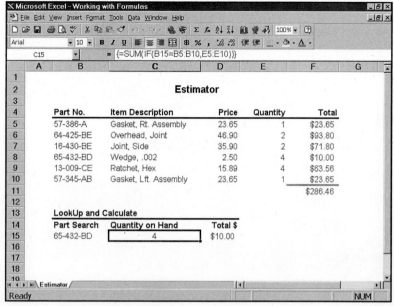

The following line shows the formula in cell C15:

> {=SUM(IF(B15=B5:B10,E5:E10))}

This formula was entered as an array formula in C15 by typing the formula and pressing Shift+Ctrl+Enter.

The formula in cell C15 uses the IF() function to compare the contents of cell B15 with each cell in the range B5:B10. When a match is found, the corresponding cell in the range E5:E10 is added to a total kept by SUM(). For this formula to work, you must enter the formula as an array formula.

The following line shows the formula in cell D15:

> =SUM(IF(B15=B5:B10,D5:D10*E5:E10))

This formula is entered as an array formula in C15 by typing the formula and pressing Shift+Ctrl+Enter.

The formula in cell D15 works almost exactly as the formula in C15 but adds an extra calculation. When a match is found between the contents of B15 and a cell in the range B5:B10, the calculation of the corresponding cells in columns D and E are multiplied. The result of this multiplication is totaled by the SUM() function. This formula must be entered as an array formula.

N O T E   You can use SUMIF and COUNTIF to sum and count data that meet specified criteria. You
can use these functions rather than the method outlined previously when you want to find
the sum of or count up specified subsets of data. To carry out other types of calculations, however,
such as averaging, on subsets of data, you still must use the method for calculating array results just
discussed.

Editing Array Formulas and Functions

To edit an array formula or function, follow these steps:

1. Move the pointer within the array range.

2. Click in the formula bar, or press F2 (the Edit key), or double-click the cell if you are
   using in-cell editing.

3. Edit the array formula or function.

4. To reenter the array, press Shift+Ctrl+Enter.

▶ **See** "Entering Worksheet Functions," **p. 612**

▶ **See** "Using the Analysis ToolPak," **p. 965**

Naming Cells for Better Worksheets

If you get tired of trying to decipher the meaning of B36 or F13:W54 in a formula, you should
use names. If you get tired of selecting the same ranges over and over for reports that you
need to print each day or each week, you should use names.

You can, for example, give an area to be totaled the name Sales_Total. You can give the print
range F19:L65 an easily recognizable name, such as Sales_Report. Named cells and ranges in
Excel are similar to range names in Lotus 1-2-3, but in Excel, you can paste names into formulas, create compound names, and even assign frequently used formulas and constants to
names.

Using names in worksheets has the following advantages:

■ Names reduce the chance for errors in formulas and commands. You are likely to notice
that you mistyped Sales.Report when you meant to type **Sales_Report**, but you may not
notice an error when you type F19:L65. When you enter an unrecognizable or undefined
name, Excel displays a #NAME? error.

■ Names are easier to remember than cell references. After you name cells or ranges, you
can look at a list of names and paste the names you want into formulas with Insert,
Name, Paste or by using the name box next to the formula bar (see "Pasting Names and
Functions into Formulas" earlier in this chapter).

- Names make formulas easy to recognize and maintain. For example, the following formula:

    =Revenue-Cost

  is much easier to understand than the following formula

    =A12-C13

- You can redefine a named reference, and all formulas that use that reference are updated.

- You can name any frequently used constant or formula and use the name in formulas. (The named constant or formula does not have to reside in a cell.) You can, for example, enter a name, such as RATE, into a formula, and then at any later time use Insert, Name, Define to assign a new value to the name RATE. The new assignment changes the value of RATE throughout the worksheet. Nowhere in the worksheet does the value of RATE need to be typed. This technique enables you to create predefined constants and formulas that others using the worksheet can use by name.

- Named ranges expand and contract to adjust to inserted or deleted rows and columns. This feature is important for creating print ranges, charts, databases, macros, and linked worksheets that continue to work no matter how a named range is expanded or contracted.

- Names make finding your way around the worksheet easy. You can choose Edit, Go To, or press F5 and select the name of the location you want to go to. Choosing Edit, Go To and then selecting Data.Entry or Report.Monthly is a time-saver.

- Using names in macros when referring to specific locations on worksheets helps make your macros more versatile. The macros continue to work on rearranged worksheets.

- Names make typing references to worksheets in other workbooks easy. You do not need to know the cell reference in the other worksheet. If the other workbook has a named cell reference, you can type a formula such as

    =YTDCONS.XLS!Sales

  This formula brings the information from the Sales cell in the workbook with the file name YTDCONS.XLS into the cell in your active worksheet.

- One set of names can be used throughout a workbook, so that when you need to reference a named cell or cell range in another sheet in a workbook, you don't need to include the worksheet reference.

- You can define names that are unique to a worksheet, so that the same name can be used in different worksheets in a workbook.

Creating Names

When the time comes to create names, you must remember a few rules. Names must start with a letter or an underscore, but you can use any character after the initial letter except a space or a hyphen. Do not use a space in a name; instead, use an underline (_) or a period (.).

Incorrect Names	Correct Names
SALES EXPENSES	SALES_EXPENSES
SALES-EXPENSES	SALES_EXPENSES
Region West	Region.West
1996	YR1996
%	Rate

Although names can be as long as 255 characters, you want to make the names as short as possible. Because formulas also are limited to 255 characters, long names in a formula leave you less room for the rest of the formula, and the full name does not show in a dialog box. Names of as many as 15 characters display in most scrolling list boxes.

You can type names in either upper- or lowercase letters. Excel recognizes and continues to use the capitalization used to create the name. Don't use names that look like cell references, such as B13 or R13C2.

Defining Names with the Insert Name Define Command   You can define names on a worksheet in two ways: you can use Insert, Name, Define or the name box in the formula bar. An advantage to using Insert, Name, Define is that you can define several names at once without having to close the Define Name dialog box.

To name a cell, range of cells, or multiple range using Insert, Name, Define, follow these steps:

1. Select the cell, range, or multiple ranges you want to name.

2. Choose Insert, Name, Define.

3. If Excel proposes an acceptable name, leave the name or type the name you want in the Names in Workbook box.

4. Leave the cell reference in the Refers to box, if it is acceptable, or type an equal sign (=) followed by the correct reference (this procedure is described later).

5. Choose OK to define the name and close the dialog box.

    You also can choose Add to define the name and leave the dialog box open.

    At this point, you can select the Names in Workbook box and type another name and then select the Refers To box and either type in a cell reference or select the cell or range of cells on the worksheet. Choose Add to define the new name. This process can be repeated as many times as you like. Choose OK when you want to close the dialog box.

You can see in Figure 24.16 that Excel often proposes a name for the cells you select. Excel looks at the left edge for a text name of a row or looks above for a text name of a column. If you select a range, Excel checks for a name in the upper-left corner of the range. If the text contains a blank space, as shown in Figure 24.16, Excel replaces the blank with an underscore to make the name legal. Excel has done this in the following figure.

Defining Names by Using the Name Box   The name box appears at the left end of the formula bar. The reference area displays the cell reference for the active cell or the name of the currently selected cell or cells, if they are named. If you click the arrow to the right of the name box, you display an alphabetical list of all defined names in the workbook (see Figure 24.17). You can select a named cell or range by clicking the arrow and selecting the name from the list. You also can use the name box to define a name and to insert a name in a formula (see "Pasting Names and Functions into Formulas," earlier in this chapter).

FIG. 24.16
Insert, Define, Name attempts to propose names for the cell or range you select.

FIG. 24.17
The name box can be used to quickly select a named cell or range or to define a name.

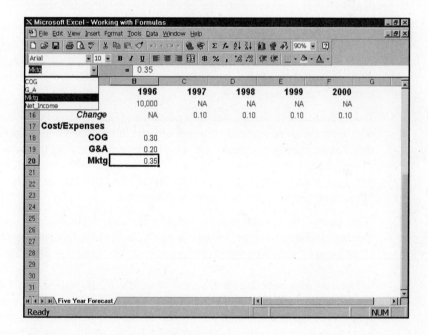

To define a name using the name box, follow these steps:

1. Select the cell or range of cells you want to name.

2. Click the arrow to the right of the name box. The active cell appears in the name box and is highlighted.

3. Type in the name for the selected cell or cells.

4. Press Enter.

If you enter a name that is already being used, the cell or range with that name is selected, rather than the current selection being given that name. If you want to redefine an existing name, you must use Insert, Name, Define.

N O T E   Excel doesn't immediately replace existing cell references in formulas with range names. You have the advantage of specifying the areas of the worksheet where formulas show the range names. This procedure is described in the section "Applying Names," later in this chapter. ▪

Workbook-Level versus Sheet-Level Names   Unless you specify otherwise, names that you define by using Insert, Name, Define or the name box are at the workbook level and apply to all the sheets in the workbook. For example, if a cell on Sheet1 is named Net_Income and you are working in Sheet2, and if you open the name box and select Net_Income in the list, Sheet1 becomes the active sheet and the cell named Net_Income is selected. When used in any formula, Net_Income refers to the contents of the named cell on Sheet1. If you define a cell or range with the name Net_Income on another sheet, the name is redefined. Using the method described here, the same name cannot be used to define cells or ranges on different sheets in the same workbook.

To use the same name to define cells or ranges on more than one sheet in a workbook, you can create sheet-level names. In this way, you can use the same name to designate related cells in different worksheets. For example, each of several worksheets representing regional sales can have a cell named Net_Income.

To create sheet-level names, you must use Insert, Name, Define. Follow the same procedure outlined in the section "Defining Names with the Insert Name Define Command," earlier in this chapter, but when you enter the name for the cell or range in the Names in Workbook box (refer to Figure 24.16), precede the name with the name of the sheet followed by an exclamation mark. For example, to define a cell with the name Net_Income in Sheet2, you would enter Sheet2!Net_Income in the Names in Workbook box.

When you use the sheet-level name on that name's sheet, you don't need to specify the sheet. You can use the name alone. To refer to a sheet-level name from another sheet, you must include the sheet name. To refer to the cell named Net_Income on Sheet2 in a formula on Sheet1, for example, type Sheet2!Net_Income. Sheet-level names take precedence over book-level names, so a name in a sheet defined at the sheet-level is used even if the same name is defined at the workbook-level. When you open the Define Name dialog box, only names for the active sheet appear in the Names in Workbook list. You can paste names from another sheet into a formula by following the steps described in the section "Pasting Names and Functions into Formulas," earlier in this chapter.

Creating Names from Worksheet Text

If you have built a text skeleton consisting of row and column headings for your worksheet, you can use the text names on the worksheet to assign names to adjacent cells. Moreover, by selecting a range of cells, you can assign a number of names at the same time. This technique of creating multiple names from text labels is important when creating well-written macros.

To assign a number of names at the same time, use the Insert, Name, Create command. You can choose whether Excel uses as names the existing text along one or more edges of the selected area.

To create names using text in the worksheet, follow these steps:

1. Select the range of cells you want to name. Be sure to include the row or column of text cells that are used as names (see Figure 24.18).

FIG. 24.18

Include text you want to use as names in the range you select.

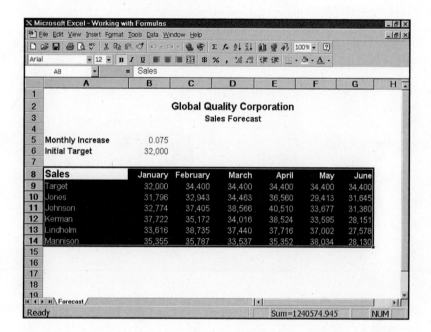

Part

VII

Ch

24

2. Choose Insert, Name, Create. The Create Names dialog box appears (see Figure 24.19).

FIG. 24.19

The Create Names dialog box enables you to choose the location of text that is used as names.

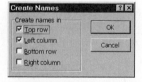

3. Select the Top Row check box to use text in the top row of the selection as names for the columns. Similarly, the Bottom Row check box uses the bottom row of text as names for the columns. The Left Column check box uses text in the left column to name the rows to the right of the text; and the Right Column check box uses the text in the right column to name the rows to the left of the text.

4. Choose OK.

In Figure 24.20, the range under the columns is selected. The names at the top of the column can be assigned by selecting the Top Row check box. In Figure 24.21, the rows are selected. The names at the left edge of the selection can be assigned to the rows by selecting the Left Column check box.

FIG. 24.20

Use the names at the top of these columns to name the cells going down.

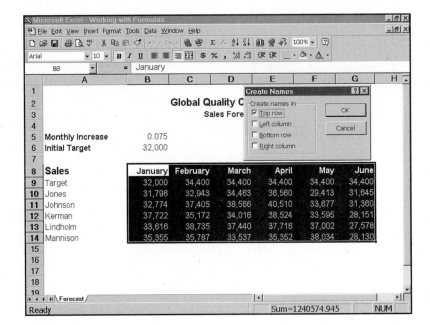

FIG. 24.21

Use names at the left of rows to name the selected cells in the rows.

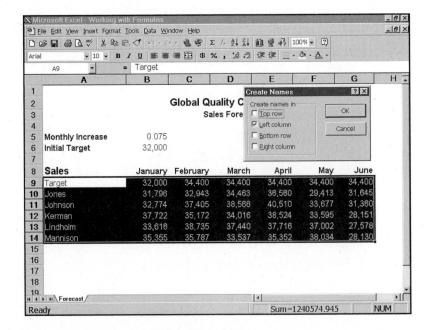

If you try to assign a duplicate name, a dialog box appears, warning you that the name is already in use. Choose Yes to update the name to the new references; choose No to retain the old name and references; or choose Cancel to retain the old name and back out of creating new names.

Text in cells used as names can include spaces. Excel automatically replaces the space with an underscore in the created name. For example, SALES RATE in a cell becomes the name SALES_RATE. You can fit longer names in a tighter space if you use a period as a separator rather than an underscore.

If you use Insert, Name, Create to name cells, try to use names that do not violate the rules for names. Remember that names cannot begin with numbers. Illegal characters are replaced with underscores, so a text label such as North %Margin results in the name North_Margin, substituting underscores for the blank and the illegal %.

You can select more than one option from the Create Names dialog box. As a result, you can name cells in different orientations with different names. If you select two options that overlap, any text in the cell at the overlap is used as the name for the entire range. If you select both the Top Row and Left Column options, the text in the cell at the top left of the selected range is the name for the entire range. The names down the left column name each row in the selected range, and the names along the top row name each column in the selected range. In the selection shown in Figure 24.18, if you select both Top Row and Left Column, the range B9:G14 will be named SALES, the names of the salespeople will be applied to the rows, and the names of the months will be applied to the columns.

When you create names using more than one option, as described in the previous paragraph, you also create intersecting names for any cell that has both a row and column heading. For example, in the selection in Figure 24.18, cell B10 would be assigned the name Jones January. When you select a cell with an intersecting name, the name is not displayed in the name box but you can use the intersecting name in the Go To dialog box to select a cell. To go to cell B10, press F5 and type **Jones January** in the Reference box. When you choose OK, cell B10 will be selected.

You can also use intersecting names in formulas. You could, for example, use the following formula to see January's sales amount for Jones:

=Jones January

The space between Jones and January acts as the intersect operator. This formula selects the cell that is common to both the row named Jones and the column named January. The result in the cell containing the formula is 31,796.

In Excel 97, you use intersecting names without explicitly defining them using the Create Names command. Any cell in a table that has both a column and row heading can be referred to in a formula by typing the row heading, a space as an intersection operator, and the column heading. For example, with a table that lists months typed across the top and sales regions down the left side, you could display the cell contents where the April column and Western row intersect with the following formula:

=April Western

However, if you want to use the Go To command to select a cell with an intersecting name, you still must create the intersecting names using the method described previously in this section.

Creating 3-D Names

You can use 3-D references when you define a name. When you enter the reference in the Refers To box in the Define Name dialog box, you include a 3-D reference of the definition. For example, to define a name that refers to cells A1:A12 in sheets Sheet1 to Sheet6 in a workbook, type **=Sheet1:Sheet6!A1:A12**. For more information on using 3-D references, see "Entering 3-D References," earlier in this chapter.

Pasting a List of Names

As part of your worksheet documentation, you should include a list of the names used. Excel can paste into your worksheet a complete list of names and the cells they name. Move the active cell to a clear area; be careful to select an area without data, or the list overwrites any existing data. Choose Insert, Name, Paste and choose Paste List. A list of all the names and corresponding cell addresses appears in your worksheet.

Changing or Deleting Names

Sometimes you may want to change a name or the cells that the name refers to. Also, from time to time, you may want to delete unneeded names. Deleting unneeded names keeps your list of names free of clutter.

To change a name or the cells that the name references, follow these steps:

1. Choose Insert, Name, Define, which is the same command you use to name a cell or range of cells manually. The Define Name dialog box appears.
2. Select from the list box the name you want to change.
3. To change the name, select the Names in Workbook box. To change the cells reference, select the Refers To box.
4. Edit the name or cell reference in the appropriate text box. Use the arrow keys, Backspace, and Delete keys to edit in the text box.
5. Choose OK.

To delete a name, select the name you want to delete and choose Delete.

CAUTION

After you have deleted a name, selecting Cancel does not undelete it.

Using Names in Formulas and Commands

Names can be used wherever you use cell or range references. In formulas, you can type a name. You also can paste a name into a formula by moving the insertion point in the formula bar where you want the name to appear, and then choosing the Insert, Name, Paste command (or pressing F3). Select the name from the Paste Name list and choose OK.

Names also can be used in dialog boxes to indicate a cell reference or range. Just type the name in the edit box requiring the reference.

If you use a name in a formula that Excel cannot find, the #NAME? error value is returned. There are several things to check for if this happens:

- The name is typed correctly in the formula.
- Names of functions are typed correctly in the formula.
- The name you are using in the formula has actually been defined.
- The name you are using was deleted.
- The name should not be enclosed in quotation marks.
- References to a cell range must include a colon; otherwise, Excel interprets the range reference as a name.

N O T E   If you copy a formula that uses a name into another workbook and that workbook already has a cell or range defined with the same name, a message box asks you if you want to use the existing definition of the name, that is, the one in the destination workbook. Answer Yes if you want to use this definition or No if you want to use the definition from the workbook you are copying the formula from. If you choose No, you must enter a new name for the cell or range in the source worksheet in the New Name box of the Name Conflict dialog box that appears. ▪

Applying Names

When you create or define names, they do not automatically appear in existing formulas in the worksheet. If you create formulas before names, you need to apply the names to the formulas. With Insert, Name, Apply, Excel gives you the capability to select where you want names applied (see Figure 24.22).

FIG. 24.22

To apply names to existing formulas, use the Insert, Name, Apply command.

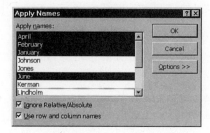

To apply existing names to formulas containing named cell references, follow these steps:

1. Select a single cell if you want to apply names to the entire worksheet, or select a range to apply names to formulas in the range.

2. Choose Insert, Name, Apply. The Apply Names dialog box appears.

   The most recently created names are selected in the Apply Names list box, but you can choose whatever names you want to apply.

3. Select the names you want applied from the Apply Names list box by clicking each name you want to apply. To select a range of adjacent names, click the first name, press the Shift key, and click the last name. To select multiple non-adjacent names, press the Ctrl key as you click the names. To select adjacent names with the keyboard, press the Shift key and use the arrow keys to select names.

   To select multiple non-adjacent names, press the spacebar to select or deselect a name, and hold down Ctrl to keep from deselecting the selected names as you use the arrow keys to move through the list.

4. Select the Ignore Relative/Absolute check box if you want names to replace absolute and relative references. Normally this box should be selected. Clearing this box applies absolute names to absolute references and relative names to relative references.

5. Select the Use Row and Column Names check box if you want Excel to rename cell references that can be described as the intersect of a named row and a named column. In Figure 24.23, cell G10 can be referenced as Jones June. (A space character is the intersect operator.) Clear this box if you want only individual cell names to apply to cell references.

FIG. 24.23

Assign frequently used formulas or constant values to a name.

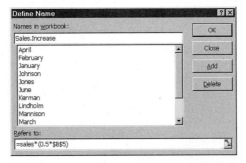

6. Select the Options button to omit row or column names when the cell containing the formula is in the same row or column as the name. The following options are available:

   Omit Column Name if Same Column

   Omit Row Name if Same Row

   After selecting Options, you also can select the order in which you want row and column names to appear. Simply select or clear the options for Name Order: Row Column and Column Row.

7. Choose OK.

Naming Formulas and Values

Your worksheets are much more readable and understandable if you create names for commonly used constants or frequently used formulas. You can name any number or formula, and then use that name in a cell or formula. The number or formula does not need to be in a cell.

Named formulas and values (constants) differ from named cells and ranges. In named cells and ranges, the name references a worksheet location. In named formulas and values, the name references a formula or value that doesn't exist on the worksheet.

To name a value or formula you enter, follow these steps:

1. Choose Insert, Name, Define. The Define Name dialog box appears.
2. Select the Names in Workbook text box and enter the name.
3. Select the Refers To box.
4. Type the constant number or the formula. Enter the formula or constant as you would in the formula bar. You can edit in the Refers To box as you edit in the formula bar.

   If you need to use the arrow keys to move around within the formula, press F2 to change to Edit mode. Otherwise, arrow keys point to cells on the worksheet.
5. Choose OK.

Figure 24.23 illustrates how a formula is assigned a name. Because the formula or constant stored in the name does not need to be stored in a cell, your worksheets stay neater and are easier for inexperienced users to work with.

If you build formulas in the Refers To box by pointing to cell references (clicking them or moving to them), Excel supplies only absolute references, such as $D$15. These references are absolute because a name usually applies to one specific location on a worksheet. You can type relative references or edit out the dollar signs to create names that act like relative references. (Named relative reference formulas can be confusing to use, so be careful.) If the active cell is C6, you can type the formula =C12 in the Refers to box. You could give the formula the name RIGHT6. You then can use the name RIGHT6 in a formula or cell to indicate the contents of the cell six cells to the right of the cell containing =RIGHT6. You can move the Define Name dialog box if it is in the way of the cell you need in a formula.

N O T E Deleting all the rows or columns that make up a named range does not delete the name. These names simply refer to cell references that no longer exist. In the Define Name dialog box, selecting an invalid name like this displays a #REF! error in the Refers To box. ■

Labeling Ranges

A new command in Excel 97 enables you to automatically label a range of cells using the row and column labels on your worksheet. For example, you can select the cells containing the column headings in a table and use the Insert, Name, Label command to name the ranges of cells adjacent to these column headings. These labels can be used instead of cell references when you are constructing a formula, making the formulas easier to read.

Part

VII

Ch

24

In Figure 24.24, the column headings were used to name the cells in the range B9:G14. In this case, the name *January* is applied to cells B9:B14, *February* to cells C9:C14, and so on. The formula in B16 was constructed using the range label *January* instead of a range reference, as shown in the Formula Bar in Figure 24.24.

FIG. 24.24

The column headings in this worksheet were used to label the adjacent ranges of cells.

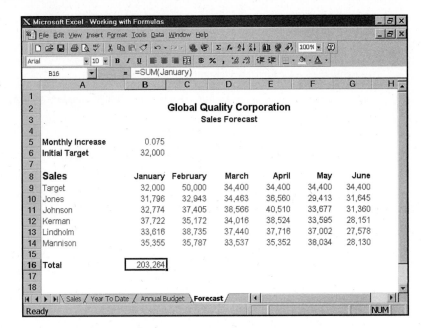

To label a range of cells using the Insert, Name, Label command, follow these steps:

1. Select the row or column headings you want to use to label a range.
2. Choose Insert, Name, Label to open the Label Ranges dialog box shown in Figure 24.25.

FIG. 24.25

Create label ranges using row and column headings in the Label Ranges dialog box.

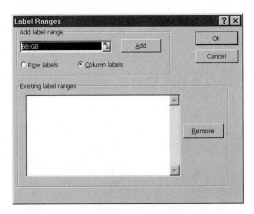

3. Click the <u>A</u>dd button to add the label range to the Existing Label Ranges box.

4. To add additional label ranges without closing the dialog box, click the Collapse Dialog button in the Add Label Range box, select the row or column headings you want to use to create the label range, click the Expand Dialog, and click <u>A</u>dd.

5. When you have finished adding label ranges, choose OK.

TIP To see the labels you have used to create label ranges, choose <u>V</u>iew, <u>Z</u>oom and enter a value less than or equal to 39 percent in the <u>C</u>ustom box. When you zoom a worksheet to 39 percent or less, a blue border appears around any row or column headings you have specified in the Label Ranges dialog box.

TROUBLESHOOTING

I labeled a range using the Insert, Name, Labels command and used the range label in a formula.
When I added new cells to the range, the value for the formula didn't change. When you use a range label in a formula and add new cells to the range, any formula that uses the range label will not update automatically. One way to update the results of the formula is to select the cell containing the formula, press F2 to open the formula bar, and press Enter.

Using Functions

Understanding Functions

Formulas allow you to do addition, subtraction, multiplication, division; formulas can also contain functions.

Excel uses prebuilt worksheet functions to perform math, text, or logical calculations or to find information about the worksheet. Functions allow you to speed up your calculations compared to writing a formula. For example, you could create a formula =(A1+A2+A3+A4+A5+A6+A7+A8)/8 or use the function =AVERAGE(A1:A8) to do the same thing. Whenever possible, use functions rather than writing your own formulas. Functions are fast, take up less space in the formula bar, and reduce the chance for typographical errors.

Functions act on data in much the same way that formulas act on numbers. Functions accept information, referred to as arguments, and return a result. In most cases, the result is a calculation, but functions also return results that are text, references, logical values, arrays, or information about the worksheet.

Functions accept data through arguments. You enter arguments, enclosed in parentheses, after the function name. Each function takes specific types of arguments, such as numbers, references, text, or logical values. Functions use these arguments in the same way that equations use variables.

If you want to write an equation to determine a mortgage or loan payment, for example, you need the following information:

Argument	Description
rate	Interest rate per period
nper	Number of periods
pv	Present value (starting value of loan)
fv	Future value (ending value at loan completion)

Because the equation for an amortized loan payment requires many complex terms, you are likely to make typographical errors if you write your own equation. Excel also solves a formula you enter more slowly than it solves a built-in function for the same operation.

So, instead of manually entering a long formula to calculate the loan payment, you can use the Excel PMT( ) worksheet function for this kind of calculation. You can type a function into a cell or insert it into a cell with the guidance of the Paste Function (covered later).

In parentheses, you enter the values or references for the information needed to do the calculation. These terms inside the parentheses are known as arguments. The PMT( ) function is entered in this form:

PMT(*rate*,*nper*,*pv*,*fv*,*type*)

N O T E   Arguments in both bold and italic, such as *rate*, *nper*, and *pv*, shown in the previous paragraph, are required. Those arguments in italic only are optional. ■

The arguments give the information needed to solve a calculation for a payment, with the addition of the argument *type*. Some functions return different answers depending on the value of *type*. In the case of PMT( ), Excel can calculate payments for different types of loans depending on the value used for *type*. An actual PMT( ) function may look like this:

    =PMT(MonthInt,A12,B36)

Here, MonthInt is the name of the cell that contains the monthly interest rate (*rate*), A12 contains the number of months (*nper*), and B36 contains the present value (*pv*). The arguments *fv* and *type* are optional and are not used in this calculation of a simple mortgage payment.

The equal sign preceding the function is required for the first function entered in the cell. You can have functions within functions. If you have a function within a function, only the first function must be preceded by an equal sign. If you wanted to calculate the *nper* argument by adding two cells, the complete function would look like this:

    =PMT(MonthInt, A12+A13, B36)

Using Arguments Within Functions

Most functions contain one or more arguments in the parentheses. If the function contains more than one argument, separate the arguments with commas. When you write a function, never include a space unless the space is in quoted text. In order to give the appearance of words, you can instead include an underscore, as in *num_chars*.

Excel uses various types of arguments for different types of information. As shown in Table 25.1, you can often tell the required types of data for an argument by the name of the argument.

Table 25.1   Argument Names and Types

Argument	Type	Sample Function and Argument Names
text	text	**LEFT(*text*,*num_chars*)** (in quotation marks or a reference)
value	value	**LOOKUP(*lookup_value*, *array*)** (text in quotation marks, a number, or a reference)
num	numeric	**RIGHT(*text*,*num_chars*)** (a number or a reference)
reference	cell reference	**COLUMN(*reference*)**
serial_number	date/time number	**DAY(*serial_number*)** (or a reference)
logical	logical	**OR(*logical1*,*logical2*,...)** (or a reference)
array	array	**TRANSPOSE(*array*)** (or a reference)

Part
VII

Ch
25

If you have a long function or formula, you can enter carriage returns (Alt+Enter) and tabs (Ctrl+Tab) to make the function more readable.

Some functions can have up to 30 arguments. This chapter shows these functions, such as the OR( ) function, with an ellipsis (…) to indicate that more arguments are possible.

Some functions have optional arguments, which are shown in the function directory (later in this chapter) in *italic type*. Mandatory arguments are shown in ***bold italic type***. If you leave out optional arguments, you do not need to enter their commas if there are no additional arguments. Commas act as placeholders so that Excel understands the position of the optional arguments that you do enter. For example, the following is the format of the PMT( ) function with all its arguments:

> **PMT(*rate,nper,pv,fv,type*)**

If you omit the *fv* optional argument, but use the *type* argument, you would enter the function as

> **PMT(*rate,nper,pv,,type*)**

While the PMT function requires values, other functions, such as LEFT, require text. Be certain that you enclose text in quotation marks (" "). Text contained in a cell and referenced by the cell address does not have to be in quotation marks. Do not enclose range names in quotation marks, and do not type spaces between the quotes. Text values in a cell, including the quotation marks, can be up to 255 characters long. If your text includes a quotation, use two quotation marks to begin and end each internal quotation. For example, to find the length of the following phrase:

> She said, "So!"

You must use

> =LEN("She said,""So!""")

NOTE To produce a blank cell display, use two quotation marks with nothing between them, as in the following example:

`=IF(A12>15,"","Entry must be greater than 15!")`

When A12 is greater than 15, the cell displays nothing because the TRUE portion of the IF( ) function returns "". When A12 is 15 or less, the cell displays the following message:

`Entry must be greater than 15!` ▪

Viewing the Parts of the Screen that Help Create Functions

Figure 25.1 shows the different parts of the screen that you can use to create functions. The function aids are in two basic places–on the Standard toolbar and on the formula bar. Both the formula bar and the Standard toolbar appear when you first load Excel. If the formula bar has been turned off, select <u>V</u>iew, <u>F</u>ormula Bar to turn it on. If the Standard toolbar has been turned off, select <u>V</u>iew, <u>T</u>oolbars, check the Standard toolbar box, and choose OK.

Entry area of formula bar   Paste Function button

FIG. 25.1

You can use elements on the Standard toolbar and formula bar to help create functions.

Range Name drop-down list

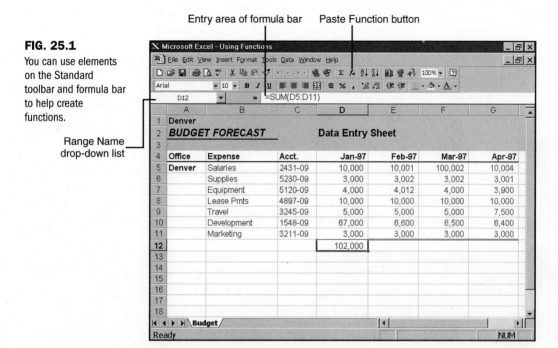

When you begin entering information in a cell, four buttons appear on the formula bar. These buttons, as well as the function-related buttons on the Standard toolbar, are explained in Table 25.2 and shown in Figure 25.1.

Table 25.2 Standard Toolbar and Formula Bar Parts Related to Creating Functions

Name	Description
Standard Toolbar	
AutoSum	Allows you to total a range. Places the SUM( ) function in a cell or number of cells.
Paste Function	Guides you through the process of creating any function.
Formula Bar	
Name box	Shows cell reference or name of active cell.
Range Name list	Displays a list of named cells or drop-down ranges.

continues

Part

VII

Ch

25

Table 25.2 Continued

Name	Description
Formula Bar	
Cancel box	Click to cancel the function.
Enter box	Click to enter the function in the cell.
Entry area	Displays formula function as you create or edit it.

Entering Worksheet Functions

You can enter worksheet functions as a single entry in the formula bar, like this:

=PMT(A12,B36,J54)

Or worksheet functions can be part of a much larger formula, including nested functions that are within other functions, as in this example:

=IF(LEFT(A12,3)="VDT",SUM(B36:B54),SUM(C36:C54))

N O T E This function looks at the first three characters of the text in cell A12. If the first three characters are VDT, the function will return the sum of cells in column B; otherwise, the function will return the sum of cells in column C.

You can enter functions by manually typing the function or by pasting the function into the formula bar (which is below the toolbar). One function, SUM( ), also can be pasted from the toolbar.

Typing Functions

You can type any function into the formula bar just as you would type in a formula. If you remember the function and its arguments, typing may be the fastest method. If you are unsure of the function's spelling or its arguments, enter the function with the Paste Function.

Using the AutoSum Button

The most frequently used function is SUM( ). This function totals the numeric value of all cells in the ranges it references. For example, SUM( ) can total all the cells between two endpoints in a column or row. Because SUM( ) is used so frequently, an AutoSum button, which you can use to total adjacent columns or rows automatically, appears on the Standard toolbar. In addition to entering the SUM( ) function, the AutoSum button selects the cells in the column above the SUM( ) or in the row to the left of the SUM( ). SUM( ) is useful for totaling columns of expenses or rows of sales by region. SUM( ) can even total subtotals while disregarding the numbers that created the subtotals.

If the Standard toolbar does not show on-screen, turn on the Standard toolbar by choosing View, Toolbars and clicking the Standard check box. If another toolbar already is displayed, you can right-click it anywhere except over a drop-down list box to display a shortcut menu from which you can choose Standard.

Figure 25.2 shows how to enter a SUM( ) function in cell D12 by using the mouse. Select cell D12, below the column you want to total, and then click the AutoSum button. Excel inserts the SUM( ) function and enters that column's range between parentheses, as shown in the figure. You can continue the formula by adding more terms, or you can enter the SUM( ) function into the cell by clicking the AutoSum button a second time or by pressing the Enter key.

FIG. 25.2

Double-click the AutoSum button to total the column above or to the left of the active cell.

AutoSum button

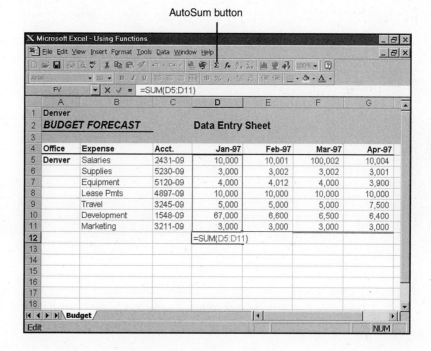

Office	Expense	Acct.	Jan-97	Feb-97	Mar-97	Apr-97
Denver	Salaries	2431-09	10,000	10,001	100,002	10,004
	Supplies	5230-09	3,000	3,002	3,002	3,001
	Equipment	5120-09	4,000	4,012	4,000	3,900
	Lease Pmts	4897-09	10,000	10,000	10,000	10,000
	Travel	3245-09	5,000	5,000	5,000	7,500
	Development	1548-09	67,000	6,600	6,500	6,400
	Marketing	3211-09	3,000	3,000	3,000	3,000
			=SUM(D5:D11)			

Part VII

Ch 25

TIP To quickly total a row or column, double-click the AutoSum button.

To select the range of cells to total, highlight the range to sum including blank cell(s) to the right or below the range. When you select the AutoSum button, Excel fills in totals. Sum totals appear in blank cells below and to the right of a range of numbers.

N O T E You can quickly enter totals at the bottom of a table of any size. If you have a table that is surrounded by blank cells, you can select the entire table, no matter how large, by clicking a cell in the table and pressing Ctrl+* (asterisk). With the table selected, double-click the AutoSum button. The AutoSum enters a total under each column in the table. ■

If you have tables of data containing subtotals, you can use AutoSum to total the subtotals. Figure 25.3 shows a simple table that contains subtotals in cells F5, F9, F13, and F17. When you click cell F18 and then click the AutoSum button, AutoSum enters a grand total in cell F18 by looking at the filled cells above the range and creating the function SUM(F17,F13,F9,F5). Cells that contain numbers are ignored so they are not counted twice.

FIG. 25.3

AutoSum also totals subtotals.

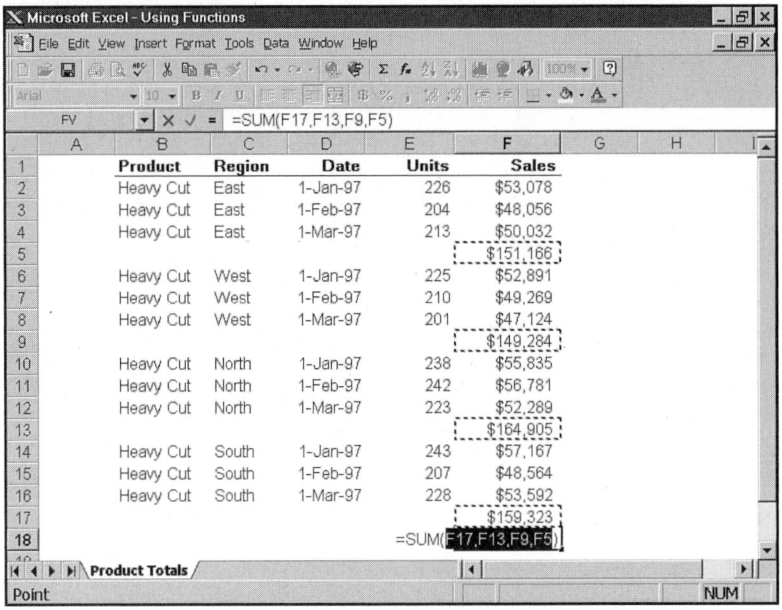

Using AutoCalculate for Quick Totals and Averages

In some cases, you may need to find a quick total in a worksheet, but that total isn't a formula you want or need to include. For example, you may want to sum a list and then use that sum in a formula. You could grab a calculator and add the figures. Or you can use Excel's AutoCalculate feature.

To use this feature, select the range you want to sum. Notice that the status bar displays the sum of the selected range. You can also average or count the selected range. To do so, right-click the AutoCalculate button and then select the function you want to use as shown in Figure 25.4. When you select the range, Excel uses this function for AutoCalculate.

Using the Paste Function

Creating functions can seem difficult, especially with the potentially different ways to spell a function name (AVG, AVE, AVERAGE) and the number of arguments available. Use the Paste Function to make your job much easier. The Paste Function guides you through the process and explains each function as well as each argument within a function.

FIG. 25.4

The AutoCalculate feature allows you to select from a variety of functions, including Sum, Average, and Count.

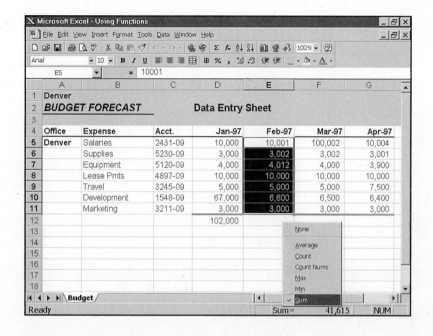

TIP In the Paste Function, use the Most Recently Used category to quickly get to functions you use frequently.

To insert a function and its arguments into the worksheet:

1. Select the cell where you want to enter the function. If you are entering a formula in the formula bar, move the insertion point to where you want the function inserted.

2. Choose Insert, Function or click the Paste Function button to display the Paste Function dialog box (see Figure 25.5).

FIG. 25.5

The Paste Function dialog box shows function names for each function category.

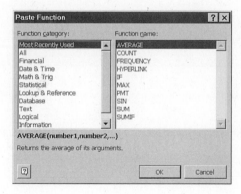

3. Select the type of function you want from the Function Category list. These categories divide the large number of functions into smaller lists. If you are unsure of the category, select Most Recently Used or All.

4. Choose the specific function that you want from the Function Name list box. Read the description in the lower part of the dialog box to verify that this is the function you want.

 T I P Scroll quickly to a function by clicking in the list and typing the first letter.

---

5. Choose OK.

6. The Paste Function displays as a pop-up window under the formula bar as shown in Figure 25.6. Enter the arguments in each argument text box. You can type the cell references or numbers, click the cell to enter, or drag across multiple cells to enter. Notice the description of each argument as you select the text box.

FIG. 25.6

The pop-up window of the Paste Function shows the required arguments in bold text and the optional arguments in normal text.

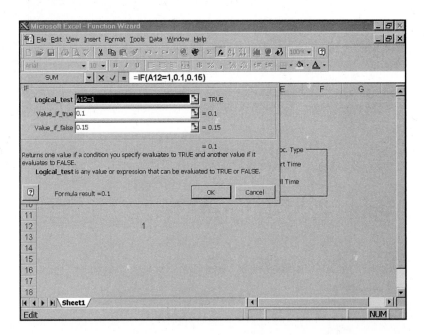

If you want to use range names in an argument text box, type the range name or select Insert, Name, Paste.

You can also create more complex functions where each argument is itself a function. Click the button next to the argument name and enter the desired formula.

7. Choose OK to complete the function and insert it in a cell.

You also can choose Cancel if you decide not to insert the function.

TIP Engineering, finance, and statistics functions are available with the Analysis ToolPak add-in described in Chapter 41, "Using the Analysis ToolPak."

Editing Functions

After you enter functions into a formula in the formula bar, you can edit them in one of two ways. You can use Paste Function to step through the functions in a formula, or you can manually edit the formula and functions.

To edit functions using the Paste Function:

1. Select the cell containing a function.
2. Choose Insert, Function or click the Paste Function button in the Standard toolbar. The Paste Function dialog box appears and shows the first function in the formula.
3. Change any arguments necessary in the first function.
4. When you finish making changes, choose OK.

To edit functions manually:

1. Select the cell containing a function.
2. Press F2 to activate the formula bar or click in the formula bar.
3. Select the argument or term in the formula you want to change.
4. Enter the new argument by typing, dragging, pasting a name, or inserting a function.
5. Choose OK.

You can move across arguments by pressing Ctrl+left arrow or Ctrl+right arrow. To select as you move, hold down Shift.

 TIP Select a term or argument in the formula bar by double-clicking it. With the keyboard, press Shift+Ctrl+arrow.

Getting Help

Excel contains extensive online Help for functions. If you forget how to use a function or want to see an example, use the Help files, which are always available.

■ To get help while you are building a function, choose the Help button from the Paste Function. This displays the Office Assistant.

■ To get help with a function that is in the formula bar, select the name of the function—for example, PMT—then press the help key: F1.

■ To access Help with functions, choose Help, Microsoft Excel Help Topics. On the Contents tab, select Reference Information and then select Worksheet Functions Listed by Category. Select the category and then the function that you want help with. If you are looking for help on a specific function, a help screen similar to the one in Figure 25.7 appears. Press Alt+F4 to close the Help window.

▶ **See** "Entering Formulas," **p. 568**

▶ **See** "Working in the Formula Bar or In-Cell," **p. 568**

FIG. 25.7
The Help window for the PMT function.

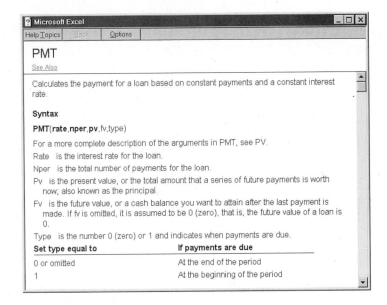

Using the Goal Seek Feature

When you know the answer you want, and you must work backward to find the input value that gives you that answer, choose Tools, Goal Seek. With this command, you specify a target value for a formula cell (the goal) and then an input cell that should be changed to make the goal cell reach this target. Excel finds the input value that results in the specific answer you want. To do so, the command operates as if it were making repeated educated guesses, narrowing in on the exact value.

The Goal Seek command saves you time when you need to *back into* solutions. You can use this command, for example, to determine the needed growth rate to reach a sales goal, or to determine how many units must be sold to break even.

When you choose Tools, Goal Seek, the cell being changed must contain a value (not a formula) and must affect the goal cell you specified. Because you cannot put constraints on the command, you may end up with input values that make no sense, or you may specify an answer for which no input value is possible. If you face situations such as these, you can use Data Tables or the Scenario Manager to test different input values, or you can use the Solver to find the optimal solution within constraints that you specify.

Seeking a Goal

Figure 25.8 shows a simple worksheet that forecasts future sales, cost/expenses, and net income. The changeable data entry cells are the rates of Change in row 16 and the Cost ratios in cells B18:B20. The rates of Change are used to project the Sales figures, and the Cost ratios are used to estimate Cost/Expenses.

FIG. 25.8

The Set Cell text box in the Goal Seek dialog box is automatically filled with the address of the active cell.

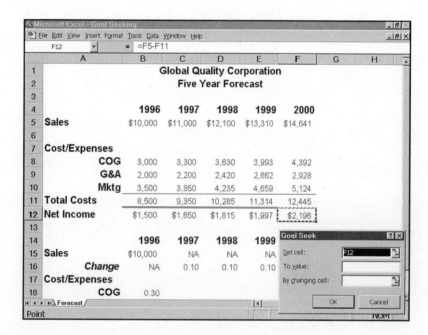

Part

VII

Ch

25

Suppose that you want to know the rate of Change for Sales that would be necessary in 1998 (cell D16) in order to reach Net income of $3,000 in the year 2000 (cell F12). You can have Goal Seek vary the value in cell D16 until cell F12 reaches the value $3,000.

CAUTION

If you have selected Precision as Displayed on the Tools, Options Calculation tab, Excel may not be able to reach the goal exactly, even though that goal would otherwise be attainable. Clear the Precision as Displayed option on the Calculation tab before you use the Goal Seek command; afterward, you can return to enforced precision.

To solve for a specific answer using Goal Seek, follow these steps:

1. Select a goal cell that contains a formula that you want to force to produce a specific value. In the example, this goal cell is F12.

2. Choose Tools, Goal Seek. The Goal Seek dialog box appears (this is also visible in Figure 25.8). Notice that the Set Cell text box contains the cell selected in step 1.

3. In the To Value text box, type the target value you want to reach. In the example, the desired target value is $3,000, so you type **3000**.

4. In the By Changing Cell text box, enter the cell reference of the input cell. In the example, the cell being changed is D16, so you type **D16**. In this instance, cell D16 contributes to the goal formula value only indirectly: It helps determine the values of Sales in row 5, and the Sales cells contribute to the Net Income values in row 12.

   Figure 25.9 shows the completed Goal Seek dialog box.

FIG. 25.9

This completed dialog box sets cell F12 to the value 3000 by changing cell D16 to an appropriate value.

5. Choose OK.

   Goal Seek begins substituting input values into cell D16. It substitutes high and low values, and converges them so that the solution becomes as close as possible to the solution you requested.

6. If you want to pause or cancel goal-seeking during a long goal-seeking process, choose Pause or Cancel in the Goal Seek Status dialog box, which is displayed during the calculations. To step through the solution iterations, choose Step in the Goal Seek Status dialog box. As you step, you see the current solution value in the dialog box. To continue at full speed after pausing, choose the Continue button.

The input cell selected in step 4 must contribute to the value of the formula in the goal cell, and must not contain a formula. To see which cells are precedents (contributors) to the goal cell, select the goal cell. Choose Edit, Go To, Special. When the Select Special dialog box appears, select the Precedents All Levels option button, and choose OK. All cells that contribute to the value of the goal cell are selected. Press Tab or Enter to move among these cells; they remain selected.

After a solution has been found, either choose OK to replace the values in the original worksheet with the new values shown on-screen, or choose Cancel to keep the original values.

Moving a Chart Marker to Seek a Goal

You can use a chart to search for a goal you want to meet. To do so, you must be in a 2D column, bar, or line chart. When you drag a marker to a new value position, the Goal Seek dialog box and worksheet appear. Excel asks which input value cell you want changed to make the chart marker's new value appear in the corresponding worksheet cell.

To find a solution graphically from a chart, complete the following steps:

1. Open the worksheet and the chart you want to manipulate. Activate the chart.

2. Click the edge of the data series marker (column, bar, or line symbol) for which you want to change the value once to select the data series and then a second time to select that marker. Black handles appear on the marker, as shown in Figure 25.10.

FIG. 25.10

Click a marker once to select its series, then click the marker edge to select the individual marker.

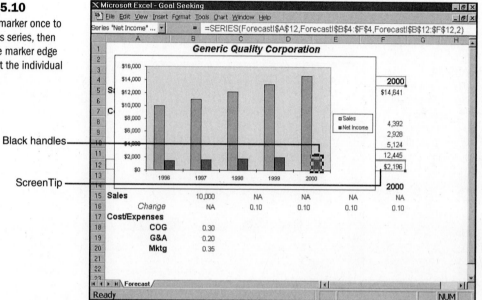

Black handles

ScreenTip

3. Drag the black handles to move the end of the marker to a new value. In this example, drag the black handles up or down to change the height of the column.

As you drag the marker, notice that the numeric value of the marker appears in a ScreenTip adjacent to the marker. This enables you to see the value as you reposition the marker.

When you release the mouse button, the Goal Seek dialog box appears (see Figure 25.11).

In the Goal Seek dialog box, the To Value text box is filled with the new value of the chart marker.

N O T E If the chart marker is linked to a cell that contains a number rather than a formula, the Goal Seek dialog box does not appear. Instead, the number in the worksheet changes to reflect the new marker value. This feature helps you to easily enter values into a worksheet when you need to make those values reflect a certain chart configuration. ▓

4. Change the To Value if you need a different value. The Set Cell box contains the worksheet cell linked to the chart marker.

Part

VII

Ch

25

5. In the By Changing Cell text box, type the cell reference you want to change or click the input cell with the mouse.

6. Choose OK.

You can use the Goal Seek options described in step 6 in the preceding set of instructions while Excel seeks the input value that most exactly produces your new desired value for the chart marker.

FIG. 25.11

Dragging a chart marker to a new value displays the Goal Seek dialog box, if the chart marker is linked to a cell that contains a formula.

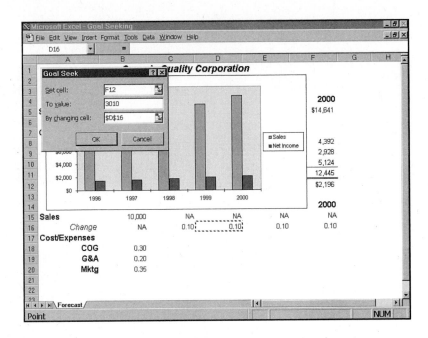

Reorganizing Your Data and Worksheets

Moving Cell Contents

Cutting and pasting is a valuable function for reorganizing your worksheet. You *cut out* a range of cells to *paste* elsewhere. This operation moves cell contents, the format, and any note attached to the moved cells.

Formulas remain the same when moved by cutting and pasting. You do not need to worry about relative and absolute cell references. (For more information on cell references, see Chapter 24, "Working with Formulas.")

Moving by Dragging and Dropping

If you have a mouse, the easiest and most intuitive way to move a cell or range is to drag the cell or range to the new location and drop it. Excel moves the cell contents and format.

To drag cells to a new location, perform the following steps:

1. Select the cell or range you want to move.

2. Move the mouse pointer over the selection's border. The pointer changes to an arrow.

3. Drag the pointer and the gray outline of the selection to the new location. Drag past the edge of a window to make the window scroll.

   Figure 26.1 shows the wide gray border that encloses the area to be moved. Notice that as you move, you see the range reference where the selection will be pasted.

FIG. 26.1

As you drag the range, you see a gray outline. After the data is in the right spot, release the mouse button.

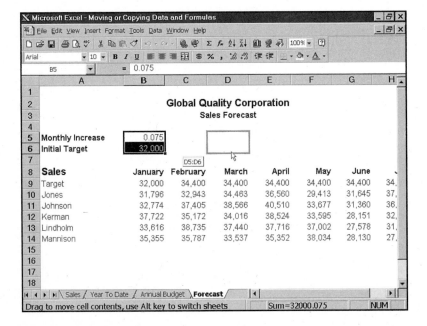

4. Release the mouse button when the gray outline is where you want to place the selected range.

The cell contents you selected in step 1 are pasted over the contents of the receiving cells. Choose Edit, Undo (or press Ctrl+Z) if you need to undo the command.

N O T E   If the pointer doesn't change to an arrow when you move it to the selection's border, choose Tools, Options. Select the Edit tab; then select the Allow Cell Drag and Drop option. Choose OK. ▪

Moving with Commands

Although the drag-and-drop technique is useful, you cannot use it to move data between different worksheets, between panes in a split worksheet, or to another application. You can make these moves with menu commands or shortcut keys.

To move a cell or a range to a new location, perform the following steps:

1. Select the cell or range you want to move.
2. Either choose Edit, Cut, click the Cut button on the Standard toolbar, or press Ctrl+X. The cells you selected appear surrounded by a *marquee*, a moving dashed line.
3. Select the cell at the upper-left corner of where you want the pasted cells.
4. Either choose Edit, Paste command, click the Paste button, or press Ctrl+V.

 T I P   You also can select the range and click the right mouse button to display a shortcut menu. Choose the command you want from the menu.

The cells you selected in the first step are cut and moved to the location you indicated. The area from which the cells were cut is blank and has a General format. If you accidentally paste over existing data or formulas, choose Edit, Undo. (Pasting over existing cells replaces the cell's previous contents and format with the pasted contents and format.)

You need to select only the upper-left corner of the new location. The move procedure is similar to moving a picture from one place on a wall to another. You do not need to describe where all four corners of the picture go; you need to specify only the upper-left corner.

As you select the range to cut, notice the reference area at the left of the formula bar, which shows the size of the range you are cutting (for example, 8R x 4C). This information helps you determine whether you can move the data without pasting over existing cells and replacing their contents.

Dragging and Inserting Cells

You also can drag and insert a cell or range so that existing cells move aside. With this procedure, you do not need to insert cells to make room for new data, and then move in the new data. This method is an excellent way to rearrange a list or move individual records in a database.

To move and insert data so that existing data moves aside, take the following steps:

1. Select the cell or range you want to move.

2. Move the mouse pointer over the selection's border. The pointer changes to an arrow.

3. Hold down the Shift key and drag the pointer to where you want the data inserted. The location where the data is inserted appears as a grayed partial cell boundary, as shown in Figure 26.2. As you drag, you also see the range reference where the selection will be inserted.

FIG. 26.2

The grayed cell boundary shows where the moved data will be inserted.

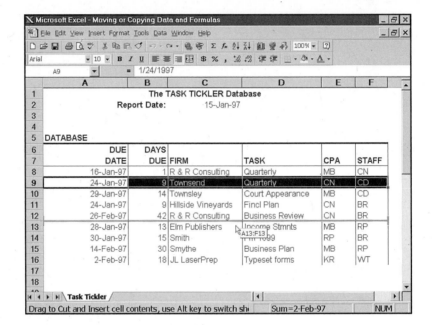

4. Continue holding down the Shift key as you release the mouse button.

5. Release the Shift key.

The cells you dragged are inserted at the location of the grayed boundary. Other cells move down or right.

Moving and Inserting with Commands

In some cases, you can move cells to a new location and move existing cells aside. This technique uses the Insert, Cut Cells command.

To insert pasted cells, perform the following steps:

1. Select the cells you want to move.

2. Either choose Edit, Cut, click the Cut button, or press Ctrl+X.

3. Select a cell in which to insert the cut cells.

   You cannot place an insert into a cell that will cause the source range of the copy to shift.

   Figure 26.3 shows a cut range and where it will be inserted.

FIG. 26.3

The marquee encloses
cells to be cut out.
Select where you want
to insert the cut cells.

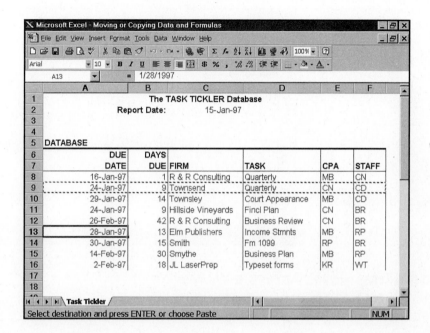

4. Choose <u>I</u>nsert, Cut C<u>e</u>lls.

5. If the Insert Paste dialog box appears, select the Shift Cells <u>R</u>ight option to shift existing cells right. Select the Shift Cells <u>D</u>own option to shift existing cells down. Choose OK. Be careful not to move cells with formulas that would create circular references.

   The cut range is inserted in the worksheet, shifting cells down or to the right. Figure 26.4 shows the database record from Figure 26.2 after it was inserted. Notice that the other cells have shifted down.

T I P To display a shortcut menu with Copy, Cut, and Paste commands, select the range you want to copy. Then click the right mouse button inside the selected range.

FIG. 26.4

The selected range from Figure 26.2 is moved to a new location. Existing cells are shifted down to make room for the data.

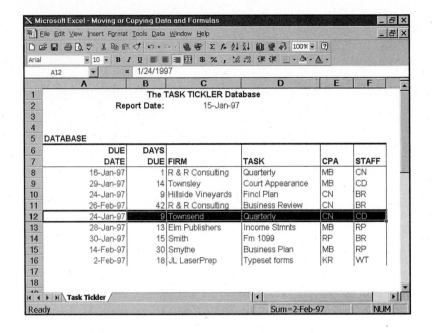

Making Moves Across a Workbook

You aren't limited to moving from just one worksheet area to another. If you need to, you also can move information among worksheets within the workbook.

To move information among worksheets in a workbook, follow these steps:

1. Select the cell or range you want to move.
2. Either choose Edit, Cut, click the Cut button, or press Ctrl+X. The cells you select appear surrounded by a marquee.
3. Select the worksheet to which you want to move data.
4. Select the cell at the upper-left corner of where you want the pasted cells.
5. Either choose Edit, Paste, click the Paste button, or press Ctrl+V.

The data is pasted in the selected worksheet. If formulas are included in the move, all references are adjusted so that the references refer to the same cells in the new location. If you want to refer to cells in the original worksheet, add the sheet name to the formula. See Chapter 24 for information on referencing cells in other worksheets in a workbook.

You can also drag a selected range to another worksheet in the workbook. To do so, hold down the Alt key and then drag the selection to the sheet tab. The sheet pops up and you can then drag the selection to the location you want on the sheet.

If you see a #REF error message, Excel cannot find a reference used in a formula.

TROUBLESHOOTING

Some of the cells now display `REF (cells)#REF.` When you move cells, any formulas are adjusted to reflect the new location. One of the formulas is probably referring to a cell that is no longer valid. Check all formulas. If necessary, adjust cell references so that they are absolute. See Chapter 24 for more information.

The pasted data overwrote existing data in the worksheet. When you paste data, it overwrites the existing data. Choose Edit, Undo to undo the paste, and then select a blank area of the worksheet for the paste. Or insert the cells, as described in the earlier section "Dragging and Inserting Cells."

> **CAUTION**
>
> You can move or copy a cell or range that contains a hyperlink within a workbook without disrupting the hyperlink, but if you try to move or copy a hyperlink to another workbook, the hyperlink will no longer work.

Filling or Copying Cell Contents

You can save a great deal of data-entry time with Excel's Copy and Fill commands and the many shortcuts that copy or fill. Rather than typing each formula in a worksheet, you can type a few formulas and copy or fill them into other cells. You even can copy the formula and format at the same time.

> **CAUTION**
>
> Because cell references in the formulas change relative to the new cell locations, some formulas don't produce the correct results when copied. Always cross-check copied or filled formulas to ensure that these formulas produce reasonable results. If you suspect an error, review the descriptions of relative and absolute cell references in Chapter 24.

Part

VII

Ch

26

Using the Fill Handle

If you use a mouse and need to fill data or formulas into adjacent cells, you need to learn how to use the *fill handle*. The fill handle is a black square at the lower-right corner of the selected cell or range. Dragging the fill handle across cells can fill the cells with copies or a data series. A *data series* is a series of data that continues a repeating pattern. To fill adjacent cells, perform the following steps:

1. Select the cell or range that contains the data or formulas.
2. Drag the fill handle so that the wide gray border encloses all cells to fill. Figure 26.5 shows an area being filled by using the mouse. Notice the shape of the pointer.

FIG. 26.5

Drag the fill handle to copy formulas into selected cells.

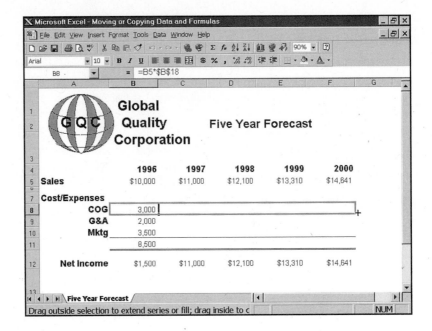

3. Release the mouse button.

Filling formulas into an area produces the same result as copying and pasting. Relative reference formulas adjust as though they were copied. Even if the formula references other spreadsheets, appropriate adjustments will automatically be made by Excel.

If you select two cells and then drag the fill handle, Excel uses the values in the two cells as "seeds" to create a series of data that fills the selection. A *series* is a sequence of data that has a mathematical, date, or text pattern. Series are useful for filling in a sequence of dates or a list of numbers. Series are described in Chapter 24.

 To fill multiple rows or columns at one time, select all the original cells, and then use the Ctrl+drag procedure to fill all the cells at one time. See the later section "Copying by Dragging and Dropping."

To turn off AutoFill, choose Tools, Options. Select the Edit tab; then select the Allow Cell Drag and Drop option. After you turn off this option, AutoFill is turned off. Choose OK.

Using Ctrl+Enter to Fill Cells

You can fill cells as you enter data or formulas if you first select the adjacent cells or ranges to fill. Next, type the formula or value in the active cell. Rather than pressing Enter, press Ctrl+Enter. Formulas and values fill into all selected cells just as though you used a Fill or Copy and Paste command. This method also works with nonadjacent multiple selections.

Using the Fill Commands

If you don't have a mouse, you need to use the Fill commands on the Edit menu to fill formulas or data into adjacent cells. You can fill cells left or right across a row and up or down a column.

To use the menu Fill commands, perform the following steps:

1. Select the range you want to fill. The cell that contains the formula or value used to fill other cells must be on the outside edge. Figure 26.6 shows cells in the worksheet selected before filling.

FIG. 26.6

Select both the original cells and the cells you want filled.

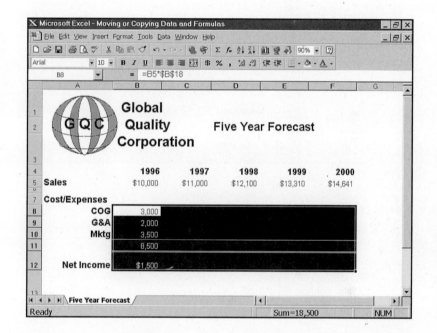

2. Choose Edit, Fill command. Then choose the direction to fill: Right, Left, Up, or Down. Figure 26.7 shows the resulting filled cells.

3. Check to see that the filled formulas produced reasonable answers.

TIP Shortcut keys for filling are Ctrl+R to fill right and Ctrl+D to fill down.

The result of an Edit, Fill command is the same as copying. Relative references adjust to the new locations. Duplicated formulas or values replace all cell contents they cover. The formatting of the original cells also copies to the filled cells.

FIG. 26.7

The Fill commands fill the original formula or value into the rest of the range.

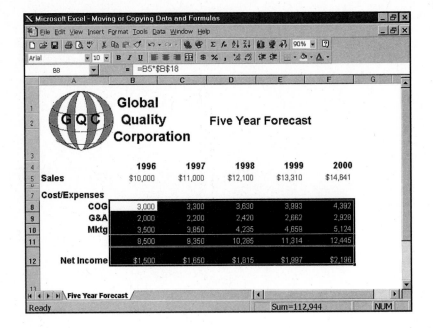

Filling Across Worksheets

If you have several worksheets that contain similar data or formulas and you have already entered the data, you can copy it to multiple worksheets in the workbook. For example, suppose that you have a monthly budget worksheet that you have created. You want to use the same column and row headings in the other worksheets in the workbook. Instead of reentering the data, you can fill it across worksheets. You can select to fill the contents, the formats, or both.

To fill data across worksheets, follow these steps:

1. Select the worksheets you want to fill. The data will be copied to all the selected worksheets. Be sure the worksheet that contains the data you want to copy across all the sheets is on top.

2. Select the range that contains the data you want to copy.

3. Choose Edit, Fill, Across Worksheets. You see the Fill Across Worksheets dialog box (see Figure 26.8).

4. Choose All to copy both the contents and the formatting, Contents to copy just the contents, or Formats to copy just the formatting.

5. Choose OK. The data is copied to the same cells in all the selected worksheets.

FIG. 26.8

Select what you want to copy across the worksheets.

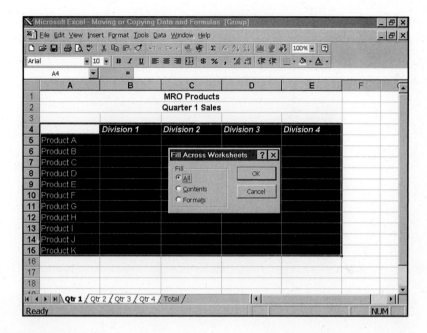

Creating a Custom Fill

If you enter the same series of data, you can create and insert a custom list. Suppose that you enter the same salespeople's names in a worksheet. You can define these names as a list, enter the first name, and then have Excel fill in the rest.

To create the custom list, follow these steps:

1. If you already typed the list in a worksheet, select the list. You then can import the list. Alternatively, you can skip this step and wait until later in this procedure to type the list manually in the Custom Lists tab.

2. Choose Tools, Options.

3. Select the Custom Lists tab.

4. If you selected text in step 1, choose Import. The Import List From Cells text box should list the selected range. You can also type in the range you want to select or click the Collapse Dialog button, select the range containing the list, and then click the Expand Dialog button. Continue with step 5.

   If you didn't select text for step 1, type the list items in the List Entries text box. Press Enter after each entry.

   Figure 26.9 shows the Custom Lists tab after a list has been added to the Custom Lists text box.

Part

VII

Ch

26

FIG. 26.9

The Custom Lists tab after a list has been imported from a worksheet.

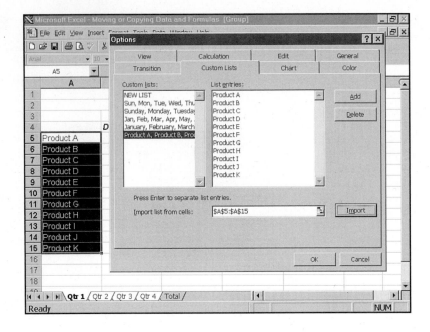

5. To add this list and keep the dialog box open, choose <u>A</u>dd, or choose OK to add the list and close the dialog box.

To insert the list, type the first item in the list and then fill, using the drag-and-drop technique (see Figure 26.10). Or you can enter the first value; select the range you want filled; then choose <u>E</u>dit, Fi<u>l</u>l, <u>S</u>eries. In the Series dialog box, select Auto<u>F</u>ill as the type; then choose OK.

To delete a list item, display the Custom Lists tab. Select the list you want to delete. Then choose <u>D</u>elete. When prompted to confirm the deletion, choose <u>Y</u>es.

Copying by Dragging and Dropping

Using the mouse, you can copy by making a selection and dragging the selection to where you want it.

To copy formulas or data with the mouse, perform the following steps:

1. Select the range of cells you want to copy.

2. Hold down the Ctrl key and move the pointer over an edge of the selection. The pointer becomes an arrow with a + (plus) sign.

3. Continue holding down Ctrl as you drag the edge of the selection to where you want the copy. The copy's location appears enclosed by a wide gray border, as shown in Figure 26.11.

4. When the gray border is where you want the copy, release the mouse button first, and then release the Ctrl key.

FIG. 26.10
Filling in a custom list.

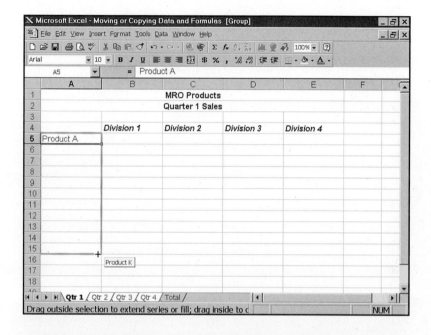

FIG. 26.11
Use Ctrl+drag to drag copies to a new location. The plus sign next to the arrow tells you that you are copying (rather than moving).

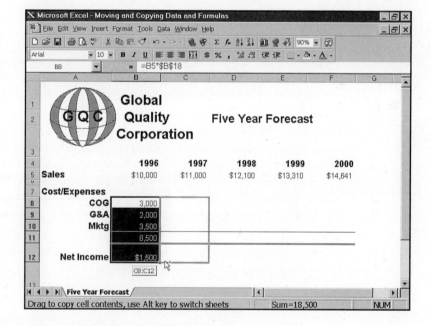

Using the drag-and-drop method, you can make only a single copy. You cannot copy to multiple locations or fill a range. See some of the preceding mouse shortcuts if you need to perform this kind of copy.

If you release the Ctrl key before you release the mouse button, the copy operation becomes a move operation; the plus sign next to the arrow disappears. You can press Ctrl again to switch back to a copy operation. As long as you don't release the mouse button, you can change your mind about whether to copy or move the selection.

Copying with Commands

Copying works well for duplicating values or formulas to cells that are not adjacent to the original cell. Copying adjusts formulas to the new locations.

 TIP As you copy, check the size of the range you are copying by watching the reference area to the left of the formula bar.

To copy a cell or range to a new location, perform the following steps:

1. Select the cell or range of cells you want to copy.
2. Either choose Edit, Copy, click the Copy button on the Standard toolbar, or press Ctrl+C. The cells to copy are surrounded by a marquee.
3. Select the cell at the top-left corner of where you want the duplicate to appear. Check to see whether other cell contents will be overwritten. If needed, cells will be overwritten; see the following section on inserting copied cells.
4. Either choose Edit, Paste, click the Paste button, or press Ctrl+V to paste and retain the copy in memory. Press Enter to paste only one time.

Because you have already established the size and shape of the copied area, you need to indicate only the upper-left corner of the paste location. Selecting the wrong size area into which you are pasting prevents Excel from pasting and displays an alert box.

Pasting Multiple Copies

You can make multiple copies of a range with a single command. Remember to select only the top-left corners of where you want each of the duplicate ranges to go. Figure 26.12 shows the marquee around a copied column of formulas and the top of each column where you are pasting the original column. Notice that pasting in multiple columns is like hanging wallpaper: You need to indicate only where the tops of each roll of wallpaper go; the wallpaper hangs down correctly. Figure 26.13 shows the pasted columns.

Figures 26.14 and 26.15 show how to copy an original row into multiple rows. Notice that only the left cell is selected where each duplicated row will be pasted.

FIG. 26.12
Select the top cell(s) where you want duplicated columns to appear.

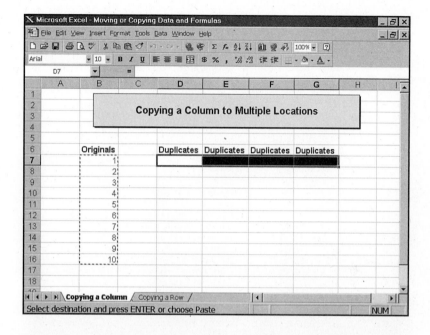

FIG. 26.13
The columns are pasted.

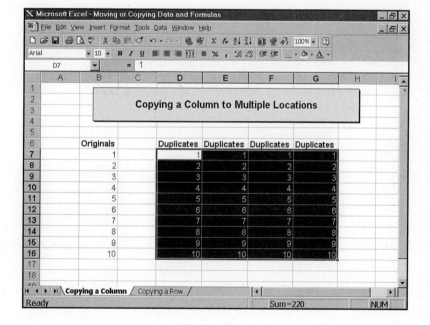

FIG. 26.14

Select the left cells where you want duplicated rows to appear.

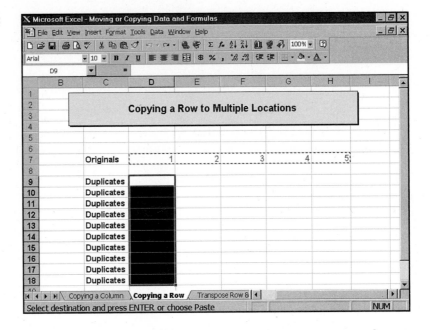

FIG. 26.15

The rows are pasted.

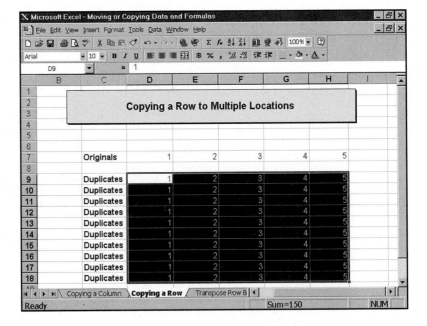

Pasting Nonadjacent Multiple Copies

Well-formatted worksheets may interfere with some of the previous methods of copying or filling formulas into a range, because worksheets may need blank rows or columns as separators for appearance. These blank rows and columns, however, prevent filling data with a single command.

Using *noncontiguous selections* (selected cells that are not adjacent), such as the selections shown in Figure 26.16, you can paste multiple copies even if the areas into which you are pasting are not adjacent.

FIG. 26.16

You can paste into multiple areas even if they aren't next to each other.

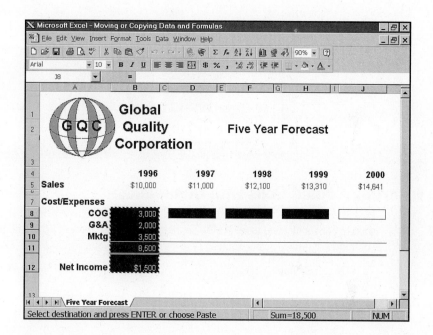

To paste into nonadjacent areas, perform the following steps:

1. Select the cells or ranges you want to copy.
2. Either choose Edit, Copy, click the Copy button, or press Ctrl+C.
3. Select the top-left corner where you want each copy to paste. With the mouse, hold down the Ctrl key as you click each cell to receive a pasted copy.

   With the keyboard, move to the first cell to receive a copy and press Shift+F8 so that the ADD indicator appears in the status bar. Move to the next cell to receive data and press Shift+F8 until ADD disappears and then reappears. Move to the next cell, and so on.
4. Either choose Edit, Paste, click the Paste button, or press Ctrl+V.

Notice that the target cells are separated by blank columns. Figure 26.17 shows the result of the paste operation.

FIG. 26.17

Pasted data is entered in nonadjacent ranges.

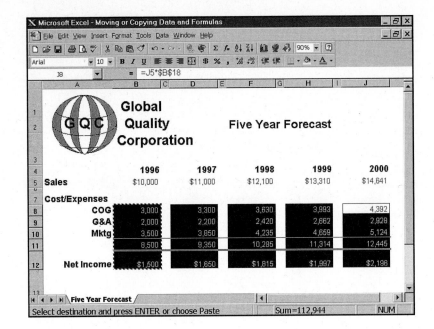

Inserting Copied Cells with Commands

Pasted cell contents usually replace the cell contents they paste over. In some cases, you may want to copy and paste to insert the copied material into the worksheet so that existing cell contents are moved aside. You can perform this technique by choosing Insert, Copied Cells.

To copy and then insert cells or a range of cells into another location, perform the following steps:

1. Select the cells or range of cells you want to copy.
2. Choose Edit, Copy.
3. Select the cell at the top left of where you want to insert your copies.
4. Choose Insert, Copied Cells.

    If Excel needs information about which direction to shift existing cells, the Insert Paste dialog box shown in Figure 26.18 appears.
5. Select the Shift Cells Right option if you want cells being pasted over to move right. Select the Shift Cells Down option if you want cells being pasted over to move down.
6. Choose OK.

 You must recopy the original data each time before you insert copied cells.

FIG. 26.18

Select which way you want to shift existing cells.

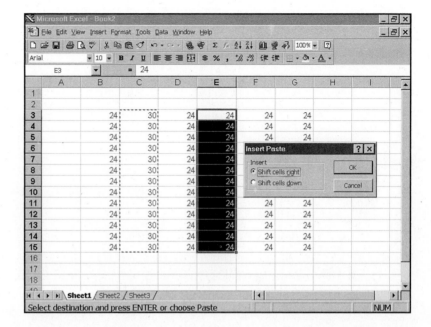

You cannot perform an Insert Paste over the original data. You also cannot perform an Insert Paste so that the original data is forced to move. If you attempt an illegal paste, Excel displays an alert box.

Copying Data Across a Workbook

To copy a cell or range to a new location, perform the following steps:

1. Select the cell or range of cells you want to copy.

2. Either choose Edit, Copy, click the Copy button, or press Ctrl+C. The cells to copy appear, surrounded by a marquee.

3. Select the worksheet to which you want to move data.

4. Select the cell at the top-left corner of where you want the duplicate to appear.

5. Either choose Edit, Paste, click the Paste button, or press Ctrl+V to paste and retain the copy in the Clipboard. Press Enter to paste one time.

The range is pasted in the new worksheet. Keep in mind that the formula references are adjusted to refer to the new location, and absolute references refer to the same cells. For 3-D moves, you may need to insert the sheet name as part of the reference. See Chapter 24 for more information on cell references.

Part

VII

Ch

26

Pasting Formats, Values, or Transposed Data

The Edit, Paste Special command is handy when copying and pasting part of a cell's attributes, such as the format or value, but not both. With this command, you can reorient database layouts into worksheet layouts and vice versa. The command also enables you to combine the attributes of cells by pasting them together. This feature is useful when you need to combine or consolidate different parts of a worksheet.

 TIP   To copy formats, select the cells with the formats that you want to copy. Click the Format Painter button on the Standard toolbar. Then select the range to copy the formats to.

To use Edit, Paste Special for any of its many operations, perform the following steps:

1. Select the cell or range of cells.

2. Choose Edit, Copy or click the Copy button.

3. Select the upper-left corner of where you want to paste.

    When transposing (flipping) rows and columns, be sure to consider which cells are covered when the pasted area is rotated 90 degrees.

4. Choose Edit, Paste Special to display the Paste Special dialog box, shown in Figure 26.19.

FIG. 26.19

Select what to paste, all operations to perform, and whether to skip blanks or transpose the data in the Paste Special dialog box.

If a Paste Special dialog box that shows a Data Type list appears, the last copy you completed was from an application other than Excel. Return to step 1 to copy and paste within Excel.

5. Select the characteristics you want transferred:

Option	Function
All	Transfers all the original contents and characteristics.
Formulas	Transfers only the formulas.
Values	Transfers only the values and formula results. This option converts formulas to values.
Formats	Transfers only the cell formats.

Comments	Transfers only note contents.
Validation	Copies data validation rules.
All Except Borders	Transfers everything except any borders applied to the selected range.

6. Select from the dialog box how you want the transferred characteristics or information combined with the cells being pasted into:

Option	**Function**
None	Replaces the receiving cell.
Add	Adds to the receiving cell.
Subtract	Subtracts from the receiving cell.
Multiply	Multiplies by the receiving cell.
Divide	Divides into the receiving cell.

7. Select the Skip Blanks check box if you do not want to paste blank cells on top of existing cell contents.

8. Select the Transpose check box to change rows to columns or to change columns to rows.

9. Choose OK.

By copying the range of formulas you want to freeze, you can convert formulas into their results so that they do not change. After copying, without moving the active cell, use Paste Special with the Values and None check boxes checked to paste the values over the original formulas.

The Transpose option in the Paste Special dialog box can save time and work if you use database information in worksheets or worksheet data in a database.

The Transpose option rotates a range of cells between row orientation and column orientation, which is useful for switching between a database row layout and a worksheet column layout. You cannot transpose over the range that contains the original data. Figure 26.20 shows an original range on the left and its transposition on the right.

The Paste Link button in the Paste Special dialog box enables you to link the pasted data to the original source. Chapter 40 covers linking data.

TROUBLESHOOTING

The Paste command is not available. You haven't selected anything to paste. You must select the range and choose Edit, Copy or Edit, Cut. Then the Paste command is available.

Nothing happens when I drag. Drag and drop may not be enabled. Choose Tools, Options. Select the Edit tab; then select the Allow Cell Drag and Drop option. Choose OK.

▶ **See** "Entering Formulas," **p. 568**

Part
VII

Ch
26

FIG. 26.20

Transposing changes rows to columns or vice versa.

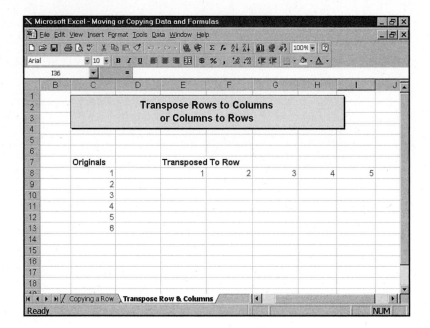

Inserting and Removing Sheets

As you create and revise workbooks, you will want to insert and remove sheets for the same reasons you insert and remove sheets in a manual workbook. You may need to add a new worksheet for data you want to include in the workbook, or you may have included a worksheet you no longer need. The following section shows how to perform these tasks with Excel.

Inserting a Sheet

In workbooks with many sheets, you may want to use more than the three that are created by default. You can insert a new sheet in the workbook at any location you want.

To insert a sheet into your workbook, follow these steps:

1. Activate the workbook into which you want to insert the sheet.

2. Select the existing sheet before which you want the new sheet inserted by clicking its sheet tab at the bottom of the workbook, or by pressing Ctrl+PgUp or Ctrl+PgDn.

3. Choose the Insert, Worksheet command.

TIP   You can also use these keyboard shortcuts: Press Shift+F11 to insert a new worksheet; F11 to insert a new chart sheet; or Ctrl+F11 to insert a new Excel 4.0 macro sheet.

N O T E You can use a shortcut menu to insert new sheets. Point to the selected sheet tab and click the right mouse button. Choose Insert, and when the Insert dialog box appears, choose Worksheet, Chart, MS Excel 4.0 Macro, or MS Excel 5.0 Dialog. ▨

You can insert several sheets of the same type at once. Group several adjacent sheets and then follow the preceding step 3 to insert the sheets. The number of sheets inserted equals the number in your group. If you grouped two existing sheets, for example, two new sheets are inserted.

Also, if you want to add a sheet to the end of the workbook, you have to insert it before an existing sheet and then move the new sheet to the end.

Removing a Sheet

If your workbook includes too many sheets, you can delete the ones that you don't need. For example, if you use only two sheets in the workbook, but the workbook contains three, you can delete the unused blank sheet. Keep in mind that if you delete a sheet that contains data, you lose all that data. Also, you cannot undo a sheet deletion. Therefore, be sure that you really want to delete the sheet. Also, be sure that none of the data in the worksheet that you are deleting is referenced by another worksheet in the workbook.

To remove a sheet from a workbook, follow these steps:

1. Select the sheet you want to delete.
2. Choose Edit, Delete Sheet.

N O T E To delete the sheet using a shortcut menu, point to its selected sheet tab, click the right mouse button, and then choose Delete. ▨

You can delete several sheets at once by grouping sheets and then following the preceding step 2. ●

Part

VII

Ch

26

CHAPTER 27

Creating Templates and Controlling Excel's Startup

Creating Workbook and Worksheet Templates

After you use Excel a while, you may find yourself making repetitive "housekeeping" changes to every document you open. Perhaps you don't like Excel's default page header, or you are always applying the currency number format to the entire workbook. By creating a special document called a *template*, you can tell Excel to incorporate these preferences in new worksheets, freeing you to focus on the task at hand.

Templates are also useful when you repeatedly create worksheets that incorporate the same data, such as labels and summary formulas. In organizations that use Excel extensively, templates can enhance accuracy and compliance with internal design standards.

If you work often with a certain document or group of documents, you may find it useful to move these files to an Excel startup folder so that Excel opens the files automatically. Finally, you can create macros and Visual Basic for Applications modules that run when Excel starts or when you open a given document.

Understanding the Concept of Templates

A template is a file used as a form to create other workbooks. Documents created from a template contain the same layout, text, data formulas, settings, styles, formats, names, macros, worksheet controls, and Visual Basic modules as the features you find in the template.

Each workbook created from a template is a repeated image of others from the template. Templates are useful for forms, such as data entry and expense accounts, or for ensuring consistency in departmental budget presentations.

A template differs from ordinary workbooks in two fundamental respects:

- Opening a template opens a replica of the template, rather than the physical template document.
- Template files use an XLT extension.

These two exceptions aside, a workbook template is like any other workbook.

Using Excel's Built-In Templates

To help get you started with templates, Excel includes several ready-to-use template files. You can use these templates to get an idea of what you can do with templates. If the templates are suited for your needs, you can use them without having to bother with creating your own. You can also customize a template so that it contains information specific to your company or business. For example, if you create invoices, you can use the Invoice template rather than create your own.

To preview and open a predefined template, follow these steps:

1. Choose File, New. Excel displays the New dialog box.
2. Choose the Spreadsheet Solutions tab. You see the templates provided with Excel.

3. To see a preview of a template, select it in the dialog box. Excel displays a preview of the selected template (see Figure 27.1).

4. If you want to use the template, choose OK.

FIG. 27.1
You can use one of the predefined templates provided with Excel.

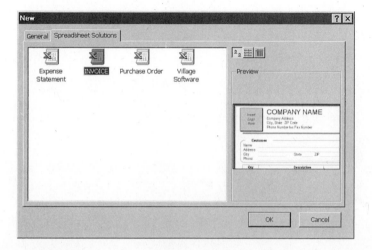

Excel displays the template on-screen. As you can see in the Invoice template shown in Figure 27.2, a template can include text, labels, formatting, formulas, and toolbars. You replace the existing information with information specific to your company. You can then save and print the worksheet as you would any regular worksheet.

FIG. 27.2
When you open a template, you see a worksheet with formatting, text, and other options set up by the template.

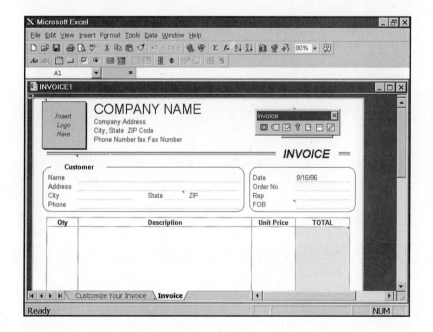

Part
VII

Ch
27

If you find that you use one of Excel's templates over and over again, you can customize it and save your changes. For example, you may want to insert your company logo on the template. Or you may prefer to use a different font. You will definitely want to replace the "filler" information (company name, address, and so on) with your specific information.

To modify a predefined template, follow these steps:

1. Display the template you want to customize.

2. Choose the Customize button.

3. Make any changes to the text or formulas for the template.

   Some templates include buttons that highlight some of the changes you can make. For instance, in the Invoice template in Figure 27.3, you can add a logo or change the font using the template buttons.

FIG. 27.3

You can customize Excel's built-in templates to fit your needs.

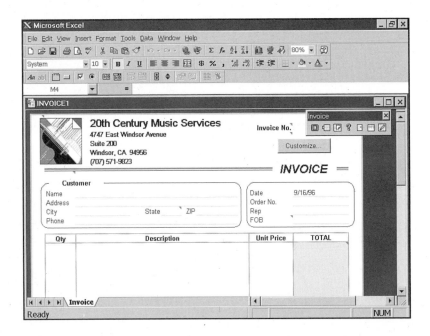

4. When you are finished customizing the template, choose the Lock/Save Sheet button.

5. In the dialog box that appears, select whether you want to lock and save or just lock. Choose OK.

6. If you elected to save the template, type a name and select a folder. Then click the Save button. You see a message stating the template has been saved.

7. Click the OK button. The next time you use this template, your changes will be incorporated.

Creating and Saving a Workbook Template

If none of the predefined templates suits your needs, you can create your own. The phrase "creating a template" is a bit of a misnomer. Actually, you start by creating an Excel worksheet, chart, or other document type. You then add data, formatting, and other desired information to the document. Finally, you save the document as a Template document type.

To create a template, follow these steps:

1. Open or create a workbook that you want the template to use as a pattern. Include the worksheet elements (such as data, formulas, formatting, and controls) you want.
2. Choose File, Save As.
3. Enter the template's name and select the folder in the usual manner.
4. Select the Template (*.xlt) format from the Save as Type list. This step adds an XLT extension (the extension for template documents to the file name).
5. Choose Save.

Excel recognizes the type of document you are saving.

N O T E   Editing a file extension to become XLT doesn't save the file as a template. You must select Template from the Save as Type list in the Save As dialog box. ▧

Creating Workbooks from Templates

Opening a template creates a new document based on the template. The template remains unchanged. The new document has a temporary name. If, for example, the template's file name is DATA.XLT, the documents based on the template are DATA1, DATA2, and so on.

You can make templates readily accessible by saving them in the TEMPLATES folder in the Microsoft Office folder. If you save the template in this folder, the template will appear on the General tab in the new dialog box. You can also choose to display the template on the Spreadsheet Solutions tab by saving the template to the MICROSOFT OFFICE\TEMPLATES\ SPREADSHEET SOLUTIONS folder. To organize your own templates so that they appear on a specific tab in the new dialog box, simply create a folder, ABC CORP. TEMPLATES for example, in the TEMPLATES folder. Then save your templates to that folder.

You can open a template stored in any folder; however, only the templates within the TEMPLATES folder appear in the new dialog box.

N O T E   You can change two important default worksheet attributes without resorting to templates. In the General tab in the Options dialog box, you can change the default number of sheets (Sheets in new Workbook) and the standard font (Standard Font). ▧

Creating Autotemplates

To change Excel's default font, formatting, protection, or other workbook attributes, create an *autotemplate*. You could, for example, create a workbook autotemplate with a footer that includes your name or the current date. If you then save the autotemplate in the XLSTART folder, it serves as the basis for all new workbooks you create. The autotemplate actually controls both the look and the contents of all new workbooks.

To create a workbook autotemplate, follow these steps:

1. Open or create a workbook that you want to use as the pattern for all new workbooks. Include the data, formulas, and formatting you want.

2. Choose File, Save As.

3. In the File name box, type **BOOK**.

4. Select the Template format from the Save as Type list. This step adds an XLT extension to the file name and changes the file's format.

5. In the list box, select the XLSTART folder, which is in the EXCEL folder.

6. Choose Save.

Now, whenever you create a new workbook (either by clicking the new Workbook button or choosing File, New), that new workbook uses the options and formatting you created in the autotemplate.

At this point, you should review the key differences between ordinary templates and autotemplates:

- Ordinary templates can be useful regardless of where they are saved or how they are named. However, you must save a template in the TEMPLATES folder if you want it to appear in the new dialog box when you choose File, New.

- An autotemplate, in general, is only useful if you save it as a template in the XLSTART folder within the EXCEL folder. With that done, creating a new workbook opens a copy of the autotemplate. It isn't necessary to display the new dialog box.

Editing Templates

From time to time, naturally, you may want to revise your templates to reflect changes in your preferences. You can edit templates as you edit ordinary workbooks.

To open a template to edit the template document, follow these steps:

1. Choose File, Open or click the Open button.
2. In the Open dialog box, change to the folder that contains the template. Then select the template you want to edit.
3. Choose Open.

After you edit the template, save by choosing File, Save. Excel saves the edited document in template format.

Inserting Sheet Templates

For some types of work, you may want to insert a worksheet based on a template into an existing Excel workbook. For example, you may be doing an analysis of a competitor's business. You need a separate analysis sheet for each major division, but you want them all within the same workbook. If you have created an analysis template, then you can open a workbook and insert as many of these blank analysis templates as you need. You can tap into your collection of sheets that you stored as a template in the TEMPLATES folder when inserting new sheets in a workbook.

To insert a sheet from a template into the current workbook, follow these steps:

1. Click the right mouse button on the sheet tab where you want to insert the worksheet, which brings up the sheet tab shortcut menu.
2. Choose Insert. Excel displays the Insert dialog box.
3. Select the template whose sheet you want to insert.
4. Choose OK.

Figure 27.4 shows a tracking sheet inserted from a template.

CAUTION

When you insert sheets from a template, Excel inserts all sheets in that template. This insertion can get messy if the template you select contains several sheets. For this reason, delete all blank sheets from workbook templates.

FIG. 27.4

The tracking sheet is inserted from the TRACKER.XLT template.

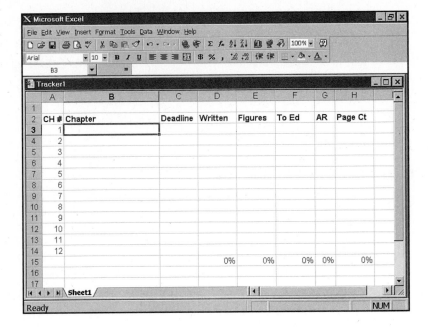

TROUBLESHOOTING

A template was created, but rather than creating a workbook with the name of the template followed by the letter "I" when opened, Excel opens the actual template document. You must have neglected to change the document type in the Save As dialog box when you first saved the template. Choose File, Save As, select Template from the Save as Type list, then choose Save.

After creating an autotemplate, every time Excel starts, it creates a workbook with the name of the template followed by the letter "I." You probably saved the autotemplate as a regular Excel workbook in the XLSTART folder. Choose File, Save As, and save the workbook as a template document.

Starting Excel with a Group of Workbooks

If you frequently work with a group of several workbooks, you can save the entire group as a *workspace file*. A workspace file is a special file that essentially contains a list of workbooks. By opening the workspace file, you open all the associated workbooks, which occupy the same window positions as when you last saved them.

To save a group of open workbooks as a workspace file, follow these steps:

1. Close all workbook files that you do not want to include in the workspace file.

2. Arrange the remaining workbooks any way you want. When you save a group of files as a workspace, you also save the arrangement of the workbooks (as shown in Figure 27.5).

FIG. 27.5

If you save this group of open workbooks as a workspace file named BUDGETS, you can later open them as a group by opening BUDGETS.XLW.

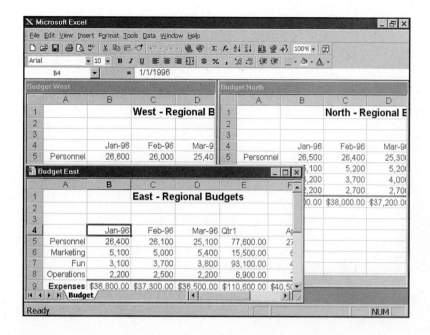

3. Choose File, Save Workspace. Excel displays the Save Workspace dialog box.

4. Enter the file name in the File name box. If necessary, select the folder in the list box.

5. Choose OK.

CAUTION

Be careful not to move files included in a workspace file to other folder locations. If you do, Excel will not be able to find them.

Printing Worksheets

Printing with Excel

Excel enables you to use the full capabilities of your printer. Excel reports printed from laser printers can look as though they have been typeset.

Figures 28.1 and 28.2 give you some idea of what you can produce. Excel can produce the equivalent of preprinted invoices or annual report-quality financial statements.

FIG. 28.1

You can produce presentation-quality reports from an Excel worksheet.

LaserPro Corporation
Balance Sheet
December 31, 1996

Assets

	This Year	Last Year	Change
Current Assets			
Cash	$247,886	$126,473	96%
Accounts receivable	863,652	524,570	65%
Inventory	88,328	65,508	35%
Investments	108,577	31,934	240%
Total current assets	$1,308,443	$748,485	75%
Fixed Assets			
Machinery and equipment	$209,906	$158,730	32%
Vehicles	429,505	243,793	76%
Office furniture	50,240	36,406	38%
(Accumulated depreciation)	(101,098)	(64,394)	57%
Total fixed assets	$588,553	$374,535	57%
Total Assets	**$1,896,996**	**$1,123,020**	**69%**

Liabilities and Shareholders' Equity

	This Year	Last Year	Change
Current Liabilities			
Accounts payable	$426,041	$332,845	28%
Notes payable	45,327	23,486	93%
Accrued liabilities	34,614	26,026	33%
Income taxes payable	88,645	51,840	71%
Total current liabilities	$594,627	$434,197	37%
Noncurrent Liabilities			
Long-term debt	$488,822	$349,253	40%
Deferred federal tax	147,844	92,101	61%
Total noncurrent liabilities	$636,666	$441,354	44%
Shareholders' Equity			
Common stock	$1,000	$1,000	0%
Retained earnings	664,703	246,469	170%
Total shareholders' equity	$665,703	$247,469	169%
Total Liabilities and Equity	**$1,896,996**	**$1,123,020**	**69%**

FIG. 28.2

What you see on-screen and in the print preview window shows you exactly how your printed page will appear.

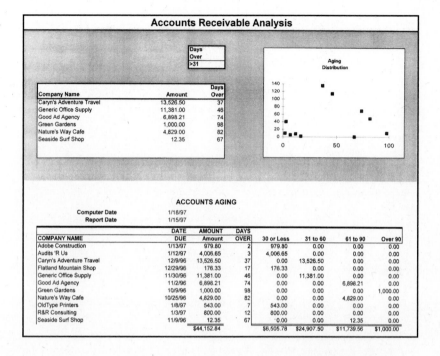

Excel saves you from the trial and error process of printing to see your results. Instead, you can preview the printed page on-screen before you send it to the printer. You also can adjust margins and column widths in the preview.

When you have many different reports or *views* to print from a worksheet, you can use the View, Custom Views command to assign a name and print settings to each different view. If your work involves multiple sheets or views that need to be printed in sequence, including sequential page numbers, use the Report Manager. The Report Manager enables you to list the different views and scenarios that you want printed. These views and scenarios are then printed as a single document. The Report Manager is described near the end of this chapter.

Defining the Page Setup

The File, Page Setup command controls all the settings you usually need in order to print. A few items controlled from the Page Setup dialog box include the position of print on the page (centered left to right, or top to bottom), paper orientation (Portrait or Landscape), headers and footers, gridlines, color or black and white, and row and column headings.

To change the page setup for the printed page, complete the following steps:

1. Choose File, Page Setup.
2. Change the page options as needed in the Page Setup dialog box (see Figure 28.3). The following sections describe these options in more detail. (Notice that the Page Setup

dialog box opens with whatever tab was last used as the active tab; it will not always open with the Page tab active, as shown in Figure 28.3.)

3. When you've set the options, choose the OK button.

FIG. 28.3

Use the Page Setup dialog box to set options for page orientation, paper size, margins, headers and footers, and the printing range for the spread-sheet.

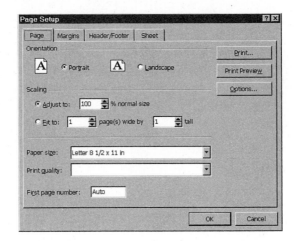

The options available in the Page Setup dialog box are grouped into separate options tabs—Page, Margins, Header/Footer, and Sheet. Usually, you need to set options on several of these tabs to set up the page.

- The Page tab enables you to select the paper size, the print quality, and the page orientation. The Page tab of the Page Setup dialog box also enables you to reduce or enlarge the size of the report or sheet that you are printing.

- The Margins tab enables you to set the top, bottom, left, and right margins for the printed page, and enables you to select how far from the top or bottom edge of the page the headers or footers are printed. The Margins tab also enables you to select whether the printed page should be centered vertically or horizontally, or both.

- The Header/Footer tab enables you to choose the content of the headers and footers that are printed on each page. The Header/Footer tab also enables you to create custom headers and footers.

- The Sheet tab enables you to set the print area, the print titles, and the order in which pages are printed. The options on the Sheet tab also enable you to choose whether to print gridlines, comments, change colors to black and white, or print row and column headings. You can also use the Sheet tab to select draft quality printing.

The remaining parts of this section describe how to use the Page, Margins, Header/Footer, and Sheet tabs to accomplish specific tasks.

Setting the Paper Margins

Excel's character width changes with each different font size. Consequently, you need to measure your margins in inches rather than by a count of characters. Table 28.1 shows the default settings for margins.

Table 28.1 Default Margin Settings

Margin	Default in Inches
Left	0.75
Right	0.75
Top	1
Bottom	1

Measure the margins from the edge of the paper inward. When you set the top and bottom margins, keep in mind that headers and footers automatically print 1/2 inch from the top or bottom of the paper, unless you change the header or footer distance from the edge of the page.

Many laser printers are unable to print to the edge of the paper. Because of this limitation, you may not be able to set margins of less than 1/4 inch. Many inkjet printers also cannot print to the edge of the paper and limit the left and right margins to a minimum of 1/4 inch, while the top and bottom margins are limited to a minimum of 1/2 inch.

To set or change the margins, follow these steps:

1. In the Page Setup dialog box, select the Margins tab to bring the margins options forward (see Figure 28.4).

FIG. 28.4

Adjust the margin settings in the Margins tab of the Page Setup dialog box.

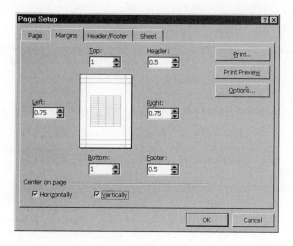

2. Set the margins options in any combination. The following table describes the available options (remember that distances are measured in inches):

Option	Effect
Top	Sets the size of the top margin.
Bottom	Sets the size of the bottom margin.
Left	Sets the size of the left margin.
Right	Sets the size of the right margin.
Header	Sets the distance from the top edge of the page at which any header will print.
Footer	Sets the distance from the bottom edge of the page at which any footer will print.
Horizontally	Centers the spreadsheet horizontally on the printed page.
Vertically	Centers the spreadsheet vertically on the printed page.

The Preview area shows how the changes you make in the margins affect the printed page.

3. Choose OK if you have finished making changes to the Page Setup options.

Setting the Page Orientation and Paper Size

If the spreadsheet document is wider than it is tall, you may want to use a landscape orientation when you print. (*Landscape* means printing across the long edge of the page. *Portrait* means printing down the long edge of the page.) Alternatively, if your printer can handle different paper sizes, you may want to print some documents on legal-sized paper (or some other size paper) rather than the standard letter-sized documents.

To change the page orientation and paper size, select the Page tab in the Page Setup dialog box to display the page options. Then in the Orientation area of the Page options, select Portrait or Landscape, as desired.

To change the paper size, select the Page tab in the Page Setup dialog box, and then use the Paper Size drop-down list to select the desired paper size. The choice of paper sizes available to you depends on the printer you have selected.

Turning Gridlines and Row or Column Headings On and Off

For most printed reports, you don't want to print gridlines or the row and column headings. If you turn off gridlines in the worksheet by using the Tools, Options command, the gridlines turn off for printed copies. You also can turn on or off the printing of gridlines in the Page Setup dialog box. To turn on or off printing gridlines or row and column headings, follow these steps:

1. In the Page Setup dialog box, select the Sheet tab (see Figure 28.5).

FIG. 28.5
Modify the print titles, print options, and page order settings in the Page Setup dialog box.

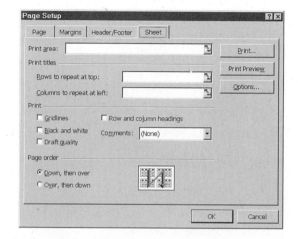

2. Set or clear the <u>G</u>ridlines check box in the Print area to turn on or off gridline printing.

3. Set or clear the Row and Column Headings check box in the Print area to turn on or off printing the row and column headings.

4. Choose OK when you finish making changes to the Page Setup options.

You probably will want to print row and column headings when you print worksheet documentation showing formulas or when you print notes entered in cells in your spreadsheet. If you use the <u>T</u>ools, <u>O</u>ptions command, select the View tab (if not already selected), and choose the For<u>m</u>ulas check box, you can display the formulas on-screen so that they print.

Creating Headers and Footers

You can create headers and footers that place a title, date, or page number at the top or bottom of each printed page of your worksheet. You also can format them with different fonts, styles, and sizes. Use headers and footers to enter a confidentiality statement, to document the worksheet's creator, to show the printout date, or to note the source of worksheet and chart data.

By default, Excel uses no header or footer. You can add headers and footers, as the following information explains.

Headers and footers always use a 3/4-inch (.75) side margin and a default 1/2-inch (.5) margin at the top and bottom. You can change the distance of the header or footer from the top or bottom edge of the page; follow the instructions on changing margins in the preceding part of this section. If you specify page setup margins that cross the header and footer boundaries, the document may print over a header or footer.

To create or change a header or footer, use the Page Setup dialog box. Open the Page Setup dialog box by choosing the <u>F</u>ile, Page Set<u>u</u>p command. In the Page Setup dialog box, select the Header/Footer tab to display the header and footer options, which are shown in Figure 28.6. The Header/Footer tab displays a sample of the currently selected header and footer.

Part
VII

Ch
28

Excel provides several predefined formats for the headers and footers. To select one of the predefined header or footer formats, use the Header or Footer drop-down lists, and choose the desired format. The same formats are available for both headers and footers.

You also can create customized headers and footers using special fonts, symbols, and text you type. To create a custom header or footer, follow these steps:

1. In the Page Setup dialog box, select the Header/Footer tab to display the header and footer options (refer to Figure 28.6).

FIG. 28.6
You can add or modify the headers and footers for a printed spreadsheet in the Header/Footer tab of the Page Setup dialog box.

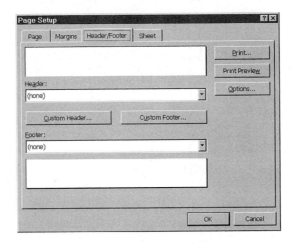

2. Choose the Custom Header button to create a customized header, or choose Custom Footer to create a customized footer. Figure 28.7 shows the Header dialog box as it first appears; the Footer dialog box, except for its title, is identical.

FIG. 28.7
Using both text and codes, you can create a customized header or footer.

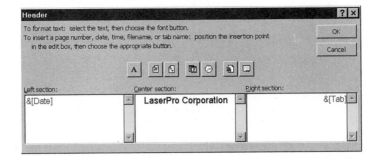

The Header dialog box contains three sections for left-, center-, or right-aligned data. The sections are labeled Left Section, Center Section, and Right Section. You enter text or codes, such as the date code, into the three sections.

3. Enter the text and codes you want for each section of the header or footer. Figure 28.7 shows the Header dialog box with text and code for a custom header.

To enter information into a section with the mouse, click a section and type. Click a code button to enter a code at the insertion point. To format text, select the text and click the Font button to display the font dialog box; select your font formatting options and choose OK. The code buttons and their results are listed in Table 28.2.

To enter information from the keyboard, press Alt+*letter* (the L, C, or R key) to move the insertion point into the corresponding section (Left, Center, or Right). Type the text and codes listed in Table 28.2, or select code buttons by pressing Tab until the button is selected and then pressing Enter. You can create multiple-line headers or footers by pressing Alt+Enter to break a line.

4. Choose OK.

TIP
To find out what an option does in a dialog box, click the Help button (a question mark at the top right corner of the window), and then click the option for which you want help. A pop-up explanation of the option is displayed.

As the following examples illustrate, you can combine the codes shown in Table 28.2 with your own text to create the header and footer you need:

Code:

Left &L&D Page &P of &N

Center &C&&BABC Investment Corp.

Right &RMortgage Banking Div.

Result:

12/24/96 Page 1 of 3 ABC Investment Corp. Mortgage Banking Div.

When you print or preview the document, the result appears. The character-formatting codes cause the text to display with the attributes and fonts you selected; the codes themselves do not display, except when you first type them.

Table 28.2 Header and Footer Codes

Button	Code	Effect
	&[Date]	Calendar: inserts the computer's date.
	&[Time]	Clock: inserts the computer's time.
	&[File]	Excel sheet: inserts the name of the file.
	&[Tab]	Excel Tab: inserts the name of the tab in the workbook.
	&[Page]	Inserts the page number.

Part

VII

Ch

28

continues

Table 28.2 Continued

Button	Code	Effect
[#]	&[Page]+#	Inserts the page number with a modified starting page number. Use the page code with the plus sign (+) to start printing at a page number greater than (by # pages) the actual page number.
[#]	&[Page]-#	Inserts the page number minus an amount you specify (#). Use the page code with the minus sign (–) to start printing at a page number smaller than the actual page number.
[#]	&[Pages]	Inserts the total number of pages. For example, the header Page &P of &N produces the result, Page 6 of 15.
N/A	&&	Prints an ampersand.

By default, headers are printed 1/2 inch from the top of the page, and footers are 1/2 inch from the bottom. If text overlaps the header or footer, use the Margins tab in the Page Setup dialog box to change the top or bottom margin or to change the distance of the header and footer from the edge of the page.

N O T E If you directly type a font name, size, and style, make sure that the font name is in quotation marks and spelled the same as it appears in the Font dialog box. Use TrueType fonts, or use font styles and sizes that are available in your printer. ▪

TROUBLESHOOTING

I can't seem to find a way to change the left and right margin settings for my headers and footers. Headers and footers always use a margin setting of 0.75 inch, regardless of your left and right margin settings in the Margins tab. You can't adjust the margin settings for headers and footers.

The font in my header doesn't match the font in the rest of my printout. If you changed the font you used in your worksheet, the font you use for your headers and footers won't match the worksheet font. To change the font used for the header and footer, choose the Font button in the Header/Footer dialog box and modify the font selections in the Font dialog box that appears.

Specifying the Page Layout Order

When Excel prints a range that is too large to fit on one sheet of paper, it prints down the range, and then goes to the columns to the right of the first page and prints down those. In some cases—wide landscape reports, for example—you may want to print so that Excel prints across the wide range first and then to the next lower area and goes across it.

To select how you want Excel to print pages, select the Sheet tab in the Page Setup dialog box. From the Page Order group, select either the Down, then Over option or the Over, then Down option.

Reducing and Enlarging Prints

If the printer supports scalable type or if you use TrueType fonts, you can print a document proportionally reduced or enlarged. By making a proportional reduction, you can fit a document to a page without losing or redoing the formatting. To scale a document, select the Page tab in the Page Setup dialog box (refer to Figure 28.3) and select the Adjust To option or the Fit To option.

 To print a sheet with the type size large enough to use as a wall chart or presentation poster, use the Fit To or Adjust To options.

Use the Adjust To option to print the document at full size or to scale the document to a specified percentage of full size. Enter the desired size in the Adjust To text box. If you enter a number smaller than 100, the page is reduced to that percentage of the original. If you enter a number larger than 100, the page is enlarged. If the printer is incapable of scaling the print job to fit the page, the Adjust To and Fit To boxes are gray.

Use the Fit To option to tell Excel to scale the document to fit a specified number of pages. In the first text box in the Fit To option, enter the number of page widths you want the document fit to. In the second text box, enter the number of pages tall that you want the document fit to. If you have a document that usually prints three pages wide and two pages tall, for example, and you want to fit it on a single page, you would enter **1** in both the first and second text box.

Printing Color or Black and White

Although worksheets and charts may use color on-screen, you need to make sure that they will look good on your black-and-white printer. Also, colors increase the print time. To substitute grays for colors, white background for patterns, and black text for colored text, select the Sheet tab in the Page Setup dialog box, and then select the Black and White check box.

Setting the Print Quality

For many printers, high quality graphics images and smooth text take quite a while to print. You often can save a great deal of printing time by using a lower printing quality. Some printers have a draft quality setting; for other printers, you select the print quality by choosing the number of dots per inch (dpi) that the printer can print. The higher the number of dpi, the higher the printing quality; a print quality setting of 300 dpi is better than a print quality setting of 150 dpi.

 If you want a draft copy, leave Print Quality (on the Page tab) set to high and select the Draft Quality check box on the Sheet tab.

To change the print quality, select the Page tab in the Page Setup dialog box, and then use the Print Quality drop-down list to select the desired print quality. The choice of print qualities available to you depends on the printer that you have selected. If the printer has only one quality setting, the Print Quality drop-down list is grayed.

Setting the Print Range

By default, Excel prints the entire worksheet unless you specify otherwise. When you need to print only a portion of the worksheet, you must define that area by using either the File, Page Setup command or the File, Print Area command. The print area can include more than one range.

If you have many print ranges on one worksheet, you may want to create named views of these print ranges and settings. You then can print a range with its settings by returning to that view. This feature is especially helpful when you print worksheets and charts on separate sheets. If you have many views that you want to print, even from multiple documents, make sure that you read about the Report Manager, which is described briefly at the end of this chapter and in Chapter 35, "Taking Advantage of Excel's Add-Ins."

N O T E When you work with databases or large worksheets, you may be tempted to put field names or column headings in the header so that you can see the labels on each page of the printout. *Don't!* Labels in the header are difficult to align with columns and cannot be positioned close to the body of the report. Instead, use the options in the Sheet tab of the Page Setup dialog box to set print titles. ▨

Setting a Print Area

The options in the Sheet tab in the Page Setup dialog box control how much of the document is printed; these options also control which cell comments are printed.

To define a single print area, follow these steps:

1. Choose File, Page Setup, and then select the Sheet tab to display the Sheet options in the Page Setup dialog box.

2. Place the insertion point in the Print Area text box.

3. Select the range of cells you want to print.

   Click the Collapse Dialog button to collapse the dialog box, make your selection, and then click the Expand Dialog button again to redisplay the dialog box.

 T I P You can also select the range you want to print and choose the File, Print Area, Set Print Area command to set the print area.

Excel enters the cell coordinates in the Print Area text box as you select the printed area.

4. Choose OK to close the Page Setup dialog box.

To print cell comments in the selected range, open the Comments drop-down list and select one of the two options for printing comments. You also can set the print area by typing the cell coordinates for the top left corner of the print area and the bottom right corner of the print area, separated by a colon, directly into the Print Area text box in the Sheet options of the Page

Setup dialog box. To set a print area to print the first three rows and the first three columns of a worksheet, for example, type **A1:F12** in the Print Area text box.

After you set the print area, Excel marks the edges of the print area with dashed lines. In Figure 28.8, you can see the dashed lines that mark the edges of the print area after the appropriate Page Setup options are chosen. Dashed lines also indicate manual and automatic page breaks. A *page break* indicates the bottom or right edge of the sheet of paper that the document prints on, and shows you where a new printed page begins. See "Setting Manual Page Breaks," later in this chapter, for more information on page breaks.

FIG. 28.8

Dashed lines mark the edges of a print area.

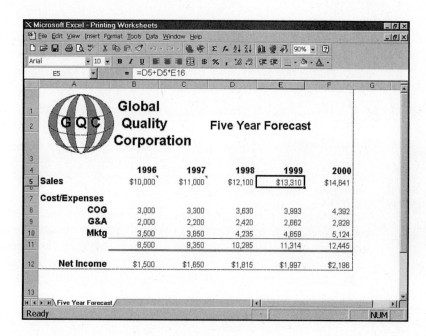

Setting the print area creates a named range called *Print_Area*. You can display this range name and its cell references with the Insert, Name, Define command.

Removing a Print Area

If you want to return to printing the entire worksheet, remove the print area. To remove a print area, choose File, Page Setup, and select the Sheet tab to display the Sheet options. Delete all the text in the Print Area text box to print the entire document, or delete only the cell coordinates for the print area you want to remove. You can also choose File, Print Area, Clear Print Area.

Adjusting How Pages Print

After you select a print area, you may want to make adjustments to fit the information on the page. For example, you may want to change the page breaks to keep related data together. You

Part

VII

Ch

28

also may want to change the margins or font size so that you can fit the information on the page.

When you set a print area with the File, Page Setup command, Excel displays dashed lines to mark the page boundaries and automatic page breaks. Automatic page breaks are determined by how much of the print area you have selected will fit within the printable area of the page.

Setting Manual Page Breaks   Sometimes you may need to insert a manual page break to override an automatic page break. When you insert manual page breaks, the automatic page breaks reposition automatically.

When you choose Insert, Page Break, the manual page breaks appear above and to the left of the active cell. Figure 28.9 shows page breaks above and to the left of the active cell. Manual page breaks appear on-screen with a longer and bolder dashed line than the automatic page breaks. Page breaks are easier to see on-screen when you remove gridlines with the Tools, Options command (clear the check box on the View tab in the Options dialog box).

To insert manual page breaks, move the active cell beneath and to the right of the place you want the break, and then choose Insert, Page Break. If you want to set vertical page breaks (that affect only the sides), make sure that the active cell is in row 1 before you choose the Insert, Page Break command. If you want to set horizontal page breaks (the breaks for only the tops and bottoms of pages), move the active cell to the correct row in column A, and then choose Insert, Page Break.

A manual page break stays at the location that you set until you remove it. Remove manual page breaks by first moving the active cell directly below or immediately to the right of the manual page break. Then choose Insert, Remove Page Break. This command appears on the menu only when the active cell is positioned correctly. Remove all manual page breaks by selecting the entire document and choosing the Insert, Remove Page Break.

N O T E   Be sure that you try to remove only manual page breaks. You can go crazy trying to remove an automatic page break that you mistake for a manual one. ▪

Using the Page Break Preview Command   A new feature in Excel 97 allows you to view your page breaks on-screen and manually adjust them using the mouse. Figure 28.10 shows the worksheet in Figure 28.9 displayed in Page Break Preview view. The page numbers are displayed in gray in the background of the worksheet, and the manually inserted page breaks are represented by solid black lines. Automatic page breaks are represented by a dashed black line, as shown in Figure 28.11.

To adjust a page break in Page Break Preview mode, move the mouse pointer over the page break line you want to adjust and drag the mouse up or down. If the page break is an automatic page break, the dashed line changes to a solid line, indicating that it is now a manual page break. You can also readjust manual page breaks using the same method.

When you drag an automatic page break up in the Page Break Preview screen, the content on the page above the manual page break is reduced, and the automatic page breaks following this page break are automatically readjusted.

FIG. 28.9
Manual page breaks appear above and to the left of the active cell.

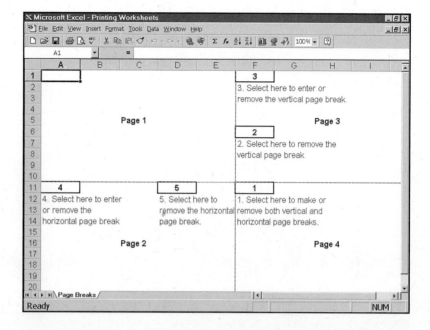

FIG. 28.10
You can preview and adjust page breaks using the View, Page Break Preview command.

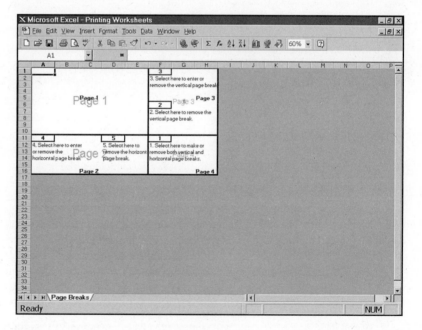

If you drag a page break down in the Page Break Preview screen to fit more on a page, Excel automatically scales down the size of the printout to fit the page contents within the manually selected page break. The entire printout is scaled down, and all of the automatic page breaks are readjusted to reflect the change in scaling.

FIG. 28.11

The Page Break Preview screen and Page tab before the automatic page breaks have been modified.

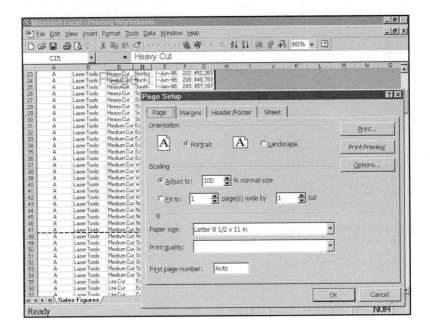

Figure 28.11 shows a worksheet in Page Break Preview mode and the Page tab in the Page Setup dialog box. Notice the automatic page break represented by a dashed line between rows 47 and 48. The Adjust To setting in the Page Setup dialog box is at 100 percent of normal size, which is the default. In Figure 28.12, the page break has been dragged down to row 61, shown as a solid line in the Page Break Preview screen. To fit the additional rows on the page, the printout was scaled down to 78 percent of normal size, as shown in the Page Setup dialog box in Figure 28.12.

To remove all manually inserted page breaks, whether you inserted them using the method described in the section "Setting Manual Page Breaks," earlier in this chapter or by dragging the page break lines in the Page Break Preview view, click the gray box at the intersection of the row and column headings (upper-left corner of the worksheet) to select the entire worksheet, and choose Insert, Reset All Page Breaks. If the printout was scaled down to fit more content on a page, the scaling is returned to the default 100 percent setting when you reset the page breaks.

Fitting More Data on a Page   You can fit more information on a page by decreasing the margins, decreasing the column widths or row heights, or choosing a smaller font size. You also can use the fit-to-page feature described in "Reducing and Enlarging Prints" earlier in this chapter.

If you used styles to format a document, you can change fonts throughout the entire worksheet by redefining the style names used in your worksheet. Normal is the style used in cells that have not been formatted. Use a small font size to fit more data on a page. Save the document before you change fonts so that you can return to the original document easily.

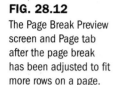

FIG. 28.12
The Page Break Preview screen and Page tab after the page break has been adjusted to fit more rows on a page.

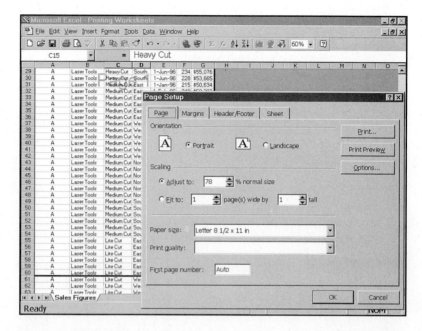

Smaller margins produce more room on the paper. Again, some laser and inkjet printers can print only within 1/4 inch of the paper's edge.

You also can narrow columns and reduce row height to fit more data on a page. To make sure that all adjustments are the same, select multiple columns before you narrow a column. All the columns will reduce simultaneously.

To fit more of a document on the page, you also can use the Adjust To option or the Fit To option found on the Page tab of the Page Setup dialog box. You can also adjust the automatic page breaks in the Page Break Preview screen. The Fit To and Adjust To options are described earlier in this chapter in "Defining the Page Setup," and the Page Break Preview screen is discussed in the previous section.

Setting Multiple Print Areas

Excel can print multiple ranges with a single print command. Although these ranges print sequentially, each range prints on its own sheet.

To select multiple print areas, follow these steps:

1. Choose File, Page Setup, and select the Sheet tab.

2. Place the insertion point in the Print Area text box.

3. Select the first area you want to print (drag the Page Setup dialog box out of the way, if necessary).

   Excel enters the cell coordinates for the selected area in the Print Area text box of the Sheet tab.

4. Type a comma (,) in the Print Area text box, and select the next area you want to print. Select areas in the order that you want them to print.

5. Repeat step 4 until you have selected all the areas you want to print.

6. Choose OK.

This technique works well for creating a single printed report from different areas of a worksheet. Each print area prints on a separate page.

You can also set multiple print ranges by typing the cell coordinates for the top left corner and bottom right corner of each print area (separated by a colon) directly into the Print Area text box in the Sheet tab of the Page Setup dialog box. Separate each set of coordinates for the different print ranges with a comma. For example, typing **$A$1:$C$3,$A$10:$C$13** in the Print Area text box sets two print ranges. The first is for the first three rows and columns of the worksheet, and the second print area contains the first three columns of rows 10 through 13 of the worksheet.

N O T E   If you frequently print the same parts of a document, save time by learning the View, Custom Views command. The Custom Views command enables you to assign names to print settings and frequently printed ranges. To print multiple views or to print the same output with different sets of input data, learn about the Report Manager at the end of this chapter. The View, Custom Views command is described in Chapter 33, "Managing the Worksheet Display."

TROUBLESHOOTING

I get only one print area whenever I try to select multiple print areas. Be sure to type a comma in the Print Area text box in between print areas. If you do not type the comma, Excel assumes that you are redefining the print area(s) and replaces the existing print area with the single new selection.

I get only one print area when I try to add another print area to an existing print area. To add one or more new print areas to an existing print area, type a comma at the end of the list of cell coordinates already in the Print Area text box *before* you select the additional print area(s). Otherwise, Excel assumes that you are redefining the print area and replaces the existing print area(s) with the single new selection.

When I set multiple print areas, they print on separate pages. How can I print nonadjacent areas on one page? To print nonadjacent areas on one page, one workaround is to hide the rows and columns that separate the areas and print them as one print area. Another trick is to copy the nonadjacent areas and place them next to each other on another part of your worksheet and select pasted copies as one print area.

▶ **See** "Saving Frequently Used View and Print Settings," **p. 804**

Printing Titles

If printed titles are repeated on each page, they can make large worksheet or database print-outs easier to read. When the worksheet is wider than one page, for example, you can repeat row titles along the left margin of each page. You can repeat column titles at the top of each page of a database that spans multiple pages. The Sheet options available through the File, Page Setup command specifies that selected rows or columns will print at the top or left side of each printed page.

To specify titles, complete the following steps:

1. Choose File, Page Setup, and then select the Sheet tab to display the Sheet options.

2. Place the insertion point in the Rows to Repeat at Top text box or the Columns to Repeat at Left text box, depending on whether you are setting row or column titles.

3. Select the row(s) or columns(s) of titles you want on each page. The rows or columns must be adjacent.

4. Choose OK.

To display the currently selected titles, press the Goto key (F5) and select Print_Titles. To delete Print_Titles, choose the File, Page Setup command, select the Sheet tab, and then clear the Rows to Repeat at Top and Columns to Repeat at Left text boxes.

You don't have to limit yourself to one row or column of titles. As long as the title rows or columns are adjacent, you can include as many as you want.

Previewing the Document

Instead of printing out your worksheet to check its appearance, you can view a display of the printout with miniature pages (see the page shown in Figure 28.13). When you want to examine a preview page up close, you can zoom into the area you want to see.

To preview pages, choose File, Print Preview or click the Print Preview button. The preview screen shows you how the pages will look when printed.

To zoom into a portion of the page, choose the Zoom button or click the mouse pointer— magnifying glass— over the portion that you want to magnify. Use the cursor keys or scroll bars to move around in the zoomed-in view. Figures 28.14 and 28.15 show the zoom-in and zoom-out views of the document. To zoom out, choose Zoom a second time, or click a second time.

To change pages in the preview mode, use the Next or Previous buttons. These buttons appear grayed if there is no next or previous page.

After you preview the worksheet, you can print it from the preview screen by choosing the Print button. If you want to change or see the Page Setup settings, choose the Setup button. To return to the worksheet, choose the Close button. To return to the worksheet and switch to

Part
VII

Ch
28

either Normal view or Page Break Preview view (whichever view was not selected when you opened the Print Preview screen), choose either the Normal Yiew or Page Break Preyiew button.

FIG. 28.13

Previewing enables you to see how the document is positioned on the printed page.

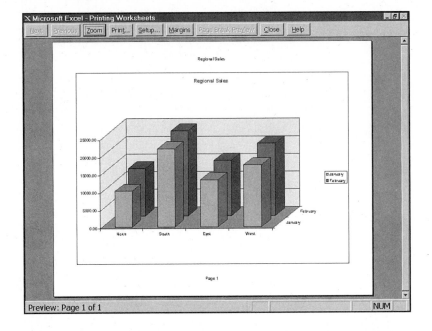

FIG. 28.14

Zoom out of a document when you want to see how your margins and columns look.

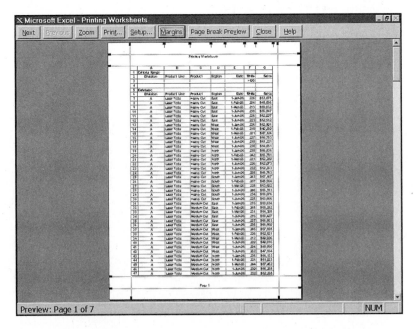

FIG. 28.15

Zoom in for a precise positioning of margins and column widths.

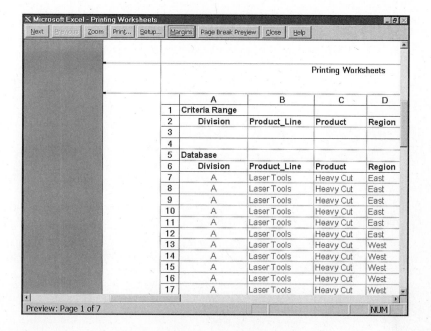

Adjusting Margins and Column Widths While Previewing

You can adjust margins and column widths while in the preview screen. Before adjusting margins with this method, save your document so that you can easily return to the original settings, if needed.

To adjust margins or column widths, complete the following steps:

1. Choose File, Print Preview.

2. Choose the Margins button. Column and margin markers appear on the preview page in full page view or when zoomed in.

3. Choose the Zoom button or click the magnifying glass pointer to zoom in or out of the preview for more accurate viewing.

4. Drag the margin handles (black squares) or the dotted line to a better position.

5. Drag column handles (black Ts) or the column gridline to adjust column widths.

6. Choose Close to return to the document with these new settings, or choose Print to print the document with these settings.

Figures 28.14 and 28.15, in the preceding section, show column and margin adjustment markers from either a magnified or full view.

Part
VII

Ch
28

Compressing Reports to Fit the Paper Size

You may have faced the problem of adjusting row heights, column widths, or margins so that your document would not have a few columns lapping over to an adjacent page or three lines hanging over at the bottom. With Excel's print-to-fit feature, you can compress a report so that it fits snugly in the space you demand.

Compressing Reports to One Page

The most basic way of using the print-to-fit feature is to compress the report enough so that a few lines from a second page move to the first page. This can turn a two-page report into a single-page report.

Compressing Longer Reports

Long reports can be compressed to prevent the last few lines from dropping over to an additional page.

To compress a tall report that is one page wide and 8 1/4 pages long so that it fits on eight pages, enter the following settings in the Fit To boxes:

> Fit to: 1 pages wide by 8 tall

To print a report that is three pages long but one column too wide so that it fits on three pages, enter the following in the Fit To boxes:

> Fit to: 1 pages wide by 3 tall

Printing Worksheet Data

With Excel, you can select the range of pages and the number of copies that you want to print. In addition, you can preview the printout on-screen before printing to paper.

After you are ready to print, choose File, Print to display the print options in the Print dialog box, as shown in Figure 28.16.

In the Number of Copies text box, enter the number of copies you want to print. Specify the range of pages that you want to print; select the All option to print the entire print area, or select the Page(s) option and enter page numbers in the From and To text boxes.

Specify what you want to print by selecting the Selection, Active Sheets, or Entire Workbook option. Selection prints only the selected cells in the selected worksheets; selecting this option overrides the print area defined in the Page Setup dialog box. Selected areas that are not adjacent are printed on separate pages. Active Sheets prints the defined print areas on each of the selected worksheets; if no print area for a selected sheet is defined, then the entire sheet is printed. Entire Workbook prints all the print areas on all sheets in the workbook; if a sheet in the workbook does not have a defined print area, the entire sheet is printed.

FIG. 28.16

Select the printer you want to use, what you want to print, the number of copies, and whether or not to collate the Print dialog box.

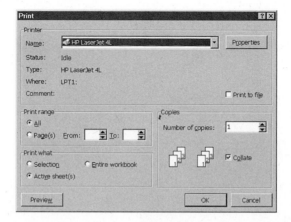

To print comments in the spreadsheet, make sure that one of the options in the Comments drop-down list in the Sheet tab of the Page Setup dialog box is selected. If you want to print cell references along with each comment, also make sure that the Row and Column Headings check box on the Sheet tab of the Page Setup dialog box is selected.

To print, choose the OK button. Make sure that your printer is turned on and is on-line.

Printing Report Manager Reports

The Report Manager automates the printing of worksheets that may have unique print ranges and different sets of input data. The finished product from the Report Manager is a report that appears to have been compiled from one all-encompassing worksheet. Read Chapter 34, "Creating Automatic Subtotals," for helpful tips on building and printing reports.

You can compile, print, and edit sequences of reports with the View, Report Manager command. The individual reports, which are compiled into report sequences, must be created from views of a worksheet and input scenarios. Views include named print areas and their associated print settings. Views are described in Chapter 33, "Managing the Worksheet Display." The Scenario Manager controls multiple sets of data used as inputs for your worksheet.

N O T E The Report Manager is an add-in installed during Excel installation. If you do not see the Report Manager command under the View menu, refer to Chapter 35, "Taking Advantage of Excel's Add-Ins," to learn how to add the Report Manager. ■

The Report Manager enables you to put together a collection of views that print in sequence as one large report. You also can print sequential page numbers. If you also have specified sets of data to be controlled by the Scenario Manager, the reports can print the result from each set of data.

Part

VII

Ch

28

Creating a Sequence of Reports

Before you can create a report, you already must have created the views you want to print. You don't need to create scenarios to use the Report Manager. Follow these steps to create a sequence of reports:

1. Choose View, Report Manager.

   The Report Manager dialog box appears (see Figure 28.17).

FIG. 28.17

Add and print reports in the Report Manager dialog box.

2. Choose the Add button. You see the Add Report dialog box (see Figure 28.18).

FIG. 28.18

Set up a report in the Add Report dialog box.

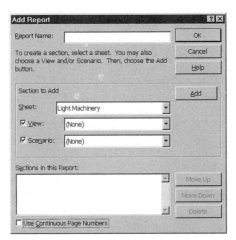

3. Type the name of the report you are creating in the Report Name box.
4. Select the sheet name in the Sheet pull-down list.
5. Select the name of the view from the View pull-down list.
6. Select the name of the scenario from the Scenario pull-down list. You do not need a scenario for a report.

   Enter views and scenarios in the order in which you want them to print in the report. You can reorder items after you have built your list.

7. Choose the Add button to add the view and scenario to the bottom of the Sections in this Report list.

8. If you want the report to print with continuous page numbers, select the Use Continuous Page Numbers check box.

9. Return to step 4 if you want to add more views and scenarios.

10. Choose OK.

Figure 28.19 shows a complete Sections in this Report list. Views appear as the first item followed by the associated scenarios.

FIG. 28.19

A complete Sections in this Report list showing views and scenarios and their order in the report.

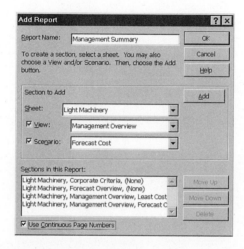

Add Report

Report Name: [Management Summary]

To create a section, select a sheet. You may also choose a View and/or Scenario. Then, choose the Add button.

OK
Cancel
Help

Section to Add   Add

Sheet: [Light Machinery]
☑ View: [Management Overview]
☑ Scenario: [Forecast Cost]

Sections in this Report:

Light Machinery, Corporate Criteria, (None)
Light Machinery, Forecast Overview, (None)
Light Machinery, Management Overview, Least Cost
Light Machinery, Management Overview, Forecast C

Move Up
Move Down
Delete

☑ Use Continuous Page Numbers

Reorganizing Report Sequences

After a sequence of views and scenarios is created, you may need to edit and reorganize it. For example, a client may prefer to see reports printed in a different order, or you may need to add or delete reports.

To edit a report sequence, choose the View, Report Manager command. When the Report Manager dialog box appears, select the report you want to edit in the Reports list and choose the Edit button. When the Add Report dialog box appears, select the view and scenarios you want to change from the Sections in this Report list. To delete a scenario, choose the Delete button. To move the selected item up or down in the list, choose the Move Up or Move Down button. Choose OK when you are finished.

Printing a Report Sequence

You can create several different report sequences. When you are ready to print one of them, complete the following steps:

1. Choose View, Report Manager.

2. Select the name of the report you want to print.

3. Choose the Print button.

4. Enter the number of copies and choose OK.

Part
VII

Ch
28

Using Excel Charts

Creating Charts

Using Excel's Charting Features

Using Excel, you can create charts appropriate for any boardroom presentation. When you analyze a worksheet or database and need to visually present the results, you can use any of Excel's predesigned formats or completely customize the chart by adding text, arrows, titles, and legends as well as changing shading, overlay, patterns, and borders. When you print the chart on a laser printer or plotter, the quality rivals charts created by graphic art firms.

This chapter explains the details of creating a chart. The following two chapters explain how to modify and format charts by using the custom formatting features available for Excel charts. After finishing these three chapters, you will be able to meet the majority of business charting needs. The final two charting chapters show some techniques for creating more complex charts and for using charts and maps to analyze your data.

Figures 29.1 and 29.2 show examples of charts you can create by using Excel. Figure 29.1 shows a chart in its own document. Figure 29.2 illustrates how you can embed charts on a worksheet. Embedded charts display and print with the worksheet.

FIG. 29.1

You can insert an Excel chart on its own sheet, separate from the worksheet you use to create the chart.

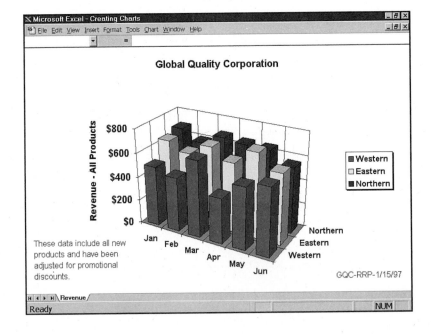

FIG. 29.2

You can embed an Excel chart on a worksheet to enhance the presentation of your data.

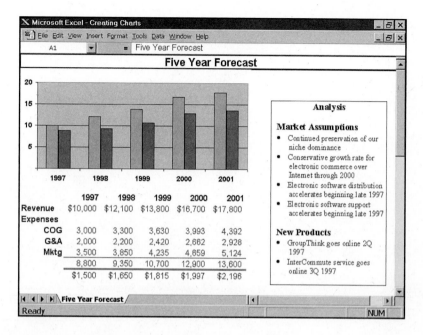

Reviewing the Charting Process

Excel creates charts from data you select. You can use the Chart Wizard to guide you through the process of creating a chart step by step. In many cases, you can have Excel draw a chart for you from the selected data. To draw the chart, the application uses certain rules based on how the data is configured. The data orientation determines which cells are used for the *category axis*, the labels along the bottom or x-axis, and which cells are used for the *legend* labels. In most cases, the rules fit standard data layout, so Excel charts come out correctly without intervention from you. You can customize the chart by using the many chart commands.

You can embed a chart in a worksheet or insert a chart in its own chart sheet. In either case, the chart is linked to the data from which it was created; if the data changes, the chart is automatically updated.

Defining Chart Terms

Excel charts contain many objects that you can select and modify individually. Figure 29.3 shows some of these objects, and Table 29.1 describes each object. When you move your mouse over an object in a chart, a tip appears that identifies the chart object (see Figure 29.3) or displays the series and value if the object is a data point.

FIG. 29.3

An Excel chart is made up of different objects that you can modify and format individually.

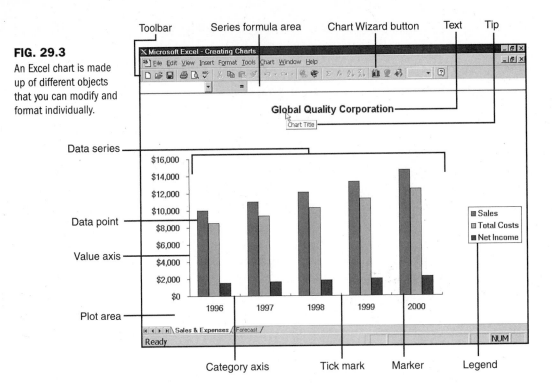

Table 29.1 The Parts of an Excel Chart

Object	Description
Axis	The *category axis* (the horizontal or x-axis along the bottom of most charts, frequently refers to time series) and *value axis* (the vertical or y-axis against which data points are measured) form the boundaries of a chart and contain the scale against which data plots. A z-axis is used for the third dimension on 3-D charts. (Axes for bar charts are reversed. Pie charts have no axes.)
Chart Wizard	Starts the Chart Wizard, which guides you through the creation of a chart.
button	Step-by-step.
Data point	A single piece of data, such as sales for one year.
Data series	A collection of data points, such as sales for the years from 1991 to 1995. In a line chart, all points in a data series are connected by the same line.
Legend	A guide that explains the symbols, patterns, or colors used to differentiate data series. The name of each data series is used as a legend title. You can move legends anywhere on a chart.

Object	Description
Marker	An object that represents a data point in a chart. Bars, pie wedges, and symbols are examples of markers. All the markers that belong to the same data series appear as the same shape, symbol, and color. In 2-D line, bar, column, and XY scatter charts, Excel can use pictures drawn in Windows graphics programs as markers.
Plot area	The rectangular area bounded by the two axes. This area also exists around a pie chart. A pie chart does not exceed the plot area when wedges are extracted.
Series formula	An external reference formula that tells Excel where to look on a specific worksheet to find the data for a chart. You can link a chart to multiple worksheets.
Text	You can edit and move titles (chart, value, and category) and data labels (text associated with data points). Unattached or free-floating text can be moved, and the box containing the text can be resized.
Tick mark	A division mark along the category (X) and value (Y and Z) axes.
Toolbar	A special toolbar is available with charting tools.
Tip	A box that identifies the object that the mouse pointer is pointing to.

Understanding How to Create a Chart

You can create two kinds of charts in Excel—embedded charts and charts that appear in a chart sheet. An embedded chart appears in the worksheet next to tables, calculations, and text. Refer to Figure 29.2 to see an embedded chart. Embedded charts make sense when you want to include a chart side by side with the data for the chart, such as in a report. Before you can embed a chart, you need to decide where the chart will appear. You may need to insert rows, columns, or cells in the worksheet to make room for the chart.

A chart also can appear in its own chart sheet within a workbook if you don't want the chart to appear with its data and you want to be able to work with the chart sheet separately from the data worksheet. When you insert a chart in a sheet, you add the chart to the active workbook and save the chart with the workbook. Charts are named Chart1, Chart2, Chart3, and so on, and can be renamed by choosing Format, Sheet, Rename or by double-clicking the tab for the chart sheet and typing in a new name. If you need to print a chart on its own, for example, to use in a presentation, creating a chart on its own chart sheet is the best approach.

A new option in Excel 97 allows you to attach a data table to a chart, as shown in Figure 29.4. This is an easy and effective way to provide the visual impact of a chart and the detailed information of a table simultaneously. The appended table is linked to the worksheet data so that its values change if you change the values in the source worksheet.

FIG. 29.4

Attaching a data table to a chart gives the user both a detailed and graphical view of the data.

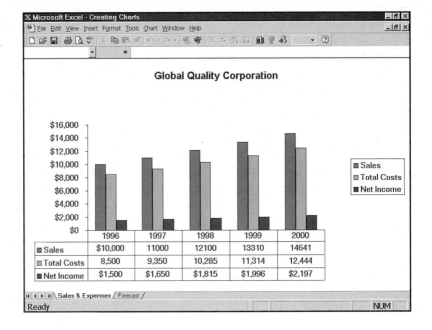

You can easily create both embedded charts and charts in chart sheets by using the Chart Wizard. The Chart Wizard guides you through the process of creating the chart step by step and gives you a preview of the chart before creating it, so that you can make any needed changes.

If you select data and press the F11 key, Excel inserts a chart in a chart sheet, using the default chart type. You then can use the chart commands to modify the chart.

Creating a Chart

The Chart Wizard and Chart menu have been reorganized in Excel 97. The four dialog boxes in the Chart Wizard are now identical to the first four menu items in the Chart menu. This makes it much easier to go back and forth between working with the Chart Wizard and using the Chart commands. In fact, you can use either the Chart Wizard or the Chart menu commands to edit a chart once you have created it. When you are creating a chart, however, the easiest method is to use the mouse and Chart Wizard. The Chart Wizard guides you through the creation process and shows a sample of the chart you are creating, so that you can see the effect of your choices before the chart is complete. This method is helpful when you use data not arranged in a layout that Excel recognizes by default.

The Chart Wizard button looks like a small 3-D bar chart. When the toolbar is docked under the menu, you see the Chart Wizard button on the right side of the Standard toolbar (refer to Figure 29.3).

Creating a Chart Using the Chart Wizard

Before you use the Chart Wizard button, select the data in your worksheet that you want to chart. Although the Chart Wizard allows you to select the data you want to chart, it is easier to do this before starting the Chart Wizard. Be sure to include the row and column headings if you want them to appear in the chart as category and legend labels.

The following steps show you the general procedure for creating a chart using the Chart Wizard. The sections that follow give a detailed description of each of the steps in the Chart Wizard. To create a chart with the Chart Wizard, follow these steps:

1. Select the data you want to chart.

2. Choose Insert, Chart or click the Chart Wizard button on the Standard toolbar. Step 1 of the Chart Wizard appears, as shown in Figure 29.5.

FIG. 29.5

In the first dialog box of the Chart Wizard, you can choose from many basic chart types.

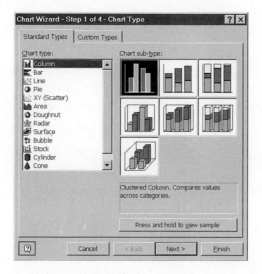

3. Select the type of chart you want to create in the Chart Type dialog box and click Next. The Chart Source Data dialog box appears (see Figure 29.6).

4. Verify that the data range is correct in the Chart Source Data dialog box and click Next.

   If you didn't select the data before you started the Chart Wizard, you can do so now. Click the Collapse Dialog button, select the data range with the mouse or keyboard, and click the Expand Dialog button to redisplay the dialog box.

   If the categories and series in the chart preview are reversed from how they should appear, select whichever of the Series In options that is not selected, either Rows or Columns.

5. Modify or add various chart options in the Chart Options dialog box, shown in Figure 29.7, and click Next.

FIG. 29.6

The second dialog box enables you to verify and change the source data for the chart.

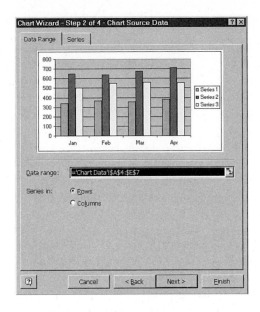

FIG. 29.7

Select among the many options for enhancing a chart in the Chart Options dialog box.

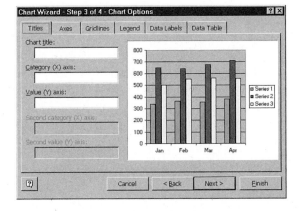

6. In the Chart Location dialog box shown in Figure 29.8, select the As New Sheet option to create a chart on a separate chart sheet. Select the As Object In option to embed the chart in a worksheet.

7. Click Finish to create the chart.

The following rules cover selecting cells for the Chart Wizard:

■ Select noncontiguous data, if necessary, by holding down the Ctrl key as you drag across each additional series of data.

■ If one series of data includes a cell with a label, then all series must include a cell in the same position, even if the cell is blank.

FIG.29.8

You can insert the chart as an object in a worksheet or on its own chart sheet.

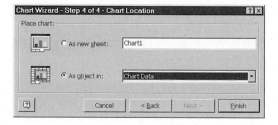

For clarification of how Excel builds a chart from different data layouts, see the section "Understanding How Excel Builds a Chart" later in this chapter.

Understanding Chart Wizard Dialog Boxes

The Chart Wizard displays a series of dialog boxes that guide you through chart-making. These dialog boxes display control buttons that enable you to move back and forth between the dialog boxes or skip over the dialog boxes and complete the chart automatically. Figure 29.9 shows one of the Chart Wizard dialog boxes.

FIG. 29.9

Use the control buttons in the Chart Wizard dialog boxes to move around in the Chart Wizard.

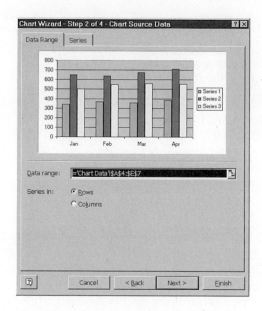

The Chart Wizard buttons control the following actions:

Button	Action
Next	Go to the next step in the Chart Wizard. You also can press the Enter key.
Back	Go to the previous step in the Chart Wizard.
Finish	Fast forward; complete the chart by using the selections made so far.
Cancel	Return to the worksheet without creating a chart.

Defining the Chart Type

The first dialog box (refer to Figure 29.5) enables you to select from the many types of Excel charts. These chart types are described in Chapter 30, "Modifying Charts." Click the chart type in the Chart Type list and then click the subtype from among the selections in the Chart Sub-Type area of the dialog box. To use the keyboard, use the arrow keys to select the chart type, press the Tab key, and use the arrow keys again to select the subtype.

N O T E Choosing Finish in the first step of the Chart Wizard creates the chart by using the default chart type. If you didn't set a default chart type, Excel creates a chart in the default format, 2-D column. See the section "Choosing a Default Chart Type" in Chapter 30 to learn how to set the default chart format. ■

Verifying the Chart Data Range

The second dialog box (refer to Figure 29.6) enables you to correct an incorrect data selection or to select the data if you did not do so before starting the Chart Wizard. You can edit the data range in the Data Range text box. Edit as you do in the formula bar. Click in the reference range, or press F2, the edit key. You can reenter ranges or cells by dragging across the cells in the worksheet. To make this easier, collapse the dialog box by clicking the Collapse Dialog button. Select the data with the mouse and then click the Expand Dialog button to redisplay the dialog box. You can select noncontiguous ranges of data using the Ctrl key. Ranges of noncontiguous data are separated in the Data Range box by a comma.

Add a data series to a chart by extending the reference in the Data Range text box in the Step 2 dialog box. Click the Collapse Dialog button to collapse the dialog box. To add a contiguous data series, hold down the Shift key and extend the data range by clicking the last cell in the series you want to add. To add a noncontiguous series, hold down the Ctrl key and select the noncontiguous range of cells you want to add. If the original data ranges included a cell with a label, the added range should include a cell. Click the Expand Dialog button to redisplay the dialog box.

The Chart Source Data dialog box also gives you the chance to verify that Excel is representing your data correctly. In most instances, Excel will correctly recognize which information should go on the horizontal Category (X) axis, which information goes on the vertical Value (Y) axis, and which cells contain the labels used for legend titles. If Category (X) Axis Labels appear in the legend, and vice versa, you can correct the problem here by selecting whichever option is not selected in the Series In group. See "Understanding How Excel Builds a Chart" later in this chapter, for a detailed explanation of the rules Excel uses to determine how to create a chart.

You can also work with the data series in the Chart Source Data dialog box. Click the Series tab to display the dialog box shown in Figure 29.10. Here you can add and remove data series and modify the range of cells containing the Category (X) axis labels. To add a data series, choose the Add button. Now click in the Name box and then click the cell in the worksheet containing the name for the new series. Next, click in the Values box and select the cells containing the values for the new data series. To remove a data series, select the series you want to remove in the Series list and choose Remove.

FIG. 29.10

Modify the information specifying the data series in the Series tab of the Chart Source Data dialog box.

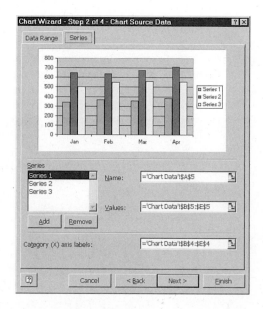

If the sample chart displays numbers as Category (X) axis labels and it should display labels, click in the Category (X) Axis Labels box and select the cells containing the labels for the Category axis. You can also modify an existing range for the Category (X) Axis Labels by editing the range specified in this text box.

After you select the range the way you need it, choose Next to move to Step 3 of the Chart Wizard.

Selecting Chart Options

The third Chart Wizard dialog box (refer to Figure 29.7) enables you to add or modify several optional features in a chart. You can add titles to the chart and axes, modify or remove the category axis, remove the value axis, and add or remove gridlines. You can also add or remove a legend and change the placement of the legend. Data labels can be attached to data points and a data table showing the source data for the chart can be added. These options are discussed in detail in Chapter 30.

Selecting the Chart Location

The final Chart Wizard dialog box (refer to Figure 29.8) is where you select the location for the new chart. If you want the chart to be embedded in a worksheet, select the As Object In option. By default, the chart will be embedded in the worksheet containing the source data. You can embed the chart in another worksheet by selecting the sheet from the drop-down list to the right of the option.

To create the chart in a separate chart sheet, select the As New Sheet option. You can enter a title for the new sheet in the text box next to this option. Otherwise, the new sheet will be given a generic name such as Chart1 or Chart2.

Figure 29.11 shows a finished chart embedded in the worksheet. The embedded chart now is part of the worksheet and will save and open with the workbook. You can position and size the chart exactly as you want. To move the chart, slide the mouse pointer up to the frame surrounding the chart and click and hold down the left mouse button. When selected, black handles will appear around the chart. Now you can drag the chart to the desired location.

FIG. 29.11

A finished chart embedded in a worksheet.

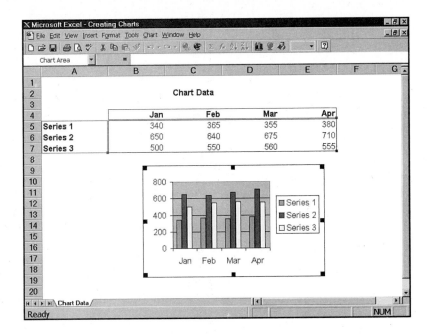

To change the size or proportions of the chart, grab the black handles along the borders (the pointer changes to a double-headed arrow) and drag until the chart is sized and proportioned the way you want. Be sure that you change the size and proportions of the chart before you open the chart to format it. If you format and enhance the chart with titles, a legend, text, and so on, and then change the size, the formatting and enhancements will be out of proportion with the chart.

 To change the size of the chart without changing its proportions, hold down the shift key as you drag a corner handle. To align a chart with cell edges, hold down Alt as you drag across where you want to establish the chart.

 If you hold down the Ctrl key as you drag one of the black handles along the side of the chart, the chart will change in size equally on that and the opposite side simultaneously. If you drag a corner handle while you hold down the Ctrl key, the chart will change in size equally in all directions.

To delete an embedded chart, select the chart and press Delete; or choose Edit, Clear, All.

To enhance the chart or make formatting changes, open the chart, as described in the section "Opening a Chart to Make Modifications," later in this chapter.

A finished chart located in its own chart sheet is shown in Figure 29.12. The chart sheet is part of the active workbook and is saved along with the workbook. You can print the chart sheet separately from the worksheet that contains the chart data.

FIG. 29.12

A finished chart located in its own chart sheet.

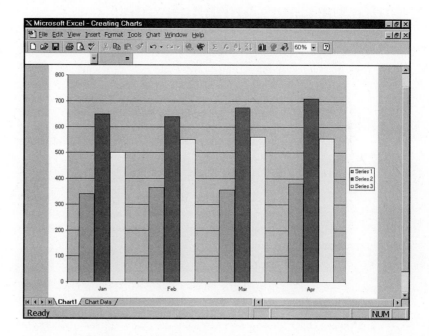

You can embed a chart that exists in its own chart sheet into a worksheet. To embed a chart from a chart sheet into a worksheet, follow these steps:

1. Select the chart sheet, and then select the entire chart by clicking along the outside of the chart.

   Black handles appear around the outside border of the chart.

2. Choose Edit, Copy.

3. Select the worksheet in which you want to embed the chart and select the cell that will be the upper-left corner of the chart.

4. Choose Edit, Paste.

The chart is embedded into the worksheet as a full-sized chart and can be resized, moved, and formatted just as you would any embedded chart.

N O T E   Excel doesn't update or redraw the chart after you change data on the worksheet. Excel may be set for manual recalculation. To update the chart by using new worksheet data, choose Tools, Options, select the Calculation tab, and choose Calc Now. The shortcut key for recalculating is F9. You can also reset the workbook to automatically recalculate by choosing the Automatic option in the Calculation tab. ▪

Creating a Chart Automatically

Although using the Chart Wizard is the easiest and most foolproof method for creating charts, you also can create a chart automatically by using the chart shortcut key. If the data is in a layout that Excel can interpret, you need only select the data and press F11 to create a chart. (Press Alt+F1 if you don't have an F11 key.)

Excel uses several rules to decide how to create a chart from the selected cells. If the cells you selected do not meet these rules, you must create the chart by using the Chart Wizard, described in "Creating a Chart Using the Chart Wizard," earlier in the chapter.

Understanding How Excel Builds a Chart

Excel can build a chart automatically from selected data and labels if the selected area follows rules. Excel uses these rules to understand what information goes on the horizontal Category (X) axis, what information goes on the vertical Value (Y) axis, and where cell labels used for legend titles are located.

Before you learn the rules, you must understand the terms, *series* and *point*. These terms describe how the data is used by a chart. Understanding how Excel builds a chart from the data on a worksheet can prevent your building charts with reversed axes or labels.

A *series* is a collection of associated data, such as the dollar amounts sold of the Global Quality bicycle, the forecast in units for specific products, or the readings from each of three specific medical instruments. When charted, the data from a series appears as a single line or as bars or columns of the same color.

A *point* is a single piece of data within any of the series. Examples of points in most charts are time sequences, such as years, quarters, or months. A point appears in a chart as a single dot on a line or one column out of a series.

You can enter labels for the Category (X) axis and legends in cells in the worksheet, and Excel uses them as labels in the chart. When charted correctly, the label for each point—month, for example—appears on the horizontal Category (X) axis. The series labels appear as titles in the legend (see Figure 29.13).

FIG. 29.13

A selection wider than it is tall plots its graph with category labels from the top row.

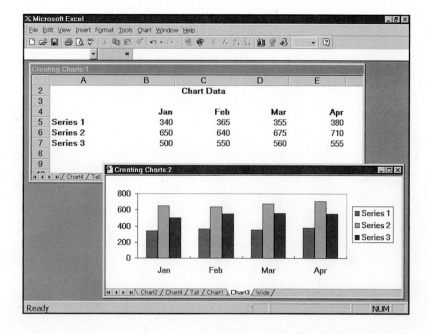

Excel uses the following rules to interpret how series and points are laid out on the worksheet:

- When Excel examines the data you selected, the program assumes that the Category (X) axis runs along the longest side of the selection. If the selection is square or wider than it is tall, as in Figure 29.13, then Excel assumes that the category labels run across the top row of the selection. If the selection is taller than it is wide, as in Figure 29.14, Excel assumes that the category labels run down the left column of the selection.

- Excel assumes that labels in cells along the short side of the selection should be used as titles in the legend for each data series. If only one data series exists, Excel uses this label to title the chart. If you select more than one data series, Excel uses the labels in these cells to title the legend.

- If the contents of the cells that Excel wants to use as category labels are numbers (not text or dates), Excel assumes that these cells contain a data series and plots the graph without category (X) labels, numbering each category instead.

- If the contents of the cells that Excel wants to use as series labels are numbers (not text or dates), then Excel assumes that these cells are the first data points in each of the data series and assigns the names Series 1, Series 2, and so on, to each of the data series.

FIG. 29.14

A selection taller than it is wide plots with category labels from the left column.

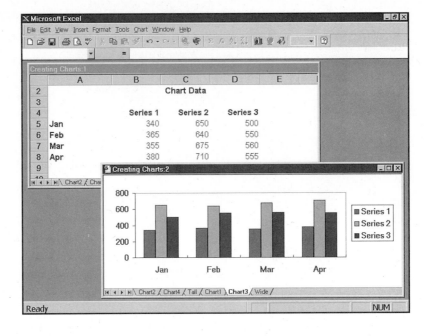

Creating a Chart Automatically with the F11 Key

To build a chart that has the correct orientation of category data along the longest side, complete the following steps:

1. Select the data and labels, as shown in Figure 29.15.

FIG. 29.15

A worksheet with three data series.

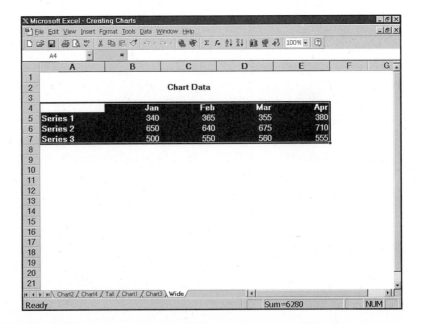

Notice that the selected range includes more data points—the months—than data series; the range has three series and four data points in each series. A data series in this example is a collection of related data—for example, all the sales for one product.

2. Press F11. (If you don't have an F11 key, press Alt+F1.)

Excel plots the data in the preferred chart type; the default is the 2-D column chart. Figure 29.16 shows a column chart created with the preceding steps.

FIG. 29.16

An example of a column chart using the data shown in Figure 29.15.

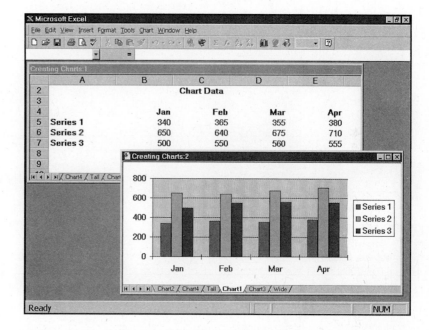

In the chart in Figure 29.16, notice that the points (months from the top row of the worksheet data) are used as category labels below the Category (X) axis. What happens if a series of data is listed down a column, as in Figure 29.17? If you select the data shown in Figure 29.17 and press F11, the chart in Figure 29.18 appears. Notice that the chart still is drawn correctly. Here, however, Excel assumes that the data series again goes in the long direction. Because the long direction is in columns, Category (X) axis labels are taken from the left column.

In the preceding two examples, Excel drew a correct chart. Excel, however, can create an incorrectly oriented chart if the data is laid out so that it doesn't match the rules Excel uses. When this happens, you need to use the Chart Wizard, described earlier in the chapter. Alternatively, you can modify the orientation of the chart using the Chart, Source Data command. Select the chart sheet, choose Chart, Source Data, and select whichever option is not selected in the Series In option group.

 TIP If a chart you create automatically is not oriented correctly, you can quickly correct it by using the By Row and By Column buttons on the Chart toolbar. Click whichever button is not already selected (the selected button is depressed) to reverse the orientation of the data series.

FIG. 29.17

A worksheet with the data series down a column.

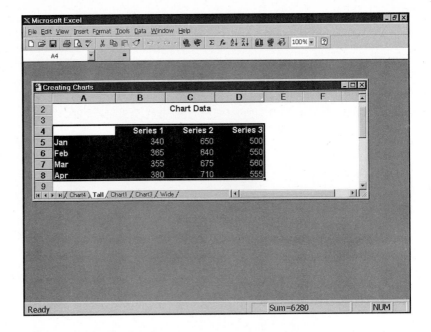

FIG. 29.18

The chart created from the vertical data series shown in Figure 29.17.

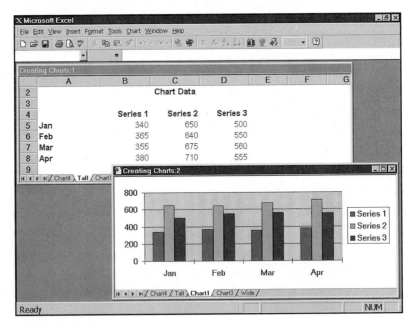

N O T E Numbers along the category axis indicate that you forgot to select category labels. If you didn't include a row or column of labels for the Category (X) axis, the chart shows a sequence of numbers that begin with 1 along this axis. ■

If you want to create a chart from data not in adjacent rows or columns, such as the selection shown in Figure 29.19, select the rows or columns by using the Ctrl and drag method with the mouse or by pressing Shift+F8 on the keyboard. Select the Category (X) axis cells; then select Value (Y) data cells in the same order in which you want the value series to appear on the chart.

FIG. 29.19
You can plot nonadjacent data by selecting the nonadjacent data and then creating the chart.

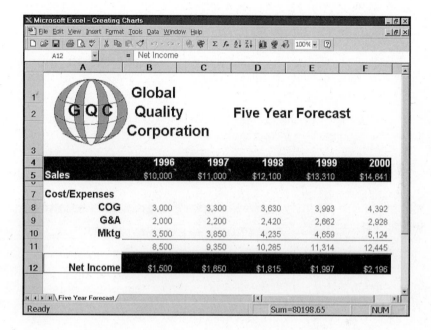

N O T E If in a table data exists that you do not want to include in a chart, you can hide the rows or columns that contain the data; or if the data is in outline form, you can collapse levels in the outline that you don't want to include in a chart. ■

▶ **See** "Controlling the Worksheet Display," **p. 800**

Saving Charts

A chart that you embedded in a worksheet is saved when you save the workbook that contains the worksheet. A chart in its own sheet also is saved when you save the related workbook. When you open a chart that was created in Excel 4 or earlier versions, it appears in its own workbook in a chart sheet. When you save the chart, you can save it in the original format, or you can update it to Excel 97 format. When you save the file, a dialog box appears and asks if you want to update the chart to Excel 97 format. Choose Yes to update the file or No to save the file in original format. Be aware that when you format and enhance a chart in Excel 97 and save it as an earlier version file, you may lose some of the formatting or enhancements due to incompatibilities between Excel 97 and earlier versions of Excel.

Changing Chart and Worksheet Links

All charts are linked to data in a worksheet. If a chart is embedded in a worksheet or if a chart in a chart sheet is linked to data in a worksheet that is part of the same workbook as the chart, then you don't have to worry about maintaining the link between the chart and the worksheet. If, on the other hand, you have linked a chart to data in a worksheet from another workbook, it is possible to break the link—for example, if you move the source workbook to a different directory, change the name of the worksheet, or delete the worksheet.

If one chart loses its link to its worksheet or if you need to link a chart to a different worksheet, perform the following steps:

1. Open the chart.

2. To establish a link with a different worksheet, open the workbook that contains the worksheet and activate the worksheet.

3. Activate the chart.

4. To display the dialog box shown in Figure 29.20, choose Edit, Links.

FIG. 29.20

Use Edit, Links to open or change source worksheets.

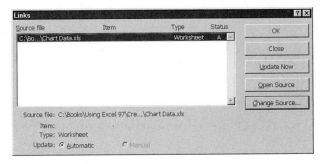

5. Select the worksheet link you want to change in the Source File list.

6. Choose the Change Source button.

7. Select from the Look In list box the name of the worksheet with which you want to establish or reestablish a link. You may need to change folders or disks to find the file. Use the same folder and drive-changing techniques you use in the File Open or File Save As dialog box.

8. Choose OK.

9. Save the workbook.

To learn more about understanding and working with links, see Chapter 40, "Linking, Embedding, and Consolidating Worksheets."

TROUBLESHOOTING

A chart that is linked to data in another workbook was opened without updating it in order to see the chart using old data. How can the chart be updated without opening the workbook? Choose Edit, Links, select the source workbook from the Source File list in the Links dialog box, and choose Update Now. Choose Close to return to the chart.

▶ **See** "Linking Workbook Cells and Ranges," **p. 942**

Opening a Chart to Make Modifications

A chart can be in a separate document window or embedded in a worksheet. You can reformat either chart.

To open or activate a chart embedded in a worksheet, click the embedded chart; black handles appear around the chart when it is activated and the menu bar changes to show the Chart menu item. After you finish formatting the embedded chart, return to the worksheet by clicking outside the chart.

You can also view an embedded chart in its own window. Click the chart to select it, then choose View, Chart Window. The embedded chart will appear in a window that is the same size as the chart on the worksheet. You can drag the window to a new location on the worksheet without affecting the location of the embedded chart. When you have finished editing the chart, click outside the window to close it or choose View, Chart Window again.

To open a chart that exists in a separate chart sheet, choose File, Open, select the workbook file that contains the chart, and choose OK. When you open a chart that is linked to data in an unopened workbook, a dialog box asks whether you want to update the chart (see Figure 29.21). If you choose Yes, the chart uses the current values stored in the worksheet file. If you choose No, however, the chart uses the values with which it was saved. Once the workbook is opened, select the chart sheet containing the chart you want to work with.

FIG. 29.21
This dialog box asks whether you want to update the chart with the information linked to the worksheet on disk.

When you create a chart on a separate chart sheet, the chart doesn't fill the chart window when it first appears. To fill the entire workbook window with the chart, choose View, Sized with Window.

To open the worksheets linked to open charts, choose Edit, Links. Select the worksheet file name in the Source File box and choose Open Source.

Printing Charts

Printing charts is similar to printing worksheets. You can print directly from the screen, or you can preview the chart before printing. Previewing a chart gives you a more accurate view of how the chart appears when printed. Charts embedded in worksheets print with the worksheets.

> **N O T E** You can print charts embedded in a worksheet by using the same techniques you use to print worksheets. You can store views and scenarios that involve the embedded charts, and then choose File, Print Report to print views with different scenarios. ■

Before you print a chart that is in a separate chart sheet, decide how large you want the chart to appear on the page. Set the size of the chart on the page by choosing File, Page Setup or choosing the Setup button in the File, Print Preview dialog box and selecting the Margins tab to display the dialog box shown in Figure 29.22. You also can change margins by choosing the Margins button in the File, Print Preview dialog box and dragging the margin lines to a new setting.

FIG. 29.22

Use the Margins Page of the Page Setup dialog box to set a chart size and other print options.

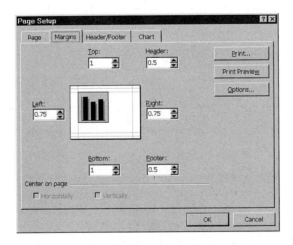

> **N O T E** If you choose fonts that the printer cannot print, the printed chart will differ from the on-screen image. To ensure that charts use fonts available in the printer, select fonts from the Font tab in the Format dialog box that shows a printer icon or the TT icon that indicates TrueType. ■

Use the chart options in the Page Setup dialog box to determine how charts react to print area margins. Choose File, Page Setup or the Setup button in the File Print Preview dialog box, and select the Chart tab to display the page shown in Figure 29.23. To expand the chart proportionally until margins are touched, select Scale to Fit Page. The results of a Scale to Fit Page setting are shown in Figure 29.24. To expand the chart in both height and width until margins in all directions are reached, select Use Full Page in the Page Setup dialog box. The same chart in Figure 29.24 is shown with the Use Full Page option in Figure 29.25.

FIG. 29.23
Specify how the chart will be fitted to the page in the Chart tab of the Page Setup dialog box.

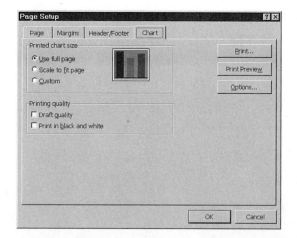

FIG. 29.24
Scale to Fit Page expands a chart proportionally until page margin is reached.

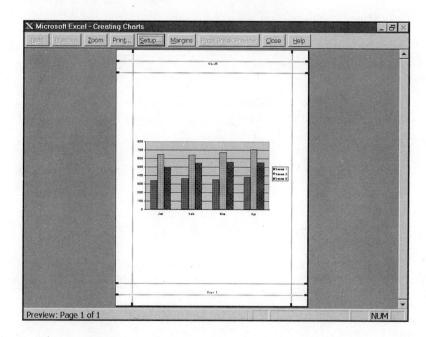

To preview your chart before printing or to use the mouse to visually adjust chart size or margins, see the steps following Figures 29.23 and 29.24.

1. Choose File, Print Preview.

2. Examine detail and positioning on the chart by zooming in or out on the page. To zoom in, move the pointer, a magnifying glass symbol, over an area of interest and click. Click the zoomed page to return to the expanded view. With the keyboard, choose the Zoom button to zoom and unzoom by keyboard.

FIG. 29.25

Use Full Page expands a chart on all sides until page margins are reached.

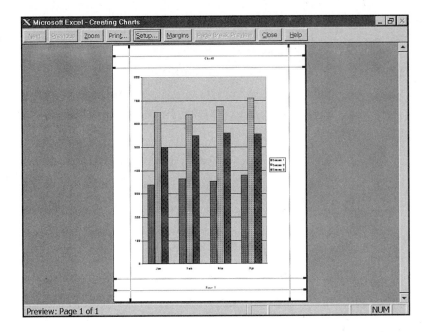

3. Return to the Page Setup dialog box by selecting the Setup button. To expand the chart in height and width, select the Chart tab and then select the Use Full Page option from the Page Setup dialog box.

4. Choose OK.

5. Adjust the margins and size of the chart by clicking the Margins button. To change margins and to change the chart size, drag the black handles shown earlier in Figure 29.24.

6. To display the Print dialog box, choose Print. To return to the chart document, choose Close.

To print the chart from the worksheet, choose File, Print (or press Ctrl+P) and complete the dialog box. Follow the same described procedures as you follow for printing a worksheet as discussed in Chapter 28, "Printing Worksheets."

TIP To quickly print a chart bypassing the Print dialog box, click the Print button on the Standard toolbar.

▶ **See** "Previewing the Document," **p. 675**

Modifying Charts

An Overview of Modifying Charts

After you have created a chart in Excel, you can modify the chart in many ways. The first modification you may want to make is to change the type of chart you are using. You may decide that you can present your data more effectively with a 3-D column chart than with the default 2-D column chart. You also can add titles, a legend, and other text to your chart to make it easier to understand. If you need to, you can add new data series or data points, or delete existing data series.

The first step in modifying a chart is selecting the type of chart you want to use to present your data most effectively. You may already have selected the appropriate chart type if you used the Chart Wizard to create your chart. You can also change the chart type after the chart is created.

After you have selected the proper type of chart, you can start inserting titles and other text, data values, a legend, gridlines, arrows, and other graphical objects to enhance your chart and make it easier for the viewer to interpret your data. You also can add data points and data series to an existing chart, or delete them from an existing chart. A new feature in Excel 97 enables you to attach to some types of charts a data table that displays the data values for the chart.

Using Shortcut Menus

In chart sheets and worksheets, clicking an object using the right mouse button displays a shortcut menu containing the most frequently used commands for that object. Figure 30.1 shows a shortcut menu for the value axis on a 3-D surface chart.

FIG. 30.1

You can quickly access commands for an object in a chart by clicking the right mouse button on the object to display its shortcut menu.

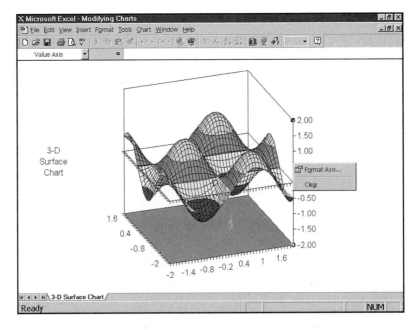

After the shortcut menu appears, you can click the left or right mouse button to choose a command. An easier way to choose a command is to click with the right mouse button (to open the shortcut menu), drag down to the command you want, and then release the mouse button.

Selecting Chart Objects

Charts are composed of objects such as markers, legends, axes, and text. When you customize charts, you either add objects—which you learned how to do in Chapter 29, "Creating Charts"—or you format existing objects with a new appearance. Before you can format a chart object, you must select it.

To select an object on the chart with the mouse, click the object. A tip that appears when you point to an object will help you select the correct object. When you see the tip for the object you want to select, click the mouse. To select a single data point in a series, click the point once to select the series, and a second time to select the point. The same procedure works with legend elements and data labels. Click the legend once to select it, and then click a legend entry or legend key to select it. Click an individual data label once to select all labels in the data series, and click a second time to select just that label. If you double-click an object, you open a dialog box that presents formatting options for that object. Just use a single click to select an object.

 TIP   If you find the tips that appear when you move the mouse over a chart object distracting, you can turn them off. Choose Tools, Options and click the Chart tab. Clear the Show Names check box to turn off the display of names of objects. Clear the Show Values check box to turn off the display of values.

You can select the two largest chart objects—the plot area and the chart background—by using the mouse. Click inside the rectangle formed by the axes to select the plot area, or click outside this rectangle to select the chart background.

To select an object on the chart with the keyboard, select the object by pressing the up- or down-arrow key. To select an individual data point or title in a legend, select the series or legend first, using the up- or down-arrow key, then use the left- or right-arrow key to select the data point or legend title.

Another method for selecting chart objects is to use the Chart Objects list at the left end of the Chart toolbar. Click the down-arrow key and click the object you want to select from the list of chart objects.

A selected object has small squares around or on top of it, and its name appears in the left end of the formula bar. Some objects can be moved and resized. If the mouse pointer changes to a double-headed arrow when you position it over any edge of the square around a selected object, you can resize that object by dragging the edge. In Figure 30.2, the plot area has been selected and the mouse pointer is positioned to resize the top line of the plot area. Titles (chart, value, and category) and data values can be moved but not resized. Press Esc to clear any selection.

FIG. 30.2

You can resize an object when the mouse pointer changes to a double-headed arrow.

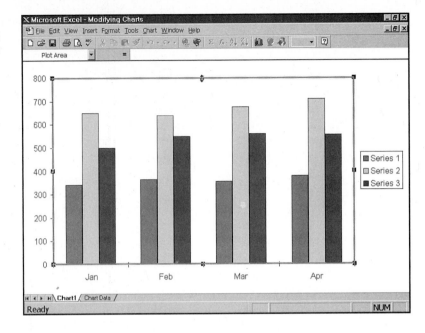

Choosing a Chart Type

Excel offers you 14 different chart types. Within each of these general types, you can select from among many subtypes. The easiest way to create charts is to select the chart type and subtype closest to the type you want. Then you can customize the predefined chart until it fits your exact needs. You should select the most appropriate chart type before you begin customizing your chart.

You can apply a chart type to the entire chart or a single data series in the chart. You can create a combination chart by applying different chart types to various data series in a chart. You can combine a line chart with a column chart, for example, to separate different types of data. See Chapter 32, "Building Complex Charts," for details on how to create a combination chart.

Using the Menu Command to Change a Chart Type

You can use the Chart, Chart Type command to change the chart type for all data series in your chart, or just for certain series. After you choose Chart, Chart Type, you can first select the chart type you want, and then select a chart subtype for that type. The Chart Type tool includes the default subtype for each of the 14 chart types and a few additional subtypes.

To change the chart type by using the Chart, Chart Type command, follow these steps:

1. Activate the chart you want to change by clicking the tab for the chart sheet, or by clicking the chart if it is embedded in a worksheet.

2. Choose Chart, Chart Type; or choose Chart Type from the shortcut menu.

The Chart Type dialog box displaying the chart types appears (see Figure 30.3).

FIG. 30.3
Select the type of chart you want in the Chart Type dialog box.

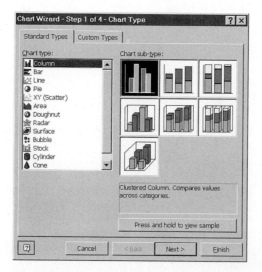

If you select a data series before you choose Chart, Chart Type, or if you click a data series with the right mouse button and then choose Chart Type from the shortcut menu, the Apply to Selection option will be selected in the Chart Type dialog box. If you want to change the chart type for the whole chart, clear this check box.

3. Select a chart type from the Chart Type list.

4. Select a subtype from the Chart Sub-Type gallery.

To view a sample of the selected chart type using your data, click the Press and Hold to View Sample button.

5. Choose OK to close the Chart Type dialog box.

 TIP If you double-click the kind of chart you want in the Chart Type dialog box, you select the default subtype for the chart and close the dialog box without choosing OK.

Using the Chart Toolbar to Change a Chart Type

You can add the chart toolbar to your screen, and click the Chart Type button to change the chart type. The Chart Type button uses the default subtype for each chart type. There are also a few additional subtypes. To select other subtypes, choose Chart, Chart Type, as explained earlier.

To use the Chart Toolbar to change the chart type, follow these steps:

1. Choose View, Toolbars, Chart or right-click any toolbar displayed on-screen, and then choose Chart from the shortcut menu.

2. Click the arrow next to the Chart Type button on the Chart toolbar to drop down a selection of chart types (see Figure 30.4). Select a chart type.

FIG. 30.4
You can select a chart type by using the Chart Type button on the Chart toolbar. The button's icon is an area chart.

If you selected a data series before this step, the selected chart type is applied only to that series.

Standard Chart Types

Excel's 14 chart types give you many options for presenting your data most effectively. For each of these chart types, there are several subtypes you can apply to your charts. This section examines how each type of chart is generally used. This information helps you to select the chart type that matches your data correctly.

Many of the chart types have 3-D subtypes. Excel's 3-D charts are attractive and work well for presentations or marketing materials. Most of the 3-D chart types do not actually add any information regarding your data. Instead, they are used to add visual depth and impact to the presentation of your data. They work well in reports, and work well to make overhead slides for presentations. When you use charts for analytical work, however, you may find exact data comparison easier on 2-D charts.

3-D surface charts do add another dimension of information. Surface charts can illuminate relationships between data that would not otherwise be easy to ascertain. Colors and patterns are used to indicate areas of the same value in a surface chart, similar to the way that shading and colors are used in a topographical map. These charts are useful for visually representing high and low points in a data set that result from two changing variables.

Column Charts

Column charts often compare separate (noncontinuous) items as they vary over time. This chart type uses vertical columns to give the impression of distinct measurements made at different intervals. Column charts frequently are used for comparing different items by placing them side by side.

In 2-D column charts, you can drag a point to a new position, and the corresponding value in the worksheet changes. If the data point plots the result of a formula in the worksheet, Excel executes the Tools, Goal Seek command to find the input value in the required worksheet to give the new result you plotted in the chart by dragging the data point. See Chapter 32 for more information on moving data points.

You can create 3-D column charts with columns adjacent to each other, or layered into the third dimension. Use 3-D column charts for the same types of data as in 2-D column charts, for added visual impact, or for comparing data series over time.

Bar Charts

A bar chart is similar to a column chart except the categories are on the vertical (Y) axis and the values on the horizontal (X) axis. For some data, this can facilitate comparing values.

In 2-D bar charts, you can drag a point to a new position, and the corresponding value in the worksheet changes. If the data point plots the result of a formula in the worksheet, Excel executes the Tools, Goal Seek command to find the input value in the worksheet required to give the new result you plotted by dragging the data point. See Chapter 32 for more information on moving data points.

Line Charts

A line chart compares trends over even time intervals (or other measurement intervals) plotted on the category axis—if your category data points are at uneven intervals, use an XY [scatter] chart. Use the line chart in production, sales, or stock market situations to show the trend of revenue or sales over time.

In 2-D line charts, you can drag a point to a new position, and the corresponding value in the worksheet changes. If the data point plots the result of a formula in the worksheet, Excel executes the Tools, Goal Seek command to find the input value in the worksheet required to give the new result you plotted in the chart by dragging the data point. See Chapter 32 for more information on moving data points.

3-D line charts are known also as *ribbon charts*. Use 3-D line charts for the same types of data as those used in 2-D line charts.

Pie Charts

A pie chart compares the sizes of pieces in a whole unit. Use this type of chart when the parts total 100 percent for a single series of data. Only the first data series in a worksheet selection is plotted. Pie charts work well to show the percentage of mix in products shipped, mix in income sources, or mix in target populations. Wedges in pie charts can be pulled out from the pie to emphasize the data point they represent. To pull out, or "explode," a slice of a pie chart, click the slice once to select the whole chart, then click a second time to select the individual slice. Drag the slice away from the pie. Release the mouse button when the slice is positioned where you want it.

If you want to compare many data points, you are better off using a column chart, because it becomes difficult to make accurate comparisons when there are more than six or eight pieces in a pie. Also, if you need to distinguish precise percentages, use a column chart so that you have a value (Y) axis from which to read percentage values.

The 3-D pie chart subtypes work well for marketing materials or presentations in which an overall impression is required. You can pull a wedge from the pie when you need to discuss that wedge's contents. Excel can show labels or calculate percentages for wedges. As with a 2-D pie chart, only the first data series in a selection is charted as a pie.

XY (Scatter) Charts

A scatter chart or XY chart compares trends over uneven time or measurement intervals plotted on the category axis (if your category data is at even intervals, use a line chart). Scatter charts also display patterns from discrete X and Y data measurements. Use scatter charts when you must plot data in which the independent variable is recorded at uneven intervals, or the category data points are specified in uneven increments. For example, survey data plotted with responses on the value axis, and ages on the category axis, can reveal opinion clusters by age. Much scientific and engineering data is charted with scatter charts.

Area Charts

An area chart compares the continuous change in volume of multiple data series. This type of chart sums the data from all the individual series to create the top line that encloses the area, giving the viewer an impression of how different series contribute to the total volume. Use the area chart for sales and production figures to show how volume changes over time, and to emphasize the amount or volume of change. The subjects of area charts are similar to those of line charts, such as units shipped per day, or the volume of orders over time.

Doughnut Charts

Similar to pie charts, doughnut charts compare the sizes of pieces in a whole unit. The arrangement of the doughnut chart, however, enables you to show more than one data series.

Again, as with pie charts, if you need to make precise distinctions between percentage values, use a column chart instead of a doughnut chart so that you have a value (Y) axis from which to read percentage values.

Radar Charts

Use radar charts to show the relationships between individual data series, and between a specific series and the whole of the other series. Unless you and those who view these are accustomed to working with radar charts, avoid this chart type. Radar charts are difficult to read and interpret.

Each category (data series label) in the chart has its own axis (spoke). Data points appear along the spoke. Lines that connect the data points define the area covered by the items. Radar charts in which each data series is a task in a given project, for example, can show how much time is spent on each task.

Each spoke on the radar chart represents time spent on a specific task. If all tasks require the same time, the chart creates a near circle. The larger the total area covered by the plot, the more total time is spent on the project.

Surface Charts

Surface charts are like topographical maps—they show high and low points along a surface. Surface charts are an excellent way to visually locate high and low points resulting from two changing variables.

The surface chart subtypes offer both wire frame and surface displays The surface chart, choice 1, shows a surface stretched between points. The color of the surface indicates areas on the surface that have the same z-value (vertical axis). A color contour chart, choice 3, acts like a topographical map by collapsing the z-axis to a flat plane, indicating elevations (z-axis values) by color alone. If you want to see the surface map from a different point of view, click one of the chart axis corners to select the axis. When black handles appear at the corners (it may take a moment), click a second time and drag the handles to rotate the chart. This procedure is described in more detail in Chapter 31, "Formatting Charts."

Part
VIII

Ch

30

Surface chart types 1 and 2 display a 3-D view of the surface. Types 3 and 4 appear more like topographical maps, which show changes in elevation with contour lines and colors. Type 2 displays data in a wire frame. The wire frame enables you to more easily compare data points that may be hidden in the 3-D chart.

The colors used in 3-D surface maps are defined by the current palette. The number of colors used depends on the scaling of the vertical axis.

Bubble Charts

Bubble charts are new to Excel 97. A bubble chart allows you to represent three variables on a two-dimensional surface. The first two variables are plotted against the Category (X) and Value (Y) axes, just as in an XY (Scatter) chart. The third variable is represented by the size of the bubble. To create a bubble chart, you need three rows or columns of values, one each for the X and Y values and one for the bubble size.

Stock Charts

Excel 97 includes four new Stock subtypes. Stock charts are used to display stock prices over time. You can display high, low, and closing prices; open, high, low, and closing prices; volume, high, low, and closing prices; and volume, open, high, low, and closing prices. When you select one of the subtypes that depicts volume as well as prices, two value axes are created: one for volume, which is represented by columns, and one for prices, depicted with vertical lines. When you set up the data for a stock chart, arrange the data series in the same order as listed at the bottom of the Chart Type dialog box when you select the subtype.

Cylinder, Cone, and Pyramid Charts

Cylinder, cone, and pyramid charts, new to Excel 97, are variations on 3-D column and bar charts. The chart markers used in these charts can add visual impact to your data. The cylinders, cones, and pyramids used in these chart types don't add any information to the regular 3-D column and bar charts.

Using Custom Chart Types

In addition to the standard types discussed in the previous section, Excel 97 includes a large collection of built-in custom chart types. You can also create your own user-defined custom chart types and save them so you can use them just as you would any chart type. You access the custom chart types by choosing Chart, Chart Type and selecting the Custom Types tab in the Chart Type dialog box.

Using Built-In Custom Chart Types

There are 19 built-in custom chart types. These chart types are based on the standard types, but have been enhanced with custom formatting and display settings. The best way to get a feel for the range of built-in custom chart types is to select each one in the Custom Types tab of the Chart Type dialog box and preview the sample displayed on the right side of the dialog box.

To select a built-in custom chart type, follow these steps:

1. Open the chart you want to apply the custom type to.
2. Choose Chart, Chart Type and select the Custom Types tab.
3. Select the Built-In option in the Select From group if it is not already selected.
4. Select a custom chart type in the Chart Type list.

   A preview of your selection appears in the Sample window.
5. When you have found the chart type you want to apply to your data, choose OK.

Creating User-Defined Custom Types

You can easily create custom chart types that are added to the user-defined list of chart types in the Custom Types tab of the Chart Type dialog box. If you have already created a chart that is formatted the way you want, use it as a template for a custom chart type. Otherwise, create a chart from scratch that is formatted the way you want, and then use it as a template for a custom chart type.

To create a custom chart type, follow these steps:

1. Activate the chart you want to use as a basis for the custom chart type.
2. Choose Chart, Chart Type and select the Custom Types tab.
3. Select the User-Defined option in the Select From area. The dialog box now appears as in Figure 30.5.
4. Choose Add. The Add Custom Chart Type dialog box appears (see Figure 30.6).
5. Type a name for the new custom type in the Name box, and type a description of it in the Description box.
6. Choose OK.

The new type is added to the Chart Type list in the Custom Types tab and can be applied to any chart the same way built-in chart types are applied. When you open the Chart Type dialog box, select the Custom Types tab and then select the Underlined option to display the list of custom chart types. To delete a custom chart type, select the type in the Chart Type list and choose Delete.

FIG. 30.5

Add custom chart types in the Custom Types tab.

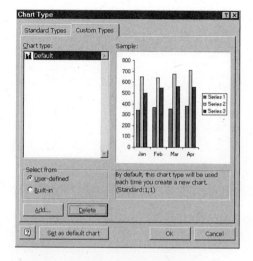

FIG. 30.6

Name a new custom chart type in the Add Custom Chart Type dialog box.

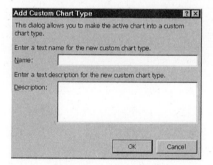

 TIP You can share a custom chart type that you have created with other users. To do this, open the worksheet containing the custom chart type on the other user's machine, activate the custom chart, and follow the preceding procedure for adding the custom chart type to the user-defined list.

▶ **See** "Formatting with AutoFormats," **p. 540**

▶ **See** "Creating Workbook and Worksheet Templates," **p. 648**

Choosing Line or XY (Scatter) Charts

Line and XY (scatter) charts can be similar in appearance, but they treat data differently. You need to be aware of the differences if you want accurate charts.

You should use a line chart when the category (X) data points are evenly spaced or when the category data points are text, and spacing does not matter. Category data should be in ascending or descending order. Line charts are most commonly used for business or financial data that is distributed evenly over time or in such categories as Sales, Costs, and so on. Category data such as time should be sequential, with no data missing.

You should use an XY (scatter) chart when data is intermittent or unevenly spaced. When Excel creates a scatter chart, the program reads the lowest and highest values in the category data and uses these values as the end points for the category axis (X). The tick marks are placed at even intervals between the end points. The data is plotted along the category axis according to the X data value, not at evenly spaced intervals as it would be in a line chart.

Figure 30.7 shows data plotted in a line chart that should have been plotted in an XY (scatter) chart. The correctly plotted data in an XY (scatter) chart appears in Figure 30.8. Notice the difference in the spacing of temperatures in the two charts.

FIG. 30.7

Intermittent data plotted in a line chart, giving an incorrect impression.

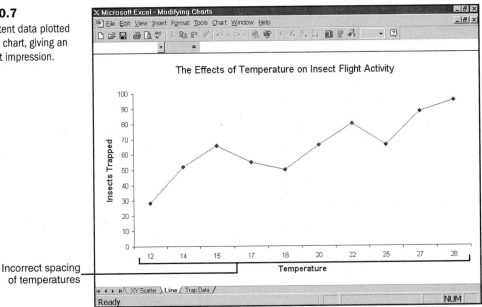

Incorrect spacing of temperatures

Choosing a Default Chart Type

If you deal with the same chart type and format regularly, you may want to designate a specific type and format for Excel to use as the default for newly created charts. Usually, Excel's preferred chart type is the first predefined 2-D column chart. You can use any of the built-in standard or custom chart types or a user-defined chart type as your default chart type.

FIG. 30.8

The same data plotted in an XY (scatter) chart, showing the correct relationship.

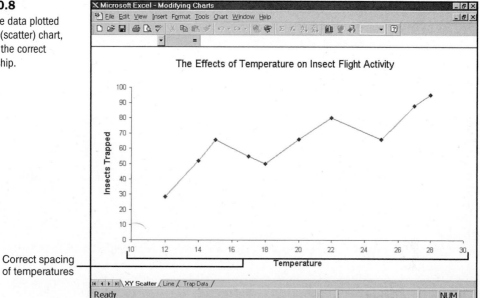

Correct spacing of temperatures

To redefine the default chart type, follow these steps:

1. Choose Chart, Chart Type.

2. Select the chart type you want to use as the default from the Chart Type list in either the Standard Types tab or Custom Types tab.

   If you want to use one of your own custom chart types as the default, select the User-Defined option in the Custom Types tab and select the custom chart type from the Chart Type list.

3. Choose Set as Default Chart.

4. Choose Cancel to close the dialog box without applying the selection to the current chart or choose OK to apply the selection to the current type.

Adding or Deleting Data

You can add data to existing charts, regardless of whether they were created automatically or manually (see Chapter 29). You can add new data series, add new data points to existing series, or change the range of data used by a chart.

There are several methods for adding data to a chart. If you are working with an embedded chart, you can select the data you want to add in the worksheet, and then drag and drop the selection onto the embedded chart. If you are working in an embedded chart that has been activated or in a chart sheet, you can use the Chart, Add Data command. You can use the Chart, Source Data command to edit existing data series or add new series. You can also use the Edit, Cut; Edit, Copy; and Edit, Paste commands to add data to either kind of chart.

Adding Data to Embedded Charts

You can add data to an embedded chart quickly by using the mouse. To add data using the mouse, follow these steps:

1. Select the data you want to add to the embedded chart.

2. Drag the data onto the chart and release the mouse button.

   To drag the selected data, move the mouse pointer up to the bottom edge of the selected data. The mouse pointer changes to an arrow. If the pointer changes to a cross, you have moved too far into the selection—move back toward the edge of the selection until you see the arrow. Hold down the left mouse button and drag the data into the chart.

If the data you select has the same layout as the original data used to create the chart, the new data is added immediately to the chart. If the data you select is such that Excel cannot determine how it should be placed in the chart, the Paste Special dialog box appears (see Figure 30.9). Specify the layout for the data, and choose OK.

FIG. 30.9

The Paste Special dialog box can be used to specify how data is used in a chart.

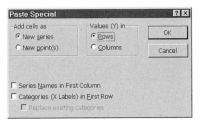

Adding Data with the Chart, Add Data Command

When you are working with an embedded chart that has been activated or with a chart on a chart sheet, you can add new data to the chart with the Chart, Add Data command.

To add new data using this command, follow these steps: ,

1. Activate the embedded chart or activate the chart sheet for the chart to which you want to add data.

   To activate an embedded chart, click it. To activate a chart on a chart sheet, click the tab for the chart sheet.

2. Choose Chart, Add Data. The Add Data dialog box appears (see Figure 30.10).

3. Select the worksheet that contains the data you want to add to the chart by clicking the tab for the worksheet.

FIG. 30.10

Specify the data you want to add to a chart in the Add Data dialog box.

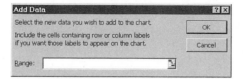

4. Select the data in the worksheet, just as you would select data in a worksheet when you first create a chart.

   Include row and column headings in the selection if you want them to appear in the chart. The reference for the data range you select appears in the Range text box.

   or

   Type the cell references for the data you want in the Range edit box.

5. Choose OK.

If the data you select has the same layout as the original data used to create the chart, the data is added immediately to the chart. If the data you select is such that Excel cannot determine how it should be placed in the chart, the Paste Special dialog box appears. Specify the layout for the data, and choose OK.

Adding Data from Multiple Worksheets

By choosing Chart, Add Data, you easily can combine data from multiple worksheets into one chart. You can, for example, create a chart that reflects data from four different quarters, although each quarter is on a different worksheet.

To combine data from multiple worksheets into one chart, follow these steps:

1. Create a chart from the worksheet data you want as the first series in the chart.

2. Choose Chart, Add Data.

3. Activate a different worksheet.

4. Select a data series. Include labels if the original data selection includes labels. (If you are adding to an XY [scatter] chart, the number of data points do not need to be the same, but you must include both X and Y data, as described earlier.)

5. Choose OK.

6. Repeat steps 2–5 for each data series you want to add to the chart.

Adding Data with the Chart, Source Data Command

You can also add data to a chart using the Chart, Source Data command. When you select this command, the Source Data dialog box appears (see Figure 30.11). This dialog box is identical to the dialog box that appears in step 2 of the Chart Wizard. Here you can change the data range used for the chart, adding either new data points or new data series.

FIG. 30.11

You can add new data points or data series to a chart in the Source Data dialog box.

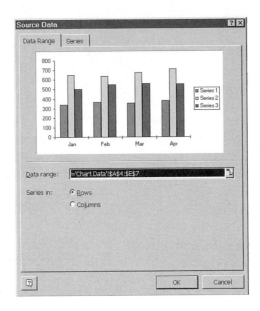

To change the data range with the Source Data command, follow these steps:

1. Activate the chart to which you want to add data.

   To activate an embedded chart, click it. To activate a chart on a chart sheet, click the tab for the chart sheet.

2. Choose Chart, Source Data. The Source Data dialog box appears (see Figure 30.11) and the data range originally selected when the chart was created is outlined with a marquee.

3. Select the worksheet that contains the data range you want to use for the chart.

   You can select a worksheet different from the worksheet that was the data source for the original chart.

4. Select the new data range for the chart.

   The new data range can include the original data used for the chart and additional rows or columns to add new data points or data series to the chart.

   To make it easier to view the source worksheet, click the Collapse Dialog button at the right end of the Data Range text box to collapse the dialog box. Select the new data range and click the Expand Dialog button again to redisplay the Source Data dialog box.

5. Choose OK.

Adding Data with the Edit, Copy and Edit, Paste Commands

To add data to charts with the Edit, Copy and Edit, Paste commands, simply copy the data from the worksheet and then paste the data onto the chart. If the original data to create the chart includes cells containing labels, the new data you copy also must include cells for labels, even if those cells are blank.

To add data with the Copy and Paste commands, follow these steps:

1. Activate the worksheet containing the data you want to add, and select the data.
2. Choose Edit, Copy.
3. Activate the chart into which you want to copy the data.
4. Choose Edit, Paste if you are adding data with a standard layout.

   If you are adding a new series that uses a standard layout and has the same number of data points as the original series in the chart, or if you are just adding new data points, the Edit, Paste command works.

   You also can choose Edit, Paste Special if the data you want to add uses a nonstandard layout and its category axis (X) is along the short side of the selection, or if a data series you are adding has fewer data points than the original data series.

   Select from the Paste Special dialog box the options that describe the layout of the data, and whether the new data should be added as a new series or as new data points. You usually must select the opposite option button from the one selected under Values (Y) in group when the box first displays. If the box appears with Rows selected, for example, you select Columns. After you change the option button, select the appropriate check boxes to describe where labels are located.

5. Choose OK.

You can use the Edit, Copy and Edit, Paste (or Edit, Paste Special) commands to add data from multiple worksheets. Simply activate the worksheet that has the data you want to add, choose Edit, Copy, activate the chart to which you are adding the data, and choose Edit, Paste (or Edit, Paste Special). Repeat this procedure for each worksheet that has data you want to add to the chart.

Deleting Data

You can delete an entire data series or points in a data series. To delete a data series, select the series in the chart. Then choose Edit, Clear, Series, or press Delete.

To delete points in a data series, delete them in the worksheet that is the source for the chart, or redefine the data range used by the chart. The latter can be done using the Chart Wizard, as described in the previous section.

▶ **See** "Filling or Copying Cell Contents," **p. 629**

▶ **See** "Analyzing Pivot Table Data with Charts," **p. 927**

Working with the Series Formula

When you create a chart, or add a data series to a chart, Excel links each data series in the chart to a data series on a worksheet. Excel creates this link with a series formula. If you use the Chart Wizard or the Chart, Source Data command to change the data used by a chart, you should understand how to use a series formula.

Part
VIII

Ch
30

Understanding the Series Formula

A series formula tells the chart several things: where the worksheet is located on the disk or network, which worksheet to use, and which cells of that worksheet contain data to be charted. Each data series has a series formula. When you select one of the markers in the data series, the series formula is displayed in the formula bar. The formula that appears in the formula bar in Figure 30.12, for example, belongs to the first data series, which is shown with squares inside the columns.

FIG. 30.12

When you select a data series in a chart, the series formula appears in the formula bar.

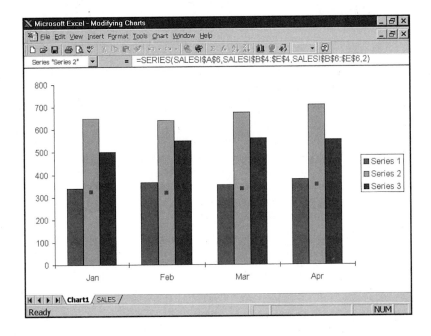

When you examine the worksheet and the related chart, you can see how the series formula works. All series formulas are constructed on the following pattern:

```
=SERIES("series_name",worksheet_name!category_reference,worksheet_name!
➥values_reference,marker_order_number)
```

The series_name is text in quotation marks or an external reference to the cell that contains the text label for the data series. An external reference to a text label in a cell is not enclosed in quotation marks. The series_name is used in the legend.

The worksheet_name!category_reference is an absolute reference to the worksheet cells that contain the category labels for the X-axis. The worksheet_name!values_reference specifies which worksheet cells contain the Y values for the data series.

The marker_order_number dictates the order of the data series. In the example in Figure 30.12, the marker_order_number is 1. The first series appears first in the legend and appears as the first series of columns in column charts. A marker_order_number of 2 would make the markers for this data series the second series of markers on the chart.

Editing a Data Series

When you extend a series of data on a worksheet, you probably want to extend the related chart as well. You can use the Chart, Source Data command to make these changes, as described earlier. Another method is to edit the series formula in the Series tab of the Source Data dialog box.

To edit the data series used in a chart, follow these steps:

1. Open the workbook containing the worksheet and chart. Activate the chart.
2. Select the data series you want to edit.
3. Choose Chart, Source Data.
4. Click the Series tab to display the dialog box shown in Figure 30.13.

Part

VIII

Ch

30

FIG. 30.13

You can add or edit data series in the Series tab of the Source Data dialog box.

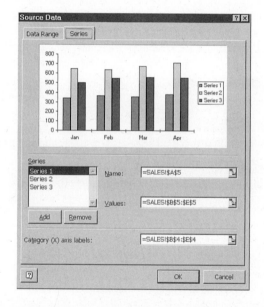

5. Select the series you want to edit in the Series box.
6. Select the Name text box and edit the external reference if necessary.

   The Name text box references the cell from which the legend name is taken. You can type a legend name directly instead of using a reference to an external cell that contains text. If you are simply adding or deleting cells from the Values range, you may not need to edit this reference.

7. Select the Values text box, and then manually edit the external reference formula or select the new data range in the worksheet by dragging across it using the mouse.

   The Values text box contains the external reference formula for the values used for the chart markers.

Manually edit the reference if it needs only minor changes. For significant changes, such as referencing a worksheet range you cannot remember or using a data series from a different worksheet or workbook, activate the worksheet and scroll to the data area. Click the Collapse Dialog button to collapse the dialog box and make it easier to select the data on the worksheet. Click the Expand Dialog button to redisplay the dialog box.

8. Select the Category (X) Axis Labels text box and edit the external reference formula or select the new data range using the mouse.

The Category text box contains the external reference used to create the category axis.

9. Repeat steps 5–8 for each data series in the chart.

10. Choose OK.

N O T E   Usually, Excel uses the names associated with each data series in the worksheet to create the names used in the chart legend. To create your own names without changing the text in the worksheet, use the Chart, Source Data command and select the Series tab. Select the series you want to edit in the Series box. To perform the replacement, select the external reference in the Name text box, type the text you want to appear instead in the legend, and then choose OK. Repeat this procedure for each data series in the chart. ▪

Rearranging the Markers

You can rearrange the order in which data series that use the same chart type are plotted in a chart.

To change the order in which data series are plotted, follow these steps:

1. Select one of the data series in the chart.

2. Choose Format, Selected Series and select the Series Order tab to display the dialog box shown in Figure 30.14.

FIG. 30.14

You can change the order in which data series are plotted in a chart.

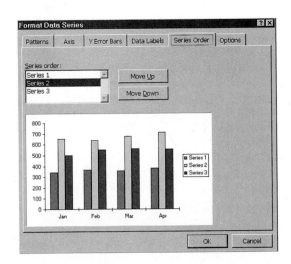

3. Select the series you want to move in the <u>S</u>eries Order list box.

4. Choose Move <u>U</u>p or Move <u>D</u>own to move the series to the desired position.

   View the chart mock-up at the bottom of the dialog box to make sure the data series appear in the order you want.

5. Choose OK.

Inserting Text

When you create a chart, Excel automatically includes labels along the category and value axes if, when you select your data, you include cells containing labels. Depending on how you select your data and what choices you make if you use the Chart Wizard to create your chart, you may also have labels for the legend and the title. You probably want to add other text to your charts—for example, a title and text annotations—to help clarify the data being presented. In this section, you learn how to add text associated with specific objects in the chart, as well as "free-floating" text.

There are two types of text you can add. The first type of text is associated with specific objects in a chart, such as the title, axes, or data points. After you insert this type of text, you can select it and revise it whenever you want, and you can reposition it. The second type of text is not associated with objects in the chart. Unattached text appears in a box that can be resized, so that the text wraps around exactly the way you want, and can be repositioned anywhere on the chart. Unattached text is useful as text labels or comments beside a chart, or for hiding portions of the screen.

You can insert titles associated with the chart and chart axes by choosing the <u>C</u>hart, Chart <u>O</u>ptions command and selecting the Titles tab. You can insert data labels that are associated with data points in the chart by choosing the <u>C</u>hart, Chart <u>O</u>ptions command and selecting the Data Labels tab. These labels can be either the value for a data point or the category label associated with the point.

You need no command to insert unattached text. Just select any nontext object in the chart—for example, a data series or the chart itself—and type the desired text. You can then move the box that contains the text to any position on the chart.

All the text you use in an Excel chart can be formatted. In Chapter 31, you learn how to format text and other chart objects.

Inserting Titles

You probably want to add to the text that Excel automatically attaches to the axes in your charts. For example, you likely want to add a chart title, and you might want to add titles to the category and value axes as well. The chart shown in Figure 30.15 has text attached to the title position and to the vertical axis.

FIG. 30.15

In this chart, text is attached in the form of a chart title and axis titles.

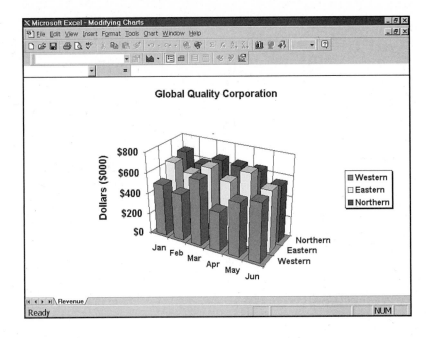

To insert titles, follow these steps:

1. Choose Chart, Chart Options—or right-click in the chart or plot area, and select Chart Options from the shortcut menu—and then select the Titles tab of the Chart Options dialog box, as shown in Figure 30.16.

FIG. 30.16

You can attach text to a chart's titles and axes.

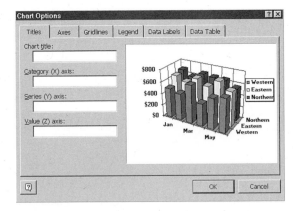

2. Select the text box for the location where you want to insert text. The following list describes these locations:

Item	Location
Chart Title	Centers the text Title above the chart.
Category (X) Axis	Centers the text X under the X-axis.

Item	Location
Value (Y) Axis Value (Z) Axis	Centers the text Y beside the Y-axis in 2-D charts or beside the Z-axis in 3-D charts.
Series (Y) Axis	Centers the text Y beside the Y-axis in 3-D charts.
Second Value (Y) Axis	Centers the text Y2 beside the Y-axis, in charts with two value axes.
Second Category (X) Axis	Centers the text X2 below the X-axis, in charts with two category axes.

Part VIII
Ch 30

N O T E   Not all selections listed in the preceding table always appear in the Titles dialog box. The selections that appear vary depending on the type of chart selected. ■

3. Enter the text for the title.

   Click in another of the text boxes to display the new title in the chart preview window.

4. Repeat 2–3 to insert additional titles.

5. Choose OK.

   The text you entered is attached to the point you specify, and remains selected. The surrounding black squares indicate that the text is selected and can be moved. You can edit the text or type over it.

6. As long as the title is selected, you can simply type over the existing text if you want to change it.

7. Press Enter or click the Enter button on the formula bar.

To edit a title by using the mouse, click the title to select it and then click inside the box that contains the text. The insertion point appears where you click. You can then use the arrow keys to move around the text, the Backspace and Delete keys to delete characters, and the keyboard to enter new text.

To make a line break to create a two-line title, or to break unattached text into separate lines, press Enter. You can remove the line break by positioning the insertion point to the right of it and pressing Backspace.

Inserting Other Text

In Excel, creating text that can be placed anywhere on a chart is easy and extremely useful. Figure 30.17 illustrates how you can use floating text in a comment box to label an arrow. See "Inserting Arrows," later in this chapter, for information on how to add arrows to a chart.

To add unattached text to a chart, follow these steps:

1. Select a nontext object. You can click the outside border of the chart or click one of the data series.

2. Type the unattached text.

3. Press Enter or click the Enter button when the text is complete.

FIG. 30.17

Floating text can be used to comment on a data point.

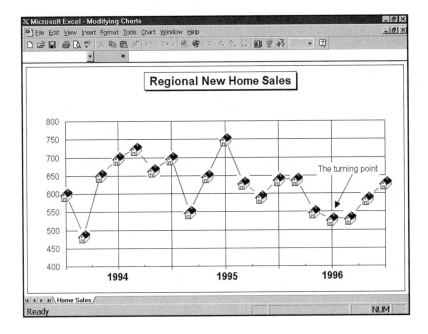

Small white squares and a hatched border surround the text on the chart. You can move and resize the text background.

To move unattached text with the mouse, click the text and then point to one of the borders. The mouse pointer should be shaped like a double-headed arrow. If the mouse pointer is shaped like an I-beam, move the pointer down slightly until it appears as a double-headed arrow. Drag-and-drop the text to the desired position. Size text blocks by selecting the text and dragging one of the white squares to expand or contract the block. Drag a corner to change two dimensions at the same time. Words within the text box wrap to fit the new block size.

To edit unattached text, click the text to select it and then click inside the box that contains the text. The insertion point appears wherever you click, and the text background turns white. You can now edit the text directly on the chart. Use the arrow keys to move around the text, the Backspace and Delete keys to delete characters, and the keyboard to enter new text. When you have finished editing the text, click outside the text box.

Checking Spelling in Charts

To check the spelling of attached and unattached text in your charts, choose Tools, Spelling. The spelling checker works the same as it does in a worksheet.

The spelling checker checks attached and unattached text. If any text in a chart is linked to a worksheet, as described in Chapter 31, use the spelling checker in the worksheet to check that text. You can check the spelling in an entire workbook by selecting all its sheets and then running the spelling checker.

▶ **See** "Formatting Text and Numbers," **p. 751**

Modifying the Axes

When you build a chart using the Chart Wizard, Excel automatically creates a Category (X) axis and Value (Y) axis. If you selected a 3-D chart type, Excel creates both a Series (Y) axis and a Value (Z) axis, as well as the Category (X) axis, to represent three dimensions of data.

You can remove any one of the axes using the Axes tab in the Chart Options dialog box. To remove an axis, follow these steps:

Part
VIII
Ch
30

1. Choose Chart, Chart Options and click the Options tab.
2. Click the Axes tab to display the dialog box shown in Figure 30.18.

FIG. 30.18

You can add and remove axes in the Axes tab of the Chart Options dialog box.

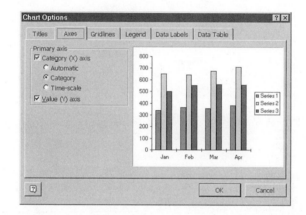

3. Clear the check box for the axis or axes you want to remove. Preview the chart to verify your selection.
4. Choose OK.

A new feature in Excel 97 is the time-scale axis. If the data for the Category (X) axis is date formatted, Excel automatically uses a time-scale axis for the Category (X) axis. With a time-scale axis, dates are displayed in chronological order with evenly spaced time units. The unit of time is determined from the smallest difference between two dates in the data series. With a time-scale axis, the data is arranged in chronological order even if the data for the chart is not arranged chronologically.

Figure 30.19 shows a chart created using date-formatted data. Notice that Excel has correctly spaced the data points over time. There are two options in the Axes tab of the Chart Options dialog box that allow you to override the Category axis created automatically by Excel (refer to Figure 30.18). If you used date-formatted data to create the chart but you want the Category (X) axis to use default categories instead of time-scaled categories, select the Category option. Figure 30.20 shows a chart created using the same data as the chart in Figure 30.19, but the Category option has been selected, overriding the time-scale axis that Excel creates automatically.

FIG. 30.19
Excel automatically creates a time-scale Category (X) axis if the category data is date formatted and correctly spaces missing days.

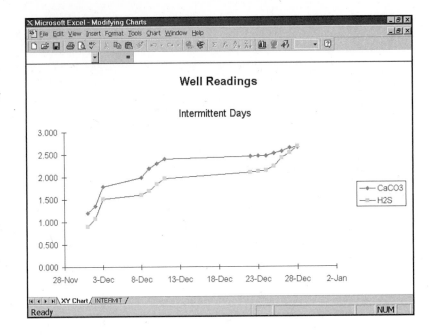

FIG. 30.20
You can select the Category option to override the time-scale axis when the data is date formatted.

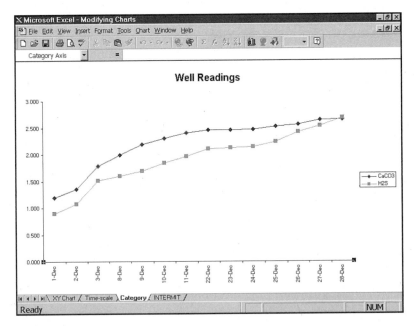

Inserting Data Labels

You can insert a label that is associated with a data point on your chart. This label can either be the value for that data point, or the category axis label associated with the data point. You can attach labels to as many data points as you want. Attaching labels to data points can help the viewer interpret the data in a chart more easily.

To insert data labels, follow these steps:

1. Activate the chart to which you want to add data labels.

2. Select the data point or points to which you want to add labels.

   To select an entire data series, click any point in the series. All data points in that series are selected, as indicated by squares that appear on each data point (see Figure 30.21). To select an individual point in the series, click a second time on that data point. The squares now appear on only that data point (see Figure 30.22).

Part VIII

Ch

30

FIG. 30.21
When you select a data series, boxes appear on each data point.

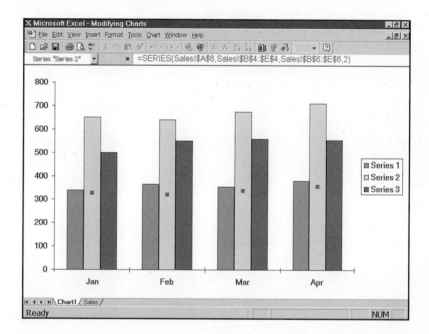

To insert labels on all data points for all series, select any object in the chart that is not a data point. For example, click outside the chart to select the entire chart.

3. Choose Chart, Chart Options. The dialog box shown in Figure 30.23 appears. Select the Data Labels tab.

FIG. 30.22

When you select one data point, a box appears on just that data point.

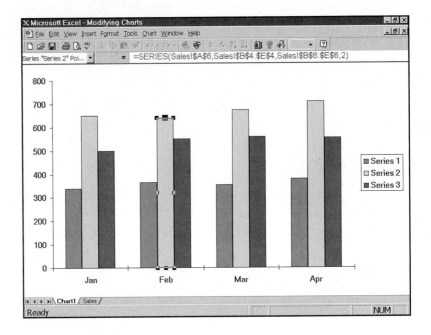

FIG. 30.23

You can insert values or labels on data points in a chart using the Data Labels tab in the Chart Options dialog box.

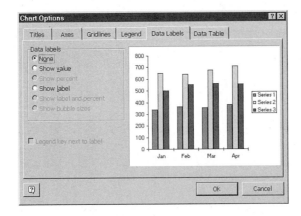

4. Select an option from the following list:

Item	Result
None	No labels are inserted with the selected data points. Previously inserted labels are removed.
Show Value	The values for selected data points are inserted.
Show Percent	The percentages for selected data points are inserted (this option is available only with pie and doughnut charts).
Show Label	The category (X) labels associated with selected data points are inserted.

Item	Result
Show Label <u>a</u>nd Percent	The percentages and associated category labels for elected data points are inserted (this option is available only with pie and doughnut charts).
Show <u>B</u>ubble Sizes	The values for the selected bubbles are inserted (this option is available only with bubble charts).

5. If you want the key from the legend to be displayed along with the data value, select the Legend <u>K</u>ey Next to Label option.

6. Choose OK.

The chart appears with data labels at the selected data points. Figure 30.24 shows a chart with data labels attached to one data series. These labels have been formatted to show dollar signs. You learn how to format chart objects in Chapter 31.

FIG. 30.24
Data labels can make a chart easier to read.

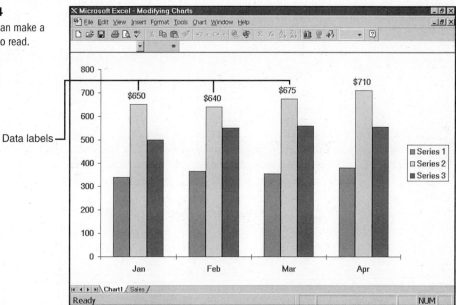

N O T E The data point values that attach to markers use the format of the corresponding cell in the worksheet. To change a number's format in the chart, you can format its worksheet cell. You can also format the data values directly in the chart using the F<u>o</u>rmat, S<u>e</u>lected Labels command. See Chapter 31 for more information on formatting data labels. ■

 You can substitute your own text for the data label that is inserted automatically when you use the previous procedure. To replace a data label with your own text, click the label once to select the labels for entire series and click it again to select the individual label. Type in the desired text.

When you substitute your own text for a data label, you break the link between the label and the worksheet cell for the data point. To reestablish the link, select the data series that you want to relink and choose Chart, Chart Options. Click the Data Labels tab, select the Automatic Text option, and choose OK.

Inserting Legends

A legend explains the markers or symbols used in a chart. Excel creates legends from the labels on the shorter side of the worksheet data series. Figure 30.25 shows an example of a legend. The legend in the figure was customized with border, pattern, and font selections. To learn about working with borders, patterns, and fonts, see Chapter 31.

FIG. 30.25

Legends explain which marker represents each data series.

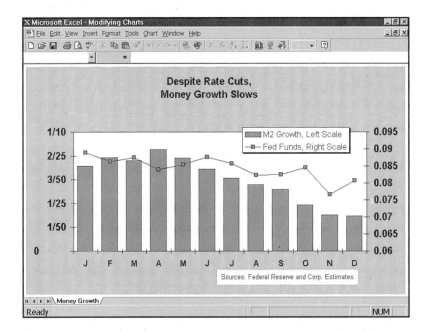

If you use the Chart Wizard to create the chart, you can add a legend by selecting the Show legend option in the Legend tab in step 3 (for additional information on the Chart Wizard, see Chapter 29). At any time, you can add a legend by choosing the Chart, Chart Options command, clicking the Legend tab and selecting the Show Legend option. You can also click the Legend button on the Chart toolbar. The legend appears on the right side of the chart. To delete a legend, select it and press Delete, or click the Legend button on the Chart toolbar.

You can move the legend to any location on the chart by selecting and then dragging the legend with the mouse. If you move the legend to a central part of the chart, the legend stays where you leave it. Figure 30.25 shows a legend over a central area of the chart. You can resize the box that contains the legend by selecting the legend, and then grabbing any of the black handles that surround the legend. Drag the box to resize the legend.

You can use the Format, Selected Legend command to move the legend to one of the pre-defined positions. Select the legend and choose Format, Selected Legend to open the Format Legend dialog box. You can also click the legend with the right mouse button and then choose Format Legend from the shortcut menu. Select the Placement tab to display the page shown in Figure 30.26. Select a location from the Type box and choose OK.

FIG. 30.26
Select the position for the legend in the Format Legend dialog box.

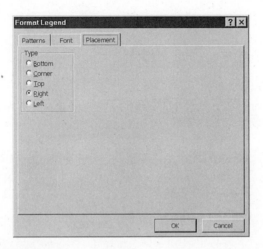

Inserting Arrows

Use arrows and unattached text to point to and identify (or explain) specific places on a chart. Headless arrows serve as straight lines. Click the Arrow button on the Drawing toolbar to add arrows to a chart.

To add an arrow or a straight line to an active chart, follow these steps:

1. Choose View, Toolbars, Drawing. Alternatively, you can click the Drawing button on the Standard toolbar to display the Drawing toolbar, or click with the right mouse button any toolbar displayed on-screen and then select Drawing from the shortcut menu.

2. Click the Arrow button on the toolbar. The mouse pointer changes to a crosshair.

3. Click the mouse in the chart where you want the tail of the arrow, hold down the mouse button while you drag across the chart to where you want the head of the arrow, and then release the mouse button (see Figure 30.27).

To remove an arrow, select the arrow you want to remove, and then press Delete.

Move an existing arrow by dragging its middle with the mouse. You can drag on the white square at either end of a selected arrow to change the arrow's size and position.

FIG. 30.27
Use the mouse to place
an arrow on a chart.

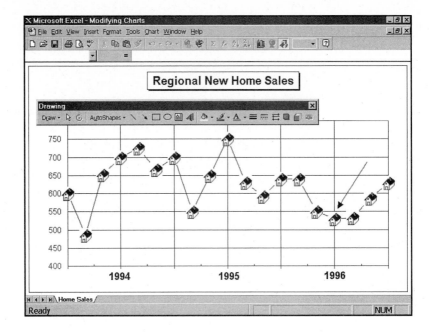

Inserting Gridlines

Gridlines help viewers compare markers and read values. You can add gridlines that originate from either the category or value axis, or both. You can choose also whether gridlines originate from only major divisions on an axis, or from points between major divisions.

To add gridlines to a chart, follow these steps:

1. Activate the chart you want to add gridlines to.

2. Choose Chart, Chart Options and select the Gridlines tab.

   Figure 30.28 shows the Gridlines tab of the Chart Options dialog box for 2-D charts, and Figure 30.29 shows the Gridlines tab of the Chart Options dialog box for 3-D charts.

3. Select the type of gridlines you want to add and preview the results in the chart preview window.

4. Choose OK.

 You can add Category Axis Gridlines and Value Axis Gridlines buttons to the Chart toolbar. See Chapter 49, "Customizing Word and Excel Toolbars, Menus, and Shortcuts," to learn how to add buttons to a toolbar. Once you've added the buttons, click either button to add gridlines to the active chart. To remove the gridlines, click the button again.

FIG. 30.28
Add gridlines to either axis in a 2-D chart with the Gridlines tab of the Chart Options dialog box.

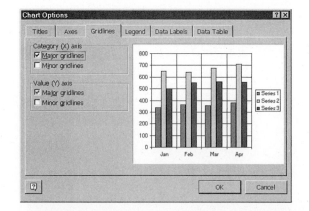

FIG. 30.29
In a 3-D chart, you can add gridlines to all three axes.

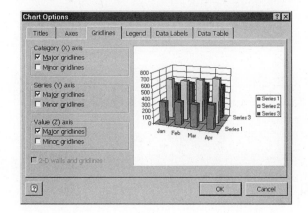

To remove gridlines from a chart, choose Chart, Chart Options, click the Gridlines tab, and clear the boxes for the gridlines you want to remove. Choose OK to close the dialog box. Too many gridlines obscure the chart, making it messy and confusing. In general, do not use gridlines if the chart is for overhead projection. You should use gridlines in printed material, where readers need to read charts more precisely. ●

Formatting Charts

Learning the Basic Chart-Formatting Procedure

After you select one of the predefined chart types, you can customize your chart. You can make it more attractive and easier to understand while emphasizing the point you want to make.

Customize charts by using the same concept you use with worksheets: Select, then do. The following procedure applies to any object in a chart. The exact formatting changes you can make vary, depending on what object in the chart you have selected. Perform the following steps to customize a chart:

1. Select the chart object you want to customize by clicking it, selecting the object from the Chart Objects list at the left end of the Chart toolbar, or by pressing an arrow key. (Refer to Chapter 30, "Modifying Charts," to learn how to select objects in a chart.)

2. To open the Format dialog box, do one of the following: Choose Format, Selected object, click the selected object with the right mouse button and select the Format command from the shortcut menu, or double-click the object.

   The Format, Selected command changes, depending on the object that is selected. If a data series is selected, for example, the Format, Selected Data Series command appears in the menu.

   The Format dialog box for the selected object appears. The Format Data Series dialog box is shown in Figure 31.1.

FIG. 31.1

You can customize the data series in a chart using the options in the Format Data Series dialog box.

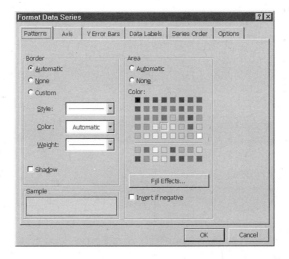

3. If the dialog box contains tabs, select the tab that contains the options you want to change.

4. Choose OK.

These steps are explained in the following sections.

Moving and Sizing Chart Objects

You can move or resize some objects in a chart. You can move the plot area, chart and axis titles, legend, data labels, slices in both pie and doughnut charts, and graphic objects that you have added to a chart, such as arrows and text boxes. Objects that can be resized include the plot area, legend, and graphic objects.

To move an object using the mouse, click the object to select it, and then point to the selected object and hold down the left mouse button. Drag the object to its new location and release the mouse button.

If you are moving the plot area, legend, or an arrow, drag from the center of the selected object. Do not drag on any of the black boxes that appear when the object is selected, or you may change the size of the object. A rectangle shows the position of the object as you move it.

To move a title, data value, or text box, position the mouse pointer just beneath the hatched gray border that appears around the selected object (see Figure 31.2). The mouse pointer should appear as an arrow. If you move the mouse pointer just inside the box, the mouse pointer changes to an I-beam. If you click the mouse button at this point, an insertion point appears inside the box, enabling you to edit the text. Press the Esc key to display the box again, and move the pointer until you see the arrow. Then drag the title or value to a new location.

Part
VIII

Ch
31

FIG. 31.2

The mouse pointer positioned to move the title in this chart.

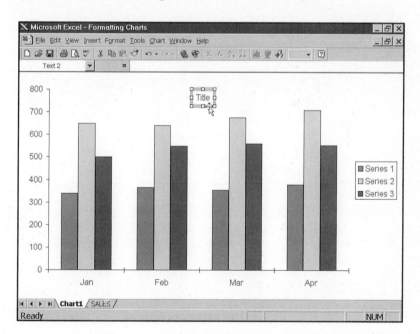

To resize an object using the mouse, select the object by clicking it. Drag one of the black boxes that appears around the selected object to expand or contract the object. Drag a handle on the edge of a text box to keep the object's other dimension the same. Drag a handle on the corner of a text box to change two dimensions at the same time. Words in a text box wrap to fit the new size.

Excel resizes pie wedges when you move them. The farther you move the wedges from the center, the smaller the wedges and pie become.

Resizing unattached text changes the size of the box the text is inside of, not the text itself. You can determine how text will wrap by changing the size of the box around the text. To resize the text itself, you need to use the Font tab in the Format dialog box to change the point size (see "Formatting Text and Numbers," later in this chapter).

Changing Object Colors, Patterns, and Borders

You can change the appearance of every object in a chart by using the formatting commands. For many objects, changing appearance consists of adding borders to the object and changing the fill pattern and color of the area around the object. You can add a shadowed border, for example, around a title and change the background color behind the title, or you can change the patterns and colors of the columns in a column chart. With the axes, you can change the appearance of the axis line and modify the tick marks.

In this section, you learn the general procedures for changing the patterns, colors, and borders of objects in a chart. In the following sections, you learn how to make other changes in the appearance of specific objects in a chart; for example, modifying the tick marks on the axes, or changing the spacing between the columns in a chart.

To change the borders, colors, and patterns of selected objects, follow these steps:

1. To display the Format dialog box, double-click the object, or click with the right mouse button on the object and choose Format. Alternatively, select the object and then choose Format, Selected object.

   The Format, Selected object command changes, depending on the object that is selected. If a data series is selected, for example, the Format, Selected Data Series command appears in the menu.

   The Format dialog box for the selected object appears. The Format Data Series dialog box is shown in Figure 31.1.

2. Select the Patterns tab if it isn't already selected.

3. Make selections from the dialog box.

   For options that are listed in drop-down list boxes, click the down arrow to display the selections.

   To select a fill effect, click Fill Effects to display the Fill Effects dialog box. The Fill Effects dialog box is discussed below.

4. When you have finished making your selections, choose OK.

Pattern dialog boxes are similar for all objects except the axes. The left group in the dialog box displays formatting for the border or line in the object. The right group in the box displays options for the area of the object, including color and fill effects. A sample of the completed format appears in the bottom-left corner. The options in the Pattern dialog boxes are described in Table 31.1.

TIP To format one marker, click the marker to select the data series; click again to select the marker, and follow the steps to the left.

Table 31.1   The Pattern Dialog Box Options

Option	Description
Border	
Automatic	Uses default settings.
None	Uses no border.
Custom	
Style	Changes type of line.
Color	Changes color of line. Choose from 56 alternatives.
Weight	Changes the thickness of a line.
Area	
Automatic	Uses default settings.
None	Uses no fill (background shows through).
Custom	
Color	Changes the color of the background color of the object. If no pattern is selected, this will be the color of the object.
Fill Effects	Opens the Fill Effects dialog box.
Sample	Shows you how your selections will appear.

Part VIII

Ch

31

The Fill Effects dialog box is a new feature in Excel 97 that enables you to select from among many customized fill effects to enhance your charts. You can use fill effects to enhance data markers, the plot and chart areas, and the walls of 3-D charts. To select a fill effect for a selected object, follow these steps:

1. Choose the Fill Effects button in the Format dialog box.

2. To select a gradient fill, select the Gradient tab and make selections in the Colors, Shading Styles and Variants groups.

   The One Color option (see Figure 31.3) uses one color, fading to black or white, to create the gradient. Select the color from the Color 1 list that appears when you select this option, and use the Dark – Light slider to change the fading from black to white.

   The Two Colors option uses two colors to create the gradient, fading from Color 1 to Color 2, as shown in Figure 31.4.

   The Preset option presents you with a selection of built-in gradients in the Preset Colors list (see Figure 31.5).

FIG. 31.3

The One Color gradient fills an object with one color, fading from light to dark.

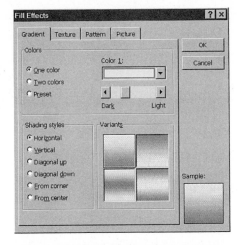

FIG. 31.4

The Two Colors gradient fills an object with two colors, fading from color 1 to color 2.

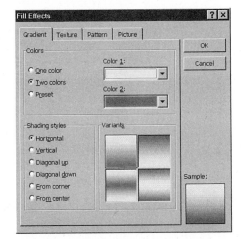

FIG. 31.5

The Preset gradient fills an object with a color gradient that you select from the Preset Colors list.

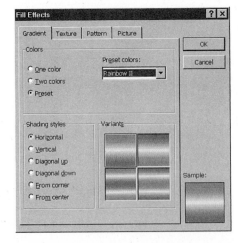

Select a style for the gradient in the Shading Styles group, and a variant on that style in the Variants group.

3. To use a texture to create a fill, select the Texture tab (see Figure 31.6) and select the texture you want to use.

FIG. 31.6

You can use a texture in the Texture tab to create a fill effect in your charts.

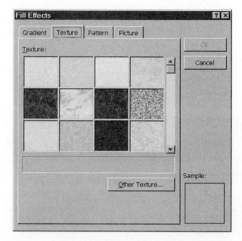

You can use your own textures to create a fill. Choose Other Texture to open the Select Texture dialog box and select the file for the texture you want to use for the fill. The texture can be stored in a bitmap (BMP, DIB) or Windows metafile (WMF), or any other graphics file for which you have installed an import filter.

4. To use a pattern to create a fill, select the Pattern tab (see Figure 31.7) and select a pattern in the Pattern group.

FIG. 31.7

Select a pattern to use for the fill in the Pattern tab.

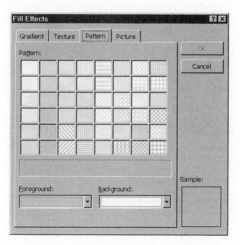

Select the foreground and background colors for the pattern in the Foreground and Background palettes.

5. To use a picture to create a fill, select the Picture tab.

   Choose Select Picture and select the file for the picture you want to use for the fill and choose OK. A sample of the picture appears in the Sample box. Select options in the Format and Apply groups.

   See Chapter 32, "Building Complex Charts," to learn more about using pictures in charts.

6. When you have finished making the selections for the fill effect, choose OK.

You can use only one type of fill effect for an object. You can experiment with the various fill effects in the Fill Effects dialog box, but only your last selection will take effect.

Pattern boxes for objects such as arrows and axes include options that specifically affect the objects. Formatting these objects is discussed in a following section of this chapter.

If you choose the Invert if Negative option, the data markers for column, bar, area, and pie charts display with the background and foreground colors reversed. This option works only if you are working with a data series that has negative values.

The largest areas in a chart are the chart background and the plot area. The chart background includes the entire chart; the plot area includes only the area within the axes. You can change the colors, patterns, and boundaries of both areas. Click the background area before choosing the format command. Figure 31.8 shows a chart with a gradient fill for the chart background and a solid white pattern for the plot area, with the text for the axes in boldface.

FIG. 31.8

A chart and plot area formatted for a standout appearance.

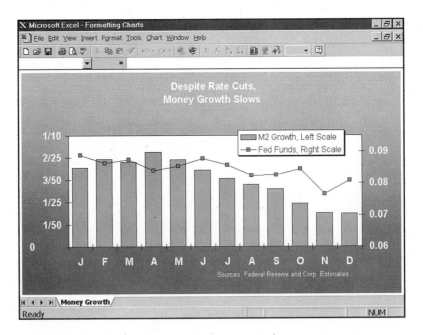

Formatting Text and Numbers

You can format any text that appears in a chart, including the axes and legend labels, any titles or data values that you have inserted, or any unattached text that you placed in a chart. You also can format the numbers that appear in a chart. You can, for example, add dollar signs to the numbers on the value (Y) axis.

Understanding How to Format Text and Numbers

To reach format commands quickly, display a shortcut menu by clicking the text with the right mouse button, and then click the Format command. Figure 31.9 shows the shortcut menu displayed for an attached title.

FIG. 31.9
A shortcut menu is displayed by clicking an object with the right mouse button.

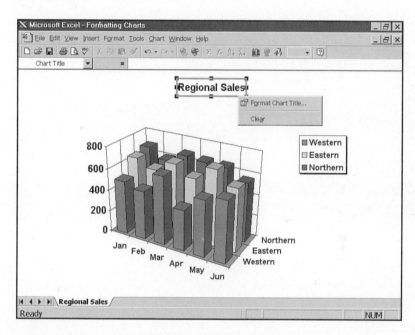

TIP If you make a change to a chart pattern or color and don't like the results, you can use the Edit, Undo command to change it back.

N O T E Several tools are available for formatting text. You can use formatting tools for changing alignment, adding bold and italic formatting, and selecting the font and font size. To add the Formatting toolbar to your screen, choose View, Toolbars, Formatting. Or click an existing toolbar with the right mouse button and select Formatting from the menu. Then, select the text in the chart and click the tool you want to use.

As an alternative to the shortcut menus, you can select the text and then choose Format, Selected object or double-click the text. When the Format dialog box opens, choose the Font tab to view the options for formatting text. If you have selected an object that has numbers—for example, the value axis—you can select the Number tab to format the numbers.

After you open the Format dialog box for a selected object and change the formatting for the text or numbers, you can select the Patterns tab to change the borders, patterns, and colors for that object without leaving the dialog box, and you can select the Alignment tab to change text alignment.

N O T E The procedure for hiding selected parts of a chart is similar to the procedure for creating unattached text. Create an empty, unattached text box by making an unattached text box that contains only one space character. (If the space appears as a blank character in the pattern, select the text and choose Format, Selected Object and select the Font tab. Next, choose Background Transparent to make the character's background invisible.) Select the Patterns tab and select a Foreground and Background color that match the area being covered. Move the box in front of what you want to hide. ▨

Changing Fonts and Styles

You can change the font, font size, and font style for any text that appears in a chart, such as in a title or along the chart axes, by making selections in the Font tab of the Format dialog box.

T I P If you choose fonts that are unavailable in your printer, the printed chart will differ from the on-screen chart. Use only TT (TrueType) or printer fonts.

To change the fonts and font style for text in a chart, follow these steps:

1. Select the object whose text you want to change.
2. Choose Format, Selected object, or click the object with the right mouse button and select the Format command from the shortcut menu, or double-click the object to open the Format dialog box.
3. Select the Font tab. The dialog box shown in Figure 31.10 appears.
4. From the Font list, choose the font you want. Check the sample box to see how that font looks.
5. From the Font Style list, choose the font style.
6. From the Size list, choose the point size. Remember that approximately 72 points equal one inch of height.
7. Choose one of the Underline options, if you want.
8. If you prefer, select one of the Strikethrough, Superscript, or Subscript options.
9. If you don't want the selected text to proportionately resize when you change the size of the object, clear the Auto Scale option.

FIG. 31.10
Select the font, font style, and point size for the selected object in the Font tab of the Format Chart Title dialog box.

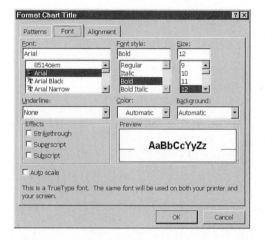

10. From the Color list, choose a color. Use Automatic for black-and-white printers.

11. Choose one of the Background options.

    You also can change the immediate background behind the text, which is useful for text that overlaps lines or patterns. Select Automatic to use the default background pattern, Transparent to let the area show through, and Opaque to remove any pattern behind characters but keep the foreground color.

 TIP To change the default font used for all text in a chart, double-click outside the border of the chart and choose the Font tab. Select the font, font style, size, and choose OK.

12. Choose OK.

Aligning and Rotating Text

You can align the text in charts. For some text objects—for example, titles—you can change both the horizontal and vertical alignment, as well as the orientation of the text. For other objects, such as the labels on the axes, you can change only the orientation. The capability of changing the text's orientation enables you to rotate axis titles or text boxes that contain explanations.

To change text alignment, follow these steps:

1. Select the object whose alignment you want to change.

2. Choose Format, Selected object, or click the object with the right mouse button and select the Format command from the shortcut menu, or double-click the object to open the Format Title dialog box.

3. Select the Alignment tab. The Alignment tab for titles is shown in Figure 31.11.

4. Select the desired alignment options from the Horizontal and Vertical drop-down lists.

FIG. 31.11

You can change text alignment and orientation in the Alignment tab of the Format Chart Title dialog box.

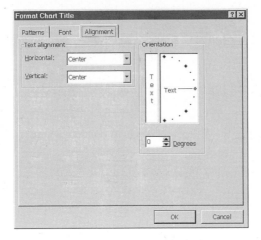

5. Drag the pointer in the Orientation box up or down to change the orientation of the text.

or

Specify a value in the Degrees box between 90 and -90 degrees.

To quickly select a stacked orientation, reading top to bottom, click the box that has the word Text in it (next to the Orientation gauge).

6. Choose OK.

Formatting Numbers

You can format the numbers in a chart just as you format the numbers in a worksheet. If the numbers in the worksheet you used to create the chart are formatted, the numbers used in the value axis in the chart are formatted the same way. You can override this formatting, however, or add formatting if the numbers in the chart are unformatted.

To format the numbers in a chart, follow these steps:

1. Select the object whose numbers you want to format.

2. Choose Format, Selected object, or click the object with the right mouse button and select the Format command from the shortcut menu, or double-click the object to open the Format Axis dialog box.

3. Choose the Number tab.

4. Choose the kind of number you want to format from the Category list.

   The options displayed in the dialog box will change depending on the category you select. If you select the Number category, for example, the dialog box will appear similar to Figure 31.12. Here, you have options to control the number of decimal places, whether or not a comma is used as a thousands separator, and a list of formats that can be used to display negative numbers. If you select the Date category, the dialog box will appear similar to Figure 31.13, where you have a list of date formats you can select from.

FIG. 31.12
When you select the Number category from the Number tab of the Format Axis dialog box, you have several options for formatting numbers.

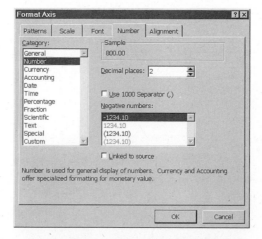

FIG. 31.13
When you select the Date category from the Number tab of the Format Axis dialog box, you can select from a list of date formats.

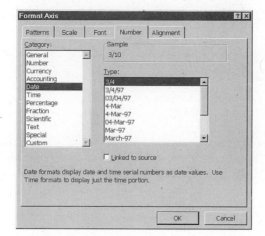

5. Select the formatting options you want to use. A sample of what the format will look like appears at the top of the dialog box.

6. To return the formatting to the numbers in the source worksheet, select the Linked to Source option.

7. Choose OK.

▶ **See** "Aligning and Rotating Text," **p. 753**

Formatting Data Series

Besides formatting the borders, patterns, and colors for the data series in your charts, you can enhance the presentation of your data by adding error bars, drop lines, hi-lo lines, and up and down bars. You also can change the gap width between the columns in a column chart, and make other formatting changes. The available options depend on the type of chart with which you are working. You access these options from the Format dialog box.

Understanding Data Series Formatting

A range of options is available for all the chart types and formats, which you access by using the Format, Selected Data Series command. To change the options for a data series, select the data series you want to format by clicking one of the data points in the series and then choose Format, Selected Data Series. Select the Options tab to display the options available for the chart type you are working with. Figure 31.14 shows the options available for column charts.

FIG. 31.14

The Options tab in the Format Data Series dialog box varies depending on the type of chart you are working with. Here you see the options for 2-D column charts.

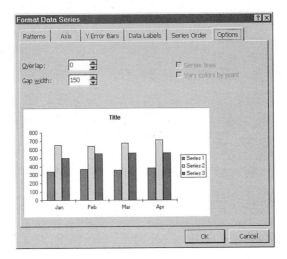

The various options that are available for the different chart types and formats are described in Table 31.2. Not all of these options are available for any one chart type. Which options are available depends on the chart type you work with. The table specifies to what chart types each option applies.

Formatting Trendlines

You can add a trendline to a series of data points to analyze the direction your data is moving, based on regression or moving average analysis. You learn how to add a trendline to a data series in Chapter 32. After you add a trendline, you can format it just like any other object in a chart.

Table 31.2 Chart Formatting Options

Option (Type of Chart)	Description
Overlap (bar and column)	Specifies how much bars or columns overlap. Enter a positive number as the percentage of overlap. 100 is full overlap. A negative number separates individual bars or columns.
Gap Width (bar and column)	Specifies the space between groups of bars or columns. Measured as a percentage of one bar or column width.

Option (Type of Chart)	Description
Gap Depth (3-D charts)	Specifies the spacing in depth between markers as a percentage of a marker. 50 changes the space of the depth between markers to 50 percent of a marker width. Because the chart depth has not changed, this action makes markers thinner. The number must be between 0 and 500.
Chart Depth (3-D charts)	Specifies how deep a 3-D chart is, relative to its chart's width. Enter a number as a percentage of the chart width. 50 makes the depth 50 percent of the width. The number must be between 20 and 2000.
Series Lines (stacked bar and stacked column)	Draws a line between types of markers in stacked bar and stacked column charts.
Vary Colors by Point/Slice (pie and charts with one data series)	Specifies a different color or pattern by category for each marker in all pie charts or any chart with one data series.
Drop Lines (line and area)	Drops a vertical line from a marker to the category (X) axis. Used on line or area charts.
High-Low Lines (2-D line charts)	Draws a line between the highest and lowest lines at a specific category. Used on 2-D line charts.
Up-Down Bars (line)	Used in stock market charts to draw a rectangle between opening and closing prices. Creates an open-high-low chart. Use only on line charts. If series are in rows, Hi data should be in the first row; Open data in the second row; and Close data in the third row.
Category Labels (radar)	Creates labels for the category axis (spokes) on radar charts.
Angle of First Slice (pie)	Specifies the starting angle, in degrees, for the first wedge in a pie chart. Vertical is zero degrees.
Doughnut Hole Size (doughnut)	Changes the size of the hole in the center of doughnut charts. 50 makes the diameter of the hole 50 percent of the diameter of the doughnut. The number must be between 10 and 90.
Area of bubbles (bubble)	Data value proportional to area of bubble.
Width of bubbles (bubble)	Data value proportional to width of bubble.
Scale bubble size to (bubble)	Proportionally changes size of all bubbles.

To format a trendline, follow these steps:

1. Select the trendline.

2. Choose Format, Selected Trendline, click the object with the right mouse button and select the Format Trendline command from the shortcut menu or double-click the object to open the Format dialog box.

Part

VIII

Ch

31

3. Choose the Patterns tab.

4. Choose the Line options you want to use for the trendline. Refer to Table 31.1 for a description of the options.

5. Choose OK.

If you need to make any changes in the way the trendline is derived and displayed, you can access the same options you used to create the trendline by selecting the Type and Options tabs.

Formatting Error Bars

You can use error bars to give a visual indication of your data's margin of error. The margin of error is a measure of the degree of uncertainty or variation in a data set. Learn how to add error bars to a data series in Chapter 32. You can change the patterns of the error bars by using the Format dialog box.

To format error bars, follow these steps:

1. Select the error bars by clicking one of the bars with the mouse.

2. Choose Format, Selected Error Bars, click the object with the right mouse button and select the Format Error Bars command from the shortcut menu or double-click the object. The Format dialog box appears.

3. Choose the Patterns tab.

4. Choose one of the Line options. Refer to Table 31.1 for a description of the options.

5. Select the type of marker you want to use in the Marker box.

6. Choose OK.

You can select the Y Error Bar tab to make changes in how the error bars are set up.

▶ **See** "Adding or Deleting Data," **p.721**

▶ **See** "Working with the Series Formula," **p.725**

▶ **See** "Automatically Analyzing Trends with Charts," **p.776**

▶ **See** "Adding Error Bars to a Chart," **p.780**

Formatting Data Markers

Besides customizing the color, weight, and style of the lines used in line charts, you can modify the color and style of the markers used to mark the data points.

To format the markers in a line chart, follow these steps:

1. Select the line you want to modify.

2. Choose Format, Selected Data Series, click the object with the right mouse button and select the Format Data Series command from the shortcut menu, or double-click the object, to open the Format Data Series dialog box.

3. Choose the Patterns tab to display the dialog box shown in Figure 31.15.

FIG. 31.15

You can format the markers used to mark data points in a line chart in the Patterns tab of the Format Data Series dialog box.

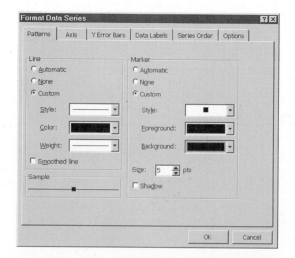

4. Choose a Line option. Refer to Table 31.1 for a description of the options.

5. Choose among the following options from the Marker group:

Option	Description
Automatic	Uses default setting.
None	No markers used at data points.
Custom	
Style	Changes the type of marker used.
Foreground	Changes the color of the outline of the marker.
Background	Changes the color of the fill in the marker.
Size	Changes the size of the marker.
Shadow	Adds a shadow effect to the marker.

6. Choose the Smoothed Line option to have Excel smooth the line between data points.

7. Check the Sample box to see whether the data point looks the way you want, and then choose OK.

Scaling and Customizing an Axis

When you create a chart, Excel uses the default settings for the axis style, tick marks, and scaling. You can customize the axis, changing the style of the line used for the axis, the tick marks, the positioning of the tick-mark labels, and the scaling of the axis.

Customizing the Format of an Axis

To customize the axes in a chart, follow these steps:

1. Select the axis by clicking one of the axis lines or by pressing the arrow keys until the axis is selected. Black handles appear at each end of the axis.

2. Choose Format, Selected Axis, or click the object with the right mouse button and select the Format Axis command from the shortcut menu (or double-click the object) to open the Format Axis dialog box.

3. Select the Patterns tab to display the dialog box shown in Figure 31.16.

FIG. 31.16

You can customize the appearance of the axes in the Format Axis dialog box.

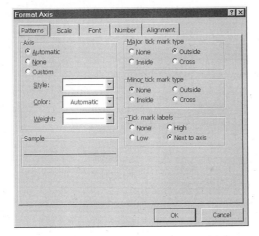

4. Choose one of the Axis options. Refer to Table 31.1 for a description of the options.

5. Choose the desired options from the Major and Minor boxes.

    Tick marks intersect the value and category axes and are used to divide the axes into equal units. They facilitate reading values from the axes. You can have both major tick marks, which display next to the labels for the value and category labels for the axes, and minor tick marks, which indicate subunits between the major tick marks.

    Select the None option to remove tick marks, the Inside option to have tick marks displayed inside the axis, the Outside option to display tick marks on the outside of the axis, or the Cross option to have tick marks cross the axis.

6. Choose an option from the Tick Mark Labels box to specify where the tick-mark labels are to be positioned.

    Tick-mark labels are used to identify the values and categories in a chart and are displayed along the axes. You can select from among four options for where the tick-mark labels are positioned. Select None to remove the tick-mark labels or Next to Axis to place the labels next to the axis, regardless of where the axis is positioned. Select Low to position the labels on the bottom (category) or to the left (value) of a chart, even if the corresponding axis is at the opposite side. Select High to position the labels at the top (category) or to the right (value) of the chart, even if the corresponding axis is at the opposite side.

7. Check to see whether the line in the sample box looks like you want, and then choose OK.

To change the formatting of the axis text and numbers, refer to "Formatting Text and Numbers," earlier in the chapter.

TIP When you change multiple axis settings, change one setting at a time, see the result, and then change another. Otherwise, the results can become confusing.

Changing the Scaling of an Axis

You can modify the scaling of the category (X) and value (Y) axes to enhance the presentation of your data. The dialog box to change the scale of an axis is different for the category and the value axes.

The Scale tab for the category (X) axis in the Format Axis dialog box, shown in Figure 31.17, enables you to change the appearance of the category (X) axis. To change the point at which the value (Y) axis crosses the category (X) axis, change the number in the Value (Y) Axis Crosses at Category Number text box. To display fewer or more labels or tick marks along the category axis, change the values in the Number of Categories Between Tick-Mark Labels and Number of Categories Between Tick Marks text boxes.

FIG. 31.17

You can change the scaling of the category (X) scale in the Scale tab of the Format Axis dialog box.

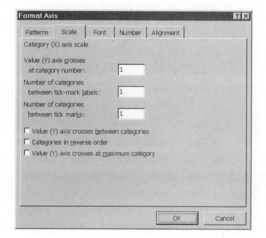

You can have the value (Y) axis cross either between or within categories by using the Value (Y) Axis Crosses between Categories option. To reverse the order in which the categories are displayed, select the Categories in Reverse Order. Select the Value (Y) Axis Crosses at Maximum Category to move the value (Y) axis to the high end of the category (X) axis.

In a Scatter (XY) chart, the Scale tab in the Format dialog box for the category (X) axis (see Figure 31.18) enables you to specify the range of the scale by changing the values in the Minimum and Maximum text boxes. By default, these values are determined automatically. To return to the default values, select the Auto check boxes.

To change the major and minor units used for the major and minor tick marks, enter new values in the Major Unit and Minor Unit text boxes. You also can change where the value (Y) axis crosses by changing the value in the Value (Y) Axis Crosses At text box.

To plot data on a logarithmic scale, select the Logarithmic Scale option. Select the Values in Reverse Order option to plot the values from high to low, instead of from low to high. To move the value (Y) axis to the high end of the category (X) axis scale, select the Value (Y) Axis Crosses at Maximum Value.

FIG. 31.18

Use the Scale tab in the Format Axis dialog box for a Scatter (XY) chart.

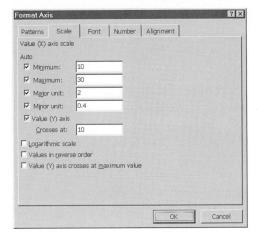

The Scale tab in the Format Axis dialog box, used for formatting the value (Y) axis, is shown in Figure 31.19. You can change the minimum and maximum values, the major and minor scaling units, and where the category (X) axis crosses the value (Y) axis. You also can choose to use a logarithmic scale, plot values in reverse order, and have the category (X) axis cross at the maximum value on the value (Y) scale. (See the previous descriptions of the category (X) axis tabs for a more detailed discussion of these options.)

FIG. 31.19

You can change the scaling of the value (Y) scale in the Scale tab of the Format Axis dialog box.

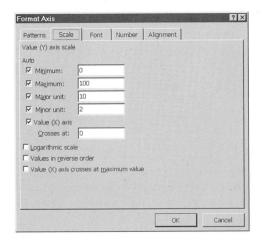

N O T E Don't crowd tick marks and axis labels. Some charts, such as charts of stock prices or instrument readings, contain so many data points that the labels and tick marks crowd one another. To reduce this clutter, choose the category (X) axis and open the Format Axis dialog box. Choose the Scale tab and enter larger numbers into the text boxes for Number of Categories between Tick-Mark Labels and for Number of Categories Between Tick Marks. The larger the numbers you enter, the more distance between individual labels and individual tick marks. ■

▶ **See** "Inserting Arrows," **p. 739**

Formatting Arrows

You can change an arrow's appearance by double-clicking the arrow to display the Format AutoShape dialog box, by choosing Format AutoShape from the shortcut menu, or by selecting the arrow and choosing Format, AutoShape. Select the Colors and Lines tab to modify the appearance of the arrow (see Figure 31.20). Notice that the Begin Style and End Style drop-down lists enable you to use many different arrowhead shapes and to change an arrow into a line.

FIG. 31.20

You can change the appearance of an arrow in the Colors and Lines tab of the Format AutoShape dialog box.

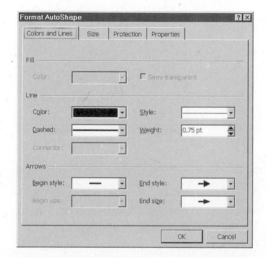

Part VIII Ch 31

N O T E Change an arrow to a line by selecting the arrow and then displaying the Format AutoShape dialog box. The dialog box in Figure 31.20 has many alternatives for the color, weight, and style of the arrow's shaft and head. To make a straight line, select the straight line from the End Style drop-down list.

Formatting 3-D Charts

Some 3-D charts may display data in such a way that some series are difficult to see. In Figure 31.21, for example, the second and third series are blocked from view. To avoid this problem, you can rotate and adjust 3-D charts by using the Format, 3-D View command. After rotation, the same 3-D chart appears as shown in Figure 31.22.

Rotating a 3-D Chart by Dragging

With a mouse, you can rotate a 3-D chart in any direction by dragging one end of an axis. To rotate a 3-D chart by dragging, perform the following steps:

1. Click at the tip of one of the axes.

   Black handles appear at the end of all eight tips (see Figure 31.23).

FIG. 31.21

A 3-D chart with data series blocked from view.

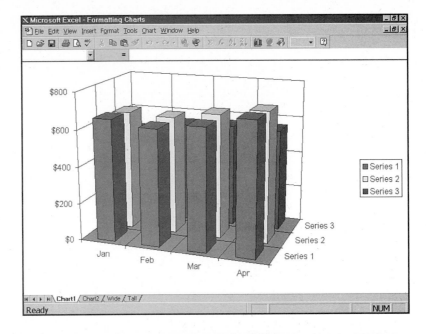

FIG. 31.22

Rotating and adjusting the perspective of a 3-D chart displays the series from a better angle.

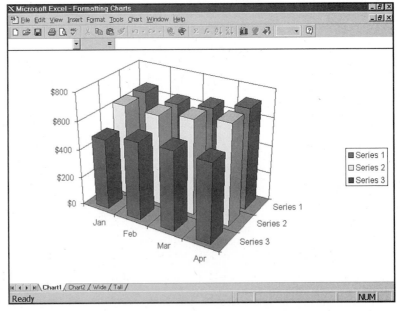

2. Drag one of the handles on the side close to you. Drag in the direction you want the chart to rotate. Imagine that the chart is in a sphere and that you are dragging the mouse along the surface of this sphere. As you drag, a wire-frame outline of the chart depicts the chart's orientation, as shown in Figure 31.24.

FIG. 31.23
Rotate 3-D charts by dragging a black handle at the tip of an axis.

Black handles

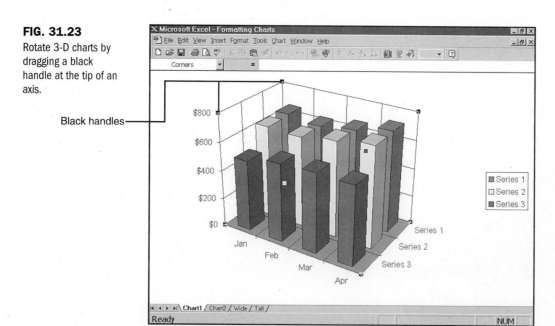

FIG. 31.24
Rotate the wire frame as though inside a sphere to change the view of 3-D charts.

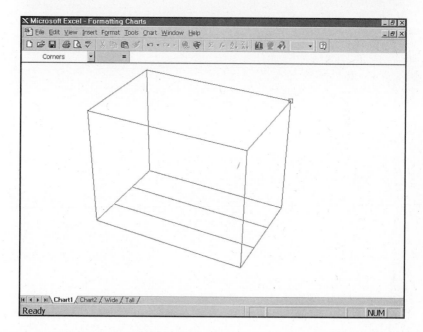

3. Release the mouse button when the outline appears in the correct orientation. Excel redraws the chart, as shown in Figure 31.22.

N O T E   Drag different handles as the chart rotates. Use one of the handles closest to you when you begin dragging the chart. After the chart passes approximately 90 degrees of rotation, you may have difficulty visualizing how the chart is rotating. Release the handle you were dragging and begin dragging one of the handles that is now in front. ■

T I P   Use the mouse to get the basic rotation and perspective for your 3-D charts and use Chart, 3-D View to fine-tune the settings.

Rotating a 3-D Chart by Command

You also can use the Chart, 3-D View command to change the perspective on 3-D charts. Using the dialog box is helpful when you need to apply the same perspective to several 3-D charts. You can use the mouse to get the exact rotation and perspective for the first chart, and then use the 3-D View dialog box to read and record the settings for that chart. Next, use the Chart, 3-D View command to apply those same settings to your other charts.

When you choose Chart, 3-D View, the dialog box shown in Figure 31.25 appears. Selections in this dialog box change the angle and perspective from which the 3-D chart is drawn.

FIG. 31.25

Rotate the wire-frame chart to rotate your 3-D chart.

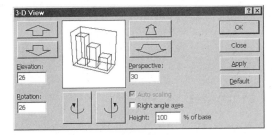

You can use a mouse or a keyboard to rotate or adjust the viewpoint shown in the 3-D View dialog box. Using the mouse is faster and easier.

If you are using the mouse to rotate or adjust the viewpoint, click the appropriate directional button to rotate or adjust the viewpoint.

To rotate or adjust the viewpoint with the keyboard, select a text box and then type a number within the range. The following table lists the available options.

Option	Effect on the Chart
Elevation	Changes the height from which you see the chart. Use an angle from -90 to +90 degrees for all charts except pie charts. Use an angle from 10 to 80 degrees for pie charts.
Rotation	Rotates the chart around the vertical (Z) axis. The range is from 0 to 360 degrees.
Perspective	Controls the vanishing point or the sense of depth in the chart. Use a number between 0 and 100 to specify the ratio of the front of the chart to its back.

Option	Effect on the Chart
Height % of Base	Controls the height of the vertical (Z) axis as a percentage of the chart width (X) axis. Enter a number between 5 and 500.
Right Angle Axes	Freezes axis angles at 90 degrees. Perspective is turned off.

When the wire-frame chart has the orientation you want, choose OK. By choosing the Apply button, you can keep the dialog box on-screen and apply the current settings to the chart so that you can see how they look. Choose the Default button to return all dialog box settings to default values.

N O T E   You can format the floor and walls of a 3-D chart using the same procedures discussed in "Changing Object Colors, Patterns, and Borders," a previous section of this chapter. You can change the border and area formatting in the Pattern tab of the Format dialog box. To open the Format dialog box, either choose Format, Selected item, or click the object with the right mouse button and select the Format command from the shortcut menu, or double-click the object. ■

Clearing Chart Formats or Contents

You don't have to create a new chart from the worksheet when you want to change all the data or formats. Use the Edit Clear command to selectively remove chart objects and data series or to remove just the formatting from a data series.

To remove a chart object and its formatting, follow these steps:

1. Select the chart object.
2. Choose Edit, Clear, All or press the Delete key.

   If you select the entire chart, all objects in the chart—including the data series—are removed, leaving a blank chart sheet or embedded chart. If you select an embedded chart, the chart is removed from the worksheet.

   You can copy and paste new data on top of a chart whose contents you deleted. The new data uses the format of the preceding chart.

To remove a data series, trendline, or error bars, follow these steps:

1. Select the data series, trendline, or error bars.
2. Choose Edit, Clear, and then choose either Series, Trendline, or Error Bars from the submenu, or press the Delete key.

   The command in the submenu changes, depending on the type of object that you selected.

To remove just the formatting for a selected series, follow these steps:

1. Select the data series.
2. Choose Edit, Clear, Formats.

   This command clears any custom formatting that has been applied to a data series and restores the default formatting that is defined by the default chart format.

N O T E   To retrieve an accidentally deleted object or data series, use the Edit, Undo command or the Undo button on the Standard toolbar to undo your mistake. ▧

TROUBLESHOOTING

When I select a single data point and use the Edit, Clear command or Delete key to try to delete that data point, the entire data series is deleted. How can I delete a single data point? You cannot truly delete a single data point on an existing chart. You can delete either the data for the point in the worksheet that is the source for the chart, or you can format the data point so you don't see it. Select the data point and choose Format, Selected Data Point. Select the Patterns tab, and select the None options on both sides of the dialog box. Depending on the type of chart, you may have to select None for both the Border and Area groups, as in a column chart, or the Line and Marker groups, as in a line chart. Formatting a data point with the None options effectively removes the point from the chart. Note that in line charts, if you remove a data point, the line connecting the adjacent points also is removed.

▶ **See** "Choosing a Chart Type," **p. 712**
▶ **See** "Choosing a Default Chart Type," **p. 720**

Transferring Chart Formats

After you create a chart, you can apply formatting from another chart. To transfer a chart format, use the Edit, Paste Special command to copy the formatting from one chart and paste it onto another chart.

To transfer a chart format, perform the following steps:

1. Activate the chart that has the format you want to copy.
2. Select the entire chart by clicking near the outside of the chart or pressing the up or down arrow key until the chart is selected. Black handles appear around the outside of the chart.
3. Choose Edit, Copy.
4. Activate the chart you want to format.
5. Choose Edit, Paste Special to display the Paste Special dialog box (see Figure 31.26).

FIG. 31.26
Use the Paste Special dialog box to copy formatting from one chart to another.

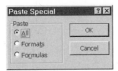

6. Choose Formats from the Paste Special dialog box.
7. Choose OK.

Building Complex Charts

When you have a situation that requires special charts or you need to go beyond the fundamentals in modifying and formatting charts, the techniques in this chapter will help you. Use Excel's powerful charting features to plot individual data sets differently on the same chart, making it easy to compare different types of data. You can add trendlines and error bars to your charts to make them even more informative. Add visual impact to your charts by replacing data points with graphics.

Creating Combination Charts

Combination charts present two or more data series on the same chart and use different chart types for the data series. For example, you can plot one series using a column chart and a second series using a line chart to make it easier to compare the two sets of data or to look for possible interactions between the data sets. You can also use a combination chart if you need to use a different axis with a different scale for plotting one or more of the data series in a chart. This might be the case if one of the data series in the chart has a range of values that differs substantially from the other data series in the chart.

Figure 32.1 shows a combination column chart and line chart created by pasting in a data series and then using the Chart, Chart Type command to change the added data to a line chart. The Goal data series is plotted as a line to separate it from the actual data for the Western and Eastern regions. This combination enables you to easily compare more than one type of data.

FIG. 32.1

Use combination charts to show different chart types in the same chart.

Figure 32.2 shows a combination chart where both charts are line charts. This combination enables you to use two value (Y) axes with different scales.

FIG. 32.2

Combination charts enable you to create two axes on the same chart.

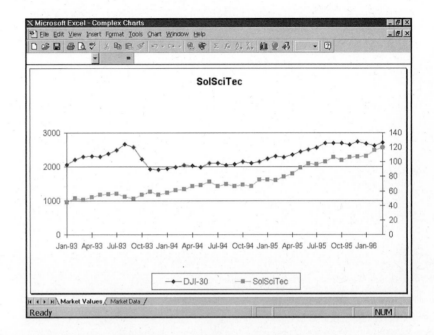

You can create a combination chart in three ways: When you are creating a new chart, you can use the Chart Wizard to create a combination chart by selecting one of the combination chart types from the Custom Types tab in Step 1; you can apply one of the combination chart custom types to an existing chart; or you can select a data series in an existing chart and change the chart type for that series.

You can choose three combination types in the Chart Wizard or the Chart Type dialog box. When you use a predefined combination chart, the data series is divided evenly, with the first half of the data series becoming one chart type and the second half of the data series becoming the other chart type. If the chart has an odd number of data series, the extra series is included in the first chart type.

The third method involves selecting one of the data series and then using the Chart, Chart Type command to change the chart type for the selected series. Once you change the chart type for a data series, you can format that series differently from the other data series by selecting the data series and using the Format, Selected Series command. You can, for example, plot the data series along a secondary axis by selecting the Secondary Axis option in the Axis tab of the Format Data Series dialog box. This is how the chart in Figure 32.2 was created.

Creating a Combination Chart from Custom Chart Types

If you are creating a new combination chart or working with an existing chart, you can apply one of the custom combination chart types to quickly create a combination chart.

To create a new combination chart using the Chart Wizard, perform the following steps:

1. Select the data you want to chart and start the Chart Wizard (see Chapter 29, "Creating Charts," for more details on using the Chart Wizard).
2. Select the Custom Type tab in Step 1 of the Chart Wizard.
3. Select one of the combination chart formats in the Chart Type list.

   The three combination chart types are Column-Area, Column-Line, and Dual Axis.
4. Complete the remaining steps of the Chart Wizard.

To create a combination chart from an existing chart that has at least two data series, using the combination chart subtypes, perform the following steps:

1. Activate the chart.
2. Choose Chart, Chart Type, or click near the outside border of the chart and choose Chart Type from the shortcut menu.
3. Select the Custom Types tab.
4. Select one of the combination chart formats in the Chart Type list.
5. Choose OK.

Whether you use the Chart Wizard or the Chart, Chart Type command, Excel applies one of the chart types to half the data series and the other chart type to the other half of the data series. If an odd number of data series exists, the first chart type receives the greater number of data series.

You can change the chart type used by either one of the data series groups created when you apply one of the predefined combination chart types. Select the data series you want to change and choose Chart, Chart Type. Select the type of chart you want to use for the selected series and choose OK.

Creating a Combination Chart with the Chart, Chart Type Command

You can create a combination chart easily from any existing chart that has two or more data series. Initially, the chart consists of one chart type. However, you can select any individual data series and use the Chart, Chart Type command to change the chart type for the selected series. The chart then becomes a combination chart. You can use this same method to change the type of chart used by any of the series in an existing combination chart.

To create a combination chart using the Chart, Chart Type command, perform the following steps:

1. Open the chart from which you want to create the combination chart.
2. Select the data series whose chart type you want to change.
3. Choose Chart, Chart Type, or choose Chart Type from the Chart shortcut menu.
4. Select the type of chart you want to use for the selected series in the Chart Type dialog box.
5. Choose OK.

Changing Chart Types

You can easily change the chart type used by any one of the data series in a combination chart. To change the chart type, select the data series you want to change and choose Chart, Chart Type. Select the type of chart you want to apply to the selected series and choose OK.

Adding a Secondary Axis

Sometimes you might want to compare two sets of data whose value ranges differ substantially. In this case, using the same category axis for both data sets will obscure the data points for the data set with the lower range of y-values. This problem can be corrected by adding a secondary category axis for one of the data sets. You can also add a secondary axis when you are comparing data sets with different units of measure—for example, dollars and number of units.

To add a secondary axis for a single data series, perform the following steps:

1. Select the series you want to plot along a secondary axis by clicking a data point in the series or by using the up- and down-arrow keys until the series is selected.
2. Choose Format, Selected Series, or choose Format Data Series from the shortcut menu, and select the Axis tab.
3. Select the Secondary Axis option.
4. Choose OK.

▶ **See** "Choosing a Chart Type," **p. 712**
▶ **See** "Scaling and Customizing an Axis," **p. 759**

TROUBLESHOOTING

When I remove the secondary axis for a data series that uses a different scale, the series for the removed axis doesn't use the scale for the removed axis. This behavior is as intended. Once you remove the secondary axis, all of the data series use the scale of the primary axis. To plot a data series with a different scale without displaying a secondary axis, select the data series and add the secondary axis, as described in the previous steps. Then select the secondary axis and choose Format, Selected Axis. Select the Patterns tab and then select the None option in both the Axis and Tick Mark Labels groups. Choose OK. The secondary axis will not be hidden, but the data series will be displayed using the scaling for the hidden axis.

Part
VIII

Ch
32

Using Charts to Analyze Data

Besides lively presentations, charts make excellent analytical tools. Excel charts are linked to one or more worksheets, so playing *what-if* games on the worksheets updates the charts linked to them. Updating can reveal profit-loss crossover points, forecast inventory quantities, or quantify trends for different scenarios.

Excel also has the powerful capability of finding a worksheet value to match changes in the chart. If you drag a bar, column, or line to a new location in the chart, Excel seeks a new worksheet input that produces the result shown in the chart. This feature provides a quick and easy way to make a visual estimate of a situation and have Excel determine the numbers that correspond.

Analyzing Charts for What-If Analysis

You can use Excel to make changes to your worksheet and watch the chart immediately reflect those changes. This capability is valuable for performing what-if types of analysis. Because you can see the effects of your worksheet changes, you can determine emerging trends, crossover points between profit and loss, and mistakes made during data entry.

As Figure 32.3 illustrates, you can position worksheet and chart windows so that all windows are visible. As you change a variable in the worksheet, the Sales versus Costs and the Itemized Cost charts reflect the changes immediately. To arrange chart and worksheet windows side by side, choose Window, New Window to open a new window for the current workbook. Next, choose Window, Arrange, select one of the options in the Arrange group, and choose OK. You can also drag the sides and title bars to arrange the windows. In one of the windows, activate the worksheet, and in the other window activate the chart.

FIG. 32.3

Open new windows and arrange them when you need to see chart and worksheet data simultaneously.

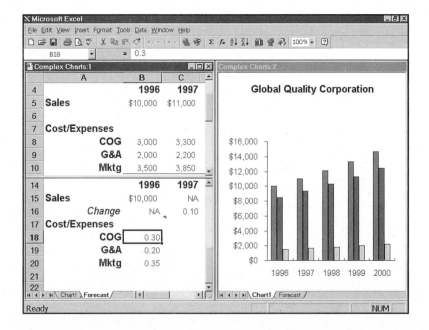

Moving Markers to Change Worksheet Values

Excel enables you to move column, bar, or line markers on a chart and change the corresponding data in the worksheet. If the data is not a value but a formula, Excel executes the Tools, Goal Seek command to find the input value that makes the worksheet correspond to the chart.

To change values on the worksheet from the chart, perform the following steps:

1. Open the workbook containing the worksheet and chart with which you want to work. Activate the chart. The chart must be a two-dimensional column, bar, line, or XY scatter chart.

2. Click once on the data point you want to change; the entire series will be selected. Click a second time on the same data point. Handles appear on the marker as shown in Figure 32.4.

FIG. 32.4
The handles for the selected data point indicate that this column can be dragged to a new height.

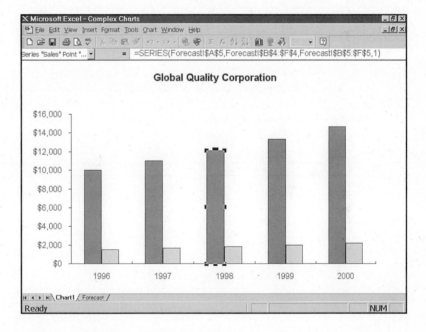

3. Drag the handle at the top of the data point to the location you want. Watch the tip that appears to see the changing numeric value for the marker. A sliding marker shows the position on the value (Y) axis. You can drag the marker past the top of the value (Y) axis if you want.

4. Release the mouse when the marker is at the location you want.

If the column, line, or bar references a number on the worksheet, that number changes in the worksheet. If the column, line, or bar references the result of a formula, Excel activates the Tools, Goal Seek command. This command activates the worksheet for the marker and displays the Goal Seek dialog box, as shown in Figure 32.5.

FIG. 32.5

The Goal Seek dialog box asks which worksheet cell should be changed to achieve the result in the chart.

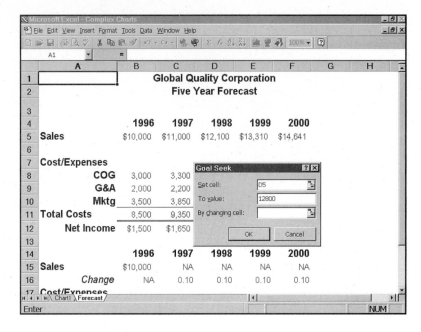

To operate Goal Seek, perform the following steps:

1. In the By Changing Cell text box, select the cell (or type the cell reference of the cell) you want to change to produce the result in the chart. The cell you select must not contain a formula.

2. Choose OK.

   Goal Seek iterates through input values to find the value that produces the result in the chart. Then, the Goal Seek dialog box displays the solution.

3. Choose OK to enter the new input value, or choose Cancel to return to the original worksheet.

When Goal Seek is complete, Excel reactivates the chart.

▶ **See** "Using the Goal Seek Feature," **p. 618**

Automatically Analyzing Trends with Charts

With Excel, there are three ways you can analyze trends and make forecasts: using the fill handles, using worksheet commands, and adding trendlines to a chart. You can add a trendline to a chart using the Chart, Add Trendline command. The trendline will show you the direction of the plotted data and can also be used to make predictions. Regression analysis is used to create the trendline from the chart data, and you can select from among five types of regression lines or calculate a line that displays *moving averages*. Moving averages smooth out fluctuations in a data series by basing a given data point on the trendline on the average of a specified number of prior data points.

CAUTION

Trendlines are a statistical tool and, like any statistical tool, can be misused or abused. If you are going to use trendlines to analyze the data in your charts, be sure that you understand the theory behind their use and that the trendlines represent a real trend in your data. It is very easy, especially with the aid of computers, to fit a trendline to data that doesn't necessarily have any statistical validity.

You can select any series of data in a chart and add a trendline, as long as the selected data is an area, a bar, a column, a line, or a scatter (XY) chart. When you add a trendline to a data series, it is linked to the data, so if you change the values for any of the data points in the series, the trendline is automatically recalculated and redrawn in the chart. If you change the chart type for the data series to a chart type other than one listed previously, the trendline is permanently deleted.

You have the option of setting the y-intercept value for the trendline and adding the regression equation and r-squared value for the regression to the chart. You can also make backward and forward forecasts for the data, based on the trendline and its associated regression equation.

Adding a trendline to a data series is a simple process of selecting the data series and choosing the Chart, Add Trendline command. You do need to know what type of regression analysis you want to use on the data.

To add a trendline to a data series, perform the following steps:

1. Activate that chart that has the data series you want to analyze.

2. Choose Chart, Add Trendline or select Add Trendline from the shortcut menu. Select the Type tab to display the Add Trendline dialog box shown in Figure 32.6.

FIG. 32.6
You select the type of trendline you want to add to the selected data series in the Add Trendline dialog box.

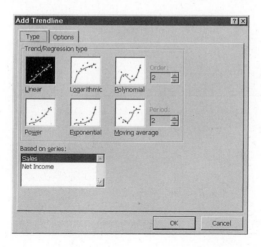

3. Select the data series for which you want to create a trendline in the Based On Series list.

4. Select from the six trend/regression types. The following table describes the regression types and how they are derived:

Type	Description
Linear	Produces a linear regression line using the equation $y = mx + b$, where m is the slope of the line and b is the y-intercept of the line.
Logarithmic	Produces a logarithmic regression line using the equation $y = c\ln x + b$, where c and b are constants, and $\ln$ is the natural logarithm.
Polynomial	Produces a polynomial regression line using the equation $y = b + c1x + c2x2 + c3x3 + \ldots c6x6$, where b and $c1$ through $c6$ are constants. Select the order of the polynomial equation in the Order text box. The maximum order for a polynomial trendline is 6.
Power	Produces a power regression line using the equation $y = cxb$, where c and b are constants.
Exponential	Produces an exponential regression line using the equation $y = cebx$, where c and b are constants and e is the base of the natural logarithm.
Moving Average	Produces a moving average, where the value for each data point on the trendline is based on the average of a specified number of prior data points (periods). The greater the number of periods used to calculate the moving average, the smoother but less responsive the resulting trendline. The equation used to calculate the moving average is $Ft=At+At-1n+\ldots At-n+1$.

5. Select the Options tab if you want to select any of the options that are available for trendlines (see Figure 32.7).

FIG. 32.7
You can customize the trendline you add to a data series in the Options tab of the Add Trendline dialog box.

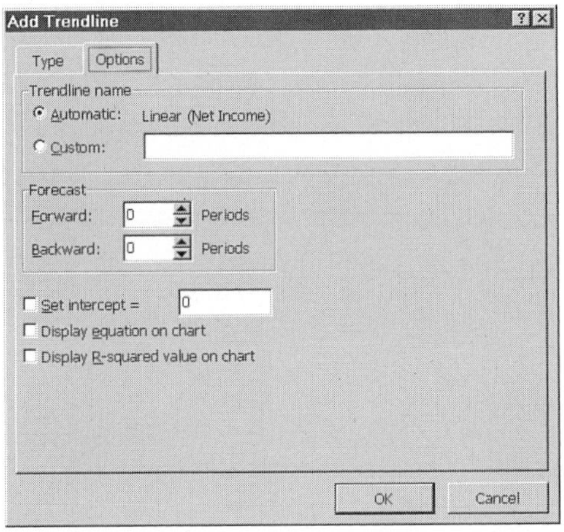

The trendlines options are described in the following table:

Option	Description
Trendline Name	
Automatic	Applies the data series name to the trendline.
Custom	Types a new name in the Custom text box.
Forecast	
Forward	Projects the trendline forward for the number of periods specified in the Periods text box.
Backward	Projects the trendline backward for the number of periods specified in the Periods text box.
Other Options	
Set Intercept	By default, the y-intercept is calculated based on the data. You can set the y-intercept to a specific value.
Display Equation on Chart	When you select, the regression-on-Chart equation for on Chart, the trendline is displayed as free-floating text on the chart.
Display R-squared value on Chart	When selected, the r-squared value is displayed as Value on free-floating text on the chart.

6. Choose OK.

Figure 32.8 shows a line chart with a linear regression trendline. The regression equation and r-squared value are displayed in the chart.

▶ **See** "Formatting Trendlines," **p. 756**

▶ **See** "Analyzing Trends," **p. 857**

TROUBLESHOOTING

I moved the trendline equation on my chart and when I changed the data for the chart, the equation disappeared. In some cases, when you move a trendline equation and change the source data for the chart, the equation will disappear. This is because the information for the position of the trendline equation is associated with its data points, so that the equation moves relative to changes in the data. Sometimes this causes the equation to move outside the plot area so it is no longer visible. The easiest way to correct this problem is to select the trendline and choose Format, Selected Trendline. Select the Options tab, clear the Display Equation on Chart option, and choose OK. Choose Format, Selected Trendline again, select the Options tab, select the Display Equation on Chart option and choose OK.

FIG. 32.8

The Insert Trendline command can be used to perform a regression analysis on a data series and add a trendline and the results of the analysis to a chart.

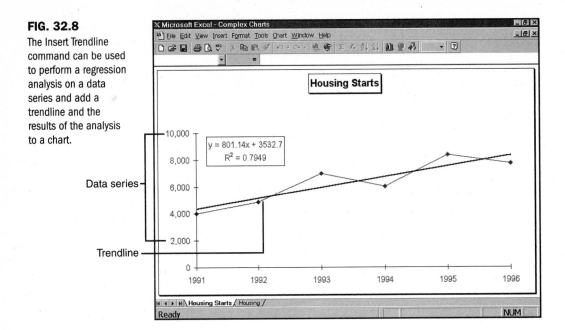

Adding Error Bars to a Chart

Error bars are used in charts to visually represent the margin of error or degree of uncertainty in a data series. Error bars are commonly used in plots of statistical and engineering data to give the viewer an indication of how reliable the data being presented is. The greater the uncertainty associated with the data points in a data series, the wider are the error bars. Figure 32.9 shows a chart with error bars inserted.

> **CAUTION**
>
> As with trendlines, do not use error bars unless you understand how to apply them correctly. Error bars should be added to a chart only if they accurately represent the statistical error in your data.

Excel enables you to associate error bars with any data series of the area, bar, column, line, or scatter (XY) chart type. If you change the data series to a 3-D, pie, doughnut, or radar chart, the error bars will be permanently lost. Scattergrams (XY-charts) can have error bars associated with both the x- and y-values.

Several options are available for deciding how Excel calculates the error bars. After you add error bars to a data series, they continue to be associated with the series, even if you change the order in which the data series are plotted; if the values for the data points change, the error bars are automatically recalculated.

FIG. 32.9

Error bars show the degree of uncertainty in a data point.

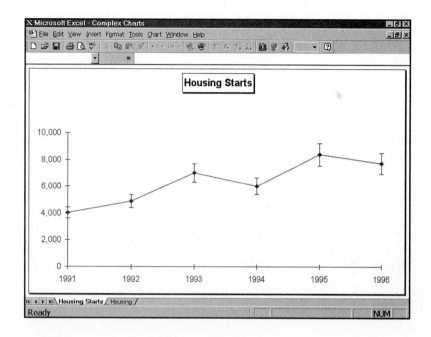

To insert error bars for a data series, perform the following steps:

1. Activate that chart with the data series you want to add error bars to and then select the data series.

2. Choose Format, Selected Data Series, or choose Format Data Series from the shortcut menu and select the Y Error Bars tab to display the dialog box shown in Figure 32.10.

   If you are working with a Scattergram (XY-chart), there will also be a tab for X Error Bars.

FIG. 32.10

Format the scale and appearance of error bars using the Y Error Bars tab in the Format Data Series dialog box.

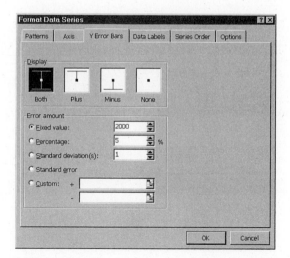

3. Select the type of error bars you want to display from the Display group.

4. Select the method you want Excel to use for calculating the error amounts in the Error Amount group. The following table describes these options:

Option	Description
Fixed Value	You enter a value that is used for the error amount for all of the data points.
Percentage	You enter a percentage that is used to calculate the error amount for each of the data points.
Standard Deviation(s)	You enter the number of standard deviations to use to calculate the error amount. The standard deviation for the plotted data is calculated automatically.
Standard Error	The standard error for the data is used for the error amount for all the data points. The standard error is automatically calculated from the plotted data.
Custom	You can either enter ranges from a worksheet in which the positive and negative error values are stored or enter the desired values for the error amounts as an array. Whether you use a range or an array, you must have the same number of error values as you have data points. Use this option if you want to specify different error amounts for each data point.

5. Choose OK.

Creating Hierarchical Charts

You can create charts that display more than one level of categories or series on the same chart. The data in Figure 32.11 has two levels along the vertical side of the data range: regions, and Sales and Net Income. When this data is plotted, a *hierarchical* series is created, as shown in Figure 32.12. The legend indicates that there are two series of data for each category (quarter). The first level is Sales; the second level is Net Income.

When you create a multilevel chart, examine the dialog box in Step 2 of the Chart Wizard carefully to be sure the correct rows and columns are being used to plot the categories and series. Change the settings in this dialog box if necessary. See Chapter 29, "Creating Charts," for detailed information on using the Chart Wizard. When you add data to a multilevel chart, always use the Chart Wizard to be sure you maintain existing category and series levels.

You also can create charts that show the multilevel categories and series in a pivot table. When you change the view of the pivot table, the chart updates. See Chapter 38, "Using the Power of Pivot Tables," to learn how to create and use pivot tables and how to create charts from a pivot table.

▶ **See** "Verifying the Chart Data Range," **p. 694**

FIG. 32.11
A worksheet showing a hierarchical data set. There are two levels of data along the vertical side of the data range: regions, and Sales and Net Income.

		Qtr1	Qtr2	Qtr3	Qtr4
East	Sales	14,331	11,353	16,713	12,425
	Net Income	10,255	14,018	11,658	15,174
West	Sales	10,000	14,230	17,011	15,515
	Net Income	13,776	11,272	15,175	12,371
North	Sales	19,792	17,906	15,421	14,272
	Net Income	20,000	19,939	12,841	14,202
South	Sales	15,808	16,346	16,580	17,364
	Net Income	10,796	11,840	12,312	15,739

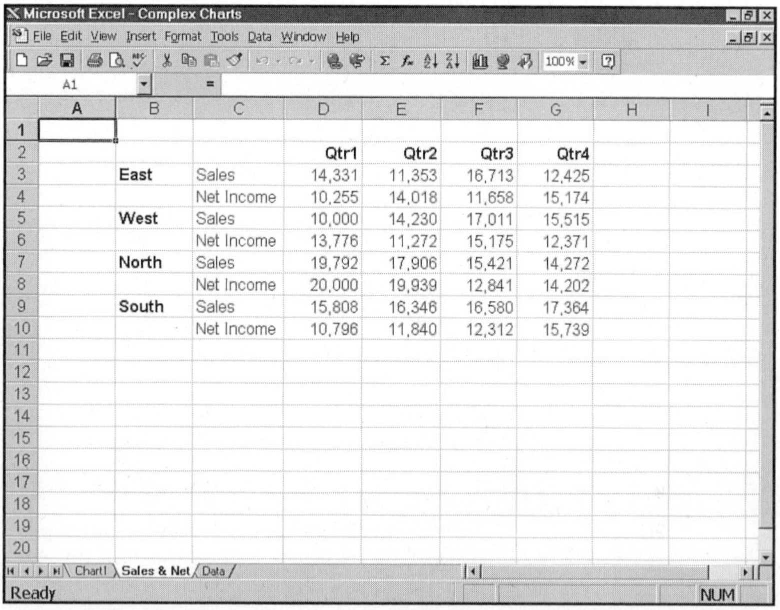

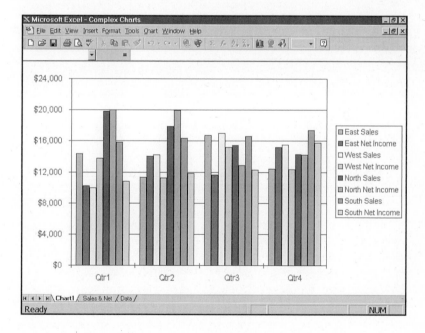

FIG. 32.12
The chart that results from the data in Figure 32.11, showing two series of data for each category.

Linking Chart Text to Worksheet Cells

The capability of linking worksheet text or numbers to attached or unattached (free-floating) chart text is helpful. You can use this technique to update chart or axis titles when titles on the worksheet change or to link comments in a worksheet cell to a chart. Figure 32.13 shows a text box that displays the contents of a worksheet cell.

FIG. 32.13

Comments, dates, or numbers in a worksheet can be linked to a chart text box.

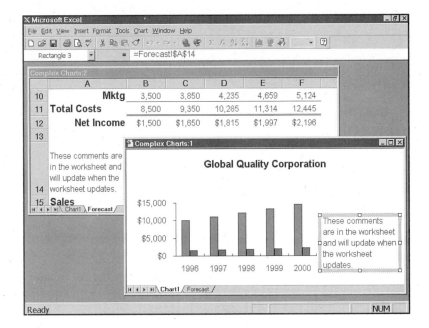

When you edit the worksheet comments, the change appears in the chart text. You also can link a worksheet cell's contents to the data series numbers that are attached to the top of columns or bars. The worksheet cell's contents then also appear at the top of the column or end of the bar.

To link a worksheet cell's contents to attached or unattached text in a chart, perform the following steps:

1. Open the worksheet and the chart. Activate the chart.

2. Create attached text, such as titles or data series numbers, if you want the cell contents to appear at these points.

3. If you want to link a worksheet cell's contents to unattached text, be certain that no text object is selected and enter an equal (=) sign; the formula bar opens.

    If, on the other hand, you want to link a cell's contents to an attached text object—say the chart title—select the attached text and type an equal (=) sign; the formula bar opens.

4. Activate the worksheet containing the cell whose contents you want to link to the chart by clicking its tab at the bottom of the window.

5. Select the cell that contains the text to link. You also can select cells that contain numbers.

   If the worksheet cell is named, you can enter the name by choosing Insert, Name, Paste, selecting the name in the Paste Name list box, and choosing OK, or by selecting the name from the Name drop-down list at the left end of the formula bar.

6. Press Enter.

7. Position, resize, and format the text as you usually do.

▶ **See** "Linking Workbook Cells and Ranges," **p. 942**

Creating Picture Charts

Excel charts can use pictures as markers in place of columns, bars, or lines. You can use this feature to make picture charts that grab the eye and then communicate the information. Figure 32.14 shows how you can use pictures in column charts. Figure 32.15 shows a drawing created in Windows Paint used as a replacement for line markers.

The new Fill Effects dialog box, which you can open from the Format Data Series dialog box, simplifies the procedure for replacing data markers with pictures in column, bar, area, bubble, 3-D line, and filled radar charts. You can use the Picture tab in the Fill Effects dialog box to select a graphic file that is stored on your computer and use it to replace the data markers for the selected data series. You can also use this command to fill the plot or chart areas with a graphic image. To replace the data markers on a 2-D line, scatter or unfilled radar chart, you need to use the Edit Copy and Edit Paste commands, as described below. The Edit Copy, Edit Paste procedure is also useful if you want to select part of a graphic image from within a graphics application to replace the data markers.

To replace columns, bars, or lines using the Fill Effects dialog box, you can use several types of graphics files, including Windows Metafile, Windows bitmap, PC Paintbrush, and GIF files. If you are using the Edit Copy and Edit Paste commands to insert the picture, you can use pictures from any Windows graphics or drawing program that can copy graphics to the Clipboard in the Windows Metafile format. Examples of such programs are Windows Paint (the free program that comes with Windows), CorelDRAW!, and Micrografx Designer. You also can use Excel's worksheet drawing tools to create pictures to copy and paste into charts. You can store frequently used pictures in a worksheet used as a picture scrapbook. Copy pictures from the worksheet by selecting them and choosing the Edit, Copy command.

Creating a Picture Chart Using the Fill Effects Dialog Box

If the graphic image you want to use to create a picture chart exists as a file on your computer, and you want to use the entire image to replace the data markers for a data series in your chart, the easiest approach is to use the Picture tab in the Fill Effects dialog box.

Part
VIII

Ch
32

FIG. 32.14
Pictures can replace columns or bars.

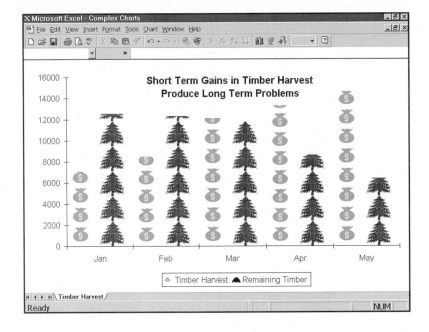

FIG. 32.15
Pictures can replace the markers on lines.

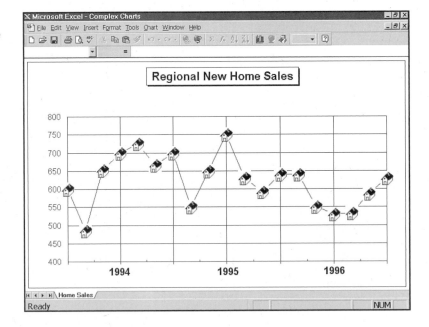

To insert a picture into a chart using the Fill Effects dialog box, follow these steps:

1. Activate a column, bar, area, bubble, 3-D line, or filled radar chart.

2. Select the data series that you want to replace with a picture.

   You can also select the plot or chart area and fill in the background with a picture.

3. Choose Format, Selected Data Series and select the Pattern tab.

4. Choose Fill Effects and select the Picture tab to display the dialog box shown in Figure 32.16.

FIG. 32.16

You can use the Picture tab in the Fill Effects dialog box to replace a series of data markers with a graphic image.

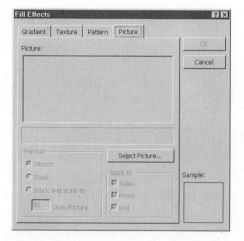

5. Choose Select Picture and change to the drive and folder where the image is stored in the Look In box.

6. Select the file for the picture you want to insert and choose OK.

   Figure 32.17 shows the Fill Effects dialog box after a picture has been selected.

FIG. 32.17

You can preview the picture you selected and change the formatting of the picture in the Fill Effects dialog box.

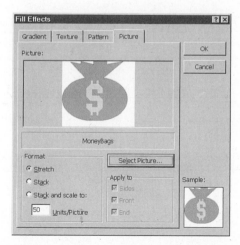

Part
VIII

Ch
32

7. Choose one of the options from the Format group, described below:

Option	Effect
Stretch	Stretches the picture to match the value for each data point.
Stack	Stacks the picture in its original proportions to match the value for each data point.
Stack and Scale to	Scales the picture's height to equal the value in the Units/Picture text box, and then stacks the picture to match the value for each data point.

8. For 3-D charts, select the options you want from the Apply To group.

9. Choose OK.

Creating a Picture Chart Using the Edit Copy and Edit Paste Commands

If you want to use part of a graphic image or replace data markers in 2D line, scatter or unfilled radar charts, you need to use the Edit Copy and Edit Paste commands.

To create a picture chart using the Edit Copy and Edit Paste commands, perform the following steps:

1. Activate a 2-D line, scatter or unfilled radar chart in Excel.

2. Switch to the Windows graphics program in which you want to draw. Click Start on the taskbar and choose the program from one of the submenus to open it, or click the program on the taskbar if it is already open.

3. Draw or open the picture you want to use in the chart. (Some graphics programs come with extensive libraries of graphics, called *clip art*.)

4. Select the picture by using the graphic selection tool for that program, and then choose Edit, Copy. Figure 32.18 shows a picture drawn in Microsoft Paint.

5. Switch back to Excel. Click Excel on the taskbar, or press Alt+Tab to cycle between programs.

6. Select the column, bar, or line series (as shown in Figure 32.19) you want to contain the picture. Click the series, or press the arrow keys to select the series.

7. Choose Edit, Paste or click the Paste button. The picture replaces the series markers, as shown in Figure 32.20. The picture may stretch to fit. You can adjust the picture later.

To stretch, stack, or stack and scale the pictures in column or bar charts, select the series containing the picture, choose Format, Selected Data Series or choose Format Data Series from the shortcut menu and select the Patterns tab. Choose Fill Effects and select the Picture tab. From the dialog box shown in Figure 32.17, select one of the picture-formatting options. See the earlier section "Creating a Picture Chart Using the Fill Effects Dialog Box" for a description of the formatting options. A stacked picture appears in Figure 32.21.

FIG. 32.18

Draw the picture in a Windows graphics program, such as Microsoft Paint.

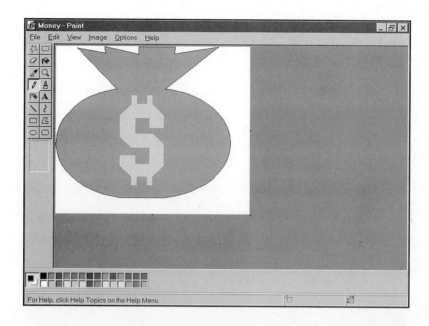

FIG. 32.19

Select the series you want to represent with the picture.

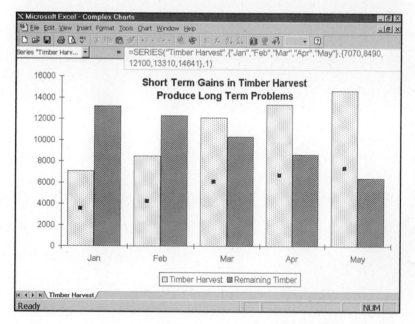

FIG. 32.20

The pasted picture replaces the series markers.

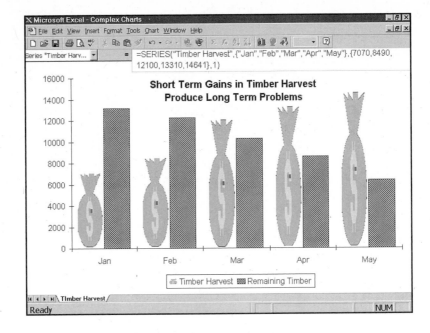

FIG. 32.21

You can stack the image you use to replace the data marker for a different look.

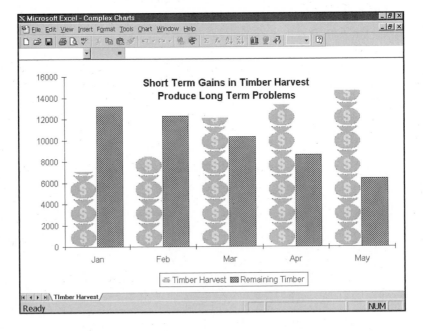

To remove a picture from a series, perform the following steps:

1. Select the series.

2. Choose Edit, Clear, Formats.

Understanding the Use of Maps in Excel

Some maps are important to good decision making but are so difficult to create and update that people avoid the task. Even though, in the past, someone was coerced into creating and keeping a map of data, it was rare that people had enough time to do "what-if" maps just as you do what-if calculations with an Excel worksheet. Using maps to model the effect of decisions on distribution, sales efforts, target marketing, population movements, and so on can be very powerful.

With an Excel worksheet, you can test different values in a business or engineering model until you find the number that produces the result you need. Excel's data mapping features produce maps from the very simple, like that shown in Figure 32.22, to the highly complex. The maps and data that come with Excel are fairly high level, but you can buy add-in maps, data, and feature extensions from MapInfo.

Part
VIII

Ch
32

FIG. 32.22

Maps make it much easier to see the relationships between data and geographic distributions.

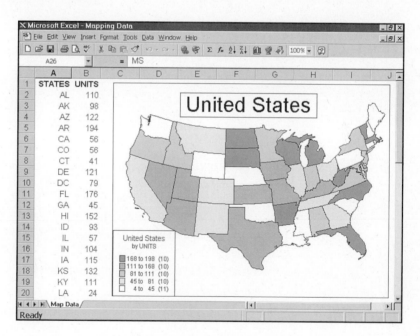

Now with data modeling you can do the same thing for marketing, finance, custom service, government, and scientific modeling where decisions are based on geographic features or regions. For example, using the data in your own databases or using demographic and geographic data from MapInfo, you can now see how

- Sales and commissions are distributed by region
- The aging of your target market will affect sales distribution
- Product revenue are distributed with respect to different types of buyers
- Ecological and environmental factors change by geographic region
- Shifting populations affect your service sector

Excel's analytical capabilities enable you to forecast future numbers and see the results geographically. You can use Excel's advanced analytical capability, such as trends analysis and pivot tables, to massage data before you display it on a map.

Maps that come with Excel are

Australia

Canada

Europe

Mexico

North America

Additional maps down to a very detailed level, as well as census data and feature data such as roads, cities, and airports, are available from MapInfo.

Creating a Data Map

Although creating a data map involves multiple steps, it's easy if you follow an organized approach to building your map. The general steps to creating your data map are

1. Organize and lay out the data in vertical columns. You can have multiple columns of data, but the leftmost column must be recognizable as a geographic identifier, such as a state or country name or abbreviation. A sample workbook, MAPSTATS.XLS, lists recognized abbreviations.

2. Select the columns of geographic identifiers and their data. Include the headings at the top of the columns.

3. Click the Map button on the Standard toolbar or choose Insert, Map and drag across the worksheet where you want the map displayed.

4. If Excel cannot recognize a specific map to use, it displays the Multiple Maps Available dialog box so you can select a map.

5. Specify the column(s) of data and which type of map you want using the Microsoft Map Control dialog box.

6. Size and format the map.

7. Add special features to the map such as pop-up labels and pushpins.

At this point your individual data map may be complete. However, if you will be creating more maps of this same map type and format, you may want to create a template from this map. A template enables you to save the map type and formatting you just created. You can then apply the map type and formatting to another map by just choosing the template from a list. You can also save as a template the information required to create a pushpin map.

Each of these steps is described in detail throughout the rest of the chapter.

Organizing the Data for a Map

Before you create your data map, you need to organize the data so that it can be read by the Data Map feature. Many maps require only two columns of information. You can make maps that display multiple columns of data and their relationship to geographic regions.

The first column contains a text description of geographic regions in the map. The additional columns contain numeric data related to each region. You can plot multiple columns of data using overlapping map types or using the Pie or Column Chart map types. The layout for a single column of numeric data is

RegionName	NumericData
Region1	Number1
Region2	Number2
Region3	Number3
Region4	Number4
Region5	Number5

Actual data that involves multiple columns of data in a worksheet might look like the following:

State	Units	Avg. Age
AZ	532	38
CA	348	32
ME	231	36
MI	621	28

The RegionName must be text or postal codes recognized by the Data Map feature. This might be full state names, state abbreviations, postal codes, country names, and so on. You can find a listing of all the regional terms that can be used in the workbook MAPSTATS.XLS. MAPSTATS.XLS also contains sample population sizes and forecasts you can experiment with. Each country's information is on a different worksheet. Move the pointer over the column headings for an explanation of the data. To find MAPSTATS.XLS on your disk, click the Start button, then click Find, Files or Folders, and then enter the file name in the Named edit box and click Find Now.

TIP The file MAPSTATS.XLS lists vendors of demographic information. This file is installed in C:\PROGRAM FILES\COMMON FILES\MICROSOFT SHARED\DATAMAP\DATA.

Part
VIII

Ch
32

When you create your map, the Data Map feature analyzes the text in the left column of the range you select and attempts to determine the appropriate map. If the left column indicates items that could be used in more than one map, a dialog box appears, giving you the choice of maps you can create.

N O T E   Numeric postal codes must be formatted as text to prevent the loss of leading zeros. To do this, select the cells, then choose Format, Cells, select the Number tab, select Text from the Category list, and then choose OK. ▨

Selecting Your Mapping Data

When you select the data to create your map, include the headings at the top of the data as well as the columns of data underneath. These headings will help Data Map automatically create legends and titles. It will also help you remember the columns of data as you work in dialog boxes. Data can be added later.

If you want to make it easy to select your mapping data, leave a single blank cell border around all sides of the region names and data. In effect, this creates a border of empty cells surrounding the data. You can then select all the cells within the island of filled cells by selecting one cell in the island, then choosing Edit, Go To, Special. Select the Current Region option and choose OK. The shortcut key for this is Ctrl+* (asterisk). (Hold down both Ctrl and Shift key as you press the 8 key above the alphanumeric keys.)

Creating a Basic Map

Once your data is selected, creating the map is as easy as a click and drag. To create your map, follow these steps:

1. Select the headings and data.

2. Click the Map button in the Standard toolbar or choose Insert, Map. The pointer changes to a cross hair.

3. Select the worksheet or workbook where you want the map, then scroll to the area where you want the map to appear.

4. Drag across the area where you want the map to appear. Figure 32.23 shows the pointer being dragged across the worksheet. Release the mouse button.

   The area you drag across will define the size of the frame containing the map. Make the frame as large as possible. Later you can resize the frame around the map, resize the map, or reposition the map after it has been created.

5. If your data uses a region name that the Data Map does not recognize, the Resolve Unknown Geographic Data dialog box appears, as shown in Figure 32.24. In this dialog box, you can type in a correct entry in the Change To box or select a region from the Suggestions list. Choose Change for your correction to take effect. Choose Discard to ignore this row of data or choose Discard All to ignore all rows containing unrecognized regions.

FIG. 32.23

Drag the pointer to create a rectangle that will contain your map.

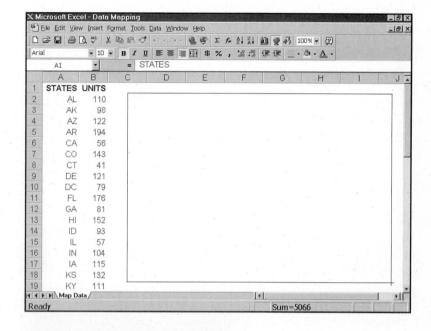

FIG. 32.24

If Data Map does not recognize a region name, you are given the opportunity to correct the name or ignore it.

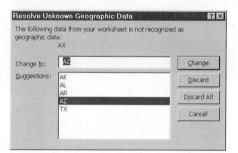

6. If the Data Map feature cannot determine a unique map to use when it analyzes the left column of data, it displays the Multiple Maps Available dialog box, shown in Figure 32.25. Select the map you want to use from this dialog box.

FIG. 32.25

If Data Map cannot determine which map to use, it presents you with a list of alternative maps.

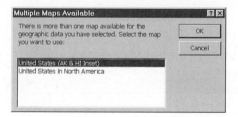

7. Once you release the mouse button and respond to any dialog boxes that appear, the map is displayed in your worksheet. The Microsoft Map Control is displayed over the map and worksheet (see Figure 32.26). The default map created is a value-shaded map using the first column of data.

FIG. 32.26

The Microsoft Map Control appears over your map, giving you the ability to select which data is mapped and to specify the types of maps.

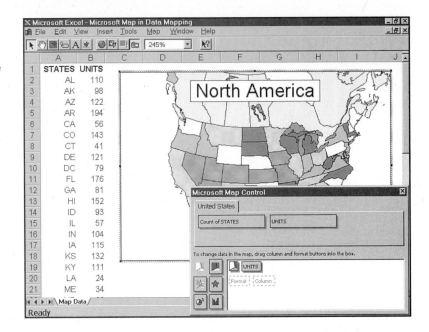

PART X

Working with Excel Subtotals, Add-Ins, and the Worksheet Display

Managing the Worksheet Display

Controlling the Worksheet Display

You can change many characteristics of Excel's worksheet display, giving worksheets and databases a custom appearance. By removing gridlines, row and column headings, and scroll bars, you can create windows that appear like dialog boxes or paper forms.

Displaying the Worksheet Full Screen

To work with the maximum amount of worksheet and reduce screen clutter, you need to know about Full Screen mode. In a normal view, like the view shown in Figure 33.1, screen elements such as formula bars and status bars take up on-screen space. As Figure 33.2 shows, the Full Screen mode rids Excel of the title bar, the formula bar, and the status bar. You can add toolbars to the full screen view by choosing View, Toolbars and selecting the toolbars you want to display.

FIG. 33.1

In a normal display, your visible work area is reduced by the title bar, formula bar, status bar, and so on.

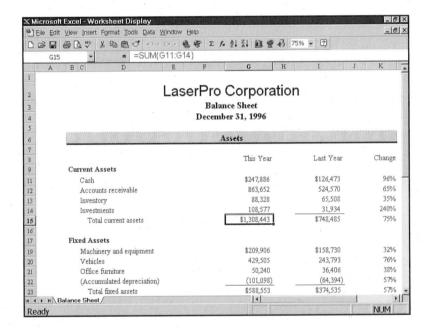

To display the active worksheet in Full Screen mode, choose View, Full Screen.

When Full Screen mode is on, a check mark appears alongside the command. To turn off Full Screen mode, either select the option again, or click the Close Full Screen button.

While you are in Full Screen mode, you want to make sure that you have in-cell editing turned on. This enables you to type or edit long entries directly into cells and see the typing or editing in the cell. To turn on in-cell editing, choose Tools, Options. Select the Edit tab and Edit Directly In-Cell.

FIG. 33.2

The Full Screen display eliminates some screen elements, letting you see more of your work.

Close Full Screen button

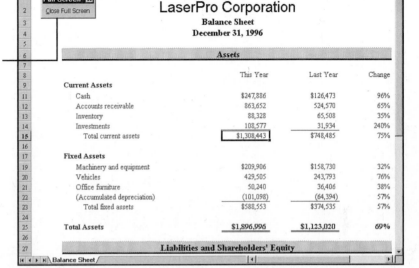

Hiding Row and Column Headings

You can create special displays in Excel for data-entry forms, on-screen information, and help screens. By removing row and column headings and gridlines, you can make windows appear as if they are not based on a spreadsheet.

When you hide row and column headings, you only hide them in the active worksheet. If you want row and column headings hidden for the workbook, you must change them in each worksheet.

To remove row and column headings on the active worksheet, follow these steps:

1. Choose Tools, Options.
2. Select the View tab.
3. Deselect the Row & Columns Headers check box.
4. Choose OK.

This action doesn't affect the row and column headings for printing. Use the Sheet tab from the File, Page Setup command to turn off row and column headings for printing.

Turning Scroll Bars On and Off

To make a window appear like a data-entry form and not allow the user to scroll in it, turn off the horizontal or vertical scroll bars. When you hide scroll bars, you are hiding them only in the active workbook.

Part

IX

Ch

33

To hide scroll bars on the active worksheet, follow these steps:

1. Choose Tools, Options.
2. Select the View tab.
3. Deselect the Horizontal Scroll Bar or Vertical Scroll Bar check box.
4. Choose OK.

Turn the scroll bars back on in a sheet by selecting the Horizontal Scroll Bar or Vertical Scroll Bar check box.

Hiding the Formula Bar, Status Bar, and Sheet Tabs

When you need more space on-screen for the display, you want to hide the formula bar, status bar, or sheet tabs. Even with sheet tabs hidden, you can change between sheets with the Ctrl+PgUp and Ctrl+PgDn keys, under the control of a Visual Basic program or with an Excel macro.

When you hide the formula bar and status bar, you hide these bars for all sheets in Excel. When you hide sheet tabs, you hide them only on the workbook that is active when you give the command.

To hide the formula bar, status bar, or sheet tabs, choose Tools, Options, select the View tab, and then deselect the Formula Bar, Status Bar, or Sheet Tabs check boxes.

Hiding or Coloring Gridlines

Turning off the on-screen gridlines gives a better appearance to data-entry forms and on-screen reports. But you may want the gridlines on while you build formulas or place text boxes and objects. To turn the screen gridlines off, choose Tools, Options, select the View tab, and deselect the Gridlines check box. Select the check box to turn them back on.

Figure 33.3 shows several of the options you can take to display or hide screen elements.

To change the color of your gridlines and headings, follow these steps:

1. Choose Tools, Options.
2. Select the View tab.
3. Make sure that the Gridlines check box is on and select a color from the Color pull-down menu by clicking the down arrow, or pressing Alt+C and using the arrow keys to select a color.
4. Choose OK.

To color individual cells, borders, or range contents, choose Format, Cells. Now select the Font tab to color content, the Border tab to color borders, and the Patterns tab to color background.

Displaying Formulas

You need to display formulas on-screen or in your printout at the following times: when debugging your worksheet (finding and correcting problems), when reviewing an unfamiliar worksheet, or when printing a documentation copy of the worksheet for future reference. To show the formulas in a worksheet, choose Tools, Options, and then select the View tab and the Formulas check box.

When printing a worksheet to show formulas, choose File, Page Setup and select the Sheet tab; then select the Row & Column Headings check box.

FIG. 33.3

Turn off scroll bars, gridlines, and other screen elements to make the display appear less like a spreadsheet and more like a graphic or paper display.

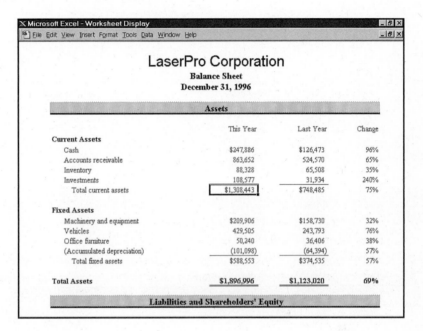

TROUBLESHOOTING

The worksheet doesn't display a formula bar, scroll bars, or other worksheet elements. How can the worksheet be returned to normal? Excel may be in Full Screen mode or individual elements may have been turned off. To see whether Excel is in Full Screen mode, choose View and look at the Full Screen command. If the icon next to it is depressed, it is in Full Screen mode. Turn off Full Screen mode by choosing the View, Full Screen command again or by clicking the Full Screen button. If this isn't the problem, individual screen elements probably were turned off. To control the individual screen elements, choose Tools, Options and select the View tab. In this tab you can select or deselect whether to show or hide the formula bar, scroll bars, status bar, and so on.

When I hide scroll bars it hides them for the entire workbook, but I need scroll bars on for some sheets and off for others. To hide scroll bars on some sheets and display them on other sheets in the same workbook, you need to open a second window on the same workbook. Open a second window by activating the workbook and then choosing the Window, New Window command. You can then use the Tools, Options command with the View tab to set one window to scroll bars off and the other to scroll bars on. If you save the file with the two windows open, it reopens with the same settings in the two windows.

Magnifying Worksheet Displays

Large worksheets or worksheets that present many different display and print areas can be difficult to get around in. If you work with large amounts of information, you need to see as much as possible on-screen. Excel's View, Zoom command can help you in both cases. It magnifies or reduces the amount you see on-screen so that you can see more or less. This command doesn't change the printed result, but it does enable you to reduce a worksheet so that you can see more of it or magnify one part to make formatting easier. Although View, Zoom changes how much of a document appears on-screen, it does not alter the font, column widths, or related features when the document prints.

N O T E   Magnifying the worksheet by zooming also makes a screen easier to read when it needs to be read from a distance; for example, when it is projected onto a screen with an LCD projection panel, projection system, or large screen monitor. Instead of reformatting the fonts in your worksheet, you can leave everything as it is and magnify the zoom so that everyone can read the content.

To change the zoom with the mouse and the Standard toolbar, pull down the Zoom box located to the left of the Office Assistant button. Select the magnification you want. If you want a custom magnification, click in the Zoom box, type the percentage, and press Enter. You can enter a custom zoom ranging from 10 percent to 400 percent.

To change the zoom with the keyboard, choose View, Zoom and the Zoom dialog box appears. Select one of the five magnifications or select one of the two custom zooms. The standard view has 100-percent magnification. The 200-percent magnification setting doubles the size of characters. The 75-percent setting presents about 30 percent more rows and columns than the standard view.

T I P   On a VGA display, try using the custom settings of 85 percent for working and 150 percent for audience display. On a Super VGA display, try 100 percent for working and 200 percent for audience display.

To select one of the standard zooms, select the option button and choose OK. The new view appears immediately. Figure 33.1 shows a document with 75-percent magnification.

When you need to magnify or reduce a screen by a percentage different than the predefined settings, choose View, Zoom, Fit Selection; or choose View, Zoom, and type a percentage in the Custom edit box. If you have a range you want to expand or contract to fit within Excel's boundaries, select the range and choose View, Zoom, and then the Fit Selection option. The range expands or contracts to fit in the boundaries. If you know approximately how much you want the normal view magnified or condensed, choose View, Zoom, and enter a percentage in the Custom edit box. To return to the normal view, select 100 percent.

Microsoft's new Intellipoint mouse enables you to scroll without using the scroll bars, pan in any direction in a window, and zoom documents to different magnifications. To use the Intellipoint mouse to zoom a worksheet, hold down the Ctrl key as you move the mouse backward and forward. The magnification of the worksheet display will increase or decrease depending on which direction you move.

Saving Frequently Used View and Print Settings

You probably use certain areas on worksheets again and again. You may need to display these areas differently or print them differently. You may be wasting a lot of time if you don't use Excel's Custom Views command.

The Custom Views command has the capability of storing the range, and the display and print settings for worksheet areas you frequently view or print. You can set up the areas with the display or print settings, position the worksheet on-screen as you want to view it, and then assign the view and settings to a name. When you save the workbook, the name and settings are saved so that you can use them later. The next time you want to see that view with the same settings, you can choose its name from the Custom Views dialog box.

To print an area that has an assigned view name, you can select and then print the view. Excel sets the print settings assigned to the name. If you have many views to print, use Excel's Report Manager to select and order the views you want printed. The named view stores the print settings saved with each view, so you don't need to change print settings with each view. You also can print views in sequence and include sequential page numbers to create a large report. The Report Manager is described in Chapter 28, "Printing Worksheets."

Naming and Saving a View

Worksheets are dynamic. You move between locations and print different areas. By using the Custom Views command, you can name different views with their display and print settings. To return to the same view or print setup, you only need to select the desired named view.

Saving views or print areas and settings with a name can be helpful in many situations, as in the following list:

- You can store the page setup, print ranges, headers, and footers for printed reports.
- You can look at the data-entry view with display settings that make the entry form appear like a paper form.
- You can set up on-screen views for reports that turn off screen elements that may clutter viewing final results. You may want to show the view—for example, with gridlines, status bar, formula bar, and scroll bars turned off.
- You can set up formula debugging views and large area overviews.

Figures 33.4 and 33.5 show before and after examples of switching between different views and settings on the same worksheet.

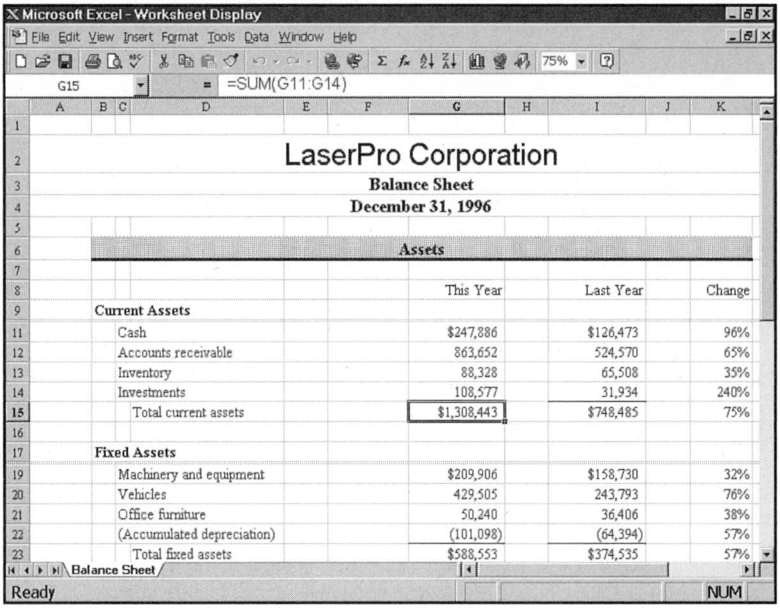

FIG. 33.4

You can assign a view such as this one a name like Working View.

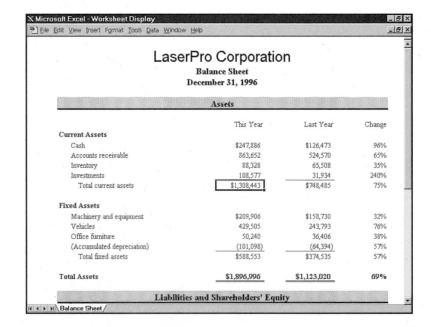

FIG. 33.5

You can assign a view such as this one a name like Presentation View.

To create a named view, follow these steps:

1. Create the worksheet or macro sheet.

2. Position the window, add panes by splitting the window, size or hide rows and columns, and set display settings as you want them in the view. If you are naming an area you will use for printed reports, specify the print area, print titles, and page setup settings.

3. Select the cells or ranges you want selected when the view appears.

4. Choose View, Custom Views. The Custom Views dialog box appears, as shown in Figure 33.6.

FIG. 33.6

The Custom Views dialog box allows you to see or add named views.

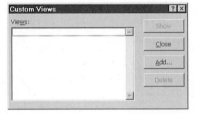

5. Choose Add. The Add View dialog box appears (see Figure 33.7).

FIG. 33.7

Enter the name you want assigned to the current display and print settings.

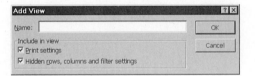

6. Type the view's name in the Name text box.

7. Select or clear the Print Settings and Hidden Rows, Columns and Filter Settings check boxes, as desired.

8. Choose OK.

To store the print and title ranges as well as the page setup settings, select Print Settings. If you have rows and columns hidden when you record the view, or if you have applied a data filter to the worksheet, and you want these rows or columns (or the filtered rows and columns) hidden when you redisplay or print the view, select Hidden Rows, Columns and Filter Settings.

To change a view you have already named, display the view. Then modify the window, display settings, or print settings as needed. Repeat the process of choosing the View, Custom Views, Add command. Enter the same name you used originally to name the view.

Displaying a Named View

To display a named view, complete the following steps:

1. Choose View, Custom Views.

2. Select the name of the view you want in the Views list, as shown in Figure 33.8.

FIG. 33.8
The Views list shows all
the names to which you
assigned display and
print settings.

3. Choose Show.

When your named view is displayed, you can work in the worksheet or print by using the File, Print or File, Print Preview commands.

Deleting a Named View

To delete a view, choose View, Custom Views. In the Custom Views dialog box, select the name from the Views list of the view you want to delete and choose Delete. Select and delete additional names, or choose Close.

Viewing a Window Through Multiple Panes

Dividing an Excel window into sections enables you to see two or four parts of a worksheet. Appropriately, each section of the window is referred to as a *pane*. Multiple panes are particularly useful when you work with databases or large worksheets. When you split the screen vertically, the two panes can be scrolled independently in the horizontal direction. Vertical scrolling is synchronized, and there is only one vertical scroll bar for both panes. Horizontal panes work just the opposite. They scroll independently in the vertical direction and are synchronized in the horizontal direction.

As an illustration, you can display both the list and criteria range for an advanced filter at the same time even if they are many rows apart. In Figure 33.9 the criteria range and the viewed portion of the list are over 260 rows apart. The multiple-pane technique enables you to enter a criterion in one pane and see the resulting filtered data in the other pane.

If you need to scroll through a long list or database, you can divide the worksheet into four panes and freeze the panes. You can scroll through the worksheet and still see the worksheet's row and column headings. As another example, you can place the data-entry area of a large worksheet in one pane and the results in another.

FIG. 33.9

The split windows are used for viewing both the list and criteria range of an advanced filter at the same time.

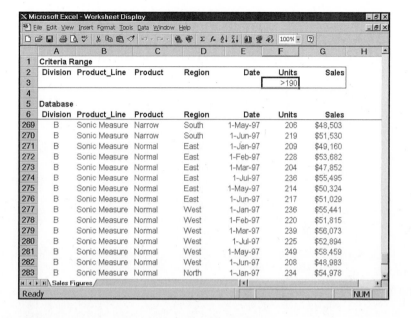

Dividing a Window into Multiple Scrolling Panes

Figure 33.9 shows a worksheet divided into two panes. Notice how the row numbers jump from 6 to 269. The upper pane shows the criteria range, the database headings; the lower pane shows the database. With this arrangement, you never lose sight of the column headings as you scroll through a database.

To split a worksheet window, follow these steps:

1. Activate the window you want to split.

2. Select a cell below and to the right of where you want the window split.

3. Choose Window, Split. The window splits above and to the left of the active cell.

   To split the window horizontally into two sections, move the active cell to column A in the cell below where you want the split, and then choose Window, Split.

   To split the window vertically into two sections, move the active cell to the first row in the column to the right of where you want the split, and then choose Window, Split.

To remove a split window with the keyboard, choose Window, Remove Split. The active cell can be in any location.

To create panes with the mouse, you use the split boxes, the solid gray boxes located at the top of the vertical scroll bar and at the right edge of the horizontal scroll bar. Try moving the mouse pointer over one of these boxes and you will see that the pointer changes to double lines with two arrows. You can then drag the split box to divide the window into panes.

Part
IX

Ch
33

To create panes with the mouse, follow these steps:

1. Drag the split gray box down the vertical scroll bar or across the horizontal scroll bar. As you drag, a gray pane divider shows where the window splits.

2. Position the gray pane divider where you want the window to split, and release the mouse button.

CAUTION

When you drag the split box along the scroll bar, it is possible to split a row or column, giving you unpredictable results. If this happens, adjust the pane by dragging the pane divider in the worksheet. When you drag the pane divider in the worksheet, you can only place the split at row or column divisions.

To resize panes, drag the split line to a new location. To remove the split, drag the solid gray bar past the arrow on the scroll bar, and release the mouse button.

TIP If you want to split a window into panes quickly, double-click one of the solid gray bars. To remove one of the splits, double-click the solid gray bar creating the split.

Freezing Headings into Position

You can freeze the panes in position so that you cannot change them accidentally. To freeze panes you already have positioned, choose Window, Freeze Panes.

When panes are frozen, the gray split bar becomes a thin solid line and you cannot scroll into the frozen area. The top or left pane cannot scroll. You can move the active cell into the frozen area by pressing the arrow keys or clicking a cell. To *thaw* the frozen panes, choose Window, Unfreeze Panes.

N O T E If you have not split a worksheet into panes, you can split the window and freeze the panes with a single command. Select a cell positioned below and to the right of where you want the panes to split and freeze, and choose Window, Freeze Panes. Choose Window, Unfreeze Panes to remove the panes.

Activating Different Panes

Using the keyboard, you can move the active cell clockwise among panes by pressing F6; press Shift+F6 to move counterclockwise among the panes. The active cell moves to the same cell it occupied the last time it was in the pane. With the mouse, you can shift among panes by clicking in the pane you want to activate. Note that jumping between panes often causes windows to reposition. You cannot move between panes like this if the panes are frozen.

Hiding and Unhiding Windows and Sheets

You do not need to keep all your windows on-screen at one time or keep all your sheets displayed in a workbook. You can hide windows from view so that the screen appears more organized and less confusing. If only one workbook is open on a window, the entire workbook is hidden when you hide the window. The sheets in a hidden window remain available to other documents with which it is linked.

To hide a window, follow these steps:

1. Activate the window.
2. Choose Window, Hide.

N O T E To move a worksheet out of the way but to keep it accessible, minimize the worksheet to an icon. To minimize a worksheet, click the worksheet's Minimize button at the top-right corner of the worksheet. To restore the worksheet icon into a window, double-click the icon. ■

To reveal hidden windows, follow these steps:

1. Choose Window, Unhide. The Unhide dialog box appears.
2. From the Unhide Workbook list box, select the title of the hidden window you want to reveal.

   You can only select one window at a time. You need to repeat this procedure for each window you want to unhide.
3. Choose OK. The hidden windows reappear in their former position and size.

If you attempt to unhide a window that is protected, you are asked for a password. The following section explains how to hide a window with a password.

To hide a sheet within a workbook, follow these steps:

1. Activate the sheet within the workbook. You cannot hide the only visible sheet in a workbook.
2. Choose Format, Sheet.
3. Select Hide from the submenu.

If you attempt to hide the last visible sheet in a workbook, a message box will appear informing you that at least one sheet must remain visible. In this case, you must either unhide or insert another sheet before you can hide the other sheet.

To unhide a sheet within a workbook, follow these steps:

1. Activate the workbook containing the sheet.
2. Choose Format, Sheet to display the Unhide dialog box.
3. Select the sheet you want to display from the Unhide Sheet list.
4. Choose OK.

Locking Windows in Position

After your windows are sized and in the proper positions, you can make sure that they stay there. Locking windows in position is a good idea, particularly if the worksheets are used by inexperienced operators or displayed by macros.

Part
IX
Ch
33

To keep a window from moving or changing size, follow these steps:

1. Position and size the window as you want it.

2. Choose Tools, Protection, Protect Workbook.

3. Select the Windows check box.

4. Enter a password if you do not want others to remove protection. (A password can be any combination of letters and numbers; letters are case sensitive. Make sure that you don't forget your password—you cannot unprotect your document if you do.)

5. Choose OK. If you entered a password, the Confirm Password dialog box prompts you to retype it.

You can scroll through locked windows, but you cannot resize or move them (notice that the sizing border disappears from a protected window). You cannot rearrange, insert, or delete sheets in a workbook if the Structure check box is selected during workbook protection.

To unlock a workbook, activate its window and choose Tools, Protection, Unprotect Workbook. If a password locks the window's position, you are asked to enter the password.

TIP   Hold the Shift key as you choose File to display Close All.

Creating Automatic Subtotals

What Are Automatic Subtotals?

Subtotals are a quick and easy way to summarize data in a list. Suppose you have a list of sales. The list includes the date, account, product, unit, price, and revenue. If you want to see subtotals by account, you can do so. You can also see subtotals by product.

With Excel's Subtotals command, you don't have to create the formulas. Excel creates the formula, inserts the subtotal and grand total rows, and outlines the data automatically. The resulting data is easy to format, chart, and print.

Creating Simple Subtotals

The subtotals provide a great deal of flexibility in the way you can summarize data. Using subtotals, you can do the following:

- Tell Excel how to group the data
- Display subtotals and grand totals for one set of groups in the list
- Display subtotals and grand totals for several sets of groups in the list
- Perform different calculations on the grouped data: count the items, total the items, average the items

After you create the subtotals, you can quickly format and print the resulting report.

Preparing for the Subtotals

For the subtotals to work correctly, you need to organize the data into labeled columns. Excel uses the column labels to determine how the data are grouped and how the totals are calculated.

You also need to sort the data into the groups to be subtotaled. If you want to subtotal the data by account, for example, then sort the data by account. You can sort on more than one field (column).

For more information on sorting data, see Chapter 44, "Sorting Data."

 T I P To select only certain rows in the data list, use a filter to display the desired rows. See "Using Subtotals on Filtered Data" later in this chapter.

Creating a Subtotal

After the data is sorted by the fields you want subtotaled, you can create the subtotals quickly by following these steps:

1. Select any cell within the list. Then choose Data, Subtotals. You see the Subtotal dialog box (see Figure 34.1).

FIG. 34.1

In this figure, DATE represents the column you want to group by and REVENUES represents the column you want to calculate.

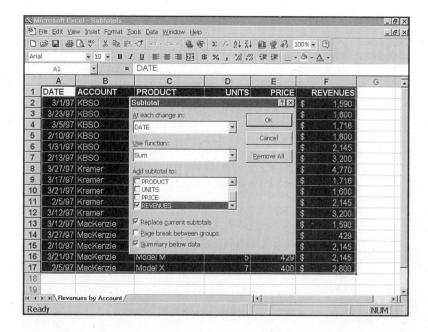

2. Select how to group the data for subtotals by selecting the At Each Change In drop-down list. This list displays the columns in your database or list. Select the column you want. If you were totaling net sales by account, for example, select Account.

   If this is the first time you selected the command, Excel selects the left-most column automatically. If you used the command before, the column you used last time is selected.

3. Select the calculation you want performed by displaying the Use Function drop-down list and selecting the function you want. The most common function is Sum, but you also can select Count, Average, Max, Min, Product, Count Nums, StdDev, StdDevp, Var, and Varp. For more information on functions, see Chapter 25, "Using Functions."

   Based on the type of data you are summarizing, Excel suggests a function. If the column you are summarizing contains numbers, for example, Excel enters the Sum function. If the column contains text, Excel enters the Count function.

4. Select data that you want calculated by selecting the check boxes in Add Subtotal To list box. This list box displays the columns in the data list. You select the column you want calculated. For example, if you want to total revenue by account, select Revenues.

   To create summary functions for more than one column, select each of the columns you want. (To perform different calculations on the same columns, see the later section "Creating Advanced Subtotals.")

5. To replace any existing subtotals, select the Replace Current Subtotals check box.

6. To insert a page break before each group, select the Page Break Between Groups check box.

Part

IX

Ch

34

7. By default, the subtotal and grand totals appear at the end of the data group. If you prefer to show these totals before the data group, select Summary Below Data to clear the check box.
8. Click OK.

Excel inserts subtotal rows for each group and performs the selected calculation (step 3) on the selected column (step 4). A grand total row is also inserted. The grand total is always the result of the detail data (not just a result of each subtotal).

Excel labels each inserted row with an appropriate title. For example, if you were totaling by Account, Excel displays the *Account Name* Total (*Account Name* would be the actual account name).

Excel also outlines the data. The outline symbols displayed after you create the subtotals enable you to quickly hide and show detail data. See the later section "Changing the Detail Level," for information on showing detail levels.

Figure 34.2 shows an example of subtotaling revenue by account.

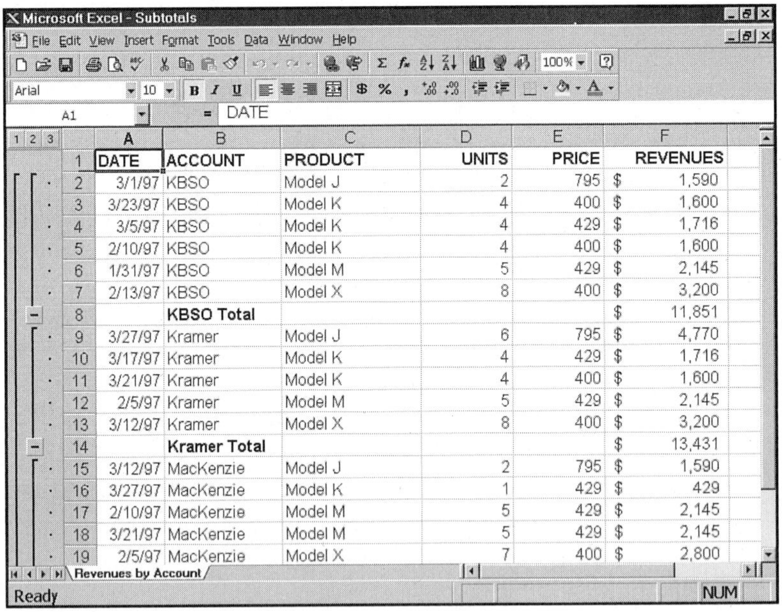

	A	B	C	D	E	F
1	DATE	ACCOUNT	PRODUCT	UNITS	PRICE	REVENUES
2	3/1/97	KBSO	Model J	2	795	$ 1,590
3	3/23/97	KBSO	Model K	4	400	$ 1,600
4	3/5/97	KBSO	Model K	4	429	$ 1,716
5	2/10/97	KBSO	Model K	4	400	$ 1,600
6	1/31/97	KBSO	Model M	5	429	$ 2,145
7	2/13/97	KBSO	Model X	8	400	$ 3,200
8		KBSO Total				$ 11,851
9	3/27/97	Kramer	Model J	6	795	$ 4,770
10	3/17/97	Kramer	Model K	4	429	$ 1,716
11	3/21/97	Kramer	Model K	4	400	$ 1,600
12	2/5/97	Kramer	Model M	5	429	$ 2,145
13	3/12/97	Kramer	Model X	8	400	$ 3,200
14		Kramer Total				$ 13,431
15	3/12/97	MacKenzie	Model J	2	795	$ 1,590
16	3/27/97	MacKenzie	Model K	1	429	$ 429
17	2/10/97	MacKenzie	Model M	5	429	$ 2,145
18	3/21/97	MacKenzie	Model M	5	429	$ 2,145
19	2/5/97	MacKenzie	Model X	7	400	$ 2,800

FIG. 34.2
Here, the entries are grouped by account. The revenues for each account are totaled.

If you edit the entries that are calculated (for example, change any of the calculated revenues), the subtotals and grand totals are automatically recalculated.

▶ **See** "Sorting by Command," **p. 1008**

▶ **See** "Using the AutoFilter," **p. 1028**

Removing a Subtotal

If you immediately realize you don't want the subtotals, choose Edit, Undo Subtotals to undo them. If Undo Subtotals is unavailable because you made other changes, choose Data, Subtotals and then click the Remove All button.

Creating Advanced Subtotals

You aren't limited to just one calculation on one set of groups. You can create subtotals for groups within the first group. For example, you might want to display subtotals for account and then for product within the account.

You also can perform multiple calculations on the columns in a group. For example, you might want to count the number of sales in a group and then total the dollar amount.

Creating Nested Subtotals

If you want additional subtotals within each group (a nested subtotal), you can create two sets of subtotals. For instance, you might want to total all accounts and also include subtotals for each product within an account.

To create a nested subtotal, be sure the data is sorted on the second key. Then, choose Data, Subtotals. Then, click the options for the first group (the largest group). Excel inserts subtotals for the first group.

Next, choose Data, Subtotals and choose the options for the next group. Be sure the Replace Current Subtotals check box is cleared (does not contain a check mark). Excel inserts a subtotal for the next set of groups.

Figure 34.3 shows revenue totals by account and unit totals by product.

Using Multiple Summary Functions

For some lists of data, you might want to do more than one calculation. For instance, you might want to total the sales (using the SUM function) and show an average of the sales (using the AVG function). You can do so with Excel.

To display two or more summary functions for the same set of data, choose Data, Subtotals and select the first function. Click OK. Excel inserts the subtotal rows. Then choose the command again and select another function. Be sure the Replace Current Subtotals check box is cleared. Excel inserts an additional subtotal row with the new calculation.

 TIP To perform a summary calculation on more than one column, select the columns in the Add Subtotal To drop-down list in the Subtotal dialog box.

Figure 34.4 shows revenue totals by account and average revenue by account.

▶ **See** "Creating a Chart Automatically," **p. 698**

Part
IX

Ch
34

FIG. 34.3
Excel created revenue subtotals for each account. The accounts then were grouped by product and a unit total was calculated.

	A	B	C	D	E	F	
1	DATE	ACCOUNT	PRODUCT	UNITS	PRICE		REVENUES
2	3/1/97	KBSO	Model J	2	795	$	1,590
3			**Model J Total**	2			
4	3/23/97	KBSO	Model K	4	400	$	1,600
5	3/5/97	KBSO	Model K	4	429	$	1,716
6	2/10/97	KBSO	Model K	4	400	$	1,600
7			**Model K Total**	12			
8	1/31/97	KBSO	Model M	5	429	$	2,145
9			**Model M Total**	5			
10	2/13/97	KBSO	Model X	8	400	$	3,200
11			**Model X Total**	8			
12		**KBSO Total**				$	11,851
13	3/27/97	Kramer	Model J	6	795	$	4,770
14			**Model J Total**	6			
15	3/17/97	Kramer	Model K	4	429	$	1,716
16	3/21/97	Kramer	Model K	4	400	$	1,600
17			**Model K Total**	8			
18	2/5/97	Kramer	Model M	5	429	$	2,145
19			**Model M Total**	5			

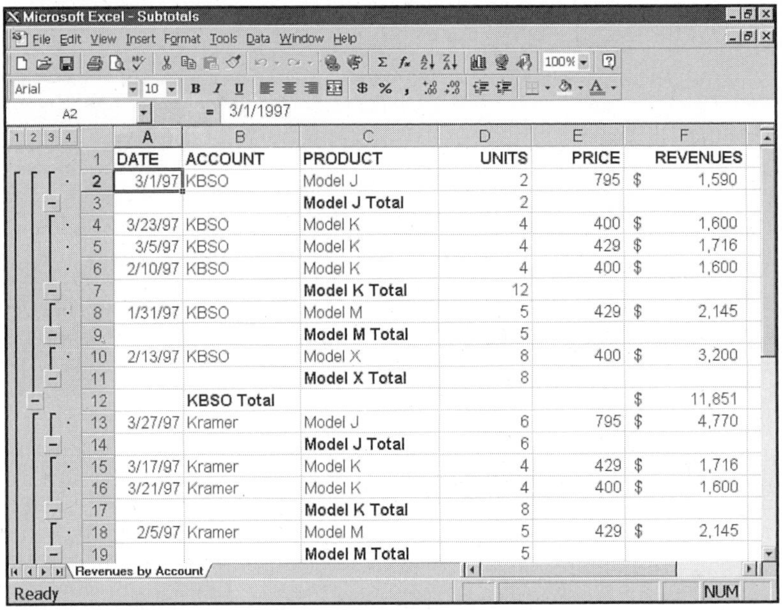

FIG. 34.4
Two calculations—a sum and an average—are performed on the account groups.

	A	B	C	D	E	F	
1	DATE	ACCOUNT	PRODUCT	UNITS	PRICE		REVENUES
2	3/1/97	KBSO	Model J	2	795	$	1,590
3	3/23/97	KBSO	Model K	4	400	$	1,600
4	3/5/97	KBSO	Model K	4	429	$	1,716
5	2/10/97	KBSO	Model K	4	400	$	1,600
6	1/31/97	KBSO	Model M	5	429	$	2,145
7	2/13/97	KBSO	Model X	8	400	$	3,200
8		**KBSO Total**				$	11,851
9		**KBSO Average**				$	1,975
10	3/27/97	Kramer	Model J	6	795	$	4,770
11	3/17/97	Kramer	Model K	4	429	$	1,716
12	3/21/97	Kramer	Model K	4	400	$	1,600
13	2/5/97	Kramer	Model M	5	429	$	2,145
14	3/12/97	Kramer	Model X	8	400	$	3,200
15		**Kramer Total**				$	13,431
16		**Kramer Average**				$	2,686
17	3/12/97	MacKenzie	Model J	2	795	$	1,590
18	3/27/97	MacKenzie	Model K	1	429	$	429
19	2/10/97	MacKenzie	Model M	5	429	$	2,145

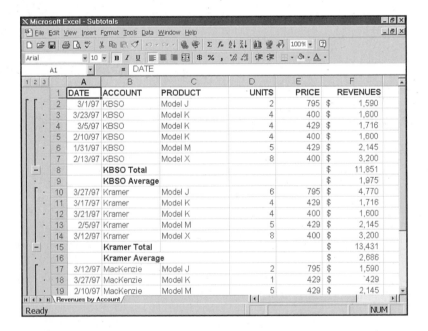

Changing the Detail Level

Depending on the level of subtotals you created, Excel creates an outline with different levels. In outline view, you can quickly display summary information. To display just the grand total and column labels, click the row level 1 symbol. If you want to display just the subtotals and grand total, click the row level 2 symbol.

You also can click the Hide Detail (-) or Display Detail (+) symbol to collapse and expand the outline.

Changing the row levels is useful when you want to perform the following procedures:

- Create a chart of just the subtotals. Collapse the detail level of the data list to show just the subtotals. Then select and chart the subtotals.

- Sort the subtotals. Display the subtotals you want to sort, and then sort the data with the Data, Sort command. All hidden rows are sorted with the associated subtotal row.

Figure 34.5 shows only the subtotal and grand total rows. All other rows are hidden.

FIG. 34.5
You can change the level of detail shown in the outline so that only the subtotals and grand total are displayed.

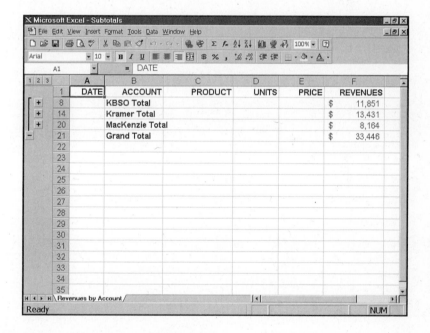

Using Subtotals on Filtered Data

There may be some rows that you want to exclude from the list. Suppose you want to summarize only sales over five units or summarize only the sales of a particular product. The easiest way to summarize only certain rows is to filter the database.

To filter the database, follow these steps:

1. Choose Data, Filter.

2. Choose AutoFilter. You should see a filter symbol beside the command, which indicates that the command is selected.

   Drop-down arrows appear next to each column head. Using these drop-down lists, you can specify the filter you want to use.

3. Click the arrow next to the column you want to use as the filter. For example, if you want to display only a certain product, click the down arrow next to Product.

   You see a list of predefined filters in parentheses, and you see each unique entry in the column listed. (All) selects all the entries in this column. (Blanks) selects blanks. (Non Blanks) selects all non-blank cells. (Custom) enables you to create a custom filter. (See Chapter 45, "Finding, Filtering, and Editing Lists or Databases," for more information on filters.) Selecting one of the entries in the column tells Excel to match this entry. If you select Model M in the Product column, for example, Excel displays only Model M products.

   After you select the filters you want, Excel hides all rows that don't meet the criteria. Now you can create the subtotals for just the displayed rows.

N O T E To turn off the AutoFilter, choose Data, Filter, AutoFilter. When the filter is activated, a filter symbol appears next to the command. Selecting the command again turns off the filter. ▪

4. Choose Data, Subtotals to select the subtotals you want calculated.

Figure 34.6 shows a database filtered by the Product column (only Model M products are displayed). The resulting list is then subtotaled by account.

 You can filter on more than one column. Just continue selecting the filters you want.

Creating Conditional Sums

A new feature in Excel 97, the Conditional Sum Wizard, enables you to sum only the data in a list that meets specified criteria. What the Conditional Sum Wizard actually does is build a SUM formula using IF statements to test if specific conditions are true. You can specify more than one condition to fine-tune your sums report. Only those values that meet the conditions are included in the sum. You could build the same formula yourself by typing it directly into the formula bar, but the Conditional Sum Wizard greatly simplifies the task, especially if you are testing multiple conditions. An example using the data list in this chapter would be to sum the total unit sales for all items with a price greater than $425.00.

FIG. 34.6

If you want to select only certain rows in your data list, filter the data first, then do the subtotals.

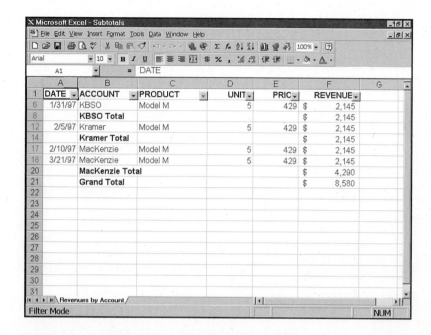

To use the Conditional Sum Wizard to create a sum, follow these steps:

1. Select any cell within the list you want to use to create the conditional sum.

2. Choose Tools, Wizard, Conditional Sum. Step 1 of the Conditional Sum Wizard appears (see Figure 34.7).

FIG. 34.7

Select the range of data that contains the values and conditional parameters you want to use to create the conditional sum.

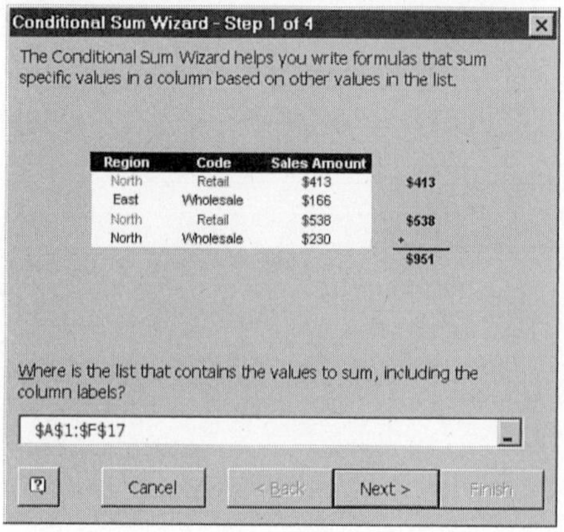

If you don't see the Conditional Sum command in the Wizard submenu, click on the arrow at the bottom of the menu to extend the list.

3. Verify the range in the text box at the bottom of the dialog box and click Next.

   If you selected a cell in the data list, the range will automatically be selected. Otherwise, you can click in the text box and select a new range in the worksheet.

4. In Step 2 of the Conditional Sum Wizard, select the column with the values you want to sum in the Sum drop-down list.

5. Select the parameter you want to use to perform the conditional test from the Parameter drop-down list.

6. Select the conditional operator from the Is drop-down list and enter a value for the conditional test in the Value text box.

7. Click Add Condition to add the condition to the box at the bottom of the dialog box.

8. Repeat steps 5–7 to create additional conditions.

9. To remove a condition, select the condition in the list box and click Remove Condition.

   Figure 34.8 shows the Step 2 dialog box set up to sum the number of units sold with a price that is greater than $425.

FIG. 34.8

Specify the column to be summed and the parameters and conditions for the conditional sum in Step 2 of the Conditional Sum Wizard.

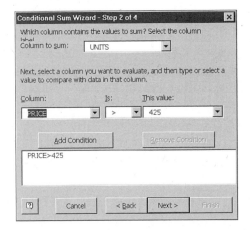

10. Click Next to display Step 3 (see Figure 34.9) and select one of the two options.

    Select Copy Just the Formula to a Single Cell if you only want to copy the sum formula resulting from the parameters you specified in the worksheet.

    Select Copy the Formula and Conditional Values if you want to also copy the current parameters to the worksheet, so you can change the parameters.

11. Click Next to display Step 4 of the Conditional Sum Wizard.

At this point, the remaining steps in the wizard will vary depending on which option you selected in the previous step 10. If you selected the Copy Just the Formula to a Single Cell option in step 10, follow these steps:

FIG. 34.9

Specify whether to include the conditional values for the conditional sum in the worksheet, allowing you to change them.

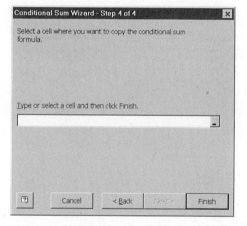

1. Specify the cell in which you want to insert the conditional sum formula in the text box in the dialog box shown in Figure 34.10.

FIG. 34.10

Specify the cell for the conditional sum formula in Step 4 of the Conditional Sum Wizard.

2. Click Finish.

The conditional sum formula is copied into the specified cell. When you select the cell, you can see the formula in the formula bar (see Figure 34.11). If you make changes in the list, the result of the conditional sum will automatically update, like any other formula.

If you selected the Copy the Formula and Conditional Values option in step 10, follow these steps:

1. Specify the cell in which you want to copy the first conditional value in the dialog box shown in Figure 34.12.

Part

IX

Ch

34

FIG. 34.11

The Conditional Sum Wizard creates a conditional sum formula and inserts it in the worksheet. You can see the conditional sum formula in the formula bar.

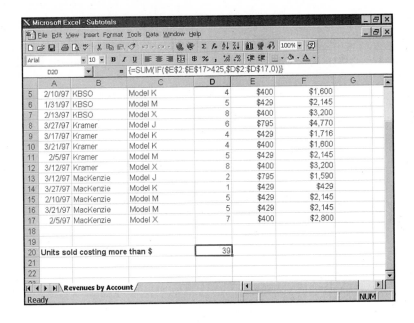

FIG. 34.12

Specify the cell where you want to copy the conditional value used in the conditional formula.

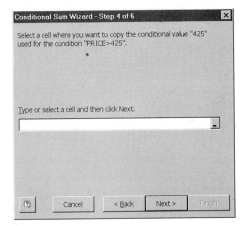

2. Click Next.

3. If there are additional conditional values in the sum formula, repeat step 1 in the dialog box that appears.

   When you select the Copy the Formula and Conditional Values option, a dialog box will appear for each of the conditional values you specified when you set up the conditions for the sum.

4. Specify the cell in which you want to insert the conditional sum formula in the dialog box shown in Figure 34.10.

The step number for this dialog box will vary, depending on how many conditional values are used in the sum formula.

5. Click Finish.

The conditional sum and any conditional values are copied into the cells you specified. Figure 34.12 shows the same conditional sum shown in Figure 34.11, but the conditional value has been copied to the worksheet. When you modify the conditional value on the worksheet, the conditional sum will recalculate.

Formatting and Printing the Report

The most likely reason for inserting subtotal rows is to produce a printed report. You can format the report quickly by using one of Excel's automatic formats. Choose Format, AutoFormat. Then select the format you want and click OK. See Chapter 23, "Formatting Worksheets," for more information on this feature.

To print the report, choose File, Print.

 TIP To print each group on a separate page, select the Page Break Between Groups check box in the Subtotal dialog box.

To print different versions of the same data, investigate creating views and using the Report Manager. Chapter 28, "Printing Worksheets," covers this topic.

▶ **See** "Formatting with AutoFormats," **p. 540**

▶ **See** "Creating a Sequence of Reports," **p. 680**

Taking Advantage of Excel's Add-Ins

Even with its ease-of-use, Excel has a more comprehensive set of features than other worksheets offer. But no matter how extensive Excel's features, special industries or special situations are bound to require more. With Excel, anyone who can record or write macros can add features, functions, and commands to Excel so that it works the way it's needed.

Excel ships with add-ins that enhance the way you work. After you install these add-ins on your hard disk during the installation process, you still need to activate the add-ins when you want to use them. These add-ins change Excel in different ways. Some add-ins provide additional items on menus. For example, Figure 35.1 shows the AutoSave command added to the Tools menu. Other add-ins increase the number of options on an existing menu or dialog box. Figure 35.2 shows the Paste Function dialog box. The Analysis ToolPak add-in adds a whole new function category, Engineering, that provides many engineering functions. The Analysis ToolPak add-in also adds functions to other function categories.

FIG. 35.1

Add-ins can add items on menus. The AutoSave add-in adds the command of the same name on the Tools menu.

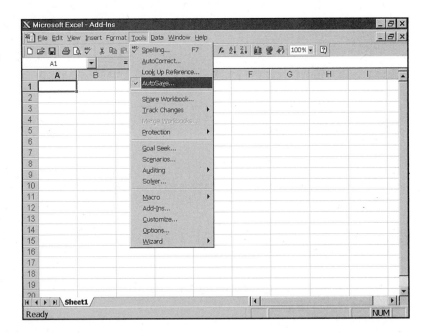

FIG. 35.2
Add-ins also can add functions. The Analysis ToolPak add-in adds a number of functions including a whole category for engineering functions.

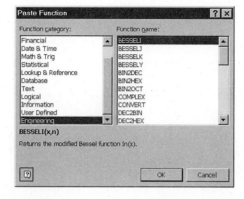

Installing Add-Ins

If you try to access an add-in and get a `Cannot find` message with the name of the add-in file (with an XLA or XLL extension), you need to install the add-in. You can check which add-ins have been installed by looking at the dialog box that appears when you choose Tools, Add-Ins (see the "Starting Add-Ins" section later in this chapter).

 For more information, choose Help, Contents and Index, select the Index tab, and type **add-ins** in the text box. Double-click Add-in Programs Included with Microsoft Excel entry in the lower pane.

When you originally installed Excel, you had three install options: Typical, Complete/Custom, and Laptop (Minimum). The add-ins installed depend on which of these options you chose and whether any changes were made after the original installation. If you chose Laptop (Minimum) installation, no add-ins were installed. If you chose Typical installation, AutoSave, Report Manager, and Solver were installed. The add-ins installed during Complete/Custom installation depend on which add-ins were deselected during the process. The default for Complete/Custom installation is for all add-ins to be installed. You can change the installed add-ins, however, within the Setup program.

To install add-ins after you've installed Excel, follow these steps:

1. Exit Microsoft Excel if it is open.
2. Using Explorer or My Computer, open the Program Files folder and then the Microsoft Office folder. Double-click the Microsoft Office Setup shortcut. The Microsoft Office 97 Setup dialog box appears (see Figure 35.3).

Part
IX
Ch
35

FIG. 35.3

The Microsoft Office 97 Setup program is separate from the Microsoft Excel program.

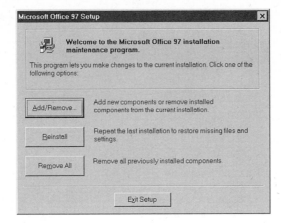

3. Choose the Add/Remove button. The Microsoft Office 97 - Maintenance dialog box appears.

4. Select Microsoft Excel in the Options list box and choose Change Option.

5. Select Add-Ins from the Options list box, as shown in Figure 35.4.

FIG. 35.4

To choose the add-ins to install, choose the Change Option button to the right of the list of options.

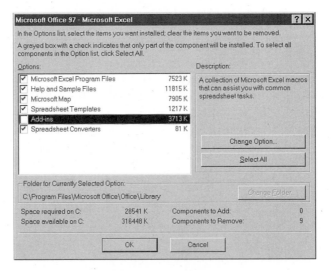

6. In the Microsoft Office 97 - Add-ins dialog box, click each option to install it, as shown in Figure 35.5.

7. After you select the add-ins to install, choose OK twice.

8. Choose Continue in the Microsoft Office 97 - Maintenance dialog box.

9. Insert the disks that the message box prompts you to insert. If you are installing from a CD-ROM, make sure the original Office 97 CD-ROM is in the CD-ROM drive.

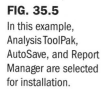

FIG. 35.5
In this example,
Analysis ToolPak,
AutoSave, and Report
Manager are selected
for installation.

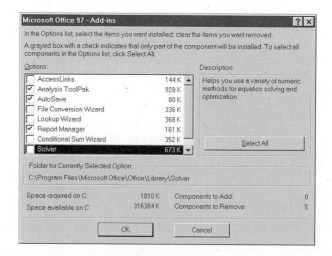

10. At the end of the process, you should get a message that the setup was completed successfully. Choose OK. If the setup was not successful, you need to start over at step 2.

When you install the add-ins, you copy the files to your hard disk. You might still need to start the add-ins, using the procedure described later in the "Starting Add-Ins" section.

Using Add-In Programs

The add-in programs that ship with Excel are stored in files ending with the XLA extension. Additional files needed by the add-ins use the extension XLL and DLL. You can find them in the LIBRARY folder in the OFFICE folder. The OFFICE folder is located in the \PROGRAM FILES\MICROSOFT OFFICE folder. These XLA files are special macros that add features to Excel as though the features were built-in. To access the add-ins, you need to install the add-in files and also activate the add-ins. In this section, you learn how to start these add-in macros and how to manage them. To learn how you can make your own recorded or written macros into add-ins, and learn more about Visual Basic for Applications programming, read *Special Edition Using Visual Basic for Applications*, also published by Que.

Starting Add-Ins

You start an add-in macro when you choose the add-in from the Tools, Add-Ins menu. Excel opens add-in files with XLA extensions. When that add-in opens, special commands, shortcuts, functions, or features available through the add-in become accessible. Although you can open XLA files with the File, Open command, they are more manageable when added to menus with the Tools, Add-Ins command. When you install an add-in with the Tools, Add-Ins command, the new feature may appear on a menu, but the add-in file does not open until you choose the command. This process makes add-ins available without using system resources unnecessarily. The add-in macros that come with Excel are stored in \PROGRAM FILES\MICROSOFT OFFICE\OFFICE\LIBRARY. Some add-in macros have their own folders in the LIBRARY folder.

Using the Tools, Add-Ins Command

The Tools, Add-Ins command helps you by opening a collection of add-ins that you specify. The Tools, Add-Ins command opens the Add-Ins dialog box (see Figure 35.6). Excel indicates active add-ins with a check mark in the check box next to the add-in name. Excel indicates available, yet inactive, add-ins with a blank check box.

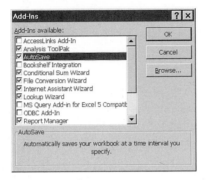

FIG. 35.6

This Add-Ins dialog box shows the add-ins that are active. Notice the description displayed at the bottom of the dialog box for the selected add-in.

To add an add-in to Excel, follow these steps:

1. Choose Tools, Add-Ins.

2. Select the add-in, or add-ins, you want by marking the check box next to the add-in, as shown in Figure 35.6.

3. If the add-in does not show on the Add-Ins dialog box, select the Browse button and search for the file. Files with XLA and XLL extensions are available as add-ins.

4. When you finish selecting add-ins, choose OK.

Using the Analysis ToolPak

The Analysis ToolPak is a must for financial, statistical, and some engineering and scientific analysis. It contains functions and models that a few years ago required minicomputers for solutions.

The Analysis ToolPak adds five Financial functions, five Date & Time functions, seven Math & Trig functions, two Information functions, and a category for 40 Engineering functions. The Analysis ToolPak also allows you to add your own functions. To access these additional functions, choose Insert, Function, and then select a Function Category and Function Name on the Paste Function dialog box (refer to Figure 35.2).

The Analysis ToolPak also adds the Data Analysis command to the Tools menu. When you choose this command, you get several statistical procedures to choose from, as shown in Figure 35.7.

For coverage of the added calculating capabilities available with the Analysis ToolPak, see Chapter 41, "Using the Analysis ToolPak."

FIG. 35.7
This Data Analysis dialog box shows some of the statistical procedures available, including Anova, Correlation, and the F-Test.

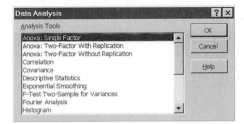

Adding an AutoSave Feature

The AutoSave add-in saves Excel files for you at the frequency you specify. This macro helps you remember to save. When AutoSave loads, it adds the AutoSave command to the Tools menu. Choose Tools, AutoSave to display the AutoSave dialog box, as shown in Figure 35.8.

FIG. 35.8
The AutoSave feature allows you to save your work automatically or to have Excel prompt you to save your work.

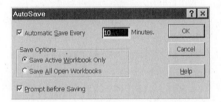

The first option on the AutoSave dialog box, Automatic Save, allows you to turn the automatic save feature on or off. If you select this check box, you can enter the number of minutes between automatic saves in the Minutes text box. In the Save Options area, you can have Excel save all workbooks or only the active workbook. The last option, Prompt Before Saving, allows Excel to prompt you before saving workbooks.

Adding the Report Manager

The Report Manager is a major feature of Excel for anyone who must print charts and reports involving multiple worksheets, multiple views, or different sets of input data. If you need to do a job like this more than once, use the Report Manager. Add the Report Manager by using the Tools, Add-In command. Use the Report Manager by choosing the View, Report Manager command. The Report Manager dialog box appears as shown in Figure 35.9. The Report Manager is described in Chapter 28, "Printing Worksheets."

FIG. 35.9
The Report Manager add-in enables you to combine worksheets, charts, and views in one report.

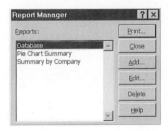

Part
IX

Ch
35

Adding Optimization with the Solver

The Solver add-in, shown in Figure 35.10, gives Excel the power of linear and nonlinear optimization. Solver not only finds an answer to a problem, it finds the best answer, given a set of cells that it can change, a set of constraints that must be met, and one cell that must be optimized for the greatest, least, or equal to solution. Use Tools, Add-Ins to add the Solver and the Tools, Solver command to run the Solver.

FIG. 35.10

Use the Solver to find the best possible solution even when there are multiple input values.

Manipulating Excel Data

Manipulating and Analyzing Data

If all Excel did was perform algebraic computations in worksheets, it would still be a powerful tool, but certain tasks need more than number-crunching. If you use Excel extensively, you will undoubtedly find situations where the result depends on different conditions. Some of these conditions may depend on specific values or a range of values in a given cell. In other situations, you may want Excel to look up an answer from a list. You may also need to summarize data in a list based on certain criteria. Excel provides a number of features to facilitate this kind of processing and analysis.

Manipulating Text

Excel enables you to manipulate text, numbers, and dates. Text manipulation is handy for combining text and numbers in printed invoices, creating titles from numeric results, and using data from a database to create a mailing list. With Excel, you can use formulas to manipulate text in the same way you use formulas to calculate numeric results.

Use the concatenation operator, the & (ampersand), to join text, numbers, or cell contents to create a text string. Enclose text in quotation marks. You don't need to enclose numbers in quotation marks. Do not enclose cell references in quotation marks. You can reference cells that contain text or numbers. For example, consider the following formula:

="This "&"and That"

This formula displays the following text:

`This and That`

N O T E Text used in a formula must always be enclosed in quotes. Excel assumes that text not in quotes is a name. This situation causes a `#NAME?` error if a name with this spelling is not defined.

You also can join text by referring to the cell address. If A12 contains the text, John, and B12 contains the text, McDougall, you can use the following formula to combine the first and last names:

=A12&" "&B12

The result of the formula is the following:

`John McDougall`

Notice that a space between the two quotation marks in the formula separates the text contained in cells A12 and B12.

You also can use the CONCATENATE function to produce the same result. The formula =CONCATENATE(A12," ",B12) also returns John McDougall.

Excel also enables you to convert a number to text. You can refer to a number as you refer to a cell filled with text. If A12 contains 99 and B12 contains the text, Stone St., use the following formula to create the full street address:

=A12&" "&B12

The result of the formula is the address:

99 Stone St.

When you refer to a number or date in a text formula, the number or date appears in the general format, not as the number or date appears in the formatted display. Suppose that cell B23 contains the date 12/25/97, and you enter the following formula:

="Merry Christmas! Today is "&B23

The result of this formula is the following:

Merry Christmas! Today is 35789

You can change the format of the number with the FIXED( ), DOLLAR( ), and TEXT( ) functions. These functions change numbers and dates to text in the format you want. With dates, for example, you can use the TEXT( ) function to produce the following formula:

="Merry Christmas! Today is "&TEXT(B23,"mmm dd, yy")

The result appears as the following:

Merry Christmas! Today is Dec 25, 97

You can use any predefined or custom numeric or date format between the quotation marks of the TEXT( ) function.

The TEXT( ) function is a handy way to trick large numbers into exceeding the width of a column without producing the #### signs that indicate a narrow column. The TEXT( ) function also is useful for numeric titles. If you want the number $5,000,000 stored in A36 to fit in a narrow column, for example, use the following formula, which displays the formatted number as text so the number can exceed the column width:

=TEXT(A36,"$#,##0")

▶ **See** "Aligning and Rotating Text and Numbers," **p. 543**

Using Formulas to Make Decisions

Excel's IF( ) function can make decisions based on whether a test condition is true or false. Use IF( ), for example, to test whether the time has come to reorder a part, whether data was entered correctly, or which of two results or formulas to use.

The IF( ) function uses the following format:

IF(*logical_test,value_if_true,value_if_false*)

If the *logical_test* (condition) is true, the result is *value_if_true*; but if the *logical_test* is false, the result is *value_if_false*. The result values can display text with an argument such as "Hello," calculate a formula such as B12*6, or display the contents of a cell such as D35. IF() functions are valuable in macros for testing different conditions and acting according to the results of the test conditions.

Consider the following formula:

=IF(B34>50,B34*2,"Entry too low!")

In this example, the IF() function produces the answer 110 if B34 is 55. If B34 is 12, however, the cell that contains the function displays this text:

`Entry too low!`

Making Simple Decisions

To make comparisons, use IF() functions. Figure 36.1 shows an Accounts Aging Analysis worksheet in which Excel checks how long an amount has been overdue. Using IF() functions and the age of the account, Excel displays the amount in the correct column.

FIG. 36.1

Use IF() functions to test ranges, such as the ages of these accounts.

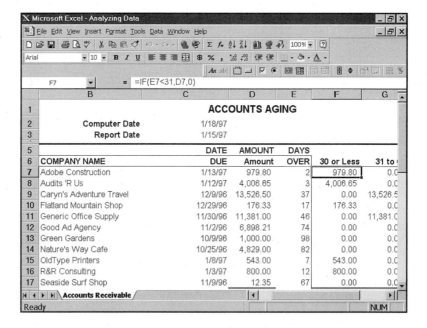

The first few times you use IF() statements, you might want to write an English sentence that states the *logical_test*, or the question you want to ask. The question also should state both results if true and if false. For example, each cell from E7 through E16 uses an IF() statement equivalent to the following sentence:

IF the value in the DAYS OVER column is less than 31, show the adjacent value in the AMOUNT DUE column, but if this condition is not true, then show zero.

The IF( ) function equivalent of this statement for cell E7 appears in the formula bar as the following formula:

=IF(D7<31,C7,0)

In this example, D7 contains the DAYS OVER for row 7, and C7 contains the AMOUNT DUE for row 7. To prevent displaying all zeroes on the sheet, choose Tools, Options, display the View tab, and clear Zero Values.

N O T E To display a blank cell for specific conditions, use a formula similar to the following:

=IF(D7<31,C7,"")

Nothing is entered between the quotation marks, so this function displays a blank cell for the false condition. Remember that Excel can hide zeroes for the entire worksheet if in the Options dialog box, you deselect Zero Values in the View tab. ■

Making Complex Decisions

In column F of the worksheet shown earlier in Figure 36.1, the IF( ) question needs to be more complex. The IF( ) functions in column F must test for a range of values in the DAYS OVER column. The DAYS OVER columns must be over 30 and less than 61:

If the value in the DAYS OVER column is greater than 30 and the value in the DAYS OVER column is also less than 61, then show the value in the AMOUNT DUE column; if this is not true, show zero.

The IF( ) functions in F7 through F17 use the following formula to check for DAYS OVER in the range from 31 to 60:

=IF(AND(D7>30,D7<61),C7,0)

The AND( ) function produces a TRUE response only when all the elements within the parentheses meet the conditions: D7>30 is true *AND* D7<61 is true. When the AND( ) function produces TRUE, the IF( ) formula produces the value found in C7.

When you want to check for a number within a range of values, use an AND( ) function as shown here; for the AND( ) function to be TRUE, all the arguments must be true. An AND( ) function is most frequently used to test whether a number or date is within a range.

An OR( ) function is another type of logical test. An OR( ) function produces a TRUE response when any one of its arguments is TRUE. OR( ) functions are usually used to match one value against multiple values. For example,

=IF(OR(B12=36,B12="Susan"),"OK","")

If the value in B12 is either 36 or Susan, then the formula results in the text OK. If the value in 36 is neither of these, then the result is nothing ("").

▶ **See** "Entering Worksheet Functions," **p. 612**

Checking Data Entry

Whether you enter data in a database form or make entries directly into the cells of a worksheet, you can prevent accidental errors by using formulas that automatically cross-check data as you enter it. Figure 36.2 shows an example of a data-entry form that uses formulas to cross-check entered data. The formula bar shows the formula used to check the data in cell D4. This formula produces no result, "", if the date entered in D4 is after 1/1/1996. However, if the date entered is prior to 1/1/1996, then the message appears in the formula's cell.

FIG. 36.2

In this data-entry form, the data in columns I and J serve as tables of valid inputs for the Item Number and Division entries in cells D6 and D8.

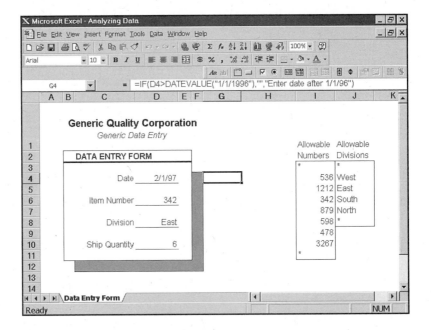

NOTE If you are creating data-entry worksheets and need to restrict the user to entering yes or no, multiple choices, or selections from a list, read Chapter 37, "Building Forms with Controls." Excel worksheets can contain items seen in dialog boxes, such as scrolling lists, pull-down lists, check boxes, and groups of option buttons. Two new data-entry devices also are available: a spinner to quickly spin through a range of numbers and scroll bars to let you drag across a wide range of numbers. The result from these devices appears in a worksheet cell where you can use it just as though it were typed. ■

Figure 36.3 shows the same form with incorrect data entered. Notice the warnings that appear to the side of the data-entry cells.

FIG. 36.3

In this data-entry form, formulas in column G display warnings when the user makes invalid entries.

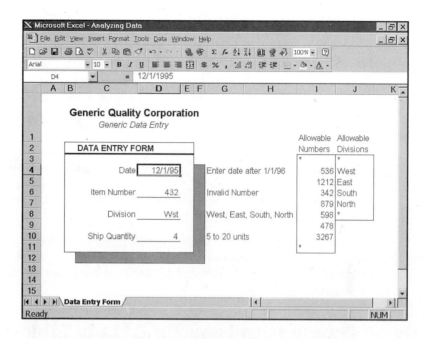

The formulas used in those cells are given in the following table:

Cell	Cross-Check	Formula
G4	Date after 1/1/96	=IF(D4> DATEVALUE("1/1/1996"),"","Enter date after 1/1/96")
G6	Item number in list	=IF(ISNA(MATCH D6,I3:I11,0)), ("Invalid Number"",")
G8	Division name in list	=IF(ISNA(MATCH (D8,J3:J8,0)),"West, East, South, North","")
G10	Range of quantities	=IF(AND(D10>4,D10<21)," ","5 to 20 units")

In each of these formulas, an IF( ) function combined with a conditional test decides whether the entry in column D is correct or not. The formula in cell G4 checks whether the date serial number from D4 is greater than the date in the IF( ) function. If the serial number is greater, the blank text " " is displayed. If the value in D4 is not greater, the function displays the prompting text.

> **N O T E** If the user needs to remember and type many different possible entries, an excellent data-entry method is the use of a pull-down list or scrolling list placed on the worksheet. This Excel feature is described in Chapter 37, "Building Forms with Controls." ■

In cell G6, the MATCH( ) function looks through the values in I3:I11 to find an exact match with the contents of D6. The 0 argument tells MATCH( ) to look for an exact match. When an exact match is not found, the function returns the error value #N/A!. The ISNA( )function detects #N/A! values when a match is not found; it displays the text warning Invalid Number. When a match is found, "" (nothing) is displayed on-screen.

Note that when you use MATCH( ), the items in the list do not need to be sorted if you use a 0 match-type argument as with the LOOKUP( ) functions. MATCH( ) also returns an error if an exact match is not found; whereas, a LOOKUP( ) function may return a near but incorrect result.

Cell G8 uses the same MATCH( ) method to check the division name against acceptable spellings. If you use large lists of possible entries, you might want to use the pull-down or scrolling lists that can be placed on a worksheet. Selecting from a list reduces the chance of typing an error or of forgetting an entry item. These pull-down or scrolling lists are described in Chapter 37, "Building Forms with Controls."

The value of Ship Quantity must be 5 to 20 units. Therefore, the formula in G10 uses an AND( ) statement to check that the number in D10 is greater than 4 and less than 21. When both checks are true, nothing is displayed. If the number is out of the range, the function displays the message 5 to 20 units.

Using Formulas to Look Up Data in Tables

You can build a table in Excel and look up the contents of various cells within the table. Lookup tables provide an efficient way of producing numbers or text that you cannot calculate with a formula. For example, you might not be able to calculate a tax table or commission table. In these cases, looking up values from a table is much easier. Tables also enable you to cross-check typed data against a list of allowable values.

Excel has two techniques for looking up information from tables. The first method uses LOOKUP( ) functions. Although easy to use, these functions have the disadvantage of giving you an answer whether or not the function finds an exact match. The list in the table also needs to be in sorted order—another disadvantage. This method is good, however, in situations such as creating volume discount tables.

The second method uses a combination of the INDEX( ) and MATCH( ) functions to find an exact match in a table, regardless of whether the list in the table is sorted. If Excel cannot find an exact match, the function returns an error so you know an exact match wasn't found. This method is good for exact matches, such as looking up the quantity on hand for a specific product. In this case, you need to find an exact part number, not the next closest item.

Using LOOKUP Functions on Tables

Excel has two functions that are useful in looking up values in tables. The VLOOKUP( ) function looks down the vertical column on the left side of the table until the appropriate comparison value is found. The HLOOKUP( ) function looks across the horizontal row at the top of the table until the appropriate comparison value is found.

The VLOOKUP( ) and HLOOKUP( ) functions use the following forms:

VLOOKUP(*lookup_value,table_array,col_index_num,range_lookup*)

HLOOKUP(*lookup_value,table_array,row_index_num,range_lookup*)

The VLOOKUP( ) function tries to match the value in the left column of the table; the HLOOKUP( ) function tries to match the value in the top row. These values are the *lookup_values*. The *table_array* describes the range that contains the table and lookup values. The *col_index* for the VLOOKUP( ) function or the *row_index_num* for HLOOKUP( ) tells the function which column or row, respectively, contains the result. The first column or row in the table is always numbered 1. The fourth argument, *range_lookup*, is optional and is explained in the next section.

The list you use for comparison in the table must be in ascending order. For the lookup function to work correctly, the cells in C11:C15, in Figure 36.4, must be sorted in ascending order. The function searches down the first column of a VLOOKUP( ) table or across the first row of an HLOOKUP( ) table until it meets a value larger than the *lookup_value*. If the *lookup_values* are not in ascending order, the function returns incorrect results.

Figure 36.4 shows an example of a VLOOKUP( ) table that locates sales commissions. The VLOOKUP( ) and HLOOKUP( ) commands are helpful for looking up data in commission or tax tables because these tables contain data that can be difficult to calculate exactly. The sales on which a commission is based, for example, may fall between two numbers in the list. The formula that finds this sales commission is in cell D5. The VLOOKUP( ) function, as shown in the formula bar of the example, is used in the following formula:

FIG. 36.4

The VLOOKUP() function finds information in a vertical table.

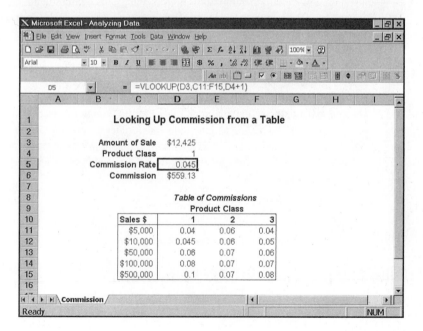

> =VLOOKUP(D3,C11:F15,D4+1)

The VLOOKUP( ) function looks down the left column of the table displayed in the range C11:F15 until a Sales $ amount larger than D3 ($12,425) is found. VLOOKUP( ) then backs up to the previous row and looks across the table to the column specified by D4+1. The formula D4+1 results in 2, the second column of the table. (Sales $ is column 1. The value 1 is added to D4 so the lookup starts in the Product Class portion of the table.) The VLOOKUP( ) function returns the value .045 from the table. The commission is calculated by multiplying .045 by the amount of sale, which is $12,425.

The VLOOKUP( ) function doesn't use the headings in row 10. These headings are shown for the user's benefit.

Finding Exact Matches

You can also use the VLOOKUP( ) and HLOOKUP( ) functions to look up data from a table and use an exact match to find the information. The data you are looking up can be text or numbers. If Excel doesn't find an exact match in the list, an error value warns you that the table contained no matches.

Using exact matches against a list is one way to prevent data-entry errors. Imagine a case in which an operator must enter an item number and an item description that belongs to this item number. To reduce data-entry errors, you might want to have the operator enter the description using a pull-down list as described in Chapter 37, "Building Forms with Controls." An Excel LOOKUP( ) function or INDEX(MATCH( )) function combination can then use the description to look up the item number from a list. This technique not only reduces typing but cross-checks the item number by displaying either an accurate description or an error message if the number is incorrect.

N O T E   While the combination of INDEX( ) and MATCH( ) is the most accurate way of matching and retrieving data from a table, it is slow when used with large or multiple tables.

The optional fourth argument (*range_lookup* in the Function Wizard) controls whether a VLOOKUP( ) or HLOOKUP( ) function looks for an exact match or the next largest value that matches. To find values that are an approximate match when an exact match is not available, use TRUE or omit the range_lookup argument. To specify an exact match, use FALSE as the fourth argument, as shown below:

> =VLOOKUP(D3,C11:F15,D4+1,FALSE)

If you entered the preceding formula in cell D5, it would return the #N/A error value because an exact match for the $12,425 in cell D3 cannot be found in the Sales $ column.

Using MATCH( ) and INDEX( ) Functions

If your source list is not sorted, the lookup functions cannot work correctly. However, in this case you can use a combination of the MATCH( ) and INDEX( ) functions to look up values. In

Figure 36.5, Excel enters the item description if the item number is entered. If the item number is nonexistent, the worksheet displays #N/A in the Description cell (C8).

FIG. 36.5

Use a combination of INDEX and MATCH to find an exact match in an unsorted table.

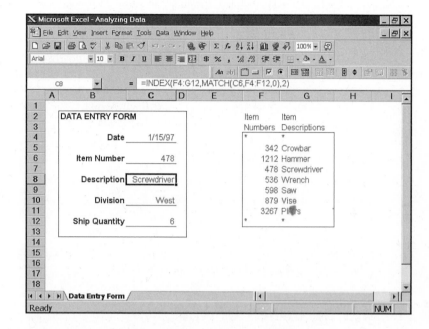

The following formula found in cell C8 looks up and enters the description:

=INDEX(F4:G12,MATCH(C6,F4:F12,0),2)

The two functions used in this formula follow this syntax:

=INDEX(*array,row_num,column_num*)

=MATCH(*lookup_value,lookup_array,match_type*)

In the INDEX() function, *array* is the entire range that contains data. (It can also be an array constant.) If you enter the INDEX() function with the Function Wizard in working through these examples, select the set of arguments that match the INDEX() arguments shown above. The *row_num* and *column_num* arguments designate the row and column that specify a value in the array. For example, for the range F4:G12, a *row_num* of 5 and a *column_num* of 2 causes INDEX() to return Wrench.

In the MATCH() function, the *lookup_value* is the value for which you are searching. In the example, this value is the item number found in C6. The *lookup_array* is an array in a row or column that contains the list of values that you are searching. In the example, this array is the column of item numbers F4:F12. The *match_type* specifies the kind of match required. In the example, 0 specifies an exact match.

In the example, therefore, the MATCH( ) function looks through the range F4:F12 until an exact match for the contents of cell C6 is found. After an exact match is found, the MATCH( ) function returns the position of the match: row 4 of the specified range. Notice that the MATCH( ) function finds the first match in the range. For an exact match, the contents of the range F4:F12 do not need to be in ascending order.

You also can omit the *match_type* or specify 1 or -1. If the *match_type* is omitted or is 1, then MATCH( ) finds the largest value in the *lookup_array* equal to or less than the *lookup_value*. If *match_type* is omitted or is 1, the *lookup-array* must be in ascending order. If the *match_type* is -1, MATCH( ) finds the smallest value greater than or equal to the *lookup_value*. If the *match_type* is -1, the *lookup_array* must be in descending order.

In the formula shown earlier in Figure 36.5, the INDEX( ) function looks in the range F4:G12. The function returns the contents of the cell located at the intersection of column 2 and row 4, as specified by the MATCH( ) function. The result is `screwdriver`.

The item numbers and descriptions in the table are outlined to identify the table. The asterisks (*) at the top and bottom of the table mark the corners of the ranges.The function continues to work correctly as long as you insert all new data item codes and descriptions between the asterisks.

▶ **See** "Entering Worksheet Functions," **p. 612**

Calculating Tables of Answers

Because of the *what if* game made possible by electronic worksheets, worksheets are extremely useful in business. Worksheets provide immediate feedback to questions, such as: "What if we reduce costs by .5 percent?," "What if we sell 11 percent more?," and "What if we don't get that loan?"

When you test how small changes in input affect the result of a worksheet, you are conducting a *sensitivity analysis*. You can use Excel's Data, Table command to conduct sensitivity analyses across a wide range of inputs.

Excel can create a table that shows the inputs you want to test and displays the results so you don't need to enter all the possible inputs at the keyboard. Using a combination of a data table and the *Dfunctions*, you can do quick but extensive database analysis of finance, marketing, or research information.

You can have more than one data table in a worksheet so you can analyze different variables or database statistics at one time.

You can use the Data, Table command in the following two ways:

- Change one input to see the resulting effect on one or more formulas.
- Change two inputs to see the resulting effect on only one formula.

One Changing Variable and Many Formulas

Among the best (and most frequently used) examples of sensitivity analysis is a data table that calculates the loan payments for different interest rates. The single-input data table described in this section creates a chart of monthly payments for a series of loan interest rates.

Before you create a data table, you need to build a worksheet that solves the problem you want to test. The worksheet in Figure 36.6 calculates a house or car mortgage payment. The following formula in cell D8 handles that task:

=PMT(D5/12,D6*12,D4)

FIG. 36.6

Build a worksheet with a result you want to analyze.

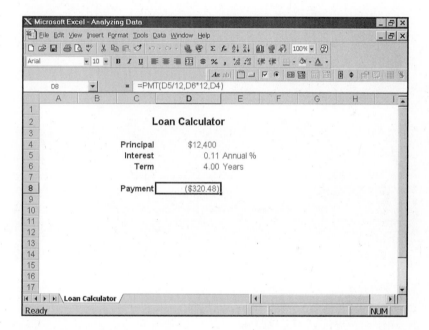

To build a data table, take the following steps:

1. Build the worksheet.

2. Enter the different values you want tested. You can enter the values in any sequence.

    Cells C11:C17 in Figure 36.7 show the interest rates to be used as inputs in the sensitivity analysis.

3. In the top row of the table, row 10, above where the results appear, enter the address of each formula for which you want answers. In this cell, you also can enter the formula directly rather than reference a formula located elsewhere.

    In Figure 36.7, cell D10 contains =D8. Therefore, the results for the payment formula in D8 are calculated for each interest rate in the table. To see the results of other formulas in the table, enter these formulas in other cells across the top of the table. For example, you can enter more formulas in E10, F10, and so on.

FIG. 36.7

The first step in creating
this table of mortgage
payments is to enter the
range of interest rates to
be evaluated.

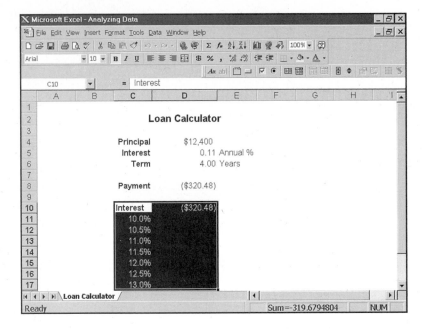

4. Select the cells that enclose the table. Include the input values in the left column and the row of formulas at the top, as shown in Figure 36.7. In Figure 36.7, you should select C10:D17. The results fill into the blank cells in D11:D17.

5. Choose Data, Table to display the Table dialog box (see Figure 36.8).

FIG. 36.8

Enter row or column
input cells in the Table
dialog box.

6. Enter a Row Input Cell or Column Input Cell. Click or point to the cell in which you want to type the variable numbers listed in the table.

   In this example, the Column Input Cell is $D$5. You should enter $D$5 in the Column Input Cell text box. The Column Input Cell is used rather than the Row Input Cell because in this table the values being tested in the table are the interest rates that go down the left-most column. If you wanted to manually calculate payment amounts, you would type these interest rates into cell D5. By entering $D$5 into the Column Input Cell, you are telling Excel to test each interest rate in the left column of the table by entering that rate into cell D5. The resulting payment that is calculated for each interest rate is then placed in the adjacent cell in column D.

7. Choose OK.

The data table fills with the payment amounts that correspond to each interest rate in the table (see Figure 36.9).

FIG. 36.9

The completed table, with results in column D for each value in column C.

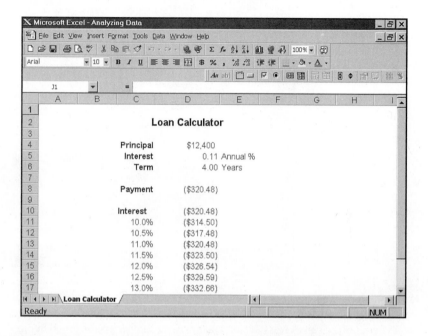

	A	B	C	D	E	F	G	H
1								
2			**Loan Calculator**					
3								
4			Principal	$12,400				
5			Interest	0.11 Annual %				
6			Term	4.00 Years				
7								
8			Payment	($320.48)				
9								
10			Interest	($320.48)				
11			10.0%	($314.50)				
12			10.5%	($317.48)				
13			11.0%	($320.48)				
14			11.5%	($323.50)				
15			12.0%	($326.54)				
16			12.5%	($329.59)				
17			13.0%	($332.66)				

TIP Use the Edit, Fill, Series command or drag the fill handle across a series to fill incremental numbers for input values.

You can enter the Row Input Cell or Column Input Cell by first clicking in the text box you want and then clicking on the appropriate cell in the worksheet. If the Table dialog box covers the cells you want to select as the row or column inputs, move the dialog box.

Two Changing Variables and One Formula

Figure 36.10 shows how to create a data table that changes two input values: interest and principal (the loan's starting amount). The worksheet calculates the result of a formula for all combinations of those values. The top row of the table, row 10, contains different principal amounts for cell D3, the Row Input Cell. The left column of the table still contains the sequence of interest rates to use in cell D4. (If you are duplicating this example, notice that cell references in the example have changed by one row from the previous example.)

Notice that when you use two different input values, you can test the results from only one formula. The formula or a reference to the formula must be in the top-left corner of the table. In Figure 36.10, cell C10 contains the reference =D7 to the payment formula to be tested.

FIG. 36.10

Data tables also can change two input values used by one formula.

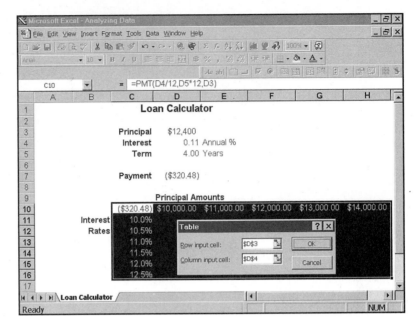

The Table dialog box in Figure 36.10 shows how the Row Input Cell is $D$3 because the values from the top row of the table are substituted into cell D3. The Column Input Cell is $D$4 because the values from the left column of the table are substituted into cell D4.

Figure 36.11 shows the result of a two-input data table. Each dollar value is the amount you pay on a loan with this principal amount and annual interest rate. Because each monthly payment represents a cash outflow, the results appear in parentheses to show that the amounts are negative and in red.

Editing Data Tables

After the data table is complete, you can change values in the worksheet on which the data table depends. Using the new values, the table recalculates. In the earlier example in Figure 36.11, typing a new Term in D5 causes new Payment amounts to appear.

You also can change the numbers or text in the rows and columns of input values and see the resulting change in the data table. In the earlier example in Figure 36.11, you can type new numbers or use the Edit, Fill, Series command to replace the numbers in C11:C15 or in D10:H10. If automatic recalculation is selected, the data table updates by default.

You cannot edit a single formula within the data table. All the formulas in this area are array formulas of the following form:

{=TABLE(*row_input,column_input*)}

To rebuild or just expand the data table, reselect the table, including new cells if you are expanding the table, and repeat the steps you used to create the original table. The new table will overwrite the old table.

FIG. 36.11
The completed data table with the results of combinations from two input values, interest and principal.

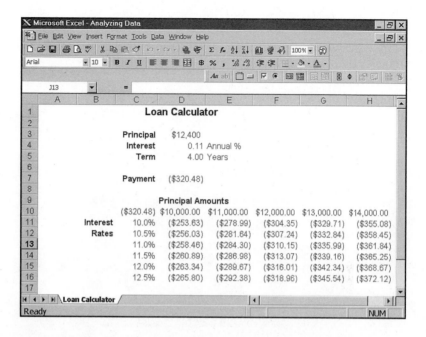

N O T E If you find data tables useful, examine the Scenario Manager, along with other more advanced methods of analysis. If you need to test a set of data inputs and find the myriad of results, then look to the Scenario Manager. ▪

Calculating Data Tables

Large data tables or many data tables may slow down calculation. If you want the worksheet— but not the data tables—to recalculate, choose Tools, Options, select the Calculation tab and select Automatic except Tables. Recalculate the tables by pressing F9 or clicking the Calc Now button on the Calculation tab to calculate all worksheets. If you want to calculate only the active worksheet, press Shift+F9 or click the Calc Sheet button on the Calculation tab. If you have selected the Manual recalculation option in the Calculations tab, and you are performing a large database analysis, you might not want the worksheet and the related tables to recalculate before saving, which is the normal process. To save without recalculating, choose Tools, Options, select the Calculation tab and clear Recalculate Before Save.

The Lookup Wizard

The Lookup Wizard is a new add-in that helps you create a formula to look up data in a list using the INDEX( ) and MATCH( )functions. To access the Lookup Wizard, select the Tools, Wizard menu. If the Lookup command is not on the Wizard submenu on the Tools menu, you need to load the add-in program through the Tools, Add-Ins menu.

An example of using the Lookup Wizard is if you wanted to create a formula that would return an inventory item's description based on the inventory item's ID number. The Lookup Wizard needs to know four things to be able to complete the formula:

■ Where the data is located

■ Which column contains the value you wish to return or look up

■ Which row contains the initial value to match

■ Where to put the results

To use the Lookup Wizard, complete the following steps:

1. Select a cell in the list.

2. Choose Tools, Wizard, Lookup. The first dialog box of the Lookup Wizard displays as shown in Figure 36.12.

FIG. 36.12

When you select a cell in the list prior to accessing the Lookup Wizard, the list's range displays in the Lookup Wizard's first dialog box.

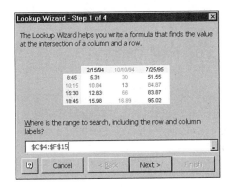

3. Verify the range is correct and click the Next button to display Step 2 of the Lookup Wizard (see Figure 36.13).

FIG. 36.13

Step 2 needs two pieces of information, which column and row contains the value to find.

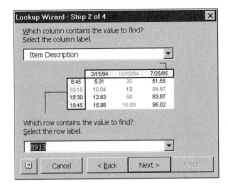

4. From the first drop-down list box, select the column that contains the value you want to return or look up.

5. From the second drop down list box, select which row contains the initial value to match.

6. Click Next. The third step of the Lookup Wizard displays (see Figure 36.14).

FIG. 36.14

Step 3 of the Lookup
Wizard gives you the
choice of displaying just
the result or including
lookup parameters.

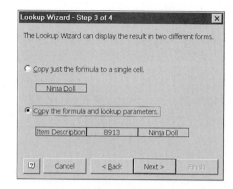

7. If you want to display just the result of the lookup, select the Copy Just the Formulas to a
   Single Cell option button. If you want to include the lookup parameters, select the Copy
   the Formula and Lookup Parameters option button.

8. Click Next to move to the fourth step of the Lookup Wizard (see Figure 36.15).

FIG. 36.15

This is the fourth step
that displays if you
select the Copy the
Formula and Lookup
Parameters option
button. This step allows
you to decide where to
place the value of one
of the lookup
parameters.

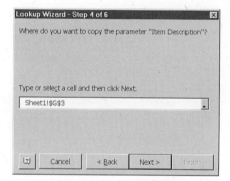

9. If you selected the Copy the Formula and Lookup Parameters option button, you are
   prompted to select which cell to copy the first lookup parameter into. Select the cell and
   click Next to move to the next step (see Figure 36.16).

FIG. 36.16

This is the fifth step
that displays if you
select the Copy the
Formula and Lookup
Parameters option
button.

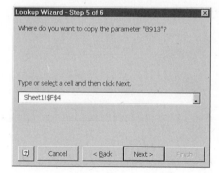

10. If you selected the Copy the Formula and Lookup Parameters option button, you are prompted to select which cell to copy the second lookup parameter into. Select the cell and click Next to move to the next and final step (see Figure 36.17).

FIG. 36.17

The final step of the Lookup Wizard is the same whether you selected the Copy the Formula and Lookup Parameters option button or the Copy the Formula and Lookup Parameters option button.

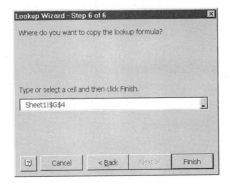

Lookup Wizard – Step 6 of 6

Where do you want to copy the lookup formula?

Type or select a cell and then click Finish.

Sheet1!$G$4

| ? | Cancel | < Back | Next > | Finish |

11. The final step of the Lookup Wizard requires you to select the cell that is to receive the formula. Select the cell and click Finish. The formula has been created based on the information you provided the Lookup Wizard as shown in Figure 36.18.

FIG. 36.18

The Lookup Wizard creates a formula to perform the lookup using the INDEX( ) and the MATCH( ) functions.

X Microsoft Excel – Lookup Wizard

File Edit View Insert Format Tools Data Window Help

Arial · 10 · B I U

G4 =INDEX($A$1:$D$21, MATCH(F4,$A$1:$A$21,), MATCH(G3,$A$1:$D$1,))

	A	B	C	D	E	F	G	H
1	Inv. ID	Department	Item Description	Price				
2	1011	Housewares	Blue Towel	4.59				
3	3012	Hardware	Hammer	6.99			Item Description	
4	2211	Garden	16" Clay Pot	5.59		8913	Ninja Doll	
5	8145	Toys	Deluxe Train Set	21.97				
6	1894	Housewares	Cow Pot Holder	2.47				
7	7001	Candy	Lollipops	1.99				
8	6541	Womens	Denim Shirt	19.99				
9	2365	Garden	Spade	9.97				
10	5565	Mens	Green Shorts	14.97				
11	1236	Housewares	4' Area Rug	23.99				
12	2987	Garden	3" Plastic Pot	2.29				
13	6037	Womens	Red Wool Skirt	24.97				
14	5203	Mens	Tube Socks	3.50				
15	7002	Candy	Gum Drops	0.97				
16	7005	Candy	Licorice	0.97				
17	8913	Toys	Ninja Doll	11.99				
18	5123	Mens	Economy Briefs	4.00				

Sheet1 / Sheet2 / Sheet3 /

Ready   NUM

To use the new formula, you can enter a different value in lookup parameters if you opted to copy them as part of using Lookup Wizard. You could, for example, enter a different inventory number and see its corresponding description.

Analyzing Trends

Excel can calculate a linear regression or best-fit line that passes through a series of data. You might remember in science class recording a number of data points on a chart and then trying to draw a line through the points so that the line gave the trend of the data with the least errors. That line was a best-fit line. Points on that line are the best-fit data.

In some cases, you can use the result of these calculations to analyze trends and make short-term forecasts. Two ways of calculating the data for these trends are available. You can drag across numbers by using the fill handles, or you can use worksheet functions.

If you need to extend existing data by a few periods (cells) but don't need the corresponding best-fit data for the existing cells, you can use the method of dragging fill handles to extend the data. You can also use the Edit, Fill, Series command to create a linear regression or best-fit line. If, however, you need both original data and the corresponding best-fit data for the same periods—for example, to show original data and a best-fit line through the data—then use the worksheet function method.

N O T E Chart the data and trend to give trends more impact and make relationships more apparent. Excel has the capability to automatically create trend lines of different types directly on a chart. To learn how to create a chart that automatically shows a trend line, read "Automatically Analyzing Trends with Charts" in Chapter 32, "Building Complex Charts." ■

Calculating Trends with Fill Handles

Figure 36.19 shows known data for regional housing starts for the years 1995 through 1998. But the future housing starts for 1999 and 2000 are unknown. If the trend from 1995 through 1998 continues, you can use a linear regression to calculate the expected starts for 1999 and 2000.

You can project this data into the empty cells to the right, 1999 and 2000, by using a linear best-fit. Select the cells as shown in Figure 36.19. To fill the data in the empty cells, use the left mouse button to drag the fill handle to the right to enclose the area you want extended, then release the mouse button. Row 4 of Figure 36.20 shows the results of this procedure.

To fill a range using a growth trend, take these steps:

1. Select the cells as shown in Figure 36.19.
2. Drag the fill handle to the right with the right mouse button. Excel displays a shortcut menu with Linear Trend and Growth Trend as commands.
3. Select Growth Trend.

Row 6 of Figure 36.21 shows the results of this procedure.

FIG. 36.19
Using linear best-fit, extend a series by dragging the fill handle.

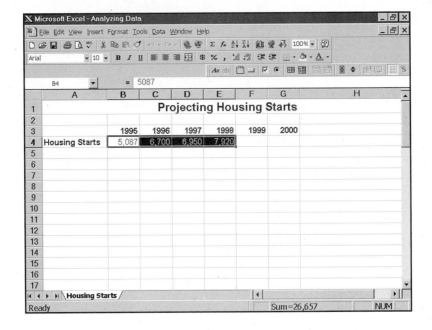

FIG. 36.20
The amounts shown for 1999 and 2000 are projections using linear best-fit.

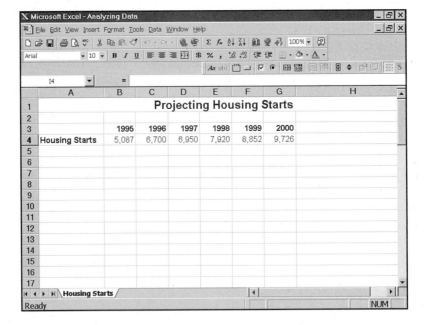

Calculating Trends with the Data Series Command

Using Excel's Edit, Fill, Series command, you can create best-fit data to replace or extend an original data set. You also can chart the best-fit data to create a best-fit line.

FIG. 36.21

Create the projections for 1999 and 2000 in row 6 by dragging the fill handle with the right mouse button, then choosing the Growth Trend command.

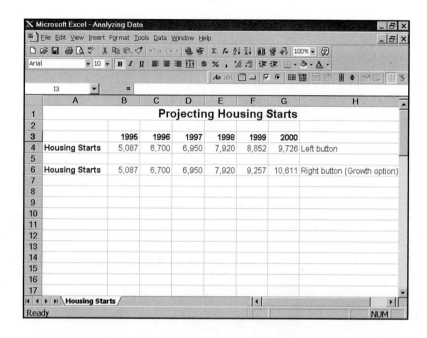

Choosing Edit, Fill, Series creates a linear (straight line) or exponential growth trend line. Using Edit, Fill, Series, you can create these two types of trend lines in two ways. Figure 36.22 illustrates the different types of trend data produced.

The original data used to produce the trends in the figure are the numbers 1, 5, and 12 shown in B4:D4. The selected range used with each command is in each of the rows from column B to column H. The different types of trend data produced use these combinations of settings in the Series dialog box:

Settings	Description of Resulting Trend
Default settings	A linear trend is produced starting with the original first data point. Calculated data replaces the original data. If charted, the trend line is forced to go through the first data point.
AutoFill	A linear trend is produced. The original data remains. Selected cells beyond the original data fill with data points for the linear trend.
Trend and Linear	A linear trend is produced and the trend is not forced to pass through the first original data point. Original data is replaced with trend data.
Trend and Growth	An exponential growth trend is produced and the trend is not forced to pass through the first original data point. Original data is replaced with trend data.

FIG. 36.22

Use the Edit, Fill, Series command to produce any of the four types of trend data shown here.

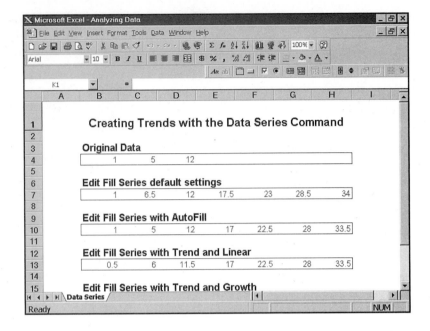

To create a trend using Edit, Fill, Series, perform the following steps:

1. Select the original data and as many additional cells as you want the trend data to extend into. In Figure 36.15, for example, the cells B4:H4 may be selected.

2. Choose Edit, Fill, Series.

3. Choose one of the options described in the previous table.

Note that, in addition to the four trend computations shown in Figure 36.15, you can produce a fifth by dragging the fill handle with the right mouse button. This produces a growth trend that does not override the original data.

Calculating Trends with Worksheet Functions

Excel's trend functions work by calculating the best-fit equation for the straight line or exponential growth line that passes through the data. The LINEST( ) and LOGEST( ) functions calculate the parameters for the straight-line and exponential growth-line equations. The TREND( ) or GROWTH( ) functions calculate the values along the straight line or exponential growth line needed to draw a curve or forecast a short-range value.

Before you use the trend analysis functions, become familiar with dependent and independent variables. The value of a *dependent variable* changes when the *independent variable* changes. Frequently, the independent variable is time, but it also can be other items, such as the price of raw materials, the temperature, or a population size. The independent variables actual data is entered as the *known-x* argument in the function, and the dependent variables actual data is entered as the functions *known-y* argument.

Imagine that you own a concrete business that depends on new residential construction. You want to plan for future growth or decline so you can best manage your firm's assets and people.

After research with the help of local economic advisory boards, you assemble statistics on housing starts in the service area for the previous five years. In Figure 36.19, row 4 shows the housing starts by year. After meeting with county planners, you are convinced that this area may continue to grow at the same or a slightly higher rate. You still need to estimate, however, the number of housing starts in 1995 and 1996.

In Figure 36.19, the independent variables of time (*known_x*) are entered in B3:E3. The dependent variables of housing starts (*known_y*) are entered in B4:E4. If the trend from the past four years continues, you can project the estimated housing starts for the next two years with the following steps:

1. Select the range of cells you want the straight-line projection to fill, B6:G6, as shown in Figure 36.23.

FIG. 36.23

Before entering an array formula such as TREND, select the entire range.

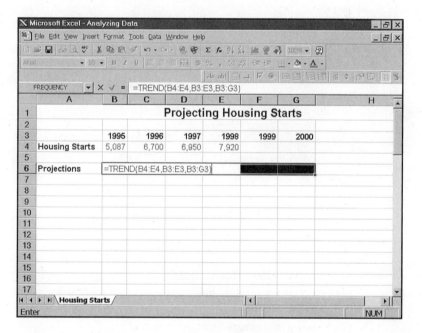

2. Enter the TREND( ) function using either the keyboard or the Function Wizard.

3. Enter the arguments for the TREND( ) function. The following line shows the correct syntax:

TREND(*known_y's,known_x's,new_x's*)

For this example: The *known_y's* argument is B4:E4. (Housing Starts are y's because these numbers are dependent on the Year value.)

The *known_x's* argument is B3:E3. (Year is the independent variable.)

The *new_x's* argument is B3:G3, which are the years for which you want to know the values that describe a trend line.

Notice that the selected area in Figure 36.24 covers the room for the resulting calculated y values.

4. To enter the TREND() function as an array function in the selected range, press Shift+Ctrl+Enter.

If the present trend continues, the result shown in Figure 36.24 illustrates that years 1999 and 2000 might have housing starts of about 8,852 and 9,726.

FIG. 36.24

The trend values in row 6 can help you make short-term projections. The TREND() function computes new values for the period of known values.

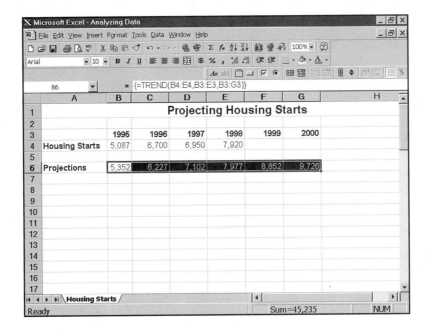

Notice that the new y values in cells B6:E6 don't exactly match the known y values in B3:E3 because the TREND() function calculated the housing starts for these years according to its trend equation (a linear regression). The real number of housing starts in each year undoubtedly will be different.

▶ **See** "Entering Worksheet Functions," **p. 612**

▶ **See** "Using Data Analysis Tools Commands," **p. 966**

Building Forms with Controls

What You Need to Know About Controls

In the past, a detriment to using a worksheet to enter data and do calculations was that complex formulas or macros were often needed to check data. Most worksheets let the occasional data entry error go rather than take the time to create data-checking formulas or data-entry macros or procedures. Also, making a worksheet data-entry area as appealing as a well-done dialog box was difficult.

You can place on a worksheet the same type of data-entry controls as you can place in a dialog box run by a macro or Visual Basic procedure. *Controls* are data-entry objects, such as scrolling lists or check boxes. When you enter a value in a control or make a selection from a control, the entry appears in a worksheet cell, and the control makes sure that you can only make valid entries.

To use controls you don't need to know how to program, you only need to know how to make selections from a dialog box.

Controls are data entry devices that can appear in a worksheet or in a dialog box. Figure 37.1 shows a form in a worksheet that uses controls for data entry.

FIG. 37.1

Controls make data entry in a worksheet more attractive and less error-prone.

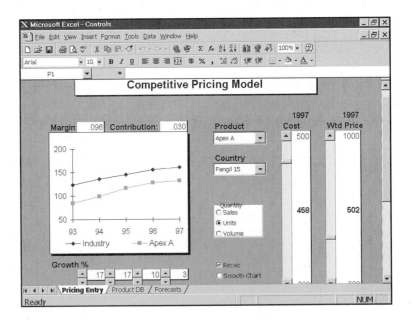

Controls used in a worksheet are linked to a cell in a worksheet. When you enter data into a control or make a selection from the control, the result of the selection appears in the linked worksheet cell. The result in this cell then can be used in standard worksheet calculations, just as though the user had typed in the cell's value.

Besides being more attractive and easier to use, you can control the values a user selects from a control. If a control is a scrolling list, for example, you can control the items in the list, which reduces the amount of formula writing you must do and reduces or eliminates data entry errors.

Differences Between Controls in a Worksheet and in a Dialog Box

The controls you use in a worksheet are just the same as the controls you place in a dialog box, however, more types of controls are available for use in a dialog box. There are also some differences, advantages, and disadvantages that exist between using a control on a worksheet to enter data and using a control in a dialog box. Table 37.1 compares some of these differences.

Part
X

Ch
37

Table 37.1 Worksheet Control Versus Dialog Box Control

Comparison	Worksheet Control	Dialog Box Control
Controls available	Label, group box, command button, check box, option button, list box drop-down list, scroll bar, and spinner	Worksheet controls plus edit box, combination list-edit, combination drop-down edit
Ease of use	Intermediate user	Advanced user
Calculation	On any selection in control	Under Visual Basic control
Accelerator (Alt+) key	Not available	In dialog sheet, choose Format, Object, then Control tab
Tab order	Not available	In dialog sheet, choose Tools, Tab Order
Results data	Simple	Advanced checking
Data manipulation	In worksheet formulas	In worksheet formulas or in Visual Basic procedure
Runs macro or VBA procedure	Yes	Yes

Using the Forms Toolbar

You draw controls on a worksheet by clicking a button in the Forms toolbar and then dragging on the worksheet to indicate the size and location of the control. Once a control is drawn, you use a formatting command to assign properties to it such as allowed values, limits, protection properties, and so on.

To display the Forms toolbar, follow these steps:

1. Choose View, Toolbars to display the Toolbars list.
2. Select Forms from the Toolbars list.

The buttons on the Forms toolbar are shown in Table 37.2.

Table 37.2   Buttons on the Forms Toolbar

Button	Name	Description
Aa	Label	Text to name items or for instructions.
ab|	Edit Box	Data entry box for text, numbers, dates, or cell references. Not available on a worksheet.
	Group Box	A border that groups option buttons. Only one option button in group can be selected.
	Button	Creates a button to run a macro.
	Check Box	Check box produces True when selected; False when cleared.
	Option Button	Only one option button from a group can be selected. Returns the number of the selected button.
	List Box	A text list. Returns the number of the item selected.
	Combo Box	A drop-down list containing text. Returns the number of the item selected.
	Combination List Edit	A text list with an edit box. Not available on a worksheet.
	Combination Drop-Down Edit	A drop-down list with an edit box. Not available on a worksheet.
	Scroll Bar	A draggable scroll bar returns a number between the range limits of the top and bottom.
	Spinner	A counter whose returned number increases or decreases in integer amounts depending on which arrow you click.
	Control Properties	Displays a dialog box for the selected control. Use the dialog box to set the control's behavior.
	Edit Code	Use to edit the code assigned to the selected control. Used in both dialog box and worksheet controls.

Button	Name	Description
▦	Toggle Grid	Turns the alignment grid in a dialog sheet on or off. Turns grid lines on or off on a worksheet.
⬚	Run Dialog	Displays the dialog box on the active dialog sheet. Used to test a dialog box you have drawn. Not available on a worksheet.

N O T E If you display the Forms toolbar while viewing a worksheet, the Edit Box, Combination List-Edit, Combination Drop-Down Edit, and the Run Dialog toolbar buttons are disabled (grayed) as a reminder that they cannot be placed on a worksheet. ▪

How Controls Affect Cell Content and Calculations

After you draw a control on a worksheet, you need to link the control to a cell in the worksheet. You use this link to transfer the value selected or entered in the control to a cell in the worksheet where the value can be used.

The control and the cell affect each other. If you make a selection in the control, the value in the cell changes. Conversely, if you change the content of the linked cell, the selection in the control changes. This linking is necessary to keep controls in sync with the worksheet. If someone manually changes a value in a cell, you expect a control linked to this cell to reflect the current state of the worksheet.

Making Worksheets Appear Like Forms

With a little formatting, you can make worksheets appear more like a paper form. You probably want to start by having the form in the same workbook as the worksheets that do the calculations, which makes it easier to create and maintain links from the controls on the form to the worksheets using the data.

To make a worksheet resemble a separate dialog box or form, but still be included within the workbook, choose the Window, New Window command. In the new window, select the worksheet tab to make the form worksheet active. Press Alt, – (minus sign found on the numeric keypad), and choose the Restore command (if the command is available) to put this worksheet in a window. Now that the form is in a separate window, you need to make it look like a form.

To make the window look like a paper form, follow these steps:

1. Choose Tools, Options to display the Options dialog box.
2. Select the View tab.

3. Select from the following check boxes in the Window Options group to affect the appearance of only the active window:

Check Box	Effect
Page Breaks	Deselect so automatic page breaks do not show.
Formulas	Deselect so results show, not formulas.
Gridlines	Deselect so gridlines do not show.
Row & Column Headers	Deselect so row and column headings are hidden.
Outline Symbols	Deselect unless your form is built in an outline.
Zero Values	Optional. Deselect to hide zeros.
Horizontal Scroll Bar	Deselect to hide the scroll bar at the bottom.
Vertical Scroll Bar	Deselect to hide the scroll bar on the right edge.
Sheet Tabs	Deselect to hide the worksheet tabs.

You can color the background area of a form with a light gray to give it a more pleasing appearance. You also can use black and white lines or overlapping black and white rectangles to give pictures, charts, or text boxes the appearance of being raised or lowered.

▶ **See** "Controlling the Worksheet Display," **p. 800**

▶ **See** "Hiding and Unhiding Windows and Sheets," **p. 810**

Adding Controls to a Worksheet

You can use different controls on a worksheet or dialog sheet, but all controls are placed on the sheet in the same way. After you draw a control on the sheet, you must format the control. Formatting the control changes protection status, how the control moves when underlying cells move, and what the data entry items or limits are. In this section, you first learn how to draw a control on a sheet and then how to format each type of control.

Before you can draw a control on a worksheet or dialog sheet, you must display the Forms toolbar. To display the Forms toolbar, choose View, Toolbars, and select Forms from the Toolbars list.

Drawing the Control

To draw a control on a worksheet or dialog sheet, follow these steps:

1. Click the button in the Forms toolbar that represents the control you want to draw. (These buttons were shown in Table 37.2 previously.) The pointer changes to a crosshair.

2. Move the cross hair to the top-left corner of where you want the control to appear and drag down and right, to where you want the form's opposite corner.

3. Release the mouse button.

When you release the mouse button, the control appears on the form or dialog sheet. If you add a button control, you see the Assign Macro dialog box. Here you can select the macro to assign to the control.

When a control is selected, black outlined boxes called handles appear at the control's corners and edges. You can then move, resize, or change the properties of the selected control.

You can move a selected control by dragging an edge. Resize the control by dragging the black handle on a corner or the black handle on one edge. Delete a selected control by pressing the Delete key or by choosing Edit, Clear.

You also can change the protection status of a selected control by formatting it. You can change how the control moves with cells, or you can set the defaults and limits for its data. To deselect a control, click a cell or object other than the selected control.

Part

X

Ch

37

 TIP Select a control and display the shortcut menu at the same time by clicking the control with the right mouse button.

Changing a Control's Format

To set a control's format, follow these steps:

1. Right-click the control that you drew on the worksheet, and then choose the Format Control command from the shortcut menu.

N O T E The Format Control dialog box used to format controls on forms may contain a different number and type of tab depending on the control that you format. ▪

2. To change the control, select one or more of the following tabs and select the options:

- *Font.* Select the font, size, style, and color for fonts used on the macro button. Fonts on other controls cannot be formatted. This tab appears the same as font tabs used elsewhere in Excel.

- *Colors and Lines.* Select border type, size, and weight. Include a fill color or pattern. The Colors and Lines page is shown in Figure 37.2.

- *Protection.* Choose whether an object can be moved, resized, or changed (see Figure 37.3). Some controls can have text protected. It takes effect when protection is turned on by choosing Tools, Protection, and then choosing Protect Sheet. A password is optional.

- *Properties.* Restrict how a control moves or resizes when the cells underneath are moved or resized (see Figure 37.4). If you do not want a control to print, deselect the Print Object check box.

- *Control.* These settings determine the default value for a control, the control's data limits, and where the entered data will be passed. The options available depend on the control selected in step 1.

FIG. 37.2
Change the fill and line color on some controls with the Colors and Lines tab.

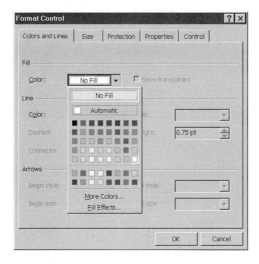

FIG. 37.3
Prevent a control from being changed by protecting it when worksheet protection is turned on.

- *Size.* The Size page controls the width and height of a control and provides you with an alternative to using the resizing handle to size the control. This makes it easier to create multiple controls with a standard size.

3. Choose OK.

FIG. 37.4
Use these options to control how a control resizes when the cells underneath change.

Adding Check Boxes for TRUE/FALSE Responses

A check box gives the user only two choices, TRUE or FALSE. The check box is linked to a cell so that the result of the check box status appears as TRUE or FALSE in the linked cell. Selecting the check box makes the cell TRUE. Deselecting the check box makes the cell FALSE. You can use an IF function that examines the TRUE or FALSE status and produces two results, depending upon whether the check box is selected.

 Double-click a selected control to display the Format Object dialog box.

To set the defaults and cell link on a check box that you draw, follow these steps:

1. Right-click the check box you already drew on the worksheet and choose Format Control.

2. Select the Control tab shown in Figure 37.5.

3. Select the default value of the check box, Unchecked for FALSE Result, Checked for TRUE Result, and Mixed for #NA Result. Choose the 3D Shading check box to add an impression of depth to the check box.

4. Select the Cell Link edit box, then click the cell in which you want to hold the results of the check box. You can use the Window menu or tab names to display other sheets to which you want to link the control.

5. Choose OK.

FIG. 37.5

The Control tab for a
check box describes the
default value and the
cell that is linked to
the result.

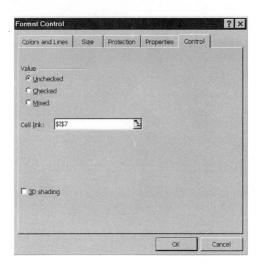

When you need the user to choose between two values, use a check box combined with an IF function. Use an IF function to convert the TRUE/FALSE result in the linked cell to one of two results. The result from the IF function can be text, date, formula, or numeric. The syntax for IF is shown in the following example:

=IF(*LinkCell,TrueResult,FalseResult*)

 For a more manageable system, type a range name in the Cell Link edit box rather than a cell reference.

If the linked cell is B35, for example, the following formula produces LOCAL when the check box is selected (B35 is TRUE), and it produces INTERNATIONAL when the check box is cleared (B35 is FALSE). Make sure you put this formula in a different cell than cell B35 that the check box is linked to:

=IF($B$35,"LOCAL","INTERNATIONAL")

Adding Option Buttons for Multiple Choice

Options buttons are used most frequently to make one and only one choice from a group of choices. Option buttons are the round buttons that usually come in groups. Option buttons are exclusive of one another—select one option button and the others deselect, which means that you can select only one button in a group at a time.

If you just draw option buttons on a worksheet, all these buttons will belong to the same group, which means that you can select only one button at a time. You can have multiple groups of buttons, however, by enclosing each group in a group box drawn with the group tool. All option buttons in the same group use the same linked cell. Drawing a group of option buttons is slightly different from drawing other controls. The result from a group of option buttons appears in one cell.

To create a group of option buttons, follow these steps:

1. Draw a group box by clicking the group box button and dragging from corner-to-corner where you want the box. While the box is selected, type a title to replace the default box title.

2. Click the option button tool and draw an option button within the group box. Type a title while the option button is selected.

3. Right-click the option button and choose Format Control to display the Format Control dialog box. Select the Control tab (see Figure 37.6 to see a completed control tab). Then select the value for the option button: Unchecked, or Checked. Remember that only one option button in a group can be checked.

FIG. 37.6

The Control tab for an option button describes the default value for the button and the cell that was linked to the result.

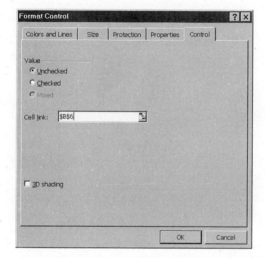

4. Select the Cell Link edit box, then click the worksheet cell that you want to contain the results from the group of option buttons.

5. Choose OK.

6. Return to step 2 to create another option button. All option buttons in a group box share the same cell reference. If you do not need to create another option button, click a cell outside the group.

When you create additional option buttons, you don't have to enter a cell reference for the Cell Link. Only one linked cell exists for all option buttons in a group. If the first button drawn is selected, the linked cell becomes 1, if the second button drawn is selected, the linked cell becomes 2, and so on.

A group of option buttons usually is used to force the user to select only one choice from many. You can use a CHOOSE function to turn the choice into different results. The syntax for using CHOOSE is shown in the following line:

```
=CHOOSE(LinkCell,Result1,Result2,Result3,...)
```

Assume that a group box contains three option buttons linked to cell B35. Selecting option buttons then would produce the numbers 1, 2, or 3 in cell B35. To convert 1, 2, or 3 into three text results, use a formula, such as the following example:

```
=CHOOSE($B$35,"Monday","Tuesday","Wednesday")
```

If the cell that contains this formula is formatted to display dates, you can choose between yesterday, today, and tomorrow's dates by adding the following worksheet function:

```
=CHOOSE($B$35,NOW()-1,NOW(),NOW()+1)
```

Adding List Boxes or Drop-Down Lists for Limited Text Choices

A list box or drop-down list restricts users to choosing from a defined list of items. The list may be product names, plant sites, employee positions, and the like. Restricting user selections prevents them from typing a mistake, entering nonexistent part numbers, or using old data. You even can use a choice from one list to look up a value from another list. Figure 37.7 shows a list box and a drop-down list.

FIG. 37.7

Use scrolling lists or pull-down lists to restrict choices.

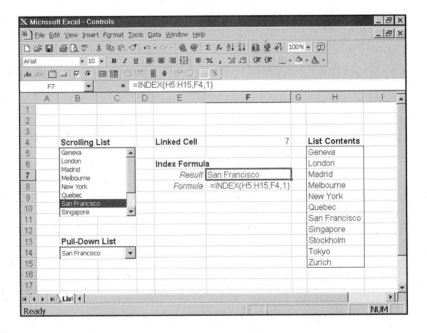

List boxes and drop-down lists produce the same result, but the appearance of these lists differs. A list box shows multiple items in the list, while the list stays the same height. A drop-down list is only one item high and has a drop-down arrow to the right side. Clicking the drop-down arrow displays the list. Drop-down lists usually are used when not enough room exists for a list box.

Use the Data, Sort command to sort the list on a sheet if you want the list to appear sorted within a control.

 For a more manageable system, type a range name in the Input Range edit box rather than a range reference.

To create a list, follow these steps:

1. On the worksheet, enter a vertical list of items you want to appear in the list. Enter one item per cell as shown previously in range H5:H15 in Figure 37.7.

2. Click the List Box or Drop Down button and draw a list box on the worksheet. If the list box cannot be made wide enough for all of the items to remain fully visible, make the list wide enough to show a readable amount of each item. Make a list box tall enough so that you can see multiple items. Make a drop-down list tall enough for one item.

3. Right-click the list and choose Format, Control to display the Format Control dialog box. Select the Control tab.

4. If you are working on a drop-down list, the Control tab resembles Figure 37.8. The Control tab looks the same for a list box but doesn't have a Drop Down Lines edit box.

FIG. 37.8

For a list, you must indicate the cells where the list is located.

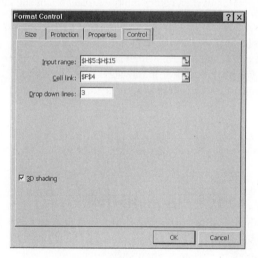

5. Select the Input Range cell, then drag across the range that contains the list. This list appears in the list box or drop-down list.

6. Select the Cell Link box and click the cell that will receive the results of the list. In Figure 37.7, the cell link is to F4.

7. If you are formatting a drop-down list, enter in the <u>D</u>rop Down Lines box the number of lines displayed when the list appears.

8. Choose OK.

The result of a selection from a list is a number that is the position of the selected item in the list. If you selected the third item in the list, for example, the linked cell will contain the number 3. In most cases you don't want to convert this number into the actual item in the list. To do this, use the INDEX function. The syntax for the INDEX function is shown in the following line:

```
=INDEX(ItemListReference,LinkCell,1)
```

Using Figure 37.7 as an example, the list of cities in the range H5:H15 is used for the range in the <u>I</u>nput Range box. The link cell for the list is F4. This cell is where the numeric position of the item selected appears. In another cell you can show the city selected with the formula:

```
=INDEX(H5:H15,F4,1)
```

This function looks down the list, H5:H15, to the row specified in cell F4. The item in that row of the list then is returned to the cell that contains the INDEX function.

As another useful technique, you can choose from one list but use a corresponding value from another list, which is useful for selecting easily recognizable named items from a list, but then letting Excel find the corresponding price for the item. You can use this technique to look up items by name or description but then return a more arcane result such as a part number, price, SKU, or weight.

To use an alternate list lookup, you need two lists (as shown in Figure 37.9). One list, H5:H15, is used for the <u>I</u>nput Range to the control, which is what the list users see. The other list is used to find the result you want to appear in the worksheet. In Figure 37.9 the formula returns a price, after the user makes a selection of a city. The formula in cell F11 is shown in the following line:

```
=INDEX(I5:I15,F4,1)
```

This formula returns the item in a specific row of the price list, I5:I15. The row is specified in cell F4, the linked cell.

Adding Spinners to Change Numbers Quickly

Spinners are controls that show two arrow heads. Each click of an arrow head increases or decreases the amount in the cell linked to the spinner. Holding down the mouse button on a spinner causes the number to change continuously.

CAUTION

The entire worksheet recalculates each time the link cell changes. When you spin through numbers with a spinner, this can cause a great deal of unnecessary recalculation, which slows both you and the computer. See the upcoming section "Controlling Recalculation" for ways to get around this.

FIG. 37.9

You can choose one item from a list (San Francisco) and display an item from an alternate list ($989).

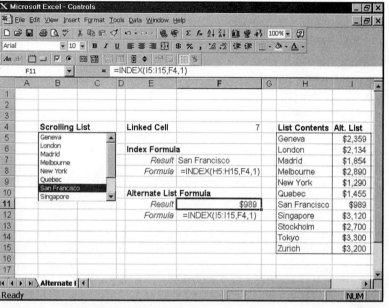

To set the defaults and limits on a spinner, follow these steps:

1. Add a spinner control to the worksheet.
2. Right-click the spinner control that you already drew on your worksheet, and then choose the Format Control command.
3. Select the Control tab, shown in Figure 37.10.

FIG. 37.10

You control the limits and change amounts on a spinner control.

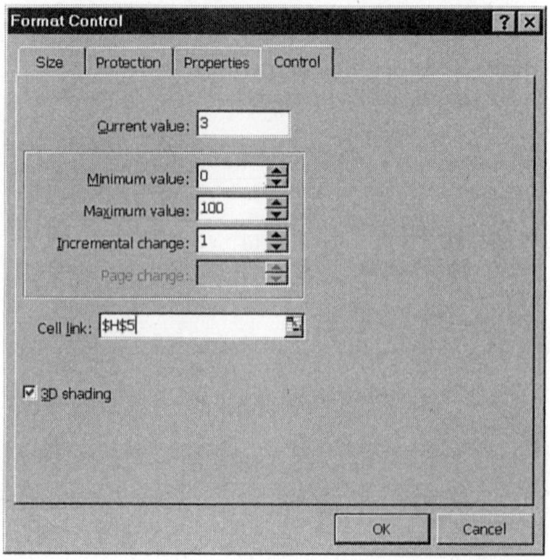

4. In the Current Value edit box, enter the amount you want the linked cell to have when the worksheet opens.

5. Enter the lowest value you want the spinner to produce in the Minimum Value box. Enter the highest value you want in the Maximum Value box. Set the amount of change for each click of the control in the Incremental Change box. The Page Change edit box is not used for the spinner control.

6. Select the Cell Link edit box and then click the cell in the worksheet that you want to receive the spinner result.

7. Choose OK.

Adding Scroll Bars to Enter Widely Ranging Numbers

Scroll bars enable users to enter a number within a wide range while getting a visual impression of where their entry lies within the range. Like other controls, the scroll bar's output is linked to a worksheet cell. To enter a number, you can click the top or bottom arrow head for incremental change, click the gray part of the bar for a page amount of change, or drag the square button in the scroll bar for a large change. The scroll bar works like the scroll bar on the right side of a window but enters numbers into a cell.

 TIP You can create horizontal or vertical scroll bars by dragging across or down.

CAUTION

Unless you follow the instructions in the later section "Controlling Recalculation," the entire worksheet recalculates each time the link cell changes. When you enter data by clicking the scroll bar, this can cause a great deal of unnecessary recalculation, which slows both you and the computer.

To set the defaults and limits on a scroll bar that you already drew on the worksheet, follow these steps:

1. Right-click the scroll bar control on the worksheet, then choose the Format Control command.

2. Select the Control tab shown in Figure 37.11.

3. In the Current Value edit box, enter the amount you want the linked cell to have when the worksheet opens.

4. Enter the lowest value you want the spinner to produce in the Minimum Value box. Enter the highest value you want in the Maximum Value box. Set the amount of change for each click of the control in the Incremental Change box. In the Page Change edit box, enter the amount of change you want when the user clicks the gray part of the scroll bar.

5. Select the Cell Link edit box and then click the cell in the worksheet you want to receive the scroll bar result.

6. Choose OK.

FIG. 37.11

Use this dialog box to set up scroll bars for entering widely varying values.

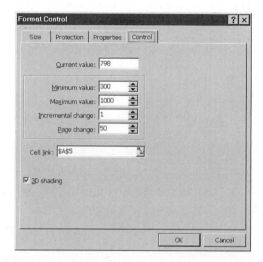

Part
X

Ch
37

Settings for the minimum and maximum values must be in the range of 0 to 30,000 and the Maximum edit box must be greater than the minimum. But this doesn't mean you have to accept these limits.

Most people are used to thermometers and having the highest number for a meter at the top of the vertical bar. The scroll bar gives results backwards to this—the top of the scroll bar results in zero. To reverse the scroll bar values, create a formula that subtracts the result from what you have set as the maximum. If the linked cell is C12 and the maximum value is 100, for example, you can reverse the minimum and maximum amounts by entering the following formula:

=100-C12

This formula belongs in cell D12.

▶ **See** "Using Formulas to Make Decisions," **p. 839**

▶ **See** "Checking Data Entry," **p. 842**

▶ **See** "Using Formulas to Look Up Data in Tables," **p. 844**

After you create controls on a worksheet, you can return to and modify them with the Control Properties button. You must select the control before you can modify it. To select a control, hold down the Ctrl key, and then click the control. To select multiple controls, hold down the Shift and Ctrl keys as you click each control you want selected. If you need to select multiple controls that are located near each other, click the Select button (an arrow) on the Drawing toolbar and drag a rectangle around the controls.

To quickly display the Format Object dialog box, right-click the object to display the shortcut menu, and then click the Format Object command.

As you design a form, you may need to move or resize controls. You even may have to delete a control. To move a control, Ctrl+click to select the control, and then drag it to a new location by its edge. To resize a control, drag one of the handles at the corner or on the middle of a side. Delete a control by selecting the control and pressing the Delete key or choosing the Edit, Clear, All command.

To align a control's edges with the grid of a worksheet, hold down the Alt key as you drag the edge or handle of a selected control.

To copy an image of a control, select the control with a Ctrl+click. Create a copy in two ways. To create a copy in close proximity to the original, Ctrl+click the original to select it, and then hold down Ctrl as you drag an edge of the original. Release the mouse button to drop the copy, and then release the Ctrl key. To create a copy that you must place farther away, select the control, and then use the Edit, Copy and Edit, Paste commands to make a copy. Copies retain the same linked cell as the original.

Enhancing Controls

Although controls are excellent for making worksheets easier to use, they work better and provide fewer management and training problems if you enhance the controls with a few design considerations.

Controlling Recalculation

When a control's result changes, the worksheet immediately recalculates. For selections from a list in a dialog box, this recalculation may not cause too much delay, because the selection probably is infrequent. Spinning through a series of numbers by holding the mouse button on a spinner, however, can cause significant delays. Each time you click a spinner, the result number changes and the worksheet recalculates.

One solution to this problem is to turn off automatic calculation by choosing the Tools, Options command, selecting the Calculation tab, and then selecting Manual. To calculate, the user then presses the F9 key or repeats the command process and chooses the Automatic option. But this requires a number of manual steps.

One way to control recalculation is to *hide* changes until you are ready to recalculate. With this method, you can leave the worksheet in automatic calculation mode. You can hide the changed number resulting from a spinner, for example, by putting the spinner result inside an IF function. The IF function then is controlled by a check box control. When the check box control is selected, the IF reveals the changed spinner result. When the check box control is cleared, the IF produces the #NA error by using an NA() function.

Figure 37.12 shows the formulas that enable one check box to hide changed results from other controls. When the check box is selected, the results pass through the IF functions and the volume calculates. When the check box is cleared, the spinner results are stopped by the IF function and the #NA cascades through all formulas that use this spinner's results (see Figure 37.13).

FIG. 37.12
Use formulas that
enable calculation
when the check box is
selected.

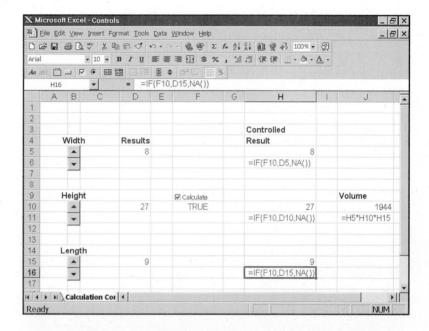

FIG. 37.13
When the check box is
cleared, calculation is
interrupted.

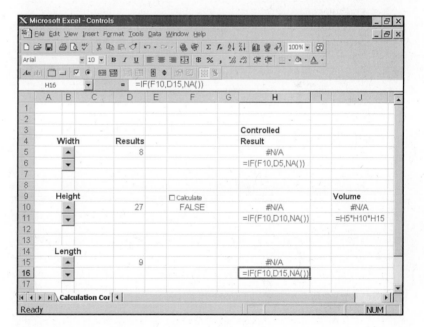

Dimming or Blanking Controls

Dimming—blanking a control so that it has no selection—is useful in a couple of ways. You can
dim a control, such as a check box, to force the user to choose between selected (True) and

cleared (False). You can create lists without a selected item to force the user to select rather than accept the default item. You even can display option buttons in a group, with no button selected so that the user is forced to make a choice.

To dim a check box or group of option buttons, type the following formula into the linked cell:

=NA( )

This function produces the #N/A error, which causes the check box to gray and removes all selections from a group of option buttons. The =NA() function also can produce a #N/A error in any formula that references the linked cell. This error lets users know that they haven't completed making selections from dimmed check boxes or option buttons.

To remove the selection from a list so that no item in the list is selected, type **0** or the following function into the linked cell:

=NA( )

Printing Forms Without the Control

When you print a worksheet that contains controls, a graphic of the control prints. If you don't want to print this image, format the controls so they don't print. To format controls to not print, right-click the control to display the shortcut menu, then choose the Format Object command. After the Format Object dialog box appears, select the Properties page and deselect the Print Object check box. While the Print Object check box is cleared the control does not print. Cell contents under the control do print.

N O T E A control can link to only one cell, but you may need to use the result in many locations. In that case, link the control to a single cell, and then enter formulas in other cells that reference the linked cell.

Protecting a Form

Forms are usually created as templates. Templates are used so a document can be opened and reused without concern for destroying or changing the original. However, even in a document created from a template, you probably will not want the user deliberately or accidentally changing formatting or erasing formulas. To prevent this, you need to protect the worksheet. Chapter 23, "Formatting Worksheets," describes in detail how to protect a worksheet.

When protecting a form on a worksheet, remember that the cells linked to controls cannot be protected. Linked cells must remain unprotected so the control can enter the new result. Having the linked cell unprotected is not much of a disability to good design and worksheet management.

CAUTION

Controls cannot be linked to protected cells. Because more forms are protected, it is a good idea to link a control to an unprotected cell on another sheet or at a distant location on the same sheet. If you need to display the value from the control next to the control, use a formula in a cell near the control to reference the unprotected cell. You may want to hide sheets that contain the unprotected linked cells. To hide them, use the Format, Sheet, Hide command.

Part
X

Ch

37

To prevent users from accidentally altering the linked cell, link all controls to cells on one sheet in the workbook. You may have controls on different sheets throughout the workbook, but all the linked cells for these controls are on the same sheet. To link a control between worksheets, display the Format Object dialog box, click the Cell Link box, activate the other sheet by clicking the tab or choosing the other sheet from the Window menu, and then click the cell in the other sheet.

After you place all the linked cells in one sheet, you can hide this sheet by activating the sheet and choosing Format, Sheet, Hide. This action hides the sheet but keeps it in the workbook, which prevents accidental changes and less knowledgeable users from making changes. Knowledgeable users can unhide the sheet with the Format, Sheet, Unhide command.

To hide the sheet so that users cannot get at it, you can use Visual Basic to change the sheet's Visible Property. For more information on this advanced technique, search the online Visual Basic Reference for Visible Property.

Using the Power of Pivot Tables

Working with Pivot Tables

Pivot tables enable you to analyze data in lists and tables. Pivot tables do more than just group and summarize data; they add depth to the data. In creating a pivot table, you tell Excel which of the fields (in the list) are to be arranged in rows and columns. You can also designate a *page field* that seems to arrange items in a stack of pages. You can rearrange the position of pivot table fields in a split second—in effect, twisting the data around. (That's where the word *pivot* comes in.)

Most Excel lists look like the one shown in Figure 38.1. These lists contain rows of information arranged in columns that hold a specific type of information. The list in Figure 38.1, for example, contains information about the sales of various products for a tool company. The data is primarily organized by product line.

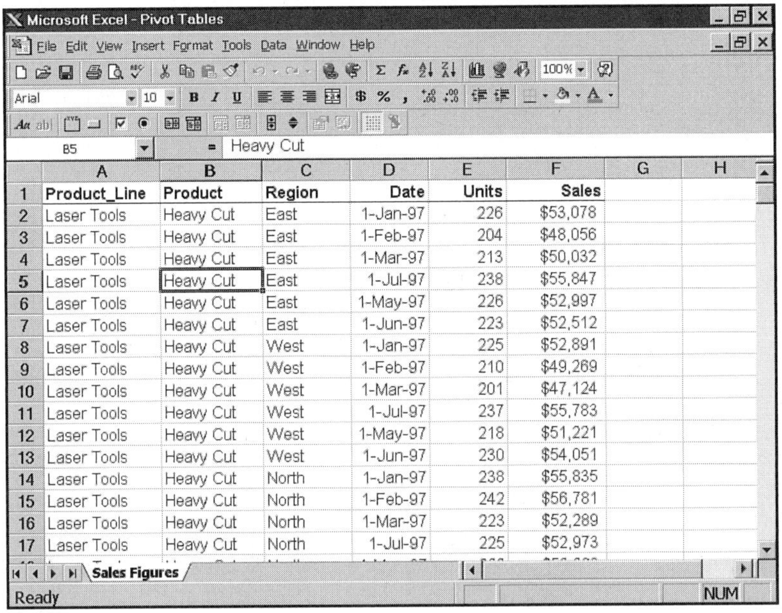

	A	B	C	D	E	F	G	H
1	Product_Line	Product	Region	Date	Units	Sales		
2	Laser Tools	Heavy Cut	East	1-Jan-97	226	$53,078		
3	Laser Tools	Heavy Cut	East	1-Feb-97	204	$48,056		
4	Laser Tools	Heavy Cut	East	1-Mar-97	213	$50,032		
5	Laser Tools	Heavy Cut	East	1-Jul-97	238	$55,847		
6	Laser Tools	Heavy Cut	East	1-May-97	226	$52,997		
7	Laser Tools	Heavy Cut	East	1-Jun-97	223	$52,512		
8	Laser Tools	Heavy Cut	West	1-Jan-97	225	$52,891		
9	Laser Tools	Heavy Cut	West	1-Feb-97	210	$49,269		
10	Laser Tools	Heavy Cut	West	1-Mar-97	201	$47,124		
11	Laser Tools	Heavy Cut	West	1-Jul-97	237	$55,783		
12	Laser Tools	Heavy Cut	West	1-May-97	218	$51,221		
13	Laser Tools	Heavy Cut	West	1-Jun-97	230	$54,051		
14	Laser Tools	Heavy Cut	North	1-Jan-97	238	$55,835		
15	Laser Tools	Heavy Cut	North	1-Feb-97	242	$56,781		
16	Laser Tools	Heavy Cut	North	1-Mar-97	223	$52,289		
17	Laser Tools	Heavy Cut	North	1-Jul-97	225	$52,973		

FIG. 38.1
Excel can accumulate large amounts of tabular data, but looking at the data in this detailed format makes it difficult to analyze.

This database contains a wealth of information, but it is difficult to form any type of a comprehensive view. That is where pivot tables come in.

Pivot tables display the finished result of a database analysis. With them, you can analyze values in a database according to related fields. The pivot table in Figure 38.2, for example, shows how each of the products is selling in each of the four sales regions. The PivotTable Wizard helps build this complex report.

FIG. 38.2
The PivotTable Wizard builds complex reports with multi-field analysis and subtotals.

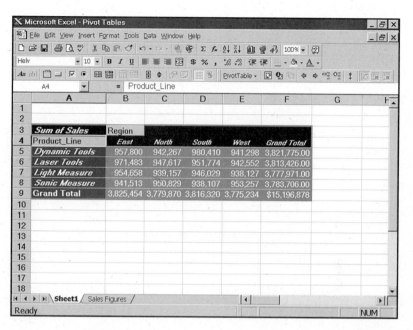

Pivot tables are analytical reporting tools that are useful for a number of purposes, including the following:

- *Creating summary tables.* As you saw in Figure 38.2, pivot tables can summarize lists and databases to provide a big-picture view of the data. They can, for instance, group a large number of transactions into account totals, or display averages and statistics for records in a list or external database.

- *Reorganizing tables with drag and drop.* Pivot tables can illustrate trends and relationships in and among data elements. Figure 38.3 shows the same pivot table shown in Figure 38.2 after being rearranged to summarize regional sales by month. You reorganize pivot tables by dragging text labels to different locations on-screen.

- *Filtering and grouping data in the pivot table.* When you are examining data, sometimes you want to see grand totals. At other times, you want to look at a subset of the data. Pivot tables enable you to zero in on the data. Figure 38.4, for example, shows the same data as in Figure 38.3, except that the sales amount for only one date, January 1, is shown.

- *Charting from pivot tables.* Pivot tables are great presentation tools, but charts can still add punch. It is easy to create charts from pivot tables (see Figure 38.5). The charts change dynamically as you manipulate the pivot table.

FIG. 38.3

This pivot table is the same one shown in Figure 38.2, rearranged to get a different view of the data.

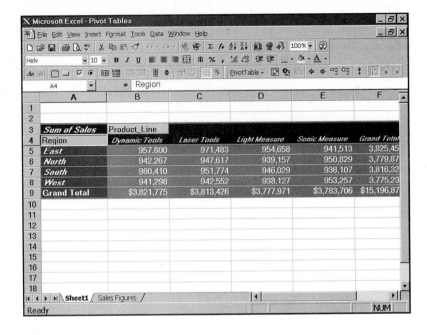

FIG. 38.4

You can define a filtered view of the data. This pivot table summarizes sales for the January 1, 1997 period.

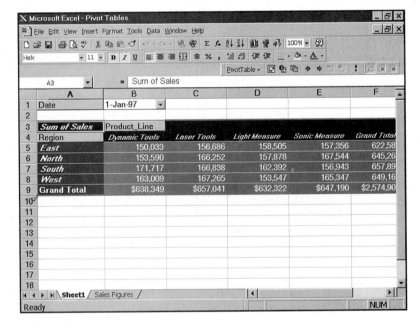

FIG. 38.5
The chart at the bottom was created from the pivot table at the top of the screen.

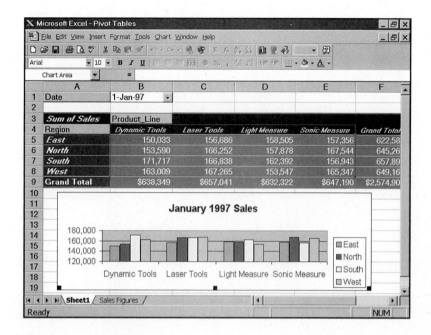

Part

X

Ch

38

Understanding Pivot Tables

A pivot table is a device for organizing data. You determine exactly how the data is organized by specifying which *fields* and *items* you want to appear in the pivot table. A field is a generic category; an item is an individual value or instance within that category. In the pivot table in Figure 38.6, for instance, *District* and *Grade* are fields; the individual districts and grade levels are items.

The source of the data can be a list or table in an Excel worksheet, or even data created in another program. Multiple data sources can feed data into a pivot table. In this chapter, the term list means a list in an Excel worksheet. Terms such as *tabular data* and *multi-column table* refer generically to data in tabular form, whether in an Excel worksheet or a file created in another program. *External data* refers to data created in another program.

When you create a pivot table, you specify row, column, and page fields. Take a look at Figure 38.7. In a normal worksheet, you can see the rows and columns only in the two-dimensional table. Likewise, in a pivot table, you can view only a single page field at a time; however, you can think of the pages as being stacked in the "through" dimension, as noted in the figure.

FIG. 38.6

A pivot table summarizing test score performance at various grade levels by district.

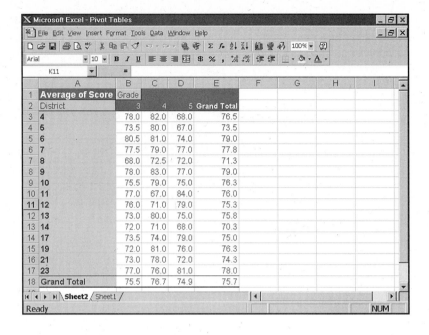

	A	B	C	D	E
1	**Average of Score**	Grade			
2	District	3	4	5	Grand Total
3	4	78.0	82.0	68.0	76.5
4	5	73.5	80.0	67.0	73.5
5	6	80.5	81.0	74.0	79.0
6	7	77.5	79.0	77.0	77.8
7	8	68.0	72.5	72.0	71.3
8	9	78.0	83.0	77.0	79.0
9	10	75.5	79.0	75.0	76.3
10	11	77.0	67.0	84.0	76.0
11	12	76.0	71.0	79.0	75.3
12	13	73.0	80.0	75.0	75.8
13	14	72.0	71.0	68.0	70.3
14	17	73.5	74.0	79.0	75.0
15	19	72.0	81.0	76.0	76.3
16	21	73.0	78.0	72.0	74.3
17	23	77.0	76.0	81.0	78.0
18	Grand Total	75.5	76.7	74.9	75.7

FIG. 38.7

Pivot tables arrange data in three dimensions, in this case, products across rows, period across columns, and regions across pages. Each dimension can contain multiple fields.

West		1-Jan-97	1-Feb-97	1-Mar-97
Laser Tools		52,891	49,269	47,124

South		1-Jan-97	1-Feb-97	1-Mar-97	48,394
Laser Tools		55,687	52,684	51,267	49,134

North		1-Jan-97	1-Feb-97	1-Mar-97	,987	61782
Laser Tools		52,690	60,125	59,987	,521	144,652

East		1-Jan-97	1-Feb-97	1-Mar-97	8,457	,775
Laser Tools		60,124	58,741	59,780	,0,185	
Light Measure		40,357	42,134	41,779	8,629	
Total		100,481	100,875	101,559		

Sum of Sales	Region				
Product_Line	East	North	South	West	Grand Total
Dynamic Tools	957800	942267	980410	941298	3821775
Laser Tools	971483	947617	951774	942552	3813426
Light Measure	954658	939157	946029	938127	3777971
Sonic Measure	941513	950829	938107	953257	3783706
Grand Total	3825454	3779870	3816320	3775234	15196878

Although the data displayed in pivot tables looks like any other worksheet data, you cannot directly enter or change the data in the data area of a pivot table. The pivot table itself is linked to the source data, and what you see in the cells of the table are read-only amounts. You can, however, change the formatting and select from a variety of computation options.

The data you want to analyze may be even more valuable when combined with a database containing geographic or demographic data. By adding census and demographic data to your own data, you can gain insights into the types of clients purchasing your products and services, the way geographic regions are growing or changing, and so forth. There are many sources for free and fee-based demographic data. A lot of data from the national census is free. To get started in mining your data, point your browser to the following Web sites:

Site Name	URL	Description
GeoWeb	http://wings.buffalo.edu/geoweb.	Locator for geographic and census data
Social Science Information Gateway Demograph Page	http://www.esrc.bris.ac.uk	World's largest source of social science resources on census, demographics, sociology studies
TIGER Mapping Service	http://tiger.census.gov	Creates census data maps while you wait (could be lengthy)
US Census Bureau	http://www.census.gov	Home page for the largest collection of US demographic data
US Gazetteer	http://www.census.gov cgi-bin/gazetteer	Search engine for state and local census data
WWW Virtual Library Demography Studies	http://coombs.anu.edu.au	Large collection of links to demography resources on the Web

Creating a Pivot Table

You create pivot tables using the PivotTable Wizard. It involves only a few steps, but it does require you to think about how you want to summarize the data. Consider the data in Figure 38.8. This workbook contains sales information for a tool company. Each record (row) in this table contains data for the fields described following Figure 38.8:

▶ **See** "What Is a List?" **p. 982**

Field	Description
Product Line	The main product categories
Product	The individual products found in the product lines
Region	The company is broken into four regions: East, West, South, and North
Date	Sales information is reported at the first of each month
Units	The number of each product sold
Sales	The sales figures for each product

FIG. 38.8

Sales Information entries in Excel are a good example of a transaction database that can be summarized with a pivot table.

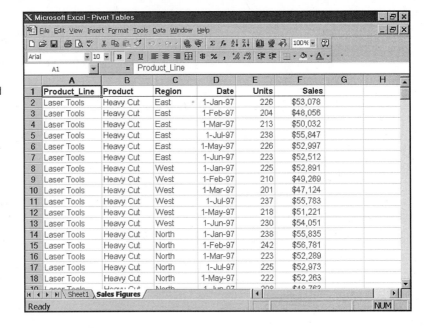

The primary purpose of recording this information is to determine the sales of each product by region. This information has other uses. Using this information, a manager could track sales trends based on the date. You'll see shortly how Excel's pivot tables are tailor-made to provide the variety of perspectives on this data required by sound business practices.

N O T E As you follow this initial example, be aware that it does not cover every option. Details of pivot table options not explained in this example are provided in subsequent examples in this chapter or in Chapter 39.

To use the PivotTable Wizard to begin creating a pivot table, follow these steps:

1. Choose Data, PivotTable Report. The first dialog box in the PivotTable Wizard then appears (see Figure 38.9). From this point until the pivot table appears in the worksheet, you are working in the PivotTable Wizard.

   The buttons along the bottom enable you to move forward or backward through the PivotTable Wizard:

Button	Result
Cancel	Cancels the PivotTable Wizard and returns to the worksheet
< Back	Moves to the preceding dialog box
Next >	Moves to the next dialog box
Finish	Uses current options and moves to the last dialog box

FIG. 38.9
The first dialog box in the PivotTable Wizard asks you to specify the source of the data you will summarize in the pivot table.

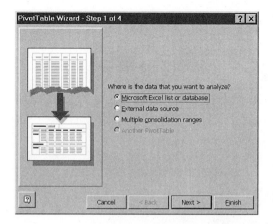

2. Specify the source of the tabular data under the heading "Where is the data that you want to analyze?"

Option	Type of Data
Microsoft Excel List or Database	List or range with labeled columns in an Excel worksheet
External Data Source	Files or tables created in other programs, such as Paradox, dBASE, Access, or SQL Server
Multiple Consolidation Ranges	Multiple ranges with labeled rows and columns in Excel worksheets
Another Pivot Table	An existing pivot table within the active workbook

Choose Microsoft Excel List or Database (if it is not already selected); then click Next > to display the second PivotTable Wizard dialog box (see Figure 38.10).

FIG. 38.10
The second PivotTable Wizard step where you select a range.

3. You can enter or select the range that contains the data in the Range box in the Step 2 box of the Wizard. If the active cell is within a range that you named Database, the Wizard selects this range. Choose Next >.

If the data source is in another workbook, you can use the Browse button to locate the workbook. See "Using a List or Database in Another Workbook," later in this chapter.

Excel now displays the Step 3 dialog box of the PivotTable Wizard (see Figure 38.11).

FIG. 38.11

The third PivotTable Wizard dialog box, where you design the layout by dragging buttons into the ROW, COLUMN, PAGE, and DATA areas.

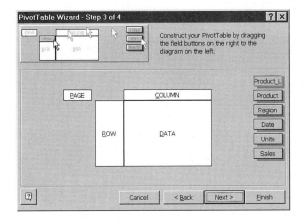

> **CAUTION**
>
> If an error message appears saying Pivot table field name is not valid, check to see if the range you specified includes a blank cell in the first row (the row containing field names).

Remember reading about row, column, and page fields earlier in the chapter? This is the place where you employ those concepts. What you do here controls what data is displayed and where it is positioned in the table. Do not be intimidated, though; the beauty of pivot tables is that whatever you do here can be modified after you display the table on-screen.

To define the layout and create the pivot table within Step 3 of the Wizard, follow these steps:

1. Determine which field contains the data you want summarized, and then drag the corresponding buttons into the DATA area. You often do not have much choice in this step. In the tool sales example, the objective is to summarize sales. Consequently, the data field must be Sales; you have no logical alternative in this case.

2. Determine how you want the data arranged:

   - To arrange the items in a field in columns, with labels across the top, drag the button for that field to the COLUMN area. Figure 38.11 needs the sales by product, so drag the Product button to the COLUMN area.

   - To arrange the items in a field in rows, with labels along the side, drag the button for that field to the ROW area. Because Figure 38.11 needs a list of regions as row headings, you drag the Region button to the ROW area.

   - The effect of using the PAGE area of the dialog box is explained later in this chapter in the section "Filtering Data by Creating Page Fields."

   - Figure 38.12 illustrates how to lay out a pivot table that creates a summary of sales by product and region.

FIG. 38.12

To lay out the pivot table, drag the field buttons into the proper places in the PivotTable Wizard Step 3 dialog box.

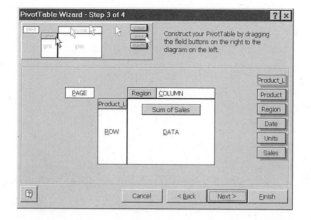

3. Choose Next >.

4. In the final PivotTable Wizard dialog box (see Figure 38.13), you tell Excel where to put the pivot table. You can put the pivot table in any worksheet in any workbook. (Just be careful not to put the table where it might overwrite data.) Enter the upper-left cell of the table in the PivotTable Starting Cell (or click the cell). One option in the final Wizard dialog box is including totals and subtotals, which Excel usually recommends. If you deselect totals, you can rerun the Wizard later and reselect this option.

FIG. 38.13

In Step 4 of the PivotTable Wizard, you tell Excel where to put the pivot table and, optionally, change some global options.

You also can save data with the pivot table. Saving the data with the pivot table stores—on the sheet with the pivot table—a copy of the data being analyzed, which has the advantage that the original source needn't be open to change the pivot table. The disadvantages are that the file containing the pivot table can grow very large. And, when you create a pivot table from a pivot table, the data will no longer be saved with the pivot table from which the new pivot table is created.

5. Choose Finish to complete the pivot table.

6. To format the pivot table, choose Format, AutoFormat and select a predefined format. Choose OK to apply the format.

T I P Putting pivot tables on a separate sheet makes them easier to find and less likely to overwrite other parts of a sheet.

Figure 38.14 displays the pivot table resulting from the specifications in Figures 38.12 and 38.13. After you create a pivot table, the PivotTable toolbar appears in the document (see Figure 38.14). (However, if you previously displayed and removed the PivotTable toolbar, Excel does not display it.) You learn how to use this toolbar later in this chapter and in the next chapter.

FIG. 38.14
The pivot table resulting from the settings in Figures 38.12 and 38.13.

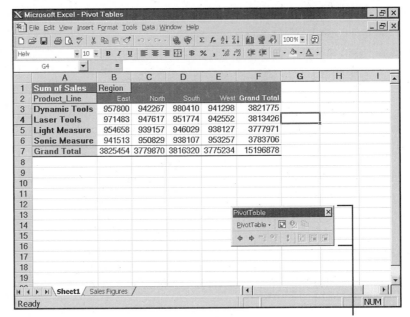

PivotTable toolbar

Editing Your Pivot Table

As you learned earlier, pivot tables are devices for displaying information, so amounts appearing in the body of the table cannot be changed. Excel does provide a number of tools to control the type of summary information, as well as the formatting, in the table. (You learn how to use those tools in Chapter 39, "Analyzing and Reporting with Pivot Tables.")

 T I P You can change the names of pivot table fields by typing over them.

You can change the names of pivot table fields and items. Simply select the field or item, and type the new name (see cell B2 in Figure 38.15). Naturally, Excel does not let you duplicate names. If you inadvertently enter an existing field or item name, Excel rearranges the pivot table, moving the item with that name to the location where you typed the name.

N O T E Changing field or item names in a pivot table does not change the names in the source list or database. ▨

FIG. 38.15
You can type new names for fields and items into pivot tables, if you do not duplicate existing names.

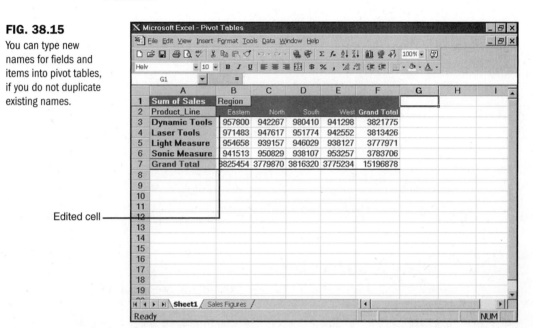

Edited cell —

Updating a Pivot Table

The pivot table display does not change when you change the data in the source list or table. You can update, or refresh, the pivot table for the following types of changes to the source data by selecting any cell within the pivot table and clicking the Refresh Data button on the PivotTable toolbar:

- Changes to data in a data field
- New or changed items
- Insertions or deletions of fields or items

If you add new fields to the source list, they do not show up in the pivot table unless you display Step 3 of the PivotTable Wizard.

> **CAUTION**
>
> Updating a pivot table after you add new fields to the source list can expand the size of the pivot table. Leave plenty of "growing room" below and to the right of pivot tables so that you do not overwrite other data in the worksheet. By putting a pivot table on a separate sheet, you alleviate this problem.

N O T E Excel does not let you insert rows into an Excel source list if those rows intersect with a pivot table because Excel protects the integrity of pivot tables. You can, however, insert a range into a source list if the range does not intersect with a pivot table. ▓

If you have changed any field or item names by direct entry into the pivot table, the changes remain in effect after you update the table.

Sometimes, you may want to preserve a pivot table in its current form although the source data may change in the future. To take a "snapshot" of a pivot table, copy it and paste it to another location by choosing Edit, Paste Special and then selecting the Values option.

> **CAUTION**
>
> Refreshing a pivot table removes any formatting applied to the cells in the pivot table, other than formats applied with the AutoFormat command on the Format menu. For more information, see the section "Formatting the Pivot Table" in Chapter 39.

Specifying the Source Data

The example presented in Figures 38.7 through 38.15 glosses over some options in Step 1 of the PivotTable Wizard, but it is now time to come back to that step. In addition to a list or table in an Excel worksheet, you can use data created in other programs as a source for pivot tables. You can also use multiple lists from one or more Excel worksheets.

Using a List or Database in the Workbook

To create a pivot table from an existing list in the current Excel workbook, select the Microsoft Excel List or Database option in the first PivotTable Wizard dialog box, if it is not already selected.

The source list must include column labels. Make sure that you include the column labels in the range you enter in Step 2 of the PivotTable Wizard. Excel uses the values in the first row of the specified range as field names.

Using a List or Database in Another Workbook

To specify a source list in another workbook, follow these steps:

1. Choose the Browse button in Step 2 of the PivotTable Wizard. The Browse dialog box then appears.
2. Select the file containing the list you want, and then choose OK to return to the PivotTable Wizard. The Step 2 dialog box reappears, with the file name in the Range box.
3. Enter the name or the range address of the source list.
4. Choose Next > to complete the remaining dialog boxes in the PivotTable Wizard.

Using External Databases

To use an external data source, select the External Data Source option in the first PivotTable Wizard dialog box, and then choose Next > to bring up the Step 2 dialog box, shown in Figure 38.16.

FIG. 38.16

The PivotTable Wizard Step 2 dialog box after selecting the External Data Source option in Step 1.

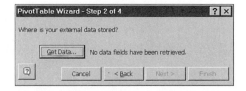

NOTE To retrieve data from an external source, you need to have installed Microsoft Query, a separate application that comes with Excel, when you installed Excel. ■

Choose the Get Data button. The Microsoft Query program starts and displays a dialog box similar to the one shown in Figure 38.17.

FIG. 38.17

The PivotTable Wizard uses Microsoft Query to retrieve data created in other programs.

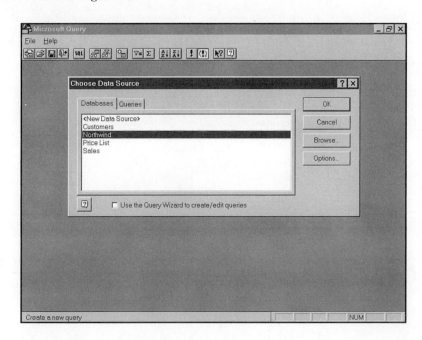

In Microsoft Query, you perform a series of operations to define the data you want to bring into Excel. Figure 38.18 shows a sample query definition table.

Part
X

Ch
38

FIG. 38.18

You fill out a query definition table to tell the PivotTable Wizard what data to retrieve from the specified source.

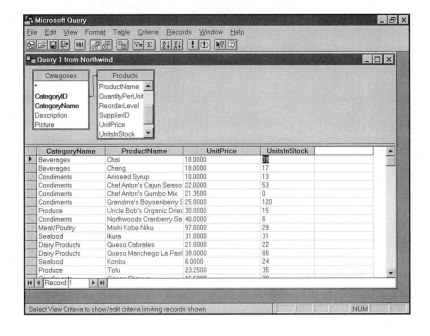

After you have defined your query, choose the Return Data to Microsoft Excel command from the Microsoft Query File menu. You then return to Step 2 of the PivotTable Wizard (see Figure 38.19).

FIG. 38.19

The PivotTable Wizard Step 2 dialog box after querying an external database.

Updating a pivot table linked to an external data source causes Excel to query the data source again.

Converting Crosstab Tables from Version 4 of Excel

If you have created crosstab tables in Excel 4, you probably want to convert them to pivot tables.

To convert a crosstab table to a pivot table, follow these steps:

1. Open the worksheet (created in version 4) that contains the crosstab table.

2. Choose Data, PivotTable. The Step 3 dialog box in the PivotTable Wizard then appears.

3. Complete the remaining steps in the PivotTable Wizard in the usual manner.

> **CAUTION**
>
> Converting a crosstab table is an irrevocable operation, so make sure that you convert from a copy if you foresee any possible need to use the crosstab table again in version 4 of Excel.

Filtering Data by Creating Page Fields

Because it is humanly impossible to read text and figures in three dimensions, all the fields you want to see in your pivot tables must be shoehorned into either the row or column position during Step 3 of the PivotTable Wizard.

▶ **See** "Paging or Filtering a Pivot Table," **p. 928**

▶ **See** "Using the AutoFilter," **p. 1028**

You can, however, set up a third dimension to provide additional flexibility in examining the data. Creating a page field creates a viewing filter of sorts. To see how this process works, look first at the pivot table in Figure 38.20. This pivot table does not display the product names because the displayed data reflects sales by product lines.

Part

X

Ch

38

FIG. 38.20

The total sales for each product line are shown by region, but detailed information for individual products is not available on this pivot table.

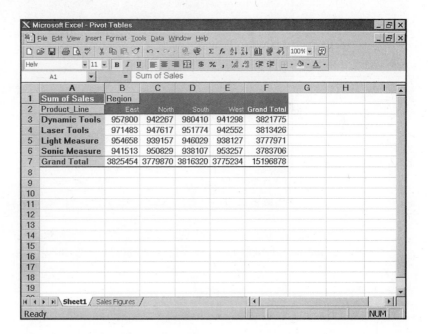

	A	B	C	D	E	F
1	**Sum of Sales**	Region				
2	Product_Line	East	North	South	West	Grand Total
3	**Dynamic Tools**	957800	942267	980410	941298	3821775
4	**Laser Tools**	971483	947617	951774	942552	3813426
5	**Light Measure**	954658	939157	946029	938127	3777971
6	**Sonic Measure**	941513	950829	938107	953257	3783706
7	**Grand Total**	3825454	3779870	3816320	3775234	15196878

To add the option of flipping through the projects or work codes to display the amounts for any individual item in either of these fields, you create a page field.

To create a page field when you create a pivot table, follow these steps:

1. Start the PivotTable Wizard and complete Steps 1 and 2 of the PivotTable Wizard's four steps.

2. In the PivotTable Wizard's Step 3 dialog box, move the field you want to filter to the Page area. It can be a field not previously displayed, or one displayed in the row or column position.

3. Choose OK, and then continue with the remaining dialog boxes in the PivotTable Wizard.

After you add a page field, the pivot table looks like Figure 38.21, which displays only the product lines that carry a version of the Heavy Cut product.

FIG. 38.21

The same pivot table as in Figure 38.20, after adding Product as a page field and selecting the Heavy Cut product from the list in the page field.

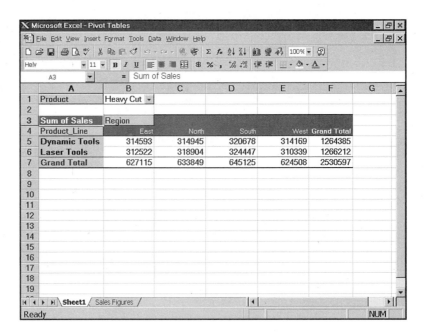

Clicking the arrow in the page field displays a list of all items in the page field along with a selection for totals. Simply select the item you want to view, and the pivot table displays that page.

Consolidating Data Using a Pivot Table

Often, the data you want to summarize is located in more than one range—sometimes even in several different worksheets. If the ranges have a similar structure and common row and column labels, you can group them together for analysis in a single pivot table.

▶ **See** "Consolidating Worksheets," **p. 953**

Figure 38.22 shows a workbook with regional sales information for a machinery company. The figures for the regions are contained in separate sheets, which are named after the respective regions.

FIG. 38.22

Each sheet in this workbook contains sales figures for a different region. You can create a pivot table that consolidates this data.

This is the only region where Sonic Measure products are sold.

Dynamic Tools are not sold in this region.

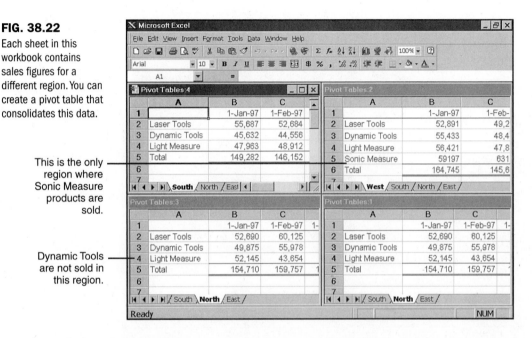

The data to be consolidated does not have to reside in separate sheets; you can consolidate data from separate ranges in a single sheet, in separate sheets, or in a combination of both locations.

Using a pivot table, you can consolidate data from multiple ranges. This process is similar to using the Data, Consolidate command; an advantage is that you can manipulate the pivot table to view the results of the consolidation in a variety of ways.

To create a pivot table from multiple worksheet ranges, start the PivotTable Wizard, and then select the Multiple Consolidation Ranges option. The Step 2a dialog box then appears (see Figure 38.23). You can have Excel create a single page field, or you can create the page field(s) yourself.

To create a pivot table from multiple worksheet ranges, with Excel creating the page field automatically, follow these steps:

1. In Step 2a, select the Create a Single Page Field for Me option, and then choose Next >. Excel displays Step 2b of the PivotTable Wizard.

2. Enter or select all the source ranges (selecting the ranges is usually faster). After you select each range, choose Add; the selected range then is added to the All Ranges list. Figure 38.24 shows the dialog box after all the ranges displayed in Figure 38.22 have been added. Choose Next >.

FIG. 38.23

When you use multiple source ranges, selecting Create a Single Page Field for Me in Step 2a of the PivotTable Wizard automatically assigns the ranges to a page field.

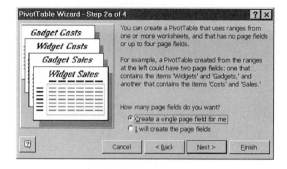

FIG. 38.24

Adding source ranges in the PivotTable Wizard.

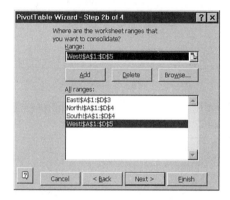

> **CAUTION**
>
> If your source ranges include totals, do not include the total rows or columns when you select the ranges; doing so causes the PivotTable Wizard to include the totals as items in the pivot table.

3. In Step 3 of the PivotTable Wizard, choose Next > to accept the default field positions. When you use multiple source ranges, Excel does not have the information it needs to determine the field names, so it uses generic descriptions ("Page1," "Row," and so on). You can specify field names later.

4. Complete Step 4 of the PivotTable Wizard in the usual manner, and choose Finish to create the pivot table.

Figure 38.25 shows the pivot table created from the sample data. Now you can enter field names in the appropriate cells. The following table lists the changes you would make to the pivot table in the example:

Field Name To Replace	Cell	New Field Name
Page1	A1	Region
Column	B3	Date
Row	A4	Product Line

FIG. 38.25

The pivot table created from the multiple source ranges shown in Figure 38.22.

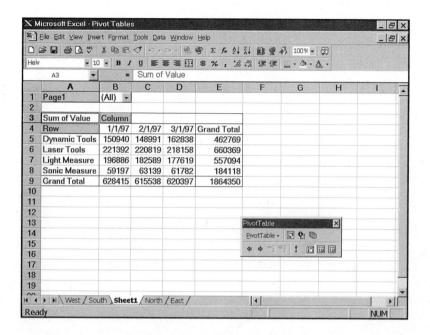

Click the arrow in cell B1. Instead of displaying the names of the regions, Excel displays place-holder names—Item1, Item2, and so on. When Excel creates the page field, you save some time initially, but you have to replace the placeholders with meaningful names—in this case, the names of the four regions. Naturally, replacing placeholders is time-consuming if your pivot table contains numerous items.

If you expect to use the resulting pivot table extensively, you should select the I Will Create the Page Fields option in Step 2a of the PivotTable Wizard. In that event, Step 2b of the PivotTable Wizard displays a dialog box where you assign names to each item in the field.

To view consolidated totals, choose the (All) option from the list adjacent to the page field button to display all products. The PivotTable Wizard uses the same intelligent consolidation method as the Data Consolidate command (for more information on consolidating, see Chapter 40, "Linking, Embedding, and Consolidating Worksheets"). The PivotTable Wizard, however, reads the text labels and correctly aggregates the totals according to the text labels, not the cell addresses.

To select the page fields yourself while creating a pivot table, follow these steps:

1. In Step 2a of the PivotTable Wizard, select the I Will Create the Page Fields option.

2. In Step 2b (see Figure 38.26), enter or select all the source ranges, and add them to the All Ranges list as explained in the preceding example.

FIG. 38.26

In Step 2b of the PivotTable Wizard, you specify how many page fields to include in the pivot table, and enter labels for the individual items.

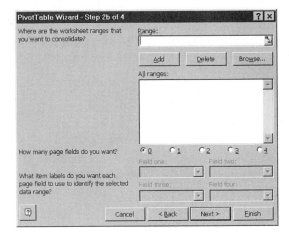

3. Select the 1 option just below the All Ranges box to indicate that you want one page field. (To create two or more page fields, select the appropriate option, or select 0 if you do not want a page field.)

4. For each of the ranges in the All Ranges list, select the range, and then type a label for it in the Field One box. After you have entered labels for the appropriate number of ranges, choose Next >.

5. Complete the rest of the PivotTable Wizard dialog boxes in the usual manner.

When Excel creates the pivot table, your labels for the ranges are included in the pull-down list adjacent to the Page1 button.

Using More Than One Field

In all the examples so far, the data field label (located above the row heading and to the left of the column heading) has shown the type of summary calculation (such as Sum of) and the name of a data field (such as Sales). This label indicates that the pivot table contains only one data field.

You can include more than one data field in Step 3 of the PivotTable Wizard. You can actually include more than one field in columns, rows and page field as well. In the sales example, for instance, you might want to view the sales for each product line along with the products in the line. Figure 38.27 shows a pivot table with two row fields, Product_Line and Product.

Chapter 39, "Analyzing and Reporting with Pivot Tables," contains information related to the specific task of adding fields to pivot tables.

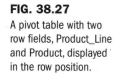

FIG. 38.27
A pivot table with two
row fields, Product_Line
and Product, displayed
in the row position.

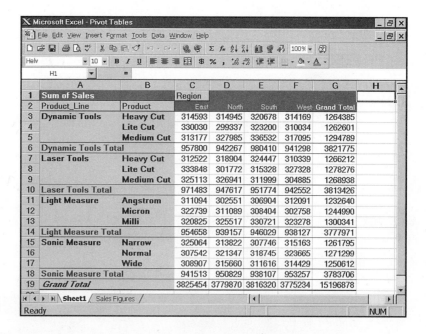

Product_Line	Product	East	North	South	West	Grand Total
Dynamic Tools	**Heavy Cut**	314593	314945	320678	314169	1264385
	Lite Cut	330030	299337	323200	310034	1262601
	Medium Cut	313177	327985	336532	317095	1294789
Dynamic Tools Total		957800	942267	980410	941298	3821775
Laser Tools	**Heavy Cut**	312522	318904	324447	310339	1266212
	Lite Cut	333848	301772	315328	327328	1278276
	Medium Cut	325113	326941	311999	304885	1268938
Laser Tools Total		971483	947617	951774	942552	3813426
Light Measure	**Angstrom**	311094	302551	306904	312091	1232640
	Micron	322739	311089	308404	302758	1244990
	Milli	320825	325517	330721	323278	1300341
Light Measure Total		954658	939157	946029	938127	3777971
Sonic Measure	**Narrow**	325064	313822	307746	315163	1261795
	Normal	307542	321347	318745	323665	1271299
	Wide	308907	315660	311616	314429	1250612
Sonic Measure Total		941513	950829	938107	953257	3783706
Grand Total		3825454	3779870	3816320	3775234	15196878

Creating a Pivot Table from Another Pivot Table

Pivot tables can become complex if you decide to display much detail—so complex that you
might want to summarize the data further by creating a new pivot table based on the existing
pivot table.

To create a pivot table using source data in another pivot table in the same workbook, follow
these steps:

1. Make sure that no part of a new pivot table is selected. (If the active selection includes
   any part of a pivot table, Excel assumes you want to make changes to that pivot table.)
2. Start the PivotTable Wizard.
3. Select the Another Pivot Table option, and then choose Next >. The PivotTable Wizard
   displays a list of pivot tables in the active workbook.
4. Select the pivot table you want to use as your data source, and then choose Next >.
5. Complete the remaining dialog boxes in the PivotTable Wizard in the usual manner.

Excel creates the second pivot table in the location you specify. The two pivot tables are updated simultaneously whenever you refresh either of them.

To create a pivot table using source data from a pivot table in another workbook, copy the
existing pivot table into the current workbook. The copied data, if it meets the definition of a
list, can be used as a source list for a new pivot table. Be aware, however, that the new pivot

Part
X

Ch
38

table loses any links to the original source data that exist for the old pivot table. As a result, you cannot manipulate the new pivot table as you would if the source data resided in the same workbook.

Creating a Chart from a Pivot Table

You can create a chart linked to a pivot table. The chart changes dynamically as you change the layout of your pivot table. Figure 38.28 shows a pivot table and a chart created from that table.

FIG. 38.28

This chart was created from the pivot table above it.

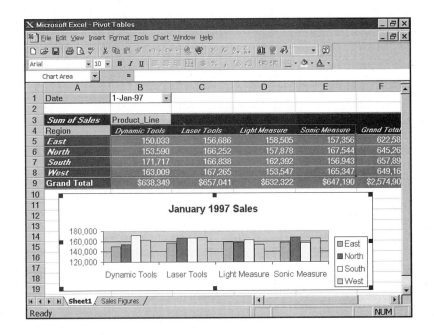

▶ **See** "Creating a Chart Automatically," **p. 698**

▶ **See** "Analyzing Pivot Table Data with Charts," **p. 927**

Notice that this pivot table has two row fields and one column field. In such cases, Excel displays the items in the column fields along the category (X) axis of the chart. It groups the chart series according to the row groupings in the pivot table, by region.

When you create a chart from a pivot table, use at most two row fields and two column fields in the pivot table to avoid confusion.

To create a chart from a pivot table, follow these steps:

1. Select the pivot table. As you do so, avoid selecting any columns containing totals. You must also avoid dragging any of the field tabs; otherwise, Excel thinks that you want to move the row field.

2. Click the Chart Wizard button on the Standard toolbar. Follow the instructions in the Chart Wizard dialog boxes.

 TIP The best way to ensure that no total amounts appear in your chart is to eliminate grand totals and subtotals from your pivot table before creating the chart.

N O T E   You can change the way Excel has grouped the series markers in the chart. (For instance, you might prefer to see the columns in the chart in Figure 38.28 grouped by product.) With the chart selected, display the Chart Wizard and change the settings in Step 2. ■

The Chart Wizard does not display items in page fields on a chart. However, if you select an item in a page field, a chart created from the pivot table changes dynamically to display the data for the selected item.

Part

X

Ch

38

CAUTION

If the pivot table dimensions change as you "page" through it (due to variations in the number of items), your chart does not adjust automatically to the changes. To avoid this situation, remove row and column totals in Step 4 of the PivotTable Wizard, and select the entire pivot table before creating the chart.

Saving Files with Pivot Tables

Sometimes files with pivot tables are surprisingly large because Excel creates a copy of the source data and stores it as hidden data with the worksheet that contains the pivot table. If your pivot table references a large amount of data in another file, you store the same data twice whenever you save the file that contains the pivot table.

To avoid this replication, deselect the Save Data with Table Layout check box in Step 4 of the PivotTable Wizard. Excel then saves the pivot table layout but omits the copy of the source data. When you make changes to—or refresh—the pivot table, Excel updates it directly from the source data. Note that when you use a pivot table that has the data saved with it as the source for another pivot table, the data is no longer saved with the original pivot table.

CAUTION

If you are working with a pivot table linked to a large list in an Excel worksheet, consider putting the pivot table in a separate workbook and linking to a closed sheet to conserve memory.

TROUBLESHOOTING

Step 3 of the PivotTable Wizard displays numbers and nonsensical field names. You've selected a part of a list and failed to include the row with the field names when you specified the source range in Step 2. Choose the Back button and redefine the range.

Excel displays a PivotTable field name is not valid message. In defining the range containing your source data, you have included a column that has an invalid field name. This happens most often when you inadvertently select a blank column in defining the range in Step 2.

The pivot table shows values of "1" in every cell. Most likely, the pivot table is showing a count of the items rather than the sum, average, or other summary function you want. See the section "Analyzing the Data" in Chapter 36, "Manipulating and Analyzing Data," for instructions on changing the summary function in a pivot table.

The pivot table is empty (or nearly empty). You get an empty pivot table when it contains at least one page field for which the value of the first item in the field is blank or zero. To see if you have a blank or zero field, select (All) in the page field list, and notice whether the pivot table displays more values.

Analyzing and Reporting with Pivot Tables

In this chapter

Adding and Removing Data

To master data analysis in pivot tables, you must understand how fields fit into the row, column, and page positions (see Figure 39.1). A field is not a row, column, or page field by nature. The Project field in Figure 39.1 is a page field only because it was defined as such in the PivotTable Wizard, or because it was positioned there after the pivot table was created. As you learn in the later section "Reorganizing the Pivot Table," dragging a field to a different position changes the layout of the pivot table.

FIG. 39.1

Positions of fields in pivot tables.

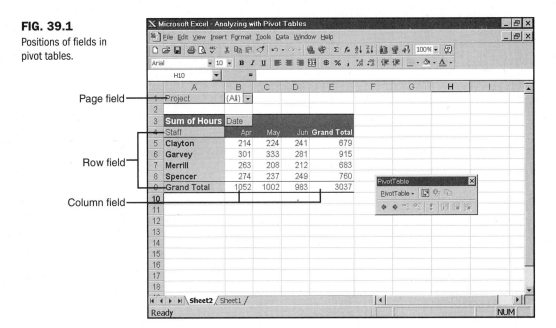

As you continue through this chapter, notice that the amounts in most of the diagrams are rounded to integers, whereas your pivot tables might display decimals. The pivot tables were formatted this way so the examples would be clearer.

Adding New Rows, Columns, or Pages

To enhance the amount of detail available in a pivot table, you add more fields. Adding row and column fields expands the pivot table and widens the view. In contrast, adding a page field narrows the scope and helps you zero in on details.

To add a row, column, or page field to a pivot table, follow these steps:

1. Select a cell in the pivot table.

2. Click the PivotTable Wizard button on the PivotTable toolbar.

3. In the PivotTable Wizard Step 3 of 4 dialog box, move the button for the desired field to the appropriate area (ROW, COLUMN, or PAGE), as illustrated in Figure 39.2.

FIG. 39.2

To add a field, move the field button to the appropriate area of the Step 3 dialog box, as shown on the left.

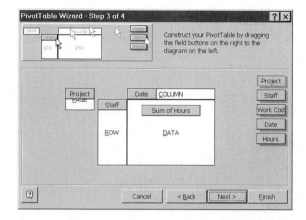

4. Click Finish.

Figure 39.3 indicates the added field in the pivot table.

FIG. 39.3

The pivot table after adding the Work Code field.

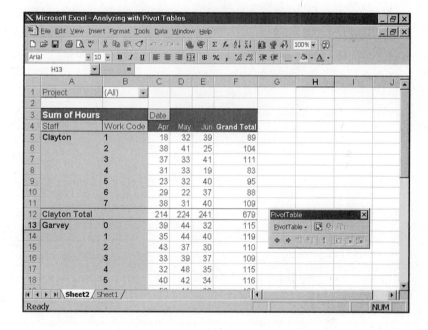

N O T E A quicker way to add a row or column field is to double-click an item in a row or column field in the pivot table. Though the pivot table displays the additional detail only for the item you double-clicked, the data for the entire field is added. If the pivot table contains more than one field in the same (row or column) position, make sure you double-click the innermost field. ▪

Removing Rows, Columns, or Pages

To remove a row, column, or page field, drag it outside the boundaries of the pivot table. A large X appears on the field as you drag it. When you release the button, the field disappears from the pivot table.

Alternatively, you can click the field tab, click the PivotTable Field button on the PivotTable toolbar, and choose Delete.

Adding Data to Analyze

Sometimes you want to look at more than one kind of data. You might want to see unit sales and dollar sales, verbal and math test scores, or blood pressure and cholesterol levels. Figure 39.4 shows a pivot table with two data fields.

FIG. 39.4

A pivot table with two data fields.

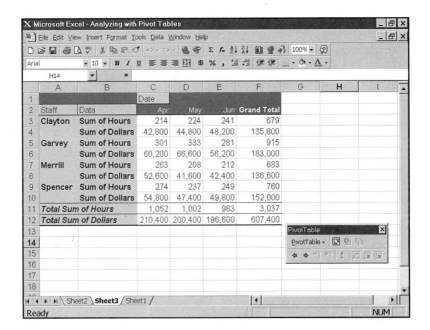

To add another data field to a pivot table, follow these steps:

1. Select a cell in the pivot table.
2. Click the PivotTable Wizard button on the PivotTable toolbar.
3. In the PivotTable Wizard Step 3 of 4 dialog box, move the button for the data field you want to add to the DATA area.
4. Choose Finish.

Reorganizing the Pivot Table

Another way to break down data in a pivot table is to change the orientation of the table. You do this by dragging the field tabs into different positions. Changing the orientation enables you to examine selected cross-sections of the data.

Flipping the Orientation

Suppose you are a project manager for a consulting firm. You are trying to find the right staff people to work on a project, and you are looking at the pivot table shown in Figure 39.5. In its current form, the pivot table doesn't provide the information you need to hunt down qualified staffers because you are primarily interested in the hours your people have spent on certain activities. You want to see a breakdown by staff and work code.

FIG. 39.5
A pivot table showing hours worked by staff and project.

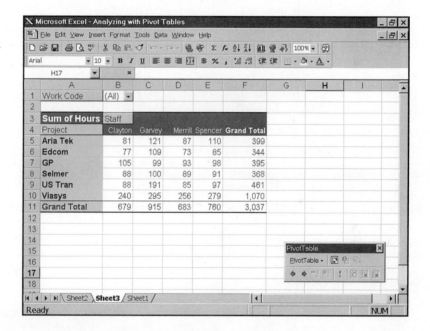

To move a pivot table field, drag the row, column, or page field to the desired position. As you do so, an insert marker appears. The shape of the marker depends on the position. Figure 39.6 shows a row field being moved to the column position. When the insert marker appears, release the mouse button.

To reorient the pivot table in Figure 39.5 to show work codes across the top, follow these steps:

1. Drag the Work Code field tab from the page position to the column position.

2. Drag the Project field tab to the page position. After the insert marker changes to an image of rectangles stacked in a staggered fashion, release the mouse button.

FIG. 39.6

Moving a row field to the column position.

Insert marker ——

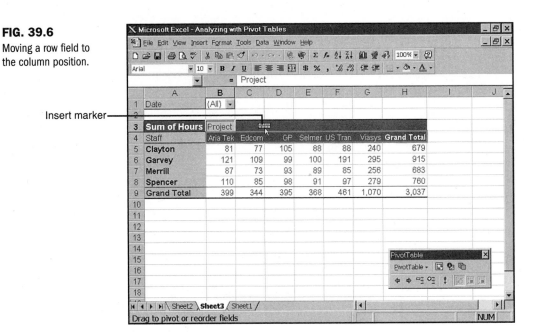

3. Drag the Staff field tab to the row position.

4. Select (All) from the page field.

The time reporting pivot table now looks like Figure 39.7.

FIG. 39.7

The pivot table from Figure 39.5, after rearranging the layout to show Work Code as the row field.

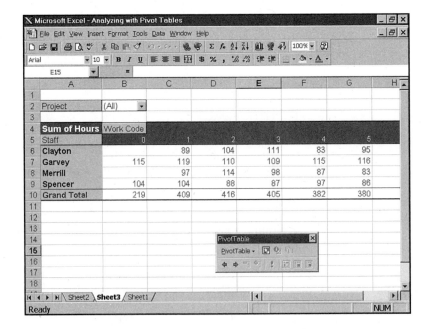

Moving Individual Items Within a Field

To change the sequence of items in a pivot table, drag them into the desired positions.

To move an item in a pivot table, simply drag the item label to another location within the same field. As you drag, a gray border appears around the item. When the border is properly positioned, release the button. Excel inserts the selected item—carrying its data with it—in the target location, moving subsequent items down or to the right.

You can also sort items in a pivot table. See the section "Sorting Items" later in this chapter.

Moving Data Fields

Ordinarily, you cannot move data fields to the row, column, or page position. However, when a pivot table contains more than one data field, you can drag the Data button from the row position to the column position and vice versa. Figure 39.8 shows the time-reporting pivot table with the data fields (Hours and Dollars) displayed in a row orientation. Figure 39.9 shows the same pivot table with the data fields in a column orientation.

FIG. 39.8

This pivot table displays multiple data fields in a row orientation.

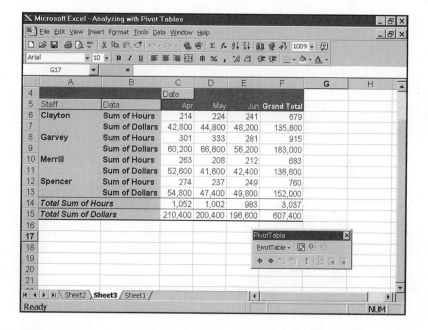

Instead of displaying multiple data fields, you can show multiple summary calculations for a single data field. You learn how to do this in the section "Using Custom Calculations" later in this chapter.

FIG. 39.9
After you move the Data button into the column position, the pivot table displays multiple data fields in a column orientation.

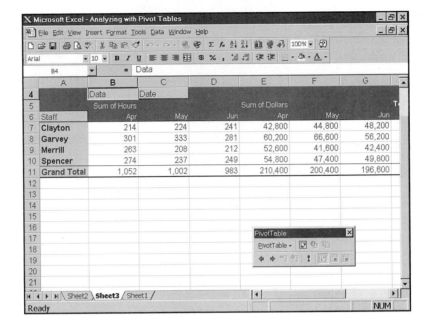

Grouping Items

Occasionally, you might have to sift through large quantities of organized data, such as financial results for a large company or demographic data from a national survey. To properly analyze such information, you have to determine the level you can work with best. Whether you need a lot of detail or want to see the overall picture, Excel's pivot tables give you the means to view only the data you need.

Grouping Items by Their Labels   Consider a large retailer with stores in several countries. At the highest level, it tracks results by country. Each country—the United States, for instance—is divided into several regions. Each region contains several states, and the company has numerous stores in every state. Store, state, region, country, and company are aggregation levels arranged in a hierarchy—with the company at the highest level. You define these grouping levels in the pivot table.

To group several items into a higher-level category, follow these steps:

1. Multiple-select the items (within the same field) you want to group together. (The best way to select numerous items is to select one item and then hold down the Ctrl key as you click additional items.)

2. Click the Group button on the PivotTable toolbar. Excel adds the new group field to the pivot table and inserts a placeholder label for the items in the new group (Group1 for the first group, Group2 for the second group, and so on).

3. Replace the placeholder labels with labels for each of the new groups.

Figure 39.10 shows a pivot table with a group field for work codes added, after new labels (Administrative and Chargeable) are added as field and group names.

FIG. 39.10
You can group items in the same field together. This pivot table aggregates subtotals for administrative time and chargeable time.

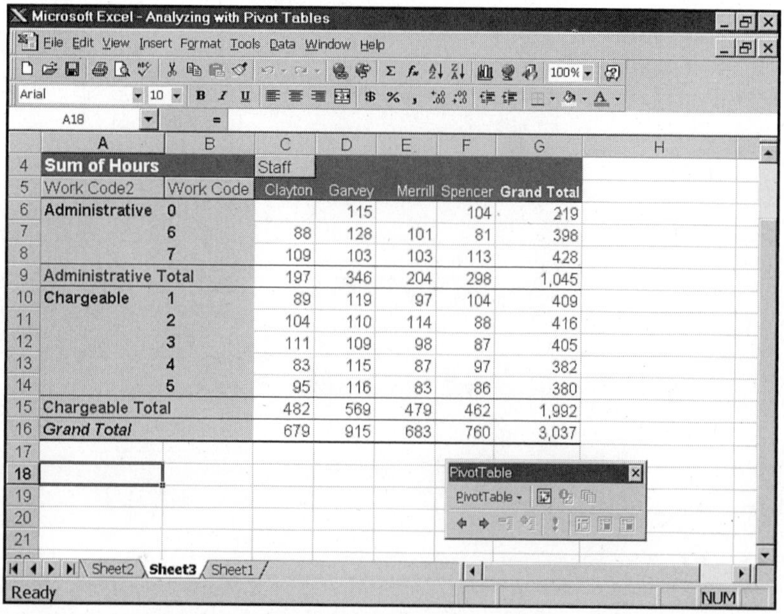

Sum of Hours		Staff				
Work Code2	Work Code	Clayton	Garvey	Merrill	Spencer	Grand Total
Administrative	0		115		104	219
	6	88	128	101	81	398
	7	109	103	103	113	428
Administrative Total		197	346	204	298	1,045
Chargeable	1	89	119	97	104	409
	2	104	110	114	88	416
	3	111	109	98	87	405
	4	83	115	87	97	382
	5	95	116	83	86	380
Chargeable Total		482	569	479	462	1,992
Grand Total		679	915	683	760	3,037

NOTE Excel cannot infer groupings from the source data. Even if your source list has fields for both city and state, Excel cannot automatically group the cities by state; you have to create the state groups yourself.

Hiding and Redisplaying Detail It's helpful to begin the process of analysis by viewing summary figures. After you have acquired the big picture, you can work your way down to a more detailed level. Excel offers a quick method for moving between detail and summary views.

You can hide or show detail in pivot table groupings. A grouping may consist of several items you have grouped together, or it can be the outermost field within a position (row or column). The higher-level groupings, or *summary items*, are located at the upper or outer edge of the pivot table. In Figure 39.10, the summary items are the group fields Administrative and Chargeable. In Figure 39.11, the Staff field contains summary items.

To hide the detail items in a summary item, double-click the summary item. Double-clicking Clayton and Garvey in succession, for example, collapses the detail for those groups, as shown in Figure 39.12.

You also can hide detail in a pivot table such as the one in Figure 39.13, which contains three geographic grouping levels (Region, State, and City). Double-clicking the summary item Pennsylvania in the State field yields the pivot table shown in Figure 39.14.

FIG. 39.11

In this pivot table, the Staff field contains summary items. The work code detail can be displayed or hidden.

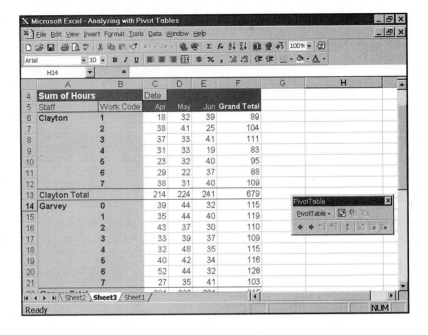

FIG. 39.12

The pivot table in Figure 39.11 after hiding the detail for Clayton and Garvey.

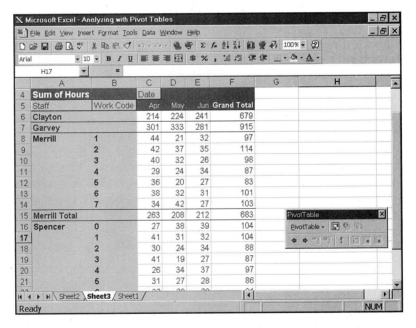

You can also use the PivotTable toolbar to show or hide detail items. To hide an item, select the item, and then click the Hide Detail button on the PivotTable toolbar. To show detail for a summary item, select the item, and then click the Show Detail button on the PivotTable toolbar.

FIG. 39.13

In this pivot table, results for cities are grouped by state, and the states are grouped by region.

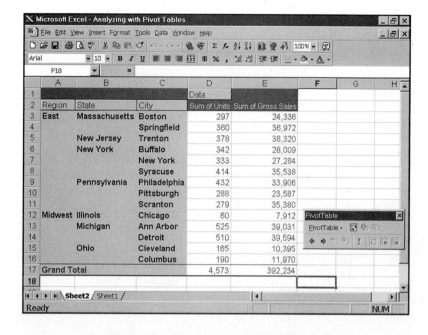

FIG. 39.14

Double-clicking the summary item Pennsylvania collapses the city detail into totals for the state.

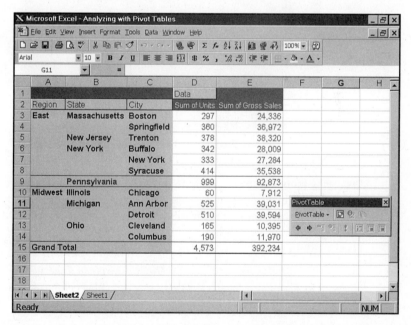

Part

X

Ch

39

To hide detail for several adjacent items, the Hide Detail button on the PivotTable toolbar is more efficient than double-clicking. You can select multiple items and then click the Hide Detail button on the PivotTable toolbar to hide detail for all selected items. This method is handy when you want to remove an entire grouping level from a pivot table. The pivot table in Figure 39.15 shows the results of selecting all items in the State field in the pivot table in Figure 39.13 and then clicking the Hide Detail button.

FIG. 39.15

The pivot table in Figure 39.13 after hiding detail for all states.

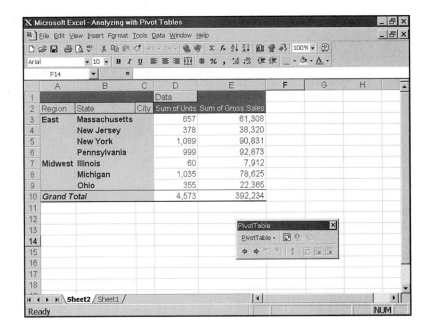

To show or hide detail items using commands, follow these steps:

1. Select the summary item whose detail items you want to hide.
2. Choose Data, Group and Outline.
3. From the submenu that appears, choose the option you want (Show Detail or Hide Detail).

Displaying More Detail   You may be surprised at how much detail you can get with the help of pivot tables. In the preceding section, you learned that double-clicking the outermost rows and columns (those containing the summary items) limits the amount of detail displayed. Double-clicking the innermost row or column has the opposite effect: It displays even more detail.

To add more detail to a pivot table, double-click the detail (innermost) row or column for which you want to show more detail. (The detail row and detail column are indicated by annotations in Figure 39.16.)

Figure 39.17 shows the result of adding work-code detail to the pivot table in Figure 39.16. (This was done by double-clicking Spencer and then selecting Work Code in the Show Detail dialog box.)

FIG. 39.16

To add more fields to a pivot table, double-click the innermost row or column.

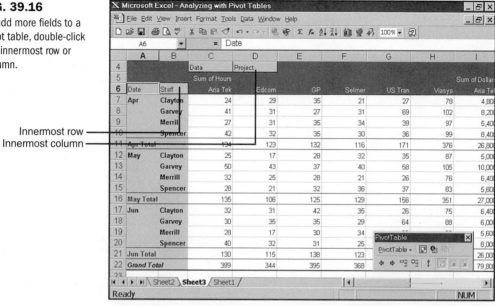

Innermost row ⎯
Innermost column ⎯

FIG. 39.17

The pivot table in Figure 39.16 after adding work-code detail for Spencer.

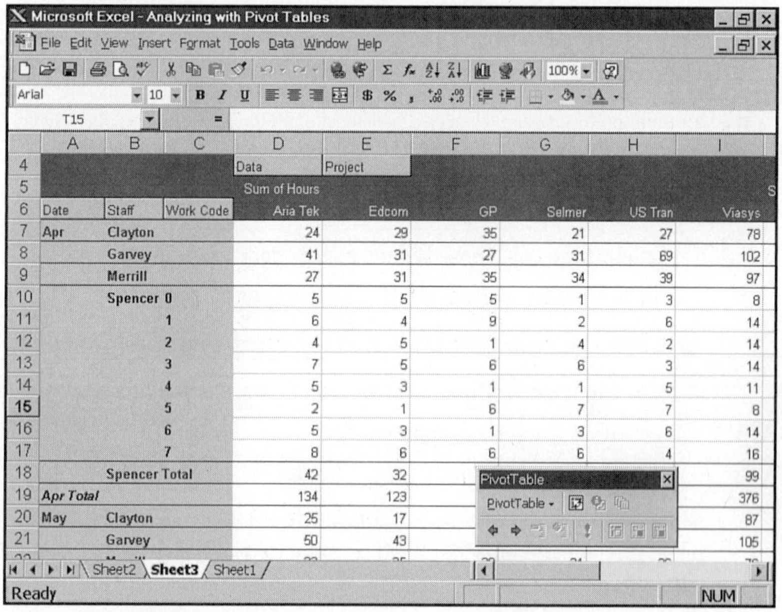

Sometimes, while viewing a pivot table, you may want to investigate the source data. Simply double-click a cell in the data area of the pivot table (the area of the pivot table excluding the field and item labels). Excel inserts a new worksheet and displays a copy of the source data that was used to calculate the value appearing in the cell. Figure 39.18 shows the displayed source data for the sales entries for Clayton.

FIG. 39.18

This pivot table was produced by double-clicking the Grand Total cell for Clayton in the pivot table shown in Figure 39.13.

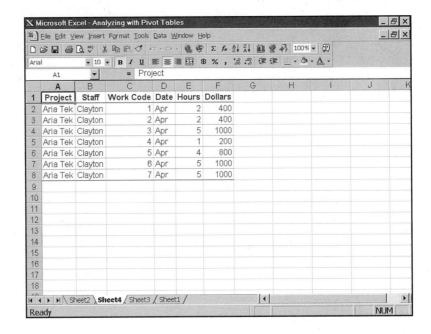

TIP The data you display is only a copy; making changes to this copy does not change the source data.

To display source data for a cell in the data area using the toolbar, follow these steps:

1. Select the cell whose related source data you want to display.
2. Click the Show Detail button on the PivotTable toolbar.

To display source data for a cell in the data area using commands, follow these steps:

1. Select the cell whose related source data you want to display.
2. Choose Data, Group and Outline.
3. From the submenu that appears, choose the Show Detail option.

Grouping Items with Numeric Labels into Ranges Sometimes you are faced with pivot tables containing items identified by numeric labels. In the example in Figure 39.19, the District field contains numeric codes. Excel can group these items into ranges based on the initial digit in the district number.

To group items with numeric labels into ranges, follow these steps:

1. Select one of the numeric item labels in the pivot table.

2. Click the Group button on the PivotTable toolbar. (Alternatively, you can choose <u>D</u>ata, <u>G</u>roup and Outline, and then choose Group from the submenu.) Excel displays a dialog box like the one in Figure 39.20.

3. Excel guesses how you want to group the items and enters proposed values in the <u>S</u>tarting At, <u>E</u>nding At, and <u>B</u>y boxes. To accept the defaults, choose OK. To define the grouping method yourself, continue with steps 4 through 7.

4. In the <u>S</u>tarting At box, enter the first number in the sequence you want to break into groups.

5. In the <u>E</u>nding At box, enter the last number in the sequence you want to break into groups.

6. In the <u>B</u>y box, enter the size of the numeric ranges you want.

7. Choose OK.

Figure 39.21 shows the pivot table created from the data list shown in Figure 39.19 after grouping the districts (using the values shown in Figure 39.20).

FIG. 39.19

A source list with numeric codes (column A).

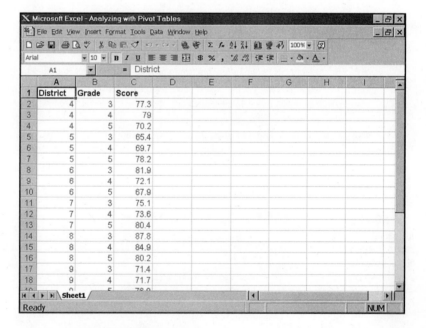

FIG. 39.20

A Grouping dialog box when the items in the group are labeled by identifying numbers with a maximum of two digits.

FIG. 39.21

The pivot table created
from the list in Figure
39.19, after grouping
the districts.

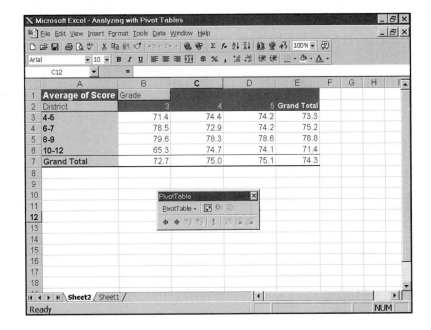

Average of Score	Grade			
District	3	4	5	Grand Total
4-5	71.4	74.4	74.2	73.3
6-7	78.5	72.9	74.2	75.2
8-9	79.6	78.3	78.6	78.8
10-12	65.3	74.7	74.1	71.4
Grand Total	72.7	75.0	75.1	74.3

N O T E The options under Auto in the Grouping dialog box are selected by default but are cleared if
you enter values in the boxes. Selecting one or both of the Auto options restores the
starting and/or ending values in the source list. ▪

Grouping Items by Date or Time Intervals   If one of your fields contains items based on time
periods, and the items you want to group are in one of Excel's date or time cell formats, Excel
displays the dialog box shown in Figure 39.22. Select the desired time interval for grouping
items from the By box.

FIG. 39.22

You can create time
period groups in this
dialog box.

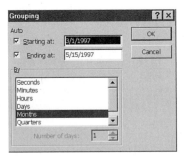

 TROUBLESHOOTING

When grouping a date field, Excel displays a message that it cannot group that selection. If the
selection includes dates, make sure all the cells in the date column in the source list are formatted in
a date or time format.

Some cells in the pivot table display the #DIV/0! error value. This error occurs when your pivot table computes averages and some necessary values are "missing" in the data source. Usually, this message means that the data range does not contain the particular combination of item values represented by the cell displaying the error. The #DIV/0! error can also result from a blank cell in the data-range column corresponding to a data field in the pivot table.

Analyzing the Data

After you get a look at your data through the pivot table, you may want to modify a number of elements to display the data in a useful and informative way. You can choose to view high-level summaries or show a lot of detail. You can change the sequence of items, and you can classify your data by values in the data area rather than by item.

 TIP It can be difficult to fit all the item labels into charts created from pivot tables. If the pivot table contains many items, substitute short names for the labels in the pivot table.

Analyzing Pivot Table Data with Charts

Moving pivot table fields to a different position can change the arrangement of data series markers in charts created from pivot tables, giving you a different perspective in the chart. Generally, the field or fields in the position (row or a column) displaying the lesser number of items occupy the chart legend.

One of the most effective ways to examine pivot table data is to add a page field and then create a chart from the pivot table. You can then flip through the items in the page field while viewing the chart to obtain a visual impression of the numbers.

Sorting Items

As you might expect, you can sort items in a pivot table field by their labels. In addition, you can sort based on values in the data fields or use a custom sort order.

When you create a pivot table, all items are automatically sorted by label in ascending order. However, if you've added new items or moved fields—or if you want to sort the items in descending order—you can redo the field.

To sort items by labels using the Standard toolbar, select the desired field, and then click the Sort Ascending or Sort Descending button, as appropriate.

To sort items by labels with menu commands, follow these steps:

1. Select the field you want to sort.
2. Choose Data, Sort.
3. Select the sort order you want (Ascending or Descending button). Notice that a thumbnail description of the sort parameters is displayed at the lower left in the dialog box (see Figure 39.23).

Part

X

Ch

39

FIG. 39.23
Choose Data, Sort while a field in a pivot table is selected to display this dialog box.

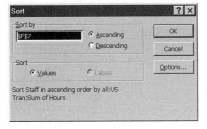

4. Choose OK.

Paging or Filtering a Pivot Table

As you learned in Chapter 38, "Using the Power of Pivot Tables," page fields selectively filter data in a pivot table. To display a particular item in a page field, click the arrow to the right of the page field, and then select the desired item from the list, as shown in Figure 39.24.

FIG. 39.24
Select an item from the list attached to a page field to display data for that item only.

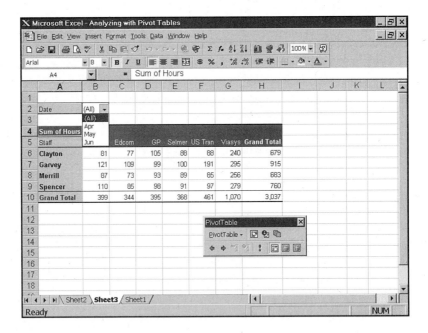

To display totals for the entire field, select (All) from the list. The displayed totals include data for all items in the field, including hidden items.

Using More than One Page Field   By adding more page fields, you can filter your data very finely. The pivot table in Figure 39.25 displays time spent by Merrill on the GP project.

FIG. 39.25

With two page fields, you can look at very specific slices of data.

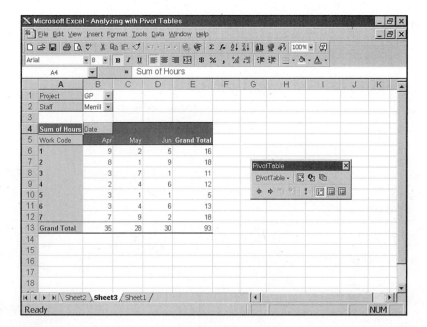

To add a page field to a pivot table, follow these steps:

1. Select a cell in the pivot table.

2. Click the PivotTable Wizard button on the PivotTable toolbar.

3. Move the desired field button to the PAGE area.

4. Choose the Finish button.

To create a page field from an existing field in a pivot table, drag the field button from the row or column past the upper-left corner of the main body of the pivot table. When the insert marker turns to stacked rectangles, release the mouse button.

Breaking Pages into Separate Worksheets You can display individual pages in a pivot table in separate worksheets. This capability is useful if you want to print all the pages or move among the pages using the worksheet tabs. Before you can display pages, however, the pivot table must already have at least one page field.

To break pages in a pivot table into separate worksheets, follow these steps:

1. Select a cell in the pivot table.

2. Click the Show Pages button on the PivotTable toolbar, or choose the Show Pages command from the shortcut menu.

3. The Show Pages dialog box displays a list of the page fields in the pivot table. Select the field whose items you want to display on separate worksheets, and then choose OK. (If the pivot table displays only one field, it is selected by default.)

Part

X

Ch

39

Excel inserts a new worksheet into the workbook for each item in the page field, naming the worksheets after the respective items. Each of the worksheets contains a pivot table with the appropriate item selected in the page field.

Managing Totals and Subtotals

By default, Excel automatically displays grand totals for rows and columns in pivot tables. If the pivot table contains multiple row or multiple column fields, it also displays subtotals, as shown in Figure 39.26.

FIG. 39.26
Excel automatically displays subtotals and grand totals in pivot tables.

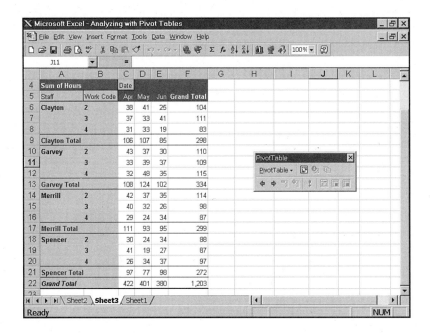

TIP Show multiple pivot tables on one printed sheet by pasting fixed copies using the Edit, Paste Special command and the Values and Formats options.

Hiding Grand Totals   To hide grand totals, turn off the first two check boxes in Step 4 of the PivotTable Wizard (see Figure 39.27).

When the pivot table contains more than one data field, it displays grand totals for each data field. You can display grand totals for all or none of the fields in the row or column position.

Hiding Subtotals   Subtotals are associated with individual fields, so you hide or display them individually.

FIG. 39.27
Turning off the Grand Totals For Rows and Grand Totals For Columns options in the PivotTable Wizard suppresses the display of grand totals.

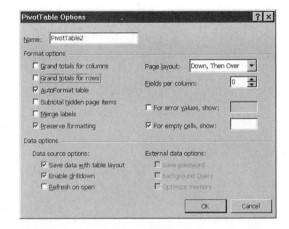

To hide subtotals for a field, follow these steps:

1. Click the PivotTable Field button on the PivotTable toolbar. (Alternatively, you can double-click the desired field in the pivot table or choose the PivotTable Field command from the shortcut menu.)

2. In the Subtotals area of the PivotTable Field dialog box, select None, and then choose OK.

To redisplay subtotals, bring up the dialog box and select Automatic.

Displaying Subtotals for Multiple Fields in a Row or Column   When a row or column contains more than one field, and automatic subtotals are selected, the pivot table displays subtotals for the outermost field only. You can, however, display subtotals for the innermost field, as shown in Figure 39.28.

To display subtotals for an innermost field, follow these steps:

1. Select the field for which you want to display subtotals.

2. Click the PivotTable Field button on the PivotTable toolbar. (Alternatively, you can double-click the button for the desired field in the pivot table or choose the PivotTable Field command from the shortcut menu.) The PivotTable Field dialog box then appears (see Figure 39.29).

3. In the Subtotals area of the PivotTable Field dialog box, select Custom.

4. Select the type of subtotal calculation, such as Sum, from the adjacent list, and then choose OK.

N O T E   You can also hide selected items in the Pivot Table Field dialog box by selecting them from the Hide Items list. ▪

FIG. 39.28

You can display block totals for the innermost field, as shown in rows 16 through 19, by creating custom subtotals.

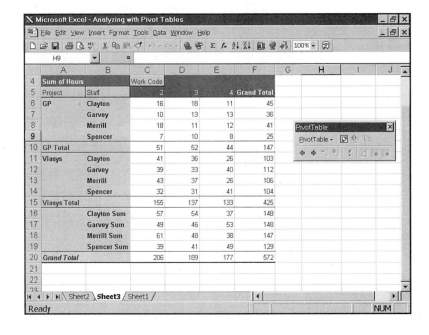

FIG. 39.29

You can change the function Excel uses to summarize data in the PivotTable Field dialog box.

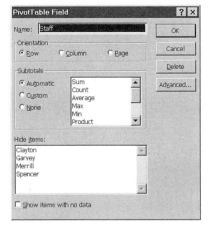

Using Other Functions for Data Analysis

Most of the pivot tables you've looked at so far have presented summary totals of the numeric values contained in the data source. Sometimes, though, you may want to view other computations, such as averages.

Changing the Summary Function Unless you specify otherwise, Excel summarizes data by summing numeric values when creating a pivot table. (If the data fields contain text, the pivot table displays counts of the values.)

You can change the summary function, or calculation type, from Sum to Average.

To change the summary calculation in a pivot table in the PivotTable Wizard, follow these steps:

1. Select a cell in the data area of the pivot table.
2. Click the PivotTable Wizard button on the PivotTable toolbar.
3. Double-click the field button in the DATA area.
4. In the Summarize By list, select the desired summary function.

    Table 39.1 describes Excel's most commonly used pivot table calculation types.

Table 39.1   Summary Functions for Pivot Tables

Summary Function	How Excel Computes an Amount in a Pivot Table from Source Data for a Given Cell
Sum	Totals all numeric values
Count	Counts all values
Average	Computes sum of all numeric values, divided by number of records in the source data
Max	Finds highest value
Min	Finds lowest value
Product	Multiplies all numeric values
Count Nums	Counts all numeric values

Part
X

Ch
39

5. Choose OK to return to the PivotTable Wizard, and then choose Finish.

Using Different Summary Functions in the Same Pivot Table You can use a different summary function for each data field in the pivot table. Figure 39.30 shows a pivot table summarizing total hours worked and average dollars (fees) generated.

You also can use a different summary function for the same data field if you add the data field to the pivot table twice.

Using Custom Calculations Sometimes you might want a pivot table to calculate values in a nonstandard way. Excel provides several calculation types that calculate values based on other values in the data area of the pivot table. Figure 39.31 illustrates a pivot table that calculates values as a percentage of the grand totals for the rows, rather than as numeric totals.

FIG. 39.30

In this pivot table, the hours are summarized using the Sum function and the dollars are summarized using the Average function.

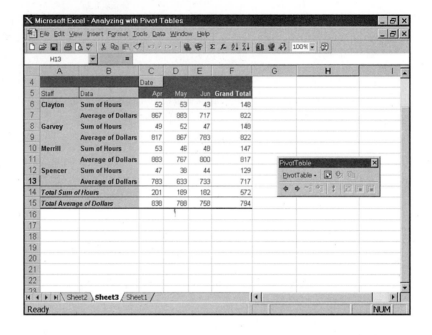

FIG. 39.31

This pivot table uses the % of row custom-calculation type.

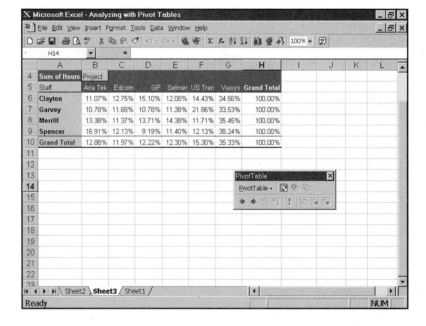

TIP Summarize the same data different ways by adding the data field twice and using the PivotTable Field button to change each summary method.

To change the calculation type for a data field, follow these steps:

1. Select a pivot table cell in the field you want to change.
2. Click the PivotTable Field button on the PivotTable toolbar.
3. In the PivotTable Field dialog box, choose Options.
4. Select the desired calculation type from the Show Data As list. See Table 39.2 for explanations of the various calculation types. Note that in the second column in the table, the term result refers to the computed result of the summary function for a given cell in the pivot table.

Table 39.2   Calculation Types for Pivot Tables

Calculation Type	What Appears in the Pivot Table Cell
Difference From	The difference between the result and a field and item you specify in the Base Field and Base Item boxes
% Of	The result divided by the specified base field and item, expressed as a percentage
% Difference From	The difference between the result and a specified field and item, divided by that base field and item, expressed as a percentage
Running Total in	For the specified base field, totals that cumulate the result for successive items
% ofrow	The result divided by the row's total, expressed as a percentage
% of column	The result divided by the column's total, expressed as a percentage
% of total	The result divided by the pivot table grand total, expressed as a percentage
Index	The value computed by the following formula:Result × Grand Total/ Grand Row Total × Grand Column Total (useful for ranking cells in the pivot table)

5. If necessary, select the field and item you want in the Base Field and Base Item boxes. (You learn how this works in a moment.) You do not need to specify a base field for the percent of row calculation type illustrated in Figure 39.31 because this calculation does not use a base field.
6. Choose OK.

To illustrate how base fields and items work, imagine you are working for a snack food company, and you are studying long-term sales trends. You have source data going back to 1990, and you want to show sales by product for that period and year-by-year percentage changes.

To display sales results over time with percentage changes, follow these steps:

1. Create a pivot table with two data fields for Sales.
2. In the Step 3 dialog box of the PivotTable Wizard, double-click the Sum of Sales2 button in the DATA area. The PivotTable Field dialog box appears.
3. Change the name of the field to Increase in the Name box.
4. If necessary, choose Options to expand the dialog box.
5. Choose the % Difference From option from the Show Data As list. The PivotTable Field dialog box then looks like Figure 39.32.

FIG. 39.32

Calculating sales as a percentage difference compared to the previous period.

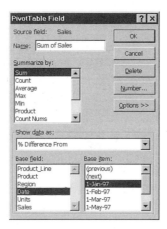

6. In the Base Field box, select Date.
7. In the Base Item box, select 1-Jan-97.
8. Choose OK.
9. Choose Finish.

Excel then displays a pivot table like the one in Figure 39.33.

Creating a Calculated Field in a PivotTable   If you don't want to use one of the built-in calculations for pivot tables, you can create your own calculated field. In the examples we have been working with, we have been limited to the fields in our original data set. What if you wanted to expand on the data set so that you could do further analysis? For example, you might want to display internal billing information based on the hours worked by each employee. Your company uses a fixed internal rate of $20. This means you could calculate the internal billing as Hours * 20. This is easy to do with the following steps:

1. Click a cell in the pivot table to activate the pivot table.
2. From the PivotTable toolbar, choose the PivotTable menu button.
3. Choose Formulas, Calculated Field. This displays the Insert Calculated Field dialog box as shown in Figure 39.34.
4. In the Name box, type a name for the calculated field.
5. Select the Formula box. Choose a field from the Fields box and choose the Insert Field button. Build your formula at this point. If you were creating the formula for internal billing, it would be =Hours * 20.
6. Choose Add, and then choose OK. The updated pivot table is shown in Figure 39.35.

FIG. 39.33

A pivot table using the % Difference From calculation type for Sales makes it easy to spot trends over time.

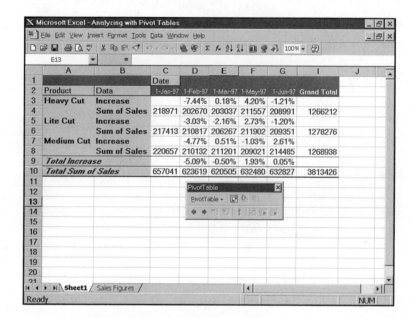

FIG. 39.34

The Insert Calculated Field dialog box allows you to add custom fields to your pivot table.

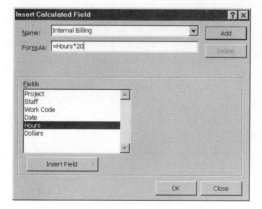

FIG. 39.35

After adding a calculated field, the pivot table has additional summary information based on the calculated field Internal Billings.

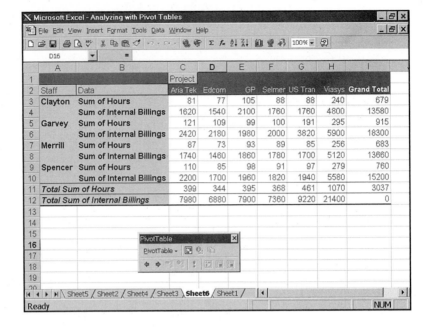

		Project						
Staff	Data	Aria Tek	Edcom	GP	Selmer	US Tran	Viasys	Grand Total
Clayton	Sum of Hours	81	77	105	88	88	240	679
	Sum of Internal Billings	1620	1540	2100	1760	1760	4800	13580
Garvey	Sum of Hours	121	109	99	100	191	295	915
	Sum of Internal Billings	2420	2180	1980	2000	3820	5900	18300
Merrill	Sum of Hours	87	73	93	89	85	256	683
	Sum of Internal Billings	1740	1460	1860	1780	1700	5120	13660
Spencer	Sum of Hours	110	85	98	91	97	279	760
	Sum of Internal Billings	2200	1700	1960	1820	1940	5580	15200
Total Sum of Hours		399	344	395	368	461	1070	3037
Total Sum of Internal Billings		7980	6880	7900	7360	9220	21400	0

Formatting the Pivot Table

The pivot table is a unique animal in the Excel menagerie. In one sense, it's simply a range of cells containing numeric constants. In another sense, it's a single unified entity that's linked to one or more other cell ranges. Pivot tables' unique characteristics dictate special formatting methods.

 TIP   Preserve the data and appearance of a pivot table by copying it and pasting it to another location using the Edit, Paste Special command. Paste with the Values option and then with Formats.

AutoFormatting Pivot Tables

Although you can apply formatting to individual cells in a pivot table, the effort usually goes for naught because Excel reformats the table as a whole whenever the layout is changed or the table is refreshed. To reformat the table, select any cell in the table, and choose the Format, AutoFormat command. Then select the desired format from the AutoFormat dialog box.

When you reorganize or refresh the pivot table, it retains the AutoFormat you applied.

 TIP   Use AutoFormat on pivot tables to preserve their appearance when they change or update.

Formatting Numbers

When you create a new pivot table, Excel applies the number format for the worksheet's Normal cell style to the cells in the data area. You can change that format, however.

To apply a different number format to the data area of a pivot table, follow these steps:

1. Select a cell in the data area of the pivot table.
2. Click the PivotTable Field button on the PivotTable toolbar. The PivotTable Field dialog box then appears.
3. Choose <u>N</u>umber to bring up the Number tab in the Format Cells dialog box.
4. Select the desired number format in the usual manner, and then choose OK.

The number format you select stays with all the cells in that field, regardless of whether the data area changes shape.

Changing Field and Item Names

You can change any of the text labels surrounding the data area in the conventional way by selecting the cell and typing a new name.

CHAPTER 40

Linking, Embedding, and Consolidating Worksheets

In this chapter

Excel enables you to work with more than one worksheet and workbook at a time. You can copy a chart or worksheet range and embed it as a picture on the worksheet. You can link workbooks so that changes in one workbook update another workbook, and you can consolidate worksheets so that data from multiple worksheets accumulates into one worksheet.

You can use linking to divide a large business system into its component workbooks and worksheets. You can test each workbook and worksheet separately, and then link the workbooks together to produce an integrated system. You can create links that always update or that update only on your request.

Excel's capability of linking pictures enables you to bring together pictures of cells and charts from different documents and arrange them on one page. This capability gives you the power to work in separate documents but organize the printed results the way you want to present them, enabling you to produce presentation-quality reports from your worksheet data.

Consolidation enables you to bring together data from multiple worksheets and workbooks into one worksheet. Consolidation is often used to accumulate budgets or forecasts from multiple divisions into a unified corporate budget or forecast. Excel enables you to fix these consolidations so that they don't change, or to link them so that the consolidations update when division data changes. Linked consolidations automatically build an outline.

Linking Workbook Cells and Ranges

Linking data enables you to avoid the problems inherent in large, cumbersome workbooks. You can build small worksheets and workbooks to accomplish specific tasks, and then link all these *components* together to form a larger *system*.

The following list describes some of the advantages of building systems composed of smaller workbooks that share data by linking:

- Data linked between workbooks passes data, numbers, and text used by formulas in the receiving workbook.

- Linked data can be formatted by using the same formatting techniques you use on any cell contents.

- Systems require less memory because all workbooks may not need to be open simultaneously. Some workbooks can be linked to workbooks that remain on disk.

- Systems composed of workbook components are flexible and can be updated more easily. You can redesign, test, and implement one component without rebuilding the entire system.

- Smaller workbooks recalculate faster than single, larger workbooks.

- You can create data-entry components that operate on separate computers or in separate locations. At a given time, filled-in components can be copied into a directory and given a filename expected by the link, which updates the spreadsheet that contains the link the next time it is opened. This arrangement has a number of advantages—more people can work on the system at once, the work can be completed faster, people can work in separate locations, and separate locations reduce the chance that an inexperienced operator can damage the overall system.

■ Systems are easier to maintain and debug when assembled in components.

■ Workbook components can be modified for use in different systems.

What You Need to Know About Links

Linking enables one workbook to share the data in another workbook. You can link one cell, a range of cells, and a named formula or constant, and sheets. The workbook containing the original data—the source of the information—is the source workbook. The workbook that receives the linked data is the *target workbook*. (You also may see the workbooks referred to as the *source* and the *target* or the *supporting* and the *dependent*.)

Source workbooks do not need to be opened for the target workbook to get the information it needs through the link. When the target workbook opens, it updates linked data that is read from the source workbook, if the source workbook is open. If the source workbook is not open, the target workbook asks whether you want to use the data the target workbook had when it was saved or whether you want the target workbook to update data from the source workbook even when it is not open.

N O T E If you have links from one workbook to a database in another workbook, the workbook that contains the link may open or close too slowly. The file size of the workbook also may become huge—too large to fit on a disk—because Excel actually is storing the last image of the database in the file, which enables you to open the workbook, not update the link to the database, and still use the workbook. Your workbook doesn't need to save this database image if the workbook that contains the database is always open with the linked sheet or if you will always be doing an update when you open the sheet. To turn off this saved image, choose Tools, Options, select the Calculation tab, and clear the Save External Link Values check box. Choose OK. ■

Part

X

Ch

40

Figure 40.1 shows workbooks linked by an external reference formula. Quarter 1 is the source for the ANNUAL.XLS target workbook. The external reference formula in ANNUAL.XLS appears in the formula bar as ='[Quarter 1.xls]Quarter 1 1996'!$E$5, which indicates that cell B5 on the ANNUAL 96 worksheet of the ANNUAL.XLS workbook is linked to the contents of cell E5 on the Quarter 1 1996 worksheet of the Quarter 1 workbook. When the contents of E5 in the Quarter 1 1996 worksheet changes, the value of B5 of the ANNUAL 96 worksheet also changes.

External reference formulas use the following form:

```
='Path\[WorkbookName]SheetName'!CellRef
```

The following formula is an example of an external reference formula:

```
='[Quarter 1.xls] Quarter 1 1996'!$E$5
```

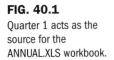

FIG. 40.1

Quarter 1 acts as the source for the ANNUAL.XLS workbook.

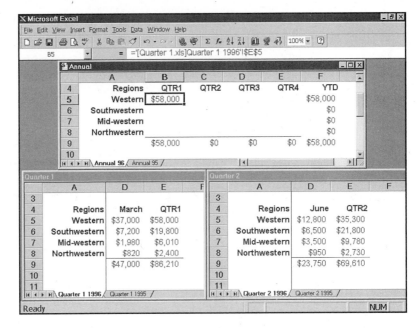

In this formula, Quarter 1 is the name of the supporting workbook that contains the data, Quarter 1 1996 is the specific worksheet in the workbook that contains the data, and $E$5 is the cell that supplies information to the link. An exclamation mark (!) separates the supporting workbook and worksheet name from the cell reference.

An external reference also can span a range of cells. The total in B9 on ANNUAL.XLS, for example, can be one formula that totals the range of cells from the Quarter 1 1996 worksheet in the Quarter 1 workbook. The formula may appear in the following way:

```
=SUM('[Quarter 1.xls]Quarter 1 1996'!$E$5:$E$8)
```

You can link a range of cells to another range of cells of the same size all at once. These links are created with the Edit, Copy and Edit, Paste Link commands as described in the next section. External reference formulas are pasted into each of the cells in the range B5:B8 on ANNUAL.XLS, with links to the supporting cells E5:E8 on Quarter 1. An example of the external reference formulas is as follows:

```
='[Quarter 1.xls] Quarter 1 1996'!$E$5
```

The external reference formula appears differently, depending on whether the source worksheet is open or closed. If the source worksheet is open, the external reference formula appears with only the workbook and worksheet names, as in the following example:

```
='[Quarter 1.xls] Quarter 1 1996'!$E$5
```

If the source worksheet is closed, the external reference appears with the full pathname, disk, directory, and filename, enclosed in single quotation marks, as shown in the following example:

```
='C:\EXCEL\FINANCE\[Quarter 1.xls]Quarter 1 1996'!$E$9
```

Because open source workbooks don't include the pathname in the external reference formula, you cannot have two workbooks open with the same name, even if both are from different folders. You can have links to source workbooks with the same names in different folders, but you can have only one workbook open at a time.

Linking Cells with Copy and Paste Link Commands

To link a cell or range in a supporting workbook to a cell or range in the target workbook, use Edit, Paste Special with the Paste Link Button. The range of E5:E8 on the Quarter 1 workbook is linked to cells B5:B8 (the rows do not have to be the same) on the target ANNUAL.XLS workbook, as shown in the following steps:

1. Open the workbooks that you want to link.

2. Activate the source workbook.

3. Select the range of cells that provide the data you want linked (see Figure 40.2).

FIG. 40.2

Select the range on the source worksheet before copying.

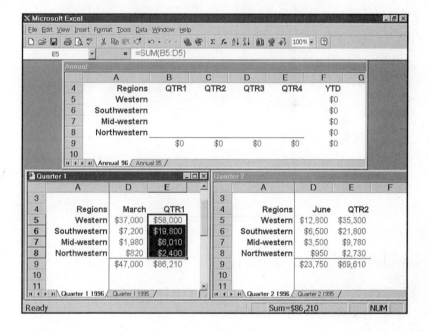

4. Choose Edit, Copy.

5. Activate the target workbook to receive the data.

6. Select the top-left cell of the range where you want the link to appear.

   In this example, you would select cell B5 on the ANNUAL 96 worksheet of the ANNUAL.XLS workbook. Do not select an entire range to paste into; doing so is unnecessary and increases the chance that you may select the wrong size of range to paste into. You need to select only the single cell at the upper-left corner of the area where you want to paste.

7. Choose Edit, Paste Special or right-click the cell and choose Paste Special. The Paste Special dialog box appears.

8. Select the Paste All option and the Operation None option.

9. Choose Paste Link.

The link appears, as shown in Figure 40.3.

FIG. 40.3

The linked cells on ANNUAL.XLS act as a group.

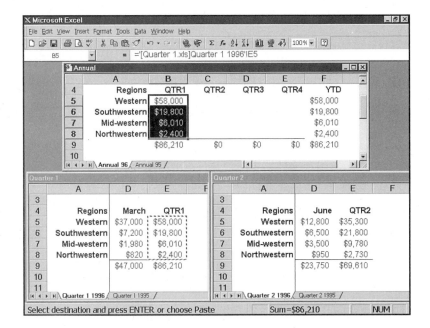

Linking Cells by Pointing

To create many links that are individual cells or are links within larger formulas, use the pointing method of creating links. You can enter external references in a formula in the same way that you build a formula within one workbook: by pointing to the cell references you want in the formula, even when the cells are on another workbook. To point to a cell or range so that it is included in a formula, click it as you build the formula, or drag across its range.

To link the target cell B5 on the ANNUAL 96 worksheet of the ANNUAL.XLS workbook to the source cell, E5 on the Quarter 1 1996 worksheet of the Quarter 1 workbook, perform the following steps:

1. Open the target and source workbooks.

2. Activate the target workbook.

3. Select the cell that you want to contain the link and start the formula. The formula may involve many terms and functions or be as simple as an equal sign (=) and the single linked cell.

   In Figure 40.4, an equal sign (=) is typed in cell B5 on the ANNUAL 96 worksheet of the ANNUAL.XLS workbook.

FIG. 40.4

Link cells by typing an = and clicking the source cell.

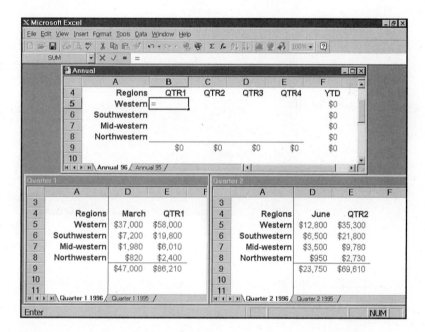

4. Activate the source workbook, Quarter 1.

5. Select the source cell or range that supplies data to the link. In the example, click cell E5 on the Quarter 1 1996 worksheet or press the arrow keys to enclose E5 in the dashed marquee.

6. Continue building the formula in the same way you build any formula, by typing another math operator (math sign) and continuing to select cells or to enter terms.

7. After you complete the formula, click the Enter box in the formula bar or press Enter.

Part
X

Ch
40

After you press Enter or type a math operator, the dashed marquee in the source worksheet disappears and the mouse pointer selects cells in the source worksheet. Figure 40.5 shows the result of the external reference formula in B5 (just after pressing Enter):

```
='[Quarter 1.xls] Quarter 1 1996'!$E$5.
```

FIG. 40.5

The resulting link is created by pointing to a cell in another workbook.

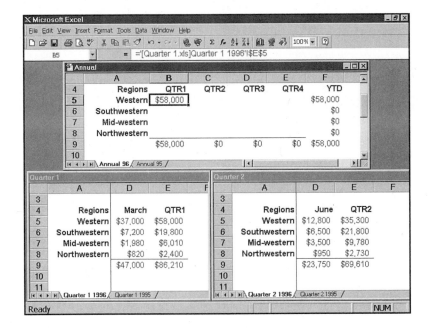

You can use the pointing method to enter external references within complex formulas such as the following:

```
=2*SIN('[READINGS.XLS]TEST 1'!$AE$5)/(B12*56)
```

You also can point to ranges on other workbooks. Consider the following formula:

```
=SUM('[QTR2.XLS]Quarter 2 1996'!$E$5:$E$8)
```

This formula was entered by clicking the AutoSum button in the toolbar and dragging across the range E5:E8 in the source workbook with the mouse. To select the range with the keyboard, hold down the Shift key and press the arrow keys until the range is selected. Type the closing), and press Enter.

Linking Cells by Typing

If you need to create links to workbooks on disk without opening the workbooks, you can type in the external reference formula. This technique can help you if the source file is too large to load with your existing workbook or if you are so familiar with the supporting workbook that you can type a reference faster than you can find and click the cell.

When you type an external reference to an open workbook, use syntax like that shown in the following examples:

```
='[Quarter 1.xls]Quarter 1 1996'!$E$5
```

or

```
=SUM('[Quarter 1.xls]Quarter 1 1996'!$E$5:$E$8)
```

or

```
='[Quarter 1.xls]Quarter 1 1996'!RangeName
```

When you type an external reference to an unopened workbook, enclose the full pathname, workbook name, and worksheet name in single quotations, as in the following example:

```
='C:\EXCEL\FINANCE\[Quarter 1.xls]Quarter 1 1996'!$E$9
```

If the source file is in the current folder, Excel enters the pathname. For example, type the following and press Enter:

```
='[Quarter 1.xls]Quarter 1 1996'!$E$9
```

Excel enters the path.

Typing external reference formulas is easiest when you use the Insert, Name, Define or the Insert, Name, Create command to name cells or ranges (or you can use the Name box in the formula bar). Suppose that cell E5 in the Quarter 1 1996 worksheet of the Quarter 1 workbook is named Qtr1.Western. If both the ANNUAL.XLS and Quarter 1 workbooks are open, you can link them by typing the following formula in the ANNUAL.XLS workbook:

```
='[Quarter 1.xls]Quarter 1 1996'!Qtr1.Western
```

This formula contains an external reference. When you type formulas that contain an external reference, the answer appears as soon as you enter the formula. (If you use a range name such as Qtr1.Western, this name must exist on the source workbook. In this example, Qtr1 in the name Qtr1.Western is not related to the workbook name Quarter 1.)

▶ **See** "Naming Cells for Better Worksheets," **p. 592**

Opening Linked Workbooks

When the workbook is opened, the linked data in a target workbook updates in different ways. If the source workbooks are already open, the target workbook updates immediately when opened. If the source workbooks are not open when the target workbook opens, the alert box shown in Figure 40.6 appears.

If you select Yes in the alert box, Excel reads the linked data off the files and updates the target workbook. If you select No, Excel retains the values the target workbook had when last saved.

If you already opened a target workbook and want to open the source workbooks that feed it, perform the following steps:

1. Activate the target sheet that contains the links.
2. Choose Edit, Links to display the Links dialog box, shown in Figure 40.7.

FIG. 40.6

When opening a target workbook, you can choose to keep the old values or update links to files on disk.

FIG. 40.7

Use the Links dialog box to change or update links between workbooks.

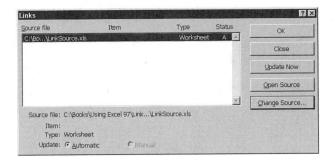

3. Select the files you want to open. Unopened files appear with their pathnames.

   To select multiple adjacent workbooks, click the first workbook and then Shift+click the last workbook. All workbooks between are selected. To select or clear nonadjacent workbooks, Ctrl+click the workbook names.

   Select multiple adjacent workbooks by pressing up- or down-arrow keys to select the first workbook, and then press Shift+arrow key to select adjacent names.

4. Choose Open Source.

 T I P   Be sure that the target workbook is active. If a workbook without links is active, the Edit, Links command is grayed and the command is unavailable.

Changing and Updating Links

To maintain a system of linked workbooks properly, you need to know how to reestablish lost links and how to update a large system of links. If source workbooks are renamed or moved to other folders, target workbooks cannot find the needed data. These links are lost and must be reestablished.

To reestablish links to a workbook or to link a target workbook to a different supporting workbook, perform the following steps:

1. Open the target workbook.

2. Choose Edit, Links to display the Links dialog box.

3. Select the files to change or update (see Figure 40.8). Unopened files appear with their pathnames.

FIG. 40.8

Selected files whose links you want to reestablish or change.

4. Choose the <u>C</u>hange Source button to display the Change Links dialog box, shown in Figure 40.9. The current link is displayed at the top of the dialog box.

FIG. 40.9

Change links by using this dialog box.

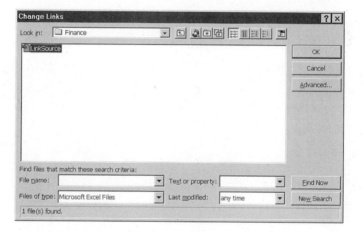

5. Select a folder and filename to indicate the folder and file of the new supporting workbook, or type the folder and filename of the file you want to establish as the source.

6. Choose OK to link to the filename you selected, or choose Cancel to ignore the change.

7. If you selected multiple source files, repeat steps 5 and 6, noting at the top of the dialog box which source workbook you are changing.

To update an active target workbook when the source workbook is unopened, choose <u>E</u>dit, Lin<u>k</u>s, select the source workbook from which the target workbook needs an update, and choose the <u>U</u>pdate Now button. You can select more than one source workbook by clicking the first workbook and then Shift+clicking the last workbook.

> **CAUTION**
>
> You can unknowingly create linked workbooks where changed data doesn't get passed to all target workbooks. This situation occurs only when workbooks involved in the links aren't open. If workbook A passes data to B, and B passes data to C, in some cases a change in A may not occur in C. If you change workbook A, but never open and update B, B cannot have the updated data to pass on to C. Therefore, you must know and update the hierarchy of linked workbooks, in order, from the lowest source workbook to the highest target workbook.

Editing a Link Manually

You can edit an external reference formula that is linked to a cell or range. Consider the following example:

```
Frequently Used='[Quarter 1.xls]Quarter 1 1996'!$E$5
```

Edit the cell as you edit any formula. Select the cell, and then press F2 or click in the formula bar to edit.

> **N O T E**   To find cells that contain external references, choose Edit, Find (or press Ctrl+F) and select the Look in Formulas option. Type an exclamation mark (!) in the Find What text box. Choose Find Next to search. This method is helpful for finding cells containing external links that need to be edited selectively.

Freezing Links

To preserve the values from a link, but remove the external reference, you can freeze the external reference portion of a formula so that portion becomes a value. To freeze an external reference, select the cell so that the formula appears in the formula bar. Click in the formula bar or press the Edit Formula key, F2, and press F9, the Calculate Now key, to change the selected reference into a value. Press Enter to reenter the formula.

You also can freeze formulas by selecting the cell or range that contains the formulas and choosing Edit, Copy (or press Ctrl+C) or right-clicking the selection and choosing Copy. Next, choose Edit, Paste Special with the Values option selected and paste directly on top of the original cell or range. This procedure replaces entire formulas with their values. If the formula is part of an array, you must select the entire array before you can freeze it.

Saving Linked Workbooks

When you save linked workbooks, first save the source workbook that supplies the data. Next, save the target workbooks. This procedure ensures that the target workbooks will store the correct pathname and filename of their source workbooks.

If you change the name of a source workbook, be sure that target workbooks that depend upon it also are open. Save the source workbook, and then resave the target workbooks. This procedure ensures that the target workbooks record the new pathname and filename of their source workbook. If a target workbook becomes unlinked from its source workbook, you can relink the workbooks by choosing Edit, Links.

▶ **See** "Entering Cell References," **p. 569**

▶ **See** "Using Names in Formulas and Commands," **p. 601**

Consolidating Worksheets

When you consolidate worksheets, Excel performs calculations on similar data across multiple worksheets and workbooks and places the results of calculations in a consolidation worksheet. You can use this capability to consolidate department budgets into one division budget; you then can consolidate the division budgets into the corporate budget. Consolidations can be more than just simple totals, however. Excel also can create consolidations that calculate statistical worksheet information such as averages, standard deviations, and counts.

TIP If you use consolidations, be sure to review outlining. A consolidation using the Data, Consolidate command can produce an outline automatically. The details within the outline are the sources of the consolidation.

TIP If your office uses a mixture of Excel and 1-2-3, remember that Excel can link and consolidate with 1-2-3 worksheets. Follow the same procedures you use for linking or consolidating with Excel workbooks.

The data in the multiple worksheets can have identical or different physical layouts. If the physical layouts of the supporting worksheets are identical, Excel consolidates data by working with cells from the same relative location on each supporting worksheet. If the physical layouts of the source worksheets are different, you can ask Excel to examine the row and column headings in supporting worksheets to find the data to be consolidated. This method consolidates data by consolidating those cells that have the same row and column headings, regardless of their physical location.

NOTE Many systems involve integrating or consolidating sheets of data from different divisions or task areas. There are three basic approaches to building this kind of system. First, you can use Excel's Data, Consolidate or Data, PivotTable command to consolidate data from different sheets and workbooks into one sheet. As a second approach, you can write a macro that copies updated worksheets into a workbook. The data sheets are copied into positions between the end points of 3-D formulas that total all the data sheets. In the third method, you create a consolidation sheet that contains links to sheets with specific filenames. Users then can copy new data sheets, with valid filenames, into the folders. The next time the consolidation sheet opens, it reads the new data sheets and updates its consolidation formulas. ■

Part
X

Ch
40

TIP You can analyze and consolidate database data from different sheets by using the Data, PivotTable command (see Chapters 38 and 39).

A common example of a consolidation occurs in corporate budgeting. A corporation accumulates all the division budget forecast worksheets into one budget forecast worksheet for the entire corporation. Each division updates its own worksheets. Each month, the corporation can consolidate the individual division budget worksheets into one corporate budget worksheet. Figure 40.10 shows 12 months of budget items from three sources, Budget North, Budget East, and Budget West, which are consolidated with the SUM function into the Consolidated Budget worksheet.

FIG. 40.10
Consolidated Budget contains a SUM consolidation of three divisional budgets.

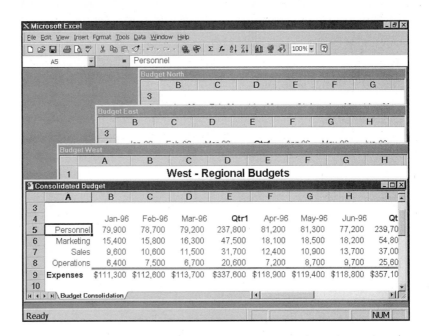

Other examples of business consolidation include sales forecasts and inventory reports. For scientific or engineering uses, consolidation can produce average or standard deviation reports. These reports can include data taken from multiple worksheets and workbooks, produced by various experiments, chromatograph analyzers, well readings, control monitors, and so on.

Consolidating with 3-D Formulas

You can create 3-D spearing formulas as shown in Figure 40.11. In our example, there are three workbooks named Sales 95, Sales 96, and Year-to-Date Sales. There are four worksheets in Sales 95 and four in Sales 96 to represent each quarter's sales. There is one worksheet in Year-to-Date Sales to represent consolidations and variances. At cell B5 in the Year-to-Date Sales, we are consolidating first and second quarter sales for the Western region for 1996. Quarter 1 sales (shown) are $58,000. Quarter 2 sales (not shown) are $35,300. The formula at B5 Year-to-Date Sales is:

```
=SUM('[Sales 96.xlsQuarter 1:Quarter 2'!$E$5)
```

FIG. 40.11

Use 3-D formulas to manually create consolidation formulas.

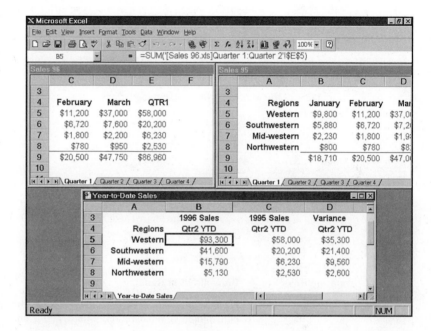

That is, the sum of the values at E5 of worksheets Quarter 1 through Quarter 2 in the Sales 96 workbook is $93,000. An easy way to enter this formula using the mouse is to select cell B5 in the Year-To-Date workbook, type **=SUM(** in the formula bar, click in the Sales 96 workbook, and select cell E5. Now press the Shift key and click the Quarter 2 tab to complete the formula and press Enter.

Understanding Consolidation

When you consolidate, Excel takes data from source areas on different worksheets and workbooks, calculates the data, and places that data onto a destination area in the consolidation worksheet. The following general steps provide an overview of consolidating multiple source areas into a destination area:

1. Select the destination area where you want the consolidation to appear.

2. Choose the Data, Consolidate command.

3. Specify the source ranges that hold the data to be consolidated in the Reference text box of the Consolidate dialog box. A consolidation can have as many as 255 source ranges. The sources do not have to be open during consolidation.

Part
X

Ch

40

4. If the physical layouts of the supporting worksheets are identical, Excel can consolidate by position. In this case, clear the Top Row and Left Column options in the Consolidate dialog box.

or

If the physical layouts of the supporting worksheets are different, Excel can use the row and column headings in the supporting worksheets to consolidate the data. In this case, select the Top Row and Left Column options in the Consolidate dialog box.

5. Select what you want the destination area to contain: fixed values that do not change or links that update when the sources change.

6. Select one of the following types of consolidation:

Sum	Average	Min
Count Nums	StdDevp	Varp
Count	Max	Product
StdDev	Var	

Consolidations are handled differently in the destination worksheet, depending on the layout of the destination area that you select, as shown in Table 40.1.

Table 40.1 Destinations and Consolidation Results

Destination Selection	Consolidation Result
One cell	Uses as much room on the destination worksheet as needed to consolidate all the categories (items) from the sources.
Row of cells	Fills the consolidation down from the selection. The destination area is only as wide as your selection.
Column of cells	Fills the consolidation to the right of the selection. The destination area is only as tall as your selection.
Range	Consolidates as many categories into the destination as will fit. You are warned if the destination area is not large enough to hold the consolidation.

Consolidating Worksheets by Physical Layout

Consolidate worksheets by their physical layout if the data items, such as budget labels, are in the same position within each source range. The actual location of the source range may be different on each source worksheet. The destination range will have the same layout as the source range. To consolidate by layout, perform the following steps:

1. Select a destination range as described previously in Table 40.1.

   Select only the data range, because text does not consolidate and because you won't want to consolidate dates used as headings.

2. Choose <u>D</u>ata, Co<u>n</u>solidate to display the Consolidate dialog box, shown in Figure 40.12.

FIG. 40.12

Consolidate open or closed sheets using the Consolidate dialog box.

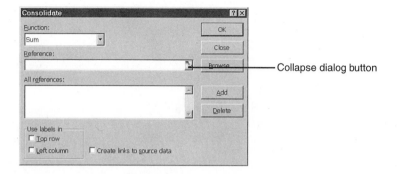

Collapse dialog button

3. Select the <u>R</u>eference text box, and select or type a source area. Use an external reference of a form like =[BudgetWest.XLS]West Budget!$B$5:$Q$8. If the source worksheet is not opened, you can type its full pathname and source area enclosed in single quotes.

   If the source worksheet is open and you use a mouse, click the Collapse Dialog button at the end of the <u>R</u>eference text box to collapse the dialog box. Click a source worksheet; or choose <u>W</u>indow to activate the source worksheet. Select the source area on the worksheet by clicking it or dragging across it and click the Expand Dialog box button to redisplay the dialog box.

   If the source worksheet is open and you use the keyboard, press Ctrl+F6; or choose <u>W</u>indow to activate the source worksheet. Select the source area by moving to it and then holding the Shift key as you press arrow keys to select, or use the F8 key to extend the selection.

   If the source worksheet is closed, choose the <u>B</u>rowse button. The standard Browse dialog box appears. Select the filename you want and choose OK. Excel enters the filename; you must type a range reference or range name.

4. Choose the <u>A</u>dd button to add the source entry to the All <u>R</u>eferences list. The Excel screen will now look similar to the screen in Figure 40.13, where the Consolidated Budget worksheet is the destination and the source area is one of the Budget division worksheets.

5. Repeat steps 3 and 4 to add all the source areas to the All <u>R</u>eferences list. If you name all your source worksheets with similar filenames and the source worksheets use the same range names, you need to edit only the <u>R</u>eference text box.

6. Select the type of consolidation you want from the <u>F</u>unction list.

7. Clear the Use Labels In <u>T</u>op Row and <u>L</u>eft Column check boxes.

   The consolidation in this procedure uses cell position within the source range, not labels in the row or column headings.

Part

X

Ch

40

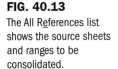

FIG. 40.13
The All References list shows the source sheets and ranges to be consolidated.

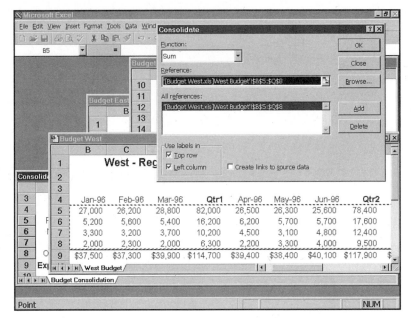

8. Select the Create Links to Source Data check box if you want the destination range to be linked to the source range.

   Linking the source ranges to the destination ranges makes the consolidation an outline. Consolidation outlines are described at the end of this chapter.

9. Choose OK.

The finished consolidation is shown in Figure 40.14.

N O T E Do not include date headings in a consolidation by position. Excel treats the serial date number in a cell as a number to be consolidated. The serial date number throws off the consolidation of numeric data. ▪

Be aware of how much space the consolidation will take if you select one cell as the destination area. One cell can use an unlimited destination area, which means that as many rows and columns are used for the consolidation as necessary. The consolidation may cover cells containing information you need.

Text and formulas within the source area are not brought into the destination area. Only values are brought in and formatted. If you are consolidating on a blank worksheet, copy text from divisional worksheets for use as headings.

You can reduce problems caused in moving or rearranging source areas. Use the Insert, Name, Define command (or the Name box in the formula bar) to name the source range on each source worksheet with the same range name. Edit the source areas in the Reference text box so that it references range names rather than cell references.

FIG. 40.14

The consolidation sheet will contain the totals derived from the source sheet.

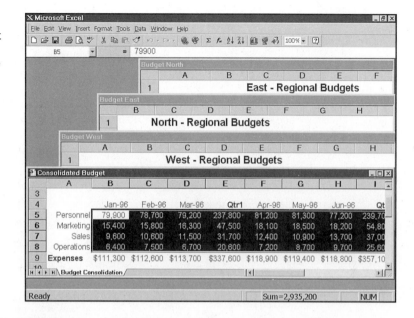

Consolidating Worksheets by Row and Column Headings

You usually don't want to consolidate worksheets by position. Doing so means that each division's worksheet must have exactly the same line items and column headings in the same order. The various divisions, for example, may have separate budget items or different sales territories selling different products. When you use the following method, source worksheets can contain different items and the headings can be ordered differently, yet the consolidation still works.

When source worksheets have data in different locations or when source worksheets contain different categories to be consolidated, use the names in row or column headings to consolidate. With this method, Excel consolidates data according to the row and column headings of a piece of data and not by the data's cell location. This method is the most flexible way to consolidate. The actual location of the data may be different on each source area.

To consolidate by headings, perform the following steps:

1. Select a destination area. If you want headings in a specific order, include the row or column headings that you want to use as consolidation categories. The headings must be spelled the same as in the source worksheets. If you do not enter headings, Excel will create them for you.

2. Choose <u>D</u>ata, Co<u>n</u>solidate.

3. Select the <u>R</u>eference text box, and then select or type a source range. Include row and column headings in the source range. You can select the source range from an open worksheet. If the source worksheet is on disk, you can type its full pathname and source range enclosed in single quotes. Use the form ='[Budget East]East Budget'!$A$4:$R$8.

If the source worksheet is open and you are using a mouse, click the Collapse Dialog button at the end of the Reference text box to collapse the dialog box. Click a source worksheet; or choose Window to activate the source worksheet. Select the source area on the worksheet by clicking it or dragging across it and click the expand dialog box button to redisplay the dialog box.

If the source worksheet is open and you are using the keyboard, press Ctrl+F6; or choose Window to activate the source worksheet. Select the source area by moving to it and then holding the Shift key as you press arrow keys to select, or use the F8 key to extend the selection.

If the source worksheet is closed, choose the Browse button. The standard File Open dialog box appears. You then can select the filename you want and choose OK. Excel enters the filename; you must type a range reference or range name.

4. Choose the Add button to add the source entry to the All References list.

5. Repeat steps 3 and 4 to add all the source areas to the All References list.

6. Select the type of consolidation that you want from the Function list.

7. Select the headings in the source areas by which you want to consolidate. Select one or both of the following: the Use Labels In Top Row and the Left Column check boxes.

8. Select the Create Links to Source Data check box if you want the destination area to be linked to the source areas. This step makes the consolidation an outline. (Consolidation outlines are described at the end of this chapter.)

9. Choose OK.

When you use headings to consolidate, you can specify which categories to consolidate and the order in which you want categories placed in the destination area. Enter the headings in the top row or left column of the destination area. Then include those headings in the selection you make before you start consolidation (step 1 in the preceding instructions).

Figure 40.15 shows a destination area with headings down the left column in an order different from the headings in the source areas. Notice that after consolidation, Excel has arranged the consolidated data in the correct rows by headings (see Figure 40.16). Notice that the Fun category from Budget East is not included in the consolidation because it was not included in the categories listed in the Consolidated Budget workbook.

Reduce problems caused by moving or rearranging source areas by editing the source areas in the Reference text box to use range names instead of cell references.

Deleting or Editing Links

You can add new source ranges to the All References list by opening the Consolidate dialog box, selecting the Reference text box, and then selecting the source range on a worksheet. Choose the Add button to add the new range area to the All References list.

Delete source ranges from future consolidations by selecting the source range in the All References list and then choosing the Delete button.

FIG. 40.15
Consolidation by heading enables you to reorder the consolidation layout.

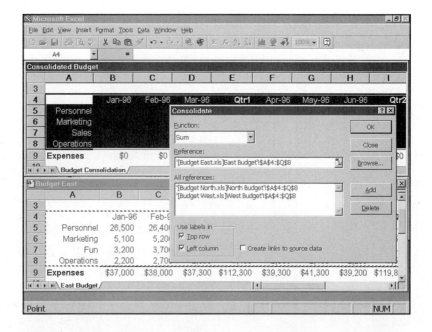

FIG. 40.16
Consolidation by labels rather than position is less error prone.

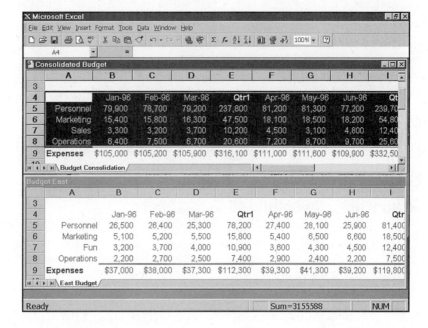

Part
X

Ch
40

Edit a source area by selecting it from the All References list, editing it in the Reference text box, and then choosing the Add button. Delete the original source area from the list, if necessary.

Linking Consolidated Worksheets

When you select the Create Links to Source Data check box, Excel consolidates and inserts detailed rows/columns that are linked to the source data in rows and columns between the consolidated results. These inserted rows and columns contain external reference formulas that link cells in the consolidation area to cells in each source area. These new rows and columns become part of a worksheet outline. The highest level of the outline shows the consolidation; the lower levels of the outline contain the links to source worksheets. Figure 40.17 shows a destination area in linked consolidation created with headings and linking selected. Figure 40.18 shows the same destination area with the outline feature turned on. The highest level of the outline is the consolidation. Lower levels contain links that feed into the consolidation.

FIG. 40.17

This destination area does not have outlining turned on.

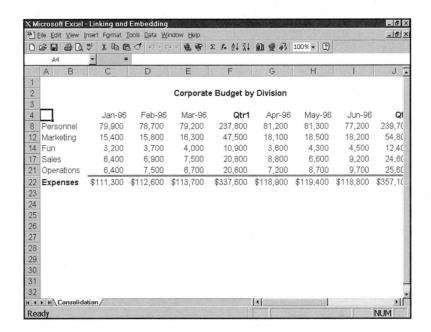

Formatting Consolidated Worksheets

You need to understand the relation of linked consolidations and outlines for two important reasons. You can give each level in an outline and the linked consolidation a different formatting style; you can expand or contract linked consolidations to show summary or detail views of the consolidated data.

By clicking the row-level buttons on the left side of the screen (shown with a plus sign, as in Figure 40.18), the outline for rows opens to reveal the links that supply the consolidated cells. Figure 40.19 shows the hidden rows revealed. The consolidation results are actually SUM() functions that total the external references in these hidden rows, as you can see in the formula bar in Figure 40.19.

FIG. 40.18
Outlining makes it easy
to show or hide detail
in a consolidation.

Row-level
buttons used
for outlines

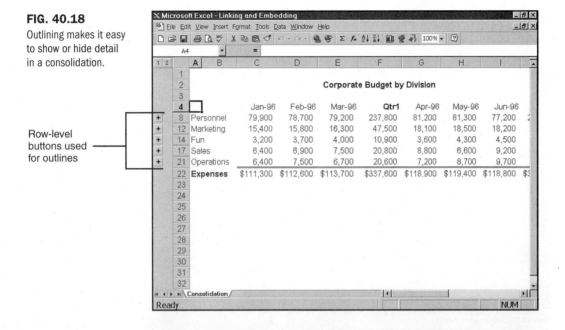

FIG. 40.19
Expanded outlines
show the detail, as well
as the link to the
source.

Part
X

Ch
40

If you double-click a cell in a detail row, its source worksheet will open and the source cell will
be selected.

To apply outline styles to an existing linked consolidation, select the destination area, choose Data, Group and Outline, Settings. Select the Automatic Styles option. Choose OK.

Consolidating Worksheets Manually

When you need to transfer only values between worksheets and you do not want these values automatically updated, use Edit, Paste Special. With Paste Special, you combine the values from one worksheet into another. Paste Special enables you to combine data by pasting values or by adding, subtracting, multiplying, or dividing values with existing cell contents. Because a link is not established, values are not updated when the supporting worksheet changes.

To consolidate data between worksheets, use Edit, Copy to copy cell contents from one worksheet. Activate the other worksheet and paste with the Edit, Paste Special command. Select the Values option to paste the values from the source worksheet. To perform a math operation with the data as it is pasted, select a math operation such as Add from the Operation option group.

▶ **See** "Redefining Styles," **p. 555**

▶ **See** "Naming Cells for Better Worksheets," **p. 592**

▶ **See** "Consolidating Data Using a Pivot Table," **p. 902**

Using the Analysis ToolPak

The Analysis ToolPak is an extensive and powerful collection of tools added to Microsoft Excel. Once added with the help of add-in macro sheets, these features are implemented using dynamic link libraries, which are fast and efficient.

Most of the commands and functions in the Analysis ToolPak are designed for specific, technical purposes. If you do not know what some mean, you probably do not need them. If you are not a highly technical user, however, do not simply skip this chapter. Some of these tools are useful for a wide variety of problems. This chapter helps you to sift through the Analysis ToolPak to find those parts you can use. Because these tools all work in a consistent way, highly technical users also learn in this chapter how to apply the tools they need.

First, you must have an idea of what the ToolPak is and how it works. The Analysis ToolPak contains two parts:

▓ Commands that are available through the Data Analysis command on the Tools menu. The ToolPak includes 17 statistical commands and 2 engineering commands.

▓ Functions that you can use from a worksheet, just like any other functions. The ToolPak includes 47 mathematics and engineering functions, 4 date and time functions, 2 information functions, and 37 financial functions.

Many statistical functions are directly built into Excel, and therefore technically are not part of the Analysis ToolPak. See Chapter 25, "Using Functions," for more information on built-in functions.

Using Data Analysis Tools Commands

Most of the Data Analysis Tools commands perform sophisticated statistical analyses on input data. These tools are for the statistician, researcher, scientist, or engineer. Hidden among these tools, however, are several tools that you can readily apply in a wide variety of situations. This section covers three common tasks you can accomplish by using the Data Analysis Tools:

▓ Creating realistic sample data

▓ Evaluating performance

▓ Smoothing time-series data

TROUBLESHOOTING

The functions listed in this chapter are not available in Excel. Make sure you have added the Analysis ToolPak add-in. These functions are not available until you use Excel's Add-In feature to add the ToolPak. How to add an add-in is described in Chapter 35, "Taking Advantage of Excel's Add-ins."

The Analysis ToolPak does not appear as one of the Excel add-ins. If you click Tools, Add-Ins to display the Add-Ins dialog box and the Analysis ToolPak is not listed, it hasn't been installed. You can re-run the Office 97 or Microsoft Excel Setup program and in Excel use the Change option to install the Analysis ToolPak. After you have installed it, use the procedures described in Chapter 24, "Working with Formulas," to add the Analysis ToolPak to Excel.

After installing the Analysis ToolPaks–VBA, there weren't any additional functions listed. The Analysis ToolPaks–VBA add-in makes the ToolPak functions available for use in the Visual Basic for Applications programming language. These functions will not be visible to worksheet users.

Creating Realistic Sample Data

Random numbers have many uses. A common use is to create realistic sample data while a model is under development. Suppose that you want to create a model to analyze Dirt Cheap's orders. You have one chart that is a histogram of the number of orders per day. Eventually, you will have actual data to put into the model, but for now you want to create a prototype chart to show your managers how the model results appear. A histogram is a table that reflects how data is distributed. A histogram is comprised of "bins," each containing a number of items that satisfy a certain requirement. The requirements usually entail a specific numeric range or a range of dates, but bins also can be used for text items. In the example, each bin holds the number of orders for that day.

You know that your company sales force makes approximately 200 calls per day, and that about 10 percent of the people who are called purchase your product, so the company averages 20 orders per day. You could just create a sample data series with average data figures for each day, but that histogram forms a single spike. You know that this pattern doesn't reflect actual daily sales. On most days, Dirt Cheap gets between 10 and 30 orders. You can use the Analysis ToolPak to create a series of random numbers between 10 and 30 to make the sample histogram appear more realistic.

To create a uniform random series, take these steps:

1. Find a location on the worksheet where you can enter the set of random numbers in a range. Note the top-left corner as well as the number of rows and columns needed.

2. Choose Tools, Data Analysis. The Data Analysis dialog box appears, as shown in Figure 41.1.

FIG. 41.1
Select a tool from the Data Analysis dialog box.

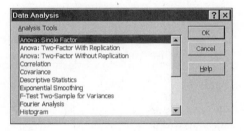

N O T E If the Data Analysis option is not available, choose Tools, Add-Ins, select the Analysis ToolPak check box, and click OK. ■

3. Select Random Number Generation from the list. Choose OK.

4. Select Uniform from the Distribution drop-down list. The Random Number Generation dialog box appears, as shown in Figure 41.2.

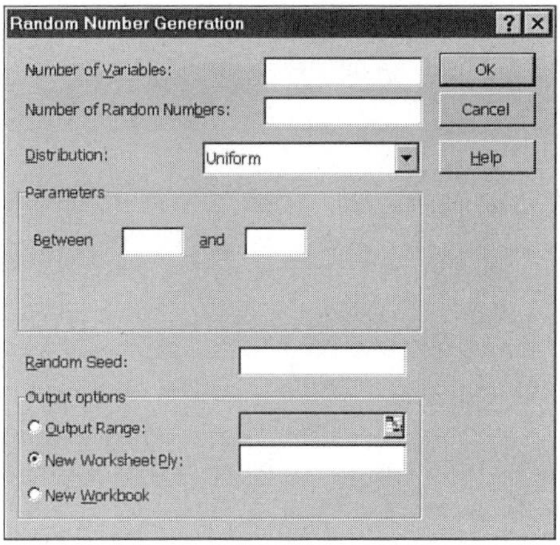

FIG. 41.2

Use settings in the Random Number Generation dialog box to specify the type of random numbers to generate.

5. Type **1** in the Number of Variables box. This is the number of columns into which you want random numbers placed.

6. Type **180** in the Number of Random Numbers box. This is the number of rows of random numbers you want to simulate six months of daily orders.

7. Type **10** and **30** for the upper- and lower-limit values in the Between box and the And box, respectively. This shows you expect between 10 and 30 orders each day.

8. Type a number in the Random Seed box if you want to create the same series of random numbers more than once. The seed can be used again to duplicate this series. Otherwise, leave the box blank.

9. Select the Output Range option and type a reference to the top-left cell of the range where you want the random numbers in the Output Range box. (You specified the number of columns and rows in steps 5 and 6.)

10. Choose OK. If data already exists in the output range, Excel asks whether you are sure you want it replaced.

Excel generates random numbers and fills the column with them. From this column, you can create a histogram that graphically shows the distribution of these numbers. The next section, "Creating Histograms and Frequency Distributions," describes how to create frequency tables and the chart shown in Figure 41.3.

The Random Number Generator can create other kinds of random numbers that may be closer to your needs. One potentially useful choice is the Normal distribution. The Normal distribution creates what is commonly known as a *bell curve*. For the Normal distribution, you specify the desired average along with a standard deviation. Most of the data falls within the standard deviation on either side of the average. The Normal distribution works well for data such as test scores or performance rankings.

For Dirt Cheap's orders, however, there is an even better choice. In this sample situation, 200 customers each day choose to order or not to order, and on average 10 percent choose to order. This situation is similar to that of tossing a coin—but it is a *loaded* coin. The Binomial distribution exactly models this situation. For the Binomial distribution, you specify how many coin tosses you want for each sample, and what percentage of them on average should be heads.

FIG. 41.3

A histogram with uniformly distributed random numbers.

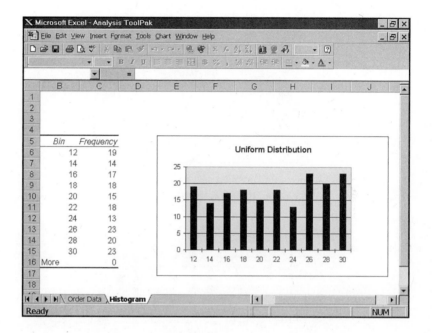

To create 180 random numbers using the Binomial distribution, follow these steps:

1. Choose Tools, Data Analysis.

2. Select Random Number Generation from the list and choose OK.

3. Select Binomial from the Distribution drop-down list. Select the distribution type before entering values for any parameters, or you may lose the parameter values. Figure 41.4 shows the Random Number Generation dialog box with the parameters for the Binomial distribution.

4. Type **1** in the Number of Variables box.

5. Type **180** in the Number of Random Numbers box.

6. Type **10%** for the p Value and **200** in the Number of Trials box. This shows that 10 percent of 200 calls result in orders.

7. Select the Output Range option and type a reference to the top-left cell of the range where you want the random numbers in the Output Range box.

8. Choose OK. Excel generates random numbers and enters them in the sheet.

When you create a histogram of these numbers, the numeric distribution is very realistic, as you can see in Figure 41.5. This chart gives management a good sense of what the final charts look like. (Creation of a histogram chart and frequency distribution table is described in the following section.)

Part

X

Ch

41

FIG. 41.4

The parameters for the Random Number Generation dialog box vary with each Distribution type.

Random Number Generation

Number of Variables: 1

Number of Random Numbers: 180

Distribution: Binomial

Parameters

p Value = 10%

Number of Trials = 200

Random Seed:

Output options
- Output Range: $C$4
- New Worksheet Ply:
- New Workbook

OK   Cancel   Help

FIG. 41.5

A histogram of random numbers created with a Binomial distribution.

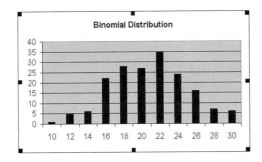

The histogram in Excel does essentially the same thing as the Data Distribution command in 1-2-3.

Creating Histograms and Frequency Distributions

Just about any performance measure compares one item with others. It is often necessary to see how people or widgets or orders per day fit into performance bands. One of the tools in Excel's Analysis ToolPak—the histogram—provides this capability. Here, a *histogram* is a table where values in a data set are counted into bins. A histogram sometimes is called a *frequency distribution*. You use histograms to get a picture of the spread of data, whether the number of orders per day or the number of students who fall into grade categories. Figure 41.6 shows a worksheet that contains random orders per day.

To categorize the orders into bins or to find out how many days had x orders placed, follow these steps:

1. Create a set of numbers to use as bins. These numbers do not have to be a regular series, but they do need to be sorted in ascending order. In Figure 41.6, the numbers defining the bins are in E4 through E14.

FIG. 41.6

Random orders per day ready to be grouped with a histogram. The bins are the numbers under the Rate heading.

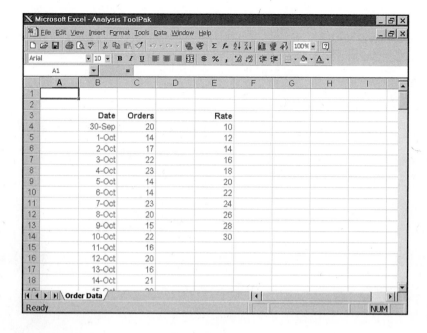

2. Choose Tools, Data Analysis.

3. Select Histogram from the list, and choose OK.

4. Type the reference $C$4:$C$183 in the Input Range box; or select the box, and in the sheet drag across the range C4:C183.

5. Type the reference $E$4:$E$14 in the Bin Range box; or select the box, and in the sheet drag across the range E4:E14.

6. Select the Output Range option and type a reference to the top-left cell of the range where you want the output in the Output Range box; or select the box, and in the sheet click the top-left cell of the range.

Figure 41.7 shows the Histogram dialog box after the cell references have been entered.

FIG. 41.7

Use the Histogram dialog box to specify how the data is analyzed.

Part
X

Ch
41

The resulting report fills down and right, so be certain that you reference an area where there is sufficient room. The Histogram command provides titles in the first row, and copies the bin values to the first column.

7. Leave the other dialog box items blank, and choose OK.

The report is generated, as shown in Figure 41.8.

FIG. 41.8

The completed histogram report shows the distribution of data in each category.

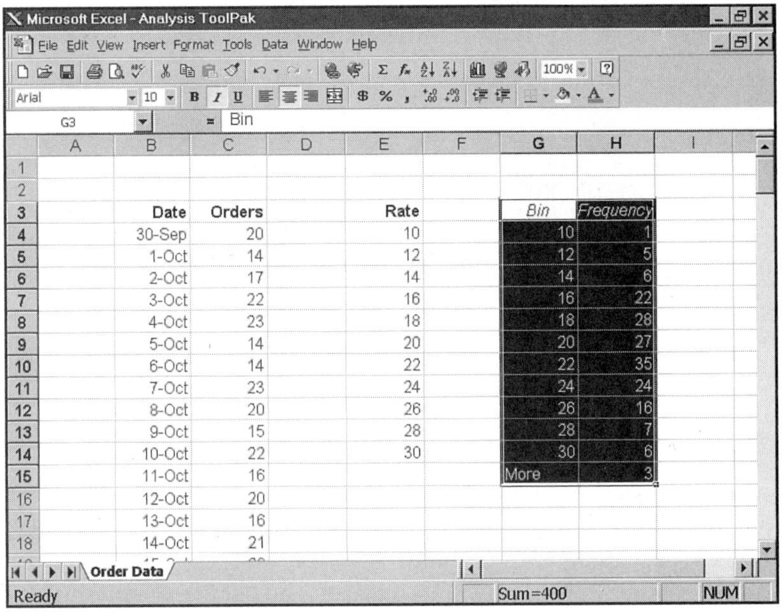

> **TIP** Let Excel create a range of evenly spaced bins by not selecting a bin range in the Bin Range box.

The check boxes in the Histogram dialog box add powerful capabilities to the Histogram command. Selecting the Pareto check box creates an extra copy of the report; that copy is sorted by the number of items each bin contains, from greatest to smallest. Selecting the Cumulative Percentage check box puts into the output report an additional column that shows the cumulative percentage of the total for each bin; if a chart is requested, the percentages are used for the chart (refer to Figure 41.7). If the Chart Output check box is selected, Excel creates a new chart based on the report results.

> **N O T E** The Analysis ToolPak add-in must be loaded for add-in functions, such as FREQUENCY(), RANK( ), and PERCENTRANK( ), to work.

The Histogram command is convenient because it walks you through the steps of creating a histogram. The values in the Frequency column of the report, however, are frozen values, not linked formulas. With a little work, you can use one of Excel's built-in statistical functions to create a hot-linked histogram that actually changes when the input data changes.

To create a histogram table with linked formulas, follow these steps:

1. Select from cell C3 to the bottom of the data. The formula is much easier to create if the input and bin ranges are named.

2. Choose Insert, Name, Create.

3. Verify that Top Row is checked and choose OK.

4. Select the range E3:E14 and choose Insert, Name, Create again. Select Top Row and choose OK. This step assigns the name at the top of each column to the cells below.

5. Select cells F4:F15. This range is where the function for the histogram is placed. This is between the Rate column and the Bin column from the previous example.

6. Choose Insert, Function.

7. Select Statistical Function Category.

8. Select FREQUENCY from the Function Name list, as shown in Figure 41.9.

FIG. 41.9

FREQUENCY specifies that you want to add the proper formula to the selected cells.

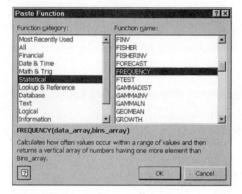

9. Choose the OK button. FREQUENCY( ) appears in the formula bar, with the data_array parameter highlighted and ready to be edited.

10. Enter **Orders**, the name of the input range, for the data_array parameter. Click the bins_array parameter to select it, and then enter **Rate**, the name of the bin's range.

11. Press Shift+Ctrl+Enter to enter the function as an array. See Chapter 24 for more information about array formulas.

TIP Press F3 to show a list that allows you to select from defined range names rather than typing the range names.

The FREQUENCY( ) function fills the cells. These values are linked to the data, however; so if the underlying data values change, the histogram is automatically updated.

Part
X

Ch
41

N O T E   Another useful command for evaluating performance is the Rank and Percentile command. This command works much like the Histogram command, but produces a report that shows both ordinal ranking and percentile ranking—the percentage of items in the sample scoring that are the same or worse than the current sample. You can use the command version in the Analysis ToolPak or, if you prefer hot-linked formulas, use the RANK( ) and PERCENTRANK( ) statistical functions. ■

Smoothing Time-Series Data

When you track data over time, "noise" in the data may make cyclical repetitions difficult to detect. You need a way to smooth out the random variations in orders to see the underlying trends more clearly. The Analysis ToolPak provides two commands to help smooth time-series data: Moving Average and Exponential Smoothing.

The Moving Average command puts the average of the previous few periods into each period. You can specify how many periods to include in this average. Exponential Smoothing averages the smoothed value for the previous period and the actual data for the previous data point. This feature automatically includes all previous periods in the average. You can specify how greatly to weight the current period.

Figure 41.10 shows a worksheet with the number of rentals per month over a few years. You can see that there is some cyclical pattern, but it's difficult to exactly tell its shape. It may be easier to see the pattern after applying the Moving Average and Exponential Smoothing commands.

FIG. 41.10

The rate of rentals over time needs to be smoothed to see whether it is periodic.

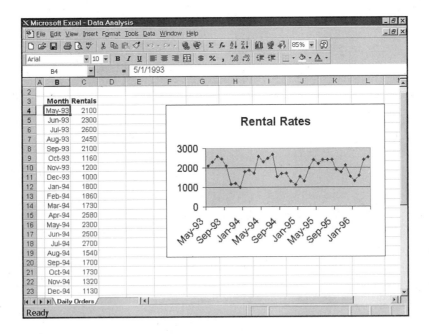

To smooth the line with a moving average, follow these steps:

1. Select the ordered data to smooth. In Figure 41.10 this is the data in column C.

2. Choose Tools, Data Analysis, select Moving Average, and then select OK. The Moving Average dialog box appears (see Figure 41.11).

FIG. 41.11

The Moving Average dialog box enables you to smooth data by averaging changes over a specified interval.

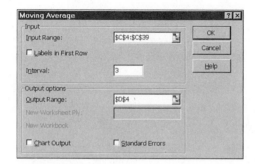

3. Edit and select boxes as necessary. Figure 41.11 shows a completed box. The following list explains some of the available options:

Input Range   Contains the data being smoothed.

Output Range   Contains the top cell where you want the smoothed data entered. The results will be one column wide and as long as the input range.

Interval   Enables you to control the number of past periods included in the average. Increasing the interval smooths the curve more but increases the inertia of the line so that the line does not reflect changes in trends as quickly. Enter **3** for the example.

Standard Errors   Creates an additional column of error statistics. Do not select this check box for the example.

Chart Output   Creates a chart. Because the example already has a chart, it is unnecessary to select this check box for the example.

4. Choose OK.

The smoothed data fills the worksheet, beginning in cell D4. The first two periods say #N/A because there were not yet three periods of data available to average. The number of #N/A reflects the number you used for the interval; until there are enough data periods to sample, the data cannot be smoothed.

Now you need to try exponential smoothing. To smooth the data using exponential smoothing, follow these steps:

1. Verify that the data to be smoothed is selected.

2. Choose Tools, Data Analysis.

3. Select Exponential Smoothing from the list, and choose OK. The Exponential Smoothing dialog box, shown in Figure 41.12, appears.

Part
X

Ch
41

FIG. 41.12

The Exponential Smoothing dialog box is used to apply weighted smoothing to a series of numbers.

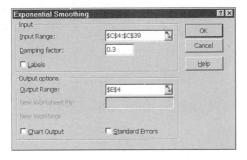

4. Select Input Range and enter the range of orders being smoothed.

5. Select Damping factor and type **0.3**. The Damping factor gives the amount of weighting to be applied to the prior average. A higher damping factor produces a smoother line.

6. Select the Output Range and click cell E4.

7. Choose OK.

The exponentially smoothed data for the example is entered, beginning in cell E4.

If you use these two lines of data (the moving average and the exponentially smoothed data) in the chart, you get something close to what is shown in Figure 41.13. With the smoothed data on the chart, you can see a more even cycle, over time. It's difficult to see in the figure.

N O T E Moving Average and Exponential Smoothing are the only Data Analysis Tools that put formulas in cells. If you change input values, the smoothed data is updated.

FIG. 41.13

The worksheet with both types of smoothing, and a chart comparing the different types of data.

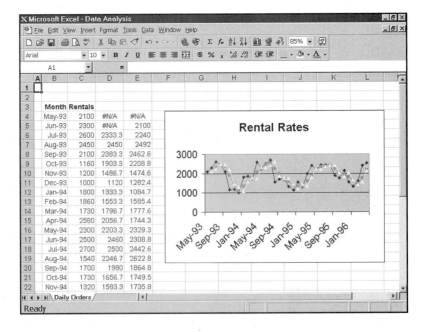

Overview of ToolPak Commands and Functions

The Analysis ToolPak contains many commands and functions.

TROUBLESHOOTING

Some of the advanced analysis functions we need are not available. Use Microsoft C++ or Microsoft FORTRAN to write Dynamic Link Libraries, DLLs, that can be used by Excel's VBA language. DLLs can give Excel the custom analysis you need.

A computer model using FORTRAN and C routines runs on our mainframe and minicomputers. Can Excel handle some of this work? Programs written in C or FORTRAN may be able to be converted to an ActiveX control (previously known as an OCX or Dynamic Link Library) making them available for use by Visual Basic for Applications programmers.

▶ **See** "Installing Add-Ins," **p. 829**

N O T E The Analysis ToolPak consists of functions available through the Insert, Function command, and commands available through the Tools, Data Analysis command. Installing the Analysis ToolPak provides access to most of these functions and commands. ▪

Part
X

Ch
41

Using Excel Databases

Designing a List or Database

This chapter helps you understand important terms used when talking about Excel lists. This chapter also explains how to choose the contents for a list, and how to lay out a list in the worksheet. Chapters 43–46 further explain the details of building and working with lists and external databases.

You are already familiar with lists of information. You probably keep lists of names and addresses, to-do lists, and shopping lists. Excel works with simple lists of information—such as a shopping list—or can work with larger, more complex lists, also known as databases. A *database* in Excel, also referred to as a list, is just a list that contains one or more columns.

With Excel's features, you can sort information in the list, find information that meets certain requirements, make copies of specific information, or even extract copies of information from larger databases located on a network or mainframe computer.

What Is a List?

The first example of a business list that most people encounter is the familiar rolling card file. You can flip through a card file quickly to find information such as a client's address, phone number, or favorite restaurant. Card files are easy to use, provided that the cards are kept in alphabetical order according to a single key word, such as the client's name. Card files can present problems, however, when you want to do more than just find a client by name. If you wanted to find all the financial analysts in San Francisco, for example, using a card file could take considerable time.

Excel's list feature handles basic functions, such as finding—quickly and easily—the kind of information you usually write on a card. Excel also handles complex jobs, such as analyzing, extracting, and sorting information in the list.

In an Excel list, the information on one file card is known as a *record*. All the information from each file card goes into one row of related information. In this row, individual items are stored in *fields*—each field is a column in the worksheet. A field contains the same kind of information for each row in the list.

Each piece of data in the record (row) must be entered in a separate cell. Kathleen Turnigan's first name, for example, goes in one cell (the First Name field), her last name in another cell (the Last Name field), the firm name in a third cell (the Firm field), and so on. To keep the information organized, each field is typed in a specific column. For example, you might put first names in column A, last names in column B, and so on. Each column is given a unique *field name*. These names, which go across the top of a list, are called the *header row*. Figure 42.1 shows how part of Kathleen's card is entered in the first record of an Excel list in row 4.

Your Excel list may have many records. When you need to find information, you need to tell Excel what field (column) to search in for matching information that you need. Using Excel's Data, Filter command, you can do this in two ways: You can use the AutoFilter feature, or you can create a Criteria Range that uses the exact field names used in the header row over your list. To find the records in a list for everyone in San Francisco, for example, you might tell Excel to search a field named City. Field names must be text or text formulas. Figure 42.2 shows how the field names and data are arranged within an Excel worksheet.

FIG. 42.1

An Excel list usually contains a header row that describes each column and data in the rows underneath.

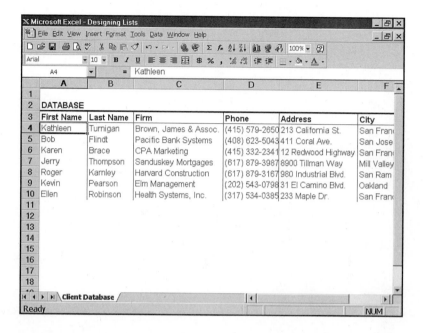

Figure 42.1 shows that the information from Kathleen's card now appears in a single record (row) of the list; each cell in the row contains a different field of data. From the field names at the top of each column, you can easily tell the data each field contains.

Your list might be simple, or it might be a multiple column list with thousands of rows of information. If you have a simple list or only need to find information using simple specifications, you can use the AutoFilter feature. To create a more robust list, you need to understand a few simple terms, as described in the following section.

Identifying the Parts of a List

To use many of the list management features, such as sorting and finding records using simple criteria, you only need to have the list itself. If you are new to working with databases, you will find that you can accomplish many database tasks using just the list and Excel's Data Form and AutoFilter features. The Data, Form command makes it very easy for you to find, add, and edit records in a list. The AutoFilter command allows even a novice user to find records in a list based on specified search criteria.

To accomplish some other tasks with lists, such as finding records using complex criteria and extracting records, you will also need criteria and extract ranges. Try working with the AutoFilter feature first, however, before you tackle the complexities of using a Criteria Range. You may find that AutoFilters are all you need for finding specific records in your data lists. Figure 42.2 shows the three parts of a fully functional list: Database, Criteria, and Extract ranges. The following list describes these ranges:

Part
XI

Ch
42

FIG. 42.2

The three parts of a fully functional list. The selected Database range contains both the field names and data.

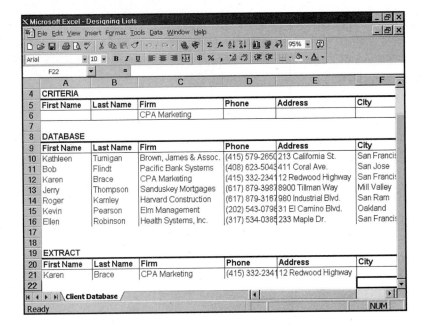

- *Criteria range*. Where you indicate what you want to find or analyze in the list by specifying criteria. This range should contain field names and an area in which you type a specification that describes the information you want.

- *Database range*. Where list information is kept. An Excel list is kept in a worksheet; related information is entered in rows. Each column of information has a unique field name.

- *Extract range*. Where Excel copies desired information from the list. When you extract information from a list, you specify a range on the sheet where the list appears where the extracted data will be copied. If you want the extracted data to appear on another sheet, you must first copy the filtered data from the sheet containing the list and then paste the filtered data into the sheet where you want the copy to go.

N O T E A list can be any table of information you select. Likewise, the Criteria range may be any range, named or selected. The range to which you copy extracted data doesn't have to be named Extract; it can be any range. The advantages and disadvantages of naming ranges with Database, Criteria, and Extract are described in following chapters. ▪

  With Microsoft Query, a database access program that comes with Excel, you can use Excel to retrieve data from databases on a hard disk, SQL server, or mainframe.

Identifying the Database Range

Before you can use a list with Excel, it must be able to find the list. Excel uses a couple of rules to determine where the list is located. Excel finds the location of the list in one of the following ways:

- If you assigned the name Database to a range in the worksheet, Excel assumes that this range is the list. The top row is assumed to be field names and the rows below the field names are data.

- If you selected a range of cells before choosing a command from the Data menu, then Excel uses the range you selected as the list, unless there is a range named Database, in which case Excel assumes this range is the list.

- If you choose a Data command that requests a range on which to operate, you can enter a range reference or a range name of a reference.

- Excel finds and selects the list you want to work on if the above rules do not apply and you selected a cell within a list. Excel examines cells above the active cell to find a row that meets the rules for text field names. All filled cells that touch and are below these field names then are selected.

The easiest way to work with Excel lists is to create lists that abide by the following rules:

- Always place a row of unique field names across the top of your list. Each column in the list must have a label at the top.

- If you have only one list in a worksheet, use the Insert, Name, Define command; or Name box on the formula bar to assign it the name Database.

- If you do not name the list with the name Database, then create each list so that it has a *moat* of empty cells above the field names and to the left, right, and below the data; or the list is bordered by the left and top edges of the worksheet with empty cells below and to the right of the list. If these conditions are met, you can use features from the Data menu by selecting a single cell within the list.

- If you cannot create or ensure that empty cells remain around each list, use the Insert, Name, Define command, or Name box in the formula bar to assign a name to each list or database range. Understand that if the user adds information to the bottom of the list, you may need to redefine the name.

After you create a list, you can add, delete, edit, sort, and find information within it. As you learn in the following chapter, choosing the Data, Form command automatically creates a database form with buttons. The form enables you to view one record at a time, and add and edit data records. Figure 42.3 shows the form created for the list in Figure 42.2. Notice that the form shows all the fields that were not immediately visible and the fields on-screen.

Part

XI

Ch

42

FIG. 42.3

Choose the Data, Form command to create a data entry and edit form for the current list or the range named Database.

With Excel you also have the ability to create two other types of data entry forms. You can create a data entry form on a worksheet and then convert that worksheet into a database entry form using the Template Wizard. The other way of creating a database entry form is to use Access database forms that you control from Excel's Data menu.

Excel's AutoFilter feature enables you to quickly find information within any list, whether or not you named the list. As Figure 42.4 shows, when you use AutoFilter, the field names in the current list change to drop-down lists. Selecting criteria from one or more of these drop-down lists in the column headers causes Excel to only display information in the list that matches your selection. The number of records matching the selected criteria is displayed in the status bar, and the drop-down arrows for columns where criteria have been selected are displayed in blue. The row headings for the filtered rows also appear in blue to indicate that you are not looking at a subset of the entire list.

FIG. 42.4

When you use AutoFilter, the field names change to pull-down lists. Selecting from a pull-down list filters the list.

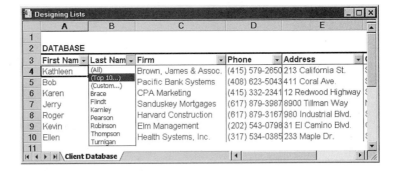

Identifying the Criteria Range

To conduct complex searches or extract a copy of information from the list, you need to specify a Criteria Range. A *Criteria Range* is where you enter the specifications that determine the records for which you are searching. The Criteria Range can be a reference, a named range, or a range named Criteria. You can use the Custom entry in an AutoFilter drop-down list to specify simple, custom criteria, in which case you don't need a Criteria Range. To do more complex searches, however, you will need to specify a Criteria Range while using the Advanced Filter command.

The Criteria Range can be any range. If you assign the name criteria to the range, Excel assumes, by default, that the criteria is contained in the range named Criteria. Figure 42.5 shows a Criteria Range selected. This range contains a simple set of criteria that is used by the Advanced Filter command to filter the list below it. Criteria are used to specify conditions to be used by the Advanced Filter command to filter information in the database so that you find or display only records (rows) in the list that match the criteria.

FIG. 42.5
When you need to filter data with more stringent specifications than AutoFilter, use a Criteria Range to specify how you want the list filtered.

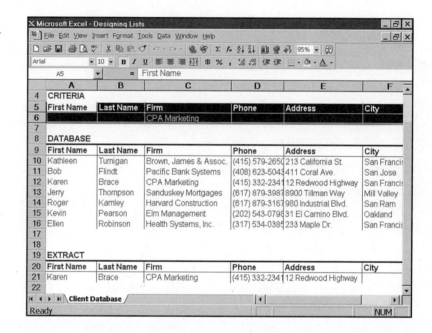

The Criteria Range must contain the field names on top and at least one blank row beneath. The Criteria Range doesn't need to include all the fields in the list; it only needs to include the field names for which you are filtering. The field names must be exactly the same as the field names in the list. In the blank row below the field names, you specify the information you want to find.

 TIP To be sure that the field names in your Criteria Range exactly duplicate the names in the list, copy and paste the names from your list to the Criteria Range.

You will learn about all the ways you can use the Criteria Range to work with data lists in the chapters that follow.

Identifying the Extract Range

The last list term you need to know is the extract range. An *extract range* is optional and is where Excel copies records that match the filter criteria you specified. You can, for example, request an extract of all addresses in a specific ZIP Code. Excel will copy the addresses into the extract range. The original list or database is left unchanged. Another excellent use of this feature is to create smaller lists or reports from the original list. The extract range doesn't have to be in the same worksheet as the original worksheet.

A *limited extract* range is a range where you define the field name row and then specify the number of rows your extract range can have. For example, if you want to limit output to 10 rows, you can select rows 21-30 as part of your extract range, with row 21 containing the field names.

An *unlimited extract* range defines only the row of field names. When you extract information from the database, Excel can fill in information from the row of field names to the bottom of your worksheet (row 16384).

Figure 42.5 shows a single row of headings (row 20 in the figure) that will be used as the row headers for an extract. The only information that will be extracted from the list or database will be rows that match the filter value in the Criteria Range (CPA Marketing in row 6) and columns that match the field names in the extract range.

▶ **See** "Using the AutoFilter," **p. 1028**
▶ **See** "Using the Advanced Filter," **p. 1034**

Choosing the Contents for a List

You can save time and trouble by planning your list before building it. As a simple checklist for what data to include in a list and how to name it, consider these points:

- *List the groups of data you want, such as Company Info and Personal Info.*

- *Break these groups of data into the smallest elements that you will ever consider using.* Address, for example, might be divided into separate fields such as Street, City, State, and ZIP. This technique makes searching the list easier and enables you to reorder data in new structures. Use only text or text formulas in field names. Do not use numeric or date values.

- *Eliminate fields you probably will never use.* For example, don't use fields that contain information you can calculate from other fields. Why waste disk space storing information that you can derive from other fields?

Choose small fields that contain the most usable part of the data. Rather than using Name as a single field containing an entire name, for example, you may want to use three fields: Prefix, First_Name, and Last_Name. This technique gives you the option of reordering the data in many different combinations. Suppose that your data looks like the following:

Prefix	First_Name	Last_Name
Ms.	Kathleen	Turnigan

From this data, you later can use Excel's text functions and concatenate cell contents to create any of the following combinations:

Ms. Turnigan

Kathleen

Ms. Kathleen Turnigan

Kathleen Turnigan

 TIP Never include postal codes in the city and state fields. Demographic and market data may be tied to the postal code. You can also lower postage costs by sorting mailings by postal code.

Stay on the lean side when including data fields. Many business information systems lie un-used because some well-meaning person wanted the list to contain too much information. The result is an expensive, time-consuming, and tedious-to-maintain database. When a list isn't maintained, it isn't used. Include only data you can use and keep up-to-date.

▶ **See** "Manipulating Text," **p. 838**

Organizing Your List

Before building a list, consider how it fits with the rest of the worksheet and how to coordinate it with other worksheets and lists for your business. Remember that you can link together Excel lists and worksheets in different files. The following list shows additional points to consider:

■ *Locate the list so that at least one empty row exists above the field names and below the last row of data.* Make sure that at least one empty column remains on the left and right side of the list, which will aid you in selecting an unnamed list. By isolating the list with blank rows and columns, you can select any cell in the list, then press Ctrl+Shift+* to select the entire list.

■ *Do not put formulas or important data to the left or right of a list.* Information on the sides of a list may be hidden when you apply a filter to the list. If important data is in these rows, you cannot see it while the filter is on.

■ *Lists may be easier to work with if you use only one list per worksheet.* Your workbook, however, can have many worksheets, each containing different lists.

■ *Draw diagrams of other lists and worksheets in your business, and notice where the data is stored twice.* Can the data be stored in separate files and recombined as needed with the aid of Excel or Microsoft Query? If you need to join lists or if the lists involve more than a few thousand records (rows), use a relational database such as Microsoft Access instead of a worksheet like Excel. Microsoft Access can store the data and then export as an Excel worksheet the filtered data you need.

■ *Be certain that nothing lies below an unlimited extract range.* Extracting to an unlimited extract range clears all cells below the extract field names.

Part
XI

Ch
42

■ *Position the list so that room is available for downward expansion.* If you use Data, Form to add records (rows) to your list, records are added without pushing down the information below the list. If not enough room (blank row) is available to insert data for the new records, the data form does not let you add a new record.

■ *If you use a list that was assigned the name Database, you need to rename the range for the list if you add data to the bottom of the database range.* If you are adding data without the data form, you can preserve the correct range if you insert cells in the middle of the list to add data or if you use the data form to add data.

Entering Data in a List or Database

Using Lists

Although Excel is primarily a spreadsheet, it has list management capabilities that can help you analyze stock market trends, track client names and addresses, monitor expense account data, and store sales figures. The combination of list functions, powerful worksheet analysis capabilities, and charting capabilities makes Excel an excellent tool for business analysis and management systems.

> **N O T E**   Excel uses the term *list* to refer to related information stored in rows and columns. If you are familiar with previous versions of Excel or with other software, you may be more familiar with the term *database*.

This chapter and chapters 44–46 describe how to build and use a list that resides in an Excel worksheet. A list is like an automated card file system that enables you to find information quickly and then edit, sort, extract, print, or analyze it. In the most simple form of an Excel list, you only need a set of information topped by a row of headings to use some of Excel's list management features.

In this chapter, you learn how to build a list and how to enter information. If you want to find and edit information in a data-entry form, you will find the discussion on the automatic data form interesting. If you want to enter information directly into a list on the worksheet, you will prefer the other methods.

Entering the Field Names

The list must have field names in a single row across the top of the list if you want to use Excel's capability of filtering out unwanted data. To use Excel's advanced filter capabilities, each field name also must be unique. The field names identify each column of data. The list must have at least one row of data directly below the field names.

Figure 43.1 shows the only mandatory part of a list: the single row of field headings (shown in row 10) and the data (shown in rows 11–19). Figure 43.2 shows a sample list and the criteria range where search conditions that filter the data are entered. The actual criteria range consists of rows 5 and 6. The formatting shown in the figure is not a requirement; it serves to enhance the list's appearance and to reduce errors. The text labels that appear in row 9 are not part of the field names. Only the row next to the data can contain the unique field names.

When you enter field names across the top of the list, keep the following points in mind:

- Field names can include up to 255 characters, but short names are easier to see in a cell.
- Only the names in the row directly above the data are used as field names. You can add explanatory names—such as the names in cells A9 and B9 of Figure 43.2—but only the field names in the row directly above the data are used by Excel.
- Names must be different from each other if you want to use Excel's data filter.
- Do not put a separate row of dashed lines or blanks under the row of field names.

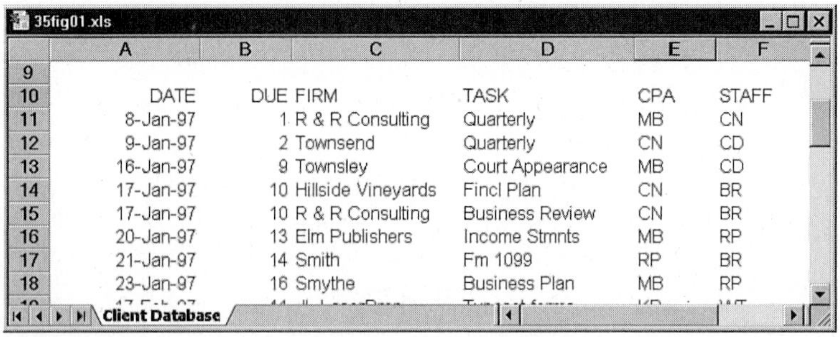

FIG. 43.1
To filter or sort data, all you need is a list with headings at the top.

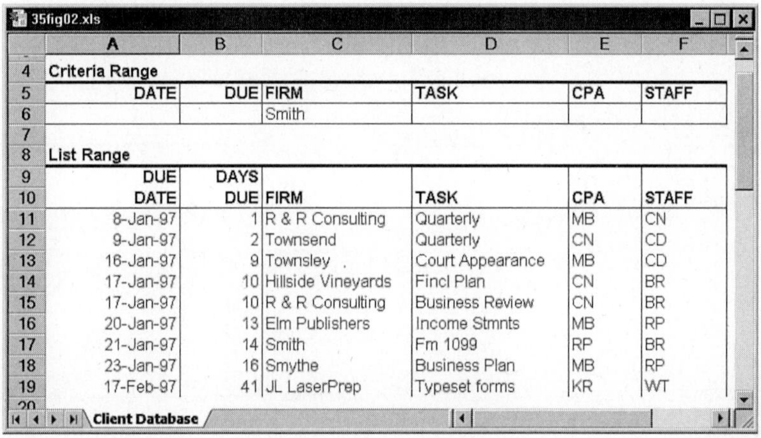

	A	B	C	D	E	F
9						
10	DATE	DUE	FIRM	TASK	CPA	STAFF
11	8-Jan-97	1	R & R Consulting	Quarterly	MB	CN
12	9-Jan-97	2	Townsend	Quarterly	CN	CD
13	16-Jan-97	9	Townsley	Court Appearance	MB	CD
14	17-Jan-97	10	Hillside Vineyards	Fincl Plan	CN	BR
15	17-Jan-97	10	R & R Consulting	Business Review	CN	BR
16	20-Jan-97	13	Elm Publishers	Income Stmnts	MB	RP
17	21-Jan-97	14	Smith	Fm 1099	RP	BR
18	23-Jan-97	16	Smythe	Business Plan	MB	RP

35fig01.xls — Client Database

FIG. 43.2
A list must have field names in the top row and one row of data. A criteria range is necessary only for advanced filters.

	A	B	C	D	E	F
4	Criteria Range					
5	DATE	DUE	FIRM	TASK	CPA	STAFF
6			Smith			
7						
8	List Range					
9		DUE	DAYS			
10	DATE	DUE	FIRM	TASK	CPA	STAFF
11	8-Jan-97	1	R & R Consulting	Quarterly	MB	CN
12	9-Jan-97	2	Townsend	Quarterly	CN	CD
13	16-Jan-97	9	Townsley	Court Appearance	MB	CD
14	17-Jan-97	10	Hillside Vineyards	Fincl Plan	CN	BR
15	17-Jan-97	10	R & R Consulting	Business Review	CN	BR
16	20-Jan-97	13	Elm Publishers	Income Stmnts	MB	RP
17	21-Jan-97	14	Smith	Fm 1099	RP	BR
18	23-Jan-97	16	Smythe	Business Plan	MB	RP
19	17-Feb-97	41	JL LaserPrep	Typeset forms	KR	WT
20						

35fig02.xls — Client Database

After you create the field names, you can start adding rows of data with standard worksheet entry techniques. Or, you can use more convenient methods of entering data, which are described later in this chapter.

Naming the List or Database Range

Excel can recognize lists and list headings without naming the database range. (Names are English text, used in place of a cell reference or range reference.) You can select a cell within a list or database and, when you choose a command from the Data menu, Excel selects the headings and data that surround the active cell.

CAUTION

If you have more than one list on a sheet but you have named one of the lists *Database*, the Data, Form command will not recognize any of the other lists, even if you select a cell within one of the other lists before you choose the Data, Form command. Use the Insert, Name, Define command to delete the name *Database* if you want to be able to use the Data, Form command with the other lists.

If you select a cell within a list range, the Advanced Filter command will automatically recognize this range as the list. The Advanced Filter command also automatically recognizes ranges with the names Criteria or Extract.

If you have many lists and decide not to use the name Database, you still may want to use names to move quickly between lists. Assign a name to one cell in each list's field names. With this capability, you can go quickly to the named cell and choose the Data command. The Data command then selects all touching cells. The following paragraph describes how to name a cell.

To name the entire list, you need to select the list range (see Figure 43.3). Notice that although two rows of titles exist in the figure, only the row of field names directly above the data is selected. Use the following procedure to name the entire list.

FIG. 43.3

The list range A10:F19 includes data and a single row of field names above the data.

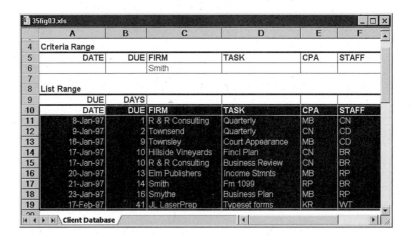

To name a single cell or the selected range that contains a list, follow these steps:

1. Select a single cell in the field names or select the field names and all the data underneath.

2. Choose Insert, Name, Define.

3. In the Name edit box, type a descriptive name. Begin with a letter and do not use spaces.

4. Choose OK.

 TIP To quickly name a range, select the range, click the pointer in the Name box in the formula bar, type the name and press Enter.

Now that you have named the range, you can select the range easily by choosing Edit, Go To, or by pressing F5, and then selecting the name from the Go To dialog box. To use the Name box to select a range, click the arrow next to the Name box and select the range name from the drop-down list.

If you want to delete the name Database, Criteria, or Extract, which were required in Excel 4 and earlier versions of Excel, choose Insert, Name, Define, select the name from the Names in Workbook list, and then choose Delete and Close.

▶ **See** "Naming Cells for Better Worksheets," **p. 592**

Entering the Data

Now that you have entered the field headings and initial data for your list, you can use many methods for entering data, including the following:

- You can use Excel's automatic data form, accessed with the Data, Form command, to enter data. This is a quick and easy method of entering data.

- You can enter data in blank rows or empty cells inserted into the list. This preserves any range name that you gave to the list.

- Use the AutoComplete and Pick from list features to speed data entry.

- Use the Access Form feature to enter data into Microsoft Access forms and have the data placed in an Excel worksheet.

- Use the Template Wizard to turn an Excel worksheet into a form. Data entered into the worksheet will be saved to a database file when you save the worksheet.

- Use Visual Basic for Applications to display a data-entry sheet or dialog box that asks for data, checks the data, and transfers the new data into a blank row of the list.

Using the Data Form

The easiest method of entering data is with Excel's automatically generated data form. You can use Excel's data form after you have created the row of field names for that list.

To enter data using an automatic form, follow these steps:

1. If you named the list range Database, skip to step 2; otherwise, select a cell within the list. A quick way to select a range is to select the name of the range from the Name box drop-down list.

2. Choose Data, Form.

    A data form similar to Figure 43.4 appears over the worksheet.

3. Choose the New button.

4. Type data in the fields. You can see, but not type, in fields containing calculated results—for example, the Due field in Figure 43.4.

    Use the Tab key to quickly move from field to field in the data form. Pressing the Enter key will open a new record, so you don't have to choose the New button after you have entered data in the last field; just press Enter.

5. To enter additional records, repeat steps 3 and 4.

6. Choose Close to return to the worksheet.

The data form displays calculated field results, but you cannot edit the contents. To hide fields in the form, hide the calculated field's column in the worksheet.

FIG. 43.4

Display an automatic data-entry and edit form by using Data, Form from within any list.

Choosing the New button places the new record you typed in the form into the list and empties the fields in the data form so you can type a new record. You can return to a record's original data by choosing the Restore button before you move to another record. After choosing the Close button, you may want to save the workbook to record the additions on disk.

The records added with the data form are placed below the last row of the list. Information below the list is not pushed down.

CAUTION

The data form does not let you add new records if there are not enough blank cells below the current list range. You receive the warning Cannot extend list or database when there is no more room to expand downward. When you create your list, choose a location in the worksheet with enough room to expand.

N O T E If you used the name *Database* to name the range of your data, then entering data through the data form automatically extends the range *Database*. ▪

You can change the data in the new record until you choose New or Close to add the record to the list. After you add the new data, use any of the filter and edit techniques described in Chapter 45, "Finding, Filtering, and Editing Lists or Databases," to make changes.

To browse through the records in the Data Form dialog box, you can use the scroll bar. To move to the next record in the list, click the down arrow in the scroll bar. To move to the previous record, click the up arrow. Clicking above or below the scroll box will move you back or forward ten records at a time. To move quickly to the last record, drag the scroll box to the bottom of the scroll bar. To move to the first record, drag the scroll box to the top of the scroll bar.

To delete a record using the data form, just display in the form the record you want to delete and then choose the <u>D</u>elete button. A dialog box asks if you are sure you want to delete the record; choose OK to confirm that you want to delete the record.

Entering Data Directly

A second method for entering data is typing the data directly into rows in the worksheet. Before you use this data-entry method, you must make room in the list for new records.

If you named the range that contains your list, insert new rows or cells between existing records (rows). Inserting new cells through the list automatically copies formats from the cells above into the new cells. For this reason, it is usually best to insert cells below the first row of data. If you insert new rows or cells below the last record of the list, those rows or cells are not included in the list range. If you insert new rows or cells directly under the field headings, the format of the heading is copied into the new row, not the format of other data cells.

> **CAUTION**
>
> Be careful when you insert empty rows in a list. If you insert blank rows and try to use the <u>D</u>ata, F<u>o</u>rm command, the records below the empty rows will not appear in the Data Form dialog box unless you have named the list Database.

If you named the list range and added new records below the last row of the existing data instead of between records, you must redefine the range name. To redefine the range, reselect the field names next to the data, including the new data, and choose <u>I</u>nsert, <u>N</u>ame, <u>D</u>efine. Retype the original name—*do not select the name from the list*—and choose OK.

N O T E To move through a list quickly from top to bottom or side to side, press Ctrl+arrow key. This action moves the active cell across filled cells until the edge of the list is reached. To select cells as you move, also hold down Shift (therefore, Shift+Ctrl+arrow key). You can move across filled cells with the mouse by holding down the Ctrl key as you double-click the side of the active cell. To select as you move, hold down Shift and Ctrl at the same time, and double-click the side of the active cell. ▪

Inserting entire rows through the list moves everything in the worksheet below that row. To move down just those cells directly below the list, select only a range that matches the list's columns before inserting rows. Insert cells in the list when you don't want to disturb areas to the right or left of the list.

In Figure 43.5, the cells of the middle two records have been selected so that they can be moved down to allow for the addition of two more records. Cells outside the list are not selected. Notice that the markers in column G indicate the cell locations outside the selected cells.

After you select cells from one side of the list to the other, press Shift+Ctrl++ (plus) or choose <u>I</u>nsert, C<u>e</u>lls (or right-click and choose <u>I</u>nsert from the shortcut menu) to display the Insert dialog box. Select the Shift Cells Down option button to insert cells and push down the list. Any data or worksheet contents below these cells are also pushed down. As the markers in column G of Figure 43.6 show, areas to the side of the inserted cells do not move.

FIG. 43.5

Select cells in the middle of a list and choose Insert, Cells to open cells for data entry while preserving a named range.

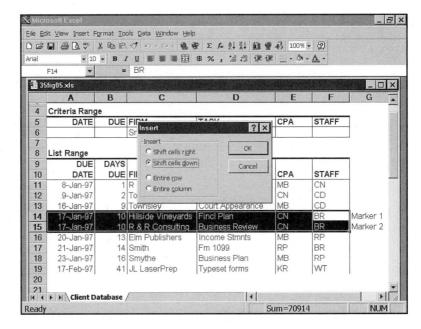

FIG. 43.6

Inserting cells through the middle of a list preserves range names, copies formats down, and does not affect cells outside the list.

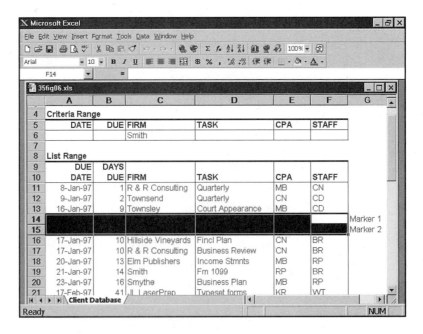

To enter data in the blank cells that you inserted, follow these steps:

1. Select the cells to receive data. If you just inserted them, they still are selected.

2. Type data in the active cell.

3. Press one of the keys shown in Table 43.1 to enter the data and move the active cell while still retaining the selected range. Return to step 2 to enter more data.

4. After all the data is entered, press an arrow key to deselect the range.

5. Format the columns of data if necessary.

6. Create and copy formulas down the appropriate columns.

While you are working within a selected data-entry range, the active cell remains in the data-entry area. The active cell wraps from one edge of the selected range to the next edge.

Table 43.1   Data-Entry Keys

Key	Action in a Selected Range
Tab	Enters data and moves right
Shift+Tab	Enters data and moves left
Enter	Enters data and moves down
Shift+Enter	Enters data and moves up

Excel has five shortcut-key combinations that can speed data-entry work. You can use these keys whenever you are working in an Excel worksheet. The key combinations are shown in Table 43.2.

Table 43.2   Shortcut Keys for Data Entry

Key Combination	Action
Ctrl+; (semicolon)	Enters the computer's current date
Ctrl+: (colon)	Enters the computer's current time
Ctrl+' (apostrophe)	Copies the formula from the cell above without adjusting cell references
Ctrl+" (quotation mark)	Copies the value from the cell above
Ctrl+arrow	Moves over filled cells to the last filled cell, or moves over blank cells to the first filled cell

Using AutoComplete and PickList to Enter Data

Excel 95 added two new features that make entering data in a list much easier. The AutoComplete feature monitors the entries you make down a column and if the first few characters of a new entry match those of an existing entry in the column, Excel will complete the entry for you. The Pick from list feature enables you to pick your entry for a cell from a list of entries. Excel builds the list from entries that you have already made in the column above the active cell.

Both the AutoComplete and Pick from list features are ideal for working with lists and databases. As you work your way across a row when you are entering a new record in a database, Excel will use the information in the column you are working in to help you complete your new entry. You will save lots of time and repetitive typing with these two new features.

To use automatic completion of entries, you must first enable this feature, using the following steps:

1. Choose <u>T</u>ools, <u>O</u>ptions and select the Edit tab.
2. Select the Enable Auto<u>C</u>omplete for Cell Values option.
3. Choose OK.

To disable autocompletion, clear the Enable AutoComplete for Cell Values option check box.

To use the AutoComplete feature, simply type the first few characters for a new entry. If an entry has been made in that column with the same characters, Excel will fill in the rest of the entry for you. You can reject the automatic entry by continuing to type over the entry. If the first few characters of more than one entry in a column match, keep typing until you have entered a character that is unique to the entry you want to make. Excel will not complete the entry until a unique character that distinguishes the entry from similar entries is made. For example, if you have already entered *Joanna Wells* and *Joan Smith* in a column, Excel will not complete a new entry based on these two entries until you have typed at least the first five characters, because the first four characters are identical.

N O T E   The AutoComplete feature only works with entries that contain some text. Number, date, and time entries are not completed because these types of entries may often start with the same characters but not be identical.

To use the PickList feature, right-click the cell you want to make the entry in and click Pick from list. A list of the entries that have already been made in that column will drop down beneath the cell (see Figure 43.7). Select an item from the list to complete the entry. Use the Pick from list command when you have many entries in a column where the first several characters are identical. In this case, picking from the list of entries will usually be faster than typing the several characters required for autocompletion of your entry.

Speeding Up Data Entry

In large lists that contain many formulas, constant recalculation can slow data entry. While Excel is calculating, you can continue to enter data; Excel stops calculation momentarily to accept an entry or command.

FIG. 43.7
With the Pick from list command, you can select an entry for a cell from a list of entries already made in that column.

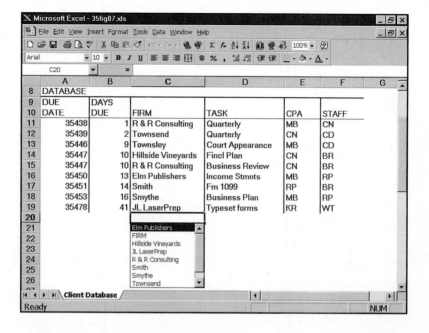

To speed data entry, turn off automatic recalculation by choosing Tools, Options, selecting the Calculation tab, and selecting the Manual option. If automatic calculation is off and you plan to read the list while it remains on disk through worksheet links or through Microsoft Query, be certain that you press F9 or choose the Recalculate Before Save check box that is in the same Calculation tab. Recalculating before the save, when the Manual option is on, ensures that the list is accurate even while saved on disk.

While Excel is in manual calculation mode, the program doesn't update the formulas as you enter data. When you make a change that affects a formula in the worksheet, a Calculate indicator appears in the status bar at the bottom of the Excel screen. When you see the Calculate indicator, do not trust formula results displayed on-screen.

To recalculate all open worksheets while staying in manual calculation mode, press F9 or choose Tools, Options, select the Calculation tab, and choose the Calc Now button. To calculate only the active document, choose Tools, Options, select the Calculation tab, and choose the Calc Sheet button.

After making list entries, you can return to automatic calculation by choosing Tools, Options, selecting the Calculation tab and the Automatic option.

TROUBLESHOOTING

The list doesn't work correctly with dates. Be certain that dates are entered in a format that Excel understands as a date. Excel can read these formats, such as m/d/yy, convert the date to a serial date

continues

continued

number, and format the cell. Without a serial date number, the column sorts as text not in date order, and list functions treat the date entry as text or as a number.

A quick way to clear a cell is selecting it and pressing the space bar. Will this cause a problem in a database or list? Blank spaces (the Spacebar character) in what appears to be a blank cell cause problems when you search or extract data. To Excel, the Spacebar character is a character, not a blank cell, which can cause problems when you sort or search. A Spacebar character, which is treated as text, also causes some list analysis and reporting functions to give what appear to be incorrect results.

Formatting Your List or Database

In Excel, a list doesn't need to look drab. You can quickly format a list to make it easier to read and more attractive. Figure 43.8 shows a list formatted with one command.

FIG. 43.8

Use Format, AutoFormat to quickly apply attractive formats to a list.

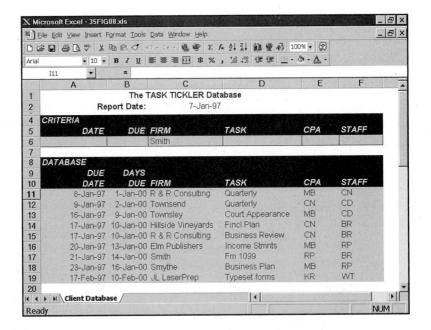

To format your list, follow these steps:

1. Select a cell within the list.

2. Choose Format, AutoFormat.

3. Select a format you like from the Table Format list. Watch the Sample area for an example of the effect.

4. For most lists, you don't want AutoFormat to affect the alignment or column width because you have formatted them manually, so choose the Options button, then deselect the Alignment and Width/Height check boxes.

5. Choose OK.

If you do not like the format you chose, immediately choose Edit, Undo; press Ctrl+Z; or click the Undo button on the Standard toolbar and try a different format.

▶ **See** "Formatting with AutoFormats," **p. 540**

Sorting Data

What You Need to Know About Sorting

Sorting organizes your data in either ascending or descending alphabetic and numeric order. Excel can sort the rows of a list or database, or the columns of a worksheet.

Excel sorts thousands of rows or columns in the time it would take you to manually sort just a few (sorting on three fields at a time in case duplicates exist in one of the sorted fields).

When you choose Data, Sort, Excel displays the Sort dialog box, shown in Figure 44.1. The items that you can select in the dialog box include the sort keys (the columns or rows that you want to determine the new order), the sort order, and whether the data has a row of labels as a header.

FIG. 44.1
Select a cell in the list or database and choose Data, Sort to open the Sort dialog box, where you can sort on one or more columns.

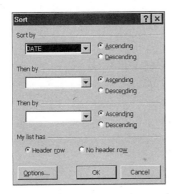

The choices in the Sort By drop-down list box determine which fields Excel uses for sorting. In a telephone book, for example, the first field sorted is Last Name and the second is First Name. If several people have the name Smith, their first names are used to put all the Smiths in sorted order. In the dialog box shown in Figure 44.2, the first sort field is the DATE column, the second field is the CPA column, and the third field is the STAFF column.

FIG. 44.2
Excel sorts up to three columns or rows at a time.

The Ascending and Descending option buttons next to each sort field tell Excel to sort in ascending (A to Z) or descending (Z to A) order. Excel sorts in ascending order from top to bottom for rows, or left to right for columns. The Descending option reverses this order (Z to A from top to bottom or from left to right). Blanks always sort to the bottom in ascending or descending sort. In addition, the program uses the following order of priority:

Numbers from smallest negative to largest positive

Text

FALSE results

TRUE results

Error values

Blanks

You can specify whether you want Excel to take case into consideration when sorting in the Sort Options dialog box. Excel can ignore the difference between upper- and lowercase letters, or it can be case sensitive. You also can adapt Excel to sort certain text lists in a non-text order—for example, Sunday, Monday, Tuesday, Wednesday, and so on (see "Sorting in a Special Order," later in this chapter). Although this order is not alphabetical, it is the order in which we expect this particular data to sort.

If you set international character settings through the Windows Control Panel, Excel sorts in the order used by the country specified.

CAUTION

Be careful when you sort lists or databases that contain formulas. When the rows in the list or database change order, formulas in the rows adjust to the new locations, which may produce references that provide incorrect results. To avoid this problem, remember that a formula in a list or database row should refer to other cells in the same row. If the formula references a cell outside the sort range, that reference should be an absolute reference or a named reference so that the reference doesn't change during sorting.

Lists of numbers and alphanumerics can sort with the numbers together or with the numbers mixed with the alphanumerics. Alphanumerics are combinations of text and numbers, such as 12b. The difference depends upon how the numbers are prepared.

If you want numbers to stay together, enter and format them as numbers in the list. Excel automatically treats alphanumerics as text.

If you want numbers to sort mixed with the alphanumeric characters, enter the numbers as text by typing an apostrophe before the number or formatting the number as text. In the following list, for example, the first three items are sorted as numbers. The other items in the list sort as text. Notice how the numbers preceded by an apostrophe sort in with the alphanumeric characters.

1	number
2	number
3	number
1	left-aligned text preceded by '
1a	alphanumeric treated as text
2	left-aligned text preceded by '
2a	alphanumeric treated as text
3	left-aligned text preceded by '
3a	alphanumeric treated as text

You also can enter numbers as text formulas, for example:

="321"

N O T E Although Excel treats numbers entered with a preceding apostrophe (') as regular numbers in some calculations, they still sort as alphabetical entries.

 T I P Excel can be case sensitive when sorting. If you want a case-sensitive sort, choose the Options button in the Sort dialog box, then select the Case Sensitive check box. In an ascending case-sensitive sort, uppercase sorts before lowercase.

Sorting by Command

Sorting is easy to use and is helpful for any list or database. In fact, you can create quick and valuable reports by sorting database-like information so that the information you need ends up in adjacent rows. Excel's Data Subtotals command also works with sorted data to create subtotals and grand totals in sorted lists.

To sort a list or database, follow these steps:

1. Choose File, Save As; or press F12. Save the worksheet with a different file name in case you scramble the data during sorting.

2. Select the cells to be sorted in one of two ways:

    To select the entire range of data when the range is surrounded on all sides by blank cells, click any cell in the data range. The sort command selects the range.

    To sort a specific portion of a range, such as a column or row, select that specific portion.

3. Choose Data, Sort.

4. If the list or database has text field names in the top row, select the My List Has Header Row option button. This ensures that the field names are not sorted in with the data. If the list or database lacks field names, select the My List Has No Header Row option button. Usually, Excel correctly selects these options.

5. Choose Sort By and select the label of the column that you want to sort first. This column is also called the *first sort key*.

   If the data lacks labels in a header row, select the worksheet column letter for the column you want to sort.

6. Select Ascending or Descending sort order.

7. Choose Then By; select the label of the column that you want to use as a second sort field.

   If the data lacks labels in a header row, select the worksheet column letter for the column you want to use.

   The second sort field is used only if duplicate data exists in the first sort field. The third sort field is used only if duplicate data exists in the first and second sort fields.

   Repeat step 6.

8. Choose Then By, and repeat the procedures in step 7 to select a third sort field.

9. Choose OK.

Part
XI

Ch
44

CAUTION

Make sure that you select the full width of a list or database before sorting. If you select manually, make sure that you get all columns, not just the columns visible on-screen. If you select a single cell and let Excel select the range, make sure that no blank columns separate the list or database. If the full width is not selected, part of the list or database is sorted and part is not, resulting in scrambled data. A database must have the full width selected before sorting, but not necessarily the full height. If you sort a list of names, phone numbers, and addresses, for example, and you select the First Name and Last Name fields in the sort area but do not include the Phone and Address fields, the First Name and Last Name cells sort into an order different from the Phone and Address cells. If you inadvertently sort a list without selecting all the columns, choose the Edit, Undo Sort command; click the Undo tool; or press Ctrl+Z immediately after completing the sort.

NOTE Use Data, Sort to be certain that all fields are selected when performing a sort. Before choosing OK in Data, Sort, click the down-arrow on the Sort By drop-down list to see which fields will be included in the sort. If some field titles are not included in the drop-down list, the entire list or database has not been selected and you will likely experience scrambled data if you continue with the sort. Instead, choose Cancel to exit Data, Sort and reselect all of your list or database fields before performing the sort. ▮

If you need to sort a list in a left-to-right order rather than a top-to-bottom order, follow the preceding procedure, but before selecting the fields to sort in the Sort dialog box, choose Options to display the Sort Options dialog box shown in Figure 44.3. Select Sort Left to Right, and choose OK.

FIG. 44.3

Choosing Options enables you to sort left to right or to require a case-sensitive sort.

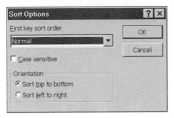

The major danger in sorting is in failing to select all parts of the database and therefore scrambling the database—having part in a different order than the rest of the database. The problem of scrambling a database occurs most frequently when the database extends past the right of the screen, and you select only the cells visible on-screen. If you sort by columns, the same problem can occur if you do not select the full column height. If you immediately recognize that the sort has created a problem, choose Edit, Undo Sort. If you cannot undo a problem, hope that you did not skip step 1. If you've scrambled your data and you do not realize it in time to use the Edit, Undo Sort command, retrieve the copy of the file you made before sorting the list.

Sorting with the Toolbar

The Standard toolbar contains two buttons that sort in ascending or descending order. These buttons show A over Z for an ascending sort and Z over A for a descending sort.

To sort a list or database with sorting buttons, follow these steps:

1. Select a cell in the column you want to use as the sort key.
2. Click the Ascending or Descending sort button.

The sort buttons sort with only one key field (the field you selected before clicking the button), sorting the list in which the cell you selected is located. They use the settings for case sensitivity, special sort order, and orientation that were last selected in the Sort Options dialog box.

Returning a Sort to the Original Order

When you want to sort a list or database but later return it to the original order, you need to add a record index to the list. A record index assigns a number to each record according to the record's position, its date and time of entry, or some other unique numeric record indicator. Figure 44.4 shows an index in column A for a database. You can insert a column or cells to make room for an index next to any list or database. (This method does not help databases that have been split by incorrect sorting.)

To index the database records so that you can return them to a previous order, follow these steps:

1. Insert a column adjacent to the list or database. (If you named the list or database range, you need to redefine the name to include the new cells.)

2. Type a number, such as **1**, in the top cell of the column. Type **2** in the second cell.

3. Select the cells containing 1 and 2 and drag the fill-handle down the length of the list. When you release the mouse button, a series of numbers fills in next to each row. These are the *index numbers*.

FIG. 44.4

A record index enables you to return the database to its previous order.

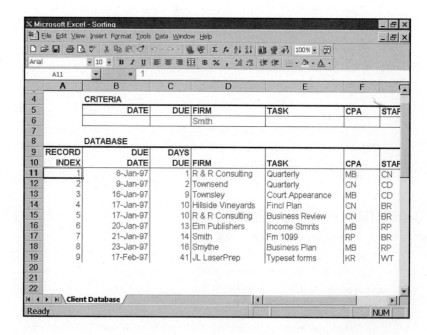

Part

XI

Ch

44

When you sort, always make sure that you include the column containing the index numbers. When you want to return to the original order, select the column of index numbers in the Sort By list and select Ascending.

Sorting in a Special Order

In some cases, you may need to sort items that should not appear in normal alphabetical order. For example, items such as the following text examples (not Excel dates) do not sort correctly if you sort in alphabetical order:

Sun, Mon, Tue, Wed, Thu, Fri, Sat

Sunday, Monday, Tuesday, Wednesday, Thursday, Friday, Saturday

Jan, Feb, Mar, Apr, May, Jun, Jul, Aug, Sep, Oct, Nov, Dec

January, February, March, April, May, June, July, August, September, October, November, December

When you are faced with these or other nonnormative sort orders, choose Options to display the Sort Options dialog box. Choose First Key Sort Order and select from the drop-down list box how you want the first key sorted, then choose OK, which works for the sort order only on the key you selected in the Sort By drop-down list box.

The First Key Sort Order drop-down list can contain user-defined lists. If you need to create a custom sort order, choose Tools, Options. The Custom Lists tab allows you to define a custom list. For more information, please refer to "Creating a Custom Fill" in Chapter 26, "Reorganzing Your Data and Worksheets."

You can return to normal sorting order on the first field by selecting Normal from the First Key Sort Order drop-down list box.

N O T E Limiting special sort orders to the first key does not prevent you from sorting in special order on any key. For example, if you want the Last Name field sorted first and the Day field sorted second using a special sort order, you first sort by the Day field only using it as the first key. After this sort, sort with the Last Name field using a normal sort order. For more information on sorting multiple times, read the upcoming section titled "Sorting on More than Three Fields." ▪

Sorting by Date and Time

Excel sorts date fields using the serial number created by dates and times entered in cells. Sorting works correctly on only dates and times entered with a date and time format that Excel recognizes or created with date or time functions. If you enter dates and times that Excel does not recognize, Excel stores them as text and sorts them in text order, unless you use a special sorting order as described in the previous section.

In many cases, you can change text dates into serial date numbers by inserting a column and entering a formula into the column that converts the adjacent date entry. Chapter 36, "Manipulating and Analyzing Data," describes several functions that may be helpful in this process. TRIM() removes unwanted blanks; DATE() converts month, day, and year to a serial number; and LEFT(), RIGHT(), MIDDLE(), and LEN() can take apart text so that pieces from within text can be used to calculate the date or time.

Sorting Account Codes, Service Codes, or Part Numbers

Sorting account codes, service codes, and part numbers can seem confusing at first because these codes can contain a prefix, body, and suffix. For example, your business may use codes, such as the following:

AE-576-12

02-88022-09

0001-6589

PRE-56983-LBL

Sorting part and service codes can be difficult because a segment of one code can overlap the character position of a different segment of another code. The result is incorrect sorting. For example, different sections of a code can have different numbers of characters for different items, such as AE-999-12 and AE-1000-12 (representing parts 999 and 1000). In this case, AE-999-12 sorts after AE-1000-12, because 1 in the 4th position of the AE-1000-12 code is less than the 9 in the 4th position of the AE-999-12 code. This sorting order is not what you want.

You can solve this problem in one of two ways. One way is to ensure that each code segment has exactly the same number of characters. You can, for example, enter the examples in the preceding paragraph as AE-0999-12 and AE-1000-12. Because you have added a zero to the middle section of the first code, both codes have the same number of characters. Another way is to have the information center (IC) download part numbers with each part code segment so that each part code segment loads into a different cell. Using the previous example, AE is in the first cell, 999 or 1000 is in the second cell, and 12 is in the third cell. You can then use Excel's capability of sorting on an unlimited number of columns to sort by all code segments or a single code segment.

Following are three methods of entering the number 0056:

What Is Typed	Numeric Format	Display
56	0000	0056
="0056"	Any format	0056
'0056	Any format	0056

The first method is a number formatted to display leading zeros, and it is sorted before text, as are normal numbers. The second and third methods change the numbers to text. The text sorts with alphabetic characters.

Sorting on More than Three Fields

With Excel's Data, Sort command, you can sort on as many fields as you want. You are not limited to three. You can re-sort on additional fields as often as necessary without losing the ordered result from previous sorts. The guideline for sorting on more than three keys is to sort the lowest levels first, working your way up to the highest level.

If you want to sort, for example, column A as the first key, column B as the second key, column C as the third key, and so on for six keys, you would need a sort like the following:

Column	A	B	C	D	E	F
Key	1	2	3	4	5	6

Although Excel has only three sort keys, you still can sort the six columns needed. Your first sort uses the lowest level columns, such as the following:

Column	A	B	C	D	E	F
Key				1	2	3

A second sort sorts the higher level columns with the following keys:

Column	A	B	C	D	E	F
Key	1	2	3			

Sorting Calculated Results

You are not confined to sorting on the entire contents of a given cell. You can include in your list or database formulas that calculate new data that represents just part of the existing data in a cell.

N O T E   When using calculated results from text entries in a database, you may want to enclose references to the data cells within the TRIM() function. The TRIM() function removes leading, trailing, and double spaces from text. ▪

In Figure 44.5, column F contains the following function:

=RIGHT(E8,5)

FIG. 44.5

You can sort calculated results as shown with this RIGHT() function that extracts a zip code from the address in column E.

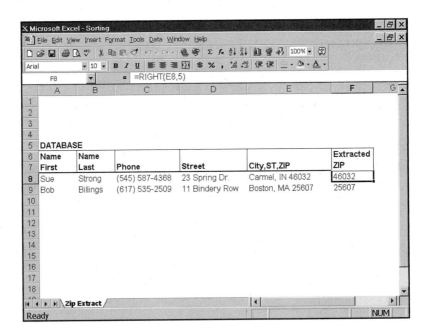

This function extracts the last five characters of cell E8, the zip. After you have the zips in column F, you can sort on column F. If you want to convert these calculated ZIPs into text permanently, copy them and paste them over the originals by using Edit, Paste Special, with the Values option selected.

▶ **See** "Manipulating Text," **p. 838**

Rearranging Worksheet, List, or Database Columns

Excel can sort columns as well as rows. This capability enables you to rearrange the columns in your list or database without extensive cutting and pasting.

Figure 44.6 shows the sample database about to be sorted into a new column order. Row 10 contains numbers indicating the desired column order. Notice that the DAYS DUE column must remain directly to the right of DUE DATE in order for the formula in DAYS DUE to calculate correctly. The formula in cell B11 of the DAYS DUE column is

=A11-$C$2

Part

XI

Ch

44

FIG. 44.6

Sort left to right on a row of numbers (row 10) to rearrange the list or database columns.

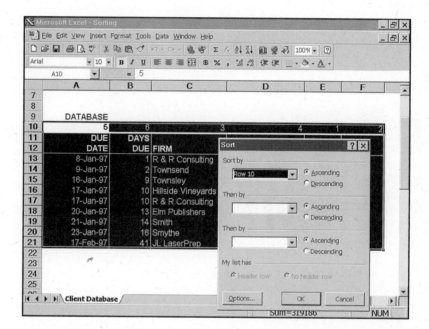

To do this sort, you must enter the numbers in row 10, then manually select the range from A10:F21. You cannot just select a single cell and let Excel do the range selection because Excel does not understand that the numbers in row 10 should be included in the sort range. To do the range selection, choose Data, Sort and the Sort dialog box appears. Choose Options and select Sort Left to Right and choose OK. The Sort dialog box looks like Figure 44.6. Notice the Sort By field is Row 10, the row containing the numeric order in which you want the columns. Choose OK in the sort dialog box.

Figure 44.7 shows the database after the columns are sorted in the order specified in row 10. If the DAYS DUE column did not stay directly to the right of the DUE DATE column, the formulas would display the #VALUE! error. This error appears because the formulas in DAYS DUE would then refer to cells containing text rather than dates.

FIG. 44.7
After sorting, the columns are in a different order.

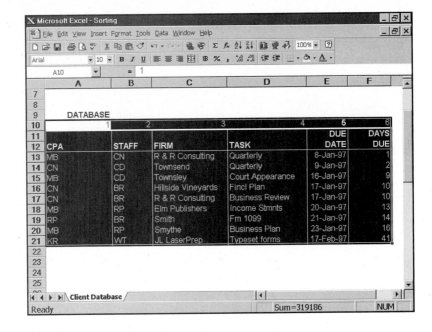

N O T E   You probably will have to adjust column widths after you reorder columns in a database. If columns are too narrow to display a number or date in the required format, the cell displays #####.

Be careful when you perform a column sort on a worksheet. After the sort, formulas refer to the same relative addresses (for example, two cells left) or absolute address that they did before the sort. When you shift worksheet columns around, the appropriate cell may no longer be where it is expected.

TROUBLESHOOTING

After sorting, the calculated data in the database shows errors or is incorrect. You can use formulas to calculate data within a list or database, but sorting can cause a problem with these formulas unless you remember two rules. First, *in most cases*, formulas that refer to other cells within the list or database should refer only to cells within the database and in the same row as the formula. Second, formulas inside the database that reference cells outside the database should use absolute or named references—for example, $G$32.

I sorted a list, but some of the records in the list did not sort. Rows or columns may have been hidden during the sort. Rows or columns that are hidden do not sort, unless they are in an outline.

Data on the left side of the records does not align with the appropriate data on the right side. The database may have split in half and been scrambled by a sort that did not include all columns. No way exists to repair the problem. Use a previously saved version.

CHAPTER 45

Finding, Filtering, and Editing Lists or Databases

Filtering a Database

Lists or databases are used most frequently to find or analyze a collection of information. Finding data in a list or database involves selecting the row or rows of information satisfying some *criteria*, a set of questions, that you ask. Frequently, you will want to see all the rows of information that satisfy the criteria. In Excel, you can also *filter* a list or database. Filtering temporarily hides all rows in the list that do not satisfy the criteria. After performing a filter, your list collapses to show only the row(s) satisfying the criteria you specified.

> **N O T E**   In Excel, the term *database* is generally the same as *list,* and the Data menu provides list
> management features that are analogous to the database management features in Excel 4
> and earlier versions.

In Excel, you can find or filter data by using three mechanisms: the data form, the AutoFilter, or the Advanced Filter. The data form is an easy way to search and edit individual records. The AutoFilter is a very easy way of collapsing a list to show only the row(s) satisfying your questions. The Advanced Filter is only slightly more complex but enables you to ask very complex questions that must satisfy multiple conditions and even calculated criteria.

Specifying Criteria

No matter which of the three methods of finding or filtering data you use, you need to learn how to specify the data you want to find. The specifications for what you want to find are called *criteria*. Criteria can be in many forms. It can be a name, such as *John*, or a comparison, such as *Amounts>500*; or it can involve a calculation, such as *=AND(B12>500,B12<1000)*.

You enter criteria in different locations, depending on whether you are using the data form, an AutoFilter, or the Advanced Filter. The concepts are all the same. Later sections of this chapter describe where to enter the information in each type of find or filter.

TROUBLESHOOTING

Data at the bottom of the list is not found or extracted. If you named the list with the name Database, Excel uses that range. However, data might have been entered below that range and the range not expanded to include the new data. Use Edit, Go To to be certain that the bottom rows are included in the database range. To display each corner of the selected range, press Ctrl+. (period). If the range does not include all records, reselect the range and use Insert, Name, Define to rename it.

Finding Simple or Exact Matches

Comparative criteria involve finding exact matches or simple ranges of greater-than or less-than comparisons. Comparative criteria do not involve mathematical calculations or logical operators such as AND or OR. You can use comparative criteria in all of Excel's data find and filter methods. If you need to use complex or calculated criteria, you must use the AutoFilter with a criteria range. (See the sections "Matching Calculated Criteria" and "Matching Compound Criteria with AND and OR" later in this chapter.)

The simplest and easiest criteria specify text for which you are searching. Figures 45.1 and 45.2 show how text criteria for the name *John* are entered in the data form (see Figure 45.1) and in the AutoFilter drop-down list (see Figure 45.2). In Figure 45.3, the same simple criteria are entered in the Criteria range before using the Advanced Filter.

FIG. 45.1

Use the data form to find and edit, using simple criteria.

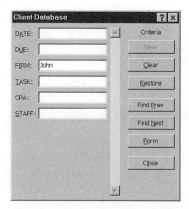

FIG. 45.2

Select what you want to see from the drop-down list in an AutoFilter.

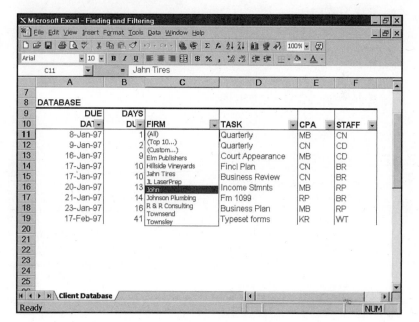

FIG. 45.3

Type a simple name or date into the Criteria range of an Advanced Filter.

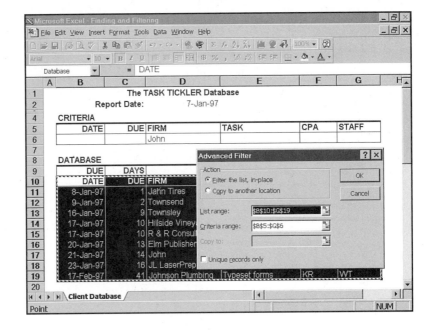

CAUTION

Do not clear cells by pressing the space bar and then pressing Enter. This procedure enters a blank character in the criteria row. Excel then attempts to find records that contain a blank character in this field.

Using Numeric Comparisons

To find an exact match for a number, enter the number in the criteria area of the data form, select the number from the drop-down AutoFilter list, or enter the number in the Advanced Filter Criteria range directly below the appropriate field name.

 You can use comparisons to find ranges of both text and numbers. For example, to find all text entries that start with T or letters after T, you can use the criteria >=T.

If you want to find numbers greater than or less than a number, enter comparison criteria, such as the criteria in Figures 45.4 and 45.5. In this case, the expression <15 tells Excel to search the DUE field (column) for records where the value is less than 15. Table 45.1 shows other comparison operators you can use in the criteria range or data form.

FIG. 45.4
Enter a simple numeric comparison in a data form.

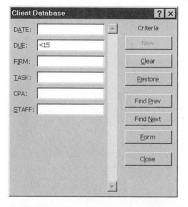

FIG. 45.5
Use the Custom AutoFilter dialog box to enter numeric comparisons.

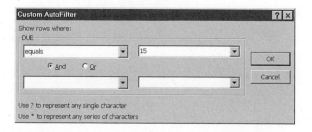

N O T E Find blank fields by using the = comparison operator followed by nothing. Find filled fields by using the not equal to operator, <>, followed by nothing.

Table 45.1   Comparison Operators

Operator	Meaning	Example	Finds
=	Equals	=200	Fields equal to 200
=	Equals	=	Fields equal to blank
>	Greater than	>200	Fields greater than 200
>=	Greater than or equal to	>=200	Fields greater than or equal to 200
<	Less than	<200	Fields less than 200
<=	Less than or equal to	<=200	Fields less than or equal to 200
<>	Not equal to	<>200	Fields not equal to 200

Finding Date and Time Matches

When you search for dates by using comparison criteria, use the comparative operators from Table 45.1. Type dates the same way you would type them in a worksheet cell. For example, to search the list shown in Figure 45.3 for dates greater than January 15, 1997, you can enter the following criteria for the DATE field in the data form, the Custom AutoFilter dialog box, or the Criteria range of an Advanced Filter:

>1/15/97

or

>15 Jan 97

You can use a date that exists in any of Excel's predefined date formats in the criteria.

TROUBLESHOOTING

The list does not work correctly with dates.   Be certain that dates have been entered with a method that produces a serial date number. Without a serial date number, list management functions treat your date entry as text or as a number.

Finding Near Matches with Wild Cards

If you are not sure of the spelling of a word in the list, or you need to find records that contain similar but not identical text, you need a couple of extra cards up your sleeve. In Excel, these cards are known as *wild cards*, and they are part of the searching game.

You can use the two text criteria wild cards: the asterisk (*) and the question mark (?). The two wild cards represent the following characters:

?   Any single character in the same position

*   Any group of characters in the same position

You can use the question mark (?) if you are uncertain how to spell the word you want to match. If a name in the FIRM field might be John or Jahn, for example, you enter the criteria as shown in the following example:

J?hn

The ? matches any single letter between the J and the h.

The asterisk (*) matches groups of characters. You can use it at any location in the text criteria: beginning, middle, or end. To locate data in a field with a name like Gallon Cans, you might use the criteria * paint. This criteria finds the following matches:

blue paint

red paint

yellow paint

If you need to find the actual symbols * or ? in a list, then type a tilde (~) before the * or ?. The tilde indicates that you are not using the * or ? as a wild card.

Matching Multiple Criteria with AND and OR Conditions

You can specify multiple criteria when you need to find records that satisfy more than one criterion. For example, in your personal contact list, you might need to find all your California clients with whom you have not talked in the last 30 days.

In the data form, you specify multiple criteria by entering criteria in more than one of the criteria edit fields. In the AutoFilter, you use a Custom AutoFilter dialog box, in which you can enter two criteria. With an Advanced Filter, you can enter many combinations of multiple criteria in the Criteria range.

Excel handles multiple criteria using two logical conditions, AND and OR. The rules for AND and OR criteria are

AND   All the multiple specifications must match for the criteria to be TRUE. Only if a record matches all the AND criteria will the record be found or displayed by the filter. (Think of the question as "This one must be true *AND* this one must be true *AND* …")

OR   One or more of the multiple specifications must match for the criteria to be TRUE. If any criteria match from the multiple criteria that are OR'd together, then the entire record will be found or displayed by the filter. (Think of the question as "Either this one must be true *OR* this one must be true *OR* …")

It is important to understand the difference between AND and OR, or you will not get the answers you want. A few general rules will help:

- If you are dealing with allowed ranges *in the same field*, for example, Amount>10 and Amount<35, you should be using an AND condition.

- If you are dealing with *separate fields where all must meet their conditions in the same record*, for example, LName=Thompson and State=CA, you should be using an AND condition.

- If you are dealing with the *same field that can meet multiple conditions*, for example, State=WA or State=NY or State=MA, you should be using an OR condition. (This one is often confused because it is different from how we speak.)

- If you are dealing with *different fields where, if any of the conditions are met, you want a match*, for example, State=WA or LName=Thompson or Due>500, use an OR condition.

When you enter multiple criteria using the data form, they are always related by the AND condition. In the Custom AutoFilter dialog box, you can relate two criteria by either the AND or the OR condition. In the criteria range used by the Advanced Filter command, you can enter many criteria and they can be related in several ways. If you enter multiple criteria in more than one row but in the same column (field), the criteria are related by the OR condition.

Criteria entered in different columns (fields) in the same row are related by the AND condition. Criteria entered in different columns (fields) and in different rows are related by the OR condition.

Choosing the Best Search Method

With three methods of finding or filtering in a list and the different capabilities of each method, it can at first seem daunting when you must decide which method to use. The following table shows some of the limits and capabilities of each method. It might help you decide when to use different methods.

Capability	Data Form	AutoFilter	Advanced Filter
Displays	Single record	List on sheet	List on sheet
Editing	Form	On sheet	On sheet
Mouse required	No	Yes	No
Single comparison	Yes	Yes	Yes
AND comparisons	Yes, simple multifield	Yes, across multiple fields	Yes, advanced
OR comparisons	No	Yes, in same field	Yes, advanced
Mixed AND and OR	No	No	Yes, advanced
Calculated/ complex comparisons	No	No	Yes
Exact match, ease of use		Easiest	
Find blanks, ease of use		Easiest	
Find nonblanks, ease of use		Easiest	
Automatic copy of found/ filtered data to another location	No	No	Yes
Limit to the number of fields (columns)	Yes, limited by form size and screen resolution	256 columns	256 columns

Using the Data Form

Excel's data form is excellent for finding and editing records that satisfy simple or multiple comparisons. You enter criteria in a blank form and request the next or previous record that matches your criteria. The data form then displays the next or previous record that matches your criteria.

Finding Data with the Data Form

To use the data form to find records, follow these steps:

1. Select a cell within the list. If the list has adjacent filled cells or has more than two rows of headings, select the range that contains the list and the row of field names next to the data.

2. Choose Data, Form to display the data form for the selected list (see Figure 45.6).

FIG. 45.6

The data form shows each of the fields in the list.

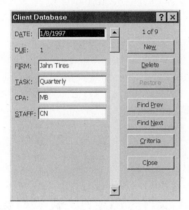

> **NOTE** If you want to see all records, ignore the next step or leave the criteria fields blank. ■

3. Select the Criteria button.

   Selecting Criteria changes the buttons on the form and clears the text box next to each field (see Figure 45.7).

4. Select the text box next to the field in which you want a criterion. Type the criterion. Click in another box or press Tab for the next box, Shift+Tab for the previous box, or the Alt+key combination for a particular field.

> **NOTE** Each key combination (Alt+A, Alt+B, and so on) is available only once. After you have used up key combinations, the field may have no key combination. For example, in Figure 45.7, CPA has no combination because C has been used for Clear, P for Find Prev, and A for the field DATE. ■

FIG. 45.7

After selecting the Criteria button, you can enter criteria.

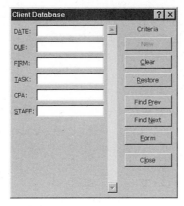

5. Choose Find Next or Find Prev to move from the current record to the next record in the indicated direction that meets the entered criteria.

Figure 45.8 shows a data form with criteria entered that will match records where the CPA has the initials MB. You also can find records that must satisfy criteria in more than one field. For example, the criteria in Figure 45.9 specify a search for records with a CPA who has initials CN, the date DUE less than 15 days, and the FIRM name starting with H.

FIG. 45.8

This simple set of criteria specifies that the CPA field must have the initials MB.

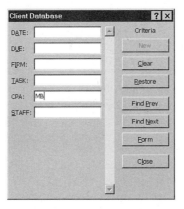

Typing multiple comparisons produces an AND condition, as described at the beginning of this chapter. All comparisons in the criteria must be true for a record to be found. For example, in Figure 45.9, the only records that will be found are those where *all three* criteria are true. You cannot do an OR condition using the data form. You can use the form to find only simple or only multiple comparisons. You cannot use the form to find calculated criteria or complex AND and OR comparisons. If you want to filter using two comparisons in the same field in an OR, use the AutoFilter. If you need an unlimited number of AND and OR conditions, use the Advanced Filter.

FIG. 45.9
These criteria specify that the CPA field must have the initials CN, the date DUE is less than 15, and the FIRM name starts with H.

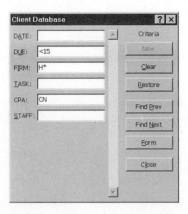

You can use the data form on only one list at a time. You can use the data form even while the list is filtered. Although you can see only filtered data on the sheet, you will be able to find, scroll through, and edit all records using a data form.

Because the data form is so easy to use, you might be able to search for data after just a few minutes of practice. If you want to see data in the worksheet while doing simple searches, use the AutoFilter. If you need to do more complex searches and see the filtered data in the worksheet, use the Advanced Filter.

CAUTION

When you enter a simple text criterion in the data form, the form assumes that the text criterion ends with the * wild card. This ensures that it finds data that might have been entered with a space at the end. However, it also means that if you type in **John**, you will also find **Johnson**.

Editing with the Data Form

The data form provides an easy way to edit individual records. If you can find the record by using the simple comparative criteria available in the data form, use the form to do your editing.

 If you click in the form's vertical scroll bar, you move to another record, but it might not be a record meeting the criteria you have specified.

To edit data using the data form, take these steps:

1. Select a cell within the database or the range containing the list.
2. Choose Data, Form.
3. Select the Criteria button.
4. Type the criteria you want and then click the Find Prev or Find Next button to find a matching record.

5. Edit the data if necessary. If you make changes and want to undo your changes before you move to the next record, click the Restore button.

6. Repeat steps 4 and 5 until you have found and edited the records you want.

7. Select Close to save the changes to the last record and return to the worksheet.

If you need to delete a record you found with the form, click the Delete button on the form. An alert message warns that you are about to delete the current record. Choose OK to complete the deletion. Keep in mind that deleted records cannot be recovered.

Using the AutoFilter

The AutoFilter gives you quick access to a great deal of list management power. By pointing and clicking, you can quickly filter out data you do not want to see or print. Unlike the data form, the AutoFilter displays the data in the worksheet. Rows of data that do not match the criteria you specify are filtered out and hidden. The entire row of data that does not match the criteria is hidden.

> **CAUTION**
>
> If you have worksheet information to the side of a list, filtering the list can hide rows within the worksheet information to the side. When rows are hidden in the list, they are hidden across the entire worksheet. To prevent a filter from hiding parts of your worksheet results, put the list in its own worksheet or be sure to keep the sides of lists clear.

When you use the AutoFilter, you can use one of three methods of finding data. You can use the drop-down lists to find exact matches. *Business Plan* is selected from the Task drop-down list in Figure 45.10. You can create simple or two-field comparisons by selecting the (Custom) subcommand from the drop-down list and using the Custom AutoFilter dialog box (see Figure 45.11). With the new Top 10 AutoFilter command in the drop-down list, you can select a specified increment of data, either by the number of items or by a percent, from the top or bottom of the list (see Figure 45.12).

Figure 45.11 shows the Custom AutoFilter dialog box in which you can enter simple or two-condition criteria. Because the AutoFilter hides rows containing records that do not match the criteria you select, row numbers appear to be skipped. The row numbers are blue in a filtered list, to indicate that you are looking at a subset of the entire list. Also, the drop-down arrows are blue in any columns in which a criterion has been selected from the AutoFilter list (see Figure 45.13).

FIG. 45.10
Click the AutoFilter's
drop-down list for exact
matches on one or
more comparisons.

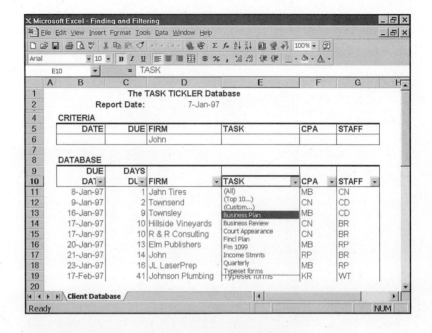

FIG. 45.11
Select (Custom) from
the AutoFilter drop-
down list to enter one
or two criteria in the
Custom AutoFilter
dialog box.

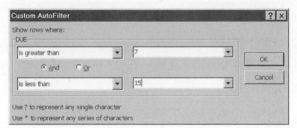

Finding Data with the AutoFilter

Before using AutoFilter, make sure that it is turned off from any previous list. Choose Data,
Filter. If there is a check mark next to the AutoFilter command, it is on for another list. Deselect AutoFilter to turn it off before using AutoFilter on another list.

To create an AutoFilter on a list, take these steps:

1. Select a cell within the list. If the list has filled cells touching it, select just the range
   containing the list.

2. Choose Data, Filter, AutoFilter.

FIG. 45.12

Filter a specified amount of data either from the top or bottom of a list using the Top 10 AutoFilter.

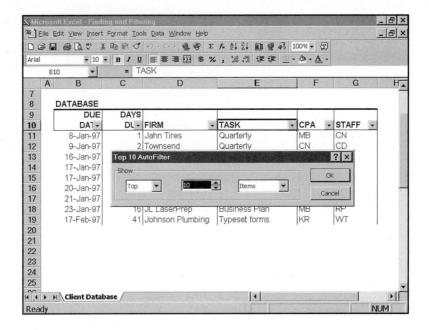

FIG. 45.13

This filter hid rows less than 15 days due. Notice the missing row numbers.

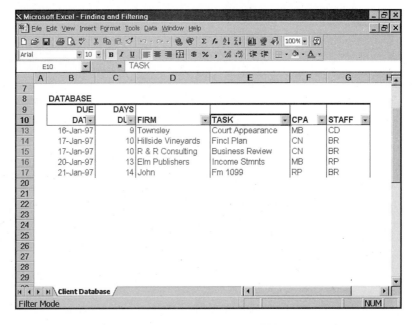

As Figure 45.10 showed earlier, the field names at the top of the list become drop-down lists.

To filter out rows that do not match your criteria, follow these steps:

1. Click the drop-down list for the column in which you want to enter criteria.

2. Select the criteria you want for that field. Select from the following options:

(All)	Allows all records in this field.
(Top 10)	Displays the Top 10 AutoFilter dialog box, enabling you to filter a specified amount of numeric data, either by percent or by number of items, from the top or bottom of a list.
(Custom)	Displays the Custom AutoFilter dialog box, enabling you to create AND or OR criteria.
Exact values	Displays only records with this exact value in this field. If you need to select more than one exact value, use the (Custom) subcommand.
(Blanks)	Displays all records with blanks in this field.
(NonBlanks)	Displays all records with nonblanks (records that contain data) in this field.

3. Complete the Custom AutoFilter dialog box if you selected the (Custom) subcommand. A description follows these steps.

4. Return to step 1 and click other drop-down lists if you want filters on other fields.

As soon as you make an AutoFilter selection from the drop-down lists, the worksheet hides rows that do not meet your criteria. You immediately see the results of your filter.

As you select criteria from each drop-down list, it is ANDed with the criteria you have selected for other fields. In other words, for a record to display, it must meet all the criteria for all the fields from which you made a selection.

N O T E Short labels used as field names can be hidden by the arrows from drop-down AutoFilter lists. To make these field names visible, select the cell and format it for left alignment by clicking the Align Left button in the Formatting toolbar or by choosing the Format, Cells command and selecting the Alignment tab. ■

If you don't like the filtered result from a selection you make, you can immediately reselect the same drop-down list and the (All) subcommand for that field.

To display all records and remove the criteria from all AutoFilters, choose Data, Filter, Show All.

To exit AutoFilter, choose Data, Filter, AutoFilter command.

When AutoFilter is on, a check mark appears in the menu next to the AutoFilter command.

TROUBLESHOOTING

Excel doesn't correctly select the list when a Data, Filter command is chosen.   Use the following checklist to troubleshoot the layout of your list:

- Check to ensure that the list is surrounded on all sides by empty cells.

- Make sure that no completely blank rows or columns exist that run through the list.

The Data commands do not work at all.   Use the following checklist of steps to find the problem:

- It may be that the list had a preexisting filter that prevented you from seeing all the data. If you are using the AutoFilter, choose Data, Filter, and choose Show All from the submenu. Then redo the filter.

- If you have named the database or criteria range, choose Edit, Go To or press F5, select the Database range name or the Criteria range, and choose OK. (You can also select the name from the Name box list in the formula bar.) Be certain that each range includes a single row of field names at the top of the selected range. The Criteria range should contain at least one row in addition to field names. The Database range should include one row of field names and all data.

- Select the rows under the field names in the criteria range, and use Edit, Clear, Contents (or press Delete) to remove any hidden space characters in the criteria range. Excel tries to find fields that match these blank characters.

- Be certain that field names in the criteria and extract ranges are spelled exactly the same as they are in the database range. Use the Edit, Copy and Edit, Paste commands to copy the names from the database range to the criteria and extract ranges.

- Check whether the data is misspelled or contains leading or internal space characters that are different from what is typed for the criteria.

Finding Near Matches or AND/OR Matches

AutoFilter is very easy to use when you want to find an exact match for one or more fields. Using its Custom AutoFilter dialog box, it is also easy to specify near matches or to match many AND and OR conditions.

To enter comparative criteria, select a comparison operator from the first drop-down list, and then type the value or select one from the list to its right. If you have a second comparison, select the AND or OR option; then select the second comparison operator and the second comparison value. Remember that if you try it and don't like the results, you can choose the (All) subcommand to remove what you entered.

The examples in Figures 45.14, 45.15, and 45.16 show some of the ways you can use the Custom AutoFilter to filter data.

FIG. 45.14
Display records where the amount Sold is greater than or equal to $85.

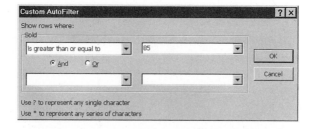

FIG. 45.15
Display inclusive dates between 18-Mar-97 and 1-Jun-97. Notice the use of And for a range.

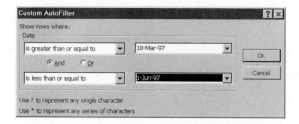

FIG. 45.16
Display records of either Heavy Cut or Lite Cut or both.

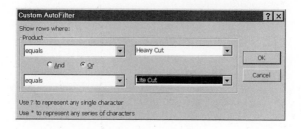

 T I P   Use AND when finding records within a range; for example, between one date AND another date. Use OR when you want one exact item OR another exact item.

Using the Top 10 AutoFilter

Excel 95 added the AutoFilter command that enables you to select a subset of records from the top or bottom of a list. You can specify the number of numeric items or percent of items you want filtered from the top or bottom of the list. For example, in a database that records sales by salesperson, you can find the records for the salespeople whose sales fall within the top 10 percent.

To use the Top 10 AutoFilter, follow these steps:

1. Click the AutoFilter drop-down arrow in the field whose values you will use to filter the list.

2. Select (Top 10...) from the list to open the Top 10 AutoFilter dialog box shown previously in Figure 45.12.

3. Select either Top or Bottom from the first drop-down list.

4. Enter or select a number specifying the value you want to use to filter the data from the spin box in the middle of the dialog box.

5. Select either Items or Percent from the drop-down list on the right.

6. Choose OK.

A subset of the list will be displayed using the criteria you specified.

TROUBLESHOOTING

There's a warning sound when I attempt to filter the Top 10, but there's no dialog box or change on-screen. The Top 10 filter works only on numeric data. If the column being filtered contains only text, you will hear a warning sound and there will be no change on-screen.

Using the Advanced Filter

Although using the Data, Filter, Advanced Filter command involves more work than using the data form or AutoFilter, the command enables you to search for data that must match calculated criteria or matches involving complex AND and OR criteria. In addition, the command prepares you to use more powerful features, such as extracting a copy of filtered data from a list. The command also uses the same concepts required for using Excel's analysis functions and data tables as described in Chapter 36, "Manipulating and Analyzing Data." It also uses similar criteria concepts to those used by Microsoft Query.

> **CAUTION**
>
> If you have worksheet information to the side of a list, filtering the list might hide rows within the worksheet information to the side. When rows are hidden, they are hidden across the entire worksheet.

Understanding the Advanced Filter

If you plan to use advanced filters, you need to create a criteria range. The criteria range specifies the conditions that filtered data must meet. The top row of the criteria range contains field names that must be spelled exactly the same as the field names above the list. You do not need to include every field name from the list in the criteria range. The criteria range also includes at least one blank row below the field names. You enter in this row criteria that the records you are searching for must match. Excel matches the criteria under a field name in the criteria range against the data under the same field name in the list.

Figure 45.17 shows a selected criteria range. (In this example, the selected cells were outlined with the Format, Cells command and the options on the Border tab.) Do not use more than one blank row in the criteria range unless you will be entering criteria in each of the rows. If you leave a line blank in your criteria range, the filter does not work, and Excel displays all data in the list. Refer to the earlier section "Matching Multiple Criteria with AND and OR Conditions" for an explanation of how criteria in the criteria range are related by the AND and OR conditions.

FIG. 45.17

The criteria range must have a blank row and field names spelled exactly like those above the list. To ensure that the field names match, use the Copy command.

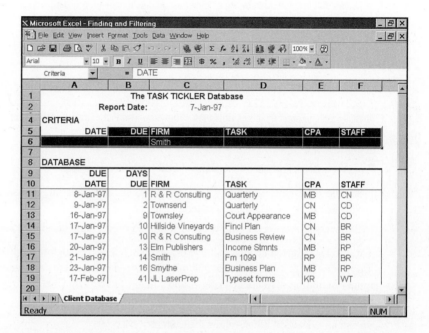

Part
XI

Ch

45

You do not need to name the criteria range, but you will find it easier to enter the criteria range—and you will make fewer errors—if you assign the criteria range a name by using the Insert, Name, Define command or the Name box in the formula bar.

N O T E If you assign the name Criteria to the criteria range, the Advanced Filter dialog box automatically picks up and enters the correct range in its Criteria Range edit box. This does not prevent you from changing the range in the Criteria Range edit box to any other range. ∎

 Excel can use text, numbers, or formula results as field names in lists and criteria ranges.

If the field names at the top of the criteria range do not match those in the list, the Data, Filter, Advanced Filter command will not work. To be certain that your criteria field names match the list field names exactly, copy them from the list with the Edit, Copy and Edit, Paste commands or with shortcut keys or toolbar buttons. You do not need to include every field name in the criteria range, and you can include the names in any order you like, as long as they exactly match the field names used in the list.

N O T E Do not include unused blank rows in the criteria range. Blank rows in the criteria range tell Excel to match against all records in the list. You can see the size of the criteria range by choosing the Data, Filter, Advanced Filter command, selecting Criteria Range, and checking the range on-screen that is surrounded by the moving dashed line. If unneeded blank rows are in the criteria range, redefine the criteria range without the blank rows.

Finding Data with the Advanced Filter

After you prepare a criteria range, you are ready to filter records in the list.

T I P AutoFilter criteria don't affect the operation of the Advanced Filter. The two methods operate independently. If the AutoFilter is on, the Advanced Filter turns it off.

To enter criteria and use the Advanced Filter, take these steps:

1. Use the Delete key, Edit, Clear command, or right-click and choose Clear Contents, to clear old criteria from the criteria range.

2. Enter new criteria in the blank row of the criteria range as shown earlier in Figure 45.17.

The criteria range can contain simple criteria, such as Smith, below the FIRM field name if you are looking for just Smith in that column. The criteria range also can contain entries that match ranges of numbers, calculate criteria, and contain TRUE/FALSE comparisons. Later sections in this chapter describe other matching conditions.

To run an Advanced Filter, follow these steps:

1. Select a cell within the list. If the list has filled cells touching it, select the range containing the list. If you select a cell within a range that has the name Database, this range is assumed to be the list you want to filter.

2. Choose Data, Filter, Advanced Filter to display the Advanced Filter dialog box shown in Figure 45.18.

3. Select the Filter the List, In-Place option so that you see only matching items in the list area of the worksheet. If you want to place the data in another area of the worksheet for printing or to work with so that you don't disturb the original data, select Copy to Another Location.

4. Select the List Range edit box and enter the range of the list if it did not automatically appear. If you named the range, you can type the name in the edit box.

T I P Enter the range references in edit boxes by first selecting the edit box and then typing the reference or dragging across the range on-screen.

5. Select the Criteria Range edit box and enter the range of the criteria if it did not automatically appear or if you want to change the displayed range.

FIG. 45.18

Use the Advanced Filter dialog box to indicate the List Range, Criteria Range, and Copy To range.

6. Select the Unique Records Only check box if you want to filter out duplicate records. This shows only the first record that meets the criteria and eliminates duplicates. If you do not select this option, all records that meet the criteria display.

7. Choose OK.

The list changes to display only those records that meet the criteria. Rows containing records that do not meet the criteria are hidden. This can hide rows on either side of the list.

If you enter a simple match in the criteria range, you might get more returned than you expected. For example, if you filter a list and have the letter L under the Product_Line header in the criteria range, Excel displays all entries for the Product_Line that start with L. The Advanced Filter acts as though there is an * (asterisk) wild card at the end of each simple match.

N O T E   When the Transition Formula Evaluation check box is selected by choosing Tools, Options and selecting the Transition tab, Excel criteria follow the database search rules used by Lotus 1-2-3. If your list does not seem to be using the rules listed here, check whether the Transition Formula Evaluation check box is cleared. ■

Using Multiple Comparisons in a Criteria Range

When using the Advanced Filter, you can enter multiple criteria on the same row in the criteria range. When you enter multiple criteria on the same criteria row, *all* the criteria must be met for a record to qualify as a match. Figure 45.19 shows a criteria range where DAYS DUE must be greater than 14 *and* CPA must be MB. Because both of these criteria are in the same row of the criteria range, a record must meet both criteria for Excel to find the record. The record in row 18 will be displayed.

To find records where one *OR* the other criterion is met, create a criteria range with more than one row. Insert an additional row in the criteria range for each criterion. Be certain that the extra row is included in the criteria range if you name the range or when you choose Data, Filter, Advanced Filter. Figure 45.20 shows a criteria range with two rows for criteria. The criteria entries shown below CPA tell Excel to find records where the CPA is MB *OR* the CPA is CN.

FIG. 45.19

All criteria on the same row must be met.

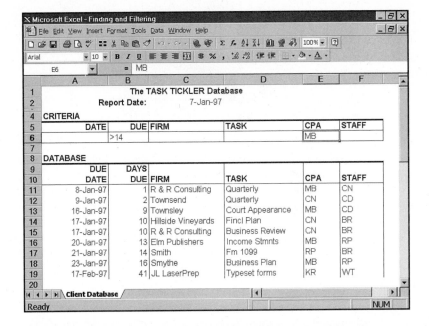

FIG. 45.20

Either one or the other criterion on separate rows can be true.

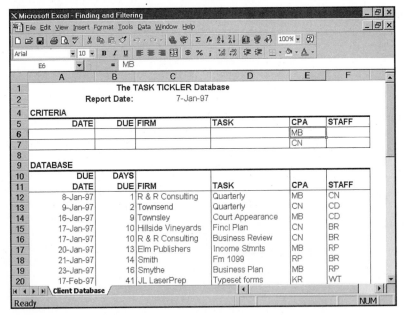

N O T E Be careful when you use two or more rows in the criteria range. A blank row tells Excel to find all records in the list. Therefore, if you leave a row blank in the criteria range, Excel filters nothing and displays all records. ▪

Figure 45.21 shows how you can combine simple criteria to ask complex questions of your list. The criteria range uses two rows so that you can find records matching one value or the other. A record must match all the criteria in one row OR the other if it is to match and be displayed. The expression following Figure 45.21 is the English equivalent of the criteria range in Figure 45.21.

FIG. 45.21

Use multiple rows with multiple criteria for complex searches.

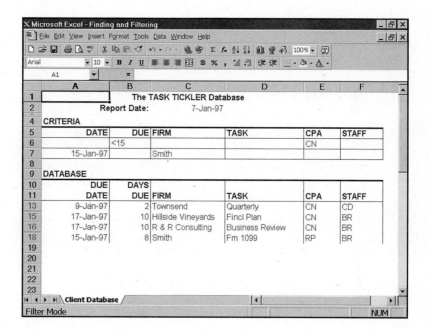

Find all records where:

> The DAYS DUE are less than 15 AND the CPA is CN.
>
> OR
>
> The DUE DATE is 15-Jan-97 AND the FIRM name is Smith.

Excel finds the records that meet these criteria in rows 13, 15, 16, and 18.

TROUBLESHOOTING

Entries in the criteria range that once worked no longer work.   Check to see whether you have changed the Transition Formula Evaluation check box found in the Transition tab of the Options dialog box. Choose Tools, Options to see this dialog box. When this check box is selected, queries use the database rules used by Lotus 1-2-3.

Calculating What You Want to Find

Using comparative criteria and ANDs and ORs through the use of additional rows in the criteria range is helpful and quick, but in some cases you need to specify more exact data. You might want to find dates between two ranges or even use formulas to calculate what you are searching for. In those cases, you need to use calculated criteria.

Matching Calculated Criteria   You can select records according to any calculation that results in a TRUE or FALSE logical value when it is tested against the contents of a record. Calculated criteria that result in TRUE are matches.

Calculated criteria are needed, for example, when you want to find records where inventory quantities are less than a calculated reorder quantity, where a range of dates is needed but some dates within the range are excluded, or where a mailing list has the ZIP code included with the City and State field.

Figure 45.22 shows an example of calculated criteria that find parts that were sold for less than 90 percent of retail price. Notice that the calculated criteria, =F9<0.9*E9, must be entered in the criteria range below a *field name that does not exist* in the list. In this example, the name Calc was inserted in the middle of the criteria range; Calc is not used as a field name in the list. You can use any text name above the calculated criteria, if it has not been used in the list as a field name.

N O T E   You must enter calculated criteria in the criteria range below names that are not used as field names in the list. Use a field name that is different from any field name in the list.

In your calculated criteria formula, use cell references that refer to a cell in the top data row of the list. Use relative reference addresses (without $ signs) for references within the list, as shown in Figure 45.22. Use absolute cell references to refer to any cell outside the list that is involved in the calculated criteria.

Calculated criteria can involve multiple fields and equations, but the result must produce a TRUE or FALSE condition. The Advanced Filter displays those records that produce a TRUE result. Some simple calculated criteria, where the first data row is row 36, are illustrated in the following table:

Criteria	Explanation
=B36=G36	Compares the values of fields in the same record. Selects the record when the value in column B equals the value in column G.
=B36<G36/2	Compares the value in B36 to one half the value in G36. Both cells are in the same record. Selects the record when the value in column B is less than half of the value in column G.
=B36–G36>10	Compares two values in the same record. Selects the record when a value in column B minus a value in column G is greater than 10.

FIG. 45.22

Use a formula to calculate criteria that can be found in no other way. (The formula for this example is visible in the formula bar, near the top of the screen.)

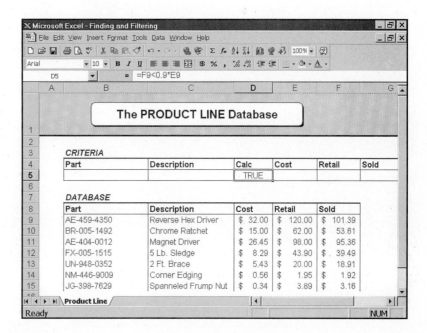

N O T E Remember that calculated criteria must compare the value found in the first row of data in the list. The filter will produce incorrect results if your calculation compares a cell that is not in the first row of data.

More complex but extremely useful calculated criteria include comparisons between values in a record with other records or with values outside the list. These types of criteria are useful when you want to compare records or use criteria calculated elsewhere in the worksheet. The following table shows some examples of these types of criteria; assume that the first data row (record) is row 36:

Criteria	Explanation
=B36–G37>10	Compares values in adjacent records. Selects the record when the value in column B of one record is more than 10 greater than the value in column G of the next record. Usually, you will want to sort the list before doing this type of comparison so that columns B and G are in an order that makes sense for the comparison.
=B36=$C$24	Compares a value in a record to a value outside the list. Selects the record when the value in column B equals the value in $C$24, where C24 is a cell outside the list. This is how you can refer to criteria calculated or entered elsewhere in the worksheet.

As you can see from the examples, calculated criteria can involve cell references that are outside the list. You must use an absolute reference or named cells and ranges to refer to any location outside the list.

TIP If you use the correct syntax when you enter a calculated criteria formula, Excel displays TRUE or FALSE in the cell after you enter the formula. TRUE or FALSE applies to the specific cells you used in the formula.

TROUBLESHOOTING

Calculated criteria do not produce an expected result. Calculated criteria must be entered in the criteria range beneath a heading that is not a field name. To use calculated criteria, create a new field heading that is *different* from any field name in the list. Replace an existing field heading in the criteria range with this new heading, or extend the criteria range to make room for the additional heading. The cell reference in the calculated criteria must be to the top data cell in the columns you are comparing. Make sure the criteria range doesn't have any extra, empty rows.

Formulas in the list that refer to values outside the list return incorrect results. Be certain that formulas referring to cells or names outside the list use absolute references or named cells.

Complex criteria using AND and OR do not work as expected. AND statements must satisfy the first condition *and* the second condition simultaneously. OR statements can satisfy *one* of the conditions *or* both conditions. Consider the following example:

=AND(A15>500,A15<750)

This formula finds records where the data in column A is between 500 and 750. Those are the only values where both conditions are true. Remember that if you are searching for values between two points, such as in a numeric or date range, use AND. If you are searching for multiple text occurrences, such as two names, use OR.

Matching Compound Criteria with AND and OR You can use Excel's AND( ), OR( ), and NOT( ) functions to create complex compound criteria. These are the AND( ), OR( ), and NOT( ) functions that are used as worksheet and macro functions. This method is useful for specifying complex criteria that cannot be handled by inserting additional rows in the criteria range. The conditions that are being matched are used as arguments within the functions. For an AND( ), OR( ), or NOT( ) function to be TRUE so that a record matches, the arguments within them must match the following conditions:

AND   All conditions (arguments) must be TRUE.

OR   One condition (argument) out of all the conditions must be TRUE.

NOT   The condition used with NOT is reversed. TRUE changes to FALSE; FALSE changes to TRUE.

Just as you can enter calculated criteria that result in a TRUE or FALSE value, you can enter AND( ), OR( ), and NOT( ) functions that evaluate to TRUE or FALSE. For example, consider the list in Figure 45.23. The following calculated criteria could be used under the dummy field name, Calc, in the criteria range. Notice that each compound criteria uses the cell reference of the first cell in the column being tested. These are all in row 11.

FIG. 45.23

The Calc field is being used as a dummy name for calculated or compound criteria.

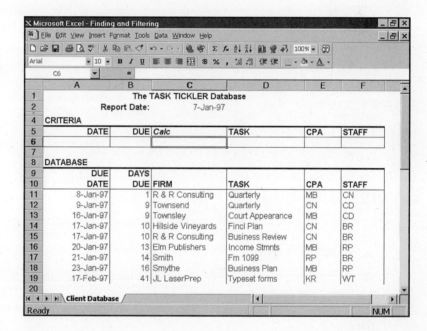

For each of the following queries stated in English syntax, the associated compound criteria formula is presented, and the resulting records that Excel finds are listed:

English statement: The CPA is CN AND the STAFF is BR.

Compound criteria: =AND(E11="CN",F11="BR")

Result: Finds the records in rows 14 and 15.

English statement:	The FIRM is Townsley OR the FIRM is Smith.
Compound criteria:	=OR(C11="Townsley",C11= "Smith")
Result:	Finds the records in rows 13 and 17.
English statement:	The FIRM is NOT Townsley AND the DAYS DUE are 9.
Compound criteria:	=AND(NOT(C11="Townsley"), B11=9)
Result:	Finds the record in row 12.

N O T E   You can make the formulas in calculated criteria much easier to read if you assign the cells in the first row of data the heading names immediately above them. In Figure 45.23, select the field names and the first row of data and choose Insert, Name, Create. Select Top Row and choose OK. Now, you can use these names instead of the cell references when you write a calculated criteria formula. For example, the first formula in the preceding examples would be written

=AND(CPA="CN",STAFF="BR")

which is much easier to enter and to read than the original formula. See "Naming Cells for Better Worksheets" in Chapter 6, "Working with Columns," to learn more about naming cells and ranges. ■

N O T E   AND( ) and OR( ) are easy to confuse. If you are searching a single field for two different text entries (for example, Smith and Jones), use the OR( ) function. An OR() function specifies that one name OR the other can be found (TRUE). An AND( ) function specifies that Smith AND Jones must be in the field at the same time—something that will not happen. ■

▶ **See** "Using Formulas to Make Decisions," **p. 839**
▶ **See** "Using Formulas to Look Up Data in Tables," **p. 844**

Viewing and Editing Filtered Lists

If you have a long or wide list, it can cover thousands of rows and more columns than fit on-screen. As you scroll down or across, the field headers at the top of the list or data in left columns scroll out of sight.

There is an easy way to prevent this. You can fix the top rows and left columns of a screen so that they do not scroll from view as you scroll any direction in the data. This enables you to see field headers at the top of a list and one or two columns of pertinent information such as names along the left side.

To freeze panes in a window so that the headers and left columns stay in sight, follow these steps:

1. Position your list on-screen so that the field headers are near the top of the screen. Any columns you want to remain in sight should be along the left edge of the screen.

2. Select the cell that is directly under the field header row and directly to the right of the columns you want to remain visible.

3. Choose Window, Freeze Panes.

The window splits into four panes. You can scroll the lower-right pane by using normal scrolling techniques. To return to normal window scrolling, choose Window, Unfreeze Panes.

To edit a filtered list, use the techniques you normally use to edit in a worksheet.

▶ **See** "Moving Cell Contents," **p. 624**

▶ **See** "Filling or Copying Cell Contents," **p. 629**

 If you have many changes to make that are the same, use the Edit, Replace command (press Ctrl+H) to search and replace through the list. If you deselect the Match Case and Find Entire Cells Only options, you can find and replace pieces within larger words, part numbers, IDs, abbreviations, formulas, and so on.

Part
XI

Ch
45

Working with Filtered Data

Editing, Sorting, Subtotaling, and Charting the Filtered Data

There are many reasons for filtering a list. You might want to examine or edit only certain information. By filtering out unwanted information, you can make a list easier to work in. After you filter information in your list, you might want to do more than just examine it. You might want to sort it, subtotal it, or create a chart from it. It is convenient and safer to work with a copy of filtered data that you have placed on a separate worksheet or workbook. Because the information in your list is probably valuable to you, you should learn how to maintain its integrity and safety.

You probably filtered a list with the purpose of doing something with it. You might need to sort, print, chart, or subtotal the list. When you work on filtered lists, you can use most Excel commands on the data displayed *after* the filter is complete.

Whether you use the AutoFilter or the Advanced Filter, you can manipulate the visible data while the filter is on. To tell if the filter is on, watch the row headings for hidden row numbers. Row numbers and the drop-down list arrows for AutoFilters in which criteria have been selected turn blue, and the status bar shows the number of records found (such as 3 of 20 records found).

Editing Filtered Data

Editing and deleting in filtered data affects only the data in which you work. While you work in Filter mode, some commands are not available to you. These commands are grayed. The editing and formatting commands that are available act as you may expect. The following table shows how these commands act while the Filter mode is on.

Command or Feature	Action
Edit, Fill	Fills visible cells. You cannot fill series of data.
Edit, Clear	Clears visible cells.
Edit, Copy	Copies visible cells.
Edit, Cut	Deletes visible cells.
Edit, Delete Row	Deletes an entire row of the filtered list.
Delete Row (Shortcut menu)	Deletes an entire row of the filtered list.
Insert Row (Shortcut menu)	Inserts an entire row through the filtered list.
Insert Paste Row (Shortcut menu)	Inserts an entire row through the filtered list and pastes in the copied data. Copy or cut a selection, select a cell in the same column as the first column in the original selection and right-click. Choose Insert Paste Row, select the Shift Cells Down option (if you are inserting a copy), and choose OK.
Format, Cells	Formats visible cells.

Sorting, Subtotaling, and Printing Filtered Data

When you sort a filtered list, only the visible records are affected. After you sort, choose Data, Subtotals to create subtotals in the filtered list. If you change the filter, the subtotals update to reflect the new set of filtered data.

When you print a worksheet, only the filtered data prints. To print the entire list, check the status bar to make sure Excel is not in Filter mode. To show all data, choose Data, Filter, Show All.

Charting Filtered Data

To chart filtered data, apply the filter to the list. Then create a chart by using any of the techniques described in Part VIII, "Using Excel Charts." If you do not want specific columns of data in a chart, hide those columns by choosing Format, Column, Hide. Then create the chart. After you change the filter, the chart updates to show the new data displayed using the new filter criteria.

If you do not want a chart to change when the criteria changes, use the Select Visible Cells button to select only the cells shown at the time of the chart's creation. Before you can do this, you need to add the Select Visible Cells button to a toolbar. Display a toolbar that you use when charting, such as the Chart toolbar. Choose View, Toolbars and then choose the Customize button. Select the Command tab and select Edit from the Categories list and drag the Select Visible Cells button onto the toolbar. Choose the Close button to close the Customize dialog box.

To create a chart that doesn't update when the filter changes, follow these steps:

1. Apply the filter to the list.
2. Select the cells you want to chart. Include field names in the selection if you want labels in the chart.
3. Click the Select Visible Cells button that was just described.
4. Draw the chart using the techniques described in Chapters 29, " Creating Charts," and 30, "Modifying Charts."

▶ **See** "Creating a Chart Using the Chart Wizard," **p. 691**
▶ **See** "Using the AutoFilter," **p. 1028**

Copying Filtered Data to a New Location

Many reasons exist for working with copies of a subset of your data. A coworker, for example, might need a filtered portion of the list. Rather than give the coworker the entire list, you can filter out the unnecessary information. You also might need to make extensive changes to the format or insert formulas, and you don't want to endanger the original list. In this case, it makes sense to use a filtered copy that contains only the data you need.

You can copy data to another worksheet in two ways. First, you can manually copy and paste, which is the method to use if you want to use a simple AutoFilter or if you have a small amount of data. Second, you can copy the data to another location by using the Advanced Filter. With

Part XI

Ch 46

this method, you can handle more complex filters. When you create a copy, you can specify that the copy contains only unique records and that all duplicates are filtered out. The original list remains intact after you extract a copy of the data that matches the criteria.

N O T E You might want to keep large lists on a disk and extract filtered portions of them using Microsoft Query. Microsoft Query comes free with Excel. Microsoft Query works with files in many formats. ■

Creating a Copy with AutoFilter

To make a copy of data, specify your criteria to filter the data by using the AutoFilter method, filter the data, and then copy and paste the filtered data to another sheet.

To copy a list using the AutoFilter, follow these steps:

1. Apply an AutoFilter to the list so that only the data you want to copy is shown. Chapter 45, "Finding, Filtering, and Editing Lists or Databases," describes how to use an AutoFilter.

2. Select the data and choose Edit, Copy (or press Ctrl+C) or click the Copy button. The Copy command copies only the data shown by the filter.

3. Activate the sheet in which you want the data.

4. Select the cell that will be the top-left corner of the new list.

5. Choose Edit, Paste (or press Ctrl+V) or click the Paste button.

Copying to the Same Sheet with an Advanced Filter

You should use the Advanced Filter method of copying data if the criteria you need to use are too complex for the AutoFilter.

To use the Advanced Filter to copy, you must use the Advanced Filter dialog box, which requires a range for the list, a range for the criteria, and a range that specifies where the copied data goes.

N O T E When you display the Advanced Filter dialog box, it recognizes the ranges it needs to know if you select a cell within the list and you previously used the Insert, Name, Define Name command to name the ranges Database, Criteria, and Extract. The Extract named range can either include just the field names or the field names and the rows for the data. If the Extract range includes only field names, you can copy an unlimited number of records. If the Extract range includes field names and a limited number of rows underneath, a dialog box will appear if you try to extract more records than will fit in the range, asking whether you want to continue copying records. ■

The Advanced Filter method of copying filtered data needs a new range in which the data will be copied—*Copy To range* or *Extract range*. In the Advanced Filter dialog box in Figure 46.1, you can see text boxes for the List Range, Criteria Range, and Copy To range. The Copy To range receives a copy of the filtered data. The Copy To edit box appears only after you select the Copy to Another Location option. For a description of the List Range and Criteria Range, refer to Chapters 42, "Designing a List or Database," and 45, "Finding, Filtering, and Editing Lists or Databases."

FIG. 46.1

The Advanced Filter dialog box. You need a List Range, Criteria Range, and a Copy To range to copy data when you use the Advanced Filter method.

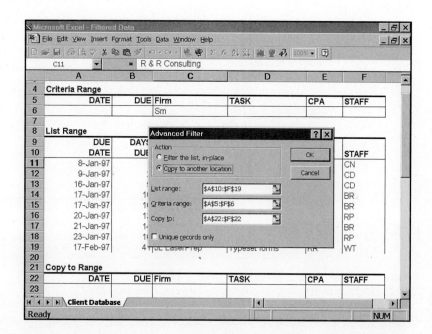

A set of field names can head the top of the Copy To range. The field names must be exactly the same as the field names at the top of the Database or List Range. These field names tell Excel which data you want extracted and how you want the columns arranged. Figure 46.1 shows a small list with the three parts that are important to extracting: the Database or List Range in $A$10:$F$19, the Criteria Range in $A$5:$F$6, and the field names for the Copy To range in $A$22:$F$22. In Figure 46.2, the data that meets the criteria that FIRM entries must start with "Sm" is copied from the list and pasted below the field names in the Copy To range.

If you specify a blank and unheaded Copy To range, a dialog box appears, asking whether you want to extract data to this range. You can accept or deny the extract.

The Copy To range is separate and distinct from the Criteria and List Ranges. In Figures 46.1 and 46.2, notice that three ranges are used. The row of field names selected as the Copy To range must be separate from the rows of field names that head the Database and Criteria Ranges.

The field names at the top of the Extract Range must be identical to the field names used at the top of the List Range. The best way to prepare your Copy To range is to copy the field names that you want from the top of the list. Normally, it is not advisable to place the Copy To range below the List Range, as shown in Figure 46.1, since it doesn't leave room for the List Range to expand.

FIG. 46.2

Data matching the criteria is copied from the List Range to the Copy To range.

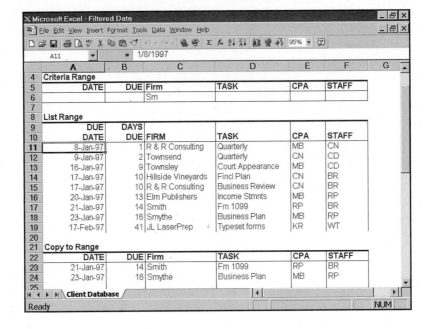

As Figures 46.3 and 46.4 illustrate, however, you don't have to include in the Copy To range all the field names from the List Range, nor must the field names be in the same order as they appear in the list. You can create reports with only the information you need and in the column order you want. Use selected field names and reorder the names as you want them to appear in the copied data. You can also repeat a field name if you want.

FIG. 46.3

Put the Copy To field names in a different order from those in the list.

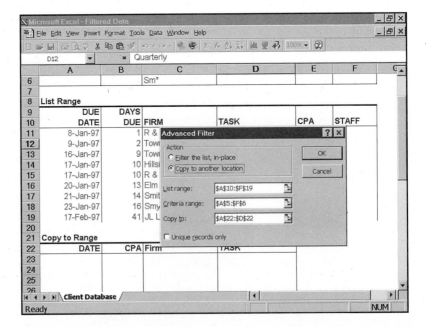

FIG. 46.4

Reordering Copy To field names enables you to structure reports by extracting columns to a new order.

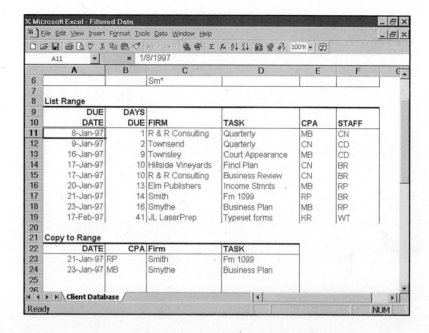

CAUTION

If you insert or delete field names in the Copy To range or Criteria Range, make sure you recheck the ranges listed in the Advanced Filter dialog box before copying data to another location. By inserting or deleting within the previous ranges, you might have moved the end points of the ranges.

You can define the Copy To range in two ways. You can use the Insert, Define, Name command (or the Name box in the formula bar) to assign a name to the Copy To range, or you can display the Advanced Filter dialog box and select the range by selecting the Copy To box and dragging it across the range on the sheet. If you assign the name *Extract* to the Copy To range, Excel recognizes the Copy To range and enters the correct cell references in the Copy To box.

You can specify two sizes of Copy To ranges, limited and unlimited. A *limited Copy To range* includes the field names at the top of the range and a limited number of cells below the names. The copied information fills only the cells available in the Copy to range. Excel leaves out copied data that does not fit but presents a message asking whether you want to continue copying records.

In an *unlimited Copy To range*, you select only the field names or name only the field names. You can fill the resulting range with data, beginning with the field names and extending to the bottom of the worksheet. If you don't know how much data will be copied, use an unlimited Copy To range.

CAUTION

The worksheet area below unlimited extracts is erased—old data or parts of the worksheet below the field names of an unlimited extract range are cleared. Do not put anything below the field names of an unlimited Copy To range. Excel does not warn you that all cells below the Extract Range headings will be cleared. After you complete an unlimited copy, Excel clears this area to avoid mingling the old data with the new.

 You might need to recalculate before you copy filtered data. If Excel is set to recalculate formulas manually and the worksheet needs recalculating, Calculate appears in the status bar at the bottom of the screen. Press F9 (Calculate).

 To copy both limited and unlimited numbers of records, create multiple names, each with the field names as the top of the range.

Use the following basic procedure to extract filtered data from the list to a new location. Each step is described in greater detail in the sections that follow.

1. Create field names for the Copy To range by copying the single row of field names from the top of the list. Arrange the field names in the order you want the columns of data to appear.
2. Enter the criteria in the Criteria Range.
3. Choose Data, Filter, Advanced Filter to display the Advanced Filter dialog box (refer to Figure 46.1).
4. Choose the Copy to Another Location option.
5. Select the List Range box and type in the range name of the list, or select the worksheet area containing the list.
6. Select the Criteria Range box and type in the range name of the criteria you created in step 3, or select the worksheet area containing the Criteria Range.
7. Select the Copy To box and type in the range name, or select the worksheet area containing the area to receive the filtered copy.

   If you want to copy an unlimited number of rows of extracted data, then select only the field names in the Copy To range.

   If you want to copy a limited number of rows of extracted data, then select the field names at the top of the Copy To range and as many rows below as you want data.
8. If you want no duplicate records, select the Unique Records Only check box.
9. Choose OK.

NOTE Use a unique copy of a filtered list to cross-check lists for typographical errors. Suppose you created a list of 320 records, with 16 different part names. To cross-check for misspelled part names, you can extract unique records by using a Copy To range that is headed by the field name containing the part names. Each of the 16 correctly spelled part names appears once in the Extract Range. Any misspelled part name appears in the Copy To range as an additional item. Use Data, Form or Edit, Find to locate the misspelled part name within the list. You can use Edit, Replace to search for and replace the mistake. ▪

Copying Filtered Data Between Worksheets or Workbooks

You often can benefit greatly from copying filtered data to another worksheet before you use the data. You can avoid contaminating original data, and the worksheet in which you are working will have a smaller list, using less memory, so it can run faster. You also can generate reports more easily because you don't have to worry about rearranging columns, changing column widths, or reorganizing the structure on a new worksheet.

 TIP Before you print hundreds of mailing labels from an Excel list, use a unique extract to make sure you don't print duplicate labels.

An easy way to copy a filtered list between worksheets is to filter the list by using either AutoFilter or Advanced Filter and then copy it from one sheet and paste it into another sheet. You can, however, use the Advanced Filter command to move filtered data between sheets.

An easy way to copy filtered data to a worksheet other than the database worksheet is to follow the same procedure you would use for extracting data to the same worksheet as the database. To specify where the filtered data will be copied, select the Copy To box, then click at the upper-left corner of the area where you want the filtered data copied.

If you need to do multiple extracts to different worksheets where each extract can use different criteria, then you will want to use the following procedure. In this procedure the list is on one worksheet and the Criteria Range and Copy To range are on a separate worksheet. All the worksheets involved must be open and the worksheet containing the Criteria must be active when you choose the Advanced Filter command.

In the following example, all items with a Quantity field greater than 10 are extracted from the list on the Flim Flam Inventory worksheet and placed in the Copy To range on the Inventory Query worksheet.

Figure 46.5 shows the two worksheets from the same workbook. The Flim Flam Inventory worksheet contains a list in the range A5:C14 that was named *Database*. Using named ranges becomes convenient when you copy between sheets or workbooks because remembering the long syntax of external references is difficult. Remembering a name is much easier.

The Inventory Query worksheet contains a Criteria Range and a Copy To range. The Criteria Range of A5:C6 was named *Criteria*. The field names that act as headings for the extract in Inventory Query are in cells A9:C9. The Copy To range, A9:C9, was named *Extract*.

To copy filtered data between worksheets, follow these steps:

1. Open the worksheets containing the List, Criteria, and Copy To ranges.
2. Activate the worksheet containing the Copy To range (see Figure 46.5). To extract only some of the columns of data, enter at the top of the Copy To range only the field names of data you want to extract.

FIG. 46.5

To do multiple different extracts, put the Criteria and Copy To ranges together on one or more worksheets separate from the list.

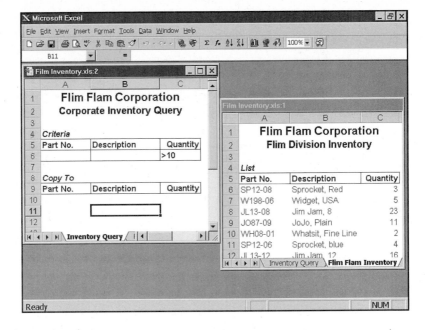

3. Select a blank cell that is not touching filled cells. In the next step this prevents Excel from attempting to find a list range on the Copy To worksheet.

4. Choose Data, Filter, Advanced Filter to display the Advanced Filter dialog box (refer to Figure 46.1).

5. Choose the Copy to Another Location option.

6. Select the List Range box and then activate the sheet containing the list. Drag across the Database Range, or click one cell in the sheet and edit the reference to include the name of the list. The external reference to the list on another sheet in the same workbook looks like

   `'Flim Flam Inventory'!$A$5:$C$14`

   where the syntax is

   `'Sheetname'!Rangename`

   If the other sheet is in a different workbook, the syntax is

   `'[Workbookname]Sheetname'!Rangename`

7. Select the Criteria Range box and enter a range by activating the sheet containing the Criteria Range and dragging across that range.

8. Select the Copy To range box and enter the Copy To range. Do this by activating the original worksheet and dragging across the field names that are at the top of the Copy To range.

9. Select the Unique Records Only check box if you want to remove duplicates. Figure 46.6 shows a completed Advanced Filter dialog box.

10. Choose OK.

Figure 46.7 shows the result of copying a filtered list on Flim Flam Inventory onto the Inventory Query sheet. The Criteria and Copy To ranges were on one sheet and the list was on another.

FIG. 46.6

Select Criteria, List, and Copy To ranges from any sheets.

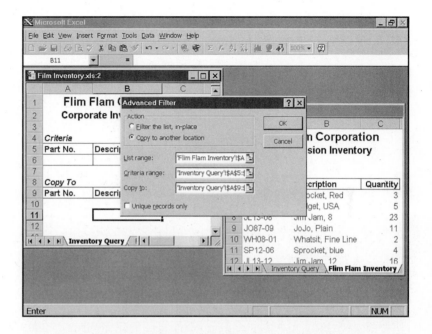

FIG. 46.7

You can copy filtered lists from any worksheet or workbook to any other worksheet or workbook.

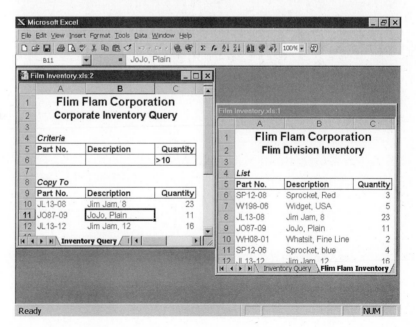

Part
XI

Ch
46

Maintaining Data

Lists have a tendency to grow. Eventually, memory and speed limitations dictate that you clean up. As part of this process, you need to make backup copies of the old information before removing it from the working list or database.

Backing Up Data

An unpleasant surprise awaits you if you continually save a worksheet to the same file name. When you choose File, Save, the current Excel file replaces the original file on disk. This practice is fine, provided that you never make a mistake. You might accidentally delete the wrong records, make a number of incorrect edits, or add some incorrect data. If you save a bad file over good, you are left with only a bad file.

If you want more security, save the list you are editing every 15 to 30 minutes by using the File, Save As command. Each time you save with File, Save As, edit the file name to make it different from the previous name. You might want to use a sequence of file names, such as the following:

> Accounting 01
>
> Accounting 02
>
> Accounting 03

The last two characters indicate the file's version number. This numbering technique enables you to return to an older file to recover previous data. When files are too old to use again, select the files in the File Open dialog box, right-click the selection, and choose Delete from the shortcut menu to erase the files from the disk. You can also use Windows Explorer to delete files.

 TIP To select multiple files in the Open dialog box, click the first file, hold down the Ctrl key, and click each additional file you want to select. Right-click the selection to open the shortcut menu.

Keep more than one copy of all important list files, and do not keep the backup copy in the same building as the original. Take the backup files to a different building or to a bank vault. If your building burns or a thief takes the computers and disks, you still have your data.

Deleting a Group of Records

Your list is of little use unless someone maintains it. You must edit, add, and delete single records, but Excel can help you delete groups of records. To delete a group of records, apply a filter to show only the records you want to delete. Select those records and then delete them with the Edit, Delete command.

If you have only a few records to delete or records that might be difficult to describe with criteria, you might want to delete them manually. Use Data, Form to find the records and then select the Delete button on the form to delete the current record.

Integrating Word and Excel

Customizing and Optimizing Word Features

Customizing Commonly Used Features

As you use Word 97, you might want to customize it to fit the way you work or to make trade-offs between increased performance and features. In Chapter 49, "Customizing Word and Excel Toolbars, Menus, and Shortcuts," you learn how to customize Word and Excel features such as menus, toolbars, and shortcut keys. This chapter contains suggestions and options to help you fine-tune Word and customize it for the way you work.

N O T E   To follow the examples in this chapter, it is assumed that Word for Windows has been installed in the C:\PROGRAM FILES\MICROSOFT OFFICE\WINWORD folder. If you have installed Word in a different folder, please substitute your Word folder's name in the following examples. ▨

Other chapters of this book discuss techniques for customizing many Word features. The following list indicates some commonly customized features and the chapters in which they are discussed:

If You Want to Customize	Refer to
Dictionary	Chapter 2, "Using Editing and Proofing Tools"
Document on startup	Chapter 1, "Using Templates and Wizards for Frequently Created Documents"
Documents that are frequently used	Chapter 1
Menus or commands	Chapter 49, "Customizing Word and Excel Toolbars, Menus and Shortcuts"
Page settings on startup	Chapter 7, "Formatting the Page Layout, Alignment, and Numbering;" Chapter 1
Paragraph settings on startup	Chapter 4, "Formatting Lines and Paragraphs;" Chapter 1
Shortcut keys	Chapter 49
Toolbars	Chapter 49

Improving the Performance of Word

Depending on the work that you do and the capability of your computer, Word may not perform as fast as DOS-based word processors. 80486 computers, minimum RAM memory, large graphics files, and long tables can make Word perform more slowly. You can make a number of trade-offs, however, to improve the speed of Word.

Modifying Word for Windows Settings

You can improve Word's performance by choosing certain options within Word. Significant performance improvements also can be made by increasing the memory available to Windows or by increasing the effective speed of your computer's hard disk.

To improve Word's performance from within Word, follow these steps:

1. Choose Tools, Options. The Options dialog box appears (see Figure 47.1).

FIG. 47.1

You can use the Options dialog box to customize many Word for Windows options.

2. Select the tab listed in the first column of the following table; then select or clear the option or check box to make the performance trade-offs you want:

Tab	Option or Check Box	To Improve Performance: Trade-off
View	Picture Placeholders	Select for faster performance; pictures display as empty rectangles onscreen.
View	Animated Text	Clear for faster performance; text animation will not show onscreen.
Print	Draft Output	Select to print faster on dot-matrix printers; the document does not use the fonts shown onscreen. Some character formatting may be lost.
Print	Background Printing	Check to be able to continue working while document is printing; clear to print the document faster.

continues

Tab	Option or Check Box	To Improve Performance: Trade-off
Save	Allow Fast Saves	Select to save more quickly by saving only the changes made to documents; files become larger and cannot be converted by other programs when saved with fast save.
Save	Embed TrueType Fonts	Clear to save more quickly; if you share your files with others who do not have TrueType fonts, they will not be able to view and print the file with the fonts used to create it.
Save	Embed Characters in Use Only	Select in conjunction with Embed TrueType Fonts to save more quickly and reduce document size; saves only the font styles actually used within the file. If you use 32 or fewer characters from a font, only those characters are embedded.
Save	Always Create Backup Copy	Clear to save more quickly; no duplicate copy (file extension BAK) is made during saves.
Save	Allow Background Saves	Select to allow continued editing while large files are saved to disk; editing commands and input may slow down slightly while Word performs a background save.
Save	Save AutoRecover Info Every	Clear to avoid being interrupted by timed saves to disk; no periodic saves are made unless you remember to make them yourself.
General Repagination	Background	Clear for better performance; page-break markers and automatic page numbering aren't correct until you repaginate.
General	Provide Feedback with Animation	Clear for faster performance; onscreen animation for actions such as saving, printing, and repaginating is not displayed.
General	Update Automatic Links at Open	Clear to open files faster; linked data is not necessarily correct unless the individual link (or the entire document) is updated.

Tab	Option or Check Box	To Improve Performance; Trade-off
Spelling & Grammar	Check Spelling as You Type	Clear for faster performance; possible spelling errors are not automatically marked as you type.
Spelling & Grammar	Check Grammar as You Type	Clear for faster performance; possible grammar errors are not automatically marked as you type.

3. Choose OK.

You also can gain a few percentage points of performance by limiting the type or number of fonts you use. Use one or both of the following methods to improve performance by way of font selection:

■ *Do not use several different fonts within a single document.* This guideline is in keeping with a general rule of desktop publishing: No more than three fonts should be used in a document.

■ *Use TrueType fonts sparingly.* TrueType fonts slow computer and printer performance slightly. Instead, use the built-in fonts provided by the currently selected printer.

Printer fonts appear in the Font list of the Font dialog box (choose Format, Font) with a miniature printer to the left of their names.

Managing System Memory

Having more memory available can make Word run faster and enable you to work more efficiently in larger or more complex documents. You can get a significant improvement in performance by increasing your computer's memory to at least 16M for Windows 95. If you are running several applications at once, adding even more memory will improve performance.

You also can improve performance (although the gains are not as significant) by making the proper selections of Word features and using wise-file and application-management practices. The following tips also can help you improve performance:

■ Exit all applications that are not being used while you are working in Word. Other applications also require memory.

■ Close unneeded documents in Word or data files in other open Windows applications. Each document and application requires a portion of Windows' limited system resources memory.

■ Close the Office Assistant if it is not being used, or customize the Office Assistant to reduce the resources it requires.

■ Use the disk defragmenting program that comes with Windows, to consolidate your hard disk so that information can be read and written more quickly. Start this program by opening the Start menu, then clicking Programs, Accessories, System Tools, and then Disk Defragmenter. Disk fragmentation occurs normally as you save and delete files. As time passes, files are saved in pieces scattered over the disk to make the best use of available space. Unfortunately, this process slows down read and write operations. Defragmenting reorganizes information on the disk so that each file is stored in a single contiguous location.

▓ Be sure to leave ample free space on the hard drive on which your Windows 95 virtual memory swap file is located. Windows 95 adjusts the size of the swap file dynamically, and you want to be sure there is plenty of room for this file to expand.

Starting Word or Documents on Startup

If you use Word as your primary Windows application, you might want it to run it each time you start Windows. You can do this by creating a shortcut for Word in the Windows Startup folder. This section explains how to do that, as well as how to create shortcuts on the desktop to start Word or load a specified document.

▶ **See** "Controlling Printing Options," **p. 274**

▶ **See** "Linking Documents and Files," **p. 1091**

Starting Word or Documents When Windows Starts

To start Word when Windows starts, you need to add Word to the Startup folder. You can do this by following these steps:

1. Open the Start menu, and click Settings, and then Taskbar. Choose the Start Menu Programs tab from the Taskbar Properties dialog box, as shown in Figure 47.2.

FIG. 47.2
Specify which programs or documents run on startup with the Start Menu Programs tab. You can also add programs to the Start menu.

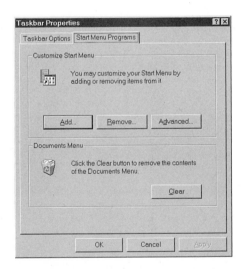

2. Click the Add button to display the Create Shortcut dialog box.

3. Click the Browse button to display the Browse dialog box. To start Word when Windows starts, open the folder containing Word and double-click the WINWORD.EXE file. This file is usually found in the C:\Program Files\Microsoft Office\Winword folder.

If you want to start a document on startup, select All Files in the Files of Type list box. Open the folder to the document and double-click the document's file. The Browse dialog box will close; the file and path name of the selected file appears in the Command Line edit box.

4. Click the Next button to display the Select Program Folder dialog box.

5. Scroll down and select the Startup folder, which is a folder within the Programs folder, as shown in Figure 47.3.

FIG. 47.3

Select the Startup folder if you want your document or application to start when Windows starts.

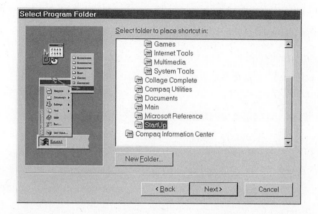

6. Click the Next button to display the Select a Title for the Program dialog box.

7. Type the name you want to use to represent Word or the document. Click the Finish button to return to the Taskbar Properties dialog box.

8. Choose OK.

The next time you start Windows, the Word program or the document you selected will open automatically.

To stop a program or document from loading automatically, reopen the Start Menu Programs tab from the Taskbar Properties dialog box. Click the Remove button. Open the Startup folder in the Remove Shortcuts/Folders dialog box. Select the program or document you no longer want to startup and click the Remove button. Choose Close and OK.

Making Menus, Toolbars, and Shortcut Keys Globally Available

If you find that a template has menus, toolbars, and shortcut keys that you use frequently, you can make them available without using the Organizer to transfer them to the NORMAL.DOT template. (The Organizer is a feature described in Chapter 1.) Instead, copy the template file (DOT extension) containing these features into the \WINWORD\STARTUP directory. The template files are usually located in folders within the PROGRAM FILES\ MICROSOFT OFFICE\TEMPLATES folder.

Part
XII

Ch
47

Make sure you copy a template into the StartUp folder. If you move a template out of the Template folder, it will not appear in the New dialog box when you choose File, New. Be careful not to copy more templates into the StartUp folder than you really need, as it will increase the time it takes to start Word.

Customizing the Workspace and Display

If you work at your computer a lot, even small things like customizing screen colors or arranging screen elements can help you reduce stress. Refer to Chapter 49 for more information.

To change the display or your Word workspace, follow these steps:

1. Choose Tools, Options. The Options dialog box appears.
2. Select the tab listed in the first column of the following table. Then select or clear the associated option or check box depending on your display preferences.

Tab	Option or Check Box	To Change
General	Recently Used File List	The number of files shown under the File menu listed as having been recently opened.
General	Measurement Units	The units used on the ruler (choice of inches, centimeters, points, or picas).
General	Provide Feedback With Sound	The status (on/off) of the audible sounds that provide feedback to indicate various actions or events.
General	Provide Feedback With Animation	The status (on/off) of the animated cursors used to indicate actions such as printing and saving.
General	Blue Background, White Text	To a white-on-blue screen, potentially reducing the eye strain caused by reading a black-on-white screen.
View	Status Bar	Whether or not the status bar appears at the bottom of the screen.
View	Horizontal Scroll Bar or Vertical Scroll Bar	Whether or not the horizontal or vertical scroll bars appear onscreen. Remove them if you use only the keyboard.
View	Animated Text	The display (on/off) of text animation onscreen.
View	ScreenTips	The display (on/off) of reviewers' comments when holding the mouse above a comment reference mark.

Tab	Option or Check Box	To Change
View	Highlight	The display (on/off) of text highlights on the screen.
View	All	The display (on/off) of nonprinting characters such as tabs, spaces, and paragraph marks.
File Locations	File Types	The location of files used by Word. Select the file type and choose the Modify button. You can change the locations for Documents, ClipArt Pictures, User Templates, Workgroup Templates, User Options, AutoRecover Files, Tools, and StartUp.

3. Choose OK.

Customizing Word for the Hearing or Movement Impaired

Windows applications can be made more accessible for users with unique needs, whether those needs are for hearing, vision, or movement.

The hearing impaired can contact Microsoft Sales and Service on a text telephone at 800-892-5234. Technical support is available on a text telephone at 206-635-4948.

CAUTION

Accessibility options are not installed with a normal Windows installation. You can reinstall Windows from your original disk or CD-ROM and select the custom installation option that will enable you to select Accessibility options.

ON THE WEB

A complete list of Microsoft products for users with disabilities can be found at the following Microsoft Website:

http://www.microsoft.com/windows/enable

Additional information and products for users with disabilities can be found at the following sites on the Word Wide Web:

http://www.adaptive-computer.com

http://www.frontiercomputing.on.ca

http://www.frontiercomputing.on.ca/sites.htm

Windows includes numerous options for people who find it difficult to use the keyboard, require larger fonts, or need visual cues and warnings rather than sounds. To access these options in Windows, follow these steps:

1. Click the Start button and choose Settings, Control Panel.
2. Double-click the Accessibility Options icon. The Accessibility Properties dialog box appears.
3. Make your selections and click OK.

The accessibility properties include the following tabs:

Tab	Description
Keyboard	Make the keyboard more tolerant and patient. Select Use StickyKeys if you need to press multiple keys simultaneously but are only able to press keys one at a time. Select Use FilterKeys to ignore short or repeated keystrokes. Select Use ToggleKeys to make a sound when you press Caps Lock, Num Lock, and Scroll Lock.
Sound	Provide visual warnings and captions for speech and sounds. Select Use SoundSentry to make Windows use a visual warning when a sound alert occurs. Select Use ShowSounds to display captions instead of speech or sounds.
Display	Select colors and fonts for easy reading. Select Use High Contrast to use color and font combinations that produce greater screen contrast.
Mouse	Control the pointer with the numeric keypad. Select Use MouseKeys to use the numeric keypad and other keys in place of the mouse. The relationship of keys to mouse controls appears in the table that follows.
General	Turn off accessibility features, give notification, and add an alternative input device. Use Automatic Reset to set Windows so accessibility features remain on at all times, are turned off when Windows restarts, or are turned off after a period of inactivity. Notification tells users when a feature is turned on or off. The SerialKey device enables Windows to receive keyboard or mouse input from alternative input devices through a serial port.

Some of these accessibility features could be difficult for a disabled person to turn on or off through normal Windows procedures. To alleviate this problem, Windows includes special *hotkeys*. Pressing the keys or key combinations for the designated hotkey turns an accessibility feature on or off, or changes its settings. To turn on the hotkeys for an accessibility feature, click the Settings button in the location indicated in the table below and check the Use Shortcut option. The following table gives the hotkeys for different features:

Feature	Hotkey	Result
High-contrast mode	Left-Alt+Left-Shift+ Print Screen pressed simultaneously (select in the Display tab)	Alternates the screen through different text/background combinations
StickyKeys	Press the Shift key five consecutive times (select in the Sticky Keys group in the Keyboard tab)	Turned on or off
FilterKeys	Hold down right Shift key for eight seconds (select in the FilterKeys group in the Keyboard tab)	Turned on or off
ToggleKeys	Hold down Num Lock key for five seconds (select in the Toggle Keys group in the Keyboard tab)	Turned on or off
MouseKeys	Press Left-Alt+Left-Shift+ Num Lock simultan- eously (select in the MouseKeys group in the Mouse tab)	Turned on or off

MouseKeys can be very useful for portable or laptop computer users and graphic artists, as well as for people unable to use a mouse. Graphic artists will find MouseKeys useful because it enables them to produce finer movements than those done with a mouse. Once MouseKeys is turned on, you can produce the same effects as a mouse by using these keys:

Action	Press this key(s)
Movement	Any number key except 5
Large moves	Hold down Ctrl as you press number keys
Single pixel moves	Hold down Shift as you press number keys
Single-click	5
Double-click	+
Begin drag	Insert (Ins)
Drop after drag	Delete (Del)

Part
XII

Ch
47

Customizing the Excel Screen

Exploring Customization Features

The graphical user interface of Windows offers the ideal environment in which to work because of its ease of use. Excel extends this capability by allowing you to customize your workspace.

As you learned from previous chapters, Excel allows you to change many of the elements of the Excel workspace, including creating custom toolbars, turning off the display of such features as the scroll bars and cell gridlines, and creating your own cell formats and styles. In this chapter, you learn how to change Windows settings to better suit your needs.

This chapter describes ways of customizing Excel that were not yet covered in this book. You might want to go back and explore the following features and topics covered in other chapters:

- *Ten-key accounting pad.* Choose Tools, Options, select the Edit tab, and choose the Fixed Decimal option so that you can type numbers on the numeric pad and have the decimal automatically entered.

- *Automatic rounding of formatted numbers.* Choose Tools, Options, select the Calculation tab, and choose the Precision as Displayed option to make Excel calculate with the formatted number you see on-screen.

- *Worksheet templates.* Create default workbook templates that you use frequently. Templates serve as the framework for creating new workbooks. Templates can contain worksheet formulas, text, graphics, formats, macros, and display settings you want. You also can create chart templates that contain the chart type, formats, and scales for each of the chart types you use frequently. Chapter 27, "Creating Templates and Controlling Excel's Startup," describes templates.

- *Toolbars.* Customize existing toolbars or create your own with the View, Toolbars, Customize command. You can add and remove buttons, design and create custom buttons and toolbars, and assign macros to buttons.

- *File loading on start-up.* Load workbooks and workspace files automatically by storing them in the XLSTART directory. When you use the same worksheets frequently, this setup enables you to get to your work quickly and easily.

- *Custom menus.* Use custom menus and commands to change the control system of Excel completely. Chapter 49, "Customizing Word and Excel Toolbars, Menus, and Shortcuts," describes how to use the View, Toolbars, Customize command to create and change menus.

- *Workspace tools.* Choose Tools, Options, and select the View tab to add or remove workspace tools, such as the formula bar, scrolling bars, status bar, sheet tabs, and so on. See Chapter 33, "Managing the Worksheet Display," for more information.

- *Hidden elements.* Choose Windows, Hide to hide active workbook windows. Choose Format, Sheet, Hide to hide sheets within a workbook. Choose Format, Cells, and select the Protection tab to hide formulas in the Formula Bar. Chapter 23, "Formatting Worksheets," and Chapter 33, "Managing the Worksheet Display," describe how to hide elements.

■ *Protection.* Use the Tools, Protection command to protect worksheets and workbooks from being altered without a password. Use the File, Save As, Options command to prevent a worksheet from being opened without a password.

Creating Your Own Colors

Excel has a palette of 56 colors available for use in worksheet and chart patterns. Although this palette is filled with a standardized set of colors when you get Excel, you can change the palette to use colors that you choose. After you define a set of colors, you can copy those colors to other workbooks or save a workbook as a template so that you can reuse the palette.

There are two ways you can change the colors in your color palette. You can select new colors from a grid of standard colors or you can create your own custom colors using the Custom tab in the Colors dialog box.

> **CAUTION**
>
> Before you change colors on the palette, consider that your changes might affect objects you have already colored. If, for example, you have created a text box with the fourth color on the palette as the background color, changing the fourth color on the palette also changes the background color of your text box.

To choose your own colors for the color palette from the standard colors, complete the following steps:

1. Open the workbook in which you want custom colors.
2. Choose Tools, Options and select the Color tab. Figure 48.1 shows the Color tab in the Options dialog box. On a color monitor, you can see the actual colors.

FIG. 48.1
The Color tab displays 56 colors you can change.

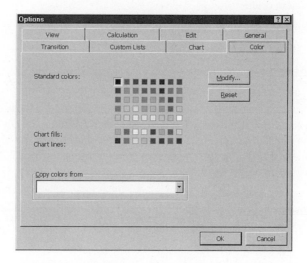

3. On the palette, select the color you want to change. Click that color box, or press the arrow keys to select the color.

4. Choose the <u>M</u>odify button to display the Colors dialog box shown in Figure 48.2. The <u>M</u>odify button is unavailable if you are using a monochrome monitor; you cannot customize the colors in the color palette.

FIG. 48.2

Replace a color on your color palette with another one of the standard colors in the Standard tab of the Colors dialog box.

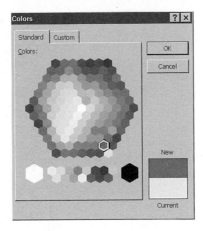

5. Select the Standard tab and select the desired color from the <u>C</u>olors grid. When you make a selection in the <u>C</u>olors grid, a box in the lower-right corner of the dialog box displays both the current and the new colors (see Figure 48.2).

6. When finished, choose OK.

7. Choose OK again.

To create a custom color:

1. Complete steps 1-4 of the previous set of steps.

2. Select the Custom tab in the Color dialog box.

3. Click in the Colors box on the color you want (see Figure 48.3).

   or

   Select the H<u>u</u>e box and enter a number from 0 to 255. Hue is the actual color. In the <u>C</u>olors box, 0 hue is the color at the left edge and 255 hue is the color at the right edge. You also can choose mixtures of red, green, and blue. To mix these colors, select the <u>R</u>ed, <u>G</u>reen, and <u>B</u>lue boxes and enter a number from 0 to 255; 255 represents the greatest amount of the color.

4. To change the luminosity, drag the pointer up or down along the right column, or select the <u>L</u>um box and enter a number from 0 to 255. Luminosity is the brightness of the color, with 0 being the darkest and 255 being the brightest.

FIG. 48.3

Create a custom color for your color palette in the Custom tab of the Colors dialog box.

5. To change the saturation of the color, select the Sat box and enter a value from 0 to 255. In the Colors box, 0 saturation is the color at the bottom edge of the color box and 255 saturation is the color at the top edge. Saturation is the intensity of the color, 0 being the least intense and 255 being the most intense.

   As you create your color, watch the sample color in the New/Current box in the lower-right corner.

6. When you are finished creating your color, choose OK to close the Colors dialog box.

7. Choose OK again to accept your color change.

If you want to return the palette to its original set of 56 colors, choose Tools, Options, and select the Color tab. Then choose the Reset button.

> **N O T E** When you copy a colored object from one workbook to another, the object carries with it the palette number of its color. When the object is pasted into the new workbook, the object uses the color assigned to that number on the palette of that new workbook. In other words, objects might change color when copied between documents that have different palettes. ■

To copy a color palette from one workbook to another, take the following steps:

1. Open both the workbook from which you want to copy and the workbook to which you are copying. Activate the workbook that will receive the new palette.

2. Choose Tools, Options and select the Color tab.

3. In the Copy Colors From list box, select the name of the document from which you are copying colors.

4. Choose OK.

Colored objects in the document receiving the new palette change to reflect the new palette.

▶ **See** "Changing Object Colors, Patterns, and Borders," **p. 746**

Setting Preferences

Excel contains a number of features that enable you to customize Excel for your work preferences. These features enable you to change such options as enabling Lotus 1-2-3 movement keys or disabling Excel features such as drag-and-drop editing. Other preferences, such as turning off the display of the status bar or changing worksheet grid colors, are described in Chapter 33.

Operating with 1-2-3 Keys

If you are familiar with Lotus 1-2-3, you can use your knowledge to learn Excel. You can modify Excel to aid you in your switch from 1-2-3.

To use operating methods similar to 1-2-3 as you learn Excel:

1. Choose <u>T</u>ools, <u>O</u>ptions and select the Transition tab (see Figure 48.4).

FIG. 48.4

Ease the transition to Excel from 1-2-3 with 1-2-3 Help.

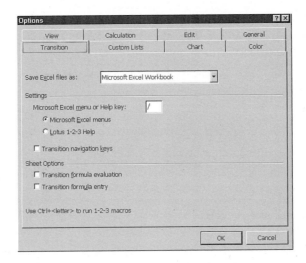

2. Type a slash character (/) in the Microsoft Excel <u>M</u>enu or Help Key text box.
3. Select the <u>L</u>otus 1-2-3 Help option and then choose OK.

N O T E To access more help when making the switch from Lotus 1-2-3, choose <u>H</u>elp, <u>C</u>ontents and Index. Double-click Switching from Other Applications and select from among the topics in the expanded list. ■

These choices will display Excel's help for users whenever you press the slash key. While in a worksheet, you can press the keys that you would use for a 1-2-3 process, and Excel will demonstrate the equivalent Excel keystrokes. This method enables you to use 1-2-3 knowledge while you continue to work productively and learn Excel.

Select the Transition Navigation <u>K</u>eys check box to use many of the 1-2-3 cell movement methods, such as End, arrow. However, Excel has all the equivalent navigation keys, so unless you are intimately familiar with 1-2-3 keystrokes, you should learn the Excel navigation keystrokes.

TROUBLESHOOTING

I have recently upgraded to Excel from Lotus 1-2-3. I was under the impression that Excel makes it easy for 1-2-3 users to make the switch, specifically, that I could use the slash (/) to get help on using 1-2-3 commands in Excel. However, when I press the slash key, it activates the Excel menu bar. Have I been misled? No, you haven't. In order to use the slash key to access help on 1-2-3, you must first let Excel know your intentions by choosing <u>T</u>ools, <u>O</u>ptions, selecting the Transition tab, choosing <u>L</u>otus 1-2-3 Help in the Settings area of the dialog box, and choosing OK. Now, when you press the slash key, the Help for 1-2-3 Users dialog box appears.

Moving the Active Cell after Entering Data

When you type data, you can choose to have Excel move the active cell to an adjacent cell after you press the Enter key. If you want the active cell to move after you press Enter, follow these steps:

1. Choose <u>T</u>ools, <u>O</u>ptions.
2. Select the Edit tab.
3. Select the <u>M</u>ove Selection After Enter option.
4. Select the direction you want the active cell to move from the <u>D</u>irection drop-down list.
5. Choose OK.

If you don't want the active cell to move after you press Enter, follow these steps:

1. Choose <u>T</u>ools, <u>O</u>ptions.
2. Select the Edit tab.
3. Clear the <u>M</u>ove Selection After Enter check box.
4. Choose OK.

TROUBLESHOOTING

When I enter data in a cell and press Enter, the active cell moves down a cell. I prefer that the active cell remain in the same place. Can I change this setting in Excel? The <u>T</u>ools, <u>O</u>ptions command enables you to change many of the operations in Excel to work in a manner in which you're accustomed, including preventing the active cell from moving when you enter data. Choose <u>T</u>ools, <u>O</u>ptions, and select the Edit tab. Select <u>M</u>ove Selection After Enter to clear the check box and choose OK.

Part
XII

Ch
48

Editing Data Directly in a Cell

When you double-click a cell entry, Excel activates the Formula Bar so that you can make changes to the entry. If you'd prefer to enter Edit mode manually, follow these steps:

1. Choose Tools, Options.
2. Select the Edit tab.
3. Clear the Edit Directly in the Cell check box.
4. Choose OK.

CHAPTER 49

Customizing Word and Excel Toolbars, Menus, and Shortcuts

Customizing the Office Shortcut Bar

By default, when Office 95 installs, it places the Microsoft Office Shortcut Bar in your Startup Folder. The typical installation of Office 97, however, does not include the Shortcut Bar. You have to return to the setup program to install the Shortcut Bar if it is not already installed. Therefore, every time you start Windows 95, the Office Shortcut Bar displays at the top of your screen (see Figure 49.1 for a customized shortcut bar). The Office Shortcut Bar gives you quick access to common Office tasks such as opening and creating documents. Using the Office Shortcut Bar, you can also add and remove Office programs and control Office settings such as the location of workgroup templates.

> **N O T E** If you are in a workgroup or have a system administrator who has configured your Office
> applications, ensure you are authorized to change these toolbar buttons and menu choices
> before doing so. In many departments, Office 97 is configured to meet the needs of the organization
> with many customized buttons and other options displayed on specific applications. Nothing irritates
> managers and administrators more than someone resetting or reconfiguring an application that has
> customized settings established. ▩

You can customize many features of the Office Shortcut Bar to better meet your needs. For example, you can do the following:

- Change the size, location, and appearance of the toolbar
- Change the names and order of buttons on the toolbar
- Hide or display toolbar buttons
- Add a button to the toolbar to load a file or program
- Add more toolbars to the Office Shortcut Bar

One of the most useful features of the Office Shortcut Bar is that it can display and manage numerous toolbars. As shown in Figure 49.1, the Office Shortcut Bar comes with six default toolbars that you can select to display or hide: Office, Desktop, QuickShelf, Favorites, Programs, and Accessories. You can customize any one of these toolbars or add your own custom toolbars.

Customizing the Office Shortcut Bar is organized into four areas: customizing the view, modifying the buttons, customizing and creating toolbars, and changing settings. The following sections explain how to customize each area of the Office Shortcut Bar.

Customizing the View

The View tab of the Customize dialog box enables you to control the color and other display options of the Office Shortcut Bar (see Figure 49.2). For example, by default, the toolbar buttons are set to a small size. You can change the button size to a larger size by clicking the appropriate check box. You can also activate features such as ToolTips, sound, and animation.

FIG. 49.1
The Office Shortcut Bar can display numerous toolbars.

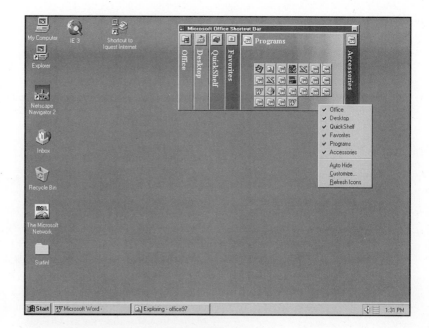

FIG. 49.2
Using the View tab of the Customize dialog box, you can modify the display of the Office Shortcut Bar.

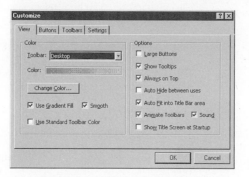

 TIP To change the position of the Office Shortcut Bar, drag it to a new location.

To customize the view features of the Office Shortcut Bar, follow these steps:

1. Right-click the Office Shortcut title bar or the background of a toolbar (not the toolbar button, but between the toolbar buttons) to display the shortcut menu.

2. Choose Customize. The customize dialog box appears with the View tab selected by default (refer to Figure 49.2).

3. Select the desired settings. Table 49.1 describes each of the view settings and options.

4. Click OK when you are done to save changes.

Part
XII

Ch
49

T I P Dragging the Office Shortcut Bar to the center of your screen helps you better navigate the shortcut menus.

Table 49.1 Options for Customizing Office Shortcut Bar View

Setting	Description
Toolbar	Specifies the toolbar name for which you want to customize the color settings.
Change Color	Displays the color palette from which you can select a color.
Use Gradient Fill	Specifies to use gradient coloring.
Smooth	When the Use Gradient Fill option is selected, the Smooth option distributes coloring more evenly.
Use Standard Toolbar Color	Changes color settings back to default colors. When selected, other color options are grayed out. When selected, the Office 97 toolbar takes on the attributes currently set for the desktop. The toolbar color is reflective of the current setting for 3D Objects.
Large Buttons	Specifies to use large buttons and icons on the currently displayed toolbar.
Show Tooltips	Specifies to show Tooltip text that describes what the button does. A Tooltip is the small pop-up message that displays when you move the mouse pointer over the button.
Always on Top	Specifies that the toolbar displays on top of any open windows.
Auto Hide Between Uses	Hides the toolbar when not in use.
Auto Fit into Title Bar Area	Adjusts toolbar size to fit inside the current application's title bar.
Animate Toolbars	Activates any animation features of the toolbar.
Sound	Activates any sound features of the toolbar.
Show Title Screen at Startup	Displays the title screen when first started.

N O T E To change the position of the Shortcut Bar when the View option Auto Fit into Title Bar is selected, use an editor, such as WordPad, to edit the MSOFFICE.INI file in the Windows folder. In the [OPTIONS] section, change the RightPos = line to a number higher than the default, which varies by the resolution of your display. ▪

Customizing the Buttons

The Buttons tab of the Customize dialog box enables you to customize toolbar buttons in the Office Shortcut Bar. You can select which files to display as buttons, arrange the order of buttons, add new files and folders as buttons, delete existing entries, and add spaces between buttons on a toolbar.

 T I P Add the MS-DOS prompt button to the Office Shortcut Bar for quick access to the prompt from any application.

To customize the button features of a toolbar in the Office Shortcut Bar, follow these steps:

1. Right-click the Office Shortcut title bar or the background of a toolbar (not the toolbar button, but between the toolbar buttons) to display the shortcut menu.
2. Choose Customize.
3. Select the Buttons tab (see Figure 49.3).

FIG. 49.3

Using the Buttons tab, you can modify the contents and layout of toolbars in the Office Shortcut Bar.

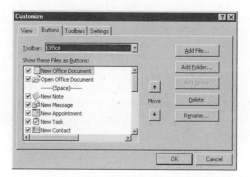

4. Modify and add toolbar buttons as needed. Table 49.2 describes each of the button settings and options on the Buttons tab.

N O T E Buttons are displayed left-to-right in a horizontal Toolbar and top-to-bottom in a vertical Toolbar. In a Toolbar palette, spaces between buttons separate buttons into rows. ■

5. Click OK when you are done to save changes.

Part
XII

Ch
49

Table 49.2   Options for Customizing Office Shortcut Buttons

Setting	Description
Toolbar	Select the toolbar to customize.
Show These Files as Buttons	Select (check) the buttons to include on the toolbar.
Add File	Select a file to add to the toolbar as a button.
Add Folder	Select a folder to add to the toolbar as a button.
Add Space	Insert a space above the currently selected button.
Delete	Delete the selected button or space.
Rename	Rename the selected toolbar.
Move [–]	Move the selected button up in the toolbar button list (to the left in the toolbar itself).
Move [˜]	Move the selected button down in the toolbar button list (to the right in the toolbar itself).

N O T E   By default, a new button displays the icon included in the program's executable file. For files and folders without a defined icon, the Office Shortcut Bar uses the standard file and folder icons. You can change the icon on a button by modifying the button properties: Right-click the button and choose Properties (make sure that the Customize dialog box is closed first). Then, select the Shortcut tab and choose Change Icon, which displays icons available in the SHELL32.DLL file found on your system. Finally, select the icon file name and icon to use, and then click OK. For another collection of icons, click the Browse button and open the MORICONS.DLL file in your Windows folder. ■

Customizing the Toolbars

The Toolbars tab of the Customize dialog box lists the files available to show as toolbars on the Office Shortcut Bar (see Figure 49.4). The checked folders display and the unchecked folders remain hidden. The Toolbars tab also enables you to add your own custom toolbars or remove toolbars.

 T I P   Create your own toolbar for quick access to frequently used tools such as spreadsheets, documents, or databases.

To add toolbars to the Office Shortcut Bar, follow these steps:

1. Right-click the Office Shortcut title bar or the background of a toolbar (not the toolbar button, but between the toolbar buttons) to display the shortcut menu.
2. Choose Customize.
3. Select the Toolbars tab (see Figure 49.4).
4. Select Add Toolbar. The Add Toolbar dialog box appears (see Figure 49.5).

FIG. 49.4

The Toolbars tab of the Customize dialog box enables you to hide, add, or remove toolbars.

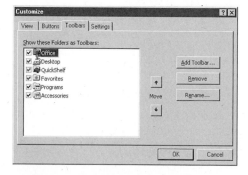

FIG. 49.5

The Add Toolbar dialog box enables you to create new toolbars.

5. To make a toolbar for a folder, type the folder name in the text box labeled Create a New, Blank Toolbar called

   or

   Type a new name in the text box labeled Make a Toolbar for This Folder (or use the Browse button to select a folder).

6. Click OK when you are done to save changes.

N O T E To remove a toolbar from the list of toolbars, select the toolbar name and click the Remove button. To rename a toolbar, select the toolbar name, click the Rename button, and fill in a new name in the Rename dialog box. ■

Customizing Settings

The Settings tab of the Customize dialog box enables you to change Office Shortcut Bar settings, such as where the user and workgroup templates are stored (refer to Figure 49.6). To modify the settings, select the Item you want and choose Modify. A settings dialog box prompts you to enter a new file location.

Customizing Application Toolbars

The process of customizing toolbars in Microsoft Office applications is much the same as customizing the toolbars in the Office Shortcut Bar. In most applications, however, you have even more options.

Part

XII

Ch

49

FIG. 49.6
You can change the
location of User and
Workgroup templates
files via the Settings tab
in the Customize dialog
box.

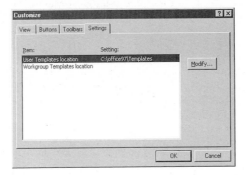

Customizing Predefined Toolbars

Each application comes with several built-in toolbars, some of which display automatically. For example, by default, Microsoft Word displays the Standard, Formatting, and Web toolbars. In addition to these, you can display a number of predefined toolbars:

- AutoText
- Control Toolbox
- Database
- Drawing
- Forms
- Picture
- Reviewing
- Tables and Borders
- Visual Basic
- WordArt
- Microsoft
- 3-D Settings
- Shadow Settings
- Shortcut Menu

Excel, Access, and PowerPoint also provide sets of predefined toolbars. You can customize any of the built-in toolbars to better meet your needs. (Microsoft Outlook provides you with two toolbars that you can display or turn off to suit your needs.) You could have a toolbar for every type of task you perform (for example, one for mail merges and one for desktop publishing) or for each user of a computer.

NOTE For even more control over your environment, Office 97 includes customizable command bars that enable you to place frequently used menu options on a toolbar. This enables you to quickly access a dialog box without navigating layers of menu options.

To customize a built-in toolbar, follow these steps:

1. Choose View, Toolbars, Customize. (You also can choose Tools, Customize.) The Customize dialog box appears (see Figure 49.7). If you want to select a new toolbar to display, click the Toolbars submenu.

FIG. 49.7

The Customize dialog box enables you to customize the view and contents of toolbars.

 To quickly customize toolbars, right-click anywhere on any toolbar and select Customize from the shortcut menu. With Office 97, you do not have to be on a blank toolbar area before you press right-click.

2. Select the Commands tab (see Figure 49.8).

FIG. 49.8

The Customize dialog box enables you to drag buttons and other items to or from any toolbar displayed on the desktop.

3. To add items to a built-in toolbar, click the category from the Categories list to display the list of commands available for that category. Then, select a command (button or other item) from the Commands list. Click the Description button to get a short description of the command button.

   Suppose that you want to add the Mail Recipient command to your toolbar. Click the File category and scroll through the list of options in the Commands list until you locate the Mail Recipient icon.

Part

XII

Ch

49

4. Drag the icon you want from the Commands section to the place on the toolbar you want it to appear.

   If you have too many buttons on your toolbar, adding more buttons to it may push buttons off the right side of the screen.

5. To remove items from the toolbar, drag the buttons or items off the toolbar. The Customize dialog box must be displayed, which can be displayed by selecting Tools, Customize.

6. To move buttons or items, drag them to a new location on the same toolbar or to a different toolbar. The Customize dialog box must be displayed.

7. Click Close to close the Customize dialog box.

Modifying Toolbar Buttons

You can change the way a toolbar icon looks, change its name, and make it perform another function by using the Modify Selection button on the Command tab. Some of the toolbar buttons you add may have only text and take up too much space on the toolbar. To minimize their space requirement, you can use a graphic as the toolbar button icon. Office 97 also enables you to attach a macro to a toolbar to make it perform specific actions you program.

To modify toolbar buttons, follow these steps:

1. Choose View, Toolbars, Customize. The Customize dialog box appears.

2. Select the Commands tab.

3. Move the mouse pointer to the toolbar button and click it. A black border appears around the button (see Figure 49.9). The Modify Selection button on the Command tab displays.

FIG. 49.9
The Modify Selection button is dimmed out until you select a toolbar button to modify.

Black border around button to modify

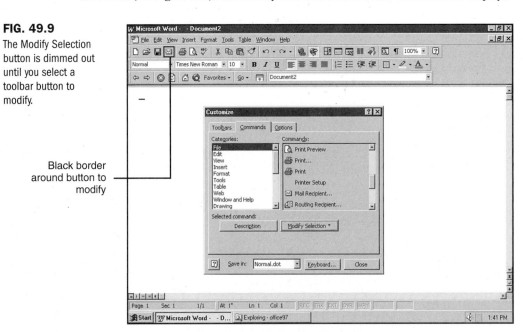

4. Click the Modify Selection button to display a menu of modification choices (see Figure 49.10). You can also right-click the button to display the same menu.

FIG. 49.10
Use the Modify Selection menu to change a toolbar button.

5. Select a menu command to change the selected toolbar button. Table 49.3 lists and describes each menu command.

Table 49.3   Options for Modifying Toolbar Buttons

Command	Description
Reset	Returns the button to its original state.
Delete	Removes the button from the toolbar.
Name	Enables you to rename the button. Use an ampersand (&) character to the left of the character you want to use as the hot key.
Copy Button Image	Places a copy of the button's image in the Windows Clipboard.
Paste Button Image	Inserts the copied image from the Clipboard to the selected button.
Reset Button Image	Returns button image to original image.
Edit Button Image	Displays the Button Editor (see Figure 49.11) so you can create, edit, and add colors to a button image. The Preview area shows the actual size of the image as you create it. Click OK when you finish the image.
Change Button Image	Displays 42 predrawn images you can choose for your button image.
Default Style	Displays the button in the default format for that application. For most buttons, this displays the button as an image only.

continues

Part
XII

Ch
49

Table 49.3 Continued

Command	Description
Text Only (Always)	Displays the button's command as a text label on the toolbar and in menus (if that command is in a menu).
Text Only (in Menus)	Displays the button's command as a text label in menus (if that command is in a menu).
Image and Text	Displays the button's command as an image and text on the toolbar and in menus.
Begin a Group	Places a group divider to the left of the button to enable you to group similar commands together.
Assign Macro	Displays the Assign Macro dialog box, enabling you to assign a macro to the toolbar button (in Excel only).
Properties	Displays the Database Control Properties for button (in Access only).

FIG. 49.11
The Button Editor lets you draw images for toolbar buttons.

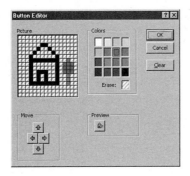

6. Click Close to save your changes.

Setting Toolbar and Menu Options

Office 97 enables you to set display options for toolbars and menus. You can, for instance, set menu animations, which cause menus to appear to unfold or slide across your screen, show toolbar ScreenTips, or display toolbar buttons as large as icons.

To set toolbar and menu options, follow these steps:

1. Choose View, Toolbars, Customize. The Customize dialog box appears.
2. Select the Options tab (see Figure 49.12). Table 49.4 summarizes the options you can select on this tab.

FIG. 49.12
The Options tab
enables you to
customize toolbar and
menu behavior.

Table 49.4 Options for Customizing Toolbars and Menus

Option	Description
Large Icons	Displays toolbar buttons as large icons. Handy for when you use high-resolution displays.
Show ScreenTips on Toolbars	Displays the name of the toolbar button when you move the mouse pointer over the toolbar button.
Show Shortcut keys in ScreenTips	Displays the two- or three-character keyboard shortcuts for each toolbar button and on menus (in Word, Access, and PowerPoint only).
Menu Animations	Controls the way menus display when you click them. You can select from None, Random, Unfold, and Slide.
Keyboard button	Displays the Customize Keyboard dialog box to create new keyboard shortcuts (in Word only).

Creating a Custom Toolbar

In addition to modifying the default toolbars of Microsoft Office 97 applications, you can create your own custom toolbar. For example, you could have a toolbar for every type of task you do, such as one for mail merge and one for desktop publishing.

N O T E   Although Excel screens are used in this section to illustrate the process of creating custom toolbars, the screens in Word, Access, and PowerPoint are similar. Any exceptions are noted. ■

To create a custom toolbar, follow these steps:

1. Choose View, Toolbars, Customize to display the Customize dialog box.
2. On the Toolbars tab, click the New button to display the New toolbar dialog box (see Figure 49.13).

Part
XII

Ch
49

FIG. 49.13

Use the New Toolbar dialog box to name your new toolbar.

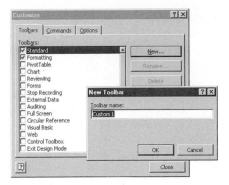

3. Enter a name for the new toolbar in the Toolbar Name text box and click OK. The new toolbar displays, but does not contain any buttons yet. Don't fret if the new toolbar is too small to read its name. It grows as you add buttons to it.

4. In Word, you have the option of naming the document template in which the toolbar is available. Click the Make Toolbar Available To drop-down list to choose a template file.

5. Select the Commands tab on the Customize dialog box.

6. Select the category that contains the buttons or other items you want to add to the new toolbar.

7. Drag the commands from the Commands list to the new toolbar (see Figure 49.14).

FIG. 49.14

The custom toolbar named Finance contains three buttons.

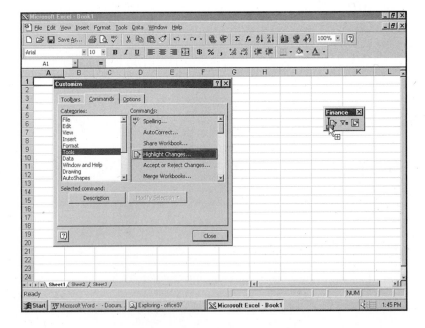

8. Repeat steps 5 and 6 until you fill your custom toolbar with the features you want (the toolbar expands to accommodate your selections).

9. Click the Close button to close the Customize dialog box.

TROUBLESHOOTING

The new toolbar I created contains no buttons. A new toolbar is empty until you add buttons. With the new toolbar visible on-screen, return to the Customize dialog box. Select the category containing the buttons you want to use and drag the button images to your custom toolbar.

Someone customized the default toolbar. I need to get the Standard toolbar back. Choose the View, Toolbars, Customize command, select a toolbar, and choose the Reset button to return to the built-in version of the selected toolbar.

Customizing Application Menus and Command Bars

You can change the organization, position, and content of default Office menus. In addition to modifying the built-in menus, you can add your own custom menus to an Office application's built-in menu bar. This feature is called command bars in Office 97. You could, for example, create a custom menu in Word that lists common tasks you perform such as using mail merges, drawing callouts, and applying font changes. The Commands tab of the Customize dialog box provides easy access to this helpful feature.

To customize or create menus, follow these steps:

1. Choose the View, Toolbars, Customize command. Alternatively, place the mouse pointer on the toolbar, click the right mouse button, and choose Customize from the shortcut menu. The Customize dialog box appears.

2. Select the Commands tab.

3. Scroll down the list of Categories and click New Menu. The Commands list displays a New Menu item (see Figure 49.15).

FIG. 49.15
Word, as well as other Office 97 applications, enables you to customize its built-in menus.

Part
XII

Ch
49

4. Select the New Menu item in the Commands list and drag and drop it on the menu bar or toolbar where you want the new menu to appear.

5. In the Categories list, click the category that contains the command(s) you want to place on your new menu. Click the Macros category to display a list of macros or VBA routines you have on your system. Click the Save in drop-down list to list macros in different templates.

 N O T E Word includes three additional prebuilt menus that do not already appear on the default menu bar — Action, Fo_nt_, and Work — you can add to your menu bar. PowerPoint includes three additional prebuilt menus that do not already appear on the default menu bar — Custom, Data, and Table — you can add to your menu bar. Excel includes several prebuilt menus you can access from the MenuWell categories. ■

T I P If you drop your command next to the New Menu item, that command becomes a new menu instead of a menu item in your new menu.

6. In the Commands list, drag the command you want on the new menu up to the New Menu item. Wait for a small, gray, square box and I-beam to appear (see Figure 49.16) and drop the new command on the box. That command now becomes a menu item in your new menu.

FIG. 49.16

Wait for the small gray box and I-beam to appear before dropping the new menu item.

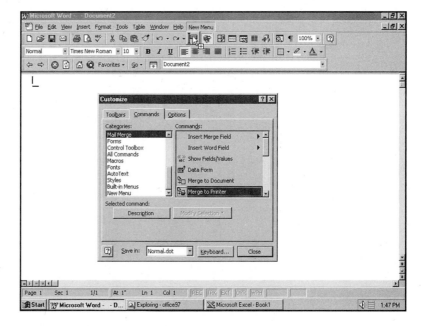

7. Continue adding new menu items until the menu is complete.

8. To assign a command to another menu, select the command from the Commands list and drag and drop it to the place on the menu where you want the command to appear.

9. To change the position of the command in a menu, select the command and drag it up or down to its new position.

10. To change the name, shortcut key, or other property of the menu item, select the command on a menu and click the Modify Selection button on the Customize dialog box. See Table 49.3 for descriptions of each of these commands.

11. To remove a menu item or menu, drag and drop the item or menu from the menu bar to the Customize dialog box.

12. In the Save in drop-down list, select the template in which you want to save the customized menu.

13. Click the Close button when you complete your changes.

TROUBLESHOOTING

I find the default Edit, Links menu command name in Word misleading. I need to change it to something more meaningful. Choose the View, Tools, Customize command and select the Commands tab. Select the Edit menu on the Word menu bar and click the Links command. On the Command tab, click the Modify Selection and change the Name field to your liking. Be sure to place an ampersand (&) in front of the character you want as the shortcut key. Also, make sure your shortcut key is unique for that menu. Click Close.

Someone customized the default menus. I need to get the standard menus back. Choose the Views, Tools, Customize command. Select the Toolbars tab and select the Menu Bar toolbar option in the Toolbars list. Click the Reset button. In Excel, click the Reset button on the Toolbars tab (a Menu Bar toolbar option is not available) and you are prompted whether you want to reset the menu bar.

I pressed Alt+Ctrl+minus sign (-), and I lost a menu item. You pressed a special shortcut-key combination that deletes menu items. Word provides shortcut keys that help you add and delete menu items as you work. Rather than open the Customize dialog box, you can press Alt+Ctrl+minus sign (-) to delete an item from the selected menu, or Alt+Ctrl+equal sign (=) to add a menu item to the selected menu. See the preceding troubleshooting item for directions on resetting the menus.

Part

XII

Ch

49

Creating Compound Word and Excel Documents

Moving Beyond Copy and Paste to Link Information

When you can reuse the same information for different purposes, in different documents, you have the opportunity to save yourself considerable time and effort. Many parts of your existing documents may be useful for information requests and for other reports and documents you might need to create. In a corporation, for example, those who might need the information include prospective customers, business partners, the press, staff, lawyers and accountants, and the board of directors. Trying to provide information to everyone is a huge task. By using Microsoft Office's capabilities to link and embed information, you can streamline the task of supplying information to a diverse audience.

You may have documents or portions of documents that you need to use repeatedly. With Microsoft Office applications, you have different options to accomplish the task of reusing the information. The first option is a simple copy and paste. Whenever you need information from one document, open the document, and select and copy the information. Then open the second document and paste the information at the appropriate point.

Although the copy and paste procedure is the easiest to master, it has two drawbacks. First, if the original information changes, you need to continually repeat the procedure if you want to keep your documents current. The second drawback is that you need to remember the application that created the information and where you put the files. If you want to edit the data, you may need to return to the original application.

To overcome these drawbacks, you have two additional options for sharing data between files (and applications). One option is to create a link between two files. Whenever the data in the source file changes, the destination file receives the update. The technical term for this is *dynamic data exchange*, or DDE.

N O T E This chapter references the *source* application and document as the application and file on disk that supply data. The *destination* or *target* application and document are the application and file on disk that receive the data.

Using Embedding to Connect Documents

Another option is to embed the information into your destination document. When you *embed* the information, you can use the source application's tools to update the information. Depending on the source application, you have two ways to get to the tools (menus and toolbars) of the source application. You can launch the source application from within the destination document, and a separate window appears with the source application showing the information to edit.

A second way to use embedded application tools is called *in-place editing*. When you select the object to edit, your menu and toolbar change to the source application, but you remain in the document and can see the surrounding text or data. The technical term for this kind of sharing is *object linking and embedding* (OLE). Embedding is discussed in more detail in the section "Embedding Information in Your Documents," later in this chapter.

▶ **See** "Linking, Embedding, and Consolidating Worksheets," **p. 941**

N O T E This chapter mentions objects. An *object* can be text, a chart, table, picture, equation, or any other form of information that you create and edit, usually with an application different from your source application. ▪

One difference between linking and embedding is where the information is stored. Linked (DDE) information is stored in the source document. The destination contains only a code that supplies the name and location of the source application, document, and the delineation of the portion of the document. Embedded (OLE) information is stored in the destination document, and the code associated with OLE points to a source application rather than a file.

In some cases, you cannot launch the source application by itself; you need to use your destination application to start the application. These applications are called *applets* (small applications) and include WordArt, ClipArt, Microsoft Graph, and others. You generally launch the source application by choosing Insert, Object.You may want to look at your existing documents and see whether you will continually use different portions in other documents. Table 50.1 lists examples of some documents that you might use in a business. Suppose that, as an office manager, you use Excel or Access to list the original document and divide the document into parts that may be used repeatedly in other documents. You decide it would be better to create separate documents for each frequently used piece required in multiple documents. You also include a column for the application that may be best for the subdocuments.

Table 50.1   Portions of Documents You Can Link to Other Applications

Portion of Document	Proposed Application	Notes and Where Else Needed
Business Plan Word Document		
Logo	PowerPoint	Use for many documents
Mission Statement	Word	Queries, brochure, many documents
New-franchise procedures	Word	Also instruct new locations
Timeline for development	Word	Goals, manage timeline, board notes
Geographic development	Word	Goals, board notes
Distribution of profits	Excel	Goals, board notes
Benefits to your company	Word	Customer presentation, brochure

continues

Table 50.1 Continued

Portion of Document	Proposed Application	Notes and Where Else Needed
Business Plan Word Document		
History	Word	Queries, press release, brochure
Equipment needed for startup	Excel	Need to update as new numbers, info received
Orgchart	Organization Chart	Will change; board notes
Budget board notes	Excel	Summary, internal management
Board of Directors	Access	Queries, phone list, mailing, board notes
Fact Sheet Word Document		
Logo	PowerPoint	Use for many documents
Purpose	Word	Queries, brochure, many documents
Product feature	Word	New-franchise notices, list
Cost sheet	Excel	New-franchise notices
Price sheet	Excel	Customers, prospects

Using Common Steps to Link Documents

The procedure for linking any kind of document in one application to any other application is essentially the same regardless of the source or destination application. You copy the source into the Clipboard and then use the Paste Link option in the Paste Special dialog box to create the link. In the Paste Special dialog box, you also can specify the type of format in which the information is presented.

Don't forget that you can use the Start button on the taskbar and the Documents icon to locate the files you most recently worked on.

Alt+Tab will cycle through the applications you currently have running. If the target application was running before you opened the source application, Alt+Tab will allow you to fast-switch back to that application.

To copy an item to the Clipboard and link the item to another document, follow these steps:

1. Select the item in the source document.
2. Choose Edit, Copy or press Ctrl+C.

3. Move to the target application and document. Position the insertion point where you want the link to appear.

4. Choose Edit, Paste Special. The Paste Special dialog box appears, as shown in Figure 50.1.

FIG. 50.1

In the Paste Special dialog box, you can choose Paste and Paste Link.

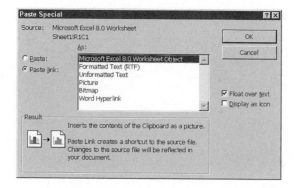

Several format types may be available, depending on the source application. Two options usually are available: Paste and Paste Link. The Paste Link option is grayed if you cannot link the source document for the selected format. Choosing Paste moves the item from the Clipboard to the target document, but does not create a link.

A check mark in the Display As Icon check box places a small picture symbol in your document.

A check mark in the Float Over Text check box pastes the object into the document in such a way that you can move it over text without disturbing the text's line and character spacing. This option is not available with the text and hyperlink formats.

The Result area gives more detail on what happens with your choices.

5. Select a format option in the As list box as described in the following paragraphs.

6. Choose Paste Link.

7. Choose OK.

The As list box shows different formats. The specific formats that are available change, depending on the source and target applications. Several different formats are available for most links. One of the formats usually is Object. In Figure 50.1, the selected format is Microsoft Excel 8.0 Worksheet Object. When you insert, or embed, an object, you can double-click the object or its icon (if the Display As Icon option is active) and then edit the object with the source application. Embedding is described in the section "Embedding Information in Your Documents" later in this chapter.

Another format option is Formatted Text. This option means that the object appears in your target document with most of the formatting (fonts, borders, and so on) from the source document. This option is different from Unformatted Text, in which the text takes on the format of the target document.

You can also add a picture of the document. The Picture option creates an image of the object. Whether the original document is a picture or text, the link becomes a picture, and you can size and move the picture as one item.

Two additional format options that you may encounter are Bitmap and Hyperlink. A bitmap format is like a picture, but it displays the linked object more precisely on the screen. It also requires more space to store, and it might not print as well as a picture format.

The Hyperlink option allows a user to open the source document (in the source application) by clicking the Hyperlink object. Functionally, this option is very similar to the Object option. In either case, the link takes you to the source document or location. The difference between the Hyperlink and Object options is that the Hyperlink is simply a way to reach the source, while the Object option actually places a view of the source in the active document.

N O T E In order for the hyperlink to take effect when you paste it, it's necessary that the source document has been saved in some location. (Else, the target application would be unable to locate the source when the user clicks it.) ▪

The Object and Hyperlink options are particularly useful when you are pasting summary information. Suppose that you use Word to create an income statement, and that you paste values such as Revenues and Costs from Excel worksheets. A user who wants to examine the underlying information—the specific revenue sources, or the particulars of the operating costs—can open and examine the supporting information in the underlying Excel worksheet.

Apart from the way that the link is stored, the most obvious difference between the Object and Hyperlink options is their appearance on the screen. For example, inserting a hyperlink means that the color of the link changes, depending on whether the user has already used the link to open the source document.

TROUBLESHOOTING

I linked my documents, but the source document isn't there. Where did it go? You may have moved your source document. In Word, check the links by turning on the field codes. Choose Tools, Options, and in the View tab, select Field codes. Then make sure your source file is in the right location. You can use Windows Explorer to find your files.

Linking Two Word Documents

When you want to link two Word documents, you can use Paste Special to create the link, or you can use the Insert, File feature. To insert a portion of a file, use the Paste Special feature, which is helpful if the source information is not a complete file. To insert an entire document, choose Insert, File. In the Insert File dialog box, make sure that you select the Link To File option under the command buttons.

To link two Word documents, follow the steps in the preceding section, "Using Common Steps to Link Documents." Select and copy the text you want to link and then move to your target document and choose Edit, Paste Special. In the Paste Special dialog box, select the Unformatted Text option in the As list box to enable the linked text from the source document to assume the format of the target document.

Table 50.1 shows that a company's mission statement might be mentioned in its business plan, fact sheet, and in most other documents. As office manager for that firm, you may want the changes to be updated in all documents containing the mission statement. Therefore, you might create the separate Word document called Mission.doc, containing a brief statement of the company's aim. Because the text is formatted differently in diverse target documents, you want to link the text using the Unformatted Text option in the As list box of the Paste Special dialog box.

Displaying the Link

When you move within the linked section, as shown in Figure 50.2, the link is highlighted in gray. Although you can edit the linked text, the editing changes disappear when the link is updated (when you open the file again, print the file, or press F9, the Update Field shortcut key). The gray highlight reminds you that your edits will not be permanent.

To toggle between a selected field code and the display of the text, select the object and press Shift+F9.

FIG. 50.2
The linked area in the document is highlighted in gray.

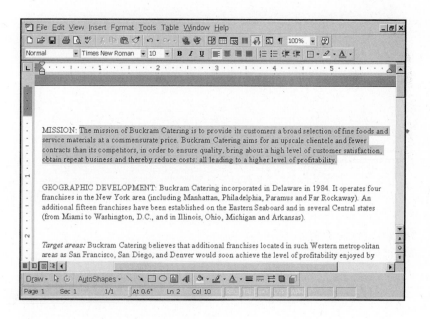

N O T E   If the linked text is not highlighted, choose Tools, Options and then select the View tab. In the Field shading drop-down list, select When selected or Always.

TROUBLESHOOTING

I can't see a field code when I press Shift+F9. You probably pasted or paste-linked the object with the Float over Text check box checked. Selecting this option when you paste or paste-link an object prevents the field codes from appearing. Place the object in the document again, but clear the Float over Text check box before choosing OK.

If you used Paste Special to establish a link (rather than Insert, File) and you want to see the name of the source document, you can display the field name codes rather than the actual text. Choose Tools, Options. In the View tab, choose the Field Codes option. (To display the text, deselect Field Codes.) Figure 50.3 shows field codes used in place of text. You can see that the file is linked to Mission.Doc, and Word 8 is the format for the file, so the source application is Word 8. The file also is linked to Logo.ppt, and PowerPoint is the source application.

FIG. 50.3

Field codes are used in place of text.

Logo.ppt link ⟶ { LINK PowerPoint.Show.8 "C:\\Buckram\\Logo.ppt" "" \a \p }

New Franchise Fact Sheet

Mission.doc link ⟶ MISSION: { LINK Word.Document.8 "C:\\Buckram\\Mission.doc" "OLE_LINK2" \a \t }

GEOGRAPHIC DEVELOPMENT: Buckram Catering incorporated in Delaware in 1984. It operates four franchises in the New York area (including Manhattan, Philadelphia, Paramus and Far Rockaway). An additional fifteen franchises have been established on the Eastern Seaboard and in several Central states (from Miami to Washington, D.C., and in Illinois, Ohio, Michigan and Arkansas).

Target areas: Buckram Catering believes that additional franchises located in such Western metropolitan areas as San Francisco, San Diego, and Denver would soon achieve the level of profitability enjoyed by

TROUBLESHOOTING

Changes in my source document aren't reflected in my destination document. The link may be an automatic link or may require manual updating (see the following section, "Editing Links"). You can also do the following:

To update any manual links, you can go to each field code by pressing F11. To update the code or link, press F9.

To make sure that your document updates any automatic links when you open the file, choose Tools, Options. In the General tab, make sure that Update Automatic Links at Open is selected.

To make sure that your document prints with the latest information, choose Tools, Options. In the Print tab, make sure that Update Links is selected.

Editing Links

When you link a document, you must subsequently maintain the source document's name, and keep the source document in the same location (drive and directory) as it was when you created the link. If you rename, delete, or (in most cases) move a document, the link is broken, and you get an error in your destination document. In some cases, you can break the link so that the source document is inserted into the target document without a link; in other cases, you can change the name of the source document.

To change links, follow these steps:

1. Choose Edit, Links. The Links dialog box appears, as shown in Figure 50.4.

FIG. 50.4

The Links dialog box enables you to update, change, or break links.

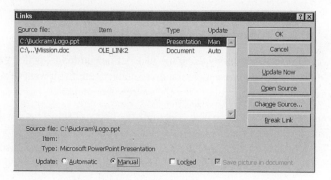

2. Select the file(s) in the Source file list box.
3. Do one or more of the following things:
    - Choose Automatic to have the link updated every time the data is available.
    - Choose Manual to require updating through the Update Now choice or by selecting the link and pressing F9.
    - Choose Locked to prevent updates to the link. If this choice is selected, Automatic and Manual choices will not be available, but will be grayed out.
    - Choose the Update Now button to update a manual link with any changes from the source file.

TIP To get out of a dialog box quickly without saving your changes, press Esc.

- Click the Change Source button to change the file name or location of the linked file in the Change Source dialog box.

- Click the Break Link button to insert the object into the document and unlink it. When Word displays a message box asking whether you are sure that you want to break the selected links, choose Yes.

4. Click OK when you finish.

TROUBLESHOOTING

I linked an Excel worksheet to my Word document, but the link won't update. You may have locked the link in the target document, which means you want to prevent updates to the link in your Word document. To unlock the link, choose Edit, Links, choose the link and uncheck the Locked check box, and then update the field by pressing F9.

Inserting a File into a Document

You also can link documents by using the Insert, File command, which enables you to insert an entire file. You might find this approach more convenient if you want to start the process from the target document, rather than from the source document.

When you use Paste Special to link a file, only the text you select before the Copy command is linked from the target file. If you later go back and insert text before or after the source document selection, the target document does not include the entire text. Insert, File alleviates this problem. The file that you insert can be from the same application or a different application.

To insert a file into a document, follow these steps:

1. Move to the position in the target document where you want to insert the file.

2. Do one of the following:

   - In Word, choose Insert, File. The Insert File dialog box appears, as shown in Figure 50.5. Keep in mind that with Word's Insert, File command, the file you want to insert must have already been saved to a disk. If you want to create a new file and insert it, use Insert, Object.

   - In Excel, choose Insert, Object. The Object dialog box appears. Choose the Create from File tab; then enter the file name in the File Name text box.

3. Identify the file you want to insert, including the drive and directory if necessary.

4. Choose the Link to File option in Word, the Link to File option in Excel, or the Link option in PowerPoint or Access.

5. Choose OK.

FIG. 50.5

The Insert File dialog box enables you to create a link between the files.

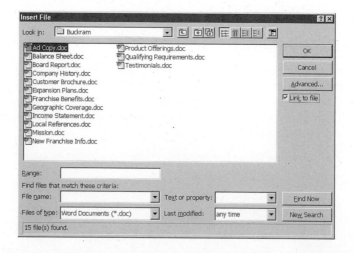

As in the Paste Special example earlier in this chapter, in Word you can display the linked document with a gray highlight or show the field codes. In Figure 50.6, the revised business plan document shows field codes for the linked documents.

N O T E If you want to insert several documents into a single larger document, give your documents a consistent appearance by using the same formats for each one. You also can use templates and styles to help ensure consistency among documents. ■

FIG. 50.6

The field code INCLUDETEXT appears for the Word documents Mission.doc, Company History.doc, Income Statement.doc, and Balance Sheet.doc.

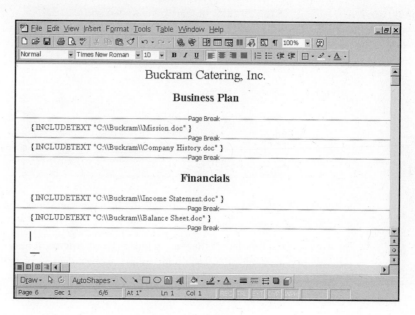

TROUBLESHOOTING

When I make editing changes in my document, why are my changes gone when I open the document again? I know I saved the file. You may be editing a document with a linked file. When you make changes in the linked field, Word will not save them (and Word will not warn you). You need to change the source document to save the changes. To view the field codes, choose Tools, Options and in the View tab select Field codes to view the field codes.

To be able to always see field codes, choose Tools, Options and on the View tab, in the Field shading option, select Always or When selected.

Linking an Excel Worksheet to a Word Document

The procedure for linking a range or an entire Excel worksheet to a Word document is the same as for linking Word documents. You can use either the Paste Special command or choose Insert, File, although formatting a document is easier when you use the Paste Special command. When you use Insert, File, the resulting table sometimes is hard to center on the page because of extra space for the last column or extra cells. In the As list box of the Paste Special dialog box, your formatting choices are different when you Paste Link than when you Paste (see Figure 50.7).

FIG. 50.7
Choose the Paste Link option to link the worksheet to the Word document.

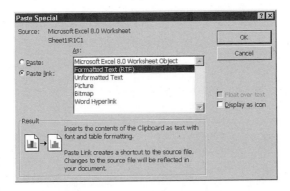

The following list describes the formatting options in the Paste Special dialog box shown in Figure 50.7. The results appear in Figure 50.8.

■ To insert the Excel worksheet as an object, select Microsoft Excel Worksheet Object. In a Word document, when you double-click the object, you activate the application's tools that created the object. You then can edit the object, using the source application's menus, toolbars, and other commands.

FIG. 50.8
You can insert the worksheet as various types of objects.

Unformatted text does not retain formatting

Selection handles used for sizing the picture

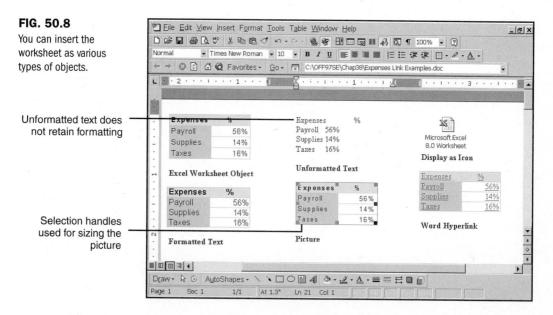

N O T E This is one of the differences between a linked object and an embedded object. When you edit a linked object, you start the source file's application itself. When you edit an embedded object, the target application's menus change to those of the source application. ▪

■ To insert the worksheet as a table in your Word document (the default choice when you choose Edit, Paste), select Formatted Text (RTF). You may need to change the column widths for the table to line up properly, as is the case in Figure 50.8.

■ To insert the worksheet with tabs separating data, choose Unformatted Text. You may need to highlight the data and change the tabs for the selection if you want the information to align.

■ To insert the worksheet as a graphic, select Picture or Bitmap. Both options insert the worksheet as a diagram, but Picture generally takes up less room in the file and prints faster. In Figure 50.8, however, there is almost no discernible difference between Microsoft Excel Worksheet Object, Picture, and Bitmap. In fact, these three options do the same thing. They all insert a picture into the Word document, and you can double-click all three options to go to Excel to edit the object.

To edit the picture, first select the picture to show the small square selection handles. To resize the picture, point to one of the handles until the mouse pointer changes to a small, double-headed, black arrow; then drag. To move the picture up or down in the document, drag the drag-and-drop white arrow and rectangle mouse pointer. To go to Excel to change the data, double-click the picture.

- To insert a hyperlink to the worksheet, choose Word Hyperlink. By means of their color, hyperlink formats can help the user determine which links have already been accessed.

- Put a check mark in the Display as Icon check box on the right side of the dialog box to place a small symbol that represents the program (or any other icon you select).

Suppose that now you need to create a quarterly report that contains text, Excel worksheets, and Excel charts. To do this, you begin by inserting some introductory text at the beginning of the report that includes the purpose and history of the organization. You could link the Mission.doc and Company History.doc Word documents to the quarterly report file. To report on the sales for the first three months, you probably want to show the amount in a table, a pie chart by type of product sold, and a column chart of sales by month.

Figure 50.9 shows a formatted Excel worksheet. Because the numbers will change, you want to link rather than paste the worksheet and the charts.

FIG. 50.9

Highlight the range in Excel and choose Edit, Copy.

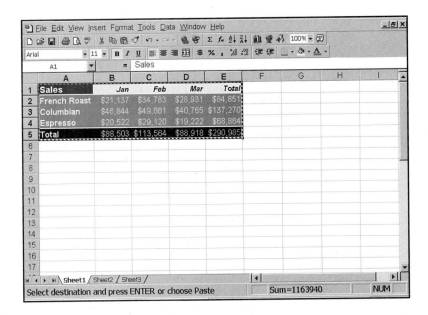

To copy this worksheet into a Word document, follow these steps:

1. In Excel, highlight the range you want to link (A1:E5).

2. Choose Edit, Copy, or press Ctrl+C.

3. Switch to Word.

4. Choose Edit, Paste Special. The Paste Special dialog box appears.

5. Choose Paste Link, and choose Picture from the As box. Then, choose OK. The result appears in Figure 50.10. Notice that the picture is left-justified.

6. If you want to center the worksheet, select the picture and then click the Center button.

FIG. 50.10
The worksheet picture appears left-justified in the Word document.

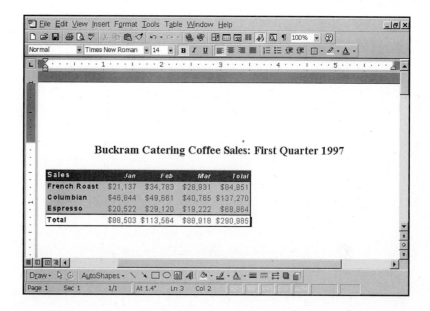

Buckram Catering Coffee Sales: First Quarter 1997

Sales	Jan	Feb	Mar	Total
French Roast	$21,137	$34,783	$28,931	$84,851
Columbian	$46,844	$49,661	$40,765	$137,270
Espresso	$20,522	$29,120	$19,222	$68,864
Total	$88,503	$113,564	$88,918	$290,985

TROUBLESHOOTING

We are working in a workgroup, and I know that my coworkers have changed the Excel document. Why aren't the links updating when I open or print the Word document? You may have one of two options turned off. Check Tools, Options, and in the General tab, make sure the Update Automatic Links at Open option is on. In the Print tab, check to make sure the Update Links option is on.

Linking an Excel Chart to a Word Document

Suppose that you want to add a pie chart and column chart to this page in your quarterly report document. You can create charts quickly by clicking the ChartWizard button in Excel's Standard toolbar.

Creating a Pie Chart

To create a pie chart, follow these steps:

1. Drag the white-cross mouse pointer to highlight the titles in A2 to A4 (refer to Figure 50.9).

2. Hold down the Ctrl button and drag to highlight E2 to E4.

3. Click the ChartWizard button. The ChartWizard dialog box appears, displaying the first of four steps.

4. Select the Pie chart from the Chart Type list box, and the 3D Pie chart in the Chart Subtype area.

5. Click Next twice to get to the Step 3 ChartWizard dialog box. If necessary, choose the Titles tab. Type **YTD Sales** in the Chart Title text box.

6. Choose the Data Labels tab. Select the Show Label and Percent option button.

7. Choose the Legend tab. Fill the Show Legend check box, and choose the Bottom option button.

8. Click Finish. The chart appears on the worksheet, as shown in Figure 50.11.

FIG. 50.11

The chart appears on the worksheet that contains the data.

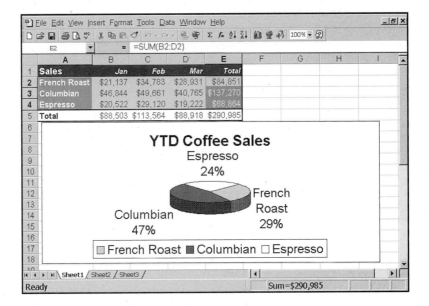

9. You can copy the chart the same way you do a range. If necessary, select the chart, choose Edit, Copy, or press Ctrl+C.

10. Return to the quarterly report document in Word.

11. Choose Edit, Paste Special. The Paste Special dialog box appears.

12. Select Microsoft Excel Chart Object, and then choose the Paste Link option. Click OK. The chart appears in the Word document, surrounded by handles. If the handles do not appear, click the chart.

Creating a Column Chart

To create a column chart in Excel, follow these steps:

1. Drag the white-cross mouse pointer to highlight the range A1 through D4 on the worksheet shown earlier in Figure 50.9.

2. Click the ChartWizard button. Step 1 appears. Select the Column chart type and Clustered Column as the chart sub-type.

3. Click Next twice to reach Step 3 of 4. In the <u>C</u>hart Title text box on the Titles tab, type **Coffee Sales by Month**.

4. Click Next to reach Step 4 of 4, and indicate whether you want to place the chart on the worksheet or on its own sheet. Click Finish.

   The chart appears with selection handles. If, in Step 4, you placed both the Pie and the Column charts on the same sheet, the second chart may appear directly over the first. You can reveal the first chart by dragging the second to the side.

5. With the chart selected, choose <u>E</u>dit, <u>C</u>opy, or press Ctrl+C.

6. Return to the quarterly report document by clicking the Word button in the taskbar.

7. Choose <u>E</u>dit, Paste <u>S</u>pecial. The Paste Special dialog box appears.

8. In the <u>A</u>s list box, select Microsoft Excel Chart Object and choose the Paste <u>L</u>ink option. Choose OK. The chart appears in the Word document, with handles.

The data range and charts in the quarterly report are shown in Figure 50.12 and 50.13. When the final numbers come in, simply go to the Excel range and edit them. Figures 50.14 and 50.15 show an updated Word document with the new number for March Espresso sales, and the result of the update is reflected in the charts.

FIG. 50.12

The Excel range and column chart appear in the Word document.

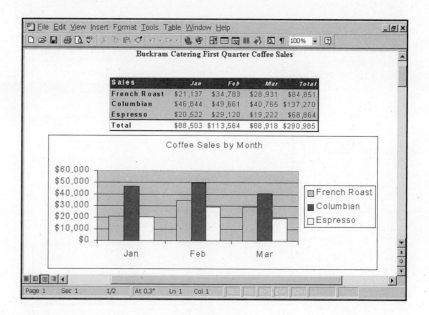

N O T E To remove the border surrounding the charts, change the charts in Excel rather than Word. In Excel, click to select the chart. Choose F<u>o</u>rmat, <u>S</u>elected Chart Area. In the Patterns tab, choose <u>N</u>one in the Border section, and then choose OK. ■

FIG. 50.13
A pie chart is useful for showing differences in percentages.

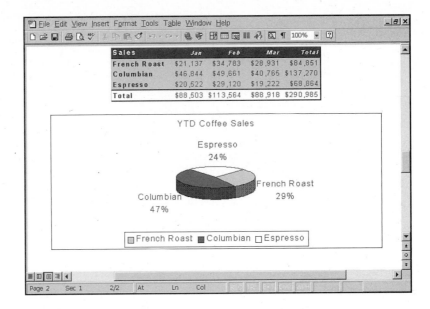

FIG. 50.14
A column chart is useful for showing differences in values.

New number in March

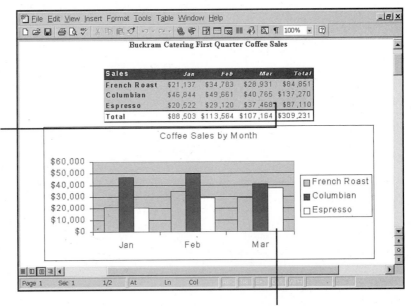

The March espresso column changes height

FIG. 50.15

After you update the Excel worksheet, the changes occur in the Word document.

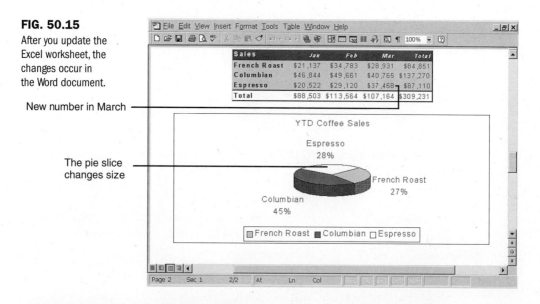

New number in March ⎯⎯

The pie slice changes size ⎯⎯

Embedding Information in Your Documents

As mentioned at the beginning of the chapter, in addition to linking information, you can embed information within a document. When you embed an object, the information resides in the destination document, but the source application's tools are available for use in editing.

For example, suppose that you have embedded a Word document in an Excel worksheet. If you now double-click the embedded Word document to edit it, Excel's menus change to Word menus, and you use the available Word commands to edit the embedded document.

You can use any of the following methods to embed information in a document. In each case, to embed the object, choose the Paste option button instead of Paste Link:

■ Copy the information to the Clipboard; choose Edit, Paste Special; select an object format. (This method was discussed earlier in the section "Using Common Steps to Link Documents," along with other Paste Special formats.)

■ Arrange two windows side by side and use drag and drop to copy information between the applications.

■ From the target application, choose Insert, Object, choose to Create from File, and open an existing file. (This method was discussed in "Inserting a File into a Document" earlier in this chapter.)

■ From the target application, choose Insert, Object, and Create New object. This section describes this method.

Inserting a New Object into Your Document

If you want to use the features of another application in your document, you can choose Insert, Object and select an application from a list. In addition to the standard Microsoft Office applications, the list contains applets and other Windows applications. Applets are small applications that cannot be run by themselves. When you purchase an application, one or more applets may be available. You may also see other applets when you install other applications such as Lotus SmartSuite.

Following is a list of some of the applets that come with Microsoft Office. If you purchased your applications separately, you may not have all the applets.

Applet	Use
Calendar Control	Inserts a calendar in your document that has drop-down arrows so that you can change the month and year.
Microsoft Clip Gallery	Inserts clip-art pictures
Microsoft Map	Inserts a map showing different levels associated with data
Microsoft Equation 3.0	Creates mathematical expressions
Microsoft Graph 97	Inserts charts from data in a table
MS Organization Chart 2.0	Creates organization charts
Microsoft Word Picture	Inserts a picture and the tools associated with the Word drawing toolbar
Microsoft WordArt	Creates logos and other special text effects

To use the tools from another application or applet within your document to create a new object, follow these steps:

1. Position the insertion point in the destination document.
2. Choose Insert, Object. The Object dialog box appears, as shown in Figure 50.16.

FIG. 50.16
The Object dialog box lists applets as well as Windows applications.

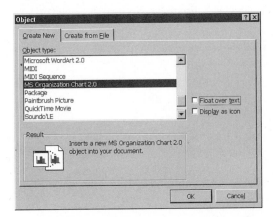

3. In the Create New tab, select an application or applet from the Object type list.

4. If you want to see only an icon for the object, put a check mark in the Display as Icon check box. If you want to put the object in the Drawing layer of your document, check the Float over Text check box (but remember that field codes will be unavailable if you do so).

5. When you finish with the Object dialog box, choose OK.

After you complete these steps, one of two things will occur. You may enter a separate window for the application or the applet, as shown in Figure 50.17. The other possibility is that you will remain in your destination document window, but the menu bar and toolbar will change to reflect the source application, as shown in Figure 50.18. For example, when you choose Microsoft Excel Worksheet, the menu bar and toolbar change to Microsoft Excel, enabling you to use Excel features such as the AutoSum button.

FIG. 50.17
When you choose Micrsoft Organization Chart, a separate window opens. After you finish with the chart program, choose File, Exit to return to the Word document.

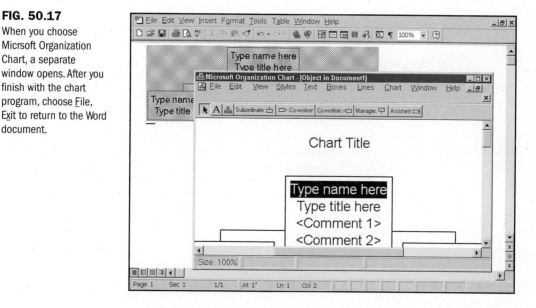

When you finish creating the object, you can exit the object in either of two ways. If you launched a separate window for the application or applet, choose File, Exit. If you stayed in your destination document, click outside the object.

Editing an Embedded Object

Regardless of which of the four methods you use to embed information into your document, you can edit the embedded object with the tools of the source application.

To edit the object, follow these steps:

1. Click the object. Handles appear around the object, and the status bar tells you to double-click the object (see Figure 50.19).

FIG. 50.18

When you choose Microsoft Excel Worksheet, in-place editing enables you to use Excel features.

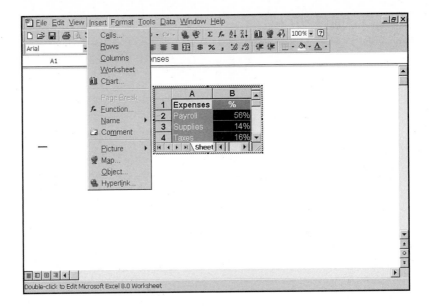

FIG. 50.19

The status bar displays instructions on how to get to the source-application tools.

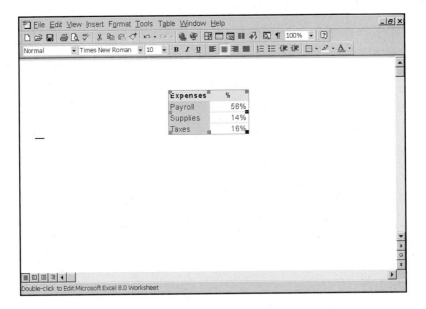

2. Double-click the object. Depending on the source and destination applications, a separate window for the program appears, or the current window's toolbar and menu bar change to those of the source application.

3. Edit the object, using the application's toolbar and menus.

4. When you finish editing the object, exit the object. If you launched a separate window for the application or applet, choose File, Exit. If you stayed in your destination document, click outside the object.

In some cases, you may be prompted if you want to update the object in your destination document. If you want to save the editing changes, choose Yes; otherwise, choose No.

TROUBLESHOOTING

Sometimes when I open a Word document with an embedded object, the object returns to its original size instead of staying the size I want. When you embed an object in Word, Word inserts the Embed field code in the document. In the Embed field code, there could be a switch \s which means return the object to its original size. To fix this problem, you need to modify the Embed field code for the object. To view the field code instead of the object, click the object and then press Shift+F9 to switch to the field code. Delete \s at the end of the Embed code.

Using Word and Excel Files on the Internet

Creating Word Documents for the Web

Opening a New Web Page

If you are creating a simple Web page that fits a predefined category, or if you are new to Web publishing, you may want to use the Web Page Wizard to help you get started. But when you want to let your creativity fly, start with a blank document and see what you can do with Word's Web authoring tools.

To open a new blank Web page and make Web authoring tools accessible, follow these steps:

1. Choose File, New to display the New dialog box, then select the Web Pages tab, shown in Figure 51.1.

FIG. 51.1

Select Blank Web Page to open a new document and access the Web authoring tools.

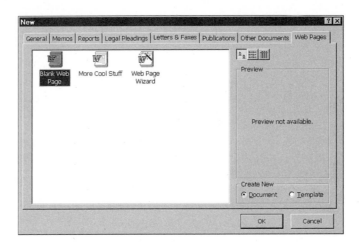

2. Select the Blank Web Page icon and choose OK.

A blank document opens. Notice that if you choose File, Save As, the Save as Type lists this document as an HTML document, not a Word DOC document. If you look through the menus, you will find that some Word menu items have disappeared and Web publishing menu items have appeared.

N O T E Word menus and menu items are available when a Word DOC document is active. Web authoring menus and menu items are available when an HTML document is active. Switching between documents automatically changes the menus and menu items to make them appropriate for the active document. ■

You can use all the Web authoring tools described in following sections to enhance this document. When you save it as an HTML document, it will become a Web page in a file with the extension HTM.

Creating a Web Page with the Web Page Wizard

When you are new to Web authoring, or if the Web page you want to create fits within one of Word's predefined categories, you can use the Web Page Wizard to save yourself work and produce pages with a uniform appearance.

To create a Web page using the Web Page Wizard, follow these steps:

1. Choose File, New to display the New dialog box, then select the Web Pages tab shown in Figure 51.1.

2. Select the Web Page Wizard icon and choose OK. The Web Page Wizard dialog box appears, as shown in Figure 51.2.

Part XIII

Ch 51

FIG. 51.2

The Web Page Wizard begins by asking you the type of page you want to create.

3. Select the type of Web page you want to create and preview the page behind the dialog box. Choose Next.

   Figure 51.3 shows that selecting the Calendar item displays the Calendar template behind the dialog box. Click Next when you find the type of page you want to create.

4. Select the style of Web page from the dialog box in Figure 51.4, then choose Finish.

   Figure 51.4 shows how the Personal Home Page selection appears with the Outdoors style. (The Personal Home Page is useful as a starting page for your Web browser.) Each style is unique and gives a different impression.

5. Choose File, Save As and give the file a name to save the HTML page. If you want to preserve this file as a template for other HTML pages, select Document Template from the Save as Type list before saving.

Once you choose Finish, the Web Page Wizard disappears, leaving you with an HTML document and the Web authoring tools. At this point you can type in your own text, reformat, insert files, add multimedia links, insert graphics, and of course create hyperlinks.

FIG. 51.3

Preview the type of page you select by watching the document behind the Web Page Wizard dialog box.

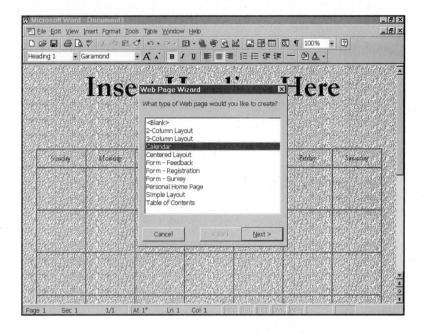

FIG. 51.4

Preview the appearance of different formatting styles.

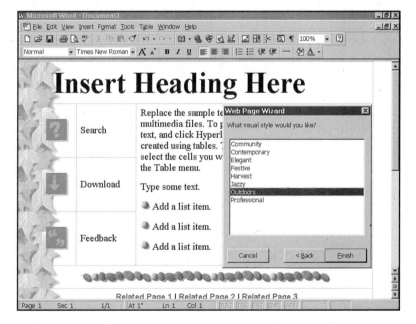

Using Word's Web Page Authoring Tools

Word's Web page authoring tools give you all the tools needed to create attractive Web pages. Your pages can be displayed with virtually all Internet browsers if you use only basic features such as formatting, graphics, and hyperlinks. Major browsers like Microsoft Internet Explorer and Netscape Navigator will also be able to display special features such as tables and scrolling text.

Viewing Your Web Page

As you work in Word, the screen displays an image close to how it will appear in Internet Explorer. However, different browsers may display the page differently: You should test your Web page against all the browsers used in your company and the major browsers used on the Internet.

To open an HTML file you have already created, double-click the HTM file and the file will open in the browser currently registered for HTM files. To see an approximation of how the HTML file appears in a browser as you are working in Word, choose File, Web Page Preview.

> **CAUTION**
>
> The view you see in Word's Web Page Preview only approximates how the page will appear in a browser. If you are creating Web pages that involve more than simple text, graphics, and tables, you should develop the page through an iterative process of working in Word and viewing on the browsers most widely used by your target audience.

Inserting Background Patterns   At any time, you can change the background pattern that is displayed behind your Web page. Although there are many beautiful patterns and textures available, have mercy on the reader's eyes. What might look pleasing as a graphic background could prevent people from even attempting to read the text.

To change the Web page background, follow these steps:

1. Choose Format, Background to display the background palette, shown in Figure 51.5.

FIG. 51.5
The first background palette shows plain colors, but patterns and fill effects are available.

2. Select a color by clicking it.

    or

    Select More Colors to display the palette shown in Figure 51.6. Select the Standard tab to choose a color or select the Custom tab to blend your own color. Choose OK.

    or

Select <u>F</u>ill Effects to display the textured and marbled backgrounds, shown in Figure 51.7. Choose OK.

FIG. 51.6
Choose from a wide variety of colors or blend your own custom color.

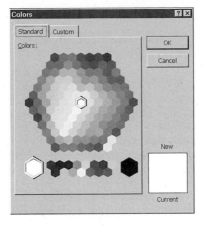

FIG. 51.7
Textured or marbled backgrounds look elegant.

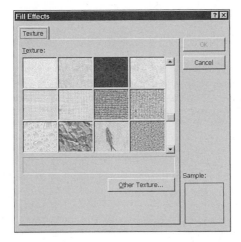

 Go to **http://www.microsoft.com/gallery** to enter Microsoft's gallery of free image and background files you can download. To download a file, right-click the graphic in your Web browser, then choose Save Picture As. Specify the folder where you want the file stored. Insert these files in your own pages or use them as Web page backgrounds.

If you want to use a picture file as the background for your Web page, choose F<u>o</u>rmat, <u>B</u>ackground, <u>F</u>ill Effect. Click the <u>O</u>ther Texture button. Select the GIF, JPG, or WMF file you want as a background, then choose OK twice. Only small files, on the order of 1K, can be used as backgrounds. If you installed Office 97, look in the CLIPART \ BACKGROUNDS folder for background files.

Formatting the Color of Body Text and Hypertext

At any time in your document, you can change the color of all body text. It's also easy to change the color of hyperlinks. Hyperlinks have two colors that can be changed: the color before a link has been used, and the color after a link has been used. Two colors are used so that it's easy to tell which links the reader has previously used.

 TIP Many designers recommend that you leave hypertext colors at their default settings because people are accustomed to seeing and reacting to the default colors.

To change the color of body text or hyperlinks, follow these steps:

1. Choose Format, Text Colors to display the Document Text Colors dialog box, shown in Figure 51.8.

FIG. 51.8
Change the color of
body text or hyperlinks
at any time.

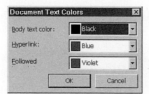

2. Select a color from one or more of the following:

Body Text Color   Changes the color of text that has not been formatted with the Format, Font command

    Hyperlink   Changes the color of hyperlink text that has not been used for a jump this session

    Followed   Changes the color of hyperlink text that has been used for a jump this session

3. Choose OK.

Formatting Selected Text

Currently, HTML does not enable you to specify the exact font and size for text as it will appear in all browsers. Instead, you specify a type of font appearance, which the browser displays according to its own capabilities and user preferences. Microsoft and other industry leaders are developing TrueType fonts for use by Web browsers, as well as cascading style sheets, which will make it easier for an author to specify exactly how text will appear.

To format a font on a Web page, follow these steps:

1. Select the text and choose Format, Font to display the Font dialog box, shown in Figure 51.9.

2. Select the font options you want applied, then choose OK.

FIG. 51.9

Font formats are more limited in HTML pages than in Word documents.

Although the Font dialog box enables you to choose a font and size that the browser displays, your finished Web page may use a different font and size. Most browsers currently do not specify exact fonts or type sizes; instead, they use a family of fonts, such as sans serif, and type sizes relative to the other type sizes on the page. If you are unsure how your font formatting will appear, choose File, Web Page Preview to see the page in your browser. If you expect the page to be viewed by browsers such as Netscape or Mosaic, then you should open the page in those browsers and examine the appearance.

Tricks for Creating Custom Font Colors

Word's Web page authoring tools have only 16 colors available for fonts and tables. If you want to add more colors, format the text with one of the 16 colors, then modify the color by going into the HTML source code and replacing the color code with a color code you prefer.

To find a color code you want to use for your fonts, you will open a blank document, change its background color to what you want, and then see what the color code is for the background. You can then use that color code to color other page elements such as the font color.

To find the code for the color you want, open a blank Web document. Choose Format, Background, More Colors. Select a color from the Standard or Custom tab and choose OK. If this is the color you want for your font, choose View, HTML Source. This displays the HTML source code for the colored Web page. Look for the HTML tag <BODY BGCOLOR="*hexnumber*">. For example, a hot pink background has the code

```
<BODY BGCOLOR="#ff0066">
```

The number in quotes is a hexadecimal number that includes some letters. Write down the number you see or select it and choose Edit, Copy. Exit the source code by clicking the Exit HTML Source button or by choosing View, Exit HTML Source.

Activate the Web page with the fonts you want to color and follow these steps:

1. Select the text you want to have the special color and format it with any color from the Font dialog box.
2. Choose View, HTML Source to display the HTML tags that compose your Web page.
3. Find the text you formatted in step 1. It should be preceded by a <FONT> tag. Within that <FONT> tag will be the COLOR parameter. Select the hexadecimal number after COLOR= and paste in or type the number you copied from the <BODY BGCOLOR> tag.

   4. Choose View, Exit HTML Source. You will be asked if you want to save your change. Choose Yes.

   The font will appear in the new color.

If you do a lot of Web pages using Word, you may want to create an HTML document that contains lines of different color fonts. You can use this document as a palette to keep your favorite exotic colors. Make sure each line of text you format contains different words, perhaps the color description, so that you can tell the text apart even when you are looking at black-and-white HTML code.

> **CAUTION**
>
> Just because you can create thousands of text colors doesn't mean you should. Consider how easy the text will be to read against the different background colors and patterns you might use.

Inserting Scrolling Text

If you really want to grab someone's attention, use scrolling text. It appears like a marquee of text traveling across the page. Be careful that you don't overuse it and make your Web look like a Las Vegas nightmare. Different browsers and different versions handle special features such as scrolling text in different ways. Test how this effect appears in your reader's browsers.

To make text scroll across your Web page, follow these steps:

   1. Move the insertion point to its own line. The scrolling text must appear on its own line in the page.

   2. Choose Insert, Scrolling Text and select the Scrolling Text Options tab to display the Scrolling Text dialog box, shown in Figure 51.10.

   3. Type the text you want as moving text into the Type the Scrolling Text Here box.

FIG. 51.10

Scrolling text travels across the page to attract attention.

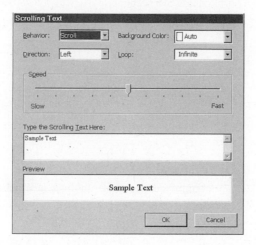

4. Select the type of action from the Behavior box. Scroll moves the text across the screen then wraps it around in a continuous loop. Slide moves the text across the screen once and stops. Alternate bounces the text between screen edges.

5. Select Right or Left from the Direction box and select a color from the Background Color box. If you choose Scroll as the behavior, you can select the number of times to scroll from the Loop box.

6. Select the Size and Speed tab, which selects the speed and size of the box through which the text moves. You can also specify how close body text appears next to the box containing the scrolling text.

7. Choose OK.

To reformat scrolling text, click the box containing the scrolling text, then choose Format, Scrolling Text.

Inserting Horizontal Lines

Make on-screen text easier to read and absorb by breaking it into chunks. These nuggets of information should be more condensed than the long passages of text we are accustomed to in printed material. If you need to express detail and depth, you can do it with hyperlinks to lengthier explanations. One way to visually break your documents into discrete chunks is to use horizontal rules or lines as demarcations between chunks of different information.

 The horizontal lines inserted by Word are actually graphic files with centered alignment. You can insert any GIF or JPEG graphic in the center of the page using this command.

The horizontal lines used in Word's authoring tools are graphic files. To insert horizontal lines, follow these steps:

1. Move the insertion point to where you want the horizontal line to be. If you put it within text, the text will be broken into two sections, above and below the line.

2. Choose Insert, Horizontal Line to display the Horizontal Line dialog box, shown in Figure 51.11.

3. Select one of the lines from the Style box, then choose OK.

   or

   Choose More. Select from the Insert Picture dialog box a graphic file that you want used as a line. If you installed Microsoft Office 97, look in the CLIPART\LINES folder. Choose Insert.

Formatting Lines with Bullets and Numbers

Web pages can have bulleted or numbered lists similar to those in Word. However, Web pages have a greater variety of bullets than Word because they use graphic images as bullets. Bullets and numbers are applied in front of the first line of each paragraph.

FIG. 51.11
A wide variety of horizontal lines are available for separating sections of your page.

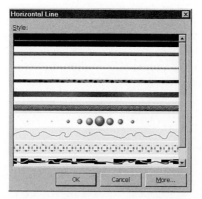

If by accident you format a line on a Web page twice with the bullets command, the line will have two bullets. To delete the bullet you do not want, select that bullet, then press the Del key.

To format paragraphs with bullets, follow these steps:

1. Select the paragraphs to be preceded by a bullet.

2. Choose Format, Bullets and Numbering, then select the Bulleted tab to display the Bullets and Numbering dialog box, shown in Figure 51.12.

FIG. 51.12
Bullets precede the first line of each paragraph.

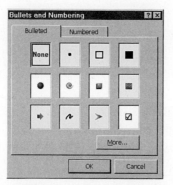

3. Select the type of bullet you want and click OK.

   or

   Click More to display the Insert Picture dialog box. The dialog opens with images in the CLIPART\BULLETS folder listed. Select an image or change to another folder and select an image, then choose Insert.

The numbering feature precedes the first line of each paragraph with numbers of different format. With the command you can also remove numbering, restart numbering, or continue the numbers from an adjacent list. To apply numbering or change existing numbering, follow these steps:

1. Select the lines or paragraphs.

2. Choose F̲ormat, Bullets and N̲umbering, then select the Numbered tab to display the Bullets and Numbering dialog box, shown in Figure 51.13.

FIG. 51.13
Numbering precedes the first line of each selected paragraph.

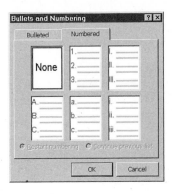

3. Select one of the following options:

None	Removes numbering from selected paragraphs.
Numbered examples	Inserts a number of the format shown in front of the first line of selected paragraphs.
R̲estart Numbering	Starts the numbering from 1 even if the selection is adjacent to an existing list.
C̲ontinue Previous List	Continues the numbering from the adjacent list.

4. Click OK.

Typing Hyperlinks to Web or Local Files

One very quick way to create a hyperlink in an HTML document is to type it directly into the document. If Word recognizes what you type as a valid URL, then it will convert your typed URL into a hyperlink. For example, the following lines will be recognized and turned into hyperlinks:

http://www.mcp.com
www.mcp.com
ftp://ftp.microsoft.com
ftp.microsoft.com
file://C:\business

Once you have typed the hyperlink, you may want to replace it with more readable and understandable text. To do this, select the hyperlink by dragging across it or by right-clicking it and choosing H̲yperlink, S̲elect Hyperlink. Once it is selected, type the text you want displayed. For example, you might want to replace

www.wsj.com

with

Wall Street Journal Interactive

Edit the hyperlink by right-clicking it and choosing Hyperlink, Edit Hyperlink. The Edit Hyperlink dialog box is described in the section "Inserting Hyperlinks to Web or Local Files."

Inserting Hyperlinks

Another method of creating a hyperlink in the Web page is with the Insert, Hyperlink command. If you are unfamiliar with the path name to a local or networked file, this method enables you to use a Link to File dialog box to find the file to which you want to link. You also can link to a specific named location in an Office document or HTML page. For detailed instructions on inserting a hyperlink using the Insert menu, see "Inserting Hyperlinks to Web or Local Files," later in this chapter.

Part
XIII

Ch
51

TIP   To create a graphical hyperlink, see the following section, "Inserting Graphics."

Inserting Graphics   Visually attractive Web pages are both a boon and a bane. They make a page more enjoyable and appealing, yet the size of the graphics increases the time it takes to load a graphic. There is both an art and a science in the use of graphics on a Web page. The art is in creating a visual layout that is appealing yet doesn't take too long to load. The science is in knowing how to create graphics that load quickly. There are special techniques you can use to make graphics of the same size load many times faster. For tips on design and how to create graphics that work well in Web pages, read these four books:

Title, Author, Publisher, ISBN	Description
Designing Business Clement Mok $60 Adobe Press ISBN 1-56830-282-7	A visually gorgeous book that fills your mind with ideas and then sets your neurons on fire with the desire to make changes. Don't read this late at night—be alert. It's about the use of design at the leading edge of technology. Includes a CD-ROM of interactive prototypes and projects.
Creating Killer Web Sites David Siegel $45 Hayden Books ISBN 1-56830-289-4	This book shows specific examples of great Web site design and how Web page design has evolved. David Siegel is one of the Web's design gods. Pay attention to the leading edge. Check out his Web site.
Designing Web Graphics Lynda Weinman $50 New Riders ISBN 1-56205-532-1	In addition to teaching step-by-step graphics techniques, Lynda does a great job of showing you how to optimize graphics for speed. Includes a CD-ROM with lots of demo software.

Creating Your Own Web Graphics with Paint Shop Pro
Andy Shafran
Dick Oliver
$34.99
Que
ISBN 0-7897-0912-0

Have you seen impressive buttons and banners on a Web page and wondered how they were drawn? This book shows step-by-step drawing techniques for great Web graphics with Paint Shop Pro.

Web pages use graphic files in the GIF or JPEG format. You can insert graphic files in other image formats that are recognized by Word, such as PCX and BMP. When you save the HTML page, Word will convert the graphics that are not GIF or JPEG into GIF format. If Word does not convert your graphic files, re-run the Office 97 or Word 97 installation and install the HTML and graphic converters.

CAUTION

Inserting a large image and then resizing it to a smaller dimension in Word will not make the Web page load faster because the full image still must be downloaded. You can use a simple graphics editor such as Microsoft Photo Editor to crop an image. If you want to create high-performance images that load quicker while preserving color and resolution, refer to the book *Designing Web Graphics*, listed earlier in this section.

 Changing a Web page in Word and then viewing it with your browser may not display the changes you have made. The browser may display the same Web page that you last viewed in the browser. This is because most browsers *cache* or save a few of their most recent pages. This improves speed but means that you might not see changes that have occurred. To see changes you have made, click the Refresh button.

To insert a graphic into your Web page, follow these steps:

1. Move the insertion point to where you want the image or picture to be.
2. Choose Insert, Picture.
3. Select Clip Art to display the Clip Gallery, shown in Figure 51.14, or select From File to display the Insert Picture dialog box, shown in Figure 51.15.
4. Select the image you want inserted, then choose Insert.

 Save graphics that you see in Internet Explorer by right-clicking the graphic, then choosing Save Picture As. Specify the file name and where you want the picture saved, then click OK. Please do not violate copyright and trademark laws.

Creating Hyperlinked Graphics   As you browse the Web, it doesn't take long to notice that many of the graphics are hyperlinked to other Web sites or documents. You can hyperlink your graphics just as easily as you created text hyperlinks. To hyperlink a graphic to a Web page or document, follow these steps:

FIG. 51.14
Select from an organized collection of images and pictures in the Clip Gallery.

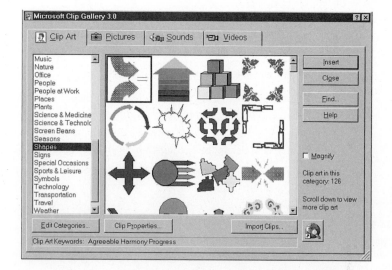

FIG. 51.15
Select files of images from the Insert Picture dialog box.

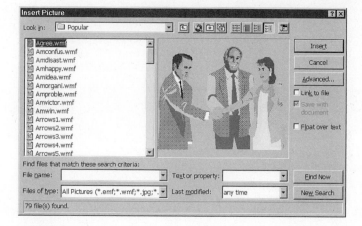

1. Insert the graphic.

2. Select the graphic by clicking it.

3. Choose Insert, Hyperlink to display the Insert Hyperlink dialog box.

4. Complete the Insert Hyperlink dialog box as described in the section "Inserting Hyperlinks to Web or Local Files."

Edit a hyperlinked graphic by right-clicking the graphic and choosing Insert, Hyperlink, Edit Hyperlink. Make changes in the Edit Hyperlink dialog box.

Creating Alternative Text for Graphics and Hyperlinked Graphics You may want to create alternative text that is displayed when graphics or hyperlinked graphics cannot display. Some browsers display only text, and a high percentage of people browse the Web with the graphics turned off on their browser so they get higher performance. For both of these types of viewers, you should create text alternatives that appear when graphics and hyperlinked graphics do not display.

To create a text alternative for a graphic or hyperlinked graphics, follow these steps:

1. Select a non-hyperlinked graphic by clicking on it. Select a hyperlinked graphic by right-clicking on the hyperlinked graphic, then choose Hyperlink, Select Hyperlink.

2. Choose Format, Picture or click Format Picture on the Picture toolbar to display the Picture dialog box. Select the Settings tab, as shown in Figure 51.16.

3. Type in the Text box the text you want to appear when the graphic does not display.

4. Choose OK.

FIG. 51.16
Picture placeholders are known as alternative text on HTML pages.

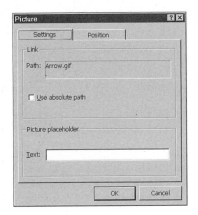

Downloading Web Art from the Internet   If you have access to the Internet, you can download free images for your Web page. To download images, choose Insert, Picture, Browse Web Art Page. If you are asked if you would like to access the Internet to browse Microsoft's Web site, click Yes. The Web toolbar will appear, and your Internet browser will access Microsoft's Web Art page.

Figure 51.17 shows one incarnation of the Microsoft Web Art page. Follow the directions on the Web page to view and download art.

Inserting and Formatting Tables

People who use Word love its table feature. You can continue to use Word's tables when creating your Web pages. Tables are an excellent way of displaying lists of related data. The *information chunking* technique that has become common on the Web fits well into a table format. While the current versions of most Web browsers can display tables, none display snaking newspaper columns. These are the multi-column layouts you might use for newsletters. If you need that type of a format, however, you can fake it with the use of two- or three-column tables that have one row per Web page. That row is as tall as the text in the column. It is up to you to cut and paste text to balance the text between columns.

FIG. 51.17
Retrieve free graphics for your Web pages from Microsoft's Web Art Page.

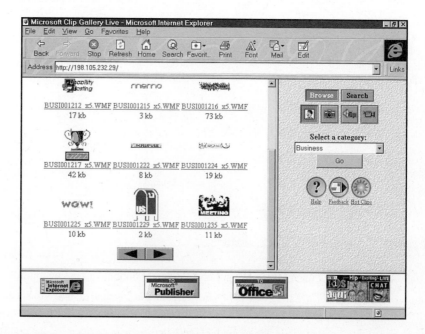

Notice that few Web pages use multiple text columns because this is hard to read. Most pages, like the Wall Street Journal Interactive or many of Microsoft's pages, use a three-column format, where the center column is reading text and the outer columns are hyperlinks.

TIP If you have a large table of numbers or calculations in Excel that need to be ported into a Web page, don't retype them; either copy and paste them into the Web page or use Excel's Internet Assistant. To save graphics or ranges as a Web page, choose File, Save as HTML. Excel's Internet Assistant will also insert graphics or ranges into existing Web pages.

To draw or insert tables, use the same table drawing command and tools you would use in a Word document. These tools are described in depth in Chapter 10, "Creating and Editing Tables," and Chapter 11, "Modifying Tables."

Format tables

Table, Cell Properties

Table, Borders

Change formatting for the entire table with Table Properties. If you want to specify how text wraps around a table or format the text's background and the space between table columns, follow these steps:

1. Select a cell within the table.

2. Choose Table, Table Properties to display the Table Properties dialog box, shown in Figure 51.18.

FIG. 51.18

Select formatting for the entire table.

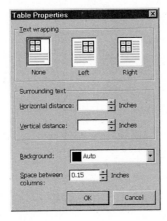

3. Click one of the table and text alignment options in Text wrapping.

4. Enter a distance in inches in Horizontal or Vertical distance to specify how close text comes to the table.

5. Format the inside of the table by selecting a color from Background and specify the distance between text in cells by entering an amount in Space between columns.

6. Choose OK.

Change the properties within individual cells with Cell Properties. If you want to specify how text aligns in cells, its color, and a dimension for cells, follow these steps:

1. Select the cells in the table you want to format.

2. Choose Table, Cell Properties to display the Cell Properties dialog box, shown in Figure 51.19.

FIG. 51.19

Select formatting for a cell within the table.

3. Select how you want cell contents to align vertically from the Vertical Alignment group.

4. Format the cell background color and dimensions with the Background, Width, and Height boxes.

5. Choose OK.

Format borders around the table by following these steps:

1. Select inside the table.

2. Choose Table, Borders to display the Table Borders dialog box, shown in Figure 51.20.

3. Select Presets, Grid to put borders around cells in the table. Select None to remove borders.

4. Select the border width from the Border Width box.

5. Choose OK.

FIG. 51.20
Put borders around the entire table.

Creating Forms with Controls

As you browse the Web, you will come across forms with check boxes, lists, text areas, and so on. These forms are used to send information back to the site that hosts the Web page. That information can then be used to customize the information you see to meet your needs, or it can be used to customize the information you see to meet what the host wants you to see.

N O T E   Form controls on a Word document do not convert to HTML form controls when you save the Word document as an HTML document. ■

To use the forms as a way of gathering information, however, you will need to use the forms with a Web site that has CGI scripts for forms. *CGI* stands for Common Gateway Interface—the programs on the Web server that add intelligence to Web pages. A CGI script will gather the information from a form and compile it into a database or return the data to you via e-mail.

   You don't have to hire a cadre of programmers and get into the expense and complexity of CGI scripts if you want to have forms on your Web. Microsoft's FrontPage 97—a Web design and management application—includes Web authoring, Web management, and forms creation, and stores the data from

continues

continued

forms in common database formats. It also manages Webs you create involving Office documents. If you want to be on the World Wide Web, you can create a Web with FrontPage and host it with all FrontPage capabilities on many Web providers.

If you will be placing a lot of controls in a form, display the Control Toolbox toolbar for quick access to the form controls.

To insert form controls in your page, follow these steps:

1. Move the insertion point to where you want the control to appear.
2. Choose Insert, Forms.
3. Select one of the following types of controls.

    The control will appear in the form. If it is the first control in the form, you will see horizontal lines marking the Top of Form and Bottom of Form. Form controls must be between these lines.

Check Box	On or off selection
Option Button	Only one selected within a named group
Dropdown Box	Display a list from a drop-down list
List Box	Display a visible list
Text Box	Enter text in an edit box
Text Area	Enter text in a scrollable text area
Submit	A predefined button that sends the current form control choices to the host Web site
Image Submit	A custom button from a graphic image that sends the current form control choices to the host Web site
Reset	A button that clears the form's settings
Hidden	Hide text
Password	Enter text without displaying the characters

4. Double-click the control to display the Properties dialog box, where you set how the control will work. A Properties dialog box displays a table of settings for the control.

    Settings in the Properties dialog box specify how the control will act and what its default contents will be. For example, check boxes are on when the checked property is true and off when it is false.

5. Close the Property sheet by clicking the Close button in the top left corner.

Copying Your Web Page to Another Location

After you create your Web page or pages, you will probably want to copy them to a Web server. If you included graphics in the Web page, you will need to copy the GIF and JPEG files for those graphics, as well as the HTML files themselves.

Using the Windows Explorer, go to the folder where you saved the Web pages and graphics. Look for files with an HTM, GIF, and JPG extensions. One of these should be the HTML file you created. Look in the same folder for files with a GIF and JPG extensions that you inserted as graphics. Graphic files that Word converted from other formats will appear with a generic file name, such as IMAGE1.GIF, IMAGE12.JPG, and so forth. When you copy the HTM file, you must copy the GIF and JPG files it uses or the graphics will not be displayed.

Understanding the HTML Behind a Web Page

Word's Web authoring tools make it much easier to create Web pages than trying to write HTML code by hand. However, you might still need to know what HTML code looks like. You might want to go directly into the HTML source code and make a correction or add a special feature that Word is not capable of creating, such as a link to a RealAudio sound file.

Web pages are written in the *Hypertext Markup Language* (HTML). HTML is made up of elements; each element contains a tag defining what kind of element it is. Most elements also contain text that defines what the element represents. Figure 51.21 displays the sample HTML page in Internet Explorer.

FIG. 51.21

The Web page displays with graphics and formatting, but the HTML source code is text.

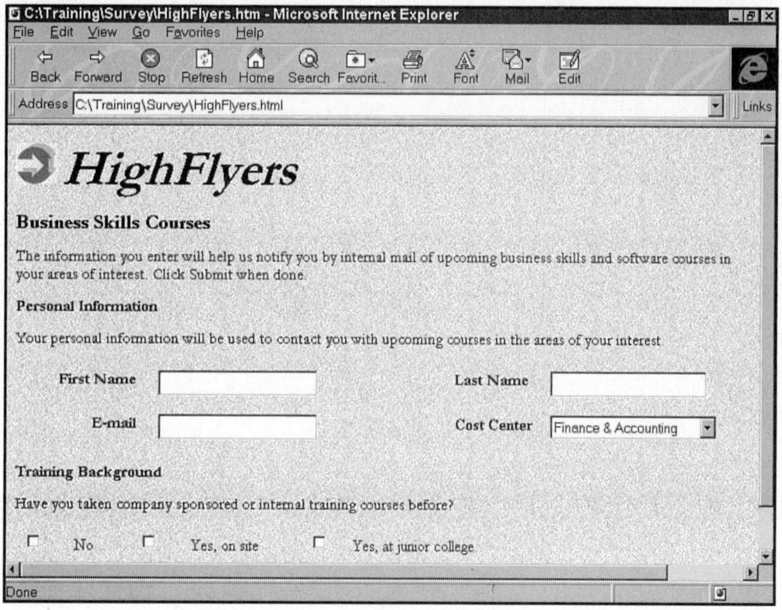

Unlike traditional desktop publishing, the user's Internet browser—not the author—controls how the document is actually displayed. The document that looks just right in your 640 × 480 Internet Explorer window may look awful to users of other browsers.

 TIP   Right-click a Web page in Internet Explorer and choose <u>V</u>iew, Source to view the HTML source.

Pages you view on the Web are intended to be well-formatted, well-presented displays. Because the page creator cannot know what type of computer or terminal the reader will use, the creator cannot use text with specific formatting information, such as fonts and point sizes, to produce these documents. To assure that everyone sees documents with approximately the same formatting, codes are inserted into a document that describe how the document should be formatted, where hyperlinks are and what they are connected to, and which graphics should be displayed. This method of inserting formatting codes in the document allows the viewer's browser to create the best display it can on the viewer's terminal or computer. These text codes that are inserted comprise the Hypertext Markup Language. The text codes, known as *tags*, are automatically inserted by Word's Web publishing tools as you create your Web pages.

How HTML Documents Are Structured

Like those nested Russian dolls, elements can contain other elements, and they can be nested several layers deep. HTML documents contain at a minimum head and body elements. Each of those elements in turn, can enclose others.

The head element usually contains a *title* element, and it may also contain comments, author information, copyright notices, or special tags that help indexers and search engines use the contents of the document more effectively.

The body element holds the actual body and content of the document. For typical documents, most of the body element is text, with tags placed at the end of each paragraph. You can also use tags for displaying numbered or bulleted lists, horizontal rules, embedded images, and hyperlinks to other documents.

Understanding Some HTML Tags

All HTML tags are enclosed in angle brackets (<>). Some elements contain two matching tags, with text or hypertext in between. For example, to define a title as part of your document's <head> element, you would put this HTML into your document:

```
<title>A Simple WWW Page</title>
```

The first tag signals the start of the title element, while the same tag, prefixed with a slash (/), tells the browser that it has reached the end of the element. Some tags do not require matching tags, such as <li>, which denotes an item in a list.

The elements most often used in HTML body elements fall into three basic categories: logical styles, physical styles, and content elements.

Understanding Logical Styles   Logical styles tell the browser how the document is structured. The HTML system of nesting elements gives the browser some information, but authors can use the logical style elements to break text into paragraphs, lists, block quotes, and so on. Like styles in Word, you can use logical styles in your documents and know that they will be properly displayed by the browser.

Table 51.1 lists some common logical styles you can use to build your document, along with examples for each one.

Part
XIII

Ch
51

Table 51.1   Logical Style Elements

Style Tag	What It Does	Sample
<p>	Ends paragraph	This is a very short paragraph.<p>
 	Inserts line break	First line Second line
<Hx>...</Hx>	Section heading	<H1>HTML Is Easy</H1>
...	Emphasis on text	Use this instead of bold text.
...	Stronger emphasis on text	THIS really gets the point across!
<code>...</code>	Displays HTML tags without acting on them	The <code><p></code> tab can be handy.
<quote>...</quote>	Displays a block of quoted text	<quote>No man is an island.</quote>
<pre>...</pre>	Displays text and leaves white space intact	<pre>E x t r a spaces are OK here.</pre>

Understanding Physical Styles   In ordinary printed documents, **bold**, *italic*, and underlined text all have their special uses. Web pages are the same way; you may want to distinguish the name of a book, a key word, or a foreign-language phrase from your body text. Table 51.2 shows a list of some common physical styles you can use in HTML documents, along with simple examples.

Table 51.2 Physical Style Elements

Style Tag	What It Does	Sample
...	Bold text	Bold text stands out.
<i>...</i>	Italic text	<i>Belle</i> is French for "pretty."
<u>...</u>	Underlined text	<u>Don't</u> confuse underlined text with a hyperlink!
_{...}	Subscript text	Water's chemical formula is H₂O.
^{...}	Superscript text	Writing "x²" is the same as writing "x*x."
<tt>...</tt>	Typewriter text	This tag's <tt>seldom</tt> seen.

Understanding Hyperlinks The key element that makes the Web different from plain documents is hyperlinking. Each link points to an *anchor*, or destination for the link. Most anchors are implied; when you specify a page as the target of the link, it is assumed that you want that entire page to be an anchor.

The basic element for hyperlinks is <a href=*"URL"*>*text description*</a>. In this case, the "a" stands for "anchor," and "href" is a hypertext reference. If you wanted a hyperlink to the file "TRAVEL/EXPENSES.HTM" on your company intranet, you would use a hyperlink in a Web page, like this:

```
<a href="TRAVEL/EXPENSES.HTM">Expense information</a>
```

The text in the middle of the link appears as a link on the browser's screen. This link points to a file named "EXPENSES.HTM" in the folder "TRAVEL".

You also could include a link to Macmillan Computer Publishing's Web page so that people visiting your page could find out about Windows 95 books. Notice that this link contains a full URL instead of the name of a local document, and the link will appear within a text phrase.

```
The <a href="http://www.mcp.com">Macmillan Publishing</a> home page has informa-
tion on Macmillan's books.<p>
```

Creating Hyperlinks in Word Documents

Hyperlinks are one of the reasons the Web is so attractive. Combined with a Web browser, such as Internet Explorer, hyperlinks make it very easy for the reader of a document to click a phrase or graphic in one document and jump to a related document. It is up to you as the author to insert hyperlinks in your documents that take the reader to related documents or Web pages.

Hyperlinks in Word documents can be between different types of Office documents, as well as to Internet or intranet sites. Clicking a hyperlink to an Office document will open the document in its appropriate application. Clicking a hyperlink to an Internet or intranet site will start your Internet browser and access the site.

The Web of linked documents and sites you create can be a simple personal Web of documents you use frequently, or it can be a complex Web of documents involving files on local computers and networks as well as sites on the Internet.

Some of the ways individuals and companies use hyperlinked documents are the following:

■ A simple Web involving hyperlinks between Word documents, Excel worksheets, and PowerPoint slides that help you switch between documents you update frequently.

■ A Web of hyperlinked Word documents that comprises a company's personnel manual. Different documents related to personnel management, rating, and hiring are all accessible from other linked documents.

■ An intranet for traveling salespeople that contains proposals and product specifications in Word documents. A client's shipping and manufacturing information is accessible through Web pages linked to ODBC database files. All users who access this Web use Windows 95 laptops.

Moving with a Hyperlink

To make a jump using a hyperlink, move the pointer over the text or graphic that is the hyperlink. The pointer changes to a pointing hand. Pause, and the path name or URL will be displayed as a ScreenTip. Click to jump to the hyperlink's destination.

If the hyperlink is to another Office document, that document's application will open and activate. The Web toolbar (see Figure 51.22) will be displayed over the document. To return to your original document, click on the Back navigation arrow. This returns you to the original document. While in the original document, you can click the Forward navigation arrow on the Web toolbar to move forward to the linked document.

TROUBLESHOOTING

Clicking a hyperlink causes an error. The two most probable causes of hyperlink errors are an incorrect path name or URL to the document and a problem in network communication.

To check the path name or URL to a document or site, right-click the hyperlink and choose Hyperlink, Edit Hyperlink. In the Edit Hyperlink dialog box, check that the path name, file name, and URL are still valid.

The other probable cause is network or communication problems. Did you see or hear your modem working correctly? If not, check the modem by trying another type of modem communication. Did the normal sign-on screens for your network connection appear? If not, check with your network administrator or attempt to access the Internet by directly using a browser. If you were trying to make an Internet connection, the Web site server you attempted to connect to may be overloaded. You might need to try that Web site again at a later time.

FIG. 51.22

Use the navigation buttons on the Web toolbar to move between linked documents.

Forward

Backward

Pasting Hyperlinks to Office Documents

In your work you may deal with documents created in different Microsoft Office applications. By adding hyperlinks to your documents, you can move between them with a single click. Figure 51.23 shows a Word document with hyperlinks to related Word and Excel documents. Clicking one of these hyperlinks opens the linked document in its native application. The text in cells containing a hyperlink appears underlined and in color.

FIG. 51.23

Hyperlinks in your documents can take you to other Office documents.

Hyperlinks can link to local Office documents

Hyperlinks can link to intranet documents

Hyperlinks can link to Internet sites

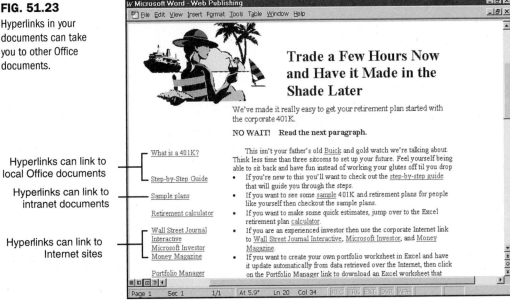

To create a link in a Word document to a specific location in another document created by an Office application, such as Excel, follow these steps:

1. Open the Word document and the document to be linked. Both documents should be saved in the folder in which you expect them to remain.

2. Activate the document you want linked and select the text or item in the document you want linked. The text or item you select at this point will be what appears in the linked document's window after you click on the hyperlink.

3. Choose Edit, Copy or right-click the selection and choose Copy.

4. Activate the Word document and select where you want the hyperlink.

5. Choose Edit, Paste as Hyperlink.

6. Click a location away from the hypertext link.

The text or worksheet cells you pasted as a hyperlink appear in the Word document. For example, if you copied and pasted a paragraph on safety training from the online personnel manuals, then that entire paragraph will appear as hyperlinked text. If you copied and pasted a range of Excel cells, then you will see a table of those cells as the hyperlink. Clicking anywhere in that hyperlinked paragraph or table opens the source document from which the hyperlinked data was copied.

One problem with this approach is that it is rare that an entire paragraph, sentence, or worksheet range from one document will fit in the context of another document. Usually you will only want a word or phrase as the hyperlink. You can retain the hyperlink and replace the lengthy text or worksheet range by following these steps:

1. Select the hyperlink by dragging across it or by right-clicking it and choosing Hyperlink, Select Hyperlink.

   If you have pasted an Excel range as the hyperlink, then use the right-click method to make sure the hyperlink is correctly selected.

2. Type the word or phrase that you want to appear as the hyperlink.

3. Click outside the hyperlink.

The word or phrase you type in step 2 will appear as a colored, underlined hyperlink. You can check or modify this hyperlink by right-clicking the hyperlink and choosing Hyperlink, Edit Hyperlink.

Inserting Hyperlinks to Web or Local Files

Another method of creating hyperlinks enables you to hyperlink to local files or Internet sites. To use this method, you need to know or be able to browse to the file's path or Internet URL.

To insert a hyperlink, follow these steps:

1. Select the cell where you want the link to appear.

2. Choose Insert, Hyperlink or click the Insert Hyperlink button in the Standard toolbar. The Insert Hyperlink dialog box is displayed as shown in Figure 51.24.

FIG. 51.24

Your hyperlink can contain a specific location in a document as well as specifying the path and file name of a document or site.

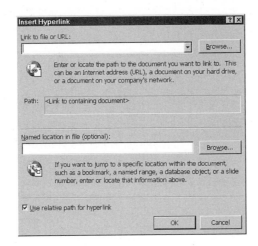

3. In the Link to File or URL box, type the path and file name or URL to the file or Web site to which you want to link.

    Enter the path name or URL like these examples:

Local document	C:\MYFILES*FILENAME.DOC*
Local program	C:\MYPROGRAMS*PROGRAMNAME.EXE*
Intranet	**HTTP://COMPANY/SALES/QUARTER.XLS**
	or
	HTTP://COMPANY/SALES/QUARTER.HTM
Internet	**HTTP://WWW.COMPANY.COM**
	or
	FTP://FTP.COMPANY.COM

    If you do not know the path or URL, click Browse. Use the Link to File dialog box to find the file. To find an Internet site, select it from the bottom of the Look In list in the Link to File dialog box.

4. In the Named Location in File box, type the named location in the file.

Some examples of named locations are named ranges in Excel, bookmarks in Word documents, database objects in Access, and slide numbers in PowerPoint presentations. HTML documents can also have named locations. When you view the HTML source code for a Web page, look for the NAME attribute within an anchor.

For example, if you are linking to an Excel worksheet containing named ranges, click the Browse button to display the Open Worksheet dialog box, shown in Figure 51.25. From that dialog box, you have a choice of selecting the entire workbook, a worksheet, or a range as the link.

5. Select the Use Relative Path for Hyperlink option if you want to be able to move all the linked files and their directories to a new location.

6. Choose OK.

FIG. 51.25

Select a document's file or an Internet site from the Open Worksheet dialog box.

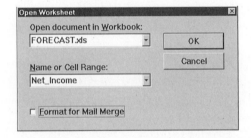

 T I P If you build Webs that must be moved to new locations, remember to select the Use Relative Path for Hyperlink option. This enables you to move all the files and their folder structures to a new drive or under a new folder.

TROUBLESHOOTING

After creating my hyperlinks, some of the files and URLs have changed. Must the links be completely re-created? You can edit your hyperlink's path, file name, URL, and document location. To edit a hyperlink, right-click the link and choose Hyperlink, Edit Hyperlink. The Edit Hyperlink dialog box will appear showing the hyperlink's current properties. Change them so they are correct.

Part

XIII

Ch

51

Linking to a Named Location in a Document

In this section, you will learn how to insert a hyperlink that will jump from one document location to another.

Hyperlinks that jump within or between documents work by jumping to text or locations that have been marked with a bookmark.

To create a hyperlink that will jump to a specific location in a Word document, follow these steps:

1. Use Insert, Bookmark to insert a bookmark at the hyperlink destination in the target document.

2. Activate the document that will contain the hyperlink and select the text that will contain the hyperlink.

3. Choose Insert, Hyperlink, or click Insert Hyperlink on the Standard toolbar. The Insert Hyperlink dialog box appears (refer to Figure 51.24).

4. Enter the path and name of the destination document into the Link to File or URL text box. If you do not know the exact name or location, choose Browse and select the file from the Link to File dialog box.

   If you are jumping to another location within the same document, leave this text box blank.

5. Enter the bookmark name into the Named Location in File text box. Choose Browse to display a list of bookmark names for the current document, or for the document listed in the Link to File or URL text box.

   Entering a named location is optional if you are linking to another file. If you leave this option blank, Word will simply open the document without moving to a specific location.

6. Select or clear the Use Relative Path for Hyperlink option. Normally, you should leave this selected.

7. Choose OK.

   The hyperlink appears in blue. Click the hyperlink to move to the destination information.

To edit or remove a hyperlink, right-click the hyperlink and choose Hyperlink, Edit Hyperlink to display the Edit Hyperlink dialog box. Make any necessary changes in the Edit Hyperlink dialog box. If you want to remove the hyperlink, choose Remove Link at the bottom of the Edit Hyperlink dialog box.

Starting Programs and Non-Office Documents with Hyperlinks

You can do more than just open other Office documents or Web sites with hyperlinks. You can create a hyperlink to programs or non-Office documents that will start the program or open the document. If Windows 95 has a program associated with a document type, then you can open that document by clicking a hyperlink to the document. You can start programs by creating a hyperlink to a program file. To do this, just enter a path to the document in the Link to File or URL box. For example, if you use the URL

C:\WINDOWS\DIALER.EXE

where Windows 95 is installed in the Windows directory on your C drive, then you will have a hyperlink that starts the Dialer program.

Some of the ways you can use hyperlinks to non-Office programs and documents are to run batch files, start communication programs, run backup programs, start agents, unzip compressed files, and so forth.

Changing the Appearance of Hyperlinks

When you insert a hyperlink and you have not selected text, the URL or path to the hyperlink appears in your document. In most cases it won't be attractive, friendly, or informative. It's better to type a text phrase that will appear as the hyperlinked text.

To enter your own text over a hyperlink, select the hyperlink by right-clicking it, then choosing Hyperlink, Select Hyperlink. Type the word or phrase that you want displayed as the hyperlink. This word or phrase will appear as underlined, colored text, indicating that it is hyperlinked. If you move the mouse pointer over the text, you will see that the hyperlink still exists.

Part
XIII

Ch
51

Creating Excel Documents for the Web

Creating Hyperlinks to Documents or Web Pages

Hyperlinks are one of the reasons the Web is so attractive. Combined with a Web browser, such as Internet Explorer, hyperlinks make it very easy for the reader of a document to click a phrase or graphic in one document and jump to a related document. It's up to you as the author to insert hyperlinks in your Excel worksheets that take the reader to useful documents or Web pages.

> **N O T E** If the Save As HTML command does not appear on your File menu, you need to install the Internet Assistant Wizard, an add-in program. Chapter 35, "Taking Advantage of Excel's Add-Ins," describes how to install Excel add-in programs. ▪

Hyperlinks in Excel can be between different types of Office documents as well as to Internet or intranet sites. Clicking a hyperlink to an Office document opens the document in its appropriate application. Clicking a hyperlink to an Internet or intranet site starts your Internet browser and accesses the site.

The web of linked documents and sites you create can be a simple personal web of documents you use frequently or it can be a complex web of documents involving files on local computers and networks as well as sites on the Internet.

Some of the ways individuals and companies are using hyperlinked documents are:

- A simple web involving hyperlinks between Excel worksheets, Word documents, and Outlook items that help you switch between documents you update frequently.

- A simple hyperlink from an Excel expense statement to a Web site on the Internet containing currency exchange rates.

- A web of hyperlinked Excel worksheets that compose an Executive Information System. Names and graphics are linked to Web sites on the Internet so executives can read competitors' business profiles, their latest Web ads, and stock analysis.

- An intranet for traveling salespeople built from Excel sales forecasts saved as HTML documents, sales proposals in native Word files so they can be edited, and product information exported to HTML documents from an Access database. All users who access this Web use Windows 95 laptops.

- An intranet for clients to track their sales orders. The Internet Assistants for Excel and Access export order tracking information as HTML documents on the intranet. Because the documents are in HTML, clients with any type of computer system can view their order information with an Internet browser.

Jumping to a Hyperlink

The following sections show you how to create hyperlinks. After you create them, you will almost certainly want to test them. To make a hypertext jump, move the pointer over the cell containing the hypertext link. The pointer changes to a pointing hand. Pause, and the path name or URL displays as a ScreenTip. Click the cell to activate the hyperlink.

If the hyperlink is to another Office document, that document's application opens and activates. The Web toolbar shown in Figure 52.1 displays over the document. To return to your original document, click the Back (left-pointing) navigation arrow. This returns you to the original document. While in the original document, you can click the Forward (right-pointing) navigation arrow on the Web toolbar to move forward to the linked document.

Forward

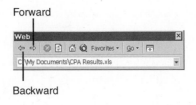

FIG. 52.1
Use the navigation buttons on the Web toolbar to move between linked documents.

Backward

TROUBLESHOOTING

Clicking a hyperlink causes an error. The two most probable causes of hyperlink errors are that the path name or URL to the document is incorrect or that there is a problem in network communication.

To check the path name or URL to a document or site, right-click the hyperlink and choose Hyperlink, Edit Hyperlink. In the Edit Hyperlink dialog box, check that the pathname, filename, and URL are still valid.

The other probable cause is a network or communication problem. Did you see or hear your modem working correctly? If not, check the modem by trying another type of modem communication. Did the normal sign-on screens for your network connection appear? If not, check with your network administrator or attempt to access the Internet by directly using a browser. If you were trying to make an Internet connection, the Internet may have been overloaded when you tried. You may need to try at a later time.

Pasting Hyperlinks to Office Documents

In your work, you may deal with documents created in different Microsoft Office applications. By adding hyperlinks to your worksheets you can move between these documents with a single click. Figure 52.2 shows an Excel worksheet with hyperlinks to related Word and Excel documents. Clicking one of these hyperlinked cells opens the linked document in its native application. The text in cells containing a hyperlink appears underlined and in color.

FIG. 52.2

Hyperlinks in your worksheets can take you to other Office documents.

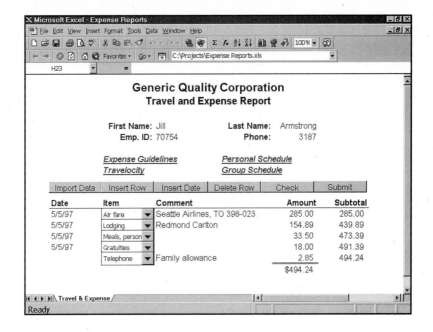

To create a link in an Excel worksheet to another Office document such as Word, follow these steps:

1. Open the Excel worksheet and the document you want to link. Both documents should be saved in the folder in which you expect them to remain.

2. Activate the document you want linked to the Excel sheet—for example, a Word document—and select the text or item you want linked. The text or item you select at this point will appear in the linked document's window after you click the hyperlink.

3. Choose Edit, Copy or right-click the selection and choose Copy.

4. Activate the Excel document and select the cell where you want the hyperlink.

5. Choose Edit, Paste as Hyperlink.

   or

   Right-click the cell and choose Paste Special. Select the Paste option, then select As Hyperlink, and choose OK.

6. Click a cell other than the cell in which you pasted the hypertext link.

   The text you selected appears in the cell containing the hyperlink. It will be colored so that it stands out from other text.

After you paste your hyperlink, the text you selected appears in the cell as the hyperlink text. In most cases, this isn't a very informative display. It usually does not explain the type of document the link is to. You can type friendlier text over the hyperlink text to produce a more explanatory hyperlink by following the directions in the section titled "Changing the Appearance of Hyperlinks," later in this chapter.

Inserting Hyperlinks to Web or Local Files

Another method of creating hyperlinks enables you to insert hyperlinks to local files or Internet sites. To use this method, you need to know or be able to browse to the file's path or Internet URL.

To insert a hyperlink, follow these steps:

1. Select the cell where you want the link to appear.

2. Choose Insert, Hyperlink or click the Insert Hyperlink button in the Standard toolbar. The Edit Hyperlink dialog box appears as shown in Figure 52.3.

FIG. 52.3

Your hyperlink can contain a specific location in a document as well as specifying the path and filename of a document or site.

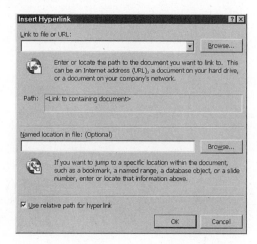

3. In the Link to File or URL box, type the path and filename or URL to the file or Web site to which you want to link.

   Enter the path name or URL like these examples:

Local document	**C:\MYFILES\FILENAME.DOC**
Local program	**C:\MYPROGRAMS\PROGRAMNAME.EXE**
Intranet	**HTTP://COMPANY/SALES/QUARTER.XLS**
	or
	HTTP://COMPANY/SALES/QUARTER.HTM
Internet	**HTTP:// WWW.COMPANY.COM**
	or
	FTP://FTP.COMPANY.COM

   If you don't know the path or URL, click Browse. Use the Link to File dialog box shown in Figure 52.4 to find the file.

FIG. 52.4

Select a document's file or an Internet site from the Link to File dialog box.

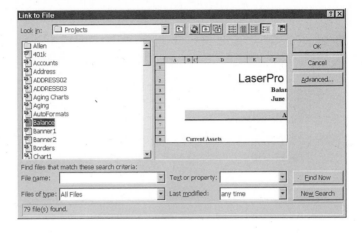

To find an Internet site, select it from the bottom of the Look In list in the Link to File dialog box. Choose OK to return to the Insert Hyperlink dialog box.

4. If you want to jump to a named location in a document, type the named location in the Named Location in File box of the Insert Hyperlink dialog box.

   Some examples of named locations are named ranges in Excel, bookmarks in Word documents, database objects in Access, or slide numbers in PowerPoint presentations.

   For example, if you are linking to an Excel worksheet containing named ranges, click the Browse button to open the Browse Excel Workbook dialog box shown in Figure 52.5. From that dialog box you have a choice of selecting the sheet or range to link.

FIG. 52.5

Link to a specific worksheet in a workbook or specific range name.

5. Select the Use Relative Path for Hyperlink option if you want to be able to move all the linked files and their directories to a new location.

6. Click OK.

TIP If you build Webs that must be moved to new locations, remember to select the Use Relative Path for Hyperlink option. This enables you to move all the files and their folder structures to a new drive or under a new folder.

If you select the Use Relative Path for Hyperlink option, the pathname you enter will be resolved to the pathname that is relative to the folder containing the worksheet. A relative path describes the location of the linked file relative to the file containing the hyperlink. This is important if you want to be able to move a group of directories together and maintain all the links between them. In a relative path, you will see the DOS notation for one folder higher is:

.. \

A relative hyperlink to a file in the same folder will appear as:

filename.XLS

A relative hyperlink to a file in the folder above the file containing the hyperlink will appear as:

..*filename*.XLS

where ..\ means next higher folder.

A relative hyperlink to a file in the folder named BUDGET below the file containing the hyperlink will appear as:

BUDGET*filename*.XLS

TROUBLESHOOTING

After building a web of linked documents, I want to move the entire web of documents to a new drive. What should I beware of? Make sure all the hyperlinks to files on the local drive use a relative path. If they do, you can move the entire folder and subfolders to a new drive and it will continue to work. If hyperlinks do not use a relative path, you must edit them to include the new pathname or redisplay the Edit Hyperlink dialog box and select the Use Relative Path for Hyperlink. See the next troubleshooting tip to learn how to edit the hyperlink.

After creating my hyperlinks, some of the files and URLs have changed. Must the links be completely re-created? You can edit your hyperlink's path, filename, URL, and document location. To edit a hyperlink, right-click the link and choose Hyperlink, Edit Hyperlink. The Edit Hyperlink dialog box appears showing the hyperlink's current properties. Change them so they are correct.

Running Programs and Non-Office Documents with Hyperlinks

You can do more than just open other Office documents or Web sites with hyperlinks. You can create a hyperlink to programs or non-Office documents. If Windows 95 has a program associated with a document type, then you can open that document by clicking a hyperlink to the document. To do this, just enter a path to the document in the Link to File or URL box.

Part XIII Ch 52

To start a program from a hyperlink, create a link to the program's EXE file. For example, clicking a hyperlink to C:\WINDOWS\DIALER.EXE opens the Windows 95 Phone Dialer in its own window.

You can also use hyperlinks to non-Office programs and documents to run batch files, start communication programs, run backup programs, start agents, unzip compressed files, and so on.

Changing the Appearance of Hyperlinks

The hyperlink text that appears in a cell may not be attractive or informative to the user of your worksheet. It displays whatever you selected in the linked document. For example, if the link is to a long paragraph about the terms in a legal document, you might want to replace the text that appears with a descriptive phrase such as *Nondisclosure terms*.

To enter your own text over the hyperlink, follow these steps:

1. Use the arrow keys to move to the cell containing the hypertext link, or right-click the hyperlink and select Hyperlink, Select Hyperlink.

2. Type an informative name in the cell and press Enter. The text you type will become the underlined hyperlink text.

You can change the font and color of hyperlink text by selecting the cell, then choosing Format, Cells. Select the Font tab, then select how you want the text to appear.

Modifying Hyperlinks

To modify a hyperlink, right-click the hyperlink, choose Hyperlink, and then choose one of the following commands:

Command	Description
Open	Opens the linked document just as though you had clicked the hyperlink.
Open in New Window	Opens the linked document in a new window.
Copy Hyperlink	Copies the hyperlink so you can paste it into another cell.
Add to Favorites	Adds the hyperlink to the Favorites list in the Web toolbar and Internet Explorer. Use this if it's a link you use frequently.
Edit Hyperlink	Opens the Edit Hyperlink dialog box that appears when you choose the Insert, Hyperlink command. This enables you to edit the file or path if folder or filenames change. The Insert Hyperlink dialog box appears in Figure 52.3.
Select Hyperlink	Enables you to select the cell by clicking rather than using movement keys to select the cell.

T I P To convert a hyperlink into the text displayed in the cell, right-click the hyperlink, choose Edit <u>H</u>yperlink, and then click the <u>R</u>emove Link button.

Creating Hyperlinks with Formulas

Put your hyperlinks under worksheet control through the use of the HYPERLINK function. By using the HYPERLINK function, you can make hyperlinks appear or disappear under specific conditions, change their link, or change their displayed text.

The HYPERLINK function has the syntax:

```
HYPERLINK(Link_location,Friendly_name)
```

The Link_location is the path and filename to the file, program, or URL that you want linked. The Friendly_name is what will appear in the hyperlink cell in place of the Link_location. This can be text or a reference to another cell's contents. Completed HYPERLINK formulas might look like:

```
=HYPERLINK("http://www.mcp.com","Computer book catalogs")
=HYPERLINK(C47,B15)
=HYPERLINK("http://www.microsoft.com",B12)
```

where B12 contains the text "Microsoft". If you put the URL in a cell, make sure you include HTTP:// or FTP:// as appropriate in front of the URL.

To make hyperlinks that turn on and off depending upon some condition in the worksheet, use a formula like this:

```
=IF(B12>15,HYPERLINK("C:\MYFOLDER\EXPENSES.XLS","Expense Report"),"")
```

In this example when the value in B12 is greater than 15, the hyperlink and its text appear; otherwise, no text (" ") appears in the cell containing the formula.

To make hyperlinks change what they are linked to, use an IF function like this:

```
=HYPERLINK(IF(B15="USA","C:\SALES\QUARTER1.XLS","HTTP://COMPANY/EUROSALES/
EUROQUARTER1.XLS")
```

In this formula, when cell B15 contains the text USA, the hyperlink opens the file QUARTER1.XLS from the SALES folder on drive C. When B15 contains anything other than USA, the hyperlink is to the file EUROQUARTER1.XLS located in the folder COMPANY/EUROSALES somewhere on the company's intranet.

Another interesting function that will change how HYPERLINK works depending upon worksheet values is CHOOSE. It enables you to make multiple decisions without nesting IF functions.

If you want to create buttons or options that will control how HYPERLINK functions work, read Chapter 37, "Building Forms with Controls."

Publishing Data and Charts in HTML Pages

A tremendous amount of valuable corporate information is stuck in programs such as Excel, Word, and Access. That information can have great value when shared with others who need it to perform their jobs more efficiently. Many companies are now creating their own intranets as a way of quickly making desktop information accessible to employees, clients, and corporate affiliates.

Although Office 97 documents are accessible over the Internet or a company intranet, reading or editing them requires users to have a computer that can run Office or one of the Word, Excel, or PowerPoint viewers. To make Office information accessible to all computer systems, Microsoft developed Internet Assistants. These are wizards that convert the data, text, and charts in Office applications into HTML pages that can be viewed by any Internet or intranet browser. The Excel Internet Assistant converts data, tables, and charts in worksheets into HTML pages. Office 97 also includes Internet Assistants for Word, Access, and PowerPoint.

Figure 52.6 shows a simple worksheet that contains a text title, a chart, and a table of data. Any or all of this can be converted into an HTML page or inserted into an existing HTML page. Figure 52.7 shows an HTML page created by using the Internet Assistant on this worksheet.

FIG. 52.6

Data, tables, or charts from Excel worksheets like this can be converted into HTML pages.

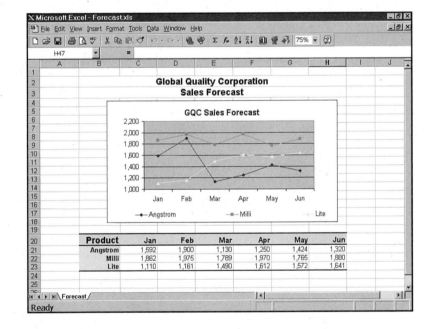

Product	Jan	Feb	Mar	Apr	May	Jun
Angstrom	1,592	1,900	1,130	1,250	1,424	1,320
Milli	1,862	1,975	1,789	1,970	1,765	1,880
Lite	1,110	1,161	1,490	1,612	1,572	1,641

FIG. 52.7

This figure shows the HTML page created with the Internet Assistant and the worksheet from Figure 52.6.

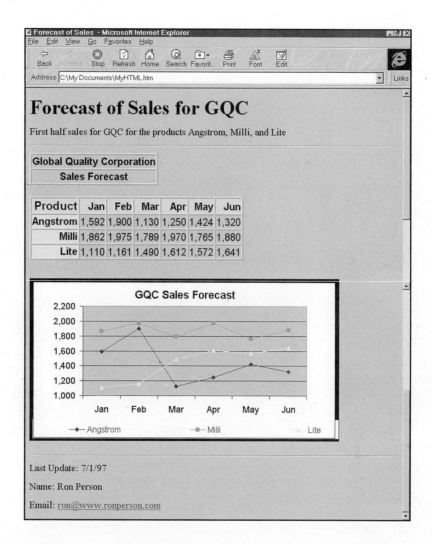

Excel's Internet Assistant is an add-in program. To see if you have the Internet Assistant loaded, choose the File menu and look for a Save as HTML command. If you do not have this command or if choosing this command produces an error, check to see if the Internet Assistant Wizard add-in is loaded. To do this, choose Tools, Add-Ins. When the Add-Ins dialog box appears, look to see if the Internet Assistant Wizard is selected. If it is not, select it and click OK. If the Internet Assistant Wizard does not show on the Add-Ins Available list, then you need to rerun the Excel or Office 97 installation, choose Custom install, and install the Internet Assistant Wizard. It won't take long—you're installing only the wizard, not the entire program.

TROUBLESHOOTING

After creating a Web page using the Excel Internet Assistant, I copied it to a new folder. The page displays, but not the charts. Small icons display where the charts should be. Charts in Web pages are stored in separate GIF or JPEG files. The Excel Internet Assistant converts Excel charts into GIF files in the same folder as the Web page you created. When you copy the HTML file the Internet Assistant creates, make sure you copy GIF files that have the same titles as your chart titles.

Publishing on a New HTML Page

The Internet Assistant will guide you through the entire process of creating an HTML page. It will create an HTML page with HTML title and header tags, divider lines, data, tables, and charts. You can specify in what order your selections from the worksheet appear. The data, tables, and charts can even come from different worksheets and workbooks. And if you want responses to your HTML page, the Internet Assistant will even insert an Internet email hyperlink to your email address.

To create a complete HTML page from data, tables, or charts, follow these steps:

1. Open the worksheet containing data you want on an HTML page.

2. Select the first range containing information you want on the HTML page. In Figure 52.6, the title area, B2:H3, was selected.

   In this case, a title on the worksheet was selected. You also can enter a title directly in a later step.

3. Choose File, Save as HTML to display the Internet Assistant Wizard-Step 1 box shown in Figure 52.8.

FIG. 52.8

The Internet Assistant opens with your selected range displayed in the List of Ranges or Charts list.

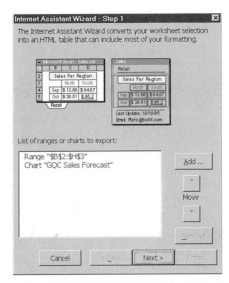

Notice that the List of Ranges or Charts to Export box displays both the range you selected and charts on the worksheet. The Internet Assistant detects charts on the worksheet and adds them to the list. You will later be able to delete the charts you do not want in the HTML page.

4. To add additional ranges to the List of Ranges or Charts to Export list, click the Add button. The Step box disappears and the range selection box shown in Figure 52.9 appears.

5. Click in the edit box and type or select on the worksheet the next range you want added to the HTML page.

   You can select individual cells as well as ranges. You do not have to include cells containing a title or description because you will have a chance to enter those directly.

   If you want to include a table, select a range that includes all the table areas you want on the HTML page. As you select a range, notice that the selection box collapses, shrinking out of the way to make it easier for you to see the range you're selecting.

   You can create HTML pages from data in different workbooks and worksheets. To switch between workbooks while the range selection box is displayed, click a worksheet or press Ctrl+F6.

   To select a range on another worksheet in the active workbook, switch between worksheets by clicking the worksheet's tab or pressing Ctrl+PgUp or Ctrl+PgDn, then select the range.

6. Choose OK to accept the range you've selected. Return to step 4 to add additional ranges.

7. Reorder ranges and charts in the order in which you want them on the HTML page by selecting a range or chart and then clicking the up or down Move button shown in Figure 52.10.

   Selecting a range in the list selects the corresponding range on the worksheet so you can tell what the range includes.

8. After the ranges and charts are ordered as you want them to appear, click Next to display Internet Assistant Step 2 shown in Figure 52.11.

9. Select the Create an Independent, Ready-to-View HTML Document option, then click Next to display Internet Assistant Step 3 shown in Figure 52.12.

   See the following sections if you want to insert your selections in an existing HTML page.

Part
XIII
Ch
52

FIG. 52.10

Selecting a range to move it to a different position also selects the range on the worksheet so you can see its data included.

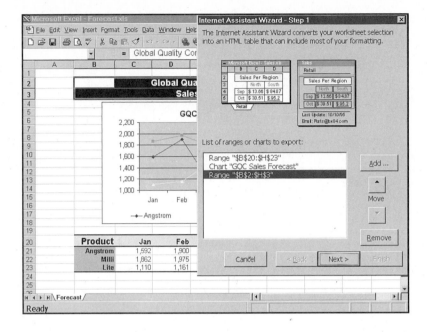

FIG. 52.11

In Step 2, you select whether you want a new HTML page or want your selections inserted into an existing HTML page.

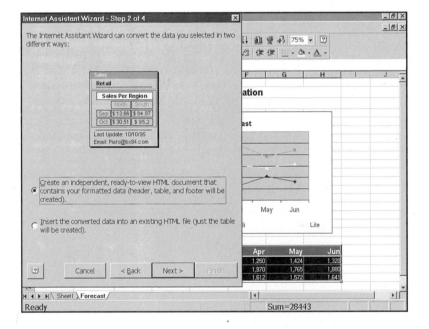

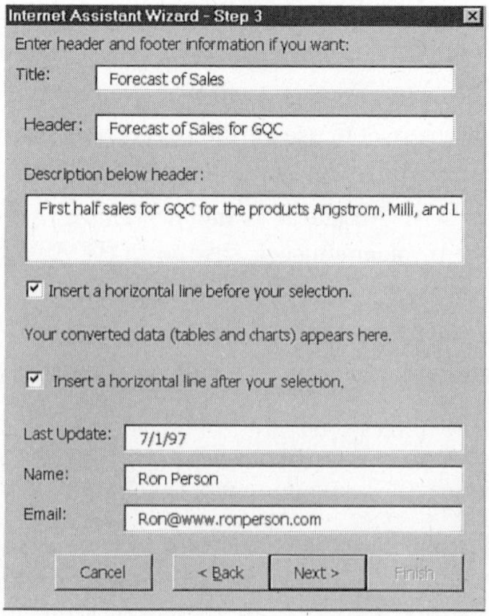

FIG. 52.12

In Step 3, you can enter a title as well as formatting lines and an email response hyperlink.

Internet Assistant Wizard – Step 3

Enter header and footer information if you want:

Title: Forecast of Sales

Header: Forecast of Sales for GQC

Description below header:

First half sales for GQC for the products Angstrom, Milli, and L

☑ Insert a horizontal line before your selection.

Your converted data (tables and charts) appears here.

☑ Insert a horizontal line after your selection.

Last Update: 7/1/97

Name: Ron Person

Email: Ron@www.ronperson.com

Cancel < Back Next > Finish

Part
XIII

Ch
52

10. In the Step 3 dialog box, enter additional HTML information such as the title, header, and description. Click Next to display Step 4, shown in Figure 52.13.

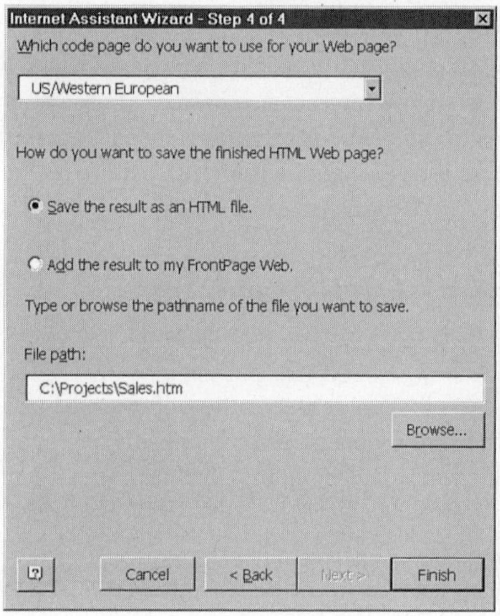

FIG. 52.13

In step 4, you decide where you want your HTML page saved and whether it should be an independent page or part of a FrontPage Web.

Internet Assistant Wizard – Step 4 of 4

Which code page do you want to use for your Web page?

US/Western European

How do you want to save the finished HTML Web page?

● Save the result as an HTML file.

○ Add the result to my FrontPage Web.

Type or browse the pathname of the file you want to save.

File path:

C:\Projects\Sales.htm

Browse...

Cancel < Back Next > Finish

The header and description will appear at the top of the Web page. The header will appear in the largest heading font and the description will appear below it in body copy font. Selecting the horizontal lines options puts lines above and below your data on the page. If you enter an Internet email address in the Email box, readers who have Internet email capability will be able to click an email hyperlink on your page to send you responses.

11. In Step 4, select the character set to use for the page. Leave the default setting unless you are creating a page for a different language computer.

12. You can choose to save the HTML file as an independent HTML file or save it within an existing FrontPage Web. If you are unsure, save as an HTML file. HTML files can later be integrated with a FrontPage Web.

To save the page as an individual HTML file, select the Save the Result as an HTML File option. Enter a path and filename for the file, then click Finish.

To save the page as part of a FrontPage Web, select Add the Result to Your FrontPage Web. FrontPage will start. Type the URL for the FrontPage Web. If you are unsure of the URL, click Browse to activate FrontPage so you can find the URL for the FrontPage Web.

Now that you have created a complete HTML page from an Excel worksheet, you may want to enhance it even more with hyperlinks, graphics, backgrounds, formatting, and so on. To enhance the Web page you've created, you can open it in any HTML editor and make modifications. If you are using the Office 97 suite, you can use Word's Web Publishing Tools. Another highly regarded HTML editor and Web manager is Microsoft's FrontPage 97.

Inserting into an Existing HTML Page

Excel's Internet Assistant Wizard produces a simple Web page, but for many projects you will want to insert Excel charts and tables into existing Web pages that have been created with Web authoring tools such as Word's Internet Assistant or Microsoft FrontPage. Inserting an Excel chart or table into an existing Web page follows almost exactly the same steps as creating a new page. However, before you can insert anything into a Web page, you must make a simple text modification to the Web page so the Excel Internet Assistant will know where you want the chart or table inserted.

Preparing an HTML Page to Receive Data   Internet Assistant inserts the data, tables, or charts into a Web page at a location you have marked with a special tag, a text code, that looks like this:

```
<!--##Table##-->
```

You don't have to use a special HTML editor to insert this tag. You can use a text editor. Or even better, some browsers, such as Internet Explorer, enable you to edit the HTML source code and view the page in side-by-side windows.

To edit a Web page that is on your hard disk or network using Internet Explorer 3, follow these steps:

1. Minimize all applications to the taskbar by right-clicking in a gray area of the taskbar and choosing Minimize All Windows.

2. Start the Internet Explorer and choose File, Open. Click the Browse button to select the HTM file, choose Open and OK. The Web page opens in Internet Explorer.

3. Choose View, Source to open the HTML source code in a separate Notepad window.

4. Display the Internet Explorer and the Notepad in side-by-side windows by right-clicking in a gray area of the taskbar and choosing Tile Vertically. The windows will appear similar to Figure 52.14.

FIG. 52.14

View and edit your Web page from Internet Explorer.

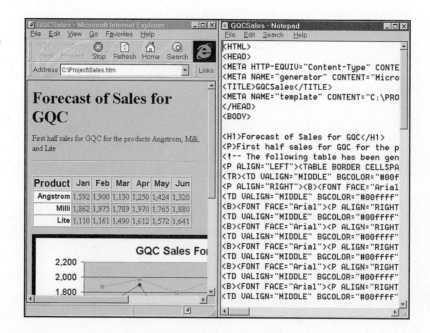

5. Scroll through the side-by-side windows matching the visual display on the Web page to the HTML source code in the Notepad. Locate the place where you want Excel's Internet Assistant to make an insert.

6. Click in the HTML source code where you want the Internet Assistant to insert code, tables, or charts and press Enter to create a new line where you will insert the code.

   Do not create the line between the start and end of a pair of tags; for example, the bold tag starts with <B> and ends with </B>. The tag must be between the tags <BODY> and </BODY>.

7. Type the code:

   ```
   <!--##Table##-->
   ```

8. Choose File, Save As in Notepad and save the HTM file to a different name. This preserves your original HTM file in case you made a mistake.

9. Close the Notepad and Internet Explorer and return to Excel to use the Internet Assistant to insert data, tables, or charts.

Inserting into an HTML Page To insert Excel data, tables, or charts into an existing Web page, you must first make a simple modification to the HTML source code as described in the previous section "Preparing an HTML Page to Receive Data." After you have made that modification, follow these steps:

1. Go to the earlier section titled "Publishing on a New HTML Page" and follow steps 1 through 8. In step 8, the Step 2 dialog box appears as shown in Figure 52.15. When that dialog box appears, return to step 2, which follows here.

FIG. 52.15

Select that you want to insert the Excel data into an existing HTML file.

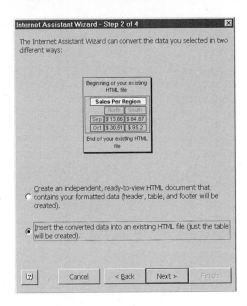

2. Select Insert the Converted Data and choose Next to display the Step 3 dialog box shown in Figure 52.16.

3. Select Open the File Directly if you are modifying an HTML file that is not part of a FrontPage Web. Enter the path of the HTML file in which you want to insert the data. Click Browse if you don't know the path. To save the page as part of a FrontPage Web, select Open the File from My FrontPage Web. FrontPage will start. Open the FrontPage Web and specify the file in which you want to insert the data. Choose Next to display the Step 4 dialog box shown in Figure 52.17.

4. Select the character set to use for the page. Leave the default setting unless you are creating a page for a different language computer.

5. Select Save the Result as an HTML File option or if you want to include the file in a FrontPage Web, select Add the Result to Your FrontPage Web.

6. Enter the path and filename where you want the file stored, then choose Finish.

FIG. 52.16

Select how you want the wizard to open the file.

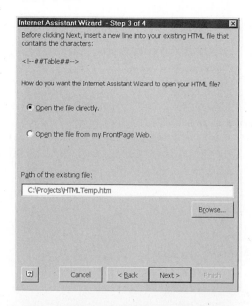

FIG. 52.17

Select that you want to save the result as an HTML file.

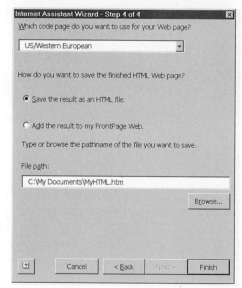

Copying Your Web Page to Another Location

After you create your Web page using Excel's Internet Assistant, you will probably want to copy the Web page to another location. If you included an Excel chart in the Web page, you will need to copy the GIF files for those charts as well as the HTML file itself.

Using the Explorer, go to the folder where you saved the Web page. Look for files with an HTM extension. One of these should be the HTML file you created. Look in the same folder for files with a GIF extension and a name that is the same as the chart's title. When you copy the HTM file, by you must copy the GIF files it uses to display graphics. If the GIF files are missing when the Web page appears, you will see a small icon with the name of the missing file instead of the chart. ●

Index

D

Complete and Return this Card
for a *FREE* Computer Book Catalo

Thank you for purchasing this book! You have purchased a superior computer book written expressly for your needs. To continue to provide the kind of up-to-date, pertinent coverage you've come to expect from us, we need to hear from you. Please take a minute to complete and return this self-addressed, postage-paid form. In return, we'll send you a free catalog of all our computer books on topics ranging from word processing to programming and the internet.

Mr. ☐   Mrs. ☐   Ms. ☐   Dr. ☐

Name (first) ☐☐☐☐☐☐☐☐☐☐   (M.I.) ☐   (last) ☐☐☐☐☐☐☐☐☐☐☐☐☐☐☐☐☐

Address ☐☐☐☐☐☐☐☐☐☐☐☐☐☐☐☐☐☐☐☐☐☐☐☐☐☐☐☐☐

☐☐☐☐☐☐☐☐☐☐☐☐☐☐☐☐☐☐☐☐☐☐☐☐☐☐☐☐☐

City ☐☐☐☐☐☐☐☐☐☐☐☐☐☐☐☐   State ☐☐   Zip ☐☐☐☐☐ ☐☐☐☐

Phone ☐☐☐ ☐☐☐ ☐☐☐☐   Fax ☐☐☐ ☐☐☐ ☐☐☐☐

Company Name ☐☐☐☐☐☐☐☐☐☐☐☐☐☐☐☐☐☐☐☐☐☐☐☐☐☐☐☐☐

E-mail address ☐☐☐☐☐☐☐☐☐☐☐☐☐☐☐☐☐☐☐☐☐☐☐☐☐☐☐☐☐

1. Please check at least (3) influencing factors for purchasing this book.

Front or back cover information on book .... ☐
Special approach to the content .... ☐
Completeness of content .... ☐
Author's reputation .... ☐
Publisher's reputation .... ☐
Book cover design or layout .... ☐
Index or table of contents of book .... ☐
Price of book .... ☐
Special effects, graphics, illustrations .... ☐
Other (Please specify): _____ ☐

2. How did you first learn about this book?
Saw in Macmillan Computer Publishing catalog .... ☐
Recommended by store personnel .... ☐
Saw the book on bookshelf at store .... ☐
Recommended by a friend .... ☐
Received advertisement in the mail .... ☐
Saw an advertisement in: _____ ☐
Read book review in: _____ ☐
Other (Please specify): _____ ☐

3. How many computer books have you purchased in the last six months?

This book only .... ☐   3 to 5 books .... ☐
2 books .... ☐   More than 5 .... ☐

4. Where did you purchase this book?
Bookstore .... ☐
Computer Store .... ☐
Consumer Electronics Store .... ☐
Department Store .... ☐
Office Club .... ☐
Warehouse Club .... ☐
Mail Order .... ☐
Direct from Publisher .... ☐
Internet site .... ☐
Other (Please specify): _____ ☐

5. How long have you been using a computer?

☐ Less than 6 months   ☐ 6 months to a year
☐ 1 to 3 years   ☐ More than 3 years

6. What is your level of experience with personal computers and with the subject of this book?

	With PCs	With subject of book
New	☐	☐
Casual	☐	☐
Accomplished	☐	☐
Expert	☐	☐

Source Code ISBN: 1-7897-1555-4

...he following best describes your

...sistant .... ☐
...or .... ☐
...dent .... ☐
...dent/CEO/COO .... ☐
Lawyer/Doctor/Medical Professional .... ☐
Teacher/Educator/Trainer .... ☐
Engineer/Technician .... ☐
Consultant .... ☐
Not employed/Student/Retired .... ☐
Other (Please specify): _____ ☐

8. Which of the following best describes the area of the company your job title falls under?

Accounting .... ☐
Engineering .... ☐
Manufacturing .... ☐
Operations .... ☐
Marketing .... ☐
Sales .... ☐
Other (Please specify): _____ ☐

9. What is your age?

Under 20 .... ☐
21-29 .... ☐
30-39 .... ☐
40-49 .... ☐
50-59 .... ☐
60-over .... ☐

10. Are you:

Male .... ☐
Female .... ☐

11. Which computer publications do you read regularly? (Please list)

_____
_____
_____
_____
_____
_____
_____
_____
_____
_____

Comments: _____
_____
_____

Fold here and scotch-tape to mail.